Brief Contents

Contents

Second Edition

THE WESTERN WORLD

A Narrative History

Prehistory to the Present

Anthony Esler
The College of William and Mary

Prentice Hall, Upper Saddle River, New Jersey 07458

Library of Congress Cataloging-in-Publication Data

Esler, Anthony.
    The Western world : a narrative history / Anthony Esler. —
Combined ed., 2nd ed.
        p.   cm.
    Includes bibliographical references (p.   ) and index.
    ISBN 0-13-495623-0
    1. Civilization, Western—History.   I. Title.
CB245.E685   1997
909'.09812—dc21   96-44445
                                                       CIP

Acquisitions Editor: *Sally Constable*
Editorial Assistant: *Maria Baynosa*
Editorial/Production Supervision and Interior Design: *Barbara DeVries*
Prepress and Manufacturing Buyer: *Lynn Pearlman*
Cover Design: *Bruce Kenselaar*
Cover Image: Dame Laura Knight, *Penzance Fair*, Signed and Dated 1919, Canvas: 46 x 59½ in.
        Richard Green, London.

This book was set 9.5/11 Galliard by Compset, Inc. and was printed by
RR Donnelley & Sons Company. The cover was printed by Phoenix
Color Corp.

© 1997, 1994 by Prentice-Hall, Inc.
Simon & Schuster/A Viacom Company
Upper Saddle River, New Jersey   07458

Printed in the United States of America

10 9 8 7 6 5 4 3 2 1

ISBN 0-13-495623-0

Prentice-Hall International (UK) Limited, *London*
Prentice-Hall of Australia Pty. Limited, *Sydney*
Prentice-Hall Canada Inc., *Toronto*
Prentice-Hall Hispanoamericana, S.A., *Mexico*
Prentice-Hall of India Private Limited, *New Delhi*
Prentice-Hall of Japan, Inc., *Tokyo*
Simon & Schuster Asia Pte. Ltd., *Singapore*
Editora Prentice-Hall do Brasil, Ltda., *Rio de Janeiro*

Maps

Preface

In this book, I have tried to outline the history of the Western World as a story, a narrative of people and events on the move, of a society evolving through time. I have also, however, allocated a substantial proportion of the book to social and cultural analysis, where so much cutting-edge historical research has been concentrated in recent years. I have tried to pay special attention to such still sometimes neglected areas as women's history and, in the second volume, to the history of the women's movement for social equality. As the author of an earlier history of the world as a whole, I have also felt a strong responsibility to deal here with the West's repeated encounters with the non-Western world; and I have tried to stress not only Western influences on the rest of the world but also a significant Western cultural debt to a number of non-Western peoples. I have made room here for both traditional emphasis on conflict between classes, creeds, and nations and for treatment of that more recently explored sense of community which defines a healthy society. And I have tried to be as up-to-date as the publishing process allows, a feature that seems particularly important in the pivotal 1990s, a watershed decade that could set the historical agenda of the Western world for decades to come.

Thanks to Prentice Hall's diligent development and production people, this book also boasts a number of special features that we hope will be helpful to its student readers. Each chapter has one or more Chronologies, listing important events in the time frame being explored. Most chapters have at least two maps, and a serious effort has been made to see to it that all places mentioned in the text are shown on the maps. At the end of each chapter is a selection of "key terms" to help students prepare for identification questions on tests. Each of the six parts of the book begins with a Time Line, which has been constructed to give a sense of sequence and of development.

In the course of assembling this book, I have accumulated a large number of intellectual debts. It is therefore my duty as well as a great pleasure to express my gratitude to some at least of those who have made the book you hold in your hands possible.

First and most of all, I must say thank you again to the scholarly and dedicated Europeanists at William and Mary, with whom I have had the privilege of working over the years—to Professors Dale Hoak, Lu Ann Homza, Gil McArthur, Jim McCord, and George Strong, as well as to some who have moved on, especially A. Z. Freeman, Harold Fowler, Bruce McCully, Maryann Brink, Dietrich Orlow, and Tom Sheppard. Thanks also to the Americanists and the specialists in non-Western history whose knowledge I have drawn upon most frequently—Cam Walker, Ismail Abdalla, Ed Crapol, Craig Canning, and Judy Ewell—and to the classicists downstairs, especially Jim Baron and Ward Jones. If I had not known that all these people were willing to let me pick their brains and paw through their books, I would probably never have had the nerve to undertake this project at all.

Next my gratitude goes to the historians at other universities who accepted Prentice Hall's invitation to read and comment on portions of this book as it has developed. My thanks then to: Douglas R. Bisson, Belmont University; Elizabeth Furdell, University of North Florida; George Huppert, University of Illinois at Chicago; James A. Jaffe, University of Wisconsin at Whitewater; James I. Martin, Sr., Campbell University; Michael Polley, Colombia College; Steven F. Sage, Middle Tennessee State University; Narashingha P. Sil,

Western Oregon State College; and Martha S. Trainer, Pellissippi State Technical Community College. All surviving errors and misinterpretations are of course mine alone.

The students themselves, finally, deserve any academic writer's gratitude. By bringing their own increasingly international backgrounds to bear in classroom discussions or simply by asking the hard questions that send the teacher back to the sources, they have contributed immeasurably to the education of their instructor.

At Prentice Hall, the most professional and hard-working selection of editors I have ever known labored over this book. It would never have been written at all if Executive Editor Steve Dalphin hadn't pried me away from another project and Senior Acquisitions Editor Sally Constable hadn't proposed this revised version. Three enormously skilled and understanding development editors, Cecil Yarborough, Virginia Locke, and Susan Alkana have given the project the benefit of their knowledge of books, book-making, and much else, and despite my sometimes negative reactions to all the rethinking and rewriting they suggested, the book is deeply in their debt. Barbara DeVries handled production deftly and bore with my seemingly congenital inability to respond to deadlines on time with remarkable calm. For copyediting that was amazingly able to pluck out inconsistencies a hundred pages apart, my appreciation to Marcia Rulfs.

Finally, I would like to acknowledge a few personal debts which can never be adequately repaid. I would like to thank my parents, Jamie Arthur and Helen Kreamer Esler for raising me with an awareness that thinking is part of life and that there is a larger world out there waiting. Thanks to my first wife Carol Clemeau Esler and to my sons Kenneth Campbell Esler and David Douglas Esler for being wonderful travelers and for finding plenty to like in European cities and villages. And thanks again to my wife Cam—Professor Helen Campbell Walker—for many years of insights and for everyplace from Skara Brae, Great Zimbabwe, Samarkand, and Lhasa to wherever we end up next year.

Anthony Esler
Harriet Tubman Drive
Williamsburg, Virginia

The New York Times and **Prentice Hall** are sponsoring **Themes of the Times:** a program designed to enhance access to current information of relevance in the classroom.

Through this program, the core subject matter provided in the text is supplemented by a collection of time-sensitive articles from one of the world's most distinguished newspapers, **The New York Times**. These articles demonstrate the vital, ongoing connection between what is learned in the classroom and what is happening in the world around us.

To enjoy the wealth of information of **The New York Times** daily, a reduced subscription rate is available. For information, call toll-free: 1-800-631-1222.

Prentice Hall and **The New York Times** are proud to co-sponsor **Themes of the Times.** We hope it will make the reading of both textbooks and newspapers a more dynamic, involving process.

Introduction: What is the Western World?

You may think this a strange question to ask, for we are all likely to believe we know the answer. If we look into a dictionary or two, to be sure, we are not surprised to note that as far back as Shakespeare's day, *Western* referred to "Western or European countries" and that more recent usage defines *the West* as "Europe and the Americas." Asked to list some characteristics of the West today, we might say that Western peoples have civil rights, democratic elections, and a fair degree of material prosperity. We might add that they also live in Europe and America or in places that have some roots in these twin centers of the modern West—Australia, say, or Iceland.

The historical core of the Western world, however, is Europe, where Western civilization was born. This brief introduction, then, will attempt to do two things: to introduce Europe itself, the historic center of the West; and to give some idea of how the larger Western world grew to its current awesome dimensions.

Both here and throughout this book, we will attempt to give the rest of the world its due. We will recognize the key role of Europe's neighbors as shapers of Western history. We will turn, at length, to the impact of the expanding West on the histories of other peoples. In dealing with recent centuries, we will see the history of the Western world blending with that of the world at large. Emphasis on *global context* is, in fact, a central feature of this particular history of Western civilization.

But this is a history of the Western peoples, of the peoples who built one of the world's half–dozen major civilizations on European land. So we will begin in Europe and move out from there.

Where the West Began

Perhaps the best way to get a sense of the European landscape today is to get away from the airplanes, and even the trains, and hike, bike, or drive through it. Go the youth hostel route; have wine, bread, and cheese in a field for lunch; and find the cheapest menus outside the brasseries and trattorias for supper on the village square. All of a sudden, Europe isn't just the Tower of London, the Louvre, and the Trevi Fountain. It's dusty roads and olive trees, a curve of the Rhine and a castle on a crag, or snowballs in the Alps. It's wine country and grain country, lakes and fjords and forests. From Ireland to the Urals, from the Mediterranean to the Arctic Circle, there's a lot of country there.

The very variety of the continent makes describing its basic geography in words no easy task. Still, we should make some effort to develop a sense of the geographical outlines of Europe today before we focus on what has happened there over the past thirty centuries and more.

There are a few basic facts, easily enough assimilated. Europe consists of the western fifth of the double continent of Eurasia. It is generally defined as the territory running from the Atlantic Ocean east to the Ural Mountains and the Turkish Straits. The Black Sea and the Mediterranean mark its southern frontier, the arctic reaches of Scandinavia and Russia its northern one. In area, it is somewhat larger than the United States.

If you were to cut out a map of Europe, it would take you quite a long time because of the many ins and outs of its coastline. Scandinavia, the Iberian countries, Italy, and Greece are all huge peninsulas, and there are many large islands in both the Mediterranean and the Atlantic, including country–sized ones like Great Britain and Ireland. Inland too, Europe is broken up by massive mountain chains—the Pyrenees, the Alps, and the ranges of the Balkans and the Caucasus. The continent is marked also by long river valleys, like the Seine in France, the Po in Italy, the Rhine–Danube line that formed the Roman frontier, and the Elbe, Volga, and other rivers of eastern Europe.

Western Europe, in particular, is a tumbled land, folded and wrinkled, with only a few plains and plateaus, like those in Spain and France. The real "great plains" of Europe lie in the central and eastern parts of the continent: a drive from Berlin to Moscow can remind you of nothing so much as a trip from Chicago to Kansas, leaving out most of the towns. But much of the rest of Europe has mountains on the horizon, gleaming rivers winding down a glen, or church spires rising over rolling hills.

In ancient and medieval times, this European land was a good deal less tidy than it looks now. Forests were heavy over much of the continent, and there was much more un-developed wasteland—undrained marshes, rocky hills, or open grasslands untenanted save by nomadic herdsmen. The great mountain ranges, not yet sown with picture–postcard ski resorts, loomed as cold and forbidding barriers to trade and travel.

There was immense potential in that European earth, heavy and black in the north, lighter in the Mediterranean south, but capable of producing bumper crops everywhere once the forests were pushed back, the swamplands drained. Properly exploited, those end-less coasts and rivers were made for trade, the streams that fed them for turning water wheels. There was plenty of timber and building stone. Minerals slept under the European earth, waiting for a later age to turn them into tools and weapons, machinery and struc-tural steel. And the climate—albeit colder and wetter the farther north you went—might serve to brace people to their duties rather than to slow their efforts.

The familiar political divisions of today were not yet there, of course. Such twentieth–century powers as Germany, France, Britain, and Russia did not exist. There were no tidy groupings of other nations, from the Scandinavian countries to the Balkans. Still, the mountain ranges, river valleys, and winding coastlines that defined later political frontiers were there. Geography was as important to Europe's future political organization as to its economic future.

To turn Europe into one of the most successful areas of human habitation on the globe was the labor of many centuries. Much of the rest of this book is devoted to exploring the achievements of these European generations.

But Europeans, like other peoples, did not limit themselves to the continent where their culture had its deepest roots. Like other peoples, they learned from their neighbors, conquered other peoples, traded with and exploited others economically, and spread their values and beliefs far and wide. We should therefore include here a brief overview of the ex-pansion of the Western world, of its interaction with other parts of the world, and of its contribution to the history of the world as a whole.

The West and the World

In the simplest territorial sense, the Western world will be seen here as a growing thing. It has expanded and spread throughout its history, swelling from the little Greek world at the eastern end of the Mediterranean to a mighty array of modern nations scattered around the world.

Some twenty–five hundred years ago—around 500 BCE—the West was a collection of tiny Greek city-states centering on the shores and islands of the Aegean Sea, a northward projection of the Mediterranean. By the time of Christ, two thousand years ago, this Greek birthplace of the Western world had given way to the Roman Empire of Caesar Augustus, ringing the entire Mediterranean, and stretching north of the Alps to encompass western Europe and the British Isles. By the year 1000 CE, the medieval West included western, central, and eastern Europe, and stretched from Spain to Russia. And by 1500 CE, five hundred years ago, the first European sailing ships to control the sea lanes of the world were already carrying European settlers to North and South America and traders to Africa and Asia. As recently as 1900, less than a century ago, Western empires were at the height of their most vigorous period of global expansion.

This process of territorial growth has been accompanied by another important characteristic of the Western world: fertile interaction with many other cultures. For Western peoples have interacted with other peoples from the very beginning, often with very significant consequences. We will thus see influences from ancient Egypt and the Near East helping to shape Greece during the earliest stages of Western history. We will visit a Roman Empire that actually included sizable slices of North Africa and Western Asia. In the Middle Ages, we will find Byzantines, Muslims, and Mongols influencing as well as threatening various parts of Europe. In modern times, we will see an imperial West coming into contact with and, increasingly, imposing its will upon other peoples around the world. And we will see how peoples from all parts of the globe have helped to build the West as we know it today, both by providing labor, goods, and ideas and by contributing energetic new citizens to many Western nations.

Overall, we will try to show that the Western world may legitimately be defined in terms of real contributions to human history as a whole. Western ideas have played a central part in modern history. The physical sciences, though derived in significant part from the thought of other peoples, emerged in their modern form in the European scientific revolution of the sixteenth and seventeenth centuries. Many of the key political, economic, and social ideas underlying the structure of modern states around the world have their roots in the European Enlightenment of the eighteenth century and in the ideologies developed in the West during the nineteenth century. The ongoing industrialization of the globe, too, has its roots in the European industrial revolution which began in the eighteenth century. It was the West which, through its structure of international trade and empire, forged the first genuinely global market and brought all the world's peoples into closer contact than ever before. These varied accomplishments are no small thing to have contributed to the world's store.

We will begin, then, with a small people at the far end of an inland sea and expand our subject until half the globe seems to be in some sense "Western." We will envision the Western world as a dynamically developing society, and one which has always been part of a larger human world. And we will follow throughout the line of historical evolution and achievement which provides the core of Western identity today.

PART I
Ancient Times

At the broadest level, the development of human society has followed a common pattern around the world. Everywhere, prehistoric hunting and food gathering societies have evolved through stone age agriculture into what we call civilization. History itself is usually said to begin with *civilization,* a society built around cities and empires, productive economies and social classes, developed crafts and literacy.

Western civilization began to take shape in southern Europe, around the Mediterranean Sea during the long millennium from approximately 750 BCE to CE 500. Borrowing from the earlier and more developed civilizations of the Near East and Egypt, Greece and Rome laid the foundations of the Western world. We will examine the political, economic, and cultural evolution of these first of Western peoples.

Politically, the Greeks developed the first Western city–states between 750 and 300 BCE. Between 500 BCE and CE 500, the overlapping Roman Empire grew to encompass the shores of the Mediterranean and much of western Europe. Both the participatory democracy developed by Athens and other Greek city–states and the order, prosperity, and sheer scale of imperial Rome greatly impressed and influenced later Western peoples.

Economically, the Greeks and Romans moved from peasant farming to large-scale commercial agriculture. They also developed handicraft industries and building skills of great sophistication. Both were trading peoples: Greek commerce spread around the Mediterranean and Black seas, and the Roman Empire became part of an intercontinental network of trade that reached as far as China.

Culturally, the Greeks are usually seen as more innovative, more intellectually adventurous, and more artistically creative than the Romans. In philosophy, science, art, and literature Greek civilization influenced all later Western cultures. The Romans, on the other hand, were masters of such practical arts as engineering, law, and government. And it was during the period of Roman rule that Christianity was born and spread from the Near East into the Western world.

A look at the map on page 106 indicates how this first formulation of Western society and civilization had spread by the time Rome fell in the fifth century CE. Greek trade and colonies were scattered from the western end of the Mediterranean to the eastern end of the Black Sea. The mighty Roman Empire had conquered almost all the peoples around the Mediterranean Sea, extending its rule well into the Near East and across North Africa. Rome had then extended its sway northward across Europe, absorbing Celtic and Germanic peoples and spreading through France, Spain, England, and parts of Germany and the Balkans.

The West of ancient times must have been a very different place from the Western world we know. Its centers were its cities, with their temples, law courts, market places, amphitheaters, aqueducts, and large tenement neighborhoods. But most early Western people lived in the country, farming or herding, following the round of the seasons to produce the food, clothing, and other things that all societies need. The Greek philosopher Socrates debating basic human values in the Athenian marketplace, Augustus Caesar ruling the Western world from the seven hills of Rome, and the unknown millions whose labor built both Athens and the Roman Empire were all part of the founding generations, the first builders of the Western world.

1

Time Line: Ancient Times

c. 3500	Sumerians build the first city–states
c. 3500	Sumerians invent cuneiform writing
c. 3200	Menes unifies Egypt, founds first nation
c. 2600	Pharaohs build the pyramids at Giza
2500–1500	Minoans build a center on the island of Crete, spread their commercial predominance around the Aegean Sea
c. 1750	Hammurabi issues Code of Laws
1500–1100	Mycenaean warriors dominate Greece, raid and trade around the Aegean
1200	Hittites introduce ironworking
1000–960	David founds kingdom of Israel
c. 800	Homer
800–300	Hebrew prophets develop monotheism
750–500	Greeks build city–states on Greek mainland, Aegean islands; Greek colonies and trade spread around Mediterranean
c. 600	Sappho
539	Cyrus founds Persian Empire
508	Cleisthenes' reforms at Athens build a more democratic political system
499–449	Persian Wars turn back Asian invaders, bring Athens leadership of the Greek city–states
469–399	Socrates
460–429	Pericles in power, completes structure of Athenian democracy, builds the Athenian Empire
400s	Classical Greek golden age—Greek drama, first historians, temples on the Athenian Acropolis
429–327	Plato
404	Sparta defeats Athens, destroys Athenian Empire
384–322	Aristotle
336–323	Alexander the Great conquers Persian Empire
323–30	Hellenistic monarchies rule eastern Mediterranean, Egypt, Near East
320–50 BCE	Hellenistic culture spreads—Hellenization of Near East
c. 300	Epicurus and Zeno
265	Rome rules all Italy
218–201	Second Punic War—Hannibal ravages Italy, but Rome emerges victorious
133–31	Roman Civil War—politicians and generals struggle for power
70 BCE–CE 19	Vergil
48–44	Julius Caesar defeats Pompey, seizes power; Caesar is murdered
31 BCE–CE 14	Augustus Caesar wins struggle for power in Rome, brings peace, prosperity
31 BCE–CE 14	Rome's "Augustan" golden age—Latin literature
31 BCE–CE 180	Roman Peace in Mediterranean and Western Europe
3 BCE–CE 29/30	Jesus
64	Nero's persecution of Christians
180–284	Third–century economic and political breakdown; Diocletian restores order to the empire under rigidly authoritarian regime
313	Constantine legalizes Christianity
378–532	Germanic invasions of Roman Empire
476	Rome falls as last Roman emperor surrenders power

— 1 —

Shadows of the Pyramids
The World Before the West

♦Prehistoric Peoples   ♦Mesopotamia and the First Cities
♦Egypt and the Growth of Centralized Monarchy
♦Persia Unites the Near East   ♦The Hebrews and Ethical Monotheism

The search for the beginnings of Western history will take us back to a time before history began—and to places outside the Western world altogether. For like all histories, that of the West began in prehistoric times. And like all cultures, Western civilization was significantly influenced by the civilizations of other peoples. These prehistoric and non–Western roots of Western history are the focus of this first chapter.

The first ancestors of all human beings apparently appeared some five million years ago in southeastern Africa. Over many thousands of generations, these early prehumans evolved and spread until modern human beings were found around the world. While our ancestors were developing biologically, they were also evolving culturally. The earliest peoples were food gatherers and hunters who made tools out of stone and lived in small roving bands. Later generations discovered how to produce their own food and settled in small agricultural villages. From these beginnings the ancient cities and larger states in which civilization was born developed not much more than five thousand years ago.

These first civilizations emerged in the fertile river valleys of Mesopotamia (Iraq today) and Egypt shortly before 3000 BCE. Around these first cities, kingdoms, and empires, many Near Eastern peoples developed their own societies: among these were the Hittites, the Phoenicians, the Persians, and the Hebrews. From the pattern of culture that took shape among these peoples around the eastern end of the Mediterranean Sea, the Greeks and the Romans, the first of Western peoples, drew freely in building their own civilizations.

♦Prehistoric Peoples♦

In the raw, stony gash of Olduvai Gorge in Tanzania, East Africa, a visitor can easily pick up—but will not be allowed to keep—fossil–bearing rock from the slopes and trails. Fossilized bone and chipped flint tools make up the majority of the evidence we have about prehistory, and Olduvai Gorge is one of the most famous of all quarries of such remains. It was the renowned archaeologist team of Mary and Louis Leakey who, in 1959, uncovered in this maze of sunbleached, broken stone, the fossil evidence that established what is believed to be the African genesis of the human race.

Archaeologists like Mary Leakey go out every day to comb the earth for these bones and stones. From pieces of rock that were not edged by nature and from bits of human bone so small that only a trained eye can recognize them, scientists have pieced together the story of our prehistoric past. The brief outline that follows will summarize that story, from food–gathering humanity to food–producing people, from the first chippers of flint to the people who reared the walls and towers of the earliest human civilizations.

Paleolithic Food-Gathering Peoples

Our prehistoric ancestry apparently goes back tens of millions of years to small lemur–like creatures who lived by picking fruit and catching insects among the branches of primeval forests. The descendants of these furry tree dwellers include many now extinct genera and species of the broad family of *hominids,* or humanlike creatures. About five million years ago, a number of prehuman types emerged in Africa, including the *australopithecines,* or "southern apemen," and the beginnings of the genus *Homo*—our own direct ancestors. Along this line of development came *Homo habilis* ("the toolmaker"), dating from approximately two million BCE; *Homo erectus* ("one who walks erect"), emerging more than one and a half million years ago; and finally *Homo sapiens* ("wise or thinking human being"), perhaps two hundred thousand years ago. The two types of *Homo sapiens* known to us are the *Neanderthals* (c. 125,000–35,000 BCE) and the *Cro-Magnons,* found at least as far back as 40,000 BCE. The Cro-Magnons are usually seen as our own direct ancestors: biologically, we differ scarcely at all from these people of forty millennia ago.[1]

Two fundamentally different ways of life evolved among these prehistoric hominids. The earliest was the food–gathering mode, which prevailed during the *Paleolithic,* or Old Stone Age (*paleo* derives from the Greek for "ancient"; *lithos* is the Greek word for "stone") that lasted from perhaps five million years ago until perhaps 10,000 BCE. The later and much shorter phase of our prehistoric social evolution was the food–producing stage called the *Neolithic,* or New Stone Age, between perhaps 10,000 and roughly 3500 BCE.

Our earliest, tree–dwelling forebears, who lived tens of millions of years ago, were probably primarily vegetarians, eating mainly nuts and berries and other fruit among the branches. When they descended from the trees, they began to eat more meat, though they continued to collect and consume vegetable food.

To operate this simple subsistence economy, these prehistoric populations made a major breakthrough early in their cultural evolution: they invented tools. At least two million years ago, Paleolithic prehumans were fashioning primitive implements out of chipped stone, later of bone and wood as well. Especially in the later Paleolithic period, "tool kits," as archaeologists call them, included sharp awls for piercing animal hides, bone sickles for cutting wild grains, stone chisels for working with wood, and spearpoints and arrowheads made of an easily–chipped stone called flint.

Paleolithic people responded to the periodic descent of the glaciers with another whole range of ingenious and practical inventions. Having first simply wrapped themselves in animal skins, they learned to construct Eskimo–style parkas, with clearly shaped arms and legs and in some cases hoods. They learned to preserve and then to kindle fire, both

Chronology 1: Mesopotamia and Egypt

c. 3500	*Sumerians build the first city–states, invent cuneiform writing*
c. 3200	*Menes unifies Egypt, founds the first nation*
c. 2700	*Old Kingdom pharaohs build pyramids at Giza*
c. 2600	*Egyptians develop large–scale irrigation along the Nile*
c. 2300	*Sargon of Akkad builds the first empire*
1750	*Hammurabi's Code of Laws*
1503–1482	*Hatshepsut encourages trade, sends expedition down the Red Sea*
1469–1436	*Thutmose III pushes into Near East, builds Egyptian Empire*
1379–1362	*Akhenaton attempts to convert Egypt to monotheism*
1200	*Hittites introduce ironworking*
c. 1300	*Moses leads Hebrews out of Egypt; Ten Commandments*
1000–750	*Phoenicians trade length of the Mediterranean*
800–300	*Hebrew prophets develop monotheism*
539	*Cyrus founds Persian Empire*

for cooking and for warmth. They not only turned caves and other rock shelters into homes, but built stone huts and rude tents out of hides draped over poles, stones, or the bones of large animals they had killed. In the later Paleolithic period, the range of the simple spear was extended first by the *atlatl*, or throwing stick, then by the bow and arrow. Fishhooks and even harpoons were used by shore–dwelling peoples. Pit traps were employed to catch some game, and other animals were driven over cliffs or into swamps to provide Stone Age hunters with a feast.

The basic food–gathering band probably comprised two or three dozen people for most of prehistory, perhaps increasing to seventy–five or a hundred in some communities in the later Paleolithic period. These small groups probably lived in relatively egalitarian societies. Where there was little material wealth or political power to contend for, there was probably also comparatively little exploitation or oppression of one person by another. Human beings, some anthropologists have urged, did not develop strong hierarchical distinctions based on class or gender until they had developed more complex societies.

Such hunter–gatherer bands, however, probably inaugurated the basic division of labor, primarily by gender, that is still found among foraging peoples today. Women, girls, and the younger boys gathered vegetable foods such as fruit, nuts, and edible roots. Men and older boys rose in the predawn hours to hunker down around a distant water hole, waiting for deer or smaller game to come within reach of their spears. Thus women may have dominated the base camp, and men the hunting grounds.

Men and women both contributed to the social cohesion of the group as a whole. Paleolithic men, operating as hunters, may have learned very early the value of teamwork. Like a wolf pack or a pride of lions today, hominid hunters probably worked together to corner and destroy their larger or faster prey. Probably, too, they divided up the meat thus secured as hunting peoples do today, awarding different portions of the kill to each member of the band according to a code based on kinship or other traditional rules. Such sharing, like teamwork in the hunt, helped to strengthen the group's social bonds.

Operating out of the base camp, meanwhile, women as gatherers probably provided the more dependable source of food for the entire band. The berry bushes, after all, were there every morning; whether the deer came by the water hole or not was more problematical. In addition, women, who bore children and had the major burden of raising them, were probably the primary educators in many basic matters. Presiding over the family and

5

providing the largest part of the food supply, women made a further contribution to the sense of community that could mean survival itself to prehistoric peoples.

Beyond these important economic, technological, and social developments, the Neanderthal and Cro-Magnon peoples, in particular, produced some surprisingly impressive artwork and the beginnings, at least, of religious beliefs. An early expression of an aesthetic sense, for example, was the development of personal adornment. It is believed that Old Stone Age people may have painted or tattooed their bodies, as many peoples have since. In addition, large numbers of prehistoric beads and other articles intended to adorn the person have been found. And if what sculpture we have from the period is to be trusted, some Paleolithic women bound their hair up in buns behind their heads, whereas others wore it in a frizzy style that resembled some modern-day hairdos.

More striking artistic achievements include the famous cave art of our Cro-Magnon forebears. The walls of caves like those at Lascaux in the Dordogne region of southwestern France and Altamira in northern Spain, for instance, glow with paintings dating to 30,000 BCE and earlier. Simple relief carvings, clay sculpture, and carved stone, bone, and ivory also reveal the artistic impulses and talents of our ancestors. Depictions of animals predominate, including such large game as horses, deer, bison, and mammoths. Not infrequently, the contour of a reindeer horn or the bulge of a painted bison's shoulder reveal both the painter's familiarity with the prehistoric world and genuine artistry.

Early religious beliefs may have included the worship of some of these animals. Among the Neanderthals, for example, the careful placement of cave–bear skulls in niches or other prominent places may indicate a "bear cult" as far back as 100,000 BCE. The fact that some of the animals painted on Cro-Magnon cave walls thirty thousand years ago are pierced by spears or arrows may reveal belief in "sympathetic magic" of the sort often practiced by hunting peoples in later times. According to this ancient faith, if the shaman or priest draws an arrow piercing a pictured animal, a real arrow will strike home in the field the next day. Small stone "Venus figurines" of women, who were often depicted as big breasted and pregnant, may be symbols of fertility designed to bring about human and animal births as well as the growth of food plants. Such fertility cults were also found among many later peoples.

Paleolithic burial customs also suggest religious beliefs. The dead of both sexes were sometimes buried in clothing decorated with beads, surrounded by tools and weapons, and painted with red ocher or even sprinkled with flowers. Such practices seem to suggest reverence and affection, perhaps even an intuition of personal immortality, an afterlife in which beads and tools might still be of use to the departed. Beliefs that would become widespread throughout human history may thus predate the birth of civilization by many thousands of years.

Neolithic Food-Producing Peoples

Cro-Magnon people carried the culture of food–gathering humanity about as far as it could go and then moved on, around 10,000 BCE to the first genuine revolution in the history of the human race. This *Neolithic Revolution* was not, of course, a political upheaval— there were no political institutions to revolutionize in those simpler societies. It was, however, a drastic transformation in the economic, technological, and social and cultural life of humankind. Its primary achievement was the invention of agriculture, a new economy involving both the cultivation of the soil and the domestication of animals.

The resulting agricultural revolution probably began hind end foremost—that is, with harvesting rather than with planting. "Food gathering," after all, is simply the harvesting of food plants found growing wild in nature. Food gatherers, who had learned when each fruit or root or wild grain would ripen, could easily have noticed that a little care—such as watering and weeding—produced a more bountiful harvest. They might also have noticed the sprouting of kernels of wild wheat or barley where grain had been stored or cast aside unconsumed. With the herds they preyed on dwindling, perhaps with the population growing, some groups of prehistoric people decided to settle down and tend the richest crops right through the growing season, from sowing time to harvest.

The most likely architects of this crucial transformation of human life were women, who as food gatherers were most likely to understand the life cycles of vegetable foods. We may imagine these prehistoric gatherers, then, watering wild barley when the band arrived at the end of a scorching summer, pulling weeds or plucking insects from the leaves, and scattering a portion of the harvest on the ground—perhaps as a form of sacrifice—to be rewarded by a new crop in the next growing season.

Although the cultivation of the soil was central to the agricultural revolution, the domestication of animals was almost equally important. Animals, like plants, could be tended and kept under human control, rather than sought out in the wild. The people of the New Stone Age thus came to herd and pen up animals and to slaughter them as needed rather than when they could be found. Sheep, goats, and pigs were among the first beasts to be domesticated in this way.

Stone was still the primary hard material used for tools by Neolithic peoples, and textiles and ceramics also came into use during this period. The knives they carved with and the sickles they used to cut their grain were still bladed or edged with stone. But it was stone worked to a new standard of excellence, no longer chipped and rough edged, but carefully smoothed and polished. The people of the New Stone Age, furthermore, learned to make pots out of clay—at first coiled by hand, then shaped on the potter's wheel—to produce ceramic jars for both cooking and storing food. The craftspeople of Neolithic times also discovered the art of weaving animal hair or vegetable fibers into cloth, and the resulting wool and linen textiles slowly replaced animal hides as human clothing.

It is likely that society remained very close knit in Neolithic agricultural villages, despite their larger populations and greater social complexity. Family and clan ties were as important as they had been in the Paleolithic period. Labor was probably still divided between the sexes, as it had been in food–gathering bands. Men now probably did much of the agricultural labor, though women joined them in the fields, and children could herd sheep or goats on the surrounding hillsides.

We know that personal adornment, music, and dancing flourished among these last generations of prehistoric people in the Near East. Although their tools were still of stone, they were already decorating themselves with beads made out of copper. We have pictures on roughly plastered walls of men dancing, beating what appear to be tambourines and waving what are clearly bows. It is apparently a hunting dance among a people who had not yet entirely abandoned the ways of their ancestors.

We may, finally, carry our educated guesses about Neolithic religion beyond what the artifacts reveal. Religion among preurban Native Americans or African agricultural villagers, for instance, tends to be animistic. Animists see all nature—plants, animals, streams, mountains, stars—as living beings, and as in some sense divine. Some of the earliest rituals and hymns of ancient civilizations also invoked, not anthropomorphic gods and goddesses, but spiritual presences within the forces of nature. Thus it seems quite likely that Neolithic farmers also prayed to natural forces, much as their Paleolithic ancestors had sought through the shaman's magic to bring the deer to the hunter's spear.

Women may have played an important part in this religious and ritual activity. There is some evidence of archaic religions in the Mediterranean region centered on a mother goddess, later shouldered aside when predominantly male–run city–states absorbed the surrounding villages. The priestesses who served this primordial goddess may have presided over annual sacrifices to ensure good harvests and abundant flocks. They may also have been shamans, serving as spirit mediums through whom the dead were believed to communicate with the living.

The Emergence of Civilization

Who has not felt the fascination of buried cities and lost civilizations? Mounds of earth, swarms of workers, and a handful of people in Bermuda shorts and pith helmets—this is modern *archaeology,* as we have come to know it from countless films, television programs, and the *National Geographic* magazine. Men and women of many nations have been excavating ancient Near Eastern sites like Ur and Babylon or Egypt's Karnak and Valley of the Kings for the past century and a half.

From Mesopotamian times on, furthermore, we begin to have *documents,* or written records of past events: prehistory gives way to recorded history. The invention of writing was a major achievement of the first civilized peoples, and the written material that survives provides the documentation on which historians have traditionally depended. From the clay tablets of Mesopotamia to Egyptian papyri, ancient tax rolls, religious texts, and the annals of royal conquests tell us much of what the builders of the first cities and empires did, thought, and believed.

From these two types of sources, archaeological and documentary, we may thus conjure up at least a hazy vision of the first *civilizations*—the first societies possessing centralized, bureaucratic governments, social classes, cities and larger states, and such skills as literacy, metal–work, and long–distance trade.

Even the first civilizations were quite a departure from the food–gathering bands and agricultural villages of earlier peoples. After so many centuries in these earlier communities, one has to ask, Why? Why did human beings put themselves to the labor of building cities and civilizations in the first place?

Population growth was certainly part of the expansion from villages to cities, in the Near East as elsewhere. Denser concentrations of people probably occurred in river valleys as swamps along the rivers dried out, producing rich farmland that could be watered from the rivers themselves. Expanding populations may also have led to feuds between cities over arable land, to wars of conquest, and hence to still larger political units, the first empires. These larger polities also typically came to be dominated by upper classes, an elite who sought to strengthen the state and to control and exploit their neighbors to advance their own interests.

As important as any of these causal factors, finally, were the state–building efforts of such charismatic leaders as Hammurabi of Babylon and Cyrus, the founder of the Persian Empire. As we will see, kings were frequently war leaders, and their victories and conquests not only expanded their realms but strengthened royal government. A militarized aristocracy and a large royal army also undoubtedly added to the power of the central state. But governments also undertook large–scale flood control and irrigation works. The benefits

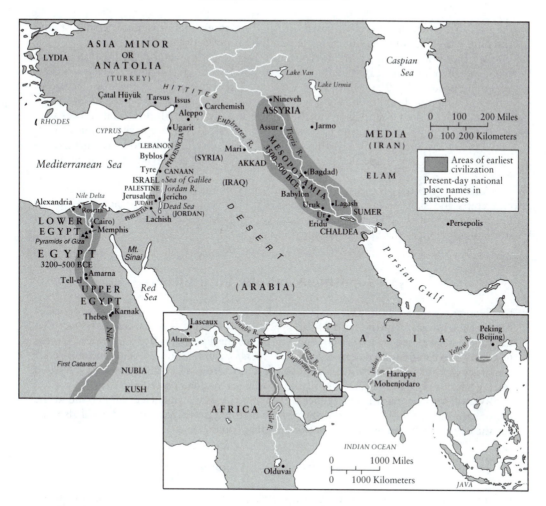

Early Centers of Civilization, 3500–500 BCE

conferred on all by the control of the river further encouraged people to accept the author-ity of the state.

The result of the coming together of all these elements was the birth of civilization it-self. The word *civilization* may be used to describe virtually any culture, from surviving food gatherers to the modern urban–industrial state. Here, however, the term is used in a strictly technical sense. Civilization was a new stage of human social and cultural evolution that produced more complex political, economic, and social structures, systems of thought, and artistic expression than was possible in earlier, simpler societies.

With civilization was born the city, the city–state, and the empire. Autocratic rulers presided over these states, generally working closely with priests and claiming divine sanc-tion for their rule. Bureaucracy developed with the officials and scribes who administered the state. Social classes emerged, based on the development of private ownership of land and on the diversity of social functions required by a more complex economy.

Another prime characteristic of civilization was a much greater diversity of crafts and skills: metalwork, large–scale building, long–distance trade, and writing. Metals—bronze beginning around 4000 BCE, iron after 1200 BCE—replaced stone in the manufacture of tools and weapons. Local exchange of goods expanded among civilized peoples into long-distance trade in such essentials as metals, fabrics, and ceramics. Monumental edifices such as city walls, temples, palaces, and tombs provide impressive evidence of the technical virtuosity of early civilizations. And writing—on clay, stone, parchment, and other materials—comes as close as any single skill can to drawing a line between civilized and precivilized peoples.

All these features—the city, the state, autocracy, bureaucracy, social classes, and complex crafts and skills—were found in the Eastern civilizations that first appeared in the fourth millennium BCE. They were also characteristics of the Western societies that evolved substantially later, in the first millennium before Christ.

✦ Mesopotamia and the First Cities ✦

Civilization, as we know it, first arose around 3500 BCE in Mesopotamia, the wide valley running northwest from the head of the Persian Gulf in what is today Iraq. The fact that the valley was watered by two rivers, the Tigris and the Euphrates, led the ancient Greeks to give this civilization the descriptive name of *Mesopotamia,* "the land between the rivers." This ancient river valley provided fertile soil for agriculture and the basis for a city–based society far more complex than the agricultural villages that had preceded it.

We will look here at the emergence of the first city–states in ancient Sumer and at the rise of early empires in Ur, Babylon, and Assyria further up the river valley. We will also survey the cultural achievements of these remarkable peoples.

The City-States of Sumer

Before human beings attempted to control them, the Tigris and Euphrates produced erratic and destructive flooding, ending in a plain of reedy swamps and pools at their juncture near the gulf. Once tamed by human works, however, the waters of the two rivers began to turn the wide flat valley between them into enormously productive agricultural land.

Some of the earliest Neolithic agricultural villages in the world had developed before 8000 BCE in the grassy uplands of northern Mesopotamia, in an area known as the Syrian steppe. Here were rain enough for farming, wild plant and animal food to fall back on as needed, and rivers that allowed for some tentative experimentation in irrigation when the rains failed. Between 5000 and 4000 BCE, some of these Neolithic farmers moved on down the rivers into the region of Sumeria, or Sumer, the southern portion of the land of the two rivers, taking with them grains and flocks of sheep and goats. Here they could harvest dates from the palm trees and spear fish in the marshes. Here, too, a little diking and draining produced rich soil, bountiful crops of wheat and barley, and a swelling population. And here, in ancient Sumer, the first cities in the world—cities with names like Ur, Uruk, Eridu, Lagash and Akkad—gradually took shape.

Specialization of labor developed as the villagers built temples to offer thanks to the gods for their prosperity. That portion of the villagers' produce intended for the gods was channeled by priests to people who, freed of agricultural labor, began to specialize in craftwork. One of the first technological breakthroughs that resulted from this specialization of labor was the production of bronze. This alloy of copper and tin proved hard enough to replace stone in tools, weapons, and other useful objects. Thus, about 4000 BCE, the Stone Age gave way to the Bronze Age, during which craftworkers began to produce beautiful jewelry, fabrics, and other luxury goods. Some of these products, furthermore, went to traders, often agents of the temples. This new class of merchants exchanged these goods with other peoples for such basic raw materials as wood and building stone, for Sumer's only natural resources were rich soil and plenty of water.

As opportunities for trade grew, people developed new and better methods of transportation. At first, merchants used mules and other beasts of burden to carry their goods. The invention of the wheel, either in Sumeria or earlier, in Neolithic times, enabled people to construct carts that could carry much greater loads. Mesopotamians also constructed crude rafts or early boats of reeds or inflated bladders, though the Nile would be the first real home of larger vessels propelled by sails.

It was around the temples of Mesopotamia that the first cities emerged about 3500 BCE. These growing communities of priests, artisans, and traders, including both their

It is traditional to call this bronze head Sargon of Akkad, history's first empire-builder, although we do not know that this casting of an Akkadian ruler is actually Sargon. The hawk-like visage and intricately dressed beard do give this face an aura of power, perhaps even menace. (Iraq Museum)

homes and places of work and worship, were protected by high walls. Some cities had popular assemblies dominated by groups of elders, a legacy from the agricultural village. City assemblies, however, served in a primarily judicial function; they had little real political power. For centuries, it was the priests, as servants of the gods, who were the most powerful element in the typical city.

Gradually, however, city governors, usually successful war leaders, overshadowed their rivals and assumed the leadership of the cities. Attacks by nomads from the Arabian desert or the Syrian steppe to the west, or from the mountains of Iran to the east, strengthened the authority of these military leaders. In time, the city governors made their power hereditary and announced that they were the chief stewards of the gods on earth. These new rulers took the title of *lugal* (literally "big man") and became the first kings in history.

The cities dominated the surrounding villages, producing a combination of metropolitan center and agrarian hinterland called the city–state. By 3000 BCE, there were perhaps fifteen or twenty such city–states, most with populations of between twenty and thirty thousand people. Few were more than a hundred square miles in extent, the size of a modern county.

A developed Mesopotamian city was laid out on a rectangular plan, with high walls, watchtowers, and tall gates. Its distinctive stepped pyramids called *ziggurats,* each crowned with a shrine to a god or goddess, dominated temple complexes and threw long shadows over the city walls and the land beyond. The sprawling royal palaces, built around a series of courtyards, included impressive throne rooms and many private chambers, thick walled, dim, and cool. Wealthy nobles and merchants lived in similarly elaborate homes. Broad avenues intended for ceremonial processions bisected the metropolis. Most streets, however, were narrow winding lanes, and most houses were little more than cubicles, crammed as close together as the living quarters of medieval Baghdad or modern Cairo.

Beyond the city walls, the tiny farming villages along the rivers were now enmeshed in a network of dikes, canals, and irrigation ditches. Wheat and barley, date palms and fruit trees stood tall against the rainless blue sky. On the road, a creaking two-wheeled cart or a caravan of donkeys laden with goods might pass. On the river, one might see a raft with a flapping sail. More rarely, there might be soldiers with long spears, or a nobleman borne in a sedan chair on the shoulders of his servants.

The Empires of Ur and Babylon

The names of city–states and kings filter down to us across the centuries, inscribed on stone or incised in clay. Although it is difficult to place people and events with precision in so distant a past, we do know that cities like Uruk, Lagash and Ur rose in the early Sumerian centuries, around 3000 BCE.

We even have the likenesses of some of the long forgotten kings of these cities, and records of the deeds of which they were proudest. There is, for instance, a broken bronze head that may represent the hawklike face of Sargon of Akkad, history's first great conqueror. Sargon, around 2300 BCE, led his Semitic peoples down from the central reaches of the Tigris and Euphrates rivers into the Sumerian cities, where they established a short–lived Akkadian rule over the southern plain.

The much excavated city of Ur seems to have been a splendid example of the developed Mesopotamian city–state. The largest of the early Sumerian cities, Ur had an elaborate system of dikes and canals that irrigated the surrounding fields. The merchants of Ur traded northward up the rivers and eastward, across the Arabian Sea, with other city–states that had sprung up along the Indus River in what is today Pakistan. The kings of Ur enforced laws, collected taxes, and around 2000 BCE briefly dominated the surrounding Sumerian cities.

Hammurabi of Babylon (r. 1792–1750 BCE), however, has over the centuries become the most famous of all Mesopotamian kings. He was the ruler of the Amorites—like the Akkadians, a Semitic people—who had established themselves at Babylon, in central Mesopotamia, where they were in a position to dominate the entire valley between the two rivers. The records we have of Hammurabi's reign illustrate the functioning of the developed Mesopotamian monarchy at its best.

We have royal correspondence on clay tablets that reveals Hammurabi supervising his scribes, a small but recognizable government bureaucracy. His public inscriptions declare that, in addition to meting out royal justice and defending the state, he built roads and kept up the all–important system of irrigation canals. But the great Babylonian ruler is best known for his code of almost three hundred laws—the earliest such developed code in history.

Hammurabi's Code has survived in the form in which he presented it to his people, inscribed on a stele (a stone slab or pillar) crowned with carvings of the king himself and of the god in whose name he claimed to speak. The legal principles thus set out included some very brutal punishments clearly aimed at retribution rather than reform. The code also emphasized class differences, prescribing one punishment for a noble, another for a commoner, and a third for slaves. Women and men of the same class, on the other hand, tended to get the same legal treatment.

But Hammurabi's Code meant more than institutionalized vengeance and rigid social hierarchy. It incorporated a sense of justice and tried to make the punishment fit the crime. Women had independent legal standing, and the laws even gave them rights against their husbands. There were economic regulations too, dealing with business contracts, debt, minimum wages, and irrigation practices. Many of these regulations were clearly built on centuries–old Mesopotamian traditions. For some historians, however, the very fact that this ancient law code was displayed in a public place, rather than remaining the special concern of magistrates or priests, is evidence that Hammurabi was a genuine reformer. There may be at least a modicum of truth in the Babylonian king's summation of his own achievements: "I promoted the welfare of the land . . . I made the peoples to rest in friendly habitations. . . . I have governed them in peace; I have sheltered them in my strength."[2]

The Assyrian Empire

The center of Mesopotamian power moved slowly up the two rivers, from Sumer in the southeast to Babylon in central Mesopotamia and finally to Assyria, in the hilly northwestern reaches of the valley of the two rivers. From their capital at Nineveh, within marching distance of the eastern Mediterranean, the Assyrians were well situated to strike at the other city–states and kingdoms that had emerged in the Near East and North Africa by this time. The Assyrian rulers thus built an empire that reached well beyond the confines of Mesopotamia early in the first millennium BCE.

During the period of greatest Assyrian power, from 900 to 600 BCE, war leaders like Sargon II (r. 722–706 BCE) and Ashurbanipal (r. 668–627 BCE) were the terror of their Near Eastern neighbors. These aggressive rulers made annual military campaigns a primary activity of the state. To acquire the rich booty depicted by their wall sculptures, to glorify their chief god Ashur, and perhaps to erect a wall of fear that would keep their enemies at bay, the Assyrian kings marched out each year to fight.

Incessant fighting imposed a semipermanent Assyrian suzerainty, or overlordship, on around the southeastern corner of the Mediterranean, including today's Iraq, Syria, Israel, and Egypt. Governors and garrisons imposed a loosely centralized administrative system supervised by the "King of the World" in Nineveh. The most famous Assyrian monarchs were also great builders: Sennacherib (r. 705–682 BCE) built a famous aqueduct, and Ashurbanipal constructed a library containing more than twenty thousand clay tablets dealing with learned subjects from history to astronomy.

Among contemporaries, however, it was the pain that was remembered. The militaristic Assyrians littered their path through history with flaming cities, deported populations, and the spectacle of leading citizens impaled, flayed, or burned alive in front of their own shattered city gates. There was no weeping when, in 612 BCE, an alliance of rival powers finally overwhelmed Assyria, and Nineveh itself was sacked and burned.

Chief among those who brought Assyria down was the last Mesopotamian power to rule the Tigris–Euphrates valley: the New Babylonian, or Chaldean, Empire. Flourishing briefly during the late seventh and the first half of the sixth century BCE, this second Babylonian hegemony extended almost as far as the Assyrian Empire had, around the Fertile Crescent through Syria and Palestine to the frontiers of Egypt. The greatest ruler of the

Gods of ancient Sumer, the oldest of all human civilizations. When Sumerian armies captured a neighboring city-state, they triumphantly carried off such clay representations of their enemies' gods into "captivity." (Oriental Institute)

New Babylonian Empire, Nebuchadnezzar II (r. 604–562 BCE), defeated the Egyptians at Carchemish, captured Jerusalem, and carried the Jews into their Babylonian captivity. He built and refurbished many temples, raised the famous walls of Babylon, and constructed the celebrated "hanging gardens," a terraced ziggurat–style royal park considered one of the wonders of the ancient world.

High Culture in Mesopotamia

We know more about the ancient Mesopotamians, however, than the physical appearance of their cities and the names and deeds of a scattering of kings. From the ruins of this oldest of civilizations, archaeologists and historians have sifted the evidence of religious beliefs, scientific discoveries, architecture, art, and literature—the cultural achievements, in short, of this vanished civilization.

Mesopotamian religion, like that of most early civilizations, was polytheistic. The people of the Mesopotamian city–states worshiped such divinities as Enlil, "lord wind," the chief divinity of ancient Sumer; Anu, the god of the sky; Ninhursag, "lady of the mountain"; Enki, lord of the waters; and Ishtar, the "queen of heaven" and goddess of war, identified with the planet Venus. Over centuries, individual divinities acquired broader religious meanings. Thus Ishtar came to preside over love, fertility, and creative power. Each city–state had its own patron divinity, and when one city triumphed over the others, its principal god was soon recognized as chief among the heavenly host. Thus the Assyrian sun god, Assur, enjoyed preeminence during the Assyrian ascendancy, as did Marduk, the patron god of Babylon, during the New Babylonian Empire.

Besides the great gods and goddesses, there were large numbers of spirits, demons, and other supernatural entities to be placated, consulted, and feared. Particularly in hard times, when floods or wars devastated the land, people flocked to their temples, consulted astrologers and diviners, and went in terror of demonic forces. Even in the best of times, Mesopotamians would not embark on a commercial venture or a military campaign, shape a brick, or bring forth a child without consultation with stargazers or prayers to the gods.

Yet Mesopotamians were also scientific observers of the heavens, creative mathematicians, and the inventors of the first developed system of writing. The ancient Sumerians were the first people we know to map the night sky, and the Babylonians were as celebrated for their astronomical knowledge as for their alleged astrological insights. They charted the constellations of the zodiac, noted the movement of the planets, and developed a calendar and a water clock to measure time. The Mesopotamian peoples invented a number system based on multiples of six and twelve, and they were the first to divide the circle into 360 degrees and the hour into sixty minutes, mathematical conventions now accepted around the world. Most important, about 4000 BCE, the Sumerians developed the first system of writing, the cuneiform ("wedge–shaped") script with which they wrote on clay.

Writing was not invented for literary purposes. In fact, the scribes who developed the first form of writing had nothing more artistic in mind than counting sheep. Sheep, cattle, measures of grain, and jars of oil changed hands repeatedly through sale, taxation, the collection of "temple fifths," and in various other ways. Writing was originally a simple tally system for recording these transactions. It began with a quick picture of a sheep, followed by a mark for each animal that passed through the gate. As civilization grew more complex and the necessary records more complicated, the number of symbols grew. The little pictures became a few conventional strokes that caught the essence of the idea: each symbol represented a thing. To these symbols were soon added characters that stood for the sounds of syllables in spoken Sumerian. Both symbols of things and symbols of sounds could then be combined to represent longer words. It is easy to see why such a system required study at a special school.

Although it was the temple, the palace, and the bazaar that utilized writing first, in time, cuneiform script did begin to be used to record early types of literature. Some of these ancient Mesopotamian literary forms were also found later in the Bible. For example, Mesopotamian proverbs foreshadow those attributed to King Solomon; Mesopotamian songs find an echo in Hebrew psalms; and there are hero tales in the writings of both peoples. Not surprisingly, the Mesopotamians, who lived in fear of river flooding, produced a flood story comparable to that of the Bible's Noah. And among the earliest pieces of literature in the world that can be attributed to a known author is a hymn to the goddess Inanna, ascribed to the poet Enheduana, the daughter of Sargon of Akkad.

The most famous Mesopotamian hero tale, however, is more often compared to the myths of the Greeks and Romans than to biblical accounts. In the *Epic of Gilgamesh*, a "Mesopotamian Hercules" kills monsters, defies the powerful goddess Ishtar, and finally sets out for the end of the world in search of the secret of eternal life. Gilgamesh fails in his quest, for he is mortal and must die; but his heroic failure remains a powerful example of human courage in the face of an inexorable fate.

♦Egypt and the Growth of Centralized Monarchy♦

West of Mesopotamia, at the northeastern corner of Africa, lay the second great center of ancient Near Eastern civilization: Egypt. In Egypt, however, social evolution beyond the village level produced not a culture of separate city–states but a strongly centralized monarchy.

This section will provide an overview of Egyptian history from the unification of the Nile valley shortly before 3000 BCE through the rise of the Egyptian Empire around 1500. It will also take a brief glance at the cultural achievements of the Egyptians, from the art of the pyramid builders to a religion that moved to the brink of monotheism.

A Kingdom Emerges Along the Nile

Like Mesopotamia, Egypt grew and flourished in a fertile river valley. The Nile valley, however, provided an even more ideal environment for the rise of a great civilization. Even without much human improvement, the Nile flooded evenly, coating the land with a rich silt accumulated over its long journey north from the lakes of central Africa. Further improved by the irrigation works of the pharaohs, the great river produced two crops a year and made Egypt the breadbasket of the Mediterranean world down to Roman times.

The Nile valley also differed from the valley created by the Tigris and Euphrates in its configuration: it was not wide and flat but long and narrow. For most of the 750 miles of its course from the waterfalls of the first cataract to the Mediterranean, the habitable valley was seldom more than 10 miles wide. The northern Nile delta did broaden out into a fan–shaped marshy area like that of Sumer. The rest of ancient Egypt, however, wound like a serpent between the Sahara and the Arabian desert. The crushing heat, the almost total lack of water or vegetation in these neighboring "red lands" made the fertile "black lands" along the river all the more precious to the Egyptians.

The narrowness of the valley and its total dependence on the Nile discouraged the development of separate centers of political power like the Mesopotamian cities. Villages lay close together all along the river, all within easy reach of the power of the ruler. There was little need for cities to develop as independent commercial centers because, at least in early times, this most fortunate of lands needed little from abroad. Thus because there were neither political nor economic reasons for the emergence of urban centers, Egypt was able to move beyond the city–state and develop a centralized monarchy larger and more long lasting than anything in the Near East.

Agricultural villagers from the Sudan and inner Africa settled the upper reaches of the Nile, while Mediterranean peoples established themselves in the delta. In early times, small territorial units comprising several villages developed along the river, each united by allegiance to a totemic animal with which the people felt a special kinship. There was also some loyalty to the "two lands": Lower Egypt, meaning the broad delta area, and Upper Egypt, the long narrow valley to the south. Cultural and social evolution along the Nile proceeded as it had along the Tigris and Euphrates. And around 3150 BCE, after a long interregional struggle, Menes, a prince of Upper Egypt, conquered Lower Egypt. He established his capital at Memphis in the delta, and become the first *pharaoh,* or king, of a united country.

Egypt remained a unified nation for most of the next three thousand years. Thirty–one dynasties, or royal families, of pharaohs—three successive historical Kingdoms called Old, Middle, and New—ruled over the valley of the Nile. Traditionally, the Old Kingdom is dated from approximately 2700 to 2200 BCE, the Middle Kingdom from 2050 to 1800, and the height of the New Kingdom and the Egyptian Empire from 1570 to about 1100 BCE.

A long decline characterized most of the next one thousand years. From about 1000 BCE on, foreign invaders repeatedly conquered and ruled the land. But until Egypt became a province of the Roman Empire in 30 BCE, the kingdom of the Nile remained the most favored of nations, and Egyptians were, in the eyes of their neighbors, the most fortunate of peoples.

Old Kingdom Egypt: The Pyramid Builders

The basic pattern of Egyptian civilization was established during the Old Kingdom dynasties that followed Menes. The Old Kingdom pharaohs were the pyramid builders, and their age was a kind of golden age of peace, plenty, and social justice, at least according to Egyptians of later centuries.

The Egyptians went one step further than the Mesopotamians in the crucial matter of divinely sanctioned rule. Mesopotamian rulers claimed to be stewards or bailiffs of the gods, but pharaohs claimed to be gods themselves. Each pharaoh was, in fact, identified with more than one Egyptian divinity. Born the son of Re, the all–powerful sun, the pharaoh was also an incarnation of the sky–god Horus, and in death, would be united with Osiris, the divine king of the underworld.

Pharaohs could thus claim truly awesome powers. The pharaohs' word was law to all their people, and their will was carried out by a large bureaucracy of trained scribes who collected taxes, supervised the irrigation system, exercised the royal monopoly of foreign trade, organized and equipped the royal armies, and built enormous public works, including royal palaces, temples, and tombs. The pharaohs themselves performed religious ceremonies that were believed to cause the Nile to flood on time and to ensure peace and order. Like Mesopotamian rulers, the pharaohs redistributed much of the wealth of the land through gifts to nobles and officials and through payments to artisans, builders, and others.

The power of Egypt's god–kings was so great that, at least in Old Kingdom times, the development of other potentially important segments of society was significantly stunted. In these early centuries, the organized priesthoods of Re and other gods were properly sub-servient to the god who walked among them. The small merchant class had little promi-nence or social prestige, since the lucrative long–distance trade was run by scribal bureau-crats. The largest structures in Egypt were the royal pyramid tombs built by pharaohs Khufu, Khafre, and Menkaure at Giza between 2600 and 2500 BCE. And the highest ambi-tion of the greatest officials and most noble princes in the land was to merit a tomb in the shadow of the pharaoh's.

It was as autocratic a society as any in ancient history. But like Hammurabi's Babylon, it was not a society without a sense of justice and human decency. Since the pharaoh's word itself was law, there was no need for codes like Hammurabi's. But the pharaoh was ex-pected to rule according to the principles of *ma'at,* a combination of social justice, order, and truth that added up to what the Egyptians saw as righteousness. If individual kings fell short of this social ideal, so have rulers in many times and lands. And there was always an-other pharaoh coming, a new son of Re to bring health and vigor once more to the land and its people.

Between the pharaohs and their hierarchy of power on the one hand and the masses they ruled on the other, there were intermediate social ranks. Skilled artisans worked in bronze, copper, and the precious metals, as well as some of the hardest stones, to produce tools, weapons, and elegant luxury goods. There were workers in cloth, ceramics, wood, and other basic materials. But no one in these middle ranks would dream of aspiring to even a modest tomb in the shadow of the god–king's.

Egyptian peasants, like their distant descendants the *fellaheen* who till the soil today, lived a life of productive toil. Some authorities see them as little better than serfs on the lands of nobles or temples, or forced laborers under the eyes of royal overseers. They did owe large chunks of their produce to the state, and, even more than Mesopotamian peas-ants, gave much labor to irrigation works or to building temples and future tombs for reigning pharaohs. On the other hand, labor on public works seems to have been paid, and hours were sensibly limited, given the blistering heat of the Egyptian sun.

Women also enjoyed more independent status than they did in some later societies. Fe-male members of the royal family had important administrative duties; other women had leading positions in temple cults. Some women practiced such skilled trades as textile man-ufacturing or served as priestesses in the temples, while others worked beside men in the fields. From the Old Kingdom to the end of Egyptian history, women had legal and prop-erty rights equal to men's. Daughters could inherit just as sons could, and women were paid equally for equal work. They were even called up for compulsory labor on government works just as male peasants were, evidence that women were considered as autonomous persons, not as dependents of men.

Middle Kingdom Egypt: Transition to Empire

Toward the end of the third millennium BCE—around 2200—this ordered system began a slow transition toward a more dynamic and expansive Egyptian Empire. This transitional era—the First Intermediate Period—began and ended with periods of social decay and disorder, but the subsequent Middle Kingdom itself pointed to an expansive future for the land of the Nile.

The decline of the First Intermediate Period was perhaps triggered by an unprecedented stretch of low Niles that left the black lands unwatered and the granaries empty. Feuds within the ruling dynasty weakened the central government, and provincial governors grew rebellious. Foreign tribes drifted in from Palestine and from Syria further to the north, sometimes challenging local authorities. Law and order broke down, and the people complained of violence, poverty, and official oppression.

After two troubled centuries, however, the First Intermediate Period ended with the reestablishment of the pharaohs' authority. As in the days of Menes, it was a dynasty from Upper Egypt that swept down the length of the river to power. Amenemhet I (1991–1962 BCE) and his successors of the twelfth dynasty moved the capital upriver from Memphis to Thebes, where the priests of the new sun god, Amen, supported their bid for power. The result was what later scholars have called the Middle Kingdom, which lasted from around 2050 to shortly after 1800 BCE.

The pharaohs of the Middle Kingdom do not seem to have enjoyed the unquestioning reverence that the people had apparently felt for the rulers of the Old Kingdom. Nobles now exercised a good deal of independent regional power. Scribes in the bureaucracy could also become powerful, rising to eminence on the basis of administrative efficiency, political skill, or the mastery of the sacred art of writing. To compensate for the decline in reverence for the monarchy, however, there seems to have been an enhanced sense of justice and public welfare. Officials were exhorted to govern fairly, to reject bribes, and to care for the people according to the ancient principle of ma'at. The pharaohs themselves were often depicted in sculpture with brows furrowed with care for their subjects.

At the same time, however, the pharaohs of the period around 2000 BCE presaged the vaster achievements of the New Kingdom of the next millennium. One hears more of the pharaoh's armies in the Middle Kingdom period, as the Egyptians fought both their African neighbors to the south and the Semitic peoples of Palestine. Trade also expanded. Egyptians had carried the art of shipbuilding beyond the rafts and reed boats of the earliest centuries of civilization to plank–built wooden sailing ships. During the Middle Kingdom, they sailed these vessels out of the Nile and around the eastern Mediterranean. Egyptians traded even as far as the island of Crete, where—as we will see in the next chapter—the seeds of Western civilization were being planted by the seagoing Minoans. What gave the Middle Kingdom its distinctive character was this foreshadowing of the more expansive New Kingdom era to come.

New Kingdom Egypt and the Egyptian Empire

The New Kingdom was the age of the Egyptian Empire, a time of far–reaching trade and foreign conquest. Powerful personalities such as the conqueror Thutmose III, the far–trading pharaoh Hatshepsut, and Akhenaton, the monotheistic pharaoh, made this an exciting time in Egyptian history.

Shortly after 1800 BCE, the Middle Kingdom collapsed as the Old Kingdom had, in a welter of weak government and rebellious nobles and governors. The domestic problems of the Second Intermediate Period that followed were compounded by a wave of intrusions by a nomadic Near Eastern people called the Hyksos. Equipped with fast war chariots and bronze weapons, the Hyksos seized power in the delta and ruled much of the country for a century. They were expelled around 1600 BCE, once again by an aggressive princely house from Upper Egypt led by the brothers Kamose and Ahmose, the younger of whom pursued the Hyksos all the way back to their base of support in Palestine.

The Egyptian victory gave the people of the Nile a new taste for foreign wars and conquests. A succession of militaristic pharaohs, including Thutmose III (r. 1469–1436 BCE) and Ramses II (r. 1290–1224 BCE), assembled a formidable empire for the New Kingdom. In so doing, they also created a new public image for the pharaohs of Egypt: the god–king as warrior, crushing his foes under the churning wheels of his chariot.

A militarized nobility eager for glory, powerful priesthoods pleased at the prestige accumulating to their victorious gods, and a nation dazzled by success and greedy for booty all supported the ambitions of the pharaohs. Equipped with light war chariots, bows, and bronze swords modeled on those of the Hyksos, their armies defeated other peoples from Palestine and Mesopotamia in the north to Nubia, south of the Nile's first cataract. At its height, the Egyptian Empire encompassed Nubia (today's Sudan), Palestine, Syria, and northern Mesopotamia. "I made the boundaries of Egypt as far as . . . the sun encircles," boasted one royal conqueror. "I made Egypt the superior of every land."[3]

Foreign trade also expanded as the Egyptian Empire grew. The pharaohs dispatched caravans and fleets of ships to bring back copper from Sinai, gold from Nubia, and exotic animals from the land of Punt, far down the Red Sea. Slaves and tribute poured in from the empire, and the divine rulers and their nobles lived luxurious lives in brightly decorated palaces and country estates.

One of the most aggressive traders among the pharaohs was Hatshepsut (r. 1503–1482 BCE), the only woman ever to govern the New Kingdom Empire in her own right. Thrusting her way to power as daughter of one pharaoh and widow of another, Hatshepsut appointed talented, ambitious newcomers to high office, encouraged foreign commerce, and was a great builder of public monuments. The trading expedition she dispatched to Punt was described admiringly by the chroniclers. There were more victories and more conquests to come, but Egypt was never wealthier and more splendid than under its great queen, Hatshepsut.

Another colorful ruler of the New Kingdom was Akhenaton (r. 1379–1362 BCE), the strange "heretic pharaoh." In an almost universally polytheistic world, Akhenaton became a monotheist, a believer in an obscure sun god called Aton. Gripped by the zeal of a convert, he denied the existence of all the other gods and sought to replace their temples, cults, and priesthoods with the worship of Aton. He prayed in open–roofed temples to the one god, visualized not in human or animal form, but as the sun disk itself as it soared over Egypt each day.

To escape the influence of the powerful priests of the traditional sun god Amen–Re, Akhenaton abandoned Thebes for a new city, built in the desert near what is today Amarna, which he intended as the center of his new cult. Here, there flourished for a brief time, a new, more human and realistic style of art, the Amarna school. Among the monuments of this style are convincing sculptures of Akhenaton's own ungainly, large–featured face and lovely likenesses of his swan–necked queen, Nefertiti, who played an important part in the new religion.

Even a pharaoh, however, could not crush so powerful an establishment as the ancient priesthoods of Egypt. After the heretic pharaoh's death, it was Aton's temples that were destroyed and Akhenaton's name that was struck from the monuments and the lists of kings. Perhaps the strangest fate, however, was reserved for Akhenaton's hapless young heir, Tutankhamen (r. c. 1361–1351 BCE). Abandoning Amarna and returning to Thebes, Tutankhamen died there while still in his teens, a thoroughly insignificant pharaoh. More than three thousand years later, the 1922 discovery of King Tut's tomb, crammed with exquisitely crafted artifacts, gave the world its most dazzling glimpse of the vanished splendor of the pharaohs.

Egypt's imperial greatness was gone by 1000 BCE. During the centuries that followed, Egypt, weakened by feuds between pharaohs and priests, became itself the victim of a series of foreign conquerors. The African kings of Kush, upriver in the Sudan, had ancient cultural ties with Egypt and strove to preserve its traditions. Most of Egypt's invaders, however, were foreign foes, including the Assyrians, already discussed, the Persians, to be surveyed shortly, and such later Western invaders as the Macedonians of Alexander the Great and the Romans of Julius Caesar.

Egyptian political greatness thus waned after 1000 BCE. Egyptian civilization, however, remained a beacon to later peoples, including, as we will see, the founders of Western civilization, the ancient Greeks.

The Culture of the Nile

The Egyptians shared the common polytheism of most early peoples. Some of their divinities were animals—cats, cows, crocodiles, hippopotamuses, hawks—creatures familiar in their land, perhaps originally the totemic animals of the villagers along the river. The chief Egyptian gods, however, were often anthropomorphic, human in shape, though they frequently retained animal heads.

The Egyptian pantheon was headed by a sun god—first Re, then Amen, and more briefly Aton. Osiris, ruler of the spirits of the dead who dwelt in the underworld, was the object of special devotion among Egyptians, who believed profoundly in life after death. Osiris's divine queen, Isis, who was believed to have brought her husband back from the dead after his murder by the evil god Set, gave hope of eternal life to growing numbers of Egyptians. Horus, the hawk–shaped sky god, was the incarnation of the living pharaoh, who was identified after death with the divine Osiris as king of the underworld. Anubis, the jackal–headed god of the graveyard, weighed the souls of the dead before Osiris and cast them into the waiting jaws of the crocodile–headed Heart Eater if they were found wanting.

Awareness of death occupied a central place in the worldview of the Egyptians and was an important characteristic of Egyptian culture and art. They developed the craft of mummification in order to preserve the body for the use of the soul, or *ka,* after death. The famous Egyptian *Book of the Dead* detailed the progress of the spirit through the underworld and described the responses that the soul should properly make to all the deities encountered along the way. Wealthy or powerful Egyptians filled their tombs with sometimes exquisite objects, from statuettes of servants to life–size chariots, for their use after they had departed. The walls of tomb passages and grave chambers were brightly painted with pictures of earthly pleasures, from banqueting to hunting, that the dead might hope to enjoy again in the other world. Even the drinking songs of the Egyptians often expressed a related theme:

> Put song and music before thee
> Behind thee all evil things
> And remember thou only joy
> Till comes that day of mooring
> At the land that loveth silence.[4]

Columns at Karnak, in Upper Egypt, tower over a modern visitor and his guide. Can you see why structures like this, built many centuries before the first Greek cities, impressed the ancient Greeks? [Courtesy of TWA]

One noticeable quality of Egyptian art is a profound conservatism. Egypt's formal writing system of hieroglyphics, inspired in part by Mesopotamian cuneiform, differed from it in that Egyptian hieroglyphics preserved many of its pictorial elements, which went unchanged for thousands of years. Egyptian "wisdom literature" ran heavily to proverbs on the virtues of tradition and obedience and encouraged the ambitious to emulate the wise men and famous scribes who had gone before. Egyptian painting followed the same formal rules century after century, depicting the human figure in profile with the eyes and shoulders shown frontally. Perhaps most strikingly, statues of pharaohs sitting with feet planted on the ground, hands resting on their knees, and wearing the traditional false beard and ancient crown of Upper and Lower Egypt, look pretty much alike down the dynasties. Only during the radical Amarna period of the New Kingdom, mentioned earlier, was some effort made to capture the individuality of a ruler.

Another characteristic of Egyptian art was monumentality, a combination of grand scale and simplicity that has made Egyptian architecture as awesome to modern as to ancient visitors. The 80–foot columns of the great hall of the temple at Karnak in Upper Egypt made this the largest temple ever built in the ancient world. Towering Egyptian obelisks have been carried off as trophies to cities as far away as Paris, London, and New York. And the three looming pyramids at Giza, on the outskirts of modern Cairo, still dwarf the antlike streams of tourists, the hawkers of souvenirs, and camel rides, who throng around them today.

Egyptian civilization was highly developed technologically. Egyptians constructed sundials, water clocks, and a calendar of 365 days. They seem to have understood the basic principles of the right–angle triangle, later formulated by the Greek Pythagorus, and were famous for their medical skill, up to and including brain surgery. The engineering genius demonstrated by this ancient people was quite remarkable. For Khufu's pyramid alone, 6 million tons of stone were carved from the living rock, moved hundreds of miles downriver and overland by barge and sledge, roller and lever, and then raised on ramps to a height of almost 500 feet above the desert. And there they sit today, inpressive monuments to the engineering skills, the social cohesion, and the focused will of the ancient Egyptians.

♦ Persia Unites the Near East ♦

The age of the founders of civilization in Mesopotamia and Egypt was succeeded by an epoch of sweeping military conquests and of ever vaster empires built by force of arms. During the second and first millennia BCE, weapons of bronze and iron replaced the ziggurat and the pyramid as symbols of a tumultuous age of violence, power politics, and empire–building on an unprecedented scale.

There were more peaceful uses of bronze and iron at this time, and the remarkable expansion of Phoenician trade represented a more long–lasting contribution to human civilization than the endless wars of the period. To contemporaries, however, the rise of unprecedented empires like that of the ancient Persians, built and maintained by military force, was the most astonishing phenomenon of the age.

The Near East in Tumult

In 3000 BCE, Mesopotamia and Egypt were the only centers of civilized living in the world. After 2000 BCE, however, two things happened: a number of other peoples began to build cities and to develop new skills, from writing and metalwork to larger social organization; and still other peoples took a more direct route to the luxuries of civilized living—they seized them by force.

Some of these invaders were heirs of the two original civilizations; for example, the Assyrians of northern Mesopotamia and the pharaohs of New Kingdom Egypt. Other ambitious peoples, however, were also pouring into the Near East—the nomads of the desert and the steppe. Of these, the Hittites were the first to forge and wield iron weapons, while the Persian troops of Cyrus and Darius the Great built the largest empire in history up to that time. In addition, the period from approximately 2000 to 500 BCE saw the rise of such dynamic new peoples as the far–trading Phoenicians and the Hebrews, whom we discuss in the last major section of this chapter.

One thing that many of the peoples who so vigorously shook up the Near Eastern world after 2000 BCE had in common was nomadic roots and a willingness to venture into new lands, as the originally nomadic Hittites and Persians did. The Phoenicians, though not nomads, pioneered long–distance trade from the Mediterranean out into the Atlantic. This urge to pack up and move on merits a brief discussion before we turn to a more detailed look at each of these vigorous new peoples.

Pastoral nomadism represented a late–developing style of life for humankind. Some groups of human beings had been unable—or unwilling—to make the full transition from the food–gathering mode to farming. Pressed by stronger neighbors into land too poor for cultivation, or simply rejecting the hard labor of farming, pastoral nomads derived their livelihood from the tending of sheep, goats, cattle, horses, and other animals. Because their herds or flocks had to be moved incessantly over their marginal land in search of pasture and water, the herders moved too. Organized in clans, highly mobile, toughened by their hard life, and led by resourceful men used to making rapid decisions in unfamiliar territory, they were dangerous enemies. Not infrequently, they cast covetous eyes on the well–watered farmland and the material plenty of the city–based civilizations.

Two groups of nomads threatened the ancient Near East: those who spoke Semitic tongues and those whose languages were Indo–European. Semitic groups included the Akkadians, the Amorites of the Old Babylonian Empire, and the empire–building Assyrians of northern Mesopotamia, all originally invaders from the dry Syrian steppe. Indo–European intruders included the Hittites and the Persians, both of whose ancestors were probably originally nomads of the vast Eurasian grasslands. Both Semitic and Indo-European groups continued to spread across the Old World, so that today both Arabs and Jews speak Semitic languages, whereas most European tongues, Persian, and Indian Sanskrit are Indo-European languages.

These restless, aggressive, often remarkably creative peoples of the steppes were at the heart of the turbulence that characterized the second and much of the first millennium before Christ. We conclude this overview of these earlier civilizations from whom the West learned so much with some account of the Hittites, the Phoenicians, the Persians, and, of even greater continuing importance, of the powerfully influential culture of the ancient Hebrews.

The Hittites and the Phoenicians

Difficult as it is to choose among the teeming peoples of the ancient Near East, the Hittites and the Phoenicians must clearly be mentioned. The Hittites introduced the use of iron; the Phoenicians carried long–distance trade to the far end of the Mediterranean and beyond.

The Indo–European Hittites had migrated down from the Eurasian steppes into the area of modern Turkey during the earlier part of the second millennium BCE. In their new home, the Hittites had established a powerful empire, fighting the New Kingdom pharaohs to a draw and oppressing the early Assyrians. The great Hittite contribution to the history of civilization, however, was the introduction of a new technology into the Fertile Crescent: the working of iron.

The Iron Age, inaugurated by the Hittites around 1200 BCE, depended on a process of pounding and then quick quenching heated ore that produced a "semi–steel" hard enough for a strong tool or a sharp–edged weapon. Before the introduction of Hittite iron technology, most weapons had been made of bronze, an alloy made chiefly of copper and tin. Since iron was much more plentiful than copper, ironworking made it possible to outfit much larger armies. Thus the bronze–armed aristocratic chariot fighters who dominated battlefields down through New Kingdom Egyptian times were replaced, in the days of Persian power, by much larger armies of iron–armed infantrymen.

The Phoenicians, a Semitic people who lived in cities along the coast of modern Lebanon, developed a brilliantly successful commercial culture in the early part of the first millennium BCE. Phoenician merchant seamen from Tyre and Sidon traded the length of the Mediterranean and even beyond the Straits of Gibraltar into the Atlantic, voyaging as far as Stone Age Britain for tin. Paper from the Phoenician city of Byblos was so famous that the very name became synonymous with *book*—and the source of our word *Bible*. Overall, the Phoenicians were the greatest traders on the Mediterranean before the Greeks.

A major Phoenician contribution to Western history was the simplest system of writing yet devised. The short easy–to–use Phoenician alphabet of twenty–two letters did not, like the Mesopotamian and Egyptian scripts, require advanced training to master. Borrowed by the early Greeks, this simple Phoenician alphabet became the basis for all Western forms of writing down to the present day.

The Persian Empire

Around the middle of the first millennium before Christ, another new people came to dominate the Near Eastern world: the Persians. The Persians and their close allies, the Medes, were an Indo–European people from the mountains of Iran whose forebears had been nomads on the Eurasian steppes. Originally the Medes were the dominant group. In the middle 500s, however, a leader emerged among the Persians who made them the builders of the largest empire in history up to that time.

Cyrus the Great (r. 559–530 BCE)—Cyrus the Shepherd to his own people—was one of the most successful conquerors in history. He led his tough cavalry, equipped with short powerful bows, to an astonishing series of victories. An early victim was Croesus of Lydia (in today's Turkey), the first ruler to produce gold coins as a medium of exchange, reputed to be the richest ruler in the world. Thereafter, the Persian warrior–king fought his way eastward from Turkey across Iran to the far cold mountains of Afghanistan. Returning to the civilized lands of the Near East, Cyrus led his battle–hardened host south to Babylon. That richest of cities shrewdly opened its gates to the Persians in 539 BCE.

When Cyrus died, fighting once more on his eastern frontiers, his son Cambyses (r. 530–521 BCE) led the Persian host still further southward to victory on the Nile. After a brief struggle for power, a third emperor, Darius the Great (r. 521–486 BCE), carried Persian rule further yet, west along the North African coast and north across the Hellespont into the Balkans, the southeastern corner of Europe.

By approximately 500 BCE, then, the Persians governed an empire that dwarfed anything seen in the world before. It included the whole sweep of the Middle East, from the shores of the Mediterranean to the banks of the Indus, in what is today Pakistan. All this, plus northeastern Africa and a bit of southeastern Europe, acknowledged the authority of the "king of the four quarters of the world" in the splendid new Persian capital of Persepolis, in what is now Iran.

The wide Persian Empire was ruled by a score of local governors called *satraps,* or "petty kings," who enjoyed a large degree of autonomy under the crown. The power of the Persian army, built increasingly now on its heavy infantry and the noble bodyguard called the Immortals, continued to be respected. There was a centralized administration, including a body of inspectors—or spies—to keep tabs on the satraps. A royal system of roads, some common laws, and a common coinage were also unifying factors. In general,

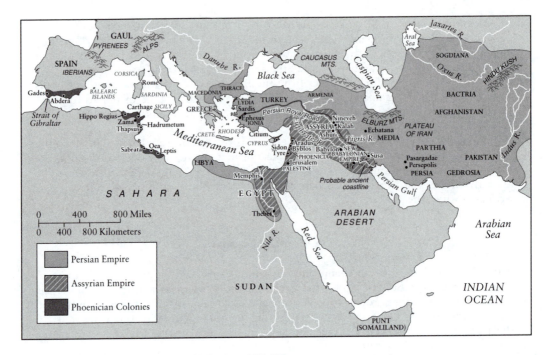

Spread of Near Eastern and North African Civilizations, 1000–500 BCE

however, the diverse subject peoples, including Egyptians and Babylonians, Greek settlements in western Turkey, and nomads in central Asia were allowed to keep their old ways and to a large extent run their own affairs.

Like the Assyrians and the New Kingdom pharaohs, the Persian emperors faced not only foreign foes but repeated rebellions and secessions. Like other early empire builders, the Persians demanded mostly taxes and tribute, and the royal writ ran no further than fear of the Persian army. Still, for more than two hundred years after the conquests of Cyrus in the sixth century BCE, the power of the Persians was awesome to behold.

They also became one of the most civilized of ancient peoples. Persian rulers built impressively, as the ruined pillars of the great palace at Persepolis remind us even today. A remarkable religious movement also took root among the hard–fighting Persian nobility, the monotheistic faith of the sixth–century BCE religious leader Zoroaster. Zoroaster preached a militant religion that pitted the god of light Ahura Mazda and his divine champion Mithras against the prince of darkness, Ahriman. Roman legionaries later learned to worship Mithras, and Ahriman served as a model for the Christian Satan.

Persian arms remained potent long after Cyrus's day. A painted relief of one of the royal guards, called *the Immortals,* shows a short trimmed beard and an elaborately decorated ankle–length robe, a wide–bladed spear, and a capacious quiver of arrows. These crack troops would soon confront the brash challenge of the Greek city–states in one of the epic confrontations of Western history. And nobody would have bet on the Greeks.

◆The Hebrews and Ethical Monotheism◆

Of all the early Near Eastern civilizations, that of the ancient Hebrews was the most influential on the future history of the Western world. The Hebrews were the founders of one of the world's oldest cultures and the ancestors of the modern Jewish community. Most important, they were the shapers of *Judaism,* the monotheistic religion of the Jews and a faith ancestral to both Christianity and Islam.

In the Judaic tradition, the Hebrews gave the world the earliest form of *ethical monotheism*. This form of religion worshiped one God rather than a pantheon of divinities. It also emphasized morality and social justice rather than sacrifice and ritual. It would be hard to overestimate the importance of this tradition on the historical evolution of Western religious life and culture.

The Rise of the Hebrews

The ancient Hebrews enter history shortly after 2000 BCE as a people on the move, drifting slowly down from northern Mesopotamia to Egypt, then back to the region in between. From about 1000 BCE, they clung to a homeland in the area known today as Israel. It is a complex and colorful story.

As the Bible makes clear, the Hebrews were nomadic herders on the desert fringe of the civilized Near East during the second millennium before Christ. They came out of Mesopotamia in the days of the patriarch Abraham, perhaps about 1900 BCE, and their wanderings down the centuries took them as far as Egypt, probably before 1600 BCE. In Egypt, they apparently became exploited laborers, a state of oppression out of which the great leader Moses led them (in "the Exodus") probably sometime around 1300 BCE. Thereafter, most of their history was lived in Palestine, the land they called Canaan and believed their god Yahweh had promised them.

Here they established themselves around 1200, first fighting and then settling down beside other peoples, including the Canaanites and the Philistines. Here, too, the Hebrews' traditional leadership of priests and judges—who were also war leaders—gave way to a typical Near Eastern monarchy around 1000 BCE. The initiator of this new regime was King Saul (r. c. 1020–1000 BCE), whose aggressive policies laid the foundations for the achievements of his successors. Under David (r. c. 1000–960 BCE) and his son Solomon (r. c. 960–933 BCE), the new nation of Israel flourished for most of the tenth century BCE. David built a capital for his new country at Jerusalem, and Solomon constructed an impressive temple there for the worship of Yahweh.

King Solomon was the most brilliant of these rulers. Revered for his wisdom in later centuries, he was in his own time a shrewd and successful Near Eastern monarch. Besides his vast temple in Jerusalem, Solomon constructed fortifications and even whole cities elsewhere in Israel. He strengthened the royal administration, fostered the use of iron for both agricultural tools and weapons, and expanded foreign trade. In the international arena, Solomon forged a marriage alliance with Egypt and took advantage of the weakness of both the Hittites and the Assyrians in his time to project Israel into the forefront of Near Eastern affairs.

Internal discord strained the new institutions, however, and before 900 BCE, the kingdom had split into two parts, Israel in the north and Judah, around Jerusalem, in the south. Both states were subsequently swallowed up by more powerful neighbors: Israel falling to the Assyrians in the eighth century BCE, Judah to the New Babylonian Empire in the sixth century. When Cyrus the Persian conquered Babylon in 539 BCE, he allowed Hebrews who so desired to return to Palestine and establish a small client state of the Persian Empire there. Thereafter, however, Israel would enjoy only brief periods of independence from the days of David and Solomon until the twentieth century CE.

Hebrew Society

Thanks particularly to the unique collection of evidence provided by the Bible, scholars have assembled a convincing picture of the social evolution of this Near Eastern people. Herders and wanderers throughout much of the first thousand years of their history, the Hebrews found a primary sense of identity in the so–called twelve tribes of Israel, which traced back to the twelve great–grandsons of Abraham. Male heads of families controlled their wives' property and had absolute power over their children. Men and women had their assigned tasks in the fields; boys and girls watched the flocks that still remained important in the economy.

After 1000 BCE, as the Hebrew monarchy took shape and Jerusalem and other towns flourished, the life of the people became still more complex. Village headmen and royal officials began to usurp much of the authority formerly exercised by the heads of tribes or families. Among the Hebrews, as among other ancient peoples, small family farms began to give way to large estates owned by nobles and worked by laborers and slaves, while in the towns, artisans practiced many crafts. After their return from Babylon about 500 BCE, some Jews became widely traveled merchants in the first of the many *diasporas,* meaning dispersals or scatterings, that would take them to all the lands of the Western world in centuries to come.

Within this society, women were encouraged to fill two traditional roles—those of wife and mother. The chronicles of the Hebrews in the Old Testament do, however, reveal an awareness that women possessed skills beyond the family circle. Women of the lower classes might function as cooks or bakers, midwives, nurses, professional mourners, and in other capacities. Hebrew women generally enjoyed property rights and increased protection within marriage. From the sixth century BCE, at any rate, Hebrew women owned property, engaged in business dealings, and took cases to court in their own names. And the Book of Proverbs hails above all the more practical skills of the "good wife":

> She considers a field and buys it; with the fruit of her hands she plants a vineyard.
> She girds her loins with strength and makes her arms strong.
> She perceives that her merchandise is profitable.[5]

It was a life, in short, rooted in the family and the household, but sometimes extending well beyond it.

The Prophetic Age

The historic significance of the story of the ancient Hebrews, however, lies in their religious development. For this small Near Eastern people evolved over centuries a complex and powerful faith which, in later centuries, would profoundly influence the spiritual life of the West.

Through all their trials and tribulations, the Jews continued to elaborate the monotheistic, increasingly moral religion of Judaism. Jewish law and the teachings of the Hebrew prophets shaped a faith built around the worship of one God and a strong commitment to his commandments. In its own right, and as a source for both Christianity and Islam, Judaism would prove to be one of the most powerful of all religious visions.

Yahweh, as the Hebrews first understood him, was not unlike the gods of other ancient peoples. The divine patron of the Hebrew people was a god of storm and war. The Hebrews carried his sacred relics about with them in a chest called the Ark of the Covenant, symbolizing his agreement to guide and protect them. They worshiped him with ceremonies and sacrifices, as gods were worshiped everywhere.

A particularly powerful element in this early Hebrew religion was Jewish law. Central to the traditional Hebrew code were the thirteenth–century BCE Ten Commandments that Yahweh was believed to have given to Moses on Mount Sinai after the Jews' Exodus from Egypt. These basic commandments glorified God, requiring his people to worship no other gods before him and forbidding them to represent him in statues or other images. The Ten Commandments also forbade a number of crimes, including murder, theft, lying, and even desiring the lands or wife of another. Over the centuries, furthermore, the Hebrews developed an intricate array of other laws, covering not only criminal offenses and civil disputes but religious duties, dietary regulations, relations with foreigners, and much else. This ancient Hebrew law had much of the rigor of Hammurabi's Code, demanding an eye for an eye and providing such harsh penalties as death by stoning for adultery.

Important advances in this religious view, however, were initiated by spiritual teachers called the *prophets* between the eighth and the fifth centuries BCE. The Hebrew prophets were not members of the priesthood but laymen inspired by the will of Yahweh. They went among the people preaching, castigating them for iniquity, warning them of impending peril, or prophesying renewal and inspiring hope.

Yahweh, as the prophets saw him, was clearly more than one divine patron among many. He was the only real God: all the gods of the Egyptians, the Mesopotamians, and the rest were mere images of wood and stone. This one true God was also the creator of the universe and the divine will that determined the course of history.

The God of the Hebrews demanded a good deal more of his followers than sacrifices, ritual worship, and observance of the letter of the law. The God of the Hebrews required both personal morality and social justice, and he punished those who committed crimes or oppressed their neighbors. The prophet Elijah, a powerful preacher in the 800s BCE, thundered against the priests of Baal, a god many Israelites had come to worship, and denounced an oppressive Hebrew king for stealing another man's land. In the 700s BCE Isaiah warned that God would send the Assyrians against the chosen people if they did not turn from their wicked ways. Jeremiah (about 626–586 BCE) urged social and political as well as religious reform, exhorting the people to love God in their hearts, and warning of the Babylonian danger even as it swept over Israel.

The Yahweh of Abraham and Moses was an awe–inspiring lord, condemning the worship of all other gods, concerned above all with his chosen people. The God of the prophets was clearly the only god and was more dedicated to fairness, compassion, morality, and justice. Throughout their history, the Jews practiced a monotheistic, morally sensitive religion, first in the time of Moses and then in prophetic times. On these Judaic foundations, Christianity rose, in its turn, to become the religion of most Western people in later ages.

Summary

A search for the beginnings of Western history has taken us back to the prehistoric past of the human race, and to the earliest of all civilizations in the ancient Near East. This first chapter has tried to survey this immense span of time and cultural development, from rooting for food in prehistoric forests to the building of the pyramids.

Perhaps two million years ago, paleolithic humans hunted wild animals and gathered vegetable food, lived in small bands and chipped tools out of flint. Around ten thousand years ago, neolithic human beings settled down in agricultural villages, cultivating the soil and domesticating animals for the first time. Five thousand years ago, people learned to build cities, work metals, and read and write—and civilization, with its bureaucracies and social classes, its empires and monumental building, was born.

The first cities emerged in Mesopotamia (Iraq today). Early empires flourished in Ur and Babylon, and the militaristic Assyrian Empire spread to neighboring lands. The first large nation was Egypt, whose pharaohs made the narrow, but immensely fertile, land along the Nile bloom for three thousand years. The largest of these ancient eastern empires, however, was that of Persia, which for a time ruled all the land between the Mediterranean Sea and the frontiers of India.

Among the many smaller peoples of these early millennia, the Hittites taught the world to work iron and the Phoenicians traded farther across and beyond the Mediterranean than any other people. But no people made a larger contribution than the ancient Hebrews, from whose early monotheistic faith three great world religions would evolve: modern Judaism, Christianity, and Islam.

By 500 BCE, then, human life on earth had already passed through many stages and ages. Against this background, we will turn next to the emergence of Western civilization in ancient Greece.

Some Key Terms

atlatl 5
civilization 1
Cro-Magnon 4
diaspora 28
ethical monotheism 27

hominids 4
lugal 12
Judaism 27
ma'at 18
Neanderthal 4

Neolithic 4
Paleolithic 4
prophets 29
satraps 25
ziggurat 12

Notes

1. Recent research suggests that because our ancestors shared the world with the Neanderthalers for thousands of years and because the two species differed little from each other biologically, we may be carrying some Neanderthal genes along with our primary Cro-Magnon heritage.

2. J. B. Pritchard, ed., *Ancient Near Eastern Texts Relating to the Old Testament* (Princeton: Princeton University Press, 1950), 178.

3. J. H. Breasted, *Ancient Records of Egypt,* vol. 2 (Chicago: University of Chicago Press, 1906), 40.

4. W. M. Flinders Petrie, *Social Life in Ancient Egypt* (New York: Cooper Square, 1970), 106.

5. *Proverbs*, 31, 10, 16–18.

Reading List

BEN–TOR, A., ed. *The Archaeology of Ancient Israel.* New Haven: Yale University Press, 1992. Archaeological underpinnings for an understanding of the ancient Hebrews.

CLAGGET, M., ed. *Ancient Egyptian Science: A Source Book.* Philadelphia: American Philosophical Society, 1995. Two volumes so far of a valuable collection of materials on an important subject.

COHEN, M. N. *The Food Crisis in Prehistory: Overpopulation and the Origins of Agriculture.* New Haven: Yale University Press, 1977. Important contribution to our understanding of a crucial topic.

COOK, J. M. *The Persian Empire.* London: Dent, 1983. Narrative and analytical history of Persia, based on Greek historians, inscriptions, and recent archaeology. See also M. A. Dandamaev and V. G. Lukonin, *The Cultural and Social Institutions of Ancient Iran,* translated by P. L. Kohl (New York: Cambridge University Press, 1989).

CUNLIFFE, B., ed. *The Oxford Illustrated Prehistory of Europe.* New York: Oxford University Press, 1994. Essays on a wide variety of preurban peoples, from prehistoric gatherers to contemporaries of the Greeks and Romans.

DAHLBERG, F., ed. *Woman, the Gatherer.* New Haven: Yale University Press, 1983. Valuable collection of essays reassessing the role of women in prehistory.

DREWS, R. *The End of the Bronze Age.* Princeton: Princeton University Press, 1993. Changes in weaponry and military tactics transform society at the end of the second millennium.

HODDER, I. *The Domestication of Europe: Structure and Contingency in Neolithic Societies.* Cambridge, Mass.: Blackwell, 1990. Sophisticated analysis of prehistoric society and culture. See also B. Campbell, *Mankind Emerging* (Boston: Little, Brown, 1979). A clear account of human evolutionary development.

GRIMAL, N. *A History of Ancient Egypt.* Cambridge, Mass.: Blackwell, 1992. A thoughtful synthesis of the history of ancient Egypt, reflecting French scholarship and intended for the non–specialist reader.

JOHANSON, D., and M. ELDER. *Lucy: The Beginnings of Mankind.* New York: Warner, 1981. Discovery, dating, and analysis of one of our oldest ancestors.

KRAMER, S. *History Begins at Sumer.* 2d rev. ed. Philadelphia: University of Pennsylvania Press, 1981. Authoritative and well–written overview, emphasizing Sumerian firsts in history.

LERNER, G. *The Creation of Patriarchy.* New York: Oxford University Press, 1986. Exploration of the emergence of male dominance in ancient society. See also B. Lesko, *The Remarkable Women of Ancient Egypt* (Berkeley: Scribe, 1978). Pioneering study of celebrated Egyptian women.

LICHTHEIM, M., ed. *Ancient Egyptian Literature: A Book of Readings.* 3 vols. Berkeley: University of California Press, 1973–1980. Translations of hieroglyphic texts, representative and readable.

OATES, J. *Babylon.* London: Thames and Hudson, 1986. Excellent survey of Babylonian history and society. See also H. W. F. Saggs, *The Babylonians* (Norman: University of Oklahoma Press, 1995). Brief but scholarly social history.

PETTINATO, G. *The Archives of Ebla: An Empire Inscribed in Clay.* Garden City, N.Y.: Doubleday, 1981. The recently discovered Syrian center of early Near Eastern civilization.

PRITCHARD, J. B., ed. *Ancient Near Eastern Texts Relating to the Old Testament.* Princeton: Princeton University Press, 1969. Standard collection of readings from both Mesopotamia and Egypt. See also H. W. F. Saggs, *The Encounter with the Divine in Mesopotamia and Israel* (London: Athlone, 1978). Stimulating cross–cultural comparisons of religious experiences.

SAGGS, H. W. F. *Civilizations Before Greece and Rome.* New Haven: Yale University Press, 1989. The ancient Near East, surveyed by a mature scholar writing for the nonspecialist.

STROUBHAL, E. *Life of the Ancient Egyptians.* Norman: University of Oklahoma Press, 1992. Good introduction. See also T. G. H. James, *Pharaoh's People: Scenes from Life in Imperial Egypt* (Chicago: University of Chicago Press, 1984). Vignettes with translations from surviving papyri.

VAUX, R. de. *The Early History of Israel.* Philadelphia: Westminster Press, 1978. A solid history of the ancient Hebrews.

WALKER, C. B. F. *Reading the Past: Ancient Writing from Cuneiform to the Alphabet.* London: British Museum, 1990. Stimulating introduction to the earliest forms of writing in western Eurasia.

2

White Cities by the Sea
The Greek City-States

•The Rise of the Greek City–States   •The Age of Pericles
•Classical Greek Culture

The history of the Western world begins in Greece. This wide, jagged peninsula in the eastern Mediterranean Sea, with its neighboring islands, became the site of the first of Western civilizations more than three thousand years ago. Greek civilization, then, will be the subject of this chapter and the following one.

The admiration of later Western peoples for "the glory that was Greece"[1] generally relates to the shining achievements of the fifth century BCE. This was the century that produced Greek democracy and much of the philosophy, art, and literature that form such an important part of the cultural heritage of the West. This chapter will climax with that astonishing era.

But there are other, earlier periods to examine first if we are to understand Greece properly, in its larger Mediterranean context. The first section below will, therefore, offer a brief account of the immediate precursors of the classical Greeks, the Minoans and Mycenaeans, who date back to the third and second millennia before Christ. This section will also evaluate the Greek Dark Age of the centuries around 1000 BCE. And it will look at the birth of classical Greece during the Greek Awakening, between 750 and 500 BCE, which saw the emergence of the Greek city–states and the growth of Greek colonies and commerce.

We will thus reach the Greeks of the fifth century BCE with a much clearer idea of the historical evolution that produced this remarkable people. The three–act tragedy of Greece between 500 and 400 BCE will then begin with the epic struggle of the Greek city–states against the colossal Persian Empire. It will rise to a high point in the Athens of the great leader Pericles. And it will come to a tragic conclusion in the terrible Peloponnesian War, pitting Greeks against Greeks in self–destructive civil strife.

The chapter will conclude, however, with an overview of the remarkable Greek cultural achievement of these centuries. In the art, literature, and thought of the early and classic phases of Greek history, we will touch on many of the reasons we continue to care about this first of European civilizations.

♦The Rise of the Greek City-States♦

The Greek people emerged slowly into history. Long before such famous Greek city-states as Athens and Sparta rose, before such celebrated Greek writers and thinkers as Homer and Plato lived, other peoples and cultures flourished on Greek land. Among these early peoples, we will look first at the far–trading Minoans of Crete (roughly 2000–1500 BCE), then at the hard–fighting Mycenaeans (1500–1100) who succeeded them, and finally at the period called the Greek Dark Age (1100–750). Thereafter, we will outline the vigorous revival, sometimes called the Greek Awakening (750–500), the period that saw the rise of the

The Greek Aegean

Chronology 2: Classical Greece

2500–1500	*Minoans build commercial center on Crete, dominate the Aegean Sea*
1500–1100	*Mycenaean warriors dominate Greece, raid and trade around the Aegean*
1100–750	*Greek Dark Age*
c. 800	*Homer composes his epics of the Trojan War*
750–500	*Greeks build city–states, spread colonies and trade around Mediterranean*
c. 600	*Sappho writes her poetry*
594	*Solon's reforms at Athens focus on social justice*
508	*Cleisthenes' Athenian reforms build a more democratic political system*
500–400	*Aeschylus, Sophocles, Euripides write their plays, Herodotus and Thucydides their histories; temples built on the Acropolis*
490–480	*Main battles of Persian War—Marathon, Thermopylae, Salamis*
469–322	*Socrates, Plato, and Aristotle shape Greek philosophy*
460–429	*Pericles in power, completes structure of Athenian democracy, builds the Athenian Empire*
431–404	*Peloponnesian Wars divide Greece*
404	*Sparta defeats Athens, destroys Athenian Empire*

classic Greek culture of the fifth century BCE, with its far–flung commerce and colonies all around the Mediterranean Sea.

The Greek World: Geography and Culture

From a rooftop terrace in a hill village on the Greek island of Evvia—ancient Euboea—a visitor can look out today across a microcosm of the Greek world of ancient times. Down the hillside beyond cypresses and eucalyptus, lies a curving bay and the Aegean beyond, the "wine–dark sea" of which Homer sang. Out on the water, smaller islands fade to the horizon. Behind, the hillside scales up to mountains sown with olive trees, shepherds, and sheep. Just over a rocky shoulder, there is an ancient quarry with a half–finished column, cut from the surrounding stone two thousand years ago, lying in the gorse. It is all there: the world the Greeks inhabited and a hint of what they made of it.

It was a poor land of thin soil over rock, indifferently watered—quite unlike the rich river plains of Mesopotamia and Egypt. Most ancient Greeks were farmers, like people everywhere, but few were rich by Near Eastern standards. And most of the time there was not enough surplus product to support so large an elite as the aristocracies, priesthoods, and monarchies of the Near East. Many Greeks had to find some other means of livelihood than the land, like handicrafts or commerce on the sea. Others were eventually driven to leave Greece entirely, establishing colonies across the Aegean or still farther away, across the Mediterranean or the Black Sea.

The sea played a crucial role in the history of the Greeks. In their divided homeland of peninsulas and islands, water was never far away. The relatively calm Mediterranean linked the early Greeks as much as it divided them, for they became seafarers early, as they are to this day. The Greeks overcame the huge Persian Empire at sea, and the Athenian Empire of the fifth century flourished all around the Aegean Sea. The greatest Greek epic poems,

Homer's *Iliad* and *Odyssey,* focused on the Trojan War, in which a Greek armada crossed the Aegean to destroy the city of Troy, and on the adventures of the Greek hero Odysseus on his long voyage home.

The world of the Greeks was thus both united and divided. Unlike the unified river valleys in the ancient Near East, the land of the Greeks was broken up by mountains and small valleys, peninsulas, and islands. It was easy and natural for Greek city–states to maintain their independence, to produce no all–powerful pharaohs or kings of kings, and to feud with each other throughout their history. These divisions also bred deep loyalty to one's own city–state, with its population of a few thousands or tens of thousands of people.

At the same time, the very geographical separateness and isolation of the Greeks may have made them cling to the common values that united them. For certain distinctive qualities—independence of mind, rationality, aesthetic sensitivity, and more dubious traits like sharp trading and contentiousness—linked all Greeks, however far they were scattered across the earth.

The culture of the ancient Greeks was also shaped by the civilizations of their still more ancient neighbors around the eastern end of the Mediterranean. Greeks of the fifth and fourth centuries BCE were well aware of their debt to these older civilizations. Classical Greek philosophers like Plato and historians like Herodotus honored the Egyptian and Near Eastern forerunners of their own culture. Greek pottery found in Egypt and Egyptian tomb paintings representing both Minoans and Mycenaeans, all dating from around 1500 BCE, give evidence of commercial and perhaps diplomatic contact between these peoples. After 1000 BCE, as we will see, Greek traders and soldiers penetrated both Egypt and the Near East, settling along the coast of Asia Minor and in the Nile delta, trading, fighting, and learning from these other cultures.

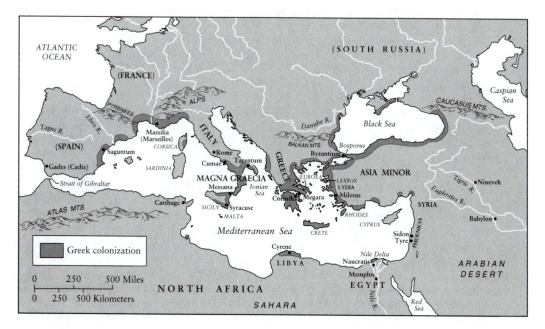

Greek Colonization, 750–500 BCE

From all these contacts, the Greeks who laid the foundations for Western civilization derived many benefits. From the Near East, as we will see, they took the Phoenician alphabet and Lydian coinage. From Egypt, they learned artistic styles and techniques, such as the creation of large imposing statues. Some scholars have further suggested that the Greeks may have derived important legal, scientific, and philosophical ideas from Egyptian sources, though the evidence for this is less clear.

Minoans and Mycenaeans

As early as the third millennium BCE, prehistoric dwellers in the area of present–day Greece built agricultural villages and learned to work metals. Around 2000 BCE, the region was invaded from the north by the first of several waves of *Indo–European* migrants from the grasslands of Eurasia. These Indo–European intruders, the earliest ancestors of the Greeks, remained relatively underdeveloped, however, until the coming of the Minoans from the Near East.

The Minoans were immigrants too, probably from Asia Minor—modern Turkey—who settled on the large island of Crete, southeast of Greece. A city–building, sea–trading people, they established trading posts all around the Aegean Sea, an area already inhabited by Greeks. This Minoan commercial predominance was probably at its height between 2000 and 1500 BCE.

The Minoan period was labeled "Minoan" by archaeologist Arthur Evans after the mythical King Minos of Crete, whose wife was said to have given birth to the monstrous Minotaur. Evans divided Minoan history into three major periods: Early Minoan (c. 2600–2200 BCE), Middle Minoan (c. 2200–1500), and Late Minoan (c. 1500–1200). Thus the seaborne Minoan culture rose early in the third millennium BCE, flourished through the early second millennium, between 2000 and 1500, and suffered some mysterious catastrophe about the beginning of the first millennium before Christ.

The Minoan Empire, then, was primarily a zone of commercial predominance, with its center at the city of Knossos on Crete. It had trading posts and commercial contacts around the Aegean, including some on the Greek mainland, as well as in Egypt, Syria, and elsewhere in the Near East. Minoan cities seem to have done without walls and moats, indicating either that their hegemony was a peaceful one or that they depended on their fleets for defense. Minoan writing appears to have developed much as Near Eastern scripts did, from pictures to a kind of writing based on syllables, and it was inscribed on clay tablets in the Mesopotamian fashion.

The sprawling, many-chambered royal palace at Knossos radiates grace and power, with its stately staircase and a red–columned throne room. There are charming wall frescoes of landscapes, the sea, and the lives of the ruling caste. The Cretan aristocracy, if we are to believe the frescoes, lived an idyllic life, strolling in flower gardens, sipping wine, or practicing the startling sport of bull leaping, in which young men and women vaulted over the horns of bulls and danced on their backs, perhaps as part of a religious ceremony.

Minoan civilization vanished with surprising suddenness, perhaps as early as 1450 BCE. The nature of the cataclysm that swept the Minoan world away, however, remains in dispute. Some historians attribute the sudden end of this civilization to some natural catastrophe, such as an earthquake or a volcanic eruption. Others interpret the visible evidence of burning and widespread destruction as proof that the state fell to foreign invaders, probably the Mycenaeans from the mainland.

The Mycenaeans were the first Greek–speaking people to leave written evidence of that language in a script known as Linear B, deciphered by scholars in the middle of the twenti-eth century. Drifting down from the north, the Mycenaeans established themselves in the wide, hand-shaped peninsula of southern Greece called the *Peloponnesus.*

This Mycenaean hegemony (c. 1500–1100 BCE) was cruder and more violent than the Minoan empire. Warriors and traders, the Mycenaeans established a power structure in southern Greece that has been called the *palace system.* In this system, scattered fortresses at Peloponnesian sites like Mycenae, Pylos, and Tiryns, and at Athens and Thebes in central Greece, dominated the countryside. These roughly built stone "palaces" were linked by roads over which the heavy chariots of Mycenaean merchants and warlords rattled with a flash of bronze armor and a glitter of weapons.

On one level, Mycenaean civilization, with its palace system and endless wars, was a coarse-grained military oppression. Yet, when archaeologists probed the graves of the Mycenaean warlords, they found startling treasures. There were game boards made of ivory, birds of crystal, gold jewelry, and golden face masks. But Mycenaean pottery was not as delicate as Minoan ware had been, and its decorative patterns were copied with increas-ing crudity from earlier work. If Minoan culture was a golden age, the Mycenaean epoch was an age of bronze.

Then, sometime between 1200 and 1100 BCE, still more waves of intruders came down from the north. Some of these invaders infiltrated into the existing society gradually, but others raided and destroyed Mycenaean settlements. The last of these migrating peoples—known to tradition as Dorians—were pastoralists, herders who even had to learn the art of farming from the villagers they overwhelmed. These still less developed people brought an-other ratchet downward for this early Greek society. The Greek Dark Age had begun.

Knowledge of agriculture did survive in this grim time, and it was during this period that iron tools and weapons replaced bronze. But there were no cities, no commercial sec-tor to speak of, and little production of handicrafts beyond objects for local use. It was life at subsistence level: days bending in the fields or climbing the rocky slopes with flocks of sheep and goats. Olive trees and grapevines grew in the light, dry soil, varieties of wheat in the small fields. It was the world of the poet Hesiod's (fl. c. 700 BCE) *Works and Days,* when the height of human wisdom was knowledge of soil and seasons, flocks and vines.

As in many preurban societies, the individual existed only as part of a defining group—age-group, family, clan. Most members had little say in their own lives. Fathers of families, leading families within a clan, and local petty kings held sway. But even they were rigor-ously guided by tradition and taboo.

By 750 BCE, in short, it must have seemed to most of these simple folk that Greece's golden age lay far in the past. For there had been a time, wandering bards like Homer (fl. c. 800 BCE) told them, when the gods spoke to human beings, when their ancestors had built great fleets and sailed east to conquer great cities in Asia. Legends of the monstrous Mino-taur in his Cretan labyrinth or of the siege of ancient Troy may have given these Dark Age Greeks a sense of what their glorious Minoan and Mycenaean past had been. They would have had no such confidence in the future.

The Greek City-States

The Greek Dark Age, however, was followed by a dynamic revival that has been called the Greek Awakening (750–500 BCE). During this period the Greeks recovered the arts of civilization, spread well beyond their Aegean homeland, and laid the foundations for the classic Greek civilization to come.

The links between the agricultural village of the Dark Age and the city–state, or *polis*, of the ages that followed are not easily traced, but some sources of this revival are becoming clear. The building of temples, and, indeed, of cities themselves, reveals increasing productivity—the achievement of a surplus beyond the daily needs of the population. And the discovery of Greek pottery and other products at sites in many parts of the Mediterranean world gives us evidence of the rapid growth of long-range trade once more.

Even the evolution of military technology and organization helps to illuminate the origins of the new social order. For it is during this time that the Greeks developed the infantry phalanx, which replaced the war chariot as their most effective fighting unit. The *phalanx* was a heavily armored infantry formation that fought in close battle order, each infantryman protecting the man beside him, all pushing together for a breakthrough. The armor of this heavy infantryman, or *hoplite,* including breastplate, helmet, shield, and greaves to protect the legs below the knee, could only be afforded by middle-rank or wealthy men—merchants, skilled artisans, well–off farmers. Not surprisingly, these well-to-do defenders of the polis came to dominate the emerging city-states in political and other ways. The close-order combat and the drill necessary to make the phalanx work, some have suggested, both reflected and generated a strong sense of community responsibility and loyalty.

The Greek city–state that began to evolve toward the end of the Dark Age had some things in common with the city–states of the Near East. Like them, the Greek polis was small in size and population. An average Greek city and its hinterland approximated the territorial extent of the Dark Age district that had preceded it. Natural frontiers, however, were perhaps more common than in the East: the boundries of a city–state were often defined by valley walls, the angle of a coastline, or the extent of a small island. The population could run to tens, even hundreds of thousands for a city and its surrounding villages: Athens, at its height during the Classical Age, may have had three hundred thousand residents.

The Greek city–states were, however, more numerous than their Mesopotamian or Phoenician precursors. Hundreds of them were distributed over the mainland, the islands, and the neighboring coasts of the Aegean. Each city presided over a number of villages in the surrounding countryside. Greeks traditionally centered their urban growth around a hill dedicated to the gods, particularly to the patron god or goddess of the state. This *acropolis*, or "high city," could also serve as a refuge in case of foreign attack. Below it was the equally essential *agora*, or marketplace. The agora, too, had other functions: it was a place for lounging and gossip, for political and, later, philosophical discussion.

What was strikingly original about the early Greek city–state, however, was not its physical plan, but its political institutions. Most city–states had an assembly, a council, and a number of elected officials. Assemblies of warriors or heads of family and councils of elders had been common in preurban village communities in many parts of the world. In Greek cities, the assembly was composed of citizens with political rights, which meant free adult males, often members of the phalanx, and property owners. Excluded from political rights were women, resident foreigners, slaves, and the poor. Limited as it was, however, this politically active Greek citizen body encompassed a larger portion of the population than enjoyed political power anywhere else in the Mediterranean.

Political power in Greek city–states included the right to vote on major matters of public policy, to elect officials to carry out those policies, and to serve as an official, if chosen.

As issues grew more complicated, a council evolved to guide the deliberations of the full assembly. The council might be chosen from the assembly itself and do little more than set the agenda. Or, it might be composed of members of the old aristocratic families and end by dominating the political life of the state. Elected officials of the city-state, finally, could include war leaders or generals, officials entrusted with religious observances, judges, and civil authorities like the Athenian *archons,* whose political clout could be substantial.

The principles on which the Greek political system was normally based seem to have included an impulse toward equality and a sense of civic responsibility. There was also an emphasis on the importance of justice, meaning the even-handed application of the traditional laws and customs, lists of which began to be inscribed on stone in public places. These principles were, of course, often breached in practice. But they led to further development of both Greek political institutions and the political ideas that undergirded them. Influential later Greek studies of government, such as Plato's *Republic* and Aristotle's treatise on *Politics* with which political scientists wrestle to this day, had their roots in several centuries of Greek experience with this uncommon system of governance.

Greek Colonies and Commercial Expansion

Supporting the mushroom growth of Greek cities and the elaboration of their political structure was a booming Greek economy. The key to this economic growth seems to lie in rapid population growth. To feed the swelling numbers, the Greek city–states imported wheat from as far away as southern Russia, and they pulled fish from the seas in increasing quantities. Most important, Greek farming at home expanded into every bit of usable land. Grain, grapevines and olive trees spread up the dry, rocky slopes, providing Greek cities with wine and oil, essentials of their own diet and major export items as well. In the cities, the manufacture of pottery, textiles, and metalware also expanded rapidly.

Commerce evidently expanded as industrial and agricultural production did. New and larger ships were built, propelled by sails and by fifty or more oarsmen. Again, technical borrowings from the Near East helped. The art of writing, lost through the Dark Age, was once more imported into the Greek world, this time from their commercial rivals, the Phoenicians. After 800 BCE, a modified Phoenician alphabet of twenty-four letters spread among the Greeks. Coinage was invented around 650 BCE in Lydia, a wealthy monarchy in Asia Minor, and the Greeks were stamping rude coins of their own by 600 BCE.

As important as economic growth to the rise of the Greeks was the spread of Greek colonies all around the Mediterranean Sea. From 750 BCE on, the population increase that crowded the small cities of the Greek mainland and the Aegean drove many Greeks out of that world altogether. People who simply could not support themselves at home set out to settle on the far coasts of the Mediterranean and beyond. This wave of colonization lasted through the seventh and sixth centuries BCE and even on into the Classical Age that began around 500. It was a great diaspora, and it established Greek cities as far afield as Spain and the Black Sea.

Not long after 800 BCE, Greek traders had begun to follow the path earlier taken by Minoans and Mycenaeans to the sources of civilization in the Near East. Over the next two centuries they moved on to Syria, where they accepted the overlordship of the Assyrian kings, and to Egypt, where the pharaohs sternly limited them to a single port. In this ancient part of the world, even the brash Greeks were impressed by the polished craftware of Syria and the monumental architecture of Egypt.

The Greeks also turned their eyes west and began the great wave of colonization in earnest. They settled most thickly in southern Italy and Sicily, a region that became known as *Magna Graecia,* Great Greece, so many were the Greek cities flourishing there. In Sicily, the Greeks began a long feud with the Phoenicians, who had already settled on the island. In southern Italy, Greek settlers helped to instruct the early Romans in the arts of civilization. Greek colonies were also established in southern France, in southern Spain, in North Africa, on the straits leading into the Black Sea, and around the Black Sea itself.

Despite this wide dispersal, however, the Greeks seem to have felt an underlying cultural unity. They were all *Hellenes,* after all, descended from a common mythic ancestor. All the Greeks spoke the same language, though there were many Greek dialects. The basic common tongue gave all Greeks a sense of being one people, no matter how far they wandered or how bitterly they quarreled with each other. Religion was another force for unity. Each polis had its own patron divinity, but all Greeks believed in the same pantheon, the great gods traditionally believed to dwell on Mount Olympus in northern Greece. Headed by Zeus, this celestial company included gods and goddesses of love and war, grain and wine, the sea and the hearth of home—things that mattered intensely to all Greeks.

Other cultural elements, some of them related to religion, also drew the Greeks together. There were Panhellenic athletic contests, of which the Olympic Games, believed to have been founded in 776 BCE, were the most famous. At Olympia in the Peloponnesus, Greeks from many cities gathered every four years to race on foot and in chariots, hurl the discus and the javelin, wrestle, and box in fierce, but peaceful, competition.

The shrine at Delphi, high in the mountains north of the Gulf of Corinth, also helped to remind Greeks of their common heritage. Here priestesses of Apollo responded to the questions of individuals or delegations from city–states with what were believed to be divinely inspired prophecies. All Greeks, finally, also shared a repertoire of artistic styles and common tastes. As we will see, Greek temples have a family likeness, and all Greeks revered Homer as the most inspired of poets.

The Emergence of Athenian Democracy

By the sixth century BCE, however, the strains of rapid social transformation had begun to show in many Greek city-states. To cope with these inevitable social dislocations, two new types of Greek leaders emerged: reformers and tyrants. Reformers sought to improve Greek society. Tyrants sought primarily to exploit it, yet often introduced changes of considerable long-term value too. Both contributed to the greatest Greek legacy to Western political life: the emergence of the earliest form of Western democracy.

Social tensions accompanied this period of dynamic growth. Landowners who had more arable land to begin with or who were more alert to the export market got richer and expanded their holdings. Less successful farmers went into debt to their neighbors, paid huge interest, and sometimes even had to sell themselves and their families into slavery to pay their debts. In cities, manufacturers of pottery, metalware, and other goods and commercial entrepreneurs competed feverishly to please the growing market with more novel and beautiful designs. But these same aggressive spirits exploited their laborers and imported increasing numbers of foreign slaves to keep up with the demand.

Resentment was often especially widespread among the middling, or hoplite class. As we have noted, the middle ranks of farmers had now been joined by representatives of the new industrial and commercial wealth to form an increasingly important bloc in society.

These people, the backbone of the economy and the defenders of the state, sometimes challenged the older wealth and power of the aristocracy. And the increasing desperation of the lowest classes, from landless farmers to rowers in the ships of the merchants, added to the growing tension.

In 594 BCE, the Athenians chose a widely respected aristocrat named Solon (c. 638–c. 558) as sole archon, or chief official, to reform the laws. Solon's reforms, which were economic as well as political, prohibited debt slavery and stimulated economic growth by encouraging production of olive oil and pottery for export and by standardizing the Athenian systems of weights and measures to conform to those of the Near East. On the political side, Solon divided the population into four classes based on landholding, assigning each class a place in the political structure. The upper two classes could hold the chief offices, both as archons and as members of the *Areopagus,* the traditional noble council, which also functioned as the highest court of law. Even the lowest rank of landholder could vote in the citizens' assembly and sit on the new *heliaea courts* of law, which in the next century challenged the aristocratic Areopagus for legal jurisdiction in Athens.

Solon's reforms were moderate, involving no such fundamental changes as land redistribution or genuine democracy. He did, however, begin to replace family connections with civic responsibility and aristocratic predominance with rule by public officials and popular participation in political affairs.

A more widespread response to social strain, however, was the seizure of power by tyrants. To the Greeks, *tyranny* meant not so much brutal oppression as illegitimate rule by individuals who held power through demagogic appeal, political intrigue, force, or a combination of all these. The tyrants of the sixth century BCE, however, commonly presented themselves as champions of the middle orders of society and protectors of the poor. To win the support of these groups, tyrants enacted reforms.

Peisistratus and his son Hippias, who dominated Athens in the second half of the sixth century BCE, were celebrated examples of the Greek tyrant of this period. This Athenian tyrant earned the support of the masses by redistributing land confiscated from noble rivals to the small farmers, and by providing work for the poor on large building projects. His beautification of Athens and his support for dramatists, poets, and artists earned the city much of the prestige it enjoyed in the next century.

The next major contribution to Athenian democracy was the reformer Cleisthenes, whose constitutional innovations were instituted in 508 BCE. Cleisthenes thrust his way to the front rank of Athenian politics soon after the fall of Peisistratus's son Hippias in 510 BCE. His approach was to break up the old centers of political power and replace them with new political units. A key change was the creation of the *deme,* a new political subdivision about the size of a country village or a ward within the city itself. The 175 demes were then combined in ten new political "tribes" which replaced the ancient ethnic tribes that had originally settled the area. Each tribe included people from the poorest hill villages, well-to-do farmers from the plains, and citizens of the most prosperous city wards. The new political tribes were thus balanced socially, economically, and regionally.

On the basis of this structure of demes and political tribes, a new council of five hundred, the *boule,* was formed. This council was composed of fifty representatives from each of the ten new tribes. Each tribe's delegation to the council of five hundred was given a turn at guiding the general operations of the government for one-tenth of the year. In 501 BCE, the army was also reorganized into ten regiments, one from each of the new tribes, each electing its own general.

Democratic participation was also advanced by the provision of financial allowances for members of the council and regular salaries for citizens who served in the large popular courts or in the army or navy. Many officials were chosen by lot, but voting continued for the board of ten generals, who increasingly became the executive heads of the government. The device of ostracism, meanwhile, allowed the assembly to send anyone perceived as a threat to the welfare of the state into honorable exile for ten years by simple majority vote.

The result was a rough-and-ready system of direct rather than representative democracy. The assembly of all citizens, which served as both the legislature and the chief court, met every ten days or so, while one-tenth of the council of five hundred were always on duty, as were archons, generals, and lesser officials. In practice, an assembly of thousands of farmers, traders, perfumed aristocrats, and sweaty laboring men must have been a bit unwieldy. Still, if we set a vision of this milling, raucous crowd alongside the bas-reliefs of Persepolis that show Darius in his embroidered robe sitting stiffly on his throne while satraps bow and marching lines of tribute-bearing subjects parade into the royal audience hall, it seems clear that Athens came a good deal closer than Persia to the modern notion of democratic government.

◆ The Age of Pericles ◆

The fifth century BCE has a symmetry and a tragic climax that give it a powerful dramatic appeal. It is the story of a genuine golden age dominated by the great Athenian statesman, Pericles, and bracketed by two terrible conflicts, the Persian and Peloponnesian wars. It was once customary for historians to present this three-act drama as a clear-cut struggle between good and evil. The freedom-loving Athenians were the heroes. They were depicted as winning a great war against the barbarous Persians in the early fifth century BCE; as bringing freedom, truth, and beauty to the West under the leadership of Pericles; and then as going down to tragic defeat at the hands of the militaristic Spartans—fellow Greeks—in the Peloponnesian War. The story thus had a clear beginning, middle, and end, as well as a disturbing moral structure.

It still makes sense to divide the century into three parts, though none of the parties involved look as simply good or bad as they once did. The Persians may not have been the barbarians, the Spartans the single-minded militarists, or the Athenians the pure champions of freedom we once imagined. But, however we reinterpret the political history of the century, the drama of fifth-century BCE Greece haunts the Western imagination still. As we will see in the last section, it provided the framework for the real beginnings of Western culture.

The Persian Wars

As we saw when we surveyed the rise of the great Persian Empire, the Middle Eastern conqueror, Cyrus the Great, seized power among the Medes and the Persians in 550 BCE and marched into Babylon in 539. His son, Cambyses, conquered the other primary center of ancient civilization by overrunning Egypt in 525 BCE, and Cambyses's son, Darius, the third of the Achaemenid line, took over the leadership of the empire after a brief civil war in 521. Persia was, in short, a young and still dynamic state in 500 BCE and one whose power had been built on the battlefield. Darius (r. 521–486 BCE), who like his grandfather Cyrus was known as "the Great," organized the conquests of his predecessors and, in attempting to preserve them, brought the empire into conflict with the Greeks.

This conflict erupted first in the Greek city–states of Ionia, scattered down the Aegean coast of Asia Minor. These Greek cities were easily absorbed into the huge Persian Empire. Suiting his rule to their traditions, Darius appointed tyrants (in the Greek sense of the term) to govern the Ionian states, choosing men who would be properly subservient to local satraps.

The trouble began in 499 BCE, when Miletus, the wealthiest, most sophisticated of all the Ionian cities, led a Greek rebellion against Persian rule. Greek cities up and down the eastern Aegean coast overthrew their Persian-backed tyrants and prepared to fight. Envoys were dispatched to mainland Greece requesting the assistance of their brothers across the sea. Athens was the only large Greek city–state to respond, sending a few ships and men. And despite early Greek victories, Persian forces soon defeated the Greek rebels.

In Athens, there was mourning for fellow Hellenes. In his many-columned throne room at Persepolis, Darius determined to discourage a recurrence by making an example of the Greek state that had dared to aid his rebellious Ionian subjects. In 490 BCE a Persian expedition involving hundreds of ships and perhaps fifty thousand men was dispatched to punish the Athenians. They drew their ships up on the shore of the mountain-fringed coastal plain of Marathon, 26 miles northeast of Athens.

Reconstructing ancient battles is not easy. All versions of this one, however, stress the contribution made by the Athenian general, Miltiades (c. 554–489 BCE), who combined a shrewd tactical sense with firsthand knowledge of the Persians, whom he had served in earlier years in Asia Minor. All authorities agree that the Greeks were outnumbered, that they attacked the Persian camp in a line of battle that was weak in the center but strong in the wings, and that it was these latter troops who drove back the Persian flanks and then closed on the Persian center, which broke and fled. When the day's fighting was over, the Greek historian Herodotus assures us, six thousand of the invaders had fallen, but fewer than two hundred Greeks.

Ten years later, in 480 BCE, the Persians came again, but this time they mounted a full-scale invasion by land and sea. Darius's son and heir, Xerxes (r. 486–465 BCE), had assembled an enormous army that may have included as many as 150,000 men and a fleet of more than six hundred ships. It was certainly the largest military force the Western world had ever seen.

But the Greeks had made plans of their own. Athens had produced another leader of genius: Themistocles (c. 527–460 BCE), the city's most ardent advocate of sea power. Themistocles was logical, persuasive, and obsessed with the crucial role he believed Athens's "wooden walls," the stout sides of its long oar-driven warships, would play in its future defense. He argued his fellow citizens into fortifying Piraeus, the harbor of Athens, and into using the windfall discovery of a rich silver lode in the mines at Laurium to build a fleet of two hundred fighting ships. These ships—called *triremes* for their three rows of oars, one above the other—ultimately provided the backbone of the Greek navy that faced the Persians in the coming war.

The first to face the Persians this time, however, were not the Athenians but the Spartans, reputedly Greece's most redoubtable warriors. The Spartan king, Leonidas (r. 490–480 BCE), thus set out with three hundred Spartans and a force of several thousand other Greeks to face the huge Persian host at the narrow northern pass of Thermopylae.

The pass at Thermopylae (literally, "the hot gates") is in some places less than 50 feet wide. The Greeks held the Persians there for two scorching days in August of 480 BCE.

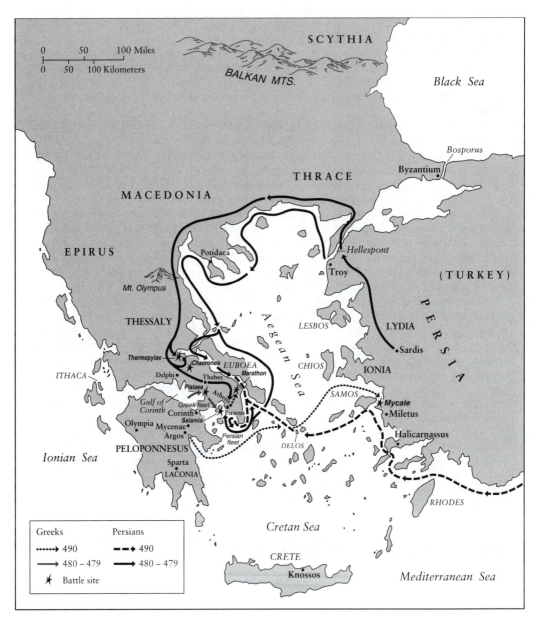

The Persian Wars, 498–449 BCE

Then a traitor showed the invaders a mountain path that enabled them to outflank the defenders. Leonidas, seeing the impending disaster, ordered most of the other Greeks to withdraw while he and his Spartans stayed, fought, and died. "Go tell them at Sparta, passerby," runs the famous epitaph for the three hundred at Thermopylae, "that here, obedient to their will, we lie."

There was now no hope of successful resistance north of the Gulf of Corinth, however, and most of the Greeks retreated to the isthmus at the eastern end of the gulf to defend the Peloponnesus. The Greek fleet anchored in the strait between the offshore island of Salamis and the mainland, only a few miles west of Athens. They were close enough to see smoke rising from the temples on the Acropolis as the Persians swarmed through the abandoned city.

It was Salamis that became the key to victory. Themistocles succeeded in tricking the Persian fleet into attacking in the narrow straits between the island and the mainland, and there, in a long and bloody day's fighting, the Greeks destroyed perhaps two-thirds of the Persian ships. Emperor Xerxes, who had set up his throne on a seaside hill to observe his victory, watched the sun set on the remnants of his fleet as it fled eastward. He knew that without his navy, which was essential to protect his supply lines, his huge army could scarcely survive in an enemy land.

Xerxes, therefore, took much of his army home with him that fall. And the next year, the Greeks won massive victories on land and sea. It was a disastrous end to the second major effort of the heirs of Cyrus to overrun the West.

The war still had thirty years to run, but it now became a very different kind of struggle. In 478 BCE Athens and a number of other seacoast and island states organized a military alliance to carry on the war. Meeting on the sacred island of Delos, the founders of the *Delian League* swore to fight shoulder to shoulder to defend the independence of the Greek cities from the Persians.

From the beginning, the Athenian fleets provided the core of the Delian League's military forces. Under Athenian leadership, the Greek peoples of the northern and eastern shores of the Aegean were freed from Persian domination. The long wars finally ended in 449 BCE with a Persian agreement to keep their navy out of Greek seas and to refrain from oppressing the Ionian city-states. In the eyes of the Greeks, at least, the peace was a victorious one, for they had accomplished their war aims.

Pericles

The structure of Athenian democracy was at this point in Greek history essentially complete. The most effective leader of the period was Pericles (c. 490–429 BCE), who dominated Athens during the middle decades of the fifth century BCE. An aristocrat and friend of intellectuals and artists, Pericles also had a reputation for honesty in financial matters and a gift for oratory. From the 460s to the 430s BCE, these qualities won him repeated election to the board of generals and swayed the assembly to accept his proposals and follow his policies. As a democrat and a patriot, Pericles combined a lifelong commitment to a broader sharing of political power in Athens with an aggressive dedication to the greatness of his city in the Greek world. He advanced the cause of democracy, rebuilt the city physically, and became the chief architect of the Athenian Empire. Pericles is thus generally credited with transforming midcentury Athens into the most honored and powerful of Greek states, both in his own time and in the collective memory of the West.

Pericles completed the structure of Athenian democracy by introducing payment for public service so that the poor could take part, as mentioned earlier. He himself appeared regularly in the assembly, carrying his policies in an atmosphere of free and vigorous debate. His democratic commitment was reflected in a famous speech in praise of Athens given toward the end of his life: "Our constitution," he told his fellow citizens, "favors the many instead of the few." The laws of Athens, he said, "afford equal justice to all," while "advancement in public life falls to reputation for capacity, class considerations not being allowed to interfere with merit; nor again does poverty bar the way."[2] It was an idealized portrait of Athenian society, but a clear statement of Pericles's ambition for his people.

Pericles also presided over the rebuilding of Athens, physically shattered by Persian attacks in 480 and 479 BCE. His inspiration is often seen behind the construction of the gleaming marble temples on the Acropolis, the elaboration of public festivals, and the flowering of Athenian drama and philosophy during the fifth century BCE. Indeed, the Athens he described in the speech just cited as "the school of Hellas" was in large part a city of his own building, an achievement which has led historians to affix his name to the age in which he lived.

Fifth-Century Greek Society

Greek society in the Age of Pericles was composed of three major groups: citizens with or without political rights, *metics*, or resident aliens, and slaves.

Politically enfranchised citizens were normally native born and always male and free.[3] Such a citizen might be wealthy, but he might also be a man of middling means or relatively poor. Such citizens had legal and political rights and a military obligation. Frequently they were farmers, the oldest and most respectable occupation. The better off city-dwelling citizens gave much of their time to government service, athletics, and such other activities as drinking parties or philosophical discourse.

Most Greek wives and daughters of the citizen class led house-bound, legally limited lives. They could not own or manage property, participate in politics, or be seen in public, except at a few religious ceremonies. The difference in age between the typical husband and wife (a groom was likely to be thirty, a bride around fifteen) may have encouraged a belief that women were less knowledgeable than men, and thus limited their lives to child rearing and household management.

Aliens were more commonly either artisans or merchants. They were not allowed to own property, participate in the deliberations of the assembly, or hold public office. Some resident aliens practiced exotic crafts indigenous to their homelands but rare and in demand in their new homes. What they were denied in political rights they compensated for by making a lot of money.

Slaves were frequently foreigners too, men and women imported to the Greek city-states as prisoners of war. A slave's legal status was comparable to that of a citizen's tangible property or his domestic animals. The conditions of their lives varied according to the type of work they performed. Slaves who worked in the state silver mines at Laurium lived a wretched life, but those who worked as house servants in Athens or Corinth were often part of a family. Nevertheless, slave labor undoubtedly helped citizens find the time to participate in the civic institutions of which they were so proud.

The Athenian Empire

Though organized as a voluntary alliance of independent Greek states, the Delian League was dominated by Athens from the beginning. A council of representatives of the allied states was supposed to set general policy, and the treasury of the league was established at the shrine of Apollo on the sacred island of Delos. In practice, however, the treasurers were appointed from Athens, and the allied navy was commanded by an Athenian admiral.

Over the quarter century that followed the founding of the league in 478 BCE, furthermore, Athenian "leadership" became something more than that. After 470, no member was allowed to withdraw from the alliance, and some were forcibly enrolled. Athens even converted some lesser states into tribute-paying colonies of its own. Still, the Athenians may have justified their actions as necessary in the broadest sense, since a strong Athens was clearly essential to the victory of the common cause.

From the 460s BCE on, Athens dictated to its allies more often than it consulted them. In 454 BCE, the treasury of the league was moved from Delos to Athens; the reason given was greater security. The annual contributions of the members, however, were soon being used to pay the salaries of oarsmen in Athenian triremes, and even to build Pericles's new temples on the Athenian Acropolis. As the century advanced, the assembly at Athens passed laws that became binding on all members of the league, including the use of Athenian coinage and weights and measures in all member states. Again, such measures could be justified by their improving the region's economy as a whole, thus further strengthening the league for the great struggle.

When the wars with Persia ended in 449 BCE, however, the Greeks were confronted with the undeniable reality of the Athenian Empire. It included most of the Aegean coastal states and almost all the islands. All told, some 170 separate city-states with a combined population of perhaps two million were ruled by a few tens of thousands of Athenian citizens who were guided in their turn by the powerful voice of Pericles.

The Peloponnesian Wars

The third act of the Greek tragedy that played itself out throughout the fifth century BCE was characterized by yet more war. The Peloponnesian Wars, whose main phase lasted from 431 to 404 BCE, were not great patriotic struggles of Greeks against a foreign foe, nor were they studded with glorious victories. These wars were fratricidal conflicts that pitted the Hellenes against each other. Greece could only emerge the loser.

The chief antagonists in this unhappy struggle were Athens, the great naval power of central Greece, and Sparta, the greatest of Greek land powers, which ruled the Peloponnesus in the south. While Athens developed along democratic lines, Sparta preserved an older, more authoritarian political structure, including not one but two kings. Most importantly, however, Spartan life, Spartan society, and Spartan history preserved the military traditions of their ancestors. In so doing, they produced the finest fighting machine that Greece had ever known.

Two crucial wars sent the course of Spartan development in this unique direction. In the later seventh century BCE, driven by overpopulation and hunger for land, the Spartans had attacked and conquered their neighbors, the Messenians. In the sixth century, these same people rebelled and had to be suppressed. Both of these wars lasted for decades and strained the Spartans to the breaking point. After the first Messenian war, the Spartans converted the entire Messenian population into serfs called *helots*. After the second, they restructured their own society to ensure that the helots would never revolt again.

What made Sparta unique, then, was not its government but its social structure. Perhaps 90 percent of the population were serflike helots, assigned to work the fields of the citizens. To keep this large oppressed majority in line, Sparta built a garrison state. At the age of seven, a Spartan male child left his parents for a state school, where he was taught basic reading and writing, turned into a perfect physical specimen, and drilled in military skills. At twenty, he joined the army, where he served for the next forty years. He could marry at eighteen but had to live in the barracks until he was thirty, slipping home in secret to visit his wife. He continued to eat with his messmates until he was sixty when, at last—if he lived that long—he was excused from further military service and allowed to return permanently to his family.

The Peloponnesian Wars, 460–404 BCE

Spartan women, on the other hand, seem to have enjoyed some advantages unique to the Greek world. Perhaps because men were so preoccupied with military matters, the women of Sparta owned and managed two-fifths of the property. They were also encouraged to participate in sports and to grow strong—in order to bear healthy sons for the state.

Toward the end of the sixth century BCE, the Spartan fighting machine began to impose its power on new neighbors. These peoples, called *perioici* ("dwellers around"), were not enslaved but were required to aid the Spartans in war. This century also saw the organization of an even larger Spartan–dominated alliance of Dorian city-states known as the *Peloponnesian League*. Members accepted Spartan leadership in foreign affairs and sent contingents to support the Spartan army in war but were otherwise self-governing. Until the Delian League was formed in the next century, the military force that Sparta assembled by drawing on the perioici and the Peloponnesian League was the largest such force ever gathered in Greece.

The common danger of Persian conquest had brought Athens and Sparta together in the opening decades of the fifth century BCE. But during the middle years of the century, while Pericles guided Athens to imperial supremacy over the Aegean, the Spartans looked on with increasing alarm. Shortly before midcentury, as the Persian Wars wound down, conflict broke out between the two leagues.

The Peloponnesian Wars raged intermittently over most of the second half of the century. The main phase, called the Second Peloponnesian War, lasted for a quarter of a century, from 431 to 404 BCE. At first, it seemed an indecisive struggle between a sea power and a land power, neither side being able to get close enough to the heart of enemy strength for a fatal blow. The Athenians struck by sea, raided the coasts of the Peloponnesus, but could not get at Sparta itself, which was located well inland. Raiding deep into Attica, the Spartans besieged Athens but, finding the city connected by long walls to its port at Piraeus, they were unable to cut Athens off from the grain supplies and imperial revenue that continued to arrive by sea.

Slowly, however, things turned against Athens. When the entire population of Attica crammed into the besieged city, a plague swept through Athens, killing tens of thousands, including Pericles himself. Then an unstable but charismatic young aristocrat named Alcibiades (c. 450–404 BCE) began to urge a new grand scheme: the conquest of Syracuse, the powerful Greek city in Sicily. He persuaded Athens to dispatch two hundred ships and tens of thousands of Athenians and others westward, but the expedition was poorly led and Syracuse proved too powerful. The result was the loss of the entire Athenian fleet and army. Alcibiades, summoned home, defected to Sparta.

For some time the Athenians, crippled as they were after the Sicilian fiasco, were still able to beat the inexperienced Spartans on the sea. Then in 405 BCE, another large Athenian fleet fell to the enemy, this one seized by the Spartans on the shores of the Hellespont while its ill-disciplined crews were inland on a foraging expedition. This humiliating defeat left Athens helpless, and the Spartan commander, the great general Lysander (d. 395), laid siege to Athens once more. The Athenians starved through a brutal winter rather than surrender, but in the spring of 404 BCE they laid down their arms at last.

The victorious Spartans required the Athenians to destroy the long walls that linked Athens to its vital port and that had made it impossible to break the city by siege for so long. They also compelled the Athenians to give up their empire and what remained of their navy and imposed a government of Athenian puppet rulers known as the *Thirty Tyrants* on what had been the most democratic people in the Greek world.

◆Classical Greek Culture◆

The Western heritage of Greek culture included the achievements of several centuries before and after the fifth century BCE. We will look here at Greek religion, history, and philosophy, poetry, drama, and art, cultural products dating back to the Greek Dark Age and forward as far as the fourth century BCE.

Does this cultural legacy matter? The books these people wrote are in your university library—more than two thousand years later. The art that remains is in museums across the Western World. And tourists are staring up at the ruined temples on the Acropolis hill in Athens today, even as you read these words.

Religion and History

As with most peoples, religion provided a framework for the culture of the ancient Greeks. In addition, however, the Greeks became the first Western people to develop a strong sense of their own history—the human side of their collective past.

In Greek religion, Zeus was universally recognized as the king of the gods and the final arbiter of human destinies. Zeus's brother, Poseidon, was god of the sea, and his daughter, Athena, was the goddess of wisdom, the crafts, and sometimes military strategy. Apollo reigned as lord of poetry, music, law, and prophecy. Aphrodite was the goddess of beauty and love, Ares lord of the battlefield, and Artemis goddess of the hunt.

These were very human gods and goddesses. Zeus had a number of sons with earthly women. These semidivine offspring were the heroes of Greek myth, like Herakles (Hercules) who slaughtered more monsters than Gilgamesh did, and Achilles, perhaps the greatest of all the heroes of the Trojan War.

Emotional new beliefs called *mystery cults* also captured the imagination of many Greeks. Among these were the cults of Dionysus and Demeter, the divinities who were responsible for the harvest of grapes and grain. Demeter also promised eternal life to initiates who attended the Eleusinian mysteries, religious ceremonies centering on rituals and dramatic spectacles so secret that they remain unknown to this day. Dionysus's death and rebirth also symbolized the annual rebirth of the crops and were celebrated with ecstatic rites, including midnight revelry and feasting on the raw flesh of a sacrificial animal. Yet Dionysus was also honored more publicly and sedately at a great annual festival at Athens, where, as we will see, the Greek theater was born.

In addition to this mythic past, however, the Greeks wrote the West's first real history books. In the fifth century BCE, they broke with supernatural accounts of human affairs to produce the first systematic, critical investigations of the human past. The pioneers of this breakthrough in human self-understanding were Herodotus (c. 484–c. 425 BCE), the "father of history," and Thucydides (c. 460–c. 400), often hailed as the greatest of ancient historians.

Herodotus's *Persian War* stands out as the work of a gifted storyteller, a genial Ionian who had traveled everywhere and was as fascinated by the exotic customs of Eastern peoples as by the motives of the Persian emperor, Xerxes, in attacking the Greeks. In its vast canvas and vivid vignettes of kings and battles, the book is often compared to a Homeric epic. Herodotus was also still religious enough to see divine punishment in the defeat of Persian hubris, and patriotic enough to see the war as a triumph of Greek freedom over Eastern despotism.

Thucydides's *Peloponnesian War* was the product of very different times and a very different man. A failed Athenian commander himself, Thucydides sees the defeat of his native Athens rooted in the failure of its democracy as the feckless multitude proved unable to carry on without the guiding genius of Pericles. As a skeptical Athenian of the later fifth century BCE, furthermore, Thucydides saw no supernatural forces at work, only fortune and human folly. With scientific objectivity, he detailed the horrors of the plague at Athens and the brutalization of the Athenians, offering no moral to his story save the grim awareness that, in real history, men are often wolves to one another.

Greek Philosophy: Socrates, Plato, Aristotle

Philosophia, literally "love of wisdom," referred in ancient Greece to freewheeling speculation on the nature of things and on the proper conduct for human beings. The first Greek philosophers seem to have devoted their energies to trying to understand the ultimate nature of the world around them.

Thus Thales (c. 625–547 BCE), the first of them all, believed that all things ultimately reduce to water, an idea perhaps derived from Egyptian or Mesopotamian thought. His pupil Anaximander (c. 610–c. 547) urged that the world is best defined in terms of the four basic qualities of hot and cold, moist and dry. Pythagoras (c. 580–500), best known for his contributions to geometry, asserted that the essence of the universe lay in numerical relationships and numerically based cosmic harmonies.

Heraclitus (c. 540–450 BCE) believed that the essence of reality is change. The world, he said, is like a leaping flame or a flowing river in which nothing is ever the same. Parmenides (b. c. 515 BCE), by contrast, asserted that beneath all appearances of difference and change lies pure being, eternal and unchanging.

A controversial breakthrough movement in fifth-century Greek thought was the rise of the *Sophists*. The Sophists were popular teachers, men who—for a fee—undertook to instruct the young sons of well-off Greeks in the sort of worldly wisdom that would guarantee them success in later life. The heart of the Sophists' formal teaching was rhetoric, or the art of winning oratory. Their enemies charged that they were teaching the young to use tricky argument to make the worse cause seem the better one. And some Sophists openly doubted the existence of the gods and declared that all things are relative, all moral principles mere matters of opinion.

Three men, however, contributed more than any others to the development of fifth and fourth century Greek philosophy: Socrates, Plato, and Aristotle.

Socrates (469–399 BCE) was an overweight, unprepossessing cracker-barrel philosopher, normally to be found lounging in the shady colonnades around the agora, arguing with judges, poets, the young, the old—anyone, in fact, who wanted to talk about the largest questions in life. Socrates saw his role in society as that of an intellectual gadfly, stinging his fellow citizens into serious thought about serious matters. The *Socratic method,* often imitated by talented teachers since, consists in rational disputation, with the object, not of defeating the opposition, but of searching for mutual enlightenment. If we argue it out, the Athenian philosopher suggested, maybe we will both learn something new. "The unexamined life," said Socrates, "is not worth living."

One of Socrates's most admiring students was a young man of noble lineage and poetic inclinations named Plato (429–347 BCE), who became the most influential philosopher in Western history. In his *Dialogues*, Plato's *theory of ideas* takes us beyond the flux and flicker and rumble of things to where, Plato agreed with Parmenides, there lies permanence—an unchanging, higher reality. Plato called that world of eternal truths the *realm of Ideas*—not ideas in your head, but Ideas with an independent existence of their own, in their own separate world of being. These eternal Ideas, forms, or absolutes can only be apprehended by human reason and thus only by a true lover of wisdom—a philosopher.

Ideas also give form and meaning to all the particular things in this material world. These "particulars," reflect, embody, or "participate in" the platonic Ideas. Individual human beings, for example, are human because they participate in the *Idea* of humanity.

On this foundation of what is sometimes called the "two–story universe"—Ideas above, particulars below—Plato based his social and ethical views. All ethical values, he declared, are absolute—not relative—because they reflect eternal forms or Ideas. On the political side, Plato argues in *The Republic*, his most famous work, that because of their superior understanding, philosophers should be the rulers of the ideal state. Under their wise rule, the other members of society would perform the tasks they were best fitted for. Peasants would farm, and soldiers would defend the state. The result would be the best of all communities, the perfect republic guided by "philosopher kings" with a unique insight into the realm of eternal truths.

Plato's most celebrated pupil and greatest rival down the centuries was Aristotle (384–322 BCE), whose knowledge was encyclopedic and who left us his ideas in the form of lecture notes on logic, rhetoric, metaphysics, physics, biology, ethics, politics, and art, to name just a few of the subjects he mastered.

A practical man with an empirical bent and a lifelong interest in biology, Aristotle developed his own theory of ideas. For him, ideas are real enough, but they exist *within* the particulars, not in some transcendent, nonmaterial realm of being. His forms, furthermore, are active forces, purposive drives in nature. These *entelechies,* as they are sometimes called, impel all things to develop to predestined ends, as an acorn grows into an oak tree.

Aristotle's ethical theory urged the *golden mean,* "moderation in all things." Virtue, he said, is not the opposite of vice, but a mean *between* vices: courage is a virtue, but both cowardice and foolhardy recklessness are vices—all extremes are wrong. Aristotle's definition of artistic beauty as "the imitation of nature," his claim that great literature produces a *catharsis,* or purging of emotional tensions, his definition of a tragic character as a noble nature doomed by a single flaw—all are familiar theories today.

Greek Poetry from Homer to Sappho

Greek poetry was invented before Greeks learned to read and write. It evolved as an oral tradition roughly comparable to the folk songs and balladry of many peoples. In the Greek Dark Age, bards chanted epic war poems; in the seventh and sixth centuries BCE, lyric poems were sung by soloists or choruses to the sound of a lyre. The Greeks thus learned to construct a gripping narrative, compress a powerful emotion into a turn of phrase, and put into words "the way life is" when literature was still a performing art. From the earlier, epic tradition, we have one giant: Homer. Of the later, lyric poetry, many fragments survive, but again one poet stands out: Sappho.

Homer was hailed by the ancient Greeks as their greatest poet, his *Iliad* and the *Odyssey* as sacred books. We know almost nothing about him, though he was traditionally described as blind and as having lived in Ionia, probably around 800 BCE. His two surviving epic poems clearly drew upon traditional tales of that most popular of Greek myth cycles, the story of the Trojan War.

This legendary conflict was believed to have begun when a Trojan prince carried a Greek queen off to the Near Eastern city of Troy, igniting a ten-year struggle between Greeks and Trojans which ended with the destruction of Troy. Homer's *Iliad*—the *Poem of Ilios,* or Troy—deals with "the wrath of Achilles," the greatest of the Greek heroes, who, after falling out with the Greek commander Agamemnon, turns his back on the war. Only when his best friend, Patroclus, has been killed trying to take his place does Achilles return to the battlefield to take a bloody revenge. In Homer's *Odyssey,* we follow another Greek hero, Odysseus (Ulysses), home from Troy. Odysseus's ten-year wandering around the Mediterranean brings him encounters with monsters and magic, seductive sirens, and violence enough to satisfy any modern audience's hunger for excitement.

If Homer hymned the soldier's death-dealing vocation, Sappho stood firmly and passionately for life. "Some say a cavalry corps, some infantry . . . are the finest sight on the

Here the bard Homer seems to be seeking another audience for the works he recited in village squares or palaces. Carved centuries after the blind poet wrote the *Iliad* and the *Odyssey,* the statue reflects the Greeks' continuing veneration of Homer. What helps us feel the poet's blindness? (Bettmann)

dark earth," she says in a famous fragment, "but I say that whatever one loves is." Sappho was an aristocratic woman who lived on the island of Lesbos off the Ionian coast around 600 BCE. She was one of the lyric poets of the seventh and sixth centuries BCE whose verse dealt often with religious and patriotic themes but who also wrote love poems, drinking songs, and other brief expressions of strong feelings.

Sappho surrounded herself on Lesbos with admiring young women, and the term *lesbian* is used today to refer to women whose sexual preference is for other women—though, again, we know almost nothing about her life. She wrote poems about beautiful women, handsome men, and her love for her child, a "golden flower" for whom she would not take a kingdom. She hymned the beauty of the Greek islands, turning moonrise over the sea into words that defy the translator yet. All we have of her verse is fragmentary, sometimes no more than a single vivid image. Yet such is the power of these shards of poems—they are so compact, direct, and delicate—that no one questions Sappho's right to stand with the greatest. She certainly spoke for herself when she wrote: "They will remember us."

Greek Drama: Tragedy and Comedy

Greek theater evolved somewhat later, and our examples come from the fifth century BCE. Archaeological remains tell us that the open-air amphitheater where the plays were presented had a round stage with a central altar to the god Dionysus. The actors wore carved masks equipped with speaking tubes so they could be heard across the huge audience and stood on high clogs so they could be seen. They shared the stage with a chorus, who danced and sang or chanted, commenting on the unfolding story. The actors sometimes sang, sometimes spoke, a vigorous thrust and counterthrust of formal argument. We really have no modern equivalent of Greek theater, but the opera probably comes closer than any other present-day theatrical form.

Greek plays were presented in groups of three tragedies, all by the same author. Skilled playwrights used familiar stories from Greek mythology to illustrate such themes of eternal human concern as the family and society, morality, religion, or human destiny. Frequently, too, these dramatic treatments reflected the attitudes and moods of the period in which they were presented.

The most honored tragedians of the fifth century were Aeschylus, Sophocles, and Euripides. Aeschylus (525–456 BCE) pioneered in developing the dramatic potential of the Greek theater. For example, he added to the number of actors permitted on stage at once in order to heighten conflict. In his plays, gods and goddesses may appear to justify their treatment of human beings. In Aeschylus's *Oresteia,* a bloody cycle of family violence and vengeance is finally ended when the goddess Athena brings young Orestes to trial before Athens' Areopagus court, taming the spirit of traditional revenge.

Sophocles (497–406 BCE), a contemporary and friend of Pericles, links human character and human destiny in plays that are still given honored productions today. Sophocles's *Oedipus the King* revolves around the moral blindness of a noble ruler. King Oedipus simply cannot bring himself to believe that he has unknowingly committed the two terrible sins of murdering his father and marrying his mother—even though, as a foundling, he could not have been expected to recognize his true parents. In *Antigone,* the heroine's crime is her stubborn defiance of her ruler in order to bury both of her brothers—a sacred obligation—even though one was killed while defending their city and the other, a traitor, while attacking it. Antigone loves and honors both her brothers and will die rather than neglect her duty to them as she sees it. The great king, Oedipus, and the noble heroine, Antigone, thus face moral dilemmas that have no easy solutions, yet their nobility stays with us after the final choral ode.

The plays of Euripides (485–407 BCE) were very different. Imbued with the skepticism of the Sophists and the bitterness engendered by the Peloponnesian Wars, he was an angry man, looking reality in the face and seeing no noble human character shining through. In *The Trojan Women,* based once more on the Greek national epic of the conquest of Troy, Euripides chose to explore not the deeds of Homer's heroes but the fate of the women of Troy, who, after seeing their husbands and sons struck down, are themselves dragged off into slavery in a strange land. The play, with its empathy for women, foreigners, and the defeated, and its angry contempt for the brutality of the Greek "heroes," demonstrates both sensitivity and honesty.

To get away from such murderous contemplation of the unthinkable you might try a comedy—but if it was by Aristophanes (450–385 BCE), you would not get away from larger concerns and public issues. In *The Clouds,* for instance, he depicts the philosopher Socrates hanging from the ceiling in a basket, floating in clouds of muddled speculation and teaching young people ridiculous arguments that would turn them against their parents. In *Lysistrata,* written 2,400 years ago, Aristophanes solved the problem of war by having the women of Greece rebel, seize the Acropolis, and refuse to have sex with their husbands until the bloody-minded male half of the population yields to an even deeper biological need than bloodlust—and makes peace.

The Art of the Acropolis

Painting, sculpture, architecture—most of the major arts of later ages were practiced by the ancient Greeks. In each case, the Greeks learned from their Near Eastern or Egyptian neighbors before going on to found a distinctively Western tradition in the arts.

Nearly all the classic Greek painting that survives is found on a wide range of pottery—from huge funerary urns and storage vessels to large jars for mixing wine and water and wide elegant cups for drinking. Early examples were decorated in simple geometrical designs. Only after learning in Asia to brighten their vases with animals and flowers did the Greeks move on to the subject that would always fascinate Greek artists more than any other: the human figure.

Pictures of gods and goddesses, scenes from famous myths or from the battles of the Trojan War soon became common on Greek vases. So did scenes from everyday life, of women talking at the well or men at drinking parties. Two basic techniques evolved: *black figure,* in which the figures were painted in black on the reddish background of the clay, and *red figure,* in which the entire vase was painted black, leaving the figures in the reddish color of the original clay. Greek vases of the Classic Period offered even more impressive examples of red-figure ware decorated with graceful figures depicting a heroic Achilles or Sappho at her lyre.

Greek sculpture also made a major leap ahead under the influence of the ancient East. Thus the crude stick figures cast in bronze during the Dark Age were replaced during the Greek Awakening by well-rounded bronze or stone animals. And then Greek sculptors also turned their attention to the human figure. Clearly influenced by Egyptian statues, with their simple forms and strong frontal poses, Greeks, too, carved life-size figures in the white marble so common in the rocky islands and hills of their homeland.

The Athenian Acropolis. Few monuments of any age so clearly symbolize Western civilization as the white marble columns of the Parthenon, shown at the right center. What aspects of Greek history and culture are illustrated in this picture? (D. A. Harrissiadis Photographic Agency)

Greek sculpture of the Classical Age reached a level of balanced excellence—a combination of realistic representation with the idealization proper to gods and heroes—that would never be excelled. The goal of the classical style was to represent in bronze or marble the inner spiritual realities that Plato called Ideas, forms, and absolutes. To accomplish this, the classical style eased the rigid poses of earlier figures and perfected the idealized proportions.

Fifth-century BCE figures from the temple of Zeus at Olympia include the often reproduced statue of Apollo, perfectly proportioned, his handsome young face radiating the grave, emotionless certainty appropriate to the god of light and truth. In Myron's *Discus Thrower,* this Greek Classical style gave us the perfect athlete poised for action, while Polyclitus's naked youths and gods radiate a spirit of strength and the potentiality of youth.

Greek architecture also emerged at the time of the Greek Awakening under Egyptian influence. Awed by Egypt's huge columned stone temples, newly wealthy Greek city–states were soon building temples in stone too. These structures were simple in design—house-shaped structures with pillared colonnades and relief sculpture under the eaves above the fluted pillars. The capitals of the columns were of two sorts: the simpler Doric, and the more elaborate Ionic—inspired by Ionian contacts with Near Eastern architecture. The basic structure remained simple post and lintel, a matter of pillars and crossbeams, like that of earlier Greek buildings.

By the fifth century, this style was capable of producing temples of exquisite artistry. The Parthenon, Athens's temple of Athena *Parthenos,* or the Virgin, was a simple rectangular building framed with columns, with painted relief sculpture beneath the gently sloping roof. The visitor today may not notice the subtle variations from straight lines and equal distances that make the Parthenon one of the most brilliantly designed pieces of architecture in the Western world. But our eyes still react with pleasure to the subtle curves and slanting lines, as Pericles's builders had intended.

One way and another, a great deal of Greek culture has had this effect on later Western peoples. For more than two thousand years, it has served as a seedbed to Western civilization.

Summary

The ancient Greeks, creators of the first of European civilizations, drifted down from the Eurasian steppes into the peninsulas and islands of the Aegean. The first people they encountered in their new home were the Minoans. This commercial people, probably Near Eastern in origin, dominated the Aegean region from their trading posts. Headqurtered on the large island of Crete, the Minoans flourished between 2000 and 1500 BCE. By 1500, however, an early Greek people, the cruder, more militaristic and piratical Mycenaeans, came to dominate the region. The period of Mycenaean predominance lasted from perhaps 1500 to about 1100 BCE. Later waves of northern immigrants toppled the Mycenaeans as they had the Minoans, and trading and raiding both gave way to a simpler village culture in the Greek Dark Age.

Between 750 and 500 BCE, however, the growing Greek population passed through the Greek Awakening, a period of city–building and commercial and colonial expansion. Learning again from advanced Near Eastern civilizations, these Greeks built a city–state civilization of their own. Led by the Athenians, they developed a relatively democratic political system, in which male, free-born citizens determined the policies of each Greek state. They also became leading traders up and down the Mediterranean and established colonies from North Africa to the Black Sea.

Shortly after 500 BCE, this first of Western peoples successfully repelled the greatest of Near Eastern powers, the vast Persian Empire. Under the guidance of the great Athenian statesman, Pericles, the Greeks also organized a military alliance, the Delian League, which soon evolved into an Athenian empire. Pericles made Athens the cultural "school of Greece" and built the temples on the Acropolis that tourists still flock to visit today.

In the second half of the fifth century, however, the southern Greek Peloponnesian League, led by Sparta, challenged Athenian predominance in the fratricidal Peloponnesian Wars. After a bloody struggle in which Greeks did more damage to Greeks than the Persians had ever done, Sparta's victory shattered the Athenian hegemony as the fifth century ended.

While they fought and built and traded, however, this energetic people had also been generating an unexcelled cultural legacy. Even before the fifth century, Homer's epics and Sappho's lyrics earned the Greeks a place in world literature. In the fifth and fourth centuries BCE, Classical Greece produced an unexcelled outpouring of original art and ideas. Greek tragedy, sculpture, and architecture inspired centuries of imitation. Greek historians, the first in the Western world, chronicled the stirring events of their own times. And the Greek philosophers of the fifth and fourth centuries BCE, especially Socrates, Plato, and Aristotle, influenced all later periods of Western thought.

Some Key Terms

Acropolis 38
agora 38
archon 39
Areopagus 41
black figure ware 55
boule 41
catharsis 52
Delian League 45
deme 41
entelechy 52

golden mean 52
heliaea court 41
Hellenes 40
helot 47
hoplite 38
Indo-European peoples 36
metics 46
palace system 37
Peloponnesus 37

Peloponnesian League 49
phalanx 38
polis 38
red figure ware 55
Socratic method 51
Sophists 51
Theory of Ideas 52
Thirty Tyrants 50
trireme 43

Notes

1. Edgar Allen Poe, "To Helen."
2. Thucydides, *The Peloponnesian War,* trans. Richard Crawley (New York: Random House, 1951), 104.
3. For some legal purposes, Athenian law declared that *both* a citizen's parents must have been citizens, by this prescription including the politically disenfranchised mother.

Reading List

Bernal, M. *Black Athena: The Afroasiatic Roots of Classical Civilization.* 2 vols. New Brunswick: Rutgers University Press, 1987–1991. Controversial study of Egyptian and Near Eastern influences on early Greek culture.

Boardman, J. *The Greeks Overseas: Their Early Colonies and Trade.* Rev. ed. London: Thames and Hudson, 1982. Thorough study of early Greek expansion.

Burkert, W. *The Orientalizing Revolution.* Cambridge: Harvard University Press, 1992. Compelling analysis of Near Eastern influences on early Greek culture.

Drews, R. *The Coming of the Greeks: Indo-European Conquests in the Aegean and the Near East.* Princeton: Princeton University Press, 1989. Brief coverage of a complex subject.

Finley, M. I., ed. *The Legacy of Greece: A New Appraisal.* Oxford: Clarendon Press, 1981. Historic contributions—and limitations—of the founders of Western civilization.

Garnsey, P., ed. *Trade in the Ancient Economy.* London: Chatto and Windus, 1983. Articles on many facets of Greek commerce, drawing on both archaeological and documentary evidence. See also A. Burford, *Land and Labor in the Greek World* (Baltimore: Johns Hopkins University Press, 1993), emphasizing landholding in the ancient city-state.

Grene, D., and R. Lattimore, eds. *The Complete Greek Tragedies.* 3 vols. Chicago: University of Chicago Press, 1960. Expert translations of all the surviving plays.

Guthrie, W. C. K. *The Greek Philosophers: From Thales to Aristotle.* New York: Harper, 1960. Survey by a leading authority, with emphasis on Plato and Aristotle. See also G. Vlastos's, highly praised *Socrates: Ironist and Moral Philosopher* (Ithaca, N.Y.: Cornell University Press, 1991).

Herodotus. *The History of the Persian War.* Trans. Aubrey de Selincourt, rev. A. E. Burn. Harmondsworth, U.K.: Penguin, 1972. Readable version of the first history book.

Homer. *The Iliad.* Translated by R. Lattimore. Chicago: University of Chicago Press, 1951. Powerful poetic rendering by a noted Greek scholar who is also a modern poet. For Sappho's poems and fragments, see *The Songs of Sappho in English Translation by Many Poets* (Mount Vernon, N.Y.: Peter Pauper Press, 1946).

Hooker, J. T. *The Ancient Spartans.* London: J. M. Dent, 1980. Spartan political history in its geographical and cultural framework, stressing foreign relations. An excellent general history is W. G. Forrest, *A History of Sparta, 950–192 b.c.* (New York: Norton, 1969).

Hornblower, S. *The Greek World 479–323.* New York: Methuen, 1983. Survey of Greek history in the fifth and fourth centuries, with many interpretive insights.

Jenkins, I. *The Parthenon Frieze.* Austin: University of Texas Press, 1994. Brief but illuminating essay on the famous sculptures.

Kagan, D. *Pericles of Athens and the Birth of Athenian Democracy.* New York: Free Press, 1991. Enthusiastic account by a distinguished historian of ancient Greece. See also D. Stockton, *The Classical Athenian Democracy* (New York: Oxford University Press, 1990), stressing participation and sense of community.

Kleijwegt, M. *Ancient Youth: The Ambiguity of Youth and the Absence of Adolescence in Greco-Roman Society.* Amsterdam: J. C. Gieben, 1991. Upper-class families and career-oriented youth.

Ober, J. *Mass and Elite in Democratic Athens: Rhetoric, Ideology, and the Power of the People.* Princeton: Princeton University Press, 1989. Uses the rhetoric employed by the elite to communicate with the citizen body to illuminate the practice of democracy.

Owens, E. J. *The City in the Greek and Roman World.* London: Routledge, 1991. Ancient cities as public places, sacred shrines, seats of royal power, and as sites of other human activities.

Palmer, L. R. *Mycenaeans and Minoans.* 2nd ed. Westport, Conn.: Greenwood Press, 1980. Revisionist approach to the two most ancient cultures of the Greek world. See also J. Chadwick, *The Mycenaean World* (New York: Cambridge University Press, 1976). Perhaps the best socioeconomic survey of the Mycenaean period.

Peradotto, J., and J. P. Sullivan, eds. *Women in the Ancient World: The Arethusa Papers.* New York: SUNY Press, 1984. Pioneering articles from the classical journal *Arethusa.* See also M. R. Lefkowitz, *Women in Greece and Rome: A Source Book in Translation* (Baltimore: Johns Hopkins University Press, 1982).

Robertson, C. M. *A Shorter History of Greek Art.* Cambridge: Cambridge University Press, 1981. Shorter version of Robertson's *History of Greek Art* (1975), with splendid illustrations.

Sealey, R. *A History of the Greek City-States ca. 700–338 b.c.* Berkeley: University of California Press, 1977. Stresses regional and personal rivalries in political conflicts. See also C. G. Starr, *The Economic and Social Growth of Early Greece, 800–500 b.c.* (New York: Oxford University Press, 1977) with some emphasis on Near Eastern influences.

Thucydides. *History of the Peloponnesian War.* Translated by R. Warner. Rev. ed. Baltimore: Penguin, 1972. Literate translation of the best of ancient histories. See also D. Kagan's four-volume history of the war, from *The Outbreak of the Peloponnesian War* (Ithaca, N.Y.: Cornell University Press, 1969) to *The Fall of the Athenian Empire* (Ithaca, N.Y.: Cornell University Press, 1987).

— 3 —

Athena and Isis
The Hellenistic World

◆Alexander the Great and the Hellenistic Age
◆Hellenistic Society   ◆Hellenistic Culture

The Greek world, shaken to its roots by the late fifth century Peloponnesian Wars between Athens and Sparta, remained turbulent and contentious on into the fourth century BCE. The Greek cities, in fact, continued to feud until a new power, the northern kingdom of Macedonia, drove south to overwhelm them all.

King Philip of Macedonia brought all the Greek city–states under Macedonian rule in the later fourth century BCE. In the 330s and 320s BCE, his son, Alexander the Great, led the Greek and Macedonian armies far across Asia, conquering Greece's ancient enemy, the vast Persian Empire. In the wake of Alexander, Greece entered a new phase of its history—the *Hellenistic Age*, which lasted from Alexander's death in 323 to the death of the famous Egyptian queen Cleopatra in 30 BCE.

Throughout this period of tumult, expansion, and change, however, the Greek creative impulse continued to astonish. In the new Greek world that was Alexander's legacy, the calm wisdom of Athena that had informed Greek classical culture gave way to the more exotic and mysterious spirit of the Egyptian goddess Isis, and Platonic reason gave way to the startling new philosophies of Epicureans, Stoics, and Cynics.

◆ Alexander the Great and the Hellenistic Age ◆

The political history of Greece in the fourth century BCE centers on the coming of the Macedonians. Through the first two–thirds of the century, the city–states continued to fight among themselves for a position of prominence. But in 338 BCE Philip, king of Macedonia, imposed Macedonian predominance on all of them. Four years later, his son, Alexander the Great, led a Macedonian and Greek army into Persia, beginning a campaign that established Greco–Macedonian rule all across the ancient Near East. It was thus above all the impact of Alexander of Macedon that turned Greek life in new directions and moved Greece into the Hellenistic Age, the last period of its ancient history.

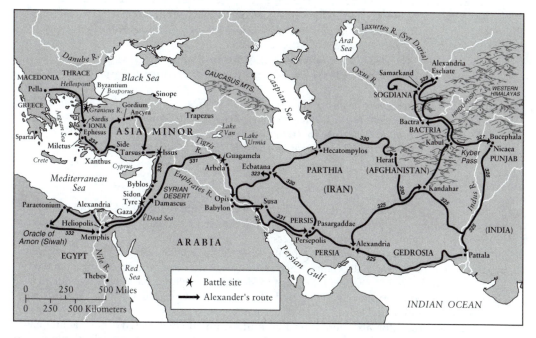

Alexander's Campaigns, 336–323 BCE

Philip Unifies Greece

Continued military conflict was not surprising. Decades of struggle in Greece had largely replaced the citizen armies of earlier centuries with professional soldiers who fought for pay. These hired troops were led by experienced military commanders to whom war was a way of life. By garnering glory, loot, and land for their people, these leaders enhanced their own power. In addition, many of the city–states' political leaders saw power as essential to their own or their constituents' interests. For decades after the Peloponnesian Wars, then, leading Greek cities continued to fight each other for *hegemony*, the position of dominant power in the divided peninsula.

The seemingly endless struggle among the city–states also had its roots in profoundly felt group interests. One continuing division was that between oligarchs and democrats, who typically represented the interests of more and less prosperous citizens, respectively. Some of these factions believed that Greece would be better off if one or another of the major contending city–states was dominant. Aegean and Ionian merchants were thus willing to accept Athenian protection once more, but others of a more conservative bent saw Sparta as the defender of sterner old Greek virtues.

The solution to the problem posed by the endless feuding of the Greek city–states came finally from a very unlikely source: the mountainous, half–civilized realm of Macedonia, looming along the northern frontier of the Greek peninsula.

To civilized Greeks, Macedonia in the fourth century BCE was the backwoods, ruled by kings who were the descendants of tribal chiefs. Macedonian rulers in the fifth and fourth centuries BCE tried to Hellenize their court with imported Greek talent and built a few new

Chronology 3: Hellenistic Greece

404–338	*Athens, Sparta, Thebes struggle for hegemony of Greece*
338	*Battle of Chaeronea—Philip imposes Macedonian hegemony on Greek city–states*
336–323	*Alexander the Great conquers Persian Empire*
323–30	*Hellenistic monarchies rule eastern Mediterranean, Egypt, Near East*
320–220	*Economic boom in Hellenistic monarchies*
c. 300	*Epicurus founds Epicureanism; Zeno founds Stoicism*
220–50	*Economic decline in Hellenistic monarchies*
47–30	*Cleopatra VII of Egypt loses last Hellenistic monarchy to Roman Empire*

cities that somewhat resembled those of their southern neighbors. Still, Macedonians were scarcely considered Hellenes even if they did speak the Greek language, and their admission to the Olympic Games was a bit of a concession.

Ambitious, ruthless, shrewd, and violent, King Philip (r. 359–336 BCE) came to power in Macedonia and substantially transformed both the country and its military machine during his twenty–two–year reign. Philip expanded trade, developed gold mines, built new cities, modernized his capital city, Pella, and got the famous Greek philosopher Aristotle to educate his son and heir, Alexander.

More important for his international ambitions, Philip constructed a new, genuinely national army. His rambunctious nobles still formed an elite cavalry corps called the royal Companions. A large infantry of tough Macedonian peasants was also organized, however, drilled in a more open formation than the Greek phalanx, and armed with a 13–foot spear that far outreached anything in use in Greece.

After years of maneuvers and countermaneuvers, the Macedonian host finally moved south in force to confront the best alliance the Greeks had been able to put together, composed primarily of Athenians and Thebans. At Chaeronea in 338 BCE, the Macedonians smashed the Greek armies and opened the way for Macedonian domination of all Greece. A key figure in the victory, commanding on the left flank, was Philip's teenage son, Alexander, whose troops shattered the Thebans and annihilated their crack "Sacred Band."

The rest of Greece accepted the inevitable Macedonian hegemony. Thebes was occupied by Macedonians and, after a subsequent revolt, leveled. Athens made terms with the victor. Most of the city–states were organized at last into a single alliance, the *League of Corinth,* sponsored and led by Macedonia. Philip, eager for still larger conquests, graciously accepted the league's request that he lead a combined Macedonian–Greek army in an invasion of the ancient common enemy, the Persian Empire.

In 336 BCE however, the Macedonian monarch was stabbed to death by a vengeful nobleman, whether in a personal vendetta or on behalf of political rivals, we do not know. Luckily for history, if not for Persia, Philip left an heir behind who was more than capable of taking over from his father.

Alexander Conquers Persia

Philip had already given his son at least two things of value: the tutorship with Aristotle, which engendered a love of all things Greek, and essential on–the–job training in the fundamentals of military command. The young noble Companions who surrounded Alexander when he led Philip's left wing at Chaeronea became the commanders of Alexander's own troops. Only twenty when his father was assassinated in 336 BCE, Alexander was ready to assume Philip's mantle.

The thirteen–year reign of Alexander the Great (r. 336–323 BCE) was one long military campaign. After burying his father, Alexander set off for the East to launch the invasion of Persia that Philip had planned to lead. It was an excellent time to strike at this traditional enemy of the Greeks. The royal court of Darius III (r. 336–330 BCE) was riddled with factions, and the satraps in the provinces were rebellious. Nevertheless, the empire still stretched for 2,500 miles across western Asia, from the Mediterranean to the Indus. Alexander spent the next dozen years fighting his way across it.

The young king's first victory, in 334 BCE on the Granicus River just across the Hellespont, was typically headlong and impetuous, Alexander leading the charge in person. Thereafter, the Macedonians marched down through the ancient Near East, defeating Darius at Issus in 333, capturing Tyre after a costly siege in 332, and continuing south through Palestine to Egypt. Returning northward, Alexander crushed Darius's army a second time at Gaugamela in 331 and took Babylon and the Persian capitals of Susa and Persepolis, looting and burning the latter. He then pursued the king of kings so relentlessly that one of the Persian's own satraps, ambitious to replace the defeated ruler, left Darius's corpse on a road in Media for the advancing Macedonians to find.

Alexander the Great, hectic and passionate, charges into battle against the Persian emperor in this Roman wall painting. Although created hundreds of years after Alexander's death, the picture captures something of the headlong rush into history that characterized the young Macedonian's meteoric career. (Art Resource)

But the wars of Alexander were not over. In 330 BCE he led his troops on to the east, up into the barbaric lands of central Asia, and then down through the Khyber Pass into India. In 326, now beyond the Indus in the Punjab, the Macedonians fought the powerful Indian army of King Porus (d. 321 or 315 BCE), whose cavalry rode on elephants. Then at last Alexander's army had enough. Worn out, ragged, thinned in numbers, they insisted on turning back across the scorching wasteland north of the Arabian Sea and traveling up the Persian Gulf toward Babylon.

There, within a year of his return, Alexander the Great died in 323 BCE of a sudden fever. At thirty–two, he was master of all the civilized world he knew. Asked by hovering lieutenants to whom he left his immense empire, the dying Alexander is supposed to have replied, "To the strongest."[1]

The Hellenistic Monarchies

"The name of Alexander," wrote the distinguished German historian, Johann Gustav Droysen, "signifies the end of one epoch of world history and the beginning of a new one."[2] Alexander's conquest of the East marked the beginning of the Hellenistic Age, and the history of this period was clearly that of Alexander's heirs and of his legacy.

Alexander left behind a new state system stretching from Greece and Egypt across much of the Middle East. These new nations were hereditary monarchies and much larger than the Greek city–states, but they were every bit as rivalrous. The political history of the Hellenistic world was, therefore, in very large part the history of conflicts between the Hellenistic kings and queens for a larger share of the world they had inherited from Alexander.

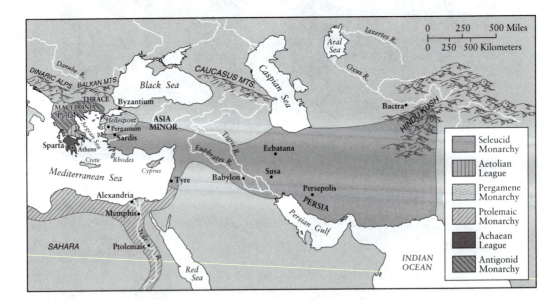

The Hellenistic Monarchies, 323–31 BCE

Within less than two decades, all of Alexander's family, including his mother and his sisters, died by violence, as did several of his generals and many of the soldiers who had marched with him. By 300 BCE, three of the chief Macedonian commanders had divided the lion's share of the empire up among themselves and were squabbling over the spoils.

Antigonus I, the One–Eyed (382–301 BCE), the grizzled veteran among the generals, came closest to taking it all. In the end, however, the *Antigonid dynasty* he founded had to be satisfied with Macedonia itself, Asia Minor (Turkey), and intermittent hegemony over mainland Greece. Seleucus I (c. 358–280), the youngest of Alexander's marshals, claimed most of the enormous expanse of the old Persian Empire. Yet in the next century, eastern Persia, and even the central provinces, cast off the Macedonian yoke, leaving the *Seleucid monarchs* mostly ancient Mesopotamia. Ptolemy I (c. 367–283), finally, whose memoirs, as drawn upon by Arrian, tell us most about Alexander, successfully established himself and his descendants as the thirty–first or *Ptolemaic dynasty* of Egyptian pharaohs.

Some of these Alexandrian successor states lasted for centuries. Among the most famous later rulers of Hellenistic dynasties were the queens of Ptolemaic Egypt. It became the custom there for the Ptolemies, like some of the earlier pharaohs, to marry their sisters, some of whom turned out to be the stronger rulers. Among the most successful was Arsinoë II (r. c. 299–c. 279 BCE). A powerful personality, she dominated the nation for three decades, expanded Ptolemaic Egypt to its greatest size, and inaugurated the golden age of the Ptolemies.

Less successful, but better known, was Cleopatra VII (r. 50–30 BCE), Egypt's last hope for freedom from the expanding Roman Empire. Determined to resist the onward march of Rome, this Cleopatra established successive alliances with two of the most powerful Roman leaders of the time, Julius Caesar and Mark Antony. Only the death of one of her Roman allies and the defeat of the other frustrated Cleopatra's efforts. She died by her own hand—to become a legendary name in history.

These *Hellenistic monarchs*, male or female, ruled Egypt, Persia, Macedonia, and other lands in a style that was without precedent in the Greek past. They assumed grand titles like Savior, Benefactor, and The Great. They built themselves huge palaces, contributed lavishly to the beautification of Greek cities and famous shrines, and staged spectacular public festivals. In the old Near Eastern style, they made law by decree and assembled hordes of officials and armies of unprecedented size to carry out their will. Frequently, they followed the ancient Eastern practice of calling themselves gods and establishing cults in their own honor. It was enough to make the democratic Greeks of an earlier age turn over in their graves.

◆Hellenistic Society◆

Greek society, as it evolved in the Hellenistic period, boasted not only strikingly autocratic government but distinctive economic and social features. From an economic point of view, the Hellenistic world appears to have been more prosperous than any Greek age before it. And the condition of women was probably better than at any earlier time. However, the gulf between the richest and the poorest yawned wider than it ever had, and tensions between the classes increased.

Wealth and Poverty

The economic history of these centuries is not all of a piece. The hundred years or so after Alexander's death in 323 BCE seem to have comprised a period of impressive economic expansion. The period following this prosperous third century, however, appears to have been a time of economic decline.

As early as the fourth century BCE, Greek merchants became even more skilled and businesslike. Trade revenues were apparently higher. The upper classes of the cities remained increasingly well off into the third century, in spite of the incessant wars. The Macedonian conquest had opened the well–filled Persian treasuries, and the new Hellenistic monarchs stamped large quantities of new coins with their own features. As a result, cash replaced barter almost everywhere and prices rose rapidly—both boons for business. In addition, the Greek–Macedonian predominance created new demands for Greek goods in the East, further expanding the volume of trade. This commercial expansion was also encouraged by the building of larger merchant ships and better harbors equipped with stone quays and lighthouses, like the famous Pharos of Alexandria. Banking also became more professional, though interest rates were extravagant, often running above 25 percent a year.

The Mediterranean market thus grew busier than ever before. Such established Greek exports as wine, olive oil, and pottery were in great demand. Luxury goods like glass, jewels, perfumes, incense, and papyrus came from the Near East. Commodities such as timber, metals, and wheat were also widely exchanged. By this time wheat was drawn from Sicily as well as from Egypt and the Black Sea. Slave labor continued to be imported from the less developed fringes of the Greek world. Meanwhile, Mediterranean merchant adventurers reached still further out during the expansive Hellenistic Age. Mariners explored the coasts of the Caspian Sea, circumnavigated Britain, and pushed down the African coast as far as the Cape Verde Islands. Though Seleucus I feuded with the Indian empire builder Chandragupta (r. c. 321–c. 297 BCE) over territory in what is today Pakistan, trade with India brought jewelry and spices along the Persian caravan routes and by sea up the Persian Gulf and the Red Sea.

After the third century, however, the economy began to shrink again, and social discord intensified once more. Inflation and the endless wars drained the wealth of the Hellenistic monarchies. Cities still glittered as relative beacons of prosperity, but the countryside sank deeper into poverty. And in the cities, too, the gap between rich and poor continued to widen. Government, especially in the Near East, still played a large part in the economic life of the period. In Ptolemaic Egypt especially, government officials continued to extract rent, taxes, and compulsory labor from the peasantry, and Greek innovations increased their burdens. The Greeks built better roads and introduced iron tools and new crops to the Egyptian community. They ran the agricultural economy even more tightly, telling the peasants exactly what to plant, providing seed in proper quantities, and collecting the grain for overseas export to enrich the treasuries of the Ptolemies. Basic industries like the production and distribution of wine, beer, and salt also remained highly profitable government monopolies.

Individual entrepreneurs—middle–class traders and artisans as well as aristocratic investors—continued to be common in the older Greek world around the Aegean. There were entrepreneurs also in the newer Greek cities of Seleucid Persia and its neighboring states. But the Hellenistic monarchies generally regulated and profited from the economic productivity of their countries as their predecessors in the Near East had done.

Social Tensions

In this enlarged Greek–dominated world of new monarchies and surviving city–states, of boom times and bad times, social discontent flared once more.

If anything, the bitterness between the classes was worse throughout most of the Hellenistic period than it was in the Classical Age. The old loyalty to the city–state that had somewhat mitigated class conflict had been badly undermined by the Peloponnesian Wars and the fourth–century BCE struggle for hegemony in which rich and poor so often found themselves on opposite sides. The individualism of the philosophical schools (see below) also undercut the growth of a community spirit that might have bridged class differences and conflicting economic interests. During most of the fourth century, furthermore, the great colonization movement of earlier periods seemed to have ended, so that there was little in the way of a safety valve for excess and discontented populations.

As pressures mounted in the fourth century BCE, conflicts between the wealthy few and the poor majority grew more virulent. The common people demanded such drastic reforms as the cancellation of debts and the redistribution of the estates of large landowners among poor peasants. The more privileged classes set up associations and clubs dedicated to the maintenance of oligarchic power in their own hands.

There was some improvement in the later fourth century. Alexander's conquests of the 330s and the 320s BCE opened up vast new lands for Greek emigration and exploitation. The economic boom of the third century further eased the pressure. The rich stayed rich, but the poor were fewer and not so badly off. Judicious distribution of festivals and other favors added to the less rebellious mood of the masses.

Then in the second and first centuries BCE, the end of Hellenistic prosperity rekindled social tensions. The wealthy, not willing to give up their privileged position, tended to make up for worsening economic conditions by expanding their landholdings at the expense of hard–hit peasants. The peasants and the urban poor responded by slacking off in their work and even by refusing to work at all—an early form of industrial strike. In Greece particularly, the cities echoed once again the shouts of the factions whose political slogans often reflected the bitter antagonisms of the social classes. If we add to this picture the tensions between Greek rulers and the non–Greeks they ruled in the East, we can see clearly the sources of weakness in Hellenistic society.

Only one bright spot remained in this picture of increasing social conflict and exploitation: the legal, educational, and economic conditions under which women lived improved dramatically in Hellenistic times. Hellenistic women had more rights in marriage than they had in earlier periods, and in some parts of the Greek world, women had as much right to own property as men did. Greek women of good family were also no longer uniformly confined to the "private sphere" of the home but moved into the larger world once reserved for men. Hellenistic women thus held public magistracies and other official positions in some city–states. There were women doctors, musicians, and painters and at least one woman architect. Women raced on foot and in chariots at the Olympic Games, and statues of victorious women began to appear at the great shrine of Apollo at Delphi.

The Hellenization of the East

A major consequence of Alexander's long march and of the Greek conquests in western Asia was what is usually called the *Hellenization* of the East. It was not as deep a transformation as was once assumed, and it did not last as long. But for several centuries, Hellenic or Greek influences had a profound impact on their neighbors in the Middle East and North Africa.

The cities the Greeks built in conquered lands were prime sources of Greek influence. Alexandria, the Ptolemaic capital situated in the Nile delta, was both the cultural center of the Hellenistic world and the largest city in the West before the rise of Rome. Scores of other Greek cities were established as military colonies all across the former Persian domains, where the Seleucids provided land, housing, and money in return for military service from the Greek colonists. There may have been as many as seventy or eighty of these new towns, some built in conjunction with existing native settlements but all dominated by a Greek ruling class.

Greek bureaucrats, soldiers, and traders further increased the Greek presence in the conquered lands. In Egypt, the ancient scribal bureaucracy of the pharaohs was now run by Greek–speaking people from the West, while for generations only Macedonians and Greeks served in Ptolemaic armies. When we add to these the great increase in the numbers of Greek merchants and artisans in Near Eastern cities, there is no doubt that the Greco–Macedonian element in these Asian areas was significantly strengthened.

This Greek style of life undoubtedly had some impact on the older world around these Western enclaves. Hercules carved in stone turns up along the Persian Gulf, and statues of Buddha in far–off India reflect the influence of Greek sculpture. In Egypt, the separation between Greeks and Egyptians eventually broke down sufficiently to permit some inter-marriage between the two cultures. Hellenized Egyptians, Syrians, or Mesopotamians probably became more acceptable in Greek society as the generations passed. There was even some cultural influence in the other direction. Such Eastern religious faiths as Persian Zoroastrianism and the cult of the Egyptian goddess Isis, as we will see, found followers first among the Greeks and later among the Romans.

Even at its height, however, Hellenization tended to be limited to urban areas or coasts. The Seleucids surrendered most of Persia to Asian rulers in less than a century, and the Ptolemies lost Egypt to the Romans in three centuries. Within a few more centuries, non–Western regimes and Asian faiths completely reclaimed North Africa and the Near East.

Yet though the Greek predominance ended and Greek cities built of brick crumbled to dust, archaeologists still find in a broken column or a scattering of Greek coins evidence of the ancient impact of the West on the East. And Western scholars in modern times found that stories about the great conqueror "Iskander" were still being told in Asian market-places more than twenty centuries after Alexander rode that way.

◆ Hellenistic Culture ◆

In the arts, literature, science, religion, and philosophy, the fourth century BCE and the Hellenistic Age that followed constituted an immensely impressive, sometimes quite star-tling period. Hellenistic high culture can be seen as largely a response to this exotic new world of autocratic monarchies, enormous wealth, sharpened class differences, and disori-enting contrasts between Greek ideas and Asian or North African cultures. Artists and writ-ers contributed to this complex reaction by representing their world in both realistic and romantically escapist ways. Greek scientists tried to explain the world in realistic terms. By contrast, philosophers and religious thinkers sought escape from troubled and confusing times in the philosophic quest for peace of mind or in the ecstatic release of cult worship.

The Arts: Realism and Sentimentalism

Greek artists plunged eagerly into the celebration of the new era. The splendor of the Hellenistic monarchies, subsidized by Persian gold and the endless bounty of the Nile, produced an unprecedented flow of commissions for statues, temples, palaces, and even new cities. Classical traditions combined with a new sense of grandiloquent scale and an enthusiasm for novelty to generate a distinctive Hellenistic style in the arts.

One element in that style was a new zeal for realism. Although the sculpture of the Classical Age was the most realistic to date in Western culture, fifth–century BCE sculptors went only so far with naturalistic representation as they needed to make their symbolic points—for example, to show Zeus as the incarnation of power or Pericles as the image of the great leader. In Hellenistic sculpture, however, the idealized proportions and Olympian calm of fifth–century statues were replaced by precise anatomical accuracy and careful delineation of individual character. Realism became an end in itself, not a means of communicating a larger truth.

Aphrodite, the goddess of love, was sculpted naked now, with a body so smooth and subtly modeled that it would be quite easy today to confuse a photographic close–up of a tautly sculptured calf or a fold of flesh with a photo of the real thing. Sculptors also showed what they could do by flinging these accurately rendered bodies into violent, twisting motion, as in the famous group of *Laocoön* and his sons crushed in the serpent's coils. Or they used swirling, clinging draperies to define the moving bone and muscle beneath, as in the great *Nike of Samothrace,* known as the *Winged Victory,* glowing today in a pool of light at the end of a long gallery in the Louvre in Paris.Realistic portraiture in stone flourished as never before. Hellenistic sculptors bring the living faces of contemporaries before us, from the sensitive Antiochus I the Great to a thuglike king of Bactria, from a thin and somber Demosthenes to an anonymous drunken old lady, every wrinkle and swollen vein in evidence. Even Socrates was sculptured as overweight and unprepossessing, as he apparently was in life, rather than as a great philosopher ought to have looked.

Another oddly contrasting element in Hellenistic style was a longing for *escape* from the very realities that this style was so good at depicting in painful detail. Sentimental subjects were as popular as realistic portraits. The public loved tragic depictions of the Dying Gaul, but also appealing statues of children in various poses, including the cliché carving of a small boy plucking a thorn from his bare foot. Equally trivial and equally charming were genre figures made of clay, like the Tanagra figurines. These miniatures depict ordinary ancient Greek people going about their everyday business: a slender young woman wearing a mantle and a fashionable hat; an old lady walking a baby that will not fall asleep. Later ages would also sentimentalize such things, but few young women in any age can have been quite so softly feminine, few grandmothers or babies so sweet.

It was in building, however, that Greek artistry rose most magnificently to the challenge of the new age of the Alexandrian successor states and their deified kings. Whether their clients were city–states seeking to preserve their heritage or monarchs aiming to awe the masses, Greek builders were equal to the task.The Greek cities distributed across the Middle East had to have their temples and their agoras like those at home, their theaters and gymnasiums dedicated to sound minds in sound bodies. Greek elites everywhere prided themselves on decorating their cities, and Hellenistic kings demonstrated their beneficence by giving a new theater or a new stoa, or pillared portico, to a favored city.

Some Hellenistic cities were dazzling sights, with their walls and terraces and two-storied stoa, their hilltop temples and palaces. Pergamum in Asia Minor set the standard for splendor, with its colonnaded agora, its great altar of Zeus and its temple of Athena, its royal palace crowning the hill, and an open–air Greek theater that held ten thousand spectators. Most splendid of all was Alexandria. The main harbor, with the Pharos, its 400–foot lighthouse, symbolized the commercial wealth of the city, while its palaces and temples revealed the presence of the divine Ptolemies. Perhaps most famous, however, were Alexandria's cultural institutions—the zoological and botanical gardens and, especially, the museum and libraries—the latter containing perhaps four hundred thousand books. Public buildings like these stood several stories high and were elaborately decorated with painted sculptures.

Reality and sentimental dreams met and mingled in these metropolitan complexes. The reality of Hellenistic power merged with the romantic dream that Classical Greek culture could be preserved forever in these exotic new homes in Asia and Africa.

Literature: From Comical to Pastoral

In Hellenistic literature, the tension between a hankering for realism and romantic escapism showed as clearly as it did in sculpture. Drama, poetry, and prose all reflected these divergent tugs on the Hellenistic psyche.

Realism was evident in such new forms as the *Characters* of Theophrastus (c. 372–287 BCE), pithy thumbnail sketches of all–too–human types with their foibles on display. And racily realistic dialogue began to appear in some popular theatrical entertainment. Perhaps most vividly, the famous comic plays of Menander (342–292 BCE), written around 300 BCE, put ordinary people of the Hellenistic world on the stage. The New Comedy, of which Menander was the foremost practitioner, differed from the Old Comedy of Aristophanes in that it deliberately eschewed large issues and political positions. Menander's characters—slaves, prostitutes, and pastry cooks, ordinary Greeks who would not know Homer from Hercules—face problems having more to do with sex, love, and money than with the great issues of the day. The actors in these plays still wore masks, though they also wore ordinary street clothes. They still spoke in verse but in a rhythm that approximated everyday speech. Menander's characters were comic stereotypes, and his endings were invariably happy, but his people were closer to real Greeks and real problems than Aristophanes's Socrates with his head in the clouds or *Lysistrata*'s women taking over the Acropolis to put an end to war.

Yet the urge to escape from reality was there too, in scholarship and literature. The museum and libraries of Alexandria were frequented by the leading scholars of the day, many of them subsidized by the Ptolemaic government. A major focus of Alexandrian scholarship was the thought and literature of the Greek past. Homeric studies flourished, producing learned and abstruse commentaries on the greatest Greek poet. Such scholarship is often seen as escapist because these Hellenistic scholars buried themselves in the literature of the past instead of producing a living literature of their own.

It was, however, the formalism of the Alexandrian poets and the idyllic pastoral poetry of Theocritus in particular that best illustrated this longing to slip away from the way life was into a variety of never–never lands. *Formalism*, or art for its own sake, became a literary

Scholars of many persuasions gathered at the great library of Alexandria in Hellenistic times. Notice the form the "books" these people read took and the way the manuscripts were stored. Why did historians in later centuries mourn the loss of this library and its contents to fire in ancient times? (Bettmann)

cult among the poets of sophisticated Alexandria. Their goal was not to offer inspired truths or insights into the human condition but to produce perfect poems. Technical perfection meant mastery of metrical forms, rhetorical devices, and all the classical models back to Homer. The Alexandrian formalists thus generated verse of a polished simplicity and an allusive wit that was quite beyond any ordinary Greek—beyond anyone, in fact, except their fellow poets.

This dream of escape to unlikely, idealized realms of poesy also affected the subject matter of Hellenistic verse. Apollonius of Rhodes (295–214 BCE) revived the epic form of Homer in his *Argonautica* to tell, not a war story, but a love story. The story of the Greek hero Jason's many adventures in his quest for the Golden Fleece in his ship, the *Argo,* and of his love for the Asian sorceress Medea might sound a bit like Odysseus's long voyage home. But Jason is no rough–hewn Homeric hero, and his voyage is so heavy with learned commentary on the local antiquities that it sometimes sounds more like a journey through a museum than a cruise to the mythical kingdom of Colchis.

The Alexandrian poet Theocritus (c. 310–250 BCE) gave expression to a more obvious escapism in his thirty *Idylls*, short poems evoking an "idyllic" pastoral world of shepherds and shepherdesses. The meticulously crafted songs of these simple folk on such subjects as love, death, and the beauties of nature could take the cosmopolitan reader far from the thronged streets of Alexandria to the half–imaginary groves of Theocritus's youth in his native Sicily. The longing of the city dweller to get "back to nature" and the belief that peasants are morally superior and lead happier, more aesthetically pleasing lives was to become a staple of literary escapism in Western culture.

The Hellenistic period also saw a significant increase in the availability of education for women. Some schools seem to have been coeducational, and a highly literate female aristocracy developed. This, in turn, led to the appearance of a number of women writers and to the presence of women in the philosophical schools.

On the literary side, the poetic legacy of Sappho was taken up several centuries later in the larger Hellenistic world. A number of Hellenistic women were honored by their cities for their poetry. Erinna of Telos, perhaps the most revered woman poet of the period, was compared to Sappho by her contemporaries. Erinna mastered the complexities of Greek verse forms at a remarkably early age and wrote the much admired *Distaff*, in which she lamented the death of a friend. Dead herself by the age of twenty, Erinna was mourned in turn by her peers.

Science: The Hellenistic Flowering

During the Hellenistic period, Greek scientists achieved enormous advances in human understanding of the material world. There had been some investigation of the nature of the physical world in earlier Greek centuries. The Milesian philosophers of Ionia, the Pythagoreans, Plato, and Aristotle all speculated on the ultimate nature of the world around us. In the sixth century BCE, Pythagoras (c. 580–500 BCE) offered mathematical insights, including the famous "Pythagorean theorem," or the formula for determining the hypotenuse of the right triangle. In the fifth century, Hippocrates (460–377 BCE), the most famous of Greek doctors, inspired new directions in medicine and proposed the Hippocratic oath, which is still taken by doctors today.

The greatest Greek breakthroughs in mathematics, astronomy, physics, and biology, however, came in the fourth and third centuries BCE. Fusing Greek and Near Eastern scientific insights and exchanging ideas in the stimulating atmosphere of Alexandria, Hellenistic scientists learned more about the universe than the West learned for the next two thousand years. It took the modern scientific revolution to match—and exceed—the Hellenistic achievement.

It was during the Hellenistic period that Euclid (fl. c. 300 BCE) summed up Greek geometrical knowledge in his *Elements of Geometry*. Euclid's elegantly logical mathematical demonstrations communicated the Greek rational spirit as effectively as Aristotle's logic did to later generations of Western people, and his book was used in schools even into the present century. Other Hellenistic Greeks studied the mathematical characteristics of circles, spirals, and conic sections.

Archimedes of Syracuse (287–212 BCE) and other Hellenistic scientists made basic discoveries in several areas of physics, including optics, acoustics, hydrostatics, and mechanics.

Archimedes calculated the value of *pi*—the ratio between a circle's circumference and its diameter—and formulated the basic principle of the lever, asserting with typical Greek panache that if he were given a long enough lever and a place to stand, he would literally move the world. Proudest of his discoveries in abstract mathematics, Archimedes was also traditionally credited with designing ingenious war machines for the defense of his city. In the end, however, he is perhaps most famous for a single word, shouted as he raced home dripping from the public baths with a new insight into the displacement of water by his own body. His cry of *"Eureka!"* ("I have found it!") is often taken as the quintessential expression of the Greek passion for truth.

In biology, the earlier Greek philosopher, Aristotle, had recognized the relationship between groups and families of living things. His empirical observations were sharp and generally so accurate that later scientists hesitated to challenge him even when he was in error. His pupil, Theophrastus, author of the satirical *Characters* that we have already mentioned, also developed a method of categorizing plants that remained standard well into modern times. With the medical insights achieved by Hippocrates and by Galen (129–c. 199 CE) later on, this biological research reflected an empirical spirit that would scarcely be seen again until the birth of modern science.

Greek scientists made their most impressive discoveries in the study of the earth and the heavens—in geography and astronomy. With their new access to Babylonian astronomical data and with the great Alexandrian libraries to draw on, the Hellenistic Greeks had a sounder empirical basis for speculation in this field also.

Greek scholars came to realize that the earth is a sphere and divided its surface into degrees of longitude and latitude. Eratosthenes (275–194 BCE) calculated the size of the earth and Hipparchus (c. 190–126 BCE) the length of the year with remarkable accuracy. The astronomer Aristarchus (c. 310–230 BCE) deduced that, though the heavenly bodies all seem to revolve around the earth, the sun is actually the center of the planetary system and the earth merely one of the planets. It was Hipparchus's earth–centered explanation of the structure of the universe, how-ever, that won general acceptance. And Hipparchus's erroneous view—in the learned, mathematically sophisticated form proposed by the astronomer Ptolemy in the second century CE—was reverently accepted until Copernicus.

Religion: Growth of the Mystery Cults

Accompanying the rise of Greek science were serious doubts about the traditional gods, already questioned by the Sophists of the fifth century BCE. Sophisticated people were amused by the mythical amours of Zeus, and some suggested that all the gods and goddesses might be legends based on half–forgotten kings and heroes. Confronted with the possibility that the gods of their fathers might never have existed at all, many people prayed instead to *Fate* or *Fortune,* to whom statues and temples were solemnly raised. Hope for good fortune was embodied in the particularly popular cult of *Tyche,* or Luck, conceived of as a goddess like Athena or Aphrodite.

Other Hellenistic Greeks, unable to confront the grim possibility that life really might be a matter of blind chance, turned to astrology, magic, and a growing number of oriental religions. Astrology built on the scientific recognition that the sun does affect the moon, the tides, and growing things, insisting that stars and planets could affect the course of human life as well. Many, including highly educated people, consulted astrologers for guidance before undertaking any serious project, just as their ancestors would have consulted oracles.

The Eastern *mystery cults,* meanwhile, came closer to replacing the Olympians than these cults had ever done before (see also Chapter 2). The faiths of Dionysus and Demeter, going back to the Greek Awakening, had never had so many initiates. Of the newer religions, the cults of the Egyptian goddess, Isis, and of Cybele, the Earth Mother from Asia Minor, were the most successful. The worship of Cybele and her consort, Attis, revived once more the ancient spirit of the fertility cult. Cybele's rituals involved ecstatic violence, climaxing on the annual "Day of Blood," when priests slashed themselves with knives before screaming crowds.

The religion of Isis, bringer of eternal life, and Osiris, lord of the underworld, which went far back in Egyptian history, was encouraged by the Ptolemies as a national religion. Often shown with a cow's horns, sometimes framing a solar disk, Isis won a cult following all around the Mediterranean. For many, Isis became, in fact, the incarnation of all the gods, the "Goddess of Ten Thousand Names," the repository of all wisdom.

The mystical wisdom of Isis was very different from the practical wisdom of grey–eyed Athena, goddess of the olive tree and protector of Athens, but it was no less valuable to Hellenistic people. Above all, Isis was the merciful divinity who brought salvation and eternal life to those who believed in her.

These oriental cults of the Hellenistic epoch thus offered the greatest escape of all from the harsh realities of life: communion with a deity who promised another, better life to true believers. Elaborate processions through the streets, ritual dramas enacting the rebirth of the god, secret initiations, hymns, and ecstasies all revealed the profound emotional hungers that "realism" could not satisfy.

Philosophy: Stoics, Epicureans, and Cynics

For the more intellectually inclined, however, escape from a world of meaningless splendor might be found in the new philosophies. Of these, Epicureanism and Stoicism had the greatest influence, though Cynicism produced perhaps the most colorful gurus. The goal of all the new schools may be summed up, however, in a single phrase: "withdrawal from reality to find peace of mind."[3]

Zeno (335–263 BCE), the founder of *Stoicism,* taught in the columned stoa around the marketplace at Athens. Urging that a rational principle orders all things in nature, Zeno concluded that all people, sharing in this basic rationality, were fundamentally equal. Slaves, women, and even foreigners were thus brothers and sisters under the skin. This was a valuable insight for Hellenistic Greeks who, unlike their ancestors, often lived in North Africa or the Near East, surrounded by people very different from themselves.

The fundamental Stoic concern, however, was to find a way of life that would help people escape the misfortunes that beset all human lives. Admitting that human affairs were often beyond human control, Zeno preached duty and emotional disengagement from the world around us. By overcoming fear, desire, and other human feelings, his followers sought what they called *apathy,* an "emotionlessness" that would free them from the worst the world could do. Thus purged of their emotions, they could do their duty and confront whatever came quite calmly—as we still say, stoically.

Epicurus (341–270 BCE), the founder of *Epicureanism,* agreed with his contemporary Zeno on the harsh nature of life in this world, but he disagreed about the formula for escape from it. Epicurus adopted the *atomism* of the philosopher Democritus (c. 460–370 BCE) as his metaphysical foundation. Everything, he said, even a god, is made of tiny identical particles of matter called atoms, drifting through space, encountering and linking up by pure chance to form the material world we know. By the philosophically dubious introduction of a willed "swerve" in the drift of atoms, however, Epicurus gave us some control over our own lives. And he told his followers how to exercise that control: through the pursuit of pleasure.

But the pleasure Epicurus preached was no eat–drink–and–be–merry sensual hedonism; it was simply the absence of pain. "The end of all our action," he declared, "is to be free from pain and fear, and once we have attained all this, the tempest of the soul is laid."[4] Death itself need hold no terrors, for it involved no afterlife but simply the dispersal of the atoms of our bodies into the universe. For this life, Epicurus and his disciples retreated to a walled garden on the edge of Athens, where they found approved pleasures in friendship, music, poetry, and the fragrance and colors of the flowers.

The ultimate philosophical withdrawal, however, was that of the *Cynics,* who sneered at society, rejected material comforts, and sought salvation in forms of "natural living" so crude that they outraged their contemporaries. The most notorious of the Cynics, Diogenes (c. 400–c. 325 BCE) jeered at money, marriage, education, and "social conventions" like the taboos on incest and cannibalism. Diogenes lived in a large jar instead of a house and, rejecting all political allegiance, declared himself a "citizen of the world." His total lack of inhibition and his refusal to be enslaved by Hellenistic social conventions earned him the contempt of many but an admiring epitaph: "Your fame will live forever, Diogenes, because you taught humankind the lesson of self–sufficiency."[5]

Among the philosophers, a number of women were disciples of Pythagoreans and some were followers of Plato, but the Stoics and the Epicureans, distinctively Hellenistic schools, offered them the warmest welcome. Epicurus saw women as fellow seekers, while Stoics recognized the divine spark of rationality in people of both sexes. There were even women in the ranks of the Cynics, perhaps the most radical of the new schools. They were apparently not always accepted easily among the disputants at the feet of the various masters. But Hipparchia the Cynic responded with proper philosophical serenity when challenged as to why she had abandoned her weaving to join the search for truth: "Do I seem to you to have come to a wrong decision, if I devote that time to philosophy which otherwise I should have spent at the loom?"[6] She might have been speaking for philosophers of both sexes who sought escape from the workaday world in the search for a higher reality.

Summary

The continuing struggle for hegemony among Greek city–states ended in 338 BCE when Philip of Macedon subdued all the feuding Greek states. The reach of Greek civilization extended even further when his son Alexander the Great went on to conquer the Greeks' ancient enemy, Persia, by 323 BCE. But Alexander's immense empire quickly fragmented into feuding Hellenistic monarchies in which the once independent Greeks became subjects of hereditary monarchs rather than self–governing citizens.

A striking feature of the Hellenistic Age was the spread of both Greek power and Greek culture across much of the Near East and parts of North Africa. Alexander's successors ruled Persia for a century and Egypt for three. These and other Hellenistic monarchies encouraged the cultural Hellenization of the eastern end of the Mediterranean from the fourth century on.

From the later fourth to the first centuries BCE, Hellenistic rulers built splendidly to project an image of their own greatness. Hellenistic science expanded Western knowledge in the fields of astronomy, physics, biology, and medicine. Stoic, Epicurean, and Cynic philosophies, as well as much of the period's sculpture, literature, and religion, however, reflected a need to escape from the tensions of Hellenistic society into sentimental art or inward-turning systems of thought.

Some Key Terms

Antigonid dynasty 65
apathy 74
atomism 75
Cynics 75
Epicureanism 74

formalism 70
hegemony 61
Hellenistic Age 60
Hellenistic monarchs 65
Hellenization 67

League of Corinth 62
mystery cults 74
Ptolemaic dynasty 65
Seleucid dynasty 65
Stoicism 74

Notes

1. Diodorus Siculus in Claire Preaux, *Le Monde Hellénistique: La Grèce et l'Orient, 323–146 av. J.-C.,* vol. 1 (Paris: Presses Universitaires de France, 1978), 127.
2. Johann Gustav Droysen, *Geschichte des Hellenismus* (Tubingen: Wissenschaftliche Buchgemeinschaft, 1952), 1.
3. Michael Grant, *From Alexander to Cleopatra: The Hellenistic World* (London: Weidenfeld and Nicolson, 1982), 234.

4. Epicurus, *Letters,* in Grant, *Alexander to Cleopatra,* 240.
5. Michael Grant, 245.
6. Diogenes Laertius, *Lives and Opinions of Eminent Philosophers,* vol. 6, 96–98, quoted in G. W. Botsford, *Hellenic Civilization* (New York: Columbia University Press, 1920), 665.

Reading List

Boardman, J., G. Jasper, and O. Murray. *Greece and the Hellenistic World.* New York: Oxford University Press, 1988. Authoritative survey of the period.

Bosworth, A. B. *Conquest and Empire: The Reign of Alexander the Great.* Cambridge: Cambridge University Press, 1988. Clear, detailed account by a leading authority.

Bulloch, A. W., E. S. Gruen, A. A. Long, and A. Stewart, eds. *Images and Ideologies: Self-Definition in the Hellenistic World.* Berkeley and Los Angeles: University of California Press, 1994. Essays on Hellenistic monarchy, religion, and philosophy.

De Sainte Croix, G. E. M. *The Class Struggle in the Ancient Greek World.* Ithaca: Cornell University Press, 1981. Strains in a slave society seen as class conflict.

Ellis, J. R. *Philip II and Macedonian Imperialism.* London: Thames and Hudson, 1976. The achievements of the first great Macedonian.

Fraser, P. M. *Ptolemaic Alexandria.* New York: Oxford University Press, 1972. Cultural life of the intellectual capital of the Hellenistic world.

Grant, M. *From Alexander to Cleopatra: The Hellenistic World.* New York: Scribner's, 1982. Colorful evocation of the age by a prolific classicist.

Green, P. *Alexander of Macedon, 356–323 b.c.* Berkeley: University of California Press, 1991. Scholarly, sharply critical biography. See also J. M. O'Brien, *Alexander the Great: The Invisible Enemy* (New York: Routledge, 1992) and R. F. Lane's very readable *Alexander the Great* (New York: Penguin, 1994). For an older, more laudatory view, see W. W. Tarn, *Alexander the Great* (Boston: Beacon Press, 1956).

Green, P. *Hellenistic History and Culture*. Berkeley: University of California Press, 1993. Good, broad account of the period.

Hansen, M. H. *The Athenian Democracy in the Age of Demosthenes: Structure, Principles, and Ideology*. Translated by J. A. Crook. Oxford: Blackwell, 1991. Describes participatory democracy operating more effectively than most would have expected.

Hornblower, S. *The Greek World 479–323*. New York: Methuen, 1983. Survey of Greek history in the fifth and fourth centuries, with many interpretive insights.

Kleijwegt, M. *Ancient Youth: The Ambiguity of Youth and the Absence of Adolescence in Greco–Roman Society*. Amsterdam: J. C. Gieben, 1991. Upper-class families and career–oriented youth.

Lloyd, G. E. R. *Greek Science After Aristotle*. New York: Norton, 1973. Clear presentation of scientific theories for the nonscientist. See also his *Early Greek Science: Thales to Aristotle* (London: Chatto and Windus, 1970).

Long, A. A. *Hellenistic Philosophy: Stoics, Epicureans, Skeptics*. London: Duckworth, 1986. Covers major Hellenistic schools.

Owens, E. J. *The City in the Greek and Roman World*. London: Routledge, 1991. Ancient cities as public places, sacred shrines, seats of royal power, and as sites of other human activities.

Peradotto, J., and J. P. Sullivan, eds., *Women in the Ancient World: The Arethusa Papers*. New York: SUNY Press, 1984. Pioneering articles from the classical journal *Arethusa*. See also M. R. Lefkowitz, *Women in Greece and Rome: A Source Book in Translation* (Baltimore: Johns Hopkins University Press, 1982).

Pollitt, *Art in the Hellenistic Age*. New York: Cambridge University Press, 1986. Recent and well illustrated. See also C. M. Havelock, *Hellenistic Art* (Greenwich, Conn.: New York Graphic Society, 1970). On later Greek art and its influence on Rome.

Pomeroy, S. B. *Goddesses, Whores, Wives, and Slaves: Women in Classical Antiquity*. New York: Schocken, 1975. A celebrated feminist survey of women's place in Greece and Rome.

Sherwin-White, S. M. *From Samarkand to Sardis*. Berkeley: University of California Press, 1992. The Seleucid Empire.

Walbank, F. W. *The Hellenistic World*. Rev. ed. Cambridge, Mass.: Harvard University Press, 1993. Excellent survey of the period.

4

The City on the Seven Hills
The Roman Republic

◆Roman Beginnings   ◆The Expansion of Rome
◆Disorder and Civil Strife   ◆Roman Culture

The great achievements of the Romans were building and ruling a vast empire. They were never quite the artists or the original thinkers that the Greeks were. But they did manage to bring not only most of western Europe, but also the Near East and North Africa, as well, under a single government. It is the only time in history this has happened.

The long-range consequences of this achievement were equally remarkable. The Romans left to later Western centuries a legacy that included not only Roman culture but much Greek and some Near Eastern civilization as well. Roman law, Greek philosophy, and the Judeo-Christian religious traditions all reached the medieval and modern West, in large part, through Rome. If Greece was the originator, Rome was the consolidator of what is properly called the Greco-Roman heritage, a major component of Western civilization.

The thousand-year span of Roman history, roughly 500 BCE–CE 500, divides in the middle at about the time of Christ. During most of the first five centuries of this history, the period of the *Roman Republic,* Rome was governed primarily by its aristocracy, the patrician ruling class that sat in the Senate and held most of the executive offices. During the second half of Roman history, the period of the *Empire,* hereditary emperors ruled the state, and the Senate became little more than a rubber stamp for imperial decrees. Both these periods, however, shared in Rome's epochal achievement, the temporary unification of the Western world and the final shaping of a Greco-Roman culture that would influence all subsequent periods of Western history.

The present chapter surveys the history of the Republic, traditionally dated from 509 to 31 BCE. It begins with an account of Rome's beginnings as a small but aggressive and ambitious city on the Italian peninsula. It traces the story of Roman territorial expansion stretching all the way around the Mediterranean Sea. And it concludes with Rome's collapse into social divisions and civil war in an anarchic period which ended with the rise of the Caesars to power in the city on the seven hills.

The Roman forum as it looks today. Here powerful orators thundered denunciations of national enemies or demanded political reforms, and huge crowds cheered. Now of this center of Roman public life only scattered columns, the shells of public buildings, and a single triumphal arch (left) remain. (Art Reference Bureau, Inc.)

Chronology 4: Rise of Roman Republic

509	*Roman Republic founded*
450	*Twelve Tables of the Roman Law*
484–287	*Struggle of the Orders divides patricians and plebeians*
265	*Rome rules Italy*
218–201	*Second Punic War—Hannibal ravages Italy, but Rome emerges victorious*
c. 150	*Hellenization of Rome begins*
133–31	*Wealth and slaves pour into Rome from Empire; class struggle divides rich and poor; politicians and generals fight for power*
133, 123	*Tiberius and Gaius Gracchus serve as consuls, seek reform*
100–86	*Long feud competition between Marius and Sulla*
70 BCE–CE 19	*Virgil*
48–44	*Caesar defeats Pompey, seizes power; murder of Julius Caeser*
31	*Octavian defeats last rivals, takes power as Augustus Caesar*

♦ Roman Beginnings ♦

Not all the remains of the ancient West lie open to the Mediterranean sun. A visitor can also find ancient history under the Church of San Clemente in Rome. While Catholic services are chanted in the nave above, you can pass down through level after level of history. There is an ancient Roman church beneath the floor of the modern one. Still further down, archaeologists have uncovered a temple of Mithras, the Persian god adopted by the Roman legions. At the deepest level, finally, dark waters swirl through a second-century alleyway far below the traffic of modern Rome. Such a descent into the past may also carry your mind still further back—back to a time before the city of Rome existed at all—back to a handful of villages scattered over green hills under a blue Italian sky.

An understanding of Rome's beginnings will involve a look at the geographical framework of Roman history. The following pages will also explore the basic structure of Roman society and, at rather more length, the formative early political history of the Roman Republic, from the influences of such developed neighbors as the Etruscans to the "struggle of the orders" for rights and power within Roman society.

Rome and the Mediterranean

Geography played as important a part in Roman history as it did in the history of the Greeks. The city of Rome, to begin with, evolved from a group of villages on the river Tiber in central Italy, and Italy is the central landmass in the Mediterranean Sea—two geographical facts that help explain Rome's rise to mastery of the Mediterranean. Another aspect of Italian geography that helped determine the course of Roman history is the fact that the Italian land is not chopped up into tiny mountain valleys or narrow promontories as Greece is. Because their land was not divided, it was much easier for Romans to move beyond the city-state than it was for the Greeks to do so. The Apennines mountain range does run the length of Italy, but it leaves large arable plains, especially in the Po River valley in the north and down the western side of the peninsula. This fertile soil, combined with much more abundant rain than Greece enjoyed, made it possible to support a larger population than the Greek mainland.

At the same time, a lack of good harbors—except in the south, where Greek colonies were already established—limited Rome's interest in the sea and the world of commerce, where Greeks excelled. Though Rome's empire ringed the Mediterranean, and Rome later built fleets and imported heavily from overseas, it was always essentially a land power. Romans became famous as builders of roads, not ships.

The Mediterranean—*mare nostrum,* "our sea," as the Romans later came to call it— did offer Rome some rich targets for conquest. The Mediterranean is the core of a water system some 2,500 miles long and includes such tributary bodies of water as the Adriatic, Aegean, and Black seas. Its coasts are eminently livable, with a subtropical climate; they have sufficient pasture to support cattle, horses, mules, sheep, and goats; and the land is fertile enough to cultivate a variety of grains and fruits. Finally, the sea itself had for centuries served as an avenue of trade for Phoenicians, Greeks, and others, and as a stimulus for cultural development through easy intercourse between peoples.

By 500 BCE, the eastern half of the Mediterranean Sea was already bordered by flourishing civilizations. From the Nile valley in North Africa around to the Turkish Straits, which separate Asia from Europe, lay the high cultures of the Near East. The cities of the Greek world stretched from the Ionian coast of Asia Minor (Turkey) across the Aegean and Adriatic seas all the way to the colonies of Sicily and southern Italy. The western half of the Mediterranean was more sparsely civilized, but it too was dotted with cities, many of them Phoenician and Greek colonies along the coasts of modern France, Spain, Morocco, Tunisia, and Algeria. As Rome grew stronger during the centuries after 500, furthermore, the Mediterranean region as a whole was growing richer. Wealth piled up in the Hellenistic monarchies to the east; prosperous cities like Syracuse in Sicily or Carthage in North Africa glittered within easy reach of Roman power.

The Mediterranean basin, as we have seen, had become over three thousand years one of the greatest centers of civilization in the world, as highly developed as the Hindu-Buddhist culture of India and the Confucian civilization of China. The imposition of political unity on one of the most affluent and brilliant centers of world civilization was Rome's first historic accomplishment.

Early Roman Society

The Romans certainly did not look like a people of destiny in 509 BCE, the traditional date of the founding of the Republic. The first Romans were an Indo-European people like the Greeks who had migrated down from the northern steppes of Eurasia around 1000 BCE. They were a tough, warlike people who moved rapidly from using excellent bronze weapons to wielding even more successful iron ones. By about 750 BCE they were living in thatch-roofed villages among the seven hills along the Tiber where the great city of Rome later stood.

They had selected a good location for their settlements, with defensible hills and a river ford, 15 miles in from the sea, that marked a key juncture on the main north-south road. The fields around their hills were fertile, and the early Romans exerted a growing influence on most of the less strategically located Latin-speaking peoples around them.

A more developed people, however, soon imposed their authority on them all. Evidence of the Etruscan culture begins to appear in the archaeological record around 800 BCE. We do not know where they came from, but their language was not an Indo-European one, and their burial and sacrificial practices point to the Near East. And as soldiers and pirates, they formed a military ruling class, forcing other Italian peoples to work their fields, mine their metals, and serve in their armies.

The Romans learned a great deal from their Etruscan neighbors and overlords. During the sixth century BCE, the villages that lay scattered among the seven hills were fused into a small city, with temples, public buildings, and walls. The Romans turned a swampy bit of low ground into the forum—a market and public meeting place like the Athenian agora. They also began to exchange goods with the colonies of what they called Great Greece, or *Magna Graecia,* further south. In fact, it was the Latin term *Graeci* that gave us the name "Greek" for the people who called themselves the Hellenes.

But it was the Etruscan influence that was paramount among the earliest Romans. Some Roman styles in building, including the arch and the vault, were modeled on those of Etruria. The Romans adopted the alphabet that the Etruscans had borrowed from the Greeks. Even the oppressive Etruscan monarchy left its mark on the political organization of the Roman Republic. The Roman Senate, for example, was originally an advisory body to the Etruscan king of Rome. The consuls, Rome's chief magistrates, took over the Etruscan symbol of ultimate authority, the bundle of rods and the ax. Together called the *fasces,* these represented royal power to order corporal punishment and execution. Even the white gown called a toga, the badge of citizenship in the Roman Republic, was borrowed from the Etruscans.

The social structure of these earliest Romans, like that of most preurban peoples, was based on a family unit over which the father had absolute authority. Broader units of social organization included the *gens* or clan, composed of a number of families claiming common—sometimes divine—ancestors. Larger still was the tribe, based on birth or place of residence.

Relations between the sexes were strongly patriarchal. Roman women of the Republic were usually subject to male guardianship. Patriarchy was enshrined in the ancient *patria potestas,* the father's life-and-death power over the rest of the family. The father's legal authority included the right to arrange a daughter's marriage, to sell any member of the family into slavery, or to sentence a wife, child, or slave to death. On the other hand, a Roman woman did acquire considerable status when she married, and the "Roman matron" could be as much admired a figure as the father of the family. Women could also inherit property in their own names, could refuse a marriage arranged for them by their parents, and could obtain a divorce relatively easily, especially in the looser atmosphere of the later Republic.

On top of older divisions based on family relations, newer social classifications founded primarily on landed property had emerged by 509 BCE. There were two such social classes in the early Republic: patricians and plebeians. The *patrician* minority boasted the most distinguished ancestors, owned the largest farms, and were the recognized leading citizens of the state. The rest of the people were *plebeians,* most of whom were poor farmers. Some plebeians, however, became men of wealth and ambition themselves in later years, leading to conflict between these two classes, or "orders," of Roman society.

Among the traditional relationships that bound the orders of society together, the highly developed system of *clientage* was central. In the earliest days and at the lowest level, this meant the almost feudal obligation of plebeians to work the estates of a patrician landowner, who, in turn, was obliged to protect and support his plebeian clients. In later republican times, clientage bound the less affluent to support the political ambitions of the great.

Similar ties across class lines often bound masters and slaves, the power of the owner being balanced to some degree by responsibility to support the unfree worker. Frequently, furthermore, slaveowners freed their slaves in later life; and such a manumission, rather than ending a relationship, created a new one, between master and freedman. A freedman's contract, in fact, often required continuing payments or other services to the former master.

Early Political Institutions

Sometime around 509 BCE, the Romans expelled the last Etrucean monarch to rule them and established their own little state. The government of this early Roman Republic resembled that of the Greek city-state. There were executive magistrates, a Senate corresponding to a Greek council, and not one but several popular assemblies. The most powerful of these assemblies in the early days was the *comitia centuriata*, an "assembly of the centuries" composed of hundred-man units in the Roman army. Like the early Greek assemblies, this gathering of Roman males under arms met periodically on their drill field to elect magistrates, pass laws, and decide basic questions of policy. In subsequent centuries, the *comitia tributa* or "assembly of the tribes" became the most important of Roman popular assemblies.

Most powerful of all was the *Senate*, an aristocratic council composed of three hundred men who were the real rulers of the state. Originally heads of the wealthiest clans and members of ancient patrician families, senators were also often former magistrates and senior statesmen. Because they spoke for the patrician ruling classes, senators tended to be conservative; because they held their Senate seats for life, they could afford to take the long view. In times of peril, senators could provide strong and steady leadership; confronted with a need for change, however, they often resisted reform.

Of the Roman magistrates, the most powerful were the *consuls,* a pair of elected officials who enjoyed the *imperium,* the absolute power, that had been wielded by the banished kings. Imperium, symbolized by purple robes and the rods and the ax, conferred the crucial authority to command armies in the field as well as the power to punish any citizen. The consuls were elected by the assembly for only a single year. In the early days, however, they were always patricians who could look forward to advancing to the Senate immediately upon completing their year's consulship.

The Struggle of the Orders

This system, putting the preponderance of power in patrician hands, generated opposition from the beginning. The first couple of hundred years following the overthrow of the kings around 500 BCE saw a long intermittent struggle by the Roman plebeians to claim a larger share of political power. This conflict, called the *struggle of the orders*, pitted the plebeian masses against their traditional betters, the patrician aristocracy.

The first clash between the orders came in 494 BCE, when the plebeians threatened a secession from the Roman state and won the right to elect two magistrates of their own, called *tribunes.* Over generations, these tribunes, whose number increased to ten, acquired extraordinary powers. They could countermand the decisions of consuls, veto legislation, and appeal any case directly to the Senate. Most important, the person of a tribune was deemed sacred, and he was thus safe from bodily harm throughout his tribuneship.

Another advance for the plebeian majority came in 450 BCE, when political pressure forced the publication of the laws for the first time. Inscribed on twelve wooden tablets, these *Twelve Tables* made public the traditional laws, customs, and legal procedures that only patrician magistrates and senators had mastered before. Other reforms followed. In 445 BCE, intermarriage between the two orders was legalized, making it possible for wealthy plebeians to marry into the prestigious patrician clans. In 367 the consulship was opened to plebeians. And in 287, laws passed by the assembly of the tribes were made legally binding on the whole Roman people.

The Senate continued to make major decisions involving war, peace, and financial matters and to guide the decisions of the assembly through personal influence, money, and even threats. But a new, broader, though still conservative, senatorial elite of old patrician and newer plebeian families came to dominate political life.

✦ The Expansion of Rome ✦

While the Romans were shaping a government that suited their conservative, pragmatic character, they were also embarking on a larger historical enterprise: the building of an empire that came to girdle the Mediterranean. As we will see, Roman expansion began as early as the fifth century BCE with the conquest of the Italian peninsula. Thereafter, this expanded Roman state fought a crucial series of wars with the North African commercial empire of Carthage for mastery of the western Mediterranean. During the last two centuries of the history of the Roman Republic, finally, Roman armies swept around this inland sea, from Greece to Egypt and beyond, to ring the Mediterranean with Roman power.

The Conquest of Italy

The instrument that built this vast empire was the famed Roman army, one of the most admired military forces in history. Like the armies of the Greek city-states, the army of the early Republic was a citizen force, composed of farmers who owned at least enough property to afford their own weapons. Roman infantrymen were armored with helmets and breastplates and armed with shields and spears in the hoplite style. Divided into the hundred-man units called *centuries,* the early army also included some cavalry and some lighter infantry. Later, Roman commanders learned to break up their military formations into small independent blocks of troops called maniples, armed with javelins rather than spears. Undergirding the strength of the Roman army was Roman discipline, tenacity, and a chauvinistic sense of Roman superiority that made Roman armies frequently victorious—and almost sure to come back again when they were not.

Rome's first foes included many peoples who shared the peninsula of Italy with this growing city-state, as well as people who had settled on the large island of Sicily to the south. Around the fifth century BCE, Rome's neighbors included other tribes who spoke Italic languages (the languages of ancient Italy, including Latin), the Etruscans and the Gauls to the north, and the Greeks and Carthaginians from North Africa to the south.

The Romans began to fight almost as soon as they were free from the Etruscans. Under Etruscan tutelage, they had attained a predominant position among their Latin neighbors, and they wanted to retain that position. Moreover, there was also a very real possibility of reconquest by the Etruscans. For both these reasons, in the first few years of the fifth century BCE, the Romans imposed alliances on the other peoples of Latium in central Italy. They also began to chop away at Etruria to the north, and in 396 BCE, after a long siege, they destroyed a major stronghold of Etruscan power, the great city of Veii.

Half a dozen years after this victory, however, the Romans suffered the greatest defeat in the history of the early Republic. Around 390 BCE, a marauding army of wild Gauls from the north overwhelmed a Roman army and sacked, looted, and held the city for ransom. The Romans picked themselves up, rebuilt their city and their alliances, and reconquered lost ground. When the Gaulish raiders next came south, they were repulsed. Rome's ultimate revenge was even sweeter, for in later centuries, Roman legions marched north to conquer not only Cisalpine Gaul but the Gauls' homeland beyond the Alps in what is now France.

Meanwhile, Rome continued to absorb neighboring Italian peoples and soon found itself intervening in the affairs of the Greek city-states to the south. One of these, the city of Tarentum, summoned a Greek king from across the Adriatic, Pyrrhus (319–272 BCE) of Epirus, to its aid. Pyrrhus had a famous mercenary army, and he beat the Romans twice at great cost to himself. In 279 BCE, surveying a battlefield littered with casualties, Pyrrhus is supposed to have groaned, "One more victory like this over the Romans, and there'll be nothing left of us." By 275 he had departed, leaving the Greeks of southern Italy to Rome and the grim phrase "a Pyrrhic victory" (a victory that is too costly) to history.

By 265 BCE, Rome was the master of Italy from just south of the Po valley to the toe of the Italian boot. But territorial expansion meant more than winning wars. It was also a matter of organizing both their newly conquered lands and their new client states into a durable structure of power. There was much to be gained by becoming, willingly or not, part of the growing Roman confederation of Italian peoples and cities. Those who accepted the status of Roman ally got Rome's protection from foreign aggression in return for providing troops for the Roman army. More fortunate peoples were made partial citizens of Rome; that is, citizens who could trade and marry in Rome but could not vote or otherwise take part in political life. The most trustworthy of the Italian peoples absorbed by Rome were made full citizens, living henceforth under Roman law, voting, and holding office like native-born Romans, in addition to accepting the citizen's obligation to pay taxes and serve in the army.

Down the centuries, defections from this structure of imperial power were remarkably few, even in Rome's hours of greatest trial—one of which was about to burst upon Italy even as the confederation was completed in the middle of the third century BCE.

The Wars with Carthage

The dramatic image of Hannibal crossing the Alps with his African army, complete with elephants, was a nightmare that haunted Romans for generations. And the three *Punic Wars* (from *Poeni* or *Puni,* the Roman word for the Phoenician ancestors of the Carthaginians) of the third and second centuries BCE in fact constituted the most dreadful military ordeal in the history of the Republic.

Carthage lay in what is today Tunisia, in North Africa, less than 100 miles across the narrow waist of the Mediterranean from Sicily. It was thus only 400 miles from Rome. Since the fall of the Phoenician city-states in the sixth century BCE, Carthage had established an extensive commercial empire of its own. By the third century, this seaborne Carthaginian Empire encompassed most of the coasts and islands of the western Mediterranean, including the North African Maghreb (stretching from Tunisia to Morocco), southern Spain, the large islands of Corsica and Sardinia, and the western part of Sicily. Besides its powerful navy, Carthage had a strong mercenary army, a great harbor, famous

Roman Expansion in Italy Under the Republic, 509–31 BCE

walls, and a government run by old commercial families through the familiar system of assembly, council, and magistrates.

The First Punic War (264–241 BCE) erupted over Sicily, the Greek buffer zone between Roman Italy and Carthaginian North Africa. The conflict began when Carthage and Rome intervened in the island to support different factions of a gang of Italian mercenary soldiers who had seized the city of Messina in northern Sicily. The Roman Senate hesitated to get involved, for Rome lacked a fleet and had, moreover, no quarrel with the Carthaginians. In the end, however, the Romans voted to build a fleet and plunged into a war that lasted twenty-three years and was the start of Rome's territorial expansion beyond the Italian peninsula.

In 241 BCE, Carthage, perhaps only slightly more exhausted than Rome, made peace and surrendered Sicily. But the rivalry between Carthage and Rome had only begun.

In the decades that followed, Rome added to its power, notably by overrunning the Po valley and imposing Roman rule at last on the Cisalpine Gauls. The Romans also learned to govern their most recent acquisitions in a new way, as provinces with appointed Roman governors. This was the beginning of Roman imperial organization.

The Carthaginian Empire, meanwhile, sought to compensate for its losses by expanding and strengthening its hold on southern Spain, and it was here that the Second Punic War (218–201 BCE) broke out, two decades after the first. Again, intervention in the affairs of other states led to a conflict between the great powers. It began with clashes in Spain between the Roman client state of Saguntum and some tribal allies of Carthage. According to a traditional Roman account, Hannibal, the Carthaginian commander in Spain, had planned a campaign of revenge against Rome for some time. Whether or not this was true, Rome declared war in March of 218 BCE, and as soon as the snows began to melt in the mountain passes of the Pyrenees, Hannibal began his overland march toward Italy with a large army, including war elephants brought around the Mediterranean from Africa.

Hannibal (245–183 BCE) is commonly ranked with Alexander the Great as one of the most successful military commanders in history. His father, Hamilcar (c. 270–229 BCE), had led the Carthaginian forces in the First Punic War and, according to tradition, had made the boy swear an oath on the altars of the gods of Carthage "to prove himself . . . an enemy of the Roman people." For the Romans, the war Hannibal brought them was "the most memorable of all wars that were ever waged."[1]

Arriving in the Po valley with an army of more than twenty–five thousand men, Hannibal easily rallied Rome's newest subjects, the Gauls, to his cause and devised a simple but devastating plan. His aim would be to meet and defeat Roman armies as often as possible, until the Roman confederation rose in revolt against its weakened overlords, destroying Roman power forever. Over the next fifteen years of fighting up and down the Italian peninsula, the African commander very nearly accomplished his goal.

In every encounter, Hannibal was the better general. At Cannae in 216 BCE, he inflicted the worst defeat Rome had ever suffered. As the defeats piled up, the Romans were reduced to arming slaves to defend the city and even resorted to human sacrifice to win back the favor of their relentless gods.

The one thing they did not do was surrender. For years they simply avoided meeting Hannibal in the field. And Hannibal, the lord of the battlefield, did not have the manpower or the siege engines to capture a major walled city like Rome. As long as Rome's allies remained loyal, final victory in Italy thus remained beyond the Carthaginian's reach.

In 209 BCE, a young Roman general named Scipio (236–184 BCE) seized the main Carthaginian base in Spain. And when Hannibal's brother Hasdrubal led a relief force into

Italy in 207, the Romans intercepted and destroyed it. This victory they announced to Hannibal by hurling his brother's head into the Carthaginian camp.

The long debilitating struggle came to an end soon thereafter. In 204 BCE, Scipio landed with a Roman army in North Africa. Hannibal returned to defend his homeland the following year. And there, at Zama in 202, Scipio earned the additional name of "Africanus" by defeating the greatest general of his age in a victory at least partially due to the defection of some of Hannibal's mercenary troops.

One more bloody war remained to be fought, however, before the vendetta between the two peoples ended at last. The Third Punic War (149–146 BCE) was one-sided and merciless. It was motivated by Roman nervousness over a Carthaginian economic revival and by the vindictiveness of Roman politicians like Cato the Elder (234–149 BCE), who made the slogan "Carthage must be destroyed" his bitter watchword in the Senate. This third war consisted essentially of a Roman siege of the great city of Carthage itself. Led by Scipio Aemilianus (185–129 BCE), an adopted grandson of Scipio Africanus, the Romans captured the city, destroyed parts of it, and sowed salt in the plowed-up ruins, a symbolic assertion that Carthage would never rise again. After 146 BCE, the Romans had a new province to add to their list, this one beyond the Mediterranean Sea in Africa.

The Conquest of the East

Meanwhile, with startling rapidity, Rome had been advancing eastward around the Mediterranean, imposing its will on the world of the Hellenistic Greeks. The Roman intrusion began in 200 BCE, just two years after the defeat of Hannibal at Zama. By 133, the lands of the eastern Mediterranean had been largely converted into Roman colonies or protectorates.

The Roman hero, Quinctius Flamininus (c. 227–174 BCE), proconsul in Greece, explained Rome's invasion of the Hellenistic East in highly idealistic terms. Rome, he told the Greeks assembled for the Isthmian Games, was the "one people in the world which would fight for others' liberties at its own cost, to its own peril . . . ready to cross the sea that there might be no unjust empire anywhere and that everywhere justice, right, and law might prevail."[2] The reality was a bit more complicated than that. Idealism may have played some role in Roman expansion into Greece itself, for many Roman aristocrats were admirers of Greek culture. Rome's early interventions in the East as a whole, however, were motivated primarily by a determination to defend Roman interests. An increasingly powerful motive, finally, was greed, as the Romans glimpsed the dazzling wealth of the East that was clearly theirs for the taking.

Rome established its paramount military position in the eastern Mediterranean by defeating the ambitious and long-reigning rulers of the two most powerful of the Hellenistic monarchies, Philip V (r. 221–179 BCE) of Macedonia and the Seleucid king Antiochus III (r. 223–187 BCE). The Romans fought no less than four "Macedonian" wars with Philip V and his successors between 215 and 146. From Syria, meanwhile, came a new threat in the person of the ambitious young Seleucid prince Antiochus III, who sought to revive the greatness of the Alexandrian successor state of Seleucid Persia.

A Roman army under Cornelius Scipio and his brother Scipio Africanus, conqueror of Carthage, crushed Antiochus at the Battle of Magnesia in 190 BCE. Later victorious struggles with real and false heirs of Philip led first to the breakup of the Macedonian monarchy into parts and finally to the absorption of Macedonia as a Roman province in 148 BCE, just

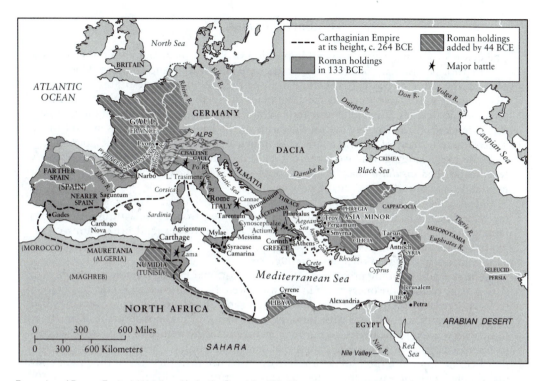

Expansion of Roman Territorial Holdings Under the Republic, 509–31 BCE

two years before the destruction of Carthage. In 133 King Attalus of Pergamum submissively left Rome his entire country in his will. Four years later, Pergamum became the core of a Roman province encompassing all the western part of Asia Minor. From the Greek city-states around to Egypt, the rest of the area was converted into a string of client states of the great city on the Tiber.

♦ Disorder and Civil Strife ♦

Even as Rome rose to mastery of the Mediterranean world, however, disorder and civil strife grew in intensity within the growing empire. Conflicts between social classes and ambitious politicians tore the land apart. In the end, this tumultuous period brought the Roman Republic down—and forged the Roman Empire in its place. Here we will look at the social and political conflicts which destroyed the Republic.

The last century of the Republic, from 133 BCE to 31 BCE, was the century of the *Roman Civil War*. It was an epoch dominated by larger-than-life characters: the reforming brothers Tiberius and Gaius Gracchus, the feuding warlords Marius and Sulla, Cicero the orator, Julius Caesar, dashing Mark Antony, and wily little Octavian, who became Augustus Caesar, the second founder of Rome. From the challenge to the traditional power structure triggered by the Gracchi brothers in 133 BCE to the triumph of Augustus in 31 BCE, this was one of the most tumultuous periods of ancient history.

Social Strains

The defeat of Carthage and the rapid imposition of Roman hegemony on the Hellenistic East transformed Roman society. The changes were interlocking and complex. Most simply phrased, the rich grew vastly richer while many of the poor became destitute. The senatorial elite gained profitable access to the grain fields of North Africa, Sicily, and Spain and to the movable wealth of the Hellenistic monarchies. They used their increased capital to expand their estates in Italy, buying up the farms of the hapless smallholders around them. These peasants, many of them veterans, sought new opportunities in the cities, particularly in Rome itself. Finding little work there, they settled at last into the crowded multistory tenements called *insulae* ("islands") in the poor sections of the city, lived on a government grain dole, and brooded over their wrongs.

Meanwhile, two new groups arose to complicate the struggle. The *equestrians*, meaning "horsemen" or "knights," actually made their money from manufacturing, trade, and moneylending at home and from tax gathering, grain growing, and other forms of exploitation in the provinces of the new Roman empire. They resented senatorial political predominance and neglect of equestrian interests.

The second expanding group was found at the bottom of society. Immense numbers of slaves, many of them prisoners taken in the wars, were brought back to Rome. Slaves soon replaced free labor on noble estates. And though some slaves, notably house servants, had sometimes warm relationships with their owners, the lot of the most brutalized of slaves, those who worked in the mines, was grim indeed. Some were trained in gladiatorial schools to fight each other at the public games that grew increasingly common. Slave rebellions thus became an even more feared form of social violence than the riots of the urban poor that erupted with increasing frequency in the last century of the Republic.

Add to this explosive mix the unhappy fact that the Romans, so successful in organizing Italy, had not yet learned how to rule the larger Mediterranean world they now dominated. Administrators of far provinces, who typically stayed only a year, took as much as they could get in bribes, gifts, and other profitable rewards before hurrying home to get on with their political careers. Equestrian exploiters squeezed taxes, lucrative contracts, and other revenues out of the conquered. Even Rome's oldest allies, the Italian peoples of the confederation, felt cheated of their fair share of land and loot and looked down upon by the arrogant new conquerors in Rome. They too simmered toward revolt.

The Roman Civil War

The result was a violent century of civil strife. Between 133 and 31 BCE, as the structure of empire was completed, the Republic was torn by foreign wars, by revolts within the empire, by desperate slave rebellions, and by riotous mobs in the streets of Rome itself. Armies were constantly on the march, demagogues shouted in the forum, and intrigue abounded in the Senate house. Attempting to guide the whirlwind were the power brokers of this age of civil war—the aristocratic Gracchi; the Roman generals, Marius and Sulla; the politicians, Pompey, Cicero, and Julius Caesar; and the final two contenders for Roman power, Mark Antony and Augustus Caesar.

Grandsons of the great Scipio Africanus, Tiberius (163–133 BCE) and Gaius (154–121 BCE) Gracchus were heirs of one of the noblest houses in Rome, yet they took up the cause of the most distressed. The tradition of aristocratic leadership for popular causes reaches back to Periclean Athens and up to the America of the Roosevelts. Charges of dema-goguery have generally accompanied popular political movements, and there have indeed often been political motives mixed with nobler impulses. There are no better exemplars of this mix of popular reform with personal political ambition than the Gracchi. Tiberius chal-lenged the system first, in 133 BCE; Gaius ten years later, in 123.

Tiberius Gracchus had seen and claimed to have been moved by the condition of peas-ants who had lost their lands and by the plight of dispossessed veterans who, he reminded the people, though "they are called the masters of the world do not possess a single clod of earth which is truly their own."[3] Elected tribune in 133 BCE, he proposed a radical land re-distribution bill that would reclaim public lands currently held by large landowners and parcel them out among the poor.

The bill threatened wealthy landowners. In addition, many senators feared Tiberius Gracchus's popularity with the plebeian masses, seeing in him a revolutionary demagogue moving to subvert the Roman constitution. Tiberius got his bill passed and some land re-distributed. But as he tried to speak to an election crowd in his second campaign for the tri-buneship, a mob of senators and their supporters burst into the meeting. In the melee that followed, the reformer's enemies beat him to death with clubs and pieces of broken furni-ture and killed several hundred of his followers.

The stunned younger brother, Gaius Gracchus, who had helped with the land distri-bution, moved from the family home on the aristocratic Palatine Hill down into the poor quarter around the forum. Elected tribune in 123 BCE, and again in 122, he pro-ceeded to reactivate the land distribution commission and to pass a law to regulate the price of grain sold to the urban masses. To win the backing of the equestrians, he spon-sored legislation opening the new provinces in Asia Minor to their ministrations as pri-vate tax collectors. He also urged the establishment of urban colonies for those of the poor who did not want to return to farming and campaigned for citizenship for the Ital-ian allies.

Again, alarmed conservative politicians rallied against what they saw as demagogic at-tacks on the traditional structure of Roman society. When violence broke out in the popu-lar assembly, Gaius's enemies in the Senate declared martial law in the city and ordered the consuls to use all necessary force to restore order. Where a few hundreds had perished with Tiberius, several thousand people were now slaughtered, many in the tenement streets of the Aventine. Gaius Gracchus asked one of his own followers to strike him down lest he die at the hands of his enemies.

Famous generals and ambitious politicians, Marius and Sulla seized center stage from a very different direction than that attempted by the Gracchi. Both were willing to use their troops to settle their political feuds in the streets of Rome. Both their careers illustrate how ambitious military leaders came to dominate Roman politics in the second and first cen-turies BCE.

Gaius Marius (157–86 BCE), a "new man" of equestrian stock, was a political outsider whom the old senatorial ruling–class elite never trusted. Lucius Cornelius Sulla (137–78 BCE), descended from an ancient but no longer wealthy patrician family, remained a staunch supporter of the Senate.

Both men held many commands and won celebrated victories. Marius rescued Rome from foreign foes by repulsing an invasion of Germanic peoples from the north, the Cimbri and Teutones, in 101 BCE. Sulla helped save the state as one of the commanders who won the Social War (91–88 BCE), a rebellion by Rome's oldest Italian allies, bitter from having been denied citizenship and otherwise discriminated against. In politics, Marius appealed to the popular assembly and dabbled in the politics of reform, while Sulla stood firmly with the conservative majority in the Senate.

Marius contributed more directly to Rome's imperial future by guiding the reorganization of the Roman army into the classic *Roman legion.* From the year 100 BCE on, each legion came to number five thousand men organized in ten cohorts, uniformly armed with javelin and shortsword. The army borrowed the famous shortsword used for close-in work from its Spanish foes. The legion was normally supported by archers, slingers, and mounted cavalry, the latter often recruited from the more flamboyant, less disciplined barbarian lands on the edge of the empire.

Even more important, soldiers no longer had to be even small landholders. They were henceforth paid regular salaries, a lure that drew many poor men into the service. But the new legions also became increasingly dependent on their commanders to lead them to rich pickings and to coerce the government into voting them land allotments on their return from the wars. The result was a more professional, full-time army, but one whose primary loyalties were more likely to be to the legions themselves or to successful generals than to the Roman state.

Competing for a military command against a Near Eastern prince, both Marius and Sulla took turns seizing power in Rome and slaughtering each others' senatorial and equestrian supporters. Sulla, in particular, saw to it that the lands confiscated from his victims were divided among his soldiers, more than one hundred thousand in number. The example he had set of building political power on military victories and deploying troops to impose his will on Rome itself was duly noted by more than one ambitious younger man.

The Rise and Fall of Julius Caesar

The next generation of Roman politicians included three of the most famous names in Roman history. These were the celebrated general Pompey, the brilliant orator Cicero, and Julius Caesar, who outdid them both.

Gnaeus Pompeius (106–48 BCE)—Pompey the Great, as he came to be called—was a protégé of Sulla's and followed the latter's military road to fame and fortune. Pompey earned a reputation as Rome's most successful military commander. He helped to smash the great slave rebellion of 73 BCE led by Spartacus, the gladiator who raised tens of thousands of slaves and terrified all Italy before the legions broke him. He swept the pirates off the sea, expanded and reorganized Rome's empire, and returned home triumphant in 62 BCE.

Pompey wanted a land distribution for his men and a formal ratification of his reorganization of the Near East. The Senate, fearful of his popularity and his army, hesitated to make him greater still by granting all his demands. Pompey waffled, backed away from deploying brute force, and looked around for political allies instead.

Marcus Tullius Cicero (106–43 BCE) wanted very much to save the battered Republic and to rise as high among its elite as he could. Trained in law, oratory, and philosophy in both Rome and Greece, Cicero was a man of immense talent. But because he was descended from equestrian stock, he was doomed to remain throughout his life a "new man"—the first in his family to rise to offices and honors. Nevertheless, his skill at public pleading made him an extremely well-off lawyer with a mansion on the Palatine. His energy, administrative ability, and sheer oratorical brilliance carried him from one magistracy to another, until, in 63 BCE, he was elected to the consulship.

By the late 60s, Cicero had also worked out an idealistic formula for the salvation of the state. The key, he felt, was "the harmony of the orders," by which he meant collaboration rather than conflict between the equestrian and senatorial classes. For the next twenty years, as senator, writer, and even in his private correspondence, Cicero preached his belief in Roman law, Roman freedoms, responsible ruling classes, and the best traditions of the Republic.

Gaius Julius Caesar (100–44 BCE), probably the most famous Roman of them all, was certainly one of the hardest to figure out. He had brains, courage, ambition, and perhaps most important, imagination. Descended from the ancient patrician Julian clan—they traced their ancestry back to the goddess Venus—and a relative by marriage of Marius, Caesar plunged into the political maelstrom in the 60s, just as Pompey and Cicero were reaching the height of their careers.

Julius Caesar was probably the second most eloquent man in Rome after Cicero, and he proved a greater general than Pompey. Of the three men, however, he was the only one with the imagination to see that the Republic had become a hollow sham, a cloak for the ambitions of its rulers, and also the only one who was willing to take a sledgehammer to the foundations of the state.

Caesar rose slowly. In the 60s, he made an informal political alliance with Pompey and a third, very wealthy politician named Crassus (c. 115–53 BCE) to advance their mutual interests. Cicero, who might have made a fourth partner, refused to join the cabal. Thanks to this so-called *First Triumvirate,* however, Pompey got the land for his troops and his Asian settlement ratified. Caesar and Crassus got military commands of their own, convinced that Pompey's military path to power was more likely to succeed than Cicero's purely political maneuvering. Thereafter, Pompey rested on his laurels, while Crassus died fighting the Parthians in the East. Caesar spent most of the next decade conquering Transalpine Gaul (roughly coterminous with modern France) for Rome.

Returning to Italy in 49 BCE, Julius Caesar faced the same hostility from the Senate that Pompey and Sulla had confronted before him. The Senate demanded that he lay down his command before he returned. Caesar's response was to cross the Rubicon, the river in northern Italy marking the legal limits of his authority in Gaul, at the head of his legions. Announcing "the die is cast," he marched against his political foes.

The Senate ordered Pompey himself to defend Rome against Caesar. Caesar routed his old ally, pursued him to Greece, and crushed his army there in 48 BCE. Pompey fled further still, to Egypt, where agents of the next-to-last Ptolemaic pharaoh cut him down, a sacrifice to Caesar's rising star. When Caesar arrived, he installed the last of the Ptolemaic line, the intriguing Cleopatra, as ruler of Egypt. He then swept victoriously across North Africa, from the Near East to Spain, and returned to Rome to decide the fate of the Republic itself.

Caesar had a sense of theater. When he reached the capital in 46 BCE, he mounted not one, but four parades to celebrate four consecutive triumphs for his conquests in Gaul, Egypt, Asia, and Africa. One parade included a decorated wagon with the famous battle report: *Veni, Vidi, Vici!*—"I came, I saw, I conquered!" Celebrating his victories in Asia, Caesar climbed the steps of the capital between two rows of forty elephants holding aloft torches to light his ascent. At the same time, he pardoned all his enemies and laid on public festivals and grain distributions of unprecedented lavishness. Then he set to work to see what he could do with the shambles of the Republic.

Caesar began by assuring his own grip on power. He accumulated a number of important offices himself, including dictatorship for life in 45 BCE. He expanded the number of magistracies and the size of the Senate and packed both with his old officers. And he provided military colonies for his troops in many parts of the empire.

A stable structure of authority thus established, he turned to more substantive changes. He divided Italy into municipal districts for more efficient administration. He extended Roman citizenship to a number of deserving regions. He announced a program of public works to repair the ravages of civil war and put the poor to work. He even found time to reform the calendar, replacing the hopelessly inaccurate lunar year with the solar calendar which, with but a single correction fifteen centuries later, we still use today.

Time, however, was the one thing Caesar did not have. Rumors that he planned to have himself crowned king—a title hated by Romans since the overthrow of the Etruscan kings—were all over Rome. The autocracy he had already put in place had drastically undermined the traditional power of the Senate. Some, like Cicero, opposed him as a matter of principle, others because he had shattered the political futures they had planned for themselves. And Caesar, whether from undue self-confidence or indifference bred of illness and weariness after the long struggle, had dismissed his bodyguard.

"The Ides of March have come," he called to an augur who had warned him of danger on that day as he entered the Senate on March 15, 44 BCE. "Ay, they have come," the soothsayer replied, "but they have not gone."[4] The conservative conspirators, led by two of Caesar's trusted aides, Marcus Brutus and Cassius Longinus, clustered around as if to greet him. And then the dagger blows rained down. He fell, the Roman historians tell us, at the very foot of a statue of Pompey the Great.

The Triumph of Augustus

The Roman civil wars that had ravaged the empire for a century did not end with the brief triumph and bloody assassination of Julius Caesar. The ultimate round of intrigues and battles dragged on for thirteen more years after Caesar's death in 44 BCE. In the end, only two contenders for the leadership of the Roman world remained. The struggle between them gave Rome another bad decade and a half before peace finally came in 31 BCE.

Caesar's deputy, Mark Antony (82–30 BCE), Plutarch reports, was "a brilliant soldier," immensely popular with the troops, among whom he ate, drank, and joked about their love affairs. He had a thick beard and "a certain bold and masculine look, which is found in the statues and portraits of Hercules." It was an image Antony assiduously cultivated, wearing "his tunic belted low over the hips, a large sword at his side, and a heavy cloak."[5] His swaggering self-confidence and his gift for bringing the Roman populace around to his point of view made him seem a likely candidate for the next dictator of Rome.

Julius Caesar's adopted heir, Octavian (63 BCE–CE 14), known to history as Augustus Caesar, was considerably less prepossessing. The contemporary Roman historian Suetonius, author of *The Twelve Caesars*, describes Augustus as having "clear and bright" eyes which "he liked to believe . . . shone with a sort of divine radiance." But "his teeth were small, few, and decayed; his hair yellowish and rather curly; his eyebrows met above [his] Roman nose."[6] He was short, he sometimes walked with a limp, he could not stand heat or cold, and he had nasty coughs and frequent stomachaches. In 44 BCE he was a sickly teenager with no military talent, facing rivals with long experience in the bloody civil wars.

When he set out for Rome to claim his inheritance, even his mother begged him not to do it.

But Octavian's ambition was made of sterner stuff, however feeble his physical equipment. Retreating to a military colony south of Rome, he told Caesar's veteran troops that his name too was Caesar. With troops and the magic name, he was soon back to demand a place at the bargaining table. The upshot was the *Second Triumvirate,* a formal public alliance this time, between Octavian, Antony, and Lepidus (d. 18 BCE), the late Caesar's Master of the Horse. The three proceeded to purge even more of their enemies than Sulla had done, including thousands of equestrians, hundreds of senators, and Cicero himself, who was murdered by Antony's minions as he sought to leave for Greece.

The army of the triumvirs met the forces led by Caesar's assassins, Cassius and Brutus, at Philippi in Macedonia in 42 BCE. Octavian, now twenty-one, but no more martially inclined than he had been, remained in his tent while Antony led the troops to victory. Brutus and Cassius took their own lives. "Very few indeed of the assassins," according to Suetonius, "outlived Caesar for more than three years, or died naturally."[7]

And the confusion and conflict of the civil wars continued. The Triumvirate proved not much more durable than the lives of the conspirators. Lepidus was shunted off to Africa by his fellow rulers. Antony took a command in the rich eastern provinces for his share of the spoils, fought new wars with the Parthians, and fell in love with Queen Cleopatra of Egypt. Cleopatra, determined to save Egypt for the Ptolemies, pinned her final hopes on the swaggering soldier who still looked most likely to emerge with Julius Caesar's bloodstained mantle around his husky shoulders.

Octavian, meanwhile, returned to Rome and plunged into politics. Although he never became a great military leader, he at least organized and dispatched the forces that defeated one rival after another.

But the great problem still remained: the ever-popular Antony, now ruling all the East conjointly with the scheming and clever Cleopatra. Octavian began cautiously and shrewdly with a propaganda campaign claiming that Mark Antony, drunk with love, had surrendered Rome's eastern empire to the Serpent of the Nile. He then raised a huge military force and turned one more weary time to march around the eastern Mediterranean.

The last battle was fought by sea off Actium in western Greece in 31 BCE. Antony's fleet, weakened by a plague and outmaneuvered by Octavian's forces, was bottled up and beaten. Mark Antony committed suicide, and Cleopatra, learning that Octavian wanted her alive to grace his triumphal procession through Rome, took her own life too. The last Hellenistic monarchy—that of the Egyptian Ptolemies—died with her. The Roman Republic, undermined by generations of corruption, class conflict, political feuds, and civil wars, was already dead.

✦Roman Culture✦

Under both the Republic and the Empire, the Romans achieved a remarkable level of cultural productivity. Rome came early under the influence of the remarkable civilization of the Greeks, their near neighbors on the Mediterranean Sea. But there was a subtlety to Roman literature and thought also, and a scale and sense of grandeur to Roman sculpture, architecture, and engineering that proved every bit as impressive as the thought and art of the Greeks before them. And the majestic edifice of the Roman law has had few parallels in Western history, before or since.

The Hellenization of Rome

The great force for cultural change in the Roman Republic was the highly developed civilization of its Greek neighbors. It has been said that the Romans conquered the Greeks and then fell captive to their new subjects—captivated by the entrancing art and startling ideas of the Hellenistic Greek world.

In the third and second centuries BCE, as their imperial horizons widened to include overseas territories, the Romans discovered Greek culture with a vengence. Shiploads of Greek statues and libraries of Greek books flooded into Rome. Greek philosophers came to lecture in Rome, spreading the ideas of Greek thinkers back to Plato. The Roman elite learned Greek the way later Europeans learned French, as the necessary "second language" for the cultured.

The result was a massive transplant of Greek culture westward to Rome. The ideas of the Greek philosophical schools and the styles of Greek literature found new homes in Roman minds. Hellenization, however, brought not mindless imitation, but a synthesis of Greek ideas and techniques with the Roman spirit. As American culture in later centuries differed in tone and spirit from the European culture from which it grew, so Romans transformed their Greek heritage.

In some cases, Roman versions were to be more influential later on than the Greek originals were. The most famous Epicurean, for instance, was the Roman Lucretius; the most celebrated Stoic was the later Roman emperor Marcus Aurelius. It was the Roman Vergil, deeply inspired by Homer, rather than Homer himself, who taught later centuries how to write epic poetry.

Roman Literature

In the later centuries of the Republic, Romans, stimulated by their brilliant Greek neighbors, began to show what they themselves could do in art and thought. This cultural flowering climaxed in the *Augustan Age*, as the reign of Augustus is called. From the oratory of Cicero to the poetry of Vergil, from impressive building to highly individualized portraits in stone, they did very well indeed.

One of the greatest poets of the period was Lucretius (96–55 BCE), whose book-length epic *On the Nature of Things* summarized the Epicurean atomist view of the nature of the universe. Profoundly aware of the violent tenor of the times, Lucretius sought to free his fellow Romans from their fear of death and supernatural forces by revealing an antiseptic universe of drifting atoms and empty space. In the end, however, his work was less philosophy or science than a great poem, replete with vigorous flashes of imagery that can still raise a living picture in the mind twenty centuries later.

The greatest lyric poet of the age was Catullus (c. 84-c. 54 BCE). Drawing his predilection for short poems and verbal wit from the Alexandrians and his subjects and themes from the corrupt high society of the last years of the Republic, Catullus transcended both his models and his subjects. His verses ranged from ribald insults directed at fellow men-about-town to passionate expressions of love for a very sophisticated woman who already had more lovers than she knew what to do with:

> My woman says she'd prefer to marry no one
> but me, even if Jupiter asked for her love.
> Ah yes: but what a woman says to an eager lover,
> write it on running water, write it on air.[8]

Roman women celebrate secret rites of the cult of Dionysus in this wall painting from Pompeii. A young matron clings to an older woman for moral support, while a celebrant clashes cymbals to the rhythm of the orgiastic dance. What elements give the painting a feeling of graceful movement? (Alinari/Art Resource)

The most admired literary voice of those last tense decades, however, was of a very different sort: the sonorous voice of Cicero, conservative statesman, eclectic philosopher, and the greatest speaker of his time. The rolling cadences that made him the most revered and imitated of all Western orators boomed with the rhythms of the Roman tongue. And the subjects he returned to again and again—freedom under law, the "harmony of the orders," and the essential soundness of the Republic—reflected a distinctly Roman dream.

Literature and history became even more closely intertwined later on, during the centuries of the Augustan peace. Both demonstrated an overriding concern with the reality and potentiality of Roman civilization itself.

Publius Vergilius Maro, known as Vergil (70–19 BCE), earned his place in cultural history with one great poem, his epic of Rome's mythic beginnings, the *Aeneid*. This long poem inspired by Homer's epics narrates the adventures of the Trojan prince Aeneas, whom most Romans believed to have been their earliest ancestor. Vergil follows his hero's wanderings over the Mediterranean in search of a new home after the fall of Troy and his struggle for a place in Italy for himself and his descendants. In one famous episode, the future founder of Rome has a tragic love affair with Dido, queen and founder of Carthage—which in later centuries became Rome's greatest foe. In another, Aeneas journeys through the underworld of the dead, where his father's spirit predicts Rome's future greatness as ruler of the Western world.

Vergil's contemporary Horace (65–19 BCE) was actually a late convert to the Augustan Empire, having struggled for years to preserve the Republic. His poems praised Augustus and Roman virtues like courage and friendship, while satirizing the lives of less noble Romans. They also demonstrated a rare mastery of poetic form that has stirred the admiration of Latin scholars and later poets ever since.

Livy's *History of Rome,* also inspired by Augustus's triumph, is quite a different production from the Greek histories of Herodotus and Thucydides. Like Herodotus, Livy (57 BCE–CE 17) celebrated the achievements of his people. But unlike his Greek predecessors, he attempted to cover, not a single recent event, but the whole history of his country. Like Vergil, however, Livy focused on earlier times—in Livy's case, on the early days of the Republic, when, he believed, civic pride and patriotism had flourished. His hope was that remembering the achievements of the founding fathers might rekindle virtue and love of country in Romans of his own age.

Ovid (43 BCE–CE 18), only a generation younger than Vergil, was born too late to take the aging Augustus seriously. Ovid's *Metamorphoses,* retelling in urbane verse many of the ancient myths (especially those involving supernatural transformations), has been a source of Roman mythology ever since. His poetry often had a flippant, cynical ring, particularly his most widely read work, *The Art of Love.* This guide to the fine art of seduction in imperial Rome got him peremptorily exiled for the rest of his life to the remotest Black Sea outpost the shocked Augustus could find.

Roman Law

A major achievement of Roman society was the impressive edifice of the Roman law. Shaped slowly over centuries in typically conservative Roman fashion, it would provide the foundations of legal systems for other Western nations in centuries to come.

The oldest Roman laws, the famous Twelve Tables, had been officially published in the fifth century BCE, at the beginning of the recorded history of the Republic. New laws and legal principles were added through three procedures. First, legislation passed by the Roman assemblies provided new laws, especially under the Republic. Second, during the imperial period inaugurated by Augustus Caesar, the decrees of successive emperors acquired the force of law. And finally, throughout Roman history, the pronouncements of magistrates and legal experts reshaped the law generation by generation. Thus the edict issued by the praetor, the government's chief legal officer, summed up the legal principles he would follow during his term of office. Even more influential were the opinions of jurisconsults, legal advisers to magistrates, whose informed judgments carried great weight in Rome.

Roman magistrates often had to deal with legal disputes between subject peoples of widely differing Asian, African, and European customs and traditions. To adjudicate in such instances, the Romans developed some general principles called *ius gentium,* "law of the peoples," many of which eventually came to be applied to Roman citizens as well. These general principles, originally attempts at fairness, were in time philosophically undergirded by the view of Greek Stoics that there exists an *ius naturale,* "natural law," transcending mere human legislation. This was conceived of as a higher law, derived from the indwelling rational principle that Stoics believed gave order to the cosmos.

To these foreign challenges and inspirations, finally, should be added the powerful Roman sense of equity. Justice—not mercy, but basic fairness—was a fundamental Roman value: "Let justice be done," the Roman legal maxim ran, "though the heavens fall." The resulting system, as we shall see, became a cornerstone of Western legal codes and thought in both medieval and modern times.

Roman Art and Engineering

A sometimes harshly honest people, the Romans had their portraits done realistically in stone. Though their models were clearly the admired Greeks, we learn more about how real Roman faces looked from their statues than we can from idealized Greek heads. There were exceptions: the physically unimpressive Augustus had himself depicted as a much more handsome man than he really was. Some of his statues may have been modeled on idealized images of Alexander the Great.

As architects, the Romans went beyond the Greeks in developing the arch, the vaulted hall, and the dome in order to roof the vast spaces of imperial buildings. The dome of the *Pantheon*, or Temple to All the Gods, at Rome became a model for architects in later ages. The splendor of Roman cities lay in these public structures—public baths, law courts, temples, palaces, circuses, theaters, triumphal arches, monuments—and the walls and columns of Rome's *Forum* or public square and the huge stadium called the *Colosseum* still stand today. Augustus boasted that he found Rome brick and left it marble—and he was only the first emperor.

For all this building, Romans developed engineering techniques of immense ingenuity and practicality. Roman construction typically combined stone facings with concrete, thus lightening the weight of the walls. Roman engineers developed basic pulleys and cranes of sorts in use as recently as the nineteenth century. The best Roman roads, built on a yard-deep substructure of gravel and concrete, were far superior to any roads built in Europe until modern times. Fourteen huge aqueducts brought enough water into the city of Rome itself to slake the thirst and wash the bodies of a million people every day. Even the *Cloaca Maxima,* the main sewer under the streets of the capital, was not matched in the Western world until the nineteenth century.

Summary

The Roman Republic began its independent history as a self–governing city-state in 509 BCE. Tough and conservative people, the Romans had learned the arts of civilization from their former rulers, the Etruscans, and from Greek colonies in Italy. Their political institutions included the Senate, several assemblies and officials, like the consuls and tribunes. Despite a long "struggle of the orders" between the ruling patricians and the commoners or plebeians which punctuated Rome's early centuries, the Republic survived and grew.

Five hundred years of war and territorial expansion carried the Romans to the conquest of the Carthaginian commercial empire and of the wealthy Hellenistic monarchies of the eastern Mediterranean. In the later Republic, Romans also crossed the Alps to conquer France and other parts of western Europe.

Meanwhile, Roman society grew more and more divided under the impact of new wealth and foreign influences from the empire. As the rich got much richer, many of the poor swarmed into the slums of Rome. The resulting social tensions, heightened by the reforming efforts of popular tribunes like the brothers Tiberius and Gaius Gracchus, led to a century of civil strife called the Roman Civil War. This conflict in turn transformed the Roman Republic, dominated by its upper classes, into the Roman Empire, founded by its first emperor, Augustus Caesar, in 31 BCE.

Among the cultural achievements of the Roman Republic were the oratory of Cicero, the poetry of Vergil, the Roman history written by Livy, and some of the most accomplished sculpture in Western history. Romans were also great builders, raising immense temples and dotting western Europe with cities and harbors, roads and aqueducts.

Some Key Terms

Augustan Age 96
century 84
clientage 82
comitia centuriata 83
comitia tributa 83
consul 83
Empire 78
equestrians 90
fasces 82

First Triumvirate 93
gens 82
imperium 83
insulae 90
ius gentium 98
ius naturale 98
patria potestas 82
patrician 82
plebeian 82

Punic Wars 85
Republic 78
Roman Civil War 89
Roman legion 92
Second Triumvirate 95
Senate 83
struggle of the orders 83
tribune 83
Twelve Tables 83

Notes

1. Livy, *History of Rome,* vol. 2, trans. D. Spillan et al. (New York: American Book, n.d.), 14.
2. Livy, trans. E. T. Sage (Cambridge, Mass.: Loeb Classical Library, 1935), 33.33.5–7.
3. Plutarch, *Makers of Rome: Nine Lives by Plutarch,* trans. Ian Scott-Kilvert (Harmondsworth, England: Penguin, 1965), 162.
4. Gaius Suetonius Tranquillus, *The Twelve Caesars,* trans. Robert Graves (Harmondsworth, England: Penguin, 1957), 45.
5. Plutarch, 274.
6. Suetonius, 94–95.
7. Ibid., 49.
8. Catullus, No. 70, in Gilbert Highet, *Poets in a Landscape* (Harmondsworth, England: Penguin, 1959), 32.

Reading List

Bradley, K. *Discovering the Roman Family: Studies in Roman Social History.* New York: Oxford University Press, 1991. Sees Roman family feeling undermined by death, divorce, variety of care providers. See also B. Rawson, ed., *The Family in Ancient Rome: New Perspectives* (Ithaca, N.Y.: Cornell University Press, 1986).

Copley, F. O. *Latin Literature: From the Beginnings to the Close of the Second Century a.d.* Ann Arbor: University of Michigan Press, 1969. Survey of Roman literature by a leading translator.

Geltzer, M. *Caesar: Politician and Statesman.* Translated by P. Needham. Oxford: Blackwell, 1968. Authoritative political biography. On

Augustus, see A. H. M. Jones, *Augustus* (New York: Norton, 1971).

Grant, M. *The Etruscans.* New York: Scribner's, 1980. Archaeological investigation of this mysterious people, for the general reader. See also P. M. Ogilvie, *Early Rome and the Etruscans* (Atlantic Highlands, N.J.: Humanities Press, 1976).

Harris, W. V. *War and Imperialism in Republican Rome, 327–70 b.c.* Oxford: Clarendon Press, 1979. Argues that Roman expansion was a deliberate policy rooted in the political ambitions of the Roman aristocracy.

Hopkins, K. *Conquerors and Slaves.* New York: Cambridge University Press, 1978. Relations between owners of large estates and their work force. See also K. Bradley, *Slavery and Society at Rome* (New York: Cambridge University Press, 1994), a very useful summary essay.

Hughes, J. D. *Pan's Travail: Environmental Problems of the Ancient Greeks and Romans.* Baltimore: Johns Hopkins University Press, 1994. The ancients also damaged the environment.

Keppie, L. *The Making of the Roman Army: From Republic to Empire.* London: Botsford, 1984. The evolution of the Roman military machine.

Kleiner, D. E. E. *Roman Sculpture.* New Haven: Yale University Press, 1992. Up to date and informative.

Lancel, S. *Carthage: A History.* Cambridge: Blackwell, 1995. Solid overview of Rome's greatest adversary. See also J. F. Lazenby, *Hannibal's War* (Warminster, England: Aris and Phillips, 1978), on geography, logistics, strategy and tactics, and N. Bagnall, *The Punic Wars* (London: Hutchinson, 1991) for a military history of all three wars.

Lefkowitz, M. R., and M. B. Fant. *Women in Greece and Rome.* Toronto: Samuel Stevens, 1977. Valuable overview of the lives of women in both societies. See also S. B. Pomeroy, *Goddesses, Whores, Wives, and Slaves: Women in Classical Antiquity* (New York: Schocken, 1975).

Livy. *The Early History of Rome.* Translated by A. de Selincourt. Baltimore: Penguin, 1960. Readable modern translation of the patriotic early books of Livy's History.

Mitchell, T. N. *Cicero, the Senior Statesman.* New Haven: Yale University Press, 1991. The defender of the Republic in his most influential years. See also his *Selected Political Speeches,* translated by M. Grant (Baltimore: Penguin, 1977).

Nicolet, C. *The World of the Citizen in Republican Rome.* Translated by P. S. Falla. Berkeley: University of California Press, 1980. Sees the citizen as an active participant in the life of the state.

Seager, R. *Pompey: A Political Biography.* Berkeley: University of California Press, 1979. The struggle with Caesar from Pompey's point of view. See also A. Keaveney, *Sulla, the Last Republican* (London: Croom and Helm, 1982) and D. Stockton, *The Gracchi* (New York: Oxford University Press, 1979), which sets the reforming brothers against the social crisis of their times.

Stambaugh, J. E. *The Ancient Roman City.* Baltimore: Johns Hopkins University Press, 1988. Useful if idealized introduction.

Syme, R. *The Roman Revolution.* London: Oxford University Press, 1967. Brilliant if still controversial interpretation of the Roman Civil War. For a more recent analysis, see M. Beard and M. H. Crawford, *Rome in the Late Republic* (Ithaca, N.Y.: Cornell University Press, 1985).

Vanderbroeck, P. J. J. *Popular Leadership and Collective Behavior in the Late Roman Republic (ca. 80–50 b.c.).* Amsterdam: J.C. Gieben, 1987. Controversial analysis of plebeian political activism.

Wardman, A. *Rome's Debt to Greece.* New York: St. Martin's Press, 1976. The impact of Greek culture, with attention to the ambivalence of Roman attitudes.

Watson, A. *The Spirit of Roman Law.* Athens: University of Georgia Press, 1995. Useful study of development and underlying principles.

5

The Power of the Caesars
The Roman Empire

•The Roman Peace   •The Decline and Fall of the Roman Empire
•The Rise of Christianity   •The Christian Church Takes Shape

Two major events bracketed the last quarter century between 31 BCE and approximately 4 BCE: the triumph of Augustus Caesar in the Roman Civil War and the birth of Jesus of Nazareth in a little town in Palestine. Augustus's victory ended the history of the Roman Republic (509–31 BCE), the period when Rome was dominated by the Senate, and began that of the Empire (31 BCE–CE 476), in which Rome was ruled by hereditary emperors. The birth of Jesus Christ brought what became the central spiritual tradition of the Western world.

Romans always said they detested crowned heads, and Augustus and his immediate successors were satisfied to be called *princeps*—"first citizen"—instead of "emperor." The *principate*, as the first two centuries of the Empire are often called, was a prosperous and relatively peaceful period in the history of Rome. The third century CE, however, saw an anarchic age of warring generals and short-lived military emperors, rather like the Roman Civil War of the first century BCE. Following this near breakdown of central authority, Diocletian and Constantine reorganized the Empire in the fourth century, adopting more of the trappings of imperial state as a means of welding the Empire together. In the fifth century CE, however, the Roman Empire collapsed at last under the combined weight of internal decay and foreign invasion.

The early Christian story is more familiar to most of us. Jesus preached to the people in the area that is today the state of Israel, faced his accusers in Jerusalem, and was executed as a sower of seditious ideas by the Roman authorities. But his disciples carried his message to other parts of the Roman Empire and, despite brutal early persecutions, triumphed in the end.

This chapter will begin by chronicling Rome's achievements of the first two centuries CE and the bumpier road that followed, from the creeping social decay of the third century, through a brief recovery, to the decline and fall of the Roman Empire in the fifth century CE. The last half of the chapter will survey the origins of Christianity and its spread across the Roman world. The Roman Empire and the rise of Christianity, between them, completed the process of laying the ancient foundations for later Western history.

✦ The Roman Peace ✦

During Augustus Caesar's own reign, now known as the *Augustan Age,* the foundations of peace, prosperity, and order were laid down. The first two centuries of the history of the Roman Empire, from 31 BCE to 180 CE, from the reign of Augustus through that of the philosophical emperor Marcus Aurelius, were in fact remarkably prosperous. This era is also often called the age of the *Pax Romana,* the "Roman Peace" in Europe—and it actually was the longest period of relative peace in Western history. And though there were outbreaks of disorder, the Augustan structure of government proved solid enough to survive even a tyrant like Nero.

This first section will offer a broad overview of the first two centuries CE. It will analyze the achievements of Augustus in some detail, and outline more briefly the reigns of the later emperors of the first and second centuries. It will also explore the structure of Roman imperial government, economic expansion, and the evolving social life of the Roman Empire.

Augustus and the Golden Age

To deal with the accumulated miseries of several generations of social dislocation and civil strife, Octavian, like Julius Caesar, was willing to undertake sweeping reforms. This was, however, modified by his own dozen years of experience and strong awareness of the need to preserve traditional forms. More practically, he commanded an immense army and was extremely rich. And he had the war weariness of all Romans working for him. People longed for peace and order once more, even if it meant sacrificing something in the way of Roman liberties.

Octavian's first priority was to establish his own power on unshakable foundations. Over the next few years, he succeeded in maintaining his position as the only warlord left in the field after the Civil War by retaining command of the army and direct rule over Syria, Egypt, Gaul, and Spain. By pyramiding his civil offices, he also acquired enormous political power, including the imperium of the consul, the immunities and popular image of the tribune, and even the religious authority of the *pontifex maximus,* chief priest. By acquiring such honorific titles as *Augustus*—meaning "revered, blessed, and inspired ruler"—he added to his air of *auctoritas,* the prestige and confidence of the maximum leader.

Even as he built his own real power, however, Augustus piously preserved the forms of republican government so dear to the conservative Roman heart. Consuls, tribunes, and other magistrates continued to be elected, though not until the "first citizen" had endorsed their candidacies. The Senate and the assemblies continued to meet, but under the guidance of special steering committees chaired by Augustus and his followers. Decisions were issued as they always had been—By Order of the Senate and the Roman People—but they were decisions formulated in Augustus's home on the Palatine Hill.

Augustus reshaped the Senate by replacing unindustrious patricians with vigorous "new men" from the equestrian order. To administer the state, he also appointed energetic equestrians to important posts and made much use of talented freedmen and slaves, the core of Rome's future professional bureaucracy. In the capital, he took steps to make the streets and tenements of the city safe by providing police and fire protection for the first time. In the provinces, he firmly asserted the right of Roman governors to enforce the laws, collect taxes, and defend the borders, but he supervised them much more closely to prevent extortion of the sort that had flourished under the Republic.

Chronology 5.1: Roman Empire

31 BCE–CE 14	*Augustus Caesar brings peace and prosperity to Rome*
31 BCE–CE 14	*"Augustan Age" in Latin literature*
31 BCE–CE 180	*Roman Peace, economic revival*
87–180	*"Five good emperors"*
161–180	*Marcus Aurelius*
180–284	*Third-century economic and political breakdown*
284–337	*Diocletian and Constantine restore order under authoritarian regime*
from 360	*Eastern and Western Roman Empires ruled separately*
455	*Vandals sack Rome*
476	*Last Roman emperor surrenders power*

Augustus's economic reforms included new but fair taxes on land and other property based for the first time on regular censuses of population and wealth. His great programs of public works and rebuilding after the long wars put large numbers of jobless plebeians to work, and he provided land allotments for one hundred thousand military veterans out of his own pocket. He improved the road system and established a sound imperial coinage to encourage trade. Beyond such basic measures, however, he kept economic regulation to a minimum. With order and confidence restored, the economic life of the Empire was soon booming again.

To protect the state he was reviving, the first Roman emperor deployed an enormous army of more than a quarter of a million men along 4,000 miles of frontier. He organized a volunteer army with a twenty-year term of enlistment, better pay, and a retirement bonus equal to more than half a soldier's lifetime earnings. Stationed in frontier fortresses, Roman soldiers also built roads, aqueducts, and other public works. In addition, Augustus founded the Praetorian Guard, nine thousand highly paid elite troops, one-third of whom served as an imperial bodyguard, a source of trouble for later rulers but a guarantee of order in Augustus's day.

Augustus also encouraged social and cultural reform and revitalization. He sponsored legislation against unduly luxurious living and in favor of decent treatment for slaves. He promoted laws that punished marital infidelity and supported marriage and the family. As high priest, he built scores of temples and encouraged the restoration of traditional religious practices. He patronized writers and artists and encouraged the poet Vergil to work on the *Aeneid,* his patriotic epic on the founding of Rome by the Trojan hero Prince Aeneas.

No wonder they voted him *pater patriae,* "father of his country," and praised him as "the savior of all mankind":

> For both land and sea are at peace, the cities are
> teeming with the blessings of concord, plenty, and respect
> for law, and the culmination and harvest of
> all good things brings fair hopes for the future
> and contentment with the present.[1]

Augustus has been seen as ruthlessly ambitious, which he surely was, and coldly hypocritical, which he probably was not. He was physically unprepossessing, yet developed the

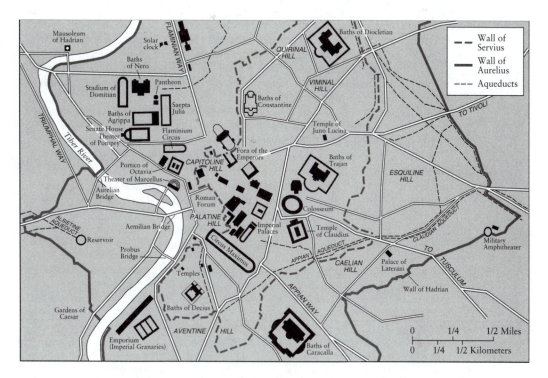

The City of Rome in Ancient Times

air of authority that impressed Romans. On his deathbed, after forty-five years in power, he is supposed to have asked those clustered round if he had acted his part well. The answer can only be yes. He had laid the political foundations for the Roman Peace that would last for two hundred years.

Emperors of the First and Second Centuries

Two dynasties ruled the Empire for most of the century after Augustus's death in CE 14: the Julio-Claudians and the Flavians. Both ruling houses included more than their share of incompetent and even vicious leaders. The second century after Augustus, the period from 96 through the death of Marcus Aurelius in 180, was, by contrast, hailed as the era of the "five good emperors."

The most successful of the Julio-Claudians was Claudius (r. 41–54) who, though lame and afflicted with a speech impediment, added significantly to his Augustan heritage. During his brief dozen years in power, he drained swamps, raised aqueducts, and built a seaport for the capital at Ostia. He followed Augustus in staffing an increasingly professional civil service with his own Greek freedmen and organized them into functional bureaus.

More typical was his successor Nero (r. 54–68), a feckless and dissolute young man whose only goals in life were to win public approbation as an athlete and a singer. For these purposes he opened a private chariot track and a private theater where he could practice his crafts before select audiences of servile flatterers. He also gave himself up to debauchery on a lavish scale. Of the greater crimes charged against him, Nero did not set fire to the city and "fiddle while Rome burned," despite the rumors that he retired to his private stage to strum his lyre and sing of the destruction of Troy while his own capital burned around him. But he did try to pin the blame for the great fire of 64 on the secretive and unpopular Christian sect, executing large numbers of them.

His reign also saw the bloody suppression of the revolts of the English Queen Boudicca (d. 60) and of the Jews of Palestine. Boudicca rebelled against Roman mistreatment of her Celtic people, while the Jews revolted against the Empire because of perceived challenges to their religious beliefs. In the end, Nero's own troops turned against him, he was deposed by the Senate and finally took his own life.

A new pattern emerged in imperial politics during the second century CE, the century of what are traditionally called the "five good emperors." Because the "good emperors" did not produce biological heirs, they adopted adult heirs to succeed them. This practice made it possible for reigning emperors to select and groom suitable successors to carry on their work. Trajan, Hadrian, and Marcus Aurelius are the best known of the "good emperors."

Trajan (r. 98–117), raised in Rome's Spanish provinces, won victories as far away as Dacia (Romania today), Mesopotamia, and Persia. A great builder, Trajan left monuments

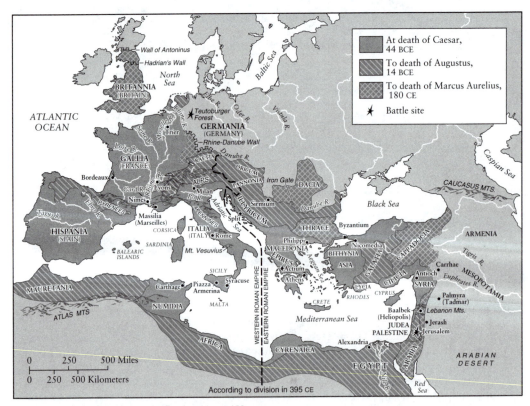

Roman Territorial Holdings Under the Empire, 44 BCE–180 CE

to his reign in a bridge across the Danube, a new city in Algeria, and a 100-foot column sculptured with his victories that can still be seen in Trajan's Forum in Rome today. Trajan also prepared his successor Hadrian for the awesome job he was to inherit by providing him with broad administrative experience.

Born in Spain like his mentor, educated at Rome, in love with Greek culture, and experienced in fighting the German barbarians, Hadrian (r. 117–138) was a man for all seasons. Over his twenty years as emperor, he undertook a number of reforms. He definitively reshaped the Augustan administrative system into a thoroughly professional civil service, including many career-minded equestrians. He encouraged the codification of the Roman laws, granted women equal legal status with men, and improved the legal condition of slaves. He also traveled the Empire, spending almost half his reign outside Italy in Britain, France, Spain, North Africa, and the Near East. He built such fortifications as "Hadrian's Wall," intended to keep the Scottish Celts out of northern England, and another line of defenses linking the fortified Rhine and Danube rivers to hold back the Germans. The Roman Pantheon, the round temple to "All the Gods" that remains so remarkably preserved today, is mostly his work.

The last of these remarkable rulers was the Stoic emperor Marcus Aurelius (r. 161–180), who spent years fighting on Rome's frontiers. His army defeated the Parthian cavalry in Persia, on Rome's eastern borders, but they also brought back a mysterious plague that caused many deaths in Europe. Toward the end of his reign, he had to face a potentially more dangerous threat on the Rhine- Danube frontier in the west, where he himself campaigned frequently against the Germans. Beset by many problems, Marcus Aurelius found in Stoicism both the strength to persevere while there was hope of success and the courage to accept inevitable setbacks when they came. His volume of *Meditations* has always been one of the most widely read of Stoic tracts.

Imperial Government

Strong leaders, however, come only sometimes into any nation's history. What the Romans had in these first two centuries of the Empire was a system—a structure—of political institutions that linked the capital to the farthest provinces. This evolving political structure could carry them through the bad reigns of profligates and tyrants. It could provide at least some degree of justice and prosperity no matter what scandalous behavior went on in the palaces on the Palatine hill or the imperial retreat on the island of Capri.

To understand the new system of governance introduced by Augustus and developed by his successors, we have to look at two things: relations between the new emperors and the old ruling class, and the continuing development of the Roman governmental administration.

Much of the trouble at the center during the first century of the Roman Peace came from the mutual hostility of the emperors and the old senatorial ruling class. By the second century CE, however, this cycle had been largely broken. Most of the five good emperors not only chose their successors wisely but won their acceptance by the senatorial class, the army, and other segments of society. Meanwhile, the emperors had been building an imperial bureaucracy that took over much of the business of ruling and did it much more efficiently than it had been done under the Republic. Under Claudius in the middle of the first century, a key step was taken with the introduction of specialized bureaus charged with such functions as the administration of justice, finances, records, and correspondence. Under Hadrian, in the first half of the second century, carefully graded career ladders in civil and military administration were opened up.

The result was an increasingly efficient system of government. The imperial bureaucracy maintained armies on the far frontiers and kept the huge capital city supplied with food from as far away as Egypt. It was the hub of a structure of increasingly uniform administration not to be matched in the West for many centuries.

If Rome was the hub, the Empire was the wheel. And the spokes that connected them included defense, politics, and social integration. The Roman Empire continued to expand during the first two centuries of the imperial period. In Europe, it came to include not only England, France, Spain, and the Low Countries, but Austria and Switzerland and the central European and Balkan territories of modern Hungary, Yugoslavia, Romania, Bulgaria, Albania, and Greece. In the East, Rome ruled most of what is today Turkey, Syria, Israel, and Jordan, as well as parts of northern Mesopotamia. In Africa, Roman authority stretched from Egypt to Morocco, from the Nile to Gibraltar. The result was an empire of unprecedented size, still roughly centered on the Mediterranean but stretching from the North Sea to the Black Sea, from the Rhine-Danube line to the Sahara. The Roman Empire at its height was over 3 million square miles in area, approximately the size of the continental United States today, and had a population variously estimated at between 60 and 100 million people.

The arches of this Roman aqueduct still tower over the city of Segovia in Spain, once a province of the Roman Empire. Like Roman roads and Roman law, Roman cities, with their many amenities, were major benefits of the only period in which the Western world has enjoyed political unity. (Spanish Tourist Bureau)

The legions had conquered all this territory, and they defended it. The process of conquest was a brutal one, involving both bloody imperial wars and subsequent suppressions of rebellions. With the passing of the generations, however, areas firmly absorbed into the Empire became the beneficiaries of Roman military power. By the second century CE, conquered peoples were beginning to staff the legions themselves, and all Roman subjects enjoyed security, relative prosperity, and generally less oppressive government than they had experienced before the Romans came.

The conquered lands were absorbed into the Roman political system as well. The Roman Senate itself was slowly expanded to include senators from Gaul and Spain, from the Near East, and from North Africa, until by the second century CE, half the Senate was provincial. Roman citizenship too was extended, until by 212, all freeborn subjects had both the rights and the obligations—such as paying taxes—of citizenship in the Empire.

Most Roman subjects worshiped their own gods, had their own social systems, and spoke their own languages. Among the wealthier and more educated elements of the provincial populations, however, a romanized stratum did evolve. The ruling classes of many lands came to dress like Romans, speak Latin, read Roman literature, and sponsor Roman-style chariot races and gladiatorial shows for the masses. The Roman Peace of the first two centuries CE thus became more than a matter of military protection and political administration: it generated the beginning of a common society as well.

The *Pax Romana* was the longest period of relative peace the Western world had yet known or would know again. The history of Europe, North Africa, and the Near East in modern times has been scarred by many terrible wars, climaxing in the world wars of the present century. When Roman legions guarded frontiers that reached from London to Constantinople, life was much more peaceful for a lot of people in between.

Economic Expansion

The economic life of the Empire followed the pattern of its political evolution, booming under Augustus and the "good emperors," declining as the Empire did thereafter. It was the framework of Roman rule, after all, that made prosperity possible. Thanks to Roman legions on the frontiers, the network of Roman roads across Europe, and the protected sea lanes crisscrossing the Mediterranean, farmers, artisans, and merchants could carry on their business in safety and confidence. The whole of western Europe and the Mediterranean basin became a vast integrated economy.

The energies of all the Roman peoples were thus unleashed in a surge of productivity and exchange. Across seas scoured of pirates, over stone roads maintained by legionaries flowed the wealth of the Empire. Grain, fruit, oil, and wine; marble, metals, timber, wool, and other raw materials; pottery, glassware, textiles of all sorts, tools, weapons, utensils, sculpture, and jewelry now circulated freely around the Roman world.

This integrated Western economy also reached out beyond the Western world to import goods from farther south and east. Trade goods came up the Nile from inner Africa, or across the Sahara on Bedouin camels. As many as 120 ships a year left Egypt for India by way of the Red Sea and the Indian Ocean; Near Eastern merchants brought goods from China along the Asian caravan trail called the Great Silk Road. From Africa came wild beasts for the arenas, ivory, gold, papyrus, purple dye, and the crystalline stone called porphyry. From Asia came spices, cottons, and precious stone from India, silks and porcelain from Han China, and metals and textiles from the Near East.

Still, most Romans lived on farms. The huge estates called *latifundia,* established during the Republic, continued under the Empire. Aristocratic landowners stressed diversified agriculture on these plantations, combining olive trees and fruit orchards, grape vines and pasture for cattle and sheep. They largely abandoned commercial grain production to Sicily and Egypt.

In the later Empire, tenant farmers on self-sufficient estates called *villas* accepted the serflike status of *coloni.* Bound to the land if not to the landowner, *coloni* received the protection of the landlord in a time when the government no longer seemed able to guarantee security.

Urban living, however, remained the ancient ideal, and cities spread far across western Europe under the protection of Rome. The towns of the western parts of the Empire were small but numerous. Army garrisons, market towns, and administrative and later ecclesiastical centers rose both north of the Alps and around the Mediterranean. It was possible in Hadrian's day to find a Roman magistrate or a regulated marketplace, to see a Roman play or a gladiatorial contest anywhere from North Africa to northern England.

In the older parts of the civilized Mediterranean zone, cities were much larger, wealthier, and more cultured. Metropolises like Alexandria and Carthage in North Africa and Antioch, Ephesus, and later Constantinople in the Near East held populations of hundreds of thousands of people. Rome itself may have harbored a cosmopolitan population of one million. It was in these older cities, and particularly in the city of Rome itself, that imperial splendors were most profusely and massively on display.

Social Life in Ancient Rome

Social life in Rome, the capital of the Western world, was as varied and colorful, corrupt and fascinating as that of any metropolis of later times. Upper and lower classes, men and women, for all their differences, shared many of the pleasures and problems of urban living.

For the lower orders, problems included such basics as housing, food, and employment. Compelled by poverty to live in overcrowded tenement buildings, the Roman masses took advantage of the warm Mediterranean climate to spend much of their time in the city's bustling streets. We have pictures of them drinking and gambling with dice, and in the ruins of Pompeii and Herculaneum, we can see the roofless remains of food stalls and cafes where ordinary citizens found refreshment. For main meals, food staples were provided at government expense in a grain dole that expanded to include free cooking oil and wine. These dangerous classes were therefore kept fed and entertained, the "bread and circuses" many governments have found it expedient to offer people not absorbed by the economy.

By way of entertainment, emperors and other wealthy citizens sponsored costly public spectacles. Tens of thousands swarmed into the Colosseum, the model for all such sports stadiums since, to watch professional gladiators, prisoners of war, slaves, and condemned criminals fight each other to the death. Even larger numbers flooded the Circus Maximus to watch two- and four-horse chariots race around a 5-mile track and to honor winning drivers, as the Greeks had Olympic athletes, with cheers, gifts, and public monuments.

The Roman upper classes, the patricians and equestrians, enjoyed an even more exciting social life than had their precursors of the late Republic. Among the major imports from Greece were public baths—huge buildings including hot and cold pools, steam rooms, gymnasiums, and refreshment booths, with separate areas for men and women. Banquets and dinner parties also grew in popularity among the upper classes. In these gatherings, men and women shared soft couches, gourmet meals prepared by foreign chefs, musical and other entertainment, wine, and conversation.

Relations between the sexes also evolved under the pressures of Roman history. Aristocratic women often exercised considerable political influence over their male compatriots. Patrician women could draw on Roman traditions of female heroism that went back to Rhea Sylvia, the mother of the city's legendary founders, Romulus and Remus, as well as on the prestige and family power that accompanied the status of the Roman matron. A woman of the upper classes could also become extremely wealthy by inheritance, especially during the long and bloody civil wars, when so many of the senatorial elite perished. Bringing family influence, wealth, and political savvy to bear on the political and military infighting of the first century BCE, such women were often in the thick of the struggle to preserve or advance the interests of husbands or families. As wives and other relatives of Roman emperors, they gained even greater power during the Empire, the first centuries CE.

Under the Empire, wealthy women seem to have lived more pleasant, luxurious lives. They could own large amounts of property in their own right, and their husbands were often pleased to have them show off their wealth. Divorce, more difficult under Augustus, became easier later. From statues, histories, and the writings of Roman satirists, we have a vivid picture of conspicuous consumption under the Empire. Wives and daughters of great houses dressed in imported silks and expensive jewelry, carefully made up with cosmetics, unguents, and perfumes, and spent hours having their hair dressed in the latest fashion in order to be properly dazzling at the banquet, the theater, or the reserved seat in the amphitheater.

Roles for upper-class women in the more serious world included social and cultural patronage and important functions in a number of the religious cults. Wealthy women, like wealthy men, earned popular acclaim and social prestige by subsidizing public entertainments or feasts, or by erecting monuments and even temples. Many daughters of good families seem to have been educated, either with their brothers or separately, and some of these women became patrons of literature and the arts. Julia Domna (c. 167–217), daughter of a Syrian high priest and wife of the emperor Septimius Severus, surrounded herself with artists and intellectuals and was herself called "Julia the Philosopher." In the religious sphere, the worship of the many female divinities was in women's hands. Particularly important was the worship of Vesta, goddess of the hearth, whose imperial shrine was tended by the Vestal Virgins, women of unrivaled prestige in Rome. A number of the foreign goddesses worshiped in the Empire, including Isis and Cybele, had female priests, as did Fortuna, the all–important incarnation of good luck.

♦ The Decline and Fall of the Roman Empire ♦

In the third century CE, weakened by political, economic, and social problems, the Roman Empire began to come apart. In the fourth, Roman emperors shored it up again by imposing a rigid authoritarian government. But in the fifth century, overwhelmed by domestic problems and barbarian invasions, the whole elaborate structure collapsed, and with it the ancient Western world. That, in three sentences, is the story to be told in the following pages. Explaining the disaster will require a more analytical approach—and more pages. Let us begin, however, with a brief survey of the events themselves.

This monumental head of the Emperor Constantine once topped a colossal thirty-foot statue long since broken in pieces. The broad face represents a later Roman symbolic style of sculpture. The simplified planes perhaps also reflect the fact that, when the head was in place on the huge body, the face would have been seen from far below. (Barbara Malter/Capitoline Museums)

Breakdown and Recovery

The rot began to spread under the last of the five good emperors, Marcus Aurelius (161–180). As we have seen, the Stoic emperor had to face foreign invasions, a plague, and other problems. His greatest misfortune, however, was to father a son. Since he had a natural heir, he broke with the second-century practice of nominating successors of proven ability, selecting instead his own son Commodus (r. 180–192), the first of a disastrous line to follow.

One obvious symptom of the decline in the quality of imperial governance was the sudden multiplication in the numbers of emperors, from five in the second century to dozens in the third. Most of these very short-term rulers were generals who, in the old pattern of the Roman Civil War, bribed their troops to support them in a bid for power only to be toppled in a few years (or months) by new contenders. The Praetorian Guard, stationed in Rome itself, played a particularly active role in the making and unmaking of emperors.

Equally disturbing was the increase in the number of successful incursions by "barbarians." These invaders ranged from the thoroughly civilized people of the Sassanian Persian Empire in the East to Germanic tribes who had not yet learned to build cities or empires in the West. The Sassanians recaptured eastern Roman provinces taken from their predecessors. In central and western Europe, the hard-fighting if undisciplined Germanic tribes broke through the Roman defense lines to occupy the Balkan provinces and raid across the Rhine into Gaul.

Demographic and economic blows also rained down on the Empire. Though reliable statistics are few, there seems to have been a sharp population decline in the third century CE. This was apparently due as much to foreign and civil wars as to recurring bouts of plague. Economic production also went down at this time, due to a complex of factors, including high taxes and the decline of the peasant and middle classes. And with all these disasters came the sort of social dislocation and psychological malaise that, though hard to footnote, can insidiously undermine an already weakened society.

Two remarkable emperors finally brought recovery in the decades around CE 300. Diocletian (r. 284–305) and Constantine (r. 312–337) reassembled at least a facsimile of the old system that held for another century. Diocletian, who usually gets the lion's share of the credit, was a Balkan provincial who had risen through the army. He imprinted his personality on the time by building huge imperial palaces and by transforming the imperial government at last into a full-fledged Eastern monarchy. Prostrate petitioners were received by Diocletian, who was dressed in elaborate silken robes heavy with gold and jewels, gold dust gleaming in his hair, wearing the purple boots that would thereafter be the symbols of imperial authority. Constantine, who fought his way to power, is best remembered for two historic acts: legalizing the Christian church after three centuries of intermittent persecution, and founding the city of Constantinople on the Straits connecting the Mediterranean with the Black Sea.

These two men faced successively the host of problems produced by the third-century breakdown. Diocletian's original solution, usually called the *Tetrarchy* ("Rule of Four") seemed at first to involve a division of power rather than further centralization. To protect the buckling frontiers, four imperial rulers divided primary responsibility among them: two senior rulers called Augusti and two Caesars, co-rulers and heirs apparent to the older men. This system, however, collapsed in Constantine's day.

More important in restructuring the Empire, however, was the great expansion and elaboration of the imperial administration. Under Diocletian and Constantine, the historic provinces were replaced by a system of four large prefectures, twelve dioceses, and ninety-six much smaller provinces. A hierarchic administration beginning with a group of imperial advisers comparable to a modern cabinet spread down through a bewildering array of grades and specializations to the local level. Among the new civil servants were numbers of spies and government agents who would be called secret policemen in a later century.

To support the top-heavy new bureaucracy and army with which they proposed to restore order and security, Diocletian and Constantine attempted social and economic regulation so rigid that it has been called totalitarian. Serious and sometimes painfully successful efforts were made to fix everyone in a hereditary economic slot—peasants to stay on the large estates, carpenters to ply their fathers' trade. Equally unpopular were regulations that forced people of substance to accept local government appointments their ancestors would have been honored to receive. In both cases, the primary goal was to establish a firm tax base for the expanded administration and defense establishment, as well as to pay for the dazzling new round of imperial building that announced the new Rome to the world.

Fifth-Century Collapse

Despite Constantine's reestablishment of rule by a single emperor, the division of authority and responsibility reasserted itself soon after his death. The job was simply too big for one

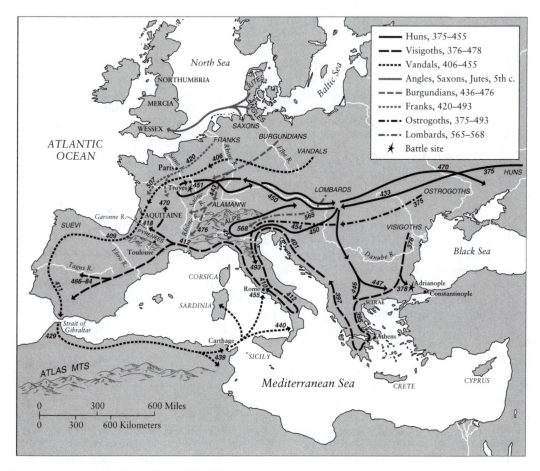

Germanic Invasions of the Roman Empire, 378–568

man, and there was no lack of candidates for the imperial purple. From the 360s on, therefore, there were frequently separate emperors for the western and eastern halves of the Empire—one centered at Rome, the other at Constantinople. Imperial authoritarianism continued to be capricious and cruel and exactions of imperial officials oppressive, undermining the people's political faith and draining their economic wealth. As a result, the political decline of the Roman Empire was far advanced before the climactic round of barbarian invasions got under way.

The triggering event was the westward thrust of a Mongol people called the Huns, who had reached the region north of the Black Sea in the fourth century CE and pushed on into Europe in the fifth. This mounting pressure from the East set the Germans into motion on the Roman borders. In the fifth century, both the Huns and the much more numerous Germans breasted and broke through the frontiers of the Western world.

They were two very different peoples. The Huns were pastoral nomads from the Asian grasslands who lived on their horses and were furious cavalry fighters. The Germanic peoples—Goths, Franks, Vandals, Saxons, and others—were village-dwelling forest tribes who inhabited much of Europe east of the Rhine and north of the Danube. These invaders came not as conquering armies, but as migrating peoples—women and children, wagons and flocks, as well as men with weapons. Some of these intruders had been infiltrating the Empire for centuries, coming to live and work in the civilized zone. Nevertheless, these massive incursions were accompanied by battles and plundering. And they did undermine Roman institutions and ways of life the Romans had introduced into Europe over the preceding four hundred years.

The first major breakthrough came in the Eastern Empire in the 370s, when a Germanic people called the Visigoths, driven from their own lands west of the Black Sea by the invading Huns, sought sanctuary inside the Roman defense lines. Unmercifully exploited by Roman soldiers and officials, the Visigoths revolted, defeated a Roman army, and killed the Eastern Roman emperor in the Battle of Adrianople (378). It was the beginning of a century of barbarian triumphs.

Arrows on a map show the confusion of the folk wanderings that followed. The Visigoths themselves pillaged their way across the Balkans and down into Italy, where in CE 410 their leader Alaric shocked the Roman world by plundering Rome itself. From Italy, the Visigoths crossed Gaul to found a Visigothic kingdom in Roman Spain. The Vandals, also jarred loose from their ancestral lands in eastern Europe by the Huns, crossed Germany, Gaul, Spain, and the Straits of Gibraltar to establish a Vandal kingdom in North Africa. From this base, they crossed the Mediterranean to sack Rome yet again in 455. When the Romans withdrew their legions from Britain to deal with these disasters, Angles, Saxons, and Jutes from Germany and Denmark crossed the Channel to invade southeastern England, where a new scattering of Germanic kingdoms soon appeared.

The Huns themselves, meanwhile, after pausing on the Danube plain, moved on into Roman Europe under the leadership of Attila (r. 434–453), who soon became known to the partially Christianized West as "the Scourge of God." Turned back by Roman troops in Gaul, the Huns headed south into Italy to pillage the rich heartland of the Empire and to camp threateningly within sight of the walls of Rome. A plague that decimated their numbers as well as Attila's own death finally turned them back into Asia. Within decades, however, they were succeeded in Italy by more Germanic peoples. In 476, the last Western Roman emperor, a youth named Romulus Augustulus, surrendered power to the German mercenary Odoacer (c. 433–c. 493), who became the first Germanic king of Italy.

There were others still to come. The hosts of Theodoric the Ostrogoth (c. 454–526) soon entered from the east and became masters of Italy in the 490s. The Lombards followed in the next century, and the region of Lombardy in northern Italy is called after them still. In the north, two powerful tribes of Franks pushed into northern Gaul and defeated the last Roman governor in the 480s. The Franks established the most powerful of the Germanic kingdoms in Gaul, which came to be called France after these conquerors.

The Eastern Roman Empire, with its capital at Constantinople, survived the fall of the Western Empire. Traditionally, however, the passing of the last Roman emperor of the West in 476 has been considered to mark the end of the Roman imperium that had begun to take shape almost a thousand years before, and with it the end of the domination of the evolving West by the ancient civilizations of Greece and Rome.

Why Did Rome Fall?

Historians are concerned not just to find out what happened in the past, but to figure out why. They have learned, furthermore, that to understand a major historical event such as a great war or a revolution one must look, not for one cause, but for a complex of inter-related historical events and conditions that together brought about the event under consideration.

Clearly, for instance, there were military causes for the fall of Rome. The Germanic invasions, sparked by the Hunnish intrusion from the East, broke through the frontiers and fragmented the Western Empire politically. There are technical explanations. The government settled the troops too comfortably into the local population and assigned them too many nonmilitary functions, from contract work for the army to subsistence farming and herding for themselves. An older, less convincing contention is that non-Italian legions lacked Roman skills or commitment to Rome, though there were many successful German, Balkan, and other provincial commanders.

Political causes are also easy to point to, though some of these too are doubtful. During the last century of their history, as we have seen, Roman emperors became noticeably more authoritarian and withdrawn, and officials also grew increasingly oppressive, rapacious, and numerous. These policies may have undermined popular dedication to the defense of a realm that must have looked as tyrannical to many as the barbarian alternatives.

Certainly economic and social factors contributed significantly to the disastrous decline of the Roman Empire. Increased taxation to support a top-heavy bureaucracy and an enormous military establishment undoubtedly drained the Empire economically. Government exactions that drove peasants to flee left land unworked, while tax penalties for success may have discouraged the growth of a productive middle class. More fundamental economic difficulties may have been rooted in Rome's large dependence on slave labor, which discouraged technological development. A system based heavily on slavery, furthermore, would have faced a dangerous labor shortage when wars of conquest, which brought in plenty of slaves, were replaced by less profitable defensive struggles on the frontiers.

What we may term ecological causes, often closely related to the state of the economy, have also been adduced. Thus droughts, climatic variations, and overworked land may have contributed significantly to shrinking agricultural productivity. The plague and other epidemic diseases may help to explain the decline in the Roman population that apparently took place. The claim that use of lead-lined vessels for food and water by the aristocracy led to slow sterilization and decline in the size of the ruling classes has not found wide-spread acceptance, since such vessels were also used in the Eastern Roman Empire, which survived handily.

Some writers have suggested that moral or ethical decline contributed heavily to the failure of the Roman Empire. For example, many have asserted that the Roman aristocracy was fatally undermined by luxurious living and debauchery. As we have seen, however, such practices were common among some elements of the Roman elite even during Rome's golden age, making it unlikely that they were a determining factor in the Empire's collapse.

Still another much-debated source of diminishing concern for the survival of the Empire is the rise of Christianity. Edward Gibbon, in his classic eighteenth-century account of *The Decline and Fall of the Roman Empire,* was one of the first to allege that the new religion drew intelligent energetic leaders away from the declining state to the rising church. The Christian faith may also have turned some people's minds from this world to the next, leaving them unconcerned for the salvation of the earthly kingdom, since eternal salvation in the heavenly kingdom lay ahead. Some early Christians and Jews did refuse both military service and the requirement that citizens express allegiance to the ruler by throwing incense on the altar of the emperor's "genius." Again, however, the Eastern Roman Empire, which became as strongly Christian as the Western Empire, found leaders and soldiers enough to preserve it for ten more centuries.

One of Gibbon's broadest assertions about the decline and fall, finally, has considerable appeal, though it would certainly be hard to document. This is the suggestion that the Empire as a whole was simply too large to survive. It had too much land, too many people to rule and defend. It devoured its resources on an unprecedented scale and had not the technical means to replenish them. A dinosaur among the nations, the Roman Empire simply fell of its own weight. The problem, as Gibbon pointed out, was not to explain the decline and fall of the Empire, but to understand how it lasted as long as it did.

♦ The Rise of Christianity ♦

The best-known ancient name of all today, however, lived far from the capital of the Western world. Jesus of Nazareth, born under Augustus, executed under his successor Tiberius, lived and died unknown except to the Jewish population of Palestine and the Roman governor and garrison who ruled there. Even Pontius Pilate does not seem to have heard of Jesus before he was brought up for trial. Yet the religion founded by Jesus Christ outlasted the fall of both the Roman Republic and the Roman Empire to provide the spiritual core of the next age of Western history.

We will look here first at the Roman background to the rise of Christianity in Greco-Roman philosophical beliefs and in the growing popularity of the mystery cults. Thereafter, this section will outline the life of the founder of the Christian faith in the context of the Jewish religion which prevailed in the Near Eastern province where he grew up. Jesus' message as it was heard in his own time will conclude this brief glance at this immensely significant spiritual beginning.

Judaism and Jesus

One important key to understanding the life and message of Jesus Christ is to remember that he was born and raised a Jew. The Hebrews, whose dedicated monotheism had made them stand out among the polytheistic Near Eastern societies of ancient times, seemed just as exotic in the Greco-Roman world. The Jews, as the Hebrews had come to be called around 500 BCE, refused to be assimilated into the world empire. To many Romans, the Christian sect looked like more of the same, only worse.

The old faith of the ancient Hebrews still burned fiercely—and with it, the spirit of rebellion. The Jews rebelled against the Seleucids, who had tried to install Zeus in the temple at Jerusalem. They revolted again on the death of King Herod, the cruel ruler who was Rome's puppet in the region. They rose in revolt against Nero in the 60s CE and against other emperors in later centuries.

The Jews of Jesus' time still believed in one God, Yahweh, invisible and all-powerful, creator of the world, whose chosen people they believed themselves to be. The personal

Chronology 5.2.: Rise of Christianity

4 BCE–CE 29–30	*Jesus founds the Christian religion*
64	*Nero's persecution of Christians*
c.67	*Execution of St. Paul*
300	*Diocletian's persecution of Christians*
313	*Constantine legalizes Christianity*
354–430	*St. Augustine*
390	*Christianity is made the state religion of the Empire*
476	*Fall of the Western Roman Empire; Christian church survives*

morality prescribed by the Ten Commandments and the sense of social justice urged by the prophets were central to the Judaic faith. Much of what Jesus later preached was part of his Judaic heritage, studied in the temple of his childhood, breathed in with the religiously charged air of this corner of western Asia. "Do not think that I have come to destroy the law or the prophets," Jesus declared. "I have not come to destroy, but to fulfill."[2]

In Jesus' time, there was a widely held belief in a coming savior or *Messiah*. Most Jews saw the Messiah as a political liberator from foreign oppression. Some, however, expected a spiritual savior, a divine Chosen One who would inaugurate a kingdom of righteousness on earth. Again, Jesus must have absorbed all these beliefs as he studied the scrolls and talked with the priests of Galilee.

There were also a number of sects and a continuing tradition of prophetic inspiration in the land of Jesus' birth. The popular Pharisees were vigorous defenders of ritual perfection and the Law of Moses, which governed every aspect of their lives. The Essenes were monkish communities, dwellers in the desert whose beliefs were revealed in detail for the first time by the discovery of the Dead Sea scrolls at Qumran in Jordan in the 1940s. These Essenes had withdrawn entirely from society to await the coming Messiah and the triumph of righteousness over wickedness.

Changes were also emerging in the larger Roman world of Jesus' time. During the last centuries before Christ and the opening centuries of what was to become the Christian era, the worship of the Roman gods—Jupiter, Mars, Venus, and the rest—had become a state function, lacking the spiritual warmth and power that many Romans needed in those tumultuous times.

For the cultured few, as we have seen, the Greek philosophical schools still offered thoughtful answers to the large questions of life. Roman Stoics like Cicero replaced the passive tone of Stoic "apathy" with a stress on doing your duty, come what might, clearly a valuable virtue for the rulers and soldiers responsible for holding the empire together. Platonism underwent even more remarkable changes, particularly in the *Neoplatonism* ("New Platonism") taught by the influential philosopher Plotinus at Alexandria in the third century CE. Plotinus (c. 205–c. 270) asserted that the greatest of all the transcendent Platonic forms (or Ideas or absolutes) was what he described as the One, the central source of all being and all values, from which these qualities radiated like light from its source. The more distant each level of being was from this spiritual source, the less reality and the less value it possessed. The material world, Plato's old world of "particulars," was the furthest removed from the spiritual core of the universe, hence the least good and the least real of all.

For those who found the philosophers too intellectual to satisfy their religious needs, finally, there were the Greek and Near Eastern *mystery cults,* including the religions of the Greek Dionysus (Bacchus to the Romans), the militant Persian Mithras (a favorite of Roman legionaries), the Egyptian Isis, and Cybele, the "Great Mother," from Asia Minor.

A major appeal of these cults, as noted earlier, was their offer of eternal life to their initiates. Among the rituals of these foreign faiths, baptism and communion were common. Christianity, too, would preach a risen God who guaranteed eternal life, who would baptize believers, and who would offer communion with God through a sacred meal. Christianity would, thus, meet many of the spiritual needs that the popularity of the mystery cults had revealed in the Roman world.

This was the spiritual world into which Jesus was born, somewhere around the year 4 CE, while Augustus Caesar ruled at Rome and the Roman golden age was just beginning.

The Message of Christ

Standing on the Arbel cliffs in northern Israel, with the flat blue Sea of Galilee spread out below and the twin-peaked mountain called the Horns of Hattin behind, a visitor may look out over the green land where Christ lived and preached. Beyond the hills to the west lies Nazareth. Below, on the western shore of the Sea of Galilee, the village of Capernaum, where Jesus recruited Peter, the fisher of men, nestles among cedars and orchards on the lake shore. Among these hills and along these roads, Jesus preached for most of his three years' ministry, before taking the long hot road south to Jerusalem.

Looking down at this first countryside to hear his words, you are struck with a sudden sense of the intimacy, the humanity of this level of communication. Word spreading from that village over there to that one just down the road. Words spoken eye to eye in the grateful shade of a palm tree tossing in the breeze from the Mediterranean. A real man walking real roads, speaking to small groups among low stone houses roofed with thatch, with the lake shore just beyond. A real man, touching the sick among the cook fires, or fixing with a gaze full of sudden force those few who would rise from their labors and follow him.

Jesus' family were apparently people of the artisan class, Joseph being a carpenter. His mother's name was Miriam, Mary in English. The first thirty years of his life are largely a blank in the record. What is recorded, including his studies in the temple as a boy and his confounding the priests with his knowledge of the faith, indicates that he was an extremely religious youth. When he was about thirty, not young in those days, he was baptized in the Jordan River by John the Baptist, a popular lay preacher in the ancient prophetic tradition. Thereafter, Jesus took up his own religious calling and began to preach to the people in his turn.

Jesus' mission probably lasted about three years, though even that is not certain. He spoke in the synagogues and disputed points of doctrine with priests and Pharisees and gained a larger following by his open-air sermons in the fields and streets of Galilee. Stories of miracles followed in his footsteps: he turned water into wine, fed multitudes on a few fish and loaves of bread, cured the sick, restored sight to the blind, and raised the dead. His message, as Christians would later come to understand it, included the two "great commandments": Love God, and love thy neighbor as thyself.

Most importantly, Jesus presented himself, not as another prophet, but as a divine being, the Son of God. And he declared that to believe in him was the only road to salvation: "I am the Way." *Christ,* the Anointed One, the Messiah so long prophesied, had come to earth. He offered to those who accepted his teaching the supreme gift of eternal life.

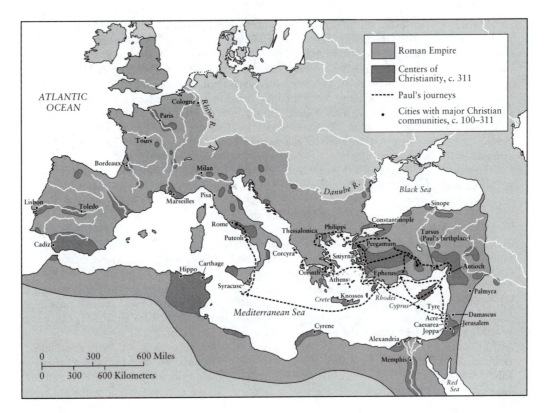

Christianity Under the Roman Empire, 29–313

The last days of Jesus' own life are reported in more detail than any other part of it in the Gospels. The story, familiar everywhere in the Western world, tells how he went south from Galilee down into Judea, entered Jerusalem to the cheers of thousands, defied the priestly hierarchy in the temple, ate a last supper with his dozen chosen disciples, was betrayed by one of them, convicted by the priests for blasphemy, and executed by the Romans for treason. Pontius Pilate, the Roman governor of Judea, had a crude sign nailed up on the cross on which Jesus was crucified, derisively labeling him "the king of the Jews." The Romans, outsiders in Palestine, probably could not distinguish between the various meanings of the term *Messiah* among the Hebrews.

And that should, by all practical Roman common sense, have been that. But history sometimes transcends common sense, and it is in fact from the crucifixion of Jesus that we date the most far-reaching spiritual transformation in the history of the Western world.

♦ The Christian Church Takes Shape ♦

Jesus had told his disciples to spread the Gospel, the "Good News" of his coming. They proceeded to do just that. The Acts of the Apostles, as recorded in the New Testament, include the martyrdoms of many, and the birth of a network of what the later world would call churches.

This final section will cover the underground centuries of persecution and the legalization of the Christian church under emperor Constantine in 313. It will also examine the development of heresies, religious views rejected by most Christians, and the rise of such Christian thinkers as Augustine and Jerome, the famous "fathers of the church," to deal with these theological problems.

Christianity Under the Sign of the Fish

The greatest of the early Christian missionaries was a man who had never seen the living Jesus: Paul of Tarsus. Paul (c. 36–67), a Hellenized Jew of the diaspora, had his own spiritual experience of the Anointed One, a vision on the road to Damascus that changed his life. Formerly a persecutor of the new sect, he became a dedicated proselytizer for Christianity. And because of his immersion in Greco-Roman culture, he was able to reach the non-Jewish population of the Mediterranean world more effectively than the more provincial Jews who had known Jesus personally could have done.

A tireless traveler, preacher, and organizer, Paul carried his message through Syria, Asia Minor, Macedonia, and Greece to Rome itself, establishing churches as he went and maintaining correspondence with all of them. Inevitably, Paul's own understanding of Christian doctrine became part of the faith as he spread it. From him came a heavy emphasis on sin as the natural human condition, a wickedness inherited from the original sin of Adam. Paul stressed three particular virtues: *faith* in the truth of Christianity, *hope* of salvation through Christ, and, above all, *love* of God. In the end, however, he saw salvation not as something to be "earned" by Christian living, but as a gift of God, conferred only by divine grace.

For Christians in early centuries, the essence of Christ's message was summed up in the Sign of the Fish. The fish was an ancient religious symbol often associated with commemoration of the dead. Christians adopted it because the letters that composed the word *ICHTHYS*, "fish" in the Greek lingua franca or common language of the Hellenistic East, were the initials of the key phrase: *Jesus Christ, Son of God, Savior.* This was the message of the enigmatic sign, a rude drawing of a fish scrawled on a wall or above a door, by which early Christians indicated their presence to fellow believers.

Christian rites were simpler and perhaps warmer with fellowship than those of other contemporary Western religions. Christians were baptized as Christ had been, symbolically washing away their sins with water in order to begin a new life in Christ's spirit. They met in private homes for religious feasts commemorating Christ's own last supper of unleavened bread and wine, feeling as they did so a sense of communion with Jesus, who had said that the bread and wine were his flesh, his blood. The sacrament of the Eucharist, or holy communion, was thus born.

It sounds a harmless regimen; yet trouble came to the new religion as early as the first century CE. Like the Jews, the Christians rejected all other gods except their own, and thus looked almost like atheists to their polytheistic neighbors. They refused to perform even the formal religious gesture of allegiance to the emperor by casting incense on the imperial altar, and thus came to be suspected of disloyalty and sedition. They met in private, a privacy that turned into secrecy as their neighbors' suspicions exploded into persecution. And secrecy, in turn, encouraged rumors that they practiced shocking rites, including incest and ritual murder. As political and social troubles developed in the later Empire, followers of the new faith were often made scapegoats for any great misfortune, human or natural.

The Emergence of the Church

For three centuries, from the death of Jesus Christ around CE 30 until official toleration came in 313, Christians were an often despised minority, attacked by mobs in the cities, and expropriated and executed by the Roman government. The worst of the persecutions came under Diocletian (r. 284–305), who restored order to Rome at the cost of rigid authoritarianism. Under his successor Constantine (r. 312–337), however, the suffering of the Christians at last came to an end. Modern historians suggest that Constantine may have hoped to use the commitment, organization, and growing wealth of the church to help hold the Empire together. While he does not seem to have abandoned the pagan cults, he did end the persecution of the Christians and even returned church property and began to build churches himself. In 313, he issued the Edict of Milan, decreeing official toleration of Christianity. Most of the succeeding emperors were themselves Christians, and the church grew rapidly in size, wealth, and prestige. In the 390s, finally, Emperor Theodosius I (r. 379–395) declared Christianity the state religion of the Roman Empire.

As early as the second century, furthermore, a hierarchy of Christian leadership was emerging. Each local congregation had its priest. The priest derived his authority from a higher official called a bishop, the recognized head of all the Christians in a diocese, a particular city or region. Bishops in turn traced their spiritual authority back to the apostles who had founded their churches, and thus to Christ himself.

Women played an important part in the early life of the Christian church. Some were widely admired leaders, prophetesses who claimed divine inspiration. Some Christians thought that these vessels of the Holy Spirit, rather than the emerging structure of bishops, should be the chief guides of the church. In many local churches, women's organizations had important functions. Groups of celibate women, virgins or widows, handled much of the material side of the church's activities, from charity to property. Their "house churches" served as central places for religious feasts and refuges for wandering preachers. The Christian assertion that in Christ "there is neither Jew nor Greek . . . neither bond nor free . . . neither male nor female"[3] continued to win the devotion of many women to the church.

As Christianity emerged from the shadow of persecution shortly after CE 300, its organizational structure developed still further. Among the many independent bishops, a few who presided over the largest cities in the Mediterranean world acquired a higher authority than others. Known as archbishops, they became the ecclesiastical heads of regions containing the churches of a number of bishops. Some few archbishops, finally, claimed even larger authority. The bishop of Rome based his claim to primacy on the fact that Peter, the disciple on whom Jesus had said he depended to build his church, had been the first bishop of Rome. In addition, both Peter and Paul were believed to have been martyred there by Nero. By the fifth century, the bishop of Rome was increasingly granted priority among the others, and the foundation of the Roman Catholic papacy had been laid.

Heresy and Schism

By the time the church was legalized in CE 313, the life of the historical Jesus was three centuries in the past. Councils of church leaders and scholars had already decided which accounts of his life and teachings were "canonical"—orthodox and true—and thus established the official text of the Bible. Church thinkers, often drawing on Greek philosophical concepts and other sources of ancient wisdom, attempted to explain "the nature of the Incarnation"—that is, what it *meant* to say that Christ was the Son of God. Some of the resulting theories were accepted and became basic Christian doctrine; others were rejected as inaccurate and heretical.

An early heresy was the view of the Near Eastern *Gnostics,* Christians who believed they possessed a "secret wisdom" (*gnosis* in Greek) concealed from others. According to the Gnostics, Christ, since he was divine, must have been a purely spiritual being, in no sense material. A purely spiritual being, however, could not have been crucified upon a material cross, could not have suffered or died as Jesus was reported to have done.

A different but equally heretical view was that of the *Arians,* followers of the Alexandrian priest Arius (c. CE 280–336). Arius insisted that if Christ was God's "begotten Son," then he could not be identical with God, as monotheistic orthodoxy asserted. Christ should be seen, then, as a creation of God's, as not eternal (since he was begotten in time), and as, in some sense, dependent on the Father. If the Gnostics emphasized the gulf between Christ and humanity, the Arians sought to broaden the gap between Christ and God.

To both, the church replied that Jesus Christ had been both God and man, divine and human. And if this was a mystery beyond our human comprehension, it was also a mystery that Christians were not at liberty to doubt.

A heresy with even broader application, with roots outside Christianity itself, was Manichaean dualism. This widely influential doctrine, which drew on the teachings of the Persian Zoroaster, was preached by a third-century Near Eastern prophet named Mani (216–276). Attempting to deal with the age-old problem of evil—how a good and powerful God could be responsible for a universe filled with suffering and sin—the *Manichaeans* absolved God of responsibility by declaring that *another* power produced the evil in the universe. This approach, depicting good and evil as independent forces in the cosmos, saw the universe as a combat zone between the two. It also, however, tended to give Satan (the Zoroastrian Ahriman) something like parity with God. This view, too, was rejected as heretical by the church.

To deal with such disputes on an authoritative level, bishops would often meet in councils, thrash out differences of opinion, and issue joint statements on policy or theology. At the first ecumenical council called by Emperor Constantine at Nicaea near Constantinople in 325, the Arian theory was declared heretical. Even more important, however, the council issued the Nicene Creed, a brief statement of orthodox Christian belief that was used as a standard for many centuries. Church councils became an essential instrument for settling disputes and solving problems within the church from 325 to the most recent such meeting, the reforming Vatican Council of the 1960s.

The Fathers of the Church

The very vigor of these disputes over doctrine in the early church honed some exceptional minds. The most influential of these early scholars and preachers, who included both Greek and Latin writers, became known as the fathers of the church.

The Greek fathers had the advantage of being able to read both the New Testament and the ancient philosophers in their original Greek. Origen (c. 185–254), perhaps the most admired of the Greek fathers, was especially celebrated for his textual study of the Hebrew Old Testament. The Latin fathers included Jerome, Ambrose, and above all, Augustine. Jerome (c. 340–420), an immensely learned man, was most famous for his translation of the entire Bible from Hebrew and Greek into Latin. This *Vulgate* version (so called because it was in the "vulgar," or popular Latin of his day) was the text used by scholars in the West throughout the Middle Ages.

Ambrose of Milan (c. 340–397) was a much-admired preacher and, as bishop of that northern Italian city, a powerful church administrator. He excommunicated Emperor Theodosius himself for having massacred the population of a rebellious Greek city.

The most influential of all the *church fathers*, however, was Augustine (354–430), bishop of Hippo in North Africa. Raised by a Christian mother and a pagan father in Roman North Africa, Augustine was an eager student of pagan learning throughout his youth and young adulthood. A successful student and then teacher of rhetoric, Augustine moved from his home near Carthage to Rome and then to Milan, where, inspired by the eloquence of Ambrose and by the Scriptures themselves, he was converted to Christianity.

Augustine's books on many aspects of Christian life and belief provided guidance for priests and inspiration for laypeople throughout the Middle Ages. His *City of God* sought to explain all history in Christian terms. Believing that God's grace was the sole source of salvation, Augustine also came to believe in predestination—that an all-powerful God has destined every human soul for salvation or damnation, and that "good works" cannot affect the outcome. The Roman Catholic church rejected this view, insisting on the equal importance of faith and works on the road to life eternal. In the early modern period, however, Protestant reformers like Luther and Calvin found warrant for their own predestinarian views in the writings of Augustine.

The history of Rome thus ended with the Christian church institutionally developed and intellectually vigorous. The Roman state withered and collapsed under the assault of less developed peoples from the north and east. The Christian faith survived, expanded still further by converting its barbarian conquerors, and emerged as the dominant force in the next stage of Western history, the age of medieval Christendom.

Summary

Augustus Caesar and the emperors who succeeded him presided over the two most successful—and relatively peaceful—centuries in Roman history. They built an efficient structure of imperial government, encouraged economic prosperity, and presided over a vibrant society, with banquets and philosophy for the elite, bread and circuses for the masses.

The third century CE, however, saw a partial breakdown of the Empire, followed in the next century by a more rigorous imperial administration under Diocletian and Constantine. Finally, in the fifth century, the Empire crumbled under a combination of internal strains and Germanic invasions from without. Attempts to explain the fall of Rome have ranged from economic problems and an unpopular government to moral decline and the rise of an otherworldly religion.

The spread of Christianity, however, had more far-reaching consequences. Jesus of Nazareth formulated his compelling beliefs in the Near Eastern atmosphere of developed Judaism. His ideas found hearers in a larger Roman world tempted to think broadly by Greek philosophers and inspired by the mystery cults to seek a supernatural salvation.

The views of Paul and the church fathers further expanded the range and influence of Jesus' teachings. Despite savage persecutions in the first three centuries after Christ, churches sprang up in many communities, and the faith grew and spread. Legalized by Emperor Constantine in 313 CE, Christianity became in the later Roman centuries the central religion of the Western world.

Some Key Terms

Arians 123	latifundia 110	*Pax Romana* 103
Augustus 103	Manichaeans 123	*principate* 102
church fathers 124	Messiah 118	Tetrarchy 113
coloni 110	mystery cults 119	villas 110
Gnostics 123	Neoplatonism 118	*Vulgate* 124
ICHTHYS 121	*pater patriae* 104	

Notes

1. *Ancient Greek Inscriptions in the British Museum* (Oxford: Oxford University Press, 1893), No. 894, trans. David Magie, *The Roman Role in Asia Minor,* vol. 1 (Princeton: Princeton University Press, 1950), 490.

2. Matthew 5:17.
3. Galatians 3:28.

Reading List

Bradley, K. R. *Slaves and Masters in the Roman Empire: A Study in Social Control.* Brussels: Latomus, 1984. Relations between owners and slaves, with an interesting attempt to penetrate the minds of the latter.

———. *The World of Late Antiquity: From Marcus Aurelius to Muhammad.* London: Thames and Hudson, 1971. Popular presentation by a gifted scholar.

Burkert, W. *Ancient Mystery Cults.* Cambridge, Mass.: Harvard University Press, 1987. Brief but readable and expert account, with some attempt to explain the appeal of the cults.

Clark, G. *Women in Late Antiquity: Pagan and Christian Lifestyles.* New York: Clarendon Press, 1993. Covers a broad spectrum of women's history, from health and work to philosophy.

Clark, M. T. *Augustine.* Washington, D. C.: Georgetown University Press, 1994. Brief account of life and ideas.

Drinkwater, J. F. *Roman Gaul: The Three Provinces, 58 b.c.–a.d. 260.* Ithaca, N.Y.: Cornell University Press, 1983. Ancient France under the Romans.

Fredriksen, P. *From Jesus to Christ: The Origins of the New Testament Image of Jesus.* New Haven: Yale University Press, 1988. Scholarly and readable work, part of a recent upsurge in books about the historical Jesus.

Garzetti, A. *From Tiberius to Antoninus: A History of the Roman Empire a.d. 14–192.* Translated by J. R. Foster. London: Methuen, 1974. Massive history of the centuries of the Roman Peace after Augustus. See also the more recent study by C. B. Wells, *The Roman Empire* (London: Fontana, 1984). Stresses economic and social affairs.

Gurval, R. A. *Actium and Augustus: The Politics and Emotions of Civil War.* Ann Arbor: University of Michigan Press, 1995. Political and literary dimensions.

Hallett, J. P. *Fathers and Daughters in Roman Society: Women and the Elite Family.* Princeton: Princeton University Press, 1984. Suggests that aristocratic women exerted significant influence on affairs.

Levick, B. *Claudius.* New Haven: Yale University

Press, 1990. Impressive life of the misfit who became one of Rome's greatest rulers.

Lewis, N. *Life in Egypt Under Roman Rule*. New York: Oxford University Press, 1983. Stylish and scholarly picture of life in this African province of the empire.

Markus, R. A. *Christianity in the Roman World*. New York: Scribner's, 1974. Christian values shape a self-confident sense of Christian identity as the Empire crumbles. See also W. H. Frend, *Martyrdom and Persecution in the Early Church* (Grand Rapids, Mich.: Baker, 1981).

Speidel, M. *Roman Army Studies*. Amsterdam: Grieben, 1984. Short papers on many aspects of the Roman military system.

Suetonius. *Lives of the Caesars*. Translated by R. Graves. Baltimore: Penguin, 1957. Colorful, critical Roman biographies, translated by a celebrated modern writer. For a more recent study of one of the more notorious emperors chronicled here, see M. T. Griffin, *Nero: The End of a Dynasty* (New Haven: Yale University Press, 1984).

Terrill, A. *The Fall of the Roman Empire: The Military Explanation*. London: Thames and Hudson, 1986. One of many explanations. For another favorite, see R. MacMullan, *Corruption and the Decline of Rome* (New Haven: Yale University Press, 1988).

Thompson, E. A. *Romans and Barbarians: The Decline of the Western Empire*. Madison: University of Wisconsin Press, 1982. Essays on the decay of the Roman imperium in the provinces; witty and learned. See also B. Cunliffe, *Greeks, Romans, and Barbarians: Spheres of Interaction* (New York: Methuen, 1988). An analysis of relations between the Mediterranean world and the rest of Europe in terms of a southern economic "core" and a northern "periphery."

———. *Romans and Blacks*. Norman: University of Oklahoma Press, 1989. Exemplary study of the evidence and the scholarly literature on race relations, which seem not to have been a problem in Rome. See also F. Snowden's seminal work, *Before Color Prejudice: The Ancient View of Blacks* (Cambridge, Mass.: Harvard University Press, 1983).

Webster, G. *Boudicca: The British Revolt Against Rome, a.d. 60*. Totowa, N.J.: Rowan and Littlefield, 1978. Brief, archaeologically informed study of the English queen and her challenge to Rome.

Williams, S. *Diocletian and the Roman Recovery*. New York: Methuen, 1985. Well-written life of the emperor who shared with Constantine the task of pulling Rome together after its third-century decline.

PART II
The Centuries of Christendom

The Middle Ages, roughly from CE 500 to 1500, marked a new beginning for Western history. As we have seen, the Roman Empire and civilization collapsed in the fifth century under both internal and external pressures. Over the next thousand years, Western peoples began again with simple agricultural villages and slowly learned to rebuild cities and larger political units. During this second cycle of Western history, which we explore in the next five chapters, Western society expanded economically and technologically once more, and constructed a sophisticated culture in which the Christian religion played a central role.

For several centuries after 500, political power fell into the hands of feudal barons, who had only a limited personal allegiance to more powerful nobles. Yet by the year 1000, larger territorial units had emerged, including hereditary counties, duchies, and larger lands. During the High Middle Ages—the eleventh, twelfth, and thirteenth centuries—feudal monarchies developed, loosely governed countries that provided the basis for the nation–states of the future.

The medieval economy evolved gradually from the subsistence agriculture of the simple manor farm in the early Middle Ages to an integrated regional or even international economy in the High Middle Ages. Merchant companies and craft guilds rebuilt the cities as centers of production and commerce. And trade once more expanded well beyond the West, reaching to North Africa, the Near East, and ultimately as far as China.

Most peasants were still bound to the land they tilled, not outright slaves but serfs owing the lord of the manor both unpaid labor and payments in kind. There were now several elite classes—the older landed aristocracy, the emergent urban middle classes, and the upper ranks of the church hierarchy—and they often feuded. Still, the Middle Ages is usually seen as Europe's great Age of Faith, when Christian beliefs infused Western thought and art. The most learned people in the Western world were religious thinkers, and the tallest building in any city was the cathedral.

Once dismissed as the Dark Ages, a time when the West was a relatively underdeveloped part of the globe, the Middle Ages actually planted the seeds of later territorial expansion. North Africa and the Near East, once part of the Roman Empire, were now absorbed into the rival Muslim family of nations. But medieval kings, merchants, crusaders, and missionaries expanded its boundaries to include more of central and eastern Europe.

Throughout the medieval period the West was influenced by many non-Western peoples: pagan Vikings from the north, Muslim Arabs from the south, and nomadic peoples from the steppes of Eurasia. The Byzantine Empire, the surviving eastern half of the Roman Empire centered at Constantinople, was medieval Europe's earliest important trading partner, and the West soon learned to trade profitably with the Muslim world as well. From many of these peoples came valuable cultural borrowings, including the Arabic numerals we use today.

Traditionally, the Middle Ages has meant castles and cathedrals, warrior kings like Charlemagne, and saints like Joan of Arc. It has also meant city streets full of busy artisans, clusters of peasant huts, and monks and nuns who preserved the cultural life of the West. All contributed to the ongoing life of the Western world, and all made their contributions to our evolving Western heritage.

Time Line: The Centuries of Christendom

from 500   Manor agriculture in Europe

527–565   Reign of Justinian—much of Roman Empire reconquered

       from 529   Monasticism spreads in Europe

       c. 565   Justinian's Code of Roman Law

       c. 565   Hagia Sophia built

       570–632   Muhammad founds the Muslim faith in Arabia

632–750   Arab Empire spreads from Indus River to Spain

771–814   Charlemagne's Empire dominates western Europe

       786–807   Harun al-Rashid rules in Baghdad—golden age of Arab Empire

       c. 800   Carolingian Renaissance

800s   Prosperity of Byzantine Empire at its height

from 850   Feudal politics established in Europe

860   Varangian princes come to rule Russia

1000–1300   Revival of trade and towns in Western Europe; "commercial revolution" at its height

       1019–1054   Yaroslav the Wise rules Kievan Rus—height of medieval Russian/Kievan civilization

1066   William the Conqueror seizes England

1077   Henry IV asks papal forgiveness at Canossa

1073–1085   Pope Gregory VII champions church reform and papal power

1095–1099   First Crusade captures Jerusalem

       1150   University of Paris founded

       1163–1235   Notre Dame cathedral built in Paris

1180–1223   Philip II Augustus builds power of French monarchy

1187   Seljuk Turks recapture Jerusalem

1198–1216   Pope Innocent III—power of Catholic church at its height

1215   King John signs Magna Carta, recognizing rights of English subjects

1220s–1240s   Mongol Goldon Horde conquers Russia

       1225–1274   Thomas Aquinas

       1265–1321   Dante

1337–1453   Hundred Years War

1348–1350   Black Death kills up to a third of European population

1350–1400   Economic decline follows Black Death

       1395–1441   Jan van Eyck

1413–1431   Joan of Arc

1453   Ottoman Turks capture Constantinople

6

Out of the Ruins
The Early Middle Ages

◆Centuries of Struggle   ◆Early Medieval Society
◆The Spread of Christianity   ◆Early Medieval Culture

Western civilization experienced the worst setback in its history during the five centuries between 500 and 1000. This period, which earlier historians called Europe's "Dark Ages," comprises the first half of the larger cycle of Western history known as the Middle Ages. Here we will label it simply the *early Middle Ages*—but by contrast with earlier and later eras, at least, it was in many ways a dark and dismal period in the history of the West.

Such periods, when things fall apart, had happened before in the histories of civilizations. The West had already had its share, in the Greek Dark Age and in Rome's chaotic third century CE. But the Western world as a whole had never experienced so deep a decline in political stability, prosperity, and culture as the centuries that followed the crumbling of the Western Roman Empire.

On the political side, as we will see in the first section below, the chieftains of the Germanic peoples who had overrun the Roman Empire established unstable kingdoms all across western Europe, from England to Spain and beyond. Even the most ambitious of these states, the French empire of Charlemagne, proved unable to preserve or revive Roman civilization. But Rome's Germanic conquerors did manage to turn back new waves of invaders, including Vikings from the north and Arabs from the south.

Section two will survey early medieval society, with its loose feudal political structure based on the personal allegiance of lesser warlords, called vassals, to more powerful ones, their feudal overlords. This society fed itself through the subsistence agriculture of the manor system, a scattering of peasant villages protected by feudal lords and worked by serfs who were bound to the land.

The Christian religion, as we will see in the last two sections, became the core of the cultural life of the Middle Ages. The bishops of Rome, who came to be called popes, were the heads of the Roman Catholic church of western and central Europe. Missionaries spread this form of Christianity further, and some degree of literacy and the arts survived in the monasteries and convents of early medieval times.

Ramshackle as it was, the feudal political structure did either stem or absorb wave after wave of barbarian invaders. Inefficient as it was, the manor system fed at least some of the people much of the time. And throughout these centuries, the church and its influence grew and spread, beacons flaring defiantly against the darkness of the early Middle Ages.

✦ Centuries of Struggle ✦

It was not for want of leadership that the Germanic kings of the early Middle Ages failed to reestablish strong and lasting government in Europe after Rome's fall in the fifth century. People like Theodoric the Ostrogoth, Charlemagne, and Alfred the Great were intelligent, determined, and had a genuine desire to recapture what had been lost when the Roman order passed, or to establish a viable substitute. But neither attempts to maintain a tribal monarchy in the old German style nor efforts to establish a new royal authority by force proved strong enough to overcome the early medieval drift toward fragmentation and anarchy. When we add to this the waves of barbarian invasions that broke over Europe with shattering force during these centuries, the failure of these early efforts to revive effective government is scarcely surprising.

Germanic Kingdoms of the Early Middle Ages

As we saw in the last chapter, a number of different German-speaking peoples flooded across the crumbling Roman Empire in the 400s and 500s. The Ostrogoths and later the Lombards established themselves in Italy; the Franks, Burgundians, and others overran France; the Visigoths set up a ramshackle kingdom in Spain; the Angles, Saxons, and others crossed the Channel to England; and the notorious Vandals rampaged on across Europe to settle in North Africa. And these were only the best known. Other Germanic peoples or federations of Germanic tribes forged lesser kingdoms in what had been Roman provinces.

Some of the new rulers did try to act more like kings than tribal warlords. In this effort, they often invoked the only model of more sophisticated government they knew, that of the Roman Empire which had just fallen to pieces under their hands. Yet none of these efforts succeeded. Two major examples from these earliest medieval years illustrate the reasons why.

Theodoric the Ostrogoth (r. 493–526), often called the Great, established the first Germanic kingdom in Italy in the late fifth century and ruled it for thirty years. He set to work to rule the heartland of old Rome in a thoroughly Roman style. "An able Goth," after all, he declared, "wants to be like a Roman; only a poor Roman would want to be like a Goth."[1] He even abandoned the customary law of the Ostrogoths and imposed Roman law on his own people—the only Germanic king to do so. He extended preferment and royal favor to Roman scholars and civil servants like Boethius, whose labors, as we will see in a later section, preserved considerable portions of the classical heritage for later centuries.

Theodoric, however, had two strikes against him from the beginning. He was a Goth, and thus never really acceptable to the Roman aristocracy whose support he needed. He was also an Arian Christian, a believer that Christ was not of one substance with God, but subordinate to him—a view which made him a heretic to the Italians he ruled. Theodoric hung onto power for his lifetime, but not long after his death another tribe of Germanic invaders, the Lombards, shattered the Ostrogothic kingdom and established a north Italian state along the Po River—Lombardy today.

Chronology 6: Early Middle Ages

378–532	*Germanic invasions of Roman Empire*
481–511	*Clovis rules the Kingdom of the Franks, founds Merovingian dynasty of France*
489–526	*Theodoric the Ostrogoth rules Italy*
from 500	*Manorial agriculture in Europe*
from 529	*Monasticism spreads in Europe*
711–925	*Arab, Viking, and Magyar invasions of medieval Europe*
711	*Arabs overrun Spain*
751–987	*Carolingians rule France*
800	*Charlemagne crowned emperor in Rome*
from 850	*Feudal politics established in Europe*
871–899	*Alfred the Great tries to unite England*
1014–1035	*Canute tries to build Danish Empire*

Failure also awaited the Frankish king Clovis (r. 482–511) in his efforts to impose a fundamentally new order in the Kingdom of the Franks—the core of modern France. Clovis was the founder of what is usually considered France's first royal dynasty, the Merovingians. By intrigue, murder, and election, Clovis made himself king of all the Franks and of parts of western Germany as well. His Frankish kingdom became the most powerful of all the Germanic states.

Rather than depending on Roman institutions, Clovis appointed many of his own royal companions as "counts" to rule large tracts of land in the king's name. Rather than feud with the Roman Catholic religious establishment, as Theodoric had, Clovis converted from paganism to Catholic Christianity. Forging a firm alliance with the church, he and his successors drew on the resources of bishops and monasteries, which provided agricultural skill, wealth, and learning.

Within a hundred years, however, Clovis's Merovingian dynasty had also declined, derided as the "do–nothing" kings of a hopelessly divided realm. For neither Clovis nor his successors had any clear idea of what a state was. They were kings of restless Germanic tribes, without a fixed capital, clear frontiers, or any sense of the territorial nation. They treated the lands they had conquered as personal property, dividing the country up among their heirs. The counts they had appointed soon became local rulers with little feeling of allegiance to the crown.

It was two and a half centuries before a Frankish king who had Clovis's energy but more vision made a serious effort to rule, not only France, but much of Europe. This was Charlemagne.

Charlemagne's Empire

Charles the Great—Carolus Magnus in Latin, Charlemagne to French- and English-speaking people—is probably the most famous of all medieval kings. His contemporary biographer, his godson Einhard, has left us a clear picture: "Charles was strong, and of lofty stature [six feet three, as was discovered when his tomb was opened in the nineteenth century] . . . his eyes very large and animated, nose a little long, fair hair, and face laughing and merry." He had a "belly rather prominent" and wore the traditional Frankish clothing: a fringed tunic and hose, a coat of otter and marten fur, a blue cloak; "and he always had a sword about him, usually one with a gold or silver hilt."[2]

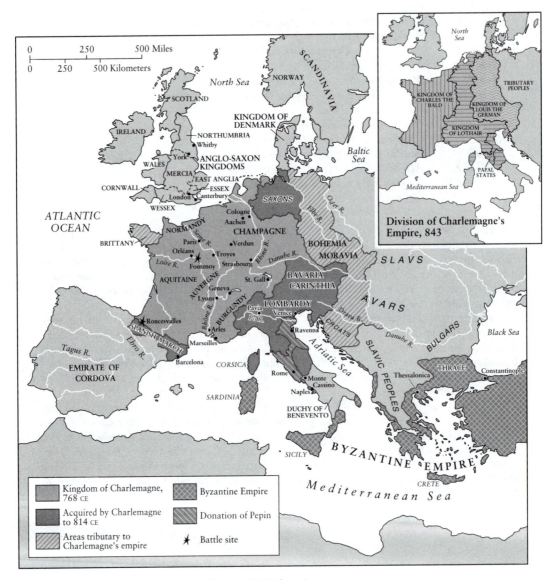

Carolingian Empire and Anglo-Saxon England, Eighth and Ninth Centuries

The king, Einhard further reports, loved to have family, friends, and dependents around him and made decisions surrounded by a motley collection of advisers in the old Germanic way. He was intelligent, spoke Latin and some Greek, was fascinated by astrology, and worked very hard at learning to write, though he made little progress because, his biographer says, he took it up too late in life. The monasteries he encouraged and the scholars who frequented his court—which he moved about but eventually centered at

Charlemagne, looking almost larger than his horse in this bronze sculpture of the period, wears the crown and holds the orb of imperial authority. Note the heavy sword under the monarch's cloak, a symbol of his many victories and conquests. Notice also the monumental feel of this representation, which is in fact only a small figurine. (New York Public Library Picture Collection.)

Aachen in the Rhineland—became the center of a revival of Western culture and scholarship known as the Carolingian Renaissance.

The Kingdom of the Franks that Charlemagne ruled was the largest and most powerful state in Europe in 800. He made it considerably larger and more powerful. If anyone could give direction to the chaotic drift of the times, Charles the Great was surely the one.

Charlemagne's ancestors had been "mayors of the palace," chief court and administrative officials to Clovis's descendants, the later Merovingian rulers of the Frankish state. Some of these officials had enhanced their own power by regulating the distribution of royal lands to other Franks or by making war on other Germanic peoples and forcing them to acknowledge Frankish authority. Charlemagne's forebears had also strengthened their ties with the Roman Catholic church by supporting missionary efforts and by serving as the pope's special protectors against the Kingdom of the Lombards in northern Italy. Charlemagne's grandfather, Charles Martel ("Charles the Hammer," r. 714–741), had performed a notable service by turning back the Muslim Arabs in the Battle of Tours in 732. Charlemagne's father, Pippin III the Short (r. 741–768), had won papal sanction for the transfer of the Frankish crown itself from the feeble Merovingian line to the virile new Carolingian dynasty, as the family came to be called after Charlemagne.

Charlemagne (r. 768–814) not only dressed like a Frank, but was a war leader in the old Frankish tradition. He reigned for forty–six years and fought in more than fifty military campaigns. Another contemporary account offers a picture of Charlemagne as he looked to his enemies, in this case the Lombards of doomed Pavia in northern Italy, that differs strikingly from Einhard's jolly, convivial ruler:

> Then they beheld Charlemagne, the man of iron, in his iron helmet, his arms covered with iron casing, his iron breast and his broad shoulders protected by an iron armor; his left hand raised up the iron lance, while the right was ever ready to grip the victorious steel. . . . His horse as well was iron in color, iron in its courage. . . . Oh, the iron. Alas for the iron! This was the desperate cry of the inhabitants [as the] iron shook the firmness of their walls and the courage of [their] youth.[3]

"Oh the iron—alas for the iron" indeed! In his endless wars, the emperor of the Franks crushed the Lombards, the Saxons, and the Bavarians. He conquered Brittany and Aquitaine. He drove the Arabs back beyond the Pyrenees and decimated the Avars— Turko–Mongol heirs of the Huns—on the Danube plain. He was capable of hanging four thousand Saxons in a single day. His grandson remembered him as a man whose "tempered severity" made "the hearts of both Franks and barbarians" tremble.[4] By the early ninth century, Charlemagne's empire included most of western Europe: modern France, Belgium, the Netherlands, and Switzerland, as well as major portions of Germany, Italy, and Spain.

It was an empire scarcely to be matched in Europe until Napoleon's day. And the Frankish king made a serious attempt to rule what he had conquered. He did this by pragmatic responses to problems as they came up and by tinkering with existing institutions, rather than through detailed planning or broad reorganization. The dukes and counts he appointed served as jacks-of-all-trades; they were military, judicial, and administrative officials of the crown in the countryside. The roving representatives, called *missi dominici*, whom he dispatched to inspect the counties, kept a check on both civil and ecclesiastical authorities and promulgated royal directives of all sorts. He also gathered the chief men of the realm, churchmen as well as nobles and royal appointees, to report to him and to hear royal decrees, called *capitularies*.

On Christmas Day in the year 800, the capstone was placed on this structure of power when Pope Leo III, grateful for Charlemagne's help against his enemies, crowned him emperor and Augustus, Christian heir of all the Caesars. The imperial title made Charlemagne equal to the Byzantine emperors in Constantinople and superior to all European rulers. It further cemented the vital alliance between the French crown and the church, linking the destiny of the still undeveloped medieval monarchy with the much more sophisticated structure of the Christian church.

But this impressive achievement, like the other Germanic kingdoms, did not last. Charlemagne died in 814, leaving his empire to his son Louis the Pious (r. 814–840), who proved more interested in cultivating his own soul than in carrying on his father's imperial tradition. In 843 Charlemagne's three grandsons divided the empire among them in the old Germanic way (see map inset, page 132), and it was soon subdivided still further. The counts and dukes ceased to be royal appointees and became hereditary local magnates instead. Charlemagne's empire had, in fact, depended as much on his endless military campaigns and on his distribution of conquered lands among his nobles as on structured administration. As a result, the Carolingian Empire scarcely survived his death.

Charlemagne's legacy was nonetheless substantial. He had successfully reasserted the importance of strong central government. Much of later medieval government drew on this Carolingian model. And even the division of Charlemagne's lands by his grandsons revealed trends of great future significance. At Strasbourg in 843, two of the grandsons, Charles the Bald (823–877) and Louis the German (c. 804–876), joined forces against the third, Lothair (795–855), and took a solemn oath of mutual support. Each swore in the language understood by the other's soldiers, and the languages the two allies used were clearly the ancestors of modern French and German. The political emergence of these two nations lay far in the future, but cultural foundations in the form of national languages were already being laid in the ninth century.

Raiders and Settlers: Vikings, Arabs, Magyars

Meanwhile, new threats to western Europe had been gathering around the unsteady states that succeeded the Roman imperium. New invaders knifed into Christendom in the eighth and ninth centuries. In the short run, these newcomers further slowed recovery from the collapse of Rome. In the longer run, they added vigorous new stock to Europe's mix of peoples. The most important of these new invaders were the Magyars, who came galloping out of the grasslands to the east, the Arabs from the southern deserts, and the Vikings, sea raiders who sailed down from the north in their long black dragon ships.

The Magyars, like the Huns before them and the Mongols still to come, were steppe nomads. Breeders of beautiful horses, taking no prisoners in combat, they were powerful cavalry soldiers. Advancing westward from the Black Sea, they established themselves in the wide valley of the Danube, modern Hungary. From this base in eastern Europe, they raided central and western Europe. In the later eighth and earlier ninth centuries, Germany, France, and Italy all suffered from Magyar depredations. Their goal was plunder, and by slaughtering whole villages they put such fear into the hearts of Europeans that other settlements bought them off with tribute without a fight. For those who resisted, there was the edge of the sword, or perhaps an Eastern slave market waiting.

From the desert lands of Arabia and North Africa to the south came Arab warriors. These invaders, however, were impelled by religious motives as well as by hope of pillage. And in some places, they came not merely to raid, but to stay.

In the early seventh century, a great religious leader named Muhammad (570–632), called the Prophet by his followers, arose in Arabia. Welding educated oasis Arabs and fierce desert Bedouins into one people with the new faith of Islam—discussed in the next chapter—Muhammad unleashed a powerful new force across western Asia and northern Africa. And less than a century after his death in 632, Muslim armies were moving against Europe as well.

Arab-led Berber forces from North Africa crossed the Strait of Gibraltar in 711, overwhelmed the Kingdom of the Visigoths in Spain, and pushed on over the Pyrenees into the Kingdom of the Franks. In 732 they were finally stopped at Tours in western France by Charles Martel, Charlemagne's grandfather; but not even Charlemagne was able to drive these invaders out of Spain. In the ninth century, meanwhile, Muslim forces from Tunisia invaded Sicily, attacked southern Italy, raided and established bases in southern France, and sacked Rome in 846. Becoming good sailors, these former desert dwellers also plundered merchant shipping up and down the Mediterranean.

Many of the Muslim invaders, however, were not merely looters, but conquerors and builders. We will look later at the civilization they constructed across Asia, Africa, and parts

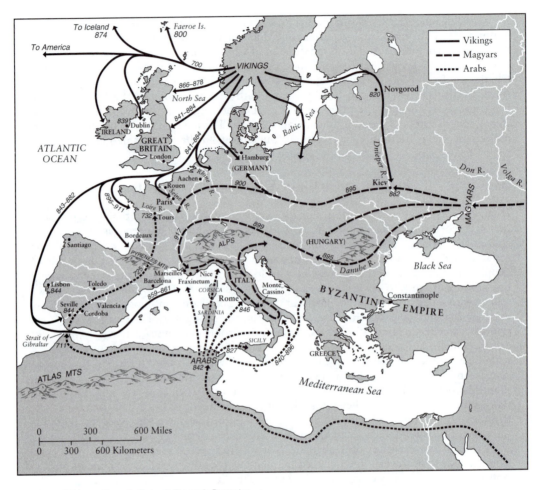

Invasions of Europe, Seventh Through Eleventh Centuries

of Europe. As we will see, one of its centers was in Spain, where Muslims ruled throughout the Middle Ages, contributing a great deal to European culture. But in the eighth and ninth centuries, Europeans saw nothing but flashing scimitars and knew nothing of Islam but the onrush of its armies. "Fight those who do not believe in Allah," the Prophet had declared, "until they pay tribute out of hand."[5] His followers were doing just that.

The most feared of all these intruders, however, were neither Magyars nor Arabs but the Vikings or Northmen who came pouring out of Scandinavia. "Good Lord, deliver us," Christians devoutly prayed in the depths of that violent age, "from the fury of the Northmen." We see them still in a rude Anglo–Saxon carving at Lindisfarne Abbey in Britain—appropriately enough on a tombstone—swinging swords and battle–axes as they advance.

Scholars dispute the causes for the Viking explosion out of Norway, Sweden, and Denmark in the eighth and ninth centuries. Suggested motives include overpopulation due to the widespread practice of polygamy; the inability of their cold northern lands, almost as unproductive as the steppes or the deserts, to feed the population; the tendency of an overthrown Viking leader to prefer emigration and foreign conquests to a subordinate position at home; and, of course, the ancient lure of plunder there for the taking.

The means they used are better understood. The Vikings were Europe's greatest seafarers and shipbuilders. They built fleets of 50–foot "dragon ships," lined with shields, propelled by long oars and a single square sail. These they manned with two– or three–score seaborne warriors to whom rivers and bays, seas and even the Atlantic Ocean were a second home. Like their warrior gods roistering in Valhalla overhead, they were joyful, savage fighting men. The toast *"Skol!"* really does mean "skull"; according to legend, it was a toast drunk from the metal–lined skull of a Viking's slain foe.

The image of the Viking wading ashore with horned helmet and unkempt beard blowing in the wind, whirling a long–handled battle–ax does, however, require considerable qualifying. The Northmen were far–ranging traders before they were pirates, and they became settlers afterward. They bartered fur, slaves, and their own ironwork as far as Baghdad and northern India. Their vessels had crossed the Atlantic by 1000, establishing settlements in Iceland, Greenland, and North America. Like the Arabs, however, they made their most vivid early impact on medieval Europe as raiders and pillagers.

In the ninth century particularly, Northmen raided the coasts of Europe, from England to Spain, and probed major rivers like the Rhine and the Seine. They also traveled from Scandinavia down the Russian rivers to the Black Sea and on to strike Constantinople. Like the Magyars, they slaughtered, looted, and wrung tribute from their victims. Like the Arabs, however, they also sometimes settled down to stay. They established kingdoms in eastern England and in northwestern France, where the Northmen's domain became known as Normandy. In southern Russia, the Vikings, called Varangians, imposed their rule on the indigenous Slavs and organized the first state in what is today Ukraine.

As the dust of this last and most violent of the great invasions began to settle in the later ninth and early tenth centuries, the Magyars dominated Hungary, the Arabs governed Spain, and the Northmen controlled southern Russia and substantial parts of England and France in addition to their native Scandinavia. As the violence ebbed for the second time, there was another chance to restore order to the battered Western world.

Efforts at State Building: Alfred and Canute

Two men who tried to reestablish a structure of authority in their overlapping areas of western Europe were the English ruler, Alfred the Great, and the Danish king, Canute.

Angles, Saxons, Jutes, and other tribes had overrun England in the fifth century. Missionaries had brought Christianity back, however, and by the eighth century, the island was divided among seven tribal kingdoms, collectively called the *Heptarchy*. Then, in the ninth century, Alfred the Great (r. 871–899), king of the West Saxon region of Wessex, imposed his authority on most of England.

Alfred organized a more efficient and mobile army and built ships and fortifications to protect his new country. His major antagonists were Danish Vikings, but in time they too came to terms, agreeing to limit themselves to the region they had already settled in northern England and to accept Christianity. Like Charlemagne and Theodoric, Alfred also encouraged scholarship and sponsored a cultural revival.

Alfred's achievement survived for the better part of a century. In 991, however, a successor paid tribute to the increasingly aggressive Danes, for which purpose a tax was levied on England, the much resented Danegeld. In 1017, under pressure of Danish invasion, the Anglo–Saxon royal council, or *witenagemot,* itself elected King Canute of Denmark to be king of England also. The emergent nation of Alfred's day had become once more a province of another's empire.

Canute (r. 1017–1035) had the vision to see England, rather than Denmark, as the center of his scattered realm and worked hard at building unity there. He gathered a mixed council of Danes and Englishmen to advise him and sought to encourage peace and even a merging of the Danish and Anglo–Saxon populations. He also worked closely with the Roman church and sponsored a revival of Anglo–Saxon law.

Yet when Canute died in 1035, he left no viable heir to his fledgling empire, and it collapsed like a house of cards. The house of Wessex reclaimed the English throne. Within a generation, however, that house was also extinguished as a new foreign dynasty swept to power—the Norman house of William the Conqueror. It was with the arrival of William of Normandy that a unified England would finally begin to emerge.

◆ Early Medieval Society ◆

In the broadest sense, European society between 500 and 1000 experienced changes that were quite different from those that occurred in ancient Greece and Rome. Early medieval people did not see one form of civilized society give way to another, as when Greek city–states lost power to Hellenistic monarchies or the Roman Republic gave way to the Empire. The early medieval period experienced a general decay of society as a whole.

Drawing on crude tribal traditions, often at war with one another and battered by new waves of invaders, Europeans seemed unable to generate strong, stable institutions. But they did begin the building of what would become some of the fundamental social structures of the Middle Ages: the feudal system, the manor system, and the medieval church.

The feudal system, which we will examine shortly, offered at least a modicum of military protection. The medieval manor farm produced a subsistence–level food supply. The church became the most impressive of all medieval institutions, contributing not only a desperately needed faith but, as we will see, some practical supports for society as well. Between them, feudalism, the manor system, and the church held the early medieval world together through these dangerous centuries.

Royal Government in the Early Middle Ages

As we have already noticed in particular cases, the Germanic successor states that replaced the Roman Empire brought their own ideas of government to the region. At the same time, however, German kings came to terms with and even borrowed from the Roman legal and political structure they found in their newly conquered lands.

The Germanic peoples were normally governed by codes of customary behavior binding on all descendants of a common divine or semidivine tribal ancestor. For their new subjects, however, and for disputes involving both Germans and Romans, the Germanic kings issued a number of legal codes based on residency rather than descent and combining Germanic, Roman, and Christian concepts. The earliest of these, the *Lex Visigothorum,* was promulgated in 483, and others were issued by the Burgundian, Anglo–Saxon, and Merovingian Frankish rulers.

The larger structure of government in the Germanic successor states is best illustrated by the empire of Charlemagne around 800. The Frankish emperor claimed for himself supreme secular and religious power, portraying himself as the heir of both the Roman Caesars and the biblical kings David and Solomon. Crowned the successor to Augustus by the pope, he saw himself as the "anointed of God," much as his Germanic ancestors had seen themselves as descendants of their own gods. The Christian doctrine of the divine right of kings to rule had first crystallized in the West in Visigothic Spain, where kings were crowned by priests. After Charlemagne's coronation by the pope in 800, divine sanction became the central justification for royal power in the Middle Ages.

For policy–making, Charlemagne summoned an annual assembly of nobles and high–ranking churchmen. This assembly was not a lawmaking body like later parliaments or other legislative assemblies, but it served nevertheless as a model for these later institutions. Like later medieval monarchs, furthermore, the Carolingian emperor usually decided what he wanted to do before he convened his advisers. He then summoned these leading dignitaries of church and state primarily to get their formal commitment to royal policies.

Below the divine–right ruler and his chief advisers, Charlemagne's administrative structure, like that of his Merovingian predecessors, was headed by members of his own household. Personal servants with governmental functions included the seneschal who managed the royal estates, the chamberlain in charge of the royal treasury, the marshal of the royal armed forces, and a chaplain who was both spiritual guide and chief secretary to his majesty. Far from the court, finally, the counts and dukes who exercised primary power in distant provinces and the *missi dominici* who carried royal authority to these outlying areas were also the monarch's personal appointees. Unlike the specialized bureaucratic jobs of later centuries, most of these functions were easily interchangeable in the early Middle Ages.

The duties of the early medieval officials, at least by the standards of modern governments, were minimal. They had to organize military campaigns, maintain a few royal law courts, collect royal tolls, build and repair the few forts, roads, and bridges for which the monarchy was responsible. Kings claimed authority in executive, legislative, and judicial affairs, with no division of powers. Strong government—where it did emerge—was essentially the execution of a monarch's decisions by his personal servants and by nobles bound to him by oaths of personal allegiance.

Women may have been accepted more easily in leadership positions in early medieval times than later on. The relative equality of husband and wife among the Germanic tribes had generated important roles for the wives of Germanic chiefs and led to the emergence of some women rulers. Among the early Angles and Saxons, for instance, women of rank were sometimes employed to negotiate peace between hostile peoples. The readier acceptance of women in positions of political authority in the Germanic kingdoms is best evidenced by the tone in which early chroniclers recount their accomplishments. Merovingian queens like Fredegund (d. 597), who began life as a servant, intrigued and fought their way to power like third–century Roman empresses. Alfred the Great's daughter, Aethelflaeda (d. 918), ruled northern England very successfully, fought the Danes, and recovered and fortified as much territory as her famous father had. And all this political activity was recorded by the chroniclers as evenhandedly as they recounted the deeds of male rulers. It was only in later medieval centuries that such exploits by a woman began to be seen as unnatural, as "manlike" or "above the nature of her sex."[6]

Feudal Politics

Despite law codes, civil servants, assemblies of notables, and monarchs making claims to great personal authority, however, strong government was not common in early medieval times. In its place, a far less centralized political structure known as feudalism gradually evolved in many parts of early medieval Europe. Feudalism was a political system in which overlords—kings, dukes, or other great men—exchanged land for the military service and political loyalty of a militarized aristocracy of lesser nobles and knights.

The concept of feudalism is much debated among modern historians, and the discussion that follows must be understood as a set of very sweeping generalizations, not as a description of any uniform or universal medieval system of feudal relations. At least in its earlier forms, feudalism may be best understood as an effort to provide minimal governmental functions—mostly military defense and police protection—over local areas when central government could no longer guarantee even these essentials. With the passing of Roman government and the failure of the Germanic successor states to provide an adequate substitute, local magnates with military experience often recruited a few lesser landowners, also trained to the sword, to defend their holdings and to restore some semblance of order. Thus elite cadres of men, devoted to arms and to the land and power they could accumulate with their weapons, came to dominate Europe. They were the early medieval substitute for effective government and, as such, essential to the survival of the Western world.

Within this military caste evolved the loose hierarchy of authority called *feudalism*. Less powerful knights and nobles offered their services to more powerful ones in return for protection and land. In a formal ceremony of *homage and investiture,* the less powerful fighting man took an oath of personal allegiance to the more powerful leader and was invested with a *fief*—an estate that included both an expanse of land and the villages full of laborers who worked it. The dependent was henceforth known as the *vassal* of the man to whom he had pledged his service and whom he then recognized as his *feudal lord*. The roots of this system of personal allegiance went back to the old Germanic *comitatus* or war band and even to the Roman system of patron and client. Feudalism, thus defined, became common first in France and the Low Countries, and later over much of medieval Europe.

The participants in the ceremony of homage and investiture probably saw it in different ways. For the lord, it was the homage that counted: the lord's military clout was increased by the addition of the new vassal with his handful of trained soldiers. For the vassal, the investiture was the heart of the matter, conferring upon him a valuable fief that would support him, his family, and his armed retainers. Feudalism was, in short, a system of land tenure based on military service. But it also meant protection for all concerned. The lord's private feudal army of vassals and their men-at-arms was so much the larger. The individual vassal could depend on his lord for help, and the peasant labor force had at least a small resident garrison of experienced fighters to guard it.

In developed feudalism, the vassal was required to provide his lord with military service, including a specified number of armed retainers, for a particular number of days—often forty—of fighting per year. The vassal also came to owe "aids," or support payments, on the occasion of his lord's oldest son's knighthood, his oldest daughter's marriage, his own departure for a foreign war, or his ransom if the fortunes of war went against him. Loyal vassals were expected to attend the lord's court, to provide wise advice, and to help try vassals who had failed in their trust. For feudal loyalty remained the essential cement that held the entire rickety system together, and breaches of fealty had to be punished.

But there was opportunity in this system for vassals to do well too. With a fief, they acquired not only labor and land but the right to establish a local law court and collect fees and fines, the right to charge tolls, and in later times, to coin their own money. Some vassals, furthermore, collected a number of such fiefs and parceled some of them out to vassals of their own, thus becoming great men in their turn. Some took fiefs from several lords, creating awkward conflicts of interest if any two of their lords should fall out between themselves. To deal with this contingency, vassals had to recognize one overlord as their *liege lord*, meaning that they would rally to his cause even against another lord to whom they had sworn loyalty. At the top of this rickety pyramid of power, the feudal allegiance of the greatest lords to their royal sovereigns was often more a formality than a fact, since a powerful duke could be his king's equal or even superior in actual feudal power.

The system became, in short, tangled and unstable. In the early Middle Ages, however, it did give Europe a loose yet flexible substitute for government, with military protection, local authority, and sometimes local baronial courts and currency as well.

The lady of the manor—the lord's wife—also played an important part in the functioning of the feudal system. Her marriage was arranged for her and had more to do with family alliances or transfers of property than with love. The crude castle she lived in was dominated by males whose main concerns were weapons and horses, hunting and fighting. And her husband, at least in the early Middle Ages, seems to have been able to treat her pretty much as he pleased, which sometimes meant brutally. A nobleman could cast off his wife for adultery or failure to produce an heir, while he himself often kept concubines.

Yet the lady of the manor had important responsibilities. Most of our evidence comes from the later Middle Ages but probably applies as well to the earlier centuries. A lord's wife had first of all to provide a male heir for her husband's lands: female heirs were less acceptable because they could not perform the military service on which most land tenure depended. The lady of the manor also had a house to run—a large one, though she had servants to help. More importantly, however, like her Germanic forebears, she had the responsibility of defending the estate when her husband was off at the wars. Since wars were common and vassals were often called on to fulfill their military service obligations, women, not infrequently, had to direct the defense of feudal castles and lands.

The idea and the very term, *feudal system*, were invented long after the Middle Ages by seventeenth– and eighteenth–century scholars who were trying to explain the remnants of feudal relations that survived in their time. So confused is the chronology, so diverse the phenomenon of historical feudalism that some recent historians have suggested simply abandoning the notion of a feudal "system" altogether. These revisionists would replace sweeping generalizations on the subject with a rich variety of "detailed descriptions of areas characterized by different forms of government and social structure."[7] In the broadest textbook perspective, however, the concept of feudalism still seems to have much to recommend it as an introductory approach to early medieval government.

Manorial Agriculture

From the top of early medieval society, we turn now to the bottom. From lords and their vassals, we shift our focus to the relationship between these members of the upper class and the serfs who labored for them. The manor system was a form of subsistence agriculture in which peasants exchanged their labor and farm produce for the protection and security of a manor village.

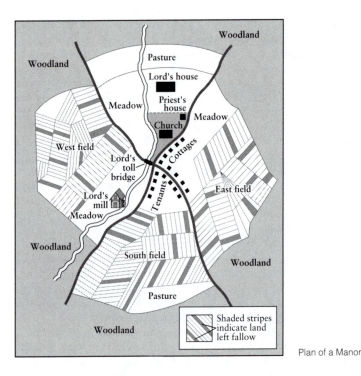

Plan of a Manor

Vassals and serfs were both committed to the service of others, but there the similarity ended. The vassal was a soldier and a landholder, committed by his own free oath to his overlord, and part of the medieval political elite. The serf was a peasant farmer, bound by tradition and law to the land he worked, and the hard–working basis of the medieval economy. Serfs provided the labor on which everything else rested. They also constituted the large majority of medieval people, 90 percent of whom lived and worked all their lives on manorial estates.

The medieval *manor*, like the feudal system, had its origins in both Roman and Germanic practices. Medieval serfs were the descendants of Roman *coloni* who had surrendered independent peasant status to a Roman landed magnate in return for land and protection. Though they were not slaves, *coloni* were bound to cultivate the land they worked as tenants or sharecroppers. From the fourth century on, they were forbidden to leave that land, as medieval serfs were later on. The early medieval manor village was thus patterned to some degree on the Roman villa or estate. But the lord of the manor also derived much of his traditional authority over his serfs from the powers enjoyed by the chief of a Germanic village. From the mixture emerged a set of agrarian institutions that were unique to medieval Europe.

This manorial pattern of agriculture took shape first in parts of France, Germany, and Italy and spread to many other parts of the continent. Peasant life on the Celtic western fringe or in Slavic eastern Europe, in sheep–herding or wine–growing areas, developed very different forms of organization. Yet the manor was prevalent enough in much of Europe to warrant our focusing on it here.

A look at a manor village from the top of a neighboring hill would not show anything like an American farming county, each substantial farmhouse and barn isolated among wide, rectangular, fenced–in fields. All the peasants on a medieval manor commonly lived together in a village. All their fields, laid out in unfenced strips, were spread out around the tiny hamlet. In northern Europe, such strips were frequently about 220 yards long (a fur- row's length, or furlong) by 16 feet wide. The traditional length was determined by the distance a draft animal could pull without tiring and the width by the space needed to turn the animal and plow around. Four such furlong strips added up to an acre, the modern unit used to measure land.

To preserve fairness, the land was either parceled out into strips as the arable land was, or used communally, as was normally the case with pasture and forest. Everybody's animals grazed and rooted on the commons, each family had some strips of the best land down by the stream, the rocky land up the hillside, and the marshy bit at the edge of the fens. The lord's strips too were typically scattered among those of his serfs.

The typical village consisted of some dozen one–room thatched–roof huts, a small church, perhaps a mill by the stream, a bakehouse, and a brewhouse in northern Europe, a winepress in the south. On the hill, the lord of the manor's stronghold in the early Middle Ages looked more like a log fort in Daniel Boone's America than the elaborate Norman castle of later medieval centuries. Inside the manor house, the lord had two rooms instead of the peasant's one. There was an all-purpose "great hall," where the men-at-arms would eat and sleep, play with the dogs, perhaps clang through a practice bout, and wait for a war. And there was a "chamber," where the lord's wife, family, and serving women could get some peace and quiet. The manor house was probably as damp and drafty as the serf's hut. For lord and serf alike, there were a minimum of material things: benches, stools, trestle ta- bles, mugs, spoons, knives, homespun clothing, leather harness, weapons, and tools.

Serfs belonged to the manor itself: to its land, its fields, its community, its customs. Though they could not be bought and sold like chattel slaves, serfs could not leave the es- tate without the lord's consent. They were subject to the lord of the manor's will in many other ways too, for he had the right to impose the discipline necessary to ensure they per- formed their many labor obligations. Normally, serfs worked perhaps three days a week on the lord's land but did extra work at harvest time. They also kept roads and bridges in re- pair and did other work around the manor, an obligation known as *corvée* labor that long outlasted serfdom itself. With what time was left them, they tilled their own strips of land. There were still some free peasants among them, and a few outright slaves. But serf labor was the backbone of the system, the bone and muscle of the manorial economy.

Serfs had other obligations too. They paid the lord a percentage of their harvest and perhaps a small head tax, or *taille*, as well. They paid a tithe—probably not literally a tenth even then—to support the church and the local priest, who probably also worked his own strips of land. They paid for the services of the mill, the bakehouse, the winepress—all of which were owned by the lord. They paid him to marry outside their tiny community or to inherit the hut and the family strips, and they paid fines to his bailiff when they were caught poaching and hauled up before the lord's court. All payments were in kind, of course: chickens, fruit, honey, and a measure of grain for the lord; a loaf of bread left to pay the baker. Peasants at the Abbey of St. Germain des Prés outside Paris, for instance, owed their landlords "three chickens and fifteen eggs, and a large number of planks to repair . . . buildings" as well as "a couple of pigs . . . wine, honey, wax, soap, or oil"; "women were obliged to spin cloth or to make a garment for the big house every year."[8]

✦The Spread of Christianity✦

Out of the tumultuous times between the fifth and the tenth centuries, only one institution in western Europe emerged clearly stronger, larger, and with a more powerful grip on the minds and lives of Western peoples. This was the Roman Catholic church. Building on intellectual and institutional foundations laid down in Roman times, the church survived the passing of the Western Roman Empire, responded vigorously to new circumstances, and carved out a unique position at the center of Western life in the Middle Ages. Three important agents of this success were early medieval popes with a broad vision of the church's role, vigorous missionaries who spread the faith, and the monks and nuns who were often the church's spiritual core.

Early Medieval Popes—Gregory the Great

The primacy of the popes, or the bishops of Rome, in Western Christendom took centuries to establish. As we have seen, Rome had some advantages from the beginning: it was the imperial see, the largest and richest diocese of the church, and the city where Peter was martyred and both Peter and Paul were buried. As early as the fourth century, the popes had begun to cite Matthew 16:18—"Thou art Peter and upon this rock I will build my church"—as evidence of Christ's intention to make the diocese of which Peter had been the first bishop the center of the entire church.[9]

During the fifth century, several aggressive and powerful popes advanced claims to papal supremacy within the church. Pope Leo I the Great (r. 440–461) urged the spiritual identity of the popes with Peter when speaking on religious matters. He also obtained an imperial edict from one of the last Western Roman emperors establishing papal jurisdiction over all Western bishops. He rejected claims of superiority advanced on behalf of the patriarch of Constantinople and dictated imperiously to church councils. Leo's alleged role in persuading Attila the Hun to spare the city of Rome also added to papal prestige. A generation later, Pope Gelasius I (r. 492–496) declared papal superiority to both the Eastern Roman emperors and church councils where matters of faith and morals were concerned. The "Gelasian doctrine" of the supremacy of priestly power over secular authority gave later medieval popes a claim to higher power than that of kings and was a crucial contribution to medieval political theory.

Perhaps the largest early medieval contribution to the rise of papal power, however, was that of Pope Gregory I the Great (r. 590–604). An ivory carving dating from the ninth or tenth century shows Pope Gregory as a saintly looking tonsured monk, writing with a quill pen in a book while a dove whispers divine inspiration into his ear. The most influential pope of these five centuries was in fact bald, dark, and hook-nosed, and at least as likely to be organizing disaster relief or negotiating with barbarians as writing his famous books. But he had been a monk, and his book *Pastoral Care* certainly seemed inspired to many later leaders of the church.

Once the prefect, or chief administrative official, of Rome, Gregory later served as the Roman church's envoy to Constantinople. By all accounts, he was a hard–driving, highly organized, and exceedingly capable man. He elevated the secular position of the papacy by feeding the populace in time of siege, caring for the sick in plague time, organizing the defense of the city, and then negotiating peace with the advancing Lombards. A prolific writer, he produced a commentary on the Bible and lives of the early saints in addition to his *Pastoral Care,* which offered guidance to bishops in the nurturing of their flocks.

As a former monk, Gregory encouraged the spread of monasticism—see below—which was coming to be seen as the most perfect form of Christian life. He also vigorously fostered missionary activity, also surveyed below, which by the year 1000 had brought most of the population of Europe at least nominally within the Christian fold. So impressive was Gregory's contribution that he came to be considered one of the fathers of the church, though he lived two centuries after the other Latin fathers, Augustine, Jerome, and Ambrose.

The rise of papal supremacy in the Western church was subsequently strengthened by the alliance between the papacy and the powerful Frankish Empire, especially under the Carolingians. Pippin the Short's donation of a large portion of central Italy to the see of St. Peter in 756 gave the popes a valuable territorial base. Charlemagne's acceptance of an imperial crown at the pope's hands in 800 seemed to indicate that the papacy had the power to confer imperial sovereignty over the Western world on a favored ruler.

The spread of the institutional power of the popes over the Christian churches of western Europe thus took several hundred years to develop. Meanwhile, the early Middle Ages saw two other major trends in the history of the church, both encouraged by Gregory and his successors. These were the missionary conversion of Europe and the rapid growth of the monastic movement.

Missionaries

Christianity, which had girdled the Mediterranean in Roman times, had spread much more thinly into Europe north of the Alps. The coming of the Germanic invaders, who were pagans or, almost worse, Arian heretics, had smothered most of what Christian communities there were in Roman provincial cities. And in CE 500, there were still large numbers of Germanic, Celtic, and other Europeans beyond the Rhine–Danube line who had never yet been touched by the Gospel.

A major achievement of this first half of the Middle Ages was the conversion of many of these inhabitants of western Europe to the Roman faith. A great step toward this goal came in 597, when Pope Gregory the Great dispatched an embassy headed by Augustine (d. 604), the first archbishop of Canterbury, to convert the pagan Anglo–Saxons of England. Augustine succeeded in bringing about the conversion of King Ethelbert of Kent (r. 560–616), who was followed to the baptismal font by his chief men, and ultimately by all his people. Roman missionaries faced vigorous competition for British converts from the Irish church, which had survived the Germanic invasions but differed from Rome on key points of ritual. At the Synod of Whitby in 664, however, the Roman rite triumphed, assuring its eventual victory over the British Isles as a whole.

Thereafter, Britain became a key base for missionary expeditions back to the continent, particularly to the Germanic tribes. But whether they came from Italy or Britain, early medieval missionaries tended to follow the procedure laid down by Augustine, converting kings first and then their peoples. Only after winning this profession of adherence to the new faith did the church proceed to the much longer, slower business of turning pagans into real Christian believers.

Women played an important part in this missionary effort. Among the unsung martyrs of the early spread of the faith were Christian women who married pagan kings in hopes of converting their husbands. Other women conducted more orthodox missionary activity, running monastic establishments in pagan areas and making many converts. Some of these, like St. Brigid in Ireland around 500, or St. Lioba, the eighth–century missionary to Saxony, were among those who attained the church's highest honor—canonization as saints.

The actual conversion of pagan populations took centuries and may never have been as total as the church desired. But through sermons and catechisms, through the legends of the saints and sharp examination of the moral and spiritual condition of Christians, priests all across Europe labored at the task. And if peasants would persist in murmuring a pagan invocation as they passed an oak tree that had once been sacred, or in leaving a bite out for the little people, lest the horses' manes be tangled in elflocks or the milk sour in the morning—well, there were more serious problems in the world of the early Middle Ages.

Monks and Nuns

The monastic life was much admired by medieval Christians, even if they could not all achieve it themselves. For monks and nuns were people who had committed their whole lives to Christ.

The ascetic tradition—withdrawing from the world into seclusion and denying the pleasures of the flesh in order to focus entirely on the spiritual life—was not unique to Christianity. There were Buddhist monks and nuns already, and there would be Muslim ascetics too. In the Christian church, the movement began in late Roman times. In Egypt, Palestine, and Syria, pious souls as early as the third century turned their backs on a society in decline and retreated to the desert to live as solitary hermits. In time, however, ascetics began to band together into communities rather than live in isolation, and the practice spread from the Near East to Europe.

The father of Western monasticism was St. Benedict of Nursia (c. 480–c. 543), the leader of a community of monks at Monte Cassino in south central Italy. Benedict compiled a set of rules for his community that, because of its logic and practicality, came to be used by monasteries all over Europe.

The *Benedictine Rule* required monks and nuns to give up the ordinary life of getting and spending and commit themselves to a lifetime of piety and labor. A day in a monastery or convent was divided into periods for worship, work, and study. There were half a dozen religious services over the twenty-four-hour day. Daily manual labor in the fields, gardens, or monastery buildings was required of everyone. And time was set aside for reading, copying, and meditating on the Scriptures and other sacred writings.

Three great vows were also required of the holy brothers and sisters: obedience, poverty, and chastity. The first meant absolute obedience to the abbot or abbess who headed the monastery or convent, although these authorities were expected to consult with their communities on important decisions. The vow of poverty required complete abandonment of worldly possessions: even the robes and sandals that monks and nuns wore were issued by the institution. Perhaps most admired by medieval people was the vow of chastity, which in time came to be taken by all priests in the Roman Catholic church.

It was a hard and demanding life. Benedict's *Rule* avoided the extreme practices that some ascetics had adopted to tame fleshly desires, such as fasting, all–night vigils, hair shirts, and even self–flagellation—lashing themselves with whips. Though some still adopted these extreme measures, the system as a whole made no such demands, channeling religious energies into the labor, study, and prayer that St. Benedict had prescribed.

Thousands of monasteries and convents, some large, some small, grew up across Europe. Monastic establishments performed many pious, charitable, and socially useful functions, from providing hospitality for travelers to caring for the poor and sick and converting the heathen. Because their people worked so hard, monasteries also made major contributions to the clearing and draining of land and to valuable experimentation with crops and breeding. Because monks had to study edifying literature, monasteries became centers of literacy and refuges for bits and pieces of classical literature as well. And because they were so much admired, monasteries and convents received many gifts and bequests, often in land, from pious Christians. As a result, orders of monks and nuns sworn to poverty came into possession of some of the largest landholdings in medieval Europe.

It was also behind convent walls that women found their most common escape from patriarchal medieval society. Women could not serve as priests in the Christian church, as they often had in pagan cults, but the monastic system was open to them. Convents, theoretically, accepted women of all social classes; but in fact, they were often largely populated by the daughters of the well-to-do, who could contribute land or other gifts to the institution. In some of these establishments, capable and ambitious women presided as abbesses over hundreds or even thousands of people and vast acreages of convent lands.

The monastic establishment, like the manor, was a self-sufficient agricultural community, and as such, it fitted the needs of the times perfectly. Islands of peace in a violent age, monasteries and convents also gave a refuge to human beings who were not suited to life leaning on a plow, coping with a household, or swinging a sword. Most important to contemporaries, monastic houses were seen as vessels of the Holy Spirit, ideal communities where men and women could lift their eyes and hearts to a higher and better world than that in which they lived.

◆ Early Medieval Culture ◆

Like the culture of the Greek Awakening, the art and thought of the early Middle Ages was perhaps most important as the foundation for a later cultural flowering. The high medieval glories of the Gothic cathedral, Scholastic thought, and the Renaissance of the twelfth century had their roots in the early Middle Ages. Yet there was a vitality, a stirring of the spirit among these early artists and thinkers that belongs to this age alone. We will see this vigor in a wide variety of early medieval literature and art, from heroic epic poems to brilliant book illustrations, from the Celtic flowering of early medieval Ireland to Charlemagne's Carolingian Renaissance.

Literature and Scholarship

Literature and thought altered drastically in character in the early Middle Ages. The replacement of an educated Roman aristocracy by a largely illiterate Germanic warrior nobility, and of Greek philosophy by Christian theology, was bound to transform the intellectual life of the new Europe.

A vigorous oral literature, today largely lost, was sung or chanted in the halls of Europe's new Germanic rulers. From the British Isles, for instance, comes the epic Anglo–Saxon hero tale of *Beowulf,* dating from the seventh or eighth century. Everything about the poem is debated by scholars, but the story itself, of the hero Beowulf's killing of the monster Grendel, and then of Grendel's even more ferocious mother, at least suggests something of the taste in tales of the Anglo–Saxon warrior elite.

Most of those who could read and write were now in the church, many of them monks, and they tended to produce books of religious edification more than anything else. St. Augustine's *City of God* remained immensely popular, as did Gregory the Great's study of the Book of Job and his collection of saints' lives.

Even books on subjects that would once have been thoroughly secular, like history, showed strong religious influences in medieval times. Thus the *History of the Franks* by Gregory of Tours (538–594) and the *Ecclesiastical History of the English Nation* composed by the Venerable Bede (c. 673–735) both reveal a historian's concern for evidence and accuracy and are essential sources for the history of the period. Yet both accept miracles in large numbers as a matter of course, and Bede became the first scholar to utilize a chronology beginning with the birth of Christ and to use the a.d. (*Anno Domini*—"Year of the Lord") dating system in a major work. History, in short, was no longer a secular subject, but part of the great intellectual crusade to glorify God in the age of faith.

The Celtic Flowering

Not all the art, literature, and scholarship of early medieval times was Germanic in origin. Indeed, the most brilliant early flowering of medieval culture came in Ireland, on the far edge of Europe's *Celtic fringe*—the areas of western Europe still inhabited by Celtic peoples.

The Irish Celts remained relatively untouched by invading peoples through much of the early Middle Ages. Neither the Romans nor the Anglo–Saxons pushed beyond the Irish Sea, and the Vikings did not establish even a temporary settlement in Ireland until the end of the eighth century. Ireland in earliest medieval times, then, developed its own society and culture. Irish social and political institutions were as simple as those of other preurban peoples, a loose structure of clans and petty kings who often feuded with each other. Culturally, however, this politically undeveloped land became a radiant center of early medieval art, literature, and learning.

One element of the larger European culture that did reach Ireland was Christianity, which followed its own line of development after its arrival in the island in the fifth century. Irish monasteries became paramount centers of learning in early medieval Europe. Irish missionaries carried their version of the faith to Scotland in the sixth century and on into the Germanic forests of continental Europe. Though Roman Catholic Christianity eventually displaced Celtic forms of worship, Irish missionaries had made an important contribution to the Christianization of Europe.

During this period, Irish decorative arts reached their peak and a unique literary tradition developed. Celtic decorative artists specialized in illuminated manuscripts like the gorgeous eighth–century *Book of Kells,* a version of the Latin Gospels with elaborately decorated capitals and illustrations for each chapter. Drawing upon Germanic styles encountered in Anglo–Saxon Britain, Irish craftworkers produced beautiful metalwork like the Ardagh chalice, an early eighth–century masterpiece of exquisitely worked silver and glass. Old Irish literature also flowered in these early centuries. Irish kings kept bards at their courts to sing the legends of their heroic ancestors. These and later sagas and hero tales, legends of early saints, lyric poems, and poetic evocations of the Irish countryside were written down in the High Middle Ages to become part of an enduring legacy of Irish history and culture.

The Carolingian Renaissance

The best examples of the sort of learning and art admired by early medieval rulers come from the Kingdom of the Franks, particularly during the Carolingian Renaissance sponsored by Charlemagne. Seeing himself as a sort of a Christian Augustus Caesar, Charlemagne seems to have taken the patronage of culture seriously. He also apparently saw the practical value of education for officials of both the state and the church. He, therefore, imported scholars from various parts of Europe and urged the production of holy books, the establishment of schools, and other cultural activities.

The emperor's chief cultural mentor was an English churchman, Alcuin of York (735–804). Alcuin headed the Palace School at Aachen and guided the preparation of new editions of St. Jerome's Latin Bible and of St. Benedict's *Rule,* which became the standard versions of these two key medieval texts. Charlemagne's interest in schooling also led to the establishment of some monastery schools and to efforts to provide book learning for the children of the Frankish nobility in the Palace School. According to his biographer Einhard, the towering emperor of the Franks did not hesitate to administer physical punishment personally to children of his greatest nobles who got their grammar wrong.

Two apparently modest scholarly achievements of the Carolingian Renaissance, however, actually had more far–reaching consequences. One of these was a determined effort to standardize church Latin. This reform gave the Roman church an international language at a time when Europe was becoming increasingly divided linguistically as separate national languages emerged. The other surprisingly valuable accomplishment of this scholarly revival was the development of a new standard script for books that added lower–case letters to the Roman capitals used up to that time. These *Carolingian minuscules* became the model for the lower–case alphabet still in use today.

Summary

During the first half of the Middle Ages (roughly CE 500–1000), invasions by Goths, Franks, Arabs, Vikings, and others combined with the weakness of the Germanic monarchies that replaced the Roman Empire to shatter political order in Europe. Despite the best efforts of such state builders as Clovis, Charlemagne, and Alfred the Great, Europe sank into disarray, a society dominated by feudal lords loosely linked by oaths of personal allegiance to warlords stronger than they.

The collapse of the Roman Empire with its integrated economy and access to the larger world reduced most of western Europe to subsistence agriculture. Cities declined and most western Europeans returned to the agricultural village, where they labored as serfs, bound to the land they worked.

Though the Roman Empire collapsed in the fifth century CE, the Roman Catholic church survived and even spread during the Early Middle Ages. Guided by popes like Gregory I the Great, the church expanded significantly, particularly through the missionary activities of dedicated monks and nuns.

Early medieval art and thought were shaped by Germanic styles, Christian ideas, and what remained of classical learning in the West. Epics like the English *Beowulf* expressed the fighting spirit of Germanic warriors. Under the patronage of the church and of a few rulers like Charlemagne, vigorously decorative art pointed toward Gothic styles to come. The writings of some Christian thinkers, from Gregory the Great to Alcuin of York, became medieval classics.

Some Key Terms

Benedictine Rule   146
Carolingian minuscule   149
Celtic fringe   148
coloni   142
comitatus   140
corvée   143
early Middle Ages   129

feudalism   140
feudal lord   140
fief   140
Heptarchy   137
homage and investiture   140
Lex Visigothorum   138
liege lord   141

manor   142
missi dominici   134
taille   143
vassal   140
witenagemot   138

Notes

1. Quoted in Michael Grant, *Dawn of the Middle Ages* (London: McGraw–Hill, 1981), 6.
2. Einhard, *The Life of Charlemagne,* trans. Samuel Epes Turner (Ann Arbor, Mich.: Ann Arbor Paperbacks, 1960), 50–51.
3. Einhard and Notker the Stammerer, *Two Lives of Charlemagne,* trans. L. Thorpe (Harmondsworth, England: Penguin, 1969), 163–164.
4. Quoted in J. Kelley Sowards, ed., *Makers of the Western Tradition: Portraits from History,* 4th ed. (New York: St. Martin's Press, 1987), 145.
5. Sura 2, verses 29 ff., quoted in Grant, *Dawn of the Middle Ages,* 63.
6. Betty Bandel, "English Chroniclers' Attitude Toward Women," *Journal of the History of Ideas,* XVI (1955), 114–115.
7. Elizabeth A.R. Brown, "The Tyranny of a Construct: Feudalism and Historians of Medieval Europe," *American Historical Review,* 79 (1974), 1987.
8. Eileen Power, *Medieval People* (Garden City, N.Y.: Doubleday, 1955), 19.
9. The name translated into English as "Peter" was the Aramaic word *kepa,* which meant "rock." What Jesus was apparently saying was that Peter's name symbolized his character and that therefore Jesus would lay the responsibility for the building of his church on this person of rocklike strength. *New Catholic Encyclopedia,* vol. 11 (New York: McGraw–Hill, 1967), 244.

Reading List

Bloch, M. *Feudal Society.* Translated by L. A. Manyon. Chicago: University of Chicago Press, 1961. Major work by a great historian seeking to recapture the "total social environment" of the age. See too G. Duby's classic *Rural Economy and Country Life in the Medieval West* (Columbia: University of South Carolina Press, 1968).

Cohen, M. R. *Under the Crescent and the Cross: The Jews in the Middle Ages.* Princeton: Princeton University Press, 1994. Jews in both Christian and Muslim societies.

Doehaerd, R. *The Early Middle Ages in the West: Economy and Society.* Translated by W. G. Deakin. New York: North–Holland, 1978. Agriculture, trade, population, and scarcity in the early medieval economy.

Fichtenau, H. *The Carolingian Empire.* Translated by P. Munz. Toronto: University of Toronto

Press, 1991. Valuable brief overview.

Godman, P. *Poetry of the Carolingian Renaissance.* Norman: University of Oklahoma Press, 1985. Latin literature of the Early Middle Ages.

James, E. *The Franks.* New York: Blackwell, 1988. Readable overview of what we know about them.

Jones, G. *A History of the Vikings.* 2d ed. New York: Oxford University Press, 1984. Exploits archaeology, art history, and other disciplines to construct a vivid narrative account.

Koziol, G. *Begging Pardon and Favor: Ritual and Political Order in Early Medieval France.* Ithaca: Cornell University Press, 1992. The power of ritual gestures to hold an anarchic society together.

Leyser, K. G. *Rule and Conflict in Early Medieval Society: Ottonian Saxony.* London: Edward Arnold, 1979. Essays on divine sanction of these German rulers, on women's wealth, and on other subjects.

Lourdaux, W., and D. Verhelst, eds. *Benedictine Culture, 750–1050*. Louvain: Leuven University Press, 1983. Essays that explore the culture and intellectual contributions of the monastic life in its broader historical and social contexts.

Mapp, A. J. *The Golden Dragon: Alfred the Great and His Times*. La Salle, Ill.: Open Court, 1974. Older but useful survey.

Marenbon, J. *Early Medieval Philosophy (480–1150): An Introduction*. London: Routledge and Kegan Paul, 1983. Christian thought under the influence of Boethius and St. Augustine.

McKitterick, R. *The Frankish Kingdoms Under the Carolingians, 751–987*. New York: Longman, 1983. Stronger on cultural matters than on political history, with revisionist emphasis on lesser Carolingians. See also her *The Frankish Kings and Culture in the Early Middle Ages* (Brookfield, Vt.: Variorum, 1995).

Randers-Pehrson, J. D. *Barbarians and Romans: The Birth Struggle of Europe, a.d. 400–700*. Norman: University of Oklahoma Press, 1983. Very well–written survey, including encounters with leading personalities of this pivotal period.

Randsborg, K. *The Viking Age in Denmark: The Formation of a New State*. New York: St. Martin's Press, 1980. The rise of the Danish empire, based as much on archaeology as on historical documents.

Reynolds, S. *Fiefs and vassals: The Medieval Evidence Reinterpreted*. New York: Oxford Universe Press, 1994. Contribution to an ongoing debate about the nature of feudalism.

Richards, J. *The Pope and the Papacy in the Early Middle Ages, 476–752*. Boston: Routledge and Kegan Paul, 1979. Sees early medieval popes as more important than traditional concentration on the developed papacy of the High Middle Ages would allow.

Wemple, S. F. *Women in Frankish Society: Marriage and the Cloister, 500–900*. Philadelphia: University of Pennsylvania Press, 1981. Engagingly written study of women's lives from the Germanic invasions to the Carolingians.

Wilson, D. M. *Anglo-Saxon Art from the Seventh Century to the Conquest*. London: Thames and Hudson, 1984. Well–illustrated survey of an impressive sample of early medieval art.

Wolfram, H. *History of the Goths*. Berkeley: University of California Press, 1988. Thoroughly researched study of Gothic tribes in Roman and early medieval times.

7

Sailing to Byzantium
Europe's Eastern Neighbors

◆The Byzantine Empire ◆Kievan Russia ◆The Arab Empire

From Europe in the early Middle Ages (500–1000), with its castles and manor villages, we move now to very different realms. This chapter focuses on the eastern edge of the Western world during the early medieval period: on the glittering Near Eastern metropolis of Constantinople, the steppes and forests of Russia, and the desert lands of the medieval Arabs. In political terms, this means a survey of the Byzantine Empire (modern Turkey), Slavic Europe (modern Russia and its neighbors), and the expanding Islamic zone, centered in the Middle East.

The medieval Byzantine Empire lives in many imaginations from William Butler Yeats's poem, "Sailing to Byzantium," with its haunting image of an exquisitely crafted bird of pure gold

> set upon a golden bough to sing
> To lords and ladies of Byzantium
> Of what is past, or passing, or to come.[1]

The glitter of gold hovers everywhere about this fantastic survival of a Christianized Greco–Roman civilization on the far eastern frontiers of medieval Europe. Gold glows in the backgrounds of Byzantine art and in the flow of trade from Constantinople into Europe. It will gleam through section one of this chapter, as we explore Byzantine imperial history from its founding in late Roman times, as well as Byzantine government, commerce, and culture.

Sprawling across the eastern margins of medieval Europe north of Constantinople, the emerging civilization of Russia was powerfully shaped by Byzantine influences. In section two, we will follow the story of Russia's origins from its Slavic beginnings in the fifth and sixth centuries through the civilizing impact of Byzantium to the heyday of Russia's Kievan period around 1000.

South of the Byzantine Empire, however, another new people rose to far greater prominence in early medieval times—the Arabs. Filled with religious fervor by the passionate preaching of the Prophet Muhammad in the seventh century, these first Muslims built the largest empire in western Eurasia and threatened the very survival of Christendom. Like the Byzantines, the Arabs also produced a marvelous civilization in the Middle Ages.

In each of these cases, we are dealing with neighboring or related cultures whose destinies were intricately intertwined with that of western Europe. Slavic eastern Europe, increasingly centered on Russia, was the other half of Europe itself. The Byzantine Empire was both protector and economic stimulus for the medieval West. Arab Islam, though Christendom's greatest adversary, would also become a trading partner and a source of cultural borrowings for Europe's later medieval revival.

♦ The Byzantine Empire ♦

No serious effort can be made in these few pages to outline the thousand–year history of the *Byzantine Empire*, which flourished around the eastern end of the Mediterranean from the fall of Rome in the fifth century to the fall of Constantinople itself in the fifteenth. After a glance at the general contours of that history and a glimpse of a powerful Byzantine personality or two, the bulk of our time must go to a general description of this exotic world of clamoring bazaars and golden churches on the near edge of Asia.

After a look at the remarkable reign of Justinian and Theodora in the sixth century, we will survey the development of autocratic government in Byzantium, the economic preeminence of Constantinople, and the distinctive art and ideas of the medieval Byzantines. Throughout, we will try to communicate at least a hint of the glamour of this land of gold at the end of the world as it must have looked to medieval Europeans ten centuries ago.

Byzantine Origins

Despite their exotic Eastern aura, both the Byzantine state and the *Greek (Eastern) Orthodox Church* evolved gradually from Western beginnings. The early history of Byzantium clearly shows its development out of the world originally built by the ancient Greeks and Romans.

The beginning of the Byzantine state may be traced back to the administrative division of the Roman Empire by Diocletian (r. 284–305), who restructured the empire in the late third century, or to the construction of much of the city of Constantinople by his successor Constantine (r. 312–337) in the early fourth century. The latter's official transfer of the imperial capital to his new city in 324 is often considered to mark the beginning of Byzantine history.

But Constantine and other early Eastern Roman emperors saw themselves as rulers of the whole Empire, not merely its eastern provinces. Not even the Germanic occupation of the Western Roman Empire in the fifth century could shake this conviction. Justinian, the great Byzantine emperor of the sixth century, continued to speak Latin and labored mightily—and with some success—to liberate the western provinces from their conquerors. Europe's Germanic conquerors were not to be turned back, however, and by the reign of Heraclius I in the seventh century, the Roman Empire in the west was history. By that time too, all the elements of medieval Byzantium were clearly in place, from oriental ceremony and autocracy to the predominance of the Greek language and the Greek Orthodox church.

Chronology 7: Byzantium, Russia, Islam

527–565	*Reign of Justinian—much of Roman Empire reconquered; Justinian's Code of Roman Law*
570–632	*Muhammad founds the Muslim faith in Arabia*
632–750	*Arab Empire spreads from Indus River to Spain*
661–750	*Umayyad caliphate*
750–1258	*Abbasid caliphate*
786–807	*Harun al–Rashid rules in Baghdad*
800s	*Byzantine prosperity at its height*
860	*Varangian Prince Rurik "called" to rule Russia*
879–912	*Oleg links northern and southern Russia in the Kievan Rus, the first Russian state*
957	*Princess Olga converted to Greek Orthodox Christianity in Byzantium; Byzantine cultural influence spreads in Russia*
c. 1000	*Seljuk Turks become dominant power in Islam, Abbasid caliphs figurehead rulers thereafter*
1019–1054	*Yaroslav the Wise rules Kievan Rus—height of medieval Russian/Kievan civilization*
1071	*Arabs defeat Byzantines at Manzikert*

The Orthodox church also took shape gradually out of origins shared with the Roman Catholic church of western Europe. From the time of Constantine's legalization of the Christian religion in 313, the bishops of Constantinople refused to recognize the growing authority of the bishops of Rome. Partly because of the rising wealth and political importance of Constantinople, its bishops, called *patriarchs,* acquired an ascendancy over the bishops of the other Eastern cities roughly comparable to the authority of the Roman popes over Western bishops. The split between the Eastern and Western churches did not become official until the eleventh century, but in fact the two main divisions of Christianity had drifted apart long before.

During the late Roman and early medieval centuries, this Eastern Empire, like western Europe, underwent significant changes. Eastern Roman emperors, from Constantine in the fourth century to Heraclius in the seventh, managed to turn back or divert the Germanic and Turko–Mongol invaders who so drastically transformed the West. But the Byzantine Empire of the Middle Ages was, as we shall see, a very different entity from the Roman Empire of the Caesars.

Justinian and Theodora

In the sixth century, Byzantium produced its greatest rulers. In Emperor Justinian (r. 527–565) and his empress, Theodora, Byzantium in fact gave the world one of the most impressive and controversial royal couples in history.

Justinian inherited the throne from his uncle, Justinus I (r. 518–527), after serving as his junior colleague for some years. Procopius tells us that Justinian was "neither tall nor short, but of normal height . . . rather plump, with a round face." He was extremely accessible—the palace was always swarming with people—"easily led astray" and "easy meat" for deceivers, above all for his controversial wife Theodora.[2] Daughter of a circus animal trainer, Theodora was a famous dancer and a celebrated courtesan when Justinian met and

The Byzantine Empire, 527–565

fell hopelessly in love with her. She had, the historian admits, "an attractive face and a good figure," but "not a particle of modesty."[3] She scandalized high society by her shocking stage performances before Justinian married her and elevated her with him to the imperial throne.

Justinian seems to have had a compulsive dedication to restoring the vanished grandeur of Rome. For thirty years, he labored to rebuild a united Empire, to codify its vast body of laws, and to turn Constantinople into a "New Rome" worthy of the Empire's ancient traditions. Sometimes faulted for exhausting the resources of the Eastern Empire in a hopeless effort to recover the West, Justinian nevertheless left behind him one of the most beautiful cities in the world and one of the most influential codes of laws in history.

Yet he might never have had the chance to do any of these things if it had not been for Theodora. "She was extremely clever," even Procopius admitted.[4] And it was she who, when a wave of political rioting threatened to drive the young Justinian from his throne, stiffened his backbone and kept him there. A tough outsider who had made it to the top and did not propose to let go, she declared: "If flight were the only means of safety, yet I should disdain to fly. Death is the condition of our birth, but they who have reigned should never survive the loss of dignity and dominion. . . . For my own part, I adhere to the maxim of antiquity, that the throne is a glorious sepulchre."[5]

Justinian's efforts to reunite the Roman Empire required many years of massive military campaigns by land and sea. His most successful generals, Belisarius (c. 505–565) and the eunuch Narses (c. 480–574), did in fact accomplish more than anyone could have dreamed possible. The Vandal regime was shattered in North Africa and almost all the southern coast of the Mediterranean reclaimed. A large slice of Spain was recaptured from the Visigoths. Most important, a pincer movement by fleets and armies liberated the old Roman heartland of Italy from the Ostrogoths and established a Byzantine viceroy at Ravenna. These wars, accompanied by long campaigns against Persia in the East, dragged on for most of Justinian's reign, exhausted even the Byzantine treasury, and left Italy, in particular, devastated by decades of war. At his death, a Roman Empire once more ringed the Mediterranean; but both the New Rome and the old had paid in terrible effusions of blood and treasure.

Justinian's codification of Roman law proved a far more lasting achievement. Roman law had been accumulating for almost ten centuries since the Twelve Tables of the early Republic. It included legislation, imperial edicts, and the legal opinions of centuries of Roman jurists. Justinian appointed a series of commissions to tackle the huge job of bringing order into this rich jumble of legal materials. The result was the *Corpus Iuris Civilis*, literally the "Body of the Civil Law," sometimes called simply Justinian's Code. The three most important elements of Justinian's Code were the *Codex* of carefully organized edicts of the emperors, the *Digest* of the legal opinions of Rome's greatest legal minds, and the *Institutes*, a basic guide to the law for students. The *Corpus Iuris Civilis*, compiled in the sixth century, reached the medieval West in the eleventh century and became the basis for the laws of a number of the new nation–states emerging in the High Middle Ages. Roman legal principles also influenced both the ecclesiastical law of the Roman Catholic church, as it began to take definitive shape in the twelfth century, and modern international law, when it began to emerge at the end of the sixteenth.

Justinian was also, finally, the greatest builder of all the Byzantine emperors. Much of this construction was composed of necessary public works across the expanding Empire: law courts, public baths, aqueducts, roads, and fortifications. He also built schools, orphanages, hospices for the sick, public recreation areas, and extensions on his own royal palaces. Above all, however, Justinian built churches. His church–building program extended from Egypt and Palestine to Greece and Italy, where such gems of Byzantine architecture as San Vitale in Ravenna and, later, St. Mark's in Venice, were constructed in the Byzantine style. Constantinople itself, however, was Justinian's special concern: his architects raised or refurbished three dozen churches in the city, including by far the largest church in the medieval world: Hagia Sophia, the Church of the Holy Wisdom.

The Power of Byzantine Autocracy

The many emperors who succeeded Justinian on the throne of the Byzantine Empire built on the foundations he had laid. We will look here at the autocratic structure of the society they built rather than at the events of their many reigns.

There was no question that the Byzantine government governed. The West would not see so successful an autocracy until the reign of Louis XIV in the seventeenth century. *Autocrat* was in fact one of the official titles of the Byzantine emperor, and the source of the word as we use it to refer to a powerful authoritarian ruler. The emperor also inherited the Roman power of *imperium,* granted to him on his accession by the army, which elevated him on a shield to indicate its acceptance of him as commander in chief. Perhaps even more important, the Byzantine autocrat enjoyed the Hellenistic monarch's aura of divinity conferred on him by the Greek Orthodox church, which anointed him with holy oil in recognition that he ruled by divine right, as God's viceroy on earth.

Byzantine emperors asserted a far–reaching authority over many aspects of the lives of their people. They regulated the economy and took a liberal share of the gross national product through taxes, customs duties, and government monopolies like the profitable silk industry, a technology that imperial agents had smuggled out of China. The emperors also claimed to be heads of the Orthodox church, appointing bishops, calling ecclesiastical councils, and passing on the resulting decisions. This doctrine of *caesaropapism,* declaring the superiority of the emperor to the head of the church, immensely strengthened the hand of the Byzantine ruler. The autocratic claims of the emperors also extended to empresses. The Empress Irene (r. 797–802), a contemporary of Charlemagne's, and the imperial sisters Zoe (r. 1028–1055) and Theodora (r. 1055–1056) guided the affairs of state as autocratically as male rulers.

The exalted position of the Byzantine emperor was embodied in the high–flown titles and elaborate court ceremonials that surrounded his person. Anyone who entered the imperial presence had to prostrate himself full length before the ruler. Hymns and trumpet flourishes heralded the emperor's approach when he went forth among his people. A day in the life of a Byzantine emperor was one long ceremony in his own imperial honor.

To turn their authoritarian claims into realities, the Byzantine rulers had a professional civil service with a tradition that went back to the days of the Roman Caesars. The treasury, staffed with shrewd products of the Greek business community, was particularly efficient at extracting taxes from the wealthy cities of the Empire. The diplomatic and intelligence services of the Byzantines were also justly famous, creating puppet rulers and supporting pro–Byzantine factions among the peoples on their frontiers.

When such intrigues failed, finally, the armed forces could generally handle the situation. Building on a Roman tradition of military excellence, Byzantine troops were normally well trained and organized, in possession of the latest intelligence on the enemy, and equipped with such up–to–date devices as signal mirrors and "Greek fire," a flammable chemical mixture sprayed on enemy vessels to set them ablaze.

Undergirding these tactical advantages was the *theme system,* which combined political organization with an effective military defense. Under this system, soldiers were granted land in various provinces of the Empire in return for accepting a hereditary military obligation. The commanders of these farmer–soldiers soon became the chief administrative authorities in the provinces, and the term *theme,* meaning a military unit, came to be applied to the provincial divisions of the Byzantine Empire. And troops and fleets defending their own farms and ports proved more effective in the field than the mercenary or even slave soldiers who preceded them.

Byzantine autocracy demonstrated its capacity for survival most impressively when facing major religious and military challenges. Religious issues certainly played a large part in Byzantine history. A particularly divisive religious dispute within the Empire was the *iconoclastic controversy.* This debate was triggered by imperial decrees forbidding the use of *icons*—images of God, the Virgin Mary, or the saints used to stimulate devotion—in churches because they encouraged "idol worship." Byzantine monks and many Orthodox Christians bitterly opposed this view and resisted its implementation for a hundred years, until the emperors relented and restored the veneration of images.

Meanwhile, disputes between Eastern Orthodox and Western Catholic Christianity, which dated back to rivalry between the bishops of Rome and Byzantium in ancient times, grew steadily worse. In 1054, as we will see in a later chapter, the schism between Eastern and Western Christendom reached its climax as pope and patriarch severed relations and excommunicated each other.

The military strength of the Byzantine Empire preserved it for many centuries in the face of increasingly high odds against its survival. Many waves of invaders assaulted Byzantium during its long history, but the most persistent of them were the Muslim peoples of the south and east. The Arabs, the first to convert to the Muslim religion of the prophet Muhammad—to be discussed below—pressed the Empire hard during early medieval times. They besieged Constantinople itself for five years in the 670s and came close to capturing the city again in 718. Then in 1071, the Seljuk Turks, who had replaced the Arabs as the most militant of Muslim peoples, crushed the Byzantine army at Manzikert. The walls of Byzantium held against the Turks, and the Byzantine Empire still had almost four hundred years of history ahead of it. But they were hard centuries.

The survival power of the Byzantine Empire had an additional effect, however: it protected the weakened West by stopping invaders from the East before they could reach western Europe. During the centuries between 500 and 1000, when the West was most fragmented and disorganized, this defensive function was particularly valuable. By the time the Byzantine Empire finally fell to foreign conquerors in 1453, at the end of the Middle Ages, Europe was strong enough to stand alone.

The Wealth of Constantinople

Economically and socially, the Byzantine Empire was as successful as it was in the political arena. And this success also benefited the economically underdeveloped nations of the West. The urban, commercial, and handicraft–industrial wealth of Constantinople thus played an important part in the history of both Byzantium and the medieval West.

The distinctive feature of Byzantine society was its urban development. And the twin keys to the prosperity of its cities were foreign trade and handicraft manufacture, which, in early medieval times, flourished there as nowhere else in Christendom.

The Byzantine Empire, unlike western Europe, inherited an urban society from Greco–Roman antiquity and preserved this legacy throughout the medieval period. Besides the capital Constantinople, Byzantine cities in the earlier period included Egyptian Alexandria, Beirut, Tyre, and Antioch on the eastern Mediterranean, and Trebizond on the Black Sea. They were crowded tangles of palaces and slums, churches and bazaars, with high walls, teeming ports, and caravansaries where caravans unloaded. They had all the problems of metropolitan areas before and since, from plague and fire to violent street crime. But they also had the capacity to generate wealth, the intellectual sophistication, and the sheer vitality of cities throughout history.

The Byzantine capital was built on one of the world's greatest natural harbors, the Golden Horn. Even more important, Constantinople was located on the main trade route between Europe and Asia, the most important commercial connection in the world. Goods came by caravan along the Great Silk Road from China, by sea across the Indian Ocean, down the rivers of Russia, or across the eastern Mediterranean from Europe to pour in a golden flood into the bazaars of Byzantium.

Into the markets of Alexandria and Antioch, Trebizond and Constantinople flowed the wealth of the world. From western Europe came textiles and weapons, iron and wood. From eastern Europe came furs and amber, wheat, honey, and slaves. Enamels, glassware, and brilliantly dyed and decorated fabrics from the Near East splashed color across the bazaars. All the way from India and Southeast Asia came precious stones, pearls, carved ivory, and the spices that scented and flavored the lives of the wealthy—nutmeg, cloves, cinnamon and ginger, pepper and sugar, aloes and musk. And from China and the Far East the most valuable of all trade items took the better part of a year to reach Byzantium: silk to clothe the bodies of the richest of the rich.

In Constantinople and other Byzantine cities, furthermore, street after street of skilled guild craftspeople labored to produce some of the finest craftware in the world. Goldsmith work, carved ivories, jewelry, and their own gorgeous purple silks were shaped by sensitive hands in Byzantine workshops. Illuminated manuscripts for scholars, incense and beautiful vestments for churches were handcrafted for local and foreign markets. Golden cups and tableware for the wealthy, icons and relic boxes for the pious, gold and silver rings, necklaces and pendants—the dazzling list had no end.

Constantinople's slums were the densest, its palaces and churches the most gorgeous. The crowds that filled the sixty thousand seats of the Hippodrome, the race track and sports stadium behind the imperial palace, could terrorize the streets if their favorite chariot drivers lost. Merchants from all parts of Eurasia had their own national enclaves in Constantinople, with their own warehouses, stables, hostelries, churches, mosques, or temples, all tolerated—if carefully policed—by the Byzantine authorities. And visiting envoys from kingdoms of Franks and Goths and Slavs prostrated themselves in awe before an emperor whose throne was flanked by handcrafted clockwork lions and shaded by a gilded tree in which sang artificial birds of bronze and gold.

"There is no estimating," said the Western chronicler Geoffroi de Villehardouin (c. 1150–c. 1213), "the quantity of gold, silver, rich stuffs [fabrics] and other valuables" in Byzantium.[6] European merchants who came sailing across the eastern Mediterranean to Byzantium came most often to tap that source of commercial exchange and handicraft production. And that wealth played its part in Western history. In the High Middle Ages, as we will see in the next chapter, trade with the Near East did much to revive Western commerce and to stimulate the revival of cities across Europe. And the source of much of that stimulus was the wealth generated in the workshops and bazaars of Constantinople.

From a rooftop in today's Istanbul, the view across the busy stretch of water called the Golden Horn is one of Muslim domes and spires rising among modern European buildings. The skyline of medieval times was quite different, of course, but one thing was as true of the medieval as of the modern city. The harbor was thick with the spars and masts of ships, the Grand Bazaar and the mercantile houses crowded with people haggling over the price of goods—just as they do today.

Byzantine Art and Thought

Byzantine palaces and craftwork were splendid, but, as in medieval Western Christendom, it was the church that dominated the intellectual and creative life of this society. The spirit of the Greek Orthodox church infused Byzantine culture from basic political concepts and scholarship to graphic arts and architecture.

A distinctive feature of the Orthodox church was the power of the Byzantine emperors to regulate its affairs. Since Constantine had sat in council with Christian bishops to rule on theological disputes in the fourth century, the rulers of the Eastern Empire had claimed supreme power over the church. Eastern emperors, while they were not priests, directed and deposed patriarchs, summoned and supervised church councils, and played a leading part in bringing about change in church practice and even in theological interpretation. The Roman popes, after the fall of the Western emperors, were free to construct a "papal monarchy" in the West; but in the East the emperors still ruled, dominated the patriarchs, and treated the church as if it were a branch of the state.

In a realm so glutted with wealth, it is perhaps not surprising that people were particularly impressed by individuals who could resist material temptations. Monks, whose monasteries were often in the heart of the cities, were thus both leading figures in the church hierarchy and popular heroes as well. In later Byzantine times, when the Empire's worldly fortunes declined, monks and other pious individuals turned increasingly to mysticism, abandoning the material world altogether in order to find in meditation a means of direct spiritual contact with God. For the majority of people, however, beautiful churches, impressive services, and moving hymns provided means of mass communion with the deity.

In an atmosphere so charged with religious feeling, theological disputes were also particularly passionate. One of the few occasions on which the Orthodox church resisted the emperors was, as we have seen, the iconoclastic debate, which also helped bring about the schism between the Greek Orthodox and Roman Catholic churches. Other theological disputes between the Eastern and Western churches had to do with differences in the liturgical ceremonies of the two churches, and/or with such practical matters as the marriage of priests, sanctioned in the East but, by the High Middle Ages, forbidden in the West. Another much-argued point was the Catholic inclusion of the word *filioque* in the Creed, indicating that the Holy Spirit proceeds from both God the Father "and the Son"—which was heresy in Constantinople. It was over the *filioque* issue that the final split between the Eastern and the Western churches took place in 1054.

In a society where monks were popular leaders and theological disputes the "great debates" of the time, it is not surprising that religious literature dominated the field. Saints' lives were as popular in the East as in the West, the most celebrated poets wrote hymns, and immense quantities of biblical commentaries, theological tracts, and other devotional works were produced. Paradoxically, however, Byzantine scholarship also treasured its heritage from ancient—and thoroughly pagan—Greece. Practically all the earliest manuscripts we have of the Greek philosophers, dramatists, and poets are Byzantine copies of long-vanished originals. The Byzantine intelligentsia seem to have been enthusiastic readers of Homer and Plato. And they certainly did the West an incalculable service by preserving this common Western heritage of Greek art and thought through centuries when even kings in western Europe were often illiterate.

Original scholarship and art also flourished in the Byzantine Empire. An outstanding example is Anna Comnena's *Alexiad*, the epic history of the reign of her father, Emperor Alexius I (r. 1081–1118). Composed in verse, Comnena's work combines thoughtful analysis with vivid description. She offers, for instance, a candid characterization of the flower of Western chivalry marching through Byzantium on their way to fight the Turks. The "Franks," as Near Easterners called Europeans, were described as famed for "their irresistible manner of attack" but also for "their unstable and mobile character" and for being "always agape for money."

All the spirituality and all the artistry of the Byzantines combined to produce the unique beauty of the Byzantine church. Gorgeous silk wall hangings, sculptured ivory, wall paintings, and mosaics all glorified the house of God. Byzantine mosaics often used small blocks of colored glass, sometimes dusted with silver or gold, instead of bits of colored stone to form their pictures. The same formal composition was used in these mosaics whether the figures looking out from the wall were divine or human, God or the emperor. Such images drew a powerful parallel between God enthroned upon the world and surrounded by the heavenly hosts and the emperor of Byzantium flanked by his imperial court. The parallel between divine and earthly power was not lost on the multitudes who flocked to the many churches of the Empire.

◆ Kievan Russia ◆

The neighbors who most resembled the western Europeans during the Middle Ages were the Slavs and other peoples of eastern Europe. In this section, we will look first at eastern Europe as a whole and the peoples who lived there in medieval times. Thereafter, we will focus on the most powerful of Slavic peoples, the medieval Russians. Shaped by Viking princes and Byzantine civilization, early Russia reached a cultural climax in the Kievan period between the ninth and eleventh centuries.

Eastern Europe and Its Peoples

Settled over most of the continent east of the Elbe and Danube rivers, the Slavic peoples were the largest of all the Indo–European groups who had populated the continent. They were also, however, culturally cut off from Europeans who spoke Germanic or Romance languages instead of Slavic ones, and who were Roman Catholic rather than Greek Orthodox. Until quite recently, these differences led to a tendency on the part of Western historians to neglect Slavic and other eastern European contributions to European history. To do so was to leave out a significant part of the story, for eastern Europe is as much a part of the historic West as the central and western portions of the European continent are.

It is easy to see the eastern half of Europe as "Slavic Europe": most of the modern countries of this region, after all, do have substantial Slavic populations. The majority of the citizens of the former Soviet Union, for instance, are Great Russians, Ukrainians, or White Russians—all Slavic peoples. So are most of the inhabitants of Poland, Bulgaria, the Czech Republic, Slovakia, Bosnia, Croatia, Serbia, and other areas in the region. On the other hand, the dominant populations of Hungary, Romania, and Albania do *not* speak Slavic languages or consider themselves Slavs, and there are non–Slavic minorities in many other eastern European lands. Despite a substantial Slav majority, in short, this half of Europe, like the western portion, is more accurately envisioned as a mosaic of peoples. In the Middle Ages, this collection of east European peoples stretched from the Baltic to the Balkans, bordered on the west by the German–speaking countries, on the north by Scandinavia, and on the south by Greece and Turkey.

Geographically, most of this half of Europe is the east European plain. This immense geological formation, which can actually be traced as far west as France or even southeast England, flows almost uninterrupted across German–speaking central Europe and east Europe all the way to the Ural Mountains. It is an enormous area. From Warsaw to the Urals is about as far as from Chicago to the Pacific, and there are no great natural barriers, like the Alps or the Pyrenees, to divide it. As a result, in early times Slavic peoples were able to migrate easily from one part of eastern Europe to another. By the same token, there was little to keep other peoples out of the area. In this chapter, we see Viking intrusion from the north and Byzantine cultural penetration from the south, both of which made important contributions to the development of Slavic society and culture. We also note the appearance of Magyars in Hungary, Vlachs in Romania, and other peoples from further east who played a major part in the history of the region. In subsequent chapters, we deal with later medieval invasions by the Germans from the west and the Mongols from the east, both crucial formative experiences for the future nation of Russia.

We focus on the Slavs in the present section, which is concerned primarily with the early history of Russia. But the descendants of Asian nomads, as well as Germans, Scandinavians, and Greek–speaking peoples, also play their part in these and later pages.

The Slavs and the Varangian Princes

From an original center in what is today eastern Poland and western Ukraine, three great branches of the original Slavic people moved east, west, and south in the fifth and sixth centuries of the Christian era. The *West Slavs* populated twentieth–century Poland and Czechoslovakia, perhaps the most westernized of eastern European countries. The *South Slavs* filtered down into the Balkan peninsula to become the basic populations of twentieth–century Yugoslavia (which means "South Slav"), Romania, Bulgaria, and other Balkan nations. The *East Slavs*, finally, occupied European Russia and became the ancestors of the Russians, Ukrainians, and Bela-, or White, Russians of today.

The East Slavs, the largest branch of the parent stem, were for the most part agricultural villagers, tilling the land with heavy horse–drawn plows and worshiping the spirits of the natural world around them. Leadership for each village as a whole—which tended to be considerably larger than the typical western European village—was provided by a chief and a council of elders. In modern terms, they were a preurban, preliterate culture, a people vast in numbers and occupying more territory than any other Indo–European people, yet unorganized beyond the level of the chiefdom. A people with an immense potential for power, they began to realize that potential under the stimulus of two neighboring peoples: the Vikings and the Byzantines.

The Viking people, called the Varangians, swept down the Russian rivers from Scandinavia. The culture of the Byzantine Empire and its metropolis of Constantinople spread up from the south. During the ninth and tenth centuries, these two forces stimulated the emergence of a new culture and even of a loose political unity among the Eastern Slavs.

Wherever there was water, the Vikings were at home. Down the Dnieper and the Volga and their tributaries, through the dark pine forests of northern Russia and across the golden plains of Ukraine drifted the dragon ships. Here and there the Varangians went ashore and built forts. They used their forts as bases for trade and tribute–gathering among the Slavic villages, taking home furs, honey, and slaves. Some of them, however, stayed, married Slavic women, lost their Scandinavian identity, and became the progenitors of Russia's emerging nobility, the *boyars*. They played an important part in the building of the first sizable trading towns in Russia, including Novgorod in the northern forests and Kiev on the southern steppes, both founded in the ninth century.

The Varangians also brought more extensive political organization to the East Slavs, though again the details are obscure. According to the *Primary Chronicle,* the greatest example of early medieval Russian historical writing, around 860 the feuding citizens of Novgorod petitioned the Vikings to restore order and become their rulers, and a Varangian named Rurik (d. c. 879) answered the call. This *calling of the princes* paved the way for Varangian political suzerainty. Rurik's successor Oleg (r. c. 879–912) united the northern and southern trading centers of Novgorod and Kiev in a loose alliance of Varangian princes that ruled all the land between. Oleg made his residence at Kiev, so that the political center of this first Russian state was actually in what is today Ukraine. In medieval times, however, this Varangian–dominated Slavic principality became known as the *Kievan Rus.* The term *Rus,* apparently originally applied to the Varangians as a people, became in later centuries the root of the name of the Russian nation itself.

The Impact of Byzantium

The establishment of the Varangian capital at Kiev in the ninth century had significant and unforeseen consequences. The original intention was probably to bring the Varangians within trading and raiding range of the Black Sea and especially of Constantinople. Viking fleets did in fact strike the Byzantine metropolis several times. But the move also brought the center of the Kievan Rus within easier reach of Byzantine influences. These influences from the civilized south proved to be perhaps even more important than the impact of the Vikings in shaping emerging Slav society. The Vikings had come with their swords and brought political unity; the Byzantines came with a missionary faith and brought a whole culture.

Greek Orthodox Constantinople became the missionary center for Slavic eastern Europe, as Rome had been for Germanic western Europe. Byzantium's first missionary efforts, however, were directed toward the West and South Slavs rather than to the East Slavs in the Rus. In 862 the ruler of the West Slav state of Moravia, in today's Czech Republic, fearful of the subversive influence of the Roman Catholic Christianity of his German neighbors, asked the Byzantine emperor to send some holy men to teach them the Greek Orthodox version of Christianity. The mission sent out to them was headed by two brothers, Cyril (c. 827–869) and Methodius (c. 825–884), later known as the "Apostles to the Slavs." The two men spoke Slavic and devised an alphabet for their converts; a somewhat later version, based on Greek and known as Cyrillic, became the Russian script of today. In the later ninth century, Bulgaria, with some reluctance, accepted Greek Orthodoxy, as in time did most of the Slavic peoples. Ironically, the Czechs, like their Polish neighbors, were eventually converted to Roman Catholicism. These peoples thus became the core of an enclave of Roman Christianity in predominantly Greek Orthodox eastern Europe.

The conversion of the East Slavs of Kievan Russia did not come until the end of the tenth century. In 957 the reigning princess of Kiev, Olga (r. 945–964), who "always sought wisdom in this world," was baptized a Christian in Constantinople.[7] When Olga's grandson Prince Vladimir the Saint (r. 980–1015) also accepted the Orthodox faith in 988, the elite of the Rus and most of the populations of the trading towns followed him into the church. The bulk of the Slavic peasantry probably remained pagan long after these royal conversions, as peasants did in western Europe. Nevertheless, the influence of the new religion, and of the intensified contact with Byzantium that accompanied conversion, was far–reaching.

The religion itself, of course, was central. Greek Orthodox priests and services were exported to Russia. Orthodox monasteries, which played an important part in the religious life of Byzantium, were founded in growing numbers among the East Slavs, and monks became the most revered holy men in Russia as they were among the Byzantines. Reverence for the religious images called icons also passed from Byzantium to the Russian Orthodox faithful.

Larger cultural influences accompanied the new faith. Literacy and the use of the Cyrillic alphabet spread not only among churchmen but among Russia's rulers and business community as well. The arts also benefited: churches were built inspired by those at Constantinople, and the making of icons became a fine art in Russia as it was in Byzantium. In centuries to come, this long–lasting Byzantine connection brought the Russians some influential Byzantine political ideas, notably the Byzantine belief in political autocracy.

The Age of Yaroslav the Wise

The Kievan Rus reached its height in the early eleventh century. The presiding spirit of this Kievan golden age was Yaroslav the Wise (r. 1019–1054), perhaps the greatest prince to rule the first Russia, revered today especially in the new independent state of Ukraine.

It is hard to say whether Yaroslav the Wise, portrayed here in one of a series of seventeenth-century paintings of early Russian rulers, was a Russian or a Ukrainian hero. He certainly played an important part in the early history of both Russia and Ukraine. (Novosti/Sovfoto/Eastfoto.)

Yaroslav, son of the convert Vladimir, was a hero to the medieval Russian monks who produced our basic source for the period, the *Primary Chronicle*. He turned back a wave of invaders from the eastern steppes and expanded his own frontiers northward into territories formerly held by the Finns. He had the traditional laws of the East Slavs assembled and codified for the first time. He achieved the formal separation of the Russian Orthodox church from the Greek Orthodox parent body in Constantinople. He made the principality of Kiev known in western Europe and negotiated alliances with some of Europe's ruling houses. Under Yaroslav, Russia was in closer contact with the western half of the continent than it was again until modern times, when Russian czars reached out once more for contact with the West.

The success of the Kievan Rus, however, was more than the achievement of one ruler, or even a succession of them. Built on solid economic foundations, this society generated some surprisingly liberal political institutions, and may have been freer than the western Europe of its day.

The economy of the East Slavs was based on agriculture but featured a bustling commercial sector as well. Russian peasants grew enough wheat to export it in significant quantities. The trading towns on the Russian rivers shipped other things too, including honey, amber, and furs. The Byzantine Empire remained the Rus's main trading partner, but Russians also exchanged goods with western Europe through Scandinavia, with Asia through the steppe nomads, and even with the Arabs, who had by that time conquered most of the Middle East in the name of Islam.

The structure of Kievan society was less rigid in some ways than that of Western Christendom at the same time. Most Russian peasants were free, though there were slaves and some serfs among them. The boyar nobility was normally attached to the retinue of a regional prince, but there was no established feudal system, and boyars could take their services wherever they pleased. Most promising, perhaps, the trading towns had free institutions, notably a municipal council, or *veche*, which governed the city with little princely or boyar intervention.

Like Charlemagne and Alfred the Great in western Europe, Yaroslav and his heirs sponsored a cultural flowering during the brief period of Kievan hegemony. Greek artisans were imported to decorate the scores of churches that sprang up in Kiev, including the Church of the Holy Wisdom, which is still to be seen there. Like their English or French contemporaries, scholarly Russian monks like Hilarion—metropolitan (bishop) of Kiev from 1051 to 1054—wrote religious tracts, including many lives of the saints. Historical writing included the *Primary Chronicle* of Russian history from the ninth to the twelfth century. The *Chronicle*, like contemporary western European histories, had a religious core, emphasizing the conversion of Russian princes and their subsequent victories over their pagan foes.

Yaroslav himself had the reputation of being a great reader, writer, and translator of works of religious edification from Byzantine Greek into the Church Slavonic used in Russia. Monastery schools apparently taught the Cyrillic alphabet to some of the children of princes and nobles. Indeed, the aristocracy of Kiev may have been more literate than the contemporary western European nobility: "For great is the profit of book–learning," as the *Primary Chronicle* says.[8]

Like the kingdoms of early medieval peoples in western Europe, however, these first state–building efforts of the East Slavs did not last. The Rus remained a loose confederation of princes in spite of the recognized headship of the prince of Kiev. A particularly unfortunate feature was the lack of a clear line of succession. In the generations after Yaroslav, an elaborate system of allotting domains to various princes on the basis of their seniority and the relative wealth of their regions led to disputes and even to wars between rulers. This system had the same effect as the division of France among Frankish princes, fragmenting the state into smaller pieces. When a powerful new nomadic people appeared out of the East in the thirteenth century, the Mongols of Genghis Khan, the divided and rivalrous princes of Kiev stood little chance against them.

The Arab Empire

South of the Byzantine Empire lived another people whose society, like that of the Slavs, was largely undeveloped at the beginning of the Middle Ages. These were the Arabs, founders of an empire that flourished from the seventh to the thirteenth centuries. And the force that turned a scattering of traders and herders of flocks into conquerors and rulers was one of the world's great religions—Islam.

Islam, still a living force in the world today, ought to be more familiar to us than the vanished civilization of Byzantium or the ill–documented early history of the Slavs. Late twentieth–century impressions of Arabs and Islamic movements, however, may actually hamper our understanding of the golden age of Arab Islam. Headlines about oil sheiks and terrorist groups scarcely prepare us for the civilizing vision of Muhammad, the Arabian Nights splendor of old Baghdad, or the spiritual peace still to be found in the courtyard of an ancient mosque.

This brief overview of early Islamic history will begin with a look at the Arabs before their new religion galvanized them and at the founder of that faith, the Prophet Muhammad. Later pages will trace the record of Arab conquests from Spain to the frontiers of India and will outline the political structure of the Arab Empire under the caliphs who succeeded Muhammad. This section will conclude with an analysis of sources of division and unity in this far–flung Islamic zone, and with at least a glimpse of the cultural flowering which was its greatest legacy.

The Desert Peoples

On today's map, Arab countries stretch from the Near East all across North Africa—through Egypt, Libya, Tunisia, Algeria, Morocco—to the Strait of Gibraltar and beyond. Arabia itself, the Arab homeland, spreads southward from the ancient Fertile Crescent between the Red Sea and the Persian Gulf into the Indian Ocean. Here around CE 600 the last of the great world religions emerged among a people who had thus far, like the Slavs and Germans, lived on the fringes of history. For them, like their northern neighbors, all that was about to change.

The twin settings of pre–Islamic Arab society were the oasis and the desert. At oases, some of which were large enough to accommodate several villages, the water table lay close enough to the surface to permit digging wells and cultivating crops, especially dates and wheat. The much larger desert areas of Arabia, by contrast, depended largely on the skimpy spring rains to produce enough grass to feed the sheep, asses, camels, and other animals herded by nomads. At the oases, farms, towns, and settled society developed; on the desert, nomadic Bedouins evolved a society always on the move to keep up with the sparse water and pasturage on which their flocks depended.

Linking the two cultures was a remarkable animal: the camel. Capable of carrying heavier loads than any beast of burden except the elephant, able to survive for long periods without water, and surprisingly fast–moving when goaded to a gallop by its Bedouin master, the camel was ideally suited to this desiccated land. Bedouin Arabs rode and herded camels, lived off their milk and meat, and used them for the rapid cavalry raids that were central to their style of fighting. Oasis Arabs used camels to import what they could not make for their own use, and for the long–distance trade in which the oases served as way stations and markets. The camel was also central to the symbiotic relationship that developed between oasis and desert: oasis Arabs bought their camels from Bedouins, and Bedouins used the camel to conduct profitable raids on the caravans of oasis–bound merchants.

Transcending these differences, however, were the cultural features shared by all Arabs. Like many peoples early in their histories, the Arabs of the seventh century were a tribal or clan–based society with an animistic religion and a vigorous oral literature. The family was the building block of Arab society, with large clans and larger tribes claiming common, often divine ancestors. The religious life of the Arabs before Muhammad centered on spirits and demons called *djinn* and on more important gods, often the patron divinities of particular clans. All these supernatural presences were associated with such natural objects as palm groves, oddly shaped rock formations, or bright stars. An immensely popular art form, finally, was Arabic oral poetry. Chanted by professional bards in fixed poetic meters, these popular ballads dealt with the blood feuds of the clans and the deeds of heroic Bedouins.

The southern sands, like the northern steppes, were a unique world and had produced a culture well adapted to this environment, if distinctly limited by it. Despite its uniqueness, however, Arabia was not cut off from the rest of the Middle East. Arabs traded and raided in the Byzantine and Persian empires and had regular contact with Palestine and Syria. They were well aware of the monotheistic religions of Judaism and Christianity that flourished in these regions. There were, in fact, scattered communities of Jews and Christians living in Arabia itself. Contact with these monotheistic peoples had already begun to make some Arabs ponder even before Muhammad came on the scene, bringing with him the third great faith to be born in this narrow corner of the Near East.

The Vision of Muhammad

> In the Name of God, the Merciful, the Compassionate
> Praise belongs to God, the Lord of All Being,
> The All–merciful, the All–compassionate,
> The Master of the Day of Doom.[9]

The man who heard these words echoing through his head and later spoke them in the market town of Mecca was in his forties, black–bearded, with intense dark eyes. Sitting alone on a mountain outside the town, he sometimes saw "a waking vision of a gigantic being on the horizon—on every horizon—on every horizon to which [he] turned his eyes— who spoke to him the words he must say."[10] His enemies among the Arabs accused him of being possessed by a djinn; more worldly Byzantines claimed he was an epileptic. The consensus of modern scholarship is that he was in any event profoundly sincere.

The Prophet Muhammad (570–632), of the Hashim clan of the Quraysh tribe, grew up as a marketplace orphan in the caravan oasis town of Mecca in west–central Arabia, not

The angel Gabriel inspires the prophet Muhammad to write the Koran, the holy book of Islam. Muhammad, who clearly had some familiarity with both Judaism and Christianity, saw himself as God's last messenger to the human race. (Edinburgh University Library.)

far from the Red Sea. Mecca, on the main north–south caravan route, was also a pilgrimage center, famous for its pagan religious shrine, the Kaaba, where idols and other sacred objects were gathered for veneration by many clans. In this atmosphere of caravans and pilgrims Muhammad grew up and became a respected businessman. He married a wealthy businesswoman named Khadijah (d. 619), who considerably enhanced his position in the trading community, and with her he had a half–dozen children. Then, in his fortieth year, he began to have visions.

Muhammad had probably encountered both Christianity and Judaism in his travels with the caravans. In middle age, he began to withdraw to a mountain overlooking the city to meditate. It was here, around 610, that he heard the great voice he identified as the angel Gabriel telling him to recite to others the religious revelations that would be vouchsafed to him. Over the next twenty–two years, Muhammad did so, reciting to growing numbers the rhythmic, vivid Arabic verses of the Koran, the Muslim holy book.

He spoke first to his own family, and his wife Khadijah became the first convert to the new religion. A few others, many of them young and not of the wealthiest classes, began to listen to him too, and then one or two of the most powerful. Most of the leading citizens of Mecca, however, were unreceptive to Muhammad's new faith, a militant monotheism that seemed to challenge all the pagan cults which drew the lucrative pilgrim trade. After a dozen years of preaching, therefore, the Prophet and his embattled followers left Mecca and moved 250 miles north to another city, subsequently renamed el–Medina, "The City," the first community to accept the Prophet's message. This "flight to Medina" became known as the *Hegira,* and the year of the Hegira, 622 by the Christian calendar, is the year 1 for Muslims everywhere.

For the last ten years of his life, Muhammad developed his ideas in the more practical atmosphere of guiding the affairs of the city that had accepted his leadership. Reaching out to the desert Bedouins, he also became more aggressive, urging believers to fight for their faith against unbelievers, something the feuding, raiding desert nomads were quite willing to do. In a long series of skirmishes and battles, the Muslims brought one Arabian tribe after another over to their side. Eight years after the Hegira, then, Muhammad had developed sufficient strength to return and set his own terms with Mecca. He cleansed the shrine of the Kaaba of its idols, retaining only the holiest of its relics, a black stone of meteoric origin, which he said was sacred to the one God, Allah. By the time of the Prophet's death in 632, two years after his triumph in his own city, virtually the entire population of Arabia had accepted his message.

The message of the *Koran* is summarized most simply by the two linked propositions: "There is no God but Allah, and Muhammad is his Prophet." *Islam* means "submission" to the will of God, and Muhammad's Koran explained Allah's basic requirements to the faithful. These included belief in the one God and his Prophet, in personal immortality, heaven and hell, and a Day of Judgment. Good Muslims were required to pray five times daily, to fast during the daylight hours of the month of Ramadan, to try to make a pilgrimage to Mecca, and to give alms to the poor. There were also some dietary regulations, including the prohibition of alcoholic beverages. Some of these ideas may have their roots in Judaic or Christian teachings, and Muhammad actually saw himself as a prophet in the line of Moses and Jesus, whose inspiration he did not deny.

On the broad social level, Muhammad, like the Hebrew prophets and Jesus of Nazareth, condemned some of the common practices of his day as immoral and unjust. Female infanticide and charging usurious rates of interest, for example, were declared to be sins in the eyes of Allah. Polygamy was permitted up to four wives, though few men could afford more than one; and women, though they lived secluded lives in the women's quarters, often found it easier to inherit and retain control of property in the Islamic world than they did in medieval Europe. The Koran and the large body of Muslim law that grew up in later centuries also offered rules for family life and business relations and a criminal code— a blueprint for Muslim society as a whole. From the visions that came to Muhammad on his mountain flowered a vigorous prescription for life on earth as well as a glimpse of paradise.

The Arab Conquests

It would not have looked like a flowering if you had been a Persian, a Byzantine, a North African, or a southern European over the next hundred years. For from the Prophet's death in 632 dates the first terrifying explosion of *jihad,* the Muslim holy war. The early victories of the Arabs spread the faith of the prophet across northern Africa and western Asia and penetrated the southern margins of Europe itself.

The motive force behind the jihad, like that of the Christian Crusades to come, was certainly in part religious. Death while fighting for Allah, Muslims believed, would be rewarded by an eternity in the gardens of paradise. But, like the later European Crusades, the jihad also had more material motives, including the traditional Bedouin raider's enthusiasm for booty. It also seems likely that overpopulation of their unproductive desert homeland encouraged Arab armies to set out, sword in hand, in search of new living space.

The Expanding Muslim Zone

They found it, with a vengeance. Unified for the first time by their common faith, oasis Arabs and Bedouins of many tribes made a powerful new force in the world. Sticking largely to the hit–and–run tactics of their raiding days, they repeatedly caught their enemies off balance, wore them down, and destroyed them. Another factor in their long string of victories was the weakness of their most formidable foes, the Byzantines and the Persians, exhausted by their own long wars. The result was a wave of conquest of almost unparalleled speed and success. (See map)

Within a dozen years, Arab armies had surged out of their sunbaked peninsula to seize the coastal provinces of Syria and Palestine and to capture Egypt—all three parts of the Byzantine Empire—and had overrun all of Sassanid Persia. As the seventh century wore on, the Arabs pushed westward across Byzantine North Africa to the Atlantic and east as far as the frontiers of India. Early in the following century, they drove on into central Asia and swung around through Asia Minor, the Byzantine heartland, to besiege Constantinople itself in 717. In the West, a force of Arabs and North African Berbers crossed the Strait of Gibraltar in 711, smashed the Visigothic Kingdom in Spain, and moved across the Pyrenees into France in 725.

Thus in the early eighth century, less than a hundred years after the death of Muhammad, Christendom found itself caught in a gigantic vice as Muslim forces pressed in on the Christian zone from both ends of the Mediterranean. With Arab armies roving through western France and camped outside the walls of Constantinople, the very survival of the West seemed questionable.

At this juncture, however, both the Byzantine Empire and the emergent Carolingian dynasty in France rose up and turned back the Arab advance. The Byzantines broke the siege of Constantinople in 718 and pushed the Muslims back to a slowly stabilizing frontier in the middle of Asia Minor. And in 732, Charles Martel defeated the Arabs at Tours. He then began the process, which his grandson Charlemagne completed, of harrying them back to a fixed frontier along the Pyrenees.

By this time, however, the Arabs had built fleets and had begun to raid Europe's southern coasts, establishing bases in Sicily and southern France, looting Rome and even raiding across northern Italy to catch Alpine merchant caravans unaware. The pagan Vikings and the Magyars, who also looted Christian lands in the eighth and ninth centuries, converted to Christianity, settled down, and became part of European society. But the Muslim world, rallying around its own potent faith, was intact and threatening still in the fifteenth century, when the medieval period ended and the modern age began.

The Arab Caliphs

The Arab rulers who succeeded Muhammad founded powerful hereditary dynasties. Like their European counterparts, the Arab Empire that resulted was prone to wars and rebellions throughout its history. Like the Byzantine Empire, however, the world of Islam achieved economic and cultural heights that were the envy of their Western rivals.

The centuries of Arab domination of the Islamic zone date roughly from 600 to 1050, though nominal Arab rule lasted until 1250. During this age of Arab supremacy in the Islamic zone they had forged, the chief Arab political and religious leaders were the *caliphs*, the "successors to the Prophet." The most important of these were the "rightly guided" caliphs (632–661), who directly succeeded the Prophet, and two longer ruling dynasties, the Umayyads (661–750) and the Abbasids (750–1258). Outside the realms of this central line of caliphs, a number of Muslim secession states also emerged during these early centuries.

The four rightly guided caliphs included Omar (r. 634–644), who launched the first great wave of Muslim expansion, and Ali (r. 656–661), whose death precipitated Islam's longest and deepest religious schism. A cousin of the Prophet, Ali won the support of the Shiite faction, who insisted that the leadership of the faithful should be vested only in members of Muhammad's own family. Ali's assassination created a division between the Shiites and the orthodox Sunni, or traditional majority, which has continued down to the present day.

The Umayyads, as we have seen, carried the first great wave of Arab conquest to its climax in the early eighth century, overrunning Spain and besieging Constantinople. They also moved the capital of the caliphate from Mecca to Damascus (today the capital of Syria). The Umayyad caliphs increasingly left religious matters in the hands of Islamic judges and theologians. Their own court at Damascus became both more secular and more sophisticated, tendencies that accelerated under their successors.

The Abbasid dynasty came to power on a tidal wave of opposition to Sunni theology and Arab oppression. Supported by Shiites and outsiders among the conquered, Abu l'Abbas (r. 750–754) seized control of the caliphate in a bloody coup that left almost all the Umayyad princes dead. The new dynasty, however, did little to change the direction of development laid down by its predecessors. Moving the capital once more, this time to the new city of Baghdad (the capital of modern Iraq), the Abbasids built over the next three centuries a metropolis to rival any in the world in size, opulence, and culture.

The most renowned of the Abbasid caliphs were celebrated for their wealth and sophistication. Harun al–Rashid (r. 786–809), known to the West as the caliph of the *Arabian Nights* tales, fought the Byzantines but also imported Greek manuscripts from them and commissioned scholars to translate the wisdom of these ancient pagans for his cosmopolitan elite. The reign of Al–Mamun (r. 813–833), Mamun the Great, was even more splendid. Mamun built libraries, a center for theological study, and an astronomical observatory, and encouraged all the sciences and many arts.

Unity and Disunity in the Muslim World

Throughout the centuries of Arab rule in Islam, the real political power of the caliphs over the far–flung community of Muslim believers was quite limited. As we see in the next section, separate caliphates flourished in Spain, Egypt, and elsewhere during this period. The hegemony of the Arabs even in the Middle Eastern heart of the Muslim zone was challenged in the eleventh century when the Seljuk Turks seized Baghdad. The later Abbasids thus became essentially figureheads in their own capital. The power of Islam, however, continued to grow under first the Seljuk and then the Ottoman Turks, who continued to threaten—and to influence—the West well into the early modern period.

Several forces contributed to the pattern of divisive violence within the Empire. One was the ancient Arab tradition of vendetta and blood feud between tribes and clans. Another was the inevitable tension between Arab conquerors and the peoples they conquered. Some heirs of proud civilizations were made to feel like second–class citizens even when they converted to the Muslim faith. Another, more diffuse source of discord was the growing gap between haves and have–nots as Muslim society grew richer and more urbanized. Most important, however, were the sectarian differences and religious schisms that arose within Islam.

Medieval Islam, like medieval Christendom, was divided by disputes over the meanings of the faith. One strong challenge to the established order came from the *Sufi* movement. The Sufis were mystic brotherhoods who cultivated an emotional form of Islam that appealed to the feelings through music, movement, chants, and ecstatic trances. They found many followers among the have–nots, the masses of the Muslim faithful.

The greatest force for schism in Islam, however, was the *Shiite* movement. Shiite Muslims, while recognizing the Koran as the central source of religious truth, rejected the large body of *Sunna* or traditions concerning the deeds and sayings of the Prophet and his companions that the Sunni majority accepted as authentic. They also rejected the rule of all the caliphs since Ali, insisting that only truly holy men directly descended from the blood of the Prophet should rule the Muslim world. Their heroes were the martyred leaders of the early Shiite movement, and martyrdom became an immensely honored destiny among them. Many believed that Allah had designated a succession of inspired leaders called *imams,* all descended from Ali, who were the true heads of the community of the faithful. The twelfth, or "hidden," imam, who disappeared in the 870s, would one day return to bring justice and righteousness to the world at last.

The forces that made for a larger unity in the Muslim world, however, outweighed the sources of discord. Besides the Muslim faith itself, unifying forces included the arabic language, the Muslim law, and long–distance trade.

Arabic, the common language of the Muslim world, was the language of the Koran and of all services in mosques. Arabic also became the language of business, literature, and government in Muslim countries, and therefore a language many non–Arabs hastened to acquire.

The basic Muslim law, the *sharia,* also served to unite the Muslim lands. This common Islamic law was based on the Koran, on the Sunna or traditions about the Prophet's views, and on the consensus of leading Islamic theologians and jurists. The sharia was administered, not by a formal system of courts, but by learned Muslim judges called *kadis.* The criminal code of the sharia could be harsh, the business law shrewd, and the rules for family relations intrusive by modern Western standards. Though polygamy was accepted and women confined to the private sphere of the harem, women were also allowed control of their own property and had the right to divorce their husbands. Recognized in all Muslim countries, the sharia meant that wherever you went, you knew the rules and the penalties— again, a feature that helped bind all these peoples.

Trade among the Islamic peoples also acted as a connecting link, giving Muslims a sense of belonging to a single international community. With their conquests across the center of the Old World, Muslims became masters of the Eurasian trade routes, including the Great Silk Road from China to Europe. Lateen–rigged Arab dhows also plied the sea routes across the Indian Ocean, from India to the Middle East, whence it was only a short haul overland to the Mediterranean.

This surge of trade and the continuing richness of Near Eastern craftwork under Muslim auspices also had the unintended effect of helping stimulate the commercial revival of Christendom in the High Middle Ages. For the Crusades brought large numbers of Europeans into contact with oriental luxuries and created a demand for them in quantities that even the Byzantine Empire could not supply. And neither Muslim nor Christian merchants hesitated to trade with the enemy between holy wars.

The Arab Golden Age

The cultural evolution of the Arabs was as rapid as their conquests had been. The illiterate Bedouins of Muhammad's day, about 600, would have been totally out of place in the Umayyad capital of Damascus around 700. And they would have been as hopelessly lost in the vast Baghdad of Harun al–Rashid in 800 as they would have been in Constantinople.

What the Arabs had done was conquer the ancient centers of Near Eastern and North African civilization, areas that had also absorbed a Greek cultural legacy in Hellenistic times. And the Arabs learned very rapidly. In some areas of art and thought, their religion limited what they could absorb. More often than not, however, toleration left the way open for profitable contact with Persian art or Greek philosophy. And in the end, it was precisely the Arabic and Islamic traditions of the conquerors that inspired their most remarkable cultural achievements.

As with Byzantium, we must look first at the cities, the treasure troves of Islamic culture. The desert Bedouin who captured cities like Alexandria and Antioch had a distrust of such places and lived instead in camps outside the ancient metropolises. But the caliphs soon not only moved into cities, but began to build their own. Mecca remained the sacred pilgrimage center, but the Umayyad caliphs moved to Damascus, and the Abbasids turned Baghdad into a city as glorious in wealth and color and sheer sprawling immensity as Constantinople itself.

The Baghdad of Harun al–Rashid was a metropolis of palaces and mosques, libraries, scholars, and poets as well as of teeming bazaars, craftshops, and caravansaries. It was said that you could buy anything in the world in the bazaars of Baghdad, and the streets described in Scheherazade's tales do echo with the polyglot life and excitement of the cities of the early caliphates.

There is little left of the monuments of old Baghdad today, and the exquisite craftwork of Persian, Byzantine, or Syrian artisans is in short supply. But the elegant pillars and courtyards, the fountains and flowering gardens of the Alhambra in Spanish Granada at the other end of the Mediterranean still give a sense of what a medieval Muslim palace could be like. And surviving ivory and metalwork, brilliantly illuminated Arabic manuscripts, and exquisite textiles indicate something of the luxury of the life of the Arab princes.

Caliphs also became eager patrons of scholarship and literature, and Arab scholars and poets took almost too enthusiastically to these pursuits. Thus histories of Muslim cities, books of travel through the Muslim world, and lives of Arab heroes and Muslim saints appeared along with the theoretical tracts of theologians and students of the sharia. But the newly civilized Arabs also became intrigued by Greek and even Indian philosophy and science. Greek ideas on medicine set the Muslims thinking, and they soon became the best doctors in western Eurasia. The study of Hellenistic science and mathematics and the far more efficient Indian system of numbers—including that marvelous aid to calculation, the zero—was permitted. And so Arabs became famous astronomers, mathematicians, astrologers, and alchemists—all valued scholarly specialties in the Middle Ages. But pagan philosophers like Plato and Aristotle raised serious problems for Muslim thinkers. The study of Greek philosophy led some Arab commentators to wonder if human reason might not be as good a tool for uncovering truth as divine revelation. It was a point of view as controversial in Islam as it was in the Christian West.

In literature, the newly sophisticated Arabs were soon moving in directions that ranged from frivolity to downright immorality. Stories like those of the *Arabian Nights*, culled from Greek, Asian, and other exotic sources and recounted by professional storytellers, were sometimes risqué and seldom spiritually elevating. Arab poetry moved from the old hero tales of blood feuds to court poetry in praise of good wine and the banquet table, or to thoroughly erotic love poetry.

Once more, the Arabs were going to pass on much of this body of achievement to their Christian rivals. Christian scholars, as hungry for new truth as Western merchants were for trade, crossed the Pyrenees to study Greek philosophy and science and learn the mysteries of "Arabic" numbers at the feet of Muslim scholars in Spain. And Arabic love poetry, serenades, and even the lute filtered insidiously across the mountains to inspire the troubadour love poetry of southern France that we look at in the next chapter.

The Muslim world, however, did not abandon its religious faith in the bright new world of urban sophistication and secular culture. Some of the most distinctive and beautiful Muslim art was actually shaped by Islamic religious requirements. Islam, for instance, prohibited images of divine personages or human beings on religious or other public buildings. While Muslims enjoyed wall paintings or illustrated books in private, mosques and palaces were therefore decorated with beautiful nonrepresentational patterns of arabesque and filigree. Designers often used Arabic script itself as a decorative motif, thus communicating a message from the Koran while patterning a wall, a textile, or a silver plate.

Most important, however, the requirements of Muslim worship created the *mosque*. There were other religious structures, including schools for religious study, tombs of saints, and shrines like the Dome of the Rock in Jerusalem, whose golden dome sheltered the spot from which Muhammad was believed to have ascended into heaven. But mosques were everywhere, with their tall minarets from which the faithful were summoned to prayer, their fountains for ceremonial ablutions, the large courtyard or hall where the believers gathered, and the glowingly decorated *mihrab,* the niche indicating the direction of Mecca, toward which Muslims faced when they knelt to pray. All these were lovingly crafted to create an atmosphere of cool peace out of the blazing sun, a twilight world conducive to religious devotion.

Even a non–Muslim can sense that peace today sitting on a worn carpet in the ninth–century mosque of Ibn Tulun in the medieval section of Cairo. Birds dart among the columns through which one can look across the courtyard at the rare stepped minaret rising against the blue. In such a place, with the sounds of Egyptian traffic muted by the heavy walls, it is easy to feel the presence of the generations of believers who for eleven hundred years have found comfort and peace among these columns.

Summary

From north to south down medieval Europe's eastern frontiers stretched three very different peoples: the Slavs, the Byzantines, and the Arabs. While western Europe slowly emerged from the early Middle Ages, all three of these neighboring peoples both evolved themselves and influenced western Europe's destiny.

Byzantine emperors like Justinian, heirs of Roman emperors, were rigid autocrats ruling a strongly centralized state. The Byzantine Empire itself, with its great port at Constantinople at the narrow juncture of trade between East and West, was one of the most industrially and commercially developed states in the world in this period. And Byzantine society, dominated by its sophisticated urban population, produced both magnificent churches and exquisite craftwork for sale in its vast bazaars.

Kievan Russia, populated largely by Slavic farmers, was ruled by a loose alliance of Varangian, or Viking, princes whose power centered in the Ukrainian city of Kiev. By the tenth century, a flourishing urban culture had developed, both at Kiev and in the northern Russian city of Novgorod. Under Yaroslav the Wise in the eleventh century, Kievan Russia reached a high level of both prosperity and culture.

In the arid lands around the southeast corner of the Mediterranean, finally, the Arab people surged to power with stunning rapidity. Inspired by the teachings of the Prophet Muhammad in the early 600s, these caravan traders and pastoral Bedouins conquered great cities and far–reaching trade routes linking northern Africa, western Asia, and parts of southern Europe. The Arab caliphs who succeeded the Prophet presided for half a dozen centuries over a politically divided, though spiritually unified Muslim zone. This Arab Empire itself produced a dazzling flow of learning and literature, art and architecture, ranging from the tales of the *Arabian Nights* to the domes and minarets of countless mosques across the Muslim world.

Some Key Terms

autocrat   157
boyar   162

Byzantine Empire   153
caesaropapism   157

caliph   171
calling of the princes   163

Notes

1. William Butler Yeats, "Sailing to Byzantium," in Alan Swallow, ed., *The Rinehart Book of Verse* (New York: Rinehart, 1953), 324.
2. Procopius, *The Secret History*, trans. G.A. Williamson (Harmondsworth, England: Penguin, 1966), 78–79.
3. Ibid, 83, 84, 91.
4. Ibid., 83, 127.
5. Edward Gibbon, *The Decline and Fall of the Roman Empire* Vol. 2 (New York: Modern Library, 1932), 491.
6. Ibn Fadlan, in Michael Grant, *Dawn of the Middle Ages* (London: McGraw-Hill, 1981).
7. Samuel Hazzard Cross and Olgerd P. Sherbowitz-Wetzor, trans. and eds., *The Russian Primary Chronicle* (Cambridge, Mass.: Medieval Academy of America, 1953), 83.
8. Ibid., 137.
9. The Koran Interpreted, trans. Arthur J. Arberry (London: Oxford University Press, 1972), 1 (sura 1, verses 1–4).
10. Marshall G.S. Hodgson, *The Venture of Islam: Conscience and History in a World Civilization*, vol. 1 (Chicago: University of Chicago Press, 1974), 161.

Reading List

Armstrong, K. *Muhammad: A Biography of the Prophet.* San Francisco: Harper, 1992. Good introduction. For early views, see U. Rubin, *The Eye of the Beholder: The Life of Muhammad as Viewed by Early Muslims* (Princeton: Darwin, 1995).

Clot, A. *Harun al–Rashid and the World of the Thousand and One Nights.* Translated by J. Howe. London: Saqi, 1989. Bagdad under the great caliph.

Collins, R. *The Arab Conquest of Spain, 710–797.* Cambridge, Mass.: Blackwell, 1989. Integrates narrative history with a critique of source materials. See also A. D. Taha, *The Muslim Conquest and Settlement of North Africa and Spain* (New York: Routledge, 1989) and A. G. Cheyne, *Muslim Spain, Its History and Culture* (Minneapolis: University of Minnesota Press, 1974).

Cormack, R. *Writing in Gold: Byzantine Society and Its Icons.* London: George Philip, 1985. Byzantine religious art as a product of Byzantine society.

Cragg, K., ed. *Readings in the Qur'an.* London: Collins, 1990. Selections usefully grouped under such headings as "faith," "society," and "law"—a good introduction to the words of the Prophet.

Donner, F. M. *The Early Islamic Conquests.* Princeton: Princeton University Press, 1981. Valuable analysis of the Arab conquests, including discussion of weapons, tactics, and motivation.

Fedotov, G. P. *The Russian Religious Mind.* Woodside, N.Y.: Northland, 1976. Focuses on the mind of the Kievan Rus.

Fine, J. V. A. *The Early Medieval Balkans: A Critical Survey from the Sixth to the Late Twelfth Century.* Ann Arbor: University of Michigan, 1983. Overview of five centuries, from the Byzantine supremacy to the rise of independent Balkan states.

Hodgson, M. G. S. *The Venture of Islam: Conscience and History in a World Civilization.* Chicago: University of Chicago Press, 1974. Impressive three–volume exploration of Muslim history, the first volume focusing on the medieval Arab Empire.

Hussey, J. M. *The Orthodox Church in the Byzantine*

Empire. Oxford: Clarendon Press, 1986. Summarizes beliefs and controversies in the framework of Byzantine history. See also M. Angold, *Church and Society in Byzantium Under the Comneni, 1081–1261* (New York: Cambridge University Press, 1995).

Lassner, J. *The Shaping of Abbasid Rule*. Princeton: Princeton University Press, 1980. Governmental development.

Magdalino, P. *The Empire of Manuel I Komnenos, 1143–1180*. New York: Cambridge University Press, 1993. Evokes the vanished world of the Byzantines.

Moorhead, J. *Justinian*. New York: Longman, 1994. Brief introduction to the life and reign. See also R. Browning, *Justinian and Theodora* (London: Weidenfeld and Nicolson, 1971).

Nicol, D. M. *The Byzantine Lady: Ten Portraits*. New York: Cambridge University Press, 1994. Brief profiles of late Byzantine ladies.

Norman, D. *The Arabs and Medieval Europe*. 2d ed. New York: Longman, 1979. Emphasizes conflict over cultural interaction.

Norwich, J. J. *Byzantium: the Decline and Fall*. New York: Knopf, 1996. For the general reader. See also D. M. Nichol, *The Last Centuries of Byzantium 1261–1453* (New York: Cambridge University Press, 1993.

Obolensky, D. *The Byzantine Inheritance of Eastern Europe*. London: Variorum, 1982. The long-term consequences of the vanished Byzantine supremacy on the eastern edge of the Western world.

Rodley, L. *Byzantium Art and Architecture*. New York: Cambridge University Press, 1994. Well-illustrated introduction to the subject.

Vernadsky, G. *Origins of Russia*. Oxford: Clarendon Press, 1959. Older but still stimulating analysis of political, cultural, and other factors that shaped medieval Russia.

Young, M. J. L., J. D. Latham, and R. B. Serjeant, eds. *Religion, Learning, and Science in the Abbasid Period*. London: Cambridge University Press, 1990. Authoritative essays on the civilization of Europe's highly developed neighbor.

8

When the Cathedrals Were White

The High Middle Ages

•The Revival of Trade and Towns   •The Feudal Monarchies
•The Medieval Church Triumphant   •High Medieval Society and Culture
•The Medieval Expansion of Europe

The interior of a Gothic cathedral is like a high–vaulted cave. Stone columns rise into dim arches far above. Candles flicker, altars and crucifixes emerge from the darkness. Shadowy figures move among tombs, massive sarcophagi on which knights and ladies repose, hands folded, stone eyelids closed seven centuries ago. Above the portals and the pillared aisles glows the jewel–like radiance of stained glass.

But look more closely at the sculptured stone scenes from Scripture and saints' lives, turn up the carved wooden seats in the choir, and you may see a very different world. Here is a simple peasant plowing, or an impudent Eve; there a crouching ape, or a devil with his tongue sticking out. Above you, leaves, flowers, and other realistically rendered vegetation cluster around the capitals of columns. If you climb the endless narrow stone stairs to the roof, you can share the view of a modern European city with the gargoyles, fantastic stone monsters that look like nothing ever seen on land or sea.

If you feel a bit confused as you descend the stairs and exit into the twentieth–century sunlight, the milling crowds and honking cars and postcard stands, it is understandable. You have just had a tour of the distinctly unmodern mind of the Middle Ages.

This chapter will survey the economic achievements, the political structure, and the religious beliefs of the High Middle Ages, the three centuries between 1000 and 1300 that marked the climax of medieval history.

During the High Middle Ages, Western civilization not only recovered lost ground but expanded and explored new terrain. The chapter will look at the economic recovery of this period, the reestablishment of strong royal government, and the zenith of medieval Christendom's central institution, the Christian church. It will also trace the expansion of that medieval world, east, west, and southward in the great Crusades launched against a rival faith, Islam. We will begin our exploration of the world of the cathedral builders with merchants making money and monarchs on their thrones. But we will end where we began, probing the subtlety and sheer power of religious faith in the High Middle Ages.

♦The Revival of Trade and Towns♦

We will begin with the economic transition from a world of manor villages to one in which proud cities and prouder kings could emerge once more. The heart of the economic recovery that fueled the High Middle Ages was probably the revival of long–distance trade. Commercial exchange, in turn, stimulated the development of handicraft industry, the rebirth of cities, and a commercial revolution of immense long–range importance. Building on this foundation, royal governments once more began to assert real authority over their lands and peoples.

Agricultural Improvements

The sources of the great economic resurgence of the eleventh, twelfth, and thirteenth centuries included significant changes in both farming technology and peasant life. The tools and techniques of agriculture improved greatly after 1000. Population increased, and as their numbers grew, some peasants began to turn to other ways of making a living as merchants and artisans.

On the technological side, later medieval plows for the first time had wheels, used an iron blade to open the clay soil more efficiently, and had a moldboard to turn the earth over. Horses often replaced oxen after 1000, for they plowed faster and pulled harder. When they were shod with iron horseshoes made in a village smithy, horses could get better traction and were less likely to injure their hooves. When the horse collar over the shoulders with a strap across the chest was introduced in later medieval times, horses could put their full weight into the operation. Where no stream flowed fast enough to turn a water mill effectively, windmills were developed to turn the grindstones that ground the harvested grain into flour.

Employing these new tools, high medieval peasants improved their own lives. By clearing wooded land, draining swamps, and bringing pasture under the plow, they increased the acreage of arable land in use and the resulting grain production. In these ways, a hard–working peasant might produce a large enough surplus to purchase his freedom from serfdom, even to make him a man of means in his little village.

The status of the peasantry as a whole began to change too. In western Europe, at least, serfdom itself was largely phased out by the end of the High Middle Ages. Lords commuted the traditional labor obligations of their peasants to rent payments instead, using the rent to pay for the luxuries they were beginning to covet. In so doing, they converted serfs bound to the land into tenants and hired laborers on a large scale.

The fundamental place of the peasantry, subservient to the landed aristocracy and providing the agricultural labor on which the rest of society depended, remained unchanged, as it did well into modern times. Nevertheless, free peasants did often become more vigorous and more productive. And some of them left the land entirely to follow other lines of work, including commerce and handicraft industry.

The Resurgence of Trade

The evolution of medieval commerce from the isolated peddler with his pack to commercial caravans, crowded fairs, and merchant vessels under sail is well illustrated in the life of a

962	*Otto the Great founds Holy Roman Empire*
987–996	*Hugh Capet founds Capetian dynasty of France*
1000–1300	*Revival of trade and towns*
1066	*Battle of Hastings—William the Conqueror establishes Norman rule in England*
1077	*Emperor Henry IV submits to Pope Gregory VII at Canossa*
1180–1223	*Philip II Augustus builds power of French monarchy*
1215	*King John signs Magna Carta, recognizing rights of subjects in England*
1212–1250	*Frederick II accepts autonomy of German princes*
1226–1270	*St. Louis IX, king of France*

medieval saint whose early years were devoted to worldly pursuits. According to the *Life of St. Godric*, this humble peasant lad "chose not to follow the life of a husbandman [farmer]" but turned instead to "the merchant's trade." Godric thus became one of many who

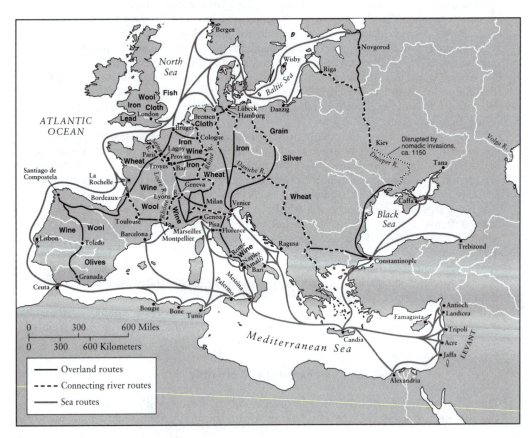

Medieval Cities and Trade Routes

began to follow the chapman's [peddler's] way of life, first learning to gain in small bargains and things of insignificant price; and thence, while yet a youth . . . to buy and sell and gain from things of greater expense.[1]

With new associates, organized for mutual protection into a company of merchants, he traveled "through towns and boroughs, fortresses and cities, to fairs and to all the various booths of the marketplace, in pursuit of his public chaffer [trade]." He even bought a ship and embarked upon still wider commerce, as so many merchants did in later medieval and modern times.

The sea lanes of the Mediterranean had been the center of Roman commerce, and some of this maritime trade had survived the fall of the Roman Empire in the West. Most important, the Italian port of Venice at the head of the Adriatic Sea had maintained a "special relationship" with Constantinople throughout the early Middle Ages, importing at least a thin stream of luxury goods for churchmen and aristocrats in the days of Ostrogothic, Lombard, and Frankish control of northern Italy. As Viking and Arab depredations decreased and population and production grew once more, this thin stream swelled into a broad current of commercial exchange.

The chief artery of European commerce in the High Middle Ages flowed north and south, from Italian ports like Venice, Naples, and Genoa up the Rhone River into France or across the Alps and down the flourishing Rhine valley to the Low Countries (the Netherlands and Belgium today). From the Low Countries, goods passed by sea to Britain, Scandinavia, and the north German towns on the Baltic. At the southern end of this commercial axis, trade also expanded, from the original Venetian connection to other ports around the Italian peninsula and beyond to southern France and Spain. Other routes developed by sea around the west coast of Europe and by land or river transport across France, German–speaking central Europe, and Slavic eastern Europe.

The goods that passed over these increasingly well–traveled routes included commodities, such as grain, timber, and furs from the Baltic, raw wool from England, and grain and wine from southern Europe. Among the most popular European manufactured goods were woolen textiles, woven in the Netherlands and then finished in the Italian cities. From Asia, came such luxury items as spices and precious stones; illuminated manuscripts, carved ivories, and goldsmith work; and silks, linens, and cotton cloth, often brocaded or embroidered.

Godric and his kind built a world for themselves separate from the manor village or the feudal castle. Theirs was the world of the open sea and the open road. But it was also a world anchored in the immensely dynamic, solidly bourgeois medieval city.

The Growth of Cities

Earlier twentieth–century historians linked the rebirth of city life directly to the revival of trade in the High Middle Ages. As these scholars saw it, the original merchant companies, after a summer spent selling their goods at local fairs and markets, settled for the winter under the walls of a castle or a bishop's palace to wait until the roads became passable again in the spring. These merchant settlements grew, attracted more free population, built permanent shops and defensive walls, and became the towns and cities of the High Middle Ages.

Many towns thus grew up largely as the result of long–distance trade. River ports like Cologne, Frankfurt, and other Rhineland cities, as well as Novgorod and Kiev on the Dnieper route in Russia flourished on these key commercial routes. Above all, seaport cities like Venice and Naples in Italy, Marseilles in southern France, Barcelona in Spain, Bruges in the Low Countries, and Lübeck and Danzig on the Baltic grew with the golden touch of trade.

This emphasis on trade led historians to see this urban rebirth occurring in opposition to the older medieval agricultural world of feudalism and manorialism, lords and peasant villages. More recent scholarship, however, has challenged this latter view. We now have evidence that both local barons and feudal monarchs fostered trade and founded protected markets around which towns might grow. Many historians also point out that it took a prosperous countryside to provide food, customers, and excess population for a growing city.

Another significant force that pushed medieval people out of the countryside was the desire of peasants to escape the servile life of the manor. Such discontented elements believed that "city air makes free." A peasant who lived in a city for a year and a day earned freedom from serfdom. In addition, cities provided the opportunity to rise by one's own efforts unfettered by a previous condition of servitude.

The dominant organizations in most medieval cities were the *merchant guilds*, originally the companies of traveling traders who had often founded the city in the first place. As the wealthiest men in town and the ones who dominated the marketplace, these merchant guildsmen were the recognized urban power elite. In time, however, medieval artisans also organized guilds to manage their affairs. These *craft guilds* were organizations of handicraft manufacturers run by the guild masters, skilled artisans who owned their own workshops. The masters employed workers called journeymen to help them and took on apprentices as trainees, and these people were also members of the guild. Journeymen could aspire to become guild masters themselves if they could produce a piece of work that would satisfy the guild as to their skill and if they could accumulate sufficient capital to open their own shops. Apprentices signed on for a term of years—typically seven—during which time they were given bed, board, and training in return for their labor.

Guilds performed a number of important functions in medieval cities besides producing needed goods. They kept up the quality of manufactures by certifying only artisans who had proved their skill to practice in the city. They controlled competition by allowing no one who was not a certified member of the guilds to open a shop. They often set wages and prices and regulated their own marketplaces. Guilds also provided a number of social services for members and their families, including basic education for children, funeral expenses for members, and support for widows and orphans. And they played an important part in the religious and community life of the town, participating in church festivals and giving banquets for their own members. Guilds were thus, in many ways, central to the economic and social life of the medieval city.

Townspeople secured the right to shape their own law and government independent of the feudal system only after sometimes bitter struggles with the traditional local authorities. If the town had grown up around a bishop's palace, citizens might rally to the cause of a religious reformer to shake the bishop's power. If a feudal baron was the local magnate, townsmen might make common cause with a distant monarch who was trying to impose his authority on the nobles from above. The towns provided financial revenues and experienced administrators—often lawyers skilled in manipulating the new laws—for the royal government. In return, monarchs conferred royal charters guaranteeing the independence of medieval cities.

On the basis of such constitutional guarantees, medieval cities organized governments typically composed of city councils or boards of aldermen and of magistrates, who served as both judges and administrators. They passed their own laws, including stern criminal codes

A French artisan family at work. The man is planing a piece of wood, the woman drawing out thread from her distaff preparatory to spinning it. Even the child seems to be cleaning up below. Throughout most of history, the family itself was the primary economic unit. (Ecole Nationale Superieure Des Beaux-Arts.)

and detailed codes of business law. They taxed themselves to keep the city walls in repair and to build almshouses for the poor, hospitals for the sick, and a guildhall for the town's leading citizens.

These urban centers of handicraft production and commercial exchange, however, nurtured two very different attitudes toward society, each with important long–range consequences. The social ethic of the craft guild reflected the general medieval emphasis on sociability, group responsibility, and corporate identity, the tendency of medieval people to see the individual as primarily a member of a larger group or collective whole. The town government and many of its laws, however, dominated by an *urban patriciate,* or elite, of leading merchants, tended to emphasize individual rights and liberties, the foundations of a more competitive, individualistic society to come.

The ideals of the craft guilds included "social solidarity, . . . brotherhood, friendship, and mutual aid."[2] From this sense of group solidarity sprang the guilds' protectionist opposition to outside competition, and indeed to anyone among themselves getting more than his "just share" of the town's business. From the general communitarian orientation of the guilds came, not only their own social services for members, but also the urban measures just mentioned, a "volume of social legislation" that one historian sees as "inviting comparison with modern welfare socialism."[3]

Medieval cities were by no means democratic societies. They often called themselves "republics," but the term did not connote popular sovereignty. Since only property owners, guild masters, or members of the town corporation could vote or hold office in a medieval town, cities were actually oligarchies run by the established business and professional elites. Still, cities were less rigidly hierarchical than most medieval institutions. And in centuries to come, commercially developed countries like England and the Netherlands were among the first to develop more liberal institutions at the national level.

The Commercial Revolution

Medieval cities also produced the *commercial revolution,* a collection of business practices and policies that became the foundation of modern capitalism in the West. A fundamental step toward a modern capitalist economy was the increasingly widespread use of money once more. From the High Middle Ages on, coins were in common use again in the West. Kings, nobles, and others had the right to mint their own coins, which found their way into the humblest manor villages. The Florentine gold florin, accepted everywhere for several centuries, was a sort of international standard currency in the later Middle Ages. This return to a money economy added immensely to the flexibility and sophistication of business life.

A related development was the gradual acceptance of the ancient practice of lending money at interest. In the Middle Ages, the Christian church officially condemned most moneylending for a profit as immoral "usury." Merchants, however, found ways of getting around this prohibition. One method was to claim that substantial risk was involved, as it frequently was, if the money was invested in trade over bandit–infested roads or stormy seas, and then to charge extra as a compensation for the risk factor. Another common expedient was to arrange repayment in another country and another currency, profiting both from the fee for money–changing and from the differences in rates of currency exchange.

Other technical advances that made business more efficient included letters of credit, bills of exchange, and double-entry bookkeeping. When a business involved a number of stages, as was the case with the manufacture of woolen cloth, a merchant might hesitate to carry bags of coins about with him, preferring to establish a credit relationship with the shearers, spinners, weavers, dyers, and many others through whose hands the wool passed. Similarly, a merchant trading in a distant country might take a bill of exchange from his own banker to a bank in the city to which he was traveling, rather than risk carrying coins on the dangerous roads.

A major step forward, finally, was the appearance of various forms of what was later called the *joint-stock company.* Such a company pooled the capital of a number of merchants for great commercial ventures that no one of them could finance alone Originally, such companies were established only by members of a single family or for a single enterprise. Medieval joint–stock companies, however, were the precursors of early modern trading combines, like the European East India Companies, and of the huge corporations of our own day.

✦The Feudal Monarchies✦

The story of the political revival of the High Middle Ages is the history of how kings, emperors, and other independent rulers gradually imposed political order on substantial portions of Europe after the year 1000. They could not know it, but these medieval monarchs were building the European nation–states of modern times. This section will outline the rise of relatively strong royal governments in two of Europe's most powerful states, France and England—and its failure to emerge in a third, the badly divided German states. In each case, we will look at the efforts of rulers both to broaden their territorial holdings and to build administrative systems in spite of the opposition of their rivals for power, the church and the nobles.

The Emergence of Feudal Monarchy

Early medieval kings, as we have seen, were typically feeble; real power was held at the local level, by counts and dukes, bishops and abbots, and later by the wealthy cities. To establish their authority, ambitious monarchs of the High Middle Ages established the principle of hereditary succession by *primogeniture*, meaning from father to first–born son. Kings also justified their expanding lands and powers by insisting on *divine sanction* for their authority. Crowned by archbishops or even popes, anointed with holy oil in cathedrals while hymns rose to the vaulting overhead, medieval monarchs saw themselves as God's viceroys in this world. Of more future significance, they tapped the riches and administrative know–how of the church and the emerging cities, and increasingly depended on salaried bureaucrats and hired mercenary soldiers to impose the royal will on the nation.

The Capetians: Philip Augustus, St. Louis, and Royal Power in France

The Capetian dynasty of France, which ruled for well over three centuries, from 987 to 1328, provides one of the best illustrations of nation building by a feudal monarchy. Hugh Capet, the founder of the dynasty, was chosen king by the powerful feudal nobility in 987. The early Capetian kings, however, really governed only a small royal domain around the city of Paris, leaving the surrounding territories in the hands of the dukes and counts who were nominally their vassals. Over the next three centuries, the Capetians both expanded their domains and began to exert some real authority over both the royal domain and the lands held by their vassals.

A basic step was the establishment of the house of Capet's hereditary right to the throne. The Capetians saw to it that their eldest sons were both elected by the barons and crowned while their fathers still lived and reigned, thus establishing the right of succession by primogeniture. By conferring lands on French bishops, French kings also got an oath of loyalty in return—and the services of such able churchmen as the twelfth–century Abbot Suger of St. Denis as royal ministers of state.

Most important, the Capetian kings pieced together the beginnings of a real royal bureaucracy. Frequently drawn from the towns and including many lawyers, this medieval civil service collected royal revenues, administered the king's justice, and kept him informed on what was happening in the provinces far from the royal court. The earlier Capetians thus laid the groundwork for the achievements of two of France's greatest kings: Philip II Augustus and Louis IX—St. Louis.

Philip II (r. 1180–1223) further strengthened the royal bureaucracy. Seeing the royal judges and tax gatherers in the provinces, called *prévôts,* becoming local landowners themselves rather than dependable royal servants, the king dispatched a new type of enforcer to the provinces. These officials, called *baillis* in northern France, *sénéchals* in the south, supervised the work of the *prévôts.* Because *baillis* and *sénéchals* were paid salaries, they tended to remain firmly attached to the interests of their royal master.

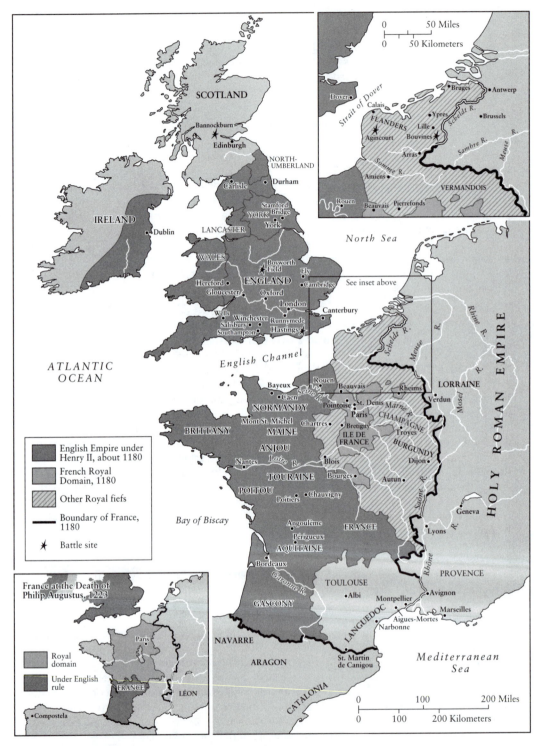

Map inset (top right)

0   50 Miles
0   50 Kilometers

Strait of Dover

Dover
Calais
Bruges • Antwerp
Ypres • • Brussels
Lille
FLANDERS
Agincourt • Bouvines ✦
Arras •
Scheldt R.
Sambre R. *Meuse R.*
Somme R.
Amiens •
VERMANDOIS
Rouen •
Beauvais • Pierrefonds

Main map

SCOTLAND
Bannockburn ✦
Edinburgh •

NORTH-UMBERLAND

IRELAND
Dublin •

Carlisle •
Durham •

Stamford Bridge
YORK
York •

LANCASTER

WALES
Bosworth Field ✦
Ely •
Hereford •
ENGLAND
Cambridge •
Gloucester •
Oxford •
London •
Wells •
Winchester •
Salisbury •
Runnymede •
Canterbury •
Southampton •
Hastings ✦

North Sea

See inset above

ATLANTIC OCEAN

English Channel

Bayeux •
Rouen •
Beauvais •
Rheims •
LORRAINE
Caen •
Seine R.
Pointoise •
St. Denis •
Verdun •
NORMANDY
Paris •
Marne R.
Moselle R.
Mont St. Michel •
Chartres •
CHAMPAGNE
BRITTANY
MAINE
ILE DE FRANCE
Bretigny •
Troyes •
ANJOU
BURGUNDY
Nantes •
Loire R.
Blois •
TOURAINE
Bourges •
Dijon •
POITOU
Poitiers •
Chauvigny •
Autun •
Geneva •
FRANCE
Bay of Biscay
Angouleme •
Périgueux •
Lyons •
AQUITAINE
Rhône R.
Garonne R.
Bordeaux •
PROVENCE
TOULOUSE
Avignon •
GASCONY
Albi •
Montpellier •
Marseilles •
Aigues-Mortes
NAVARRE
LANGUEDOC
Narbonne •
ARAGON
St. Martin de Canigou
Mediterranean Sea
CATALONIA

HOLY ROMAN EMPIRE
Rhine R.
Meuse R.
Scheldt R.
Saône R.
Rhône R.

Legend

■ English Empire under Henry II, about 1180
■ French Royal Domain, 1180
▨ Other Royal fiefs
— Boundary of France, 1180
✦ Battle site

Inset (bottom left)

France at the Death of Philip Augustus, 1223

■ Royal domain
■ Under English rule

Paris •
FRANCE
LÉON
Compostela •

0   100   200 Miles
0   100   200 Kilometers

France and England, Eleventh–Thirteenth Centuries

Philip's great territorial concern was with the English domination of the western half of France. He weakened the English by supporting the English King Henry II's rebellious sons, Richard the Lion–Hearted and John, against their father. When John inherited the English throne in 1199, Philip moved to confiscate John's French possessions, including Normandy, Anjou, and Brittany. At the Battle of Bouvines in 1214, Philip Augustus defeated John and his allies and made good his claim to the northern half of England's possessions in France.

The most admired of all the Capetian kings, however, was Philip Augustus's grandson, Louis IX (r. 1226–1270). Louis became famous for keeping the peace and meting out equal justice to rich and poor. He surrounded himself with holy friars, personally led two Crusades against the Muslims of northern Africa, and was canonized as a saint shortly after his death. For all his Christian piety, however, Louis IX was a strong defender of royal authority. He added a new layer to the bureaucracy he inherited from Philip Augustus—officials called *enquêteurs* who checked up on the work of all lower officials. He also issued royal ordinances that were valid throughout the country. Defying the traditional view that kings were only "first among equals" when surrounded by their feudal vassals, he declared that "there is only one king in France."[4]

From William the Conqueror to the First Parliament in England

Another of the major feudal monarchies evolved in the island kingdom of England. In this relatively small and self–contained area, William of Normandy, who conquered the country in 1066, and his successors were able to construct a model feudal monarchy. At the same time, however, other political changes in England laid the foundations for the rise of parliamentary or representative government in modern times.

William the Conqueror, sometimes called William the Bastard in his own day, was the duke of Normandy, a tightly organized feudal state on the French side of the English Channel. He also claimed the throne of England, however, and in 1066 crossed the channel at the head of his knights to make good his claim against his rival, Harold the Saxon. The two armies met on what became one of the most famous of medieval battlefields, a few miles from Hastings.

William depended on his Norman barons, armed with long lances and experienced in massed cavalry charges. According to a famous story that may even be true, the French minstrel Taillefer led the first charge, singing war songs and tossing his sword into the air and catching it again as he rode. William himself galloped into battle with a string of holy relics around his neck. Harold, the last Saxon king of England, died fighting, felled by an arrow through the head. William the Conqueror (r. 1066–1087) had himself crowned King William I of England on Christmas Day of 1066.

As in France, the growth of royal power in England was a complex process. William left the Anglo–Saxon system of shires or counties intact and continued to utilize the traditional sheriffs as local administrators and law enforcers. He replaced the *witenagemot,* the chief Anglo–Saxon council, with its continental equivalent, a *curia regis,* or royal council. From the continent also came the feudal structure of vassals and subvassals in its Norman form, with the monarch himself firmly established at the apex of the feudal pyramid.

As a step toward increasing royal revenues, in 1086 William ordered a national census of population and property, the first such national survey in any European country. This compilation, known as the *Domesday Book,* attempted to list every lord and serf, every acre of arable land, plow, and pigsty the compilers could find. The Domesday Book has been a gold mine of information for historians in later centuries.

Under William I's successors, the royal administration became more specialized. A secretariat charged with foreign correspondence emerged and a treasury department called the Exchequer grew up. Henry II also dispatched itinerant judges, called *justices of eyre* (*eyre* meant "to travel"), to circulate through the shires trying cases. These circuit judges followed the traditional procedure of calling up groups of informed local people to give information about crimes and to indicate who they thought was responsible—the origin of the modern *jury trial*. The judgments offered by these royal judges, furthermore, grew into a body of legal precedent and principle rooted in local practices, yet applicable all over England—the beginnings of the English *Common Law.*

Difficulties with both the church and the nobility, however, slowed the rise of royal power. William I's grandson King Henry II (r. 1154–1189) and Archbishop Thomas Becket (c. 1117–1170) fell out over *benefit of clergy,* the principle of the church's canon law that all clergymen must be tried in church courts rather than royal courts for any offenses. When the archbishop excommunicated those who supported the king, Henry angrily expressed the wish that he could be rid of this defiant priest. Four of Henry's knights took his wish for a command and stabbed Becket to death one night after vespers in his own cathedral at Canterbury. The martyred Thomas Becket, however, won the last round. Public outrage and papal pressure forced the king to abandon his efforts to bring the clergy under English law, and Becket himself was canonized two years after his murder.

Like the leaders of the church, English nobles sought to impose legal limits on royal power. The two most important early steps toward this goal were the Great Charter— *Magna Carta*—of 1215 and the beginnings of the English Parliament in the later 1200s.

In 1215, King John (r. 1199–1216) had already been forced to back down by the powerful Pope Innocent III (r. 1198–1216) in a struggle over the appointment of a new archbishop of Canterbury. He had also been outmaneuvered by Philip Augustus, who took half his lands in France. Seizing on this moment of weakness, his own barons forced John to sign the Magna Carta—an agreement to refrain from exploiting his noble vassals financially and trying them illegally. The Great Charter also required him to recognize the right of the church to choose its own bishops and the right of the towns to their traditional liberties. In modern times, this essentially medieval document would be reinterpreted as protecting the rights of *all* citizens, not just those of the aristocracy and the church.

A similar future significance lay ahead for the English version of the common medieval practice of summoning leaders of the main "estates"—churchmen, nobles, and the wealthier common people—to consult with the monarch, especially when kings wanted to impose taxes on them. In thirteenth-century England, such meetings were often called *parliaments*, meaning "discussions."

The first such gathering to include townsmen and country gentry as well as nobles and bishops was the so-called *Model Parliament* called by Edward I in 1295. This set the pattern for later parliaments in which titled aristocrats and high churchmen met together as the House of Lords, while two knights from each shire and leading citizens from selected cities met in the House of Commons. In modern times, a more democratically elected House of Commons would make Parliament the center of Britain's democratic government.

Imperial Power in Germany: Otto the Great, Frederick Barbarossa, and Frederick II

The *Holy Roman Empire*, the loose collection of German–speaking states that sprawled across central Europe during the High Middle Ages, was one of the great centers of medieval civilization. Yet in the end, the Holy Roman emperors failed to establish their power as other feudal monarchs did.

When the last Carolingian to rule in the eastern part of Charlemagne's empire died in 911, the great German duchies—Saxony, Bavaria, Franconia, Swabia, and Thuringia—emerged as the real centers of power. As in France, the dukes who ruled these territories—originally Carolingian military commanders—elected one of their own as king. They objected, however, when kings tried to impose real royal authority on them. Both these great German magnates and many lesser German nobles, knights, archbishops, and new commercial cities soon acquired a sense of independence that proved very difficult for German emperors to overcome.

In the tenth century, however, Otto I the Great (936–973) moved to strengthen imperial power. He established his own relatives as rulers of the other German duchies and brought the German church under imperial patronage and control, using bishops as imperial administrators. His eleventh–century successors would make use of laymen as royal bureaucrats, *ministeriales,* whose dependence on the crown was absolute.

Otto the Great also developed an aggressive foreign policy. He spread Christianity among the Slavs on the eastern frontiers—the beginning of Germany's traditional *Drang nach Osten* or "drive toward the East" into Slavic lands—and led his armies over the Alps, beginning three centuries of German intervention in the affairs of Italy. Like Charlemagne a century and a half before, Otto went to Rome in 962 to support the pope in a struggle with Italian nobility—and was crowned Holy Roman Emperor by the pope in return. The imperial title gave the German emperors unrivaled prestige in Europe. *Holy* because of their papal sanction, *Roman* in their ambition to revive Roman imperial glory, the emperors would for centuries claim the place at the head of the table when the great powers gathered to determine the fate of Europe.

The German emperors expected the same sort of subservience from the pope that monarchs expected from "their" archbishops and bishops. The emperors also sought to tap the wealth of the northern Italian cities, which were among the richest in Europe. In the eleventh, twelfth, and thirteenth centuries, however, they faced determined opposition from a militant new breed of pope and increasingly independent north Italian cities.

In 1075, Pope Gregory VII (r. 1073–1085), a longtime crusader for both church reform and papal power, officially condemned the widespread practice of *lay investiture*, the granting of authority to churchmen by secular rulers. Henceforth, Gregory declared, only the pope should invest bishops with the symbols of their spiritual authority. Emperor Henry IV (r. 1056–1106) responded by convening his German bishops to reject the papal decree. Pope Gregory struck back by excommunicating Henry, declaring him deposed as emperor, and releasing his subjects from their obligation to obey him. Eager to undermine imperial power still further, the German princes gathered to judge the emperor and asked the pope himself to take the chair. Gregory, a hot–eyed crusader for his cause, accepted and set out for Germany.

Henry IV's response to this challenge was either brilliant or humiliating, depending on your interpretation. He intercepted the pope at Canossa in northern Italy, pleaded for forgiveness, and waited for three days in the snow, clad in sackcloth and humility, until

Medieval Germany and Italy, ca. 1375

Gregory relented and lifted the ban of the church. The vivid image of the emperor submitting to the pope at Canossa became a symbol of the power of the medieval papacy. In fact, however, Henry had effectively deprived the pope of his most powerful weapon by getting the excommunication lifted. When the frustrated German magnates rebelled, he suppressed the revolt. He then turned on Pope Gregory and drove him into exile, where one of the most famous of all popes died a defeated and embittered man.

The German nobility, however, remained unrepentant, and in the twelfth and thirteenth centuries, they challenged two of the greatest of all Holy Roman emperors with considerably more success: Frederick I Barbarossa and Frederick II.

Frederick I (r. 1152–1190), popularly known as Barbarossa, meaning "Redbeard," faced growing resistance from the north Italian cities, noble opposition at home, and a renewed tendency toward *particularism,* or strongly felt regional loyalties, in Germany. Frederick Barbarossa met these challenges over his forty–year reign by laboring to restore the imperial image, to reorganize Germany along the lines of a classic twelfth–century feudal monarchy, and to establish imperial dominion over the wealth of northern Italy once and for all.

Barbarossa strengthened his image as a leader by his many military campaigns, including aggressive drives into Slavic eastern Europe. He reconstructed the imperial administration and established an official feudal hierarchy for his vassals, exalting the higher ranking German magnates at the expense of the lesser nobility. He failed, however, in Italy, where the popes continued to resist imperial control and the *Lombard League,* an alliance of north Italian cities, administered a crushing defeat to imperial forces at Legnano in 1176.

Frederick Barbarossa's successor, Frederick II (r. 1212–1250), nicknamed *Stupor Mundi,* "the Wonder of the World," took up the struggle with the popes one last time— and lost most of his power in Germany as a result.

Literate in six languages, a patron of poets and scholars, and a Christian ruler who even tolerated Muslims, Frederick II was a rare medieval monarch indeed. The child of a diplomatic marriage, Frederick was born and bred in Sicily and constructed a tightly organized nation–state in southern Italy. He concentrated all his energies on trying to win control of the rich northern Italian cities, came into repeated conflict with the Roman popes, and paid little attention to his German possessions.

To prevent trouble in the north, Frederick granted German princes, nobles, bishops, and abbots almost total freedom from imperial control. They were allowed to mint their own coins, operate their own courts, collect customs duties at their frontiers, and run their own states without imperial interference. From the mid–thirteenth century onward, the Holy Roman Empire remained little more than a loose confederation of separate German states. There would be no truly unified German nation until modern times.

◆ The Medieval Church Triumphant ◆

As we have seen already, the world the kings and merchants made in the eleventh, twelfth, and thirteenth centuries was one in which religious organizations and church leaders played a central role. Popes defied kings, bishops served them, and religious issues like "benefit of clergy" and "lay investiture" could divide governments and nations. For the leaders of the high medieval church did not believe in separation of church and state, in religious toleration, in religion without dogma or heaven without hell. They thrust their way into every sphere of life, challenging kings and tending lepers, reforming religion and inventing the Inquisition.

The source of this renewal of papal power lay in the great campaign for church reform with which the High Middle Ages began. Facing a deeply rooted crisis of corruption within the church, the eleventh–century pope Gregory VII and his successors built a papal structure of power capable of challenging the might of kings. By the time of Innocent III in the thirteenth century, the papacy could claim, with some justification, to be the greatest power in Europe.

Corruption, Heresy, Friars, and Inquisitors

By 1000, worldliness and corruption had reached as high as the see of St. Peter itself. Some popes became more deeply involved in the secular affairs of the territories they ruled in central Italy, known as the Papal States, than in the spiritual affairs of Christendom. Powerful Italian noble families feuded for control of the papacy, and a rebellion in the streets of Rome could decide who the next pope would be.

Reform was clearly needed at all levels. The ecclesiastical administration sometimes seemed more secular than religious in the High Middle Ages. Lawyers and accountants proliferated in the church, men often more at home with law or numbers than with theology. Some archbishops, bishops, and other church leaders, appointed by kings or emperors, focused their energies on affairs of state or were tempted into worldly living by their close ties with the secular establishment. Even monasteries and convents too often became sunk in soft living and vice. Some were filled with the worldly children of aristocratic families, younger sons who would not inherit land, or daughters without doweries. Other religious houses, renowned for their piety, attracted huge gifts—which in turn tempted the monks and nuns to a more luxurious style of life.

In the twelfth and thirteenth centuries, some Christians began to do something about the challenge of church corruption. Some of those who demanded change were condemned as heretics; others were canonized as saints.

The most challenging heresy, or refusal to accept orthodox Christian views, was that of the Cathars ("purified ones" in Greek). Better known as *Albigensians* from the city of Albi, a major center of Albigensian activities in southern France, these dissenters flourished in the twelfth and early thirteenth centuries. The Albigensians were dualists, seeing the world as a battleground between God and Satan, a doctrine that went back to Persian Zoroastrianism, with its struggle between light and darkness. Satan, Albigensians believed, had created and ruled the material world. Christ was pure spirit, and so had never been "made flesh" at all, nor really crucified. The purified Cathar elite, called *perfecti,* who did not eat meat or marry, found many followers in the easygoing cities of southern France and the worldly commercial centers of northern Italy.

But revulsion against worldly corruption inspired more orthodox Christians to action too. This new piety produced both new monastic orders and an entirely new approach to the religious life—the wandering friars.

One new beginning came at Citeaux in Burgundy, where the *Cistercian order* was founded in 1098. The Cistercian goal was to escape from worldly temptations by rejecting the luxurious style of life of other orders. The Cistercians were also very disciplined workers who made their monastery lands very productive—and thus brought themselves once more within reach of temptation.

A more daring new approach to reform was the foundation of the Franciscan and Dominican orders of friars. Franciscans and Dominicans lived like monks, but in the world, not out of it. Rather than seeking escape from temptation in isolated monasteries, they lived and worked among the suffering, sinning masses of humanity, protected from contamination only by the armor of their faith.

Obeying a visionary call to "repair God's church," St. Francis of Assisi (c. 1181–1226) preached absolute poverty, service to one's fellow beings, and joyous love of God. He also expressed a childlike love of the natural world, manifested in a sermon to the birds or in a hymn to the sun. Begging his way through Italy, Francis won thousands of converts to the *Franciscan order*, which was officially recognized by Pope Innocent III around 1210.

Like Francis—whom he much admired—St. Dominic (1171–1221) founded a mendicant, or begging, order. *Dominicans,* however, took as their particular mission the preaching of true doctrine to combat heresy and save souls from hell. To achieve this mission, Dominic's followers became deep students of theology, including in the next century such brilliant theologians as Thomas Aquinas. Dominicans also became leading figures in the *Inquisition,* the church's agency for the suppression of unorthodox religious beliefs.

The Holy Office of the Inquisition was itself a product of these times. To deal with the spread of heresy, seen as threatening the salvation of both the heretic and all who might be exposed to heretical doctrine, Pope Gregory IX founded the Holy Office in 1233. The ecclesiastical judges of the Inquisition worked with local bishops to ferret out spiritual contagion.

The Inquisition became notorious in later centuries for its persecution of heretics, Jews, witches, and others whose views differed from those of the church. The inquisitors' methods included unspecified accusations, secret testimony from unidentified witnesses, and torture to secure confessions. Among the punishments inflicted were fines, imprisonment, and, for lapsed heretics (those who repented but later returned to their heretical views), public execution by burning at the stake.

Church Reform and Papal Power:
From Gregory VII to Innocent III

The swelling demand for religious renewal, reflected at the grass roots by heretics as well as by monks and friars, also found ardent champions in Rome. The transformation of the papacy began with the reform movement led by Pope Gregory VII and climaxed in the pontificate of the most powerful of medieval popes, Innocent III.

The revival emerged under Pope Leo IX (r. 1049–1054). Leo's particular targets were those ancient vices, simony and clerical marriage—the selling of church offices and the sexual indulgence of priests. Leo gathered like–minded spirits, including monks, at Rome and gave them important positions in the church. His spirit and determination survived his time in this band of dedicated reformers, sometimes called the Hildebrandine party after its leader, Hildebrand—the future Gregory VII.

The Hildebrandine party turned its attention particularly to strengthening the power of the papacy. In 1059, they established the right of the College of Cardinals, a body of leading churchmen, to elect future popes. This reform advanced the goal of an independent papacy, free of Italian noble or German imperial control.

This preoccupation with papal power also inspired the formal break with the Eastern Orthodox church in 1054. Certain of the rightness of their own theological views,

Chronology 8.2: The Age of Faith

1073–1085	*Pope Gregory VII champions church reform and papal power*
1095–1099	*First Crusade captures Jerusalem*
1089	*Cistercian order of monks founded*
1098–1179	*Hildegard of Bingen*
1130–1204	*Maimonides*
1150	*University of Paris founded*
1163–1235	*Notre Dame cathedral built in Paris*
1210	*Francis of Assisi founds Franciscan order of friars*
1198–1216	*Pope Innocent III carries power of Catholic church to its height*
1225–1274	*Thomas Aquinas*

reforming churchmen excommunicated the Greek patriarch Michael Cerularius (c. 1000–1059), the head of the Greek Orthodox half of Christendom. The patriarch responded by excommunicating the Roman pope in his turn, completing the great divide in medieval Christendom.

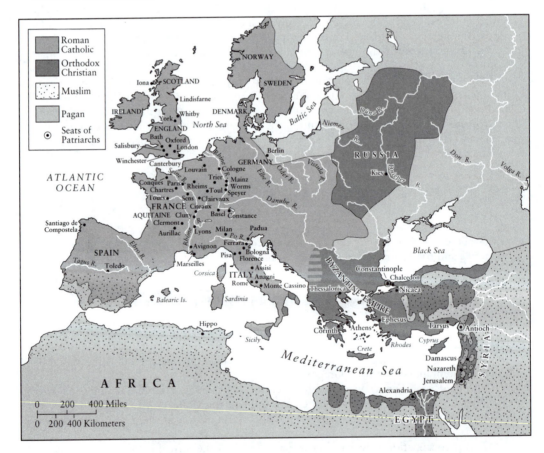

Christianity and Its Neighbors in the Western World

In the last quarter of the eleventh century, the new zeal for reform brought Hildebrand himself to the papal throne as Gregory VII (r. 1073–1085). Hot tempered, unbending, and absolutely convinced of the righteousness of his own cause, Gregory was "eaten up with . . . one burning passion: to restore the glory of the Apostles" Peter and Paul, both buried at Rome—to establish both the moral regeneration and the power of the popes.[5] The result was the *Gregorian reform.*

As we saw in earlier sections, Gregory's demand for an end to lay investiture seemed a direct challenge to the secular monarchs' sovereign power to run their own states. To get his way with Emperor Henry IV, Gregory made use of powerful but purely spiritual weapons: excommunication, expelling the emperor from the church, and interdict, forbidding the performance of any church services anywhere in Henry's realms. Both were powerful because medieval Christians believed that the popes, as vicars of St. Peter, held the keys to salvation, and because the German princes could use this condemnation of the emperor as a pious excuse to rebel against him.

In the end, Henry IV had the troops, and he used them to drive Pope Gregory into exile in southern Italy where he died, lamenting the earthly fate of those who fight for righteousness. Still, the spiritual weapons of papal power had brought an emperor to his knees at Canossa, however temporarily. And the power of the papacy had not yet reached its height.

The drive for papal power to reform both church and society continued. In 1095, as we will see, Pope Urban II preached the First Crusade, a great military campaign to liberate the Holy Land from Muslim rule, which provided a release for still–building religious passions and rekindled popular support for the reformed papacy. A more practical twelfth–century development that greatly strengthened the papacy was the codification and widespread application of the church's *canon law.* Inspired by the recent establishment of law schools like that at Bologna which taught Justinian's code of Roman law, the architects of church law set out to codify Christian doctrines that had accumulated over centuries. This meant collecting, comparing, and validating scriptural injunctions, decisions of church councils, papal decrees, and statements of the fathers of the church and other respected Christian thinkers. Where there were apparent differences of opinion, canonists declared that whatever view had earned papal approbation was probably the correct one.

Marshaling Christian armies and codifying Christian law, the papacy built its power. Then at the very end of the twelfth century came the most powerful of all medieval popes, Innocent III.

A thirty-seven-year-old canon lawyer, unanimously elected by the cardinals of the church, Innocent III (r. 1198–1216) had an exalted sense of the papacy's place in Christendom. He described his position as that of "the vicar of Jesus Christ, successor of Peter . . . set between God and man, lower than God, but higher than man, who judges all and is judged by no one."[6] During his eighteen years on the throne of St. Peter, he enacted reforms, fought heresy, and challenged the greatest princes in Europe.

Innocent's major contribution to church reform was the *Fourth Lateran Council* (1215), a gathering of leading churchmen as important as the fourth–century Council of Nicaea. The Fourth Lateran Council produced the definitive list of seven sacraments, the sacred rites of the church, to be discussed below. The council also offered an official explanation of the most important of the sacraments: the Mass. The Mass or communion service, was defined as a mystical transformation of the communion wafer and wine into the spiritual body and blood of Christ. The thrust of all the council's decisions was to elevate the clergy, who alone could perform these sacred rites.

Innocent III favored preaching and example to bring heretics back into the fold, and to this end he officially recognized the Franciscan and Dominican orders of friars. In 1208, however, following the murder of a papal legate, Innocent proclaimed a holy war against the Albigensians that effectively—and bloodily—suppressed these southern French heretics. Innocent also authorized the Fourth Crusade in 1204, and when the crusaders seized and plundered Greek Orthodox Constantinople instead of attacking the Muslim Turks, he saw in the incident God's hand smiting the Orthodox heretics.

So powerful was Innocent III that the papacy he commanded is sometimes called a "papal monarchy," as powerful as any secular government. He manipulated Holy Roman emperors, including the brilliant Frederick II. He compelled the hapless King John to accept a papal choice for archbishop of Canterbury. He also continued the vigorous moral crusades begun in the days of the Gregorian Reform against simony, clerical marriage, and other forms of conduct unbefitting the church as he envisioned it.

Women in the High Medieval Church

Women played a variety of roles in the renovated church. This came about in spite of the fact that the ecclesiastical developments of the High Middle Ages sometimes seemed to undermine women's place in the church. The high medieval church took control of local church affairs out of the hands of landed magnates—some of whom were women—and emphasized the role of the ordained priest, a role closed entirely to women. Reformers also closed down double monasteries, which included women as well as men, and put convents under the supervision of male church officials. The rise of cathedral schools and universities, by shifting the center of medieval learning from monasteries and convents to all–male episcopal establishments, closed the doors of scholarship to many women.

But there were orders of nuns still—five hundred convents in Germany alone. Many of these nunneries followed the rigid convent rule originally devised by Hildegard of Bingen (1098–1179), a widely admired writer, mystic, and adviser to popes. In time, Franciscan and Dominican religious houses for women emerged. There were also independent groups of dedicated laywomen called Beguines who labored to help the poor in Rhineland cities.

Other women, denied scope for their talents in the Catholic church, were swept up in heretical movements. The Albigensians of southern France included a female as well as a male elite, and some women were leaders of the movement. In the desperate defense of Toulouse against the anti–Albigensian forces, women and young girls fought beside the men. The leader of the attacking "crusaders," Simon de Montfort (c. 1165–1218), was killed by women.

High Medieval Society and Culture

Infused with this sort of religious passion, and with such other central medieval ideas as community and social hierarchy, knightly chivalry and courtly love, life in the High Middle Ages was very different from anything known in the modern West. A visit to a high medieval village or to one of the new cities, an encounter with a knight and his lady or a guild master behind his counter on a cobbled medieval street would surely emphasize the difference a few centuries can make. Much as we might admire the cultural achievements of the Age of Faith—the cathedral architecture, sculpture and luminous stained glass, the subtlety of scholastic thought, and the music of troubadour poetry—we would find their world a very strange place indeed.

This section will begin with a survey of the splendid cultural achievements of the Age of Faith. It will then look at the lives of medieval people, from the knightly elite to the peasants and townspeople who did the world's work, including the most significant minority, the Jews of medieval Europe.

The Religious Culture of the Age of Faith

For medieval people, the center of the Christian religion remained salvation through Christ. As they saw it, Adam and Eve had sinned by defying God's commandment in the Garden of Eden, and all their descendants had inherited this primal sinfulness. But Christ, by taking the sins of the human race upon his shoulders, had made salvation possible for those who lived Christian lives.

A multitude of saints also loomed large in the medieval mind. The saints were the great martyrs, preachers, and spiritual leaders of the past, from Peter and Paul in Gospel times to Francis of Assisi in their own days. Their relics, the bones of apostles and martyrs, had the power to cure the sick and work miracles, and the roads of Christendom filled with pilgrims every spring, traveling to their shrines. The Virgin Mary, Mother of Christ and Queen of Heaven, was the great intercessor, pleading at the throne of God for suffering sinners here below. Most of the great cathedrals were dedicated to her, and were therefore called *Notre Dame,* churches of Our Lady.

The religious life for most Christians was centered around a series of moments of contact between the material and spiritual worlds, rites of passage called the seven *sacraments.* The seven, formalized by Innocent III's Fourth Lateran Council in 1215, were baptism soon after birth, confirmation as a member of the church in adolescence, marriage for most young adults, ordination for priests, the Mass or communion service, confession of sins and penance, and the last rites for the dying. At each of these important moments in a human life, priestly words and gestures, hymns, holy water, holy oil, or the consecrated wine and wafer inspired a sense of contact with the realm of the spirit.

It is a vivid image of the West in the grip of a great world religion. In recent years, however, study of Inquisition records and medieval sermons has unearthed a surprising amount of pre-Christian folklore and magical practice among medieval Europeans. That pre-Christian folk beliefs survived in larger numbers than was once suspected now seems indisputable. To suggest, however, that Christianity scarcely reached beyond the cities and a priestly elite, as some do, seems to most medieval historians to be going too far in the other direction. To face the myriad material and spiritual problems of life, Christian faith must have seemed essential to most medieval men and women.

Gothic Architecture and Art

The most awesome expressions of the faith of medieval Christendom were the great *cathedral* churches of the High Middle Ages. Sometimes called "Bibles in stone," these churches used the arts to tell Bible stories and saints' lives and to communicate basic doctrines such as the sovereignty of God and the coming Last Judgment. Such churches were built in astonishing numbers during the High Middle Ages. In France alone, eighty cathedrals and five hundred other large churches were constructed, along with many thousands of parish churches. Cathedrals were the largest buildings in the West since Roman times: the cathedral at Amiens, with 200,000 feet of floor space, could hold the city's entire population.

The style of building changed significantly during this period, from Romanesque during the tenth and eleventh centuries to Gothic in the twelfth and thirteenth. The Romanesque style, in which such monastic churches as that at Cluny were built, was characterized by massive walls and round arches.

More widespread, especially in northern Europe, was the high–towered Gothic style of church–building. Gothic churches combined three features—the pointed arch, ribbed vaulting, and the flying buttress—to create larger and much loftier buildings. Ribbed vaulting carried much of the weight of the roof, and graceful flying buttresses provided further bracing from the outside. The pointed arch lifted the roof still higher and gave the cathedral its sense of reaching upward toward heaven. Since the ribs and buttressing supported so much of the weight, the walls could be pierced for large areas of stained glass.

Carefully carved stone statuary represented Christ, Mary, and other biblical personages, saints and kings, depicted in relatively realistic proportions and graceful draperies. Stained glass windows were assembled like mosaics of separate pieces of colored glass fitted between leadings to form a picture, which was then set in an iron frame to fit the window space. The stained glass itself was mixed with oxides to create brilliant ruby reds, emerald greens, or blues unreproducible today. The huge arched windows glowed with a radiance like precious stones when the sun shone through them, as they still do.

Any tour of Gothic cathedrals should include the first, Abbot Suger's abbey church of St. Denis located in what is now a grimy Paris suburb; Notre Dame de Paris on its island in the Seine; and perhaps Westminster Abbey in London. But all pilgrim roads lead at last to Chartres, where classic sculpture frames the portals and Our Lady of the Beautiful Glass looks down from the most gorgeous window in the world.

Scholasticism and the Twelfth–Century Renaissance

The high medieval intellectual revival sometimes called the *Twelfth Century Renaissance* centered in a new institution of higher learning: the university. In the early Middle Ages, most education was offered by monastery and cathedral schools. These schools taught Latin and a smattering of what were called "the seven liberal arts"—the *trivium* of grammar, rhetoric, and logic; and the *quadrivium* of arithmetic, geometry, astronomy, and music. From these cathedral schools evolved the ancestors of modern universities.

Universities were organized by students in southern Europe and by teachers in the north. Students, gathering in growing numbers to hear famous lecturers, banded together to force the professors to cover the material and to treat them fairly on examinations. Professors organized themselves into four faculties based on their specialties—law, medicine, philosophy, and theology—to maintain control over curriculum and teaching degrees.

The typical class saw a professor reading a text aloud and commenting on it while students dutifully copied everything down. In this way poor students got both a copy of the book and a scholarly commentary on it. Boards of professors examined students orally for the bachelor's, master's, or doctor's degree, much as guild masters tested the skill of journeymen who sought the status of master.

Europe thus began to recover a substantial portion of the wisdom of the ancient Greeks and Romans that had been preserved among Europe's more civilized neighbors for

In this medieval university classroom, as in its many descendants of our own time, the teacher lectures and the students take notes. Unlike today's typical college student, however, the students here are all men and mostly mature individuals with careers already begun in the church. (Bettmann.)

centuries. From Byzantium came Roman law, in the form of Justinian's Code. From Muslim Spain came much of the philosophy and science of ancient Greece, including the voluminous works of Aristotle, which quickly became the backbone of university teaching.

Dozens of universities were founded in Europe in the High and later Middle Ages, including Paris, Oxford, Cambridge, Heidelberg, Prague, and Bologna. University students were often accused of intoxication and riotousness, yet the best of them became the intellectual leaders of their age.

These "schoolmen" or *scholastics* were medieval thinkers who used Aristotelian philosophical ideas to push back the frontiers of religious understanding. The most important of them, such men as Albertus Magnus ("Albert the Great") and Thomas Aquinas, are known as the "doctors" of the church and are ranked with the church fathers in theological understanding.

Scholasticism shone most brilliantly at the University of Paris, the Athens of the High Middle Ages. There, in rude lecture halls on the left bank of the Seine, professors began to lecture at five in the morning and students sat in the straw to take notes. The air of this "Latin Quarter" of Paris—so called because Latin was the language of the schools—was electric with intellectual excitement.

The source of this explosion of philosophical and theological enthusiasm was the coming together of two great streams of Western thought: the Judeo–Christian tradition and Greek philosophy, particularly the works of Aristotle. Pagan reasoning sometimes seemed to challenge Christian faith, but the Scholastics insisted that philosophy could actually illuminate faith, bringing new depth to Christian understanding.

Yet tension between pagan and Christian was still there. Albertus Magnus (c. 1200–1280) dared to assert that, while "in matters of faith and morals Augustine is to be believed rather than the philosophers," nevertheless, "if one speaks of medicine, I should rather believe [the Greeks] Galen or Hippocrates, or if of the nature of things, I believe Aristotle . . . who is expert in the nature of things."[7] And the brilliant French iconoclast Peter Abelard (c. 1079–1144) detected so many conflicts between Christian authorities that he summarized them in a daring book called *Sic et Non*—"Yes and No."

A new synthesis of faith and reason, of St. Augustine and Aristotle, did finally emerge in the works of Thomas Aquinas (c. 1225–1274), later canonized for his religious insights. In his *Summa Theologica* and many other works, Aquinas used Aristotelian logic to solve theological problems. Through precise definition of terms, clear distinctions, consideration of authoritative views on each side of the issue, and rigorous deductive reasoning, Aquinas reached what seemed to the scholastics to be irrefutable conclusions.

Chivalric Culture and Courtly Love

While church thinkers constructed elaborate theological systems, the secular leadership explored values appropriate to their role in society and their style of life. The bulk of the ruling class in the High Middle Ages were the military elite of knights and titled nobles. These feudal descendants of the Germanic warriors of Roman times had provided most of what real power there was in the earlier Middle Ages. During the high medieval period, this militarized ruling class developed a unique code of conduct known as *chivalry*. Ladies of this class, meanwhile, formulated a doctrine of *courtly love* intended to improve relations between the sexes. And both these views found exciting literary expression in medieval poetry.

Over the medieval centuries, an idealized code of aristocratic conduct evolved: the code of chivalry. In its first form, chivalry was a largely military and feudal ethic, requiring the military qualities—courage, strength, and skill with weapons—usually summed up as chivalric prowess. In addition, a true knight was expected to fight fairly, not attacking an unarmed opponent or otherwise taking advantage. Feudal loyalty was also a crucial virtue, since only the network of feudal allegiances held the whole system together. The church of the High Middle Ages added the requirements that a true knight must protect the Christian church, serve his prince, and defend the state.

Most striking, finally, was the medieval cult of courtly love that was grafted onto the chivalric ethic in the twelfth century, originally by the aristocratic ladies of southern France. In real life, knights apparently did not hesitate to beat their wives and often seem to have saved their passion for mistresses and prostitutes, both common around feudal courts. Some noblewomen responded by broadening the concept of chivalry still further, to incorporate the notions of courtesy, tenderness, and romantic love.

The perfect knight, the doctrine of courtly love urged, must be a faithful lover who adored a high–born lady. His love would double his prowess as he sought to win the favor of his lady fair. He should also develop courtesy and sophistication, wash more often, dress elegantly, and talk wittily and entertainingly. He might even learn to write love poems, or at least to sing them, accompanying himself on a lute.

The courtly love ethic was propagated by troubadour poets and minstrels, particularly at the courts of women like Marie of Champagne (1145–1198). At such courts, young knights, ladies, and noble youths gathered to debate intricate questions of courtly love and knightly honor or to listen to the romantic songs of the troubadours.

The most highly developed literary forms of the age were the feudal epics called *chansons de geste* ("songs of deeds"), the courtly love lyrics of the troubadours, and the more elaborate romances of later medieval poets. All were composed and sung in the "vernacular" languages, early versions of French, English, and other modern languages, rather than in the Latin favored by the universities.

The "songs of deeds" were intended for audiences of old–fashioned fighting barons and celebrated the older chivalric virtues of courage and skill, honor and loyalty. Thus the famous *Song of Roland* narrates the heroic death of the French knight Roland, ambushed while leading Charlemagne's rear guard home from a campaign against the Muslims in Spain. Roland's refusal to blow his great horn to summon help until his troops have been wiped out and he himself is mortally wounded epitomizes a twelfth–century soldier's view of combat as a matter of personal honor.

Jewish Life and Culture

One group constituted a genuine social and cultural minority in medieval Christendom: the Jews of the diaspora. Few in numbers but well established in many parts of western Europe, Europe's Jews now encountered mounting religious persecution. This increasing pressure drove many to migrate into eastern Europe or even beyond.

The Jewish diaspora, or "dispersal," of Roman times had taken many Jews far from their Palestinian homeland. In the earlier Middle Ages, the Jewish communities of Europe had enjoyed a considerable degree of liberty and relative prosperity. They sometimes functioned as traders between Europe and the Muslim zone of the Near East and Africa, where most Jews still lived. Excluded from Christian communities, European Jews moved into a variety of commercial and handicraft industrial trades. They also practiced medicine, served as bankers, and often engaged in small–scale moneylending.

From the tenth century on, however, popular antipathy to Jews in the Western world became more apparent. The religious resurgence of the High Middle Ages bred dark suspicions that Jews were agents of Antichrist. Superstitious people blamed them for natural disasters like famine or epidemic disease. Crusades against Muslim peoples often began with massacres of Jews in Europe itself. Another dark period of persecution was triggered by the Black Death, the terrible plague that reached Europe just before 1350, for which Jews were also often quite irrationally blamed.

Expelled by royal decrees from England in the thirteenth century, from France in the fourteenth, and most disastrously from Spain in the later fifteenth century, Jews moved steadily eastward. Some found new homes in the emerging civilization of Poland and other Slavic lands. These Jews did not return to western Europe in large numbers until modern times.

And yet, this persecuted minority produced its own vibrant intellectual life during this period. Learned rabbis studied the *Torah,* a body of holy wisdom centered on the first five books of the Hebrew Bible (the Christian Old Testament). Jewish thinkers also immersed themselves in the *Talmud,* a massive body of rabbinical writings based on close reading of the Torah. And like both Muslim and Christian scholars, some Jewish students mined the thought of Plato and Aristotle for philosophical insights.

Medieval Jewish culture north of the Mediterranean flourished most brilliantly in Muslim Spain. The *Sephardic Jews* of Spanish Andalucia, led by a "courtier class" of Jewish administrators in the service of the Muslim rulers, generated a remarkable outpouring of scholarship and literature. In the twelfth century, however, waves of Muslim fanaticism destroyed this island of civilized living, converting Jews by force or driving them into exile, as a similar surge of religious hysteria was doing in Christian Europe at the same time.

One who fled from Spain in the later twelfth century was the most honored of all medieval Jewish thinkers, Moses Maimonides (1130–1204). A brilliant scholar and religious philosopher, Maimonides wandered across North Africa and the Near East before settling in Cairo. After making contributions to the study of logic, astronomy, ethics, the Talmud, and the Torah and composing an unrivaled multivolume commentary on Jewish Law, Maimonides wrote his most controversial work, the *Guide of the Perplexed*. Drawing on biblical and rabbinical ideas, the *Guide* explored a wide range of intellectual concerns, from the relative value of faith and reason to prophecy, divine providence, and the existence of God.

For Jews as for medieval Christians, then, this was a great age of religious faith. And the same zeal that drove Christians to persecute the Jews among them, impelled them to take up arms against pagans and Muslims in a powerful surge of Western expansionism.

◆ The Medieval Expansion of Europe ◆

In the early Middle Ages, Europe had been feeble and backward by comparison with its glittering neighbors, the Byzantine Empire and the far–spreading world of Islam. Europe had been in somewhat the position of an underdeveloped nation today, fearing its more powerful neighbors yet drawing on the economic and cultural achievements of these more technically advanced peoples.

In the twelfth century, however, this relationship between the West and the near ends of Asia and Africa began to change. A new age of Western expansion got under way as aggressive Western warriors pushed east, west, and south. The age of the Crusades had begun.

The *Reconquista* and the *Drang nach Osten*

As we have seen, Germany's *Drang nach Osten* began in the reign of Otto the Great. In 955 Otto had turned back the marauding Magyars of Hungary at the Battle of Lechfeld. To strengthen the frontier against renewed incursions, he established fortified colonies and marches, or military border lands, running from the western Baltic in the north down to the head of the Adriatic. He then supported church efforts to move into the area to convert the pagan Slavic population to Christianity. A degree of economic integration also resulted, since both the German military and the monastic establishments made use of Slavic labor, while German cities grew up near the Baltic, serving as bases for further German expansion.

For the next three centuries, this broad eastward push continued. The agricultural expansion of the High Middle Ages motivated some German lords and peasants in need of new agricultural land to move into the territories beyond the Elbe river. In the thirteenth century, the Teutonic Knights, a chivalric order based in Prussia, took the lead in this "drive to the east" along the Baltic, while others pushed east along the Danube.

A first hint that the western Europeans might meet their equal in these eastern lands came when a Russian prince, Alexander Nevsky (c. 1220–1263), grand duke of Novgorod, defeated the German knights on the ice of Lake Peipus in 1242, temporarily stalling the German drive. In the next century, however, the Hanseatic League of German trading cities formed on the Baltic, and Prussia, the core of modern Germany, emerged there in early modern times. And German pressure on eastern Europe would continue to grow.

The *Reconquista* or "reconquest" of Spain from the Muslims was the core of a larger Western drive southward into the peninsulas and islands of the western Mediterranean. Restless land–hungry Norman knights first invaded Sicily in the later eleventh century, then added the southern half of Italy in the early twelfth century. As they did in England, the Norman conquerors combined imported feudalism with existing governmental institutions. In this case, they adopted Muslim political structures to create a most efficient feudal monarchy, the Kingdom of Sicily. It was in Muslim–dominated Spain, however, that this European push centered.

In a sense the *Reconquista was* the history of medieval Spain. Muslim invaders from North Africa invaded Spain in 711, and the last of them were not expelled from Spanish soil until 1492, the year Columbus sailed. Most of the area of modern Spain and Portugal, however, was reconquered during the thirteenth century. In the course of their centuries–long struggle, powerful and independent groups of Spanish knights grew up, fierce fighters dedicated to "honor and faith," to fighting the enemies of Christ and liberating Spanish land.

By 1250, the Moors, as Spain's Arab and North African rulers were called, were penned into a southern strip of land running from the mountains around Granada down to Gibraltar. They would occupy this narrow area for the next three centuries. On the liberated land, meanwhile, three major Christian kingdoms emerged: Castile, Aragon, and Portugal.

The power of the Spanish kings, however, was weakened by the rough independence of their knights and by their own policy of offering self–government to Jews and Muslims in return for their surrender. Soon the rulers of the Iberian kingdoms, like the kings of England, were consulting with representatives of their subjects in a regional *cortes,* the rough equivalent of an early English parliament.

The Crusades

The most important manifestation of the medieval expansion of Christendom, however, was the crusading movement that began at the end of the eleventh century and lasted through the thirteenth. The *Crusades,* Christian holy wars against the Muslims of the Near east and North Africa, took Europeans farther and provided more experience of foreign conquest than any other events in the Middle Ages.

As we have seen, militant tendencies were emerging throughout Christendom at this time. The same surge of religious feeling that brought cathedral building, church reform, aggressive popes and the Inquisition also encouraged military campaigns against the Muslims.

"A grave report has come from the lands around Jerusalem and from the city of Constantinople," Pope Urban told a huge crowd at the Council of Clermont in 1095, "that a foreign race, a race absolutely alien to God . . . has invaded the land of those Christians, has reduced the people with sword, rapine, and flame . . . and has . . . razed the churches to the ground. . . . On whom, therefore, does the task of avenging this fall . . . if not on you, upon whom . . . God has bestowed outstanding glory in arms?"[8] So Robert of Reims recorded the Pope's words 900 years ago.

"When Pope Urban had with urbane delivery said these things," the chronicler reports, "everyone, moved by the same feelings, shouted in unison, 'God wills it! God wills it!'"[9] A venerable French bishop knelt before the pontiff to beg permission to go, and hundreds more surged forward. These details may not be strictly accurate, even though the author was there, but this account does capture the spirit of the First Crusade.

The Muslim Arabs, who had conquered Palestine in the seventh century, had generally tolerated pilgrims to Jerusalem and other Christian holy places. Christians, after all, were "people of the Book" too, and Muhammad had recognized Jesus as a fellow prophet. In the eleventh century, however, the Seljuk Turks, steppe nomads and new converts to Islam, had established control over the Near East. In 1071 they had crushed the Byzantine army at Manzikert, and in 1095 the Byzantine emperor, Alexius I Comnenus (r. 1081–1118), had pleaded with Pope Urban to send help before Constantinople, the eastern bastion of Christendom, should fall.

The Crusades offered both solutions to social problems and economic opportunities. The pope himself saw Crusades as an answer to overpopulation and resulting pressure on the food supply in Europe. Crusading offered an outlet for the violence of the military aristocracy, and for the land-hunger of younger sons who could not inherit estates. Crusades also presented Italian trading cities with the opportunity to provide transport, supplies, and

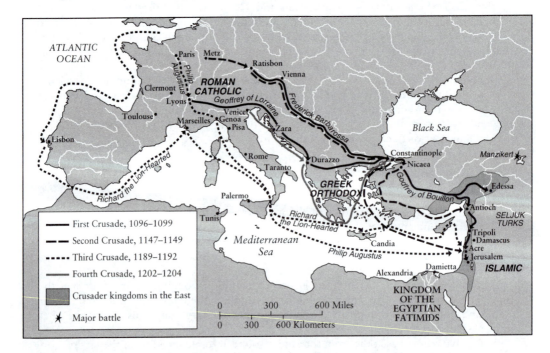

The Crusades, Eleventh–Thirteenth Centuries

naval support in exchange for commercial concessions in Muslim lands. Even crusading knights like the Templars (so called because their headquarters was set up next to the Temple of Solomon in liberated Jerusalem) became very wealthy by offering protection to visiting pilgrims in the Holy Land.

Yet the *First Crusade* seems to have been driven to a great extent by religious motives. Donning shirts marked with the cross of Christ, many simple Christians "took the Cross" (*Crux* in Latin) and became *Cru*saders. As they set out for the Holy Land, some may even have confused Jerusalem with Heaven and believed "they were marching directly to the city of eternal bliss."[10]

In fact, two crusading hosts set out in 1095: the People's Crusade, composed of peasants and the very poor, and the real army, composed of four contingents of heavily armed knights from Normandy, Flanders, southern France, and Sicily. The so-called People's Crusade, an ill–organized horde of peasants and beggars led by charismatic orators like Peter the Hermit (c. 1050–1115), was hurried across the Bosporus by the shocked Byzantines and quickly slaughtered by the Turks. The real army was led by soldiers like Godfrey of Bouillon (c. 1060–1100) and his brother Baldwin (c. 1058–1118), Raymond of Toulouse (1042–1105) from the south of France, and Bohemond (c. 1050–1111) from Taranto in Italy. These were experienced fighting men, hungry for loot.

They caught the Muslims at a moment of weakness, torn by divisions between Turks and Arabs and Sunni and Shiite sects. Despite the hardships of desert warfare, the armies of the First Crusade captured Jerusalem in 1099. The savagery that followed is often cited as an illustration of the cruelty of holy wars. "The Crusaders," in the words of a standard account, "maddened by so great a victory after such suffering, rushed through the streets and into the houses and mosques killing all they met, men, women, and children alike. All that afternoon and all through the night the massacre continued."[11]

◆The Crusader States◆

The victorious Christian knights established the *Crusader States* in the Near East. To defend this 500-mile-long strip of land, much of it desert, the conquerors built huge castles like the famous *Krak des Chevaliers* in Syria. The most powerful fighting forces in the Christian enclave were the knightly crusading orders, including the Templars and the Teutonic Knights.

Both knights and states, however, tended to squabble among themselves in the time–honored way of feudal barons, sometimes even forming alliances with neighboring Muslim rulers to support their claims against each other. It is not surprising, then, that once the Muslims achieved some degree of unity and developed strong leadership, the position of the Crusader States deteriorated rapidly. Trying to maintain their power in the Near East and North Africa, Christian Europeans launched a number of new crusades, only a couple of which need be mentioned here.

In the 1180s, the great Muslim leader Salah ad–Din (1138–1193), known to the West as Saladin, decisively turned the tide. Uniting Egypt, Mesopotamia, and Syria, he closed in on the Crusader States and overran the Kingdom of Jerusalem itself in 1187. The three most powerful rulers in the West responded to this challenge. The German emperor Frederick Barbarossa and the French and English kings Philip Augustus and Richard the Lion–Hearted all joined the *Third Crusade*. But Barbarossa drowned in Asia Minor; and Philip and Richard, archfoes at home, could not work together against the common enemy in the Near East. Nevertheless, the chivalrous Saladin agreed to allow pilgrims access to their holy places once more.

The worst debacle of all occurred in 1204, when the *Fourth Crusade,* preached by Pope Innocent III, turned to attacking Christians instead of Muslims. The knights agreed to help a pretender to the Byzantine throne, Alexius IV Angelus, to win his empire. But when their candidate was overthrown and killed in 1204, the Crusaders sacked Constantinople and took over the Byzantine Empire themselves for sixty years. Later in the thirteenth century, the Muslims mopped up the remnants of the Crusader States. They recaptured Antioch in the 1260s, Tripoli in the 1280s, and Acre in 1291—massacring tens of thousands of Christians in their turn.

There were, however, some long–term gains for the West from this high medieval burst of expansion. In eastern Europe, the size of the Holy Roman Empire doubled between the tenth and thirteenth centuries. Most of the Iberian peninsula—modern Spain and Portugal—had been reoccupied by Christian peoples by the end of the thirteenth century. Trade, already revived by the Byzantine connection through Italy, was further stimulated by the establishment of European distribution centers in the Crusader States. And in general, Westerners gained some experience with organizing large–scale overseas ventures—experience that became useful three centuries later when the West began to expand once more, this time on a global scale.

Summary

Europe's High Middle Ages—the eleventh, twelfth, and thirteenth centuries—saw a remarkable revival of trade and towns, strong royal government, and the triumph of the medieval church.

On the reborn long–distance trade routes of Europe, cities reappeared as merchant companies settled down, craft guilds appeared, and city walls and city government rose once more. In these bustling new urban centers, a "commercial revolution" forged many of the techniques and tools of modern capitalism.

During the period between 1000 and 1300, Europe also began to build strong government in the form of feudal monarchies. Royal governments based on hereditary succession and divine sanction assembled small administrative systems capable of overcoming the power of the feudal nobility. Monarchs like Philip Augustus in France and William the Conqueror in England laid the foundations for modern nation–states to come.

Perhaps even more impressive was the triumph of the Roman Catholic church under powerful reforming popes like Gregory VII and Innocent III. Combining religious reform with vigorous assertion of the Europe–wide power of the papacy, popes challenged even royal power. The high medieval church also sowed Europe with cathedrals, filled the lives of Christians with meaning, suppressed corruption and heresy, and oppressed the continent's largest minority, the Jews.

High medieval society provided a pleasant life for the knightly elite, a busy commercial world for townspeople, and a more productive agrarian style of life for the peasant majority. The culture of the Age of Faith centered on cathedrals and scholastic thought, but also produced a colorful chivalric literature and a flowering of Jewish thought even in dangerous times.

The High Middle Ages, finally, resumed the territorial expansion of the West begun by the Greeks and the Romans. Pushing into eastern Europe and reclaiming Spain from the Muslims, Christians also launched crusades into the Near Eastern and North African Islamic zone. In the end, the Crusaders failed to sustain early victories. But they did provide a valuable rehearsal for European imperialist expansion overseas in the modern period.

Some Key Terms

Notes

1. *Life of St. Godric,* trans. G.G. Coulton, in *Medieval Europe,* eds. William H. McNeill and Schuyler O. Houser (New York: Oxford University Press, 1971), 91–92.
2. Antony Black, *Guilds and Civil Society in European Political Thought from the Twelfth Century to the Present* (Ithaca, N.Y.: Cornell University Press, 1984), 13–14.
3. Ibid., 46.
4. Quoted in Robert Fawtier, *The Capetian Kings of France: Monarchy and Nation, 987–1328* (London: Macmillan, 1962), 26.
5. Richard Southern, *The Making of the Middle Ages* (London: Hutchinson, 1967), 139.
6. "Sermon on Consecration of a Pope," in *The Crisis of Church and State, 1050–1300,* trans.

Brian Tierney (Englewood Cliffs, N.J.: Prentice-Hall, 1964), 132.
7. In *New Catholic Encyclopedia,* vol. 12 (New York: McGraw-Hill, 1967), 1156.
8. Robert of Reims, *Historia Iherosolimitana,* in Louise and Jonathan Riley-Smith, *The Crusades: Idea and Reality, 1095–1274* (London: Edward Arnold, 1981), 44.
9. Ibid.
10. Hans Mayer, *The Crusades,* trans. John Gillingham (London: Oxford University Press, 1972), 12.
11. Steven Runciman, *History of the Crusades,* vol. 1 (Cambridge: Cambridge University Press, 1951), 286–287.

Reading List

Baldwin, J. W. *The Government of Philip Augustus: Foundations of French Royal Power in the Middle Ages.* Berkeley: University of California Press, 1986. Imaginative interweaving of narrative and institutional analysis.

Baron, S. W. *A Social and Religious History of the Jews.* 18 vols. 2d ed. New York: Columbia University Press, 1952–1983. Standard work on the subject, with detailed coverage of the Jews in medieval Europe.

Bartlett, R. *The Making of Europe: Conquest, Colonization, and Cultural Change, 950–1350.* Princeton: Princeton University Press, 1993. Readable synthesis.

Benson, R., et al., eds. *Renaissance and Renewal in the Twelfth Century.* Cambridge, Mass.: Harvard University Press, 1977. Authoritative essays on many aspects of the Twelfth Century Renaissance. See also the pioneering work of C. H. Haskins, *The Renaissance of the Twelfth Century* (Cambridge, Mass.: Harvard University Press, 1977).

Brooke, R. C. *Popular Religion in the Middle Ages: Western Europe 1000–1300.* London: Thames and Hudson, 1984. Introduction to a burgeoning field of research. See also: R. C. Finucane, *Miracles and Pilgrims: Popular Beliefs in Medieval England* (New York: St. Martin's Pres, 1995). For medieval theology, see J. Pelikan, *The Christian Tradition* 5 vols. (Chicago: University of Chicago Press, 1983), Volume 3.

Contamine, P. *War in the Middle Ages.* London: Blackwell, 1984. Highly recommended general study of medieval warfare. See also K. DeVries, *Medieval Military Technology* (Lewiston, New York: Broadview, 1992).

Douglas, D. C. *William the Conqueror: The Norman Impact upon England.* Berkeley: University of California Press, 1964. Excellent study of William I and his achievement. On his successors, see R. V. Turner, *Men Raised from the Dust: Administrative Service and Upward Mobility in Angevin England* (Philadelphia: University of Pennsylvania Press, 1988). On the civil service, see Alker's brief recent summary, *The Normans in Britain* (New York: Blackwell, 1995).

Duby, G. *The Age of the Cathedrals: Art and Society, 980–1420.* Translated by E. Levieux and B. Thompson. Chicago: University of Chicago Press, 1981. Stimulating impressionistic study of the cathedrals as products of a shift in medieval mentality. See also C. M. Radding and W. W. Clark, *Medieval Architecture, Medieval Learning: Builders and Masters in the Age of Romanesque and Gothic* (New Haven: Yale University Press, 1992). Interaction of ideas and art in the age of faith.

Ennen, E. *The Medieval Town.* Translated by N. Fryde. New York: North–Holland, 1979. Excellent overview, with attention to regional differences. For a comparative study, see R. H. Hilton, *English and French Towns in Feudal Society* (New York: Cambridge University Press, 1992).

Epstein, A. *Wage Labor and Guilds in Medieval Europe.* Chapel Hill: University of North Carolina, 1991. Broad geographical coverage. See also H. Swanson, *Medieval Artisans: An Urban Class in Late Medieval England* (New York: Blackwell, 1989). Stresses conflicts with merchant elites. A. Black, *Guilds and Civil Society in European Political Thought from the Twelfth Century to the Present* (Ithaca, N.Y.: Cornell University Press, 1984). Emphasizes conflict between corporate guild ethos and the competitive ethic of modern capitalism.

Erler, M., and M. Kowaleski, eds. *Women and Power in the Middle Ages.* Athens: University of Georgia Press, 1988. Essays on the exercise of power by medieval women of different social classes. See also S. M. Stuard, ed., *Women in Medieval Society* (Philadelphia: University of Pennsylvania Press, 1976). The many roles women played in medieval society.

Herlihy, D. *Medieval Households.* Cambridge, Mass.: Harvard University Press, 1985. Family structure and social class in a world of growing populations and a limited food supply. See also his *Opera Muliera: Women and Work in Medieval Europe* (Philadelphia: Temple University Press, 1990). Concentrates on work that was performed outside the home. And see C. N. L. Brooke, *The Medieval Idea of Marriage* (Oxford: Oxford University Press, 1989). A synthesis of legal, social, and religious ideas.

Kean, M. *Chivalry.* New Haven: Yale University Press, 1984. Positive evaluation of the cult of chivalry. See also C. S. Jaeger, *The Origins of Courtliness: Civilizing Trends and the Formation of Courtly Ideals, 939–1210* (Philadelphia: University of Pennsylvania Press, 1983). Sees chivalry as restraining knightly proclivities toward violence.

Le Goff, J., ed. *The Medieval World.* Translated by L. G. Cochrane. London: Collins and Brown, 1990. Scholarly essays on medieval social ideas.

Pacaut, M. *Frederick Barbarossa.* Translated by A. J. Pomerans. London: Collins, 1970. A clear exposition of the long conflict between popes and emperors.

Phillips, J. R. S. *The Medieval Expansion of Europe.* Oxford: Oxford University Press, 1988. Useful survey of the activities of crusaders, merchants, missionaries, and other forerunners of later Western imperial expansion. See also J. Prawer, *The Latin Kingdom of Jerusalem: European Colonialism in the Middle Ages* (London: Weidenfeld and Nicolson, 1972), which views the most developed crusader state as the model for later Western colonies overseas, and H. Kennedy, *Crusader Castles* (New York: Cambridge University Press, 1994).

Reynolds, S. *Kingdoms and Communities in Western Europe, 900–1300* (New York: Oxford University Press, 1984). Focuses on the traditional sense of community in village, guild, and parish and the medieval consensus on good government and royal power.

Spufford, P. *Money and Its Use in Medieval Europe.* New York: Cambridge University Press, 1988. Thoroughly researched study of the medieval money economy. See also R. Unger, *The Ship in the Medieval Economy, 600–1600* (London: Croom Helm, 1980). A useful overview, based on underwater archaeology as well as written sources.

Straw, C. *Gregory the Great: Perfection in Imperfection.* Berkeley: University of California Press, 1988. Sophisticated exploration of Gregory's contributions to Christian thought and sensibility.

9

Apocalypse

The End of the Middle Ages

◆Plague, Depression, and Social Strife ◆The Hundred Years' War
◆The Church Divided ◆Mongol and Muslim Attacks
◆The Survival of the West

> Day of wrath and doom impending
> Heaven and earth in ashes ending . . .

Dies Irae ("Day of Wrath"), a thirteenth–century hymn commonly sung in services for the dead, powerfully expressed the sense of overwhelming disaster in which the Middle Ages ended. For in the fourteenth and the earlier fifteenth centuries, it seemed very much as if God's wrath was indeed pouring down upon Christendom, as if the Day of Judgment was at hand, the Four Horsemen of the Apocalypse thundering across the sky.

Even a brief catalog of the major disasters to be confronted in this chapter should give some sense of the precipitous decline that ended the second great cycle of civilization in Western history. The first section will describe perhaps the best–known catastrophe of the period between 1300 and 1453, the plague called the Black Death, which reached Europe in 1347. Section two will chronicle the Hundred Years' War between England and France (1337–1453). The third section will deal with the Avignon papacy and the Great Schism in the history of the Catholic church (1305–1417), while the fourth will include the capture of Constantinople by the Turks in 1453. When we add to these a late–medieval economic decline, civil strife in the new cities and nations of the West, and a steep decline in European population, the Western preoccupation with death and judgment during these centuries is clearly understandable. If there was ever an age that looked like the end of the world, surely this was it.

It is true that a new stage in the history of the Western world was coming into existence even as the Middle Ages sank into chaos. The great revival known as the Renaissance was in fact beginning in Italy even as medieval institutions fell into disarray north of the Alps. Nevertheless, it is the sense of doom impending that must concern us most as we see this second great phase of Western history coming to its end.

◆Plague, Depression, and Social Strife◆

A complicated network of factors, including epidemic disease and dwindling population, poverty and civil strife, contributed to the decline of the fourteenth and fifteenth centuries.

In this first section, we will explore some of the ecological, social, and economic elements in the complex of catastrophes that scarred the Middle Ages. The *Black Death* itself, sweeping over Europe in the late 1340s, contributed to many of these problems. The late medieval depression which followed also helped bring on the social conflicts of this period. Rebellions like the Peasants' Revolt in England and the Jacquerie in France in the later 1300s also added much to the feeling many Europeans had that their society was crumbling, their world coming to an end. When things started to come apart in the late Middle Ages, they came apart everywhere at once.

The Black Death

In the fourteenth century, a microscopic creature now called *Yersinia pestis* inhabited the digestive tract of the flea that lived in the fur of small rodents like the Asian black rat, native to the eastern end of Eurasia. One might think that medieval Europeans half a world away would have been safe from micro–infected rats native to the crowded cities of China. This

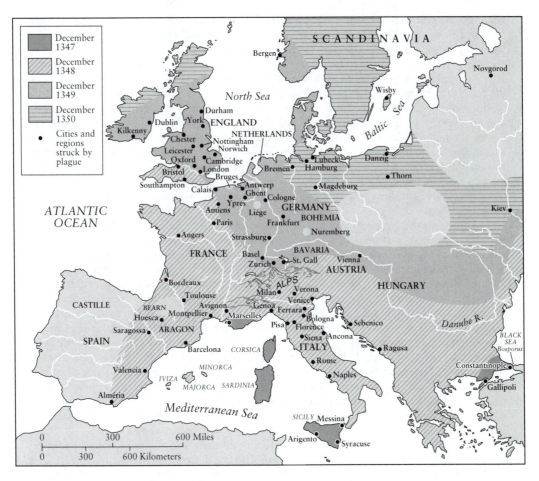

Spread of the Black Death, in the Fourteenth Century

Chronology 9: Late Middle Ages

1220s–1240s	*Mongol Golden Horde conquers Russia*
1265–1321	*Dante*
1300–1326	*Othman leads Ottoman Turks in attacks on Byzantine Empire*
1305–1378	*Popes in Avignon*
1337–1453	*Hundred Years War*
1348–1350	*Black Death kills up to a third of European population*
1350–1400	*Economic decline follows Black Death*
1358, 1378 1381	*Jacquerie revolt in France, Ciompi revolt in Italy, Wat Tyler's revolt in England*
1378–1415	*Papal schism divides church*
1395–1441	*Jan van Eyck*
1415	*Battle of Agincourt—Henry V defeats French*
1413–1431	*Joan of Arc—French rally against English*
1453	*Ottoman Turks capture Constantinople*

bacillus, however, was about to undergo one of the great ecological odysseys of human history and to devastate medieval Europe. The Chinese were already dying in large numbers when the whole ecological complex began to move west.

Some of the fleas changed hosts, transferring to the clothes, packs, and persons of busy East Asian merchants who traveled the Silk Road from China to central Asia and the Middle East. Other fleas continued to inhabit the fur of rats who found new homes in the small wooden cargo vessels of those times, especially those carrying shipments of grain. In 1347 a grain ship from the Crimea in southern Russia carried rats, fleas, and bacilli over the last leg of their journey, across the Black Sea and the eastern Mediterranean to the port of Messina in Sicily. From there, thanks to the busy roads and sea lanes of Europe's commercial revolution, rats, fleas, and their microbial parasites spread to a whole new world of human habitations as densely populated as the cities of East Asia.

Everywhere the fleas once again shifted to human hosts, and when their insect jaws punctured human skin, the bacilli passed into the bodies of medieval people. The infection spread through the lymphatic system. Painful swellings, the *buboes* for which the *bubonic plague* was named, appeared at the throat, under the arms, and in the groin. Soon, black patches or spots of blood appeared under the skin. In the variant known as *pneumonic plague*, the bacilli spread through the bloodstream to the lungs, causing pneumonia. The infected person was racked by terrible coughing and spat blood; sputum, sweat, and feces emitted a strong smell. Medieval people called it *atra mors*—"the dreadful death"—a phrase later mistranslated as "Black Death," the name it has been known by ever since.

In the Western world, pain, terror, pandemonium reigned. Where the plague escalated to the pneumonic strain, coughing spread the bacilli directly through the air. One flea bite thus rapidly infected a whole household, and the household in turn infected the narrow street outside. Friends who came to help, priests who administered the last rites, all carried the fleas or the bacilli away with them to their own households and to the next home they visited. Recognizing the pattern, people shunned the homes of the sick, leaving family after family, street after street to care for its own—and die. Cities were filled with fear and funeral corteges; mass graves were opened up for the dead.

Those who died in largest numbers were city dwellers and the poor, who lived most closely packed together, and the caring citizens who continued to bring them comfort. The wealthy, and others who could afford to leave, abandoned the cities and waited for the in-

"The Triumph of Death," as this painting is called, was a common theme in the later Middle Ages. Here corpses laid out for burial force these aristocratic passers-by to confront the fact that the same fate awaits even the most fortunate. (Alinari/Art Resource.)

fection to pass. No one knew the cause of the plague, which was blamed on a variety of factors from "bad air" to the wrath of God punishing humankind for its sins. Equipped with very limited medical knowledge, city and royal governments were helpless. And the plague advanced inexorably northward across Europe. After decimating a few Italian coastal cities in 1347, it moved on to Italy, France, and Spain in 1348, to England and western Germany in 1349, and to Scandinavia and the Baltic in 1350. Naples, Rome, Florence, Marseilles, Paris, Barcelona, London, Vienna, Hamburg—the cities that had been reborn in the preceding three centuries were stricken one by one. Medieval statistics remain patchy and unreliable, but the most common estimate is that a third of the population of Europe died of the Black Death.

The epidemic waned after 1350, but it was not gone. The plague returned in the 1360s and the 1370s, and again around 1390. This was in fact the beginning of a pandemic of bubonic plague, which would recur again and again over the next three centuries. One of the most vivid documentary–fictional accounts of a city gripped by the contagion is Daniel Defoe's *Journal of the Plague Year,* written in the seventeenth century, more than three hundred years after the arrival of the pestilence. The impact was greatest during the late medieval period, however, when everything from economic life and social relations to culture and religion was affected by one of the most terrible calamities ever to afflict the Western world.

The whole tone of society was colored by the omnipresence of death. In a stricken city, many abandoned their shops, their homes, and their responsibilities and gave themselves over to alcohol and debauchery. Others, seeing the plague as a divine punishment, turned to extreme mortification of the flesh. Wandering through the land in long lines of flagellants, they lashed themselves with whips as penance for the sins of the world. A powerful new theme emerged in the art of the age: the *Dance of Death*, depicting dancing skeletons leading aristocrats and merchants, peasants and paupers alike to their graves—a grim reminder that death spares neither high nor low. Tomb sculpture often reflected a bizarre fascination with death and decomposition. In place of the dignified representations of the dead on earlier tombs, realistically carved corpses now began to appear on the lids of late medieval sarcophagi.

Economic Decline and Stagnation

The most obvious consequences of the loss of a third of the labor force were economic. Production declined drastically in many places. Laborers profited from the situation by demanding and often getting much better terms from employers and landlords, but the latter suffered commensurately. And with the cost of labor going up, prices went up too. The Black Death thus played a large part in the economic dislocations of the late Middle Ages.

The medieval economy did in fact decline drastically during the later fourteenth century and stagnated through the first half of the fifteenth. It seems likely that the economic expansion of the High Middle Ages had reached its natural limits by 1300, before the disasters of the fourteenth century struck. A population decline of more than 30 percent, however, left many fields unworked and goods unsold in every shop. Agricultural and handicraft–industrial production, as well as volume of trade, declined precipitously, international commerce perhaps by as much as 60 percent. But this decline in production and commerce was only the most evident of the economic problems of the age.

Although more people in the lower classes died from disease, those who survived found themselves in a fortunate economic situation. The drastic shortage of labor meant that farm workers could demand excellent terms from their landlords to keep them on the land. It meant that urban workers could get much higher wages—sometimes three or four times what they had been paid before. The labor shortage also led to a greater mobility of labor, as workers moved in search of the most favorable terms. It even gave some of the surviving laborers access for the first time to such luxuries as meat, fruit, and good wine and beer.

On the other hand, the economic crisis hurt landlords and merchants, for both of whom labor costs were rising rapidly at a time of sharply declining demand. Knights and noblemen were caught in a vise between the chivalric virtue of largesse and the baronial lifestyle on the one hand, and dwindling returns from their land on the other. Businesses that had prospered in the twelfth and thirteenth centuries collapsed during the fourteenth as labor costs rose, the number of customers diminished, and profit margins shrank.

Under these circumstances, landholders and traders fought back in a variety of ways. Landed aristocrats discovered that by converting labor–intensive arable land into sheep pastures, they could cut their need for expensive labor to a few shepherds. This of course meant depriving many peasants of their homes and livelihoods. In the towns, guilds began to limit membership—often to the relatives of existing masters—in order to restrict destructive competition. Again, this hurt journeymen who had hoped to rise in the business and outsiders who could not even be admitted to apprenticeship.

European political leaders did try to deal with the economic chaos, usually by attempting to defend the old system. The governments of England and France and of the kingdoms of Castile and Aragon in Spain passed laws regulating wages and limiting worker mobility. Italian towns and some other cities outlawed journeymen's associations, workers' organizations intended to fight guild control. The Hanseatic League of Baltic German towns, like other associations of commercial cities, tried to establish a trade monopoly of its region and to bargain as a group with trading partners elsewhere. Typically, the league's functions were defensive: to protect the interests of Lübeck, Bremen, Cologne, Hamburg, and other members in troubled economic times.

Between the landed aristocracy and the peasantry, between the merchant oligarchies of the towns and their work force, bitter social tensions thus emerged in the fourteenth century. In this way, class conflict was added to the list of woes besetting the people of the later Middle Ages.

Social Disarray

Peasant revolts had occurred even in the High Middle Ages, but they became more common and more violent in the later medieval centuries. Two of the most terrible were the French *Jacquerie* of 1358 and the Peasants' Revolt in England in 1381.

"Jacques Bonhomme" ("Jack Goodfellow") was a nickname coined by the French upper classes for their stereotype of the good–hearted average peasant—a decent fellow, basi-

The savage reaction triggered by the Jacquerie was in many places more violent than the original revolt. Why would the knights tend to have the better of it when the lower classes revolted? (Bibliotheque Nationale.)

cally satisfied with his lot. Great was the horror, then, when thousands of Jacques Bon-hommes revolted in 1358, attacking and burning chateaus, killing landlords, raping their wives, and leaving a trail of death and destruction across northern France. The peasantry, already ravaged by the Black Death and frustrated in their demands for improved labor conditions, had been pushed beyond the limits by the Hundred Years' War, which brought high taxation, the ravages of mercenary armies, and unsuppressed banditry.

Unfortunately, the French peasants had little effective leadership and no clear program for social change. Although the aristocracy were caught off balance by the suddenness and savagery of the outburst, they soon rallied and crushed the rebellion, massacring perhaps as many as twenty thousand peasants in the process.

The even larger *Peasants' Revolt* in England more than two decades later grew from some of the same economic discontents, although the English peasants framed their issues more clearly and demanded specific social changes. The immediate causes of this revolt included new taxes, the ravages of the war and other rural violence, and the reluctance of landlords to modify manorial labor obligations. These deeper grievances were further expressed in peasants' demands for a final end to serfdom and for the confiscation of the wealth of the church. Their leaders, about whom not much is known, included a laborer named Wat Tyler and a popular priest called John Ball whose social radicalism was expressed in the jingle:

> When Adam delved and Eve span [spun wool],
> Who was then the gentleman?

In 1381, then, peasant rebellion exploded across southeastern England, the normally prosperous area around London. A peasant army burned manor houses, killed a number of leading citizens, including the archbishop of Canterbury, and attacked royal officials. In this desperate situation, King Richard II (r. 1377–1399), still a youth of fifteen, risked his life by going to the peasants with an appeal to disperse and a personal assurance that their demands would be met. When they did disperse, however, England's landholding elite counterattacked and slaughtered many of the rebels. Both Tyler and Ball were executed. And King Richard, feeling that commitments made to a rabble under duress need not be binding, quickly forgot his promises of social change.

In both the Jacquerie and the Peasants' Revolt, elements of the urban population supported the rural rebellions. In Paris, a merchant named Etienne Marcel (c. 1316–1358) engineered a widespread strike and called for the removal of unpopular royal advisers. In London and other English cities, journeymen and apprentices rebelled, demanding that their opportunities to advance through the guilds be unblocked once more. But urban discontent did not need the excuse of rural violence. Violent social conflict also broke out in the handicraft–industrial cities of Flanders (modern Belgium) and in Florence in the 1300s, climaxing in the Florentine Ciompi Revolt of 1378.

Conflict between artisans and merchant elites exploded at the very beginning of the fourteenth century in Flanders. Artisans of the three great wool–producing cities of Bruges, Ypres, and Ghent bitterly resented the defensive policies of merchant oligarchs, who kept wages low, outlawed journeymen's associations, and blocked efforts on the part of the poorer industries to organize guilds of their own. Two outside feudal powers also played a part in the struggle: the counts of Flanders, who used the artisans' cause as an excuse to try to impose their authority on the merchant oligarchy, and the king of France, whose help the merchants sought.

In 1302 the artisans of Bruges murdered their royal governor and a number of the town's leading merchants, and even defeated a French army in the field. A quarter century of class conflict followed, before an alliance of the merchant elite, the French king, and the count of Flanders—who had changed sides—defeated an artisan army and massacred many workers. Despite this setback for the rebels, the bloody struggle dragged on through most of the rest of the century, until a paternalistic duke of Burgundy intervened to foster the development of the lucrative wool–producing cities as a whole in the 1380s.

Florence, the wealthiest of Italian cities at the beginning of the fourteenth century, was also torn by simmering social conflict that lasted for decades. Florence was dominated by an oligarchy of woolen cloth manufacturers, bankers, and export merchants, who operated through the city's wealthiest merchant guilds and controlled city government. The poorer and less prestigious guilds and the poorest day laborers, the *ciompi,* or wool carders, struggled for the political power necessary to improve their economic standing. Feeling the economic pinch of the century, the Florentine business elite laid off workers, clamped a ceiling on wages, and, like the merchants of Flanders, prohibited laborers' associations. An initial revolt as early as the 1340s was firmly suppressed, but the coming of the Black Death later in that decade contributed to the growing tensions.

The climax came with the *Ciompi Revolt* of 1378, when the poorest workers seized the city hall and forced the oligarchy to accept their terms. These included increased production (which increased the number of jobs available), the legalization of new guilds among the *ciompi* and their allies, and the appointment of some of the poorest guild workers to government offices. Again, however, the workers' gains did not prove lasting. Within four years, the city's patrician overlords had outmaneuvered the inexperienced rebel leaders, regained control of the government, and begun to renege on earlier concessions. The bitterness continued into the following century, until the Medici family, Renaissance Florence's most famous bankers and political bosses, saw the need to take the interests of the lower orders into consideration as well.

Demographic disaster and economic decline thus combined with the policies of landlords and merchant oligarchs to touch off both peasant and urban rebellion. But there was violence on a larger scale too, for this period also witnessed a sudden international upsurge in warfare and political disorder.

♦ The Hundred Years' War ♦

The widespread wars and political dislocations of the fourteenth and fifteenth centuries, like the demographic, economic, and social disasters, centered on one or two major events. What the Black Death and the contraction of the late medieval economy were to the social and economic history of the period, the *Hundred Years' War* (1337–1453) was to the military and political trends of the times. For that prolonged struggle between England and France kindled civil wars in the most unified and powerful of medieval nations.

The English and the French battered each other mercilessly for more than a century, and neither the early English victories achieved by Edward III and Henry V nor the revival of French fortunes under the inspiration of Joan of Arc could bring a definitive victory for either side. As that century of struggle wound down in the middle 1400s, marauding bands of mercenary soldiers and ambitious feudal barons further challenged central authority in both countries.

Causes of Conflict

A search for the deeper causes of the Hundred Years War has uncovered a variety of factors. Medieval people saw the issues as dynastic, a feud between the royal houses of England and France. Modern historians have emphasized economic causes. And a third causal element was the first glimmering of national feeling in both England and France.

Proponents of the old dynastic interpretation point out that in the early fourteenth century, the king of England still controlled Gascony and other territories in southwestern France. He was, however, the French king's vassal for these lands, and frictions inevitably

The Hundred Years' War and English Rule in France

developed between a French ruler trying to assert his authority over his vassals and an English ruler demanding his feudal right to govern his French fiefs as he saw fit. The tension increased when the ancient French royal house of Capet failed to provide an heir, and the crown therefore went to a first cousin of the last of the Capetians, Philip VI (r. 1328–1350) of the house of Valois. Among the disappointed claimants to the throne, however, was Edward III of England (r. 1327–1377), a nephew of the last Capetian king. Edward's claim was tainted in feudal eyes by the fact that it came through a woman, his French mother, but the English king continued to assert his rights with vigor. This agitation, combined with conflict over administration of England's French territories, escalated into a struggle for the French crown itself—and moved inexorably from the law courts to the field of battle.

Recent historians, however, have noted some important economic motives, including Anglo–French rivalry over the wealthy cities of Flanders. The French kings, as overlords of the county of Flanders, demanded their rightful dues from the region. The Flemish nobility resisted these demands and turned for help to England, which depended on the area as a market for English wool and a source of finished woolen cloth. This lucrative economic connection repeatedly involved English kings in political struggles between the Flemish cities and in feuds between Flanders and the French monarchy.

A third important motive, particularly for the continuation of the war once it was begun, was the development of something resembling modern nationalism in both England and France. Each royal contender quickly attributed the war to the perfidy, greed, and cruelty of the other side and spread this version through official pronouncements, church sermons, and by other means. The people of both countries rallied to popular war heroes like Edward III, Henry V, or Joan of Arc, whom they increasingly saw as symbols of the nation as a whole. The two peoples also groaned under the heavy burdens imposed by the war, from loss of property and human life to the immense financial costs—all of which they tended to blame on the national enemy rather than their own rulers. This traumatic national experience thus produced the rudiments of national feeling which, combined with a passion for chivalric glory and a lust for loot, helped to perpetuate the war for half a dozen generations.

Edward III and English Victories

With beating drums and blaring trumpets, fluttering pennants and flapping banners, the kings of England and France thus went forth to war in 1337. France, three times as populous and much richer than the island nation of England, looked far the stronger. But the English benefited from a series of alliances with rebellious French subjects—in this first phase, with the wool towns of Flanders. Their chances were also improved by better leadership and discipline, and by the deployment of an unexpectedly potent weapon: the English longbow. Six feet long, requiring a strong arm to draw and years of practice to master, this traditional English peasant weapon could be fired three times as fast as the crossbows used by the French infantry and had the power to penetrate all but the heaviest plate armor. It was not superior English chivalry that won the day in battle after battle in France, but sturdy English peasants wielding this fearsome medieval missile weapon.

Over the first twenty years of the war, then, the armies of Edward III won one encounter after another. In 1340 the English triumphed in the naval battle of Sluys, winning the control of the channel Edward needed to operate across the water in France. In 1346 the English met the French knights at *Crécy* in northern France in what became the paradigm battle of the war. The French were worn out from their hot pursuit of the invaders, yet hurled themselves upon the foe with the sort of impetuosity that minstrels and troubadours admired. The English simply held firm while a blizzard of arrows littered the field with screaming horses and helpless or dying French knights. The following year, the key port of Calais fell to the English, giving them ready access to northern France for future campaigns.

The coming of the Black Death caused a temporary halt in the human carnage, but ten years later, in 1356, the English won an even more stunning victory at Poitiers in central France. The rain of English arrows took an even greater toll than at Crécy. Knights, nobles, and even allied sovereigns perished, and the French king himself—Philip's successor John (r. 1350–1364)—was taken prisoner and held for an enormous ransom.

Edward III died in 1377 after a fifty–year reign, leaving England exhausted by decades of fighting. France, meanwhile, though even more battered by the conflict, had acquired one of the more competent French rulers of the war, Charles V the Wise (r. 1364–1380). Thanks also to a series of financial and governmental reforms and to the skill of one of France's greatest commanders, Bertrand du Guesclin (c. 1320–1380), the French pushed the English back. By 1380, England held only a string of French port cities along the Channel, from Calais down to Bordeaux. Both sides, however, were nearing collapse from the terrible strain of the contest. As a result, both avoided major campaigns for the next thirty–five years, though an endless series of raids, sieges, and skirmishes continued.

Henry V, Joan of Arc, and the Turn of the Tide

It would have been an excellent time to bring the struggle to an end, with honor satisfied on both sides. Efforts, indeed, were made in that direction, including the marriage of an English prince to a French princess in 1396. Early in the next century, however, a fiery new English king, seeing France convulsed by what amounted to a civil war, was tempted across the Channel once more.

Charles the Wise had been succeeded by the intermittently insane Charles VI (r. 1380–1422). With a mental incompetent on the throne, ambitious French princes of royal blood were soon feuding for power. One of these, Louis, duke of Orléans (1372–1407), gained effective control over the king himself; another, John the Fearless, duke of Burgundy (1371–1419), promptly allied himself with the English. Against this background, England's young King Henry V (r. 1413–1422) resolved to reassert his rights in France.

In 1415 Henry invaded Normandy and met the French army in the celebrated battle of Agincourt. Even without the support of the Burgundians, the French substantially outnumbered the English. But the field was thick with mud, slowing the French cavalry charges, and the deadly hail of English arrows rained down once more. The French were routed again, the victorious invaders proceeded to overrun the rest of Normandy, and the Burgundians occupied Paris.

Henry V then showed himself as shrewd a diplomat as he was a successful military commander. By the Treaty of Troyes in 1420, Charles VI agreed to legitimize all Henry's conquests in northern France, disinherit his own son, and name the young English king heir to the throne of France. For a dazzling moment, it looked as if the most extravagant dreams of Edward III were to be realized at last, as if a single monarch might come to rule both of the most powerful nations in medieval Europe.

Two years later, however, both the feeble–minded French sovereign and the virile young English monarch died within a few months of each other. The new English king,

Henry VI (r. 1422–1471), was an infant, unable to assert his rights under the Treaty of Troyes. Charles VI's disinherited son declared himself King Charles VII (r. 1422–1461) but seemed militarily incapable of making good his claim in the face of the powerful English–Burgundian alliance. The stage was set for more decades of grinding war.

Into this hopeless situation came what seemed to the French like a miracle from heaven—the young girl known to history as Joan of Arc (c. 1412–1431). Daughter of a devout and prosperous farming family from the village of Domrémy in Lorraine, Joan began in her teens to hear the voices of saints and angels summoning her to save France from the unending wars. With the English and their Burgundian supporters occupying northern France—including Paris—and much of the southwest as well, Joan's mission could only be accomplished by force. And the only source of an army was the apparently feckless Charles VII, still uncrowned seven years after his father's death, his troops dispirited, his cause seemingly hopeless. Nevertheless, it was to Charles that the seventeen–year–old peasant girl turned in the spring of 1429.

What Joan accomplished in less than a year was, in its way, as miraculous as her later reputation. It is doubtful that she really convinced Charles and the worldly men around him that she was, as she said, "the Maid sent from God."[1] Still, Charles allowed her to ride out with the soldiers that he sent to relieve the besieged city of Orléans, as she had asked. She certainly had a galvanizing effect on the troops, who broke the English siege. And when Joan returned victorious, she moved Charles himself to risk everything by marching off—under her escort—to be crowned king at last in the traditional ceremony in the cathedral at Reims, in the heart of the English–occupied zone.

Anointed and crowned, with the miraculous maid by his side, Charles VII suddenly began to look like a king to the French people. From that point on, things moved slowly but inexorably in his favor. In the 1430s, he made at least a temporary peace with the duke of Burgundy and began the reorganization of the French army. Garrisoning his cities with regularly paid soldiers, he also provided them with a new weapon more devastating than the English longbow: artillery. Gunpowder, known in China centuries before, found military application in Europe in the early fourteenth century, although cannons did not become effective weapons of war until the fifteenth. Charles VII's new army included professional artillerymen and trains of siege guns. By 1453, his forces had driven the English out of both Normandy in the north and Gascony in the south, leaving the invaders only the isolated port of Calais to show for 116 years of intermittent warfare.

Joan had not lived to see the glorious French victories. In 1430, the year after her triumphs at Orléans and Reims, she had been captured by the Burgundians. Turned over to the English, she was tried for witchcraft and heresy by the French ecclesiastical courts in the occupied zone. She was convicted and burned alive in 1431, still insisting her inspiration was divine, not diabolical.

An illiterate peasant demanding the right to command armies, a girl who cut her hair and wore men's clothing, a teenager who led her elders by the nose, Joan remains in some ways one of the most astonishing of medieval people. In one great respect, however, she was not atypical at all: true believers in divine inspiration never seemed to be in short supply in the age of faith.

Marauding Mercenaries and Bastard Feudalism

Violence, too, was never lacking in the Middle Ages; yet there seems to have been even more of it than usual during the fourteenth and fifteenth centuries. Besides the major campaigns of the Hundred Years' War, later medieval times were afflicted by baronial factionalism, bastard feudalism, and marauding mercenaries. Once the dogs of war were unleashed, they could not easily be brought to heel, as even the most powerful monarchs soon learned.

Mercenary soldiers—called *free companies* because they had no fixed feudal ties but sold their services to the highest bidder—multiplied during the Hundred Years' War. Both sides found these professional troops, efficiently commanded by captains with an eye out for profit, to be more effective fighting forces than the traditional feudal levies. The free companies, however, tended to live off the land, showing no more respect for the people they were defending than for their enemies. During the long periods between campaigns, furthermore, mercenaries often turned into bandits, establishing themselves in fortified castles, imposing tribute on the surrounding countryside, and frequently robbing travelers and looting villages and even cities. It was a throwback to the anarchistic days of the early Middle Ages, and it devastated parts of France for generations.

The feudal system itself was corrupted during the fourteenth and fifteenth centuries into what is sometimes called *bastard feudalism*. The feudal bond, once based on a personal oath that often reflected genuine respect and loyalty to one's overlord, became in later medieval times increasingly a matter of cash payments. Nobles, like kings, simply hired fighting men, clothing them in their own colors and maintaining them at their own expense. They used these private armies both to meet their feudal military obligations to their overlords and to settle disputes in their own provinces by force of arms. Feudal display had never been more grand, outdoing even that of the High Middle Ages with lavish feasts, elaborate tournaments, new knightly orders, and other manifestations of enthusiasm for the chivalric ideal. Too often, however, a veneer of chivalry concealed crass mercenary greed or unseemly aristocratic ambition.

Not surprisingly, baronial factionalism also experienced a powerful resurgence in the later Middle Ages. The most successful high medieval monarchs had worked hard to bring their vassals to heel, suppressing private feuds and fortified castles. But a century of intensified warfare, inevitably accompanied by defeats for one king or the other, brought feudal rebelliousness and factional conflict back with a vengeance, as we will see in the next section.

The Monarchies Challenged

In the war–torn fourteenth and fifteenth centuries, finally, the feudal monarchy itself seemed to be under fire. The Hundred Years' War and the ensuing climate of social disarray, mercenary violence, and bastard feudalism all contributed to this challenge to royal power. Even more important was the rebelliousness of ambitious nobles, whose intrigues and private wars divided not only royal courts but whole countries. Beyond this, it has been suggested, lay structural problems of the medieval monarchy as an institution. Among these were the loose feudal organization of much political power, the limited authority of monarchs to tax wealthy landholders, and the decline of landed wealth itself under the impact of war, plague, and general economic decline.

These historic disasters and institutional weaknesses interacted with the personal failings of individual rulers to bring the powerful monarchies of earlier centuries to a low ebb in the earlier 1400s. This happened not only in war–ravaged France and England, but also in Spain, the Holy Roman Empire, and parts of eastern Europe. Let us glance briefly at some of these areas.

In France, the English more than once encouraged the great royal vassals to defect from the French king, promoting secession by wealthy Flanders, by the peninsular duchies of Normandy and Brittany, and most importantly by the ambitious dukes of Burgundy. The French royal court became a hotbed of intrigue, and powerful nobles and royal favorites plundered the country remorselessly. The policies of the French rulers themselves also contributed to the crumbling of royal power over the great fiefholders. Attempting to keep their vassals in line, French monarchs gave large areas of land to princes of royal blood. These became the most aggressive and ambitious of all the "*overmighty subjects*" who challenged the authority of their sovereigns.

In the early fifteenth century, then, with the mentally incompetent Charles VI as France's nominal ruler, the dukes of Burgundy and Orléans were able to divide much of the French ruling class into two bitterly opposed factions. Louis, duke of Orléans, was assassinated in 1407; John the Fearless, duke of Burgundy, in 1419; and all France was plunged into civil war even as the country reeled under the renewed English invasion led by Henry V. Under Joan of Arc's protégé Charles VII, the French monarchy began to recover and then to extend the centralizing power it had enjoyed in the twelfth and thirteenth centuries. But the challenge of the fifteenth century brought France's kings very low indeed before recovery began.

England also suffered from feudal factionalism and royal weakness during the 1400s. Military setbacks and the immense cost of the war enabled the ambitious English noble house of Lancaster to overthrow Edward III's incompetent successor Richard II in 1399. Half a century later, in the wake of its final expulsion from France, England also slid into a prolonged bout of civil strife known as the *Wars of the Roses* (1455–1485). For three decades, the powerful baronial houses of Lancaster and York, symbolized by red and white roses respectively, fought each other up and down the land.

The strongest champion of the house of Lancaster was Queen Margaret (1430–1482) wife of the Lancastrian king Henry VI (r. 1422–1461), the heroic Henry V's mentally incompetent son. A strong–willed dynast, Margaret fought doggedly for many years to hold the throne for her family. The Yorkist claimant Edward IV (r. 1461–1483) seized power after a series of bloody battles, but was himself for some years seen as a virtual puppet of the ambitious "kingmaker" Richard Neville, earl of Warwick (1428–1471), who had helped the young king to his crown. Warwick subsequently fell out with Edward, shifted to the Lancastrian camp, and briefly restored Henry VI to the throne in 1470. But Edward and the Yorkists recovered and counterattacked; Warwick died in battle, and hapless Henry VI perished in the Tower of London.

The climax of this carnival of civil strife came in the brief, bloody reign of Richard III (r. 1483–1485), Edward IV's brother and the last Yorkist king. Richard, the witty hero–villain of one of Shakespeare's most popular plays, imprisoned and probably murdered Edward's young son and heir Edward V (1483), along with a number of other Yorkist rivals. It was only when Richard himself fell on the battlefield at Bosworth (1485) that another Lancastrian claimant, Henry Tudor, brought to power a royal family capable of reasserting authority in the realm—the famous Tudor dynasty of Henry VIII and Queen Elizabeth.

In the German states of the Holy Roman Empire, meanwhile, central power also continued to deteriorate rapidly in the later Middle Ages. In this vast, predominantly German–speaking area of central Europe, as we have seen, the emperors had failed to establish strong royal government in the fourteenth century. The fifteenth saw the decline of political power at the next level down, among the great princely families who had defeated the centralizing efforts of the emperors. Ruling families like the Habsburgs of Austria and the

Wittelsbachs of Bavaria still suffered from the old German custom of dividing the realm among the various members of a princely clan. In addition, all the German princes faced aggressive challenges from below as insurrectionary nobles and knights, independent towns, and rebellious peasants repeatedly rose against them.

The election of Frederick III (r. 1440–1493) of the house of Habsburg as Holy Roman emperor in 1452 brought to the German imperial throne a family that continued to hold that title until the Empire itself was abolished in the nineteenth century. Earlier Habsburgs had ruled Austria and other German states, as well as Hungary and Bohemia, but had been handicapped by feuds within the family and by the opposition of other German rulers. Only with the reunion of the Habsburg territories and the ascendancy of Emperor Maximilian I (r. 1493–1519) did the power and prestige of the German emperors begin to grow once again.

✦ The Church Divided ✦

Even in the worst of times, afflicted by wars, rebellions, and the decline of royal power, medieval people had their religion to console them. At the end of the Middle Ages, however, even that consolation seemed to be denied them as the papacy sank into division and disrepute and heresy stalked the land once more.

These religious problems began at the center of Western Christendom, with two grievous shocks to the Roman papacy. Through the first three–quarters of the fourteenth century, from 1305 to 1378, the popes shifted the center of the Catholic church from Rome to the city of Avignon, on the southern frontiers of France. There worldliness, corruption, and charges of subservience to the French monarchy greatly weakened the moral authority of the papacy. Worse yet, the later fourteenth and early fifteenth centuries, the period from 1378 to 1417, saw the Great Schism, when two and sometimes three men claimed to be the true pope, further undermining the credibility of the institution. As Christians lost faith in the institutional church, some turned to the more personal devotions known as lay piety, while others fell into heresy once more.

The Avignon Papacy

By the beginning of the fourteenth century, the Roman church was once again in need of rehabilitation. The great days of the Gregorian reform were more than two centuries in the past. High offices were once again bought and sold, and worldly friars were as common as worldly monks. It was at this juncture that the most outspoken of all champions of papal supremacy, Boniface VIII, challenged one of the most determined builders of royal power, Philip the Fair of France—and lost.

Boniface VIII (r. 1294–1303) was not a pope of the stature of Gregory VII or Innocent III. He was deeply involved in Roman aristocratic politics and the butt of scandalous rumors. Nevertheless, he responded vigorously when France's King Philip IV (r. 1285–1314), called the Fair (meaning "Handsome") challenged papal control over the Catholic church in his country. Without prior consent of the pope, Philip attempted to tax the French church to pay for royal wars. Boniface forbade the tax. Philip responded by prohibiting the export of gold and silver from France, effectively cutting off all papal revenues from Europe's richest country. At this point, Boniface gave way, allowing the king to levy a tax on church property, at least in a legitimate emergency such as a just war.

But Philip the Fair went further: he brought a French prelate to trial for treason in a French court. Philip thus raised again the vexing question of clerical immunity from trial in secular courts. And this time Pope Boniface did not back away. He issued instead the most sweeping of all assertions of papal supremacy over secular rulers, the bull *Unam Sanctam* in 1302. (A bull is an official document or decree, often one issued by the Church; the term is derived from the word *bulla* for the imperial seal affixed to such a document.) The sword of secular authority wielded by earthly monarchs, the pope decreed, was subordinate to the sword of spiritual power held by the heirs of St. Peter. "Therefore we declare, state, define, and pronounce that it is altogether necessary to salvation for every human creature to be subject to the Roman Pontiff."[2]

King Philip, a notable aggrandizer of royal power in France, did not hesitate to strike back at the great monopolist of international power. Conspiring with the pope's enemies in Rome, he dispatched a band of royal agents led by Guillaume de Nogaret (c. 1260–1313) to seize Boniface at Anagni in 1303 and bring him to trial as a false pope. The scheme misfired as ordinary Italian townsmen rallied to the pope and expelled the foreigners. But Boniface, a man in his sixties, psychologically and perhaps physically battered by Philip's henchmen, died within a month of their visit.

But the relentless French king was not through. To prevent further papal interference, he engineered the election of a Frenchmen, Clement V, to the papacy in 1305 (r. 1305–1313). Clement, furthermore, did not go to Rome, but settled at Avignon, on what was then the southeastern border of France. Thus began a seventy–year period of papal exile from Rome (1305–1378) known as the *Avignon papacy.*

Seven French popes ruled the church from the sunny southern city of Avignon, on the Rhone. Seen by many Christians as a "second Babylon" of worldliness and corruption, Avignon did become the site of a splendid new papal palace and a brilliant court. Through the first half of the Hundred Years' War, the English and others declared that the Avignon popes were captives of the French king. But Avignon was not part of France; it was a papal enclave. And the popes of this exile, though they appointed many French cardinals, seem to have worked for the interests of the church as a whole. Nevertheless, the reputation of the Avignon popes as subservient to a secular monarch did damage to papal prestige.

Another charge leveled against the Avignon papacy had more substance. The Avignon popes were widely seen as worldly, even venal men, more concerned with squeezing the Christian faithful for church revenues than with providing spiritual leadership. And in fact the Avignon papacy did help to develop the well–oiled machinery of church administration, a primary purpose of which was the collection of revenues from the international church and its holdings. These revenues, furthermore, were often used for such unspiritual ends as maintaining cardinals in splendor at Avignon or armies to defend the Papal States in Italy. Altogether, even if Avignon was not as sunk in corruption as its enemies averred, it was not the fount of spiritual guidance and consolation many Christians needed in those tortured times either.

Strolling the streets and squares of Avignon today, you will find one of the most pleasant of the cities of Provence, France's sunny south. The palace of the popes, with its crenellated towers and its peaceful view across the river Rhone, looks thoroughly medieval. Little remains of the sinful city condemned by the fourteenth–century poet Petrarch or of the throbbing center of papal administrative organization extolled by modern historians. But Avignon was both. And the Avignon papacy opened the way to an even more disturbing chapter in the history of western Christendom.

The Great Schism

When the papal sojourn in Avignon ended in the later 1370s, it was replaced by something even worse: the *Great Schism* (1378–1417). Modern dictionaries define a *schism* as a division brought about by religious differences. At the end of the Middle Ages, the Great Schism split the Roman papacy and the Catholic church itself for half a century. It was a sad decline after the international power of such high medieval popes as Innocent III.

Pope Gregory XI returned to Rome, where he died in 1378. Under pressure from a Roman mob determined that the papacy should not again repair to Avignon, the predominantly French College of Cardinals elected an Italian pope, Urban VI (r. 1378–1389). Urban, however, immediately launched a hot-tempered assault on the luxurious living, financial abuses, and other sins of the ecclesiastical hierarchy. The French cardinals thereupon withdrew from Rome, elected a new, French pope, Clement VII (r. 1378–1394), and returned to Avignon. Urban, meanwhile, appointed an Italian College of Cardinals and remained in Rome.

Western Christendom was thus confronted by the disturbing spectacle of two popes, each claiming to be the legitimate heir to St. Peter, the bearer of the keys of heaven. Both demanded revenues from the churches of the West. Each excommunicated the other, putting the soul of any Christian who supported the wrong claimant in mortal danger. It was precisely what a Europe reeling under the hammer blows of plague and war did not need.

Rulers and their nations had to choose a pope to support: the French defended the Avignon line; the English accepted Rome; the Holy Roman Empire favored first one and then the other. Many Christians, already dismayed at the worldliness into which the church was sinking once more, turned away from the official church to private devotions or even to new heresies. Many others must have lapsed into deep cynicism at the spectacle.

Yet most Christians, including their rulers, remained profoundly troubled. The only practical solution religious thinkers and leaders could come up with was the *conciliar movement* of the first half of the fifteenth century. The conciliar movement was based on the conviction that a church council could both end the Schism and reform the church, and that conciliar government might even replace papal rule in the Catholic church. Such gatherings as the Council of Nicaea of 325 and Innocent III's Fourth Lateran Council of 1215 had successfully resolved great problems before. Surely God would inspire such a conclave in this dark hour of Christendom.

In the first half of the fifteenth century, a series of councils was held. The first, the Council of Pisa in 1409, did not augur well for the conciliar approach. After firmly announcing that both the Roman and Avignon popes had been deposed, the assembled dignitaries chose a new one. Unfortunately, neither the Roman nor the Avignon pontiff accepted his dismissal, and western Europe had three popes instead of two.

The Council of Constance (1414–1418) was somewhat more productive. Called at the insistence of the Holy Roman emperor and supported by such powers as the kings of France and England, this gathering of theologians and princes of the church did succeed in at least some of its objectives. The council managed to depose both the Roman and Pisan popes, and by depriving the Avignon papacy of all support, forced its collapse within a dozen years. These actions paved the way for a conclave that elected a new pope, Martin V (r. 1417–1431), who settled a single papacy once more in Rome. On the other hand, the Council of Constance did not effect any reforms, since the new pope promptly dissolved it. Nor did conciliar authority ever replace papal power in the church.

Mysticism, Lay Piety, and Resurgent Heresy

Even in this dark, bewildering time, however, religion did not perish. In many parts of Europe, Christians found their way to a sense of God's presence in their lives through mysticism, private devotions, or the new heresies of Wycliffe and Hus (explored later). Religious belief survived, but the isolated mystic, the small groups of devout laypeople, and the peasants who responded to the anticlerical preaching of the new heretics all in their various ways challenged the unity of medieval Christianity, for they sought God outside the traditional framework of the Roman church.

Individual people who were towers of religious strength and often had a highly developed mystical gift were found in many lands. In the fourteenth century, the Italian St. Catherine of Siena (1347–1380) and St. Bridget of Sweden (c. 1303–1373) took leading roles in bringing the papacy from Avignon back to Rome. In the fifteenth century, the earthy English mystic Margery Kempe (c. 1373–c. 1440) chronicled her visions and pilgrimages—which took her as far as Rome and Jerusalem—in a popular autobiography that became one of the first classics of the genre in English. But it was in the Low Countries and in Germany that the revival of religious devotion found its most intense and influential expression.

In the shadows of the great cathedrals that followed the winding course of the Rhine from the Netherlands down through western Germany, individuals and small groups of Christians now lived an intense religious life, but in private homes. Mystical spirits like Master Eckhart (c. 1260–c. 1328) urged the faithful to find God within themselves through meditation or, in the words of an immensely popular tract attributed to Thomas à Kempis (c. 1380–1471), through a personal *Imitation of Christ* (1425). Theologically orthodox, these spiritual leaders pointed out an emotional path to the religious life that transcended dogma and had no need of relics or pilgrimages, priests or prelates.

Emotional religiosity and private devotions also characterized the movements toward lay piety called the *devotio moderna*, the "modern devotion" that flourished in the Low Countries and the German states. The most famous of these movements, the Brethren of the Common Life, was patterned on the teaching of the Flemish mystic Gerard Groote (1340–1384), "the apostle of his country," as a follower described him, "who kindled the fires of religion in the cold hearts of men."[3] The Brethren, living communally, breaking bread and working together, encouraged each other in prayer and fasting, study and worship. The Sisters of the Common Life were also disciples of Groote and of his successor as leader of the movement, Florence Radewijns (1345–1400), who restructured and expanded the array of brother and sister houses. Although these groups functioned outside all the official monastic orders, they lived much like monks and nuns, and because their views were orthodox, the church could not move against them. Yet the humble piety of these laymen did contrast disturbingly with the worldly lives and theological quibbles of the feuding followers of the rival popes.

Other individuals and groups who carried their search for God over the line into heresy did incur the wrath of the authorities. Wycliffe in England and Hus in Bohemia (the Czech Republic today) followed this dangerous road. Both men were university professors who stirred less educated Christians to religious dissent.

John Wycliffe (c. 1320–1384) of Oxford University declared that faith bloomed in the hearts of those who were divinely predestined to salvation. He believed that all religious truth was to be found in Scripture rather than church dogma, and that priests had no special spiritual powers that were not available to any Christian. Writing in the middle of the

Hundred Years' War, Wycliffe particularly denounced the Avignon papacy, urging that Englishmen refuse to contribute revenues to a sinful papal court that danced to the tune of the French king. Wycliffe's message, however, went far beyond war–kindled patriotism, moving men and women of the lower orders of society to read translations of Scripture and to probe their own souls for signs of predestined salvation without the help of the official church. This underground movement, called *Lollardy,* survived to provide support for the Reformation two centuries later.

Jan Hus (1369–1415) of the University of Prague was a student of Wycliffe's views but developed his own passionate style, denouncing the wealth and corruption of the church to *Hussite* crowds of Bohemian townsmen and peasants. Like Wycliffe, Hus insisted that priests were not a separate caste with special prerogatives and powers. His demands for church reform and his doctrinal heresies brought him into conflict first with his archbishop and then with the Council of Constance. Although the council's members shared Hus's dedication to reform, they rejected his theology, and in the age of faith, this rejection was paramount. Hus was condemned and burned for heresy in 1415.

Wycliffe and Hus both encouraged the use of the living vernacular languages in religion, rather than church Latin, and followers of Wycliffe translated the Bible into English. The new heretics, like the mystics and the Brethren of the Common Life, were strongly anticlerical, rejecting priestly mediation between God and the individual worshiper and condemning the wealth and worldly concerns of the church. Despite their deeply religious nature, then, both the heresies and the lay piety of the later Middle Ages reflected the crumbling of the religious unity of the Roman church—another symptom of the decline of medieval Christendom.

♦ Mongol and Muslim Attacks ♦

Against a Europe thus weakened and divided in so many ways came perhaps the greatest threat of all in the later Middle Ages: invaders from Asia. From the four–fifths of the Eurasian continent that lay east of the Urals came waves of Mongol horsemen and the powerful armies of the Ottoman Turks. Between them they shattered both of the medieval "shields of the West"—Kievan Russia in 1240 and the Byzantine Empire in 1453. As the medieval cycle of Western history drew to a close, it did not seem at all unlikely that the story of Western civilization might be ending too.

The Decline of Kievan Russia and the Byzantine Empire

We have encountered these peoples of the Eurasian steppes before. The Indo–Europeans who populated most of Europe were originally steppe nomads who penetrated Europe and the Near East in the second millennium before Christ. Turko–Mongol invaders from the steppes had included the Huns who reached the walls of Rome in the last days of the Empire. In the thirteenth, fourteenth, and fifteenth centuries, however, the most formidable of all these Asian intruders broke into eastern Europe: the Ottoman Turks, marching under the banner of Islam, and the Mongols of Genghis Khan.

The realms of Eastern Christendom against which they marched no longer constituted the substantial bastions they had once been. The Kievan Rus, never strongly unified, was even more divided and weakened by outside pressures when the Mongols appeared out of the Eastern grasslands in the thirteenth century. The Byzantine Empire, powerful enough in Justinian's day to undertake the reconquest of the Mediterranean, was only a narrow strip of land on each side of the Bosporus when the Ottomans moved against it in the fourteenth and fifteenth centuries. A brief look at the decline of Eastern Christendom on the eve of invasion helps to explain the terrifying breakthroughs of Turks and Mongols at the end of the Middle Ages.

Even in the great days of Yaroslav the Wise in the eleventh century, the Kievan Rus had been more an alliance of princes than a centralized monarchy. The practice of parceling out royal lands to princely heirs had proved as fatal to national unity in Russia as in western European nations. As early as the eleventh century also, Turkish nomads called the Cumans had begun to raid the southern steppes, the heartland of Kievan Russia. Instead of uniting to resist these incursions, however, feuding Russian princes had often taken them on as mercenaries in their endless petty wars with each other.

By the twelfth and thirteenth centuries, many East Slavs were withdrawing to the west and north to escape the Cumans and the endemic warfare of the steppes. Those who moved westward became the ancestors of the White Russians (or Belarussians) and the Ukrainians of modern times. In the late Middle Ages, however, they fell temporarily under the rule of the Catholic Kingdom of Poland or the still pagan Grand Duchy of Lithuania and were thus lost to Russia for hundreds of years. East Slavs who moved northward to settle in the scantily populated forests contributed to the development of the great Russian trading city of Novgorod and founded other cities, including Moscow. In this forest zone of European Russia, Muscovy soon emerged, the core of modern Russia. But first there was the Mongol conquest to face and to endure.

The Byzantine Empire far to the south had, as we have seen, already lost large portions of its territory. The Arabs in the seventh century and the Seljuk Turks in the eleventh had conquered most of the Near East. In 1204 the Fourth Crusade had turned against its Byzantine allies and occupied the once-great Empire itself through the first half of the thirteenth century. Even after the restoration of the Greek emperors by Michael VIII Paleologus (r. 1259–1282) in 1261, bitter struggles between rival claimants to the throne undermined the political strength of the Empire. Economically, meanwhile, Venetian and other Italian merchants had come to dominate the commerce of Constantinople, while oppressive imperial tax collectors and the reduction of the peasantry to serf status by rapacious landlords had further weakened the state.

Religious disputes completed the disarray of the Empire that claimed the leadership of the Greek Orthodox world. The split between the Greek Orthodox and Roman Catholic churches had been made official by mutual excommunications in 1054. Byzantium's need for Western aid in the face of military threats from the East, however, kept alive the issue of reunification with the Roman half of Christendom, an issue that caused bitter divisions in Constantinople. Even more disturbing, the Orthodox church was riven by a resurgence of mysticism and the rise of new monastic movements in the fourteenth century. The most important of these, called *Hesychasm*, the search for inner peace, centered around the ancient tenth-century monasteries on Mount Athos in Greece. The monks of Mount Athos— who are still there—cut themselves entirely off from the surrounding countryside, excluded women and even female animals from their mountaintop cloisters, and gave themselves up wholly to meditation and scholarship. New monastic foundations in Constantinople itself divided between those devoted to the preservation of their cultural heritage, including ancient Greek philosophy and literature, and those committed to a mystical search for a spiritual "inner light" of salvation. Still other Byzantine religious thinkers, meanwhile, saw signs of the impending end of the world—a presentiment that, as far as the Byzantine Empire was concerned, was not far from right.

The Yoke of the Golden Horde

Mongolia today is a barren land between Russia and China. Modern cities and collective farms have largely squeezed out the herding, tent–dwelling life led by *Mongols* well into the present century. Looking at a forlornly flapping felt tent on that cold northern plain today, it is hard to remember that seven centuries ago the ancestors of these people built the largest empire the world had ever seen.

Turko–Mongol peoples had for hundreds of years harassed the ancient civilizations of Asia just as the Germanic peoples had harassed the Roman Empire. Pastoral nomads, expert archers, and totally at home on their shaggy Mongolian ponies, these tribes and clans of the northern steppes had repeatedly broken through the Great Wall of China or pushed through the passes of the Northwest Frontier into India. Then, shortly after 1200, a remarkable leader arose among them: Temujin, hailed by his followers as Genghis Khan, Lord of All Men. Genghis Khan (r. 1206–1227) imposed unity and organization on the Mongol peoples for the first time and led them in a series of sweeping conquests where they had only conducted sporadic raids before. Within a couple of generations, he and his successors had overrun the Chinese Empire, central Asia, the Muslim Middle East, and a substantial chunk of eastern Europe.

A probing expedition penetrated into Kievan Russia in 1223, defeating the Russian princes in a battle on the Kalka River near the Sea of Azov. In the 1230s, after Genghis Khan's death, his grandson Batu Khan (r. 1235–1255) led a major invasion of the lands of the East Slavs, devastating Kiev and many other Russian cities in 1240 and galloping on to burn and pillage in Poland, Hungary, and Bohemia. Thereafter, the Mongols established a capital at Sarai on the Volga and settled down to exploit a conquered Russia.

The Mongols were skillful and ruthless fighters, plundering and putting captured cities to the torch, slaughtering whole populations in order to fill their enemies with fear. Europeans, like the Chinese and Muslim peoples who faced them, recounted stories of half–human savages destroying all in their path. Ruling an empire that stretched from China to the frontiers of the Holy Roman Empire, from Moscow to Baghdad, the Mongol Khans certainly looked unstoppable.

Once victorious, the Mongols proved less oppressive than might have been expected. The *Golden Horde,* as the Mongol khanate that governed Russia was called, actually required little of their Slavic subjects beyond regular tribute, occasional drafts of Russian recruits for their armies, and the humble submission of each Russian princeling before he could exercise authority over his city or principality. Still, the two centuries of the Mongol yoke did cut most of Russia's budding commercial ties with the West. The Mongols also habituated the Russians to a more rigorously authoritarian rule than most European peoples experienced. For the Golden Horde—so called from the color of their tents—were always ready to ride when any Russian principality was dilatory with its tribute or slow to make submission. And raids into other eastern European lands continued, putting the fear of the Mongols into European hearts well beyond the khanate of the Golden Horde.

Despite the economic destruction of Russia, however, the most important consequence of the Mongol predominance for Eurasia as a whole was the reopening of the trade links between East and West that had flourished in ancient Roman times. Protected by Mongol rulers whose linked realms stretched from China to Russia, merchants once again traveled the Silk Road from China through central Asia and down through the Middle East to the Mediterranean and the Muslim and Christian worlds of western Eurasia and North Africa. It was, as we see, a harbinger of better times for Europeans as well as for Asians.

The Fall of Constantinople

Another and even more terrible threat, however, seemed to loom over Christendom as the Middle Ages drew to a close. This was the menace of the *Ottoman Turks,* the third great wave of followers of the Prophet Muhammad, after the Arabs and the Seljuk Turks, to march against the West.

The collection of Turkish clans that would come to be known as the Ottoman Turks descended from the steppes of central Asia into the Muslim Middle East in the thirteenth century. Refugees like many others from the irresistible advance of the Mongols of Genghis Khan, they were nomads and spoke a Turko–Mongol language. Eastern Islam remained in the hands of the Seljuk Turks against whom the Crusades had been launched a century earlier, though an Arab caliph still presided as a figurehead in Baghdad. Converting to the Muslim faith, the Ottoman Turks followed the pattern of their predecessors, serving in the wars against Byzantium, carving out a place for themselves in the violent world of the *ghazis,* the Muslim frontier fighters who pushed insistently against the eastern wall of Christendom.

In 1300 their great leader Othman (r. 1300–1326) became an independent sultan and founded the Ottoman dynasty. His son Orkhan (r. 1326–1360) conquered much of Anatolia, the plateau of inland Turkey today, and then went on to take most of what remained of the Byzantine Empire in Asia. From the Byzantines, the Ottomans learned the subtleties of governmental administration—a skill for which they showed a notable knack. It was, for instance, Othman's son Orkhan who first organized the *janissary corps.* These Christian slaves, converted to Islam and trained from childhood as an elite corps of soldiers and administrators, played a key role in the great Ottoman Empire to come.

In the middle of the fourteenth century, the Ottomans outflanked the Byzantine capital and pushed northward, up through the Balkans toward central Europe. The great Battle of Kossovo in 1389, in which they defeated an alliance of Bulgarians, Romanians, and Serbs (founders of twentieth–century Yugoslavia), gave them most of the Balkans. As they paused on the borders of Hungary, a crusading army from France and the German states rushed to the aid of the Hungarians. The Ottomans wiped them out.

At the beginning of the fifteenth century, there seemed little to stop the advance of Turkish Islam into the heart of Christendom. First, however, they turned their attention to the areas they had bypassed earlier. In the 1440s they completed the conquest of Greece. In the 1450s they marched against the fragment of the Byzantine Empire that remained—the legendary city of Constantinople. Under a twenty–three–year–old sultan, Muhammad II (r. 1451–1481), known thereafter as the Conqueror, the Ottomans closed in on their prize.

It was no nomadic horde that moved against Constantinople in the spring of 1453. The Ottoman Turkish force was by this time a well–organized army, equipped with the largest siege guns in the world. It advanced with skill and prudence, fortifying the Straits to prevent resupply by water and ringing the walls of the city with seventy thousand veteran soldiers. The Turks even transported a fleet overland into the Golden Horn, Constantinople's famous harbor, a remarkable feat for the military engineering of the time.

At the end of May, the huge Turkish artillery breached the walls, and the Turks poured in. The last Byzantine emperor, Constantine XI (r. 1449–1453), died fighting. Muhammad the Conqueror rode through the carnage to Justinian's great Church of the Holy Wisdom, where he heard an Islamic sermon even before the building was reconsecrated as a mosque.

The year 1453 is often used to mark the end of the Middle Ages. To thunderstruck Christians in the West, the fall of Constantinople seemed to threaten more than the end of an age. It seemed to presage a renewed Muslim assault that could sweep all Christendom into the trash bin of history.

◆The Survival of the West◆

The terrible shadow of the Black Death stretched far across Europe, returning again during the late medieval centuries. Hunger and other suffering resulting from the economic decline of the later Middle Ages added much to the misery. Wars, both international and civil, were endemic through the 1300s and 1400s. Death itself came early for many individuals and seemed to threaten Western civilization as a whole as this age drew to a close.

Confronted not for the first time with impending doom, however, Western humanity once again demonstrated a remarkable range of survival skills. In one area of human endeavor after another, later medieval people adapted, coped, and even developed in response to the shocks of the fourteenth and fifteenth centuries. This section will outline some of the positive achievements of the time in the fields of government, society, and the arts. For monarchs began to rebuild their royal administrations before the Middle Ages was over. Individual businessmen did well in spite of the widespread economic downturn. And the late medieval period actually saw a significant cultural revival, from brilliantly realistic Dutch painting to the work of such celebrated Italian and English poets as Dante and Chaucer.

The Growth of Government

The kings who fought so many wars also had countries to run, and some did so with growing efficiency under the pressure of war and their own ambitions. At the same time, however, governmental institutions increasingly reflected the interests of such other powers in medieval society as the aristocracy, the towns, and the church.

Later medieval rulers continued the efforts of their predecessors to strengthen royal bureaucracy, particularly in the fields of law and finance. In France around 1300, Philip the Fair employed growing numbers of *gens du roi*—king's men—to impose his will. In particular, he sent his own judges and lawyers from the Parlement of Paris fanning out over the country to establish the preeminence of the king's justice and to undermine the surviving baronial courts. In England in the mid–1300s, Edward III used different means to achieve the same end, appointing local landowners to serve as his *Justices of the Peace* with a combination of judicial and administrative duties. These "JPs" were to serve for centuries as royal agents in the shires. On the financial side, both English and French monarchs were compelled by their long wars to increase their revenues drastically. Despite the resistance of traditionalists who thought that kings should live on the profits of their own estates, Charles VII secured the right to levy a regular tax, or *taille,* on the whole French nation. By Henry V's time, the English royal budget was six times what it had been before the Hundred Years' War began. As far away as eastern Poland and Hungary, as far south as the Kingdom of Naples, monarchs worked to expand their administrative power and their financial resources.

The increasing need for money, however, also led the kings of the late Middle Ages to make concessions to the wealthiest and most powerful of their subjects. These concessions frequently took the form of granting a voice in the royal government itself to these traditional enemies of centralization. In France, the power–hungry Philip the Fair convened the first French *Estates General* in 1302 in order to get these great men of the realm to vote him taxes for a war. This assembly, purporting to represent all three estates of medieval society—clergy, knights, and commoners—in fact resembled the original English Parliament, which had also consisted of three groups: the leaders of the church, bishops, and abbots; dukes, counts, and other landed magnates; and merchants and lawyers from wealthy towns.

The Parliament in England, established in the preceding century, grew stronger, particularly during Edward III's long war–torn reign (1327–1377). During this period, Parliament divided into upper and lower chambers—the House of Lords, consisting of the church hierarchy and the nobility just mentioned, and the House of Commons, where townsmen and untitled country gentry met together, beginning a partnership of historic significance. During this period also, the parliamentary practice of petitioning the king evolved into genuine legislation as those petitions the king granted were duly registered as laws. Perhaps most important, the House of Commons acquired the exclusive right to initiate revenue bills. This *power of the purse* gave Commons a great deal of political clout in centuries to come.

In later medieval and earlier modern times, monarchs normally manipulated these occasional conventions of their ruling classes in their own interests. The powerful prelates, landed aristocrats, and wealthy merchants assembled in the Parliament, the Estates General, the Spanish *cortes,* and similar bodies seldom seriously challenged the authority of the crown. In one case, however, the great magnates were able to extract major concessions from a monarch as early as the fourteenth century. This occurred in the Holy Roman Empire, where the emperor surrendered most of the real power to the individual German states by the *Golden Bull* of 1356.

The basic pattern for the delegation of imperial power had been established in the thirteenth century by the formidable emperor Frederick II, whose main interests lay in Italy and who willingly sacrificed power in Germany to free himself for an active policy in the south. In the mid–fourteenth century, Emperor Charles IV (r. 1355–1378), whose primary concern was to strengthen his hereditary kingdom of Bohemia, won the consent of the German princes to his efforts by issuing the Golden Bull. This fundamental document formally granted the right to choose each successive emperor to seven princely electors—the duke of Saxony, the count palatine of the Rhine, the margrave of Brandenburg, the king of Bohemia, and the archbishops of Cologne, Mainz, and Trier. It also vested broad independent powers in all the German princes and lesser magnates, including rights to coin money, run their own courts, control mineral rights, and otherwise operate free of imperial intervention.

In the fifteenth century, finally, the Habsburg dynasty of Austria—whose members were elected Holy Roman emperors from 1452 until the abolition of the Empire in 1806—followed the policies established by Frederick II and Charles IV. The Habsburgs thus concentrated on building the power of the dynasty in its hereditary domains, centered this time in Austria, and allowed the princes, nobles, churchmen, knights, and towns of the Holy Roman Empire almost complete autonomy to run their own domestic affairs.

Business Recovery

The fourteenth–century depression and the stagnation of the economy through the first half of the fifteenth century was an economic and social calamity for most Europeans. Yet there were some businesspeople who managed to prosper even in hard times. In so doing, furthermore, they added significantly to the West's economic base and to its armory of business skills and techniques.

Despite the passing of the expansive economy of the High Middle Ages, it was still possible for an aggressive entrepreneurial spirit like the French merchant, manufacturer, and financier Jacques Coeur (1395–1456) to grow very rich indeed. Born poor, this late medieval merchant prince rose through the mining industry, textile manufacturing, and Mediterranean trade to become one of the richest men of his time. He built an immense mansion, dressed in velvets and multicolored robes like a nobleman, and became a financier to kings. His financial empire was finally destroyed by political enemies, who charged him with extortion, poisoning, and other offenses. Jacques Coeur may have lacked political savvy, but no one questioned his ability to make money, even in depressed times.

Other businessmen also built themselves private palaces, erected impressive Gothic guildhalls, and continued to contribute lavishly to civic charities and church building. They stayed afloat and even prospered by fine–tuning business techniques developed earlier, by moving into new lines of profitable endeavor, and by building new and more dynamic centers of business activity in hitherto less economically developed parts of Europe.

Thus partnerships and larger companies began to be established on a more permanent basis and to employ professional agents in distant cities to further their interests. Improved bookkeeping methods, letters of credit, and bills of exchange became more common, the use of Arabic numerals even more widespread. Some merchant families began to circulate Europewide newssheets, precursors of today's business press, to help them keep abreast of changing conditions in those politically and economically troubled times.

New businesses also emerged in the late Middle Ages. These included the development of luxurious new fabrics in the wool–manufacturing towns of the Low Countries, an immense armaments industry in Milan, and mining and metallurgy in Austria and Hungary. Most important was the expansion of banking and other financial operations. These included collecting taxes for kings and princes, serving as financial agents for the church, currency dealing, and of course moneylending at a healthy rate of interest. Such loans could go spectacularly bad, especially when bankers financed the sometimes extravagant ambitions of kings. But they could also make a financier like Jacques Coeur extremely rich.

Even in times of economic decline or stagnation, some parts of Europe exhibited real economic growth. Southern Germany and Switzerland, for example, developed extensive commercial and financial sectors in this period. Flanders gradually gave way to the Netherlands as a center of industry and commerce, and Bruges took second place to the bustling Dutch city of Antwerp. On the Baltic, as noted, the Hanseatic League made the fortunes of Lübeck, Hamburg, and dozens of other cities.

Some European merchants, finally, found ways to take advantage even of some of the more disturbing trends of their times. A few European traders explored the Eurasian caravan routes reopened by the Mongols. The Venetian Marco Polo (c. 1254–c. 1324) was the most famous merchant traveler to take that long road east and back again. With his father and his uncle, Marco Polo journeyed across the Middle East and central Asia to China, where for some years he served the most famous Mongol ruler of China, Kublai Khan. Polo's account of the wonders of the Asian civilizations he had seen during his seventeen years at the other end of Eurasia influenced Christopher Columbus, Vasco da Gama, and other European explorers who set out to reach East Asia by sea at the end of the fifteenth century.

Most Europeans remained inward looking and parochial, battered by the late medieval economic decline, as the Middle Ages drew to a close. The conservative guilds of earlier centuries survived to protect the interests of most urban craft workers, and the vast majority of peasants never looked beyond the village and the economic niche in which they were born. But the future belonged to those who were willing to take a chance on something new.

Late Medieval Art

Even in a Europe under siege from so many directions, art and literature did not vanish. As long as there were wealthy merchants, self–glorifying kings, and popes in Rome or Avignon, artists found work.

Gothic cathedrals continued to be built, some of them exploding into the elaborate *flamboyant* ("flaming") style, a profusion of stone traceries, fan vaulting, buttressing, turrets, and finials. The Gothic style also spread to secular structures, including guildhalls, urban mansions, and the castles of great magnates. We have only an exquisite miniature painting of the long–vanished palace of the fourteenth–century French duke of Berry, for example, but it shows the fairy–tale elaboration of towers and turrets that gave their special charm to the chateaus of the fifteenth and later centuries.

Architecture, the dominant art in the days of the high medieval cathedral builders, lost its central place in the fourteenth and fifteenth centuries. Among arts now developing rapidly was painting, the fine art that would play a central role in the Renaissance. A major technical breakthrough was the fifteenth–century invention of oil painting, a medium that was thick, slow drying, and exceptionally rich in color. At the same time, the flatness and linear quality of Byzantine mosaics and stained glass began to give way to fully rounded, carefully modeled faces and figures. Both oils and the new naturalism would come into their own in the painting of the Renaissance.

Late medieval painting north of the Alps reached its highest development in Flanders, especially in the work of such masters as Jan van Eyck (c. 1395–c. 1441) and Rogier van der Weyden (c. 1400–1464). The fidelity of Flemish artists to realistic detail made them the most admired painters of portraits, a new and burgeoning field. They also did altarpieces and other religious paintings, however, which shine with the spirit of the lay piety that also flourished in the Low Countries. The mourning figures in Van der Weyden's *Descent from the Cross,* for instance, radiate the sorrow and devotion of the *devotio moderna*.

The Climax of Medieval Literature: Dante and Chaucer

A later medieval development that had a profound impact on Western literature was the emergence of the vernacular, or modern languages, as literary vehicles. This change made possible the rise of national literatures in the West, including the work of such brilliant later medieval writers as Dante and Chaucer, François Villon and Christine de Pisan.

Latin remained the language of serious thought in the church, the universities, and the scholarship of the emerging Renaissance. From the thirteenth century on, however, some versions of the spoken tongues of the European peoples began to be recognized as legitimate "literary languages" also. Literary traditions thus grew up in the dialect of the Paris area of northern France, in the Tuscan Italian spoken in Florence, in the southeastern English of London, in the Castilian Spanish of Spain's leading kingdom, and so on. Literature in these languages had the advantage of being available to a much broader cross section of the national population than the handful of churchmen and scholars who were literate in Latin. The new vernacular literatures thus played an important role in the slow development of national cultures and national consciousness in Europe.

Dante Alighieri (1265–1321), universally hailed as Italy's greatest poet, was the son of a bourgeois family in the wealthy commercial city of Florence. Drawn into the feuds of the papal and imperial political factions that divided northern Italy, Dante was driven into exile for the rest of his life in 1302. His works included a eulogy of the Italian language and a thoughtful tract *On Monarchy* discussing the relative claims of pope and emperor to the allegiance of contemporary Europeans. One of his most popular works was his *Vita Nuova* ("New Life"), a poetic evocation of the beauty and virtue of Beatrice Portinare (1266–1290), whom he loved all his life and converted into a symbol of idealized perfection.

It was his epic poem, *The Divine Comedy* (1312–1321), however, that earned Dante his place among the three or four greatest of Western poets. This vision of a journey through Hell, Purgatory, and Heaven offers a panoply of medieval people, real and fictional, facing the consequences of their earthly lives in the other world. Sinners, saints, and many in between, they are assigned their punishments and rewards with Scholastic logic and depicted with vivid imagery, some condemned to the infernal underworld of hell, others exalted to the heavenly spheres beyond the stars. Introduced to the other world by the Roman poet Vergil and guided by his beloved Beatrice to his final discovery of celestial bliss, Dante offers an unparalleled journey through the spiritual "other world" of the age of faith.

Geoffrey Chaucer (1340–1400), England's most admired poet before Shakespeare, was, like Dante, of middle–class origins. Descended from a family of London leatherworkers and winemakers, Chaucer himself became a royal civil servant under Edward III and his successors. Around a successful career as a diplomat and comptroller of customs, he produced poems that combined earthy humor with love and high idealism. Drawn like Dante to the great literature of ancient times, the English poet produced a translation of Boethius's *Consolations of Philosophy* and a tragic love story in verse, *Troilus and Criseyde,* set against the background of the Trojan War. Far and away his most popular work, however, is his *Canterbury Tales,* dating from the 1390s. Here again, a motley array of medieval people of all sorts and conditions pass before our eyes, this time not in the other world but threading a very real pilgrim road from a London suburb to Canterbury Cathedral. The tales the Canterbury pilgrims tell to pass the time range from sermons to animal fables, from chivalric romances to bawdy stories. Each is suited to its teller, each a further revelation of the range and humanity of Western people in that time of trial, survival, and new beginnings.

In the French poets Christine de Pisan (1364–c. 1431) and François Villon (1413–1463), we have two strikingly original spirits whose writing expressed awareness of deep currents of distress in the fifteenth century. Christine de Pisan was a woman intellectual whose verse and prose commanded respect. Her allegorical *Book of the City of Ladies* (1405) raises such startlingly modern issues as education for women and the sexual double standard, which condemns women for sexual behavior that is acceptable for men. Villon was even further out of the mainstream of courtly verse and chivalric romances. Born in poverty, he discovered his intellectual gifts as a roistering university student, became a bandit, and was nearly executed for murder. His poems, written in the slangy French of the late medieval Parisian underworld, give us a glimpse of that community of the damned—criminals, prostitutes, beggars, and others who lived their lives at the bottom of society. A modern note—the celebration of society's victims—is clearly struck once more. Yet there is a sense of loss here also, of a medieval world as much myth as reality, indubitably vanishing as the fifteenth century wore on, in Villon's most haunting refrain: "But where are the snows of yesteryear?"[4]

An age was dying. Despite the sulfurous imagery of Dante and the flame–lit Last Judgments on the walls of late medieval churches, however, the end of the world was not yet. Those apocalyptic days took their toll, yet in the end they passed by.

Summary

A Europe stunned by the Black Death, which swept over the continent for the first time just before 1350, was soon mired in a related economic downturn and a series of social upheavals in town and country. Over this same period, the bloody Hundred Years War (1337–1453) tore at the vitals of England and France, leaving both nations in a state of disarray.

Between the early 1300s and 1415, meanwhile, Western Europe faced the deeply troubling Avignon papacy and the Great Schism, which further divided the church. And on the eastern fringes of Europe, the Mongol Golden Horde conquered Russia and the Muslim Ottoman Turks overwhelmed Constantinople in 1453.

Some late medieval rulers did strengthen their governmental machinery in the later 1400s, however. Institutions speaking for the wealthiest and most powerful of their subjects, including the English Parliament, exploited the royal need for funds to increase their rights and powers. And new forms of art and literature, including realistic painting and the poetry of Dante and Chaucer, pointed toward the work of early modern times.

Some Key Terms

Avignon papacy   225
bastard feudalism   222
Battle of Crécy   219
Black Death   210
Ciompi Revolt   217
conciliar movement   226
Dance of Death   214
devotio moderna   227
Estates General   232
free company   222

gens du roi   232
Golden Bull   233
Golden Horde   230
Great Schism   226
Hesychasm   229
Hundred Years' War   217
Hussites   228
Jacquerie   215
janissary corps   231
Justices of the Peace   232

Lollardy   228
Mongols   230
Ottoman Turks   231
overmighty subjects   223
Peasants' Revolt   216
power of the purse   233
taille   232
Unam Sanctum   225
Wars of the Roses   223

Notes

1. The Trial of Jeanne d'Arc, trans. W. P. Barrett (London: Routledge, 1931), 165.
2. *Unam Sanctam,* in *The Crisis of Church and State,* trans. Brian Tierney (Englewood Cliffs, N.J.: Prentice Hall, 1964), 189.
3. Maurice Keen, *The Pelican History of Medieval Europe* (Harmondsworth, England: Penguin, 1968), 283.
4. "Ballade des Dames du Temps Jadis," in *Oeuvres,* ed. André Mary (Paris: Editions Garnier Frères, 1951), 31.

Reading List

Atkinson, C. W. *Mystic and Pilgrim: The Book and the World of Marjorie Kempe.* Ithaca, N.Y.: Cornell University Press, 1983. The work and milieu of the remarkably worldly late medieval mystic.

Chaucer, G. *The Canterbury Tales.* Boston: Houghton Mifflin, 1974. Medieval people brought vigorously to life in verse.

Dante Alighieri. *The Divine Comedy.* Translated by J. Ciardi. New York: Norton, 1970. Poetic journey through the other world.

Gies, F. *Joan of Arc: The Legend and the Reality.* New York: Harper & Row, 1981. Many views of the most famous of French saints.

Gottfried, R. S. *The Black Death: Natural and Human Disaster in Medieval Europe.* New York: Macmillan, 1983. Relates the bubonic plague to human ecology and outlines the broad economic and psychological circumstances in which it occurred.

Guenee, B. *States and Rulers in Later Medieval Europe.* Translated by J. Vale. New York: Blackwood, 1985. Comparative study of royal governments in western Europe.

Hicks, M. *Bastard Feudalism.* New York: Longman, 1995. The late medieval decay of the feudal ideal.

Holmes, G. *Europe: Hierarchy and Revolt, 1320–1450.* London: Harvester Press, 1975. Brief yet comprehensive overview of the end of the Middle Ages, with glances ahead at the early modern period.

Howell, M. C. *Women, Production, and Patriarchy in Late Medieval Cities.* Chicago: University of Chicago Press, 1986. Productive women in male–dominated institutions.

Huizinga, J. *The Waning of the Middle Ages.* Garden City, N.Y.: Doubleday, 1956. Famous portrait of a dying age, focusing on France and the Low Countries.

Lambert, M. *Medieval Heresy: Popular Movements from Bogomil to Hus.* New York: Holmes and Meier, 1976. Broad historical summary of the major medieval heresies.

Leff, G. *The Dissolution of the Medieval Outlook: An Essay on Intellectual and Spiritual Change in the Fourteenth Century.* New York: New York University Press, 1976. Brief but illuminating interpretation of late medieval thought.

Le Roy Ladurie, E. *Montaillou: The Promised Land of Error.* Translated by B. Bray. New York: Braziller, 1978. Startling account of life in a late medieval village, including candid confessions of heretical beliefs and sexual peccadillos, based on Inquisition records.

Nicol, D. M. *The Last Centuries of Byzantium, 1261–1453.* London: Hart–Davis, 1972. The decline of the Byzantine Empire to its final fall to the Ottoman Turks. See also his *The Immortal Emperor: The Life and legend of Constantine Palaiologos, Last Emperor of the Romans* (New York: Cambridge University Press, 1992). A brief, sympathetic life of the last Byzantine emperor.

Poos, L. R. *A Rural Society After the Black Death: Essex, 1350–1525.* New York: Cambridge University Press, 1991. Sees strong similarity to early modern country life.

Ross, C. *Richard III.* Berkeley: University of California, 1961. Good introduction to a controversial ruler of England.

Seward, D. *The Hundred Years War: The English in France, 1337–1543.* New York: Athenaeum, 1982. Clear and informed narrative account of the war, stronger on events than analysis.

Sumption, J. *The Hundred Years War: Trial by Battle.* Philadelphia: University of Pennsylvania, 1992. Grim picture of the horrors of war. See also A. Curry, *The Hundred Years War* (New York: St. Martin's Press, 1993). Emphasizes international relations rather than battles.

Turberville, A. S. *Medieval Heresy and the Inquisition.* Hamden, Conn.: Archon, 1964. Balanced account. R. I. Moore, *The Formation of a Persecuting Society: Power and Deviance in Western Europe, 950–1250* (New York: Blackwell, 1987). Sees religious persecution as intrinsic to medieval society.

Vale, M. *War and Chivalry: Warfare and Aristocratic Culture in England, France, and Burgundy at the End of the Middle Ages.* London: Duckworth, 1981. Sees more vitality in fifteenth–century chivalry than is commonly believed.

PART III
The Early Modern West

The early modern period, with which this part of the book is concerned, is commonly dated from the fifteenth century for most of Europe and from the fourteenth century for Italy, where the rebirth of arts and letters called the Renaissance began. Just as the fall of Rome in the fifth century has traditionally been seen as marking the divide between the ancient and medieval periods, so the fall of Constantinople in 1453 has often been taken as a convenient point at which to end the Middle Ages and begin the modern age. We also follow the common practice of marking the end of early modern history with the reign of the great French king Louis XIV, who died in 1715. This part of the book thus deals primarily with the 1400s, 1500s, and 1600s.

For the now rapidly expanding Western world, these were the turbulent centuries of such innovative spirits as Columbus and Leonardo daVinci, Martin Luther, Copernicus, Shakespeare, and Isaac Newton. They were times of change and challenge not only for the West but for humankind itself.

In the political arena, the early modern period saw the development of the strongest central governments since ancient Rome in the "new monarchies" of the fifteenth and sixteenth centuries and the "absolute monarchies" of the seventeenth. But the seventeenth century also witnessed the emergence in England of the constitutional monarchy, the forerunner of more democratic forms of government. In addition, these were the centuries of the birth of Europe's vast overseas empires, which brought much of North, South, and Middle America under western European rule and scattered Western trading posts around Asia and Africa. Early modern times thus saw the Atlantic powers become the prosperous center of a flow of silk, spices, and slaves from Asia and Africa and of gold, silver, sugar, and tobacco from the Americas.

The European core of the Western world also exhibited a new level of social mobility after 1500. Few European peasants were serfs any longer, and the commercial middle class gained a new importance. A few brilliant individuals mastered so many arts and skills that we still reserve the label "Renaissance person" for an individual with a multiplicity of interests and talents.

But it is the intellectual and artistic life of this period that has most dazzled later observers. The Renaissance revitalized Western culture, partly by a major recovery of ancient arts and ideas, partly by inventing new art forms of its own. The Reformation divided western Europe spiritually but ended by fostering a spirit of toleration not seen in the West since ancient Rome.

In terms of territorial expansion and of contacts with non-Western peoples, the early modern period marked a great leap forward in the history of the West. Although, even in the Americas, much of this expansion was limited to coastal areas and islands, and though Africa remained largely unpenetrated and Asia unconquered, the mere presence of Western soldiers, traders, settlers, and missionaries in so many parts of the world was unprecedented. The global rise of the West had begun.

Time Line: The Early Modern West

1400–1500	Rise of Medici business empire in Florence
1450–1500	Economic recovery in Europe
1452–1519	Leonardo da Vinci—paints the *Mona Lisa* and *The Last Supper*
1474–1504	Isabella and Ferdinand unify Spain, expel last Muslim rulers, sponsor Columbus's New World voyages
1475–1564	Michelangelo—sculptor (*David*), painter (*Creation* on Sistine Ceiling), architecture (dome on St. Peter's)
1486	Pico's humanist tract *On the Dignity of Man* celebrates unique qualities of humanity
1492	Columbus reaches the Americas
1498	Da Gama reaches India
1517	Luther's *Ninety–Five Theses* challenge indulgences—and papal rule of the church
1519–1522	Magellan's expedition circumnavigates the world
1519–1555	Charles V rules vast Habsburg Empire—Holy Roman Empire, Spain, parts of Italy, and New World colonies
1520s	Cortez conquers Aztec Empire of Mexico for Spain
1530s	Pizzaro conquers Inca Empire of Peru for Spain
1536–1564	Calvin at Geneva becomes center of international Protestant movement
1543	Copernicus's *On the Revolutions of the Heavenly Bodies* replace earth–centered universe with sun–centered one
1545–1564	Council of Trent prescribes moral reforms, defends Catholic theology
1558–1603	Elizabeth I becomes less militant leader of Protestant cause
1560s–1609	Wars of religion in France, Netherlands
1564–1616	Shakespeare
1572	St. Bartholomew massacre in France
1618–1648	Thirty Years War ravages the German States
1642–1649	Civil War pits Cromwell against Charles I in England
1643–1715	Louis XIV, "the Sun King," becomes model absolutist monarch
1649	Charles I is beheaded; Cromwell rules through "Kingless Decade" of 1650s
1687	Newton's *Mathematical Principles of Natural Philosophy* proposes law of gravity
1688	Glorious Revolution brings constitutional monarchy to England; English Bill of Rights, 1689
1690	Locke's *Two Treatises of Civil Government* preaches natural rights, social contract
1700–1721	Great Northern War—Peter the Great builds St. Petersburg, his "window on the West," on conquered land
1607	English establish first colony at Jamestown
1608	French establish first colony at Quebec

—10—

The West Reborn
The Renaissance

◆Economic Revival ◆Renaissance Princes
◆An Evolving Society ◆Humanism and Literature
◆Renaissance Art

The Western world got a new start in the centuries around 1500, and the core of that new beginning was a remarkable social and cultural revival we call the *Renaissance*. The word *renaissance* means "rebirth," and the period carrying that name, which began in Italy in the 1300s and climaxed across much of western Europe in the 1500s, has often been seen as the springtime of the modern world. Although this view has been challenged and reinterpreted by a number of historians over the past century and a half—and we will explore some of these objections—the fundamental strength of this conception justifies structuring this chapter around the notion of a Western rebirth.

In the present chapter we deal first with the economic expansion and social dynamism of the age as a whole, and with the aggressive "new monarchs" and "princes" of the Renaissance who restored political power to the center of the European states. Thereafter we will turn to the great cultural achievements in thought and scholarship, literature and the arts for which the Renaissance is renowned. It is an archetypal age of contrasts, producing political opportunists like the notorious Cesare Borgia, wealthy patrons of the arts like Lorenzo de' Medici, and such towering talents as the painter Leonardo da Vinci and the pious and learned scholar Erasmus.

Later chapters in this part of the book will focus on other innovative, even revolutionary events that began at this time, including the Reformation of the 1500s, the scientific revolution of the 1500s and 1600s, and the first great age of European overseas expansion that began with Columbus and stretched from 1492 into the 1700s. But here we will try to present a political, economic, and cultural framework for an understanding of this age of rebirth and new beginnings as a whole.

◆Economic Revival◆

The economic history of the Renaissance period is one of dynamic change after the decline and stagnation of the later Middle Ages. Demographically, commercially, financially, and in terms of overall production, the West was expanding once more in the later fifteenth and sixteenth centuries, as it had been in the twelfth and thirteenth. Many historians have felt that the whole turbulent history of the Renaissance was to a significant degree built on this great early modern expansion in the material wealth of the West.

Renewed Population Growth

A primary source of this first modern surge of productivity, power, and creativity may be found in the demographic statistics of the age. The population of the West, which had grown rapidly in the centuries between 1100 and 1350, had been flung into a precipitous decline by the plagues and wars of the later Middle Ages. Around 1450, however, a demographic recovery began that was to last some two hundred years. By 1500, Europe's population was probably approaching that of 1350 once more. By 1600, population gains of perhaps 50 percent had been registered across much of the Western world.

Cities grew particularly rapidly. Only four European cities had populations of over 100,000 in 1500, three of them—Venice, Milan, and Naples—in Renaissance Italy. By 1600, five cities—those just listed, plus London and Paris—had more than 150,000 people. Several others, including Rome and Palermo in Italy, Antwerp and Amsterdam in the Low Countries, and the Spanish and Portuguese imperial ports of Seville and Lisbon, now had populations over 100,000. All such figures for this early period are estimates at best. Nevertheless, if the demographic recovery and advance just outlined is even broadly accu-

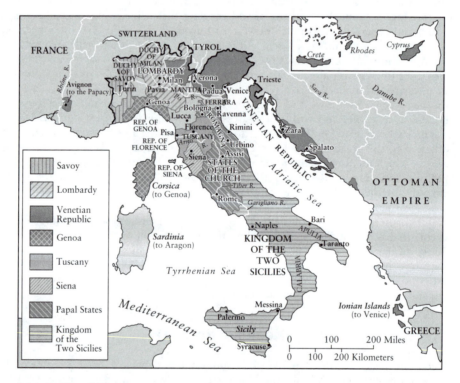

Italy in the Fifteenth Century

Chronology 10: The Renaissance

1304–1374	*Petrarch begins both Renaissance humanism (in Latin) and Renaissance love poetry (in Italian)*
1450–1500	*Economic recovery in Europe*
1452–1519	*Leonardo da Vinci—paints Mona Lisa and The Last Supper*
1455	*Gutenberg printing press*
1461–1483	*Louis XI, the Spider King, revives royal power in France*
1462–1505	*Ivan III establishes Moscow's domination of Russia*
1474–1504	*Isabella and Ferdinand unify Spain, expel last Muslim rulers, sponsor Columbus's New World voyages*
1475–1564	*Michelangelo—sculptor (David), painter (Creation on Sistine ceiling), architect (dome on St. Peter's)*
1485–1509	*Henry VII founds Tudor dynasty in England*
1509	*Erasmus's Praise of Folly exposes follies and vices of the age*
1513	*Machiavelli's The Prince gives ruthlessly realistic view of Renaissance rulers*
1516	*More's Utopia describes imaginary perfect society*
1564–1616	*Shakespeare—his plays include Hamlet and Romeo and Juliet*

rate, its impact on the Western economy must have been considerable. More mouths to feed necessitated expanded agricultural production. Handicraft manufacturing and larger industrial ventures were also stimulated by increased demand. And commercial exchange inevitably expanded to effect the necessary distribution of this increased production to the growing numbers of customers. The rapid economic expansion of the Renaissance was thus in large part caused by the increased demand created by population growth.

Agriculture, Trade, and Technology

European agriculture grew in part because of demographic recovery. With more people to feed, woodlands, swamps, and rocky hillsides abandoned by farmers when the Black Death swept through were once again brought under the plow. Especially notable was land reclamation from the sea. Centering in the Low Countries—the Netherlands and Belgium today—this campaign by lowland dwellers to push back the sea produced large amounts of new arable land in northwestern Europe. Methodical and determined, the Dutch, in particular, had been raising dikes and draining land since the High Middle Ages. By the sixteenth century, these massive engineering projects had reclaimed thousands of acres of *polders*—table-flat land scored by irrigation canals, guarded by immense dikes, and drained by slowly turning windmills.

Another factor in the agricultural growth of this period was the controversial type of land organization often called *enclosure*. Under this system, lands formerly plowed in uneconomical strips by medieval villagers were enclosed in large blocks by landowners for more efficient utilization. Enclosure usually involved a shift from cropping the land to pasturing sheep for wool production. The enclosure system required less labor—only a few shepherds rather than villages full of peasants. This feature made enclosures more profitable for landowners in later periods. Enclosures, which continued to become more common, especially in England, made land more economically productive than it had been.

There were important drawbacks. In a Europe whose population was growing once again, enclosures had the unfortunate effect of driving large numbers of peasants off the land where their labor was no longer required. These "sturdy beggars" (so called to distinguish them from cripples who begged because they were not physically able to work) thronged the roads and swelled the populations of the cities, creating new social tensions there.

A more positive consequence of enclosure was a renewed expansion of cloth manufacturing, the oldest and largest of Western industries. Production not only of woolens but of linens, silks, and other fabrics grew. Some of this hand manufacturing was cottage industry, done on cottage looms and spinning wheels by peasants. Their labors were coordinated by traveling merchants who provided the raw materials and picked up the roughly woven cloth in what became known as the *putting–out system.* This form of domestic production presided over by a merchant capitalist is, as we will see in a later chapter, often described as *proto–industrialism,* the precursor of the Industrial Revolution.

Metallurgy was another industry that made great strides in the later fifteenth and sixteenth centuries. New techniques for driving mine shafts deep into the earth, for shoring them up against cave–ins and pumping out water seepage made possible the exploitation of iron, copper, silver, and other metals from strata that were unreachable before. Heavy mechanical hammers were developed to pound metal into required shapes. Water wheels, long used for grinding grain, were brought into play here to provide power for draining mines and operating bellows and triphammers in foundries. Mining and metalworking thus reached new levels of productivity, especially in central Europe.

Renaissance Cities

With both population and productivity growing rapidly once more, commerce also flourished in the Renaissance. Merchants were the middlemen who got goods from producers to consumers, stimulating both production and consumption, and growing exceedingly rich in the process. Italy was the center of this resurgent capitalism, but cities flourished in the north as well.

Commercial methods originally pioneered in the Middle Ages were further developed. Coinage itself, reestablished in Europe during the twelfth–century commercial revolution, expanded further in the fifteenth century, thanks to the increased amount of silver available. Such business practices as the letter of credit—safer than carrying coins—and double–entry bookkeeping were also more widely used, and commercial insurance for long and dangerous trading voyages became common. The family firms and joint–stock companies of the fifteenth century, sometimes smaller than their medieval predecessors, were better organized to respond flexibly to changing times.

Cities remained the centers of Renaissance trade, and their growth reflected the commercial expansion of the era. Italian commercial preeminence continued throughout the fourteenth and fifteenth centuries. Among the large and prosperous Italian cities of the Renaissance were Milan, Genoa, Naples, Rome, and most admired of all, the venerable commercial metropolis of Venice and the newer center of wealth and culture, Florence.

The Venetian Republic, a key connection between Europe and the Near East since the Middle Ages, now commanded a coastal and island empire that stretched from northern Italy down the Adriatic and across the eastern Mediterranean as far as Cyprus. It still imported luxury goods from the Near East and beyond. Its industries included the famous Venetian arsenal, dedicated to shipbuilding and weapons manufacture for defense, which employed some ten thousand men and women by 1500, making it the largest single employer in Europe. The city of canals that the tourist sees today, with its splendid townhouse facades and tangled commercial streets, dates largely from this period. Most dazzling of all, however, was Florence, the economic as well as the cultural capital of Renaissance Italy. Still a major trade emporium and a center of woolen manufacture, Florence in the fifteenth century was also perhaps Europe's leading banking and financial center. The Florentine florin was an international currency, the dollar of its day, and branches of Florentine banks were found in all the great cities of Europe. Its patrician business community included some of the leading patrons of Renaissance art and learning, wealthy people who surrounded themselves with mural paintings and statuary of bronze and marble and who subsidized poets and philosophers.

In northern Europe, the revival of commerce was perhaps most vividly embodied in the rise of Antwerp, which emerged as the trading center of the Netherlands in the later fifteenth century. Like Venice, Antwerp benefited commercially from its location at the meeting of major trade routes. The city stood at the northern end of the Rhine–Alpine axis, with easy access to the North Sea and the merchant roads of Germany and northern France. Again, however, a farsighted business community made a central contribution. In particular, Antwerp's merchant patriciate opened what became Europe's most famous *Bourse,* or stock exchange and money market, in the early sixteenth century.

Renaissance Merchant Bankers

Two of the greatest names among Renaissance merchant bankers were the Italian Medici family of Florence and the German house of Fugger, headquartered in Augsburg. The former were among the most successful businessmen in fifteenth–century Italy; the latter were the wealthiest financiers in all Europe in the sixteenth century.

The Medici, the best known of Renaissance business clans, rose to prominence in the early 1400s when they began to give more of their attention to banking than to their established trading activities. In the middle of the century, the most successful of them, Cosimo de' Medici (1389–1464), made the Medici bank one of the biggest in Renaissance Italy and the centerpiece of an international business empire. The Medici family was involved in such key industries as wool processing and silk manufacture and in foreign trade, from the importation of Near Eastern spices to the large–scale export of cloth to France. Above all, however, their wealth was built on the far–flung branches of the family bank, which were to be found not only in the Italian metropolises of Venice, Milan, and Rome, but north of the Alps in the southern French cities of Lyons and Avignon, in Bruges in the Low Countries, in the Hanseatic city of Lübeck, in London and Barcelona and elsewhere. Profiting from loans to businessmen, noblemen, princes, and popes, the fifteenth–century Medici earned their reputation as the greatest financial dynasty in Renaissance Italy.

The Fugger family of Augsburg, in southern Germany, became Europe's most successful financiers in the 1500s. Jakob Fugger (1459–1526), called "Jakob the Rich," who had learned his trade in Venice, built the fortunes of the family. Their enterprises eventually stretched from Naples to Flanders and from Spain to Poland and deployed ten times the capital of the Medici bank in its heyday. Leading manufacturers of linen and fustians, masters of the iron, copper, and silver mines of central Europe, and traders in spices, jewels, and other luxury products, the Fuggers, like the Medici, still made most of their money from the trade in money itself. They were most famous for their loans to the ruling houses of Europe. Fugger money paid for military campaigns and for the elaborate ceremonial

Jakob Fugger with his chief accountant. The labels in the background are the names of major European cities, beginning with Rome and Venice, where the great international house of Fugger had commercial and financial dealings. (Herzog Anton Ulrich, Museum Braunschweig.)

occasions beloved of Renaissance sovereigns, bribed the electors who chose German emperors, and influenced the election of popes.

◆Renaissance Princes◆

The most famous of Renaissance political thinkers, Niccolò Machiavelli (1469–1527), whose views are discussed below, is best known for a brief manual of statecraft called *The Prince*. By "prince," Machiavelli did not mean the son of a king and queen, but simply an independent ruler, of either sex and any title. The duke of Milan, the Holy Roman emperor, Queen Elizabeth, and the pope were all "princes" in this sense. Because Renaissance politics revolved around such leaders, we pay considerable attention here to princes in all their decadence and grandeur.

The Revival of Political Power

Renaissance princes governed through both formal and informal institutions. Among the central institutions of early modern government was the informal gathering of power brokers and cronies called the *princely court*. More formal and more lasting were the growing centralized administrations and the beginnings of modern diplomatic corps, armies, and navies.

The courts of princes were social institutions that gathered the chief people in the realm about the ruler. Ministers of state, great noblemen, ambitious soldiers of fortune, charming hangers–on, the prince's friends and lovers, artists, entertainers, and servants in large numbers clustered around a powerful ruler. They came to make their fortunes—to become princely favorites (or favorites of favorites), to acquire lucrative posts or lands, to win knighthoods or noble titles. In return, they were willing to serve the prince by doing the work of government—some as judges or treasury officials or royal secretaries, others by carrying out diplomatic missions or commanding armies in the field.

Competition for royal favor and rewards was rife at court, and competing factions could paralyze a government or divide a nation. A shrewd ruler, on the other hand, could play chief favorites off against one another and get the most work out of all of them. Women found more power at court than elsewhere, either as sovereigns themselves or as wives or mistresses of princes. Satirists like the Italian wit Aretino (1492–1556)—a onetime courtier himself—sneered at princely hangers–on as sycophants condemned to "wait at table, stand about at their master's pleasure in a state of exhaustion, clean out privies [or] pimp for a happy young lord."[1] Moralists denounced the Renaissance court as a cesspool of worldliness and vice. Nevertheless, the courts got much of the governing done in early modern times.

Among the more formal institutions, courts of law and departments concerned with princely revenues continued to develop as they had in the medieval period. The handling of government business was increasingly routinized, a commonly cited sign of professionalization. The sheer number of officials grew, and their work was more and more specialized. It was increasingly common to make a lifetime career as a public official, as it had been in ancient Rome. Both at the center of power at the court or capital and in far–off provinces, professional administrators began to make the will of the prince a reality once more.

Renaissance Despots: The Medici and the Borgias

In the fourteenth and fifteenth centuries particularly, the Italian city–states produced a new type of ruler who became a model for the new monarchs of the nation–states to the north: the Italian Renaissance despot. Like tyrants in ancient Greece, the *Renaissance despots* of early modern Italy were not necessarily cruel or oppressive rulers. *Despot,* like *tyrant* in earlier centuries, meant simply an illegitimate ruler, one who governed without a traditional or constitutional basis for power like that enjoyed by the hereditary, divinely sanctioned monarchs of the north.

The Italian political scene was changing during the 1300s and 1400s, and many despots were the products—or the perpetrators—of those changes. In the High Middle Ages, the long struggle for control of Italy between the Holy Roman emperors and the Roman popes had the effect of preventing either from establishing an undisputed hegemony. The resulting power vacuum had fostered the growth of a large number of small but prosperous commercial and handicraft–industrial city–states. At the same time, however, these urban republics, or *communes,* were often torn by internal feuds between upper and lower classes and between partisans of either the pope or the emperor. In addition, they tended to be violently competitive and were frequently at war with each other, hiring mercenary companies to do most of the fighting but suffering themselves from sieges, unsafe roads, and ravaged countryside.

To restore order, the city–states sometimes turned to powerful autocratic rulers. In other cases, the head of one faction or a hired mercenary commander, a *condottiere,* might seize power. One way or another, during the Renaissance, despotism increasingly replaced the oligarchic merchant republic of the High Middle Ages.

In order to rule without clear constitutional sanction, the Italian despots became skilled practitioners of the art of politics. They imposed their will through military or monetary power, through political intrigue and manipulation. Some dominated politics by their personal popularity or by engaging in lavish programs of public building. Some used art patronage for political purposes, lavishing largesse on poets and artists who glorified them in verse and prose, paintings and statues. This was the political scene that Machiavelli observed around 1500, the world whose fundamentally amoral tone he communicated with such startling honesty in *The Prince*. It was a political world with no chivalric illusions, no lingering sense of the unity of Christendom, dedicated to the single–minded pursuit of power through war and politics.

Two examples of Italian political dynasties will illustrate the variety of Renaissance types. The Borgia clan built their power on control of the papacy, the Medici on financial preeminence.

The Papal States, stretching across central Italy from Rome to the Adriatic, had largely slipped out of papal control during the Avignon papacy and the Great Schism. In the later 1400s and the early 1500s, however, a series of thoroughly worldly and politically ambitious popes turned their attention to recovering control of the Papal States, adding the neighboring lands of the Romagna, and feuding with other Italian rulers. One of the most aggressive of these political popes was the notorious Borgia pontiff, Alexander VI (r. 1492–1503). Scion of a Spanish family and father of the much romanticized Cesare and Lucrezia Borgia, Pope Alexander founded a family that became notorious for plots, poisons, and alleged sexual irregularities. He spent lavishly and intrigued ruthlessly to reassert papal power in central Italy and to impose papal authority on the lands and mountain strongholds of the neighboring Italian nobility.

Cesare Borgia (c. 1475–1507), an unprincipled politician and celebrated soldier, became duke of Romagna and looked to Machiavelli like a man who might have it in him to unite all Italy, as in the days of the Roman Caesars. Lucrezia (1480–1519), lovely in her youth and devoutly religious in her later years, married three times in order to advance the family's dynastic ambitions, and was more likely a pawn than a participant in her relatives' nefarious schemes. Only the sudden death of Pope Alexander—attributed by many to poison—and Cesare Borgia's subsequent imprisonment and later death in battle put an end to the ambitious machinations of the Borgias.

The most famous of Italy's Renaissance rulers, however, were the heads of the Medici family of Florence, whose economic success was discussed above. Cosimo de' Medici built his political power on the family's wealth. Following his father's advice, he dominated political life by appealing to the less prestigious craft guilds while playing leading businessmen off against each other in the ruling councils of the Florentine Republic. In foreign affairs, it was Cosimo who organized a triple alliance of Florence, Milan, and Naples that restrained the more aggressive, expansionist power of Venice and the Papal States for more than forty years, from 1450 to 1492.

Cosimo's grandson Lorenzo (r. 1469–1492), called "the Magnificent" for his style of life and lavish art patronage, found both political power at home and the international balance of power harder to maintain. A rebellion in Florence led by a rival banking family and a war with both the Papal States and Naples, Florence's erstwhile ally, scarred the middle years of Lorenzo's tenure of power. Like his grandfather, however, he continued to rule, without doing drastic violence to the republican constitution of Florence, through influence, intrigue, and manipulation. Subsequent Medici formalized their power by turning Florence into a dukedom and going on to provide both queens and popes for early modern Europe.

The Spider King and the First Tudor

The kings of the north also prospered during the Renaissance period. Reestablishing the royal power that had been shaken by the troubles of the later Middle Ages, they laid solid foundations on which later monarchs might build. It is with the first of these, the so-called *new monarchs* of the later 1400s, that the present section is primarily concerned. Their newness lay in their sometimes ruthlessly pragmatic policies, their growing tendency to claim absolute power over their subjects, and their sheer success as builders of centralized government. Some gave at least lip service to the chivalric and crusading ideals of their medieval predecessors, but almost all were primarily dedicated to expanding the power of the monarchy in the Renaissance world.

Of all the celebrated sovereigns whose names and fame come crowding at us out of this segment of the past, Louis XI of France (r. 1461–1483)—the Spider King—was one of the least glamorous. Where other princes gloried in feats of arms and royal pageantry, King Louis preferred manipulation and intrigue, bribing allies and waiting out his foes. Organizing and conspiring, he wove intricate webs that were sometimes too clever to succeed. But his approach was far more suited to the times than was the much admired chivalry of his great rival, Charles the Bold (r. 1467–1477) of Burgundy.

With the English invaders of the Hundred Years' War expelled from France by Louis's predecessor, Louis XI's most dangerous antagonist was his powerful vassal Charles, duke of Burgundy. The ambitious duke had a grand scheme: to construct a new state stretching

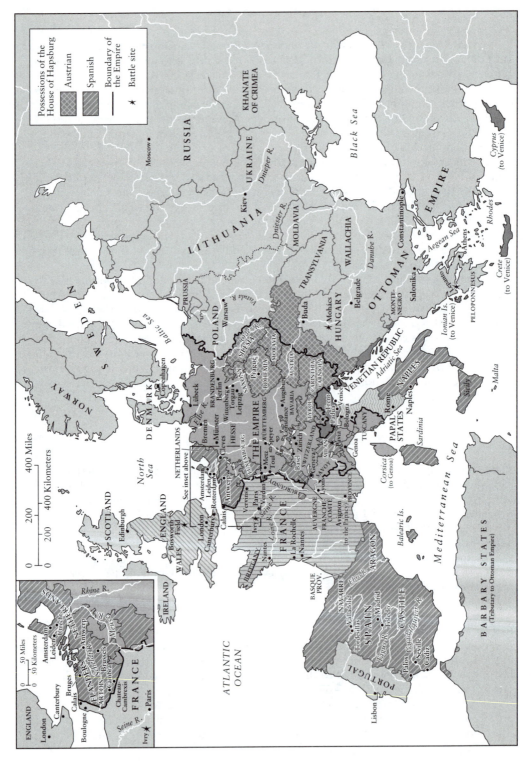

Possessions of the House of Hapsburg
- Austrian
- Spanish
- Boundary of the Empire
- ★ Battle site

RUSSIA

KHANATE OF CRIMEA

Moscow

Black Sea

Cyprus (to Venice)

UKRAINE

Dnieper R.

LITHUANIA

Dniester R.

MOLDAVIA

WALLACHIA

TRANSYLVANIA

Danube R.

OTTOMAN EMPIRE

Aegean Sea

Rhodes

Constantinople

Athens

Crete (to Venice)

Salonika

MONTE-NEGRO

Belgrade

PELOPONNESUS

Ionian Is. (to Venice)

PRUSSIA

Vistula R.

POLAND

Warsaw

Buda

Mohács ★

HUNGARY

SILESIA

MORAVIA

BOHEMIA

Prague

AUSTRIA

CARINTHIA

CARNIOLA

VENETIAN REPUBLIC

Adriatic Sea

Venice

NAPLES

Naples

Sicily

Malta

Rome

PAPAL STATES

Sardinia

BRANDENBURG

Berlin

SAXONY

Torgau

Leipzig

Wittenberg

Lübeck

Bremen

Münster

Elbe R.

HESSE

Cleves

THE EMPIRE

WÜRTTEMBERG

Augsburg

BAVARIA

Speyer

TYROL

Constance

Trent

Padua

Bologna

TUSCANY

Genoa

Corsica (to Genoa)

DENMARK

Copenhagen

Baltic Sea

NORWAY

SWEDEN

North Sea

NETHERLANDS
See inset above

Amsterdam
Leiden
Rotterdam

Antwerp

Calais

LUXEMBURG

Metz
Toul
Verdun

Cateau-Cambrésis

Paris

Rhine R.

Marne R.

Ivry ★

Seine R.

BURGUNDY

SWITZERLAND

Basel
Zürich

MILAN

Marignano

SAVOY

Lyons

PROVENCE

Avignon (to the Papacy)

FRANCHE-COMTÉ

AUVERGNE

FRANCE

Loire R.

La Rochelle

Nantes

BRITTANY

Nantes

SCOTLAND

Edinburgh

ENGLAND

Bosworth Field

London

Canterbury

WALES

IRELAND

ATLANTIC OCEAN

BASQUE PROV.

NAVARRE

ARAGON

Ebro R.

CASTILE

Madrid

Toledo

Valladolid

Tordesillas

Tagus R.

Guadalquivir R.

Seville

Cádiz

Palos

SPAIN

Balearic Is.

Mediterranean Sea

BARBARY STATES
(Tributary to Ottoman Empire)

PORTUGAL

Lisbon

Scale
0   200   400 Miles
0   200   400 Kilometers

Inset (Netherlands):
0   50 Miles
0   50 Kilometers

Rhine R.

FRIESLAND

NETHERLANDS

Amsterdam
Leiden

Antwerp

Ghent
Bruges

FLANDERS

ARTOIS

Calais

Boulogne

Cambrai

Cateau-Cambrésis

Meuse R.

Brussels

Maastricht

BRABANT

FRANCE

Paris

Seine R.

Ivry ★

ENGLAND

London

Canterbury

Europe in the Sixteenth Century

north and south along the Rhine between France and the Holy Roman Empire. Supported by the fighting prowess of the Burgundian knights and the wealth of the Netherlands—also ruled by the house of Burgundy—it was not an impossible dream. Had Charles succeeded, he could have stripped the French monarchy of half its lands and created a powerful new state in the heart of Europe.

Louis the Spider, however, responded to Charles's martial challenge by subsidizing the redoubtable Swiss, then the most effective mercenaries in Europe, who were also threatened by Burgundian expansionism. The Swiss, then, did the French king's fighting for him, defeating Charles the Bold three times. They finally killed him at the Battle of Nancy in 1477, while Louis sat smiling in the center of his web, reaching out to absorb most of Burgundy once the duke was dead.

Additional territorial acquisitions under Louis XI included the large Angevin lands in the west and south, which he inherited, and two provinces pried away from Spain. He thus left the French monarchy twice the size of the kingdom he had inherited.

Louis also left it stronger and more centralized. He reasserted his authority over the remaining lands held by independent princes of royal blood, promoted and supported middle–class officials, and expanded the royal army (though he tended to keep it in reserve rather than committing it to battle). He increased taxation and encouraged the development of handicraft industry in France. He left the country prosperous and powerful, fully recovered from the disasters of the Hundred Years' War.

England also recovered from its late medieval trauma of foreign and civil strife. The Hundred Years War (1337–1453) was followed in England by the Wars of the Roses (1455–1485), which had seen the land torn by factions of feuding nobles led by the houses of Lancaster and York. This long civil war, in turn, had ended dramatically with the Battle of Bosworth Field in 1485. The victor was the Lancastrian Henry Tudor, a shrewd, industrious Welshman much closer in spirit to Louis the Spider than to the chivalrous warriors of the Middle Ages. The royal house of Tudor that he founded became England's most admired—and romanticized—dynasty: Henry VII (r. 1485–1509) was the father of Henry VIII and grandfather of Queen Elizabeth I. The first Tudor spent his quarter of a century on the throne strengthening and enriching the kingdom they would inherit.

Like Louis XI, Henry VII generally preferred diplomacy to warfare. He strengthened England's international position by marrying his daughter to the king of Scotland and his two sons (in succession) to the same Spanish princess, a daughter of the powerful King Ferdinand and Queen Isabella. To promote domestic tranquillity, Henry VII himself had married Elizabeth (1465–1503), the heiress of the house of York. To strengthen his own hand, he increased the powers of the justices of the peace in the shires and promoted burghers and churchmen to high official posts in the central government.

Coming from the unprosperous land of Wales, Henry Tudor was particularly conscious of the importance of money. He worked diligently with his councilors to expand the wealth of both the kingdom and the monarchy. Through the confiscation of the lands of rebels against the crown and through the heavy exactions imposed by his notorious Court of the Star Chamber, he accumulated an unprecedented treasury surplus of more than a million pounds. He also provided official support for the cloth trade, England's biggest export, and signed commercial treaties with states as far away as Florence. Like Louis XI, Henry VII thus left his country unified and prosperous.

Ferdinand and Isabella

As medieval monarchies that had been evolving for hundreds of years, France and England were old players of the power game. The unification of most of the Iberian peninsula into the powerful Kingdom of Spain took longer. Surrounded on three sides by water (the Atlantic, the Strait of Gibraltar, and the Mediterranean), the territory that became Spain was isolated from the rest of Europe by the Pyrenees mountain range. Overrun by the Moors in the eighth century, divided geographically, linguistically, and politically, and home to Christians, Muslims, and Jews alike, this corner of Europe had experienced none of the unifying trends of medieval France and England. Isabella of Castile (r. 1474–1504) and Ferdinand of Aragon (r. 1479–1516), whose marriage began the process of Spanish unification, had their work cut out for them.

Married as teenagers in 1469 in what may have been that rarity among royal marriages, a love match, the two inherited the thrones of their respective kingdoms in the 1470s. The result was a personal, but not an institutional, union of the two largest Iberian monarchies. Castile (by far the larger) and Aragon remained separate entities, each with its own internal administration, regional characteristics, and independent feudal nobility. Two unifying factors, however, did bind Castilians, Aragonese, and most other Spaniards: a common enemy in the Moors, who still ruled the Kingdom of Granada in the south, and the loyalty of a crusading people to the militant Catholic church. Isabella's intelligence and religious piety and Ferdinand's crafty aggressiveness helped them to parlay these factors into strong royal government and international power.

To bring their feudal aristocracy under royal control, the new rulers minimized noble participation in the *cortes* (assemblies) of Castile and Aragon. To control the towns, the determined pair appointed royal officials to replace elected magistrates and councils in Spanish cities. Ferdinand and Isabella also created a group of powerful councils on the national level to deal with finances, justice, and international and religious affairs. Staffing the new councils mostly with lawyers, they ruled in large part through these central institutions. *Los reyes católicos*—"the Catholic kings," as they came to be called—also used medieval religion and the church to strengthen the state. They made good use of Isabella's astute chief adviser Cardinal Ximenes, transforming the Spanish Inquisition into a virtual branch of the government. And by equating Christianity with patriotism, the Catholic kings used the strong religious feelings of the people as an ideological cement to hold the new nation together.

In the 1480s, the new rulers gained a special grip on the loyalty of most Spaniards by launching a crusade to expel the last Muslims from western Europe. They achieved this goal with the conquest of Granada in 1492. This was also the year in which Isabella received the aspiring navigator Christopher Columbus for the first time—in her camp outside the walls of the last Moorish stronghold—and provided the support that led to the founding of the Spanish Empire in the New World. Ferdinand, meanwhile, expanded the Aragonese power base already established in Naples and Sicily into a greater Spanish presence in Renaissance Italy. The Spanish sovereigns also arranged a series of carefully calculated diplomatic marriages into the ruling houses of France, England, and the Holy Roman Empire. Through war, diplomacy, and gambling on Columbus, they thus elevated their still only half–unified nation to the rank of one of Europe's greatest powers.

Ferdinand and Isabella also implemented a fiercely orthodox religious policy, and one that is difficult for us to understand today. They required the large Muslim and Jewish populations to convert to Christianity, persecuted them through the Inquisition, and finally expelled both groups. The expulsion of the Jews in particular cost Spain many of its wealthiest merchants, most skilled artisans, and most brilliant intellectuals. But the rigorously Catholic nation that remained was prepared to lead the forces of Western Catholicism in the impending struggle with the Protestant Reformation and to launch the conquest of the pagan New World with special zeal.

Czars and Emperors

On the other side of Europe, across the wide central and east European plains, north to the Baltic Sea and south into the mountain ranges of the Balkans, the Germans, Slavs, and other peoples of central and eastern Christendom had evolved their own monarchies by the end of the Middle Ages. The most important of these central and eastern European states were the medieval Holy Roman Empire in what is today Germany and the new state of Muscovy just taking shape in northern Russia.

Among the more prominent eastern European nations, Poland, Lithuania, Hungary, and Bohemia shared some common problems and patterns of development. Most of these states faced foreign pressure, either from the Germans of central Europe or from the Ottoman Turks advancing up the Balkan peninsula after their conquest of Constantinople. Most of these states also felt the familiar strains of conflict between ambitious monarchs and the traditional noble ruling class. In Poland, the nobles succeeded in largely emancipating themselves from their kings, gaining tax exemptions, absolute authority over their peasants, and legislative supremacy through the *diet,* or assembly, which they controlled. In Hungary, the gains of the Magyar nobles were only temporarily reversed by King Matthias Corvinus (r. 1458–1490). This strong–willed, shrewd Renaissance prince built up his army and his financial strength, imported Italian artists and scholars to glorify his capital at Buda, and for a time made Hungary the most powerful nation in eastern Europe.

But the future lay with the slowly stirring might of Muscovy. The slow crumbling of the hegemony of the Mongol Golden Horde left two north Russian states as the most likely candidates for supremacy: Novgorod and Moscow. Novgorod in the northwest, with access to the Baltic Sea, developed as a typical medieval commercial city, with a patrician merchant class running the expanding principality through its assembly, the *veche.* Moscow, more centrally located in European Russia, evolved in closer contact with the Mongols and under the influence of Byzantium.

A fourteenth–century prince of Moscow, Ivan I (r. 1328–1341), known as "Moneybags," became chief collector of revenues for the Golden Horde and made Moscow the wealthiest of all the Russian states. Another Muscovite prince, Dmitri of the Don (r. 1359–1389), earned an immense reputation by defeating the Mongols at the Battle of Kulikovo in 1380. It was a century later, however, before Ivan III the Great (r. 1462–1505) turned back the last Mongol advance on Moscow in 1480, emerging as the first real ruler of the state that became the core of modern Russia. Ivan the Great also established Russia's claim to be the true heir of the Byzantine tradition. He married a niece of the last emperor of Constantinople, took the imperial titles of autocrat and caesar, or *czar,* and established the Byzantine policy of caesaropapism, or subordination of the Russian Orthodox church to the czarist state. It was Ivan, finally, who first declared that Muscovite Russia was the "Third Rome," the modern heir to ancient Rome and medieval Byzantium, with a comparable right to universal and absolute authority.

Under Ivan III, the ambitious Muscovite state overwhelmed and absorbed the rival principality of Novgorod in the 1470s. In so doing, Moscow added substantially to its territory, which Ivan expanded still further by seizing parts of eastern Lithuania and Poland. The result was a Muscovy extending as far north as the Arctic and as far east as the Ural Mountains. Perhaps more important, however, the victory of Moscow over Novgorod meant the virtual severing of Russian contact with western Europe. Novgorod's Western–style commercial middle classes, with their local assembly and trade with the West, gave way to a more autocratic regime with traditions rooted in Russia's unique connections with the Mongols and Byzantium.

Russian autocracy in 1500, however, was in some ways more claim than reality. Russia's boyar nobility clung to its traditional right to hold land free of military service or to change princely overlords at will. Even the caesaropapist Russian Orthodox church defended its lands against czarist encroachment. A direction had been laid down by the Muscovite czars; but it took centuries to build the czarist state that had the reputation of being the most autocratic in the Western world.

"The Holy Roman Empire of the German Nation," as it was first officially called in the fifteenth century, had never attained a centralized organization comparable to that of England or France. Germany did produce a strong—if in the end less successful—ruler in this period. A chivalric prince who loved the knightly virtues, Maximilian I (r. 1493–1519), displayed an old–fashioned idealism that made him much more popular than either Louis XI in France or Henry VII in England. But the Austrian Habsburg emperor also saw the need for more centralized authority over his ramshackle confederation of principalities, free cities, and independent knights and bishops, and he labored toward that end. Maximilian's centralizing efforts were aimed at imposing imperial authority on the *Reichstag*. This assembly, inherited from the earlier fifteenth century, brought together the seven imperial electors, the chief German princes, and the leaders of the free cities of Germany. The emperor's new schemes for governmental reform included an imperial council with real executive powers over the separate German states, imperial law courts and coinage, an end to private wars, and even a system of imperial taxation. The courts and the imperial council were in fact created, but because these institutions were largely controlled by the electors and the princes, they did not increase the power of the Holy Roman emperor after all.

In the tradition of his medieval predecessors, Maximilian led a series of imperial armies over the Alps into Italy. These indecisive campaigns added little to his international position, at least in material terms of territory or wealth. Through a series of fortunate diplomatic marriages, however, he did lay the groundwork for the Habsburg international supremacy of the sixteenth century. His own marriage to Mary of Burgundy (1457–1482), daughter of Charles the Bold, brought him the wealthy commercial and industrial centers of the Netherlands. The marriage of his son Philip (1478–1506) to Juana the Mad (1479–1555), daughter of Ferdinand and Isabella, brought the vast Spanish possessions in Europe and the New World into the hands of the Habsburgs in the next generation. Through such politically astute marriage alliances, the Habsburgs, who could not impose centralized authority on the German states, nevertheless emerged as the most powerful dynasty in Europe as the sixteenth century began.

There was a bustle and a stirring among the political rulers of the West in 1500. Despots in Italy and the new monarchs in Europe north of the Alps were laboring mightily to establish more powerful governments than the most successful of medieval sovereigns. Yet there was a sweaty intensity, a driven quality about this commitment to power that disturbed at least one shrewd contemporary commentator. They were, admitted the Spider

King's biographer Philippe de Commines (c. 1447–1511), "great men [who] labored so much to aggrandize themselves and to acquire glory." And yet, he wondered, "would it not have been better, both for them and all other princes, and for men of middling rank who have lived under these great men . . . if they had . . . striven less hard, . . . undertaken fewer enterprises and . . . been more afraid of offending God and of persecuting their subjects and neighbors?"[2]

♦ An Evolving Society ♦

The social history of Renaissance Europe saw a notable intermingling of new and old patterns, medieval and early modern folkways. The period saw the emergence of a new aristocracy and new opportunities for at least some women. But both city and country life were still heavily influenced by earlier traditions, and the social scapegoating of Jews continued to oppress Europe's largest minority.

The New Aristocracy

The social ideal of the Renaissance ruling class was outlined in so-called *conduct books.* Most of these were Italian, and the most famous of all was Baldassare Castiglione's (1478–1529) *Book of the Courtier* (c. 1516). According to Castiglione, such medieval physical skills as mastery of sword and spear, stylish horseback riding, hunting, and other sports like wrestling and tennis (played with smaller rackets and on an indoor court) were essential parts of the genteel life. The perfect Renaissance gentleman was also expected to have the social graces first cultivated in the high medieval courts of love: the ability to sing, play the lute or some other musical instrument, dance such athletic Renaissance dances as the galliard, and perhaps most of all, carry on the sort of elegant, witty conversation fashionable in Renaissance princely courts.

The major new emphasis, however, was the requirement that a Renaissance gentleman possess a civilized knowledge of the "humane letters," meaning the ancient classics. The Renaissance aristocrat was also expected to be both familiar with the revival of classical studies called *humanism* and sensitive to the art and literature of the Renaissance itself.

Two qualities of Renaissance character, finally, have been perhaps clearer to modern historians than they were to Renaissance people themselves. The first of these was a widely admired blend of individualism and what Machiavelli called *virtù*—a combination of the ability to stand on one's own feet and the will and capacity to fight one's way to the top. Though the Renaissance condemned social climbing in theory, successful climbers were often admired, and suitably aristocratic ancestors could usually be found for the individual who did win high place and reputation without the advantage of gentle birth. The Second and most striking quality is the many–sidedness of such rare Renaissance individuals as Leonardo da Vinci, versatile geniuses whose many talents have earned them the label of "universal." Leon Battista Alberti (1404–1472), for instance, was a multifaceted Florentine, perhaps best known as an architect and the author of books on the subject, but also celebrated for his writings on painting, moral philosophy, geography, language, and secret codes! When we call a contemporary a *Renaissance person,* it is this quality that is usually meant: a dazzling mastery of many fields which expands our sense of human capabilities.

Women in the Renaissance

The ideal education of a Renaissance lady in many ways resembled that of a Renaissance gentleman. She, too, could study the ancient poets and philosophers, learn to play, sing, dance, and draw and to excel in the elegant, urbane conversation of the court. Many up-per–class women also acquired skill in riding, in hunting with hawks, and in other vigorous activities.

There, however, the resemblance ended. Women did not engage in the more violent sports or learn to use weapons. Instead, the Renaissance lady, like her medieval forebear, was encouraged to practice such "feminine accomplishments" as skilled needlework and embroidery. A number of traditional personal qualities were also part of the image of the ideal woman around 1500. Religious piety, moral virtues, and social submissiveness to par-ents and husbands were still commonly praised traits.

Joan Kelly–Gadol, in her classic essay "Did Women have a Renaissance?" drew on a close reading of literary evidence to suggest that the Renaissance actually represented a net loss in power and prestige for women.[3] The ladies of medieval romances, Kelly–Gadol urged, at least commanded the devoted service of enamored knights. The more decorative, less active ladies in Renaissance courtly literature did not. Underlying these differences in the literary image of women, Kelly–Gadol detected a decline in real power for both noble women and the women of the urban patriciate in the Renaissance. The rise of despotic princely power seized by force or guile and most often exercised by men led to an increas-ingly passive and subservient role for women in Renaissance society. There was a revival of the ancient Athenian distinction between "an inferior domestic realm of women" and a "superior public realm of men," a "division between personal and public life" that became the basis for "the modern relation of the sexes" for the next five centuries.[4]

And yet, despite the commonplace that woman's role was subordinate, aristocratic gentlemen and ladies are depicted as exchanging wit and repartee on a basis of evident equality in such popular Renaissance works as Shakespeare's plays and the bawdy tales of the Italian writer Boccaccio. Certainly more respect and admiration seem to have gone to gifted women in the Renaissance than in the Middle Ages, and there were probably more powerful women in the later period too. Queen Elizabeth herself was fluent in a half–dozen languages, including Latin and Greek. Italian Renaissance ladies like Isabella d'Este (1474–1539), hailed by poets as "first lady of the world" for her exquisite taste, were among the most discriminating patrons of Renaissance art. Caterina Sforza (1463–1509), countess of Forlì, is cited in Kelly–Gadol's essay as a female Renaissance prince who rose through "skill, forcefulness, and ruthless ambition" like her great adver-sary Cesare Borgia.[5] Renaissance sovereigns like Queen Elizabeth I of England and others probably changed the history of their times more than any medieval queen did.

Cities and Villages

Communities, from the agricultural village to the bustling city, were also of great impor-tance to Renaissance people. Indeed, our awareness of Renaissance individualism and the glittering achievements of individual Renaissance rulers and artists has perhaps blinded us to the communal life of most Renaissance people.

The homes of early modern villagers showed few advances beyond those of their me-dieval forebears, though chimneys and snug rainproof thatching were more common in the north. The watermill or windmill, the smithy, and the parish church still stood out among the clustered huts, and there was often a manor house or castle on a neighboring hill. But there were also more deserted villages, thanks to enclosure. "Sheep are devouring people," they grumbled in England as villages emptied of people and sheep proliferated in the fields the villagers had once tilled.

Most Renaissance cities rose on medieval or even ancient foundations. Clustered thickly around crossroads, riverbanks, or hilltops, their streets, houses, churches, and public buildings were crammed within a concentric ring of centuries-old, still expanding city walls. Cobblestoned streets and multistoried buildings were common by now. Italian cities were often lower and more open, with airy squares and two–story buildings predominating; French or German cities had taller overhanging houses shading their narrow medieval lanes.

Neighborhoods were still often defined by the guilds that practiced there, and towering churches were still the main landmarks, proudly added to by guilds and merchant princes. City halls, guildhalls, hospitals, almshouses, schools, and buildings used by the community at large also reflected the intensity of civic pride. Vegetable gardens were sandwiched in between the houses, and chickens, goats, and milk cows were raised in crowded city streets. The result was a colorful, if not always healthful, scene as garbage and sewage still lay heaped in city streets or trickled along open sewers.

Power relations in both villages and cities also resembled their medieval precursors. Though serfdom had largely vanished from western Europe in the Renaissance, peasant villages were still often dominated by local landowners. In many places, the lord's bailiff still administered local justice, and compulsory corvée labor and other holdovers from the medieval manor were still common. The relative political independence characteristic of medieval cities persisted, and the superior quality of urban life continued to draw immigrants from the countryside.

The sense of community was widely expressed in the public celebrations, civic functions, church festivals, and popular entertainments of all sorts that frequently filled the streets of Renaissance towns. Crowds gathered for weddings and funerals, for the installation of officials and the arrival of visiting dignitaries, and for the whipping, mutilation, or execution of criminals. Processions, feasts, and festivals highlighted the church calendar also, celebrating saints' days of local significance, Christmas and Easter, the New Year, Epiphany, and especially the gaudy carnival time that preceded Lent. Such occasions were celebrated with elaborate processions and feasts, with entertainment in the form of plays, puppet shows, jugglers, and acrobats. There was also plenty of dancing and singing, drunkenness, casual sexual encounters, and sometimes wanton violence.

The Jews in the Renaissance

As noted in earlier chapters, the hysteria accompanying religious crusades and the disasters that threatened medieval Christendom in its last centuries often led to violent attacks on the Jews of Europe. Long blamed for the death of Christ, suspected of bloody secret rites, and resented as moneylenders, Jews were particularly made to serve as scapegoats to satisfy the desperate need for someone to blame when the world goes wrong.

As early as the thirteenth century, Louis IX of France—St. Louis—had rigorously enforced anti–Jewish regulations, and in 1290 the Jews were expelled entirely from England. Waves of persecution included killings by gangs of German *Judenschläger* ("Jew beaters") in the 1330s and 1340s, and in the once tolerant Spain, the murder of many Jews in a wave of forced conversions in the 1390s.

Even through these violent centuries, however, successful Jews played important roles in the business, professional, and political life of the West. France repeatedly had to allow the return of exiled Jews because of the skills and wealth they brought with them. Highly placed "court Jews" helped finance the Holy Roman Empire, and Jews like Don Isaac Abranavel (1437–1508) were among the most trusted advisers of Ferdinand and Isabella of Spain. In Spain and particularly in Italy, highly educated Jews pursued successful careers in government service, law, the universities, and in other professions and crafts.

Learned Renaissance Christians, furthermore, added to their passion for the pagan Greco–Roman classics a new interest in the Hebrew language and the Hebrew Old Testament. Renaissance scholars like Pico della Mirandola became fascinated by the Jewish mystical tradition of the *Cabala*, which sought occult meanings in the sacred writings of ancient and medieval Judaism. In the later sixteenth century, however, the intensified religious feeling kindled by the Protestant and Catholic Reformations led to renewed persecution of Jews, even in Italy. Harried from country to country and always under threat of confiscation of property or personal attack, the oldest Western minority managed only by a remarkable tenacity of purpose both to survive and to preserve its faith intact.

◆ Humanism and Literature ◆

It is in the manipulation of the written word, from poetry to political thought, that the Renaissance was most clearly a revival of ancient culture. We look first at humanism, a conscious campaign to recapture the vanished literary styles of the Romans and the Greeks, which flourished from the 1300s to the 1500s. But Renaissance writers were creative people too, and the same period saw new literary forms take shape in the vernacular languages. From the Italian Renaissance poet and humanist scholar Petrarch in the 1300s to Shakespeare around 1600, this was an age of brilliant literary artists.

Rediscovering the Classics

The *humanist movement*, which extended from the middle 1300s to the early 1500s, was a shared passion for the ancient classics and a determined effort to recover—and to imitate—lost masterpieces. Humanist writers spent little time on metaphysics, logic, and theology, which were the central concerns of the medieval university. Instead, they concentrated on what seemed to Renaissance scholars to be more "human" literary subjects: poetry and rhetoric, ethics, history, and government. The new movement thus became known as *studia humanitatis*—"human studies," or as we say today, "the humanities"—and those who pursued these studies were called humanists.

Humanist scholars began as early as the fourteenth century to dredge up forgotten manuscripts of Latin classics from dusty monastery shelves. These rare finds were edited and annotated by their triumphant discoverers. As printing presses—discussed later—sprang up in many European cities, publishers like the Aldine Press of Venice made printed copies of these works available to students, teachers, and an increasingly literate aristocracy. For those whose Latin was not up to the originals, translations into the major languages were made, and collections of selected literary gems and wise sayings were widely published.

As private tutors or heads of elite schools, humanists taught the ancient classics to Europe's aristocracy. Renaissance despots and the new monarchs alike, meanwhile, demanded higher education in their officials and ministers of state, who had to cope with the increasingly complex business of governing a modern state. Thus for the first time since antiquity, Europe acquired an educated ruling class.

The first humanist was Francesco Petrarca (1304–1374), known as Petrarch in English, a dedicated poet and scholar often described as the first "Renaissance man." Trained in the law at Bologna, Petrarch was much more interested in poetry. He pioneered in two basic humanist directions: ferreting out manuscripts of ancient Roman writers, and writing original works in classical literary Latin rather than in the church Latin of the Middle Ages. Yet he had a strong medieval otherworldly streak himself and was as great an admirer of St. Augustine as of Cicero and Vergil. His fame as scholar, moralist, and poet was so great that King Robert of Naples (r. 1309–1343) revived the ancient custom of rewarding excellence with a laurel crown to make Petrarch the first modern poet laureate in 1341.

Among the leading humanists who carried on the effort in the fifteenth century were Valla, Ficino, and Pico della Mirandola. Lorenzo Valla (1407–1457) epitomized the new movement at its most daring. Valla demonstrated through stylistic analysis of the text that the Donation of Constantine, which had provided a basis for the pope's claims to rule the Papal States and to sovereignty over Christendom as a whole, was a forgery. Marsilio Ficino (1433–1499) translated Plato's works and founded the Platonic Academy in the Florence of the Medici. He also explored the ideas of the third–century Neoplatonic philosopher Plotinus and fathered the influential notion of "platonic"—really Neoplatonic—love, a spiritual passion of one person for another.Giovanni Pico della Mirandola (1463–1494) immersed himself in Hebrew and Arabic as well as Latin and Greek and wrote the famous *Oration on the Dignity of Man* (1486), a confident assertion of pride in human achievement and of conviction that human beings are masters of their fates.

Northern humanism, the work of scholars living north of Italy, had a more moralistic and overtly Christian focus than the humanism of the sunny south. The most famous northern humanist was Desiderius Erasmus (1466–1536) of Rotterdam, a wandering scholar who earned the reputation of being the most distinguished intellect in the Western world. His most famous work was the satirical oration called the *Praise of Folly* (1509), which exposed the follies of sixteenth–century people of every class and condition. Erasmus's major concern, however, was to apply humanist scholarship to the great books of the Christian tradition. He propounded what he called "the philosophy of Christ," based on faith, Christian love, and ethical behavior rather than on dogma and ritual. He applied this humanistic creed to the education of European aristocrats and rulers in such books as *The Handbook of the Christian Knight* (1503) and *The Education of a Christian Prince* (1516).

Humanist Social Thought

Modern social thought can be traced to humanist origins in the fifteenth and sixteenth centuries. In two unique works by humanists, Machiavelli's *Prince* and More's *Utopia,* lie the origins of some basic modern ideas of how human society is or should be run.

Niccolò Machiavelli (1469–1527), diplomat and secretary of the ruling council of Florence for fifteen years, knew many of the political leaders of the Renaissance personally. Though *The Prince* (1513) earned him a reputation for cynicism, it was more a realistic account of politics in his own time than anything else.

In the real world as he knew it, Machiavelli felt that only a shrewd and ruthless prince could govern successfully. He therefore advised such policies as brutal repression (fear is more dependable than popularity); governmental deception (lying may be necessary to gain the prince's ends); and manipulation of religion and law to keep the people in order and to improve the prince's image. A successful prince, Machiavelli believed, would have to play the fox and the lion, sly and strong enough to survive in the jungle of politics and international relations. *The Prince* is a book about this sort of political power, a manual of statecraft without a moral, and the rumored bedside book of every modern autocrat and dictator from Frederick the Great to Stalin.

The *Utopia* of Thomas More (1478–1535) was all moral—an account not of the way things are, but of how an ideal state *ought* to be run. It established the genre of modern "utopian" writing that traces its roots to Plato's *Republic* and has continued into our own century. Yet like Machiavelli's *Prince*, More's *Utopia* (1516) was unique.

A lawyer and an admired humanist, Erasmus's friend and Henry VIII's chancellor, More tried to put his ideals into practice. And he died for his beliefs: he was beheaded in 1535 for refusing to accept King Henry's headship of the English church during the Reformation.

More's *Utopia* describes the ideal state, imagined as an island in the Ocean Sea, where Columbus and his successors had made so many new discoveries. More's Utopians shared their material goods and used gold for such ignoble purposes as making chamber pots. Reasonable, well educated, and socially disciplined, the citizens of Utopia had built a hard–working and well–ordered community. The weakness of this glowing vision, however, was revealed in the title itself. *Utopia* means "Nowhere." As critics have repeatedly pointed out, there was no such community. To label a social ideal as "utopian" has thus been to dismiss it as unrealistic—as a social vision too perfect for this world—ever since.

Innovative Spirits: Petrarch to Cervantes

The writers of the Renaissance include some of the great names of English, French, Spanish, and Italian literature. We will have space here for only a select few of those literary giants, including the poet Petrarch; the essayist Montaigne; Cervantes, creator of the immortal Don Quixote, and William Shakespeare, whose plays still challenge us today.

The two most critically acclaimed and influential of Italian Renaissance writers both wrote in the fourteenth century, at the beginning of the new era. Petrarch, already discussed, was not only the founding father of Latin humanism but an enormously influential poet in Italian. His fame in Italian literature was based on his *Sonnets to Laura* (1360), a collection of lyrical love poems addressed to the great love of his life, who had died in the plague. The Laura of these poems is both physically beautiful and the symbol of a higher perfection. This intriguing duality, and the beauty of Petrarch's verse, won him hordes of imitators all over Europe. By the end of the Renaissance, the Petrarchan conventions of golden hair and hopeless love began to seem a little silly even to Renaissance readers. But for many generations, Petrarchism in poetry was as satisfactory to that age as the romantic conventions of our time are to us.

A very different attitude toward love and sexual passion was taken by Petrarch's contemporary and friend Giovanni Boccaccio (1313–1375). Son of a Florentine merchant, bored with business and law, Boccaccio gave himself over to a life of pleasure and poetry in Renaissance Naples. Returning to Florence in time to witness the ravages of the Black Death in 1348, Boccaccio soon thereafter wrote the *Decameron,* the collection of one hundred witty, often bawdy tales on which his reputation largely rests. Presented as stories told by ten spritely young ladies and gentlemen who have fled the ravages of the plague to a country retreat, the book has a vitality that earned it immense popularity both during and long after the Renaissance.

Michel de Montaigne (1533–1592), gentleman, judge, and mayor of Bordeaux, showed few signs of literary aspirations until he retired to his country chateau to jot down his thoughts on life. But the resulting three volumes of *Essays* (1572–1580) became French classics and established the essay as a literary genre. Montaigne brought his substantial classical learning to bear on the world around him, providing thoughtful comment on everything from friendship and skepticism to the new fashion of horse–drawn coaches and the nature of the New World's "noble savages." Montaigne's motto, "What Do I Know?" reflected the maturity of an age whose choicer spirits were coming to terms with human fallibility.

Miguel de Cervantes (1547–1616), the greatest Spanish writer of this "golden century" in the history of Spain, said goodbye to his age with a laugh. Cervantes himself had aspired to military glory, fighting the Turks in the great naval battle of Lepanto, but he ended his military career as a prisoner of war. In the two volumes of *Don Quixote* (1605), however, Cervantes created one of the great books and two of the archetypal characters of modern fiction. The insanely idealistic knight Don Quixote and his peasant squire Sancho Panza who set off in search of chivalric adventures in a thoroughly postchivalric century are the stuff of great comedy, from slapstick to social satire. But Cervantes' creations are also unforgettable symbols of the fate of high ideals in the real world, the nobility of "quixotic" quests in a world of tawdry realities.

Shakespeare and the English Renaissance

The Renaissance came late to Britain, Europe's offshore islands to the west. But the literary flowering of the Elizabethan Age (1558–1603) was worth waiting for. In the plays and poems of William Shakespeare of Stratford–upon–Avon, the age of Elizabeth produced the best writing the English language has yet seen.

There were other giants in the Elizabethan age. Christopher Marlowe (1564–1593) died young in a tavern brawl but left half a dozen plays that incarnated the overweening self–confidence and exalted aspiration of the Renaissance. *Dr. Faustus* retells the medieval legend of the man who sold his soul to the Devil in return for supernatural power. Most memorable of all, however, is the moment when Faustus faces death and eternal damnation in the powerful verse of Marlowe's "mighty line."

William Shakespeare (1564–1616), his fellow playwright Ben Jonson said with much truth, was "not for an age, but for all time." His plot lines were very often borrowed from history books or the works of earlier writers. His characters—in *Romeo and Juliet, Macbeth, Henry V, Richard III, Hamlet, Julius Caesar, Othello, King Lear, The Tempest,* and so many others—while larger than life, were also embodiments of such universal human passions as love, ambition, heroism, jealousy, revenge.

As modern producers quickly see, Shakespeare's plays still *work* dramatically. He knew how to construct taut scenes, build tragic tension, and plunge his characters into the ordeal that will test them to the utmost. His poetry has been heard on the lips of the most celebrated actors of each age in turn. His words and phrases, from throw–away lines's like "something's rotten in Denmark" to such ultimate questions as "to be or not to be?" have become part of the language.

✦Renaissance Art✦

Renaissance artists, like Renaissance writers, tried to learn from ancient models. In architecture and sculpture, they borrowed heavily and praised what they learned. In painting, however, Renaissance artists were innovators of the first order. Beginning in Italy once more, let us look at the most familiar achievement of the age: the art that produced Leonardo's Mona Lisa smile, Michelangelo's dome on St. Peter's church in Rome, and a dazzling array of other masterpieces.

Renaissance Painting

In painting and other graphic arts, Renaissance artists had little choice but to be original. No ancient paintings had survived to be imitated—or none that the Renaissance knew about, since the buried city of Pompeii still slumbered unknown under many feet of volcanic ash. The fundamental goal that Renaissance painters set for themselves was that urged by Aristotle and illustrated by ancient sculpture: art as the imitation of nature. The contemporary art historian Giorgio Vasari (1511–1574) offered as his highest critical commendation the accolade of "lifelikeness," and much of the innovative energy of the age went into perfecting new techniques to achieve this end.

A basic method pioneered in the Renaissance was drawing and sketching from life. It was said of Leonardo da Vinci that "whenever he saw a strange head or beard or hair of unusual appearance . . . he would follow such a person a whole day, and so learn him by heart,

Michelangelo's *Creation of Adam* from the ceiling of the Sistine Chapel in Rome is one of the best-known of all Western paintings. The throbbing vitality of God's extended forefinger contrasts strikingly with the languid finger of Adam waiting for the ultimate gift of life. (The Vatican, Rome.)

that when he reached home he could draw him as if he were present."[6] Among the artists of the northern Renaissance, Albrecht Dürer's often–reproduced praying hands are as utterly convincing in their gnarled piety as they were when he drew them four and a half centuries ago. Another technical innovation was the careful exploitation of highlights and shadows—*chiaroscuro*—as form–revealing elements. Shadows defining the folds of clothing or the curve of a painted cheek make Renaissance faces and figures stand out in naturalistic relief from the surface of canvas or wall.

Two basic devices above all, however, made Renaissance painters the masters of graphic realism. These were anatomically accurate figure drawing and a firm command of perspective.

Really convincing *figure drawing* became a prerequisite for success in painting for the first time in the early modern centuries. Renaissance artists sketched from the living model, learning through many painstaking hours of practice to render human bodies convincingly. Leonardo initiated the practice of studying the mechanics of human anatomy by sketching dissected corpses. Figures depicted nude or partially clothed thus looked far more lifelike; but so did figures swathed in heavy robes, since clothing hanging from realistically conceived bones, muscles, and flesh was inevitably more convincing.

The art of *perspective* drawing was another part of the course of study at the new art academies that sprang up for the first time in the sixteenth century. Atmospheric perspective enabled the artist to give a picture depth by depicting distant objects as dimmer, grayer, and bluer than people and things in the foreground. The basic techniques of perspective drawing, however, involve various forms of linear or mathematical perspective. This approach is based on the easily observable fact that, as the eye perceives them, nearer objects seem larger, more distant ones smaller. By imposing a checkerboard grid on the world as they sketched and painted it, Renaissance artists learned to represent figures, buildings, and cities with proper placement and foreshortening and in the correct relative size depending on their distance from the observer.

The result of combining this array of skills was art with a new degree of lifelikeness. With the exception of the great modernist rebellion of our own century, Western artists have been using these Renaissance techniques ever since.

Italian Painters: Giotto to Titian

Giotto di Bondone (c. 1267–1337), whose life overlapped that of Petrarch, is sometimes heralded as the first Renaissance painter. His series of frescoes depicting the life of St. Francis, on the walls of the Arena Chapel in Padua, broke with the flat style of medieval painting. Neither perspective nor anatomical detail are strongly evident in Giotto's pictures, but their solidity and the use of chiaroscuro cause his people to stand out from the surface of the wall.

Sandro Botticelli (c. 1444–1510) was profoundly affected by the humanistic, philosophical, and religious currents of his time. Botticelli is now best known for his *Birth of Venus* from the sea and his *Primavera (Springtime)*. Both were symbolic, almost allegorical paintings, done with a nearly calligraphic line. The elegant goddesses have a freshness that often seems to radiate the enthusiasm of the Renaissance Florence of Botticelli's patron, Lorenzo de' Medici.

The most famous of all Renaissance painters was Leonardo da Vinci (1452–1519). A many–sided genius, Leonardo combined scientific speculation with artistic brilliance, a light hand on a lute with the strength to bend an iron bar. His speculative designs for such technological breakthroughs as flying machines and submarine boats remained unknown until others had developed more practical designs. But Leonardo's surviving work both illustrates and transcends the artistic trends of his age. His smoky chiaroscuro shows in the enigmatic *Mona Lisa,* the portrait of a lady whose smile has become the best known in Western art. In his *Last Supper,* Christ looks straight out at you from the center, while the twelve apostles turn to each other in stunned disbelief at the master's announcement that one of them will betray him to his enemies. The picture embodies Leonardo's conviction that everything—expression, gesture, even the model chosen, costume, and accessories—should help to convey the artist's message.

Michelangelo Buonarotti (1475–1564), despite his lifelong concentration on sculpture, also painted some of the most magnificent of Renaissance frescoes in the Sistine Chapel of the Vatican in Rome. His immense panorama of the biblical book of Genesis, from the creation through the flood, on the ceiling of the Sistine took four years of excruciating labor to create. The 350 biblical and classical figures were deliberately executed with bodies hugely out of proportion, in order to radiate superhuman spiritual power. And the most famous composition, God infusing life into Adam with the touch of a finger, is still perhaps the most widely reproduced detail in Renaissance art.

The sixteenth century flung up so many famous names in Italian painting alone that it is hard to keep the list of greats from growing into a catalog. Raphael Sanzio (1483–1520), best loved for his charming Madonnas, is admired by critics for his large compositions. *The School of Athens* gathers all the great philosophers and scientists of ancient Greece, with Plato and Aristotle in the center, majestically framed by a series of monumental Roman arches receding in Renaissance perspective into the background. Titian, or Tiziano Vecellio (c. 1487–1576), was one of the most long lived and successful of all artists. A leader of the Venetian school of "colorist" painters, he was as interested in rich hues as in perfect forms. In his many brilliant portraits, living faces look out at us with a realism that goes beyond the physical to give us a sense of the personality of the individual before us.

Northern Painters: Dürer to El Greco

In the sixteenth century especially, Renaissance Italian styles in painting and the other arts spread out across Europe, as classical humanism and Italian literature had before them. As they spread, Renaissance artistic styles both evolved and interacted with such powerful currents as the Protestant and Catholic Reformations in the lands beyond the Alps. The result was an enriched and distinctive art of the Northern Renaissance.

The greatest German artist of the age was Albrecht Dürer (1471–1528), sometimes called "the German Leonardo." An eager learner during visits to Italy, Dürer combined German, Italian Renaissance, and Reformation influences in his work. His passion for Renaissance naturalism shows in his famous small paintings of some of nature's more modest creations—a large brown hare, a tuft of grass—infused with trembling life by Dürer's sensitive brush. An admirer of Martin Luther and a Lutheran during his later years, Dürer also produced enigmatic allegorical works like *The Knight, Death, and the Devil* and powerful evocations of such religious themes as *The Four Horsemen of the Apocalypse.* Such works combined a Renaissance eye for accurate detail with a Reformation awareness of the supernatural forces, divine and diabolical, that the people of his century imagined all about them.

The greatest Spanish painter of the sixteenth century was born Doménikos Theotokópoulos in Crete, studied in Renaissance Venice, but lived and worked for forty years in Spain, where he was known as El Greco—"The Greek" (1541–1614). El Greco's paintings illustrate the late Renaissance style called *mannerism*—an abandonment of the classic harmonies of High Renaissance art for strikingly personal styles, aiming at singularity and strangeness. The narrow hands, flamelike figures, and cold greenish skin tones for which he is famous served as compelling expressions of the spiritual exultations of the Catholic Reformation. His *Burial of Count Orgaz* contrasts the earth where the funeral takes place with heaven above—opening in triumph to receive the soul of the pious count—in a work of medieval force and mannerist expressiveness. More eye–catching today is his phantasmagoric *View of Toledo;* seen under swirling black clouds and the glare of lightning, it is one of the first great landscapes in modern Western art.

Architecture and Sculpture

The Renaissance Italian ruling classes began the practice of collecting not only the manuscripts of ancient books but statuary and other artifacts dating back to classical times. The writings of the Roman architect Vitruvius were also taken up and studied by Renaissance builders. The result was a wave of emulation of Roman architecture and Greco–Roman sculpture that transformed the art of early modern times.

Renaissance architects rediscovered the beauty of the classical orders of columns and colonnades and the Roman art of roofing vast spaces with huge domes. With the Pantheon as a living model, Filippo Brunelleschi (1379–1446) raised a dome over the cathedral of Florence that proved the possibility of building such structures once more and inspired many imitators. The most influential Renaissance architect was Andrea Palladio (1508–1580), whose palaces and country villas, churches and government buildings rose in a number of north Italian cities. In Palladio's work, stately colonnades and elegant Ionic and Corinthian capitals once more featured prominently. In later centuries, his widely read *Four Books on Architecture* (1570) spread such influential devices as the Palladian portico—a porch graced by two–story columns—as far north as the stately homes of Britain and as far west as the white–pillared mansions of the American south.

The most admired single architectural achievement of the Renaissance, however, was Michelangelo's dome on St. Peter's Church in Rome. Designed in the master's later years and erected after his death, the dome towers 435 feet above the floor, setting the scale of a church designed for giants. The majesty of the great dome is a fitting legacy from the Renaissance to the age of the baroque that followed, combining Roman majesty with the power of the Catholic Reformation in which baroque art was born.

In sculpture, as in architecture, a modern tradition grew from the Renaissance fascination with the Greco–Roman legacy. In the fifteenth century, Donatello (c. 1386–1466), the first great Renaissance sculptor, produced statues very different in spirit and technique from their medieval predecessors. In his *Gattamelata,* a bronze glorification of a celebrated condottiere, Donatello cast the first large equestrian statue made since ancient times. His series of statues of *David* offered the first great free–standing male nudes since antiquity. At least as impressive, however, was the sculptural range of Benvenuto Cellini (1500–1571). In his colorful *Autobiography* (1558), Cellini reveals a vivid Renaissance personality combining vanity, sensitivity, and even mysticism. He also gives us some idea of the labor and difficulty of casting a huge bronze statue in the sixteenth century. His famous representation of *Perseus,* showing the mythical hero with sword in hand, raising the severed head of the monster–woman Medusa, offers a mix of Greek anatomical realism with the distinctive grace of the later Renaissance. Cellini also worked in gold, fashioning for King Francis I of

France the world's most celebrated saltcellar. In this foot–wide masterpiece, a reclining Neptune and a sea goddess confront each other across a miniature world of curling waves, seahorses and mermaids, a tiny temple, and a minute boat (for the salt) wrought of gold, jewels, and shell.

But the greatest of Renaissance sculptors, perhaps the greatest of all carvers of stone, was Michelangelo Buonarotti. The young Michelangelo studied ancient statuary in the gardens of Lorenzo the Magnificent in Florence and did early statues of classical subjects. His view of art was shaped by Platonic and Neoplatonic doctrines, which led him to declare that the "form" of the statue was already present in a block of marble before he laid a chisel to it. Inspired by a Platonic vision of the beauty within, he saw the artist's job as simply to chip away the excess stone to lay bare that perfect indwelling form.

Michelangelo was, however, a devout Christian, and his most famous work is on Christian themes. His remarkable early *Pietà*—Mary mourning over the body of the crucified Christ—shows a youthful and lovely Virgin with the Savior stretched across her lap, a totally unlikely pose, yet compositionally perfect and deeply moving. His taut *Moses* incarnates the fierce power of the Old Testament patriarch, from the turn of the bearded head to the great hands clutching the Tablets of the Law. And Michelangelo's giant *David*, three times the size of a normal man, combines youth and strength, the face of a classic Apollo with the hard–fingered hands of the shepherd boy who struck down Goliath. If any single work of art may be said to embody the proud confidence of the High Renaissance, it is the *David* of Michelangelo.

Women and Renaissance Art

The position of women in Renaissance art deserves special note. Although women have excelled in all the arts in later modern times, there are few female names in the lists of Renaissance painters and other artists. Women were not apprenticed to the goldsmiths' and other guilds that traditionally trained artists during the Renaissance period, nor were they admitted to the later Renaissance art academies. They were not allowed to learn figure drawing by sketching male nudes as men did. Since the ordinary avenues of artistic training were closed to them, only a few exceptional women managed through special circumstances to learn these professions.

One of these was Sofonisba Anguissola (c. 1532–1625). The talented daughter of a northern Italian nobleman, she moved beyond the sort of amateur skill at art Castiglione recommended for young ladies and gentlemen to become a successful professional painter. Her work, mostly portraiture like *The Artist's Sisters Playing Chess,* was characterized by vivid personal expression. Michelangelo offered critiques of her work, and she was finally summoned to Madrid to become a court painter to Philip II.

Common prejudices and institutional limitations on their training would continue to handicap women in the arts for centuries to come. Nevertheless, as we will see, women artists would become more numerous and prominent in art from this time on.

Summary

Europe around 1500 experienced a vigorous economic revival after the late medieval depression triggered by the Black Death. As populations began to grow again, enclosure made land use more efficient, and the volume of trade expanded. Cities also began to grow once more, and merchant bankers like the Medici and the Fuggers led the West into an era of expanding mercantile capitalism.

Renaissance rulers restored centralized political power to the growing nation–states and smaller principalities of Europe in the fourteenth, fifteenth, and sixteenth centuries. Italian Renaissance despots like the Medici in Florence governed informally but firmly. Aggressive "new monarchs" like the Tudors in England and Isabella and Ferdinand in Spain both ruled forcefully themselves and began to build stronger administrative structures to strengthen the monarchy as an institution.

In this changing economic and political framework, a literate new elite emerged in Renaissance Europe. This elite did include some educated Renaissance ladies, although in general the role of women was severely restricted. Most Renaissance people, of course, were still the products of the family and the village or neighborhood community in which they lived.

The literary and artistic "rebirth" which earned the Renaissance its name was inspired by the rediscovery of Europe's Greco–Roman heritage. Classically–oriented humanists like Petrarch and Erasmus exercised a central influence on this cultural flowering of the fourteenth, fifteenth, and sixteenth centuries. Renaissance writers, however, included such innovative spirits as Cervantes and Shakespeare. And Renaissance artists soon went beyond their classical models, especially in painting, where the work of Italian artists like Leonardo da Vinci and Michelangelo, and such northern painters as Dürer and El Greco became themselves models for future generations.

Some Key Terms

Bourse 245
Cabala 258
chiaroscuro 263
commune 248
conduct books 255
condottiere 248
cortes 252
czar 253
enclosure 243

figure drawing 263
humanist movement 258
mannerism 265
new monarchs 249
northern humanism 259
perspective 263
polder 243
princely court 247
proto–industrialism 244

putting–out system 244
Reichstag 254
Renaissance 241
Renaissance despots 248
Renaissance person 255
los reyes católicos 252
utopia 260
virtù 255

Notes

1. John Larner, "Europe of the Courts," *Journal of Modern History*, 55 (1984), 676–677.
2. *Memoirs: The Reign of Louis XI,* trans. Michael Jones (Harmondsworth, England: Penguin, 1972), 417–418.
3. Joan Kelly–Gadol, "Did Women Have a Renaissance?" in *Becoming Visible: Women in European History,* 2d ed., eds. Renata Bridenthal, Claudia Koonz, and Susan Stuard (Boston: Houghton Mifflin, 1987).
4. Ibid., 177, 197.
5. Ibid., 186.
6. Giorgio Vasari, *Lives of the Artists,* trans. E.L. Seeley (New York: Noonday Press, 1957), 148.

Reading List

Baumgartner, F. J. *France in the Sixteenth Century.* New York: St. Martins, 1995. Recent survey. On political evolution, see J. R. Major, *From Renaisance Monarchy to Absolute Monarchy: French Kings, Nobles, and Estates* (Baltimore: Johns Hopkins Press, 1994).

Bonner, R. *The European Dynastic States 1494–1660.* Oxford: Clarendon Press, 1990. A valuable volume in the *Oxford History of the Modern World* series.

Braudel, F. *Afterthoughts on Civilization and Capitalism.* Translated by P. M. Ranum. Baltimore: Johns Hopkins University Press, 1977. Briefly summarizes the main themes of Braudel's multivolume study of *Materialism and Capitalism* between 1400 and 1800. See also J. N. Bell, *Markets and Merchants: The Expansion of Trade in Europe, 1500–1630* (New York: St. Martin's Press, 1977). Examines political conflicts, business methods, and precious metals from the New World.

Brucker, G. *The Civic World in Early Renaissance Florence.* Princeton, N.J.: Princeton University Press, 1977. Public life in the most renowned of Renaissance city republics. On class conflict between the urban patriciate and working–class neighborhoods, see S. K. Cohn, *The Laboring Classes in Renaissance Florence* (New York: Academic Press, 1980).

Cervantes Saavedra, M. de. *The Portable Cervantes.* Harmondsworth, England: Penguin, 1976. Includes *Don Quixote* and other vigorous Renaissance writing by Cervantes.

Eisenstein, E. L. *The Printing Press as an Agent of Change: Communications and Cultural Transformations in Early Modern Europe.* 2 vols. New York: Cambridge University Press, 1979. Assigns a crucial role in both the Renaissance and the Reformation to the new communications technology produced by the invention of movable type.

Farr, J. R. *Hands of Honor: Artisans and Their World in Dijon, 1550–1650.* Ithaca, N.Y.: Cornell University Press, 1988. Working men and women, with emphasis on community and the "cohesive culture" of sixteenth– and seventeenth–century artisans.

Ferguson, W. K. *The Renaissance in Historical Thought: Five Centuries of Interpretation.* Boston: Houghton Mifflin, 1948. The evolution of historical understanding of the Renaissance period as a reflection of the shifting perspectives of later centuries.

Gutman, M. P. *Toward the Modern Economy: Early Industry in Europe, 1500–1800.* Philadelphia: Temple University Press, 1988. Popular attitudes and social structures interact with economic and demographic factors to produce proto–industrialism. See also F. F. Mendels's seminal "Proto-industrialization: The First Phase of the Industrialization Process" (*Journal of Economic History,* vol. 1 [1972], 241–261).

Hale, J. R. *Civilization of Europe in the Renaissance.* London: HarperCollins, 1993. Valuable as survey and reference.

Hartt, F. *History of Italian Renaissance Art: Painting, Sculpture, Architecture.* New York: Abrams, 1994. Well illustrated standard source. For social ramifications, see G. Holmes, *Art and Politics in Renaissance Italy* (Oxford: Oxford University Press, 1993). Impressively illustrated.

Hillgarth, J. N. *The Spanish Kingdoms, 1250–1516.* 2 vols. Oxford: Clarendon Press, 1988. A comprehensive survey: see Volume 2 for the fifteenth century and the "Catholic monarchs."

Hook, J. *Lorenzo de' Medici.* London: Hamilton, 1984. Readable brief life.

Huizinga, J. *Erasmus of Rotterdam . . . With Selections from the Letters.* Translated by F. Hopman and B. Flower. London: Phaidon, 1952. A classic life. For a revisionist view of the humanist Pico, see W. G. Craven, *Giovanni Pico della Mirandola: Symbol of His Age* (Geneva: Droz, 1981).

Kemp, M. *Leonardo da Vinci.* London: Dent, 1981. Illustrated life of the famous artist. On Michelangelo, see R. S. Liebert's scholarly *Michelangelo* (New Haven: Yale University Press, 1983) and U. Baldini, *The Complete Sculpture of Michelangelo* (London: Thames and Hudson, 1982).

King, M. L. *Women of the Renaissance.* Chicago: University of Chicago Press, 1991. Scholarly study of the social and cultural aspects of the position of women in the Renaissance. See also C. Jordan, *Renaissance Feminism: Literary Tastes and Political Models* (Ithaca, N.Y.: Cornell University Press, 1990). Renaissance discussions of the position of women as precursors of modern feminist ideas.

Klapisch–Zuber, C. *Women, Family, and Ritual in Renaissance Italy.* Translated by L. Cochrane. Chicago: University of Chicago Press, 1985. Quantitative, ethnographic, and other studies by an expert in the new social history.

Machiavelli, N. *The Prince, Selections from 'The Discourses,' and Other Writings.* Translated by A. Gilbert. London: Fontana, 1972. Good selection of representative works.

Mattingly, G. *Renaissance Diplomacy.* Harmondsworth, England: Penguin, 1973. Basic study of the subject by a historian who can make institutional history intriguing reading.

More, T. *Utopia.* Edited by E. Surtz and J. H. Hexter. New Haven: Yale University Press. The first modern account of a "Utopian" society.

Shakespeare, W. *The Complete Works.* Edited by C. J. Sisson. London: Oldhams Press, 1953. Includes authoritative introductory essays. Any paperback edition of individual plays, however, will serve the purpose, especially if read aloud.

ⵎ 11 ⵎ

Faith and Fury

The Reformation

•The Lutheran Revolution
•Calvinism and the International Protestant Movement
•The Catholic Reformation   •The Nation-States in the Sixteenth Century
•The Wars of Religion   •The Reformation Wars

The Age of the Reformation filled the 1500s with religious conflict between Catholic and Protestant Christians. As a rebellion against orthodox views—in religion rather than the arts—the Reformation resembled the Renaissance which it overlapped chronologically. From another perspective, however, the Reformation represents less an extension of Renaissance rebelliousness than a medieval reaction *against* the worldliness of the Renaissance. For preachers like Martin Luther, though they disagreed violently with the popes over religion, were after all reasserting the medieval priority of spiritual over worldly concerns, of the next world over this one.

The first two sections of this chapter will focus on the *Protestant Reformation,* the religious revolt that began in 1517 and led to the secession of most of northern Europe from Roman Catholic Christendom. The third section will show how the Catholic church, partially in reaction against the Protestant revolt, proceeded to reform itself in the Catholic Reformation beginning in the 1530s. The reigns of most of the later new monarchs of the sixteenth century—which will be discussed in section four—were shaped by the strains and conflicts generated by the conflicting Reformations. Much of western Europe, finally, was swept by terrible wars of religion between Protestants and Catholics, especially in the later 1500s. These wars, and the beginnings of religious toleration that resulted, will be the subject of the final section.

✦The Lutheran Revolution✦

The Lutheran revolt that set off the Protestant Reformation in 1517 is one of the most dramatic of historical confrontations between conflicting belief systems. Both the rebels and the defenders of the old order based their stands on Christian beliefs. The Protestant Martin Luther's ringing defiance of Emperor Charles V—"Here I stand!"—is matched by the Catholic Thomas More's defiance of King Henry VIII, which cost More his life. At the same time, however, more material interests were at work among both Catholics and Protestants in this great conflict.

We will look here at the decayed state of the church in Luther's day, at the sources of Luther's revolt, the content of his ideas, and the spread of his Protestant faith. We will also note the worldly motives which moved some at least of his many supporters.

Martin Luther's Religious Crisis

The son of an upwardly mobile German miner of solid peasant stock, Martin Luther (1483–1546) had a university education and was destined for law school. Then, at the age of twenty–two, he had an experience that changed his life. Returning to the University of Erfurt in 1505, he was caught in a terrific thunderstorm and, with lightning and thunder crashing around him, cried aloud to the saints that, if he were spared, he would give his life to the church. Such oaths in the grip of a sudden panic were not rare in that age; but young Luther perhaps took the experience more seriously than most. He went on to Erfurt, but instead of law school he entered the highly intellectual order of Augustinian monks.

A closer look at young Luther's character and at the church in his time will help us understand his religious vocation and its impact on western Christendom. A totally committed Christian, educated by the Brethren of the Common Life, he also had both a powerful theological mind and a remarkable gift for eloquence. He went on to earn advanced degrees in theology, to become a formidable debater, and to pen impassioned pamphlets and tender hymns with equal success.

The church Luther sought to serve was still in the deep spiritual decline that had followed the Avignon exile (1305–1378) and the Great Schism (1378–1417). "The popes of the Renaissance," as the *Catholic Encyclopedia* puts it, "had become Italian princes among other Italian princes, who warred and intrigued for worldly interests. Excessive pomp, luxury, and tolerated immorality set the tone of the papal court."[1] Worldliness, ignorance, and selected vices infected the Renaissance church at all levels, corrupting cardinals and bishops, monks and village priests. One reaction was the spread of such societies of pious laypeople as the Brethren of the Common Life. This groundswell of popular resentment at the corruption of the church would provide growing support for Luther's revolt.

Luther's early years in the monastery were a time of deep spiritual trouble, filled with fears of his own worthlessness and sinfulness. Though he lived a Christian life and performed many good works, he did not feel saved. Then he discovered his own salvation— and the beginning of his Protestant vision—in a passage in St. Paul's Epistle to the Romans. Salvation, he suddenly understood Paul to be saying, was "the free gift of God" and came "by faith," not through the good works. "Thereupon," he recorded the great moment, "I felt as if I had been born again and had entered Paradise through wide–open gates. Immediately the whole of Scripture took on new meaning for me."[2] Before he was through, it would take on new meaning for half of western Christendom as well.

The Religious Core of Protestantism

Among Martin Luther's most influential Protestant ideas were his views on salvation, religious authority, the priesthood, and what he saw as the dark role of the popes in history. Luther's moment of truth had come when he discovered that salvation was possible even for sinners through faith in Christ. This doctrine of *salvation through faith* alone contrasted

1517	*Luther's Ninety–Five Theses challenge indulgences—and papal rule of the church*
1521	*Diet of Worms—Charles V outlaws Luther, brings him political supporters in the German states*
1534	*Anabaptists in Munster*
1534–1549	*Paul III launches Catholic Reformation*
1536–1564	*Calvin in Geneva—supports militant Protestants in France, Netherlands, Scotland, and elsewhere*
1540	*Loyola founds Jesuit order*
1545–1564	*Council of Trent prescribes moral reforms, defends Catholic theology*
1556–1598	*Philip II becomes champion of Catholic Counter–Reformation*
1558–1603	*Elizabeth I becomes leader of Protestant cause*
1562–1598	*Wars of religion in France*
1568–1609	*Wars of religion in Netherlands*
1572	*St. Bartholomew massacre in France*

sharply with the church's traditional view that both Christian faith *and* a Christian life were necessary for salvation. For Luther, and for most Protestants, however, salvation came as the free gift of divine grace. Those who had been given this greatest of gifts would be capable of faith, and from faith would spring the life of a true Christian.

Another key Lutheran view that won almost universal acceptance among Protestants was belief in the unique *authority of the Bible*. The church had for centuries taught that God revealed his will to human beings through the Old and New Testaments but also through church councils and the pronouncements of the popes. Luther, however, insisted that only the Scriptures had been divinely inspired. As printed books became more available in the sixteenth and seventeenth centuries, the Bible joined the sermon as the center of Protestant worship.

A third crucial Lutheran emphasis was the doctrine of the *priesthood of all believers*. The church had taught that priests possessed special spiritual powers, derived from those of the Apostles and passed on to priests through the "laying on of hands" by a bishop. Luther, however, declared that all Christians had direct access to God through prayer. Priests were simply individuals delegated to care for the spiritual needs of the congregation full time; they had no special power denied to any other true believer. To some, this view seemed to call in question the necessity of the whole hierarchy of the church as mediator between humanity and God.

A larger step in that direction was the doctrine of *papal usurpation*, which as we see grew directly from Luther's struggle with Rome. Luther and most early Protestants came to believe that the papacy had usurped its position as head of the church. Many believed that the pope was in fact the Antichrist himself.

Martin Luther's powerful voice is most familiar today from the Bible he opened to Germans for the first time and from such hymns as his "A Mighty Fortress Is Our God," sung in many tongues. But he was a thinker too, a theologian like Augustine or Aquinas, and his crucial role in setting the course of Protestant belief is the core of the claim that he was the indispensable man of the Protestant Reformation.

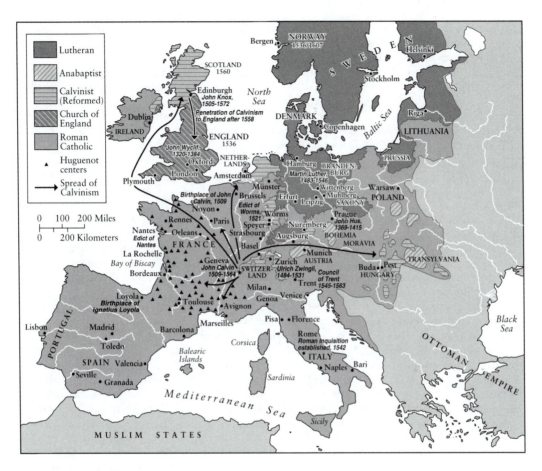

Catholic and Protestant Centers in Sixteenth-Century Europe

The Spread of Lutheranism

Certainly he was the core of it, the eye of the hurricane during the first half of the sixteenth century. The reborn Luther's first clash with his ecclesiastical superiors came in 1517, when he challenged what he saw as the unjustified sale of *indulgences*. According to the late medieval doctrine of the "treasury of merit," Christians could earn remission of punishment for their sins in purgatory by contributing financially to the good works of the church. By making such contributions, the faithful tapped into the bottomless reserves of merit accumulated by the good works of Christ and the saints. Though the church required real repentence, many thought they could buy forgiveness of their sins, and some indulgence "salesmen" encouraged the view that

> As soon as the coin in the coffer rings,
> The soul from purgatory springs![3]

In 1517, Luther, outraged at what he saw as the shameless exploitation of gullible people, published his famous *Ninety–Five Theses* against indulgences—according to tradition, by nailing them up on the church door at Wittenberg.

Luther's contention that Germans were being bilked under the cloak of false doctrine was widely discussed in the German states, and receipts from the indulgence campaign fell off drastically. Ordered by a papal representative to withdraw some of his theses as heretical, Luther refused to do so, and he began to suggest that even the pope could be wrong. When Pope Leo X signed a bull excommunicating Luther from the church, Luther burned it in a public bonfire. When Emperor Charles V called Luther before an imperial diet, or assembly, at Worms to lay the ban of the Empire on him if he would not recant, Luther replied with his most ringing declaration of defiant faith: "I cannot and will not recant anything, for to go against conscience is neither right nor safe. . . . Here I stand. I cannot do otherwise."[4]

Concealed by supporters in the secluded castle of Wartburg, near Eisenach, Luther carried on his work in safety. He had already completed such widely read pamphlets as *To the Christian Nobility of the German Nation,* which urged the princes to reform the church in Germany and to resist the exactions of a foreign pope. At the Wartburg castle in 1521, Luther began the German translation of the Bible that became his most widely read work and influenced German prose style for centuries.

All over Germany, preachers were drawing crowds to hear Luther's reform doctrines, and sometimes to go considerably beyond them. In some places, statues and stained glass windows in churches were smashed by mobs who equated all images with idol worship. German knights launched the Knights' War against their archbishop of Trier in the name of feudal rights and Lutheran religious doctrines. A peasant revolt called the Peasants' War demanded the abolition of serfdom and manorial dues as well as the right to choose their own pastors, as Luther had said. Protestant extremists called Anabaptists (discussed below) rejected infant baptism and urged such "primitive Christian" practices as common ownership of property. And soon the revolt spread beyond Germany to other parts of northern Europe.

Luther was neither a political nor a social radical: in this world, he favored social order and respect for political authority. He urged the suppression of the "thieving and murdering peasants" and apparently initialed orders for the execution of at least a few Anabaptists. Drawing steadily closer to his princely protectors, he and his followers organized Lutheran churches across north Germany and in many imperial cities. The kings of Denmark and Sweden were converted to the new faith and imposed Lutheran reforms on their own churches.

The Lutheran churches all rejected papal authority and recognized the local prince as head of the church. The result was the state church, common all across Europe from the sixteenth through the nineteenth century. And when in 1529 a group of German princes signed a "protest" against an imperial decree prohibiting innovations in religion, the wave of religious reform had its name: *Protestantism.*

From the 1530s on, the center of the religious revolt shifted elsewhere, to Switzerland, the Low Countries, France, and Britain. Luther himself married a former nun named Katharina von Bora (1499–1552) and, with their children, established the pattern of the Protestant minister's family. Against all odds, he lived to an honored old age, hailed by Protestants as the man who had started it all. He had, in fact, started more than he knew, and more than he intended.

Secular Sources of Revolt

Luther's case against the sixteenth–century church was a powerful one, powerfully put. But the widespread support he commanded was also rooted in other factors, including ideology, politics, social problems, and economic concerns.

Luther's pamphlet *To the Christian Nobility of the German Nation* appealed to the half–developed nationalist feeling that the German states were being exploited by Italian popes. Nationalism also increased the strength of the Reformation in the Low Countries, where Dutch patriots resisted the Catholic policies of their foreign overlord, the king of Spain.

Lutheranism also found support in political forces. Particularism, the traditional demand for regional autonomy, moved the north German rulers who rallied to Luther's cause. The political maxim *cuius regio eius religio*—roughly, "the prince's religion is the people's religion"—became the rule all across the German states as well as in Scandinavia. Elsewhere, other political motives played a part. In France, for example, both the Protestant and Catholic factions were led by ambitious dynasties competing for the throne.

As noted above, peasant social grievances were at least as compelling as their religious commitments in the German Peasants' War. And there were other religious movements in which social causes loomed large. A famous Catholic case was that of the so–called Pilgrimage of Grace, a revolt in the north of England that Henry VIII savagely suppressed despite the religious banners borne by the rebels.

Economic motives of the crudest sort also moved some to join the Reformation crusade. Secular princes in the German states often saw Luther's denunciation of the worldliness of the church as warrant for the princes themselves to divest local churches of their wealth and property. Rulers in other lands, including England and the Scandinavian countries, also moved against the wealth of the church. Henry VIII's seizure of the lands of the English monasteries not only filled his own coffers, but enabled him, through judicious distribution of the confiscated property, to ensure support for the newly established Anglican church.

Ideology, politics, social grievances, and greed all contributed to the spread of the Reformation. Yet religion was the heart of it, and the religious ideas of Martin Luther were the central cause of the Protestant revolt.

✦Calvinism and the International Protestant Movement✦

The rebellious spirit of the Reformation leaped from city to city across the Germanies, from nation to nation across northern Europe after Luther's declaration of 1517. Within a few years, major outbreaks flared from Switzerland to Britain, with many lesser conflagrations flickering in between. The man who brought some order to this chaos of Reformation upheavals was John Calvin, who lived and labored in Geneva, Switzerland, from the 1530s to the 1560s. Around the fringes of the Lutheran and Calvinist movements, meanwhile, a host of more radical sects emerged. Altogether, this proliferation of Protestant sects produced, by midcentury, a crescendo of trumpets heralding the coming of the New Jerusalem.

Calvin's Theology

Unlike Luther, John Calvin (1509–1564) looked his part. A famous sketch of Calvin preaching, done in his later years, shows the archetypal religious zealot, lean and goat bearded, hollow of cheek and eye. An iron will and an incisive mind, known to college classmates as "the accusative case," Calvin was a man to respect, but not an easy one to love.

The son of a French lawyer with ecclesiastical connections and a devoutly religious mother, young Calvin had a broader, in some ways more sophisticated, educational background than the German peasant's son. He studied law and never lost the grasp of legal logic and rigorous organization he gleaned from his legal training. He studied ancient languages, first as a humanist, and would put this learning to good use in his religious researches. He studied theology in Paris, became a priest, and was soon interested in the ideas of the reformers.

In the earlier 1530s, Calvin joined the streams of religious refugees already in motion across a religiously divided continent. In 1536, he published the first small edition of his book *The Institutes of the Christian Religion*, which would become a key Protestant manual of religious organization. And in that same year he settled in the Swiss city of Geneva, recently converted to the Protestant faith. Over the next thirty years, he not only reshaped religion in Geneva but also brought order to much of Protestant Europe.

The ideas of John Calvin included many of Luther's basic convictions, among them salvation by faith, the authority of the Bible, papal usurpation, and the priesthood of all be-

Martin Luther's most important successor in the next generation of Protestant reformers was John Calvin. This portrait shows Calvin about the time he arrived in Geneva, in the 1530's—young, intense, fiercely intelligent and totally committed to his cause. (Musée Historique de la Reformation.)

lievers. But two distinctively Calvinist views—his emphasis on divine sovereignty and his belief in the predestination of each human soul to salvation or damnation—particularly distinguished Calvinism among the Protestant sects.

The center of Calvin's faith was his certainty of the *sovereignty of God*. For Calvin, God's majesty, beneficence, and power towered over the universe. Human beings, by contrast, were powerless and sunk in sin: all the descendants of Adam and Eve were "sinners from our mothers' wombs . . . all born to the wrath and retribution of God."[5]

Calvin thus became the most vigorous spokesman for *predestination* among the reformers. God the all–knowing, the all–powerful, had predestined each human soul to salvation or damnation. This hard doctrine might have bred apathy or even libertinism, since nothing we did in this life could affect our ultimate destination. In fact, however, the Calvinists' conviction of being themselves "the elect," the chosen few destined for the right hand of the Lord, made them militant crusaders for God's kingdom here on earth.

Calvinist Geneva

The Calvinist church at Geneva was run by four orders of officials, two clerical orders and two of laypeople. The pastors were the Calvinist priests, possessing no magical powers but charged with leadership, the preaching of sermons, and the care of souls; in fact, these were very powerful people indeed. The teachers were the intellectuals, responsible both for the study of theology and for the teaching of catechisms and creeds to the faithful. Elders and deacons were lay officials, the former responsible for disciplining any of the faithful who fell from grace, the latter caring for the physical fabric of the church and ministering to the sick, the elderly, the infirm.

The civil government of the prosperous city–state of Geneva during Calvin's leadership of the church is sometimes seen as a rare example of a modern theocracy—a state ruled by its priests. The political structure actually functioned through a cooperative committee of devout laymen and pastors called the *consistory,* on which Calvin wielded immense personal authority. Laws were passed making religious and moral offenses civil crimes, and people were punished by the state for questioning the theology of John Calvin.

The style of life of Calvinist Geneva was very puritanical by modern standards. Calvinists were forbidden to read light literature, attend stage plays, dance or sing popular songs, blaspheme, buy a round of drinks at a tavern, or work on the Sabbath. A Spanish fugitive from the Inquisition named Michael Servetus (1511–1553) who sought refuge in Geneva was promptly put on trial for heresy, convicted, and burned alive.

Protestant refugees from many lands, however, found Calvin's city a haven of Reformation piety. Calvin's *Institutes,* with its detailed instructions for church governance, was read and heeded all over Protestant Europe. By the time John Calvin himself died in 1564, Calvinism flourished among the French Huguenots, in the Dutch Reformed church, in the Scottish kirk led by the eloquent John Knox (1513–1572), among the English Puritans, and in many other lands.

Anabaptists and Other Sects

Luther and Calvin were not the only preachers of the new dispensation. Many others emerged as preachers, prophets, and leaders of religious movements. All added to the confusion of voices demanding—and making—changes in the life of faith as the Reformation century roared on.

Ulrich Zwingli (1484–1531) was a contemporary of Luther who paved the way for Calvin and other second–generation Protestant leaders. After laboring for the cause in the Swiss cantons through the 1520s, Zwingli was killed in a war between Protestants and Catholics in 1531. Zwingli rejected the Catholic view of the Mass or communion service, seeing communion as a purely symbolic act, a commemorative service reminding us of Christ's sacrifice, in which the wafer and wine underwent no mystical transformations at all. Zwingli also provided a model for the stripped–down Calvinist church by insisting that sacred images, candles, incense, and elaborate vestments were all pagan distractions from true piety.

The most extreme of the new believers, however, were the sectarians now called religious radicals, then often lumped together as *Anabaptists,* a blanket term of condemnation. Literally, the term meant "rebaptizers," referring to the Anabaptist practice of baptizing adults because baptism had no spiritual vitality unless the baptized understood the teachings of the church—which no baby could do. Some of the sects described as Anabaptists also practiced a primitive form of communism, as they believed the early Christians had, and some tried to reinstitute the Biblical practice of polygamy.

The most notorious Anabaptists were those who took over Münster in northern Germany in 1534. Winning power in the city through an appeal to the poor and the humbler craft guilds, they finally drove both Catholic and Lutheran citizens into exile and announced the New Jerusalem. Led by Jan of Leiden (c. 1509–1536), whom they hailed as King David reborn and rewarded with a harem, the Anabaptists of Münster instituted primitive communism and Old Testament polygamy and prepared for the end of the world. It came, in the form of a combined force of Lutherans and Catholics who took the city and slaughtered the Anabaptists.

The label of Anabaptist, however, also covered many peaceful and pious Christians who espoused such modern principles as toleration, freedom of conscience, and separation of church and state. Denominations like the Mennonites and Amish—the Baptists and Quakers of today—can trace their spiritual ancestry to these quiet unworldly groups who tried to lead Christian lives amid the more strident trumpets of the sects and the drumbeats of resurgent Catholicism.

Protestantism and Society

Protestantism in general has been associated with a variety of social attitudes that began to emerge about this time. We note here the doctrine of the calling, Protestant attitudes toward the family, and the role of women in the Reformation.

An extremely influential Calvinist doctrine was the Calvinist version of *the calling.* The Roman church had for centuries declared that some few Christians had a divine *vocation,* or "calling," to the priesthood. Protestants, and Calvinists especially, asserted that all Christians had a calling to practice whatever trade they followed in a Christian spirit—honestly, industriously, thriftily, and soberly. Businesspeople in many lands, told that they too had a calling and a way to heaven, found Calvinism a particularly satisfying doctrine.

Protestantism also imputed a particular significance and dignity to the Christian family. The medieval Catholic church had seen celibacy as the noblest human condition, demanding it of priests, monks, and nuns, and glorifying the Virgin Mary in a thousand churches.

For Luther, marriage was the highest human condition, and the ideal Protestant union was what we now call a "companionate" marriage, in which two helpmeets share interests and work together for the happiness of the family unit.

Many courageous and talented women also played active parts in the Reformation movement. In some radical sects, women became public preachers and leaders. Perhaps the most important such case was that of Margaret Fell (1614–1702), wife and patron of George Fox (1624–1691), the father of the Society of Friends—the Quakers—in seventeenth–century England. Margaret Fell's country estate of Swarthmore became the center of the new sect, and she herself was one of its founders.

◆The Catholic Reformation◆

Though many Catholics were horrified at Luther's attack on the church, the hunger for religious revival was also strong on the Catholic side. The result was a major counterattack against the Protestant revolt and a great drive for reform within the church. Seen as a reaction against Protestantism, this movement is often called the *Counter–Reformation*. As a profound expression of Catholic religious feeling, it is known as the *Catholic Reformation*. This section will explore the reform activities of the Reformation popes, the great Council of Trent, and the Jesuit order founded by Ignatius Loyola.

The Reformation Popes

As in past centuries, papal leadership played a crucial part in the Catholic Reformation. After the so–called Renaissance popes of the decades around 1500 came the "Reformation popes" of the half–century after 1530. These vigorous papal reformers organized and increasingly inspired the renewal of the faith.

The first of the Reformation popes, Paul III (r. 1534–1549), was a relatively secular Renaissance character himself who nonetheless inaugurated the moral and spiritual revitalization of the church. His reform–minded appointees both fostered the spread of the Catholic Reformation and ensured a succession of reforming popes to carry on the work. Paul himself recognized the Jesuit order in 1540 and called the Council of Trent in 1545—both major counterattacks against the Protestant movement to be discussed in a moment.

The Rome of Martin Luther's day was a worldly Renaissance city ruled by secular and often corrupt princes of the church, a city of great art but little religious spirit. Half a century later, the Rome of the Catholic Reformation was as holy a city in its different way as the Geneva of John Calvin, filled with lay societies devoted to good works and pious prelates dedicated to the greatness of Mother Church.

The Catholic Counterattack

The Catholic side of the great religious revival of the sixteenth century was also, however, a counter reformation, a vigorous attempt to turn back and overcome the Protestant revolt. As such, it involved the mobilization of a number of institutions for struggle as well as for reform.

The *Council of Trent*, which met off and on for twenty years between 1545 and 1564, was one of the most influential of all church councils. By and large, this gathering of leading churchmen reaffirmed traditional theological views even as it recognized the need for reform in church practice. Thus, for example, the council denied Luther's claim that faith alone was sufficient for salvation, insisting that both Christian faith and good works were necessary. Trent also rejected Zwingli's and Calvin's view of the Mass as a purely symbolic commemoration of the Last Supper, insisting on the real metaphysical presence of the body and blood of Christ in the wafer and the wine. On matters of religious faith, in short, the church would not compromise.

The assembled churchmen, however, did recognize the urgent need for reform in church practice. Trent therefore renewed the old assault on clerical concubinage, simony, nepotism, and other manifestations of worldliness in the lives of the clergy. The council also provided for a new system of seminaries to train priests to debate successfully with Protestants and to communicate more effectively to their own congregations.

The Catholic Reformation also offered some important opportunities for women. While Protestants closed down hundreds of convents as they did monasteries, Catholics continued to support these institutions, in which women held high offices. The militancy of the Catholic Reformation also encouraged lives of Christian commitment that earned sainthood for some of these devout women.

Perhaps the most loved of these was the Spanish nun Teresa of Avila (1515–1582). A vigorously practical woman, St. Teresa developed a rigorous new regimen for her Carmelite order and traveled about Spain reorganizing convents and founding new ones. She was also a mystic whose *The Interior Castle* (1577) and other works described, in moving detail, the visions she believed brought her into the presence of the risen Christ himself.

For those who rejected the church's message, the Holy Office of the Inquisition was revitalized. This system of church courts charged with suppression of heresy still made use of secret testimony and torture to extort confessions. It still punished heretics with prison and confiscation of property and those who later returned to their heretical beliefs with death. The *auto da fe* ("act of faith") was the public ceremony in which the Inquisition judged and sentenced a heretic. Often culminating in death by fire, this act was one of the most dreadful expressions of this age of powerful religious passions.

The *Index of Forbidden Books,* finally, was a branch of the Holy Office that proved particularly important in the new age of the printing press. Responding to the large number of books made available by the new print technology, the Index sought to prevent the circulation of books of pornography, sorcery, and even early modern science. The primary target of the Index of Forbidden Books, however, was the heretical theology of Luther, Calvin, and other leaders of the Protestant Reformation.

Loyola and the Jesuits

Perhaps the most influential saint of the Catholic Reformation was Ignatius Loyola (1491–1556), founder of the Society of Jesus, an order of friars commonly called the *Jesuits* and seen as the shock troops of the Catholic Counter–Reformation. A Basque knight from the mountainous border country of northern Spain, Loyola was lamed for life in combat. He saw religion in crusading terms and organized the Jesuit order along the military lines of the knightly crusading orders of the Middle Ages.

After spending some time as a hermit, Loyola studied theology and then gathered a small band of equally dedicated men around him—the first Jesuits, officially recognized by Pope Paul III in 1540. His immensely influential book, the *Spiritual Exercises* (1523–1535), became the meditation manual of his new order. This course of Christian meditation, requiring concrete visualization of a series of spiritual objects, from the pains of hell to the glory of the risen Christ, was intended to fortify the Jesuits for the struggle to which they were committed. The result was an elite corps of Catholic crusaders, as dedicated and totally convinced of their own righteousness as the most militant Calvinists were of theirs.

Standards for admission to the order were high, requiring dedication, discipline, and intelligence. Jesuit schools and colleges came to be recognized as among the finest educational institutions in Europe. Jesuit missionaries carried Christianity to the indigenous peoples of North and South America and to the sophisticated courts of India and China. Within Europe, some Jesuits became spiritual counselors to princes, advising them to take a militant stand on religious issues. Others traveled in disguise to Protestant countries to provide an underground church for Catholics.

Luther, Calvin, and Loyola, with legions of other Protestant and Catholic reformers, thus fanned the flames of religious passion. Religious fervor, however, was soon interacting with the political trends of the sixteenth century, which are outlined in the following section. The result was the terrible wars of religion that scarred the second half of the century, as we will see in the last section.

✦The Nation–States in the Sixteenth Century✦

The sixteenth–century successors to the "new monarchs" of the fifteenth century combined aggressive foreign policies with further strengthening of royal authority at home. During the earlier 1500s, these included Henry VIII of England, Francis I of France, and Emperor Charles V of Spain and the Holy Roman Empire—the subjects of the first three subsections below. In the later 1500s, two long–ruling monarchs dominated western European affairs—the Protestant Queen Elizabeth I of England and the Catholic leader Philip II of Spain—while Ivan the Terrible built autocracy in emerging Russia.

Henry VIII and the English Reformation

In many ways the most successful sixteenth–century monarchy was Tudor England. Generally united and prosperous, the island kingdom found strong leadership in Henry VIII during the first half of the century and in Elizabeth I during the second half.

Henry VIII (r. 1509–1547) faced the greatest challenge of his reign when his queen, Catherine of Aragon (1485–1536), failed to produce a male heir. Most historians today feel that the fault was probably his rather than hers. Nevertheless, Henry sought the solution in a royal divorce and remarriage to an ambitious and attractive lady–in–waiting, Anne Boleyn (c. 1507–1536). Only the pope, however, could annul a royal marriage—and the reigning pope, influenced by Queen Catherine's kinsman, Emperor Charles V, refused to grant the annulment.

Henry's solution was typically extravagant and, in a Europe already in an upheaval over the Reformation, seemed just daring enough to work. He declared the English church independent from Rome and himself the head of it, freeing him to see to the annulment of his marriage himself—and to marry whom he pleased.

To legalize England's secession from the church of Rome, Henry VIII convened what became known as the *Reformation Parliament* (1529–1536). But there were other religious forces at work in the land, including medieval anticlerical feeling and growing enthusiasm for Reformation religious ideas. Over a period of seven years, then, this activist Parliament accomplished the king's purpose—and in the process brought the Reformation to England, something the religiously conservative king had *not* intended.

In the 1530s, the Reformation Parliament made the king "supreme head" of the Church of England, thus creating the Anglican church. Responding to dubious charges of immorality in the English monasteries, Henry's agents closed them down and confiscated their immense lands and wealth. By redistributing these assets among England's ruling classes, the king won the support of the English aristocracy for his religious policy. He also executed such leading opponents of the Reformation as Chancellor Thomas More (1478–1535), the humanist, who refused to recognize Henry's leadership of England's Christians and was subsequently canonized as a martyr by the Catholic church.

Besides taking over the English church, Henry VIII strengthened the royal government by reorganizing six major bureaus and encouraging increased professionalism in the royal administration. Parliament, however, also increased its own power, especially during the seven years of the Reformation Parliament. The elected House of Commons in particular, bringing country squires and townsmen from all parts of the country together to debate matters of immense national interest, acquired a growing sense of its own powers, duties, and importance. In later centuries, Parliament would challenge the monarchy itself for power in England.

King Henry, meanwhile, married Anne Boleyn, who gave him a daughter rather than the male heir he had sought, and had her executed for adultery soon thereafter. He married four more times and was survived by two daughters and one son. Edward VI (r. 1547–1553) plunged the country deeper into Protestantism, while Mary (r. 1553–1558) veered back toward Catholicism. Mary martyred several hundred Protestants before dying childless and leaving the throne to her Protestant sister, Elizabeth I, to be discussed below.

Francis I and the French Monarchy

Francis I (r. 1515–1547), the gallant Valois king of France during the first half of the sixteenth century, was a lavish patron of Renaissance art, a lover of tournaments and battles, and a womanizer with a string of beautiful mistresses. Inheriting the refurbished French government of Louis XI, the late medieval "spider king," Francis himself made only modest contributions to the institutional growth of the French monarchy. He did increase the number of civil servants, streamline the treasury, and establish royal supremacy over the French church, winning the right to appoint bishops and abbots and to enjoy a share of church revenues.

Most of Francis's contributions, however, were informal ones. He bound the French nobility to him by by distributing provincial governorships, pensions, and other rewards and by being a chivalrous comrade–in–arms to France's old "nobility of the sword." He also expanded the sale of government offices, enhancing royal revenues and opening judgships, and hence places in the nation's "nobility of the robe," to bourgeois citizens who could afford them.

Charles V and the Habsburg Predominance

Charles V (r. 1519–1556), the Habsburg Holy Roman Emperor, was not as flamboyant as either Henry VIII or Francis I. Small and thin, with a long bony face and sad eyes, Charles had the jutting lower jaw that distinguishes Habsburg portraits from the thirteenth century to the twentieth. He inherited the wealth of the Netherlands in 1506, Spain with its growing New World empire in 1516, and finally secured election as Holy Roman Emperor of the German states in 1519—all before he was twenty years old. To this hard–working, duty–bound little man fell the task of governing the largest empire any European prince had ruled since Charlemagne.

In Spain, which proved to be the real power center of the Habsburg domains in the sixteenth century, Charles faced his first great problem: the revolt of the Spanish townsmen called the *comuneros*. The *comuneros* (members of communes, or incorporated towns) opposed Charles—who had been raised in the Netherlands—as a "foreign" ruler and demanded such social reforms as an end to the traditional preeminence of the landed aristocracy. The outraged Spanish nobility crushed the *comuneros* revolt.

Charles and his chief Spanish adviser, the industrious Francisco de los Cobos (d. 1547), responded to this upheaval by constructing a Spanish administrative system of unrivaled size and complexity. A central Council of State was established for Spain, for Spanish holdings in southern Italy, and for Spain's expanding American colonies. Subsidiary councils, originally developed by Ferdinand and Isabella, were organized into a dual system,

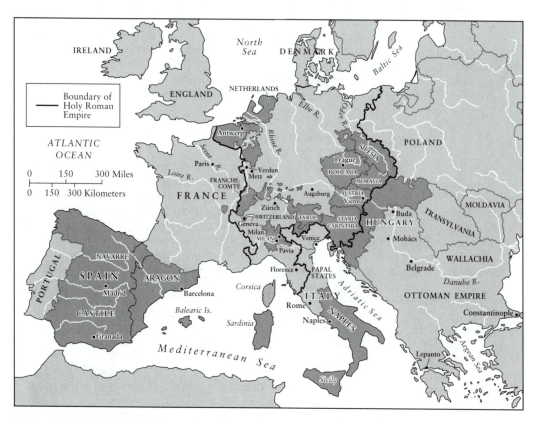

Empire of Charles V (excluding American colonies), ca. 1550

some by function—treasury, war, religion—and some by region, each of the latter governed by a royal viceroy. Townsmen dominated the councils; nobles filled the viceroyalties.

The Holy Roman Empire, the other epicenter of Habsburg interests, was by contrast, hopelessly divided and normally out of control. The German states of the Holy Roman Empire—"the Germanies" as they were sometimes called—included powerful princes, independent knights, ecclesiastical states ruled by archbishops, and many free cities bound by charter to the crown. What unifying institutions there were for this medieval agglomeration of territories, including the imperial *diet,* or assembly, and an imperial council, were controlled by the German princes rather than by the emperor.

To add to Charles's problems, the Lutheran heresy had spread rapidly within this feeble political structure, adding to demands for autonomy among the princes and free cities of north Germany. The Knights' War, the Peasants' War, and waves of Anabaptist agitation soon shattered the peace of the Empire. Some Lutherans, led by Luther's lieutenant, Philip Melanchthon (1497–1560), sought reconciliation with both the emperor and the pope through the moderate *Augsburg Confession* of 1530. But when Charles V rejected the document, the German princes of the north organized the *League of Schmalkald* in 1531 to defend their interests and their new religion by force.

Imperial armies defeated the Schmalkaldic League in 1547, but the emperor's subsequent efforts to impose a Catholic settlement on the Protestant principalities failed. And in the early 1550s, the Schmalkaldic League reorganized, formed a key alliance with the king of France, defeated the aging Habsburg ruler, and forced him to sign the Peace of Augsburg in 1555. This historic document allowed each prince to choose the faith of his own principality *(cuius regio eius religio)* and recognized the privilege of dissenting subjects to move to another German state in which their creed was the law of the land. It was a major victory for Protestantism and for the rights of princes against their emperor.

Good Queen Bess

Elizabeth I (r. 1558–1603) was one of the two most important rulers of the later sixteenth century. She was masterful like her father, Henry VIII, prudent and frugal with the public's money like her grandfather, Henry VII, and probably more intelligent than either. She was also a natural politician, using jeweled gowns and annual royal progresses through the countryside to stir the admiration and affections of her people, assuring them that she was "a princess to whom nothing . . . was so dear as the hearty love and good will of her subjects."[6] Though she depended on industrious administrators from the gentry class and especially on Sir William Cecil (1520–1598), Lord Burghley and lord treasurer of the realm, she was, in the end, always the one in charge.

Queen Elizabeth faced many problems and dealt successfully with most of them.

Like her father, Elizabeth had a political problem with the succession to the throne. Unmarried on her accession, she refused all advice to marry and provide an heir. Instead, she converted her unwed condition into a diplomatic advantage by dangling the possibility of a marriage alliance before one European royal house after another.

A problem that was all her own, however, was that of female governance in her day: how was a woman to rule a court and country dominated by men? Improvising as she went, she soon learned to manipulate rival courtiers, to balance opposing points of view, and to be by turns haughty and gracious with her Parliaments. She invented her own style of government, and she made it work.

Queen Elizabeth I is shown here surrounded by symbols of her power. Note the crown to her right, the globe under her hand, and the pictorial representation of her naval strength on the wall behind her. (Cooper-Bridgeman Library.)

As the age of the Reformation evolved into a half–century of religious wars, Queen Elizabeth also faced a series of religious problems. The "Elizabethan settlement" of the Church of England was typically middle of the road. The church retained its hierarchy of bishops and archbishops with the queen at the top as "Supreme Governor," as well as elaborate Catholic liturgies and vestments. At the same time, however, Elizabeth retained a Protestant Prayer Book and promulgated a set of moderate Protestant doctrines, the Thirty–Nine Articles.

Though most English Christians accepted this compromise settlement, Catholics hoped for a return to papal supremacy, while Protestant militants, the Puritans, dreamed of a Calvinist England. The Puritans would not become a revolutionary force until the next century. Catholic militancy, however, coalesced in Elizabeth's reign around the romantic Catholic exile Mary Queen of Scots (1542–1587), who had a hereditary claim on the English throne.

Raised in Catholic France and briefly queen of that country, Mary returned to rule Scotland in 1561—only to be driven into exile once more by the Calvinistic Presbyterian church and the Scottish nobility, who disliked her foreign ways and entourage. Forced to seek asylum across the border in England, she became the Catholic candidate to replace Queen Elizabeth herself.

Elizabeth prudently had the Scottish queen taken into custody and, when Catholic zealots plotted to put Mary on the throne, ordered her execution. Mary's execution, in turn, led King Philip of Spain, self–appointed champion of Europe's Catholics, to dispatch the *"Invincible Armada"* of 1588 against England. This immense force, 130 ships and 25,000 men, was intended to link up with a Catholic rebellion, overthrow Elizabeth, and destroy the greatest Protestant state in Europe. The revolt, however, never materialized; Elizabeth rallied her people to defend their country; and her most skilled naval commander, Sir Francis Drake (c. 1540–1596), harried the Armada up the English Channel. The English weather did the rest as heavy seas and a stormy "Protestant wind" sank a third of the Spanish galleons and sent the rest limping home in defeat.

Besides preserving England from the ravages of foreign wars, Elizabeth presided over a half–century of increasing prosperity. For the Elizabethan Age saw not only England's rise to naval prominence, but the beginnings of its great commercial outreach. English merchant companies traded from Russia to the Mediterranean. English privateers like Drake, equipped with licenses to steal from the queen's enemies, seized Spanish merchantmen and raided the coasts of the immense Spanish American empire. Elizabeth's knighting of Sir Francis Drake on the deck of the *Golden Hind,* in which he had sailed around the world— raiding Spanish colonies all the way—had a symbolic meaning. For England would soon begin to build the largest world empire in history.

When Queen Elizabeth died in 1603, her ministers quickly bundled her cousin James VI down from Scotland to take her place on the throne. James, however, lacked Elizabeth's gifts; and as things rapidly came apart in the new century, the hawk–faced old woman in her jeweled gowns quickly became Good Queen Bess, her reign a golden age in the collective memory of her people.

Philip II and the Power of Spain

The Habsburg Emperor Charles V divided his vast realms into two parts, leaving the Holy Roman Empire to his brother Ferdinand and Spain, southern Italy, the Netherlands, and the New World to his son Philip. Philip II (r. 1556–1598), the other dominant ruler of the later sixteenth century besides Elizabeth, was a natural autocrat and a devout Catholic. His autocratic temper compelled him to expand still further the centralized government his father left him. His piety led him to pour the blood and treasure of Spain into the religious wars triggered by the Reformation.

Philip expanded the Spanish structure of councils and viceroyalties, depending increasingly on a group of powerful royal secretaries, typically commoners by birth, popularly called the *junta de noche,* the "night council." To staff the administration as a whole, Philip turned to university–trained *legados,* officials with legal expertise, who imposed some order on the vast system.

Two major economic problems confronted the king throughout his reign: a massive indebtedness rooted in his endless wars, and the persistent inflation that multiplied prices in Spain four times over. The wars and other expenses drained the nation even more rapidly than its vast resources could replenish it. The century–long inflation was the result of huge annual imports of silver and gold bullion from the American colonies. The influx of bullion put too much coinage into circulation, and too much money chasing too few goods produced a steady rise in prices.

Philip continued to accumulate wealth through taxes, royal monopolies, and the "royal fifth" he took of all New World treasure, but he also continued to spend it in military campaigns against enemies of his country or his church. This brought him some great victories. In 1571 his fleets triumphed over those of the Ottoman Turks at Lepanto and temporarily swept the Mediterranean of Muslim raiders. In 1580, he seized neighboring Portugal and its great spice–trading empire in the Far East, uniting almost all of Europe's overseas colonies under his rule. But the cost was great, and when Philip died in 1598, Spain was drained, its golden age slipping into the past.

Ivan the Terrible and the Growth of Russian Autocracy

The isolation and relative backwardness of Russia were still striking in the later sixteenth century, the period of the reign of Ivan IV the Terrible (r. 1547–1584). Ivan's nickname has become a joke—"the Dread" or "Dreaded" is a better translation of *Groznyi*. But Ivan, tormented, talented, pious, brutal, and perhaps psychotic, was no joke to contemporaries.

The most powerful Russian ruler before Peter the Great and Joseph Stalin, Ivan IV came to the throne at the age of three. The result was a traumatic childhood, scarred by bullying, thieving Russian princes and boyars—the ancient independent nobility of Russia—and by the death of his mother, perhaps poisoned, as she struggled to hold his throne for him. Taught and guided thereafter by Metropolitan Makarios (1482–1583), the head of the Russian Orthodox church, Ivan grew up pious, profoundly insecure, determined to crush the boyar nobles and to impose his own absolute rule on the frighteningly chaotic world of his early years.

Guided by a small group of friends and advisers, the czar imposed a new code of laws on Muscovy as a whole. In 1549 he convened the first *zemsky sobor,* or "assembly of the land," bringing together boyars, bishops, and royal officials, not to advise but to carry out their ruler's will. Like his western European contemporaries, he tried to expand his still modest bureaucracy and forged a small standing army, the musket-armed *streltsy* ("shooters").

More important, his reign saw an acceleration of the process of bringing Russia's princes, boyars, and peasants under more rigorous control. By Ivan's time, all rival princely houses were gone, and the princes of his own blood had definitively lost the right to a share of the family domains. The boyars, denied the right to change overlords by the elimination of other rulers, were also at least nominally the czar's men. In addition, Ivan expanded the system of *pomestie,* or military fiefs, granted to noblemen in exchange for direct service to the crown. The peasant masses of Russia, finally, came under stricter overlordship as Ivan issued an edict forbidding the formerly free peasantry from leaving the estates of their royal or noble masters except during a brief period each year. This limitation was an important step in the growth of serfdom in Russia, an institution that had all but disappeared in western Europe by this time.

The czar's campaign against the boyars reached its climax in the violent period dominated by the *oprichniki* (1565–1572). Created to deal with alleged traitors and with other anticzarist elements, the *oprichniki* have been compared to the political police of modern authoritarian states. In fact, they were members of a unique institution that could have existed only in the still medieval Russia of early modern times. Headquartered at a monastery east of Moscow, they were a special order of armed black-robed royal agents who were given absolute control over the central and northern half of the country. Alternating periods of ecstatic religious devotions with wild orgies, the *oprichniki* were then turned loose on the country where they executed and expropriated the property of boyars and even looted whole cities as punishment for suspected disloyalty. Only after seven years of this reign of terror was the organization disbanded, leaving the ancient boyar aristocracy shattered—for the time at least.

Ivan's last years were filled with capricious cruelty and periods of mental imbalance. His first wife, Anastasia Romanovna (d. 1560), was a woman of character and beauty who restrained some of his worst impulses for many years. After her death, however, he remarried several times, lashed out violently at those around him, killing his own son and striking down others he saw as threats. When he died in 1584, he left Russia filled with discontent and simmering rebellion. But he had also added to the Russian experience of authoritarian government that began with Byzantine and Mongol influences and would continue down to the twentieth century.

✦ The Wars of Religion ✦

Philip II was not alone in paying a great price for the large–scale violence of the war–torn sixteenth century. Wars and rebellions, many of them rendered more violent by religious passions, challenged all Europe's rulers. Riven by the Habsburg–Valois wars during the first half of the century and the wars of religion in the second half, torn by revolutions and spattered with massacres, the age of Michelangelo and Shakespeare was also perhaps the bloodiest of Western centuries before our own.

The Habsburg–Valois Wars

The central strand of European international relations between the 1490s and the 1550s was the chain of conflict that began with the struggle for Italy and evolved into the prolonged Habsburg-Valois wars. This archetypal dynastic conflict pitted the strengthened monarchies of France and Habsburg Spain against each other, frequently over the wealth of Renaissance Italy.

Both powers had what their rulers regarded as perfectly legitimate claims on major portions of Italy. The house of Aragon, fused with that of Castile in the Spanish monarchy, had ruled parts of Sicily and Naples—the southern half of Italy—since the fourteenth century. In 1494 Charles VIII (r. 1483–1498), the Valois king of France, led a large professional army across the Alps and temporarily occupied Milan, Florence, and Naples, thus vigorously asserting the French right to intervene in the affairs of the peninsula. His successor Louis XII (r. 1498–1515) also intervened in the south, and Spanish and German soldiers were soon fighting there as well.

As the sixteenth century advanced, however, the struggle simplified to a basic conflict between the Valois and Habsburg dynasties and shifted north of the Alps, to focus on the virtual Habsburg encirclement of France. This great strategic advantage accrued to the Habsburgs as Charles V first inherited the Netherlands, then the Spanish throne with its claims in Italy, and finally won election to the throne of the Holy Roman Empire in 1519. Threatened by Habsburg power looking down at him from the Pyrenees, the Alps, and across the Low Countries and the Rhineland from Germany, Francis I fought back with more energy than his pleasure–loving image suggested. His worst setback came when he was defeated and captured by Charles V at Pavia in 1525. In the 1540s, Henry VIII, intermittently allied with the emperor, invaded and ravaged large tracts of French territory, while in 1544 Charles's own troops advanced to within 50 miles of Paris. But Francis hung on and in the end preserved the territorial integrity of France despite all Charles V and his allies could do.

The long struggle finally came to an end in the 1550s, when both Francis and Charles were in their graves and their sons, Henry II of France and Philip II of Spain, had finally wearied of the wars. By the Treaty of Cateau–Cambrésis of 1559, France abandoned Italy to Habsburg Spanish domination, while the French kept claims on key Rhineland outposts, including Metz and Verdun. The Medici and other powerful dynasties also acquired title to new territories in northern Italy.

It was not much for either side after more than sixty years of intermittent struggle. But there was worse to come as the great wars of religion broke over Europe in the 1560s.

✦The Reformation Wars✦

Religion and politics made a potent mix in the Age of the Reformation. For sixteenth–century Christians, as we have seen, religious faith was not a matter of opinion but of truth and falsehood; each side was absolutely certain it was right. Protestant and Catholic forces each believed they alone were the legions of the Lord and that their opponents had enlisted under the banner of Satan. The most costly consequences of this revival of the medieval crusading spirit were the waves of religious warfare that began in Luther's day and continued for more than a century.

In the broadest sense, the *wars of religion* encompassed three great waves of religious conflict. A series of relatively small and scattered struggles began in the 1520s and stretched through the 1550s, a period that included the wars of the Schmalkaldic League in the German states, conflicts between Swiss cantons, and other nasty little wars. From the 1560s into the early 1600s raged the great wars of religion in France and the Netherlands and the naval war between Elizabethan England and Philip II's Spain. During the first half of the seventeenth century, finally, religious differences contributed to both the Thirty Years' War (1618–1648) on the continent and to England's Civil War (1642–1649). In the remaining sections of this chapter we will concentrate on the bloodiest of these contests, the revolutions in the Netherlands and France in the later sixteenth century. We begin, however, with a few generalizations about all these encounters.

All involved bitter propaganda campaigns, each side condemning the other as heretical and immoral enemies of the true faith. In these wars of words and images, the recently invented printing press played a key role. Religious arguments, suitably simplified, became for the first time accessible to millions through crudely printed tracts and pamphlets, illustrated with woodcut drawings depicting the pope as Antichrist or Luther as a limb of Satan. It was a true struggle for the hearts and minds of the West.

Another feature of the religious conflicts of the Reformation period was the fact that they were frequently civil wars. The Holy Roman Empire, France, the Netherlands, and England were all torn by sectarian strife at one time or another during this century and a half. Nations, towns and villages, even families were thus divided against themselves by religious differences.

International wars between the great powers also figured importantly, however. Neither Philip II nor Queen Elizabeth hesitated to intervene in the civil wars of France or the Netherlands in support of co–religionists. Soon, as we have seen, England and Spain themselves were engaged in sporadic warfare that reached to Spain's overseas colonies and raged up the English Channel and across the Atlantic. In the next century, the Thirty Years' War, which began with a Protestant revolt in Bohemia, soon came to involve virtually all the great powers of Europe.

In all these cases, finally, religious motives were thoroughly mixed with other, more material concerns. Economic and social factors triggered peasant rebellions that took the color of religious revolts. A desire for pillage could inspire such disparate crusaders as Philip II in the Netherlands and the Elizabethan privateers on the high seas. Political rivalries between ambitious dynasts were also often important, as in the French wars of religion, while particularist politics drove the German princes into the wars of the Schmalkaldic League.

This combination of creeds in conflict with more material interests, of propaganda, revolution, and big–power rivalries recurred in various forms throughout modern history. A closer look at these first modern wars of the true believers thus provides a useful foundation for much of what is to come.

The French Wars of Religion

The religious wars in France (1562–1598) were an immensely complicated sequence of civil struggles involving half a dozen wars separated by ineffectual truces, four feuding factions ranging from radical Protestant to reactionary Catholic, three French kings, and two generations of leaders. Simplified, these wars were a struggle between Huguenots and Ultra–Catholics. The Ultra–Catholic faction included most of the peasantry, a large part of the urban masses, and probably a majority of the higher nobility, led by the ambitious house of Guise. The Calvinist Huguenots included many bourgeois citizens and a growing portion of the nobility, and were led by the Bourbon dynasty of Navarre, destined to rule France itself for the next two centuries. In between, the rapidly declining royal house of Valois struggled to survive under three feeble kings guided by the strong–willed queen mother, Catherine de Médicis (1519–1589). In its later phases, finally, the civil struggle was exacerbated by the intervention of Philip II on the Ultra–Catholic side and Elizabeth I in support of the Huguenots.

The long civil and religious crisis began to take shape when King Henry II (r. 1547–1559) was killed by a splintered lance in a tournament held to celebrate the Treaty of Cateau–Cambrésis. He left three sons to succeed him: Francis II (r. 1559–1560), a fifteen–year–old who was carried off by illness in a year and a half; Charles IX (r. 1560–1574), a nervous, sickly nine–year–old who died within 15 years; and Henry III (r. 1574–1589), twenty–three, strong and quick witted, but politically foolish and dissolute even for those times, shocking Catholic and Calvinist alike. To hold the monarchy together through such hopeless reigns became the lifework of their mother, Catherine de Médicis.

A daughter of the great Medici family of Florence, Catherine was a vigorous and intelligent woman and a determined dynast. A foreigner—"the Italian shopkeeper's daughter"—in France and largely excluded from influence during Henry II's life by his powerful mistress Diane de Poitiers (1499–1566), Catherine played a central role in French history during the reigns of her sons. Surrounded by men as ambitious as she was, she was nevertheless all that stood between the crumbling French nation and total collapse.

The Huguenots had hoped for some remission in the persecutions ordered by Francis I, and Catherine in fact issued edicts of toleration in the early 1560s. In 1562, however, François, duke of Guise (1519–1563), after escaping a Bourbon plot, slaughtered a Protestant congregation at Vassy, and the Huguenots sprang to arms. The civil war Catherine had tried to avoid thus broke out; it lasted, with intervening truces, for thirty–five years.

Ambushes and sieges, pitched battles, mob violence, and massacres marked the bloody course of the conflict. Churches were burned on both sides, lands denuded, private scores settled, and personal ambitions advanced in the name of religion. The leaders of the first generation, including the duke of Guise who had initiated the struggle and the militant Huguenot leader Admiral Gaspar de Coligny (1519–1572), were killed in battle or assassinated. The most notorious atrocity of the French wars of religion was the *St. Bartholomew's Day Massacre* in 1572. This horror took place when Queen Catherine, fearing Admiral Coligny's growing influence on young Charles IX, sanctioned a plot by Henry the new duke of Guise (1550–1588) to murder Coligny. The assault soon expanded to include more Huguenot leaders, and mobs began killing Protestants indiscriminately, some three thousand in Paris and several times that in the provinces. The pope had a mass of thanksgiving sung in Rome, and according to legend, Philip II of Spain laughed.

The seemingly endless bloodshed reached a garish climax in the 1580s War of the Three Henrys. The three were Henry III, the last of the Valois line and unlikely to produce any heirs; Duke Henry of Guise, architect of the St. Bartholomew's Day Massacre and organizer of a nationwide Catholic League against Protestantism; and the knightly, debonair young Henry of Navarre, leader of the militant Huguenot faction after Coligny's death. As heir of the princely Bourbon family, Navarre was also next in line of succession should the Valois dynasty become extinct. In a tangle of shifting alliances and escalating bloodshed, Duke Henry of Guise was murdered at the king's order, Henry III was assassinated by an Ultra–Catholic Dominican monk, and Henry of Navarre declared himself King Henry IV (r. 1589–1610). But when Henry IV learned that Paris, the heavily Catholic capital city of France, would never open its gates to a Protestant ruler, the Huguenot leader abandoned his faith in return for the submission of his new capital. "Paris," he is reputed to have declared, "is worth a Mass."

If Protestants were disturbed by Henry's casual renunciation of his faith, Catholics were soon outraged when the new king issued the *Edict of Nantes* (1598). This royal dispensation granted the Huguenots religious toleration, civil liberties, and the right to retain their arms and garrison a number of cities for their protection. The religious question flared up again, and Henry IV himself in the end died by violence. But the great wars of religion were over in France after more than three decades of death and destruction.

The Dutch Revolt

The Dutch Revolt (1568–1609) bathed the plush and comfortable Netherlands in blood for more than forty years. And like the French wars of religion, the revolt of the Netherlanders against their Spanish overlords ended without satisfying true believers on either side.

Besides religion, the clash in the Low Countries involved the great wealth of the Dutch and Flemish cities and the local patriotism of their citizens. Mobilized against the increasingly Calvinistic Netherlands were the professional armies of Philip II, their legal ruler who had inherited this portion of the Habsburg domains, along with Spain, from Charles V. Philip, desperate for funds to support his many crusades, tried to squeeze more taxes out of the commercial and industrial cities of his Netherlands provinces. In so doing, he ignored or rode roughshod over the local power structure of these seventeen separate city–states: the elected councils and magistrates of the cities, the respected nobility of the countryside, and the estates general that loosely bound the seventeen states together. As a champion of the Catholic Reformation, Philip also sought to wipe out the Lutheran, Anabaptist, and particularly the new wave of Calvinist heresy spreading rapidly through the Low Countries in the 1560s. A regency council under his sister, Margaret of Parma (1522–1586), was established to collect the king's taxes. The Inquisition went in to destroy the Calvinist "field preachers," or open–air evangelists. When he was confronted by a vigorous defense of local liberties led by the nobles, and when destructive iconoclastic attacks were mounted on Catholic churches, Philip sent in a Spanish army under the veteran duke of Alva (1507–1582) to maintain order and royal authority in the Netherlands.

Alva, who had fought in the Habsburg–Valois wars and who subsequently seized Portugal for his king, seemed the ideal man to suppress unrest in the Low Countries. He replaced Margaret of Parma's regency with a rigorous council of his own—soon dubbed the Council of Blood by the Netherlanders—and executed thousands for refusing to abide by his decrees. His victims included not only Anabaptists and other Protestants from the lower orders of society, but also leading citizens like the counts of Egmont (1522–1568) and Horn (c. 1524–1568). When Dutch and Flemish nobles petitioned for their rights, Alva dismissed the petitioners as "beggars," a nickname they wore proudly for the rest of the war. In the end, Alva was summoned back to Spain in disgrace, while the revolt raged on.

Over four decades, four famous generals in succession were sent out to crush the insurrection. The rebels found a leader in William of Orange (1533–1584), a nobleman widely admired for his wise counsel, who was made stadtholder, or chief magistrate, of the Netherlands in 1580. The Spanish regiments, veterans of many wars and reputed to be the best soldiers of Europe, won almost every battle. But the rebels developed a potent naval arm in the "sea beggars," merchant sea captains turned privateers, who cut the Spanish supply lines by sea and attacked ports held by royal troops.

Violence, inflamed by religious passions on both sides, grew more and more savage. Catholic churches were vandalized by image–breaking mobs, monasteries and convents stripped and closed, bishops imprisoned, priests murdered. To kill a Spaniard, Calvinist preachers told their congregations, was no sin; for the rough–and–ready sea beggars, to kill a priest was half a joke and half a pious act. On the other side, hundreds of Protestants were burned by the Inquisition or executed as traitors by Alva and his successors, while Spanish armies burned and looted the wealthy cities of the Netherlands. The terrible "day of the Spanish fury" at Antwerp, one of the greatest financial and commercial metropolises in Europe, was vividly described by a Protestant source:

> They neither spared age nor fortune . . . person nor country; young nor old; rich nor poor. . . . They slew great numbers of young children. . . . Within three days Antwerp, which was one of the richest towns in Europe, had now no money nor treasure to be found therein, but only in the hands of murderers and strumpets; for every Don Diego must walk jetting up and down the streets with his harlot by him in her chain and bracelet of gold.[7]

On a Sunday in 1584, a Catholic assassin shot William of Orange dead in his own garden; a Protestant multitude watched approvingly while the assassin was publicly tortured to death with red–hot pincers and nearly lynched a woman who was sickened by the spectacle.

The outcome, again, was less a clear–cut victory than a compromise solution. In 1579 the ten southern provinces, where Catholicism was still strong, signed the Treaty of Arras, withdrawing from the rebellion and accepting Spanish protection of their religion against the zealots from the north. The seven northern provinces fought on, finding new leadership in Johan van Oldenbarneveldt (1547–1619). In the 1580s, Queen Elizabeth dispatched modest military aid, and in 1588 a Spanish plan to use troops from the Netherlands under Alexander Farnese (1545–1592), duke of Parma, to invade England was frustrated by the defeat of the Spanish Armada. At an international peace conference in 1609, Oldenbarneveldt won a truce that provisionally recognized the independence of the United (Northern) Netherlands "for purposes of negotiation." Despite renewed fighting in the Thirty Years' War, this became essentially the final settlement. The predominantly Catholic southern states became the Spanish Netherlands, later Belgium. The Protestant northern states emerged as the Dutch Republic—the republic of Rembrandt, the Netherlands of today.

The Birth of Toleration

Somehow, out of this welter of wars and revolutions, persecution and martyrdom, the modest beginnings of modern religious toleration began to appear. This complex shift in the modern religious mind has been attributed to a variety of factors.

The official position of Protestants and Catholics alike during the Reformation was that expressed by the Calvinist leader Theodore Beza (1519–1605): religious freedom was "a most diabolical dogma because it means that everyone should be left to go to hell in his own way."[8] Bitter disputes therefore continued about the right way to salvation, not only between Catholics and Protestants, but within both camps, dividing Jesuits from other Catholic orders, Lutherans from Calvinists, and disputatious theologians within each sect from each other. Meanwhile, religious warfare and persecution also went on, ravaging western Europe.

As early as the middle of the sixteenth century, some few had objected on purely religious grounds to religious persecution. Could God really want such numbers of his creatures to suffer simply because they did not understand his Word properly? Thus Sebastian Castellio (1515–1563) wrote in the 1550s:

> When scourged, spat upon, mocked, crowned with thorns, and crucified shamefully. . . . Thou didst pray for them who did Thee this wrong. . . . [D]ost Thou now command that those who do not understand Thy precepts . . . be drowned in water, cut with lashes to the entrails, sprinkled with salt, dismembered with the sword, burned at a slow fire, and otherwise tortured? Dost Thou, O Christ, command and approve of these things?[9]

An ancient and powerful current of Christian opposition to persecution on dogmatic grounds came from the mystical strain in Christianity. Religious mystics, after all, rooted their faith less in doctrine and dogma than in visionary experience, in direct, often powerfully emotional contact with the Godhead. Among mystic Catholic saints, visionary Anabaptists, or Quaker followers of the Inner Light, religious experience was ineffable—unstatable in words—so that persecution over differing dogmatic formulations made little sense.

Outside the religious realm altogether, meanwhile, cosmopolitanism and skepticism began to emerge as challengers to both doctrinaire religion and intolerance in its name. Renaissance humanists had already detected much good in the pagan philosophers of pre–Christian Greece and Rome, and such daring spirits among them as Pico della Mirandola had begun to seek truth even in Jewish and Muslim sources. This cosmopolitan open-ness even to non–Christian creeds was reinforced, as the sixteenth century advanced, by some degree of familiarity with the very different cultures of Asia and the Americas. People who saw truth in many creeds could not approve of persecuting others for their beliefs.

Meanwhile, a few politicians began to oppose religious conflict and repression on purely practical grounds. Some European rulers began to reject policies that produced nei-ther peace nor victory, but only martyrs (who would not abandon their religious convic-tions) and hypocrites (who would only pretend to). Queen Elizabeth remained a staunch Protestant but tended to shrug off most controversial doctrines as "nonessentials" and in-sisted she would "make no windows into men's souls" to check on their beliefs. In France, a faction called *politiques* remained good Catholics but put the national recovery of their country first, substituting a political faith in absolute monarchy for religion as a means of holding the nation together. The Protestant queen of Navarre, Jeanne d'Albret, issued an edict on freedom of religion as early as 1564. By the end of the century, many who had wearied of crusades that settled nothing and repression that failed were coming to share her point of view.

In the seventeenth century, finally, new currents of ideas, notably the beginning of modern secularism, further advanced the slow process of tamping down the fires of sectar-ian enthusiasm that had raged across Europe for a hundred years. Reflective minds simply turned to other subjects besides theology. The scientific revolution, for instance, was ad-vancing to its climax in the work of Newton. A new interest in political theory was stimu-lated by royal absolutism and the rise of constitutionalism. Modern philosophy took its be-ginnings in the 1600s in the thought of Bacon and Descartes. Religious bigotry still lived, but Western peoples, weary of religious bloodletting, grew increasingly willing to let their neighbors follow Christ as they pleased.

Summary

The sixteenth century saw a final surge of medieval religious feeling in the Protes-tant and Catholic Reformations. The Ger-man monk Martin Luther ignited the Protestant revolt in 1517, protesting the increasing worldliness of the Roman church and proposing such new doctrinal emphases as salvation through faith and the Bible as the sole source of religious truth. The rigorous mind and organizing talents of John Calvin made the Swiss city of Geneva a model for Protestant militants everywhere.

The Roman church, meanwhile, re-sponded by generating its own spiritual re-newal in the Catholic Reformation. The first Reformation pope, Paul III, convened the Council of Trent, reinvigorated the In-quisition, and encouraged the labors of the new Jesuit order, restoring religious piety to the Catholic church and stemming the tide of Protestant secession.

Another major trend of the sixteenth century was the continuing development of royal government in the European nation–states. Such strong–willed rulers as Henry VIII and Elizabeth I in Tudor England, the Habsburg sovereigns Charles V and Philip II in Spain, and Francis I of France all strove to increase their authority over their people.

Many of these rulers mobilized their new powers to fight long and bloody inter-national wars, like those that pitted the Habsburgs against the Valois dynasty or Elizabeth I against Philip II. Even more de-structive, however, were the wars of religion, civil struggles such as the French religious wars or the Dutch revolt which divided families, communities, nations, and the Western world itself. By the end of the sixteenth century, an exhausted Europe began to see the virtue and even the necessity of religious toleration.

Some Key Terms

Anabaptists 278
Augsburg confession 284
authority of the Bible 272
auto da fe 280
calling 278
Catholic Reformation 279
comunero 283
consistory 277
Council of Trent 279
Counter–Reformation 279
cuius regio eius religio 275

Edict of Nantes 291
Index of Forbidden Books 280
indulgences 273
Invincible Armada 286
Jesuits 280
junta de noche 286
League of Schmalkald 284
Ninety–five Theses 274
papal usurpation 272
politiques 294
predestination 277

priesthood of all believers 272
Protestant Reformation 270
Reformation Parliament 281
St. Bartholomew's Day
    Massacre 291
salvation through faith 271
sovereignty of God 277
wars of religion 289
zemsky sobor 287

Notes

1. W. S. Barron, "Reformation, Protestant (On the Continent)," *New Catholic Encyclopedia,* vol. 12 (New York: McGraw–Hill, 1967), 183.
2. Quoted in De Lamar Jensen, *Reformation Europe: Age of Reform and Revolution* (Lexington, Mass.: D.C. Heath, 1981), 46.
3. Roland H. Bainton, *Here I Stand: A Life of Martin Luther* (New York: New American Library, 1955), 60.
4. Ibid.
5. Calvin, *Instruction in Faith,* vol. 2, trans. Paul Fuhrman (London: Butterworth Press, 1949), 36, 37.
6. Quoted in Lacey Baldwin Smith, *Elizabeth Tudor: Portrait of a Queen* (Boston: Little, Brown, 1975), 118.
7. George Gascoigne, *The Spoyle of Antwerpe* (London: Richard Jones, 1576), [Bvii recto]–cii recto.
8. In Roland H. Bainton, *The Reformation of the Sixteenth Century* (Boston: Beacon Press, 1952), 211.
9. *On the Coercion of Heretics,* in Roland H. Bainton, *The Age of the Reformation* (Princeton, N.J.: Van Nostrand, 1956), 186.

Reading List

Bainton, R. H. *Here I Stand: A Life of Martin Luther.* New York: New American Library, 1962. Readable and authoritative, by a leading Protestant scholar.
———. *The Reformation of the Sixteenth Century.* Boston: Beacon, 1956. An earlier version of the Reformation, with much of the flavor of the age.
Cameron, E. *The European Reformation.* Oxford: Clarendon Press, 1991. Solid survey, emphasizing power of an alliance of clergy and variously motivated secular leaders in launching the Reformation.

Daniel–Rops, H. *The Catholic Reformation.* New York: Dutton, 1962. Good overview by a Catholic historian.
Dickens, A. G. *The English Reformation.* New York: Schocken, 1964. Standard work.
Dunn, R. S. *The Age of Religious Wars, 1559–1689.* New York: Norton, 1979. Covers the rise and decline of the sectarian crusading impulse in early modern Europe. See also P. Zagorin, *Rebels and Rulers,* 2 vols. (New York: Cambridge, 1982). Classifies rebellions from palace coups to civil wars.

Geyl, P. *The Revolt of the Netherlands, 1555–1609.* New York: Barnes and Noble, 1980. Thorough account by a leading Dutch authority.

Haigh, C. *English Reformations: Religion, Politics, and Society Under the Tudors.* New York: Oxford University Press, 1993. Valuable recent analysis.

Heller, H. *Iron and Blood: Civil Wars in Sixteenth–Century France.* Buffalo, N.Y.: McGill–Queens University Press, 1991. Links the wars of religion to earlier civil strife, emphasizing class conflict rather than religious differences. See also B. Diefendorf's more focused study, *Beneath the Cross: Catholics and Huguenots in Sixteenth Century Paris* (New York: Oxford University Press, 1991).

Hsia, R. P.–C., ed. *The German People and the Reformation.* Ithaca, N.Y.: Cornell University Press, 1988. Methodologically sophisticated essays on the social history of the Reformation. See also A. Friesen, *Thomas Muenzer, a Destroyer of the Godless: The Making of a Sixteenth–Century Religious Revolutionary* (Berkeley: University of California Press, 1990). A collection of useful essays on the intellectual shaping of a religious radical.

Kamen, H. *The Rise of Toleration.* London: World University Library, 1972. The emergence of the modern view in the aftermath of the religious wars.

Lynch, J. *Spain Under the Habsburgs.* 2 vols. New York: New York University Press, 1981. Volume 1 of this impressive study covers the century of Charles V and Philip II.

MacCaffrey, W. *Elizabeth I.* London: Arnold, 1993. Political history of the reign by a leading authority. See also J. E. Neale's classic life, *Queen Elizabeth I* (New York: Doubleday, 1957) and A. Somerset, *Elizabeth I* (New York: Knopf, 1991).

McGrath, A. E. *Reformation Thought: An Introduction.* Oxford: Blackwell, 1993. Religious, humanistic, and other writings.

Meissner, W. W. *Ignatius of Loyola: The Psychology of a Saint.* New Haven: Yale University Press, 1992. Challenging anaylsis. See also W. W. Meissner, *Ignatius of Loyola: The Psychology of a Saint* (New Haven: Yale University Press). The latest psychological study.

O'Connell, M. R. *The Counter–Reformation, 1559–1610.* New York: Harper & Row, 1974. Surveys all aspects of the second half of the century.

Ozment, S. *When Fathers Ruled: Family Life in Reformation Europe.* Cambridge, Mass.: Harvard University, 1983. Draws on personal documents and contemporary books on how to run a household to paint a picture of shared parental authority. See also E. Carlson, *Marriage and the English Reformation* (Cambridge: Blackwell, 1994).

Pettigree, A., et al, eds. *Calvinism in Europe, 1540–1620.* New York: Cambridge University Press, 1994. Essays on Calvinism in various countries and cities.

Potter, D. *A History of France, 1460–1560: The Emergence of a Nation State.* New York: St. Martin's Press, 1995. Solid survey of the period. See also R. J. Knecht, *Francis I* (London: Oxford University Press, 1982). Political history of the reign of the flamboyant French king.

Scarisbrick, J. J. *Henry VIII.* Berkeley: University of California Press, 1968. Standard life, with the warts left in.

—12—

I Am the State
The Age of Absolutism

•The Crisis of the Seventeenth Century
•The Triumph of Absolute Monarchy: France
•Absolutism in Central and Eastern Europe
•Constitutional Government: England and the Netherlands

The seventeenth century, sometimes called the *critical century* in modern European history, may be seen as a key period in the long transition from medieval to modern times. This transition, which began with the Renaissance before 1500 and reached its climax in the French Revolution of 1789, passed through a critical phase in the 1600s. During this century, Europe faced a series of social crises and found temporary political solutions to them—above all, the rise of absolute monarchies with more political power than their medieval predecessors had ever dreamed of.

The first section will cast a wide net over early seventeenth–century problems. These will include a range of social disasters, from wars and epidemics to a cruel wave of witch hunting.

The next two sections will analyze the rise of several of the powerful new absolute monarchies as a reaction to the disorders and social pathologies of the time. For it was during this century that Louis XIV in France, Peter the Great in Russia, and other rulers seemed finally to have overcome their medieval rivals in the churches, the nobility, and other once independent power centers.

The final section, however, will discuss a very different response to the crises of the seventeenth century. This was the emergence of less autocratic constitutional government in England and the Netherlands.

The idea of a "critical century" is still a theory, though by the end of the chapter we may agree with historian Theodore Rabb that during the years around 1650 especially, "Europe entered a new era" with "a change of direction more dramatic than any . . . between the beginning of the Reformation and the French Revolution."[1] What is clear is that Louis XIV spoke for his age when he declared that "*I* am the state!" Confronted by an awesome range of threats, most of Europe had granted supreme power to the crowned heads who ruled the nations.

•The Crisis of the Seventeenth Century•

The crisis of the seventeenth century meant a number of things. Armed conflicts ravaged the continent throughout the first half of the century, most centrally the terrible Thirty

Years' War (1618–1648) in the German states. Around mid–century, the English Civil War (1642–1649) and the upheaval called the Fronde (1648–1653) in France challenged royal authority once more. Economic depressions, famines, and outbreaks of plague further jolted European society in the 1600s. One response to this string of misfortunes was the wave of witch–hunting which also reached its bloody climax during these decades.

Reacting to these often catastrophic breakdowns in public order, Europe's nobles re-asserted their traditional claims to be the natural ruling class of the West. At the same time, however, growing royal bureaucracies intruded more and more into the lives of all European people—and the aristocracy itself accepted a place below that of Europe's newly absolute monarchs.

Defining a crisis is not an easy thing to do. But the sense of mounting tension, followed by a decisive event and at least some sort of resolution, does seem to recur in one field after another. The crisis may be a war, a revolution, an economic decline, or a savage round of social scapegoating, but the pattern of critical moment followed by at least a temporary solution is the same.

The Thirty Years' War

The Thirty Years' War (1618–1648) began as a civil war between Protestant and Catholic factions within the Holy Roman Empire and ended as an international conflict that involved most of the great powers of Europe. It ravaged the German states of central Europe so terribly that it was sometimes seen as having put Germany a century behind the rest of the continent. It may be seen as the last and goriest of the religious wars—or as the first of the historic series of general European conflicts that included the wars of Louis XIV and Napoleon and climaxed in the two world wars of the twentieth century.

In the half–century after the Peace of Augsburg (1555) that recognized Lutheranism within the Holy Roman Empire and strengthened the independence of the German princes, the religious situation in central Europe had become more complex and more volatile. Calvinism had spread to many states, while militant Jesuits helped to reclaim others for Catholicism. By 1609, two leagues of princes—one Catholic, one Protestant—had been organized within the Empire. Then in 1618 the Habsburg prince Ferdinand, a devout Catholic, became king of Bohemia (today's Czech Republic), which had a substantial Calvinist community. When Ferdinand moved to suppress Protestantism in Bohemia, Bohemian nobles responded by hurling Ferdinand's agents out the window of a castle in Prague. This act, known as the "defenestration of Prague" (from the Latin *fenestra*, for "window") ignited the Thirty Years' War. The Bohemian Calvinists then chose the most militant Protestant prince in the Germanies, Elector Frederick of the Palatinate (r. 1610–1632), in western Germany, as their new king. Ferdinand, meanwhile, was chosen Holy Roman emperor (r. 1619–1637).

In the early phases of the war that followed, Emperor Ferdinand's forces, supported by troops and money from Habsburg Spain, defeated his foes on all fronts. His ally Prince Maximilian of Bavaria (r. 1597–1651) crushed the rebellious Bohemians at the Battle of the White Mountain in 1620 and overthrew Elector Frederick, whose short reign in Bohemia earned him the nickname of "the Winter King." Frederick's own domain in the Palatinate was conquered and occupied by the Spaniards in that same year.

These striking imperial gains, however, cloaked serious weaknesses. For one thing, Emperor Ferdinand had to depend largely on the armies of his subjects, including the Catholic League of German princes, the Catholic Prince Maximilian, and, most importantly, the opportunistic and brilliant mercenary captain, Albrecht von Wallenstein

Chronology 12: The Age of Louis XIV

1618–1648	*Thirty Years War ravages the German states*
1624–1642	*Richelieu strengthens French monarchy*
1630s–1640s 1665	*Plague in the German states, England*
1640–1688	*Frederick William, the great Elector, strengthens Prussian monarchy*
1640s–1650s	*Chill of "Little Ice Age" hurts agriculture across Europe*
1642–1649	*Civil War in England—Cromwell defeats and executes Charles I*
1643–1715	*Louis XIV, "the Sun King" becomes model absolute monarch*
1648–1653	*The Fronde shakes royal power in France*
1657–1705	*Emperor Leopold I builds new Danubian Empire for Austria*
1662–1683	*Colbert imposes mercantilist royal regulation on French economy*
1667–1714	*Four wars of Louis XIV against coalitions of rival powers*
1682–1725	*Peter the Great begins to modernize Russia, builds St. Petersburg, his "window on the West"*
1688	*Glorious Revolution brings constitutional monarchy to England;*
1689	*English Bill of Rights*

(1583–1634). These forces lived off the land—Catholic lands as well as Protestant ones—and soon became independent of imperial control, looting and conquering to line their own pockets or advance their leaders' ambitions.

Another problem was created by Emperor Ferdinand's growing determination to crush all the Protestant princes, a policy which, combined with his support for Habsburg Spain's attempt to reconquer the Netherlands, aroused the fears of neighboring states, Protestant and Catholic alike. France in particular, guided by the brilliant statesman Cardinal Richelieu, once more feared Habsburg encirclement, while the newly independent northern Netherlands—the United Provinces—naturally opposed Spanish use of the captured Palatinate as a staging area for Spanish troops coming north from Italy. Both Catholic France and the Protestant Netherlands therefore soon began to subsidize Emperor Ferdinand's Protestant foes. By the 1620s and 1630s, these foes in the field included two ambitious Scandinavian kings, Christian IV of Denmark (r. 1588–1648) and Gustavus Adolphus of Sweden (r. 1611–1632)—both Lutheran, both distrusting Habsburg expansion, and both soon ambitious themselves to seize control of north Germany and the Baltic Sea.

King Christian invaded the northern German states in the later 1620s, but proved unequal to the task and was driven back by Wallenstein, who then invaded Denmark itself. The Swedish monarch, Gustavus Adolphus, however, proved to be made of sterner stuff. A devout Lutheran, a military innovator, and as skillful a field commander as Wallenstein, "the Lion of the North" drove the imperial forces back and won perhaps the greatest victory of the war at Breitenfeld in 1631. King Gustavus had reorganized and trained both his infantry and his cavalry with emphasis on battlefield mobility and the use of light artillery. Allied with both Protestant north Germans and some Catholic princes, Gustavus Adolphus pushed into southern Germany and defeated Wallenstein himself at Lützen in 1632—a bloody and ultimately pyrrhic victory, for the Lion of the North himself perished on the field. The enigmatic Wallenstein's ambitions soared, but he was killed in 1634, assassinated at the behest of his apprehensive employer, Emperor Ferdinand.

The surging tides of battle seemed to be turning once more in favor of the emperor. The French and the Dutch, however, contrived to keep the Swedes in the field with money and supplies even after the Swedish king's death. In 1635 France declared war on Habsburg Spain, and in 1636 French armies invaded the Holy Roman Empire to prevent further Habsburg gains. Most of the major powers were thus swept into what became the climactic phase of the Thirty Years' War.

Crisscrossed by warring armies, Germany bled. The new tactics and more effective firepower littered the battlefields with casualties. Foreign and German mercenary armies alike burned crops and villages, slaughtered stock, and tortured and butchered peasants all across central Europe. German cities were pounded by artillery, stormed, sacked, and gutted: at the taking of Magdeburg in 1631, as many as twenty thousand people were killed in battle or massacred afterward. All told, as much as a third of the population of the Germanies may have died in the thirty–year holocaust.

When peace finally came at Westphalia in 1648 it was a peace involving most of the great powers and a number of the lesser European states. It was also a genuine attempt to settle all outstanding issues in order to prevent the recurrence of such an outbreak of warfare again. France and Sweden, which had pounded away at bleeding Germany the longest, were the biggest winners; the Habsburgs, who had for so long threatened to dominate Europe, were the primary losers.

By the Treaty of Westphalia and the later Peace of the Pyrenees (1659) with Spain, France acquired territory on both its frontiers, including portions of Alsace and Lorraine on its German border. With the decline of Spain and the Habsburgs, France soon emerged under Louis XIV as the greatest power in Europe. Sweden acquired territory on the Baltic and went on to fight an even more titanic struggle with Peter the Great's Russia for domination of the north. The Habsburg emperors, meanwhile, had to acknowledge the legitimacy of Calvinism as well as Lutheranism and Catholicism in the imperial domains. They were also compelled to accept the almost total independence of the German princes, who now added control of their own foreign policy to their separate governments, armed forces, coinage, tariffs, and state churches. In addition, the Habsburg rulers recognized the complete independence of the Dutch United Provinces and the Swiss Confederation (today's Netherlands and Switzerland). With the Habsburg attempt to assert imperial authority over central Europe thus decisively defeated, the way was open for the rise of another powerful German dynasty: the Hohenzollerns of Brandenburg–Prussia, the future founders of modern Germany. Meanwhile the Habsburgs built a new Danubian Empire around their remaining stronghold in Austria that included the non–German peoples of Hungary and Bohemia.

The Midcentury Rebellions

The revolutions of the midcentury decades, which coincided with the climax of the Thirty Years' War, constituted as powerful an assault on the unity of the individual nation–states as the long war did on the larger international order. We examine some of these upheavals, including the Fronde in France and the Puritan Revolution in England, in more detail later. Here, however, we will venture a few generalizations on this crisis of national governance between the 1620s and the 1660s.

Since the rise of the new monarchs of the later fifteenth century, the central governments of the European nation–states had resumed their high medieval effort to impose law, order, and royal authority on the nations they ruled. Throughout the intervening two centuries, rulers had deployed expanding bureaucracies and larger and more effective armies against the traditionally autonomous towns, regions, and above all the independent aristocracy, which still demanded recognition of its time–honored prerogatives and powers. The resulting resentment of the governed against their increasingly powerful monarchical governments reached a climax in the uprisings of the middle seventeenth century.

In a brief overview, these rebellions look like a rather motley array. In France, many elements in society joined the revolt called the Fronde (1648–1653), but nobles recently returned from the carnage in Germany took the lead. In England, Puritan clerics provided spiritual leadership for the revolt of the 1640s, but the gentry, England's country squires, provided the effective leadership of the revolt. During that same decade, Spain was shaken by a struggle in which Castilian domination was challenged by other provinces and regions, including Catalonia, Portugal, and the Spanish–ruled Italian territories of Naples and Sicily. In the United Provinces, the merchant elite, led by the province of Holland, resisted the power of the noble house of Orange, urging a policy of trade and peace against the stadtholders' pressure for Calvinist rigor and war with the Catholic powers. The Thirty Years' War itself was, in its internal imperial dimension, a struggle between the Holy Roman Empire and its nominally subordinate princes and aristocracy. In Poland, a Cossack rebellion cost that country its domination of the Ukraine in 1648. In Russia two decades later, another Cossack revolt freed serfs and ignited peasant rebellions all along the Volga before it was suppressed.

Everywhere, the aggressive centralizing policies of early modern governments thus went through a final time of testing. The results varied from victory for the monarchy, as in France, through an alliance between monarchy and landowning classes, as in England, to a rare victory for the nobles and princes, as in the Holy Roman Empire. Overall, a resolution in favor of the crown in collaboration with the aristocracy was most common.

The victorious monarchies continued to expand their administrative systems: the number of bureaucrats in Europe may have multiplied as much as four times over between the early sixteenth and the later seventeenth centuries. The main purpose of this increasingly elaborate governmental machinery continued to be the collection of revenues and the mobilization of standing armies for war. In addition, however, these strengthened central governments intruded into the lives of provinces and towns to administer royal justice, regulate the economy of the state as a whole, distribute food in time of famine, and in other ways begin the long process of habituating Western peoples to bigger, more powerful government.

With centralizing monarchies thus increasingly accepted in the nation–states and with aristocrats staffing the top spots in government, the structured society that came to be called the *ancien régime*—the "old order" of Western society before the French Revolution—took its final shape. Again the nations of Europe had survived a major crisis—the midcentury revolutions—and Europeans believed a permanent structure had been established in the political order.

Famine, Depression, and Disease

The tendency of twentieth–century historians to seek economic causes for many things is difficult to apply to the crisis of the seventeenth century. There appears to be no clear correlation between the economic doldrums of the century and the wars and revolutions just inventoried. Yet both the demographic and economic trends of the times do seem to have followed the general pattern of crisis, resolution, and acceptance of what was perceived as a new status quo.

The problem for historians seeking to establish a midcentury "crisis" in the economic and demographic history of the period is that famine, depression, outbreaks of plague, and related disasters tended to be localized in an area and to occur at different times in different places. Some historians have seen the greatest economic reverses beginning around 1620, others around 1680, while a few regions, like the Netherlands, enjoyed a golden age of prosperity and growth pretty much throughout the century. If the seventeenth century as a whole is set in the larger context of the early modern period, however, a broad pattern of critical setbacks and survival does emerge.

Overall, the 1600s constituted a period of relative economic stagnation and a striking slowdown in population growth. By contrast with the sixteenth century, with its economic and demographic expansion, and the eighteenth, which saw the agricultural and industrial revolutions and the beginning of the modern population explosion, the 1600s look like grim times indeed.

As in the later Middle Ages, seventeenth–century Europe was visited by a pandemic of disasters. The wars and civil wars we have discussed ravaged agricultural land, ruined prosperous cities, and sometimes made drastic inroads into populations. The central European population may have fallen by as many as six or seven million people, and the economic development of Germany was probably retarded by generations. Outbreaks of plague and related catastrophes killed an estimated half a million Spaniards, a million Italians, and a fifth of the entire Danish population during the century, ravaging such cities as Naples and London with particular ferocity. Local famines were not less brutal simply because they were less widespread. All European agriculture suffered from the so–called Little Ice Age of short, cool growing seasons that was most noticeable in the 1640s and 1650s. Economic downturns may not have been Europewide, but the century as a whole saw a slackening of economic growth and even declines in some fields, from bullion exports to agricultural production. Overall, population, which had doubled in the sixteenth century, scarcely increased by a third in the seventeenth, while agricultural and industrial growth, commercial exchange, and other signs of economic health slumped badly in the 1600s.

In the later fifteenth and sixteenth centuries, the continent had rebounded vigorously from the series of catastrophes that had beset late medieval Europe. In the eighteenth, the West was launched on the unparalleled trajectory of modern growth and expansion. In the disturbed century between, these ascending graph lines wavered, and the Western world seemed as likely to slide backward as to continue its growth. The seventeenth century was thus as critical a century in the material history of the modern West as in the areas of domestic and foreign politics.

The Great Witch Craze

The international military, political, economic, and demographic crisis of the seventeenth century had its social aspects too. The later sixteenth and earlier seventeenth centuries saw the climax of a unique wave of social violence. This was the great surge of witch hunting, the *witch craze* as it is often called, which peaked between 1550 and 1650.

Medieval and early modern witches, sometimes called "wise women" or "cunning men," were probably most often herb healers who combined spells and charms with their folk remedies. Most were women (though about a fifth were men), and more were old than young. Those accused of witchcraft frequently came from the marginal elements of society: beggars, poor widows without families, midwives (commonly blamed for high infant mortality). They were often outsiders in other ways—quarrelsome neighbors, people known to be disrespectful of authority, emotionally disturbed people. Only when a local witch hunt was in full cry did suspicion reach as high as the middle or upper classes of society.

European views of witchcraft had undergone a drastic transformation in the fifteenth century. The Inquisition had decided that witches were actually agents of Satan and as such a major threat to Christendom. Books like *The Hammer of the Witches* (1487) by Heinrich Kraemer and Johan Sprenger spread the notion that these local weavers of spells and cures had gained their magical powers by swearing allegiance to the Devil. In return, they had received "familiars," demons in the guise of animals, to do their will, as well as the powers traditionally assigned to witches: the ability to conjure up storms, ruin crops, kill livestock, cause illness or death in humans, and transform themselves into animals. Satan's servants were also believed to rub themselves with a salve that allowed them to fly through the air to the Witches' Sabbath, where they paid obscene homage to the Devil, feasted, danced, and flung themselves into orgiastic sex in defiance of all the laws of God and man.

Using torture to gain confessions to these crimes, both ecclesiastical and civil courts burned or hanged tens of thousands of alleged witches during the 1500s and 1600s. This savage persecution has been interpreted in many ways. It has been seen as an attempt to suppress a genuine witch cult (a view not now generally accepted), as scapegoating of social outsiders made to take the blame for misfortunes like illness or bad harvests, or simply as a form of mass hysteria. The witch craze has also been characterized as an expression of widespread male hatred and fear of women. Some scholars see the willingness to believe in a diabolical conspiracy of witches as a product of a feverish religious temper. Perhaps three-quarters of the persecutions occurred in the German states, the Swiss cantons, and France, all areas of intense religious conflict, and as Reformation religiosity waned, this brutal campaign against the "witches" also came to an end.

◆The Triumph of Absolute Monarchy: France◆

The odor of politics hangs thick over the seventeenth century. Monarchs in conclave with great ministers of state, leaders in parliaments or estates general all talked the language of power. The winners, successful state builders like Richelieu and Cromwell, stare flintily at us out of darkening portraits. The losers often paid with their lives for their failure.

The primary form of government to emerge from these struggles was the absolute monarchy epitomized by France's all-powerful Louis XIV (1643–1715). *Absolute monarchy* was government by hereditary kings and queens who made the extravagant claim to be the first and final source of power in the state. As we will see in the following pages, Louis XIV built the first absolute monarchy on foundations laid by predecessors like Henry IV and the great statesman Cardinal Richelieu in the earlier seventeenth century. His splendid royal court, his paternalistic control of the French economy, and his huge military establishment became the model for other royal governments across Europe.

"I Am the State"

"L'état, c'est moi!" Louis XIV (r. 1643–1715) is reputed to have snapped when a statesman referred to "the French state" as if the nation were an independent entity: *"I* am the state!"

The Sun King's formulation may stand as the central political maxim of the age. Absolute monarchy, the most widespread political form among the larger states of the seventeenth century, represented the height of royal power.

In the absolutist state, both Protestant and Catholic clergymen reasserted with new vigor the medieval doctrine of the divine sanction for royal rule. Expanding bureaucracies and standing armies gave the monarch the real power to impose the royal will on the nation. The people as a whole looked up in awe—if not always with enthusiasm—to the splendor of the royal courts, housed in vast new palaces like Louis XIV's Versailles, or in cities like Peter the Great's new capital of St. Petersburg.

It was a hard–won predominance, achieved after centuries of struggle and the critical conflicts of the seventeenth century itself. And its greatest achievement came in France under the Bourbon dynasty of Louis XIV.

The founder of the Bourbon dynasty, Henry of Navarre, both ended the sixteenth–century wars of religion and revived the will to power of the French monarchy. As leader of the Huguenots in the late 1500s, Henry was the chivalric "white plume of Navarre," always visible where the fighting was fiercest. As Henry IV (r. 1589–1610), he turned Catholic to win entry into his capital but also issued the Edict of Nantes (1598) granting toleration to Protestants. Thereafter, he and his finance minister, the duke of Sully (1560–1641), labored to rebuild the battered nation. They reclaimed wastelands for agriculture, built roads and canals, founded France's silk industry, and even piled up a surplus in the treasury.

To reestablish the authority of the monarchy, Henry IV brought the rebellious "nobility of the sword" into the central Council of Affairs or retired them to their estates with large cash settlements. He allowed the "nobility of the robe," judges and chief administra-

King Louis XIV was the living embodiment of royal absolutism. His palace, his court, his lavish life style, and his arrogant assertion that "I am the state" served as models for other monarchs all across seventeenth-century Europe.

tors, to purchase not only these top offices, but also guaranteed succession to the position for their sons. To undercut the French Estates General, which had been a center of dissent, Henry never convened it at all during his two decades on the throne.

Murdered by a fanatical Catholic in 1610, Henry left nine–year–old Louis XIII (r. 1610–1643) on the throne and a foreign queen mother, Marie de Médicis, as regent. Almost at once, the French nobility grew rebellious, the Huguenots more restive. For the last two decades of his reign, however, Louis XIII found a royal minister who took up the task of strengthening the monarchy with vigor. Jean Armand du Plessis, Cardinal Richelieu (1585–1642), brought the French nobility under control by requiring the destruction of their fortified strongholds while at the same time offering them top jobs in the government, the diplomatic service, and the army. He handled the Huguenots by capturing their garrisoned towns and disbanding the armed companies granted them by the Edict of Nantes, but leaving them free to worship as they pleased. To advance royal power across the land, finally, Richelieu developed the system of *intendants,* royal officials who thrust aside local and noble power to collect taxes, administer justice, and generally carry the king's will to distant provinces.

When the all–powerful Richelieu died in 1642 and his ineffective king followed him in 1643, they were succeeded by another royal minor, King Louis XIV, aged five, and another powerful royal minister, the Italian–born Cardinal Mazarin (1602–1661), personally groomed for his post by Richelieu. Mazarin, however, was greedier than his illustrious predecessor and less able. Accumulated resentments soon exploded in the great rebellion known as the *Fronde,* meaning "sling," the favorite weapon of Paris street kids.

Set off by a constitutional dispute between the Parlement of Paris and the crown, the Fronde soon expanded to include not only the prestigious Paris Parlement but the provincial parlements as well; some of the highest nobility; the Huguenots; the overtaxed bourgeois of Paris, Bordeaux, and other cities; and peasants caught in a vise of famine and depression that afflicted many parts of the kingdom. The insurrection drove the boy Louis XIV from his capital and Cardinal Mazarin out of the country.

By a combination of force, bribes, and Machiavellian tactics Mazarin gradually reasserted control. But Louis XIV learned a lesson on the importance of royal power that he never forgot.

The Sun King

Louis XIV was never really lovable, even in his youth, when he was known as an inveterate womanizer who prowled the palace roofs in search of unbarred windows into ladies' bedchambers. In his later years, under the influence of his devout mistress and secret wife Madame de Maintenon (1635–1719), the king became increasingly obsessed with his own majesty. Narrowly religious, he revoked the Edict of Nantes in 1685, expelling fifty thousand highly productive Huguenot families from the country. Certain of his own rights in every international dispute, he plunged the nation into four immensely costly wars.

Louis XIV was also, however, a serious–minded man, hardworking and determined to make ruling France his full–time occupation. Daily meetings with his chief ministers and close attention even to minor documents were other qualities of this archetypal royal absolutist. Convinced that God had put him on his throne, he accepted labels like the Sun King or *le Grand Monarque* as no more than his due as ruler of Europe's greatest nation.

Absolutist government during Louis XIV's seventy years on the throne meant both curtailing all other authorities and asserting royal power all across the land. Thus the nobles, competing for royal favor at Versailles, lost their roots in the countryside. Independent towns were increasingly run by officials who had bought their jobs at court, while city guilds became enforcers of royal economic regulations. The provincial parlements, which traditionally ruled on the constitutionality of royal edicts, learned to rubber stamp the king's decrees. The potentially troublesome Estates General was never convened once during Louis' reign. The French Catholic church's "Gallican Liberties," officially drawn up at this time, rejected papal jurisdiction over French ecclesiastical affairs, leaving Louis in control of his church.

On the positive side, absolutism meant delegating power to skilled royal appointees like the finance minister Colbert and the war minister Louvois. It meant utilizing Richelieu's system of intendants to impose the king's will on the provinces. It meant, in short, battalions of bureaucrats, a mounting flood of paper, and a nation perhaps halfway to the big government of today.

Finally, Louis XIV's absolutism meant the huge royal palace at Versailles, a third of a mile long, with space to house ten thousand. It meant endless acres of formal gardens, lavish meals, splendid entertainments, and pompous ceremonies filling each day of the Sun King's reign. But Louis knew the importance of cultivating an image of splendor in an age of absolute royal power.

Mercantilism and War

Economic controls and an aggressive foreign policy were two central features of absolute monarchy in France. Colbert and Louvois were the architects of Louis XIV's economic policies and military adventures.

Jean–Baptiste Colbert (1618–1693) was committed to the policy of economic regulation called *mercantilism*. A financial genius and a dedicated organizer and planner, Colbert was convinced that government could and should foster economic development. Mercantilists believed that national wealth should be measured in terms of gold and silver bullion. To guarantee an inflow of precious metals in the form of coins, a favorable trade balance was essential. Production must rise and exports must exceed imports, the surplus to be paid for in money. These goals in turn required paternalistic government intervention in the national economy.

To encourage production, Colbert sought to develop such natural resources as timber, minerals, and agricultural land through reforestation, iron mining, and land reclamation. To encourage luxury industries, he imported lace makers and glassblowers from Venice and converted the Gobelin tapestry works into a state industry. To further stimulate the economy, he built roads, bridges, and canals.

Colbert also sought to develop France's overseas colonies as parts of a closed mercantilist system. He committed government funds to develop sugar, tobacco, and chocolate production overseas. He prohibited French colonial trade with foreign powers and required that all shipping between the colonies and France be in French vessels. To protect French industry from foreign rivals, he levied heavy tariffs on imports. To encourage exports, he developed monopolies and state subsidies and imposed quality controls on French goods sold overseas.

With such support and guidance from above, France became the most productive nation in Europe. The resulting prosperity, however, was sadly drained by Louis's exhausting wars.

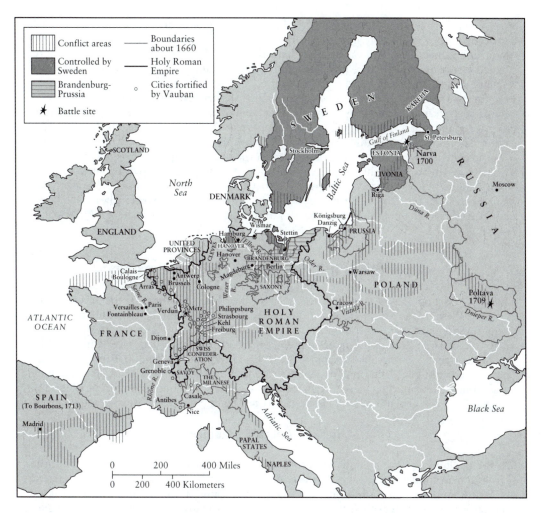

The Wars of Louis XIV and Peter the Great, 1660–1725

Louis XIV's commercial and colonial expansion brought him into competition with the Dutch and other rivals. His quest for defensible frontiers on the Rhine and the Alps brought conflict with France's ancient rivals, the Habsburgs, in Spain and central Europe. The French king thus depended heavily on his dedicated war minister, the marquis de Louvois (1639–1691), his renowned military engineer Sébastien Vauban (1633–1707), and an army that reached the unheard–of size of four hundred thousand men.

The other great powers responded to French expansionism by organizing a series of military alliances against Louis. These coalitions were led by Louis's implacable foe, William of Orange, stadtholder of the Netherlands and later King William III of England (r. 1688–1702). The wars that resulted brought misery and exhaustion to Louis XIV's France.

Louis's armies actually performed brilliantly in the 1660s and 1670s, though French gains from these wars were limited. From the Dutch War (1672–1678) in particular, the Sun King gained a string of valuable border fortresses and the territory of Franche–Comté, which barred Spain's corridor from Italy to the Low Countries. It was a clear indication of Spain's decline and the rise of French power.

In the 1680s and 1690s, Louis's military efforts were repeatedly frustrated by another international alliance organized by William of Orange. William's accession to the English throne in place of the Stuart heir whom Louis had supported was another setback for Louis's ambitions. The War of the Spanish Succession (1702–1714), finally, resulted from the Grand Monarch's effort to establish a Bourbon ruler on the throne of Spain. This diplomatic move, which could have established French domination of Europe, triggered a fourth coalition which roundly defeated the aging French autocrat. When peace came at last, Louis XIV's grandson did become king of Spain, but only on condition that the two branches of the Bourbon dynasty should never be united—terms Louis could have had before the war broke out.

♦Absolutism in Central and Eastern Europe♦

Louis XIV's France was the great exemplar of absolute monarchy in the seventeenth–century West. Many other European sovereigns, however, sought to emulate the Sun King's regime in their own countries. The Austrian Habsburgs, while retaining their shadowy title of Holy Roman Emperor of the Germany states, built themselves a new and far more centralized empire in the south, with Slavic, Hungarian, and Italian subjects. In north Germany, the Prussian Hohenzollern dynasty began the process of state building that would climax in the emergence of modern Germany two hundred years later. And in Russia, Peter the Great (1682–1725) began to construct the modern Russian state.

The New Habsburg Empire

At the beginning of the seventeenth century, Habsburg sovereigns reigned over both the Holy Roman Empire and Spain. By the end of the century, Habsburgs had been replaced by Bourbons on the Spanish throne, and Habsburg imperial authority in German–speaking central Europe was weaker than ever. Yet the Austrian Habsburgs had by 1700 also succeeded in constructing a new and impressive empire for themselves among non–German neighboring peoples.

The decline of the Spanish Habsburgs was one of the most striking features of the seventeenth century. The nation that had towered over Europe in the sixteenth century tumbled into the ranks of the second–class powers in the seventeenth.

The sources of Spain's decline went back at least to Philip II's time. In the century after Columbus, Spain had built the largest overseas empire in the world, but much of the profit had gone to others. Foreign bankers, merchants, and artisans had skimmed off the wealth of Spain's new world mines and plantations. A ruinous inflation had also accompanied the influx of so much precious metal. Above all, Philip II's enormously costly wars, fought to advance his dynastic interests and to defend the Catholic faith, had exhausted even Spain's vast resources by the end of the sixteenth century.

Under his seventeenth–century successors, Philip III (r. 1598–1621), Philip IV (r. 1621–1665), and Charles II (r. 1665–1700), these trends continued. Declining imports of silver combined with increased taxation to leave the people impoverished. Regional loyalties flamed into open revolt in Catalonia, Portugal, and Spain's Italian holdings, especially during the 1640s. And Philip IV's powerful minister Gaspar de Guzman, count–duke of Olivares (1587–1645), poured the nation's resources into the Thirty Years' War, with results as draining as the wars of Philip II had been. Forced to raise taxes and to borrow heavily, the Spanish crown was soon paying out half of its annual revenues in interest on the national debt. In addition, Spain's once victorious regiments finally began to lose in the field. The Dutch naval victory in the Battle of the Downs (1639) and the crushing French triumph over the Spanish army at Rocroi in 1643 shattered Spain's dream of hegemony over Europe.

In central Europe, the rise of Habsburg imperial absolutism had been repeatedly undercut by princely autonomy, local independence, and geographical and cultural differences. To overcome these handicaps, ambitious German dynasties depended on armed force, on new arrangements with the nobles, and on centralized administrative systems. In the seventeenth century, the Austrian Habsburgs deployed armies to build a new empire on the Danube, came to a profitable arrangement with their aristocracies, and depended increasingly on modern bureaucratic machinery to govern an increasingly diverse group of peoples, many of them in the Danube river valley to the south.

The independence of the German princes from the Holy Roman emperor had been established definitively in the Thirty Years' War. From their capital at Vienna, the Habsburgs therefore directed their ambitions toward non–German dependencies: Slavs in Bohemia, Magyars in Hungary, Italians in the Lombard plain of northern Italy. In 1620 the Bohemians, whose revolt had set off the Thirty Years' War, were decisively defeated in the Battle of the White Mountain. In 1683 Emperor Leopold I (r. 1657–1705), after repelling a last Turkish siege of Vienna, drove the Ottoman Turks out of Hungary and added this territory to his new lands. And in 1713, after the long war with Louis XIV over the Spanish succession, Austria took over the Lombard lands and cities south of the Alps. From these territories, the Austrian rulers fashioned at last the centralized monarchy they had been unable to impose on their fellow German princes in centuries of trying.

The new Habsburg Empire that resulted was a federated state still, with local authority remaining in the hands of the provincial diets or estates general and much power still held by the ancient nobility, especially in Magyar Hungary. But there were centralized bureaus in Vienna directing some administrative, legal, and financial affairs. Austrian settlement in these non–German lands and imperial support for increased noble control of the serf populations that still existed east of the Rhine further strengthened Habsburg power. In addition, this new Danubian Empire increased the leverage of the ancient dynasty in the Holy Roman Empire itself, adding substantially to the remarkable revival of the fortunes of the dynasty.

The Rise of the Hohenzollerns

Within the Holy Roman Empire, however, the Habsburgs faced a new rival for dominance in central Europe. This was the Hohenzollern dynasty of Brandenburg–Prussia. Stretching east and west across the valleys of the Elbe and the Oder rivers in north Germany, the principality of Brandenburg centered on the town of Berlin, provincial capital of the Hohenzollerns since the fifteenth century. In the course of the seventeenth century, this prominent north German dynasty acquired a number of other scattered territories. These included the Rhineland duchy of Cleves in the west, a stretch of Baltic coastline, and East Prussia in northern Poland. By the end of the century, these noncontiguous holdings added up to more territory than that held by any other German prince except the Habsburg emperor himself. Because the Hohenzollerns were also imperial electors—among the seven rulers who chose the Holy Roman emperors—they would have been men of consequence in the Germanies in any case. In the middle 1600s, however, Brandenburg–Prussia was ruled by the stern–faced and determined Frederick William (r. 1640–1688), the "Great Elector," who devoted his life to building the family domains into a European great power.

The Great Elector's achievement was one of discipline and determination over circumstance. The lands he inherited were economically poor, geographically divided, politically independent minded, and in 1640 thoroughly ravaged by the Thirty Years' War. Over the following half–century, Frederick William hammered together a well–trained and rigidly disciplined army and built one of the most efficient centralized administrative systems in Europe. The army earned him a profitable place in the diplomatic intrigues and military struggles of central Europe and gave him a powerful tool to impose his authority on his scattered territories. That authority was then implemented by the effective royal bureaucracy centered in Berlin. His landed aristocrats, the *Junkers,* willingly staffed the higher ranks of both army and administration in return for the Elector's support for their own control over the peasantry. This powerful interlocking alliance proved even more successful at binding geographically separated territories together than the Habsburgs had been at uniting their culturally disparate domains. When the Great Elector's successor, Frederick I (r. 1688–1713), secured the title of king from the Habsburg emperor in return for military support against Louis XIV, the Hohenzollern kings were well positioned to begin the long competition with the emperors that brought them mastery of all Germany two centuries later.

Peter the Great

While Louis XIV made France Europe's greatest power and the Habsburgs and Hohenzollerns dominated central Europe, a new great power emerged in eastern Europe around 1700: the Russia of Peter the Great (1682–1725).

A half–educated giant, almost seven feet tall, and a tremendous eater, drinker, and worker, Peter had a powerful practical intelligence and no patience at all with time–honored traditions. He was possessed by a driving will to transform Russia from a backward medieval land into a modern state second to none in Europe. He found Russia a backwoods anachronism; he laid the foundations for Russian power in the Western world.

The sprawling land he inherited had not stood entirely still since the death of Ivan the Terrible a century earlier. There had been a "Time of Troubles" around 1600, a period of economic decline, domestic discord, and foreign invasions. After a Polish occupation of Moscow in 1610, an assembly of notables, the *zemsky sobor,* chose Michael Romanov, a boyar noble, as the new czar. The Romanov dynasty would rule Russia for the next three hundred years, until the monarchy itself was overthrown in 1917.

The early Romanov czars were not strong leaders, but they did preside over national recovery and the beginning of new directions for Russia. Not all the trends they imitated were positive. They let the *zemsky sobor,* Russia's embryonic national assembly, die out in the middle of the seventeenth century. They promulgated the law code called the *Ulozhenie* of 1649, which completed the process of imposing serfdom on the Russian peasantry after that medieval institution had died out in western Europe. They also commissioned the patriarch Nikon (1605–1681) to attempt a sweeping reformation of the Orthodox church—which drove many Russians out of the official church entirely into a fundamentalist backwoods sect called the Old Believers.

On the other hand, the early Romanovs did pursue the valuable policy of encouraging foreign tradespeople, artisans, and military officers to settle in Russia, bringing their skills with them. And it was among these skilled foreigners that young Peter the Great acquired the fascination with things western that would become the focus of his life and reign.

Peter I came to the throne after outmaneuvering two siblings and their supporters and led a couple of military campaigns against the Turks. In 1697, he set out on what was to become a legendary European tour. Determined to see western Europe for himself, the young czar visited industrial establishments, hospitals, schools, and shipyards, where he took a job himself as a carpenter. Filled with admiration for the practical, technical side of Western civilization, Peter returned home and set to work.

Demanding that his courtiers wear Western clothes and go clean shaven as western Europeans did, Peter even took the shears to some boyar beards himself. Threatened by a rebellion of the *streltsy*—the musketeer regiments who had become a reactionary force in Moscow politics—he suppressed them and ordered many executions—sometimes taking the headsman's ax in his own large hands. Then he turned to building his new Russia.

The Founding of Modern Russia

To restructure his country, Peter needed to bring every Russian under the authority of the crown, the only real force for change in a deeply conservative land. He therefore demanded government service of everyone, from noble to serf. Peasants were ordered into military service or mobilized for labor on roads, canals, port facilities, and the czar's new capital at St. Petersburg. The nobility served in special guards regiments or as government officials, encouraged by a new Table of Ranks assigning precedence on the basis of service to the state rather than an ancient boyar name. The resulting *service nobility* earned its place by devotion to Western models and dedicated service to the czar.

Peter reorganized his government, creating a powerful new nine–member Senate and reorganizing the chief government bureaus under new boards or "colleges," a modern form borrowed from his archenemy, Sweden. He reformed and expanded taxation until townspeople and peasants felt taxed on everything they used or did, produced or consumed. He abolished the office of patriarch—the head of the church—and replaced him with a lay *procurator,* the emperor's own appointee, who ran the church virtually as a branch of the government. He even changed his own title from czar to emperor, which he saw as more suitable to the head of a modern state.

The economy also felt the impact of Peter's efforts to expand production and trade and to import Western technology. Commerce with western European lands flowed in increased volume through the Baltic ports Peter acquired in war. The iron mines he fostered in the Urals, at the other edge of European Russia, soon became Europe's most productive.

Peter may have made many of these changes with an eye to strengthening Russia for what was after all his most common year–to–year preoccupation: the wars he fought with the Turks, the Swedes, and others. Peter's early efforts to push through the lands held by the Turks in the south to the Black Sea proved a costly failure. But in the north, his tenacity of purpose brought him his greatest success against the Swedish warrior–king Charles XII (r. 1697–1718). Peter fought this "Great Northern War," as he fought the Turks in the south, to reach the seacoast—in this case, the Baltic, with its even more direct access to western Europe. Defeated at Narva in 1700 by Charles XII—a worthy successor to Gustavus Adolphus–Peter reorganized and came back to win a smashing victory at Poltava in 1709. It was the end of Sweden's century of predominance in the north and the beginning of Russia's rise, first to great–power status in the eighteenth century, then to become for a time the most powerful nation in Europe in the twentieth.

On the long stretch of Baltic lands he thus acquired, Peter built his new capital and prime seaport, St. Petersburg. This city was an outstanding illustration of Peter's determination to transform Russia and of the power of absolute monarchy. Built on land conquered by Russian armies, raised on a poisonous swamp by Russian peasant labor at a cost of many lives, the new capital was peopled by reluctant nobles who were simply ordered to build townhouses in the emperor's new city. St. Petersburg thus came into existence, quite simply, because Peter the Great willed that it should. With the passing of generations, it became Russia's great "window on the West," the most civilized of Russian cities, and one of the most beautiful in Europe.

Yet the Russians of Peter's day hated St. Petersburg; and Peter himself, like Louis XIV, was not mourned when he passed to his reward. Boyars saw him as a traitor, and Orthodox Old Believers were convinced he was the Antichrist himself. A British observer could only marvel that "the providence of God . . . has raised up such a furious man to so absolute authority over so great a part of the world."[2]

✦Constitutional Government: England and the Netherlands✦

In the repeated clashes between the forces of centralization and those who resisted royal power, the centralizers most commonly won out. At the national level, absolute monarchy thus became the archetypal governmental form of the later seventeenth century. In some places, however, those who resisted the further growth of royal power succeeded, sometimes to a surprising degree.

In England, an alliance of country gentry and urban merchants, inspired by Puritan clergymen, forced their Stuart kings to abandon absolutist claims and accept the limited power of a *constitutional monarchy,* royal government limited by law. In the Netherlands, the merchants who ran the commercial cities reached an uneasy compromise with the landed aristocracy to produce a state without a monarchy at all—the Dutch Republic.

Challenge to Royal Power in England

Conflicts between ruler and ruled in England were likely from the start. Dying without an heir in 1603, Queen Elizabeth was succeeded by her cousin King James Stuart of Scotland—ironically the son of her old rival, Mary, Queen of Scots. James I and his descendants, Charles I, Charles II, and James II, lacked both the Tudor gift for public relations and empathy for English ways. They also had to face the piled–up grievances of Puritans, members of Parliament, and others who had not dared confront Queen Elizabeth with their complaints. All four Stuarts, finally, believed totally in royal absolutism and in their own divine right to rule, a view that made compromise extremely difficult as demands for reform escalated toward revolution.

Leadership for the opposition to the crown seems to have come from the gentry. England's thousands of landholding but untitled country squires were used to independence and to taking the lead; many were justices of the peace or members the House of Commons. Many of them were also *Puritans,* willing to accept the spiritual guidance of the preachers who demanded change in the Church of England. Puritans tended to be militant Calvinists, either Presbyterians who wanted a national church like that of Scotland or Congregationalists who sought total independence for each congregation. They shared a passion to purify the church of "Catholic" practices like organ music, candles, and incense and to end immorality at court and such popular vices as maypole dancing and theater going. Some merchants, particularly those from London and the port cities, opposed the Stuarts over high taxes and wasteful spending both at the royal court and on futile foreign wars.

Country squires and other opposition leaders were soon challenging the monarchy on a variety of policies. They spoke for Puritanism against high church tendencies, resisted the "tyranny" of the archbishops and bishops, and even feared a reestablishment of Catholi-

The English parliament, which in the seventeenth century challenged the Stuart kings and began to impose limits on the power of the monarchy. (The Folger Shakespeare Library.)

cism in England. They were disgusted with Stuart attempts to draw England closer to such absolutist Catholic states as England's old enemy Spain. They opposed royal attempts to collect taxes not authorized by Parliament. And increasingly, opposition leaders spoke up for the right of Parliament's House of Commons to free elections, free debate, and control of such key matters as taxation and government expenditures.

Both James I (r. 1603–1625) and his successor Charles I (r. 1625–1649) defended their right to rule as continental kings did. James was an irritable and pedantic spokesman for royal absolutism, Charles an emotional believer in high church rule and ritual. These early Stuarts responded to parliamentary challenges with vigor. They forbade debates, arrested members, and dissolved parliaments. Charles I tried for over a decade in the 1620s and 1630s to govern by royal prerogative, without summoning Parliament at all, as the Bourbons were doing without the Estates General in France.

Then in 1637, Charles attempted to impose the Anglican prayer book on the rigorously Calvinist Scottish national church. The Scottish lords promptly rose in rebellion— and ignited a civil war in England too.

Cromwell and the English Commonwealth

In need of funds to field an army against his Scottish subjects, King Charles in 1640 summoned what became known to history as the Long Parliament. Once convened, this Parliament remained in intermittent session for most of the next two decades. Inspired by long–term foes of royal autocracy like John Pym (1584–1643), the "uncrowned king of Parliament," the House of Commons used the king's desperate need for funds as a club against him. They forced him to back away from high–handed policies on taxation and governance. They compelled the impeachment and execution of leading royal advisors, including the archbishop of Canterbury, William Laud. In a final clash, King Charles led troops into Parliament himself in an attempt to seize radical leaders by force. The radicals escaped, and the parliamentary opposition openly took up arms against the king.

In the Civil War (1642–1649) that followed, the king and his hard–riding Cavalier courtiers expected to have it all their own way. The *Cavaliers*—swashbuckling duelists with flowing locks, real–life English equivalents of the "Three Musketeers"—looked forward to cutting through these stodgy country squires and their Puritan chaplains like a knife through butter. But Oliver Cromwell (1599–1658), both a Puritan country squire and a successful military commander, organized a disciplined New Model Army whose "Ironside" cavalry—so called because they charged into battle as though bullets would bounce right off them—proved more than a match for the king's Cavaliers. After years of maneuvering and fighting up and down the length of England, they defeated the royal army and captured King Charles. In 1649, to the horror of absolutist monarchs everywhere, the victorious revolutionaries tried and executed their king.

Royalists, of course, turned at once from the martyred Charles I to his exiled son, Charles II. Regrouping on the other side of the Channel, they mobilized attacks on the Celtic fringe of the Commonwealth in Scotland and Ireland. Cromwell beat back all assaults, often with great brutality. Meanwhile, a series of splits fissured the ranks of the victorious rebels themselves. The differences between Presbyterians and Independents on church organization surfaced as soon as the common enemy was defeated. Political differences also developed between the gentry leadership, who assumed that England would continue to be guided by its traditional ruling class, and a radical element called the

Levellers, who dared to dream of a nation ruled by all Christian men. There were even a few primitive communists, the so–called *Diggers,* who urged the sharing of property as they believed New Testament Christians had done.

The clearest and most devastating division, however, was that between two power centers: Cromwell's victorious New Model Army, where radicals found a platform, and the Parliament, whose political leadership began to seem too conservative to those who had fought and bled for the cause. The result was a series of defections from and purges of the Long Parliament. In 1649, there were only sixty members left, the so–called Rump Parliament, to bring Charles I to trial before the special court that sentenced him to death. After 1653, finally, Cromwell ruled as Lord Protector of the Commonwealth, dividing the country into military districts and governing through major–generals in each.

Cromwell's wars and the changes in government he imposed, however, brought crushing taxes and social turmoil. Puritan efforts to abolish theaters, taverns, and May Day celebrations further angered the citizens. Less than two years after Cromwell's death, one of his own major–generals conspired to turn the nation back over to Charles II (r. 1660–1685). The people, who had once cheered for the revolution, now cheered King Charles back to his kingdom. Cromwell's corpse was disinterred, his head stuck on a pole on top of Westminster Hall in London, where it remained throughout Charles II's reign.[3]

The First Bill of Rights

In 1660 a struggle that had begun in 1603 seemed to have come full circle, ending as it had begun with a Stuart king welcomed into London. Charles II, a romantic but prudent prince, had no desire to go back into exile, and therefore did not press too drastic a reaction on the country. The Anglican church was restored with the monarchy, and Puritans suffered such civil disabilities as being prohibited from holding public office. The pastimes and pleasures the Puritan regime had outlawed were revived, particularly by the pleasure–loving king and his courtiers. Charles, furthermore, had come under Catholic and absolutist influences during his years overseas. He set out to forge an alliance with Louis XIV— who was his first cousin. Raised by a Catholic mother, he was probably converted to Catholicism himself before his death in 1685.

He left the crown to his elderly brother, James II (r. 1685–1688), an avowed Catholic who soon claimed the right to "dispense," or suspend, the laws of the realm and established a 30,000–man standing army to garrison it. The fears of "popery" and royal tyranny that had set the revolutionary spiral in motion at the beginning of the century were thus stirred up once more. Within three years of his accession, James II fell victim to what came to be called the *Glorious Revolution* in English history—the expulsion of the last Stuart king and his replacement by the first real constitutional monarchs, William and Mary, in 1688.

The architects of what was really more a political coup than a popular revolution were the leaders of the second James's parliamentary opposition. By 1688, members of this strong antiroyalist faction were being called *Whigs* by their enemies, while the more conservative defenders of royal policies were labeled *Tories*—colorful tags for Scottish and Irish rogues, respectively. The Glorious Revolution was triggered by the birth of an infant son to James and his Catholic queen, an event that seemed to threaten a long line of Catholic sovereigns on the throne of Protestant England. The Whig leaders reacted by circulating the rumor that the child was not the elderly king's but a commoner's brat smuggled into the queen's bed in a warming pan. They also turned to King James's Protestant daughter Mary and her husband William of Orange, stadtholder of the Netherlands, who was both ruler of a constitutional state and the moving spirit behind the international coalition against Louis XIV. William, eager to channel the wealth of England into the struggle against absolute monarchy, landed by prearrangement with a Dutch army. Abandoned even by his Tory supporters, James Stuart fled once more into exile, and William III (r. 1689–1702) and Mary II (r. 1689–1696) were crowned joint sovereigns of England early in 1689.

As a condition of being crowned, however, William and Mary were required to accept a set of English constitutional principles enacted by Parliament in 1689. The Whigs thus pushed through *England's Bill of Rights,* the first such legislation to appear in the Western world. Explicitly or implicitly, this remarkable seventeenth–century document guaranteed many of the rights for which Parliament had been fighting for many decades. The sovereigns were compelled to agree to parliamentary control of government revenues, the right to free elections and regular meetings, freedom of debate, and freedom from arrest during a session. Other supports for the rights of the governed included an independent judiciary in which judges could not be cashiered for their political views; relative freedom of religion; and implied support for the rights of all subjects to life, liberty, and property. William of Orange, who as stadtholder had functioned for years as constitutional ruler of the Netherlands, was willing to accept these terms. Across the Channel, Louis XIV was horrified that any monarch—even his longtime archenemy William of Orange—would accept a crown at the cost of such constraints on his divine right to rule.

The Glorious Revolution of 1688 and the Bill of Rights of 1689 did not bring democracy to England. The House of Lords, filled with titled noblemen and high churchmen, could still veto any bill passed by the Commons. The House of Commons itself was composed of gentry, merchants, and lawyers elected by a small minority of the population. Nor did the Bill of Rights deprive the crown of power, since the monarchs still retained a preponderance of authority. But what began to grow in 1689 was constitutional monarchy, government by a loose alliance between the king and the aristocracy under strict legal limitations. In the following centuries, the English Parliament became both more representative and more powerful; and in the twentieth century a democratic House of Commons became the real seat of power in Britain, the monarchy no more than a symbol of national unity.

The Golden Age of the Dutch Republic

In continental Europe, however, another people had gone even further than the English down the road toward a more liberal political order in the seventeenth century. Culturally and economically, this century was the golden age of the Netherlands, the century of Rembrandt and the Dutch overseas empire. Politically, it was also a time when the United Provinces offered more opportunity for citizen participation than any other power in Europe. Theirs was a political system founded on an immense prosperity and precariously balanced between disunity and autocracy. But it produced a freer, more tolerant society than could be found anywhere else—a freedom that in return made its contributions to the economic progress and the cultural brilliance of the Dutch golden age.

Economically, centuries of industrial, commercial, and financial development reached their climax in the wake of the successful revolt of the United Provinces against Spain. The tidy, solidly built cities of the northern Netherlands had been a hive of productivity since the High Middle Ages. They were centers of shipbuilding, textile manufacturing, diamond cutting, book publishing, and a dozen other crafts, including the production of Delft china

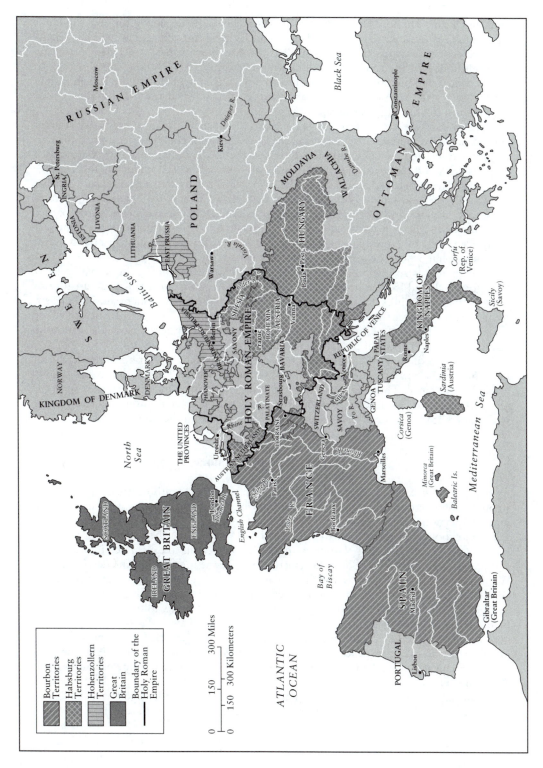

Europe in 1715

and Dutch gin. The low Dutch polders bloomed beneath the slowly turning windmills. The Dutch city of Amsterdam replaced the Flemish city of Antwerp as Europe's most active financial center, Dutch fishing vessels trolled the North Sea banks, and Dutch merchantmen outnumbered the shipping of all other states combined. In the colonial realm, the Dutch shouldered the Portuguese out of southern Asia, competed with the British and the French in North America and the Caribbean, and established one of the West's most long–lasting colonial outposts in South Africa.

The political structure of the Netherlands was an unstable compromise between urban autonomy and domination by the nobility. The seven United Provinces were urban republics with elected councils and magistrates on the medieval pattern. They were loosely joined by an *Estates General* that had little authority over the affairs of the member provinces. The Dutch leaders Jan van Oldenbarneveldt, who played a leading part between 1587 and 1618, and Jan de Witt, prominent between 1653 and 1672, guided the United Provinces through some of their most prosperous times. They spoke for the urban patriciate of the cities whose goals were prosperity above all; toleration, which unleashed the productive energies of Protestants, Catholics, and Jews alike; and control of affairs by the Estates General, where the urban oligarchy dominated.

But there was another center of power in the United Provinces: the noble house of Orange, which had led the northern Netherlands to freedom and enjoyed an aristocratic prestige that went back to the Middle Ages. From William the Silent during the sixteenth–century Dutch Revolt to the rule of that William of Orange who became King William III of England, leaders of this Dutch dynasty were regularly chosen as stadtholders, or overlords, of most of the Dutch provinces.

The leaders of the house of Orange, however, tended to be more rigorously Calvinistic than the merchants and more fearful of the "Catholic menace," first of Spain and then of Louis XIV's France. They were also typically more eager for war, in which they were the recognized leaders. An internal tension was thus set up in which power swayed from the stadtholders at the center to the cities and back again through the century.

The Rewards of Freedom

As the English overthrew their monarchs twice in the seventeenth century, so the Dutch Republic went through the same cycle twice during this critical century. Oldenbarneveldt secured the twelve years' truce with Spain that first recognized the United Provinces in 1609 and took the leading role thereafter. In 1619, however, the reigning head of the house of Orange, Maurice of Nassau, found a religious reason to execute Oldenbarneveldt and plunged the Netherlands into the Thirty Years' War against Spain. The descendants of William the Silent prevailed for the next quarter of a century. In 1648, however, Jan de Witt led the peace forces who finally and permanently negotiated the independence of the United Provinces. More than twenty years of peace and prosperity followed under De Witt before Louis XIV broke into the republic in 1672. Outraged at de Witt's lack of preparedness, a mob of his fellow countrymen then murdered their venerable leader, and William of Orange took up the reins of leadership for the rest of the century. King of England after 1689, William also embodied the triumph of centralized authority over the provinces in his own country.

Many factors, however, limited the power of the nobles in the United Provinces. There was neither an autocratic royal tradition nor a powerful centralized bureaucracy. The economic power of urban mercantile interests was great. Provincial loyalties were strong, and a high proportion of the citizenry participated in the political life of these prosperous cities. It was, finally, a remarkably open society, welcoming immigrants of any faith: Protestant refugees from Catholic countries, Catholics fleeing Protestant countries, and Jews from everywhere.

The French philosopher René Descartes, one of many freethinkers who sought a haven in the Netherlands, hymned the virtues of the country: "What other place could one choose in the world," he wrote to a friend, "where all the comforts of life . . . may be so easily found as here? What other country where one may enjoy such perfect liberty?"[4] There was a harsher side to the Dutch dominion in its far–flung colonies, where, as we will see in a later chapter, they could be as brutal as any other imperialists. But the solid middle–class qualities Descartes applauded—comfort, security, liberty—were major achievements too. In the long run, the modern West looks more like the Dutch Republic than any other seventeenth–century state.

Summary

The misfortunes of the "critical" seventeenth century were many. The period was jolted by a series of rebellions and civil wars in such great nations as England and France. It also faced severe economic problems, including regional depressions, famines, and economic stagnation between surges of growth in the sixteenth and eighteenth centuries. If we add plagues and the divisive social scapegoating of the witch hunts, it is easy to understand the feeling many Europeans had that strong, even absolute monarchy was necessary as a means of restoring order to a shaken continent.

Powerful absolutists like Louis XIV in France, the Habsburg and Hohenzollern rulers in central Europe, and Peter the Great in Russia thus emerged supreme in the later 1600s. They increased royal power at the expense of the traditional prerogatives and liberties of nobles, towns, provinces, and other once autonomous groups and institutions. In England and the Netherlands, by contrast, decades of political struggle produced a rough partnership between the king and Parliament in England, and between stadtholder and Estates General in the Netherlands. In these relations lay the beginnings of modern constitutional government.

Some Key Terms

Notes

1. Theodore K. Rabb, *The Struggle for Stability in Early Modern Europe* (New York: Oxford University Press, 1975), 3–4. For a brief summary of the debate over "the crisis of the seventeenth century," see Chapter 13.
2. Bishop Gilbert Burnet, in B. H. Sumner, *Peter the Great and the Emergence of Russia* (New York: Collier, 1962), 41.
3. Today the lord protector's statue guards the Parliament House in Westminster.
4. Petrus Johannes Blok, *History of the People of the Netherlands,* vol. 4, trans. Oscar A. Bierstadt (New York: Putnam's, 1907), 102.

Reading List

Anderson, M. S. *War and Society in Europe of the Old Regime, 1618–1789.* New York: St. Martin's Press, 1988. A useful introduction to a field of growing interest to historians—the role of warfare in Western society.

Ashley, M. B. *The Golden Century.* New York: Praeger, 1969. Good place to begin on the seventeenth century.

Braudel, F. *Capitalism and Material Life, 1400–1800.* New York: Harper, 1974. Thoughtful exploration of the material lives of early modern people.

Carsten, F. L. *The Origins of Prussia.* Westport, Conn.: Greenwood, 1982. The beginnings of modern Germany, through the Great Elector.

Cole, C. W. *Colbert and a Century of French Mercantilism.* Hamden, Conn.: Archon, 1964. Thorough survey of the mercantile system at its most developed. See also E. F. Herkscher, *Mercantilism,* 2d ed. (New York: Macmillan, 1962). A provocative analysis.

Corvisier, A. *Armies and Societies in Europe, 1494–1789.* Translated by A. T. Siddall. Bloomington: University of Indiana Press, 1979. The army as an instrument of state power, as part of society, and as a subculture of its own.

Coward, B. *Oliver Cromwell.* New York: Longman, 1991. A readable, concise, and up to date life of the English revolutionary leader.

Elliott, J. H. *Richelieu and Olivares.* New York: Cambridge University Press, 1984. Comparative biographies of the two rival statesmen, seen in the context of their times and the problems each faced.

Friedrichs, C. *The Early Modern City 1450–1750.* New York: Longman, 1995. Solid survey, centering on the sixteenth and seventeenth centuries.

Gentles, I. *The New Model Army in England, Ireland, and Scotland, 1645–1653.* Cambridge, Mass.: Blackwell, 1992. Scholarly account of the Puritan army.

Hill, C. *The Century of Revolution, 1603–1714.* New York: Norton, 1982. Admired overview of the England's "century of revolution," with social and economic emphasis.

Klaits, J. *Servants of Satan: The Age of Witch Hunts.* Bloomington: University of Indiana Press, 1985. Synthesizes views on a much discussed subject. See also B. P. Levack, *The Witch Hunt in Early Modern Europe* (New York: Longman, 1995).

Mousnier, R. E. *The Institutions of France under the Absolute Monarchy, 1598–1789: Society and the State.* Chicago: University of Chicago Press, 1980. Interaction of government and people from the century of Richelieu and Louis XIV to the French Revolution.

Rabb, T. K. *The Struggle for Stability in Early Modern Europe.* New York: Oxford University Press, 1975. Extends the crisis of the seventeenth century back to the sixteenth, seeing it as a conflict between central government and the regions.

Raeff, M., ed. *Peter the Great Changes Russia.* Lexington, Mass.: D.C. Heath, 1972. Essays on the impact of the controversial founder of modern Russia.

———*The Well-Ordered Police State: Social and Institutional Change in the Germanies and Russia, 1600–1800.* New Haven: Yale University Press, 1983. Comparative study of emerging autocracy, going below institutional structures to administrative routines and political attitudes of elites.

Ranum, O. *The Fronde: A French Revolution,*

1648–1652. New York: Norton, 1993. Analyzes a series of "revolutionary moments" in this mid–century upheaval.

Roosen, W. J. *The Age of Louis XIV: The Rise of Modern Diplomacy.* Cambridge, Mass.: Schenkman, 1976. Analyzes the diplomatic system of Louis XIV's day in terms of institutions, personnel, and practice.

Stone, L. *The Family, Sex, and Marriage in England, 1500–1800.* New York: Harper & Row, 1977. Documents a drift in family organiza-tion from loose structure through the patriarchal private family of the seventeenth century to a more affectionate nuclear family in the eighteenth.

Wedgwood, C. V. *The Thirty Years War.* New York: Methuen, 1981. The bloodiest war of the century vividly retold. For a more analytical approach, see T. K. Rabb, ed., *The Thirty Years War: Problems of Motive and Effect* (New York: University Press of America, 1981).

—13—

Michelangelo's Dome and Newton's Apple

The Birth of the Modern Mind

•The Beginnings of Modern Political Thought
•Expanding Horizons of Art   •The Scientific Revolution
•Impact of the New Science

"Tis all in pieces," lamented the poet and preacher John Donne, looking around him at the confused and fragmented intellectual world of the early 1600s, "all coherence gone."[1] The crisis of the seventeenth century, which shook society and transformed the state, inevitably had its impact on the thought and art of the period. Sensitive spirits like Donne were no longer able to find answers to all their questions in classical and Christian sources as Renaissance humanists and Reformation preachers had done. They were also challenged by the scientific revolution, which had begun in the middle of the preceding century and reached its climax in the later seventeenth century. Overwhelmed, thoughtful people fumbled for new certainties. As state builders from Louis XIV to Cromwell imposed order on society, so thinkers and artists strove to reassemble an intellectually acceptable picture of the world and of humanity's place in it.

Through their labors the modern Western worldview began to take shape. During the 1600s, as we will see in the first two sections of this chapter, Western people began both to entertain more modern political views and to see the world artistically through more realistic eyes. In the last two sections, we will see how these same generations began to understand nature and nature's laws in modern scientific terms.

It was only a beginning in political thought, in the arts, and in the new sciences. But it was a level of achievement that has earned for the critical century another appropriate label: the "century of genius" in the history of the Western mind.

♦The Beginnings of Modern Political Thought♦

The deep political divide between absolutist and constitutional governments in the seventeenth century was reflected in the political thought of the time. From this conflict between the political vision of Louis XIV and that embodied in the English Bill of Rights came the seminal ideas of Thomas Hobbes and John Locke: Hobbes asserting the need for stronger central government, Locke defending the rights of the governed. Both these ideals have echoed down the modern centuries as formulations of two key views of how Western people ought to be ruled or to rule themselves.

The Concept of Sovereignty

The political thought of the age certainly felt the impact of the atmosphere of crisis that enveloped the times. In an age of rebellion and the reassertion of royal power, many political thinkers continued to draw on ancient and medieval ideas, while others found support for their theories in the emerging physical sciences and in new views of human nature. The result was a war of words between rigidly absolutist and radically constitutionalist doctrines in which modern political science was born. We look at the theory of royal absolutism in this section and at constitutionalist ideas in the section that follows.

To support the claims of early modern rulers to unprecedented power over the people, apologists for absolute monarchy drew on sources such as the aristocratic Greek views of Plato and Aristotle, the Roman imperial experience, and the medieval concept of divine right. Views older than Plato that "the people" were sheep in need of a shepherd, or wild beasts requiring a strong hand to tame them, echoed convincingly in the ears of thinkers who had seen the Fronde or the excesses of the Puritan Revolution. Images of Roman imperial grandeur surrounded the Sun King in stone and glowing pigment. Above all, seventeenth-century thinkers developed and vigorously asserted the medieval concept of the monarch's divine right to rule. Phrases like "God, by whom kings reign" came naturally to their lips.[2] King Charles II of England, speaking for the battered Stuart monarchy, said this to a university audience at Cambridge in 1681, only half a dozen years before the Glorious Revolution:

> We will still believe and maintain that our kings derive not their title from the people, but from God; that to him only they are accountable; that it belongs not to subjects, either to create or to censure but to honor and obey their sovereign.[3]

Other political thinkers explored the concept of *sovereignty,* the authority to govern, attributing an unprecedented degree of power to the royal governments of the seventeenth century. As a political concept, sovereignty had traditionally meant the highest level of authority *within* a particular institution or subdivision of society. The church, the legal system, provinces and towns all had their own sovereign or supreme authorities. In the depths of the French wars of religion, however, Jean Bodin (1530–1596) in his *Six Books on the Republic* (1576) offered a new definition of *maiestas,* or "sovereign authority." Sovereignty for Bodin was no longer relative to a particular subdivision of society, but absolute, supreme over the whole of the body politic. Such absolute sovereignty, furthermore, was necessary to the health of the state, since only *maiestas* could hold together the component parts of the nation. It was an argument that had as much appeal to the crisis–torn seventeenth century as to the sixteenth, and was freely cited by defenders of absolute monarchy.

Hobbes and the Leviathan State

In a longer perspective, however, the most important supporter of absolutist government was the eccentric English conservative Thomas Hobbes (1588–1679), whose concept of the Leviathan state was used later to explain far more authoritarian regimes in our own century.

Chronology 13: Science and Culture

1543	Copernicus's **On the Revolutions of the Heavenly Bodies** *replaces earth-centered universe with sun-centered one*
1598–1680	Bernini's sculpture, **Ecstasy of St. Teresa,** *exemplifies baroque capacity to excite belief*
1606–1669	Rembrandt's painting—**Anatomy Lesson, Supper at Emmaus**— *transcends middle-class market*
1607	Monteverdi's **Orfeo**—*first important opera—demonstrates potential of baroque music*
1608–1667	Milton's poetry—**Paradise Lost, Samson Agonistes**—*combines classical style with religious themes*
1610	*Galileo's telescope sees mountains on moon, Saturn's rings*
1637	Descartes' **Discourse on Method** *rejects authorities in favor of rational investigation*
1639–1699	*Racine's classical tragedy* **Phèdre**
1651	*Hobbes's* **Leviathan** *urges absolute government*
1561–1626	*Bacon becomes first to prophesy great value of science*
1670	Moliere's **Bourgeois Gentleman** *mocks middle-class pretensions*
1687	Newton's **Mathematical Principles of Natural Philosophy** *proposes law of gravity*
1690	Locke's **Two Treatises of Civil Government** *preaches natural rights, social contract*

Horrified by the Puritan Revolution in England, Hobbes had fled to France, where his book *Leviathan*, a "Discourse of Civil Government Occasioned by the Disorders of the Present Time," was published in 1651.

Hobbes's view was based not on Christian or classical sources but on the materialistic philosophy that underlay the scientific revolution which, as we will see, reached its apogee in this century. His materialistic analysis produced a grim picture of human beings driven by selfish motives of desire and fear, locked in a perpetual struggle for survival, the "war of all against all." He began his analysis with a look at life in *the state of nature*—a key concept in early modern political thought, meaning the condition in which human beings would live if there were neither government nor laws to restrain them. Hobbes described this condition as bleak and brutal, deprived of the skills and comforts, arts and sciences of civilization. Human life was thus naturally, as an often quoted passage puts it, "solitary, poor, nasty, brutish, and short."

To end this anarchic and mutually destructive situation, Hobbes asserted, human beings sooner or later formulate a *social contract*—another basic conception of modern political analysis. Social contract theory asserts that structured society exists by virtue of a tacit contractual agreement among its people. In Hobbes's view, such a social contract requires the people to surrender all their personal power to a central government that, by ruling over them all alike, will protect them all from each other. Leaving the state of nature behind, people thus create organized society—and absolute sovereignty at the same time. For in order to carry out its primary function of protecting the governed from their own baser instincts, government must have great power. It must possess not only lawmaking and police powers, but control of state revenues, of the armed forces, of the printing press and the pulpit; in short, it must have ultimate authority over every institution and every individual in the state. We are driven by our basic natures, Hobbes said, to erect the *Leviathan state,* a society as powerful and all–encompassing as Leviathan, the biblical monster of the deep— and to more liberal thinkers in later centuries, every bit as frightening.

The absolute monarchs of the seventeenth century understandably preferred divine right and grandiose Roman parallels to Hobbes's grim justification of their supreme power. Later modern political thinkers, however, have made Hobbes's book a classic. And many people since have seen in Hobbes's *Leviathan,* as in Machiavelli's *Prince,* some uncomfortable intimations of the way human beings and human governments too often really are.

Locke and Government by Consent of the Governed

In the long run, however, the most influential political thinkers of the seventeenth century proved to be those who spoke for the constitutionalist side in the century's great debate. Phrases and philosophies well known from America's own eighteenth–century Declaration of Independence and Constitution, for example, could be heard on the lips of the Levellers during the English Civil War and from John Locke at the time of the Glorious Revolution.

The *Levellers,* who flourished briefly in the 1640s, got their name from those who charged they wanted to "level" a naturally hierarchic society to confer an unnatural social equality on all people. Part of the extremist fringe in revolutionary England, the Levellers were yeomen farmers and others even lower on the social scale, people who would never serve as magistrates or sit in Commons. But they had heard much talk about "rights"—the rights of Parliament, the rights of judges to try cases without royal interference, the rights of the rather abstract "freeborn Englishmen" the orators defended. Religious Independents (Congregationalists) and leaders among the rank and file of the Puritan Army, these radicals began to demand some rights of their own.

"The poorest he that is in England," thundered Thomas Rainborough in a public debate with Cromwell, "hath a life to live as well the richest he; and truly, sir, I think it is clear that every man that is to live under a government ought first by his own consent to put himself under that government."[4] The leaders of the parliamentary revolution were horrified at these radically democratic demands. Cromwell suppressed the Levellers as firmly as any sovereign in Europe would have done.

John Locke (1632–1704) came several decades after the Levellers, publishing his *Two Treatises of Civil Government* in 1690 and declaring that the work was intended "to establish the throne of our great restorer, our present King, William, to make good his title in the consent of the people . . . the only one of all lawful governments."[5] Locke's epochal *Second Treatise* though written some years earlier, thus appeared in the wake of the Glorious Revolution that put William and Mary on the throne as England's first real constitutional monarchs. This essay also became the first classic of the liberal political tradition, and Locke the original prophet of government by consent of the governed—though his definition of "the governed" was not so radical as that of the Levellers.

Locke, a physician by training, shared Hobbes's enthusiasm for science and rooted his political theory also in distinctive views of human character, "the state of nature," and an ideal "social contract." Locke's account of all three, however, differed strikingly from the views of his countrymen a couple of generations earlier.

Human character, Locke believed, was not innately selfish and vicious, but infinitely malleable, a *tabula rasa* ("blank slate") on which childhood training, education, and later experience inscribe the character of the adult. Nurture, not nature, said Locke, makes us what we are. This view implied also the doctrine of human perfectibility: the belief that by transforming the social environment, human beings can effectively change human nature—or at least human behavior—and produce a better society, a happier world. It was a vision of humanity that proved central to all the reformist and revolutionary ideologies of the modern world.

In the state of nature, Locke declared, mild–mannered human beings live not in a war of all against all, but relatively peacefully much of the time. Even before the creation of an ordered society, furthermore, humans enjoy both the use of reason and their most precious possessions, their *natural rights*—particularly, the rights to life, liberty, and property. Because intermittent outbreaks of injustice and aggression could occur even in Locke's state of nature, however, institutional support for these rights would in the long run prove beneficial. Thus for the preservation of their natural rights, Locke argued, rational people will enter into a social contract, establishing the state. But this Lockean state will be very different from Hobbes's Leviathan.

Legitimate government, John Locke believed, would be limited in its powers, would be restrained by law, and would exist only by the consent of the people it governed. The powers of the state, far from being absolute, were strictly limited to the protection of the rights of the people. Government was also to be restrained by its own laws, as William and Mary were restrained by the Bill of Rights from ruling by decree or riding roughshod over law and tradition. Above all, any legitimate government should be controlled by the governed themselves, making their power felt through an elected legislature like the House of Commons in the English Parliament. And if an illegitimate government arose, one that suppressed rather than protected the natural rights of the governed, then the people had the ultimate "right to revolution," the right to overthrow such a government and replace it with a new one.

Locke saw two other elements as essential to a free society: private property and toleration of dissent. He felt that those who own land or other material possessions have a larger *stake in society* than those who have nothing to lose. An active share in government should therefore be limited to those who, because they owned property, have "something to lose" if society fails to function properly—people with a "stake" in the success of the body politic. Locke also believed strongly, however, in toleration for minority views and in freedom of expression. His support for tolerance was originally intended to apply to religious minorities like the Puritans, but it provided support for freedom of thought more broadly conceived in later centuries.

◆ Expanding Horizons of Art ◆

The arts in the seventeenth century, like so much else, reflected that period's critical place in Western history. Artists and writers looked back for inspiration to the glories of ancient art uncovered in the Renaissance and to the religious passions unleashed by the Protestant and Catholic Reformations. Like their predecessors in earlier times, seventeenth–century writers and artists catered to the tastes of their patrons in church and state. At the same time, however, literature and art responded to the attitudes of increasingly prosperous and educated middle–class Europeans.

To appeal to the old powers of church and state, seventeenth–century artists and writers produced splendid baroque and subtle classical art, both rooted in the elegant traditional styles of the Greco–Roman and Renaissance periods. For the rising middle classes, new schools of art and literature developed such realistic contemporary genres as Dutch landscape painting and the English novel.

Baroque Art

As the religious passions of the preceding century cooled toward toleration and political thinkers debated the relative merits of absolute and constitutionally limited government, the arts also responded to these trends of the times. This was particularly the case with later sixteenth– and seventeenth–century styles like the baroque and classicism. Behind the triumphant notes of baroque trumpets, the sweep of St. Peter's Square in Rome, or the fourteen hundred playing fountains of Versailles gleamed taut calculations of power and politics in an age of crisis.

The word *baroque* may derive from *barroco*, a term of perhaps Arabic origin meaning "an irregularly shaped pearl." Baroque architecture, painting, sculpture, and music did depart from the balanced, logical norms of Renaissance art. It did so in order to stir the emotions rather than to impress the intellect. Its object was to move its audience powerfully by any means possible, from movement and color to sheer breathtaking scale. Baroque art thus answered the uncertainties of the age by an overwhelming assertion of the will: be-

Bernini's 85-foot *Baldacchino* or tabernacle fills the huge space beneath the dome of St. Peter's. Modeled on the canopy placed over the sacrament, the *baldacchino* matches the immense scale of the expanded baroque St. Peter's.

lieve, accept, and Donne's disoriented world, "all coherence gone," will make sense once more.

Such a powerful style had an instant appeal to both church and state in a time when both were challenged. Baroque thus became the art of the Catholic Reformation in the later 1500s and of absolute monarchy in the 1600s. Authorized by the Council of Trent to make use of carved and painted images, music, and gorgeous decorations to draw waverers back to the faith, Catholic church leaders built, rebuilt, or refurbished hundreds of baroque churches during the sixteenth and seventeenth centuries. They commissioned thousands of paintings and statues of saints in ecstasy, Mary ascending into heaven, and the Passion of Christ on the cross, all aimed at reviving belief by sheer emotional impact. Royal absolutists built ornate palaces surrounded by vast formal gardens and splendid vistas for the same reason. Such structures served as awesome settings for ceremonies that restored belief, in this case in the sovereign's authority and divine right to rule.

The baroque style in a variety of media was perfectly suited to these ends. Baroque painting combined drastic foreshortening, asymmetrical composition, bright colors, and swirling movement of draperies and straining limbs. These visually exciting elements were typically organized around an inward–driving diagonal to focus dramatically on a wonder–working saint or a king in his glory. The Flemish master Peter Paul Rubens (1577–1640) thus filled his huge canvases with bodies turning, gesturing, guiding the eye from lower left to upper right through waves of color to a heroic St. Francis, or to Mary offering the infant Jesus to the adoration of the three kings.

In Spain, the court painter Diego Velázquez (1599–1660) and the church artist Bartolomé Murillo (1617–1682) concentrated their great talents in the service of the monarchy and the church. A close friend of Philip IV, Velázquez painted the Spanish Habsburg king, the royal family, and such historic events as *The Surrender at Breda* with an accuracy, powerful composition, and a control of brush strokes that compelled belief. His contemporary Murillo became perhaps the most admired of all baroque religious painters, loved particularly for his moving depictions of the Virgin, from the child Mary to her ascent into heaven.

In Italy, the dramatic paintings of Caravaggio (1573–1610) and of Artemisia Gentileschi (1593–1652) exploited realism and violently contrasting chiaroscuro to further intensify the viewer's reactions. Caravaggio (real name Michelangelo Merisi) was himself a violent person, exiled from Rome for killing a man in a brawl. Though his realistic depiction of disciples like St. Matthew as rude peasants disturbed some, his tenebrist (deeply shadowed) chiaroscuro, with its focused lighting and enveloping areas of darkness, stirred powerful emotional responses in many viewers.

Artemisia Gentileschi was the daughter of a well–known artist—the most likely route for a woman into the arts. Like Caravaggio's life, Gentileschi's had its dramatic moments, including her rape by the man her father had engaged to teach her and the humiliation of the resulting trial, in which she—not her attacker—was tortured to ascertain the truth of her testimony. One of the best known artists of her generation, Gentileschi, like Caravaggio, composed her pictures in dynamic contrasts of light and darkness. Her psychological realism shows in her savage pictures of the biblical heroine Judith decapitating the tyrant Holofernes, images in which some critics have detected a violence born of her own traumatic life experiences.

Baroque sculpture could become almost painterly in its effort to achieve emotionally stirring effects, combining stone, metal, glass, and colored light in an intensely illusionistic art. The famous statue of *The Ecstasy of St. Teresa* by Gianlorenzo Bernini (1598–1680) in the church of Santa Maria della Vittoria in Rome, for instance, features golden metal rays and filtered yellow light from above flooding over the marble figures of the swooning saint, head thrown back, and the smiling angel posed to thrust the arrow of divine love into her heart.

Baroque music was also eminently suited to the sumptuous culture of court entertainments and gorgeous church ceremonial in which it was born. Richly dramatic church music, dazzling in counterpoint and fugue, made baroque worship a stirring aesthetic experience. Opera and ballet flowered as suitably splendid entertainments for a society of aristocrats and kings.

The first generally recognized ballet was a French court entertainment of the 1580s. Depending heavily on costume and scenery for their effect, ballets were often performed by noble courtiers and even kings until Louis XIV established the first school to train professional dancers in the 1660s. From this Royal Academy of Dance and its imitators across Europe came rigorously trained, highly athletic artists who could perform feats no dancers had ever before attempted.

The first important opera was the Italian *Orfeo* of Claudio Monteverdi (1567–1643), produced in 1607. Opera developed as a form of musical drama combining choral and solo singing, much as ancient Greek tragedy had done. The powerful solos called *arias* in particular, expressing a character's passion, anguish, or other intense feeling in an intricate flood of melody, tested the range and mastery of the most gifted singers of the age. Built around slender stories and extravagant characters, baroque opera depended on spectacle and glorious music to hold first courtly and then popular audiences spellbound.

Perhaps most impressive of all, baroque architecture, integrated with sculpture and painting, sounded a powerful reaffirmation of the grandeur of church and state. Ornate and elaborate in Italy, Austria, and Spain, more stately in France, baroque building combined Greek columns and capitals with Roman arches and domes, replaced balanced rectangles with sweeping curves, and aimed at giving a sense of vast spaces mastered by the architect.

A single room in the opulent immensity of Versailles, like the Salon of War, blends huge scale with a profusion of art. Dominated by a marble relief of Louis XIV triumphant on horseback, the chamber is resplendent with richly colored paintings, marble fireplaces, huge chandeliers, and carving everywhere, generating awe in even the most footsore visitor. It was the effect the baroque aimed at everywhere—the glory of the reformed Catholic church, the splendor of the absolutist state.

Classical Art

Also rooted in Greco–Roman and Renaissance sources, but very different in spirit from baroque art, was the *classical* tradition that flowered in the seventeenth century.

The Renaissance had brought the modern West back into contact with its ancient roots, and Renaissance art had profited thereby. Seventeenth–century *classicism* turned to ancient culture with even greater dedication, building with Greek and Roman columns and capitals, filling pictures and plays with characters out of Greek myth and Roman history, writing epics, lyrics, satires, and tragedies because the ancients had. Drama followed the three unities of action, place, and time derived from Aristotle. Poetry found its ultimate authority in the *Poetic Art* (1674) of Nicholas Boileau (1636–1711), a vigorous defender of classical models against the "moderns." In the arts, Louis XIV became the official patron of the French Academy of Painting and Sculpture in 1667. Here the royal painter Charles le Brun (1619–1690) held regular lecture–discussions of art works designed to formulate fixed "academic" standards of artistic excellence.

The classic art and literature that resulted cultivated traditional subjects and styles and aimed at refinement, rationality, and high seriousness. Often contrasted with the baroque style, classicism sought balance and tranquility where the baroque stressed movement and dynamism; simplicity and clarity where baroque was full of life and action; hard–boned structure in contrast to the rich color of the baroque. The surging crowds and driving diagonals of Rubens, for example, vanish in the calm landscapes with a few quiet classical figures of Nicolas Poussin (1594–1665), in whose arcadian scenes a single musing shepherd may be all that breaks the golden–age tranquility of a perfectly balanced landscape of horizontal meadows and vertical trees.

In the classical tragedy of Pierre Corneille (1606–1684) and especially of Jean Racine (1639–1699), noble heroes and heroines discuss their emotional crises—usually involving a clash between love and honor, passion and loyalty—in chiseled diction, balanced rhetorical arguments, and elegant six-beat verse. That such rigorous standards need not drain literature of emotional power is clear in the work of Racine, the most admired of all French dramatists. His tragedy of *Phèdre* (1677), for example, follows the mythic queen of Athens who falls hopelessly in love with her own stepson as she warps and destroys the lives of others.

Towering over all other English poets of the later seventeenth century, John Milton (1608–1674) has been described as the last great Renaissance writer, as the poetic voice of Puritan England, and as a clearly baroque poet in the sonorous power of his verse. Yet Milton's deep involvement in all the traditions of the Western past—biblical and Greco–Roman, medieval and Renaissance—makes him a striking exemplar of the classical spirit too.

A pious youth, Milton acquired a classical education at Cambridge, traveled Italy in the afterglow of the Renaissance, and participated as a pamphleteer in the Puritan revolt. He wrote his greatest poems in his later years, however, when he had seen both his revolution and his eyesight fail and had to dictate his lines to the daughters who cared for him. His epic *Paradise Lost* (1667) and his verse drama *Samson Agonistes* (1671) draw on ancient Hebrew and Christian subject matter, the fall of Adam and Eve in the garden of Eden and the last days of Samson, blind and beaten like the poet himself. In form, these great poems reverberate with the classical literary models with which Milton was so familiar. Scenes, characters, speeches, epic similes and mythological allusions, the very Latinate power of the verse itself, all echo the great poetry of Western antiquity.

Art for the Middle Classes

In a new wave of art and literature aimed at middle–class Europeans, finally, the century showed a sense of growing confidence, a feeling that the world was good, a worthy stage for the decent lives of decent people. Sensible Englishmen like the diarist Samuel Pepys, solid Dutch burghers like those Rembrandt painted, faced few of the ideological and spiritual torments addressed by political theorists or by the high art of court, church, and academy. But theirs was, in a sense, the art of the future, the culture of the coming bourgeois predominance in the Western world.

From the urban patrician and the high–ranking civil servants at the top through merchants, artisans, doctors, lawyers, and growing numbers of officials, they reached down through the ranks to servants and half–literate clerks at the bottom. This broad middle range of society wanted art to include an exciting narrative, human sympathy, respectability, virtue triumphant. Above all, their view of the world respected the world: the material frame itself, the fascinating variety of people in it, the lives and interesting experiences of real people like themselves. Unlikely to identify with saints in ecstasy or kings in their glory, or to be interested in classical themes, the middle–class public wanted simpler, solider fare. They got it in the English literature of "prose and sense" or the paintings of the Dutch realists of the seventeenth century.

There was clearly a moral dimension to the middle–class view of the world. Good Christian families read their Bibles or attended Mass, prayed and sang hymns. Printed volumes of spiritual edification found substantial numbers of bourgeois readers. In France, Italy, and the Spanish Netherlands, the almost Calvinist vision of the Catholic Cornelius Jansen (1585–1638), stressing human wickedness and the need for divine grace, emphasized rigorous moralism. In England, the middle classes made the *Pilgrim's Progress* (1678) of John Bunyan (1628–1688) one of the all–time English bestsellers. It was an allegory for people seriously concerned about the moral and spiritual dimensions of life, tracing the progress of the pilgrim Christian through life, passing through the Slough of Despond, the Valley of the Shadow of Death, and the worldly temptations of Vanity Fair to reach the Celestial City.

Middle–class literary staples included a flood of books in straightforward prose written by a new class of professional writer. These "Grub Street" literary artisans (so called for the London street where they worked and lived) were not supported by aristocratic patronage like Renaissance writers or like the makers of high culture in their own time, but by the bookshop sale of their works to ordinary people. Adventurous prose fiction, travelers' tales of far places, recent history, biography and autobiography, popular science, and the newly invented newspaper perused over a coffeehouse table—these were what stirred the imaginations of the prosperous and progressive middle ranks. The French comic dramatist Jean–Baptiste Molière (1622–1673) appealed more to the Paris bourgeoisie than to the Versailles courtiers for whom he wrote. These solid citizens immensely enjoyed his satires of social pretense in high society, of religious hypocrisy, and even of the ambitions of some tradesmen to pass as cultured gentlemen. The verbal wit of Molière's *Misanthrope* (1666) and *Bourgeois Gentleman* (1670) was brilliant, but Molière offered high farce too, and he remains to this day the most popular writer of all the galaxy of talent that sought the patronage of France's Grand Monarch.

The greatest example of the sort of painting the middle classes enjoyed and commissioned was the work of the *Dutch realists,* the portraitists and the landscape and still–life painters of the Dutch golden age. These artists offered homely scenes of parlor and kitchen, images of grapes you could pluck off the sideboard, cheeses that look good enough to eat. In the level polders, verdant countryside, and tidy towns of the Low Countries, Dutch artists also founded the first famous school of European landscape painters. No mythical gods or heroes were needed to justify these pleasant stretches of countryside with their drifting clouds and shady trees, a cart and horse in the foreground, in the distance a gleam of sunlight off a weathervane or steeple.

Among the leading Dutch painters, Franz Hals (c. 1581–1666) was famed for his vigorous brushwork and vital portraits, particularly of jolly peasants, happy parties, and other scenes from everyday life expressing the cheerful confidence of his people at the height of their golden age. Often compared with Hals was Judith Leyster (1609–1660), a versatile painter of portraits and genre scenes, who excelled in representing the materials and textures of the solid Dutch world around her. She also showed a striking originality of treatment, as in her woman's–eye view of *The Proposition,* an atypical picture showing, not a cheerful prostitute accepting her money, but a woman bent over her needlework, studiously ignoring the lascivious proposals of the man who bends over her. The calm, carefully finished canvases of Jan Vermeer (1632–1675) imparted an almost classical dignity to the lives of the urban patriciate, depicted at such everyday tasks and pastimes as reading a book or writing a letter, playing a meticulously rendered musical instrument or just pouring milk.

But the Dutch golden age left its most moving legacy to future generations in the art of Rembrandt van Rijn (1606–1669). The whole of Rembrandt's seventeenth–century world comes vividly to life in the paintings, prints, and drawings of this, perhaps the most beloved of all the "old masters." There are *Beggars Receiving Alms* at someone's front door and *The Board of the Clothmaker's Guild* meeting around a red–plush covered table, complacent in their suits of sober black. Rembrandt's golden light gleams on the intense faces of the physicians pressing around the pale corpse of *The Anatomy Lesson of Dr. Tulp* and radiates from the quiet face of Christ in *Supper at Emmaus.* Without using pigment at all, Rembrandt could capture in drawings or etchings the colorful streets and synagogues of Amsterdam's Jewish community or freeze forever a simple field of tufted grass or three trees against a flood of light just bursting through the clouds.

The arts of this period drew upon the past to cater to the tastes of the seventeenth–century present. Early modern science, to which we now turn, pointed above all at the future, reshaping Western views of the world we live in from that time to the present.

◆ The Scientific Revolution ◆

What is sometimes called the first *scientific revolution*—our own century has seen the second—was a collection of new scientific attitudes toward truth, new research methods, and new conclusions about the natural world. Its sources, as we shall see in the section below, lay in the felt need for a new worldview around 1500. It began with the astronomer Copernicus's theory of the sun–centered universe in the first half of the sixteenth century and climaxed with Isaac Newton's formulation of the law of gravity in the second half of the seventeenth. The revolution spread to other branches of science also, laying the foundations for more knowledge of the world around us than human beings have ever had before.

The Need for a New Paradigm

The way from the older science to the new, from Aristotle and Ptolemy to Nicolaus Copernicus and Isaac Newton, was paved by a number of continuing trends and significant new developments in Western thought. Both older approaches and new attitudes toward learning helped to bring about the scientific revolution of the sixteenth and seventeenth centuries.

Some of the roots of modern science may be traced back to the superstitions and pseudo-sciences of earlier times, approaches that mingled mysticism with experiment and empirical observation. Some astrologers did observe the heavens closely and plotted the paths of the planets among the constellations in the effort to calculate their influences on human life. Alchemists undertook long and painstaking experiments in their laboratories, becoming experienced with simple apparatus and knowledgeable of the properties of metals and chemicals.

Another source of the new science lay in changing modern attitudes toward the inherited body of ancient science. Humanist editions of Aristotle's scientific writings, for instance, sometimes dared to update the master by introducing plants or animals the Greek thinker had never seen, or even by hesitantly pointing out errors that had crept into his work. Some thinkers of the late sixteenth and the seventeenth centuries were willing to challenge and even attempt to go beyond the Greeks and the Romans. Aristotle was openly rejected by the scientist Galileo, the philosopher Francis Bacon, and others. The broad seventeenth–century dispute over the relative merits of "ancients and moderns" did not demolish the former, as the popularity of classicism in the arts made clear. But the dispute itself indicated a growing confidence that mere modern minds could hope to compete successfully with the giants of antiquity.

Among the earliest believers in the possibility of improving on the ancient knowledge of the material world were technical workers of various sorts. Lacking classical educations these surgeons, ballistics experts, engineers, and others were not overwhelmed by the achievements of the ancients. Impressed by progress in their own trades, such practical men as the surgeon Ambroise Paré saw the possibility of further improvement in the future. From the modest books they produced, the influential philosopher Francis Bacon (discussed later) drew some of his faith in scientific progress. From such views also grew the confidence that modern science could drastically improve our understanding of the world we live in.

Central to the emergence of the new science, finally, was what the philosophical historian of science Thomas Kuhn calls a new scientific *paradigm*. Kuhn borrows the term and the basic concept from the grammatical paradigm, the model conjugation or declension that illustrates the patterns followed by a whole class of verbs or nouns. In the same way, "recognized scientific achievements . . . for a time provide model problems and solutions to a community of scientific practitioners."[6] Breakthrough theories, experiments, or demonstrations capable of serving as new paradigms, many students of the subject feel, are necessary to any significant advance in the sciences.

Such revolutionary shifts in goals and methods are only likely when so many anomalies—failures of accepted theory to explain the observed workings of nature—have piled up that a radical break with past science seems necessary. In Copernicus's day, just such anomalies had accumulated as astronomers tried to use the elaborate Ptolemaic system to explain planetary locations, the sequence of the equinoxes, and other problems. As a colleague of Copernicus's declared, "No system so cumbersome and inaccurate" as the Ptolemaic view, particularly after centuries of revisions and additions, "could possibly be true of nature."[7]

It was time for a radical break with the science of the ancients, for daring assumptions and new methods. From the work of Copernicus and his followers sprang a new scientific paradigm and with it the scientific revolution that is central to the modern mind.

The Copernican Breakthrough

A Pole, a German, and an Italian were the chief contributors to the first century of this explosion of new knowledge. Copernicus inaugurated the great transformation; Kepler methodically elaborated it; and Galileo's combative genius and determination to see with his own eyes advanced the new science in several directions at once.

Nicolaus Copernicus (1473–1543) was the Columbus of the scientific revolution. A Polish clergyman who had studied for a decade in Italy, best known in his own lifetime as a physician, and well versed in law, mathematics, and even economics, Copernicus was a multi-faceted intellect of the sort the Renaissance admired. His book *On the Revolutions of the Heavenly Bodies,* on which he labored intermittently for thirty years, was published in 1543, the last year of his life. It is as important a date in the history of modern science as 1492 is in the history of Western global expansion. It was the beginning.

The revolutionary assertion of the book was, quite simply, that the sun, not the earth, is the center of the universe. Earth, Copernicus suggested, is merely one of the planets, revolving around the sun once a year. It is because our planet rotates on its axis once in every twenty–four hours that the universe as a whole seems to revolve around us. For the better part of two thousand years, the *geocentric* view of earth's central place in the universe had held the field. Now for the first time it was challenged by Copernicus's *heliocentric,* or "sun–centered," interpretation.

In other ways, Copernicus's views were actually rather traditional. He retained such astronomical conventions as circular orbits and the sphere of the fixed stars at the outer edge of the universe. But the heliocentric theory was a red flag to the conservative scientific, philosophical, and religious establishment, and a rallying point for the scientific revolutionaries, for the rest of the century.

The German Johannes Kepler (1571–1630), the next in this succession of scientific geniuses, was a more single–mindedly professional man of science. His career carried him from a post as assistant to Tycho Brahe (1546–1601), the foremost astronomer of the day, to a position as court mathematician to the Holy Roman emperor. Kepler's contributions were based on long years of empirical observation and meticulous mathematical calculation—two keys to the success of the scientific revolution. Yet even in this solid, almost modern–sounding man of science, there was ample evidence of the influence of premodern views. He believed, for instance, in the "music of the spheres" produced by the harmonious movements of the heavenly bodies, and in the possibility that angels rode the planets in their orbits.

Kepler became the first well–known astronomer openly to support the Copernican heliocentric theory. Even more important, he added to it the three laws of planetary motion which, unlike much of Copernicus's theory, have survived intact to the present day. Working with Tycho in the best observatory in Europe, Kepler had collected detailed data on planetary motion for many years, giving him much better evidence to work with than his predecessors had. Like others in the latter part of the century, he was also more willing to break completely with ancient authority than anyone in Copernicus's generation had been. When the observed positions of the planet Mars simply could not be made to fit a circular orbit, as both Ptolemy and Copernicus insisted it must, Kepler took the eminently scientific step of trying another hypothesis. He theorized that the paths of the planets might be ellipses rather than circles. Orbits calculated on the basis of elliptical paths, with the sun at one of the foci of the ellipse, fit his observations. The first law of planetary motion thus entered the astronomy books with impeccable scientific credentials: it fit the facts, and the numbers checked. The other two laws, defining the varying velocity of planets in their orbits and the length of time it takes each planet to revolve around the sun, are even denser with detailed data, mathematical relationships, and scientific concepts as complex as the metaphysics of the ancients.

The Italian Galileo Galilei (1564–1642), the first telescope astronomer and a trailblazer in both physics and astronomy, gave the new movement a genuinely colorful personality. An even more wide–ranging Renaissance man than Copernicus, Galileo studied philosophy and medicine and was a skillful painter and musician. Like Kepler, however, he became a professional mathematician and a passionate advocate of the new science. A university professor in north Italian universities and a protégé of the Medici family of Florence, Galileo published frequently in Italian rather than scholarly Latin, making his treatises accessible to educated nonscientists. When the Inquisition finally reined him in at the end of his long life, the confrontation simply added to the legend of a man who had done more than anyone before him to make the scientific revolution part of the life of the Western mind.

Galileo's earliest formulations, in physics, included the law of the pendulum: he discovered that each swing, whether it covers a longer or a shorter arc of space, takes the same amount of time—the basic principle of the pendulum clock. He also worked out the first hydrostatic balance for establishing the density of an object by weighing it in water. Probably Galileo's most celebrated discovery in physics, however, was the law of falling bodies, which challenged Aristotle's view that heavier bodies fall faster, lighter ones more slowly. By rolling small metal balls down an inclined plane—a kind of controlled free fall—Galileo was able to measure distances covered and times elapsed when an object falls more precisely than anyone before him. He thus demonstrated that all falling bodies, heavy or light, fall at a velocity that accelerates at a rate of 32 feet per second every second. Expressed in the mathematical formula $V=32n$ (n being the number of seconds the object falls), this principle, like Kepler's laws of planetary motion, had the quantitative precision of modern hard science.

As an astronomer, Galileo's great contribution was less mathematical than empirical. Learning of the experiments of a Dutch optician in combining lenses in a tube in order to magnify distant objects, Galileo applied the principle to celestial observation and produced the world's first astronomical telescope. His were thus the first human eyes to see the mountains on the moon, sunspots on the sun, the larger satellites of Jupiter, the rings of Saturn, and the multitudes of stars that make up the hazy path of light across the night sky we call the Milky Way.

His announcements of these discoveries, combined with his vigorous defense of the heliocentric theory, brought Galileo into conflict with the scientific establishment and finally to the attention of the Holy Inquisition. Church tradition and even the language of Scripture seemed committed to the view that the earth stood at the center of things while the sun moved through the sky around it. Compelled to recant his heretical views in his last years, Galileo before the Inquisition became a symbol of the modern struggle between free thought and "thought police," of whatever faith or ideology.

Newton and the Law of Gravity

Sir Isaac Newton (1642–1727) became for many the master intellect who finally put it all together, explaining the way the universe worked in scientific terms as convincing and coherent as medieval theology and ancient philosophy had been in their day. Science grew and changed drastically over the centuries that followed, and even Newton's master concept, the law of universal gravitation, was restructured by Albert Einstein in our own century. Yet as a major contributor and as the widely admired embodiment of the scientific spirit, the English scientist deserves his preeminent position in the history of the scientific revolution.

Newton was not particularly good in school, nor was he distinguished as a Cambridge university student in the 1660s. The celebrated episode of the falling apple occurred, if at all, while he was taking tea in a Cambridge garden. But he filed away his unorthodox conclusion—that the force that pulled the apple to the ground might also be the force that bound the planets—for twenty years. Only in 1687, when he was prevailed on by a scientist friend to publish his *Mathematical Principles of Natural Philosophy,* did Newton's name become synonymous with the scientific revolution. As professor of mathematics at Cambridge and virtually lifetime president of the British Royal Society, Newton seemed the incarnation of the scientific spirit. And yet, he remained a man of his age: he never lost his enthusiasm for theology, biblical chronology, and alchemy. Personally an ambitious, arrogant, and contentious man, avid for the fame his discoveries brought him, Newton nevertheless described all his investigations as mere child's play beside "the great ocean of truth" that was yet to be explored.

From a scientific viewpoint, Newton had the two essentials: "a grasp of mathematics" and an understanding of "experiment as a systematic procedure."[8] Among his major achievements are usually listed his development of calculus and his invention of the reflecting telescope, which uses a mirror as well as lenses, as all large modern telescopes do. The first accomplishment was a mathematical breakthrough, the other a great leap forward in empirical observation.

Newton's work in optics is often ranked second only to his insights on gravity. By breaking up light through a glass prism into its component chromatic spectrum, he revealed that ordinary white light is in fact composed of all the colors of the rainbow. He also became the father of modern spectroscopic analysis of everything from chemicals on earth to the composition of the most distant stars.

But it was Newton's law of universal gravitation that became the linchpin of early modern science. Every object in the universe, he suggested, exerts an invisible attraction on every other chunk of matter. The force of attraction between any two bodies varies directly with the masses of the two bodies: the greater the masses, the more powerful the gravitational pull between them. The force also varies inversely, he added with the mathematical precision essential to the new approach, with the square of the distance between the two bodies. Because his formulation could be applied equally to apples and planets, it served as a unifying principle, tying the new physics to the new astronomy. Seen as the binding force that held the universe together, the *law of gravity* seemed to many to make sense out of the world once more.

Progress in Other Sciences

The major achievements of the scientific revolution came in astronomy and physics, from Copernicus through Kepler and Galileo to Newton. Yet there were advances by other important scientists and in other sciences as well. In this other work too, we have a mix of some very unscientific early modern ideas with some truly remarkable scientific contributions.

Among astronomers and physicists, the Italian Giordano Bruno (1548–1600) and the English scientist William Gilbert (1544–1603) both added significantly to our understanding of the material world while working to varying degrees within the mystical tradition of the sixteenth century. Gilbert's classic study of the compass pioneered in the study of magnetism; yet he also believed in a "world soul" at the heart of the cosmos. Bruno rejected Aristotle, supported Copernicus, and was an early proponent of the view that the traditional sphere of the fixed stars was actually a vast expanse of star–spangled space, that there might in fact be an "infinity of worlds" like our own. But Bruno was also a believer in mathematical magic and in humanity as a microcosm of the universe—a philosopher so un-orthodox that he was rejected by the Calvinists, excommunicated by the Lutherans, and finally burned at the stake by the Catholic Inquisition.

In other sciences, the celebrated Swiss physician Paracelsus (Theophrastus von Hohen-heim, c. 1493–1541), who had a reputation for well–nigh miraculous curative powers, be-came a pioneer of modern chemotherapy in his advocacy of the use of mercury for the treatment of one of the scourges of the century, syphilis. Even more important additions to Western scientific knowledge, however, came from the Flemish anatomist Andreas Vesalius (1514–1564) and the English doctor William Harvey (1578–1657). Vesalius's book *On the Structure of the Human Body* (1543) provided the first detailed, empirically accurate study of human anatomy; it was as revolutionary for biology as Copernicus's book of the same year was for astronomy. Harvey, a physician to King James I of England, was the first to offer an accurate description of the functioning of the heart and the circulatory system as a pump and a conduit for the flow of blood through the human body, another major ad-vance.

Abstract mathematics also made striking progress in the sixteenth and seventeenth centuries. Mathematical insights from ancient Greece and medieval Islam and from India by way of the Muslim world had reached Western scholars in the Middle Ages. In the early modern period, however, European thinkers made breakthroughs that form the founda-tion of mathematics today.

In the sixteenth century, for example, a group of Italian thinkers made major advances in the study of algebra. A single book by Gerolamo Cardano (1501–1576), *The Great Art, or the Rules of Algebra* (1543), summed up the achievements of two generations of Italian mathematicians, stirring widespread interest in the mysteries of algebraic equations. Later in the century, others further developed the ability to manipulate algebraic variables and symbols and increased Western understanding of decimal fractions.

In the seventeenth century, modern geometry at last moved well beyond Euclid in the work of Newton and the philosophers René Descartes and G. W. Leibniz, both discussed below. Descartes made his greatest scientific contributions in the early development of ana-lytic geometry. Newton and Leibniz were early explorers of the intricacies of calculus. By the end of the century, mathematics had thus far surpassed the work of earlier periods and stood ready to serve the other sciences in centuries to come.

✦Impact of the New Science✦

The impact of the new scientific discoveries would be far greater than the scientists them-selves could have imagined. The new attitudes engendered by the scientific revolution, as we will see in this final section, spread to philosophers and to growing numbers of educated laypeople. As philosophers explained the larger relevance of the new scientific ideas, ordi-nary citizens developed an unprecedented enthusiasm for the new view of the material world. We will deal here with only the beginnings of the influence of scientific ideas on the thought and life of the Western world. For science is still shaking the fabric of Western ideas and Western society today.

The Philosophers of the Scientific Revolution

Drawing larger meanings from the new science was primarily the work, not of the new scientists themselves, but of the philosophers of the seventeenth century. We have already seen the impact of scientific attitudes on political thought in the ideas of Hobbes and Locke. Other leading thinkers of the period developed even broader views of the world under the influence of the new "natural philosophy," as science was often called. Indeed, the origins of modern philosophy are usually seen in the problems explored and the startling solutions propounded by such thinkers as Descartes, Spinoza, Leibniz, and Francis Bacon.

René Descartes (1596–1650), a Frenchman of independent means who lived most of his productive life in the freer intellectual atmosphere of the Netherlands, is often hailed as the founder of both modern philosophy and the stream of philosophic thought called *rationalism*. As a rationalist, Descartes exhibited an immense faith in human reason—in the validity of ideas clearly and distinctly held and logically developed. He also revealed a radical willingness to start over from scratch in the human effort to understand ourselves and our world. His famous maxim, *Cogito, ergo sum,* "I think, therefore I am," summed up the single certainty with which he began his sweeping investigation of the nature of things. All traditional authorities, he declared, even the testimony of our senses *might* be wrong; but the very fact that he could *think* this proved that he, as a thinking center of consciousness, did exist. It was the kind of daring new start that the scientific revolution was making, and it earned his *Discourse on Method . . . Seeking Truth in the Sciences* (1637) an enthusiastic reception from many thoughtful people.

From this single certainty, the existence of the thinking mind, Descartes proceeded to demonstrate the existence of both a highly rational God and of a radically divided world.

As a philosopher of science and the founder of European rationalism, René Descartes, portrayed here by Frans Hals, was one of the giants of modern philosophy. (New York Public Library Picture Collection.)

The universe, he asserted, was composed of two basic substances: mind (immaterial, "thinking substance") and matter ("extended substance," which occupies space). These two realms of being were so different that it was difficult to see how they could interact at all, as they must in human beings, composed of both mind and matter. But Descartes found a point of interaction for them in the hitherto apparently functionless pineal gland of the human brain. Times had indeed changed: it is difficult to imagine Plato or Thomas Aquinas concerned about the precise part of the human body in which ideas and particulars, soul and body interact; but for the founder of modern philosophy, such a question was only natural.

If Descartes was arguably the most admired philosopher of the age, Baruch Spinoza (1632–1677) was probably the most controversial. A Jewish lens grinder of Amsterdam, the independent–minded Spinoza, like Descartes, benefited from the intellectual toleration of the Netherlands. Deeply impressed by the logical coherence of mathematics, he constructed a system of ethics that sought to be as rigidly logical as Euclid's geometry. Disturbed by the Cartesian problem of interaction between the mental or spiritual world and the world of matter, Spinoza evolved a philosophy resembling pantheism in which both mind and matter were seen as "attributes" of God. Pantheism, heretical in both Judaism and Christianity, seemed one way at least to restore unity to a Cartesian world in which matter, the realm of the sciences, had achieved virtual parity with mind in the Western worldview.

Another radical philosophy seeking to solve the problem of interaction in a metaphysically divided world was that of the great German philosopher Gottfried Wilhelm Leibniz (1646–1716). An intellectual prodigy in his youth, Leibniz became a leading logician and mathematician, the inventor of an early calculating machine, and an organizer of both the Prussian and Russian academies of science. His unique vision posited a universe of *monads*, totally independent centers of consciousness, each a microcosm of the world as a whole, none having any causal contact with the others at all. The appearance of causal interaction, Leibniz declared, was the result of a "preestablished harmony" between their actions that was decreed by God. It was an extreme solution, and with its corollary that the universe God had made must be "the best of all possible worlds," was savagely satirized by Voltaire in the following century.

Philosophers thus sometimes followed the implications of the scientific revolution far from the concrete world of scientific experiment and observation. The leading English thinker of the early seventeenth century, however, made his highly influential contribution precisely by honoring empiricism and glorifying scientific achievement. This was Francis Bacon (1561–1626), essayist, lord chancellor of England, and prophet of a "Great Renewal" in human understanding and control of the world we live in.

A bitter opponent of the logic–chopping authoritarianism of the medieval Scholastics, Bacon spoke for the new thinkers of this pivotal age when he urged the intellectual community "to try the whole thing anew upon a better plan; . . . to commence a total reconstruction of sciences, arts, and all human knowledge."[9] In this call for a new beginning, Bacon was a precursor of Descartes. By contrast with the Cartesian continental emphasis on mathematics and rational clarity, however, Bacon stressed empirical observation and experiment as the road to new truth. He proposed the collection and sifting of evidence, the formation of possible explanations, and the testing of these hypotheses by more empirical evidence before a general theory could be deemed proven. This *inductive* emphasis, building large truths on a foundation of accumulated data, contrasted with the *deductive* method of inferring lesser truths from some larger authoritative proposition. In his fictional account of the utopia he called *The New Atlantis* (1627), the English philosopher stressed the value to society of large–scale state–supported research institutions and insisted that scientists and inventors, not kings and generals, should be recognized as the heroes of the human race.

Above all, Bacon saw the immense power over the world that scientific knowledge could give to humanity. Through science, he said, we may acquire an unprecedented "dominion over natural things" and "extend more widely the limits of the power . . . of man."[10] Francis Bacon thus became the first prophet of human and scientific progress, envisioning a brave new world of social improvement through research and development. Like a conquistador of the mind, he set a new goal for the Western world: the conquest of nature through science and "the enlargement of the bounds of human empire [control], to the effecting of all things possible."[11]

The Rage for Science

As the seventeenth century advanced, the new science found a growing audience, at least among an educated elite. What classical studies had been to the Renaissance and religion to the Reformation, a passion for the natural sciences was for the later seventeenth and the eighteenth centuries.

In the 1600s, some educational institutions began to teach modern mathematics and science. Descartes acquired some of the latest mathematical theories at the Jesuit school he attended. Individual scholars at Gresham's College in London gathered privately to discuss "natural philosophy" in the 1640s. Such leading men of science as Galileo lectured on these subjects at universities. Educational emphasis still fell heavily on Christian teaching and ancient languages, but it was at least possible in seventeenth–century educational institutions to learn something of the scientific breakthroughs that had begun a hundred years before.

Another important source of scientific knowledge was the printed book. As print technology had spread the new learning of the humanists and the religious views of the reformers, so books now played a large part in the success of the scientific revolution. Most important, printing assured the accumulation of the new knowledge: discoveries were not lost, and knowledge of them reached scientists in other parts of Europe through books like those of Copernicus, Galileo, and Newton. In addition, laypeople could get some idea of the new scientific theories, particularly from the works of scientists and philosophers like Galileo, Descartes, or Bacon, who were willing to publish in Italian, French, or English rather than in the scholarly Latin used by Copernicus and Newton.

Scientific societies, finally, came into being in the seventeenth century for the specific purpose of disseminating knowledge to an educated public. The earliest of these organizations were private gatherings, like the Accademia dei Lincei in Rome, founded in 1603, or the meetings at Gresham's College. And in the latter part of the century, rulers like Charles II in England and Louis XIV in France added science to the arts and literature as worthy subjects of royal patronage. The Royal Society of London for Improving of Natural Knowledge was thus officially founded in 1660, the Academy of the Sciences in Paris in 1666. These organizations brought interested people together at regular meetings to hear and discuss scientific papers or to watch scientific demonstrations. The leading scientists also became fellows of the academies, and their work was often published in the scientific journals the societies sponsored.

In this increasingly hospitable atmosphere, scientific knowledge accumulated rapidly and spread to a small but supportive public. In the next century, we will see, these circles of scientifically informed laypeople grew to include practically minded businesspeople and technicians, with the result that science, technology, and production came together in another great breakthrough–the Industrial Revolution.

The New Worldview

By 1700, then, scientists and philosophers had given the Western world a new vision of the world we live in. The new methods they employed, the conclusions they drew, and the glimpses they had of a universe without limits were key elements in the new scientific paradigm that resulted from the Copernican revolution.

The methodological innovations of the scientific revolution have already been noted. Instead of turning to ancient authority as the inevitable source of truth, the scientific revolutionaries looked at the facts of the physical world around them. Experiment in physics and close observation in astronomy provided an empirical foundation for knowledge that neither ancient philosophy nor medieval theology had possessed. Equally important, the new breed of scientists abandoned the Aristotelian logic practiced by the medieval Scholastics in favor of the quantitative logic of mathematics. By recording their results in quantitative terms, rather than in terms of vaguely defined "qualities," they gave science a greater degree of precision. And in fact the defining features of modern science became the empirical and quantitative dimensions that distinguished the modern search for truth from that of any other period.

Not surprisingly, from these early probes emerged a very quantitative and essentially material vision of the nature of things. Observed in numerical terms, the world came to be seen primarily in dimensions of space and time, its most readily measurable characteristics. Time and space were thus accepted by the modern West as *the* basic dimensions of the physical universe.

The seventeenth century also revived the metaphysical *atomism* of the Greek Epicureans, especially as presented by the Roman poet Lucretius in *On the Nature of Things.* In this interpretation, the material world was believed to be made of "atoms and the void," minute bits of matter drifting through empty space, bumping and clustering into the larger chunks that compose the physical world as we know it. The real, or "primary," qualities of matter were those of the atoms and their configurations: size, shape, mass, motion, and number (quantifiability). All other apparent qualities—colors, sounds, smells, and other characteristics absorbed by the senses—were dismissed as "secondary," existing only in the mind of the observer, not in the real or objective world at all.

At the level of the infinitely large as well as at the atomic level, the scientific revolution developed a new view of the world. As we have seen, the only real martyr to the scientific faith, Giordano Bruno, was burned for his conviction that there are an infinite number of planets like our own in the cosmos. Without going so far, seventeenth–century astronomers went further than Copernicus had: they rejected the sphere of the fixed stars and projected a much larger size for the universe. Not only the earth, but the solar system itself was looking less and less like the center of God's world, and the stars seemed to stretch on forever, without pattern or obvious meaning.

To some, it was a chilling vision. The French mathematician and religious thinker Blaise Pascal (1623–1662) was deeply disturbed: "The eternal silence of these infinite spaces," he said, "terrifies me." Others saw in Newtonism the basis for a mechanical model of the cosmos, an orderly if rather inhuman universe presided over by a distant, aloof divinity—God the great geometrician who had designed it all. However they responded, theirs was a new and astonishing view of the world we live in. It was to be a crucial Western contribution to the life of the human mind as whole.

Summary

In the intellectual history of the West, the seventeenth century saw important advances in political thought and produced new styles in the arts. Perhaps most important, however, this period saw the climax of the first scientific revolution and the birth of the modern scientific worldview.

The beginnings of modern political thought were stimulated by the political turmoil of the sixteenth and seventeenth centuries. Most serious seventeenth–century political theory, including Hobbes's argument in his *Leviathan,* focused on the concept of sovereignty in an effort to justify strong monarchical government. Locke's *Two Treatises* on government, by contrast, sought to justify the constitutional monarchy just emerging in England, defending limited government and the rights of the governed.

Both dynamic, emotionally compelling baroque art and classicism rooted in tradition responded to the tastes and propaganda needs of the revived Catholic church, the aristocracy, and the new absolute monarchies. By contrast, Rembrandt and the Dutch realists produced art that suited middle–class taste in its convincing representations of their everyday world.

The scientific revolution of the sixteenth and seventeenth centuries began with the Copernican revolution in astronomy, grew with the work of Kepler and Galileo, and climaxed with Newton's law of gravity. It transformed the Western worldview, replacing a tidy earth–centered universe with a sun–centered planetary system set in an endless universe of stars. With additional contributions in physics, some basic biology, and other advances, science began to replace art and religion as a focus for philosophical speculation and educated concern.

Some Key Terms

aria 329
atomism 341
baroque style 327
classicism 329
cogito, ergo sum 338
deduction 339
Dutch realists 331
geocentric theory 334
heliocentric theory 334

induction 339
law of gravity 336
Levellers 325
Leviathan state 325
maiestas 323
monad 339
natural rights 326
paradigm 333
rationalism 338

scientific revolution 332
social contract 324
sovereignty 323
stake in society 326
state of nature 324
tabula rasa 325

Notes

1. *An Anatomie of the World: First Anniversary,* line 213.
2. Herbert H. Rowen, ed., *From Absolutism to* *Revolution, 1648–1848* (New York: Macmillan, 1963), 30.
3. Ibid., 33.

4. John Bowle, *Western Political Thought: An Historical Introduction from the Origins to Rousseau* (London and New York: Methuen and Barnes and Noble, 1961), 345. The "poorest she" is not yet mentioned, and women's political rights were not discussed until the time of the French revolution a century and a half later.

5. In *Locke on Politics, Religion, and Education,* ed. Maurice Cranston (New York: Collier, 1965), 10.

6. Thomas S. Kuhn, *The Structure of Scientific Revolutions* (Chicago: University of Chicago Press, 1962), x.

7. Ibid., 69.

8. Jacob Bronowski and Bruce Mazlish, *From Leonardo to Hegel* (New York: Harper & Brothers, 1960), 189.

9. "Proemium" to *Instauratio Magna,* in *The Works of Francis Bacon,* vol. 8, ed. James Spedding (London: Longman, 1857–1874), 18.

10. *New Atlantis,* in *Works,* vol. 8, 260; *Novum Organum,* ibid., vol. 8, 147.

11. *New Atlantis,* in *Works,* vol. 8, 297.

Reading List

Armitage, A. *Copernicus: The Founder of Modern Astronomy.* London: Allen and Unwin, 1933. Still useful older biography.

Bazin, G. *The Baroque.* New York: Norton, 1978. Stimulating analysis of this complex and controversial phase of Western history.

Burtt, E. A. *The Metaphysical Foundations of Modern Physical Science.* Rev. ed. Garden City, N.Y.: Doubleday, 1931. The philosophical underpinnings of the scientific revolution.

Dreyer, J. L. E. *A History of Astronomy from Thales to Kepler.* 2d ed. New York: Dover, 1953. Locates the Copernican revolution in the context of ancient and medieval astronomical and cosmological thought.

Friedrick, C. J. *The Age of the Baroque, 1610–1660.* New York: Harper & Row, 1952. Broadens the scope of the baroque to encompass the tone of society and politics.

Galilei, G. *Discoveries and Opinions of Galileo.* Edited and translated by S. Drake. New York: Doubleday, 1957. Galileo's vigorous presentation of his controversial views. On the continuing controversies over his ideas, see C. L. Golino, ed., *Galileo Reappraised* (Berkeley: University of California Press, 1966).

Guerard, A. *France in the Classical Age: The Life and Death of an Ideal.* Rev. ed. New York: Brazillier, 1956. Subtle analysis of the classical spirit in life and art.

Hall, A. R. *The Scientific Revolution, 1500–1800.* Rev. ed. New York: Beacon Press, 1960. Older but still valuable survey, stressing the emergence of the scientific way of seeing the world. H. Butterfield, *The Origins of Modern Science, 1300–1800,* rev. ed. (New York: Free Press, 1965), puts the discoveries of the sixteenth and seventeenth centuries in a larger framework of thought about nature, from Scholasticism to the Enlightenment.

Hobbes, T. *Leviathan.* Edited by C. B. Macpherson. Harmondsworth, England: Penguin, 1981. Handy edition of the monumental, still surprisingly relevant work.

Hunter, M. *Science and Society in Restoration England.* New York: Cambridge University Press, 1981. Widely praised account of the absorption of the scientific revolution in later seventeenth–century England.

Kearney, H. F. *Science and Change, 1500–1700.* New York: McGraw–Hill, 1971. Good survey of the scientific revolution.

Kuhn, T. S. *The Copernican Revolution: Planetary Astronomy in the Development of Western Thought.* Cambridge, Mass.: Harvard University Press, 1957. Thoughtful analysis of the long–range implications of the new scientific paradigm.

Locke, J. *Two Treatises of Government.* Edited by P. Laslett. New York: New American Library, 1966. Seminal essays for the emergence of a more liberal order.

Milton, J. *The Portable Milton.* Edited by D. Bush. Harmondsworth, England: Penguin, 1976. Reveals the range of thought of the poet of Puritan England.

Molière, J. B. de. *The Misanthrope and Other Plays.* Translated by J. Wood. Harmondsworth, England: Penguin, 1959. Accessible English version of Molière's comedies.

Sarton, G. *Six Wings: Men of Science in the Renaissance.* Bloomington: University of Indiana Press, 1957. Probes by an eminent historian of science.

Vickers, B., ed. *Occult and Scientific Mentalities in the Renaissance*. New York: Cambridge University Press, 1984. Essays drawing a generally sharper distinction between occult studies and early science than do some other scholars.

Webster, C. *From Paracelsus to Newton: Magic and the Making of Modern Science*. New York: Cambridge University Press, 1982. Brief exposition of the close ties many see between magical thinking and the birth of modern science.

Westfall, R. S. *Never at Rest: A Biography of Isaac Newton*. New York: Cambridge University Press, 1980. Scholarly life by a leading expert, interweaving scientific, religious, and other strands of his evolving ideas.

White, C. *Rembrandt*. London: Thames and Hudson, 1984. One of many introductions to the life and work, with good reproductions of paintings, prints, and drawings.

14

Empires Beyond the Seas
The Rise of Western Imperialism

◆The Beginnings of Western Imperialism
◆Sixteenth–Century Empires: The Iberian Powers
◆Seventeenth–Century Empires: The North Atlantic Powers
◆Global Impact of Western Expansion

We come now to the story of how, during the two centuries after 1492, the Western world first moved out on a massive scale to confront the rest of the world. For us, for whom the rest of the globe is no further away than the nearest television screen, this early modern time seems very remote indeed. It is difficult to imagine a world in which only a tiny handful of Western voyagers had ever ventured westward from Europe across the Atlantic or traveled from Europe to Asia. Yet that time was only a score of generations ago. It is only a tick of history's clock back to those days of wooden caravels wallowing in heavy seas and camel caravans plodding along the old Silk Road to China.

During the 1500s and 1600s, then, while Western peoples struggled with tradition and change through the Renaissance, the Reformation, and the crisis–torn seventeenth century, they were also beginning an unprecedented campaign of global conquest. This great wave of Western imperialism would carry Europeans in large numbers to the Americas and to smaller trading posts in Africa and Asia.

The first part of this chapter will be concerned with the new technologies, the powerful motives, and the forms of Western colonialism that made this unprecedented imperial outreach possible. The next two sections will chronicle the conquests of the Iberian powers, Spain and Portugal, and the later expansion of three North Atlantic nations, England, France, and the Netherlands. The final part of the chapter will analyze Western gains and look at the changes to the world wrought by this first surge of Western imperialism.

◆The Beginnings of Western Imperialism◆

The Western Age of Discovery, as it is often called, is actually something of a misnomer: the more recent term *Age of Encounter* comes closer. During the two centuries between Columbus's first voyage of 1492 and the death of Louis XIV in 1715, Europeans did encounter lands they had never seen before. But they were "discovering" territories quite familiar to the native inhabitants of these lands. Great civilizations like those of India and

China, as well as many flourishing village societies, had existed around the world long before Westerners began to intrude on their lives.

This first section of the chapter begins with a brief survey of that larger world as it was and as it looked to Europeans around 1500. It then outlines the motives that impelled Western people to set out in search of lands beyond the seas, as well as the technology and social organization that made these ventures possible. Finally, we will discuss the phases and forms of Western overseas expansion during the first two centuries of Western imperialism.

The World Beyond the West

In Western civilization textbooks, the West often looks like the center of the world. Understandably, a history of Western peoples must focus on its subject, necessarily reducing the rest of the world to a peripheral role in the story. Unfortunately, this approach sometimes leaves the impression that nothing of importance was happening outside the chosen subject area. And that was certainly far from true in 1492.

Even a very rapid survey of the non–Western world on the eve of the Western intrusion should make this clear. When Columbus set sail from Spain, major centers of civilization around the globe included the sprawling Islamic zone, Hindu India and Southeast Asia, China and its sphere of influence in East Asia, and a number of kingdoms and empires in northern Africa, Mexico, and Peru. Nor was Christian Europe obviously the most impressive of the developed civilizations in 1492. The Muslim zone was then considerably larger than the Christian one, extending from North Africa to Southeast Asia. For many centuries Hindu India had been developing a great civilization of its own, teeming with prosperous trading cities and the cultured courts of cultivated rajahs. Still further east, China under the Ming dynasty was a Europe–sized empire powerful enough to send fleets of Chinese junks westward across the Indian Ocean half a century before Vasco da Gama crossed it the other way in 1497. The trading cities of East Africa and the empires of the West African grasslands were flourishing, while across the Atlantic, the Aztec military machine had unified most of Mesoamerica before 1500, and the Inca emperors ruled the Andes from their capital in Peru.

In the year Columbus sailed, however, almost all of this larger world was essentially *terra incognita,* or unknown land, to Western peoples. Europeans had traded with, and learned from, Near Eastern and North African peoples, including ancient Egyptians and Persians and medieval Arabs. The West had also traded with East Asia since Roman times, and Western merchants like Marco Polo had reached China directly in the Middle Ages. Nevertheless, the sun–blasted Sahara and the stormy Atlantic had cut Europeans off from most of Africa and the Americas, and the very density of Asian civilization had limited European penetration there. Few Westerners ever left their end of Eurasia at all, and only the most dubious information was available about the world outside.

Motives for Imperial Expansion

Then, shortly before 1500, this isolation ended. First Portuguese and Spaniards, then Dutch, French, and English—all the major powers of Europe's Atlantic seaboard—dispatched armed flotillas and commercial fleets, first to the Indies and Cathay, then to the newly discovered Americas. The result was an unprecedented five centuries of Western

Chronology 14: Rise of Western Imperialism

1400s	*Europeans develop maneuverable, heavily–armed ships with improved navigational aids*
1419	*Henry the Navigator sets up Sagres research and development center for overseas exploration*
1492	*Columbus reaches the Americas, claims region for Spain*
1593	*Treaty of Tordesillas divides non–Western world up between Spain and Portugal*
1492–1600	*Spain and Portugal dominate overseas imperialism*
1498	*Da Gama reaches India, establishes Portuguese trade*
1510	*Albuquerque organizes Portuguese commercial empire around Indian Ocean*
1519–1522	*Magellan's expedition circumnavigates the world*
1520s, 1530s,	*Cortez conquers Aztec Empire of Mexico for Spain, Pizzaro conquers Inca Empire of Peru for Spain*
1600–1715	*Dutch, French, and English build overseas empires*
1602	*Dutch East India Company organized for trade with Asia— headquarters established at Batavia in Java*
1607, 1620	*English establish first colonies at Jamestown and Plymouth*
1608	*French establish first colony at Quebec*
later 1600s	*French and English establish bases on coasts of India*

◆—◆

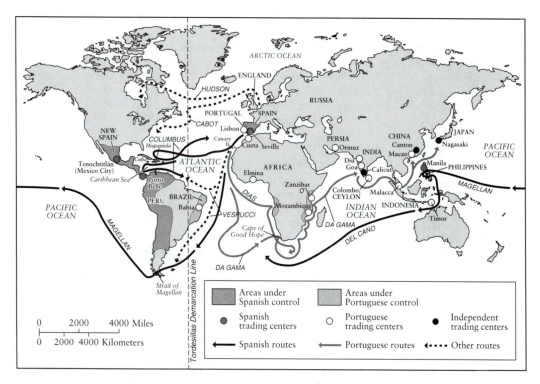

Europe Encounters the World: Voyages from 1487 to 1610

global imperialism which would shape both Western and world history in the modern period.

Most of the hard–bitten men who carried the banners of the West beyond the seas were impelled by some combination of three motives. These were desire for material gain, the missionary impulse, or a thirst for fame and reputation—gold, God, and glory.

Golden idols in heathen temples, gold and silver mines, the pearls and precious stones that were rumored to litter the beaches and line the rivers of the New World drew Europeans like a magnet. The most vivid myth of the Spanish conquistadors was the dream of El Dorado, the legendary "Golden Man" and his fabulously wealthy city somewhere in South America. The Portuguese and Dutch merchants who pioneered the sea trade with India and Southeast Asia were drawn by the immense profits to be made from silks and cottons and spices.

The religious motive inspired the Spanish and Portuguese friars who founded missions in the jungles of South America or the deserts of the southwestern United States, the French Jesuits in Canada or China. These missionaries were spreading Western influence as they spread the Christian creed. But it was the apostolic faith itself that compelled them to undertake such perilous missions to the far places of the earth.

Glory, finally, was a powerful motive for these early empire builders. The leaders of these enterprises tended to be soldiers, avid for the combination of public honors and immortal fame they called *honor*. They longed to be welcomed home by cheering crowds and immortalized by poets and historians as founders of new empires. The same sort of lust for honor that led these cavaliers to seek their reputations in European wars inspired Cortés to conquer Mexico and Sir Walter Raleigh to found what became the Lost Colony in North Carolina.

Such motives were often mingled in a single individual. Christopher Columbus promised Ferdinand and Isabella the wealth of China, Japan, and the East Indies if they would finance his effort to reach the East by sailing west. But he also saw himself as carrying the true faith across the ocean and coveted such grand titles as "Admiral of the Ocean Sea." Cold–eyed calculators with an eye on the bottom line, saints and fanatics, brave and brutal soldiers, they were a driven lot of men.

The Technology of Empire Building

Their success was partly the result of some remarkable technological advantages in such matters as ships, maps, and guns. But there were other advantages rooted in the structure of western society itself as the modern age began.

Europe's sturdy little fifteenth–century *caravels,* combining medieval square sails with Arab triangular lateen ones proved remarkably maneuverable, capable of tacking across and even into the wind. The galleons of the sixteenth century and the lumbering seventeenth–century East Indiamen multiplied the carrying capacity of European ships. Such improvements in design gave the West superiority at sea over all other peoples.

European explorers, traders, and conquerors also developed a number of invaluable navigation aids. The compass was first employed in China, but Europeans perfected it for their own use at the end of the Middle Ages. By means of the *astrolabe,* an instrument for measuring the altitude of the sun above the horizon, Western mariners learned to determine latitude north or south of the equator. Using a knotted rope, a floating log, and an hourglass to estimate the speed with which the ship left the log behind, they were able to calculate how far they had progressed in a day and thus work out their longitude. Map–maker Gerardus Mercator (1519–1594) worked out the *Mercator projection,* which spread the curved surface of the earth onto a flat map, enabling navigators to plot their locations more accurately than ever before.

Another major technological advantage was the rapid improvement of *gunpowder weapons* in the war–torn West. The Chinese had used gunpowder for centuries, and the Ottoman Turks had leveled the largest siege guns in the world against Constantinople in 1453. From the sixteenth century on, however, European artillery rapidly outdistanced all rivals, and muskets and rifles gave Western infantry an increasingly devastating advantage. Though some Muslim peoples, the Japanese, and others adopted the new weapons, the West continued to set the global pace in the development of firepower.

But Western success was also rooted in the very structure of western society around 1500. European business organization had developed impressively from the commercial revolution of the High Middle Ages on. By pooling the investment capital of many merchants in large *joint–stock companies,* European traders accumulated sufficient capital to undertake the global ventures of the Renaissance and later centuries. Western governmental organization also improved greatly in early modern times. Europe's administratively complex, increasingly powerful political institutions could channel the energies of whole peoples into centuries–long efforts at empire building.

To the strengths derived from technological advances and organizational sophistication, we should perhaps add the traditional competitiveness of many Western peoples. The very fact that Europe was divided, not united as China was, bred an urge for that competitive edge in European traders, military captains, and kings. When the Chinese emperor decided to stop dispatching fleets of junks westward across the Indian Ocean, those great voyages ended. It is difficult to imagine any force capable of stopping the floods of European freebooters, merchants, missionaries, and competing mercantilist monarchs who exploded across the oceans of the world in the centuries after 1492.

Phases and Forms of Imperialism

Two major phases in the history of Western expansion have been distinguished: the old and the new imperialism. The so–called *old imperialism,* with which we are concerned here, stretched from the late fifteenth century to the late eighteenth, from Columbus's historic voyage of 1492 to the American Declaration of Independence from Britain in 1776. The *new imperialism,* which will be discussed in later chapters, filled the later nineteenth and the first half of the twentieth centuries, from the 1870s to the collapse of the major European overseas empires after the end of World War II in 1945.

The pioneers of the old imperialism were the Spanish and Portuguese who planted the first colonies and laid the foundations for Western control of world trade during the fifteenth and sixteenth centuries. After 1600, "interlopers," Dutch, French, and English, defied Iberian claims and soon established their own colonies and trading centers around the world. Throughout this period, finally, Russia was also expanding, though by land rather than by sea, in an eastward sweep across northern Eurasia that was as impressive in its way as the seaborne empires.

Historians have distinguished two major forms of Western expansion during the age of the old imperialism: settlement empires and trading empires. A *settlement empire* meant the establishment of colonies overseas, with European governors and garrisons, plantations, mines, fishing and trapping industries, and other profitable overseas ventures. Such colo-

The Taj Mahal in Agra, India, built in the early seventeenth century by the Mughal emperor Shah Jahan as a tomb for his beautiful wife, the Mumtaz Mahal. High civilizations existed in many parts of the world when the West began its long campaign of overseas empire building. (Air India.)

nial empires were most common in the New World. The Spanish and Portuguese settled much of South America, Middle America (Mexico plus Central America), and the Caribbean, as well as western North America. English, French, and Dutch settlers colonized eastern North America and some Caribbean islands.

Trading empires were more common in Asia and Africa. In Asia, large and well–established empires effectively discouraged large–scale Western settlement. In Africa, inhospitable geography and unfamiliar disease germs made conquest and Western settlement difficult. On these two continents, then, Europeans established trading posts, signed treaties with local rulers, and took home steady and growing profits from trade in Asian luxury goods and African slaves. The Portuguese established the first such trading empire in around 1500, followed by the Dutch, British, and French after 1600.

New forms of imperial control evolved further in later centuries. But the Western presence in much of the rest of the world was an accomplished fact throughout the early modern period.

♦ Sixteenth–Century Empires: The Iberian Powers ♦

The Spanish and the Portuguese were ideally situated to become the first architects of Western overseas imperialism. From the *Iberian* peninsula, the westernmost extension of the European continent, they dispatched the explorers and conquerors, the merchants and missionaries who carved out Europe's first intercontinental empires in Asia and the Americas.

This section will begin with the Portuguese seamen who led the way eastward to Asia, but will concentrate on Spain's immense conquests in the Americas. For three hundred years these Spanish American domains would constitute the world's largest empire.

The Portuguese in Asia

Under the able royal house of Aviz, Portugal had established its independence from its much larger Spanish neighbors at the end of the Middle Ages. By 1400, the Portuguese had a centralized government capable of mobilizing the resources that exploration and empire building required. In the early fifteenth century, Prince Henry the Navigator (1394–1460) had established a research center at Sagres to seek African gold mines and an alliance with a fabled Christian ruler called Prester John against Africa's Muslim peoples. He and his successors built ships, collected maps and reports, and pushed steadily further down the west coast of Africa. In 1497 King Manuel I the Fortunate (r. 1495–1521) sent out four ships under a nobleman named Vasco da Gama to make the final push.

Vasco da Gama (c. 1460–1524) was tough, shrewd, persistent, brutal—clearly the man for the job. He sailed his little flotilla down the length of Africa, around the Cape of Good Hope, and up the eastern side of the continent to the latitude of modern Kenya. With the help of a Muslim pilot, he then crossed the Indian Ocean to Calicut, on the Malabar coast of India. As the battered Portuguese vessels dropped anchor in the Indian harbor in May of 1498, two Muslims from North Africa greeted them from a bobbing small boat, calling, "A lucky venture! A lucky venture! Plenty of rubies, plenty of emeralds! You owe great thanks to God for having brought you to a country holding such riches!"[1]

Most Arab traders were not so happy to see these intruders into their traditional Indian Ocean trade route. In the teeth of Arab intrigues, the contempt of Indian buyers for European trinkets and trade goods, however, da Gama assembled a cargo of spices and made his way homeward. Despite hostile native populations and pirates, storms and scurvy, he made it back. At the cost of half his ships and a third of his men, he returned to Lisbon after a two years' voyage—with a cargo valued at sixty times what the expedition had cost.

The Portuguese quickly constructed an extensive trading empire in the Far East. Organized by the grizzled commander Affonso de Albuquerque (1453–1515) around 1510, this zone of Portuguese predominance included supporting bases along the east coast of Africa and around the Indian Ocean, enclaves in India and southeast Asia, and commercial contacts as far east as South China. Seeking to convert this ancient center of commercial exchange into a Portuguese lake, the Portuguese seized and burned both Arab vessels and the ships of European interlopers caught on the trade routes they now controlled.

In the long run, however, this pioneering imperial venture faced insuperable problems. Portugal was small, and the East was large: increasingly, numbers told against the Portuguese. The logistics of imperial control also proved tremendously costly in lost ships, in graft, in the sheer expense of maintaining bases and trading posts so far from home. By the beginning of the seventeenth century, finally, other European nations could no longer be kept out of the empire itself. The French and British pushed into India, the Dutch into the islands of Southeast Asia. Portugal's pioneering days in Asia were ended.

The Spanish in the Americas

Spain's predominance in the Americas would last considerably longer. Spanish sovereigns, from Isabella and Ferdinand through Charles V to Philip II, built a vast American empire in the 1500s. More than anything else, it was the discoveries of explorers and the victories of conquistadors under the Spanish flag that made the sixteenth century Spain's *siglo de oro* or "golden century."

Christopher Columbus (1451–1506), who started it all, was of course not Spanish but Italian. A long-faced, red-headed, ungenteel, he was a self-educated seaman from the ancient Italian port of Genoa. His knowledge of geography was scrappy, and he became fixated on the erroneous theory that the earth was so small in size that China was really within a few weeks' sailing time of Europe—if you sailed west around the world instead of east. Doggedly determined, he bombarded the Portuguese and Spanish courts with petitions year after year, until Ferdinand and Isabella, flushed with victory over the Moors, agreed to provide the money he needed to test his theory.

Columbus sailed with a fleet of three small ships in early August of 1492. After a voyage of a bit over two months' duration, he made his first landfall in the Caribbean at the island of San Salvador (Watlings Island) in the Bahamas. The scene is vivid in every schoolchild's imagination: caravels in the middle distance, men in doublets and hose splashing through the surf to kneel beneath flapping banners to take possession of a wide white beach in the name of the Catholic kings. From further up the palm-fringed shore, naked Indians may be imagined watching the curious spectacle. "I found very many islands filled with people without number," the Admiral of the Ocean Sea reported, "and of them all I have taken possession for their Highnesses, by proclamation and with the royal standard displayed, and nobody objected."[2]

In this and three subsequent voyages, Columbus explored the Caribbean and adjacent coasts of Middle and South America, always under the illusion he was in East Asia. Later explorers and geographers, however, soon realized they were dealing with unknown lands. Early maps called it first the "New World," then "America" after the Italian explorer Amerigo Vespucci (1452–1512), who had explored thousands of miles of South America and realized that this was not Asia.

Later navigators, still determined to reach the rich markets of the East by sailing west, sought a way around this vast geographical barrier. In 1520, Ferdinand Magellan (1480–1521) found it.

A Portuguese in Spanish service, Magellan sailed in 1519, equipped with five old and battered ships and crews recruited from the dregs of half the ports in Europe, in search of Cathay, the Spice Islands, and the biblical lands of Tarshish and Ophir. This small fleet crossed the Atlantic, rounded the southern tip of South America through what became the Straits of Magellan, and sailed on across the wide Pacific. Passing through the islands of Southeast Asia, the survivors crossed the Indian Ocean, rounded Africa, and headed north once more to Spain. Storms and scurvy, maggoty ship's biscuit and foul water, mutiny, hostile natives and rival European imperialists all took their toll. Magellan himself was killed in the Philippines. Of all his fleet, only one ship, the tiny *Victoria* under the Basque captain Sebastián del Cano (1476–1526), and a crew of eighteen, completed the three-year voyage—the first circumnavigation of the earth in human history.

The Conquistadors

The Spanish monarchy, meanwhile, had been guaranteeing its imperial future against its Portuguese competitors diplomatically. In 1494, after securing a papal decree and renegotiating its contents with the Portuguese, Spain signed the Treaty of Tordesillas with Portugal. The agreement gave Portugal the right to explore, exploit, and colonize everything east of a line that included Brazil, Africa, and Asia to the eastern edge of China. Spain had similar exclusive rights to the west of the demarcation line, which as it turned out meant most of North and South America. No Native Americans, Africans, or Asians, of course, were consulted.

Within a generation, Spanish *conquistadors* (conquerors) built a New World empire for Spain. Between 1520 and 1550, as one authority sums it up, "a few thousand down–at–heels swordsmen . . . the products of [Spain's] Moorish wars, possessed themselves of most of the settled areas of both Americas and established the first great European land empire overseas."[3] Theirs was a more orthodox breed of heroics, and a more brutal one. The Aztecs of Mexico and the Incas of Peru, themselves conquering peoples who had only recently imposed their authority on their neighbors, ruled ancient and highly developed civilizations. Cortés, Pizarro, and their mercenary followers destroyed both the rulers and the civilizations.

The *Aztecs* were a military elite who had intrigued and fought their way to mastery of ancient Mexico and part of Central America only a few generations earlier. Their religion required them to sacrifice large numbers of human beings on the altar of the sun in Tenochtitlán, their capital city. Their stone–and–adobe cities, however, were large, beautiful, and cleaner than most European ones, their society almost crime free, the arts and sciences they inherited from Mayan and earlier cultures highly sophisticated. Dominated by priests and nobles, limited by the lack of large beasts of burden and by their failure to develop iron tools, the Aztecs were nevertheless impressive builders and agriculturalists, effective rulers, and fierce fighters.

Against them came, in 1519, "as devoted a gang of desperadoes as ever engaged in a desperate venture," the freebooting band of conquistadors led by Hernán Cortés (1485–1547). Dashing lover, rare university man among the rough men he led, Cortés proved also to be an inspiring and fearless leader, a clever diplomat, and a ruthless conqueror.

With the aid of an Indian woman, Doña Marina, he formed alliances with disgruntled Indian peoples against their Aztec rulers, exploited Mexican legends of returning gods, and maneuvered his way to the heart of Tenochtitlán to seize the person of the Aztec emperor, Montezuma II (r. 1502–1520). Expelled from the city with huge losses following a Spanish massacre of Aztec nobles, Cortés stubbornly regrouped. He turned Spanish troops sent against him by a rival conquistador into reinforcements for his cause; he mobilized his Indian allies, who stuck with him even in defeat. Taking the offensive once more, he returned to central Mexico, crushed the Aztecs, reduced their beautiful capital city to rubble, and established the Spanish colony of New Spain on the ruins of the Aztec Empire.

The feel of the conquest emerges vividly from Cortés's third dispatch to Charles V, telling the bloody story of the capture of Tenochtitlán. The final clause in particular sums up the impact of the European onslaught in many imperial wars to come:

> Seeing that the enemy was determined to resist to the death, I came to [the conclusion] that they would force us to destroy them totally. This last caused me the greater sorrow, for it weighed on my soul. I reflected on the means I might use to frighten them so that they would realize their mistake and the injury they would sustain from us; and I kept on burning and destroying their houses and the towers of their idols.[4]

Far to the south, the empire of the *Incas* stretched for more than 3,000 miles from what is today Colombia through most of Chile. The empire was bound together by the awesome Royal Road through the Andes, with way stations every few miles and hundreds of suspension bridges swinging over mountain gorges. Indian towns, scattered the length of the realm, "replete with administrative centers and Sun Temples . . . , stone–laid palaces, temples for Sun Virgins, official storehouses, and fortresses, . . . for the sheer mass of building almost equaled the Roman."[5] Having seized power by force even more recently than the Aztecs, the Inca elite had welded many peoples into a centralized state, with a divine emperor, an elaborate administration, and social services that have been compared to those of a modern welfare state.

Into this Andean civilization in 1532 came the grim, illiterate, and thoroughly unprincipled Francisco Pizarro (c. 1475–1541), with his three brothers and a couple of hundred colonial fortune hunters at his back. By exploiting an Indian civil war, by holding the Inca emperor Atahualpa (r. 1530–1533) for a huge ransom and then killing him, and by making murderous use of their superior steel and gunpowder weapons, Pizarro and his conquistadors won a gold–rich empire beyond their wildest dreams. Pizarro himself was murdered less than a decade later in the bloody feuding over the spoils that soon divided the victors. Again, the Indian civilization itself crumbled and vanished, plunging these new subjects of Western rule into centuries of deprivation and misery.

Other would–be conquerors from Castile crisscrossed their newfound lands in search of more Aztec or Inca realms to plunder. Crossing the deserts of the North American southwest or painfully tracing the Amazon to its mouth, they performed prodigies of exploration, but found no more El Dorados. Claiming most of South America, Central America and the Caribbean, and southwestern North America from California to Texas, the Spanish set out to make what they could from the lands and peoples they had conquered.

Climbing up to Machu Picchu today, by train, bus, and foot from the old Inca capital of Cuzco, you get a vivid sense of what these adventurers destroyed. Perched among cloud–crowned peaks high above the jungle floor, Peru's most famous lost city lies roofless and open to the elements now. But its buildings of stones precisely cut, carried to this lofty pinnacle and fit together so accurately that a knife blade cannot be inserted between them, provide ample evidence of the capacities of the society Western empire builders shattered in these mountain fastnesses.

Spain's American Empire

The freebooting rule of the original conquistadors soon gave way to a more bureaucratic structure of government, with its headquarters in Spain, at the great port of Seville and in Madrid itself. From Madrid, viceroys and royal governors were dispatched to the two capitals of Spanish America—the booming colonial metropolises of Mexico City (on the site of the vanished Tenochtitlán) and Lima, Peru—as well as to lesser provincial centers. In the colonies, royal governors were aided by local councils called *audiencias* with advisory and judicial functions. Colonial cities also had municipal assemblies which expressed the views of the Spanish colonial population.

Developed in the spirit of European *mercantilism*, the colonies provided Spain with agricultural products and a diminishing flow of gold and silver bullion. Though they were required to trade exclusively with the mother country, colonists could not be prevented from illegal trade with other countries. Economic production, meanwhile, was carried forward under a system of land grants called *encomiendas*, in which colonial landholders lived off the labor of Indian or African fieldhands, cattle herders, or miners.

Socially, the bulk of the colonial population was divided hierarchically along essentially color lines. "Peninsulars" sent out from Spain headed the government and the church. Descendants of Spanish settlers ran ranches, plantations, and mines. *Mestizos,* of mixed Spanish and Indian origin, though sneered at by people of unmixed Spanish descent, occupied a productive middle stratum of society. Indians and Africans provided most of the labor force and had the least social prestige.

European women in Spanish or Portuguese territories were frequently relatives of men settled in the colonies. As in their Iberian homelands, those colonial women often lived cloistered lives, jealously guarded behind high garden walls and shuttered windows. At the same time, there were opportunities and advantages for women in the Iberian colonies. A leading authority on the European conquest of Latin America refers to "many examples of women who fought alongside and encouraged their menfolk, nursed the sick and wounded, and displayed a spirit of exemplary self-sacrifice."

The fate of the Amerindian peoples of the New World remains one of the most tragic in the whole story of Western global predominance. The so–called *black legend* of particular Spanish cruelty to the Indians, circulated by European enemies of Spanish power, painted a grim picture of hunting, torturing, and burning Indian resisters to death. There was some substance to this "legend," though Spain was not alone in savage treatment of the Native Americans. More important, however, repressive rule, unfamiliar labor discipline, and above all smallpox and other diseases to which they had no immunities caused Indian populations to decline precipitously. The native population of Mexico dropped from perhaps nineteen million to between two and three million in the course of the sixteenth century, while the Indians of the Caribbean virtually disappeared. Some Spanish churchmen, most notably Bartolomé de las Casas (1474–1566), "Father of the Indians," fought for their interests, and laws were passed protecting the original inhabitants and even making them wards of the crown. The Spanish colonists, however, often ignored such laws, as did Western settlers in many other parts of the world.

As the seventeenth century advanced, Spain declined and the Spanish Empire was no longer in the forefront of Western colonial expansion. The causes of this Spanish decline included Spain's losses in the Thirty Years' War, growing English competition for overseas empire, and shrinking revenues from Spain's New World mines. The Spain of Philip II had been the greatest power in sixteenth–century Europe; a hundred years later, Louis XIV's France had replaced it. The Spanish–American Empire remained prosperous enough that other European powers fought for the right to trade with it. But the Spanish colonies now expanded only slowly on their internal frontiers, while other European powers took the lead in the continuing expansion of the imperial West.

✦Seventeenth–Century Empires: The North Atlantic Powers✦

The North Atlantic maritime powers—the Netherlands, France, and England—who followed the Iberians onto the world stage after 1600 were called *interlopers,* "intruders" into a non–Western world to which the Iberian states claimed exclusive rights. We will look first at the remarkable Dutch commercial empire, then at the rise of the French Empire, which extended the power of Louis XIV beyond the seas, and finally at the origins of the British Empire, which would eventually become the largest in world history.

The Dutch Commercial Empire

The Dutch were the first to breach the Iberian monopoly of overseas empire in a large way. With centuries of experience as one of Europe's leading commercial centers and as leaders in seaborne enterprise, the merchants and seamen of the Netherlands were ideally suited to reach beyond the ocean to the world at large. Beginning by marketing the overseas products brought to Europe by the Iberian powers in the sixteenth century, the Dutch began to trade with the outside world directly in the seventeenth. They soon became the world leaders in oceanic commerce.

The Dutch Empire, like that of the Portuguese, was essentially a trading rather than a settlement empire. It differed from Portugal's, however, in being a private enterprise empire, founded by consortia of businessmen organized in great trading companies, rather than by the central government. The Estates General of the United Provinces, like royal governments elsewhere, did charter the East and West India Companies in 1602 and 1621, granting them monopolies of trade in these regions. But it was the initiative, efficiency, and determination of Dutch businessmen that built the seventeenth–century Dutch supremacy on the seas of the world.

The first Dutch fleets set sail for what were still nominally the Portuguese East Indies in the 1590s. Within a few years, the aggressive Dutch had expelled the Portuguese from island Southeast Asia (Indonesia today) and had established themselves as masters of the spice trade.

On the route east, the Dutch established a colony at the southern tip of Africa (the modern Republic of South Africa) that rapidly became a profitable way station for ships of all nations traveling to the Far East. Dutch traders also set up the only Western trading post in Japan before the nineteenth century. But their headquarters in the Far East became the city of Batavia (today's Jakarta) on the island of Java, a tidy port of white high–gabled Dutch houses and canals like those of Amsterdam in the tropical southern seas. A visitor to the old port today will find its jetty lined with the largest fleet of old–fashioned commercial sailing schooners still afloat, now owned and operated among the islands of Indonesia by skilled Javanese seamen.

The Dutch West India Company had a harder time of it. Expansive plans to take Brazil and African Angola from the Portuguese and to monopolize the slave trade between Africa and the Americas failed. But Dutch colonies were successfully planted in North America and in the Caribbean. Basing their claims on the explorations of Henry Hudson (c. 1550–1611), an Englishman sailing in Dutch employ, they founded New Netherland in what is today New York State, and demonstrated the celebrated Dutch commercial acumen by buying Manhattan Island from the Indians for gifts and commodities once valued at $24. Further south, the island of Curaçao gave them a valuable base in the Caribbean, an area already settled by Spaniards as well as by English and French interlopers. From these two centers, Dutch traders proceeded to sell better goods at better prices to colonists of all nations in the Americas, openly defying mercantilist regulations limiting all trade to the colonists' respective mother countries.

"To beat the Dutch" became the dream of European leaders as diverse as Cromwell and Louis XIV. Both absolutist France and constitutionalist England fought essentially commercial wars with the Netherlands in the seventeenth century, and by the end of it, the Dutch Empire was in fact fading. Its small size, like that of Portugal, made it harder for the Netherlands to absorb the inevitable losses that went with such extended commitments. The attrition of repeated wars with European rivals also told. Portugal's recovery of Brazil from the Dutch and the seizure of New Netherland by the English were setbacks from which the Dutch Empire never recovered. They remained masters of the Dutch East Indies and firmly established in South Africa, but from shortly after 1700 on, they ceased to compete with France and England for global supremacy.

The French Mercantilist Empire

The French began with half–hearted and unsuccessful efforts at overseas expansion in the sixteenth century, but constructed the most fully developed mercantilist government–regulated empire of all in the seventeenth. Centrally involved in all the major conflicts of western Europe, the French could not commit themselves to overseas activity as fully as the Iberian powers on the western edge of Europe, or as single–mindedly as the Dutch, whose fundamental activity in the world was commercial exchange. France did make efforts to acquire its share of trade and empire beyond the oceans, particularly in intervals of relative peace, when it was not mired in the Renaissance Italian wars, the wars of religion, or the Thirty Years' War. Only in the seventeenth century, however, under state builders like Cardinal Richelieu—one of the last great political churchmen—and the mercantilist finance minister Colbert, did France really begin to construct an overseas empire worthy of the Sun King.

Sixteenth–century French colonial ventures in the Americas, including Huguenot settlements in Brazil and Florida, were destroyed by the Portuguese and the Spanish. Only Jacques Cartier's (1491–1557) explorations of Newfoundland and the St. Lawrence and his founding of Montreal in what became eastern Canada had future significance. Shortly after 1600, Samuel de Champlain (c. 1567–1635) further expanded this wedge into northern North America, founding Quebec and signing treaties of alliance with the Indians around the Great Lakes. But the number of settlers, mostly fur traders and Jesuit missionaries, remained small.

Under Richelieu, these small beginnings in French Canada were expanded somewhat, and profitable Caribbean plantations were established on the islands of Guadeloupe, Martinique, and later Haiti. To work the land in the Caribbean, now bare of its original Native American inhabitants, the French, like the Spanish and the Portuguese before them, imported large numbers of black slaves from Africa. Louis XIV's great minister Colbert, finally, sought to integrate the American colonies into a unified mercantilist empire. Transferring the Canadian settlements from private operation to royal control, Colbert augmented the population and organized it under landholding seigneurs and peasant tenants, as in France. Explorers like Father Marquette (1637–1675) and the ambitious Robert Cavelier de La Salle (1643–1687), meanwhile, traveled down the Mississippi and claimed this whole swath of inner North America for France, naming it Louisiana after Louis XIV. A broad vision of a French North American presence from the St. Lawrence and the Great Lakes down the Mississippi to the Gulf of Mexico and the Caribbean was thus projected, though settlers on the ground remained few, and claims larger than colonial realities.

In Africa and India also, the French made significant beginnings in the seventeenth century. The French traded regularly in India after 1600. In the later seventeenth century, the French East India Company established trading posts and bases in India itself, with a center at Pondicherry on the eastern coast. The power of the *Mughal* emperors of India was so great, however, that the interior of the subcontinent remained closed to the French, as to other Europeans. In fact, their position remained that of respectful dependents of Aurangzeb (r. 1658–1707), the last great Mughal ruler, throughout the later 1600s. Here also, however, a French presence was established and ready to expand as the Mughals declined in the following century.

The Rise of Britain's World Empire

In both East and West, the main competition the French faced was that of the rising imperial power of England. Even slower to start than the French, the English came on with a rush in the seventeenth century once they threw themselves into the empire–building game in earnest.

In the sixteenth century, then, England's imperial involvement was largely limited to piracy. Elizabethan privateers raided the Caribbean and prowled the Atlantic, burning Spanish colonial cities and lying in wait for Spanish treasure fleets from the New World or Portuguese spice ships from the East Indies. Sir Francis Drake (c. 1540–1596), the most famous of these raiders, became the second captain to circumnavigate the globe in 1580, looting the coasts of Spanish America on the way.

Not until the seventeenth century did English enterprise successfully follow the Dutch and French in shattering the Iberian colonial monopoly and beginning the construction of an English Empire beyond the seas. As in the Netherlands and to a considerable degree in France, English imperialism was undertaken by private companies and individuals, rather than by the crown. In England, these empire builders included not only joint–stock companies of "merchant adventurers" but also groups seeking a religious haven in the New World. And though the royal government did soon impose governors and regulations on the colonies, English settlers remained more self–governing than most.

The first permanent English settlements in what became the United States were established at Jamestown, Virginia (1607) and at Plymouth, Massachusetts (1620). The Jamestown settlement was funded by a commercial corporation, the London Company of Virginia, which hoped to find gold and settled for tobacco, the American south's first plantation crop. The Plymouth colony was set up by a group of Puritan Independents, traditionally known as the Pilgrims, fleeing the religious climate of Stuart England. They were soon absorbed by the Massachusetts Bay Puritans, who arrived later but were much more numerous. These English efforts north and south both survived, thanks to the rigorous discipline of military commanders like Captain John Smith (c. 1580–1631) in Virginia and the flinty determination of the Puritans in New England. The colonists also had essential early help from neighboring Indian tribes, with whom they were soon at war.

Subsequent English settlements in America followed these two patterns of religious or commercial settlement. Expansion and secession spread Puritans to other New England states; Catholics led by Lord Baltimore (1580–1632) and Quakers under William Penn (1644–1718) sought refuge in Maryland and Pennsylvania, respectively. Meanwhile, speculators undertook to colonize the Carolinas, and England took over New Netherland—thereafter New York—in the 1660s. Far to the south, English settlers moved into the West Indies, filling a string of islands from Barbados to Jamaica with slave–operated sugar plantations.

In the Far East too, the English appeared in increasing numbers. The British East India Company, organized in 1600, initiated an immensely profitable commerce with the East. The English established trading posts on the west coast of India, across the subcontinent from the French settlements. Like the French, however, the handful of English imperialists in India remained mere clients of the Mughal emperors until that powerful dynasty fell into decay after 1700. Thereafter, both the British and the French East India Companies began to involve themselves more aggressively in the political and military affairs of India and to clash with each other in an intensifying feud for Indian empire.

Women were much more visible in the emerging English Empire than was realized until recently. The first successful English settlement at Jamestown in 1607 soon requested women, hoping their presence would make the male colonists more content to stay on that barbarous shore. By the eighteenth century, there was nothing strange about the petition from the English colony in Georgia for "thirty head of women . . . who would soon get husbands and be an inducement to those soldiers to settle in the colony when the time of their service should expire."[6] The need was not sexual—Western soldiers or settlers quickly found consorts, willing or unwilling, among the indigenous population—but social, the desire to create stable European communities beyond the seas.

Many English immigrants came as part of families. Those who came alone were usually indentured servants, bound to work four or five years to pay for their passage before being free to make their own lives in the colonies. For most, this meant marriage and the establishment of a family, the basic social and economic unit on the frontiers of the expanding West as it was in Europe. Like Spanish women, however, women in England's new colonies also seem to have "played a much greater variety of roles than their contemporaries in England," perhaps because challenging frontier conditions "often made de facto partners of husbands and wives."[7] One still debated thesis suggests that English colonial women were commonly considered "deputy husbands," expected to be able to conduct business for the family just as the husband did and to carry on a number of trades including "blacksmiths, silversmiths, tinworkers, shoemakers, shipwrights, tanners, gunsmiths, barbers, printers, and butchers, as well as . . . teachers and shopkeepers."[8]

England's empire in the old imperial period thus centered in the New World, in the string of colonies running down the east coast of North America and extending into the Caribbean islands. A vigorous town life, crafts, trade, and many farms flourished in Puritan New England, while a single–crop plantation economy emerged in the south and on the islands. It was not as splendid as the baroque churches and ornate colonial palaces of Spanish America to the south, and the English did not get along with the Indians as well as the French north of them did. But there were a quarter of a million English settlers in America already in 1700, and their prosperous colonies were growing fast. In India, meanwhile, the agents of the East India Company could live like rajahs in their trading compounds and come home rich, hailed as "moguls" (Mughals). But the glory days of the company in India still lay ahead. And it would be another century and a half before Victorian imperialists turned the once great Mughal Empire into the largest and most populous colony in the world.

Russia's Eastward Expansion

So far, we have emphasized the unique overseas character of Western imperialism, based on Europe's mastery of the world's oceans. One great exception to this rule must be included here as well: the expansion of Russia across the Eurasian continent to the Pacific.

East of Moscow, east of the Ural Mountains, Eurasia stretched away some 6,000 miles to the Bering Straits. North of the civilized centers of the Middle East, India, and China, these endless reaches of steppe grass, barren tundra, and dark pine forest supported only a scanty population of Mongol tribesmen. It was open country for horsemen, traveled by nomadic herdsmen for many centuries. In addition, a series of great rivers, with their networks of tributaries, offered a water road for those experienced in river transport. A people well suited to both means of moving east were readily available in early modern Russia: the *Cossacks*.

These unique subjects of the autocratic czars lived in independent bands on the steppes. They made their own rules and bought their freedom by serving Moscow as an elite cavalry corps, as ready to repress rebellious Russians as to fight their country's foes. Famous horsemen and skilled river travelers as well, the Cossacks of the Don and Volga river basins and other areas also became the frontier vanguard of Russia's centuries-long eastward expansion.

Under Ivan the Terrible in the later sixteenth century, the Cossack leader Yermak (d. 1584) routed the last Mongol khan and offered western Siberia to the czar. In the seventeenth century, under the early Romanovs, Cossack raiders and fur traders boated and portaged eastward up and down the Russian rivers—the Ob, the Yenisei, the Lena, the Kolyma—to reach the Russian Far East by midcentury. The Cossacks pushed on to explore the Amur River, north of Manchuria. In 1689 the Treaty of Nerchinsk between the Romanovs and the Manchu emperor of China delineated Russia's border with the Chinese Empire a century before the Middle Kingdom, as the Chinese called their ancient realm, officially recognized the existence of any other European power. Further north, Vitus Bering (1681–1741), a Danish navigator engaged by Peter the Great, explored the strait between eastern Siberia and Alaska that was later named for him.

By the early 1700s, Russia had explored and laid claim to more land than any European monarch had ever ruled on the Eurasian mainland. Throughout most of these eastern lands, however, there were very few Russian settlers. The Cossacks and the occasional Russian collector of taxes or tributes from the indigenous population were often looked on more as marauders than as agents of a legitimate government. Independent regimes, especially in central Asia and the Caucasus, still remained for soldiers and proconsuls of empire to conquer in later centuries. Nevertheless, in terms of territory claimed if not yet occupied, Russia in the days of Peter the Great was already the largest country in the world.

◆ Global Impact of Western Expansion ◆

The European settlers and traders established on four other continents brought the West unique rewards. In this section we focus first on the benefits accruing to Europeans from their new intercontinental empires, highlighting the flow of luxury goods from Asia, the rise of the African slave trade, commodity imports from North America, and the flood of silver and gold that reached Europe from Latin America. Equally important was the unprecedented impact of Western power upon the rest of the world. This impact also—ecological, demographic, economic, and cultural—will be examined here.

Asian Imports and the African Slave Trade

Europeans who visited or established themselves around the fringes of Asia and Africa during this period found rich pickings of very different kinds. From Asia came traditional luxury goods; from Africa, enslaved human labor.

Having reached the East by sailing east, Europeans had direct access to the luxury goods they had been importing through Asian intermediaries for centuries. These included large quantities of silk, porcelain, and tea from China; cotton textiles and gems from India; spices like cloves, cinnamon, and pepper from the islands of Southeast Asia; and coffee, drugs, indigo dye, and saltpeter for gunpowder from the Middle East.

These luxury goods had large effects on Europe's economy and society. Thus the tastes Europeans acquired for overseas products led Europeans to produce imitations of Chinese porcelain or Indian cottons. Coffee and tea became national drinks in European countries,

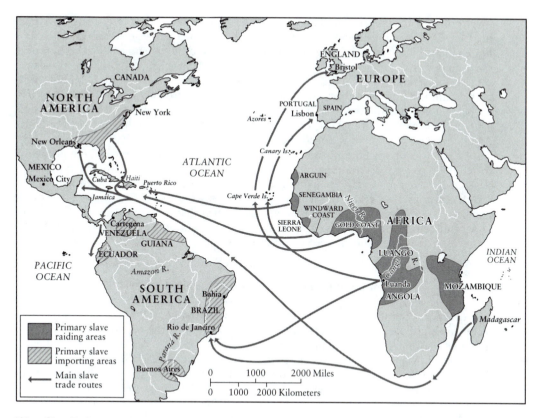

African Slave Trade

and tea shops and coffeehouses emerged as social and cultural centers where news was exchanged, business transacted, opinions formed. European ladies and gentlemen sipping tea or coffee from "china" cups—with sugar imported from the West Indian colonies—thus benefited from overseas empires in some very subtle ways.

The sugar had almost certainly been harvested by Africans in Europe's New World plantations. Africa exported a variety of products to the West, including gold and ivory and some spices, including pepper and cloves. Africa's major contribution to the wealth of the West, however, was enslaved labor, bought in Africa and sold in the Americas.

The decimation of Amerindian populations and their inability to adapt to the brutal labor conditions of the mines and plantations created a pressing labor shortage in the American colonies. The Portuguese were the first large–scale importers of slaves, but the Spanish bought large numbers, and the British, French, and Dutch were soon both trading in slaves and using them on their own Caribbean and American plantations.

The result was a triangular trade route linking Europe, Africa, and America. From Europe, liquor, guns, iron, jewelry, and textiles went to Africa, where they were exchanged for slaves. From Africa, the slaves were then transported to the New World. In the Americas, the products their labor produced, including rum, tobacco, and sugar, were shipped off to European markets.

Apologists for the trade in human beings have pointed out that slavery and slave raiding were established institutions in Africa, as in many other parts of the world. They have not emphasized the great increase in slave taking sparked by the annual visits of European slave ships to the long western coast of Africa, from Senegal to Angola. For more than three centuries, Africans carried off from their villages by slave–raiding neighbors were packed into the European slave ships, two hundred and more into a tiny hold where 10 to 25 percent could easily die from overcrowding and disease during the Atlantic crossing. The survivors were auctioned off at the slave markets of the West Indies or North or South America and set to work in Europe's New–World colonies.

In purely economic terms, these African workers contributed greatly to the growth of the colonies of the Western hemisphere. Estimates of the numbers of Africans imported as slaves range from ten to twenty million people over the sixteenth, seventeenth, and eighteenth centuries. By the time of the first national censuses in the 1790s, almost a fifth of the population of the new United States and well over half that of Brazil were at least partially of African descent. It was by any standards a massive addition to the economic life of this first great extension of the Western world overseas.

Produce and Precious Metals from the Americas

The Americas contributed many commodities to the expanding Western economy. These included fish, tobacco, and sugar—as well as gold and silver, the precious metals that had fired the avarice of the first conquistadors.

Codfish from the Newfoundland Banks and the New England shore, salted or dried for preservation, provided a vital component of the European diet, especially on the many religious fast days, but also for general consumption during the winter.

Of more debatable value but extremely profitable nonetheless was tobacco, a widely used Amerindian product which quickly caught on in Europe. While some saw it as an exotic drug, others claimed medicinal properties for it, and tobacco soon became a regular part of European theater, taverns, coffeehouses, and even domestic life.

A third valuable American product was sugar, the main support of a booming Brazilian and Caribbean plantation economy in the 1600s. Introduced by the Spanish and Portuguese from Asia, sugar was used as a sweetener, especially for tea or coffee, and was also the basis of other food products. It was commonly shipped home in the form of molasses—like tobacco, believed to have medicinal value—or rum, which became one of the most destructive alcoholic drinks of Europe's poor.

Throughout the sixteenth and the first half of the seventeenth centuries, finally, American silver and gold poured into Europe. First taken as booty or in trade, later from the legendary mines of Guanajuato in Mexico and Potosí in Bolivia, Latin America's tribute tripled the European supply of silver and gold in the 1500s. The European economy, low in precious metals for centuries due to the outflow to Asia for luxury goods, had only begun to make up its needs with late fifteenth–century finds in central Europe. The new flood of bullion from overseas was therefore a powerful stimulus for the European economy.

This influx of gold and silver had, as noted in an earlier chapter, a powerful inflationary effect, combining with increased demand due to population growth to produce higher prices across much of Europe. This sixteenth–century inflation finished off the late medieval depression and brought—for some at least—a boom comparable to that of the High Middle Ages. Prices doubled in France and England and tripled in Spain over the century.

Native Americans forced to labor in a West Indian sugar mill. Can you follow the process from raw sugar cane in the upper right hand corner to the large jars being carried out for shipment home at the far right? (New York Public Library Picture Collection.)

Middle–class businessmen profited greatly, especially in labor-intensive industries like mining, shipbuilding, or cloth making. Landowners seeking profit from rising cloth prices enclosed their fields and took up sheep raising. Wage workers, however, found that their salaries seldom kept up with inflation, and many peasants were turned out of their villages entirely by enclosures. Once more, the influence of Europe's imperial expansion on European society was extensive and complex.

Ecological and Demographic Impact

Some of the most striking effects of Western imperialism were ecological and demographic in nature. These included such terrible visitations as the decimation of the Native American population of North America and such long–range benefits as the spread of Indian corn to other peoples around the world. All alike were consequences of the growing Western presence in so many foreign lands.

On a map of the Western overseas empires around 1700, it is evident that Europeans were still largely limited to coastal areas, islands, or, in some places, inland rivers or lake shores—areas, in short, that were accessible to their remarkable ships. Nevertheless, these little sailing ships moved goods and people around as never before, causing, among other things, unprecedentedly rapid ecological changes.

Seeking to make their New World colonies pay, for instance, Europeans transplanted cash crops like sugar, coffee, and cotton from the Old World to the New. They also exported large domesticated animals, a major lack in the Western hemisphere, including horses, donkeys, cattle, and sheep. From the Americas, finally, they brought back crops that would flourish in various parts of the Old World, including Indian corn, potatoes, tobacco, and other valuable plants. Many of these were soon growing in Asia and Africa as well as in Europe. Again, the impact was eventually immense: Indian corn, originally developed in ancient Mexico, helps to feed half the world's populations today.

Demographic changes were greatest in the Americas. There, the world's most ethnically homogeneous population was replaced by the world's most heterogeneous one. As we have seen, Western wars, mistreatment, and the "biological invasion" of Western disease germs caused a sharp decline in the Native American population. The introduction of African slaves in large numbers established an important new element in the demographic mix. When we add the European invaders themselves, we have a region of the globe uniquely divided among the three main human families: Mongoloid Native Americans, Negroid Africans, and Caucasoid Europeans.

Impact of Western Ideas and Economic Power

Even this early, the world also began to feel the economic weight of the European predominance. On the positive side, commercial exchange on a global basis became possible for the first time, thanks to European merchants and seamen. Asia's empires experienced only a modest influx of Western products, but Africa got more manufactured goods than ever before, and the Native Americans were introduced to them for the first time. And as overseas imports changed European society, so the introduction of the iron ax into the Brazilian rain forest, or of the horse to the plains Indians of North America, exercised a transforming effect on these cultures.

On the negative side, however, Western economic penetration also began to undermine the native economies. In the New World, Western conquest had destroyed the two most developed American empires, stopping their economic evolution in its tracks and condemning masses of Indians to a grim future as second–class citizens in European–dominated lands. In Africa, the ready availability of Western manufactured goods in exchange for slaves both encouraged the economically counterproductive "export" of human labor and discouraged the development of manufacturing in Africa.

Even ideas were transported to new parts of the globe by the Western intrusion. Of these, by far the most important in the period of the old imperialism was the Christian religion. Again, Asia resisted most strongly. The handful of Jesuits in China were largely cocooned in Peking, while the Japanese shoguns became so alarmed at the potentially subversive effect of the Western religion that they all but destroyed the Christian convert community in Japan. Africa's defenses against Christian missionary activity and other forms of Western penetration consisted of difficult geography and alien microbes. Thick coastal forests and swamps, rivers blocked by rapids or falls, and other geographical barriers combined with malaria, yellow fever, and other germs to which Europeans had no immunities to discourage major efforts at missionary activities.

In North America, the Puritans seem to have seen the Indians as limbs of Satan more often than as potential Christians. French Jesuits in Canada and the Spanish mission fathers of California and the Southwest, however, did make many converts to Catholicism. And in Latin America, the Spanish and Portuguese churches and missionary orders exercised an even wider influence, reshaping the religious lives of many of the surviving native population.

The West at the World's Center

For better or worse, by 1700 the world had a center for the first time in its history. This centrality is what we have been describing as an emerging Western *hegemony*, the unprecedented predominance of one of the world's peoples over all the others. In the most focused sense, the core of this Western global predominance can be located in western Europe. In a broader sense, however, what was beginning was a larger Atlantic–centered Western predominance that would last through most of modern history.

This Western domination of global affairs over the last five centuries has been described by Immanuel Wallerstein as the *modern world system*.[9] In the view of Wallerstein and his adherents, this system is a worldwide network of nations and peoples dominated more by Western economic and political power than by military strength. The "core" of the system was originally the handful of western European Atlantic seaboard nations we have studied in this chapter. In later centuries, however, the core expanded across the Atlantic Ocean to include North America, particularly the United States. The "periphery" of the system was originally composed of European colonies and of other peoples with whom early modern Europeans traded; today it is said to include most of the Third World. Within this "world system," proponents of this theory believe, the West provided capital and control, while the rest of the world contributed labor, raw materials, and agricultural products. Western political hegemony, Western economic exploitation, and Western "cultural imperialism"—the spread of Western ideas and values—have thus shaped the global history of the last five hundred years.

Whether this theoretical formulation accurately defines the basic relationship between the West and the rest of humanity over the past five centuries or not, it does reflect the growing Western preeminence in modern times. And, as we have seen throughout this volume, this wave of Western expansion is only the latest stage in a pattern of Western territorial growth that goes back to our earliest beginnings.

The Western world had been expanding, despite setbacks and periods of paralysis, throughout its history. From a cluster of Greek city–states in southeastern Europe, it had spread around the Mediterranean Sea and thrust north into western Europe in Roman times. During the Middle Ages, Western civilization, though losing its grip on the African and Asian shores of the Mediterranean, had consolidated its position in western Europe and spread through the central and eastern portions of that continent as well. And in early modern times, as we have seen in this chapter, the West expanded once more, this time across the oceans of the world to colonize the Americas and establish commercial beachheads in Africa and Asia.

Western global expansion had only begun as the seventeenth century drew to a close. But a pattern of imperial conquest, economic penetration, and cultural domination had been established. The future held even more astonishing developments in store, as the West transformed an emerging hegemony into a virtual mastery of the rest of the world in later centuries. It was a global supremacy which, when it ended with the collapse of those empires in the later twentieth century, left the world transformed and evolving in directions undreamed of at the beginning of the modern age.

Summary

During the sixteenth and seventeenth centuries, the time of the so-called old imperialism, Western powers became the first of the world's peoples to construct vast overseas empires. In the 1500s, the Iberian powers, Spain and Portugal, led the way. In the 1600s, the North Atlantic interlopers, England, France, and the Netherlands began to build their own intercontinental empires.

In the sixteenth century, Spain conquered the Aztec and Inca empires and imposed its rule on the southern parts of the New World. Portugal, meanwhile, established commercial colonies in southern Africa, the Indian Ocean, and Southeast Asia. In the seventeenth century, the Netherlands set up trading colonies in South Africa, Southeast Asia, and the Americas, while both France and England established themselves in North America, the Caribbean, and India.

Europeans reaped lavish rewards from these early intercontinental empires. They imported luxury goods from Asia; sugar, tobacco, and other commodities from North America and the Caribbean; silver and gold from Mexico and South America; and from Africa, slave labor for their New World colonies.

Western imperialism also moved peoples, plants, and animals around the globe to an unprecedented degree. Most importantly, many historians believe, Western imperialism created a "world system" of power and economic exchange centered in a western European core with much of the rest of the world as its periphery.

Some Key Terms

Age of Encounter 345	gunpowder weapons 349	*mestizo* 355
astrolabe 348	hegemony 365	modern world system 365
audiencia 354	Iberians 350	Mughals 357
Aztecs 353	Incas 353	new imperialism 349
black legend 355	interloper 355	old imperialism 349
caravels 348	joint-stock companies 349	settlement empire 349
conquistador 353	mercantilism 354	trading empire 350
encomienda 354	Mercator projection 349	

Notes

1. E. G. Ravenstein, ed., *A Journal of the First Voyage of Vasco da Gama* (London: Hakluyt Society, 1898), 49.
2. "Columbus's Letter on His First Voyage," in Samuel Eliot Morison, *Christopher Columbus, Mariner* (New York: New American Library, 1955), 149.
3. J. H. Parry, *The Establishment of the European Hegemony, 1415–1715* (New York: Harper & Row, 1961), 60.
4. *Conquest: Dispatches of Cortes from the New World*, ed. Irwin R. Blacker and Harry M. Rosen (New York: Grosset and Dunlap, 1962), 125.

5. Victor W. von Hagen, *Realm of the Incas* (New York: New American Library, 1957), 147, 150.

6. Julia C. Spruill, *Women's Life and Work in the Southern Colonies* (Chapel Hill: University of North Carolina Press, 1938), 18.

7. Susan F. Bailey, *Women in the British Empire* (New York: Garland, 1983), 83.

8. Laurel Thatcher Ulrich, *Good Wives: Image and Reality in the Lives of Women in Northern New England 1650–1750* (New York: Oxford University Press, 1983), 35.

9. Immanual Wallerstein's *The Modern World System* (New York: Academic Press, 1974–) has now reached three volumes and the eighteenth century.

Reading List

Andrews, K. R. *Trade, Plunder, and Settlement: Maritime Enterprise and the Genesis of the British Empire, 1480–1630.* New York: Cambridge University Press, 1984. Very readable account of voyages by the English to many parts of the world.

Boxer, C. R. *The Dutch Seaborne Empire, 1600–1800.* New York: Humanities Press, 1980. Solid overview by a leading authority. See also J. I. Israel, *Dutch Primacy in World Trade, 1585–1740* (New York: Clarendon Press, 1989).

Cronon, W. *Changes in the Land: Indians, Colonists, and the Ecology of New England.* New York: Hill and Wang, 1983. An interdisciplinary student–oriented summary of the interaction of cultures and countryside.

Crosby, A. W. *The Columbian Exchange: Biological Consequences of 1492.* Westport, Conn.: Greenwood, 1973. Highlights microbial interchange and its impact on Amerindian and Western peoples.

Davies, K. A. *Landowners in Colonial Peru.* Austin: University of Texas Press, 1984. Good example of the burgeoning literature on the rural landowning elite that dominated colonial Latin American society.

Elliott, J. H. *The Old World and the New, 1492–1650.* Cambridge: Cambridge University Press, 1972. Essays on the impact of the American colonies on Europe.

Gunder Frank, A. *World Accumulation, 1391–1789.* New York: Monthly Review Press, 1978. The consequences of Western capital accumulation and domination of the world market on colonial and other peripheral areas.

Lach, D. F. *Asia in the Making of Europe.* 3 vols. Chicago: University of Chicago Press, 1971–1977. Volume 2 offers encyclopedic treatment of the cultural influence of Asia on sixteenth–century Europe.

Leon–Portilla, M. *The Broken Spears: The Aztec Account of the Conquest of Mexico.* Translated by L. Kemp. London: Constable, 1962. History from the viewpoint of the Amerindians of Mexico.

Morison, S. E. *Admiral of the Ocean Sea.* 2 vols. Boston: Little, Brown, 1942. Classic highly readable account of Columbus's voyages by a mariner and naval historian who explored the fifteenth–century navigator's problems in his own vessel.

Parr, C. M. *So Noble a Captain.* Westport, Conn.: Greenwood, 1976. Magellan and the first circumnavigation of the globe.

Parry, J. H. *The Age of Reconnaissance.* Berkeley: University of California Press, 1981. The European voyages, by a leading authority. See also his *The Establishment of the European Hegemony, 1415–1715: Trade and Exploration in the Age of the Renaissance* (New York: Harper & Row, 1963).

————. *The Spanish Seaborne Empire.* New York: Knopf, 1966. Sweeping overview of the largest of the early empires.

Prescott, W. H. *The Portable Prescott.* New York: Viking, 1964. Extracts from both his vivid nineteenth–century narratives, *The Conquest of Mexico* and *The Conquest of Peru.*

Quinn, D. B. *North America from Earliest Discovery to First Settlement.* New York: Harper & Row, 1977. Vivid retelling of early Western penetration of North America.

Reid, A. *Southeast Asia in the Age of Commerce, 1450–1680.* New Haven: Yale University Press, 1993. Dutch impact on the islands.

Sale, K. *The Conquest of Paradise: Christopher Columbus and the Columbian Legacy.* New York: Knopf, 1990. Depicts European imperialism as a ruthless ravaging of the planet, perhaps idealizing non–Western peoples in the process.

Sweet, D., and G. Nash, eds. *Struggle and Survival in Colonial America.* Berkeley: University of California Press, 1981. Biographies of a score of Europeans and Amerindians, illustrating the conflicts between them.

Trudel, M. *The Beginnings of New France, 1524–1663.* Translated by P. Claxton. Toronto: McLelland and Stewart, 1973. Good introduction to the beginnings of France overseas.

Wallerstein, I. *The Modern World–System.* Vol. 1, *Capitalist Agriculture and the Origins of the European World–Economy in the Sixteenth Century.* New York: Academic Press, 1974. Widely discussed study of the structure of the Western economic hegemony of the globe.

PART IV
The Eighteenth Century: New Directions

For some historians the eighteenth century is the "real" beginning of modern times. Politically, we certainly see trends toward a more familiar world. In continental Europe, the absolute monarchs of the preceding century metamorphosed into "enlightened despots," benevolent rulers claiming, at least, to be the servants of their people. But, first in Britain's thirteen colonies in North America and then in France, Europe's greatest power, there were outbreaks of revolution that promised something much more radical—representative government that guaranteed the rights of the governed.

Economically also, the eighteenth century saw some astonishing beginnings. In the early 1700s, an agricultural revolution significantly increased productivity in parts of Europe. The early part of the century also saw the beginning of the remarkable modern population explosion that has since spread around the world. And from about 1760 on, the Industrial Revolution began the unprecedented material transformation of the Western world, the consequences of which are everywhere today.

Eighteenth-century society also faced some startling changes. An increasingly educated and wealthy middle class grew in self-confidence and began to take a hand in politics. But western Europe's peasant masses were often underemployed or displaced entirely by agricultural changes. In central and eastern Europe and in the Americas, serfs, slaves, and other unfree laborers did much of the work. And in the cities of the Western world, unemployment and miserable wages were rife.

The cultural and intellectual history of the eighteenth century also reflected the churning uneasiness of a society in the throes of change. Kings, nobles, and the Catholic church continued to support elegant poetry and music, to commission portraits and country homes, and to build impressive palaces and churches. Middle-class citizens, by contrast, demanded relatively realistic novels, genre paintings of everyday life, and other forms of bourgeois expression. The subversive ideas of the Enlightenment, meanwhile, challenged all aspects of the status quo, ridiculing nobles and churchmen and rejecting many of the values the Western world had inherited from ancient and medieval times. In place of these ideas the leaders of the Enlightenment proposed such radical notions as liberty, equality, and democracy—and they began to get a hearing in the West.

The Western world in the eighteenth century, finally, was vastly larger than it had been in ancient and medieval times and was increasingly involved politically and economically with the rest of the globe. The Western imperial powers emerged from early modern times with large settlement empires in the Americas and trading posts and other colonial holdings dotted around the coasts and islands of Africa and Asia. Little was added to these holdings during the 1700s, and at the end of the century Britain lost its most prosperous colonies in North America, as Spain later lost its South American territories. But Western rule and Western economic and cultural dominance would continue to grow for most of the next two centuries.

Time Line: New Directions

1700–1750	French literary salons
1721–1742	Walpole develops prime minister's office, cabinet system in Britain
1740	Richardson's *Pamela*—early middle-class novel
1740–1748	War of the Austrian Succession—Frederick the Great vs. Maria Theresa
1740–1786	Frederick II the Great rules Prussia
1748	Montesquieu's *Spirit of the Laws* offers rationalistic analysis and evaluation of political institutions
1751–1772	Diderot and d'Alembert publish the *Encyclopedia*
1756–1791	Mozart—operas like *Don Giovanni* challenge convention
1759	British defeat French at Quebec, winning Canada; British capture Pondicherry, assuring dominance in India
1760	Industrial Revolution begins in Britain
1762	Rousseau's *Social Contract* urges democratic political reforms
1762–1796	Catherine II the Great rules Russia
1776	Adam Smith's *Wealth of Nations* explains economics in terms of the free market
1775–1783	American Revolution
1776	American Declaration of Independence
1782	Watt's steam engine adapted for many industrial uses
1788	United States Constitution ratified
1789	Estates General convened to deal with problems—demands reforms; fall of Bastille; march on Versailles; Declaration of Rights of Man and the Citizen
1792–1794	The Terror—Robespierre's Committee of Public Safety turns back foreign invaders, but executes many "enemies of the people" in France itself
1794	Thermidorean reaction ends the Terror by executing its leaders
1796	Napoleon's Italian campaign makes him a national hero
1799–1814	Napoleon seizes power; makes himself emperor (1804); strengthens French government and legal system (Napoleonic Code)
1805	Battle of Austerlitz brings Napoleon within sight of ruling all Europe
1815	Battle of Waterloo—Napoleon is defeated and exiled to St. Helena

⟶ 15 ⟵

The Pillars of Civilization
Europe in the Old Regime

◆The Great Powers of Europe   ◆The Power Structure
◆Classes and Communities   ◆Wars and International Relations

"After me," said the eighteenth–century French King Louis XV, "the deluge!" But then, he added, brightening, "The old machine will last our time." It did—but barely. For the society known to later generations as the *ancien régime*, the "old order" in Europe, was struck at the end of the century by a flood as overwhelming as the biblical deluge—the great French Revolution of 1789.

This chapter's first three sections will look at the nations of Europe, their political organization, and their classes and communities during the 1700s, the century before the Age of Democratic Revolutions began with the American Revolution of 1776 and the French Revolution of 1789. The last section will then turn to the foreign relations of that vanished Europe, with its international wars, intercontinental empires, and burgeoning overseas trade.

A doomed world like that of Europe's old regime seems an unrewarding subject for historical study. Eighteenth–century society, with its tiny villages and pre–industrial cities, its kings and queens and ancient aristocracies, even its still rising, not yet risen middle classes, is not the society we know. The eighteenth–century's international rivalries, alliances, and colonial empires are no part of the twentieth–century international scene.

And yet, a look at that vanished society may help us to understand the Europe which succeeded it in the nineteenth century—and the Western world of today. For our society is as structured, in its way, as that one was, and the interests of great powers continue to shape international relations today as they did then. This anatomy of the old regime may thus serve as a model for our understanding of later times.

◆The Great Powers of Europe◆

The survey of the major European states that follows serves as an introduction to the main players on the political stage of eighteenth–century Europe. It will focus on Europe's great powers—France under the heirs of Louis XIV, Britain and its emerging parliamentary gov-

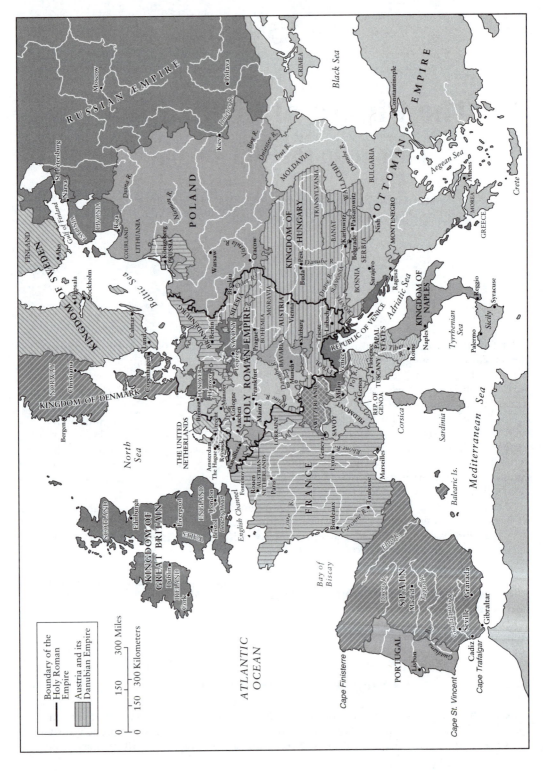

RUSSIAN EMPIRE

Moscow •

• Poltava

Dnieper R.

St. Petersburg •
• Narva
Gulf of Finland
ESTHONIA
LIVONIA
Riga •
Dvina R.
COURLAND
Kiev •
Bug R.
Dniester R.
Prut R.

FINLAND

Åbo •
• Uppsala
• Stockholm

KINGDOM OF SWEDEN

Baltic Sea

Calmar •

Königsberg •
PRUSSA
Niemen R.
LITHUANIA
Warsaw •
Vistula R.
Cracow •

POLAND

MOLDAVIA
WALLACHIA
Danube R.
TRANSYLVANIA
Karlowitz •
BANAT
Passarowitz •
Belgrade •
SLAVONIA
SERBIA
BOSNIA
Sarajevo •
Nish •
MONTENEGRO
Ragusa •

BULGARIA

Constantinople •

OTTOMAN EMPIRE

CRIMEA

Black Sea

Aegean Sea

Athens •
GREECE
MOREA

Crete

KINGDOM OF HUNGARY
Buda • • Pest
Danube R.
Drave R.
Save R.
Temesvar •

BRANDENBURG
Berlin •
SILESIA
Breslau •
Oder R.
SAXONY
Leipzig •
MORAVIA
BOHEMIA
Prague •
Frankfurt •
Main R.
BAVARIA
Munich •
AUSTRIA
Vienna •
Salzburg •
Danube R.
Linz •
Innsbruck •
TYROL
Trieste •

HOLY ROMAN EMPIRE

REPUBLIC OF VENICE
Venice •
Milan •
Adriatic Sea

Bremen •
HANOVER
Hamburg •
Hanover •
Münster •
Cologne •
Aachen •
Rhine R.

THE UNITED NETHERLANDS
Amsterdam •
The Hague •
Utrecht •
Antwerp •
Ostend •
AUSTRIAN NETHERLANDS
Rouen •
Fontenoy •
Paris •

Danube R.
Elbe R.

Po R.
Genoa •
REP. OF GENOA
PIEDMONT
SAVOY
Geneva •
SWITZERLAND
Rhone R.
Lyon •

Florence •
REP. OF TUSCANY
PAPAL STATES
Rome •
Tiber R.

KINGDOM OF NAPLES
Naples •
Reggio •
Syracuse •
Sicily
Palermo •
Tyrrhenian Sea

North Sea

Bergen •

KINGDOM OF NORWAY
Christiania •

KINGDOM OF DENMARK
Copenhagen •

LORRAINE
Mainz •

FRANCE
Loire R.
Bordeaux •
Garonne R.
Toulouse •
Marseilles •

Corsica
Sardinia

Balearic Is.

Mediterranean Sea

English Channel
Beachy Head
Dover •

SCOTLAND
Edinburgh •

KINGDOM OF GREAT BRITAIN

ENGLAND
Liverpool •
London •
Bristol •

IRELAND
Dublin •
Cork •

Bay of Biscay

Cape Finisterre

ATLANTIC OCEAN

Ebro R.
SPAIN
Duero R.
Madrid •
Tagus R.
Guadiana R.
Seville •
Guadalquivir R.
Cadiz •
Granada •
Gibraltar •

PORTUGAL
Lisbon •

Cape St. Vincent
Cape Trafalgar

Boundary of the Holy Roman Empire

Austria and its Danubian Empire

0   150   300 Miles

0   150   300 Kilometers

Europe in 1715

Chronology 15: The Eighteenth Century

1701	*Frederick I makes Prussia a kingdom*
1707	*Queen Anne unifies England and Scotland, forming Britain*
1713–1740	*Frederick William I builds Prussian army*
1720s–1740s	*Walpole and Fleury foster peace and economic development for England and France*
1721–1742	*Walpole develops prime minister's office and cabinet system in Britain*
1715–1774	*Louis XV lets social problems multiply in France*
1740–1780	*Maria Theresa defends and reforms Austrian Empire*
1740–1786	*Frederick II the Great expands and reforms Prussia*
1740–1748	*War of the Austrian Succession—Frederick the Great wins Silesia from Maria Theresa*
1756–1763	*Seven Years War—Pitt leads British to victory over French, winning Canada and assuring dominance in India*
1768–1774	*Catherine II the Great defeats Turkey, expands Russian frontiers to Black Sea*
1771	*First partition of Polish territory among Russia, Prussia, Austria*
1793, 1795	*Second and third partitions of Poland divide the entire nation up among the three great powers*

ernment, Austria and its new Danubian empire, the rising power of Prussia, and the Russia Peter the Great had built. In each case, the section will outline the national resources upon which the nations could draw, indicate their weaknesses, and point out the main issues that divided them against each other.

France and the Legacy of Louis XIV

An English visitor describing the city of Paris at the beginning of the eighteenth century hailed it for its tree–lined streets, its "infinite Number" of coaches and carriages, its elegant fashions, eloquent academies, and many learned women ("there are some of 'em who write and make Books").[1] Perhaps most striking of all, however, were the amazing street lamps of the French capital:

> The Invention of illuminating *Paris* during the Night–time, by an infinite number of Lamps, should invite the most distant Nations to come and see. . . . The lights enclosed in Lanthorns of glass, hung in the Air . . . shine the whole Night [and are] of mighty benefit to all People.[2]

The greatest of all the Western great powers in the eighteenth century—the United States of the age—was France. Heir to the European predominance of Louis XIV, France enjoyed some unrivaled advantages. Endowed with an excellent balance of agriculture, industry, and commerce and with the largest population of any Western country, the French had developed a powerful central government, Europe's largest army and second–largest navy, and a far–reaching overseas empire, stretching from India to Canada. Even the later Bourbons, pleasure–loving Louis XV and the ineffectual Louis XVI, could not entirely dissipate such strengths.

Louis XV (r. 1715–1774), great–grandson and heir of Louis XIV, reigned for sixty years but seldom actually ruled at all. Indolent, unable to stick to a firm policy line, and addicted to every form of courtly pleasure, he inherited all of Louis XIV's sociability but none of his dedication to the hard work of governance. He had one great minister of state, Cardinal Fleury, and a number of beautiful and powerful royal mistresses, including Madame de Pompadour and Madame du Barry. Enmeshed in the intrigues of his mistresses, favorites, and courtiers, Louis proved hopelessly inadequate to all challenges.

The aged cardinal André Fleury (1653–1743) dominated policy for almost twenty years, from 1726 to 1743. By encouraging new industries, building roads and bridges, attempting to stabilize royal revenues and to keep the country out of war, Fleury gave France a period of peace and prosperity during the first half of Louis XV's reign. From the 1740s to the 1760s, the most powerful personality in the realm was the king's mistress, Madame de Pompadour (1721–1764). Remembered today for the upswept hairdo still called by her name, Pompadour was actually as intelligent as she was beautiful, a discriminating patron of the arts and an influential shaper of French policy.

Throughout his reign, Louis XV was beset by the efforts of a resurgent nobility to recover some of the independent power of which Cardinal Richelieu and Louis XIV had stripped them in the preceding century. The main instruments of the aristocracy were the

Madame de Pompadour, royal mistress and one of the most powerful women at Louis XV's court, looks relaxed and confident in this portrait by François Boucher. Her political influence, her views on foreign policy, her taste and openness to new ideas all helped shape the reign. [François Boucher. *Madame de Pompadour.* Reproduced by permission of the Trustees of the Wallace Collection.]

parlements, the prestigious law courts of Paris and the provinces. Staffed by the nobility of the robe, the titled families who provided the state with its judges, generation after generation, the parlements had the ancient right to rule on the constitutionality of royal decrees. Louis XV's failure to dominate or even abolish the parlements opened the way to the Revolution of 1789 under his unfortunate successor, Louis XVI.

Britain and the First Prime Minister

In the eighteenth century, Britain was just entering its period of global greatness. A leading builder of overseas empire since the 1600s, Great Britain had the largest navy and merchant fleets. A leader in both the agricultural and industrial revolutions of the 1700s, Britain became Europe's wealthiest state. Ruled by a foreign dynasty for most of the eighteenth century—Georges I, II, and III of the German house of Hanover—Britain remained Europe's most important constitutional monarchy.

After the passing of William and Mary, who had come to power in the Glorious Revolution of 1688 and who agreed to share power with the ruling class through Parliament, England was ruled by the last Stuart monarch, Queen Anne (r. 1702–1714). Anne signed the *Act of Union* in 1707, binding England and Scotland into one nation, modern Britain. When all her children predeceased her, the British crown passed to her cousin George, elector of Hanover and founder of Britain's Hanoverian dynasty, whose descendants have reigned there ever since.

Both George I (r. 1714–1727) and George II (r. 1727–1760) were Germans born and bred, neither deeply versed in nor centrally concerned with British affairs. Both therefore left much of the political power in the hands of Robert Walpole (1676–1745), England's first prime minister and architect of the *cabinet system* of parliamentary government that has prevailed ever since.

The English *Parliament,* like the estates generals, diets, and other assemblies on the continent, was more a convention of the ruling classes than a democratic body representing the population as a whole. Titled aristocrats and leaders of the Anglican church met in the House of Lords; country gentry, lawyers and businessmen in the elected House of Commons. During the revolutionary seventeenth century, the House of Commons had compelled England's kings to recognize its rights to free elections, freedom of debate, and control of government revenues. The Whig and Tory factions, corresponding very roughly to later Liberal and Conservative parties, had emerged in the later 1600s. It was thus an organized and powerful body that Robert Walpole came to dominate in the 1720s.

A Norfolk country squire with long experience in Parliament, Walpole was the recognized leader of the Whig party. He served as chief minister to George I and George II for more than twenty years, from 1721 to 1742, a period corresponding to Fleury's tenure of power in France. Like his French counterpart, Walpole favored peace and economic growth and opposed foreign military adventures. His major historical achievement, however, was to establish a pattern of rule by leading members of one political party through a "cabinet" of royal ministers headed by a *prime minister,* or "first" minister of state.

Walpole depended for his authority on a combination of royal favor and ruthless manipulation of patronage, using political appointments, government contracts, and other rewards to keep Whigs in line and Tories out of power. The Whig party he led was unified less by allegiance to common political principles than by family ties, political alliances, and "special interests" concerned with agricultural prices, foreign trade, overseas plantations, and the like. Nevertheless, Walpole's long and successful tenure of office established a tradition of political authority in the hands of prime ministers representing one party and ruling through a disciplined cabinet.

Austria's New Empire

Vienna, filled with baroque palaces and churches, elegant townhouses, opera houses, coffeehouses, and wonderful pastry shops, was one of the loveliest capitals in Europe in the eighteenth century. Yet the serene beauty of Vienna cloaked a fundamental weakness. Despite their intermittent efforts in earlier centuries, the Holy Roman emperors had failed to convert their exalted title into real power. They exercised only a shadowy ceremonial authority over the more than three hundred independent secular and ecclesiastical principalities, free cities, and individual knights of the empire.

In the decades around 1700, however, the Habsburg rulers assembled a new domain for themselves outside German–speaking central Europe. This *Danubian Empire,* so called because its east–west axis was the broad Danube River valley, was a multinational realm centering on the Habsburg territory of Austria. It included Bohemia (later Czechoslovakia), Hungary, and portions of northern Italy. In these areas, the Austrian rulers set out to establish the real power that had eluded them in the Germanies. They suppressed two major rebellions in the first half of the eighteenth century, one in Hungary (1703–1711), the other in Bohemia (1740–1741). They encouraged Germans to settle on confiscated land in their new realms and imposed centralized bureaucratic government staffed by German–speaking officials.

Besides the national diversity of his subjects, Emperor Charles VI (r. 1711–1740) had no male heir to inherit this diverse collection of lands and peoples. He therefore spent much of his reign trying to win consent from both foreign powers and subject peoples for his highly competent, religiously devout, and dedicated daughter, Maria Theresa (r. 1740–1780), to inherit his throne. The Pragmatic Sanction of 1713 granted the formal consent he sought. But, as we will see, Charles was scarcely in his grave before his heiress was under assault by enemies eager to dismember the territories of one of Europe's oldest dynasties.

The Rise of Prussia

Perhaps the most dynamic of all the powers was the emerging north German state of Prussia under the Hohenzollern dynasty. Challenging Habsburg Austria for primacy among the German states, the Prussia of Frederick the Great was also paving the way for the unification of Germany and for its emergence as the greatest power in Europe a hundred years later.

The Hohenzollerns of the eighteenth century were the heirs of the state–building efforts of their seventeenth–century precursor, Frederick William, known to history as the Great Elector (r. 1640–1688). Beginning with a scattering of noncontiguous Hohenzollern lands scattered across northern Germany, the Great Elector had taken major steps toward uniting these areas territorially by acquiring the principalities in between. By military force and administrative reorganization, he also strove to impose a single unified government on them all, in the teeth of local traditions of independence. To accomplish these dynastic goals, Frederick William forged a strong alliance between the crown and the

Junker aristocrats who staffed his exemplary civil service and served as officers in his well–trained, well–equipped army.

Frederick William's successors, Frederick I (r. 1688–1713) and Frederick William I (r. 1713–1740), added the new title of "king," transformed the provincial Hohenzollern city of Berlin into a royal capital, further disciplined their officials, and doubled the size of their army. Frederick William I, famous for his grenadier guards regiment composed entirely of strapping soldiers over six feet tall, actually avoided wars, at least in part to spare his famous army.

Frederick II the Great (r. 1740–1786) thus inherited a royal title and budding culture on the one hand, an efficient bureaucracy and an army of eighty thousand well–trained fighting men on the other. As we will see in a later section, he would prove to be both more cultured and a greater military leader than any of his predecessors.

Russia: The Heritage of Peter the Great

The largest and most backward of the powers in the eighteenth century was Romanov Russia. Peter I the Great (r. 1682–1725) had thrust his country into the front ranks at the turn of the century.

Peter had transformed his vast medieval land. He had brought the Orthodox church and the *boyar* nobility into the service of the state, imported industrial crafts and foreign experts from western Europe, and forged an army that made Russia the greatest power in eastern Europe. His heavy hand on noble and serf alike and his contempt for old Russian ways, however, alienated many Russians. Between his death in 1725 and the accession of the equally powerful Catherine the Great in 1762, Russia in large measure marked time.

Politically, Russia in the mid–century decades was tormented by the tyranny of royal favorites, by noble intrigues, and by palace coups. Many of Peter's reforms were rejected, and even his new capital of St. Petersburg was temporarily abandoned. The economy stagnated while the new industries introduced from western Europe faltered and the local power of the boyars and their oppression of the serf majority increased.

There was some recovery under Peter the Great's popular daughter Elizabeth (r. 1741–1762), when the Petrine *service nobility,* ennobled for service to the state, regained lost ground. The next real step toward building Russian greatness, however, would, ironically, be taken by a German princess steeped in the French Enlightenment—Catherine II the Great (r. 1762–1796). The combined efforts of Peter I and Catherine II would produce a Russia as aggressive, pushy, and potentially powerful as Prussia was.

♦ The Power Structure ♦

Despite the real differences indicated above, the great powers and many smaller states of Europe in the 1700s did share some basic structural similarities. This section will look more deeply into the power structure of the Western nations in the eighteenth century. Such a survey must begin with the royal governments of Europe's great monarchies, many of them claiming the absolute power achieved by Louis XIV and his fellow rulers in the preceding century. This section will also look at surviving centers of resistance to royal authority—and at other institutions which joined the monarchies in an interlocking directorate of power.

The Royal Center

The eighteenth century was the last great age of kings and queens, when the dynasts who had built the modern national states still enjoyed unquestioned supremacy. Indeed, most Europeans were simply incapable of imagining a political order that was not built around a royal center.

The heads of all the great powers and many lesser states were hereditary, divine–right monarchs, many of them claiming absolute power over their peoples. Royal authority was in practice limited often by the traditional autonomies and privileges of Europe's nobility and churches, towns and provinces, to be discussed below. Sometimes monarchical power was also constrained by constitutional guarantees like those prevailing in Britain. But most attempted to emulate the French model established by Louis XIV. They insisted not only on their medieval right to rule through heredity and divine sanction, but also on the absolute sovereignty wielded by the Sun King.

The medieval political theories that supported royal government were still widely accepted in the eighteenth century. Royal claims to rule by divine right, still preached from pulpits across Europe, undergirded the power of kings and queens. Crowned in cathedrals, anointed with holy oil, monarchs could point to warrant for the power of princes in the Scripture. Like their predecessors, they claimed to be God's viceroys on earth, and masses of eighteenth–century peasants still believed them.

More sophisticated subjects saw strong monarchical government as essential to the very survival of organized Western society. The most widely recognized centers of authority, monarchs were believed to be the only guarantee of public order and domestic tranquillity. Related by marriage, by traditional dynastic alliances and enmities, Europe's "cousinhood of kings" also organized international relations on a relatively predictable, if not always peaceful, basis. The power of the royal center was symbolized, and sold to the people, by the magnificent style of life that Europe's crowned heads enjoyed. Louis XIV's seventeenth–century legacy, the immense palace of Versailles, housed ten thousand and provided a stately setting for the pomp and pageantry of royalty. Peter the Great's new eighteenth–century capital city, St. Petersburg, incarnated both his will to power and his determination that Russia should turn westward to play a leading part in European affairs. Royal palaces were consciously constructed, in the words of Louis XIV's chief minister Colbert, to "compel the people to look on them with awe."[3]

Ministers and Servants of the State

To translate these claims into realities, rulers depended on powerful royal ministers of state and on steadily expanding royal bureaucracies.

Chief ministers of state were appointed by the monarchs they served, and continued to serve only as long as they enjoyed the confidence of their sovereigns. Some were gifted commoners like Britain's great midcentury war minister, William Pitt (1708–1778); others, like Austria's brilliant foreign minister Count Wenzel von Kaunitz (1711–1794), were titled noblemen; and at least one, France's Cardinal Fleury, was a churchman in the service of the state. All, however, depended on royal patronage for their high positions and authority.

The policies formulated by monarchs and their ministers were carried out by growing numbers of officials, the bureaucrats whose increasing power would be a feature of all modern government. From a handful of clerks in the Middle Ages, European civil servants had become both more numerous and more professionalized in early modern times. Trained in law, languages, or finances, building lifelong careers in the service of the state, bureaucrats were increasingly specialized in their functions. They brought system, routine, and more efficient organization to the governments of the Western nations.

The most impressive bureaucracies did not approach those of later centuries in size: there were regiments, but not yet armies, of civil servants. Personal ambition, corruption, and inefficiency could and did infect governments as they did other human institutions. By and large, however, the eighteenth century European bureaucracy at its best was probably the most effective to be found anywhere in the world.

Centers of Resistance to Royal Power

The underlying conflict of eighteenth–century political and constitutional history was the ongoing struggle between the royal center and the rest of the country, between growing state power and traditional local claimants to rights and privileges. Medieval and earlier modern monarchs had slowly gained control over the feudal nobility, the church, the towns, independent provinces, and other rival centers of power. Nobles and churchmen, towns and provinces nevertheless retained a strong sense of their traditional rights and privileges and remained alert to royal weakness which might allow them to assert those rights once more.

The churches in the eighteenth century were not famed for piety. Fox–hunting parsons who liked their pint of ale and bishops who made their reputations as church administrators or salon wits displayed little of the spirituality of a St. Francis or a Martin Luther. Still, the common people often loved their priests and pastors, and the wealth of the churches still gave them considerable clout.

Europe's hereditary aristocrats now made their careers in the service of their princes. But they also held a virtual monopoly of the highest positions in government, the church, the diplomatic corps, and the military. In the German and Italian states, independent princes and nobles were virtually independent rulers, and almost everywhere, the landowning elite still dominated the lives of the peasant majority.

In the cities, merchants and bankers, guild masters and professional people—especially lawyers—loomed large. In the older urbanized areas of Italy, the Netherlands, the Rhineland, France, and Britain, business families served as mayors and magistrates, members of boards of aldermen and town councils. Here again, despite the intrusion of royal authority, local power structures still held considerable sway.

Everywhere, provincial assemblies, judicial systems, and law codes embodied a sense of regional autonomy, and local authorities sought to defend the customs of the country against royal officials and decrees. In many European countries, such bodies as estates general, diets, or the British Parliament resisted royal power. In Britain, as we have seen, government had in fact become a partnership between crown and Parliament.

The resulting power structure of the old regime was a delicate balance of tensions and mutual support involving a range of recognized elites and powerful institutions. For most of the century, the ruling orders of society managed to work together in uneasy harmony. At the end of it, the tensions that had been building beneath the surface exploded in a series of revolutionary upheavals centered on the French Revolution of 1789.

✦Classes and Communities✦

No trip to Europe is complete without a few visits to stately homes and royal palaces, and some of the most stately and palatial were built in the eighteenth century. The homes of the wealthy were full of gilt and velvet, portraits and chandeliers and canopied four–poster beds. The houses of ordinary people were much simpler, furnished with crude benches, stools, and shelves with a bit of crockery, and equipped with tools—a spinning wheel, a plow and harness in the shed.

The pages that follow will anatomize the differences between the aristocracy and the bourgeoisie, the peasantry and the urban poor. But they will also survey Europe's *communities,* the ties that bound Europe's villages and preindustrial cities in a web of common values and mutual needs.

Aristocracy and Bourgeoisie

At the glittering apex of the social pyramid stood the hereditary aristocracy. Resplendent in powdered wigs and elaborate coiffures, in knee breeches and buckled shoes or flowing gowns and glittering jewels, they were the cynosures of all eyes—and the targets of many resentments.

About 3 percent of the population qualified as aristocrats, but there were many differences among these leading citizens. The cultivated French seigneur, the stiff–necked Prussian Junker, the haughty Spanish don, and the wild Russian boyar had little in common but their status at the top of their respective societies. In Spain and in eastern Europe particularly, many nobles actually lived like peasants, without land, servants, or even decent coats on their backs, yet clung to the pride and pretensions of their caste. The more affluent of the nobility owned wide–lawned mansions in the country and sometimes tall townhouses on fashionable squares in the capital, with the clothes, carriages, servants, and manners that befit a ruling class. A few were great magnates: several dozen south Italian aristocratic families, for instance, owned lands and villages inhabited by ten thousand or more peasants.

The roots of this aristocratic predominance lay in the land. Most aristocrats held large tracts of it, and many seldom left it at all. Backcountry British gentry were often content to stay on their estates year round, farming, hunting, and depending on rustic fairs and country–house parties for entertainment. Others used their lands primarily as sources of revenue, disbursing their rents lavishly in Paris, Vienna, St. Petersburg, and other royal capitals. The lives of city and court nobility were full of balls and banquets, theater, opera, and ballet, as well as gambling, drinking, amorous intrigues, and other pastimes. Some sought new thrills in bizarre directions. The notorious marquis de Sade (1740–1814) explored disturbing byways of sexual exploitation and physical torment, and produced some even more shocking books. At the opposite extreme, Queen Marie Antoinette (1755–1793) had a peasant village built on the grounds of the palace of Versailles where she and her ladies-in-waiting could dress up as milkmaids and try to recapture the innocence of an idealized country life. Such were the varieties of the "sweet life" that the aging diplomat Talleyrand remembered with a sigh when the *ancien régime* had passed into history. The marquis de Sade ended his days in a madhouse; the queen ended hers under the blade of the guillotine.

Ranked just below the aristocracy, the middle class, or bourgeoisie, had become increasingly complex over the centuries since its emergence during the Middle Ages. We might distinguish, for example, between the commercial, financial, and handicraft–industrial middle classes on the one hand and the bureaucratic and professional middle classes on the other. The former type was considerably more common in western Europe and in parts of central Europe, the latter in much of central and eastern Europe. Among the commercial-financial-artisan middle classes, the most eminent were the established merchant families of the older cities of northern Italy and the Netherlands, the Swiss cantons, and western and northern Germany. As the hereditary elite of cities as old as the oldest noble families, this urban patriciate of merchant princes wielded unchallenged power in these centers of productivity and wealth. Dominating the economic and political life of their towns, they were as proud and lived as sumptuously as all but the highest hereditary aristocrats. Other groups of traders who waxed wealthy and confident in the eighteenth century were the leading business houses of booming port cities like Bristol and Liverpool, Bordeaux and Marseilles, Hamburg in Germany, and Leghorn in northern Italy.

The cream of these economic middle classes were the wealthy import–export merchants, the great banking houses and insurance brokers, and the middlemen who handled finances for the crown, the aristocracy, and the church. Less wealthy but still thoroughly respectable were local traders and the guild masters who supervised the handcrafting and sale of goods in their own shops. In an increasingly prosperous Europe, there was also a clearly distinguishable class of *rentiers*, those who lived without working at all by investing their capital in the productive labor of others.

Less familiar, perhaps, were the middle–class groups who had little direct connection with manufacturing and trade. These included doctors and lawyers, government officials at all levels, and most of the recognized intellectuals of the age, from scholars to distinguished writers and even some artists. Perhaps the most important of these were the growing numbers of officials, local, provincial, and national. The German states in particular were already producing vast numbers of meticulously trained and efficient civil servants. In eastern Europe, the typical bourgeois citizen was not a merchant at all, but a state servant.

Europe's middle classes had their own styles of life, their own values and social outlook. These qualities included precision, respect for contracts and law codes, social and moral respectability, frugality, thrift, and shrewd practicality. Their lifestyles, however splendid, were infused with a strong awareness of the value of money. Wealthy bankers and merchant princes were always alert to costs and value-for-money—"tradesman's" attitudes sneered at by the casually free–spending nobility.

Indeed, even the wealthiest cloth manufacturer or the head of the oldest firm of merchant bankers could feel some resentment over the social prestige and special privileges accorded to the aristocracy. Many, comparing their own productive work and respectable lives with the parasitical and often libertine lives of the aristocracy, saw serious flaws in their eighteenth–century world.

Urban Workers and Peasants

Many working people were journeymen and apprentices, lower–ranking members of the medieval guilds that still performed many of the skilled crafts on which society depended before the coming of the machine age. Others were manual laborers, vendors and peddlers, and servants of various sorts. At the very bottom were beggars, prostitutes, thieves, con artists, and criminals, as well as large numbers of unemployed slum dwellers, never far above the hunger line.

Bakers are shown at work in this copper engraving. The dough is kneaded, shaped into loaves of various shapes, baked in the large oven in back and displayed for customers out front. (Bettmann.)

The guilds were still run by the masters, as in medieval times. Guilds still excluded competition, regulated training and marketing, and kept up quality as they had for centuries. In big commercial cities like Paris and London, guilds could inhibit progress by stifling innovation and throttling vigorous competition. A system designed to provide security in the troubled Middle Ages was increasingly out of phase in the expanding economy and changing technology of the eighteenth century.

Urban workers often felt even more oppressed and exploited than peasants did. The wages or piecework rates on which laborers depended were generally controlled by guild masters, municipal authorities, or merchants. Journeymen were frequently prevented from becoming masters by exorbitant fees or the limitation of masterships to the relatives of current masters. They might fight back by doing illegal piecework in their garrets, by organizing illegal journeymen's associations, or even by resorting to work stoppages in hopes of better treatment. In the long run, however, city workers had no more chance against their middle–class masters than peasants did against the landed aristocracy.

Three–quarters, four–fifths, and even larger proportions of the populations of most European states were, as they had always been, peasants, laboring on the land. Agricultural labor by most humans was still necessary to support the higher culture for their social superiors in the eighteenth century. Conditions of life and labor did differ from one part of Europe to another, however, becoming increasingly harsh as one moved from the economically developed west to the less developed east.

In western Europe—England, France, the Low Countries, western Germany, northern Italy, and Spain—most of these peasant populations were small independent landowners, tenant farmers, or hired agricultural laborers. Peasant laborers worked for low wages in the fields of large landholders or helped peasant proprietors who owned small farms themselves. Farm tenants lived on the landlords' estates, paid rent in cash or kind, or share-cropped for a percentage of the produce. Even peasants who owned their own land often owed fees or charges to the local magnate and were still subject to the legal jurisdiction of baronial law courts, as in medieval times. They also had to accept such traditional aristocratic privileges as the lord's exclusive right to hunt for meat animals, and their own ancient serf obligation to perform the compulsory work, called corvée labor, on local roads, bridges, and other facilities.

In central and eastern Europe, most of the peasantry were still serfs in the eighteenth century. In the Habsburg lands and Prussia, in Russia, Poland, and elsewhere east of the Elbe, the crown, the church, and the aristocracy still owned most of the land, while the peasantry were bound to their villages and to labor for their overlords. Like medieval peasants, they worked half the week on the lord's fields and owed him payments in cash or in the produce of their own plots. In Russia, where serfdom reached its height in the eighteenth century, many peasants were closer to chattel slaves than serfs. They were called *souls,* dependent populations whom the lord could sell, give away, or lose at cards. Russian peasants faced such grim possibilities as assignment to the mines, lifetime conscription into the army, and the omnipresent knout, the wire and leather–thonged whip used to discipline troublesome serfs.

Women, Work, and the Family

In the eighteenth century, almost all women, like almost all men, worked very, very hard for most of their lives. The work lives of both men and women, however, were closely integrated into the life of the family.

A key factor in the changing status of women's work was the emergence of *wage labor* as the standard in an evolving capitalist economy. Medieval guild shops and farms—the family firm and the family farm—had rewarded members by shares in the food, clothing, and housing they all produced. Then came early modern merchant capitalists, operating on a money basis, buying raw materials and hiring labor. Women, however—the peasant's or guild master's wife and daughters—still worked as in the old days, unsalaried. Since work was increasingly defined as labor for which one was paid, women's work was devalued, redefined as not "real work" at all.

Meanwhile, the work actually done by women also changed. Where medieval guilds had included some women, early modern guilds refused women membership. While medieval journeymen had often worked alongside the master's wife and daughters, male workers now demanded an end to female participation in production. Fear of female competition—for customers or jobs—was an important motive for this relegation of women to domestic chores. But theories about women's "limitations"—their alleged irrationality, weakness, and "natural" place in the home—provided the rationale.

Women's work outside the domestic sphere of course continued nonetheless, in the fields and in the cities. In the latter area particularly, however, women were increasingly limited to spinning thread for cloth, selling food or secondhand items bought from the poor, and working in service industries, from health care, including midwifery, to laundries.

At all levels of society, the family in preindustrial Europe was both the institution that shaped the lives of its members in crucial ways and the building block of society itself. The twentieth–century model of a society composed of separate, competitive individuals living alone or in public institutions intended for particular groups, from school to retirement home, was almost nonexistent in the eighteenth century. Instead, the individual lived and functioned socially as part of a family—indeed the individual could scarcely survive outside of the family group.

The structure of the European family varied significantly across the continent. In western and central Europe, the nuclear family—parents and children, totaling five or six people—was almost universal. In eastern Europe, by contrast, serf households often followed the pattern of the extended family, with three or more generations and even the families of several brothers living together. Older relatives normally chose promising spouses for young people, usually on such practical bases as physical strength, work skills, wealth, or family connections.

At all social levels, the family remained the basic social institution. At the top of society, royal dynasties and aristocratic family connections guided the political lives of the nations. Among the vast majority, the close fellow–work of the integrated family was quite simply essential for survival.

In the peasant household, husbands did the plowing and sometimes worked as weavers or carpenters as well. Peasant wives presided over the household, earned extra cash by selling eggs or produce from the vegetable garden, and fed and clothed the family. Wives often joined their husbands in the harvesting, while peasant children watered animals, carried food to parents in the fields, and learned basic tasks themselves.

Among urban artisans, husbands were normally the master craftsmen, while wives kept the books, sold the goods in the shop out front, and often prepared materials for their husbands to finish. Children, again, fetched and carried, cleaned, and performed other simple chores.

The households of the middle and upper reaches of society could be large and splendid establishments, with many servants and hangers-on. Valets and chambermaids, secretaries and tutors, butlers, footmen, cooks, grooms, and gardeners—all had their places in the elaborate hierarchy of the great estate or the urban mansion. And though the social distance between master and servant remained great, all shared a community of interest that made the great family, too, a living organism and an essential part of the larger society.

The Village and the Preindustrial City

Beyond the level of the family, the next largest communities were the village and the city. As we will see, however, these were not the leafy suburban villages of later centuries, nor were the cities the vast concrete hives thrown up by the coming industrial revolution.

As they had for ten thousand years, most human beings ate the grain they grew, dressed themselves in woven fibers from the backs of their own sheep, and built houses of local stone, clay, wood, and thatching. Most peasants lived together in central or "nucleated" villages, with the fields stretching around them. Most peasants, unfortunately, possessed too little land to support their families without renting or sharecropping, borrowing, or undertaking additional paid labor.

The villagers assembled en masse to discuss and decide when to plow, plant, and harvest, and other matters of common concern. Some peasants were more prosperous and hence more influential than others. By accumulating land, lending seed grain and renting draft animals to their fellows, these rich peasants became a sort of rural middle class, sometimes more dominant in the community than the seigneur.

Private morality was also often regulated by the villagers acting as a group in defense of traditional values. Peasants might stage a *charivari,* a derisive and sometimes terrifying midnight serenade, to publicly humiliate the husband who beat his wife—or let her dominate the family. By and large, they were a very conservative lot. Peasants might resent the tithes, fees, dues, and rents that they still paid the priest and the landed magnate, yet they often respected the village priest or pastor and still habitually removed their hats or pulled a forelock when the squire rode by.

There were peasant revolts somewhere in Europe almost every year, but most of these were directed against what were perceived as specific local abuses rather than against the system as a whole. The village, the church, and the landlord's stately home remained a genuine rural community.

Even before the Industrial Revolution, cities were many times larger than agricultural villages, and infinitely more complex. And they too were communities in the broadest sense of the term.

By 1800, there were perhaps twenty European cities with populations of over one hundred thousand. Paris had more than half a million people, and London probably a million. Even the largest of these urban complexes were likely to have medieval cores, warrens of small shops and slum tenements pressing close along unpaved streets, noisy and jostling by day, unlit and haunted by thieves and prostitutes by night. But now there were magnificent modern squares as well, lined with the tall Renaissance houses of merchants, baroque palaces and churches, government buildings, banks and stock exchanges.

Urban guilds often provided the setting for celebrations and fellowship, vocational training, and care for widows and orphans. Taverns were the focus of neighborhood life for the poor, as coffeehouses were meeting places for the bourgeoisie and the elegant salon was for the aristocracy.

A traditional morality flourished among the urban laboring masses as it did among the peasantry. A *bread riot* might punish an extortionate baker—and redistribute the confiscated food at what the mob deemed a fair price. Mob violence also expressed popular prejudices against Protestants in Catholic countries, or against Catholics in Protestant ones.

As in the rural environment, finally, the upper and lower classes existed in a sort of symbiosis. The moneyed classes created a lucrative market for the services of craft workers, merchants of food and wine, wet nurses, and the "link boys" who lit the respectable citizens through the streets at night with torches. The whole grimy anthill swarming with humanity was actually a nexus of communities and, in the largest sense, a vast community itself. For most of the eighteenth century, these ties of community outweighed the differences between subcultures and classes, and the city continued to flourish, verminous, raucous, and dynamic, at the center of the old regime.

The Jewish Community: Persecution and Assimilation

By the eighteenth century, there was not one but a collection of Jewish communities scattered across the continent. Descendants of the Jews of the ancient Roman diaspora, the Jews of the Western world practiced a different religion and cultivated a different culture from those of the Christian majority. Persecuted in ancient and medieval times, Jews were traditionally outsiders who nevertheless often flourished in Western society. This period saw the beginning of one of the greatest ages of Jewish history—and of the first major effort to integrate the Jews into mainstream Western culture.

The Jewish communities of early modern times were close–knit, built around the family and the synagogue. Jewish culture encouraged education and industry, traits with survival value for them and of general value to the larger society. Jews governed themselves, organized their own guilds, developed hereditary crafts, and regulated their own social and economic affairs. Jewish rabbis pored over the Torah, the five books of Moses that also formed the beginning of the Christian Old Testament, and the Talmud, the vast body of law, commentary, and tradition on which orthodox Judaism was built.

Typically, these enclaves of minority culture in a still strongly Christian West were confined to *ghettos,* the Jewish sections of European cities. Sometimes *pogroms,* murderous anti–semitic riots, exploded in the ghettos or in Jewish villages in the countryside. More often, however, Jewish and Christian communities lived in uneasy or even friendly coexistence. Jews constituted a generally law–abiding and productive, if separate, segment of Western society.

In the later Middle Ages, as we have seen, the Jews had been largely expelled from western Europe by a series of brutal persecutions. Some settled in the German cities of central Europe. Many found new homes in eastern Europe, particularly in Poland. When Poland was partitioned in the later eighteenth century, most Polish Jews became subjects of the Russian Empire.

By that time, however, the Jewish diaspora across Europe had reversed its direction, from an eastward drift into sparsely settled Slavic lands to a westward migration back into lands from which they had once been expelled, where booming centers of capitalist economic development now had need of their talents. Jewish communities grew in London, Paris, and Amsterdam, in German cities like Hamburg, and in northern Italian cities from Venice to Florence.

In many places, the Jewish people prospered in the eighteenth century. Many were artisans or small traders, but some rose to great wealth. They helped develop trade in the Mediterranean and were involved in the East India Companies of the North Atlantic powers, Britain, France, and the Netherlands. So-called "court Jews", Jews who served German princes in particular, helped to rationalize government administration, to establish central control over formerly independent territories, and to supply luxury goods for princely courts and provisions for princely armies.

In general, the eighteenth century saw Jews tolerated, their rights recognized in the relatively liberal Netherlands and Britain. In continental absolute monarchies, however, Jews were pressured to abandon their traditional culture and accept absorption into the modern state. Governments in Poland and elsewhere abolished independent Jewish councils and other institutions. At the same time, relatively enlightened and tolerant western European aristocrats welcomed wealthy and educated Jews into the cultural life of the Western world's increasingly cosmopolitan elite.

A drift toward assimilation thus emerged as early as the 1700s. Jews in many places began to speak the language of the nation in which they lived. Intermarriage between Jews and Christians became more common. A Jewish Enlightenment saw some Jewish scholars turning from exclusive absorption in religious texts to secular studies and applying the same rationalistic principles to Judaism that other philosophers were applying to Christianity. Most Jewish communities in eastern European villages or in the ghettos of European cities were not yet affected by this trend. Some, confronted with pressure for assimilation, reacted with a vigorous reassertion of Jewish traditions. Thus, the fundamentalist Hasidic movement emphasized emotional forms of worship linking this world with a higher spiritual realm through passionate prayer. But in central and western Europe, Jewish business leaders, court Jews, and Jewish intellectuals were already playing important parts in the shaping of Western society as a whole.

♦ Wars and International Relations ♦

The eighteenth–century international scene was dominated by the powerful nations discussed above—the imperial powers Britain and France, the central European rivals Austria and Prussia, and Russia, the emerging giant of eastern Europe. The following pages will first outline the general patterns of international relations that existed in the eighteenth century in terms of the balance of power, imperial rivalries, and the role of diplomacy and military force. We will then turn to the great wars that filled the mid–century decades—the War of the Austrian Succession (1740–1748) and the Seven Years' War (1756–1763)—and to such international crises as the partitions of Poland in the 1770s and 1790s. Dusty names and unfamiliar dates—yet clear examples of the ruthless power which great modern nations were already able to deploy in pursuit of their national interests hundreds of years ago.

States and Empires

On a continent ruled by the cousinhood of kings, dynastic struggles based on the rivalries of the great European ruling houses were still causes of conflict in the eighteenth century. Territorial claims, inherited or acquired through royal marriages, and conflicting commercial and imperial interests overseas were thus often causes of international wars. These aggressive policies were summed up by the French phrase *raison d'état—reason of state*. In that hard-nosed age, as Frederick the Great put it, "the fundamental rule of governments is the principle of extending their territories."[4] The powerful took what they could get, the weak went to the wall, and self–aggrandizement was the one motive that everybody understood.

To impose any sort of order on this international anarchy, major alignments of force were necessary. Such alignments included shifting international alliances and conscious attempts to maintain the balance of power between the nation–states of early modern Europe.

Alliances were a traditional device for attaining diplomatic ends. They usually had specific objectives and lasted no longer than they served the interests of the nations involved. Such agreements implied no warm friendship between peoples, no similarity of political principles, no goals higher than the winning of wars, the acquisition of territory, or the humbling of a common foe. Nevertheless, treaties of alliance did impose a modicum of order on the chaos of a world of mutually suspicious, self–aggrandizing states.

Another way of limiting the potential for mutual destruction inherent in a world of sovereign states was the *balance of power*. This diplomatic ploy went back to the city–states of Renaissance Italy and had flourished ever since among the nation–states north of the Alps. The primary objective of power–balance politics was to restrain aggressive states by confronting them with an alliance strong enough to discourage aggression. Sometimes several European powers would combine to restrain a single superstate—like Louis XIV's France—that was threatening them all. Sometimes, two large rival alliance systems would confront each other, often in arms. Balance-of-power diplomacy was also used to compensate one major power for another's gains, thus maintaining the balance between them.

In the 1700s, a number of Western nations also held large empires beyond the seas. These also provided grounds for international conflict.

Of the two older Iberian empires, Spain held most of South and Central America, Mexico, and much of the Caribbean, as well as what are today California, Texas, Florida, and the southwestern United States. Portugal retained its coastal enclaves in southern Africa and scattered trading posts in South and East Asia; its largest colony, however, was what is today Brazil. The Dutch, the first of the "interlopers" to challenge the Iberian imperial monopoly in the seventeenth century, were masters of much of the East Indies as well as of Ceylon (Sri Lanka today) and the tip of South Africa.

The most powerful eighteenth–century imperialists, however, were the British and the French, both, like the Dutch, interlopers who had accumulated most of their colonial possessions in the preceding century. In the 1700s, both Britain and France had colonies in North America, the Caribbean, and India. France's thinly settled North American empire centered in eastern Canada, though its explorers had descended the Mississippi to found New Orleans and had laid claim to the entire midwestern region of the future United States. France also had profitable plantation islands in the Caribbean—notably in what is today Haiti—and the trading center of Pondicherry on the coast of India. Great Britain had thirteen populous and thriving colonies down the east coast of North America, from Massachusetts to Georgia. Its Caribbean possessions included Barbados, the Bahamas, and Jamaica; and it had trading posts in India, at Madras and Bombay.

Mercantilism, the paternalistic economic theory that reached its fullest development in the age of royal absolutism, saw overseas colonies as objects of competition and struggle. The goal of mercantilistic policy was a favorable balance of trade and payments in gold and silver—which inevitably meant deficits for competitors. To achieve these ends, colonies were to be part of a closed economic system, providing natural resources and agricultural products for the mother country and serving as a market for its manufactured goods. Rival imperial powers were to be excluded from the system by an elaborate structure of protective tariffs, trade monopolies, shipping laws, and coast guards patrolling colonial waters.

In the colonial competition of the eighteenth century, the oldest imperial powers, Spain and Portugal, no longer expanding, were content to hang onto what they had, especially their large Latin American colonies. The Dutch had also lost momentum, failing in efforts to establish themselves in both New Netherland (New York) and Brazil, though they continued to profit from their mastery of the Dutch East Indies. Britain and France, the strongest of the European great powers, were thus also the main contestants for overseas empire. In North America, in the islands of the Caribbean, and on the coasts of Mughal India, they made the far places of the earth their battleground.

The War of the Austrian Succession

The history of Europe in the eighteenth century began, ended, and was divided in the middle by major outbreaks of warfare among the great powers. The century began with the last wars of Louis XIV (r. 1643–1715) and ended with the first of the Napoleonic wars (1796–1815). In between, the general conflicts of the 1740s, 1750s, and 1760s both divided Europe and reached to the most distant colonies. These midcentury great–power struggles included the War of the Austrian Succession between Prussia and Austria and the Seven Years' War, which involved both a continuation of the Austro–Prussian conflict and rivalry for colonies between Britain and France. From these struggles, the aggressive Prussia of Frederick the Great and Britain under its great war leader William Pitt emerged with expanded territories and enhanced prestige.

Frederick II the Great (r. 1740–1786), the most famous of Prussia's kings, was in his youth more interested in French poetry and playing the flute than in the Prussian army. Brutally punished for this un–Hohenzollern behavior by his father, Frederick William I, Prince Frederick accepted his royal responsibilities, including the Prussian army, yet always remained fascinated by French culture. Frederick the Great thus became both a leading enlightened monarch and the most celebrated military commander of his age.

His great rival was the ruler of the other great power of German–speaking central Europe, Empress Maria Theresa (r. 1740–1780). An able monarch whose right to the throne had been internationally recognized by the Pragmatic Sanction of 1713, Maria Theresa nevertheless soon found herself surrounded by enemies eager to seize some or all of the Habsburg domains. Her chief antagonist in the resulting *War of the Austrian Succession* (1740–1748), however, was Frederick II.

Soon after both of them had been crowned in 1740, Frederick dredged up a Hohenzollern family claim to the rich Habsburg province of Silesia and mobilized his troops. In the eight-year struggle that followed, other powers lined up on one side or the other as their interests dictated. France, an ancient enemy of the Habsburgs, allied itself with Prussia in hopes of picking up some scraps of territory. France's imperial rival, Britain, whose Hanoverian king feared Prussian aggression against his own home state of Hanover, supported Austria against France and Prussia.

It was in this War of the Austrian Succession that Frederick II first earned his reputation as a military leader of genius. Ignoring the plodding chessboard campaigns and by-the-book battles typical of the age, he made rapid night marches and oblique flank attacks that overwhelmed armies much larger than his own. In the conquest of Silesia, he gained a province rich in iron and coal, textiles, and manpower, an addition that guaranteed Prussia's status as a great power.

Through shrewd political maneuver and diplomacy, however, Maria Theresa and her foreign minister, Wenzel von Kaunitz (1711–1794), emerged from the struggle much more successfully than might have been expected. The empress retained both Hungary and Bohemia, where rebellion still simmered, and gained general recognition of the imperial title. She even maneuvered Frederick II into a separate peace, leaving his allies in the lurch.

The Seven Years' War

The mid–century wars, however, were only half over. The *Seven Years' War* (1756–1763) both continued the Austro–Prussian struggle and pitted Britain against France beyond the seas.

Empress Maria Theresa, a devout Christian, the "mother of her country" and of a dozen children of her own, radiates an appealing innocence. In fact, she was an intelligent and practical ruler who labored indefatigably to strengthen her government and

Legend

- Kingdom of Prussia
- Austria (Habsburg Dominions)
- Holy Roman Empire Boundary
- ★ Battle site

Scale:
0   150   300 Miles
0   150   300 Kilometers

KINGDOM OF GREAT BRITAIN

SCOTLAND — Edinburgh, Berwick, Preston, Marston Moor, Manchester, Naseby

ENGLAND — Liverpool, Nottingham, London, Bristol, Dover, Thames R.

ULSTER — Drogheda, Dublin

IRELAND — Limerick

ATLANTIC OCEAN

RUSSIA — Smolensk, Kiev, Dnieper R., Dniester R.

INGRIA — St. Petersburg, Novgorod, Narva, Pskov

FINLAND — Gulf of Finland

KARELIA

LIVONIA — Riga, Nystadt

COURLAND

LITHUANIA — Vilna

POLAND — Warsaw

SWEDISH EMPIRE — Stockholm

Baltic Sea

NORWAY — Oslo

DENMARK — Copenhagen

SWEDISH POMERANIA

BRANDENBURG — Königsberg, Danzig

HOLY ROMAN EMPIRE

SAXONY, SILESIA, MORAVIA, BOHEMIA — Prague, Blenheim

Berlin, Elbe R., Hamburg, Bremen, Hanover, Kassel, Hesse, West Phalia, Aachen, Rhine R.

AUSTRIA — Vienna, Buda, Pest

BAVARIA — Augsburg, Baden, Würzburg

STYRIA, CARINTHIA, CARNIOLA, TYROL

SWITZERLAND — Geneva

UNITED NETHERLANDS — Utrecht, Nimwegen, Ryswick

AUSTRIAN NETHERLANDS — Ypres, Oudenarde, Brussels, Malplaquet

HUNGARY — Karlowitz, Belgrade, Passarowitz

TRANSYLVANIA — Danube R.

MOLDAVIA, WALLACHIA

BULGARIA — Salonika

MONTENEGRO, Ragusa

OTTOMAN EMPIRE — Constantinople

Black Sea

Aegean Sea

Adriatic Sea

REPUBLIC OF VENICE — Venice

PAPAL STATES — Rome, Tiber R.

TUSCANY — Florence, Leghorn

MILAN, PARMA — Genoa

PIEDMONT, SAVOY — Turin

Corsica (to Genoa; to France, 1768)

Sardinia (to Austria, 1714; to Savoy, 1720)

NAPLES — Naples

Sicily

Mediterranean Sea

FRANCE — Paris, Versailles, Metz, Toul, Blois, Orleans, Nantes, Bordeaux, Lyon, Marseilles, Avignon (to the Papacy), Narbonne, Rouen, Rossbach

ALSACE, LORRAINE, FRANCHE-COMTÉ

Rhône R., Saône R., Garonne R., Seine R.

PYRENEES MTS.

SPAIN — Madrid, Barcelona, Valencia, Seville, Granada, Ebro R., Tagus R., Guadalquivir R.

Minorca (Br.), Balearic Is., Gibraltar (Br.)

PORTUGAL — Lisbon

Europe After the Mid-Century Wars: 1763

army with a view to revenge on Prussia. In the 1750s, her foreign minister Kaunitz set out to build a powerful new alliance against Frederick. The resulting *Diplomatic Revolution* reversed the alliance structure of the 1840s. Britain's King George II, convinced Austria could no longer guarantee his Hanoverian lands, allied himself with Prussia. France's Louis XV, detecting a Prussian sellout to his imperial rival, Britain, responded positively to Kaunitz's proposal of an Austro–French alliance. Kaunitz then completed the Diplomatic Revolution by winning the support of Empress Elizabeth II (r. 1741–1762) of Russia.

The Seven Years' War on the European continent saw Frederick the Great's finest hour as a military commander. Attacked from all sides by Austria, Russia, and France, he darted back and forth across the scattered Hohenzollern lands, repelling first one and then another of his foes. Commanding the most tightly disciplined and rigorously trained of European armies, he could depend on his troops to march farther and faster than their enemies, to stand their ground under the most withering fire, and to load and discharge their own muskets more rapidly and effectively than any other soldiers. Always willing to risk his troops in battle despite the enormously high casualties incurred, Frederick repeatedly defeated the more conservative commanders who opposed him. In the end, Prussia outlasted them all.

Overseas, meanwhile, the Seven Years' War marked a major shift in the imperial balance of power between Britain and France. Britain's prime minister William Pitt (1708–

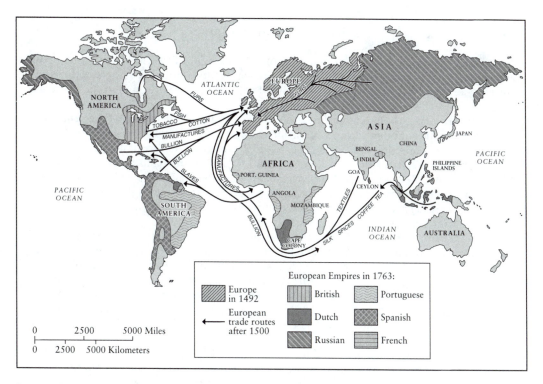

European Empires After the Mid-Century Wars: 1763

1778) revealed a broader and surer strategic vision, including a shrewd awareness of the centrality of sea power in a struggle between intercontinental empires.

The key to Britain's victory was its seizure of the initiative at sea. Thanks to an early British victory at the Battle of Quiberon Bay (1759), the French were unable to supply or reinforce their colonies. The British thus moved with confidence against the French overseas in both Canada and India.

In North America, the French were settled in Canada and down the Mississippi to New Orleans and could depend on the support of the Native–American population. Nevertheless, after initial setbacks, the British overran the French holdings, capturing Quebec, the chief city of French Canada, in 1759.

In India, the conflict evolved into a duel between two highly competent and aggressive leaders, Robert Clive (1725–1774) of the British East India Company and Joseph Dupleix (1697–1763) of the French one. Directing native troops and manipulating alliances with Indian princes, the two commmanders attacked each others' bases on the Indian coast. In 1759 Clive captured the French headquarters at Pondicherry and effectively destroyed French influence in the Mughal Empire.

In the Peace of Paris of 1763, then, the mid–century wars finally ended. Frederick the Great won formal acceptance of his claim to Silesia, and like Maria Theresa in the 1740s, Frederick won a measure of victory simply by surviving. Britain gained French Canada and unchallenged predominance in India, setting the British Empire on its way to the global preeminence it would enjoy in the nineteenth century.

Victims: Poland and Turkey

Two other important international changes of the later 1700s further illustrate the harshly self–aggrandizing spirit of foreign affairs in the eighteenth century. These were the complete absorption of Poland by its neighbors and the Russian breakthrough to the Black Sea at the expense of the once–great Ottoman Empire.

The Ottomans, though in decline in the 1700s, still controlled most of the southeastern corner of the continent, from Greece and the Balkans to southern Russia. It was in the latter area that Catherine the Great (r. 1762–1796) enjoyed her greatest successes in the 1770s and 1780s. Attacking by sea and by land, Catherine shattered the Turkish navy in the Aegean in 1770 and sent her armies deep into the Balkans and down the broad Crimean peninsula in the Black Sea. By 1783, Russia had gained both the northern shores of the Black Sea and the Crimea and the right to passage through the Turkish straits out into the Mediterranean.

The dismembering of Poland by the three great powers of central and eastern Europe was accomplished largely by diplomatic means in the three *partitions of Poland* of 1772, 1793, and 1795. The Polish monarchy, weak and without a large royal army, could only give way when Prussia, Russia, and Austria, acting in concert for once, made their first territorial demands in 1772. Frederick the Great acquired Polish lands between isolated East Prussia and the main portion of the Hohenzollern realm; Catherine the Great took much of what is today Belarus; and Maria Theresa and her son Joseph II, co–rulers of Austria, got the rich province of Galicia.

Two further partitions of Poland took place in the 1790s, the final one erasing Poland from the map of Europe for more than a century. It was a triumph of the sort of calculation and ruthless reason of state for which the eighteenth century was famous.

Partitions of Poland, 1772, 1793, 1795

Summary

Five major powers dominated the Western world in the eighteenth century. The older, established European nations were France, in many ways Europe's leading power since the days of Louis XIV; Britain, France's great rival and Europe's leading constitutional monarchy; and Austria under the Habsburgs, rulers of both the German Holy Roman Empire and a new multinational Danubian empire to the south. Two new great powers were the efficient, aggressive Prussia of Frederick the Great and Russia under the Romanovs, a vast peasant land that Peter and Catherine the Great labored to drag into the modern world.

By the eighteenth century, hereditary monarchs in many lands claimed absolute power, which they exercised through appointed ministers of state and large numbers of officials. Traditionally independent elements such as the church, the aristocracy, and the vigorous middle classes, though always eager to reassert former rights and prerogatives, normally operated in conjunction with the monarchies as an interlocking directorate of power.

The traditional classes still flourished. These included landowning aristocrats now clustering in cities or royal courts; an ambitious bourgeois class of merchants, bankers, professional people and bureaucrats; urban workers; and large numbers of peasant farmers and farm laborers, the latter still serfs in eastern Europe. Most women as well as men were integrated into this world of work, as the family was integrated into the larger society. Important communities in this society were the traditional village, the preindustrial city, and Europe's now partially assimilated Jewish community.

Relations among the five great powers of eighteenth-century Europe were often competitive and coldly calculating, governed by national self-interest. Conflicts frequently broke out, triggered by dynastic rivalries and competing commercial and imperial interests. A long midcentury series of wars, including the War of the Austrian Succession in the 1740s and the Seven Years' War in the 1750s and 1760s, involved such power players as Frederick the Great of Prussia, Maria Theresa of Austria, Catherine the Great of Russia, and William Pitt, Britain's celebrated war leader.

Some Key Terms

Act of Union 375
alliances 387
ancien régime 371
balance of power 387
bread riot 385
cabinet system 375
community 380
Danubian Empire 376

Diplomatic Revolution 391
ghetto 386
mercantilism 388
parlement 375
Parliament 375
partitions of Poland 393
pogrom 386
prime minister 375

reason of state 387
rentier 381
service nobility 377
Seven Years' War 389
wage labor 383
War of the Austrian Succession 389

Notes

1. Matthew Prior, *The Present State of the Court of France, and City of Paris* (London: E. Curll, 1712), 15.
2. Ibid., 46–47.
3. Jean-Baptiste Colbert, quoted in E. A. Gutkind, *Urban Development in Western Eu-rope*, vol. 5 (New York: Free Press, 1970), 115.
4. Frederick the Great, quoted in Isser Woloch, *Eighteenth Century Europe: Tradition and Progress, 1715–1789* (New York: W. W. Norton, 1982), 27.

Reading List

Anderson, M. S. *Europe in the Eighteenth Century, 1713–1783.* London: Longman, 1976. Clear introduction to the history of the century. See also R. Zeller, *Europe in Transition, 1660–1815* (Lanham, Md.: University Press of America, 1988).

Browning, R. *The War of the Austrian Succession.* New York: St. Martin's Press, 1993. Highly readable narrative history of the first half of the mid–century pandemic of wars.

Craig, G. A. *The Politics of the Prussian Army, 1640–1945.* Oxford: Oxford University Press, 1964. A well-known overview of an important aspect of modern German history.

DeVries, J. *European Urbanization, 1500–1800.* Cambridge, Mass.: Harvard University Press, 1984. A challenging book on European urban growth, pushing the modern industrial city back into the old regime.

Earle, P. *The Making of the English Middle Class: Business, Society, and Family Life in London, 1660–1730.* Berkeley and Los Angeles: University of California Press, 1989. Penetrating account, stressing family accumulation.

Furber, H. *Rival Empires of Trade in the Orient, 1600–1800.* Minneapolis: University of Minnesota Press, 1976. A solid survey of this important center of imperial competition.

Hill, B. *Women, Work, and Sexual Politics in Eighteenth-Century England.* New York: Blackwell, 1989. Women in the family economy of preindustrial England.

Joeres, R. E. B., and M. J. Maynes, eds. *German Women in the Eighteenth and Nineteenth Centuries.* Bloomington: Indiana University Press, 1985. Women and women writers in the German states.

Kahan, A. *The Plow, the Hammer, and the Knout: An Economic History of Eighteenth–Century Russia.* Chicago: University of Chicago Press, 1985. Social as well as economic analysis.

Langford, P. *A Polite and Commercial People: England, 1717–1783.* New York: Oxford University Press, 1989. Wide–ranging and up-to–date analysis of eighteenth–century English society and politics. See also H.–C. Mui and L. H. Mui, *Shops and Shop–Keeping in Eighteenth–Century England* (Kingston, Ont.: McGill–Queen's University Press, 1989).

Lis, C., and H. Soly. *Poverty and Capitalism in Preindustrial Europe.* Translated by J. Coonan. Atlantic Highlands, N.J.: Humanities Press, 1979. Traces a pattern of polarization.

Mousnier, R. E. *The Institutions of France under the Absolute Monarchy.* Chicago: University of Chicago Press, 1984.

Raeff, M. *The Well–Ordered Police State: Social and Institutional Change Through Law in the Germanies and Russia, 1600–1800.* New Haven: Yale University Press, 1983. Comparative study of developing autocracies in central and eastern Europe.

Ritter, G. *Frederick the Great.* Berkeley: University of California Press, 1968. Scholarly treatment by a German historian.

Rodger, N. A. M. *The Wooden World: An Anatomy of the Georgian Navy.* Annapolis, Md.: Naval Institute Press, 1986. Revisionist look at the British navy in the eighteenth century, seeing less brutal conditions than most treatments suggest.

Snell, K. D. M. *Annals of the Laboring Poor: Social Change and Agrarian England, 1660–1900.* Cambridge: Cambridge University Press, 1985. See also P. Goubert, *The Ancien Regime: French Society, 1600–1750,* translated by S. Cox. (London: Weidenfeld and Nicolson, 1973). A good account of peasant society.

Spear, Percival. *The Nabobs: A Study of the Social Life of the English in Eighteenth Century India.* London: Oxford University Press, 1963. Older but readable account of westerners overseas.

Thomson, G. S. *Catherine the Great and the Expansion of Russia.* London: English Universities Press, 1961. A useful survey of the reign and achievements, particularly in foreign policy.

Vardi, L. *The Land and the Loom: Peasants and Profit in Northern France, 1680–1800.* Durham, NC: Duke University Press, 1993. Close interaction of local industry and peasant agriculture in the eighteenth century.

Wallerstein, I. *The Modern World System,* vol. 2: *Mercantilism and the Consolidation of the European World–Economy, 1600–1750.* New York: Academic Press, 1980. Analytical study of the global system of economic and power relationships.

—16—

The Age of Reason
The Challenge of the Enlightenment

+The Eighteenth–Century Philosophers   +Enlightenment Social Thought
+The Enlightened Absolutists   +Eighteenth–Century Culture

The greatest intellectual movement of the eighteenth century was the Enlightenment, the powerful critique of the old regime that climaxed in the later 1700s. The Enlightenment is sometimes also called the Age of Reason because of its emphasis on reason as the standard for judging all human institutions. In this profoundly influential movement we will find both the source of governmental reform in the eighteenth century and the seedbed of the revolutionary trends of later centuries as well.

Flourishing between 1760 and 1790, the eighteenth-century *philosophes* (philosophers) were the intellectual leaders and the leading social thinkers of the Enlightenment. They were not revolutionaries: their solution for the problems of the age was to "enlighten" the nobility and the absolute monarchs of Europe, thus encouraging them to govern in the public interest. These intellectual reformers typically shared the pleasant life of the ruling classes, a cultivated world of art and music, elegance and wit. Yet the disturbing ideas they disseminated among the top people of the age did help bring on the great French Revolution of 1789.

This chapter will offer an overview of the thought of the Enlightenment and of its impact on contemporary politics, society, and culture. We will begin with a glance at such leaders of the movement as Voltaire and at some of the most common assumptions of these enlightened intellectuals. We will then outline the major ideas of such key social critics as Montesquieu, Rousseau, and Adam Smith. Thereafter we will examine the influence these social critics had on such enlightened despots as Frederick the Great and Catherine the Great. The chapter will conclude with a glimpse of the cultural life of this pivotal century.

Subsequent chapters will make clear how the Enlightenment opened the floodgates of change in the Western world. For the philosophes' dream of a better world designed by human beings nurtured the revolutionary ideologies of the next two hundred years. Through the nineteenth and twentieth centuries, liberals, socialists, nationalists, and other social critics and political activists offered their own charts of the road to utopia. But their faith in the possibility of building a better world for us all to live in was born in the minds of the eighteenth–century philosophes.

◆ The Eighteenth-Century Philosophers ◆

The *Enlightenment* was a movement in European thought that pinned its faith in human reason, both to understand the world we live in and to solve its problems. Like the humanist movement of the Renaissance, the Enlightenment was spread by intellectuals—the philosophes—totally convinced of the value of their insights. Drawing on modern science and urging the rule of reason, these unconventional thinkers proved urbane and witty propagandists for their cause.

This introductory section will concentrate on the leading spirits of the Enlightenment and on some general principles to which most of them adhered. The section will begin with an outline of the Age of Reason as a whole and with a close–up look at Voltaire, the most celebrated of all the philosophes. It will then examine both the philosophes as a group and the *salonières* or salon hostesses who directed the salon discussions which were the major intellectual forums of the age. This overview will conclude with a few words about such central Enlightenment concerns as reason, nature, and progress.

Voltaire and the Enlightenment

The most celebrated exemplar of the Enlightenment spirit was François–Marie Arouet, known everywhere by his pen name of Voltaire (1694–1778). Born in the reign of the greatest of all absolute monarchs, Louis XIV, Voltaire lived through the first years of the American Revolution, which began in 1776. A cosmopolitan man of the world, he wrote in praise of liberal England, served or corresponded with such leading enlightened rulers as Frederick the Great of Prussia and Catherine the Great of Russia, and jocularly wrote the pope to demand the ears of the chief of the Roman Inquisition. A brilliant satirist and salon wit, he was the most famous subversive critic of society of the eighteenth century.

The son of a bourgeois father with court connections and a mother who came from the provincial nobility, Voltaire was raised on the lower fringes of the ruling class. Thrown into the Bastille prison for sneering in verse at high court personages, beaten in the streets by a nobleman's servants for putting on aristocratic airs, Voltaire was finally driven into exile in England. There he gathered material for his *Philosophical Letters* in praise of the relative freedom of England. His latter travels included years at the court of the enlightened despot of Prussia, Frederick the Great. He spent the last decades of his life at Ferney, an estate located conveniently near the Swiss border in case, as he said, he should need to emigrate again. From Ferney, he issued a stream of tracts, pamphlets, books, and letters directed against the major social abuses and intellectual follies of his day.

Voltaire launched his barbs at corruption and inefficiency in government, at arbitrary laws and cruel punishments, at religious fanaticism, social inequality, official tyranny, and a host of other social evils. His best–known work, the satirical novel *Candide* (1759), exposed the hypocrisies of just about every social class, established institution, and intellectual pretension of his time. The naive Candide wanders from the German wars to Portuguese Inquisition to Spain's South American colonies, foolishly trying to see a society soaked in folly, crime, and pointless misery as "the best of all possible worlds."

Chronology 16: The Enlightenment

1685–1750	*Bach brings baroque music to its climax*
1700–1800	*French literary salons provide centers for intellectual discussion*
1721	*Montesquieu's* Persian Letters *ridicule society of Louis XIV*
1732–1806	*Fragonard paints idealized court life*
1740	*Richardson's* Pamela—*early middle–class novel*
1748	*Montesquieu's* Spirit of the Laws *offers rationalistic analysis and evaluation of political institutions*
1751–1772	*Diderot and d'Alembert publish volumes of the* Encyclopedia
1755–1842	*Vigée–Lebrun paints stars of French court*
1756–1791	*Mozart operas like* Don Giovanni *challenge conventions*
1759	*Voltaire's* Candide *lampoons claims that the old regime is "the best of all possible worlds"*
1760s–1800	*"Bluestockings" provide intellectual centers in England*
1762	*Rousseau's* Social Contract *urges democratic political reforms*
1776	*Adam Smith's* Wealth of Nations *explains economics in terms of the free market*

Philosophes and Salonières

Voltaire was the most famous of the *philosophes*. To the traditionally minded majority, these eighteenth–century philosophers were mockers and scoffers, jeering at ancient institutions and eternal verities. They tended to see themselves as new brooms, sweeping the cobwebs out of a musty attic, dissipating the shadows of deception and ignorance. Their goal was to cast light into the dark corners of a corrupt society.

Sometimes scientists, university lecturers, or poets, the philosophes were more often wide–ranging writers and intellectuals like Voltaire. One thing they seldom were, however, was systematic thinkers of the sort whose work is commonly considered philosophy today. The lions of that portion of the educated elite who prized advanced ideas, they had little in common with the academic philosophers of their own or later times.

The philosophes' goal, as they saw it, was a higher one. They sought to improve society by enlightening the ruling classes and inspiring Europe's crowned heads to turn their hands to reform. Particularly by serving or corresponding with rulers, or by tutoring youthful princes in their duties to their future subjects, the philosophes hoped to produce a race of enlightened autocrats. It was Plato's dream of a world ruled by philosopher–kings once more.

To reach the middling and lower orders of society, the philosophes made varied and effective use of the printing press. Solid bourgeois citizens, for instance, might buy copies of Voltaire's *Philosophical Dictionary* (1764) or subscribe to the famous *Encyclopedia* (1751–1772) edited by Denis Diderot and Jean d'Alembert. In such works, mingled with more straightforwardly informative entries and articles, they would find critical treatment of such institutions as the Inquisition, or even carefully veiled support for such radical political notions as popular sovereignty. Even the half–literate artisan, meanwhile, might be stirred by often anonymous pamphlets urging amelioration of some social injustice. And all France could learn to laugh at the attacks on aristocratic pomposity or priestly hypocrisy that called into question all the exalted claims and special privileges of the top two orders of society.

There were other forums for reaching the public besides the printed word, however. The most distinctive vehicle for the spread of enlightened ideas to the aristocracy, was the unique social institution called the salon.

The *salon* was a social gathering designed to bring the intellectual and social elites together. Held in the elegant drawing room, or salon, of a noblewoman or a member of the upper bourgeoisie—a marquise or a banker's wife—these evenings at home featured good conversation instead of more formal entertainment. Seventeenth–century salons often emphasized literary readings and discussions, and a writer's reputation could be made by a scintillating performance under these discriminating eyes. In the eighteenth century, the assembled intellectuals came to include scientists and thinkers concerned with social questions as well as the literati. As the French Revolution came on in the later 1700s, some salons became hotbeds of radical talk, affecting a more austere republican decor and listening to proposals for new constitutions and passionate harangues by colorful extremists like Jean–Jacques Rousseau.

The guiding spirit of the salon was the *salonière*, or hostess, whose interests and talents determined the concerns, set the tone, and directed the course of the discussions. In the later eighteenth century, the middle–class salonière became more common than in the aristocratic seventeenth century. Some saw the "moral tone" of the salon declining at this time, when some hostesses trotted out their distinguished lovers as the lions of their salons, as Julie d'Espinasse (1732–1776) did the encyclopedist Jean d'Alembert. In the later 1700s also, hostesses like Madame Necker, wife of the banker and reform minister to Louis XVI, became notorious for encouraging a daringly liberal tone in their gatherings.

There were salons in the German and Italian states, in Britain and elsewhere as well as in France. Jewish women with a passion for ideas ran some of the most intellectual salons of Berlin. Learned Italian women further held positions as university professors and were members of academies or scientific societies. In Britain, intellectual women called *bluestockings* not only hosted cultural discussions but dominated their membership. In such groups, women like the novelist Fanny Burney (1752–1840), and Elizabeth Montagu (1720–1800), hailed as "the queen of the blues," exchanged ideas with the learned and witty Samuel Johnson, the painter Joshua Reynolds, and other leading figures. The most famed of French salonières, however, was Madame Marie–Thérèse de Géoffrin (1699–1777). Widow of a wealthy businessman, a devout Christian, and a woman of impeccable reputation, she gathered some of the most radical spirits of the century around her table. Her Monday evenings for artists and, particularly, her Wednesday suppers for intellectuals and men-of-letters brought some of the best minds of the Enlightenment together with the cream of liberal–thinking European society. Like many of her guests, Madame de Géoffrin corresponded with the crowned heads of other nations, while foreign visitors to Paris clustered around her chair to catch what was rumored to be the most brilliant conversation to be heard anywhere in Europe.

The Enlightenment Faith in Reason

In confronting the problems of their age, eighteenth–century thinkers and social critics made use of a tool honed and sharpened in the seventeenth century: human reason. Rational inquiry, the philosophes believed, was the key both to understanding society and to improving it.

To understand the nature of things, the French rationalist René Descartes (1596–1650) had asserted as early as the 1630s, "clear and certain reasons" must be sought. The capacity for rational thought was the essence of human nature, and "this truth, *I think, therefore I am*" was "the first principle of . . . philosophy."[1] A century and a half later, the great German philosopher Immanuel Kant defined intellectual enlightenment itself as

> man's release from his self–incurred tutelage, [his] inability to make use of his understanding without direction from another. . . . *Sapere aude!* [Dare to think!] "Have courage to use your own reason!"—that is the motto of enlightenment.[2]

The heart of the eighteenth–century Enlightenment was this faith in reason. The human mind, the philosophes asserted, could comprehend all things, solve all problems. It was a conviction not unique to the 1600s and 1700s, of course. The ancient Greeks had seen philosophical reasoning as the road to truth, while the Scholastic thought of the Middle Ages had offered rational theological explanations for all things on this earth and beyond it. The seventeenth and eighteenth centuries, however, pinned their faith in a new kind of reason: *scientific* reasoning, rooted in empirical observation and mathematical analysis.

The basis of the Enlightenment's faith in human reason was the remarkable success of the scientific revolution of the sixteenth and seventeenth centuries. The ability of scientists like Galileo and Newton to explain and even predict the behavior of the natural world, from the behavior of bodies on this earth to the movement of the heavenly bodies above, had a profound effect on educated opinion. Societies of interested laymen, like the French Académie Royale and the English Royal Society, both founded in the 1660s, gathered to hear scientific lectures and observe experiments and demonstrations. In the 1700s, groups like the English Lunar Society formed among the middle classes, sometimes bringing amateurs of the new science together with technicians and manufacturers. As James Keir declared in his *Dictionary of Chemistry* (1789), "The diffusion of a general knowledge, and of a taste for science, over all classes of men, in every nation of Europe, or of European origin, seems to be the characteristic feature of the present age."[3]

Faith in the rational, scientific approach to truth had broader consequences. A method that had done so much to enhance our understanding of the physical world, some thought, might help also in other spheres of human knowledge. It might, for instance, guide us to a clearer comprehension of the way society itself works. It might even enable us to improve the social world in which we live. This conviction of the larger value of scientific reason sparked the eighteenth century's belief in progress and generated the revolutionary ideologies of the nineteenth and twentieth centuries.

Scientific discoveries continued to be made in the 1700s, and many scientists of the later part of the century were themselves hopeful about the contribution the new knowledge might make to the improvement of society. Joseph Priestley (1733–1804), best known for his discovery of oxygen in 1774, became a leading English supporter of the French Revolution in the 1790s. Antoine Lavoisier (1743–1794), hailed as "the father of modern chemistry," for his research on combustion, oxidation, and respiration, emphasized the value of science for agriculture and guided early studies of weights and measures that led to the adoption of the metric system in Revolutionary France. And Edward Jenner (1749–1823), the physician who discovered that inoculation with cowpox could prevent a human being from catching the cruelly disfiguring disease of smallpox, was hailed in later centuries for this fundamental medical advance.

Like the first airplanes more than a century later, this early hot-air balloon built by the Montgolfier brothers stayed aloft only a few minutes. Like early satellites, it carried animals rather than people—a sheep, a duck, and a rooster. Can you see how such experiments could create interest in science? (Culver Pictures, Inc.)

Science had learned to predict, and technology was learning to control the material world around us. Some social analysts argued that, by following the same rational methods, people could learn to predict and control the behavior of human society. A brave new world lay within our grasp, attainable through the application of reason to the solution of social problems.

Nature, Humanity, and Progress

Human reason was also the source of new truths that would help humankind find its way into the most promising of futures. For the philosophes, perhaps the most important of these truths were the laws of nature, the law of progress, and the perfectability of humanity.

From the eighteenth century to our time, *nature* has repeatedly been invoked as the standard of what is true and right. During the Enlightenment itself, this concern with nature and nature's laws took many forms. We have already mentioned the spreading belief in natural law, both in the physical sciences and in the emerging social sciences. As we will see, many enlightened individuals turned to "natural religion," replacing sectarian Christianity with faith in God as the divine designer of the universe. Advanced political thinkers preached John Locke's seventeenth–century theory of natural rights, while the eighteenth–century economist Adam Smith analyzed the natural laws of the marketplace. Again and again, the Enlightenment turned to humanity "in the state of nature" as the basis for analyzing modern society.

It was in this context that the belief in *social progress,* most influentially preached by Francis Bacon in the seventeenth century, began to find adherents in the eighteenth. The doctrine of progress asserted that, guided by scientific understanding of nature and society, human life would inevitably improve, building toward a just, humane, and happy social order to come. This doctrine was a startling reversal of the ancient belief that the best times lay in the past, in the Greco–Roman golden age or the Christian Garden of Eden. It offered hope for an earthly millennium, a utopia built by human hands in some future time.

Accompanying this faith in social progress was an equally unprecedented belief in the *perfectibility of human nature.* Again, this was a reversal of traditional views, notably the Christian doctrine that Adam's sin had been inherited by all his seed, leaving the whole human race depraved by nature. Many modern people, by contrast, came to believe that changes in education or social institutions would produce better human beings, a perfected species freed of the benighted behavior of our ancestors. This better breed of humans also lay in the not-too-distant future.

Human virtue and human happiness were for the philosophes the true end of social thought and institutions. The Middle Ages had seen obedience to God's will as humankind's highest duty and heaven as the goal of life. For the new age, however, human happiness and human welfare in this world became the objective. In the nineteenth century, this exaltation of human beings to the center of the picture produced the "religion of humanity" adhered to in various forms by the founders of almost all the new ideologies. In our own century, human welfare and human rights have become the recognized goals of peoples around the world—an impressive legacy from an age whose leading intellectuals called themselves "the party of humanity."

Nature, humanity, and progress thus became central organizing concepts in Western thought. Increasingly, nature became the criterion and human welfare the end toward which Western society labored, while the law of progress guaranteed the success of those labors.

♦ Enlightenment Social Thought ♦

The Enlightenment was both a subversive and a creative movement. Building on its faith in the human rational faculties, the enlightened leaders of Western thought launched a wide–ranging critique of the traditional institutions and conventional ideas of the old regime. At the same time, some among them formulated original theories of a more positive nature in political, economic, and social thought.

After a brief overview of the Enlightenment critique of Western society in the 1700s, this section will survey the original theories of a number of leading social thinkers of the Enlightenment. It will look at Montesquieu's views of the legitimate powers of government, at Rousseau's theory of the social contract between the government and the governed, and at Adam Smith's influential ideas about the natural laws of the free market. The final pages will summarize Enlightenment thinking about two other large subjects—the rights of women and the role of religion in a free and rational society.

The Enlightenment Critique

The eighteenth–century philosophes saw inequities, anachronisms, and hypocrisy on every side. Voltaire's *Candide,* for example, lampooned aristocrats who worshiped their own pedigrees yet cheated at cards and heroic soldiers steeped to the elbows in rapine and slaughter. Voltaire scoffed at priests of all faiths, including Protestant clergymen who preached charity but emptied their chamberpots over the beggar at the door and Catholic prelates who saw a mass burning of heretics as a sure cure for earthquakes. He mocked even his fellow philosophers, who misused logic to prove that this unhappy universe was "the best of all possible worlds."

A more substantial monument to the philosophic spirit of the time was the *French Encyclopedia* (1751–1772) edited by Denis Diderot (1713–1784) and the mathematician Jean d'Alembert (1717–1783). Diderot, like Voltaire, was a man of wide–ranging interests and talents whose books had been banned and who had spent time in the Bastille. The *Encyclopedia* included articles by many other members of the party of humanity, among them such leading social critics as Voltaire, Rousseau, Montesquieu, the economic theorist François Quesnay, and the political reformer Jacques Turgot. Thanks to Diderot's twenty-year labor and the supportive efforts of the salonière Madame de Géoffrin and the influential Madame de Pompadour, the two dozen volumes were published despite church opposition and the royal censors.

The goal of the mammoth production was to present "advanced ideas" on all subjects and thus, as the preface candidly explained, "to change the general way of thinking."[4] The *Encyclopedia* included some of the latest and most unorthodox theories of government, economics, human nature, and human society, from Quesnay's "physiocratic" economic views to Rousseau's radical ideas on government by the general will of the people, both of which we will explore shortly. The skeptical, critical treatment accorded to important religious institutions and ideas disturbed the devout. The thorough and approving treatment given to scientific subjects, by contrast, showed where the sympathies of the editors lay. And the detailed accounts of the latest technology, with many pictures of machinery and descriptions of technical processes, dignified the labor of artisans still often considered beneath the notice of the upper classes of society.

Religious institutions, in particular, were prime targets for the Enlightenment critique. To the philosophes, ignorant, superstitious, or licentious priests, unproductive monks, and university theologians still spouting Scholastic logic all reeked of the unscientific spirit of the Middle Ages. Church control of education, censorship, and the mind of the masses made churchmen the particular enemies of the new free spirit. Voltaire regularly concluded his letters with the phrase, "Crush the infamous thing!"—meaning the French Catholic church. Here above all, reason was seen as the great liberating force. Rational analysis, the philosophes averred, would free people's minds from the ignorance and superstition on which the churches throve. It would liberate humanity from religious fanaticism, which could still stir the ignorant to the persecution of Protestants in Catholic countries or of Catholics in Protestant ones.

Montesquieu and the Powers of Government

While it took the scalpel of reason to the conventional wisdom of the age, the eighteenth century also provided the first broad audience for some of the most important new political ideas of modern times. During this period, the seventeenth–century theories of human rights and constitutional government propounded by John Locke (1632–1704) found acceptance among advanced thinkers on both sides of the Atlantic. At the same time, the new notions of Montesquieu and Rousseau sowed the seeds of further political innovation in the West.

Although automatic acceptance of social hierarchy and divine–right monarchy remained the rule in the 1700s, Locke's radical notions did gain much wider attention than they had received in the preceding century. In the *Second Treatise of Government* (1690), written during the last phase of England's century of revolution, Locke had claimed that human beings possess natural rights to liberty, equality, and property. The proper government, he declared, ruled on the basis of a constitution or *social contract* guaranteeing the people free exercise of these rights. Although the word *people* tended to be used in a very limited sense, referring only to educated, property–owning people with a stake in society, Locke's ideas proved seminal. In the late eighteenth century, they found a place in the basic documents of both the new United States and revolutionary France, becoming articles of faith for generations yet unborn.

Charles de Secondat, baron de Montesquieu (1688–1755), was hailed as a "social Newton" when his monumental work, *The Spirit of the Laws* (1748), came out at the middle of the eighteenth century. A lifetime student of law, history, and science and a leading philosophe, Montesquieu combined many years of historical and social research with political theory in his vast analysis of human governance.

Drawing on his knowledge of a variety of European and non–European cultures, Montesquieu discussed the essential spirit of the main forms of government and the basic powers of all governments—executive, judicial, and legislative. Perhaps his most influential idea was his assertion that in the ideal government these three powers would be separated and balanced against each other. This system of *checks and balances,* intended to prevent total power from falling into the hands of a single group or individual, became an important element of the United States Constitution.

Montesquieu's methods, however, were almost as important as his conclusions. For Montesquieu's theories were not purely logical constructs, like Plato's *Republic*; instead, they derived from the study of real societies, including ancient Greece and Rome, medieval Germany and Britain, and China and America in his own time. Montesquieu also took climate, geography, and the ways in which people earned a living into consideration in *The Spirit of the Laws*. The book thus embodied some of the emphasis on the empirical and the concrete that would be central to the social sciences of the future.

Rousseau and the Social Contract

In Jean–Jacques Rousseau (1712–1778), the Enlightenment found its most colorful—and atypical—spokesman. Intensely emotional in a century dedicated to reason, sincere and poetic in an age of satire and cynicism, Rousseau sometimes looks more like a nineteenth–century romantic than a leading spirit of the Enlightenment. Taking a barmaid for a mistress and urging a return to the simple life in an age that loved its comforts, he struck some of his contemporaries as a bit of a wild man. Certainly his *Confessions* (1768) constituted the most psychologically penetrating autobiography since St. Augustine's. And his belief that education should not be a matter of rote memory but should develop the capacities of the individual student through direct exploration of the natural world remains influential today.

Rousseau's most controversial and influential work, however, was *The Social Contract* (1762), his contribution to the political thought of the Enlightenment. The ideal state, Rousseau asserted, would be one governed, not by divine–right monarchs or enlightened despots or even by a Lockean majority of those with a stake in society, but by

Jean-Jacques Rousseau was at once a social and cultural critic, a political thinker, an
educational theorist, and a romantic novelist.
In his autobiography, in particular, he revealed many personality characteristics that
baffled his contemporaries. (National Gal-
leries of Scotland.)

the general will of all the people. In the Lockean liberal state, each citizen would vote his
or her own self–interest. Under Rousseau's version of the social contract, the community
as a whole would consciously put the *general will,* the collective welfare of all, ahead of
the separate interests of its individual members. The state would thus be guided by the
best conscience of the people to do what was best for all of society. So central was this
general will that individuals who resisted it should be compelled to accept it—"forced,"
as Rousseau enigmatically put it, "to be free." For "only the general will can direct the
energies of the state in a manner appropriate to the end for which it was founded, i.e., the
common good."[5]

Phrases like "forced to be free" and the glorification of Rousseau by some of the most
violent leaders of the French Revolution have raised questions about the true tenor of his
thought. He has even been seen as an early defender of something suspiciously resembling
modern totalitarianism. In his own time, however, Rousseau was rated as the most radical
of democrats, preaching popular sovereignty in an age of kings.

Adam Smith and the Laws of the Free Market

The economic thought of the Enlightenment did not build on seventeenth–century precursors but reacted against them. Eighteenth–century economics, developed by the enlightened French school of economic thought called the *physiocrats* and by the English

thinker Adam Smith, challenged the paternalistic mercantilism of the age. Smith, in particular, became the first modern proponent of free-market economics.

François Quesnay (1694–1774), leader of the physiocratic school, did not set out to defend the interests of commerce. Rejecting the mercantilist view that wealth consisted of gold and silver bullion flowing into the nation, Quesnay declared that the only real wealth was that produced by the earth itself. Only agriculture and the other "extractive industries"—mining, fishing, and other drafts upon nature's bottomless bounty—really added to the total wealth of the world. Manufacturing was the mere processing of natural resources, trade nothing more than exchanging these products. Because neither added substantively to the world's material wealth, the physiocrats urged, tariffs on trade and taxes on industry should be abolished. In their place, a single tax should be levied on the true source of wealth—the land and its produce. *Laissez faire, laissez passer* (Let people make what they will, let goods pass freely), they urged—let the manufacture and exchange of goods go on unimpeded by governments.

Like Montesquieu, Quesnay offered a method that ultimately proved to be almost as important as his conclusions. The physiocratic leader's famous *Economic Table* (1758) was an early example of the presentation of economic ideas in graphic form. This elaborate flow chart showed the distribution of wealth across France in a typical year, demonstrating the blessings brought by the year's newly created wealth—primarily the annual harvest—to every sector of the population. With its dependence on quantification and its graphic presentation, Quesnay's economic table pointed toward the social sciences of the future as clearly as did Montesquieu's empiricism.

The real founder of free-market thinking, however, was Adam Smith (1723–1790), who is commonly recognized as the father of modern economics. In *Wealth of Nations* (1776) this Scottish philosophy professor produced a book as revolutionary in its way as the American Declaration of Independence that was being hammered out in that same year on the other side of the Atlantic.

Smith propounded a number of seminal ideas about human getting and spending. For him, the source of real wealth was neither the favorable balance of trade the mercantilists sought nor the rich harvests of the physiocrats, but human labor—the labor that produced material things, and the amount of labor that these products could in turn command in the marketplace. Before the Industrial Revolution was well under way, Smith detected the immense productive advantages of the division of labor, which assigned each worker a small and repetitive job rather than allowing each to handcraft his or her own finished article. Smith's most important contributions to economic thought, however, were the economic laws of the *free market,* as he called the unregulated economy. These natural laws of human economic behavior, he believed, were the key to the present welfare and future progress of the race.

Like many of his contemporaries—as noted above—Adam Smith believed in an underlying harmony between the apparently diverse and conflicting sectors of society. Human beings, he admitted, were by nature self-interested and competitive. Yet the sum total of human competition for products and jobs, low prices and high profits, would be the general welfare of society. Not mercantilistic government regulations but the law of *supply and demand,* the natural economic tendency of supply to follow demand, would bring about this happy state of affairs.

In this view, public demand would stimulate profit-hungry producers to supply whatever the public wanted in sufficient quantity to meet public demand. On the other side of the counter, consumers would buy at the lowest price they could get, keeping prices and profit margins reasonable. And even workers, the group most likely to be victimized, would refuse jobs that paid too little, compelling employers to offer a living wage. Everywhere, as though directed by an "invisible hand," the wealth of nations would increase if intrusive government regulation were ended and the natural laws of the free market were allowed to function unimpeded. Many nineteenth-century liberals—and twentieth-century conservatives—would agree with Adam Smith that "the quantity of every commodity brought to market," as well as the market price, wages, and profits would be naturally determined by "the effectual demand"—if only government would leave the marketplace alone.[6]

Enlightenment Ideas About Women

The eighteenth century also saw significant—if contradictory—shifts in ideas about women and the family. Some of these emerging views were rooted in the rationalism of the Enlightenment, some in the emotional sentimentalism of the end of the century.

Ever since Descartes in the preceding century, some advanced thinkers had come to admit that women, as human beings, were quite as rational as men. Poulain de la Barre, a seventeenth–century follower of Descartes, had pithily summed up a fundamental eighteenth–century attitude: "Intelligence," he wrote, "has no sex."[7] Enlightened spirits of the 1700s favored improved education for women, as they did for artisans and others who were at that time denied the opportunity to develop their rational faculties to the fullest. The activities of salonières in France, bluestockings in England, and other intellectual women strongly supported this Enlightenment attitude.

The sciences of medicine, anatomy, and physiology, however, took a rather different view of female character. Increasingly, doctors and anatomists saw women's reproductive capacities as their defining physical features. The wide pelvic bone structure designed for childbearing, breasts for nursing, and other sex–specific features suggested to these (mostly male) scientists that women's rational capacities might be conditioned, even limited, by their physical nature. The old claim that women were more sensual than men resurfaced, now based on the anatomical allegation that women had more nerve ends to enjoy physical sensations than men did.

This "scientific" interpretation of female sexuality was accompanied by a sentimental rediscovery of the "natural" joys of family life and a reemphasis on motherhood. In the last decades of the eighteenth century, concern for slaves, convicts, and other sufferers was accompanied by a more positive attitude toward children and a greater sensitivity to the value of warm family life. Caring parents have left many touching letters expressing their concern for the health, education, and future of their children. Rousseau advocated breast feeding as a source of natural closeness between mother and child. In *Emile* (1762), he also became a leading advocate of educational reform, urging that rote learning be replaced by an attempt to tailor education to the nature of the child. And Julie, the heroine of his emotionally charged novel, *The New Héloïse* (1761), survives an unhappy love affair in youth to come into her own as a married woman, mother, and benefactor of the community.[8]

Yet this focus on family life was more than simply a reemphasis on women's domestic role. The Enlightenment, looking ahead toward a better society, tended to see a larger social dimension to motherhood. Some saw a loving family as an essential source of comfort and support for the male citizen, the free individual of the utopian future. Women, as mothers, were also seen as performing a vital duty to society as a whole, shaping future citizens for the republic of virtue. Adam Smith saw the true source of all human goodness in the family, where children should be nurtured with intelligence as well as with love. From the nurturing family, virtue might radiate out into a society otherwise guided by the coldly competitive self–interest of the marketplace.

Despite this attempt to see the domestic sphere in a larger social context, however, the immediate result was to stress once more the view that woman's natural place was in the home. With the prestige of medical science and the Enlightenment added to Christian idealizing of this role, middle– and upper–class women at least were being elevated to that "pedestal" from which many women in later centuries would determinedly descend. In its recognition of the centrality of reason to all human character, however, the Enlightenment had also provided a tool that would make it easier for women of later generations to explore a wider variety of options than that of wife, mother, and shaper of new generations.

Religion and Philosophy

Religion and philosophy also felt the touch of the Enlightenment. The new faith in human reason produced a variety of spiritual and metaphysical responses, ranging from skepticism and atheism to "natural religion" and the abstruse philosophy of the German idealists.

Perhaps the most typical religious formulation of the century was *deism*, sometimes called natural religion. Deists admitted the existence of God as creator of the complex and wonderful universe the scientists explored. They believed, however, that once the divine artificer had built the remarkable world machine and laid down the natural laws that governed it, he took no further hand in its operation. Miraculous intervention, divine revelation, and sectarian dogma had no place in natural religion. Thus a Muslim or a Hindu who believed in a divine creator was as true a worshiper of nature's God as a Protestant or a Catholic.

A few truly radical spirits, like Julien de la Mettrie (1709–1751) or Baron d'Holbach (1723–1789), carried the materialism and science worship of the Enlightenment still further, daring to suggest that there might be no God at all. For such extremists, human beings were not immortal souls clothed in an envelope of flesh, but simply infinitely complex natural mechanisms. La Mettrie suggested in his *Man a Machine* (1748) that "the soul is but an empty word," the human body a mere mechanism with "a few more wheels, a few more springs" than lesser works of nature.[9] Such out-and-out atheism was still rare and deeply disturbing in the 1700s. Once again, however, it did point ahead to such later and more far–reaching movements as nineteenth–century philosophical materialism and twentieth–century existentialism.

Another reaction to deism was not to take the approach further, but to return with passion to the Christian fold. *Pietism* in Germany and *Methodism* in Britain reflected this approach. The Pietists reacted to the staid and ritualistic tendencies of contemporary Lutheranism by preaching a warm and emotional Christianity of the heart. Methodism was originally an Anglican sect whose most powerful preacher was John Wesley (1703–1791). The Methodists were particularly concerned to bring their healing, heart–warming version of the faith to the poor in the open fields, cities, and coal mines of an industrializing England. Both Pietists and Methodists hurled jubilant hymns and hallelujahs in the teeth of what they saw as the impious rationalism of the Enlightenment.

Systematic philosophy also responded in a variety of ways to the world of the scientist and the philosophe. Preeminent among the more systematic thinkers who wrestled with the problems posed by the growing faith in science and reason were the celebrated Scottish skeptic David Hume (1711–1776) and the outstanding proponent of German idealism, Immanuel Kant (1724–1804).

For most Greek philosophers and medieval Christian theologians alike, it had been axiomatic that the human mind or soul was capable of understanding the world in which we live. This conviction was strengthened for many by the discoveries of the scientific revolution and by the Enlightenment's faith in reason. But the new science also for the first time elevated the human senses to parity with human reason as a source of truth. The result was to open up a buzzing hive of philosophical problems about the relationship between reason and observation, between the world as experienced and the world as it really is, and between human moral conduct and God.

David Hume put sense experience first and asserted a thoroughgoing skepticism about the claims of reason to understand the deeper reality of things. All we know about the world, he declared, is that certain things or events resemble each other, occur close together, or in other ways seem to relate to each other. Human reason is not justified in going beyond these basic observations, however. We may assume a cause-and-effect relationship, for instance, when one event occurs before another one: all we know is that the one comes before the other in time. Even the existence of God cannot be proven—though neither, the great skeptic added, can his nonexistence be proved by human experience, our only guide.

Immanuel Kant, the abstruse Königsberg University professor, took a different view. In his *Critique of Pure Reason* (1781), Kant insisted that the human mind itself structured reality-as-experienced according to elaborate interpretive patterns, "categories" of thought by which the mind comprehended and interpreted the world as we observe it. Kant's idealism was a faith in the reality and efficacy of Ideas that could be traced back to Plato. Unlike the Greeks or the medieval Schoolmen, however, Kant denied the capacity of human reason to break through its own network of interpretations to the world at large, the "thing-in-itself." For the rationalist Kant as for the empiricist Hume, the world as it really is remained beyond our ken.

Unsure though they might be about human understanding, however, both men remained confident of human decency. Hume believed in the natural good will or benevolence of human beings toward each other. For him, morality leads to action conducive to social utility and personal happiness. Kant, raised in a strong Pietist tradition that emphasized the love of God, insisted that all humankind has a *categorical imperative* or absolute obligation to love and obey the moral law. This imperative, he declared, requires us always to act in accord with principles that we would like to see the whole world obey. It was a philosophical version of the Golden Rule that appealed strongly to the Age of Reason.

♦ The Enlightened Absolutists ♦

The later 1700s saw the royal rulers of the Western world themselves taking up the Enlightenment's call for better government and expressing their desire to serve the great cause of reform. The Prussian king Frederick the Great defined his role as merely "first servant of the state," while Empress Maria Theresa of Austria presented herself as "the mother of her people." Words like "freedom," "rights," "welfare," and "happiness of man" were constantly on the lips of Europe's enlightened autocrats in the later eighteenth century.[10]

The image of the ruler as the benefactor of his or her people is of course not new. But this princely self–image took a new and more modern form in the eighteenth century—that of the enlightened despot or enlightened absolutist, the absolute monarch who used his or her autocratic power to bring about modern, rational reforms.

After a brief summary of the spread of at least some degree of enlightenment among eighteenth–century Europe's crowned heads, the following pages will look more closely at some important examples. These will include Frederick the Great of Prussia, Catherine the Great in Russia, the empress Maria Theresa and her son Joseph II in Austria, and a number of less powerful but perhaps more genuinely enlightened rulers elsewhere in Europe.

Enlightenment and Absolutism

"Not until philosophers are kings," Plato had written more than two thousand years earlier, "or the kings and princes of this world have the spirit and power of philosophy . . . will this our State have the possibility of life and behold the light of day."[11] The dream of philosopher–kings, of rule by the wisest and the best, has haunted the mind of the West ever since. In the 1700s, Voltaire—and his fellow philosophes—agreed that "the happiest thing that can happen to men, is for the prince to be a philosopher."[12]

Good government means different things to different times. In the twentieth century, Western people tend to see representative democracy—election of the rulers by the people themselves—as a basic ingredient of any legitimate form of government. Educated eighteenth–century people, however, had never seen a large democracy successfully run and had no faith in what they saw as the half–literate, priest–ridden masses of their time to run a nation. Living in an age of royal absolutism, at the end of a thousand years of kings, even advanced political thinkers turned to monarchy for any realistic solution to the political problems of the day.

Despite some theorizing about popular sovereignty, then, good government in the eighteenth century tended to mean guaranteeing the rights, welfare, and happiness of the people through some form of monarchy. Royal absolutism was a given: what was needed was a more enlightened, efficient, and benevolent absolutism than any that had yet prevailed.

Enlightened absolutism sums up what was wanted: absolute power directed to enlightened ends. It seemed a viable option during the second half of the century, particularly between 1763 and 1789, the three decades between the end of the Seven Years' War and the outbreak of the French Revolution. Impressive lists of enlightened autocrats who ruled during these years have indeed been assembled. Among them are such powerful rulers as Frederick the Great of Prussia, Joseph II of Austria, and Catherine the Great of Russia, as well as such lesser princes as Leopold II of Tuscany, Charles III of Spain, the Portuguese chief minister the marquês de Pombal, and Gustavus III of Sweden. Distinguished as much by style as by the substance of their reforms, these eighteenth–century rulers represented the last chance of absolute monarchy to provide the sort of effective modern government the evolving Western world required.

Absolute monarchs like Philip II in the sixteenth century or Louis XIV in the seventeenth had labored assiduously to provide more efficient government and to foster agriculture, industry, and trade. The enlightened absolutists of the later eighteenth century differed from their predecessors partly in the simple fact that they were or claimed to be "enlightened," imbued with the free and beneficent spirit of the new age. Sometimes tutored by philosophes, frequently corresponding with them or taking them into the royal service, these monarchs gave the impression of being new–fashioned rulers, responsive to the needs of their time. Like the Renaissance princes who patronized humanistic scholars, the enlightened absolutists benefited from the up-to-date image they projected and from the public approval of the intellectual leaders of their age.

It would be oversimplifying and overly cynical, however, to dismiss the enlightenment of these eighteenth–century absolutists as purely a matter of public relations. For some, such as Catherine the Great, concern with cutting–edge ideas was more a matter of intellectual pleasure and personal vanity than a serious influence on her public policy. For Frederick the Great and many others, the rationalization of government meant basically a stronger administrative system, one more capable of foreign conquests as well as of domestic reforms. In a few, like the Habsburg emperor Joseph II, the Enlightenment did kindle real concern for the hard lot of peasants and other long–suffering subjects—though even Joseph II had other motives for reform. In each case, as we will see, the doctrines of the philosophes were adapted to historic circumstance in the realms of Europe's would–be philosopher–kings.

Frederick the Great

It would be hard to come up with a more fascinatingly self–contradictory ruler than Frederick the Great of Prussia (r. 1740–1786). Relentless general, tireless administrator, philosopher, musician, and poet, Frederick II combined an unlikely array of talents. Sensitive and witty, cynical and ruthless, he possessed both a real dedication to social progress and a strongly felt contempt for human nature. He was a Prussian nationalist before loyalty to a nation, as opposed to loyalty to its ruler, was generally understood in Europe. His description of himself as first servant to the state was thus probably heartfelt—as was the absolutist rigor with which he imposed his royal will upon his country.

In some ways, Frederick II's domestic policies, like his foreign aggressions, were clearly in the old Hohenzollern dynastic tradition. Like his predecessors, he depended on and considerably strengthened the Junker aristocracy as the prime instrument of royal power. Junkers staffed the officer corps of the Prussian army and dominated the Prussian bureaucracy, both fabled for their efficient discharge of their duties. The aspirations of the middle classes, by contrast, the king either ignored or rebuffed, and most of the peasantry continued to languish in serfdom throughout his reign.

Yet Frederick's reputation as an enlightened reformer was not without foundation. To strengthen the agricultural base of the Prussian economy, for instance, he drained swamps, encouraged large–scale immigration, introduced such important new crops as the potato, and distributed seed and tools to peasants left destitute by the Seven Years' War. A deist in a Lutheran nation, he showed remarkable toleration for Catholics and members of other sects, though he continued to impose rigorous restrictions on Jews in his realms. Perhaps most important, he strove to construct a genuine *Rechtsstaat*, a state founded on the rule of law. Under his rule, laws were simplified and impartially administered, justice dealt out swiftly and fairly. The Prussian civil service, which he personally directed and endlessly inspected, was probably the most efficient, honest, and industrious in Europe.

For Frederick, enlightened despotism meant above all the rational restructuring of government to enhance the effectiveness of the absolutist state, on which he believed the welfare and progress of the people depended. He was first servant to the state in that he worked hard for a better life for Prussians; but Prussia remained as much his personal fiefdom as France had been Louis XIV's.

Maria Theresa and Joseph II

Maria Theresa (r. 1740–1780) and Joseph II (r. 1765–1790) of Austria were a unique mother-and-son team. Maria Theresa, often seen as too old–fashioned an absolutist to be considered "enlightened," was nonetheless responsible for many reforms, as we will see. Joseph, by contrast, was perhaps the most dedicated "philosophical" reformer of all the enlightened autocrats.

Maria Theresa, "the mother of her people," or, as Catherine the Great sarcastically described her, "lady prayerful," was totally committed to the Habsburg dynasty and the Roman Catholic church. Hard–working, strong–willed, and proud, she could be a stern ruler and as aggressive as her great rival Frederick when she saw a chance for a slice of a neighbor's territory. Joseph II, her co–ruler for fifteen years and successor for ten, was considerably more open to newfangled ideas and radical reform. Impatient of opposition, puritanical in his passion for social amelioration, Joseph tried to be guided in everything by the spirit of the Enlightenment. Sometimes called "the peasants' emperor," he traveled incognito among his people to learn their problems, then flooded the Habsburg Empire with new laws and reform decrees. Yet the son built on the changes initiated by his mother; and in some ways hers were the more lasting contributions to the future of Austria.

Among the transformations wrought by this odd couple were reforms affecting the nobility, the church, and the peasant masses. Maria Theresa took a strong line with the aristocracy, increasing their tax burdens and undercutting the power of the provincial assemblies they dominated. Joseph II further undermined aristocratic preeminence by replacing noble with middle–class administrators at the top of the bureaucracy and by drastically reducing the power of the nobles over the peasantry. The empress, devoted as she was to her religion, nevertheless increased taxes on the wealth of the Catholic church and even confiscated some church lands. Her son, far more tolerant of other faiths, allowed Protestants freedom of worship and eliminated the taxes and restrictions imposed on Jews. At the same time, however, he asserted his own authority over the Catholic establishment, confiscated the property of hundreds of "unproductive" monasteries and convents, and used the proceeds to build public hospitals. Perhaps most strikingly, Maria Theresa eased the burden of taxation and labor imposed on serfs, while Joseph II actually abolished serfdom—though this radical decree was rescinded not long after his death.

Joseph's highhandedness, his doctrinaire attempts to impose enlightened ideas by imperial decree through a centralized bureaucracy proved largely unsuccessful. Peasants resented his attacks on the church, nobles his attacks on the nobility. Many of his reforms thus proved as transitory as his attempt to free the serfs. Other accomplishments, however—like the hospitals and schools he opened in Vienna—survived as evidence of the sort of social and cultural advancement that was possible through enlightened absolutism.

Catherine the Great

Further still from Paris, the capital of the Enlightenment, stretched the vast expanse of Russia, the backward colossus of eastern Europe. Yet Russia also produced one of the most celebrated—and controversial—of all the enlightened autocrats: Catherine the Great (r. 1762–1796).

Catherine II, born the princess of an obscure German principality, was also related through her mother to the Romanov dynasty of Russia. Thanks to this connection, Catherine was carried off to St. Petersburg at the age of fifteen to marry the Russian prince who subsequently became Emperor Peter III. In 1762, young Peter, unprepossessing and not overly bright, was overthrown and murdered in one of the many conspiracies and coups that had tormented the Russian royal court since the death of Peter the Great in 1725. Empress Catherine, who had probably been involved in her husband's overthrow, was soon restoring order and direction to the Russian government after four decades of dislocation and weakness.

It is sometimes said that if Peter the Great inaugurated the westernization of the body of Old Russia, Catherine the Great began the westernizing of the Russian soul. She was certainly one of the most colorful and dynamic of all Russian rulers, and of all Europe's enlightened despots.

As a foreigner, Catherine was even more of an outsider in that tradition–bound land than the iconoclastic Peter had been. Avid to enjoy all sides of life, she followed the European royal custom of taking a long string of lovers, though like most powerful rulers she never allowed her personal pleasures to interfere with the business of governing. A much more sophisticated person than the uncouth Peter the Great, she used her eager involvement in the culture of the Enlightenment to enhance Russia's image and advance Russia's interests among the great powers.

A voracious reader, eager to keep up with the latest cultural trends from her exile on the east European plain, Catherine wrote plays and satires, edited a magazine, and composed a striking autobiographical memoir. She corresponded with famous philosophes, became the much–admired patron of Voltaire and Diderot, and assured them all of her desire to implement their ideas in Russia. Early in her reign, she convened a Legislative Commission to modernize the empire's antiquated laws, herself contributing a set of *Instructions* (1767), studded with concepts gleaned from Montesquieu and Beccaria, to guide their deliberations. She even expressed opposition to serfdom decades before Joseph II attempted to abolish it in the Habsburg lands.

But Russian realities frustrated any enlightened intentions Catherine may have entertained. When a massive serf rebellion led by the Cossack Emelian Pugachev (1726–1775) exploded across southern and eastern Russia, Catherine turned the army loose on the serfs, had Pugachev brought to Moscow in a cage for execution, and thought no more of liberating the peasant masses. Realizing that, practically speaking, her absolute power depended on noble support, she freed the aristocracy from taxation and compulsory government service, rewarded them with lands confiscated from the Russian Orthodox church, and gave them almost total power over their serfs. Some reorganization of provincial and municipal government, a degree of religious toleration, and some support for education were the modest fruit of Catherine the Great's attempts at enlightened government in her huge but still underdeveloped empire.

♦ Eighteenth-Century Culture ♦

"Life, liberty, and the pursuit of happiness," declared the founding fathers of the American republic, were the natural goals of human beings. Happiness of mind and spirit, but also of the senses and the flesh, preoccupied the witty, bawdy, eighteenth century. The literature and graphic art, the architecture and music of the century sometimes seemed, in fact, to have no higher goal than the giving of pleasure.

This section will examine the arts of two key social groups—the aristocracy and the bourgeoisie. We will first analyze the neoclassical and rococo arts of the aristocracy, eighteenth–century descendants of the classical and baroque styles of the seventeenth century. We will then turn to the continuing development of the more realistic arts of Europe's middle classes and to the spread of a vigorous popular culture among the masses.

Neoclassical and Rococo Art

The arts of the aristocracy provided an exquisite setting for—and expression of—the pursuit of pleasure, intellectual and sensual. Neoclassicism on the intellectual side and rococo as a direct appeal to the senses both illustrate this tendency.

Eighteenth–century *neoclassicism,* or "new classical" art, carried the formal tendencies of seventeenth century classicism to their extremes. Aiming at an eternal perfection achieved only by the greatest artists of earlier centuries, neoclassicists took Greek, Roman, and some Renaissance masters as their models. Greek architecture, illustrated in trend-setting sketches of Greek ruins, influenced a wide range of art forms, from architecture and interior decoration to ceramics and furniture design. Classical rules were laid down for every art, from painting to play writing, while ancient forms of poetry—lyric and epic, eulogies and elegies—still dominated literary practice.

Eternal themes, traditional forms, and subject matter derived from Greco–Roman myth and history combined to strengthen a sense of aristocratic superiority, and to give pleasure to aristocratic viewers. And though much of neoclassical art seems a little formal and cold to twentieth–century viewers, it could stir a powerful intellectual enthusiasm in its own day.

Rococo art (from *rocaille,* a fanciful French shell design) was equally artificial in its lighter, more frivolous way, and much more directly pleasing to the senses. A playful, decorative style, rococo provided a graceful setting for such pleasures of the nobility as salon conversation and chamber music, a high–stakes game of cards or a leisurely seduction. Deriving from the powerful, sometimes pompous baroque of the preceding century, rococo was an art, not of pageantry and ceremony, but of intimate occasions.

Painters associated with this exquisitely frivolous style give us our most vivid, if highly idealized, impression of the "sweet life" of Europe's aristocracy in the century before the revolution. Élisabeth Vigée–Lebrun (1755–1842), one of the most respected—and best paid—painters of her time, reflect the more respectable side of the life of the upper classes. Her *Marie Antoinette and Her Children* was a deliberate attempt to improve the frivolous, even immoral image of the queen by depicting her as a royal mother. By contrast, such canvases as Antoine Watteau's (1684–1721) *Pleasures of the Ball* or Jean–Honoré Fragonard's (1732–1806) *The Swing* set courtly pleasures or frankly amorous dalliance in dreamlike palaces or gardens. Watteau's fairy tale images of an oddly innocent aristocracy at play look more like figures out of old romance than lusty eighteenth–century gentlemen and ladies. In Fragonard's *Swing,* by contrast, carved little gods of love watch knowingly as a fatuous old man swings his young bride high over the bushes where a young gallant reclines, looking up the young lady's fluttering gown as she flashes overhead.

Middle-Class Realism in the Arts

The art of the rising middle classes projects a very different image of the age. Like aristocratic art, however, bourgeois art offers immediate enjoyment to the eye and a pleasing reassurance of the specialness of those for whom it was intended. Once more, these were paintings people liked to look at, books people liked to read.

Like the Dutch burghers of the seventeenth century, English, French, German, and other bourgeois citizens were increasingly wealthy, educated, and self–confident in the eighteenth century. Like their predecessors, they patronized art and literature that reflected their own realistic and moralistic vision of their world. We can thus depend on the accuracy of the details of London drawing rooms and taverns shown in William Hogarth's (1697–1764) prints and paintings and of the peasant homes depicted by Jean–Baptiste Greuze (1725–1805). But the morals are also clear in such evocations of domestic virtue as Greuze's *Village Betrothal* or such graphic condemnation of immorality as Hogarth's celebrated series, *The Rake's Progress* or *The Harlot's Progress,* both following their subjects from a first moral slip to ultimate degradation.

At a deeper level, the genre scenes of Jean–Baptiste Siméon Chardin (1699–1779) combined moral judgment and fidelity to nature with pure pleasure in the everyday world. A master of still life, intimately familiar with the daily life of bourgeois Paris, Chardin offers totally convincing glimpses of a middle–class family at dinner, a little girl being dressed by her nurse, a boy spinning a top. In addition, pictures like *Grace Before Meat* carry a firm conviction of the moral worth of the bourgeois style of life. This attitude contrasts strikingly with the frivolous cupids and rococo curlicues affected by the aristocracy.

In literature, also, bourgeois taste found its own unique expression. Drama on middle–class themes appeared in France and Germany, and in Britain the English novel took shape in direct response to middle–class demand. Again, bourgeois realism and moralism are clearly detectable, but so is a genuine enjoyment of the material world.

Generally masquerading as collections of letters, these epistolary novels appealed to a strong desire for verisimilitude, for a true-to-life feel in fiction. They dealt with familiar, even commonplace subjects: the adventures of a young man in Henry Fielding's (1707–1754) *Tom Jones* (1749) or the attempted seduction of a servant girl in Samuel Richardson's (1689–1761) *Pamela* (1740). Clear descriptions, plain narrative, and language like that of common discourse predominated in a fiction free of rhetorical decoration or classical allusion. The social types and psychological reactions of the characters, strange though their moral earnestness and tender sentimentality may seem to us, were pleasantly familiar to their bourgeois readers.

Women both wrote and read many novels from the emergence of the genre. The colorful fictions of the later seventeenth–century writer Aphra Behn (1640–1689) are sometimes read as precursors of Defoe in their sense of place and time. More celebrated was Fanny Burney (1752–1840), whose early novels *Evelina* (1778) and *Cecilia* (1782) earned her fame and fortune. Burney's work appealed to the interest of middle–class women in good manners, sentimental relationships, and the eventual triumph of virtue. Between them, Defoe and Burney summed up the attitudes of bourgeois men and women of the age.

Popular Culture

The popular culture of the eighteenth century also found its expression in the arts. Its roots ran deep into the past and were still firm in the traditional society, beliefs, and pastimes of the rural and urban masses. Impoverished and often grueling though the existence of this majority of Western people was, there was pleasure in their lives and in their arts as well.

The pastimes of most Europeans, like their social organization, were still focused around local groups and places: the family, the age group, the village and the neighborhood, the peasant hearthside and the urban tavern. Major celebrations included church festivals, the festivals of local saints, celebration of the harvest, and midwinter carnival immediately preceding Lent. Community events of more recent origin were urban fairs, with their acrobats, freaks, and conjurers, and such increasingly commercialized sports as cockfighting, horse racing, and boxing, where upper and lower classes often mingled.

Among the art forms prominent in this popular culture were a traditional oral literature and a cheap printed literature of chapbooks and tracts. Centuries–old oral forms included popular ballads and longer epics, comic plays like the Italian *commedia dell'arte,* puppet plays, parodies of sermons and trials, and plays based on Bible stories and saints' lives that went back to the Middle Ages. English chapbooks and the French "blue library" offered cheaply printed versions of entertaining adventure stories and humorous narratives, religious catechisms and devotional tracts, books on supernatural and occult subjects, and how–to books.

Through many of these forms of entertainment, meanwhile, ran strong veins of violence and bawdy humor shared by upper and lower classes alike. Warrior tales, Punch and Judy shows, animal fights, boxing, and public brawls revealed a traditional taste for combat. Sexual and scatological humor in poems, plays, tales, and carnival presentations, like the bawdy behavior of May Eve and carnival nights, spoke of even deeper and more universal human passions.

Summary

The *philosophes* of the eighteenth–century Enlightenment believed that human reason could both understand and control the world. In print and through the personal contacts of the salon, these social critics both attacked the society of the *ancien régime* and expressed their faith in nature, humanity, and progress. Eighteenth–century philosophers also offered blueprints for a better society, including Rousseau's idealistic social contract, Montesquieu's emphasis on limiting the powers of government, and Adam Smith's free–market theory that the economy should be allowed to operate according to the natural laws of supply and demand.

Some of Europe's rulers, the so–called enlightened absolutists, claimed to be disciples of the philosophes and to rule in the spirit of the Age of Reason. Frederick the Great of Prussia, Catherine the Great of Russia, and Joseph II of Austria, among others, did discuss and even institute a variety of political, economic, and social reforms. Often, however, these changes were intended to make government more efficient and absolutist rulers stronger rather than to improve the lot of the ruler's subjects.

Culture in the eighteenth century aimed to please both the intellect and the senses. Neoclassical art recognized the great models of the past, while the rococo style offered cheerfully frivolous settings for the social life of the aristocracy. Middle–class realism, by contrast, glorified real life, bourgeois morality, and the new sentimentalism of the later 1700s.

Some Key Terms

bluestocking 399
categorical imperative 409
checks and balances 404
deism 408
enlightened absolutism 410
Enlightenment 397
free market 406
general will 405

human perfectibility 402
laissez faire 406
Methodism 408
nature 401
neoclassicism 414
philosophe 398
physiocrats 405
Pietism 408

Rechtsstaat 411
rococo 414
salon 399
salonière 399
social contract 404
social progress 402
supply and demand 406

Notes

1. René Descartes, *A Discourse on Method,* trans. G. B. Rowlings (London: Walter Scott, 1901), 38.

2. Immanuel Kant, "What Is Enlightenment?" in *The Portable Age of Reason Reader,* ed. Crane Brinton (New York: Viking Press, 1956), 298–299.

3. James Keir, *The First Part of a Dictionary of Chemistry* (Birmingham: Elliot & Kay, 1789), iii.

4. Quoted in Isser Woloch, *Eighteenth Century Europe: Tradition and Progress 1715–1789* (New York: W. W. Norton, 1982), 241.

5. Jean–Jacques Rousseau, *The Social Contract,* trans. Willmoore Kendall (Philadelphia: Henry Regnery Co., 1954), 33.

6. Adam Smith, *An Inquiry into the Nature and Causes of the Wealth of Nations,* ed. Ludwig von Mises (Chicago: Henry Regnery Co., 1953), 101–112.

7. Poulain de la Barre, quoted in Paul Hoffman, "L'Héritage des lumières: Mythes et modèles de la femininité au XVIIIe siècle," *Romantisme: Revue du Dix–Huitieme Siecle,* nos. 13–14 (1976): 8.

8. Rousseau himself, however, abandoned all his own children to a foster home.

9. Julien Offray de la Mettrie, *Man a Machine* (La Salle, Ill.: Open Court, 1912), p. 128.

10. Leonard Krieger, *Kings and Philosophers, 1689–1789* (New York: W. W. Norton, 1970), 253.

11. Plato, *The Republic,* Book V, in *Five Great Dialogues* (Toronto: D. Van Nostrand, 1942), 362.

12. Voltaire, "The Philosopher–Prince," in *Enlightened Despotism: Reform or Reaction?* ed. Roger Wines (Boston: D. C. Heath, 1967), 19.

Reading List

Beales, D. *Joseph II.* New York: Cambridge University Press, 1987. Promises to be the definitive biography. See also T. Blanning, *Joseph II and Enlightened Despotism* (London: Longmans Green, 1970), for a short introduction and E. Crankshaw, *Maria Theresa* (New York: Viking, 1969). A solid life of the ruler.

Berlin, I., ed. *The Age of Enlightenment: The Eighteenth Century Philosophers.* Salem, N.H.: Arno, 1956. Useful collection of works by leading thinkers, edited by a prominent twentieth–century intellectual historian.

Cassirer, E. *The Philosophy of the Enlightenment.* Princeton, N.J.: Princeton University Press, 1951. Magisterial analysis of fundamental principles of the Enlightenment.

Darnton, R. *The Literary Underground of the Old Regime.* Cambridge, Mass.: Harvard University Press, 1982. Essays on aspects of popular culture in France.

Gagliardo, J. G. *Enlightened Despotism.* Arlington Heights, Ill.: Harlan Davidson, 1967. Handy brief introduction.

Gay, P. *The Enlightenment.* New York: Simon and Schuster, 1974. Insightful overview.

Goodman, D. *The Republic of Letters: A Cultural History of the French Enlightenment.* Ithaca: Cornell University Press, 1994. Literature and life in the Enlightenment. See also R. vanDulmen, *The Society of the Enlightenment* (New

York: St. Martin's Press, 1992) on the German middle class and the new ideas.

Guehenno, J. *Jean–Jacques Rousseau*. New York: Columbia University Press, 1966. Masterful account of a complicated figure whom no one seems confident of "getting right." See also M. Hulliung, *The Autocritique of the Enlightenment* (Cambridge: Harvard University Press, 1994) and Rousseau's *The Social Contract*, translated by G. Hopkins (Oxford: Oxford University Press, 1971).

Held, J., and D. Posner. *Seventeenth and Eighteenth Century Art*. Englewood Cliffs, N.J.: Prentice Hall, 1972. Broad coverage of styles during these two centuries.

Krieger, L. *Kings and Philosophers, 1689–1789*. New York: Norton, 1970. Perceptive discussion of rulers, thinkers, and the interaction between them.

Madariaga, I. de. *Catherine the Great: A Short History*. New Haven: Yale University Press, 1990. A brief life drawing on the latest research, for nonspecialist readers.

May, H. F. *The Enlightenment and America*. New York: Oxford University Press, 1976. Wide–ranging assessment of the impact of the Enlightenment on American ideas and attitudes.

McClellan, J. W., III. *Science Reorganized: Scientific Societies in the Eighteenth Century*. New York: Columbia University Press, 1985. Multiplication of state–supported scientific societies during the Enlightenment century.

Schonberger, A., and H. Soehner. *The Age of Rococo*. London: Thames and Hudson, 1960. Lavishly illustrated.

Smith, B. G. *Changing Lives: Women in European History Since 1700*. Lexington, Mass.: Heath, 1989. Perhaps the best survey of women's experience in Europe over the past three centuries.

Till, N. *Mozart and the Enlightenment*. New York: Norton, 1993. Enlightenment ideas and the operas.

Voltaire. *Political Writings*. Ed. by D. Williams. New York: Cambridge University Press, 1994. The most revered radical intellectual of the century speaks out on government. See also his *Candide*, many editions.

Wilson, A. M. *Diderot*. Oxford: Oxford University Press, 1972. Best biography of Diderot, who possessed one of the most wide–ranging minds of all the philosophes.

— 17 —

Revolutionary Beginnings

The American Revolution and the
Industrial Revolution

◆The Agricultural Revolution and the Population Explosion
◆The Industrial Revolution   ◆Political Revolts in Europe
◆The American Revolution   ◆Colonial Revolts in Latin America

A landslide of change in the Western world began shortly after the middle of the eighteenth century. The eighteenth was the first of the truly modern centuries, and revolutionary change—in society, economics and politics, in Europe and the Americas—has been a central feature of the modern age ever since.

We have seen the Enlightenment challenge to the old order, climaxing in the decades between 1760 and 1790, and the response of Europe's enlightened despots. But the process of change, once begun, accelerated more rapidly and spread to more aspects of eighteenth–century society than anyone had anticipated. Among the radical changes of the 1700s were the modern agricultural revolution, the beginnings of the population explosion, and the great Industrial Revolution, as well as rumblings of political revolt in Europe and in the American colonies. During the next two centuries, the 1800s and the 1900s, these new trends swept away both the old economic system and the political order of the ancient régime, totally transforming the life of the West.

The first of these changes, the agricultural revolution, actually began in the later 1600s, but reached its flood tide in the early 1700s. The population explosion began not long before 1750, and the greatest surge of population growth came during the later 1700s. The Industrial Revolution got under way around 1760 in Britain and spread to the continent in the next century. Political challenges to the ancien régime, finally, gathered momentum in the 1770s, when peasants revolted in Russia, angry mobs surged through the streets of London, and the American Revolution exploded in Britain's North American colonies.

These material and political changes were only the beginning. Agricultural and industrial expansion continued for the next two hundred years, while the population explosion, brought under control in the West, spread to the rest of the world with devastating impact. The political revolts mentioned in the last paragraph, meanwhile, were followed by the great French Revolution (1789–1799), the Latin American Wars of Liberation (1810–1824), waves of revolt across Europe between 1820 and 1848, the shattering Russian Revolution of 1917, and other ideological upheavals around the world in the twentieth century. The revolutions that began in the 1700s thus pointed the way to a revolutionary future that would last two centuries at the least.

◆ The Agricultural Revolution and the Population Explosion ◆

The story of the sweeping changes that gathered momentum in the 1700s begins on the most changeless of European scenes: in the country houses and peasant villages of Europe. Here a handful of large landowners and tenant farmers began to try new methods of growing things. From this burst of improvements in soil cultivation and stock raising called the *agricultural revolution,* new patterns of life on the land began to emerge.

A related phenomenon was the beginning of one of the most amazing features of modern history—the global *population explosion,* a rapid acceleration in population growth that began in the eighteenth century and continues to the present day. We will look here at both the eighteenth–century agricultural revolution and the eighteenth–century beginnings of the population explosion.

Agricultural Improvements

Need for reform was certainly there. Farmland separated into strips in the medieval way might divide good and bad land equally among peasants. But it also wasted land on footpaths and strip dividers, led to endless disputes over rights and ownership, and produced holdings too small for more than subsistence living. Country people also contributed to their own plight by clinging to outworn practices like leaving a third of their strips fallow each year to restore fertility or burning as fuel cow dung that could have been used much more profitably as manure.

As early as the seventeenth century, industrious Dutch and Flemish farmers had introduced a number of innovations. The Low Countries were famous for having painstakingly reclaimed much of their land from the sea with their dikes. They also combined smaller holdings into larger, more efficient ones and combined crops and stock in mutually supportive ways.

The most influential pioneers of the agricultural revolution of the first half of the eighteenth century, however, were English. Jethro Tull (1674–1741), for example, urged the planting of clover and turnips on land formerly left fallow, a practice which both restored fertility and provided pasturage for stock. Tull also invented the seed drill, which enabled farmers to deposit seeds in regular rows of holes rather than wastefully scattering them over the surface of the land.

Other successful agricultural reformers included Lord Charles ("Turnip") Townshend (1674–1738) and Robert Bakewell (1725–1795). Townshend's experiments led many landlords to adopt the basic rotation of turnips, barley, clover, and wheat, alternating periods of soil enrichment with seasons of planting traditional grains. Bakewell, a tenant farmer himself, became an immensely successful stock breeder. He led in the movement to breed sheep and cattle for meat rather than exclusively for their wool and milk and in developing thick–bodied, shorter–legged horses for farm work.

The English example was admired and followed in other parts of Europe, particularly where dense population created a demand for increased agricultural output. In the Nether-

Chronology 17: Political and Economic Revolutions

1700–1750	*Agricultural Revolution*
1750	*Population explosion begins*
1760	*Industrial Revolution begins in Britain*
1760s	*Early factories point toward much larger industrial complexes to come*
1763–1774	*"Wilkes and liberty!" agitation in London*
1765	*Hargreaves's spinning jenny speeds up spinning process*
1773–1775	*Pugachev's rebellion in Russia*
1775–1783	*American Revolution*
1776	*American Declaration of Independence*
1782	*Watt's steam engine adapted for many industrial uses*
1785	*Cartwright's power loom speeds up weaving by using steam power*
1788	*United States Constitution ratified*

lands, the Rhineland, northern Italy, and some parts of France, the new methods were adapted to local conditions. For those who were able to use them successfully, production—and profits—rose rapidly.

Not everyone was overjoyed at these agricultural breakthroughs. Most cottagers simply could not afford the investment in fencing or seed needed to join the agricultural revolution. And enclosure of land for large–scale grain cultivation, like enclosures for grazing sheep two centuries earlier, drove many peasants off the land altogether.

In many parts of western Europe, however, less productive smallholdings were replaced by middle–sized and larger farms run by farmers with capital, knowledge, and enthusiasm for experimenting. The overall result was burgeoning agricultural production, improvements in the quality and quantity of livestock, and the expansion of commercial rather than subsistence farming.

Causes of the Population Explosion

The world's human population had taken tens of thousands of years to reach perhaps three–quarters of a billion by 1750. In the brief two and a half centuries since, that population has multiplied almost eight times to five and a half billion and is still growing rapidly. How this unprecedented population surge began in Europe is one of the stickiest problems of modern Western demography and social history.

Quite suddenly, in the middle decades of the eighteenth century, population figures began to rise. Despite the lack of national census data before 1800, it seems likely that this was the most dramatic spurt of demographic growth in Western history. Attempts to explain this remarkable fact have produced a flow of theories and disputes that, like the population explosion itself, continues to the present day.

Both declining death rates and increases in births probably contributed to population increases in the 1700s. Declining mortality was probably due to the disappearance of bubonic plague shortly after 1700, to the relative decline in the ferocity of eighteenth century wars as a result of better discipline, to improved food production, and to a scattering of advances in sanitation. Rising birth rates may have been rooted in the undermining of the power of landlords and guild masters, freeing young people to marry earlier and thus to have more children. It has also been urged that the Industrial Revo-

Population Density in Eighteenth-Century Europe

lution, providing jobs that even children could do, created incentives for raising larger families. Some have even seen a new surge of family feeling encouraging larger families.

Soaring Population Figures

One way or another, an astonishing rise in the population of the West got under way in the mid–eighteenth century. Even a few rough figures will indicate that this demographic acceleration deserves its explosive label. Because national censuses were rare before 1800, we have only fragmentary figures for most countries in the preceding century. These figures, however, certainly suggest that the demographic growth of early modern times resumed with unprecedented vigor after 1750.

The population of France, Europe's most populous nation in 1700, grew from perhaps 18 million at Louis XIV's death in 1715 to 26 million at the time of the French Revolution in 1789. The British, who numbered something over 5 million in 1700, were almost 9 million strong in 1800, and Prussia doubled in size in the century of Frederick the Great. Europe as a whole may have had as many as 120 million people at the beginning of the eighteenth century and 140 million in 1750, when the population explosion really took off. By 1800, the total was probably pushing 190 million, the most rapid half–century increase in Western history.

Parson Thomas Malthus (1766–1834), writing just before 1800, became the first to alert the Western world to the grim implications of such accelerated population growth. In his *Essay on Population* (1798), Malthus predicted that at present growth rates, population would tend to double every quarter century. Despite improvements in agricultural methods, however, food production could never keep up with such population growth rates. The result of these *"Malthusian ratios"* between rapid population growth and slower growth in food production would be hunger, disease, and bare subsistence living for the masses.

In the eighteenth century itself, the impact of the population explosion was particularly great on the personal lives of women. The proliferation of too often unwanted children led some poor women to abort the fetus or kill the infant. Well–off women frequently employed wet nurses or shipped infants off to rural foster homes. In either case, unsanitary conditions, neglect, and such practices as the use of gin or laudanum (opium) to quiet crying led to early death.

But not all the growing numbers of new human beings were rejected by a society not yet able to cope. The later eighteenth century, after all, did welcome Rousseau's vision of childish innocence and of the importance of careful individual attention to a child's education and individual development. Dolls, toys, and a distinctive children's literature proliferated in the later eighteenth century. Well–off parents posed for painters cuddling their children, and domestic letters are full of affectionate concern over childish ailments, careers, and marriages. What has been called "the age of the child" in Western social history had begun.

◆ The Industrial Revolution ◆

Most impressive of all these socio–economic transformations was the *Industrial Revolution*—traditionally dated 1760–1830—that began in Britain and subsequently spread to continental Europe, the Americas, and the rest of the world. The core of this epochal change is usually seen as technological in nature, the replacement of hand tools by power–driven machines in manufacturing. These machines, in turn, led to the birth of the factory system, mass production, modern transportation and communication, and other technical shifts.

On the economic side, the Industrial Revolution led to the rise of industrial capitalism, the emergence of the industrial city, and the development of a society dominated not by agriculture but by industrial production. The birth of modern industrial society was thus clearly one of the most important transformations of material life in human history.

This section will examine the background and probable causes of the Industrial Revolution. It will then follow its development in the British cotton–textile and iron and coal industries, and look at its early impact on women workers and on society at large.

Causes of the Industrial Revolution

Before the Industrial Revolution, manufacturing was, literally, the "handmaking" of tools, clothes, objects of everyday use and luxury goods of all sorts. In 1700, the material things humans wanted were being handmade in two ways. Since medieval times, urban guilds of highly trained workers had crafted many things, particularly the expensive, high–quality goods demanded by the wealthy. The second type of manufacturing enterprise was *cottage industry* based on the putting–out system that had emerged in early modern times. In this system, particularly important in the textile industry, merchants purchased raw wool, distributed it to peasant cottagers for spinning and weaving, and then picked up the hand-made cloth for resale at a considerable profit.

A peasant family typically divided up the labor, the wife and other female relatives spinning the short fibers into long thread, the husband weaving the threads into cloth. As increasing numbers of peasants became involved, the resulting "thickening" of the putting–out system has sometimes been called *protoindustrialism*. Prevalent in southeastern and northern England, in parts of the Netherlands, France, and Germany, protoindustrial rural manufacturing may be thought of as a transitional stage to modern industrial organization.

The great change in the economic life of the West—and the world—was first defined more than a hundred years ago in Arnold Toynbee's book on *The Industrial Revolution* (1884). Toynbee saw this transformation as characterized by "great mechanical inventions," "the substitution of the factory for the domestic system," "the new class of great capitalist employers," and "the Misery which came upon large sections of working people."[1] No single cause can adequately account for such a complicated and far–reaching change. As with a chemical experiment, a number of ingredients were necessary. Among them were resources, labor, demand, capital, technology, and entrepreneurship.

Two fundamental requirements were natural resources and an available labor force. The key raw materials for early industrial development were coal, the crucial power source, and iron, of which the new machines were to be built. Because both resources were heavy, it was helpful if they were located in close geographical proximity to one another or near rivers or canals on which they could be cheaply transported. As for labor, in the eighteenth century, two factors combined to generate unprecedented numbers of laborers in need of work. The population explosion drastically increased the sheer numbers of people, while the agricultural revolution rendered many of them redundant on the farms. Labor was thus available in increasing quantities to staff the new industries.

Basic economic essentials included a sufficient *economic demand* for larger quantities of goods and a supply of capital sufficient to pay for the new industrial plants. Demand, like labor, resulted in part from the population explosion: more people meant a need for more things. Equally important, significant segments of Europe's upper and middle classes could afford to pay for them. Large sums were also needed for *capital investment* in the industrial plant itself. Profits from foreign and domestic trade and from overseas empire, accumulating in eighteenth–century banks, provided immense reserves of capital for this purpose. Forms of business organization imposing only "limited liability" for the company's debts—liability limited to the amount of each investor's investment rather than to his total resources—also encouraged large–scale commitment of funds for business purposes.

The most obvious key to the industrial takeoff, however, would seem to have been the technological innovations of the century. Inventors were now called upon to solve problems that made the existing technology inadequate to meet the growing demand. Their solutions would both add to the total technology on which others might draw and create new

Manufacturing in Eighteenth-Century Europe

problems demanding new technical solutions. The result was the modern process of *technological development,* an upward spiral stimulating both industrial growth and economic expansion.

The guiding spirit of this great change, however, was the industrial *entrepreneur* who brought together all the other factors—resources and labor, demand, capital, and technology—to make industrialization happen. Like the catalyst in a chemical experiment, entrepreneurship triggered the transformation. Entrepreneurs also developed division of labor, large-scale production, and modern marketing practices. Many exploited the labor force and resorted to shady tactics to defeat competitors. Yet they did provide the catalytic element in the complicated mix that, sometime around 1760, exploded into the Industrial Revolution.

England and the Industrial Takeoff

In Britain all these elements came together in the later part of the eighteenth century. The nation that had developed the first large constitutional monarchy and had outdistanced all rivals in the race for overseas empire thus also took the lead in industrial development as the nineteenth century began.

The necessary ingredients were actually all there by the mid–1700s. Parts of the British midlands and the north were vast coalfields pocked with iron deposits. The agricultural revolution had flourished in Britain, producing increasing numbers of laborers and contributing to burgeoning economic demand. Wealth had piled up in the British Isles from domestic and foreign trade and from the growth of empire: Britain in fact enjoyed both the largest internal free–trade zone in Europe and the largest overseas empire. This wealth both increased economic demand and, as it accumulated in economic institutions like the Bank of England, provided capital in large quantities. Technical ingenuity was encouraged by a liberal patent law and by a weakened system of mercantilistic regulation of domestic industry. Entrepreneurial ambitions and hustle were stimulated by a flexible social system in which a gentleman could invest or even engage in "trade" without a hopeless loss of status and in which business people could hope for some degree of acceptance in respectable society.

It is easy to exaggerate Britain's lead in industrial development during the takeoff phase of the Industrial Revolution. Other European states, including the Austrian Netherlands (Belgium today) and France, were expanding their industrial output, generally without benefit of steam power and the new machinery. France, using preindustrial methods, was still producing more iron than Britain as late as the 1780s. Even in Britain, not more than a few hundred steam engines were "on line" as late as 1800, perhaps 5,000 horsepower altogether. The vast majority of British workers still labored in urban guilds or in their own cottages rather than in the handful of new factories as the century ended.

Yet something decisive had happened in Britain. A fundamentally new system of industrial production was at least taking shape, beginning in the textile industry and pointing toward the coming predominance of steam power.

Cotton, Coal, and Iron

The beginning of the Industrial Revolution came in the cotton textile industry. But the progress essential to all industries came in iron and coal, and in the crucial development of the new power source involving both: the steam engine.

The textile industry, one of the oldest in the world, employed a larger percentage of British workers than any other trade. Many textile workers, furthermore, were in the protoindustrial sector of merchant–capitalized cottage industry. Of the cloth thus manufactured in Britain, woolens were the largest, the old medieval standard. But cotton had become increasingly popular since cotton textiles had begun to be imported in quantity from India in the seventeenth century. And it was in the relatively new cotton industry that the Industrial Revolution began.

The basic technological problem was a need to accelerate cotton production to meet expanded demand. Inventions to achieve this end came first in the weaving, then in the spinning side of the industry. The *flying shuttle* invented by John Kay (1704–1764) speeded up the weaver's work by lifting alternate threads and "throwing" the shuttle across, pulling transverse threads between them. Faster weaving, however, created a need for technological advances in the spinning of thread. Breakthroughs in this area included the *spinning jenny,* perfected by Richard Hargreaves (d. 1778), which replaced the traditional cottage spinning wheel with a number of spindles which spun several threads at once. The *water frame,* developed by Richard Arkwright (1732–1792), hooked up first horses and then water power to these multiple spinning machines. Because these devices gave spinners the clear advantage, Edmund Cartwright (1743–1823) designed the first power loom to speed up the weaving process. And increasingly, all these textile machines were grouped in long factory sheds and hooked up, not to traditional power sources like horses or water mills, but to the new steam engines, motors powered by burning coal.

As with the component technologies of cloth production, the coal and iron industries advanced in tandem through a process of problem solving and interacting development.

Britain's iron industry lagged behind that of the continent because Britain, having burned off its forests, had to use coal for fuel—and coal could not be used for smelting iron. Early in the 1700s, however, Abraham Darby (c. 1678–1717) devised a process for smelting pig iron with coke produced by the burning of coal. Later in the 1700s, Henry Cort (1740–1800) invented the "puddling" process for manufacturing malleable iron—easily shaped into objects—that was soon being used by ironmasters all over Britain. By the end of the century, visionary ironmaster John Wilkinson (1728–1808) had bored iron cylinders of unexampled precision for cannon, had built the first sizable iron bridge, more than 100 feet long, and could foresee the day when carriages would run on iron rails and iron ships would sail the seas.

The most fateful single technological breakthrough, however, was the development of the *steam engine* by the Scottish instrument maker James Watt (1736–1819). Coal-powered steam engines had been constructed earlier, but only for pumping water out of the coal mines themselves. Watt built a much more fuel–efficient model and developed a rotary version that could be hooked up to a much wider variety of industrial operations. This new power source would transform the industrial world in the next century.

Women in the Industrial Revolution

Women did their share of the labor that built the new industrial society. With their husbands, and often their children as well, women moved from work on the farm or in the family shop to labor outside the home as part of the new industrial work force. More commonly employed in some industries than in others, women found many jobs in the textile mills, fewer in ironworking. But they also worked in mines and performed other physically demanding jobs.

Like men, women sometimes lost traditional jobs to the new machines, while in other cases they found new areas of employment opening up thanks to technological change. In France, women who had been employed for two hundred years as "drawgirls," positioning threads for weaving in the brocade industry were, in the later eighteenth century, put out of work. As power looms spread to France after 1790, however, growing numbers of women were employed to run the new machines, displacing the men who had monopolized the weaving trade in the days of handlooms.

Women were often considered more adaptable to the rigorous requirements of the new machinery than men. Women were more careful and more likely to accept direction than men used to working on their own schedules or on no schedule at all. However, both women and the children who were often employed in factories were treated brutally by

Hargreaves' spinning jenny greatly speeded up the spinning of thread for textiles. When women, who had traditionally done the spinning in cottages, moved into factories, they also ran these machines. (Culver Pictures, Inc.)

foremen determined to force them into the artificial rhythms of the throbbing power looms. In some English mills, children were compelled to sing popular hymns to keep them awake and alert as they hurried from machine to machine.

In the cramped, dirty quarters without plumbing and with very little furniture where the new industrial workers congregated, women also had to keep their families fed and clothed. Younger, unmarried women may have had a somewhat less difficult role. Like the young men who came to work in the mills, they had only themselves to care for and may have enjoyed escaping from the prying eyes of parents and other village authorities. The "factory girl," like the male mill hand, was part of the army of laborers who turned an agrarian West into the first modern industrial society in the world.

The Dawn of Modern Industrialism

In 1800, the consequences of the Industrial Revolution were still modest in the century that gave it birth. The new machines would not really begin to transform Europe until the nineteenth century. Yet travelers from the continent who got a glimpse of what was going on in the north of England or the wilds of Wales two centuries ago sometimes had a sense at least of a strange and even frightening new age dawning. Thus, a French mineralogist wrote in awe, after visiting a British ironworks in 1784, of wandering through a maze of "huge cranes, every kind of windlass, lever, and tackle for moving heavy loads," deafened by "the piercing noise of the pulleys, the continuous sound of hammering. . . . There is," he declared, "such a succession of these workshops that the outer air is quite hot; the night is so filled with fire and light that . . . we do not know whether we are looking at a volcano in eruption or have been miraculously transported to Vulcan's cave, where he and his cyclops are manufacturing lightning."[2] Three years after the last battle of the American Revolution, five years before the French Revolution broke out, Britain thus had a revolution of its own in full swing. In the long run, it was perhaps the most consequential revolution of all.

◆ Political Revolts in Europe ◆

Shaken by the agricultural and industrial revolutions and the population explosion, the eighteenth century was also a time of increasing social and political tension all across Europe. As we will see below, pressures for change came from many directions—social, political, and economic. These tensions in turn led to peasant revolts, to mobs in city streets, even to bourgeois or aristocratic conspiracies against the status quo. A number of these upheavals will be dealt with in the following pages.

Pressures for Change

The political structure of the eighteenth century, a loose interlocking directorate of monarchs, aristocrats, and clergy, had dominated most of Western society since the Middle Ages. In the 1700s, however, pressures began to build against these political components. The power of the absolute monarchs, even when channeled toward "enlightened" ends, could weigh heavily on eighteenth–century society. Europe's aristocracies frequently felt financial pressure to squeeze more revenues out of their peasants and to defend their traditional privileges and prerogatives against royal bureaucrats. A worldly clergy, under heavy attack from the philosophes, might retain the support of the peasantry but commanded little respect from the enlightened elites.

Other elements of society also felt the pressures building in a Western world on the eve of monumental changes. Members of the commercial and professional middle classes, prosperous, educated, and increasingly self–confident, resented aristocratic pretensions and were moved by commitment to enlightened ideals. Peasants had more concrete problems, from the spread of enclosures in western Europe to the tightening of serfdom in eastern Europe, as well as royal taxes and noble exactions everywhere.

In Europe's growing number of large cities, finally, discontent was often on the verge of boiling over. By 1800, there were perhaps twenty cities with populations of more than a hundred thousand, while Paris reached well over half a million and London a million people. In the medieval slums of these preindustrial urban centers, even the working poor could be driven over the brink of violence by a simple rise in the price of bread.

Peasant Revolts and Urban Turbulence

Across later eighteenth–century Europe, many groups reacted to the pressures of the times by erupting into rebellion. Much, though by no means all, of this domestic turbulence involved the lower levels of society, the peasantry and the urban poor.

Peasants lived lives deeply rooted in tradition and largely dependent on their ability to extract a meager living from the soil. In England, they rioted against enclosures instigated by improving landlords who expelled tenants from their lands. In the Austrian Habsburg empire, they rebelled against heavy taxes, the *robot* or labor service owed their overlords, and other survivals of medieval serfdom. In czarist Russia, dozens of serf rebellions climaxed in the reign of Catherine the Great with the massive revolt led by Emelian Pugachev (1726–1775).

Pugachev's rebellion raised a heterogeneous host of runaway serfs, religious dissenters called Old Believers, independent Cossack bands, Mongol tribesmen, and others who had collected in the Volga region of southeastern Russia. Pugachev himself, an illiterate Cossack claiming to be Catherine's murdered husband Peter III, won popular support by announcing the abolition of serfdom but offered no positive programs or plans to unite his diverse horde. He raised the banner of revolt in 1773 and ravaged much of southern Russia until he was finally defeated by the imperial army in 1774. He was sent to Moscow in an iron cage to be executed. In fact, his ill–organized rising had little chance of success. Like most peasant revolts, it was a symptom of rather than a solution to the far-reaching problems of Europe's peasant majorities.

In other parts of Europe, the laboring classes and large numbers of indigents who congregated in the cities also exploded in urban uprisings. In Britain, urban unrest could reflect the most up-to-date political ideas, as in the tumult over *Wilkes and Liberty!* in the 1760s and 1770s. John Wilkes (1727–1797), a journalist and fashionable man-about-town with political ambitions, emerged from a running series of squabbles with George III and his ministers as an unlikely popular hero. Whether he was opposing the royal peace that ended the Seven Years' War, composing a diatribe against women, or fighting Parliament's efforts to exclude him from his seat, Wilkes had the common touch. The surging crowds

Emelian Pugachev, pictured here after his capture, led a massive peasant revolt against Catherine the Great. Such upheavals occurred many times in Russia and elsewhere in Europe but seldom succeeded. (Bildarchiv Preussischer Kulturbesitz.)

chanting "Wilkes and Liberty!" may not have understood the fine points of constitutional law involved, but they marched with him, voted for him, and put his picture up in half the pubs in London.

Aristocratic Resistance and Bourgeois Agitation

Aristocratic resistance to royal absolutism, particularly to enlightened despotism, could take the form of court intrigue or of the manipulation of such traditional institutions as estates general or law courts. But it could also go well beyond such traditional ploys, exploding in violent political confrontations and even leading to political assassination.

A colorful example of this aristocratic reaction was the struggle between Gustavus III (r. 1771–1792) and the aristocracy of Sweden. Confronting noble discontent head on, King Gustavus seized control of the legislative Diet that the nobility dominated. He also imposed a written constitution on the country—one that gave the crown still more power. Gustavus's continuing attacks on aristocratic inheritance of land, control of high office, and other prerogatives moved experienced intriguers among the nobility to plot his downfall. In 1792, Gustavus III was melodramatically assassinated during a masquerade ball.

The middle ranks of society, too, were capable of violent political agitation and even action. In the 1780s, for instance, the Habsburg emperor Joseph II (r. 1765–1790) tried to impose an autocratic if enlightened regime on the old established merchant families of the Austrian Netherlands. The commercial oligarchs of these Flemish cities responded by organizing secret societies, and in 1789 two of the ten provinces declared their independence from the Austrian emperor. The attempt was frustrated by divisions between the patriciate and the less–affluent and prestigious burghers, followed by an invasion of the provinces by the armies of the French Revolution. The solid commercial bourgeoisie of the Low Countries, however, had clearly demonstrated their revolutionary potential.

In Britain also, middle– as well as upper–class radicals demanded changes and supported revolution, though usually in someone else's country. From the 1770s through the 1790s, radicals enthusiastically defended first the American, then the French Revolution, preached such drastic parliamentary reforms as universal male suffrage, and even urged the replacement of Parliament by some more representative body. In the 1790s, middle–class English radicals provided leadership for tumultuous working–class political societies that seemed on the verge of triggering revolutionary violence in Britain itself. In the 1790s, erstwhile reformer William Pitt the Younger (1759–1806) invoked rigorous treason and sedition laws to suppress radical meetings and exile the radical leaders.

✦The American Revolution✦

Revolts in Europe's American colonies contributed significantly to the political ferment that swept across the Western world in the later eighteenth century. There were rebellions in both North and South America, but it was the insurrection in Britain's thirteen North American colonies that astonished and inspired Europeans of a radical bent. The result of what began as a colonial revolt was the most successful of all the democratic revolutions—the American Revolution that began officially in 1776.

Seeds of Revolt in North America

The twentieth–century American image of the colonial cause in 1776 as that of an embattled David in conflict with a British Goliath does not reflect the real balance of forces. Britain's North American colonies were in fact prosperous, populous, and to a considerable degree self–governing even before the Revolution broke out. A century before India became "the jewel in the crown" of the British Empire, eastern North America occupied that place in Britain's global holdings. It was actually challenges to the freedom and prosperity already achieved by the colonists that lit the flames of revolt. And the colonies stood a much better chance than David did.

The string of colonies that ran from New England down through New York and Pennsylvania to Virginia and the deeper south had a population of three million, fully a third of that of the mother country. The colonists enjoyed a developed commerce, some local handicraft industry, and immense land resources. Unlike the European peasantry, most freeborn Americans owned enough land to feed their families—the indispensable prerequisite for political freedom in the eyes of such democrats as Thomas Jefferson. Basic literacy, rooted in Protestant religious emphasis on Bible reading, was widespread and helped produce a more informed citizenry—and thus one that could more readily be reached by the propaganda of revolt. All the colonies, furthermore, possessed elected legislative assemblies capable of successfully resisting the will of their appointed royal governors. A century and a half after the first settlements in the wilderness, in short, the British Americans had a very good thing going.

Then, in the aftermath of Britain's victory over France in the Seven Years' War, young, aggressive George III (r. 1760–1820) and his ministers began to exert new pressures on their New World colonies. Attempting a general overhaul of what was after 1763 the world's largest overseas empire, the government headed by Lord North (1732–1792) sought to strengthen the traditional ties of mercantilist control. Concerted efforts were made to suppress smuggling, a practice common in all the overseas colonies. Troops intended for the future defense of the overseas territories were quartered there at the expense of the colonials. And an ill–considered succession of new taxes and customs duties were levied on a range of common articles of daily use, from newspapers to tea. In London, such royal measures seemed fair enough, particularly considering the cost to the government of defending the colonies from the French and their Indian allies in the late war. In the bustling streets of colonial Boston or New York, or in the more rustic Virginia capital of Williamsburg, however, the new policies seemed tyrannical infringements of traditional colonial rights.

As in Europe, American expressions of discontent drew upon the radical political ideas of the Enlightenment. All kinds of contemporary ideas were in fact in circulation among educated settlers. Colonials of a scientific bent like Benjamin Franklin (1706–1790) conducted experiments and founded societies for scientific studies like those in Europe. And well–read Americans such as Thomas Jefferson were aware of the natural–rights doctrines of John Locke and of the Lockean theory that legitimate government should be founded on a "social contract" involving both the governors and the governed. The radical Tom Paine (1737–1809) saw the revolt in the American colonies as having "sowed the seeds" of the French Revolution that broke out fourteen years later. But Paine's *Common Sense* (1776) and *The Rights of Man* (1791–1792) won large audiences on both sides of the Atlantic by preaching natural rights, representative government, and popular sovereignty. By the later 1700s, such views were common among radical and liberally inclined people all across the Western world.

Material grievances and subversive social theories, then, combined in North America as in Europe to spark an unprecedented political upheaval, the American contribution to the surge of revolutions with which the eighteenth century ended.

Minutemen, Liberty Boys, and the Continental Congress

The dozen years between the end of the Seven Years' War in 1763 and the skirmishes at Lexington and Concord that ignited the Revolutionary War in 1775 saw one of the most remarkable movements of a revolutionary age take shape in the American colonies. By the time the Declaration of Independence was passed by the Continental Congress in 1776, these prosperous colonies had been transformed into a hotbed of sedition, ready for armed resistance to the tyranny of kings.

As in Europe, the revolutionary spirit in the colonies took different forms among different segments of the population. Brilliant radical tacticians like Samuel Adams (1722–1803) in Massachusetts and eloquent orators like Patrick Henry (1736–1799) in Virginia orchestrated the response of the merchant and planter elites. Laborers, artisans, small shopkeepers, and backwoods farmers were more likely to react with violent action than with words to what they perceived as royal oppression. There were moderates in the opposition movement, demanding only the rescinding of oppressive royal policies and parliamentary acts. There were also increasing numbers of radicals who called for armed resistance and denied the right of the British crown to govern the colonies at all. In the end, British blunders, colonial tactical ingenuity, and the momentum of events swept the thirteen colonies into open revolt.

Subversive organizations proliferated at all levels through the 1760s and early 1770s. As London sought to tighten mercantilist controls, Americans reacted by turning colonial legislative assemblies into conduits for petitions and demands. Riotous gangs of so–called Liberty Boys attacked royal officials and their homes. Farmers' militias stockpiled weapons and drilled on village greens, prepared to stand to arms at a minute's notice—these were the *Minutemen* of American revolutionary legend. Activists from New Hampshire to Georgia coordinated their efforts through Committees of Correspondence, which shared information, ideas, and support up and down the long coastline.

Subversive words and organizations were accompanied by increasing amounts of physical violence. In 1770, British soldiers defending themselves against mob harassment in Boston opened fire on the crowd, killing half a dozen in what radicals like Sam Adams and Paul Revere quickly dubbed the "Boston Massacre." In 1772, Rhode Island saw the seizure and burning of the *Gaspee,* a British warship that had been too zealous in the suppression of smuggling. When Parliament attempted to impose a duty on imported tea in 1773, Liberty Boys and radical organizers prevented the landing of the tea in colonial ports, while at Boston a mob unconvincingly disguised as Indians boarded a ship full of the offensive commodity and hurled 340 chests of tea leaves into the harbor.

Goaded beyond endurance by the "Boston Tea Party," the Parliament in London put Boston under military rule, closed the port until the tea should be paid for, restructured the government of Massachusetts to give the royal governor more power, and imposed a series of other Coercive Acts (1774) designed to bring the insurrectionary colonies to heel. Angered at this new act of despotism and fearful that what could be done to Massachusetts today could be done to any other colony tomorrow, the colonists responded with vigorous political action, and then with military force.

Stimulated by the Committees of Correspondence, colonial legislatures in Massachusetts, Virginia, and elsewhere called for a gathering of representatives of all the colonies to coordinate American countermeasures. The result was the First *Continental Congress* of 1774. While ordinary citizens of many colonies sent food and fuel to help beleaguered Boston, the congress met at Philadelphia. Composed of solid middle– and upper–class citizens but dominated by the more radical element among them, the congress denounced the Coercive Acts, denied the right of the British government to interfere in the domestic affairs of colonies, and announced a boycott, not only of tea, but of all British goods. Then, in the spring of 1775, British troops dispatched from Boston to seize stockpiles of weapons in the nearby towns of Lexington and Concord met armed resistance from the Minutemen—the famous "shot heard round the world" that triggered the American Revolution.

The War for Independence

It was a revolution made with quill pens and clanking old–fashioned printing presses, with flintlock muskets and cannon balls. The ideals it espoused were not original, but part of the common Western heritage of Enlightenment radicalism. The scale of armed conflict, involving usually a few thousand combatants, was meager by comparison with European battles. But the American Revolution did produce the first and most long–lasting victory of the Age of Democratic Revolutions.

The most impressive achievement of the war of words was the *Declaration of Independence,* drafted by Virginia's Thomas Jefferson (1743–1826) and passed by the Second Continental Congress in Philadelphia on July 4, 1776. The ideas were those of the Lockean tradition of natural rights and social contract, but the words have a resounding revolutionary eloquence still:

> We hold these truths to be self–evident, that all men are created equal, that they are endowed by their Creator with certain unalienable Rights, that among these are Life, Liberty and the pursuit of Happiness—That to secure these rights, Governments are instituted among Men, deriving their just powers from the consent of the governed— That whenever any Form of Government becomes destructive of these ends, it is the Right of the People to alter or abolish it, and to institute a new Government.[3]

Besides thus committing the American colonies both to revolution against the crown and to republican principles of government, the most important decision made by the Continental Congress was the appointment of a wealthy Virginia planter to command the unified colonial army. Picked to reassure the moderates that the Revolution was not in the hands of rabble–rousers and to convince the southern colonies that it was not just New England's war, George Washington (1732–1799) revealed prudence, patience, and a determination that made a major contribution to the ultimate victory.

The war in the field, which dragged on for six long years, from 1775 to 1781, centered first in the north, then in the south, with the turning point coming in the middle colonies in 1777. The British had the advantages of money, ships, and trained professional soldiers, many of them German mercenaries. The rebellious colonies, however, had larger numbers of fighting men available, knowledge of the terrain, and the zeal that went with defending their own land. In the later stages, they also had the essential help of Europe's greatest power and Britain's greatest foe, the France of Louis XVI.

During the early years, the British won almost all the battles and captured the major cities, including Boston, New York, and Philadelphia. Colonial militiamen, however, controlled the countryside, and Washington's small but increasingly professional regular army had continental distances across which to maneuver. Then at Saratoga, New York, in 1777, a British army invading from Canada under General "Gentleman Johnny" Burgoyne (1722–1792), worn down by the harassing tactics of what he called "a rabble in arms," surrendered to the Americans. This first major colonial victory had even greater repercussions across the sea, where it convinced the French that Britain could be beaten and led to the signing of a Franco–American alliance against their common enemy.

In 1778, the center of the struggle shifted to the southern colonies. Supported by British control of the sea, a royal army captured the port city of Charleston, South Carolina—and a large American army with it—and moved slowly north through the Carolinas into Virginia. Tormented as usual by the hit-and-run tactics of the colonials, the British general Lord Cornwallis (1738–1805) sought to bring matters to a successful conclusion by overrunning Virginia, the colony which, with Massachusetts, was the heart and soul of the rebellion. At this juncture, however, the French alliance came decisively into play. Washington, currently besieging New York, marched south to join the young marquis de Lafayette (1757–1834) confronting Cornwallis on the narrow peninsula between Virginia's James and York rivers. At the same time, the French admiral François Joseph de Grasse (1722–1788) drove off a British naval force on its way to support the British army. Trapped between the American and French armies and the French navy, Cornwallis capitulated at Yorktown in October 1781. As the red–coated troops of the largest empire in the world surrendered their weapons to the American "rabble," a band played a popular tune of the day: "The World Turned Upside Down."

The Oldest Constitution

The first revolutionary goal envisioned by the American Declaration of Independence—liberation from Great Britain—was achieved by the victory at Yorktown at the beginning of the 1780s. The second implied objective—an effective republican government for all the former colonies—took the rest of the decade to accomplish.

During and after the Revolutionary War, the separate colonies, now called states, continued to be ruled primarily by their own elected assemblies. To provide some central authority for the new nation, the so–called Articles of Confederation were drafted in 1781 and continued in force for most of the 1780s. The Americans, however, felt a deep distrust of central government—they had just fought to free themselves from one such, after all—and therefore conferred little power on their Confederation. As a result, the new government proved unequal to many of the problems that confronted the new nation in the 1780s. A worthless continental currency and a wave of foreclosures drove many farmers off their lands. These events, in turn, generated rumblings of social discontent that made the merchant and planter elite fearful of new uprisings, this time of poor Americans against rich ones. Large and small states feuded, particularly over the extensive claims to western lands made by some of the former. When attempts at reform within the framework of the Articles of Confederation failed, therefore, yet another congress was called—the Constitutional Convention that met in Philadelphia in 1787.

Through that sweltering summer, a number of divisive issues were settled by compromise and ingenuity. Large states wanted strong central government with representation proportional to their larger populations, while small ones favored autonomy for the individual states with equal voting power for each. Some doubted that so large a republic was workable at all, pointing to the failure of the Cromwellian Commonwealth in England in the seventeenth century and to the autocratic drift of the Dutch Republic. Others were simply fearful that any strong central government would lose touch with the distant states and become as authoritarian as the European monarchies. In the end, however, the plan urged by James Madison (1751–1836) of Virginia, modified to assuage the fears of the smaller states, was passed by the Constitutional Convention and, after extended public debate, ratified by enough of the states to bring it into effect by 1788.

The *Constitution of the United States* incorporated some of the most radical ideas of the century. It was a genuine Lockean social contract, establishing a government by the consent of the governed. It made use of the separation of powers urged by Montesquieu to prevent the concentration of too much authority in individual hands. Its three divisions—executive, legislative, and judicial—provided for a president with real executive powers; a two–house legislature (the Senate, in which all states were equally represented and the House of Representatives, in which representation was proportional to population); and federal judges with authority in all the states. Yet the powers of the president, Congress, and the federal judiciary were circumscribed by built–in checks and balances, such as presidential power to veto laws, congressional authority to reject presidential appointees, and the power of the Supreme Court to rule on the constitutionality of legislation (established early in the nineteenth century). Fears of tyranny also led to the first ten amendments to the Constitution, the *American Bill of Rights.* These additions guaranteed the "unalienable rights" of the people to freedom of speech, press, and assembly, to religious freedom, jury trial, private property, and other prerogatives deemed essential for citizens of a free republic.

Looking back from the perspective of two centuries, it is possible to see distinct limitations to this pioneering effort. A fifth of the people of the "land of the free," for instance, were black slaves with no rights at all, and the female half of the population could neither vote nor hold office. Even among white males, local and federal suffrage was generally limited to property owners or taxpayers. But most white male Americans did in fact own some land, and after two revolutionary decades they had a good deal of experience in thrashing out public issues and choosing political leaders. And America was at least free of some of the thorniest challenges to democracy to be found in Europe. Divine–right monarchy, a titled aristocracy, and an established church, with its grip on the mind of the masses, were nonexistent in the United States.

It was not, in short, a bad beginning, this American Constitution that came into effect just as the French Revolution was getting under way. With many modifications, it is still working two centuries later. It is the oldest written constitution in the world.

♦ Colonial Revolts in Latin America ♦

Discontent fermented in Central and South American society, as it did in Europe and the North American colonies. In Latin America, however, these tensions did not generate large–scale revolutions until the early 1900s. We will look here at the sources of discontent and at the more localized rebellions which did erupt before the end of the eighteenth century.

Reforms and Discontents

The Latin American settlement colonies were ruled by a thin layer of Spanish or Portuguese *peninsulars*—Latin Americans born in Europe—sent out as viceroys, provincial governors, bishops, and other officials. The colonial population they ruled, however, was a richly varied social mix simmering with suppressed resentments.

Just below this small peninsular elite were the *creoles,* European descended but American born. Creoles owned the plantations, ranches, and mines, dominated the commerce of the port cities, and ran the economies of the colonies. Yet, like the European bourgeoisie, they bitterly resented the privilege and prestige accruing to the colonial ruling class of viceroys, ecclesiastics, and others dispatched from Europe to govern them.

At the bottom of society, the native Amerindians and black Africans imported as slaves did the heavy labor in the fields and mines. These *peons,* the peasant masses of Latin America, resented their servile condition and their poverty, oppressive officials, crushing taxation, and other forms of exploitation. At the next social level up, *mestizo* and mulatto inhabitants were caught between dismay at the oppression of their Indian or African parents and resentment at the contempt of their European parents. Struggling for a foothold in a society dominated by the Europeans, they made their livings often as peddlers or petty officials. Yet the mestizos, in particular, would take the lead in the Latin American society of the next century.

Paradoxically, the later eighteenth century—the eve of the Latin American revolutions—saw considerable improvement in the condition of the three-century-old Latin American colonies. In the later sixteenth and seventeenth centuries, the overseas territories of Spain and Portugal had shared in the decline of their mother countries into sleepy backwaters. After 1700, however, they experienced a distinct economic revival. And in the later 1700s, the Bourbon reforms in Spanish America and benign neglect in Portuguese Brazil brought what looked like a dynamic new era.

A revival of gold and silver production contributed significantly to Latin America's eighteenth-century prosperity. As early as the 1680s, the silver mines of Mexico and Bolivia began to produce heavily once more. In the 1690s, the discovery of gold and later of diamonds in the "backlands" of Brazil generated both a mining boom and rapid expansion to the interior. Increased amounts of gold and silver coinage led to rising prices and lubricated the wheels of commerce on both sides of the Atlantic.

Political reform also came to Spanish America in the latter part of the century. Spain's enlightened despot, Charles III (r. 1759–1788) attempted both to rationalize the government and to free the economy of his overseas colonies as well as of his European realms. These reforms included territorial reorganization, the establishment of local creole militias, and the abolition of some oppressive lower-ranking officials. On the economic side, they involved lower taxes, freer trade among the colonies, and an end to commercial monopolies held by certain Spanish cities. The reforms also included some reluctant opening up of Spain's colonies to trade with Britain, the United States, and other foreign nations. Traders and owners of haciendas (plantations) and mines, formerly driven to large-scale smuggling, benefited greatly from the reforms instigated by their Spanish Bourbon rulers.

Another enlightened measure, the royal attack on the Jesuits and other missionaries, proved less salutary. The suppression of the Jesuits left Indian populations, who had been protected from enslavement by the benevolent if autocratic fathers, open to colonial slavers in Spanish America. In Brazil, benign neglect of the backlands by Portugal allowed rapid development of the interior of that vast country as the mines were opened up. There too, however, colonial slave raiding among the Native–American population increased, as did disruptive rivalry between the coastal plantations and the mines of the interior.

Into this changing colonial society there filtered some new ideas and some startling news at the end of the century. The radical theories of the Enlightenment, particularly Rousseau's emphasis on popular sovereignty, stirred the imaginations of young creoles. News of the successful North American revolution and of the freer and more profitable economy that resulted reached Latin American traders through their Yankee counterparts and aroused considerable interest. And older problems and discontents remained, in spite of the Bourbon reforms. The colonists resented the stronger administration with which Charles III replaced corrupt local bureaucrats. Colonial merchants wanted the eradication of all, not just some, mercantilistic restrictions on trade: "Commerce," said one, "ought to be free as air."[4] The ideas of the French Revolution found converts in Latin America, and translations of the U.S. Declaration of Independence circulated in the Iberian colonies to the south. Revolutionary solutions to social problems found passionate advocates in South as well as in North America.

Indian Uprisings and Slave Revolts

The first Latin American revolutions came among the lowest and most long–suffering of classes: Indians, black slaves, and some of the most oppressed of laboring people. Yet their leaders tended to be middle or upper class, and the resulting outbreaks spanned most of the range of late eighteenth–century revolt.

The Peruvian Indian uprising led by Tupac Amarú (1742–1781) was as innocent of ideology or detailed program for social change as any European peasant revolt. A descendant of the last Inca, wealthy, educated, and honored with a Spanish title, Tupac Amarú first sought reforms and then, in 1780, led his fellow Native Americans in a rebellion that temporarily won control of large parts of Peru, Bolivia, and northern Argentina. The ensuing bloodbath cost many Spanish lives and many more Indian ones—including those of Tupac Amarú and his family—and accomplished no more than Pugachev's Rebellion had in Russia a few years before.

In 1789, the year of the French Revolution, an abortive conspiracy led by an unlikely revolutionary called "the Toothpuller" attempted to raise Brazilian miners, priests, and underpaid soldiers against the Portuguese monarchy. A self–educated jack-of-all-trades, including dentistry, Joaquim José de Silva Xavier (1748–1792), was popularly known as *Tiradentes,* "the Toothpuller." He had become familiar with much of the radical literature of his day, from the constitutions of the North American states to the theories of the French philosophes. His revolt was stillborn, however, and after mounting an eloquent defense, including appeals for Brazilian independence, the abolition of slavery, and the founding of a university, the Toothpuller was executed for sedition in 1792.

A third rebellion came in the Caribbean, where in 1791, Toussaint L'Ouverture (1743–1803), a well–educated Haitian slave who claimed descent from an African king, led the black slaves of French Haiti in revolt. The insurrection was triggered by a decree of the French Revolution outlawing slavery, and Toussaint L'Ouverture produced a model constitution for his countrymen. But Haiti, with its huge sugar plantations and half–million African slaves, was France's most valuable colony—too valuable for France to let go. A French expedition captured the black leader by treachery, and he died in a French prison. His successors, however, did win their independence in 1804, making Haiti the first American colony after the United States to gain its independence.

Haiti's was the only victory among this first string of Latin American revolts. Tupac Amarú has since been made a national symbol in Peru, and the Brazilian Congress meets today in the Toothpuller Palace. In their own day, however, they perished as martyrs to the democratic impulse that was spreading across the Western world.

Summary

A series of seismic changes began in Western society in the eighteenth century. The population explosion expanded Europe's population more rapidly than at any other time, from 120 million to 190 million in a single century. The agricultural revolution created many deserted villages but also provided food enough to feed millions of new mouths. And the Industrial Revolution, beginning in Britain around 1760, multiplied textile production and brought coal and iron into the center of European manufacturing. Over the next two centuries, Europe, the Americas, and much of the rest of the world would be transformed by these unprecedented technological, economic, and demographic changes in ways that contemporaries could never have imagined.

Political life also began a period of unparalleled change in the eighteenth century.

In Europe, these upheavals were local and, before 1789, usually suppressed. Still, Pugachev's Rebellion in Russia, popular agitation for "Wilkes and Liberty!" in Britain, and a scattering of bourgeois and aristocratic coups and rebellions revealed the range of political discontent in later eighteenth–century Europe.

In Europe's American colonies, similar discontents led to similarly violent outbreaks. Slave revolts and Indian uprisings south of the Rio Grande, like their European counterparts, failed in the years before 1800. But the American Revolution that produced the fledgling United States did succeed. And provincial though this colonial revolt seemed to many in 1776, the new nation that emerged across the Atlantic would in time create a second epicenter for the Western world as a whole.

Some Key Terms

agricultural revolution 420	economic demand 424	population explosion 420
American Bill of Rights 436	entrepreneur 425	protoindustrialism 424
capital investment 424	flying shuttle 426	Pugachev's Rebellion 430
Constitution of the United States 436	Industrial Revolution 423	spinning jenny 427
	Malthusian ratios 423	steam engine 427
Continental Congress 434	mestizo 437	technological development 425
cottage industry 424	Minutemen 433	water frame 427
creole 437	peninsular 437	Wilkes and Liberty! 430
Declaration of Independence 434	peons 437	

Notes

1. Arnold Toynbee, *The Industrial Revolution* (Boston: Beacon Press, 1956), 7, 63, 65, 66.
2. Faujas de Saint–Fond quoted in P. Mantoux, "Coal and Iron," in *Europe and the Industrial Revolution*, ed. Sima Lieberman (Cambridge, Mass.: Schenkman Publishing Company, 1972), 124–125.
3. "The American Declaration of Independence,"

in *Readings in World Civilization,* ed. Kevin Reilly, vol. 2 (New York: St. Martin's Press, 1988), 96.

4. E. Bradford Burns, *Latin America: A Concise Interpretive History* (Englewood Cliffs, N.J.: Prentice Hall, 1982), 68.

Reading List

Alexander, T. *Autocratic Politics in a National Crisis: The Imperial Russian Government and Pugachev's Revolt, 1773–1775.* Bloomington: University of Indiana Press, 1969. Thorough, thoughtful account.

Bailyn, B. *The Ideological Origins of the American Revolution.* Cambridge, Mass.: Harvard University Press, 1967. Highlights the importance of ideas in a revolution that is often seen as free of "ideology."

Barton, H. A. *Scandinavia in the Revolutionary Era, 1760–1815.* Minneapolis: University of Minnesota Press, 1986. Transformation of northern Europe during the Age of Democratic Revolutions.

Cipolla, C. M. *An Economic History of World Population.* 6th ed. Baltimore: Penguin, 1974. Brief, older book that is full of insights on the intertwined growth of production and population.

Fischer, D. H. *Paul Revere's Ride.* New York: Oxford University Press, 1994. Vastly detailed analysis of both the ride and the misinterpretations of it that have appeared since.

Flexner, J. T. *George Washington.* 3 vols. Boston: Little Brown, 1968–1972. Standard life. On Jefferson, see the new, more human figure revealed in W. S. Randall's *Thomas Jefferson: A Life* (New York: Henry Holt, 1993).

Flinn, M. W. *The European Demographic System, 1500–1820.* Brighton, England: Harvester, 1981. Brief technical discussion of population patterns in early modern times. See also W. R. Lee, ed., *European Demography and Economic Growth* (London: Croom Helm, 1979). Socioeconomic aspects of European population trends.

Gilmour, I. *Riot, Risings, and Revolution.* London: Pimlico, 1993. Upheavals in eighteenth-century Britain.

Higonnet, P. L. R. *Pont-de-Montvert: Social Structure and Politics in a French Village, 1700–1914.* Cambridge, Mass.: Harvard University Press, 1971. Microcosm of peasant life over two centuries.

Jones, E. L. *The European Miracle: Environments,* *Economies, and Geopolitics in the History of Europe and Asia.* Cambridge: Cambridge University Press, 1981. Seeks elements in European society that explain its economic breakthrough.

Kriedke, P. *Peasants, Landlords, and Merchant Capitalists.* Leamington, N.H.: Berg, 1983. Economic changes undermine European peasant life.

Landes, D. *The Unbound Prometheus: Technological Change and Industrial Development in Western Europe from 1750 to the Present.* Cambridge: Cambridge University Press, 1969. The long view of the industrialization of western Europe.

Martinez–Alier, J. *Laborers and Landowners in Southern Spain.* London: Allen and Unwin, 1971. By a noted student of agrarian societies in both Old and New Worlds.

McEvedy, C., and R. Jones. *Atlas of World Population History.* Harmondsworth, England: Penguin, 1978. Indispensable guide to population history.

Middlekauff, R. *The Glorious Cause.* New York: Oxford University Press, 1982. Highly readable yet scholarly account of the American Revolution.

Mullin, M. *Africa in America: Slave Acculturation and Resistance.* Urbana: University of Illinois Press, 1992. Impressive study of tactics developed by enslaved Africans.

North, D. C., and R. P. Thomas. *The Rise of the Western World: A New Economic History.* Cambridge: Cambridge University Press, 1973. A useful overview of economic changes.

Rude, G. F. E. *Wilkes and Liberty: A Social Study of 1763 to 1774.* Oxford: Clarendon Press, 1962. An expert on the crowd in history analyzes the social background to the Wilkes phenomenon.

Senghaas, D. *The European Experience: A Historical Critique of Development Theory.* Translated by K. H. Kimmig. Leamington, N.H.: Berg, 1985. Tests theories of Third World economic development against earlier European experience.

Te Brake, W. P. *Regents and Rebels: The Revolutionary World of an Eighteenth–Century Dutch City.* Cambridge, Mass.: Blackwell, 1989. Deventer—a small city in a revolutionary age.

─18─

From the Bastille to Waterloo

The French Revolution and Napoleon's Empire

◆The Roots of Crisis
◆The Revolution of Liberty, Equality, and Brotherhood
◆The Reign of the Guillotine   ◆Napoleon's European Empire

The American Revolution of 1776 stirred excitement and admiration in enlightened circles in Europe. But it was the French Revolution of 1789 that shook the old regime to its foundations. And it was the upheaval in France that established a distinctive new revolutionary paradigm in history: that of the modern *ideological revolution,* the mass revolt driven in large part by belief in radical new ideas about society and aimed at the construction of a new and better world.

The American revolt cost Britain some valuable colonies, but the French upheaval plunged France itself—Europe's greatest power—into chaos, uprooting ancient institutions and inspiring new political passions. In Europe as a whole, the French Revolution triggered two decades of warfare, pitting the France of Napoleon Bonaparte against all the other great powers. In the longest perspective, finally, the French Revolution of 1789 became the model for ideological revolutions throughout the next two centuries.

This chapter will probe the root causes of the French Revolution in both the real problems and radical ideas of the eighteenth century. It will then follow the course of the great upheaval, from its constructive early stages of idealistic reform through the violence of the Reign of Terror and the corruption of its last years. A concluding section will briefly outline the meteoric career of Napoleon, enlightened dictator of France, conqueror of Europe, and the revolution's most astonishing offspring.

◆ The Roots of Crisis ◆

The French Revolution of 1789 was rooted in the broader history of its time. The social and constitutional strains, the tensions between classes and estates, the ideas and commitments that produced it were not limited to France alone. It was, however, in France that the conflicts that beset the old regime came most dramatically to a head. This section will try to explain how the radical Enlightenment ideas discussed in an earlier chapter interacted with genuine social problems, a series of economic blows, and a major political crisis to ignite the explosion of 1789.

Social Problems of the Old Regime

The philosophical critique of the old order, as we have seen, included some scathing criticisms of the ancien régime. This attack undoubtedly undermined public confidence in traditional institutions and values. The philosophes heaped scorn on the teachings of the church, the prestige of the nobility, the efficiency and honesty of royal officials. By so doing, these intellectual radicals prepared the way for the French Revolution. Real social problems, however, also contributed to the coming explosion. The deeply held grievances of major subdivisions of society progressively undermined public enthusiasm for the status quo as the century drew to a close.

In eighteenth–century French society, the first and second estates, the clergy and the nobility, enjoyed a privileged status denied to the *third estate,* which comprised the middle and lower classes. Thus the French peasantry, the largest part of the third estate, resented the traditional payments required of them—seigneurial dues, church tithes, and royal taxes like the taille—as well as their labor obligation, the *corvée,* imposed upon them since medieval times. These burdens were increased by the effort of the resurgent aristocracy to search out and reimpose a variety of lapsed financial obligations on their tenants. The population explosion added to this weight of rural misery by requiring the division and redivision of peasant holdings to provide for increasing numbers of surviving children until no child's share could support a family. Most of the French peasantry, like peasants everywhere

A heroic image of the Paris *sans-culottes,* radiating dedication and strength. How do the pose, the flag in one hand, the lighting of the figure, and the low angle from which we look up at the face of this political activist contribute to the impression the picture makes? (The Mansell Collection Limited.)

Chronology 18.1: The French Revolution

1770s–1780s	*Economic decline; French government debt triples*
1788–1789	*Bad harvest, high prices, food riots*
1789	*Estates General convened, demands reforms; fall of Bastille; march on Versailles; Declaration of Rights of Man and the Citizen*
1789	*Night of August 4 brings end of aristocracy's feudal rights*
1790	*Civil Constitution of the Clergy nationalizes church*
1791	*Constitution of 1791 converts absolute monarchy into a constitutional monarchy with limited powers*
1792	*Austria and Prussia attack revolutionary France*
1792–1794	*The Terror—Robespierre's Committee of Public Safety turns back foreign invaders, but executes many "enemies of the people" in France itself*
1793	*Vendee revolt—peasants rebel against the Revolution*
1794	*Thermidorean reaction ends the Terror by executing its leaders*
1794–1799	*The Directory brings opportunists to power—corruption at home, more victories by revolutionary armies abroad*

in the Western world, remained fundamentally conservative at heart, dedicated to traditional beliefs and patterns of life. In 1789, however, peasant resentments temporarily carried the day: many contributed their complaints to the lists of grievances which, as we will see, were carried up to Versailles as the Revolution began.

The most incendiary element in the population, however, was the urban poor. City workers, including small shopkeepers, artisans, clerks, apprentices, manual laborers, and street peddlers, spent half their meager incomes on the bread that was the backbone of their diet and lived in perpetual fear of unemployment, hunger, and beggary. In Paris, these discontented urban masses included five hundred thousand of the city's population of six hundred thousand people. Radically politicized during the early years of the French Revolution, these thronging crowds of *sans-culottes* (people too poor to afford culottes, the fashionable knee breeches of their betters) pressed for new and more drastic measures at each stage of the Revolution. As the "Paris mob" of the Reign of Terror, they became one of the most famous crowds in history.

The French bourgeoisie were once seen as the leaders of a capitalist revolt against a feudal order dominated by landed interests. In fact, members of the upper middle class, at least, were often able to buy tax exemptions, secure government posts, and even acquire landed estates for themselves. Still, the bourgeoisie did resent the special privileges and snobbishness of the hereditary nobility, as well as the social prestige that went with an ancient family name. These productive and prosperous citizens—bankers and merchants, lawyers and office holders—felt an inevitable discontent with a society based on hereditary privilege rather than on productivity or wealth.

The French aristocracy itself, finally, had reasons for discontent with the old regime. Economically, this unproductive elite felt the pressure of price inflation, pushing up the cost of periwigs and velvet gowns, carriages and Paris mansions. They also resented both the aspirations of social–climbing "tradesmen" below them and the absolutist claims of the monarchy above. In fighting back against royal absolutism, defending their traditional privileges, and working for the restoration of their exalted medieval status, this most favored of classes also became one of the most potent enemies of the status quo.

Economic and Financial Disasters

The complex crisis of the late 1780s, explored only with difficulty by later historians, was baffling and terrifying to those who lived through it. As the century drew to a close, economic and financial problems gathered like thunderheads over France. In the spring and summer of 1789, the storm burst over the land.

After several decades of prosperity, a period of economic decline began in the 1770s and 1780s, rapidly increasing the suffering of the lowest social classes. In 1786, a commercial treaty with Britain badly hurt rural handicraft industries and combined with rising prices to throw many out of jobs in Paris as well. In 1788, a bad harvest conjured up the terrible possibility of famine. By the spring of 1789, more than 10 percent of the peasantry were indigent, and as many as half the country's handicraft industrial workers may have been unemployed.

A reeling economy thus helped to ignite the great conflagration. The year 1789 saw skyrocketing food prices trigger bread riots in the cities. In the provinces, when the government failed to distribute adequate grain in the emergency, gangs of peasants seized government grain, then began to loot and burn isolated chateaus. Assaults on high–priced bakers or grain hoarders expanded to include attacks on unpopular landlords and royal officials. There were rumors of profiteering and official collusion in a deliberate conspiracy to starve the people, and then of armed bands marching to destroy the villages. In the summer of 1789, what became known as the Great Fear leaped from one village to another. And when fear of the "famine conspiracy" and of imminent attack led the peasants to arm themselves, other elements in society were filled with terror of impending revolution.

While these economic disasters pyramided and intermittent violence spread, a government financial crisis was building inexorably toward its climax. The root cause of the French government's fiscal problems lay in the tax exemptions enjoyed by the clergy and the nobility, who between them controlled much of the wealth of the land. Deprived of the right to tax the upper two estates, the royal government could scarcely tap the real wealth of one of Europe's most prosperous nations. To finance an extravagant court, some enlightened road building and land improvement, and a series of costly wars, the government had to resort to borrowing. As a result, during the 1770s and 1780s, the national debt tripled. By 1789, interest payments alone consumed more than half the total royal revenues. Running a substantial deficit each year, the royal government was by the end of the 1780s confronting the ultimate financial catastrophe: bankruptcy.

The Political Crisis of 1789

Neither France's monarchs nor the government they headed was up to handling the crisis. Neither of the French kings of the eighteenth century—Louis XV and XVI—had Louis XIV's passion for power or dedication to duty. Louis XV (r. 1715–1774), who gave over much of his long reign to indolence and pleasure, is supposed to have summed up the situation with a biblical allusion: "After me, the Deluge!" Louis XVI (r. 1774–1792) was one of those well–meaning but indecisive people who should never be put in charge of anything, least of all a government. He was an honorable young man who wanted his people to be happy, and the nation had high hopes of a change when he inherited the throne from his grandfather in 1774. But the vacillating prince soon succumbed to the influence of his self–serving courtiers and his lovely but frivolous Austrian queen, Marie Antoinette (1755–1793). While Louis devoted himself to his hobbies of hunting and repairing clocks, the royal court grew increasingly profligate, the royal administration more inefficient and corrupt.

The benevolent but ineffectual sovereign had made fitful efforts to deal with the rising sea of troubles over the first fifteen years of his reign. He had appointed and sporadically supported a series of reform–minded ministers of state, including the physiocratic administrator Jacques Turgot (1727–1781), the Protestant banker and financial wizard Jacques Necker (1732–1804), and the enlightened archbishop Etienne Charles de Loménie de Brienne (1727–1794). These men, among the best practical minds of the Enlightenment, readily saw that either expenses must come down or taxes must rise, and preferably both. The resurgent French aristocracy, however, repeatedly frustrated their efforts. Exploiting their domination of the parlements, especially the prestigious Parlement of Paris, the nobility successfully denied the constitutionality of royal plans to tax the first and second estates. Influential courtiers, meanwhile, secured the dismissal of the reformers one after another.

The government's economic and financial crisis thus became a political one. Desperate royal ministers and an exasperated king tried a variety of expedients, including efforts to abolish the parlements. In 1787, Louis XVI summoned an ad hoc Assembly of Notables to validate tax reform, but the aristocrats who dominated the Assembly responded by denouncing all such expedients as "royal tyranny" and by setting themselves up as defenders of the nation against the excesses of absolutism. In the late 1780s, they insisted that only the Estates General—which theoretically represented the nation as a whole but which they themselves fully expected to dominate—was qualified to pass on such a fundamental innovation as the taxing of the upper estates.

With bread riots in the cities and hunger and unemployment in the countryside, with the nobility demanding the restoration of its medieval prerogatives and the royal government on the verge of bankruptcy, Louis XVI gave up. He announced that the ancient Estates General, which France's absolute monarchs had not convened for 175 years, would meet in the spring of 1789. It was, though he could not have known it, the beginning of the end for his reign, his dynasty, and a system of governance that had dominated the Western world for almost a thousand years.

♦ The Revolution of Liberty, Equality, and Brotherhood ♦

The French tradition of representative government and concern for social justice, the French flag and the French national anthem were all forged in the fires of the French Revolution that filled the tumultuous decade between 1789 and 1799. Dramatic incidents like the storming of the Bastille, ringing slogans like *Liberté, Égalité, Fraternité*—Liberty, Equality, Brotherhood—have spread beyond the land of their birth to become part of the popular history of the Western world.

This section will narrate the stirring events of the early years: the summoning of the Estates General, the fall of the Bastille, the march on Versailles, and the systematic dismantling of the old regime itself. It will conclude with a reformed constitutional monarchy in place in France—and the worst stages of the Revolution still to come.

The Estates General

On May 5, 1789, more than 1,100 delegates to the reconstituted *Estates General,* France's traditional representative assembly, paraded through the streets of Versailles to their open-

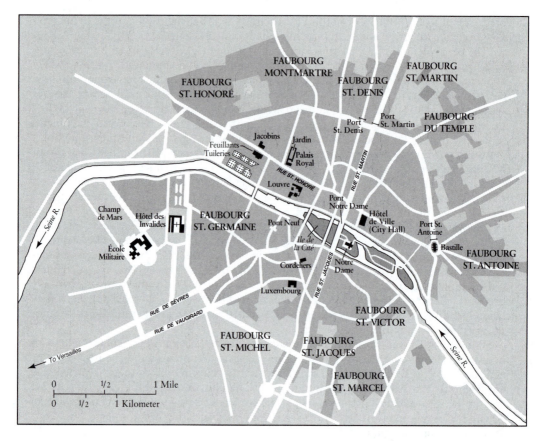

Revolutionary Paris

ing session. The nobles were splendid in gold braid, lace, and feathered hats, the clergy more quietly opulent in their best robes. The representatives of the third estate—the large majority of the king's subjects—marched in the same plain coats and knee breeches their predecessors had worn the last time the estates had met—in 1614. Most of the delegates of the third estate, chosen by a complicated system of indirect voting that gave men of means a clear advantage, were lawyers or civil servants, leavened by a sprinkling of acknowledged intellectuals. They were professional talkers, organizers, and thinkers. Only a handful were capitalists or businessmen, and there was scarcely a peasant or an urban worker to be seen.

Louis XVI had summoned them primarily to deal with the financial problems of a bankrupt government, but they came full of larger concerns. Many of the delegates carried *cahiers*, notebooks full of the grievances of the peasants and other royal subjects. Many of them had read the writings of the philosophes and had been impressed by the achievements of the American Revolution, whose leaders had just completed a new Constitution for that nation. Many were imbued with the latest theories about human rights and with dreams of crafting a political constitution for their own country.

Thanks to a royal concession intended to curtail the power of the fractious nobility, the representation of the third estate had been doubled, so that it roughly equaled the number of delegates of the nobility and the clergy combined. Numerically, in fact, the position of the third estate was even stronger, since the more enlightened nobles and many underpaid priests or village curés supported some of the third estate's demands for change. These initial advantages, however, were canceled out when Louis ruled that the three estates should sit separately and vote as three separate units rather than sit in one body and vote together. Louis thus enabled the first and second estates to outvote the third two to one.

It was not a good way to begin, and other troubles multiplied as the summer advanced. The Great Fear and the resulting peasant outrages spread through the provinces. The price of bread doubled, sending angry mobs prowling the streets of the cities. The most radical of the delegates at Versailles were dreaming of a constitutional monarchy; but in Paris, travelers heard common citizens talking openly about establishing a republic *à l'américaine* in France.

Then, after six weeks of haggling over organization and procedures, the leaders of the third estate acted. On June 17, the "third" announced that it spoke for the nation as a whole and urged the other two estates to join it in a National Assembly. This the clerical delegates, a majority of whom were village priests, subsequently did. When the king responded by locking them out of their meeting hall, the Assembly convened in a nearby indoor tennis court and took the famous *Tennis Court Oath* never to disband until it had drawn up a new constitution for France. In the panoramic painting of this historic moment by the contemporary artist Jacques–Louis David, the people themselves are shown gazing symbolically down from the high windows as delegates all through the hall embrace, cheer, and raise their right hands to take the historic oath.

The Fall of the Bastille and the March on Versailles

Accepting the situation, Louis XVI ordered all the members of the other two estates to meet with the third estate in the National Assembly. At the same time, however, he ordered more troops brought into the capital. In August 1789, the Assembly itself produced the first major flower of its deliberations: the *Declaration of the Rights of Man and the Citizen*, the French Bill of Rights. "Men are born and remain free and equal," this document boldly declared. "The purpose of all political associations is the preservation of the natural . . . rights of man. . . . All citizens have the right to take part personally or through their representatives in the making of the law."[1] Freedom of thought, public control of taxation, the right to private property—all Enlightenment ideas—were thus laid out as the foundations of the new society. For divine right and absolute monarchy were to be substituted liberty, equality, and the brotherhood of all people. It was a good start for France's equivalent of the American Constitutional Convention, which had met in Philadelphia only two years before.

In the sprawling metropolis of Paris, meanwhile, wild rumors and real deprivation fed a growing clamor for still more drastic action. When the king, foolishly reversing himself yet again, dismissed the popular royal minister Necker, political activists in Paris organized a new city government and a National Guard with the marquis de Lafayette as its commander to protect the National Assembly. On July 14, crowds of citizens, seeking arms to defend themselves against a rumored counterattack, assaulted the forbidding towers of the *Bastille*.

A royal prison and a fortress believed to be well stocked with weapons, the Bastille was a massive symbol of royal tyranny. When the smoke settled at the end of the day, scores of citizens were dead, half the small garrison had been killed, and half a dozen prisoners—

none of them locked up for political offenses—had been freed. The symbolic significance of this assault on royal authority, however, was immense. The Bastille was subsequently leveled, its key ceremoniously sent to George Washington across the sea. Two centuries later, Bastille Day, the fourteenth of July, is still celebrated as France's independence day.

Another blow to royal power was the *march on Versailles* by the women of Paris in October 1789. Furious at the price and scarcity of bread and at a rumor published in the radical press that Marie Antoinette had responded to the bread shortage by ignorantly replying "Let them eat cake!", a mob of Parisian women marched on the royal palace of Versailles. Led by the city's fishwives, but including other market women and even some well–dressed bourgeois housewives, and followed by other working people of Paris and by Lafayette and the National Guard, the demonstrators constituted a cross section of the urban populace. They were inflamed, not only by desire for an end to food shortages, but by a determination to get Louis XVI away from the "counterrevolutionaries" in the royal court and bring him back to the center of more radical feeling in the capital.

Breaking first into the National Assembly, then into the palace of Versailles itself, the demonstrators demanded that the king and queen return with them to Paris. Royal guards were killed, and the women confronted the king, forcing him to agree to all their demands. The mob returned to the city the next day in a long procession in which women rode on the barrels of rumbling cannon followed by carts full of grain, disarmed royal guards, a hundred members of the National Assembly, and a carriage bearing the royal family itself. Henceforth King Louis would live and the Assembly would carry on its debates in the heart of Paris, surrounded by the turbulent populace.

Dismantling the Old Order

In this tumultuous atmosphere, then, the new National Assembly labored for two years to right the wrongs of centuries and to forge a new government for France. Between 1789 and 1791, it in fact struck major blows at the aristocracy, the clergy, and the monarchy—the three main pillars of the old regime.

On the wild *Night of August 4,* in 1789, the nobility, frightened by peasant uprisings and urged on by the more enlightened among them, voted to sacrifice the seigneurial privileges they had struggled so long to defend. They gave up the feudal dues and payments still required from their tenants, peasant labor obligations, surviving manorial courts, hunting preserves, and other vestiges of medieval serfdom. They agreed to pay taxes on their land like other citizens and abandoned their exclusive right to high posts in the military, the church, and the state. "Adjourn the session," a secretary hissed to the president of the Assembly as the wild night reeled on from one concession to the next, "Everyone is mad!"[2] There was some calculation behind the aristocratic collapse of the Night of August 4, however. The rights of private property were preserved by a requirement that the nobles were to be compensated for their losses. And the peasantry, thus placated by the abolition of their medieval obligations, became increasingly conservative thereafter.

The French Catholic church also shook under the assaults of the National Assembly. In late 1789, the delegates decided to pay off the debt that had brought the royal government to the brink of ruin by confiscating the immense property of the church. And in 1790, the *Civil Constitution of the Clergy* made priests and bishops civil servants paid by the state. When clerics protested, they were further required to take a special oath of allegiance to the government. Most of the bishops and more than half the village curés refused to take the oath. Like the peasants, these "nonjuring" clergy soon turned vigorously against the Revolution.

The *Constitution of 1791,* finally, dealt a crippling blow to royal absolutism by transforming the government into a constitutional monarchy. By the new Constitution, laws were to be passed by a legislative assembly elected by tax–paying, property–owning males. The historic provinces of France were abolished and replaced by a system of eighty–three "departments," roughly equal in size, rationally subdivided into smaller administrative districts, and run, not by royal agents, but by elected officials.

In June 1791, Louis XVI and Marie Antoinette, disguised as a valet and a chambermaid, actually tried to flee the country. Caught at Varennes and brought back before they could reach the border, the royal family were literally prisoners from then on. The transition of France from a royal absolutist state to a constitutional monarchy seemed complete.

There were many, however, who thought the Revolution had not gone nearly far enough—and others who were equally convinced that it had gone much too far. The result was an unstable period, dating roughly from the promulgation of the Constitution in September 1791 to the suspension of the monarchy in August 1792. During this uneasy year, France was torn by splits in the ranks of the revolutionaries and bombarded by counterrevolutionary pressures from abroad.

Feverish political activism flared up across the land, particularly in Paris and many provincial cities. Radicals organized revolutionary political clubs like the Jacobins and took over the Paris "sections," as the city's wards were now called. Political pamphlets poured out by the hundreds, and popular political newspapers were read everywhere. The tricolor cockade and the red "liberty cap," revolutionary songs and dances, parades and public meetings reflected the excitement of a nation drunk on politics and its new freedom.

In Paris, where the Legislative Assembly of the newly established government first met in the fall of 1791, feuding political factions quickly emerged, each with its eloquent leaders and passionately held political convictions. The *Jacobins,* who got their name from the former monastery of St. Jacques where they met in Paris, were the most radical. They urged that the Revolution should move on, expanding the suffrage beyond the propertied classes and eliminating the monarchy altogether to give France, not a constitutional monarchy, but a republic. Dynamic Jacobin leaders like Maximilien Robespierre soon rose to prominence. Like "Roundhead" in seventeenth–century England, the very name of "Jacobin" became a symbol of ideological extremism in revolutionary France.

Another faction, the *Girondins,* whose leaders came from the Gironde in southwestern France, proved more moderate. Their presiding spirit was Madame Jeanne Roland, who made her salon a center of Girondist ideas, and her husband, Jean–Marie Roland, a leader in the Assembly. The Girondins were willing to give the constitutional monarchy a chance to prove itself. They were also, however, fiercely nationalistic, demanding a great crusade to spread the French Revolution and destroy the old regime all across Europe. There were other splinters as well, some even further to the left than the Jacobins. Among these were the *enragés* (madmen), who demanded controls on grain prices to feed the hungry populace of Paris.

Many aristocrats and Louis XVI's own royal brothers had already emigrated to neighboring countries. There these *émigrés* spread horror stories and dire warnings that stimulated opposition to the Revolution. Prussia and particularly Austria, which was ruled by Marie Antoinette's nephew, the rigid absolutist Francis II (r. 1792–1835), talked publicly of invading France to rescue Louis XVI and his Austrian queen.

In the spring of 1792, the French warhawks had their way: France declared war on Austria and Prussia. But the ill–organized French troops, many of whose original officers were among the *émigrés,* were defeated in early encounters, and the Prussians were soon marching on Paris. In August 1792, Jacobins from the Paris sections seized the *Hôtel de Ville* (City Hall) and installed a new government for the capital, the *Paris Commune.* The national Legislative Assembly thereupon voted to dissolve itself and called for new elections and a new government empowered to deal more forcefully with the escalating crisis. The most dramatic and terrible chapter of the Revolution was about to begin.

♦ The Reign of the Guillotine ♦

It is the *Reign of Terror,* the period of savage political repression which we may date from the September Massacres of 1792 to the fall of the terrorist leaders themselves in the Thermidorian Reaction of July 1794, that has left us our most vivid images of the French Revolution. For this was the period of Robespierre and his ruthless Committee of Public Safety, which sentenced thousands of counter–revolutionaries to execution, and of the Paris mob that jeered these "enemies of the people" to their deaths under the blade of the guillotine. The Terror also put an end to a surge of revolutionary activity by women and produced the final phase of the revolution—the Directory.

The Reign of Terror began as an escalating effort to save the Revolution. It ended with the Revolution victorious over its foreign foes but apparently bent on destroying itself.

The Committee of Public Safety

In the fall of 1792, with Prussian forces advancing on the French capital and rumors of royalist plots rampant in the city, the intensely politicized Paris sections struck again. In the bloody September Massacres, militant sans–culottes broke into the prisons to slaughter accused enemies of the new state. The Jacobins and other extremist factions, meanwhile, took control of the National Convention, as the new assembly was called. The Convention promptly abolished the monarchy altogether and set to work on a new constitution for the Republic of France.

The Convention was the arena where passionate debates were fought out and broad policy decisions made throughout the next two years. The Paris sections and the Commune headquartered at the Hôtel de Ville continued to clamor for vigorous action and radical change. More and more, however, real power fell into the hands of a new revolutionary body, the twelve–member *Committee of Public Safety.* Led by dedicated Jacobins, the Committee dominated the Convention and proved as willing as the Commune to resort to drastic measures. Its chief figures included Lazare Carnot (1753–1823), military engineer and chief organizer of France's victory over its foreign foes; Louis–Antoine Saint–Just (1767–1794), the handsome young firebrand they called "the angel of death;" the eloquent, opportunistic warhawk Georges Danton (1754–1794); and Maximilien Robespierre (1758–1794), a lawyer in his thirties, maximum leader of the Jacobins, hailed as "the incorruptible." There were other influential spirits among the sans–culottes as well. Of them all, Robespierre, with his attention to detail and to duty, his rigor, ruthlessness, and total commitment to the cause, best embodied the spirit of modern ideological revolution.

The Reign of Terror

With unremitting rigor, then, the Committee of Public Safety took the lead in mobilizing the entire nation for defense. Their enemies included not only the Austrians and Prussians, but soon the British, Dutch, and Spanish as well. Within France itself, embittered nobles, outraged priests, and rebellious peasants, especially those from the hills and forests of the *Vendée* region, defied the new government.

Against this mounting reaction, the Revolution sought to mobilize the French people as a whole. Under the direction of Carnot, all males of an age to bear arms were made liable for military service and drafted into the huge revolutionary armies. Other *citoyens* and *citoyennes* (the egalitarian new title "citizen" was used by men and women alike) were set to work to manufacture arms and equipment for the troops. To stabilize the economy, the Committee of Public Safety prescribed maximum prices and wages. The result was what has been called the first mobilization for total war in modern history.

The enormous new armies produced by the draft were ill disciplined and poorly trained. Nevertheless, deployed as snipers or in aggressive new column formations that exploited their numbers, and led by ambitious new officers, they began to turn the tide against the enemies of the Republic. Expelling the Prussians and the Spanish, invading the Low Countries and the Rhineland, they rapidly conquered more territory than Louis XIV had won in all his costly wars. Infused with a new patriotic spirit, marching under the tricolor flag of the Revolution and singing the "Marseillaise," the new national anthem brought up from the sunny south by the Marseilles contingent, the armies of the Republic loomed suddenly as a threat to every monarchy in Europe.

In Paris, meanwhile, tribunals sentenced hundreds of alleged counterrevolutionaries and foreign agents to die each month under the blade of the guillotine. In the Vendée, rebellion was suppressed with great savagery; thousands of captured rebels were shot or even drowned in mass lots. Under the Reign of Terror, all three main pillars of the old regime faced a final series of devastating attacks. The monarchy was abolished, Louis XVI and Marie Antoinette executed. Aristocratic titles were forbidden, landed estates confiscated to fill the coffers of the Revolution, and many nobles were also condemned to death by revolutionary tribunals. Even the Catholic church was briefly abolished and replaced by a Cult of Reason, while hundreds of nonjuring priests were trundled through hooting crowds to the guillotine.

Nor did the momentum of the Terror stop with priests, nobles, and the monarchy. Under the influence of Robespierre and the implacable young Saint–Just, the tribunals were soon sentencing fellow revolutionaries to death also. The Girondins, considered too moderate, and the radical *enragés*, whose demands for economic help for the poor went beyond the Jacobin program, were both decimated by executions. The once–admired leader Danton, accused of corruption by his rival Robespierre, was also purged. The Girondins died singing the "Marseillaise" in a dwindling chorus as one by one they mounted the steps to put their heads under the blade of the guillotine. "O liberty," said Madame Roland as she approached the scaffold, "what crimes are committed in thy name!"

The climax of the Terror came when personal enemies accused even the incorruptible Robespierre, the inexorable Saint–Just, and other Jacobin leaders of treason to the Republic. In July 1794—the month of Thermidor in the new revolutionary calendar—they, too, went under the knife. In this *Thermidorian reaction,* as enemies of the Republic gleefully pointed out, the Revolution "devoured its own children."

The Directory

Thanks to the national emergency and the de facto rule of the Committee of Public Safety, the democratic Constitution of 1793 never went into effect. In its place, a third revolutionary reorganization, embodied in the Constitution of 1795, established the rule of another board, the five–man *Directory* (1794–1799). For the next five years, less fanatical but ambitious and often corrupt politicians presided over a period of reaction and resurgent greed. Only in the military victories of the armies of the Republic did the spirit of 1789 still seem to burn brightly through this uninspiring final half–decade.

In the aftermath of Thermidor, the demands of the militant Paris sections were rejected, their riotous demonstrations crushed by armed force. Jacobins and others associated with the Terror were rooted out and destroyed. Staunch supporters of the older order, meanwhile, emerged once more. Nonjuring priests, who had refused to accept the Civil Constitution of the Clergy, were nevertheless allowed to return to their country parishes. The peasants of the Vendée challenged the government again, and this time won concessions—amnesty, religious freedom, even indemnity for their earlier suffering.

Economically, the ideals of revolutionary equality and fraternity gave way to glaring disparities of wealth. Bad harvests, the end of price controls, and the suppression of sans–culotte power combined to send the price of food skyrocketing and left the poor more miserable than they had been since the late 1780s. A new elite of government contractors, war profiteers, and speculators, meanwhile, emerged in the later 1790s.

Only in their foreign wars did French citizens find much to be proud of under the Directory. Operating now well beyond the old Bourbon frontiers, the armies of the French Republic had taken the offensive on all fronts. From the Netherlands to Italy, a string of annexations and satellite republics thus extended French power north and south. The Austrian Netherlands (Belgium today) and several other territories were annexed outright. The Netherlands, Switzerland, and northern Italy became French client states. In all these lands, princely houses were overthrown, established churches were disestablished, and the principles of liberty, equality, and brotherhood were vigorously asserted.

The most successful of these builders of the new French predominance that grew out of the Revolution was a young Corsican general named Napoleon Bonaparte. So rapidly did Napoleon's reputation grow, particularly after his dazzling victories in Italy in 1796, that ambitious politicians at home began to see him as a valuable ally. In November 1799, then, the young general and several co–conspirators mounted a successful coup against the Directory. In the new government, called the Consulate, Napoleon became first consul. In five years, he was emperor of France.

Women in Revolt

In the wide–ranging enthusiasm of the Revolution's creative period, women as well as men flung themselves into public demonstrations, radical journalism, political clubs, and fiery debates on the issues of the day. As early as 1789, as we have seen, the fishwives of Paris marched to Versailles to bring Louis XVI and Marie Antoinette to the capital. As the Revolution progressed, some educated women further radicalized the traditional salon, a tactic employed by the Girondist leader Madame Roland and the noted intellectual and writer Germaine de Staël. Others formed women's political clubs, like the Society of Revolutionary Republican Women, or joined clubs open to both sexes. Still others petitioned or spoke for women's rights before the revolutionary assemblies.

Some of these revolutionary women began to demand specific rights for their half of the population. Applying general revolutionary principles of liberty and equality to their own particular grievances, they insisted on women's rights to own and manage their own property, to obtain education comparable to men's, to have equal access to divorce, and to possess the basic civil rights of all citizens. And by and large, the Revolution seemed disposed to grant their demands—for a while.

The reforms that were granted, however, were generally intended to strengthen the power of the Republic itself at the expense of the church, or other traditional centers of power, which also happened to be patriarchal. Thus marriage was made a civil ceremony and divorce facilitated as a blow at the church, which saw marriage as an indissoluble sacrament. All children, female as well as male, were allowed to inherit equal shares of their parents' property in order to prevent large concentrations of wealth and power in individual hands.

Much more important for the future of feminism than these reforms, theoretical tracts on the rights of women began to appear in print. Of these, the most famous produced in France was the *Declaration of the Rights of Woman* (1791) published by the revolutionary journalist and activist Olympe de Gouges. Gouges's ringing assertion still resonates today:

> Woman is born free and her rights are the same as those of man. The law must be an expression of the general will; all citizens, men and women alike, must participate in making it, either directly or by means of representatives; it must be the same for all. All citizens, be they men or women, being equal in its eyes, must be equally eligible for all public offices, positions, and jobs. . . . [Women] have the right to go to the scaffold; they must also have the right to go to parliament.[3]

Appealing to a fundamental principle of the Revolution, this militant French revolutionary demanded equal participation by women in the new social order, including parity in property rights, educational opportunity, and the right to hold government office, as well as equal tax liability and equal punishment for crimes.

In Britain the writer and bluestocking intellectual Mary Wollstonecraft (1759–1797) championed female emancipation in her celebrated book, *A Vindication of the Rights of Woman* (1792). Wollstonecraft, who had written on educational reform and in support of natural rights in general, saw a strong education, developing both intelligence and character, as an essential preparation for women's rights. Women should develop, not the charming social graces that made them decorative adjuncts to male lives, but the rational faculties and strength of character that would make them effective participants in public life.

It was an early stage of feminist awareness and demand for reform—too early for success. Gouges was executed during the Terror. Wollstonecraft died of childbirth complications following a series of unhappy relationships with men, only the last of whom—the reformer William Godwin—appreciated her brilliance. And in 1804, the Napoleonic Code reimposed male supremacy on French society. Nevertheless, in Gouges, Wollstonecraft, and other women and men of the revolutionary era who spoke up for women's equality, future generations of feminists would find both inspiration and models.

This portrait of Mary Wollstonecraft, author of *A Vindication of the Rights of Woman,* shows both strength of character and a thoughtful disposition. Like many European radicals, Wollstonecraft hoped for more from the French Revolution than it would deliver. (John Opie/National Portrait Gallery, London.)

♦ Napoleon's European Empire ♦

Military genius, emperor of France, and for a dazzling moment in the early 1800s master of most of Europe, Napoleon Bonaparte was a product of the chaos and conflicts generated by the French Revolution. This section will trace Napoleon's rise to power in the 1790s, his many victories, his reorganization of France itself, and his conquest of most of the rest of the continent, before following him down the last long road to defeat at Waterloo in 1815.

Though Napoleon declared the Revolution at an end when he seized power in 1799, his marching armies spread the principles of 1789 all across Europe. Despite determined conservative efforts to restore the old regime in the nineteenth century, the Western world would never be the same again.

The Rise of Napoleon

The meteoric rise of Napoleon Bonaparte (1769–1821) could never have happened under the old regime. Indeed, the story of Napoleon's career vividly illustrates the revolutionary turmoil of the end of the eighteenth century, when anything was possible and history, so it seemed, was about to begin again at the year one.

France's greatest national hero was not French, but Corsican, born on that Italian-speaking Mediterranean island, which had been acquired by France just before his birth. Like many Corsicans, he was not tall—only five and a half feet in his boots—but was

Chronology 18.2: The Napoleonic Era

1796	*Napoleon's Italian campaign makes him a national hero*
1799	*Napoleon's coup makes him ruler of France*
1804	*Napoleon becomes emperor; strengthens French government and legal system (Napoleonic Code)*
1805	*Battle of Austerlitz brings Napoleon within sight of ruling all Europe*
1805	*Battle of Trafalgar shows British determination to resist Napoleon's ambitions by sea*
1812	*Russian campaign burns Moscow, fails to defeat Russians*
1814–1815	*Congress of Vienna meets to control France, restore old regime*
1815	*Battle of Waterloo—Napoleon is defeated and exiled to St. Helena*

aggressive and competitive from birth. A member of the minor Corsican aristocracy, he attended the elite French military academy at Brienne, where he studied the most up-to-date military tactics, with emphasis on rapid mobility and the new light, easily transported field artillery. When the Revolution broke out in 1789, Napoleon was an ambitious artillery lieutenant in the French army, not yet twenty years old.

The revolutionary policy of "careers open to talent" gave him his chance. During the Terror, he skillfully used his field guns to dislodge the British from the port of Toulon. Under the Directory, he deployed his artillery once more, this time against a royalist mob in the streets of Paris. Crushing the revolt with what he casually described as "a whiff of grape–shot," he won the chance he had been waiting for.

Bonaparte's reward was a major general's rank at twenty–five and the command of the French armies currently fighting the Austrians in northern Italy. In 1796, in a series of brilliantly planned and daringly executed campaigns, he overwhelmed the Austrians in battle after battle—a dozen major engagements in as many months. He forced one Italian state after another to accept French suzerainty and to pay millions in war indemnities into the French treasury. In 1797, he forced the the Austrian Habsburgs to make peace and won for France new territory in the Rhineland, allies in Italy, and the right to intervene in the affairs of Germany. He returned to Paris a conquering hero, already dreaming of a still larger role in the affairs of nations.

Over the next two years, Napoleon became involved in a French effort to strike at Britain through its Indian empire—which in turn was to be reached by way of the Mediterranean and Egypt. Napoleon did defeat both Egypt's Mameluke warrior elite and the once–mighty Ottoman Turks. In the end, however, he was frustrated by the British admiral Horatio Nelson (1758–1805) who, by destroying the French fleet on the Nile, cut the French expeditionary force off from reinforcements and supplies. Napoleon thereupon abandoned his army, slipped through the British squadrons patrolling the Mediterranean, and returned to France and his rendezvous with history.

General Napoleon

The coup d'état of November 1799 ended the ten years of political tumult that had begun when the Estates General met in 1789. For the next fifteen years, France would have a strong hand on the helm. And Europe would have a problem the like of which it had not faced since Charlemagne, or perhaps Julius Caesar.

Napoleon, as we shall see, proved to be as remarkable a ruler as he was a general. Governing for five years as first consul (1799–1804), then for ten years as emperor of France (1804–1815), the former artillery lieutenant extended his power until he became also the de facto ruler of most of Europe. In so doing, however, he triggered modern Europe's inevitable response to every great power that has threatened the continent with a single, universal hegemony. Again and again the other powers—Britain, Austria, Prussia, and Russia foremost among them—allied themselves against France, determined to overwhelm the would–be ruler of the Western world. Again and again, General Napoleon drove them back and restlessly redrew the map of Europe, parceling out thrones to his brothers, sisters, and generals. It took two decades for the other great powers to pull him down.

Four times the European powers organized alliances to smother the French explosion across Europe. The first of these coalitions, originally formed to suppress the French Revolution, was finished off by the young Napoleon in Italy in 1796. Napoleon overwhelmed the Second Coalition soon after he became first consul of France in 1801: the Treaty of Amiens (1802) brought peace for a little over a year to war–torn Europe. Despite a second crucial naval defeat by Admiral Nelson at Trafalgar off the coast of Spain in 1805, Napoleon crushed the Third Coalition in a stunning series of victories, defeating the Austrians and Russians at Austerlitz in 1805, the Prussians at Jena in 1806, and the Russians definitively at Friedland in 1807. In a famous summit meeting with Czar Alexander I at Tilsit (1807), Bonaparte divided continental Europe between France and Russia. After French setbacks in Spain and particularly in Russia in 1812, however, the Fourth Coalition finally overpowered the emperor at the Battle of the Nations at Leipzig in 1813 and again in 1815 at a hitherto uncelebrated little village south of Brussels called Waterloo. Master of a nation at thirty and of a continent at forty, Napoleon was a has–been at forty–six, exiled to the rocky island of St. Helena off the African coast for the rest of his days.

It was, to put it mildly, an astonishing career. Efforts to unravel the "secret" of Napoleon's military success are endless. Certainly the large, battle–hardened armies of the French Revolution and the cadres of officers who had risen through talent provided Bonaparte with a superb military instrument. Certainly, too, he made effective use of his advanced French military training and of the new light artillery—"the god of war" as he called it—which he deployed with devastating efficiency. Even the all–weather roads built by the enlightened despots who preceded him facilitated the rapid marches that enabled Napoleon to show up in force halfway across Europe long before his enemies expected him.

In the Battle of Austerlitz in 1805, perhaps his masterpiece, Napoleon faced the combined armies of Austria and Russia some 70 miles north of Vienna. Luring his foes into attacking his apparently overextended right wing, the emperor then split the allied armies with an assault on their center, which had been weakened in order to press the attack on his right. Thereafter, he rolled up the left and right wings of the Austro–Russian host, destroying them in detail as they broke and fled. At the end of the day, the French had lost eight thousand men, their opponents twenty–six thousand, and the allied army "had ceased to exist" as a fighting force.[4] The Russian emperor Alexander I (r. 1801–1825) was in full retreat, and Austria's emperor Francis II was ready for unconditional surrender. "Never," as Admiral Nelson wrote that same year, "was Europe more critically situated than at this moment, and never was the probability of universal monarchy more nearly being realized than in the person of the Corsican."[5]

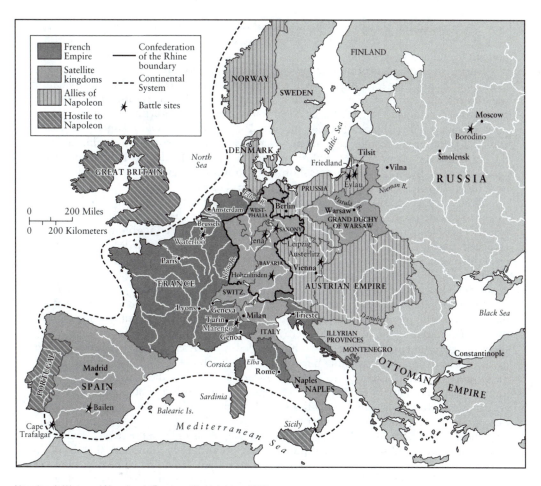

Napoleon's Wars and Napoleon's Empire at its Height, c. 1810

Napoleon and France

Napoleon summarized his own political ambitions to a French liberal not long before Waterloo. "I desired the empire of the world," he said, "and to insure it, absolute power was necessary to me."[6] As an organizer of power on a national and international level, he has had few peers.

Judged on his domestic reforms, Napoleon has sometimes been described as the enlightened despot France had failed to produce in the eighteenth century. He proceeded early to convert the French Republic created by the Revolution back to an autocratic monarchy. To this end, he had himself made first consul for life in 1802 and then, in 1804, hereditary emperor of France. The elected legislature inherited from the revolutionary Republic was abolished, and the most important governmental body became an appointed Council of State responsible, not to the people, but to the emperor. In the departments that had replaced the ancient provinces, elected officials were replaced by appointed prefects and subprefects. Even the mayors of village communes were henceforth to be appointed from Paris.

During the early years of his rule, however, Napoleon did often use his immense power to rationalize government, frequently in the interests of the governed. A prime example was the reform of the French legal system carried out under his sponsorship. The *Napoleonic Code* made all French citizens equal under the law and guaranteed their rights to private property, free choice of career, and freedom of religion. Old distinctions of caste and class, local privilege and religious persuasion were thus swept aside. Again, however, the more liberal reforms of the Revolution were abandoned. Under the new regime, wives and children were once more made subordinate to husbands and fathers, and all citizens were more directly subservient to the state than ever before.

The French economy flourished, at least in the earlier years of the Napoleonic Empire. Bonaparte made tax collection both more efficient and more honest than it had ever been before. He even managed to balance the budget, partly by plundering foreign lands. He established a central Bank of France and stabilized the French currency. Military contracts brought profits to businessmen, and laws against strikes and labor organizations further benefited the bourgeoisie. These changes, however, were not welcomed by the laboring people who had once thought that they, too, had a place in the revolutionary Republic.

Even education was improved—in a practical way—by the Napoleonic regime. Most schools were still operated by the church, and the broad promises of public education for the masses offered by the Revolution were not implemented. But the emperor did create a system of government–run secondary schools called *lycées*. The *lycées* maintained high standards of scholarship and discipline; but they admitted only those who could afford the tuition, and they were intended to produce future servants of the state. Napoleon also founded the University of France and gave it general supervision of all education, lay and ecclesiastical. He thus laid the foundations for the centralized national education structure that developed in France over the next two centuries.

Those who dissented in Napoleonic France got short shrift from the strong–willed emperor. His censors and secret police suppressed the political press and political clubs of the 1790s and harassed or arrested extremists of left and right. Most French people, however, acquiesced willingly enough in a strong government that brought them tranquillity and prosperity at home and victories abroad and asked only that they surrender their recently acquired liberties in return. When Napoleon submitted his own elevation to emperor to a plebiscite, 3,572,329 French citizens voted aye, only 2,579 against. Even allowing for some intimidation and manipulation, it was an impressive vote of confidence in the government of Napoleon Bonaparte.

Napoleon and Europe

Increasingly, however, the object of this impressive organization became, not the rationalization of the state, but the greater glory of its ruler. More and more convinced of his larger imperial destiny, Napoleon saw himself as a second Charlemagne and dreamed of imposing new order on Europe as a whole.

To that end, Napoleon converted the satellite republics he inherited into satellite monarchies and added others, from Spain to Poland. On the thrones of these client kingdoms, he placed his own brothers and other relatives. He divorced the great love of his life,

Joséphine Beauharnais, for her failure to provide him with an heir to his emerging empire. In her place, he married an Austrian Habsburg princess, Marie–Louise (1791–1847), daughter to the oldest and most prestigious ruling house in Europe.

Meanwhile, creating new nations and crippling old ones with a wave of his scepter, Bonaparte reorganized the state system of Europe. He abolished the ancient Holy Roman Empire of the Habsburgs, with its hundreds of autonomous principalities, and replaced it with a Confederation of the Rhine allied to France. He confiscated half the territory of Hohenzollern Prussia, converting much of it into a revived Polish state, the Duchy of Warsaw. In 1807, he met with Alexander I of Russia on a raft in the Niemen River to reorganize the continent as a whole. The resulting Treaty of Tilsit recognized Napoleon's restructuring of western and central Europe, leaving the east to Russia. Five years later, however, the restless French emperor marched once more against Alexander, determined to have eastern Europe as well.

Only one of the great powers successfully resisted this Napoleonic drive for mastery of the Western world. Britain, safe on its offshore islands, refused to accept the new French predominance. Rulers of a global empire, masters of the new industrial system and of the world's largest navy and merchant marine, the British stood against Napoleon year after year. The emperor's dream of invading the British Isles was shattered when Admiral Nelson destroyed half the French fleet at Trafalgar in 1805, guaranteeing the British control of the seas for the rest of the war. In 1806, therefore, Napoleon determined to break the islanders economically by compelling all Europe to sever its ties with "the nation of shopkeepers." This so–called *Continental System* also required his satellites and allies to trade heavily with France instead, thus further strengthening the imperial center.

Britain, however, reacted by instigating a massive commercial blockade of Europe and seizing thousands of neutral vessels attempting to trade with France or its allies. The result was costly for both sides. The British lost many customers and faced widespread depression and public disorders at home. French ports and manufacturers, deprived of trade and imported resources, suffered grievously. And the emperor's client states groaned under the impact of the conflict, losing many ships to the British and seeing their commerce increasingly dominated by the French.

Napoleon's far–reaching efforts at the imperial reorganization and control of all Europe were thus not undergirded by the sort of support he enjoyed in France. The rumblings of defeated foes and exploited allies grew louder. The Grand Empire that looked so splendid in 1810 was gone five short years later.

The Road to Waterloo, 1815

The tides of history turned slowly but inexorably against Napoleon through the last years of his reign. A variety of forces and factors contributed to this end. The Continental System not only failed to bring Britain to its knees but ignited open conflicts between Bonaparte and his unwilling allies. Militant nationalism, which had earlier inspired the French to the defense of their homeland, flamed up now in nations conquered by France. And the sheer attrition of two decades of war cost Napoleon the best of his troops and exhausted even Europe's greatest power. Nevertheless, in the end it took the most impressive of all the coalitions raised against him to bring him down.

Napoleon became embroiled in the Peninsular Wars when he sent armies into Portugal in 1807 to impose the Continental System on that country. He stirred up violent opposition in Spain when in 1808 he put one of his brothers on the Spanish throne and began stripping Spanish grandees and churchmen of their traditional privileges. A draining five–year guerrilla war in Spain resulted, supported by a British expeditionary force under Sir Arthur Wellesley (1769–1852), later known as the duke of Wellington, the title he earned for his leading part in Napoleon's overthrow.

At the other end of the Grand Empire, Russia also failed to live up to the costly terms of the Continental System. Napoleon responded in his usual impetuous style—by marching on Moscow in 1812. He defeated the Russians at the epic battle of Borodino and captured their capital, but Alexander I refused to make terms, and Bonaparte found himself stranded in Russia with winter coming on. Russian guerrilla attacks and scorched–earth tactics—they even burned Moscow itself around his ears—joined with impossible logistics and the crushing cold to decimate Napoleon's army on the long march home.

Close on the heels of the disastrous Russian campaign, the Wars of National Liberation broke out in the German states. Repeated defeat and occupation by the French had kindled powerful national feeling in Prussia and in the smaller principalities that Napoleon had so cavalierly reorganized in his Confederation of the Rhine. A new wave of enlightened reforms in the early 1800s had strengthened both the national will and the social fabric of Austria, Prussia, and the other central European states, and they were ready and eager to fall upon the French emperor in the aftermath of his debacle in Russia.

With Russian armies closing in from the east and Britain's Spanish expeditionary force breaking through from the west, Bonaparte faced the armies of the Fourth Coalition at Leipzig in 1813. Overwhelmed in the so–called Battle of the Nations, he was deposed and exiled to Elba, a small island off the coast of Italy, while his victorious opponents met at Vienna to pick his empire to pieces.

Within a year, he was back. Landing on March 1, 1815, at Cannes in southern France with a tiny handful of the faithful, he found the Napoleonic magic working for him still. Hailed by his old soldiers and welcomed by a French populace apprehensive of its fate at the hands of the Congress of Vienna, he marched across France and entered Paris in triumph. In three hectic months—the famous "Hundred Days," from March 20 to June 29—Napoleon Bonaparte recaptured his throne, raised yet another army, and marched off once more to meet his destiny—at Waterloo. In this bloody daylong encounter on June 18, 1815, the staying qualities of Wellington's British troops and the nick-of-time arrival of Prussian reinforcements under General Gebhard Leberecht von Blücher (1742–1819) defeated Napoleon in his last battle. Abdicating for a second time, the French emperor was again banished, this time to the far more distant British–ruled island of St. Helena in the South Atlantic. Six years later, he was dead, probably of cancer, perhaps of arsenic poisoning, in his island exile.

Napoleon was thus both an autocrat and a reformer. The child of the French Revolution, he was one of a long line of subverters of revolutionary dreams. Yet his astonishing career is perhaps the best evidence of all of the new dynamism unleashed in European history by the revolutions of the eighteenth century.

Summary

The French Revolution of 1789 inaugurated a tumultuous decade of political change, domestic terror, and foreign wars.

The revolutionary decade also produced the amazing career of Napoleon Bonaparte, who restructured French government and conquered most of Europe before going down to defeat at Waterloo.

The old regime in France had reached an economic, financial, and political crisis in 1789. Facing depression, bad harvests, and impending bankruptcy, the royal government desperately needed to tax the wealth of the nation. In search of a solution, Louis XVI summoned the Estates General, France's medieval assembly, for the first time since the early seventeenth century. Both these politicians and the radical elements in the population of Paris were soon up in arms, storming the Bastille and marching on the royal palace at Versailles.

The resulting French Revolution, launched in the name of such high ideals as liberty, equality, and brotherhood, began with a surge of political achievements. It eliminated the surviving feudal rights of the nobility, brought the French Catholic church under state control, and transformed France's absolute monarchy into a constitutional one.

When the royal governments of other European powers attacked France, however, the revolutionary regime fell into the hands of Jacobin extremists. Robespierre and the Committee of Public Safety repelled the foreign invaders but also imposed a reign of terror on France itself. The Reign of Terror that followed abolished the monarchy and executed both the king and queen and their reactionary supporters and those revolutionaries who resisted further radical change. When the revolutionaries themselves executed Robespierre and the Jacobin leadership, France fell into the hands of the corrupt Directory.

In 1799, the Directory gave way to the reign of Napoleon Bonaparte. An autocratic military man, Napoleon quickly became the enlightened despot France had missed in the eighteenth century. The greatest general of his age, Napoleon repeatedly defeated the other great powers—Britain, Austria, Prussia, and Russia and imposed his will on Europe. Though no revolutionary himself, Napoleon made Europe's peoples aware of the ideals of liberty and equality, careers open to talent, and other revolutionary principles. Only in 1815 did a final European alliance pull him down at Waterloo.

Some Key Terms

Bastille   447
cahiers   446
Civil Constitution of the
   Clergy   448
Committee of Public Safety   450
Constitution of 1791   449
Continental System   459
Declaration of the Rights of Man
   and the Citizen   447

Directory   452
émigrés   449
enragés   449
Estates General   445
Girondins   449
ideological revolution   441
Jacobins   449
Liberté, Egalité, Fraternité   445
march on Versailles   448

Napoleonic Code   458
Night of August 4   448
Paris Commune   450
Reign of Terror   450
sans-culottes   443
Tennis Court Oath   447
Thermidorian reaction   451
third estate   442
Vendée   451

Notes

1. The Declaration of the Rights of Man and the Citizen, quoted in D. G. Wright, *Revolution and Terror in France, 1789–1795* (London: Longman, 1974), 108.

2. Leo Gershoy, *The French Revolution, 1789–1799* (New York: Henry Holt and Company, 1932), 21.

3. Olympe de Gouges, quoted in *Not in God's Im-*

age: Woman in History, ed. Julia O'Faolain and Lauro Martines (London: Virago, 1979), 319–320.

4. R. Ernest Dupuy and Tor N. Dupuy, *The Encyclopedia of Military History* (New York: Harper and Row, 1970), 749.

5. Horatio Nelson, quoted in Felix Markham, *Napoleon* (New York: New American Library, 1963), 120.

6. Napoleon Bonaparte, quoted in David L. Dowd, *Napoleon: Was He the Heir of the Revolution?* (New York: Holt, Rinehart and Winston, 1957), 12.

Reading List

Bertaud, J.-P. *The Army of the French Revolution: From Citizen–Soldiers to Instrument of Power.* Translated by R. R. Palmer. Princeton, N.J.: Princeton University Press, 1988. Evolution of the army that would conquer much of Europe under Napoleon's leadership.

Church, W. H. *The Influence of the Enlightenment on the French Revolution.* 2d ed. Lexington, Mass.: Heath, 1972. The role of ideas in the Revolution.

Connelly, O. *Napoleon's Satellite Kingdoms.* New York: Free Press, 1966. The first, brief unification of much of Europe since Roman times—under the Bonaparte dynasty.

Doyle, W. *The Oxford History of the French Revolution.* Oxford: Clarendon Press, 1989. Solid survey, more critical of the Revolution and heavy on revolutionary violence than most scholars have been.

Geyl, P. *Napoleon For and Against.* London: Cape, 1949. Considers the debate over Napoleon's character and contribution to history.

Godechot, J. *France and the Atlantic Revolution of the Eighteenth Century, 1770–1799.* Translated by H. R. Rowen. New York: Free Press, 1965. France's place in the larger series of revolutions on both sides of the Atlantic.

Greenlaw, R. W., ed. *The Social Origins of the French Revolution.* Lexington, Mass.: Heath, 1975. Essays exploring the extent to which the French Revolution was essentially a bourgeois revolt. See also the succinct analysis in W. Doyle, *The Origins of the French Revolution* (Oxford: Oxford University Press, 1980).

Holtman, R. B. *The Napoleonic Revolution.* Baton Rouge: University of Louisiana Press, 1979. Institutional changes under Napoleon.

Johnson, D., ed. *French Society and the Revolution.* Cambridge: Cambridge University Press, 1976. Scholarly essays on the social dimension that many historians have seen as central to the story of the Revolution.

Kennedy, E. *A Cultural History of the French Revolution.* New Haven: Yale University Press, 1989. Sees the Revolution having little immediate impact on French high or popular culture.

Levy, D. G., H. B. Applewhite, and M. D. Johnson. *Women in Revolutionary Paris, 1780–1795.* Urbana: University of Illinois Press, 1979. Reveals a much more active role by women than was once assumed.

Lyons, M. *France Under the Directory.* Cambridge: Cambridge University Press, 1975. Scholarly treatment, including aspects of society and culture.

Markham, F. M. H. *Napoleon and the Awakening of Europe.* Harmondsworth, England: Penguin, 1975. Brief but recommended, emphasizing the spread of revolutionary ideas in Napoleon's empire.

Palmer, R. R. *Twelve Who Ruled: The Year of the Terror in the French Revolution.* Princeton, N.J.: Princeton University Press, 1978. Riveting biographical approach to the Committee of Public Safety.

Schama, S. *Citizens: A Chronicle of the French Revolution.* New York: Viking, 1989. Mammoth panorama of individuals and events; some emphasis on the role of the enlightened nobility.

Soboul, A. *The Sans–Culottes and the French Revolution.* Princeton, N.J.: Princeton University Press, 1980. Arrest records show the sans–culottes to have been much more solid citizens than the legendary "mob." See also G. Rudé, *The Crowd in the French Revolution* (Oxford: Clarendon Press, 1959).

Thompson, J. M. *Napoleon Bonaparte: His Rise and Fall.* Oxford: Oxford University Press, 1969. Older, but perhaps still the best biography of Napoleon in English.

Thomson, G. *The Babeuf Plot: The Making of a Republican Legend*. London: Kegan Paul, 1947. Facts and fictions on the Conspiracy of Equals.

Tilly, C. *The Vendée*. New York: Wiley, 1967. A provocative consideration of the motivation that underlay the peasants' decision to rebel against the Revolution.

Vouvelle, M. *The Fall of the French Monarchy, 1787–1792*. Cambridge: Cambridge University Press, 1984. Emphasis on social history and collective attitudes.

PART V
The Nineteenth Century: Western Supremacy

Economically and technologically, the Western world changed more dramatically than ever before during the century between Waterloo in 1815 and the outbreak of World War I in 1914. The Industrial Revolution, which began at the end of the preceding century, accelerated after 1815 and spread eastward across Europe and westward across the Atlantic to the Americas. An unpredicted consequence of industrial and economic growth was the emergence of big business, with its huge corporations and globe-girdling cartels, in the later nineteenth century. New ideologies, meanwhile, paved the way for major transformations to come. Conservatives resisted all radical change but retreated slowly before the onslaught of the new ideas of liberals, socialists, nationalists, and smaller but no less militant groups of utilitarians, feminists, and anarchists.

Politically, this century was dominated by two new notions in particular: liberalism and nationalism. In the early 1800s, liberal and nationalist revolutions flared across central, southern, and eastern Europe and spread across the Atlantic to Latin America. Although most of the revolutions of the 1820s, 1830s, and 1848 in Europe were suppressed, the Latin American revolts of 1810–1825 succeeded.

In the second half of the century, Britain was transformed by a wave of reforms, France became a republic, Austria confronted rising tides of nationalist feeling among its subject peoples, and the Russian czars faced down futile assaults by radicals and revolutionaries. Brilliant diplomatic maneuvers combined with growing nationalism to forge two new great powers in Germany and Italy.

Masters of machines and money, nineteenth-century entrepreneurs and industrial organizers began to make themselves heard in politics as well. The laborers in mines and mills, meanwhile, struggled to organize labor unions or to throw their support to political candidates who would defend their interests. And women began to seek jobs created by the Industrial Revolution and to demand education and political rights equal to those enjoyed by men.

The cultural history of the nineteenth century can be largely divided into a passionately romantic movement in the first half of the century and a harshly realistic, even materialistic trend in the second half. Romanticism, rooted in the arts, emphasized an emotional response to the world. Realism, impressed by scientific breakthroughs like Darwin's theory of evolution, claimed to face the world honestly, without rose-colored glasses. The same century thus saw romantic poets reveling in love, beauty, and sometimes despair, and realistic novelists anatomizing the grim new social order of factories and slum tenements.

In the later decades of the nineteenth century, finally, Europe launched an important new wave of imperial expansion upon the world. The new imperialism brought most of Africa and Asia under the control of Britain, France, and other Western nations. In addition, expanding Western nations like the United States and Russia absorbed vast tracts of sparsely populated territory on their frontiers. Most of the rest of the world submitted to an unprecedented Western hegemony of the globe.

Time Line: The Western Supremacy

1790   Burke's *Reflections on the Revolution in France* formulates conservative critique of radicalism

1791   Gouge's *Declaration of the Rights of Women* demands equal rights for women

1798   Wordsworth and Coleridge, *Lyrical Ballads* celebrates simple peasant hearts

1810–1825   Latin American Wars of Liberation create republics in Middle and South America

1814–1815   Congress of Vienna tries to restore the old regime

1820   Revolts in southern Europe—Spain, Portugal, Naples, Piedmont—are suppressed

        1829   Chopin's debut introduces new kind of romantic music

        1830   Delacroix's *Liberty Leading the People,* a romantic painting hailing the Revolution of 1830

1830   First steam airway

1830   July revolution in France overthrows Bourbon dynasty; revolts in Belgium succeed; revolts in Poland and the Italian states suppressed

1832   Reform Bill of 1832 begins democratizing British Parliament

1840   First ocean-going steam ship

1846   Repeal of "Corn Law"—tariff on imported grain—brings triumph of free trade in Britain

        1847   Emily Bronte's *Wuthering Heights*—lost romantic lovers in a wild romantic setting

        1848   Marx's and Engels's *Communist Manifesto* formulates Marxist revolutionary socialism

1848   British Chartist movement suppressed

1848   February revolution in Paris establishes republic; revolutionaries seize power in Italian and German states, including Prussia and Austria

1848–1849   Monarchs and armies restore order in Italian and German states; some limited constitutions are granted

        1850   Courbet's *The Stonebreakers* realistically showcases life of the working poor

        1859   Darwin's *Origin of Species* raises furor over theory of biological evolution

1859–1860   Unification of Italy

1860–1865   Civil War in the United States

1870–1871   Unification of Germany

1870s   Rise of big business—giant corporations and cartel agreements

1870s–1914   New Imperialism partitions Africa, imposes European hegemony on Asia

1871   Republic established in France

        1871–1893   Zola's Rougon-Macquart series traces lives of French people of all classes, seen as products of biology and environment

        1874   First Impressionist show, artists paint light, not things

1880s   Welfare legislation in Germany

        1885   Nietzsche's *Zarathustra* announces the "death of God."

        1885–1890   Van Gogh's major paintings reflect his tortured spirit

1890s   Chamberlain urges superiority of Aryan "race"

1890s–1900s   Women's suffrage campaigns in Britain

1894–1906   Dreyfus case divides France

        1895   Freud's *Studies on Hysteria* reveals existence of unconscious drives at heart of human psyche

1900   Boxer Rebellion tries to drive Westerners out of China

— 19 —

Power and Principles
The Rise of Industrialism and Ideology

♦The Industrialization of the West   ♦Free Enterprise and Big Business
♦A Changing Society   ♦Conservatism and Liberalism
♦Nationalism, Socialism, Feminism

Industrialism and ideology played central roles in the shaping of nineteenth–century Western civilization. This first chapter on the century will therefore survey both the accelerating industrial development and the new ideological theories of the years between 1815 and 1914. We will begin with a look at the spread of industrialization from Britain to Europe and the Americas and at the further technological evolution of the Industrial Revolution, from coal–powered steam engines to hydroelectric power and petroleum.

The next section will trace the changes in economic organization that resulted, from the decline of mercantilism and the rise of free enterprise to the emergence of big business. Thereafter, we will look at Western society in terms of classes and social change, the ongoing population explosion, migrations to industrial cities and around the world, changes in gender roles and in the interaction of age groups.

While the material lives of Europeans changed, their views of themselves and their world changed as well. Particularly influential were the new political, economic, and social theories we call *ideologies*. The last two sections of this chapter will attempt a broad survey of the formation of the major ideologies of the last two centuries: Conservatism and liberalism, nationalism and racism, socialism of various types, feminism, anarchism, and related concepts.

English poets complained even before 1800 that the "dark, Satanic mills" of the new industry were blackening the green hills with coal dust. A half–century later, true believers hailed the violent ideological revolutions of 1848 as "the springtime of the peoples." Both the power unleashed by the new technology and the "self–evident truths" which gripped generations of ideological revolutionaries would play key roles in the history of the nineteenth century—and of the twentieth.

♦The Industrialization of the West♦

Although the industrialization of the West began in Britain, it quickly spread to continental Europe and to North America. By the end of the 1800s, both Germany and the United

States were challenging Britain for mastery of the new industrial world. But the West as a whole was an industrial powerhouse.

The Industrial Revolution began in an age of steam and textiles; by the end of the century, oil and electricity, steel, chemicals, and a flood of other new products had transformed the Western economy. From the steam locomotive to the electric telegraph, new technological marvels studded the history of the century.

Britain and the Age of Steam

"Steam," they said in the nineteenth century, "is an Englishman," and Britain was "the workshop of the world." The British Isles, where the Industrial Revolution began, retained many of its eighteenth-century economic advantages through most of the nineteenth century as well.

Economic historians, indeed, have increasingly identified the nineteenth century as the time when the Industrial Revolution really took hold in Britain as well as elsewhere. Emphasizing the undoubted fact that most British people continued to work in agriculture or in industries not affected by industrialization, they have tended to push even the British Industrial Revolution back well into the 1800s. Here we will consider industrialization as an ongoing process, beginning in the single industry of British cotton manufactures in the late eighteenth century and spreading from one industry to another and from one country to another through the nineteenth century.

In this approach, Britain still retains its vanguard role. British society, with its vigorous middle class and a working class that was dependent on wages and open to new skills, had

An early iron-hulled steamship, the *Great Eastern* of 1861 combined traditional sails with the paddle wheels that had been used earlier on river boats. The most striking thing about this pioneer ocean liner, however, was its size. (The Granger Collection.)

Chronology 19.1: Spread of Industrialism and Big Business

1815–1850	*Spread of industrialization to Europe and North America*
1830	*First steam railway*
1840	*First ocean–going steam ship*
1844	*First telegraph*
1846	*Repeal of "Corn Law"—tariff on imported grain brings triumph of free trade in Britain*
1860s	*Open–hearth furnaces for steel making; dynamos and hydroelectric power*
1869	*Transcontinental railroad in United States*
1870s	*Rise of big business—giant corporations and cartel agreements*
1880s	*Petroleum challenges coal as industrial power source*
1891	*Trans–Siberian railway in Russia*

greater social mobility and faced less prejudice against "trade" than much of European society. As a result, England continued to provide a hospitable environment for business growth. The Bank of England was a rock–solid source of financial support for industry, and many middle–class Britons, tempted by exciting new industries from railways to hydroelectric power, began to invest in business enterprise in the nineteenth century, channeling their modest personal surpluses into industrial expansion. The nation's own domestic market combined with markets in its vast overseas empire and in the new American republics to create an immense demand for cheap, mass–produced goods. And the technological innovations England had achieved in the later eighteenth century gave Britain a long lead in developing the means to supply that demand.

Britain continued through much of the nineteenth century to be the home of aggressive entrepreneurs and ingenious inventors. It produced more efficient steam engines and larger textile mills, new applications of steam power to transportation and new processes for the smelting of steel. Though much of the country remained rural, Britain continued to be the most heavily industrialized of nations and to enjoy the highest per capita income of all the Western powers. Only at the end of the century was this predominance challenged— by nations that had acquired much of their industrial know–how from the British.

Industrialism Spreads to Europe and the Americas

After 1815, the British experience began to influence a number of European states. Nowhere, however, was the British model followed exactly. In each country and region, social conditions and traditions focused the process of industrialization in distinctive ways. Britain was the great teacher, but each pupil learned in its own manner.

The spread of the new industrial economy to Europe was a regional phenomenon. Industrialism spread first, between 1815 and 1850, around areas of resource concentration, most notably the coalfields and iron pockets of Belgium, northern France, western Germany, and parts of the Austrian Empire. During the second half of the century, from 1850 to 1914, industry spread also to backward Russia and resource–poor Italy, to Switzerland and Scandinavia. Continental industrialists, furthermore, had the latecomer's advantage of being able to draw upon the developed technology of those who had gone before. Importing machines, skilled workers, and even entrepreneurial talent from Britain, Europeans could leapfrog whole stages of industrial development.

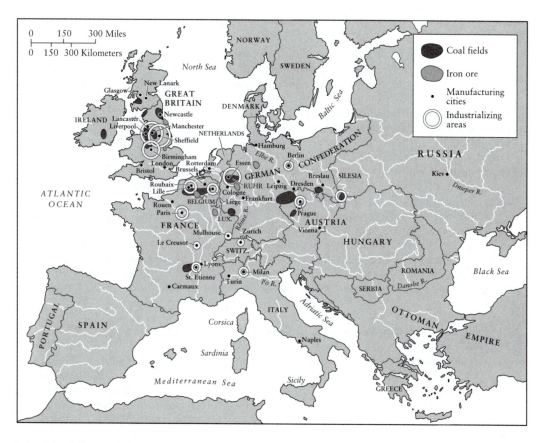

Industrialism in Europe, 1860

For example, for laying railway lines or building steel mills based on the new smelt-ing techniques, Europeans needed immense capitalization. Such a scale of investment was often possible only if governments guaranteed the loans or if the largest banking and other financial houses were drawn upon. The result, especially in Germany, was a bigger scale of business venture, and one in which both government and high finance played a more important part than that originally played by individual entrepreneurs in Britain.

Industrialism began to spread to North America at about the same time that it reached continental Europe, during the first half of the nineteenth century. It was during the sec-ond half of the century, however, that the new industrial society boomed in the United States and began to develop in Latin America as well.

The new republics across the Atlantic boasted a wide variety of natural resources and rapidly growing populations of labor composed of European and Asian immigrants as well as African Americans and Native Americans. Like continental Europe, furthermore, the Americas benefited from developed British technology, capital, and trade. British capital poured into the United States, for instance, to finance that nation's immense nineteenth-century railroad network. And after the Latin American Wars of Liberation

(1810–1825), British commerce and capital replaced Iberian economic stimulation in the new southern America republics too.

In North America, an expanding society rapidly constructed an infrastructure of roads and canals in the first half of the century, transcontinental railroads in the second half. The newly developed steamship and telegraphic communications further linked the nation's economic regions and bound the United States to European markets. The result was astonishingly rapid industrial growth, especially after the Civil War ended in 1865. Early textile mills and other manufacturing centers were concentrated in New England. As the century advanced, however, manufacturing, mining, food processing, and other industries spread westward to cities like Pittsburgh and Chicago, while San Francisco on the west coast became a major port. In the United States as in Europe, textiles, coal, and iron were soon rivaled by oil, steel, railroads, and high finance as growth industries. And total output grew even more rapidly in the New World than in the Old.

Latin America, however, developed less rapidly. Liberated politically half a century after the United States, the republics of Middle and South America continued to function primarily as suppliers of raw materials and agricultural produce. In exchange for Argentine beef and wheat, Brazilian coffee, Chilean nitrates, and Mexican oil, these nations bought most of their manufactured goods from Britain or the United States. In most of South and Middle America, large–scale industrial development was thus deferred until the twentieth century.

Power Sources, Transportation, Communication

Even as industrialization spread from its first home in Britain to the rest of the Western world, the Industrial Revolution was itself changed and expanded. The eighteenth–century British Industrial Revolution had focused on textiles, iron, coal, and steam power. The broader industrialization of the nineteenth–century West expanded from steam to electricity and petroleum as power sources. It also saw major advances in steel making, chemicals, transportation, and communication.

Both of the two new power sources introduced during the nineteenth century, the *electrical generator* and the *internal combustion engine,* were developed in the 1860s. Electrical energy was applied to lighting streets and buildings after American inventor Thomas Edison (1849–1931) developed the incandescent lamp in the 1870s. Oil– or gas–powered internal combustion engines, developed first in Germany and France, were used for pumping and for marine and land transport, including early automobiles. Electricity would find many more uses after 1900, and as early as 1875, a farsighted engineer declared that the gas engine would become "the real power–machine of the masses"[1] in the next century.

The modern steel industry also emerged in the nineteenth century. Iron masters had learned to make much cheaper iron and steel by using hotter–burning coke (partially burned coal) before 1800. But it was nineteenth–century demand for steel for machine tools, bridges, and above all for railroads that produced Henry Bessemer's (1813–1898) *Bessemer converter* in the 1850s and Karl Wilhelm Siemens's (1823–1883) *open hearth process* in the 1860s. Steel thus quickly became the basic structural material in everything from steamships to the first skyscrapers.

More futuristic still was the emergence of industrial chemistry in the later nineteenth century. German chemical plants led the way in maintaining research laboratories and keeping in touch with university chemists. Among the products that resulted were medicines and photographic equipment, chemical fertilizers, aniline dyes for clothing, and even the first plastics. A major breakthrough in the chemical industry came in the 1860s, when the Swedish industrialist Alfred Nobel evolved a powerful yet stable explosive called dynamite, which had many industrial and military uses.

Most striking to contemporaries, however, were the astonishing changes in transportation and communication between 1815 and 1914. The first steam locomotive to pull both freight and passenger cars on rails went into service between the port of Liverpool and the industrial city of Manchester in Britain in 1830. By the century's end, tens of thousands of miles of track crisscrossed Europe and spanned the United States and Russia from coast to coast. Cheap steel made much larger and more seaworthy steamships possible, and screw propellers, developed in the 1840s, gave steamers a dependability that even the most streamlined clippers under masses of canvas could not match. The cutting of great ship channels like the Suez Canal in 1869 and the Panama Canal in 1914 enabled steamships to move between the world's oceans without going around Africa or South America.

Communications also made advances unprecedented in history, thanks to the application of electricity. The first public telegraph line carrying messages by dot-and-dash code was put into service between Washington and Baltimore in 1844. Undersea telegraph cables were soon laid beneath the English Channel and the Atlantic, bringing virtually instantaneous communication between nations and continents. Alexander Graham Bell (1847–1922) transmitted the first telephone message in the United States in 1876, and Guglielmo Marconi (1874–1937) developed the first radio communications in the 1890s.

The rattle and clang of early eighteenth–century spinning machines thus rose to a roar as the nineteenth century progressed. And the roar of the machines signaled an unprecedented great leap forward in the ancient human enterprise of producing goods and services to meet our multiplying needs.

✦Free Enterprise and Big Business✦

If the scale of industrial production was unparalleled, so was the scale of economic organization that produced it. Accompanying the amazing technological growth of nineteenth-century industrialism were crucial developments in the history of Western capitalism. These included both the emergence of modern free enterprise and the mushrooming growth of what the next century would call "big business."

The earlier nineteenth century, particularly the period between 1820 and 1870, saw growing faith in the unalloyed virtues of free competition. In the last third of the century, however, the giant corporations and cartels that some called monopoly capitalism seemed to threaten to eliminate competition in some sectors of the economy altogether.

The Rise of Free Enterprise

In medieval and early modern Europe, trade and particularly manufacturing had traditionally been controlled, fostered, and regulated by authorities beyond the individual merchant or artisan. Local guilds had controlled training, limited competition, set standards of quality, fixed prices and wages. Mercantilist monarchs had assigned monopolies, chartered trading companies, and established protective tariffs.

Industrialism in the United States, 1860

In the nineteenth century, however, industrial entrepreneurs spearheaded a determined drive to free business from these restraining shackles. The central thrust of this drive was the great campaign for free trade. This crusade, first in England and then in other parts of Europe, demanded the shattering of the tariff barriers that hamstrung commercial exchange across the Western world.

There were other battlegrounds in the struggle to free economic activity from any control but that of the laws of the free market. Industrialists fought outdated guild rules, particularly apprenticeship regulations requiring years of craft training that were now irrelevant to the labor of factory hands. Entrepreneurs demanded *freedom of contract*—the right to negotiate wages, hours, and other terms with individual employees without deferring to guild traditions or the new labor unions. But free trade was the main focus of the nineteenth–century free–enterprise movement in Europe.

In Britain, the *free–trade movement,* led by Richard Cobden (1804–1865) and John Bright (1811–1889), fought for the abolition of protective tariffs, particularly tariffs on grain. Free traders insisted that grain tariffs kept food prices high and deterred foreigners, who could not export agricultural products to Britain, from buying British manufactured goods. In 1846, during the terrible Irish potato famine of the "hungry forties," Prime Minister Robert Peel (1788–1850) finally repealed the corn laws in order to allow the importation of desperately needed cheap grain. By midcentury, Britain stood as a model of free trade to the world.

Continental Europe proceeded more slowly along this road. In Germany, Prussia led in establishing a customs union, the *Zollverein,* which abolished tariff walls between most of the three–dozen German states during the first half of the century. In France, Emperor Napoleon III signed the Cobden–Chevalier commercial treaty with Britain in 1860, lowering customs duties and benefiting French industry. Everywhere, progressive businesspeople saw free competition as the wave of the future. With producers competing for trade in the free market, the public was sure of getting the best product at the cheapest price. Free competition, they argued, was "the law of progress and the life of trade."

Corporations and Cartels

Then, over the last third of the century, there came a startling change. Technically, it was called *industrial combination;* to its enemies it was "monopoly capitalism." In America, its architects were the *robber barons,* the aggressively successful, but too often unscrupulous, businessmen whom cartoonist Thomas Nast depicted as bloated plutocrats with dollar signs on their stomachs. In Europe, believers in free competition saw the emerging corporate giants as the greatest threat to free enterprise since the heyday of mercantilism.

There had been problems with free competition, even in its midcentury golden age. For every winner, there were always losers, firms that could not compete and went bankrupt. The nineteenth century also saw the *business cycle* of boom and bust—good times followed by industrial depressions—assume its rhythmic modern form, bringing steep economic downturns every decade or so.

Modern big business thus arose in the 1870s as a response to the dangers of fang-and-claw competition and devastating periodic depressions. Through corporate mergers or business agreements, the builders of the gigantic new industrial combines sought to limit or even eliminate competition between rivals.

Some of the architects of the corporate empires of the later nineteenth century were hard–driving individuals like Alfred Krupp (1812–1887), Alfred Nobel (1833–1896), or John D. Rockefeller (1839–1937). Dynasties like the Krupps pyramided their assets into business enterprises larger than anything the world had ever seen before. But even the largest family firms soon gave way to giant joint–stock companies, owned by large numbers of stockholders, capitalized by large banks and other financial institutions, and run by professional managers.

Economists see two basic forms of nineteenth–century industrial combination: corporate amalgamation and cartel agreements. In the business *corporation,* an aggressive entrepreneur or company simply bought up weaker rivals. This method of combination sometimes involved the establishment of a *holding company* that might not make anything at all itself but simply owned a number of operating companies that did. In general, however, corporations came in two basic forms, usually described as "horizontal" and "vertical" amalgamation. In a horizontal merger, rivals in the same line of business combined to create a corporate giant. In this way, Alfred Nobel brought producers of explosives in several European countries together in the Nobel Dynamite Trust. In vertical amalgamation, a company bought up enterprises that were *related* to its own operations, often stages in a single process. Thus Alfred Krupp, the German steel manufacturer, bought up iron and coal mines, fleets of ore boats, and such users of his steel as machine–tool works, railway manufacturers, and the armaments factories for which the firm was best known.

A *cartel* was an agreement by rival firms intended to eliminate competition between them. Such treaties might fix common prices for particular products, establish production levels and assign quotas to each member, or divide up market areas between the signatories. A single syndicate, for example, came to control the policies of the independent coal producers of the Rhineland through such an agreement. And by 1900, an international shipping cartel had come close to setting freight rates on the sea lanes of the world.

Economic Integration and Growth

Another important feature of the nineteenth–century economy was *economic integration* and the contribution this made to the remarkable technological and economic growth of the West as a whole. Medieval feudalism, with its patchwork of local lords and free cities, all with their own fees, tolls, coinages, units of measurement, and commercial regulations, had greatly limited the possibilities of national economic integration. As the nation states grew, mercantilism had fostered trade barriers and bitter competition between European powers. It was only in the later eighteenth and the nineteenth centuries that these obstacles were overcome, and Western economic integration could expand at all levels.

In the decades around 1800, the French Revolution stepped up roadbuilding, abolished local tariffs and tolls, and established a national system of metric weights and measures and a national commercial code. Napoleon's victories carried these reforms to other lands and inspired still other governments to emulate this rationalization of the economic system.

Through the nineteenth century, Britain led the way to free trade. Customs unions like the Zollverein were negotiated between Italian states, states of the Austrian Empire, and other neighboring principalities. The British established the gold standard, pegging the value of the pound sterling to that of gold, a policy followed by the newly united German Empire, the United States, and other nations, so that all the major currencies became easily convertible and international trade much simpler. The export of industrial technology and know-how from developed industrial societies to less-developed European (and American) countries, the free flow of capital, particularly to finance railway building, and labor migration all made their contributions to the elaborate network of economic ties between nations and peoples across the West. Evidence of growing economic integration may also be found in the rash of conferences and agreements on matters of international concern, including railways, international river navigation, communications such as the telegraph, health and epidemic disease, and the slave trade.

The result was a network of expanding trade and spreading technological and economic development. The core was western and central European, with a strong American center emerging in the second half of the century.

◆A Changing Society◆

Western society as a whole was deeply affected by the technological and economic changes outlined above. This section will show how the Industrial Revolution carried the middle classes to a dominant position in Western society, how new classes of industrial workers struggled to capture a share of the new wealth, how old aristocracies faded and peasants survived in the new era. It will also explore other trends in nineteenth–century society, including patterns of population growth and migration, life in the new industrial city, and changes in the lives of both women and young people.

Classes in Conflict

In western Europe, the heart of the middle class was the business elite—the great industrialists, merchants, and financiers who dominated the new productive machinery. There were other members of the modern bourgeoisie—civil servants, professional people, shopkeepers—but the most admired and imitated were the English entrepreneurs, the French bankers, the German captains of industry, and the heads of international commercial houses who were seen as the architects of the century's phenomenal economic growth. Their values filtered down, and their preeminent place in society was widely acknowledged, even by their enemies.

Admirers of the bourgeoisie insisted that through ability, hard work, and respectable character, anyone could rise in the business world. "In the manufacturing districts," Lord Palmerston assured the crowd at an industrial exposition in 1865, "no man can go even for a few days . . . without hearing of great wealth acquired by men who started with little, but by their talents and genius raised themselves and their families to opulence."[2] The nineteenth was thus a century of middle–class predominance, when wealth was proud to call itself "self–made," and "rising in society" was a badge of honor.

By contrast, the traditional upper classes, the European nobility, became increasingly marginal as the nineteenth century advanced. Europe's aristocratic families still owned vast tracts of land and played a leading part in the social life of the Western nations. Some were still prominent in governments. But the real power was increasingly money power. Ancient families were thus driven to marry their children into "new–rich" families or even sending their sons into trade to preserve their stately homes a generation or two longer.

Unable to compete in wealth, fading aristocrats increasingly defined their superiority in terms of birth, education, taste, accent, and manner. They still swirled through glittering balls, galloped after the hounds, and lived in sprawling mansions waited on by old family retainers. But they were living on borrowed time.

Major changes were also taking place in the condition of the European peasantry. The French Revolution had liberated peasants from manorial exactions and had given many of them freehold control of the land they cultivated. During the early 1800s, serfdom was finally eliminated in Austria and Prussia, and in 1861 in Russia. Though the packets of land they acquired were often minuscule, many European peasants thus gained the dream of farmers down the centuries: ownership or at least free tenantry of the land they lived by.

Everywhere, peasants were drawn into modern economies by the increased demand created by the population explosion, the impact of railroads and steamships opening up distant markets, and the slow introduction of new farming methods. Other factors that helped end the ancient isolation of peasant villages included seasonal migration to the city for work, the spread of mass–produced goods to the villages, and the appearance of grow-ing numbers of middle–class peasants eager to imitate the lifestyles of the city.

The emerging industrial working classes, finally, faced unprecedentedly hard times in the nineteenth century. Everywhere in the industrializing West, men, women, and chil-dren worked twelve or more hours a day at the lowest wages the market would bear. They filled their lungs with lint or phosphorus fumes and ran a terrifying risk of industrial accidents that could cost an eye, a limb, or a life. At night they stumbled home to crowded, smelly, and unsanitary tenements for a few short hours of sleep before rising once more to another day of grinding labor. They were the first generations to submit to the iron discipline of the factory whistle and the mechanical, implacable rhythm of the machines.

Some historians have challenged this traditionally grim picture of the condition of the nineteenth–century working classes, pointing out that peasants also labored for long hours at exhausting jobs. Nevertheless, it seems clear that the working people who labored in the mines, factories, and railways of industrializing Europe were at least as exploited as any la-borers in Western history.

Population and Migration

The population explosion, which had begun in the eighteenth century, roared on through the nineteenth. The overall growth in population of Europe more than doubled, from 190 million in 1800 to 425 million in 1900. The population of industrializing Europe was thus the fastest growing in the world.

As in the preceding century, both a rise in fertility and a decline in the death rate helped cause these surging population figures. The figures are complicated, however. The increase in the birth rate was highest for only some countries early in the century, and there was even a widespread decline in family size in the last quarter of the century, due to later marriages and increasing use of birth control.

Explanations for population growth in this period commonly focus on declining death rates. Despite epidemic diseases in overcrowded industrial cities and some of the last famines in European history, death rates did clearly decline. Causes included greater avail-ability of food thanks to new agricultural methods, railroads, and lowered tariff barriers, as well as better sanitation, housing, and clothing in the latter part of the century.

Medical breakthroughs also made an increasingly important contribution. Among these medical advances were the introduction of anesthetics in 1846 by the American dentist William Morton (1819–1868) and of antiseptics in 1877 by Dr. Joseph Lister (1827–1912). Disease prevention also became more effective than ever before. Louis Pas-teur (1822–1895) discovered the basic mechanism of microbial infection in 1870, and Robert Koch (1843–1910) uncovered the tubercle bacilli that had wreaked so much havoc on European populations in the 1880s.

Another increasingly important feature of Western population history in the nine-teenth century was migration. In a massive outflow of peoples, some 40 million Europeans left the continent—never to return. Their most important destinations were the nations of North and South America, especially the United States, Canada, and Brazil.

Some European migrants were driven by religious persecution or social discrimination or fear of official oppression. Some fled military conscription or punishment following a failed revolution. Many more left for economic reasons, such as the potato famine of the

1840s, the great depression of the last quarter of the century, and the continuing lure of cheap land in the Americas.

Emigration could be very painful for the uprooted migrants. But it did ease pressure on strained resources at home. Many migrants sent money back to relatives who remained in the "old country." And as the new settlers developed their talents in their new North or South American homes, they were strengthening the sinews of the expanding Western world as a whole.

The New Industrial City

A primary focus for migration, in either Europe or the New World, was the city, especially the new industrial cities of the West. Many of the new urban complexes sprang up around factories or mines, railway hubs or seaports. The resulting influx of working people produced some of the worst slum conditions ever known as multistoried tenements clustered around tiny courtyards or were crammed in among the warehouses, railway yards, or factories where the people worked. Whole families lived in one small room. Toilets were in outhouses used by far too many families, and water might be available only from a distant public pump. Under such conditions, epidemic diseases from cholera to tuberculosis flourished.

The novelist Charles Dickens vividly described such a grimy working–class city as "a town of machinery and tall chimneys [with] a black canal in it . . . that ran purple with ill–smelling dye, and vast piles of building . . . where there was a rattling and a trembling all day long as the piston of the steam engine worked. . . ."[3]

This was the image of urban blight for generations: a world of jammed and fetid slums, unsanitary tenements, dirt, drunkenness, enforced idleness, and crime.

There was another side to life in the nineteenth–century city, however. The city also meant opportunity, entertainment, and excitement—electric trolley cars, restaurants, cafes, and a glittering array of shops. As the century advanced, furthermore, the "respectable poor" of regularly employed workers acquired better clothing, less–crowded housing, and access to the social life of the cafe or the public park.

At the top level of society, finally, the great houses of the nobility were joined by the tall, overdecorated mansions of new millionaires. Broad avenues were hacked through the medieval slums and lined with expensive shops and restaurants, past which the rising business elite as well as the old aristocracy paraded in their fashionable carriages. The boulevards offered a splendid stage on which the rulers of a bourgeois age, ladies swathed in yards of satin or taffeta, gentlemen top–hatted and frock–coated, might flaunt their sober splendor.

Women and Work in the Nineteenth Century

The lives of women were also undergoing significant change in the nineteenth century. Many changes, in women's work in particular, accompanied the emergence of full–blown industrial society. When women moved to the cities in search of work, they found it increasingly segregated by gender; employment opportunities for women were limited to the lower–paying occupations.

In industry, for example, women were heavily concentrated in textile mills. Later in the century, many women were caught up in sweatshop labor, stitching garments together or hand–fashioning goods of all sorts, from artificial flowers to cigars.

In the 1800s service work also absorbed increasing numbers of women who arrived in the cities from the country. As more and more men were drawn into industry, domestic service—work as servants in middle and upper–class homes—became increasingly a female occupation. In the latter part of the century, other service trades and professions also opened up to women, from sales jobs in shops to teaching and nursing in the growing numbers of public institutions devoted to these functions. These occupations too came to be both dominated by women and relatively low paid.

It was during this century also that Western society began to emphasize the role of women as homemakers with more vigor than ever before. The traditional tendency to associate women with the domestic sphere, men with the public one, was reinforced by the eighteenth–century discovery of the joys of family life and Rousseauian enthusiasm for motherhood. Looking at the problem from this perspective, many social reformers lamented the necessity for women to work at all. Employers found it profitable to assume that working women were only seeking to supplement the salaries earned by their husbands, the "natural" breadwinners, an assumption that justified paying women workers half or a third what men received. Thus the sweated garment industry, in which women labored

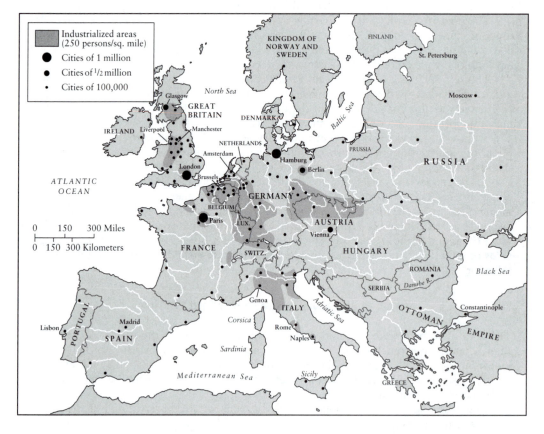

Urbanized Areas of Nineteenth-Century Europe

for a pittance in their own tenement rooms, could be presented as a method of enabling women to be gainfully employed without leaving their natural sphere, the home.

The theory that work beyond child care and housework was not natural for women flourished particularly among the middle and upper classes, whose growing affluence made it possible for them to spare bourgeois wives and daughters the rigors of work. The nineteenth century was thus the period that saw middle–class women elevated to the social "pedestal" which their descendants so vigorously rejected in the next century.

In an age of machinery and money–grubbing, the "pedestal" theory alleged that women were made of "finer clay" than men: they deserved to be admired, like statues on pedestals, but were not suited to taking a more active part in life.[4] The sensitive natures of women, it was claimed, made them natural wives and mothers, helpmates to their husbands and loving shapers of the young. Beyond the family, the female temperament was suited to religious piety, to maintaining the moral tone of society, to the patronage of the arts. Business, politics, and other work involving rationality, firmness of purpose, and related "masculine" virtues were believed to be unnatural to delicate female natures.

Some women, of course, broke free of these unrealistic constraints. There were strong women like the English nurse Florence Nightingale (1820–1910), the famous "lady with the lamp." Nightingale's lifetime of dedication to the improvement of hospital care and of the nursing profession climaxed in her mission to take charge of the English wounded during the Crimean War of the 1850s. An international consultant widely honored for her lifelong struggle against infection and primitive care in nineteenth–century medical facilities, Nightingale pioneered as a woman in the medical profession. Nevertheless, it remained extremely difficult for a woman to get into a medical school throughout the nineteenth century.

A Subculture of Youth

The lives of the young were also changed significantly by the drift of social history in the nineteenth century. Again, the main thrust was toward isolating this group more sharply from many aspects of society than ever before.

A primary cause of the changing nature of youth as a stage of life in the West was the decline of the sheltering environments of village and family. Many young people left their families and their native villages in search of work in the cities. The introduction of public education on a large scale—primary schools for everyone, secondary schools like the French *lycée* and the German *Gymnasium* for the middle classes—also helped to segregate the young from the rest of the population. So did the conscription of young men into the large standing armies that became increasingly common in the later part of the century.

The transmission of traditional values was much more difficult under such circumstances. Growing up away from the restraints exerted by parents, pastors, and other local authorities, young people were free to follow their own impulsive inclinations. The influence of adults on young people was increasingly replaced by the peer pressure of school classmates, army pals, or workmates. Under such conditions, the young were educating *themselves* rather than learning from their elders.

Such circumstances were conducive to drastic shifts in values and styles of life. The image of country youth corrupted by big-city ways entered the folklore of the Western world

Chronology 19.2: Spread of Ideologies

1790s	*French revolution spreads radical ideas across Europe*
1790	**Burke's** Reflections on the Revolution in France *formulates conservative critique of radicalism*
1791	**Gouge's** Declaration of the Rights of Women *demands equal rights for women*
1815–1819	**Burschenschaften** *(Student Unions) spread nationalism in German states*
1820–1860	**Risorgimento** *(Italian liberation movement) spreads nationalism in Italy*
1830s	*Utopian socialism begins to spread as Industrial Revolution does*
1848	**Marx's and Engels's** Communist Manifesto *formulates Marxist revolutionary socialism*
c. 1850	*Mill and de Tocqueville preach a more democratic liberalism*
1870s	*Bakunin preaches anarchism*
1890s	*Chamberlain urges superiority of Aryan "race"*

at this time. Another consequence was to render young minds and hearts particularly open to the influence of the new ideologies to be discussed below. The result was yet another new stereotype of youth: the image of the youthful barricade fighter or bomb thrower, of youth as the revolutionary stage of life.

♦ Conservatism and Liberalism ♦

Ideologies are theories about society. They are attempts to explain how human beings behave in groups, communities, nations, classes. But they are more than explanatory theories: they are programs for social action. The real point for the true ideologue is not to understand society, but to change it. To accomplish this goal, ideologues publish explanations of their theories, organize parties and movements, and sometimes take more direct action to bring about change.

Like the new industrialism, the new ideologies of the nineteenth century had their roots in the later eighteenth century. And like industrialism, these new theories had a transforming effect on Western society in the nineteenth and twentieth centuries.

This section looks at two of the most influential of the new creeds: conservatism and liberalism. Both these "isms" have changed significantly since they were first formulated, but both also retain some of the key points of view that first defined them almost two centuries ago.

The Conservative Reaction

The conservative impulse was—and is—the urge to conserve or restore traditional beliefs, practices, and institutions that are believed to be of great value and are perceived to be under attack. Modern conservatism arose in response to radical assaults on the status quo, first by the Enlightenment and the French Revolution, then by middle–class liberalism, and finally by the industrial working class and its socialist champions. In general, then, *conservatism* may be defined as "support for the status quo and opposition to fundamental changes in a social system."[5]

The widely admired conservative Edmund Burke (1729–1797) developed his dislike of radicalism by observing the French Revolution. Though he had supported the American Revolution, he was horrified at what he saw as the excesses of "the assembly of pettifoggers run mad in Paris" in 1789.[6] His *Reflections on the Revolution in France* (1790) became a powerful conservative commentary on revolution in general.

Burke and other early conservatives contrasted the seething mobs in the streets of Paris with the stability that came with divinely ordained royal rulers, established churches, and traditional aristocratic leadership. Conservative leaders like Prince Klemens von Metternich (1773–1859), the Austrian foreign minister, tried to reestablish these pillars of the old regime all across Europe.

Burkean conservatism also asserted that all great political truths were already known and that existing institutions were the result of a long historical evolution directed by God's providence. Urging the proven value of time–tested traditional ways and stressing the duty of each generation to pass on this heritage, conservatives allowed only slow and carefully considered change. Revolution, they said, would lead to moral confusion and despair, and could in the end be accomplished only by force. The utopian dreams of revolutionary ideologues were dangerous: human beings were neither smart enough nor good enough to build a brave new world.

Support for these conservative views came, understandably enough, from aristocrats, the chief beneficiaries of the old regime. But many peasants defended the old order, too. Faithful to traditional religion, they supported local priests and sometimes even rallied to country squires who remained the leading citizens of the provinces. Peasants could even idealize a far–off emperor or king, blaming oppression on evil advisors.

After 1850, however, many conservatives learned to compromise with some of the new isms in order to survive. In Britain, Tory prime minister Benjamin Disraeli (1804–1881) urged "Tory democracy" in order to woo voters away from the Liberal party. In Germany, Chancellor Otto von Bismarck (1815–1898), while suppressing socialist political organizations, co–opted their issues by giving the German Empire the most advanced system of social welfare legislation in the world.

Nineteenth-Century Liberalism

Rooted in the teachings of John Locke (1632–1704) and Adam Smith (1723–1790), early nineteenth–century *liberalism* emphasized political freedom and free enterprise as the twin roads to progress. The liberal goal was the political and economic liberation of the individual. "The worth of the state in the long run," declared John Stuart Mill (1806–1873), one of the premier liberal thinkers, "is the worth of the individuals composing it."[7] Centuries of preoccupation with maintaining order in society were thus challenged by a ringing assertion of the immense creative potential that would be unleashed by the liberation of the people.

From Locke came liberal acceptance of the natural rights to liberty, equality, and property and belief in the social contract as the only sound basis for government. Both natural rights and the contract theory, however, took specific forms in the hands of nineteenth-century liberals. To them, liberty meant freedom of speech, assembly, and the press. Equality referred to equal treatment before the law and to equal economic opportunity. The social contract, as embodied in such models as the United States Constitution or the still–evolving British parliamentary system, should provide for a government freely elected by the people to defend the people's basic rights.

On the economic side, many nineteenth–century liberals were strong believers in Adam Smith's laws of the free marketplace. Liberals were sure that demand would stimulate supply as self–interested producers sought to make a profit by selling what the public wanted. Many liberals therefore championed free trade to expand the market for the producer's goods. Many also believed that economic freedom also meant that each worker should negotiate an individual contract with his or her employer, "free" of labor union interference—or support.

"Bourgeois liberalism," as it was called, was in fact often taken up by middle–class businesspeople or politicians as a potent weapon in their struggles with aristocrats above them and laborers below. To these liberals, "government by the people" meant political participation expanded beyond the aristocracy to include the educated, property–owning middle classes—not the masses. Many of these liberals also admired the economic theories of David Ricardo (1772–1823), who showed how, as business investment expanded the economy, the population would grow, and increased demand for food would mean wholly undeserved profits for the landed aristocracy. Some liberals also thought Parson Thomas Malthus's grim population predictions had proved that population would grow faster than food supply, no matter what wages were paid, so that nothing could be done to save the working classes from misery, disease and famine.

Democracy and Welfare

Then, as the century advanced, liberal doctrines, like conservative thinking, began to change. This new liberal ideology was much closer to the democratic, social welfare liberalism of the twentieth century.

A number of factors combined to cause this leftward drift of liberalism. Some liberals were simply swept along by the momentum of their own rhetoric, talking so much about rule by the people that they became committed beyond their power to pull back. John Stuart Mill thus suggested that the interests of such groups as workers and women would never be adequately served by government until there were some women and workers in Parliament to present their case with the passion that came from personal involvement. Liberalism thus became increasingly democratic as the century advanced.

Liberals also became more and more willing to use the power of government to benefit the governed. Some liberal politicians were as willing as conservatives to offer social reforms in order to win lower–class votes. Like Bismarck in Germany, the British Liberal party laid the foundations of that country's welfare institutions in the early 1900s.

Another source of this shift was the movement known as *utilitarianism*, which valued institutions for their *utility* or usefulness as tools for improving human life. By urging liberals to use government for social betterment, utilitarians helped to make social reform part of the expanding liberal agenda. Jeremy Bentham (1748–1832), the eighteenth–century founder of utilitarianism, is best known for his formulation of the utilitarian *happiness principle*. The goal of all human institutions, he declared, should be human happiness, specifically "the greatest happiness of the greatest number" of people. Bentham's many nineteenth–century disciples, of whom John Stuart Mill is the best known, thus supported a wide variety of social reforms, from poor relief to public health.

◆Nationalism, Socialism, Feminism◆

Conservatives and liberals did not long have the political stage to themselves. Other ideologies flooded out pell-mell as the 1800s advanced. Among them were modern nationalism, several varieties of socialism, and early formulations of feminism. The following section will serve as an introduction at least to this flood of new isms.

Cultural and Political Nationalism

Nationalism, the sense of allegiance to one's nationality we often call "patriotism" (especially when we are speaking of loyalty to our own country), has become so widely accepted that it is hard to think of it as an ideology. Haven't people always and quite naturally felt a sense of loyalty to their homelands?

Western people, like other peoples, have of course often felt a sense of loyalty to their communities. They have seen themselves as "belonging" to an agricultural village or a city–state, for example, or to a clan or feudal overlord, even to a sovereign or a dynasty. But allegiance to a *nation* that was still a hazily conceived abstraction to masses who had never left their native villages did not become a powerful force until the 1800s.

Like Bentham, the influential German nationalist Johann Gottfried Herder (1744–1803) was a prophet of the preceding century. Disturbed by the widespread French influence in the three hundred independent German principalities of his time, Herder preached a purely *cultural nationalism,* concerned only with the recovery of Germany's lost national culture.

God himself, Herder believed, planted the seeds of nationality in all of us, and geographical environment and common historical experiences, customs, language, and literature brought those seeds to fruition. It was, Herder further urged, every person's duty to reject foreign influences and develop his or her national spirit and national character.

The French Revolution of 1789 turned enthusiams for national culture into *political nationalism,* a form of national feeling that insisted people who shared a common national culture should also have their own political state. The leaders of revolutionary France told the French people that the nation was now *their* country, to be ruled and defended by them. Other peoples realized what it meant to be Spanish, German, or Russian when they were occupied by Napoleon's armies. As the nineteenth century advanced, this new sense of nationality moved Germans and Italians to demand the national unification of their politically divided realms. Slavic and other peoples who had been absorbed into the Austrian, Russian, Turkish, and other empires also became fervent political nationalists, demanding independence from foreign rule.

The eloquent and tireless Italian nationalist revolutionary Giuseppe Mazzini (1805–1872) thus bitterly opposed the division of the Italian peninsula into separate countries and its domination by Habsburg Austria. A student activist in his youth, Mazzini joined and later organized secret societies dedicated to expelling the Austrians and unifying Italy by force. An admirer of the Roman Empire and an eager reader of Dante, he believed that the Italian people, fired by prophets like himself, would not only liberate itself from foreign rule, but would lead all Europe into the climactic age of human history, the Epoch of the Peoples. In this last age, each people would recognize its true national mission and begin to play its part in a free and pluralistic world.

North
Sea

NORWEGIANS

SWEDES

FINNS

FINNS

Baltic Sea

ESTONIANS

LATVIANS

LITHUANIANS

GREAT RUSSIANS

GERMANS

DANES

ENGLISH

BELORUSSIANS

DUTCH

GERMANS

POLES

UKRAINIANS

KALMUKS

FLEMINGS

WALLOONS

CZECHS

SLOVAKS

ALSATIANS

FRENCH

SWISS

MAGYARS

SLOVENES
CROATS

ROMANIANS

Black Sea

GEORGIANS

GREEKS

SERBS

BOSNIA

ITALIANS

BULGARIANS

ARMENIANS

KURDS

ALBANIANS

TURKS

GREEKS

Aegean Sea

GREEKS

GREEKS

ARABS

ARABS

Mediterranean Sea

ARABS

Red
Sea

Ethnolinguistic groups

Germanic	South Slavic	Greek
Baltic	Finno-Ugric	Turko-Tatar
East Slavic	Romance	Armenian
West Slavic	Albanian	Mongolian

0   250   500 Miles

0   250   500 Kilometers

Nationalities in Central and Eastern Europe, 1914

Chauvinism and Racism

By the last decades of the century, however, nationalism had evolved still further. National feeling had generated a range of concrete symbols and abstract concepts, many of them easily exploited by proponents of two new isms: *chauvinism* and *racism.*

Among the most widely accepted symbolic evocations of strong national loyalty were national flags, like Britain's Union Jack or the Stars and Stripes, and such national anthems as "The Star Spangled Banner" or France's stirring "Marseillaise." Other emblems of nationhood included "native soil" and the "blood" of a people—the "black earth" of Russia or the superior "blood" that was believed to flow in French, German, or Anglo–Saxon veins.

At the same time, many people came to endow national spirit with an almost mystical reality, as Germans believed in the *Volksgeist* or "folk spirit" that was the metaphysical incarnation of their Germanness. Many others believed in their own "national character" in a simpler sense, seeing themselves as more practical, and commonsensical, more cultured, or more resourceful than other peoples.

These symbols and abstractions particularly served the advocates of *chauvinism,* an aggressive political nationalism that seemed to be spreading as the century turned. For chauvinists, to be a patriot meant to see one's own nation as superior to others—and to be ready to fight to prove it. German chauvinists bellowed out their new national anthem, *"Deutschland über Alles"* (Germany over All), while the new motto of French nationalism became *"France d'abord!"* (France First!). Britons coined the term *jingoism* on the basis of a popular music hall song that greeted the possibility of war with a surge of self–confidence:

> We don't want to fight, but by *jingo* if we do,
> We've got the ships, we've got the men, we've got the money too![8]

In the next century, nationalists of all stripes would have plenty of opportunities to demonstrate their loyalty in combat.

A related phenomenon of the later nineteenth century was the spread of modern *racism.* Ideological racism asserted the primary importance of one's racial identity rather than one's nationality. Nineteenth–century racists typically divided the human species into classifications based on physical features (e.g., white, black, and yellow races), on language group (e.g., Slavic or Semitic races), or simply on nationality (e.g., "the French race," "the German race"). Reacting to later nineteenth–century enthusiasm for biological science, racists detected inherited psychological and behavioral traits in the various races.

Among the most influential devotees of racism was the English social theorist Houston Stewart Chamberlain (1855–1927). Chamberlain's integral racialism urged that all social and cultural achievements were rooted in a racial "life force." He developed a version of social Darwinism (see Chapter 22) in which the survival of the fittest race would determine the future of civilization. For Chamberlain, the fittest was the "Aryan" or German race.

Racism tended to focus on the inferiority or the menace of races other than one's own. It helped Europeans feel superior to the "lesser breeds" encountered by Western imperialists in Asia and Africa during the later nineteenth–century (see Chapter 23). At the same time, racism could produce paranoid reactions toward Jews (conceived of as a "Semitic race") in Europe and African Americans (the "black race") in the United States. For believers, racism would justify such horrors as the lynching of African–Americans in the early 1900s and the Holocaust of European Jews in the 1940s.

Utopian Socialism and Marxism

Socialism was an ideological response to the dark side of the Industrial Revolution. It was a reaction to the painful paradox that most of the new machine–made goods went to the middle and upper classes, while the men and women who labored at the machines languished in poverty. The socialist solution to "the social question," as it was called, was to demand that the machines and factories, the mines and railways should be owned by the workers themselves, rather than by entrepreneurs or capitalist investors. Only in this way, socialists averred, would a fairer distribution of the new wealth be achieved.

Utopian socialism, the earliest form of this ism, projected a powerful, quasi–religious vision of humankind united in love and labor in the socialized world of the future. Human beings were not naturally self–interested, profit–hungry, and competitive, as liberals believed. By nature, people were cooperative and concerned for the welfare of their fellows. One had only to eliminate the competitive economic institutions of capitalist society for humanity to show its true colors.

"The secret," wrote Charles Fourier (1772–1837), perhaps the most influential of the utopian socialists, "lies in Association." People of all classes should live and work together in small communes, called *phalansteries,* in which shared ownership, labor, and produce would soon wipe out all differences among them. Fourier described his ideal commune in such mouth–watering detail that some of them were actually built in Europe and America. Etienne Cabet's *Voyage to Icaria* (1842) was a fictional account of a socialist utopia so attractive that some working–class readers believed that Icaria was a real place and longed to book passage to the perfect society.

In *The Communist Manifesto* (1848), Karl Marx (1818–1883) and Friedrich Engels (1820–1895) took a much more hard–boiled view of the road to the socialist future. *Marxism* described the socialist society to come as the product of economic forces and of the conflict between social classes, a conflict which the working class would inevitably win. Marx, the primary architect of the form of socialism that bears his name, was a former German philosophy student and journalist who had come under the influence of the French utopians on his way into exile in London. With the help of Engels, son of a German industrialist who owned a factory in Britain, Marx gave his life to research and writing on the workers' struggle and how it would be won.

"Society," Marx and Engels asserted, "is more and more splitting up into two great hostile camps directly facing each other: bourgeois and proletarian."[9] Marx defined the capitalist bourgeoisie as those who owned the means of production, the proletariat as the workforce, who did not even own the tools they worked with. Since workers needed higher wages and capitalists wanted to pay the lowest possible wages in order to maximize their profits, the conflict between them was irreconcilable. It would end, not in utopian harmony, but in world revolution.

The struggle between the classes would take political form as the workers rebelled against the capitalists whose money power dominated all bourgeois–liberal governments. Once the political revolution was accomplished, however, the real economic revolution must come: the socialization of the means of production. Only when the people's state owned land and factories, banks and railroads, would a truly "classless society," the communist millennium, be possible.

The Rise of Social Democracy

The history of socialism, like that of other isms, is however a tale of many compromises with other ideologies and with changing realities. As we will see in a later chapter, the Europe socialists confronted as the nineteenth century drew to a close was a different place from the Europe of 1848, when the *Communist Manifesto* was published. In western and central Europe, at least, labor unions, liberal reform legislation, a free press and the right to vote all opened other roads to a better life for working people than the world revolution.

Under such improved circumstances, *social democratic socialism* emerged. Evolutionary rather than revolutionary, social democrats determined to work through a relatively democratic, reform–minded system for piecemeal changes in society. Accepting liberal political ideas—though not liberal free–market economics—the new socialists were committed to constitutional government. Dedicated reformers, they worked for public health insurance, unemployment compensation, public housing for the poor, and government pensions for all citizens. Public ownership of the means of production might remain a long–range goal, but for now they would be satisfied with a law limiting the working day to eight hours, or with municipal ownership of a local trolley line.

Child labor in the nineteenth century could be every bit as horrendous as it sounded in contemporaneous literature and reformist tracts. (The Illustrated London News.)

Less romantic than the utopians, less apocalyptic than revolutionary Marxists, social democratic socialists became the mainstream of the socialist movement. It was not until 1917 that a serious challenge to social democracy reemerged in the revolutionary Marxism of the Russian Communists.

To the left of virtually everything else, finally, were the linked ideologies of *anarchism* and *syndicalism*. Followers of both movements agreed with many socialists that existing institutions were the instruments by which the rich exploited the poor. Both, therefore, worked for the destruction of these institutions. Anarchists, however, convinced that "property is theft," demanded a mass uprising to overthrow the state, the church, private property, and other oppressive institutions by force. Syndicalists urged strikes, industrial sabotage, and other forms of violent action to paralyze the existing society and replace it with a social order based on a loose federations of labor unions.

The Emergence of Feminism

Feminism—the crusade for equal rights for women—emerged with most of the other ideologies around the time of the French Revolution. As we saw in an earlier chapter, the British radical Mary Wollstonecraft (1759–1797) insisted in her *Vindication of the Rights of Woman* (1792) that women's alleged weakness of character and intelligence were the result of the political, social, and intellectual limitations imposed on them by a male–dominated society. It is "from the tyranny of man, I firmly believe, [that] the greater number of female follies proceed. . . . Let women share the rights," therefore, and women would "grow more perfect when emancipated."[10] In France, Olympe de Gouges's (1748–1793) *Declaration of the Rights of Woman* (1791) sought to extend the Rights of Man to the other half of humanity. Both economic and political power, this French revolutionary leader insisted, should be available to women as well as to men. During the 1830s and 1840s, further manifestations of feminist consciousness surfaced among the more radical elements, particularly in France. The Saint–Simonian socialists preached the political, social, and moral equality of the sexes. When their commune at Ménilmontant closed down, a small group of Saint–Simonians under Prosper Enfantin set out for Egypt in search of the "Woman Messiah."

Much of the feminist thought of the nineteenth century, however, was what has been described as *relational feminism*.[11] Where later feminists would concentrate on the rights of women *as individuals* to political, economic, and social equality, relational feminism saw women's rights in the context of society as a whole, of women's established relations with men, and of their traditional central role in the family. This approach demanded parity and true partnership with men. It often emphasized the image of the "mother–educator," depicting women as shapers of new citizens for new, more democratic societies. It frequently led women to give their first allegiance to some even larger social cause, such as national independence or unity, the victory of liberal principles, or the advancement of the working class.

Examples may be found in the work of the utilitarian liberal John Stuart Mill and the Marxist socialist Friedrich Engels. In *The Subjection of Women* (1869), Mill, deeply influenced by his wife Harriet Taylor, who was also an intellectual and a reformer, condemned the injustice of society's failure to accord women all the rights and opportunities open to men in a liberal age. The widely read essay, however, was as much a liberal as a feminist document, focusing on middle–class women rather than the working majority and accepting unquestioningly such Victorian conventions as women's central commitment to the family. Engels and other socialists, meanwhile, looked at the "woman question" from their own point of view. Engels's *Origin of the Family, Private Property, and the State* (1884) considered women in bourgeois society as essentially property, their liberation as part of the struggle to overthrow capitalism. Both liberals and socialists thus subordinated the aspirations of women to other ideological concerns. Nevertheless, discussion of the woman question did prepare the way for the rise of a women's movement demanding legal, social, economic, and political equality for women in the last years of the nineteenth century. This and other waves of organized political action mentioned above will be examined in the next two chapters.

Summary

The nineteenth century saw the Industrial Revolution, which had begun in the late eighteenth century in England, spread to Europe and the Americas. Though coal remained an important power source, petroleum and hydroelectric power were also harnessed to new and ever more complex machinery. Chemicals, steel, and other new products joined railroads, steamships, and the telegraph among the wonders of modern technology.

Free enterprise produced a Europe of vigorously competing small industries in the early 1800s but gave way to huge industrial combinations—corporations and cartels—in the later nineteenth century. Industrial combinations thus sought to limit or eliminate rivals, although competition among the giants remained an important characteristic of modern "big business."

Class conflict and social change rapidly reshaped nineteenth-century society. The industrial, commercial, and financial middle class rode accelerating industrialization to wealth and increasing political influence. The working class, often brutally exploited, struggled to find their way in the new industrial society. The aristocracy lost ground to the rising bourgeoisie, while Europe's peasantry began to become integrated into national communities. The continuing population explosion encouraged large-scale migration to the cities and beyond the seas.

In response to these challenging economic and social changes, a number of new ideologies flourished in the nineteenth century. These theories purported to explain both the way society actually worked and the way it ought to work.

Nineteenth-century conservative thinkers still supported the power structure of the old regime—kings, aristocrats, and priests—and opposed rapid social change of any sort. Liberals believed in Locke's theory of natural rights and the social contract and in Adam Smith's laws of the free market, though late in the century they moved toward an increasingly democratic suffrage and more social reform. Political nationalists saw the formation of a nation-state as the ultimate goal of all nationalities, while racists focused on larger racial groups. Utopian socialists believed people should live together in communal harmony; Marxists, seeing the social classes locked in conflict based on opposing economic interests, urged revolution; and social democrats sought a better life for workers through the ballot box. Feminists demanded political rights for women but emphasized "relational" virtues, seeing women as part of the traditional family. Anarchists denounced the state as tyranny and sought to break up society into small communities.

Some Key Terms

anarchism 488
Bessemer converter 470
business cycle 473
cartel 474
chauvinistic nationalism 485
conservatism 480
corporation 473
cultural nationalism 483
economic integration 474
electrical generator 470
feminism 488
freedom of contract 473

free–trade movement 473
happiness principle 482
holding company 474
ideology 480
industrial combination 473
internal combustion engine 470
jingoism 485
liberalism 481
Marxism 486
nationalism 483
open hearth process 470
phalanstery 486

political nationalism 483
racism 485
relational feminism 488
robber barons 473
social democratic socialism 487
socialism 485
syndicalism 488
utilitarianism 482
utopian socialism 486
Volksgeist 485
Zollverein 473

Notes

1. Carlyle, quoted in W. O. Henderson, *The Industrialization of Europe, 1780–1914* (London: Thames and Hudson, 1969), 59.
2. Lord Palmerston, quoted in P. Thane, "Social History, 1860–1914," in *The Economic History of Britain Since 1700,* ed. Roderick Floud and Donald McCloskey, vol. 2 (Cambridge: Cambridge University Press, 1981), 208.
3. Charles Dickens, *Hard Times* (London: Oxford University Press, 1924), 23.
4. This theory, it should perhaps be noted, applied only to middle– and upper–class women; no one suggested that women textile workers or scullery maids were unsuited by nature to taking an active part in the world of work.
5. William R. Harbour, *The Foundations of Conservative Thought* (Notre Dame, Ind.: University of Notre Dame Press, 1986), 1–2.
6. Edmund Burke, *An Appeal from the New to the Old Whigs,* in *Maxims and Reflections of Burke,*

ed. F. W. Rafferty (London: T. Sealey Clark and Co., 1909), 94.
7. John Stuart Mill, *On Liberty* (London: George Routledge and Sons, 1910), 172.
8. G. W. Hunt, "Song," 1878.
9. Karl Marx and Friedrich Engels, *The Communist Manifesto,* in Marx and Engels, *Basic Writings on Politics and Philosophy,* ed. Lewis S. Feuer (London: Collins, 1969), 48–49.
10. Mary Wollstonecraft, *A Vindication of the Rights of Woman,* ed. Elizabeth Robins Pennell (London: Walter Scott, 1892), 280–281.
11. See Karen Offer, "Liberty, Equality, and Justice for Women: The Theory and Practice of Feminism in Nineteenth Century Europe," in *Becoming Visible: Women in European History,* ed. Renate Bridenthal, Claudia Koontz, and Susan Stuard, 2d ed. (Boston: Houghton Mifflin, 1987), 355–373.

Reading List

Beecher, J. *Charles Fourier.* Berkeley: University of California Press, 1986. Discusses both Fourier's utopian socialist ideas and his early feminist views. See also the standard summary, N. V. Riasanovsky, *The Teachings of Charles Fourier* (Berkeley: University of California Press, 1969).

Crowder, G. *Classical Anarchism: The Political Thought of Godwin, Proudhon, Bakunin, and Kropotkin.* New York: Oxford University Press, 1991. Traces origins of nineteenth–century an-

archism to eighteenth–century rationalism, scientism, and Rousseau. For a developed anarchist movement, see N. Pernicone, *Italian Anarchism, 1864–1892* (Princeton: Princeton University Press, 1993).

Goodman, D., and M. R. Redclift. *From Peasant to Proletarian: Capitalist Development and Agrarian Transitions.* New York: St. Martin's Press, 1972. Key changes in society over two centuries.

Heilbroner, R. *The Worldly Philosophers.* New York:

Touchstone, 1980. Spritely survey of primarily nineteenth–century economic thinkers. See also A. Smith's *An Inquiry into the Nature and Causes of the Wealth of Nations* (Oxford: Clarendon Press, 1978). Scholarly edition of the eighteenth–century study that shaped the economic ideas of nineteenth–century liberals and twentieth–century conservatives.

Hobsbawn, E. J. *The Age of Capital, 1848–1875.* London: Weidenfeld and Nicolson, 1975. Crucial role of investment in Western economic growth.

Hoppit, J., and E. A. Wrigley, eds. *The Industrial Revolution in Britain.* Cambridge, MA.: Blackwell, 1994. Valuable essays on the much discussed pattern of British industrialization.

Lichtheim, G. *Marxism: An Historical and Critical Study.* New York: Columbia University Press, 1982. Solid history of the evolving views of Marxist socialists. For Marxism in the founder's own words, see K. Marx and F. Engels. *Basic Writings on Politics and Philosophy.* Edited by L. S. Feuer (Boston: Peter Smith, 1975). For the spread of his ideas, a good example is S. Pierson, *Marxist Intellectuals and the Working Class Mentality in Germany, 1887–1912.* Cambridge: Harvard University Press, 1993.

Kirk, R., ed. *The Portable Conservative Reader.* Harmondsworth, England: Penguin, 1982. Useful compendium of extracts from conservative thinkers.

Lee, W. R., ed. *European Demographic Growth.* London: Croom Helm, 1979. Socio–economic aspects of the population explosion in Europe, 750–1850.

Manning, D. J. *Liberalism.* London: Dent, 1976. Brief summary of the liberal perspective. See also the writings of J. S. Mill, especially *On Liberty* (New York: Norton, 1975) and his *Autobiography,* ed. J. Stillinger (London: Oxford University Press, 1971). The intellectual development of his younger years.

Milward, A., and S. B. Saul. *The Economic Development of Continental Europe, 1780–1870.* London: Allen and Unwin, 1973. Outstanding study of the industrialization of Europe in nations other than Britain. See also their *The Development of the Economies of Continental Europe, 1850–1914* (Cambridge, Mass.: Harvard University Press, 1977).

O'Brien, P. *Peaceful Conquest: The Industrialization of Europe, 1760–1970.* Oxford: Oxford University Press, 1981. Authoritative summary and assessment of research. See also W. O. Henderson, *The Industrialization of Europe, 1870–1914* (New York: Harcourt, Brace and World, 1969) and a collection of classic essays on the subject edited by O'Brien, *The Industrial Revolution in Europe.* 2 vols. (Cambridge, MA.: Blackwell, 1994).

O'Brien, P., and C. Keyder. *Economic Growth in Britain and France, 1780–1914: Two Paths to the Twentieth Century.* London: Allen and Unwin, 1978. Contrasting growth patterns, France owing less to Britain than was once thought.

Pearson, R. *European Nationalism 1789–1920.* New York: Longman, 1994. Useful survey of the evolution of this powerful ism. For an authoritative examination of the origins of one of the earliest and most powerful of modern nationalisms, see L. C. Snyder, *Roots of German Nationalism* (Bloomington, Ind.: Indiana University Press, 1978). On Italian nationalism, see D. Mack Smith, *Mazzini* (New Haven: Yale University Press, 1994).

Pollard, S. *Britain's Prime and Britain's Decline: The British Economy, 1870–1914.* London: Edward Arnold, 1989. Exploration of the end of the British predominance.

Rendell, J. *The Origins of Modern Feminism: Women in Britain, France, and the United States, 1780–1860.* New York: Schocken, 1984. Best comparative study of the rise of feminist attitudes on both sides of the Atlantic. For a contemporary voice, see also H. Taylor, *Enfranchisement of Women* (London: Virago, 1983).

Sewell, W., Jr. *Structure and Mobility: The Men and Women of Marseilles, 1820–1870.* New York: Cambridge University Press, 1985. Women's work–related migrations in industrializing France. For material on German women, see the essays in J. Fout, ed., *German Women in the Nineteenth Century: A Social History* (London: Holmes and Meier, 1984). For documentary material on British women in the new industrial economy, see E. O. Hellerstein, L. P. Hume, and K. Offen, eds. *Victorian Women.* Stanford: Stanford University Press, 1981.

Stearns, P. N. *The Industrial Revolution in World History.* Boulder, Colo.: Westview Press, 1993. Emphasis on social impact of the great change.

Williams, T. I., ed. *A History of Technology.* 7 vols. Oxford: Clarendon Press, 1978. Carries the story of technological advance through the twentieth century. On the key source of power for the earlier Industrial Revolution, see Richard A. Hills, *Power from Steam: A History of the Stationary Steam Engine* (New York: Cambridge University Press, 1989).

— 20 —

The Springtime of the Peoples

Revolution and Reaction 1815–1848

The last chapter surveyed two of the central strands of Western history in the nineteenth century—industrialism and ideologies. Beyond these economic and intellectual developments, we move now to the political history of the 1800s. This chapter will survey the waves of revolution that filled the first half of the century, the years between 1815 and 1848, with turmoil. The next chapter will analyze the reshaping of Western society and of leading Western nations that marked the second half of the century.

We left the European political scene at the end of one of the continent's greatest revolutionary upheavals, that which exploded in Paris in 1789 and generated the bloody Napoleonic wars that ended at Waterloo in 1815. As we take up the story, the Western world teetered on the brink of three decades more of rebellion and reaction. This chapter will offer an account of the European revolutions of the 1820s, the 1830s, and of 1848, the continent's most revolutionary year. These pages will also look at the Wars of National Liberation that freed the Latin American colonies from their European rulers and explore the dramatic demands for reform that echoed through other Western lands during this turbulent half–century.

"The conduct of the Parisian population during these last days of testing," proclaimed the white–haired marquis de Lafayette at the height of France's revolution of 1830, "makes me prouder than ever to be at their head. Liberty will triumph," he declared, "or we shall perish together: long live liberty! long live the fatherland!"[1] The aging "hero of two worlds," who had fought beside George Washington in the American Revolution of 1776 and played a part in the French Revolution of 1789, was a living link between those late eighteenth–century revolts and their sequels in the first half of the nineteenth century. In 1830, he spoke as the young barricade fighters did of "the people," of patriotism and liberty, and of revolution as the key to a better tomorrow. How far he was right, how far he was unduly optimistic we will see in the following pages.

♦The Vienna Settlement♦

A chapter on nineteenth–century revolutions must begin with a section on reaction. For the century began historically with the triumph of the Congress of Vienna in 1815 and the reactionary peace it imposed upon a Europe shaken by the French Revolution and the Napoleonic wars.

At Vienna the great powers both redrew the map of Europe and strove to restore the pre–revolutionary society of the old regime. And as later waves of political revolt broke across the continent between 1815 and 1848, the powers invoked the spirit of Vienna and responded with renewed political reaction. The Vienna settlement stabilized Europe's boundaries until 1914, but it also bolstered a reactionary social order against which revolutionaries would hurl themselves for half a century.

The Congress of Vienna

The *Congress of Vienna* has a wonderfully romantic, if somewhat misleading image in European history. As the story used to be told, the Vienna peacemakers, the most glittering international assemblage of glamorous names in a hundred years, dickered and danced through the winter of 1814–1815. Hundreds of miles away, Napoleon, gambler with the fate of nations and the greatest general of his age, escaped from his Mediterranean exile in the spring of 1815 and returned to shatter the peace of Europe for a last astonishing hundred days. At Waterloo, he lost the last throw of the dice. While the beaten would–be emperor of Europe was shipped off to his final home on St. Helena, the feuding statesmen at Vienna resolved their differences. Reminded by Napoleon's return of both the recent French imperium and the threat of revolutionary French ideas, they redrew the map of Europe and turned the clock of history back to the status quo as of 1789, before the fall of the Bastille and all that followed. That is how the colorful story used to go, but, as always, the facts were a bit more complicated.

What is commonly called the *Vienna settlement* was actually hammered out in three separate agreements. Following Napoleon's defeat at the Battle of the Nations in 1813, a first Peace of Paris was signed in the spring of 1814. In June 1815, the Vienna treaty was signed. And finally, after Waterloo, a second Peace of Paris was signed in the fall of 1815, imposing harsher terms on France. The so–called Congress of Vienna, furthermore, was not exactly a congress, for no plenary session of all those in attendance was ever convened. Nevertheless, while many of the invited diplomats, courtiers, and crowned heads danced and gossiped away their days, delegations of the great powers did work long, hard hours rearranging European boundaries and redirecting the course of European history.

They were an interesting assortment of personalities. Austria's Habsburg emperor Francis I (r. 1792–1835) wisely turned over the head of the table to his foreign minister, Prince Klemens von Metternich (1773–1859). Handsome, aristocratic, a bit pompous, the Austrian minister was dedicated to two things: conservative principles and the eighteenth–century ideal of balance and stability in international affairs. Metternich played such a central role in the effort to preserve the Vienna settlement over the next thirty–five years that the period is often called the Metternich era in European diplomatic history.

Britain's Viscount Castlereagh (1769–1822), more of a pragmatist than Metternich, pressed for international consultations on specific matters and worked for the protection of British commerce. Russian Emperor Alexander I (r. 1801–1825), despite his reputation as a reactionary, here proved an odd mix of mysticism, liberalism, and determination to advance Russian power. Alexander joined Prussia's King Frederick William III (r. 1797–1840) and his chief spokesman, the celebrated reformer Karl August von Hardenberg (1750–1822), in making aggressive territorial demands for parts of Poland and the German states.

Chronology 20: Revolutions of the 1820s, 1830s, and 1848

1814–1815	*Congress of Vienna tries to restore the old regime*
1810–1825	*Latin American Wars of Liberation create republics in Middle and South America*
1820	*Revolts in southern Europe are suppressed*
1821–1832	*Revolt in Greece leads to freedom from Turks*
1825	*Decembrist revolt in Russia is crushed*
1830	*July revolution in France overthrows Bourbon dynasty; most other revolutions are suppressed*
1832	*Reform Bill of 1832 begins process of democratizing parliamentary system*
1840s	*"Hungry forties" breed discontent in Europe*
1848	*British Chartist movement suppressed*
1848	*February revolution in Paris establishes republic; June revolt leads to suppression of workers*
1848	*Revolutionaries seize power in Italian states, compel rulers to make concessions in German states*
1849	*Monarchs and armies restore order in Italian and German states; some limited constitutions are granted*
1851–1852	*Napoleon III, elected president of French republic, makes himself emperor—but promises reforms*

◆—◆

Defeated France, finally, was represented by one of the most celebrated diplomats of the age, Charles Maurice de Talleyrand (1754–1838). A shrewd, cynical man who in half a century served virtually every French government from royalist to revolutionary, Talleyrand operated with his usual brilliance at Vienna. Exploiting the resentment of the lesser states at their exclusion from decision making, dividing the victorious great powers against each other, he earned his defeated country a leading place at the peace table.

Out of the haggling and haranguing, the moral posturing and hard bargaining of this assorted group came the Vienna settlement. It was one of the most diplomatically successful, if politically repressive, peace treaties of modern times.

Redrawing the Map of Europe

The most obvious object of the negotiations was the traditional diplomatic one of depriving an aggressive great power of the capacity to impose its hegemony on the powers again. To this end, France was deprived of all its revolutionary and Napoleonic foreign conquests, shrinking it back to its boundaries of 1790. Thus weakened, France was hedged in by carefully strengthened neighboring states, including a larger and more powerful Austria, an expanded Prussia, a new Kingdom of Holland enlarged by the addition of the Austrian Netherlands (today's Belgium), a more unified Switzerland, and an enlarged Kingdom of Piedmont in northern Italy.

Beyond the containment of France, however, the victorious allies had conflicting long–term ambitions of their own. With all of Napoleonic Europe to reorganize, the peace-makers advanced these ambitions by helping themselves to substantial chunks of territory.

Russia, whose armies had followed Napoleon all the way to Paris, sought to expand its permanent influence as far as possible into Europe. In a vigorous dispute that dominated the earlier stages of the conference, Alexander I acquired much of the Polish territory that

Europe in 1815

KINGDOM OF NORWAY AND SWEDEN

RUSSIAN EMPIRE

FINLAND (to Russia, 1808)

Oslo

Stockholm

Åland I.

St. Petersburg

Moscow

Volga R.

Don R.

Dnieper R.

Dniester R.

Riga

Kiev

Odessa

Sevastopol

CRIMEA

Sea of Azov

Black Sea

OTTOMAN EMPIRE

ANATOLIA

SYRIA

Beirut

Acre

Cyprus

Alexandria

Cairo

EGYPT

Smyrna

Constantinople

Adrianople

Salonika

Sofia

Athens

GREECE (Ind. 1829)

Crete

BULGARIA

WALLACHIA (Aut. 1829)

SERBIA (Aut. 1829)

BOSNIA

MONTENEGRO

Belgrade (Aut. 1829)

TRANSYLVANIA

MOLDAVIA

BESSARABIA (to Russia, (1812)

MORAVIA (Aut. 1829)

Baltic Sea

DENMARK

Copenhagen

SCHLESWIG

HOLSTEIN

Hamburg

Danzig

EAST PRUSSIA

POLAND

Warsaw

Cracow

Vistula R.

Pressburg

Budapest

Vienna

AUSTRIAN EMPIRE

HUNGARY

CROATIA

DALMATIA

Laibach

Buda

Pest

TYROL

Trieste

Venice

Verona

Milan

LOMBARDY

PIEDMONT

Genoa

PARMA

LUCCA

MODENA

TUSCANY

PAPAL STATES

Rome

KINGDOM OF THE TWO SICILIES

Palermo

Sicily

Sardinia

Corsica

Malta (Br. 1800)

Mediterranean Sea

North Sea

ATLANTIC OCEAN

KINGDOM OF NORWAY AND SWEDEN

UNITED KINGDOM OF GREAT BRITAIN AND IRELAND

SCOTLAND

Edinburgh

IRELAND

Dublin

WALES

ENGLAND

London

THE NETHERLANDS

BELGIUM (Ind. 1831)

LUXEMBURG

Cologne

Elbe R.

Rhine R.

HANOVER

Berlin

PRUSSIA

SAXONY

THURINGIAN STATES

Prague

Troppau

Danube R.

Munich

BAVARIA

WÜRTTEMBERG

BADEN

Strasbourg

SWITZERLAND

Berne

FRANCE

Paris

Rouen

Seine R.

Tours

Loire R.

Bordeaux

Garonne R.

Toulouse

Lyon

Rhône R.

Marseille

Barcelona

Balearic Is. (Sp.)

SPAIN

Madrid

Burgos

Valencia

Ebro R.

Seville

Cadiz

Gibraltar (Br.)

Tagus R.

PORTUGAL

Lisbon

had been partitioned in the later 1700s and converted to a Napoleonic puppet state in the early 1800s. This new *Congress Poland* became a separate nation with a liberal–sounding constitution, but with the Russian emperor as its ruler. In compensation for its lost share of Poland, Prussia got two–fifths of Saxony as well as much of the Rhineland. These concessions satisfied Frederick William III's hopes for a revival of Prussian power in north Germany after the mauling Prussia had suffered from Napoleon.

Habsburg Austria, finally, gained nominal control over Germany as a whole and real power over Italy. The former Holy Roman Empire, abolished by Napoleon, was replaced by an equally feeble Germanic Confederation of thirty–nine states headed by Austria. The north Italian principalities of Lombardy and Venetia were annexed to Austria, and the rest of the Italian states were bound to the Habsburg monarchy by a web of dynastic ties and treaties. This restoration of Austrian power after its sharp curtailment by Napoleon was vigorously supported by the British. Alarmed by the strength the Russian Empire had demonstrated against Napoleon, Britain's leaders saw Austria as a potential buffer against both Russian and French power.

Britain itself, whose interests lay beyond the European continent in colonies and commerce overseas, made no territorial demands, and defeated France could expect nothing from the negotiations. Nevertheless, the restructuring of Europe by the Congress of Vienna was as radical as that imposed by Napoleon, and the most drastic before the First World War transformed the map of Europe a hundred years later.

Restoring the Old Order

The conservative impulse, however, was as strong among the powers at the Vienna Congress as the diplomatic imperative to restrain aggression and advance national interests. The desire to restore legitimate monarchs and with them the old aristocracy and the established churches thus also shaped the Vienna settlement. In addition, some conservative leaders worked for a permanent alliance to maintain the reestablished status quo. The result was the Europe–wide *Restoration* of the first half of the nineteenth century.

Austria's Metternich was a leading proponent of these policies at Vienna and for three decades thereafter. Metternich's stance was partly a matter of conservative principle, partly a consequence of the unique vulnerability of the Habsburg realms to revolutionary ideologies. Composed of a number of national groups—Germans, Hungarians, Czechs, Poles, Italians, and others—the Habsburg Empire could easily disintegrate if nationalism spread among its peoples. A ramshackle structure held together mostly by an autocratic monarchy, the empire was also particularly vulnerable to the spread of liberalism, which might undermine the autocracy that provided its only cement. These two isms, which were joined by socialism as industrial development spread slowly into central Europe, made the Habsburg monarchy a natural champion of the restoration of the old regime in nineteenth–century Europe.

The European Restoration was a sweeping one. After 1815, "legitimate" rulers—pre–Napoleonic and prerevolutionary—were returned to their thrones. Preeminent among these was Louis XVIII, brother of the martyred Bourbon king Louis XVI of France.[2] Emigré noblemen, expelled from France and the lands it controlled by the Revolution and Napoleon, also hurried home to purge those who had replaced them and to take up their traditional leading roles in society. In some places at least, state churches were able to reestablish the ancient alliance between throne and altar. Everywhere, a noble title became once more the best guarantee of political advancement, while priests and clergymen rode a postwar wave of religious revival to renewed popularity with the European masses. Liberalism seemed in full retreat, nationalism frustrated, and discontent of the working classes suppressed.

The Concert of Europe

To support this attempt at an across–the–board restoration of the old order in Europe, the conservative masters of the continent depended on two overlapping coalitions after 1815. Emperor Alexander I organized the so–called *Holy Alliance,* an agreement by legitimate Christian monarchs to defend the Restoration against any revival of the revolutionary spirit in Europe. Britain's Castlereagh, meanwhile, depended on the *Quadruple Alliance* of 1815, by which the four victorious great powers guaranteed to maintain the terms of the Vienna settlement by force if necessary. This pact was soon expanded to include France itself under the restored Bourbons. The rather vague Holy Alliance, however, never won widespread support, and soon both Alexander and Castlereagh were working primarily through the expanded Quadruple Alliance to achieve their ends.

The ends themselves were controversial from the beginning. The pragmatic British saw the alliance primarily as a vehicle for periodic consultations among the great powers over conflicts of interest among them. Governing through a more open parliamentary system than the autocracies of central and eastern Europe, the British were much less enthusiastic than continental Europeans about using the coalition as a tool for the suppression of radicalism everywhere in Europe. Metternich and Alexander, by contrast, believed that the powers should be ready to intervene directly in the internal affairs of other nations to extinguish the flames of ideological rebellion before they spread. If this had only been done in 1789, they argued, Europe might have been spared all the blood shed in the wars of the four coalitions against France.

The two views, however, did coincide on one point: it was the responsibility of the great powers to preserve the peace and guide the affairs of Europe. In this conviction, diplomats after 1815 went considerably beyond the eighteenth century's dependence on the balance of power to preserve peace and the independence of nations. The acceptance of regular consultations and great–power responsibility for international concord evolved into the nineteenth–century doctrine of the *Concert of Europe,* each nation pursuing its own ends yet all contributing to a common harmony. Discords were in fact common, as we shall see. Nevertheless, the Concert of Europe was a step beyond balance–of–power politics as a means of countering the international anarchy that had prevailed since the emergence of the nation–states.

Successes and Failures of 1815

The Vienna settlement was one of the most important peace settlements in European history. It is often ranked with the Peace of Westphalia (1648) that ended the carnage of the Thirty Years' War, the Treaty of Utrecht (1713) that ended Louis XIV's decades–long reach for European ascendancy, and the Peace of Paris (1919) after the First World War. The agreements achieved in 1814 and 1815 had one thing in particular to recommend them: in many ways, they worked. The terms imposed on France were not severe, and France was soon readmitted to the councils of the great powers. For half a century, the

Vienna settlement kept the major nations from each others' throats. For almost a hundred years, from 1815 to 1914, there was no great war in Europe like those associated with Louis XIV or Napoleon.

As an attempt to control the revolutionary spirit, however, the Vienna peace was much less successful. The radical ideas of the Enlightenment and the French Revolution could not be smothered so easily after decades of turmoil. And the continuing social changes brought about by the spread of the Industrial Revolution and the development of the nine-teenth–century ideologies repeatedly challenged efforts to restore the eighteenth–century world order. It is this revolutionary impulse in nineteenth–century Europe that will con-cern us for most of the remainder of this chapter.

◆ 1820: The Fringe Revolutions ◆

Though the Congress of Vienna may be judged a success in terms of limiting international warfare, it was much less successful at reestablishing a tranquil and traditional society. The first of three great waves of revolutionary tumult began in Europe in 1820, only five years after the Vienna peace itself. Other revolutions, which had already broken out in Europe's Latin American colonies, also reached their conclusion during the 1820s. We will begin this brief survey in the European core, then move out to the imperial periphery to look at the triumphant revolutions in the Spanish American colonies.

Rumblings of Discontent

The Restoration outlined above may sound more formidable than it was. Granted, the old order was reestablished by the eighteenth–century interlocking directorate of kings, priests, and nobles and guaranteed by a nineteenth–century alliance of all the great powers. But the hold of the resurrected conservative establishment was much weaker than it seemed.

Rumblings of discontent with the Restoration began almost at once. Liberals every-where in Europe denounced the Vienna settlement and all its works. They condemned the Holy Alliance as a vehicle for the reestablishment of royal tyranny and cast the Russian czar or Prince Metternich as the presiding evil genius of reaction. Metternich and other conser-vatives were right to fear that "the spirit of revolution" was not dead. Indeed, during the immediate postwar years, a number of indignant radicals and other discontented groups took to the streets once more.

In Britain, the economy was already strained by the boycott imposed by Napoleon's Continental System and by the unemployment created as the Industrial Revolution re-placed hand labor with machinery. When many thousands of demobilized soldiers poured back into the job market after Waterloo, further unemployment contributed to political re-sentment. Workers smashed machines, demonstrated in the streets, and cheered the speeches of radical orators. In 1819, at St. Peter's Fields outside Manchester, troops fired on such a crowd, killing eleven. Liberals at once filled their newspapers with denunciations of the "Peterloo Massacre," a conservative crime to set beside the conservative Welling-ton's victory at Waterloo four years earlier.

In German–speaking central Europe, patriotic young veterans of the German Wars of Liberation against Napoleon felt cheated by the new order established in Germany by the Congress of Vienna: a feeble Germanic Confederation of thirty–nine virtually independent

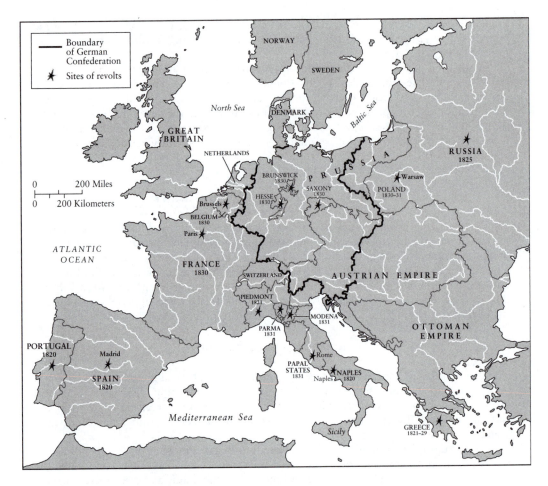

European Revolutions of 1820s and 1830s

states chaired by Austria. This, they angrily told each other, wasn't the glorious German fatherland they had fought for. Enrolling in the universities with which Germany was so liberally endowed, they organized militant *Burschenschaften* (Student Unions) at many universities and soon linked them up into a single national Student Union all across north Germany. Demanding a united German nation purged of princes and governed by a liberal constitution, the liberal–nationalistic youth horrified the older generation. When one of their number murdered a conservative German writer rumored to be a czarist secret agent, the Germanic Confederation unanimously passed the repressive Carlsbad Decrees of 1819, suppressing the *Burschenschaften* and bringing universities under much closer government control. But nationalism in the Germanies did not die with the Student Unions.

Thus compromised and opposed from the outset, the conservative Restoration faced an even more jolting series of challenges in the next decade. The most direct early defiance of the Vienna peace settlement came on the fringes of the Western world. Revolutions blazed up along the southern and eastern margins of Europe, from the Iberian and Italian peninsulas around through Greece and up into Russia, while far to the west, the revolt of the Latin American colonies also reached its climax in the 1820s. All these rebellions occurred in small or backward states far from the centers of Western civilization in London and Paris, Vienna and Berlin.

Rebellions in Southern Europe

Revolutions broke out in all three of the sleepy southern European peninsulas jutting down into the Mediterranean in the early 1820s. There were revolts in Spain and Portugal in 1820; in two of the Italian states, Naples and Piedmont, in 1820 and 1821; and in the Greek provinces of the Ottoman Turkish Empire in 1821. And in several of these cases, the leaders of the conservative coalition did feel impelled to take direct action.

The targets of the majority of the Iberian and Italian revolts were reactionary kings put into power by the victors at Vienna. Important causes of unrest included efforts to reestablish the power of aristocrats and priests, a retreat from hoped–for reform measures, and the persecution of liberals in these nations. The rebellions were often led by half–pay army officers, some of them disturbed by the possibility that they might be dispatched to Latin America to suppress the colonial revolts. Middle–class businessmen also supported the revolutions, demanding liberal political institutions. Thus motivated by a variety of discontents, rebels from Spain to southern Italy won startling initial victories against the feeble local power structures.

Most continental conservative leaders, including Metternich and Alexander I, were horrified at this revolutionary "contagion" spreading across the southern littoral of Europe. They therefore mobilized the congress system of big–power consultations to discuss action. And though the British strongly dissented, intervention was finally agreed upon in most of these cases. In 1821, Austrian troops crossed the Alps to overthrow the revolutionary regimes in Naples and Piedmont. In 1823, a French expedition crossed the Pyrenees to crush the revolution in Spain and restore the brutally reactionary government of Ferdinand VII. The flames of rebellion thus flickered out across most of the south.

The interventions, however, also led to the fissuring of the conservative alliance and the early end of regular conferences to control international affairs. In the series of congresses called to deal with the crises of the early 1820s, the British repeatedly and publicly dissented. Castlereagh and after him foreign minister George Canning (1770–1827) denied the right of any nation to intervene in the internal affairs of a sovereign state, even to suppress a revolution. After 1822, Britain sent no more representatives to such conferences. Canning thus became the chief architect of what was to become Britain's nineteenth–century policy of "splendid isolation" from long–term European alliances.

The collapse of the series of post–Vienna congresses did not destroy the Concert of Europe. The rulers of the great powers, including Britain from time to time, continued to feel an obligation—and a right—to guide the affairs of Europe as a whole. To this end, they consulted each other frequently through regular diplomatic channels and met in major international conferences when crises arose throughout the nineteenth century. But the united conservative front against ideological revolution effectively ended in the 1820s. This was particularly clear in the tangled and long drawn–out negotiations surrounding the Greek revolution that broke out in 1821 and did not end—in a qualified victory for the rebels—until 1832.

Greece was an exotic special case in the 1820s. Overrun by the advancing Ottoman Turks at the end of the Middle Ages, the Greeks had been cut off from most of Europe for centuries. Within the Turkish Empire, however, they had enjoyed freedom to practice their Orthodox Christian religion, had dominated eastern Mediterranean trade, and had even held a privileged position in the Ottoman administrative system. But in the early 1800s, nationalism had spread even this far into eastern Europe. A secret society called the Friends of Greece had been formed to work for independence from the Ottoman Empire, and a leader had emerged in Prince Alexander Ypsilanti (1792–1828). In 1821, rebellions erupted at the Greek end of the Balkan peninsula.

The resulting struggle was much complicated by the rivalries and ambitions of the European powers in this area. In various ways, Russia, Britain, and France all hoped to benefit from the slow crumbling of the Ottoman Empire, which had been declining throughout the eighteenth century. Both big–power involvement and the crumbling of Turkish power continued through the nineteenth century. Europeans in many countries, meanwhile, admired Greece as the seedbed of Western civilization. Some could even see the Greek revolution as a Christian crusade against Muslim oppression. In the course of the revolution, there were atrocities on both sides, but the Turkish massacre of tens of thousands of Greeks on the island of Chios had the greatest impact on European opinion. The martyrdom of the romantic poet Lord Byron, who died of exposure in Greece while helping to organize the rebels, further inspired European liberals to rally to the cause.

In the later 1820s, then, Britain, France, and Russia intervened on the side of the Greek rebels. An Ottoman fleet was destroyed in 1828, and Turkey was forced to grant Greece its independence. The appointment of a Bavarian prince as king of the new nation in 1832 was a concession to the conservative belief in monarchical government. But nationalism, one of the most dangerous of the new isms, had clearly won a victory over one of the oldest established monarchies in western Eurasia.

The Russian Revolution of 1825

Liberalism suffered a signal defeat in another part of eastern Europe in the 1820s. The Russian Empire, victorious over Napoleon and a leading force in the councils of nations, remained the most backward of the powers in 1815. An unexpected byproduct of the postwar Russian occupation of parts of France, furthermore, was the exposure of educated, aristocratic young army officers to radical French ideas and to the jarring fact that, even in defeat, the average French peasant was much better off than the typical Russian serf. On their return home, some of these young men organized secret societies and began to dream wild dreams of a Russia economically and politically as advanced as the nations they had marched through to the west. One of the most colorful of these subversive young men, an officer named Pavel Pestel (1793–1826), projected a vision of Jacobin dictatorship over Russia, including in his plans government confiscation of all productive land and other measures similar to those actually taken by Russian revolutionaries a century later.

The death of Czar Alexander I in December 1825 gave these men—known thereafter as the *Decembrists*—a chance to do something more than dream about this radical future. Alexander left no children to succeed him, and there was confusion over which of his two surviving brothers was his intended heir. In this rare moment of weakness in czarist autocracy, the Decembrist officers decided to act. Picking the more distant brother Constantine—then in Poland—to support, the revolutionary officers marched their troops into the square in front of the palace at St. Petersburg chanting their demand for "Constantine and a Constitution." The actual heir, Nicholas, responded by rallying loyal troops and mowing down many of those drawn up before the palace. Other rebellious army units, mobilized by Pestel and the southern branch of the Decembrist underground in the Ukraine, were similarly dealt with, though it took a little longer to run them down. Hundreds of rebels were imprisoned or bundled off to exile in Siberia. Five of the leaders, including Pavel Pestel, were hanged.

The Decembrist revolt was a futile gesture. Its most immediate consequence was to convince the new emperor, Nicholas I (r. 1825–1855), of the necessity for autocratic government in Russia. The attempt also revealed the gulf between a westernized, politically aware elite and the masses of Russians, who did not rise in support of the young officers. The insurrection of December 1825 did, however, provide a beginning—and a first crop of martyrs—on the long revolutionary road that led to 1917.

The Latin American Wars of Liberation

As we have seen, earlier revolts in Latin America, such as that of the Peruvian Indian Tupac Amarú in 1780 and the Haitian slave Toussaint L'Ouverture in 1791, had occurred at the time of the North American and French revolutions. The full flood of the Latin American Wars of Liberation, however, came during the early nineteenth century, roughly paralleling

Simón Bolivar, the Venezuelan liberator of half of South America, was a dedicated idealist. A man of action, Bolivar was the most widely admired symbol of the Latin American Wars of Liberation. (New York Public Library Picture Collection.)

the European revolutions of the 1820s. From Father Hidalgo's call to arms in Mexico in 1810 to the final victory of Simón Bolívar's forces at Ayacucho in 1824, it was a violent decade and a half, rich in colorful heroes and heroic deeds. And while distinctively American problems, classes, and institutions played a central part, so, too, did the common core of Western ideas that had first taken shape in the Old World.

It began with yet another revolt of the wretched of the earth, the New World equivalents of Pugachev's hordes or the sans-culottes of Paris. When the Mexican reforming priest Father Miguel Hidalgo (1753–1811) rang the church bell at Dolores on September 16, 1810, he summoned the poverty-stricken Indians and mestizos of his parish to rebellion against the Spanish rulers, who were resented by creoles, mestizos, and Indians alike. The revolt, launched in the wake of an unsuccessful creole conspiracy in which Hidalgo had been involved, swept across central Mexico to the suburbs of the capital itself in 1810, only to be crushed the following year, its leader executed. But Father Hidalgo's *grito de Dolores,* his ringing cry *[grito]* for "Independence and Liberty," had inflamed poverty-stricken Mexican Indians and mestizos.[3] The mantle of leadership was taken up almost at once by an even more revolutionary priest, Father José María Morelos (1765–1815). A mestizo himself, Morelos defined the revolutionary struggle as one for the rights of the masses and the overthrow of aristocracy and wealth. After four years of revolt, however, Morelos, too, was taken and executed, the popular uprising finally suppressed.

When victory for the revolution did come in Mexico, half a dozen years later, it was won, less by radical mestizos or Indians than by creoles and Spaniards. The liberal revolt in Spain itself in 1820 left the colonial elites fearful of liberal reforms that might be imposed on them by the new government in Madrid. To avoid such a revolution from above, a Mexican cabal headed by the creole army officer Agustín de Iturbide (1783–1824) seized power in the colony. Iturbide, however, was overthrown in his turn by a republican faction in 1824. Mexico thus emerged as a republic at last by a route as tangled as that of the French Revolution. Nor did the new creole-dominated government of Mexico show any more serious concern for the welfare of the mestizo and Indian people than the French Directory had shown for sans-culottes and peasants.

The revolts in South America, like that in Mexico, were initially triggered by patriotic colonial reaction against Napoleon's imposition of a French king—his brother Joseph—on both Spain and its colonies in 1808. From the resulting confusion of local juntas in various parts of South America, the Venezuelan revolutionary Simón Bolívar (1783–1830) emerged preeminent. Widely traveled in Europe and much influenced by the ideas of Locke and the philosophes, Bolívar opposed slavery and social oppression as well as the political domination of the colonies by Madrid. With the help of Venezuela's hard-riding *llaneros* (cowboys), supplies from liberated Haiti, a volunteer British Legion, and his own sweeping strategic vision, Bolívar, "the liberator" freed a wide swath of northern South America, from Venezuela to Ecuador, from Spanish rule.

Upheavals in Argentina, meanwhile, opened the way for the rise of the talented soldier José de San Martín (1778–1850). Seeking to strike at the center of Spanish power in Peru, San Martín organized and led an epic march across the Andes to liberate Chile, then swung north toward Lima. In Peru, he and Bolívar linked up, preparing for a final assault on Spanish power in South America. When the two leaders found that their personalities and goals clashed irreparably, however, it was San Martín who gave way, leaving the field to the more charismatic Venezuelan. It was thus Bolívar's forces who defeated the Spanish decisively at Ayacucho, Peru, in 1824.

Out of this revolutionary ferment, there emerged half a hemisphere of new nations. Brazil was a monarchy still, though independent from Portugal, and small European colonies survived on the islands and coasts of the Caribbean. Some of the new polities, like the Confederation of Central America and Bolívar's Gran Colombia in northern South America, proved unstable and subsequently fragmented into smaller nations. Nevertheless, by 1825 most of Latin America, from Mexico in the north to Argentina and Chile in the south, consisted of republics, replete with liberal constitutions, free economies, and guarantees of the rights of the governed. Though the democratic niceties were often violated by power–hungry Latin American warlords called *caudillos,* the new republics, like the United States to the north, represented clear victories for the revolutionary spirit.

There was some talk of European intervention to restore the authority of Madrid and Lisbon beyond the seas. In 1823, President James Monroe (president, 1817–1825) of the United States responded to this possibility by issuing what became known as the Monroe Doctrine, prohibiting European intervention in the Americas. The European great powers, however, were more significantly deterred by the British stand on the issue. Britain, determined to maintain its burgeoning commercial ties with the new Latin American countries, firmly opposed any attempt to return these lands to their former European rulers, whose mercantilistic policies had excluded British trade in earlier centuries. And since the British navy was the world's largest, no intervention was possible in the face of British opposition.

These setbacks for conservative principles, however, came a hemisphere away from Europe. They caused little loss of sleep in the courts of St. Petersburg or Paris, and few crisis meetings in Metternich's offices in Vienna.

◆ 1830: Revolution Returns to the Center ◆

In the 1820s, the conservative Metternich system had been forced to accept the triumph of revolution in Latin America and Greece. But the conservative powers had vigorously suppressed revolutions in Spain, Italy, and Russia.

In the 1830s, however, a new wave of political violence swept over Europe. These upheavals came much closer to the centers of European civilization than Russia or the New World. They included a revolution in Paris, a tumultuous reform campaign in Britain, and revolts in Belgium, Poland, and several German and Italian principalities. By and large, the conservative system contained these revolutionary outbreaks also. But it did so only at the cost of concessions to the liberal bourgeoisie—perhaps the least threatening opponents of the conservative order, but opponents nevertheless.

Unsolved Problems of the Restoration

The underlying causes of the revolutions of the 1830s were apparently of two sorts: worsening socio–economic conditions and political tensions. Both worked against the perpetuation of the Restoration order.

In 1830, the Industrial Revolution had only begun to exert its transforming influence on Europe. More powerful factors in the early nineteenth century were accelerating population growth and the continuing expansion of the commercial economy. An expanding population put pressure on all sectors of the economy, creating new mouths to feed and a need for new jobs that were simply not available in the traditional economy. Seeking to meet these growing demands, commercial agriculture and business expansion pushed deeper into Europe's traditional society of village and artisan workshops, challenging and disrupting old ways. At the end of the 1820s in particular, bad harvests raised the cost of food in some parts of Europe. Unemployed men and women paying higher prices for food could not afford to buy much of anything else. The result was a further decline in handicraft and factory production, business failures, and more people out of work in these sectors. Jobless and underfed men and women made inflammable tinder for the revolutionaries.

Politically, meanwhile, the apparently solid conservative front of 1815 had visibly deteriorated by 1830. And in some countries, inefficient administrations combined with favoritism to the aristocracy and established churches to drive even the least incendiary middle–class citizens to the brink of militant action. "It is notorious," said a Belgian politician in February of 1830, "that Europe is in the grip of a new crisis. It is more difficult to grasp . . . its nature than to know the theater in which it will be played. Each of us feels in himself that this theater must be France."[4]

The July Days in Paris

France, the centerpiece of the entire conservative Restoration, was governed between 1815 and 1830 by the most important of restored monarchs, the elderly Bourbons Louis XVIII (r. 1814–1824) and Charles X (r. 1824–1830). And Paris, swollen with provincial immigrants and just beginning to feel the dislocation that accompanies industrialization, was the metropolis of France. Here the most important European revolutionary drama since 1789 reached its climax in the violent *July Days* of 1830.

Both the Bourbon brothers who reigned in turn during the fifteen years after Waterloo were strong conservatives, but Louis XVIII was the more prudent. Trundled ingloriously into his capital "in the baggage train of the allies" in 1814, he brought with him a Charter of French Liberties intended to buy him at least some support from his people. Among the rights granted by the Charter were a number that his subjects had enjoyed at least intermittently since the Revolution. These included a legislature elected by a small number of property–qualified voters and royal ministers who were to be held "responsible"—but whether to the elected legislature or to the hereditary monarch was not clearly specified. For the next decade and a half, political parties jousted in the legislature and in the vigorously partisan Paris press. The ultraroyalists—more royalist than the king—sought to repeal the Charter and further restore the prestige of nobles and priests. French liberals—most prominent among them politicians, journalists, bankers, and industrialists—demanded political rights for the bourgeoisie and ministerial responsibility to the elected legislature. On the sidelines, growing numbers of nonvoting workers and students agitated. The workers wanted help with their economic grievances; the students demonstrated for a radical political dream—a return to the French Republic of the 1790s.

In July 1830, Charles X, more autocratic and less cautious than his predecessor, precipitated a crisis. Appointing a reactionary chief minister who could not command a majority in the legislature, closing down opposition journals, and circumscribing still further the right to vote, Charles seemed to be moving toward final abrogation of the Charter. In response, liberal politicians and journalists defied him openly. Workers, often led by students, barricaded the streets and unfurled the Tricolor, the long–banned flag of the Republic. In three hot and bloody days in late July, this impromptu alliance drove the royal troops from the capital and expelled the last Bourbon from his throne.

The Paris barricades of the Revolution of 1830 are vividly evoked in this dramatic yet real-istic nineteenth-century painting. Note the ramshackle barricade and the heaps of *pavés*, or paving stones, which were used both as the foundations of the barricade and to hurl at attacking soldiers. (Culver Pictures, Inc.)

But that was as far as it went. Alarmed at the specter of a Jacobin republic and radical democracy, middle–class political and economic leaders hastily offered the crown to Louis Philippe of the house of Orléans. A royal kinsman shrewd enough to assure the bourgeois politicians that he would uphold the Charter, Louis Philippe was a clever choice. Pointing with pride to his own youthful liberalism in the days of the Revolution of 1789, he ap-peared publicly with the ancient marquis de Lafayette, wrapped himself in the Tricolor, and within days emerged as king of the French.

Over the next few years, youthful republicans organized secret societies, while workers manned hopeless barricades and read their first socialist pamphlets in a series of futile insur-rections against this hijacking of the revolution of 1830. Many French people, however, ac-cepted their "bourgeois king" and his claim to embody the best of the tradition of 1789. The more ambitious among them enthusiastically took up the injunction of François Guizot (1767–1874), Louis Philippe's most successful chief minister, to "enrich your-selves!" It was a maxim that came opportunely as the Industrial Revolution spread across France.

The revolution of 1830 in France had overthrown a dynasty and offered a larger share of power to the bourgeoisie. But it brought no revolutionary transformation to the coun-try at large.

Britain's Reform Bill of 1832

In London, also, political conflict boiled over in the early 1830s. The struggle over the *Reform Bill of 1832* was not as violent as the July Days, but it was almost as disturbing to conservative Britons.

Dominated by the Tory (Conservative) party ever since Waterloo, Britain nevertheless saw some important reforms in the 1820s and 1830s. So–called Liberal Tories, utilitarians, and other reformers lowered some tariffs, granted Catholics the right to participate in politics for the first time since the Reformation, and improved local government. More controversial was the creation of the first British police force by Liberal Tory Robert Peel—called "bobbies" in his honor and initially seen as tools of social repression. As bitterly contested were the new workhouses for the indigent, supported by the utilitarians but very often quite as horrible as Charles Dickens depicted them in his novels. The resurgent reform impulse, however, reached its first climax in the yearlong struggle over the parliamentary reform act that was finally passed in 1832.

Parliamentary reform, urged for half a century, was long overdue. A hundred and fifty years after the Glorious Revolution of 1688 had created Britain's constitutional monarchy, the right to vote or sit in the House of Commons was still largely limited to a small minority of country squires and property–holding citizens of the older towns. So–called rotten boroughs, once important towns now shrunk to insignificance, still sent members to Parliament, while huge new industrial cities like Manchester and Birmingham had no representation. The members of Britain's opposition Whig party, like the conservative Tories, were for the most part landowning aristocrats and country gentry. Nevertheless, the Whigs prided themselves on being the true heirs of the Glorious Revolution of 1688, and in 1831 their leaders in the House of Commons, the prime minister Lord Grey (1764–1845) and the eloquent liberal Lord John Russell (1792–1878), introduced a bill to reform the lower house.

The struggle that followed lasted for a year and a half and filled the streets of London and other British cities with marching supporters of this move toward a broader distribution of political power. Operating with their first majority since 1783, the Whigs passed the bill in the House of Commons. Then at Whig insistence, King William IV (r. 1830–1837) forced the reform through the House of Lords by threatening to create enough new Whig peers to carry the bill if the Tory Lords did not accept it. Mobs paraded through the streets of London and actually seized control of the city of Bristol for a short time. With visions of the recent revolution in France flickering through their heads, the Tories capitulated, and the Reform Bill of 1832 became law.

Like the July revolution in France, the Reform Bill did more for the liberal middle ranks of society than for the democratically inclined lower orders. Scores of rotten boroughs lost their seats in Parliament, while some of the new industrial cities at last won representation. Property remained a requirement for political participation, but the number of eligible voters grew from 430,000 to 800,000 (out of a potential voting population five times that). Middle–class citizens did begin to get a share of political clout in the commonwealth. Working–class Britons, however, found their new appetite for a voice in government whetted. They turned toward universal manhood suffrage, a radical measure by nineteenth–century standards, and one that still lay far in the future. As in France, then, only modest changes were achieved in the 1830s, but the seeds of a more radical trial of strength in the next decade were sown.

Other Revolutions of 1830

Echoes of France's revolution of 1830 were heard all across the continent as upheavals in a half–dozen countries made that a year of revolutions. But revolutionary outbreaks in Belgium and several north German states shared a fate similar to that of the French: apparent victories for liberals cloaking very limited real change.

The rapidly industrializing Belgian provinces in the new Kingdom of Holland—created in 1815 to help contain any future French expansion—differed in language and culture from their Dutch overlords. Liberal opposition and worker unrest due to an economic downturn combined with a student revolt inspired by the July revolution in France to overthrow Dutch rule in the south. The new Belgian nation took shape as a constitutional monarchy, but one in which fewer than fifty thousand very well off citizens could vote. In several north German states, revolts in 1830 and 1831 also produced somewhat more liberal government under continuing princely rule.

In Poland and the Italian states, as yet scarcely touched by industrialization and its problems, opposition came from liberals and nationalists. Liberal opposition to authoritarian government and nationalist resentment of Russian rule spread among Polish student clubs, military secret societies, and some of the landed nobility. The Polish revolution of 1830, however, lacked the support of the peasant masses and was brutally suppressed in 1831. Revolts in three of the Italian principalities, including the Papal States, suffered a similar fate. Inspired by the July Days in Paris, Italian rebels toppled a couple of local princes and seized control of the pope's own domains. But Austrian arms crushed the Italian rebellions for the second time in a decade.

The Vienna system had held once more. The "international revolutionary conspiracy" Metternich was forever warning of was again substantially frustrated in 1830.

♦ The Advance of the Revolutionary Spirit ♦

The greatest assault on the Restoration settlement, however, still lay ahead. During the two decades between 1830 and 1848, an articulate and organized opposition grew up in Europe—the subject of this section.

Over these two decades, the conservative social order of the Vienna settlement changed, growing more flexible in some places, more rigid in others. At the same time, liberals joined forces with radicals in western Europe, with nationalists in central and eastern Europe. During these years too, new social problems arose, encouraging the rise of a new ideological challenge—socialism. The following pages will chronicle these changes, emphasizing their contributions to the revolutionary upheaval to come.

Changes in the Conservative Order

There were significant changes in both the ruling elements and the opposition ideologies over the score of years between 1830 and 1848. After 1830, the establishment included liberal as well as conservative regimes. Socialism began to develop, and working–class opposition movements grew more powerful in western Europe. Rebellious nationalism spread further in central, southern, and eastern Europe.

Britain and France, the two constitutional monarchies among the great powers, were both ruled by comparatively liberal governments that, nevertheless, had no use for revolutions or radical change. Whigs dominated the British Parliament for most of the 1830s and 1840s, and the accession of seventeen–year–old Queen Victoria (r. 1837–1901) inaugurated what would later look to many like Britain's longest golden age of prosperity, power, and reform. In France, Louis Philippe (r. 1830–1848) concealed a shrewd and even ruthless love of power beneath his affable, umbrella–toting "bourgeois king" exterior. Liberal politicians and journalists dominated French political life, while liberal businessmen took Guizot's advice and got richer.

In the more conservative Europe that stretched from the Rhine to the Urals, the power structure moved further to the right. In Prussia, King Frederick William III was replaced by King Frederick William IV (r. 1840–1861), who saw himself as a Christian monarch out of an idealized Middle Ages. He believed that he had the duties of a Christian prince to his subjects—but also that they owed him their reverent obedience. In Russia, Emperor Nicholas I (r. 1825–1855) went from suppressing the Decembrists to turning Russia into an even more rigid autocracy run by officials, soldiers, and secret policemen and limited only by its own monumental inefficiency. In Austria, the feeble–minded Ferdinand I (r. 1835–1848) reigned but could not rule, signing whatever documents his ministers put in front of him. Metternich, a leading figure among those ministers, grew gray in power. Though he sometimes seemed to dominate all Europe through his intricate diplomacy, he insisted that he never governed the Austrian Empire itself, a tangle of peoples and problems that he regarded as essentially ungovernable.

Liberalism and Radicalism in Western Europe

Those who opposed the Vienna settlement changed, too, during the 1830s and 1840s. Different varieties of liberalism evolved in both western and eastern Europe. Socialism began to find adherents in the Western nations, and nationalism spread further, especially in the east and south. Peasants remained fundamentally conservative, but a genuine working–class movement took shape in Britain and other industrializing countries.

In western Europe, all liberals were believers in constitutional, representative government. But liberals in power retained an oligarchical grip on it, while those in opposition urged a modest expansion of the suffrage in order to outvote the oligarchy. English utilitarians like John Stuart Mill were willing to cooperate with the elite of the laboring classes against the "governing classes," particularly the landed interests, Whig or Tory. In France, the so–called party of movement among the liberal bourgeoisie sought a tentative alliance with the radical republicans against Louis Philippe and his moneyed supporters.

In both countries, however, a more radical fringe also developed. Drawing their primary support from the working classes, these radicals soon alienated the nervous liberals. In the industrial north of England, early labor unions, workers' cooperatives, and finally Chartism, a movement for further expansion of the suffrage, carried opposition too far to the left for most liberals. In France, the radical republicans set up subversive organizations like the Society of the Rights of Man, allied themselves with rebellious workers, and more than once mounted futile barricades against the "bourgeois king" during the 1830s. Among the coal miners, weavers, and iron– and steelworkers of northern England or the silk weavers of Lyons, genuine working–class movements thus emerged. Such workers were willing to listen to union organizers and radical political agitators, to read socialist tracts, and even to rise in revolt against bourgeois liberal governments.

Liberalism and Nationalism in Central and Eastern Europe

Liberalism in central and eastern Europe took very different forms. Here liberals were often still agitating for what had already been achieved in western Europe: constitutional limitations on royal authority, elected legislatures, freedom of press and political organization. There was also a larger academic leadership, especially in central Europe, emphasizing constitutional forms and the rule of law. In Prussia, for example, middle–class Rhineland liberals encouraged Frederick William IV to abandon traditional Hohenzollern dependence on the Junker aristocracy and the Prussian bureaucracy. Instead, they urged the king to grant a constitution with limited suffrage, thus also depriving radicals of bourgeois liberal support. In the Russia of Nicholas I, those liberals who survived the purges that followed the Decembrist debacle retreated to their country estates. Here they read subversive radical literature imported from western Europe, expressing their discontent in print only in the "Aesopian language" of parables, dark hints, and other circumlocutions. Liberals, let alone radicals, saw themselves as "superfluous" in a land of autocracy and serfdom.

There were radicals east of the Rhine and south of the Alps, too, but they tended to disappear into prisons or flee into exile, as Marx did from Prussia, Bakunin from Russia, and Mazzini from Italy. In central and southern Europe, a working–class movement did begin, spawning strikes on the new railroads and some bloody riots such as a revolt of Sicilian weavers in the 1840s. By and large, however, extremists in the east and south tended to focus their grievances around a sense of nationality rather than a class identity.

Multinational empires like those of Austria and Russia and such politically divided peoples as the Germans, Italians, and Slavs provided fertile ground for nationalist agitators. Relatively modest industrial development, by contrast, limited the likelihood of strong socialist or working–class movements in the first half of the nineteenth century. In Germany, students continued to dream of a united German nation, while businessmen found in railways and a tariff union some commonsense reasons to favor national unification. In Italy, some leaders of the nationalist movement called the *Risorgimento* (Resurgence) encouraged Italians to rise and unify their land, while others turned for leadership to the papacy or the industrializing, liberal Italian Kingdom of Piedmont.

In the Austrian and Russian empires, rebellious national minorities grew increasingly clamorous. Polish nationalists, far from accepting their suppression in 1831, were among the most eloquent of nationalists. They saw theirs as a nation of martyrs to the cause of national self–determination, a people who would one day yet be free. In the Habsburg Empire, Magyar gentry and professional people became chauvinistic Hungarian nationalists. Czech intellectuals began to write their own history and study their own language instead of those of their Austrian rulers. Even smaller Slavic peoples founded ardent nationalist movements to demand freedom from their German or Russian overlords, and sometimes the right to impose their will on minorities within their own territories.

A variety of dissatisfied groups and militant ideologies—liberal, socialist, and nationalist—thus emerged in the 1830s and 1840s. In 1848, when Paris rose in revolt once more, revolution quickly spread from one discontented minority to another until half of Europe seemed to be up in arms.

Economic and Political Grievances

The causes of so important an event as the upheaval of 1848 have of course been of considerable historical concern. From one point of view, each separate explosion had its own peculiar circumstances. So many similar upheavals occurring at once, however, suggest some common causes at work. And since it is precisely the number of revolutionary outbreaks occurring at one time that gives the Revolutions of 1848 their historic significance, these common causes are of particular importance.

One of the more general causes was the spread of radical ideologies. In a classic study, Sir Lewis Namier called the revolts of 1848 "the revolution of the intellectuals," and various forms of liberalism, nationalism, and working–class discontent with the status quo did in fact play a leading part.[5] Around these passionately held isms, many of the opposition movements crystallized.

Another much–discussed set of causal factors was primarily economic in nature. In 1845, a potato blight destroyed this basic staple from Ireland through the Low Countries into Germany. In the following year, the grain harvest, especially in France and the German states, was drastically reduced by drought. In 1847, a credit squeeze set off a wave of bankruptcies and plant closings, especially in France. Rapidly rising food prices due to the poor harvests were thus accompanied by mounting unemployment in the later 1840s.

The revolutions of 1848, however, took place not at the depth of this economic downswing but just as recovery was taking hold. The contribution of these economic factors, then, was probably to undermine confidence in governments and their ability to deal with social problems like those of the "hungry forties." In so doing, the disasters of the decade reminded Europeans of other, long–held discontents with the states of Europe under the Metternich system. "The crisis . . . 'revived every grievance'; it intensified and unified discontent."[6]

The immediate cause of the widespread rebellions in 1848 was thus apparently political. It was popular resentment of the oppressive structure of government in the Restoration states and in a few somewhat more liberal regimes across Europe. Absolutism, bureaucracy, censorship, domestic spying and police terror, an out–of–date aristocracy clinging to vestiges of power, and a rapacious bourgeoisie with no thought for the public welfare—all had combined to create sullen resentments across Europe. In 1848, hungry victims of an economic downturn were at last angry enough about a multitude of long–festering woes to take up arms against the system as a whole.

The final stimulus was the spark provided by the French revolution of February 1848. France had since 1789 been the revolutionary bellwether nation. When barricades went up in the streets of Paris, the young and disaffected of other lands started prying up the cobblestones and overturning wagons in the streets of their own capitals.

◆ 1848: The Springtime of the Peoples ◆

We can list the "causal factors" of the revolutions of 1848, but in the end, we must face the experienced reality. And "the springtime of the peoples," as supporters called this wave of revolutionary new beginnings that swept across Europe in 1848, vividly illustrates the sense of starting over that is the essence of the revolutionary experience.

The following section will survey the revolutions of 1848 in France, Prussia, Austria, and a number of other German and Italian states, as well as reactions in liberal

Britain and reactionary Russia. These pages can only offer glimpses of a few of the fifty or so uprisings of 1848. But they will attempt to convey something of the sense of taking history by the throat that can make a revolution perhaps the headiest of all historical experiences.

The Two French Revolutions of 1848

France in the late 1840s was gripped both by mounting unemployment and a severe agricultural crisis on the one hand and by political demands for governmental reform on the other. A campaign of public banquets at which opposition leaders demanded a reform of the suffrage led the government of King Louis Philippe to bar any further banquets. The liberal politicians who had scheduled a climactic meeting for February 22 canceled it; but workers demonstrating in the streets clashed with royal troops, and demonstrators were killed. In the ensuing wave of protest, radical students and young members of the secret societies mobilized angry Paris workers to raise the barricades once more.

As in 1830, the violence was initially confined to a few days of street fighting in the capital, while the major decisions were made by rapidly maneuvering politicians. Louis Philippe, like Charles X two decades earlier, tried to save his dynasty by abdicating in favor of his heir. But a provisional government of opposition leaders quickly took up residence in the *Hôtel de Ville* (City Hall), the traditional headquarters of alternative governments since the 1790s. This group, whose most eloquent spokesman was the poet Alphonse de Lamartine (1790–1869), included dynastic opponents of the king, liberals both moderate and radical, and even a couple of socialists, the utopian Louis Blanc (1811–1882) and a metalworker known to history only as Albert.

Then, only three days after the first clash, a more radical force of militant workers led by secret society revolutionaries marched on the Hôtel de Ville. Determined not to allow another king to be imposed on them, as in 1830, revolutionary workers forced the liberal leadership to declare the Second Republic in France. As prime victims of the economic downturn, they also demanded the creation of a ministry of labor to provide work and to regulate conditions of labor.

The *February Days* were filled with exultation and hope. "People who did not see Paris that evening," declared the *Gazette de France* on February 27, "where all was good order, concord, and majesty in the very midst of the sublime disorder of the barricades, will never have any idea how fine the idea of the sovereignty of the people really is."[7]

The concord, however, did not last long. Instead of a powerful ministry of labor, the bourgeois provisional government appointed the Luxembourg Commission, which, under Louis Blanc and Albert, collected evidence on the gravity of the economic situation and made unsatisfactory efforts at reform. Laws regulating hours and wages did not help the jobless, of whom there were many in 1848. The most radical relief measure, a group of National Workshops to create public works jobs for the people, provided too few jobs to solve the workers' problems and looked too much like make–work to the middle classes. When elections for a constitutional convention were held at Easter time, the left received a decisive setback as the majority voted for traditional liberal leaders rather than for the Paris radicals. The militant workers of the capital invaded the new constituent assembly as soon as it met, demanding further changes. The liberals, however, retained control, accepted the resignations of Blanc and Albert from the Luxembourg Commission, and closed down the National Workshops as a hotbed of idleness and sedition.

Ideological passions were polarized and intense on both sides. Many leaders of the secret societies and the new political clubs had been arrested, but there were enough left to summon the working–class population to the barricades once more. The people who took up arms during those *June Days* of 1848 were in part the victims of the recent economic crisis: "Ah! Monsieur Arago," one such interrupted a liberal speaker, "you have never been hungry!" But they were also gripped by an intensely held workers' belief in "justice, happiness, and life" as a working person's due. Unfortunately, the supporters of the new government believed with equal passion in the bourgeois liberal ideals of "order, property, and liberty."[8] The resulting carnage was the bloodiest France was to see between the Terror of 1793 and the Paris Commune of 1870.

The insurrection of the June Days pitted metalworkers, construction workers, cobblers, the laboring masses of Paris's eastern slum districts against the bourgeoisie. Some peasant proprietors, fearful that the rebels were "socialists" who might confiscate their land, also rallied to the government. It was, as the liberal Alexis de Tocqueville agreed with

European Revolutions of 1848–1849

the socialist Karl Marx, "not the work of a group of conspirators, but the rising of one part of the population against the other." It was, in short, "a class war"—and it sent a chill down the backs of Europe's propertied classes everywhere.[9]

The workers lost. But the battle lines were clearly drawn. Tensions between laborers and owners would simmer through the rest of the century and well into the present one.

The New Napoleon

Thereafter, however, the French revolution of 1848 followed a totally unforeseen path of political alliances and manipulation from which a single charismatic personality emerged as the man of the hour.

The parties who jockeyed for power after the June Days included a self–styled party of order and a more radical opposition. The party of order, composed of moderate liberals who formed an alliance of convenience with conservatives dedicated to the restoration of the monarchy, used censorship, imprisonment, and electoral manipulation to decimate the ranks of the radical left.

The real contest, then, was for the leadership of the liberal–conservative party of order. And here the wildest of wild cards leaped suddenly from the pack to dominate French history for the next twenty years. Louis Napoleon Bonaparte (1808–1873), nephew of the great Napoleon, had played no part in the revolution of 1848. But he had been imprisoned for earlier revolutionary activity, he had written a book on *The Extinction of Poverty,* and he claimed to care for the people and their problems. At the same time, he let the monarchist factions think they might use him as a means of restoring monarchial government. Above all, perhaps, Louis Napoleon had the charisma of the Napoleonic cult that had grown up in France around the memories of his uncle's famous victories.

A new constitution was adopted in November 1848, creating the Second French Republic and providing for universal manhood suffrage. Louis Napoleon won 75 percent of the vote in the presidential elections held in December. In the next couple of years, the heir of the great Napoleon solidified his position with the people, and, in 1851, he mounted a coup from the top, arresting thousands of his political opponents, including two hundred members of the national legislature. Thereafter, in 1852, he followed in his famous uncle's footsteps by having himself crowned emperor of the French. Both these last two moves, furthermore, were ratified by 90 percent of the electorate in nationwide plebiscites.

A repressive atmosphere and some electoral manipulation had something to do with this victory at the polls. But most of those who voted for Louis Napoleon were voting for a carefully nurtured image. They voted against radical change and revolutionary violence and in favor of order, authority, and modest reform from above, all hedged about with glimmerings of Napoleonic glory.

The Revolutions of 1848 in Italy

The revolutionary spirit had manifested itself even earlier in the Italian states. There domestic grievances had combined with resentment of Austrian predominance to produce decades of subversive agitation. In 1846, Pope Pius IX (r. 1846–1878) himself had unwittingly encouraged unrest when he embarked on a series of reforms in the Papal States, relaxing censorship, releasing political prisoners, and even summoning a "consultative" assembly that could have been a first step toward a legislature. In Vienna, an aging Prince

Metternich, convinced that reforms only encouraged more radical demands, sent troops south—an act that further increased nationalistic resentments and demands for political freedom.

In January 1848, a revolt broke out in Sicily and quickly spread to the mainland. King Ferdinand II (r. 1830–1859) of Naples and Sicily was forced to introduce a parliament and grant a constitution, and peasants began to seize land from aristocratic landholders. In central Italy, Pius IX's reforms filled Rome with radicals, political clubs, and an inflammatory press. In November 1848, the pope's efforts to reassert his authority touched off an uprising that forced him to flee into exile. Radicals seized power, announced a new Roman Republic, and appointed Giuseppe Mazzini (1805–1872), back from his long exile in London, as first triumvir—the most prominent of a three–man political junta—to rule the new Rome. Farther to the north, the radical Venetian lawyer Daniele Manin (1804–1857) became the spark that set off the revolution. "Sometimes," he shouted to a crowd assembled in the Piazza San Marco, "there come moments when insurrection . . . is not only a right but a duty!" Five days later, he proclaimed the Venetian Republic from the top of a cafe table while mobs "went through the town with flaming torches, tricolor banners and cockades, shouting *Viva la republica di San Marco!*"[10]

Among the Italian rulers who granted constitutions was Charles Albert of Piedmont (r. 1831–1859), who set himself at the head of the movement for independence from Austrian control. In Milan, the workers themselves manned barricades and forced the Austrian garrison to withdraw northward to an impregnable array of fortifications called the Quadrilateral, in the shadow of the Alps. Everywhere, liberal bourgeois citizens and enlightened nobles joined radicals and working people against their reactionary local rulers and the overarching foreign power of Austria. And for a time, they had their way.

But the current soon turned against them, and the new year 1849 proved an unmitigated disaster. In southern Italy, King Ferdinand rallied the *lazzaroni,* as the royalist and religiously inflamed rabble of Naples were called, against his own reforms. He rescinded the constitution and suppressed the parliament that had been extorted from him earlier. In the north, King Charles Albert declared war on Austria, drew enthusiastic support from all over Italy—and lost. The Austrians then reoccupied Milan and Venice, with brutal reprisals against the revolutionaries. And in central Italy, the French army expelled Mazzini and his fellow triumvirs from Rome and restored Pius IX. The embittered papal reformer remained a champion of political reaction for the rest of his days.

The Revolutions of 1848 in Germany

In the German states, on Austria's northern flank, insurrection also multiplied in the miraculous year. The spirit of revolution shook even that most efficient of conservative regimes, Hohenzollern Prussia.

Surviving relics of manorialism, the growing pains of industrialism, and the potato famine of 1846–1847 all laid the groundwork. Then came the February Days in France, inspiring a rash of uprisings on the other side of the Rhine as it had south of the Alps. In Bavaria, Baden, Hesse–Darmstadt, and elsewhere across south Germany, peasants seized land and burned landlords' country houses, while urban crowds demonstrated for political rights. Frightened princes responded by granting wider political representation, a freer press, and the final abolition of manorial dues. In western Germany, the Rhineland exploded in working–class violence, destroying factory machinery that had replaced workers and attacking river steamboats that were displacing bargemen. Politicians from this relatively liberal part of Germany, bordering on revolutionary France, scurried to Berlin to plead for reforms.

By then, however, Berlin itself had collapsed into revolutionary violence. In March 1848, Frederick William IV (r. 1840–1861) had promised a constitution, an end to censorship, and a more democratic legislative assembly. But when a crowd gathered to cheer his decision and to urge him to withdraw the military garrison from his capital, the king instead ordered the troops to clear the square in front of the palace. Outraged artisans responded by flinging up barricades. Many were killed before the king, shocked at having shed the blood of his "dear Berliners," withdrew the soldiers and appointed a liberal ministry to oversee political reforms. He even provided work on railways and canals for unemployed laborers in his zeal to prove himself the benevolent medieval monarch he had always imagined himself to be.

In May, meanwhile, an all–German assembly convened at Frankfurt, in western Germany, announcing its intention to produce a liberal constitution for a united German nation. The *Frankfurt Assembly* was dominated by liberal nationalist intellectuals, many of them civil servants, jurists, or university professors. Their goal was a German constitutional monarchy, headed by either the Austrian emperor or the Prussian king.

"Hand in hand," a leaflet circulated in the streets of Berlin trumpeted, "burghers, artisans, students, artists, laborers . . . thus we advance our age!"[11] In fact, however, divisions were deep. The laboring masses felt themselves oppressed by the artisan elite. Middle–class burghers rallied to the Prussian monarchy as a guarantor of order and property. And academic liberals, from students in the streets to the dignitaries of the Frankfurt Assembly, soon found that they had little support from either the Habsburg and Hohenzollern rulers or the peasants and bargemen.

In November 1848, the Prussian army marched back into Berlin, and Frederick William IV re–asserted his authority and imposed a strictly limited suffrage. Prussian troops also put down armed revolts in Bavaria, Baden, and other states that had earlier made concessions to radical change. The Frankfurt Assembly, after endlessly debating the relative merits of a *grossdeutsch* empire ("large German," including Austria) with an Austrian ruler and a *kleindeutsch* kingdom ("small German," excluding Austria) headed by the royal house of Prussia, found that neither sovereign would accept the crown at their hands. Many gave up and went home, and the rest were expelled from Frankfurt by Prussian bayonets.

Revolution Reaches the Land of Metternich

Meanwhile the Austrian Empire, the center of the Metternich system, saw some of the most dramatic upheavals of all in 1848. In Vienna, Prague, and Budapest, in a dazzling display of activism and eloquence, liberals, radicals, and revolutionaries seized power—and then lost it to armed force.

Idealistic students were prominent in many of the revolutions of 1848, and nowhere more so than in Vienna. The youthful *Academic Legion* of the University of Vienna was thus hailed at the height of the uproar in the Habsburg capital:

> What comes here, with daring stride—
> Their weapons flash, their banners fly—
> It closer comes, with roll of drums—
> The Uni–ver–si–ty![12]

With their beards, long hair, wide–brimmed plumed hats, and clanking sabers, their talk of freedom, a constitution, and "a United States of Germany," the Academic Legion were an inspiring sight. Elsewhere, liberal nationalists in the Czech and Hungarian portions of the empire were the prime movers. And unemployed factory or railroad workers from the new industrial suburbs of Vienna, or Hungarian peasants resentful of the surviving medieval *robot* (labor service), provided much of the real clout.

The first upheaval came in Vienna itself. In March, student leaders from the University of Vienna demanded a constitution and the dismissal of the archreactionary Metternich. Fired on by troops during a demonstration, the students were quickly supported by the workers. Within days, the whole system of Habsburg rule began to come apart before their eyes.

Metternich, stunned to see the infamous "spirit of revolution" he had fought so long burst forth even in Vienna, abruptly resigned and slipped out of the city in disguise, heading for exile. Surviving court politicians, speaking for the feeble–minded Emperor Ferdinand, forthwith promised a constitution. Meanwhile, the passionate oratory of liberal nationalists like the Hungarian journalist Lajos Kossuth (1802–1894) stirred up rebellion in both Budapest and Prague. Czech Bohemia won a more democratic legislature, and the Hungarian Diet declared that nation an independent republic with Kossuth as president.

Smaller national minorities did not do so well, however. Some of the emperor's Slavic subjects—Czechs, Poles, Slovaks, Slovenes, and others—demanded their own independent states. Others urged autonomy within a reformed Habsburg empire, or dreamed of a huge Russian–led Slav empire. But neither the German–speaking Austrians nor the Magyars who dominated Hungary paid any attention to these nationalistic demands. Hungary's rulers even imposed a rigorous policy of Magyarization on their ethnic minorities, while the Austrian government continued its eternal game of playing one nationality off against another to maintain its own authority.

In fact, repressive forces soon came surging back all over the empire. In June, defiance of imperial authority in Prague led the emperor—or his handlers—to send in the Austrian army, which bombarded and captured the Bohemian capital. When the Hungarian Magyars embarked on their drastic nationalization program, some Slavs rose in rebellion, and the Austrian government invited Czar Nicholas I to send in Russian troops to help crush the Magyars. The Austrian army, meanwhile, marched on Vienna itself, where they besieged, shelled, and captured the Habsburg capital. The student revolutionaries fled into exile, some as far as the United States in search of political freedom, while the revolution was liquidated everywhere in the Habsburg lands.

British and Russian Responses to Radicalism

At opposite ends of Europe, two great powers were spared: Russia and Britain, the most reactionary and the most liberal of the major powers in 1848. Both had at least a taste of radical activism, however—the Russians from a handful of dissident intellectuals, the British from the militant mass movement called Chartism.

In Russia, the legacy of the Decembrist revolt of 1825 was the rigid autocracy of Nicholas I (r. 1825–1855). Russians with an interest in radical intellectual or social questions were reduced to reading German philosophy or French utopian socialism and debating these western ideas in informal discussion groups. During the 1830s and 1840s, however, a major controversy with long–range consequences arose between the "Westernizers" and the "Slavophiles" among the Russian intelligentsia. The *Westernizers* urged the view, popular with an enlightened minority since Peter the Great's day, that Russia must modernize its society by adopting western European ideas and technologies. The *Slavophiles,* by contrast, insisted that Russia should pin its faith in the Russian Orthodox church and Old Russian ways, which they saw as authentic expressions of the Slavic soul. Both, however, were critical of the Russian present and dreamed of change, the Westernizers seeing hope in a utopian socialist future, the Slavophiles favoring a return to the village commune of the past and the pre–Petrine Orthodox church.

A few Westernizers, like the radical propagandist Alexander Herzen (1812–1870), actually moved to western Europe and smuggled radical publications back into their own country. Then in 1848, the czarist secret police, alarmed at the convulsions that gripped the rest of Europe, swept up a couple of "subversive" discussion groups and sent them off to prison or Siberian exile. The best–known of these groups, the *Petrashevsky Circle,* was guilty of discussing Charles Fourier and his phalansteries a little too enthusiastically for the inevitable police spy in their midst. Among the Petrashevskyites bundled off to Siberia was young Fyodor Dostoyevsky, who later became one of Russia's most celebrated—and most antirevolutionary—writers.

Britain faced a much more direct and potentially violent challenge in 1848. The People's Charter had first been proposed a decade earlier, in the 1830s. The half–dozen points of this simple document would have required a reform of Parliament going well beyond the Reform Bill of 1832, including universal manhood suffrage, annual elections, and salaries for members of Parliament. It would, in short, have opened the way to the participation of the poor in government. The *Chartists* who organized the campaign to petition Parliament to this effect included early labor leaders and members of working–class cooperatives, as well as middle–class London radicals and popular orators like the Irish radical journalist Feargus O'Connor (1794–1855).

The petition to incorporate the Charter into the British constitution, submitted with a million signatures in 1839 and again with a claimed three million in 1842, had been rejected both times. Resubmitted at the height of the 1848 revolutions across the Channel, it was supported by radicals drilling with weapons and conspirators plotting arson and barricades. Sent off to Parliament with a claimed six million signatures—Parliament counted only two million—the People's Charter was once more turned down, the conspiracies were exposed, and the agitation was left to wither away.

The fact that it did fade away left many Britons smugly convinced of the superiority of their relatively liberal system of government. The Russians were equally certain of the superior wisdom of crushing revolution in the egg, before it could grow. Both countries, like the rest of the Western world, would in fact change radically over the next half–century.

Summary

The Western world in the first half of the nineteenth century was swept by three great waves of political revolutions, most of them in the 1820s, in 1830, and in 1848. Although these revolts frequently succeeded in overthrowing established governments for a short time, they were generally either suppressed in the longer run or taken over by politicians more moderate than the barricade fighters who made the revolutions.

This short half–century began with the reactionary Vienna peace conference of

1815, which attempted to restore the old regime to power in Europe. Within five years, however, the revolutions of the 1820s challenged this restoration in Europe's southern and eastern fringes and in the Latin American colonies overseas. Though the great powers successfully put down most of the European revolts, the southern American colonies did make good their independence.

Ten years later, in the 1830s, a wave of revolutions swept across western and central Europe, challenging regimes and toppling dynasties in France and Belgium, the German and Italian states. Again, most of the revolutions were suppressed, though a new and more liberal king did come to power in France and Britain accepted the Great reform Bill of 1832.

The next two decades saw growing opposition to the social order established in 1815 as liberals allied themselves with radicals in western Europe and with nationalists in central and eastern Europe. The spread of industrialism also helped create more social tension and made its contribution to the climactic explosion to come.

In 1848, then, the revolutionaries rose once more, in as many as fifty places across the continent. Governments fell or were forced to make concessions in France, the German and Italian states, and other places. In 1849, however, the forces of reaction once more came surging back, recovering power almost everywhere.

Some Key Terms

Academic Legion 517	February Days 513	Quadruple Alliance 498
Burschenschaften 500	Frankfurt Assembly 517	Reform Bill of 1832 508
Chartists 519	*grito de Dolores* 504	Restoration 497
Concert of Europe 498	Holy Alliance 498	*Risorgimento* 511
Congress of Vienna 494	July Days 506	Slavophiles 519
Congress Poland 497	June Days 514	Vienna settlement 494
Decembrists 502	Petrashevsky Circle 519	Westernizers 519

Notes

1. Marquis de Lafayette, quoted in Sébastien Charléty, *La Restauration, 1815–1830* (Paris: Librairie Hachette, 1923), 377.
2. Louis XVI's young son, hailed by legitimists as Louis XVII after his royal father's execution, had died in the dungeons of the Revolution in 1795.
3. John Lynch, *The Spanish American Revolutions, 1808–1826* (London: Weidenfeld and Nicolson, 1973), 308.
4. Quoted in Clive L. Church, *Europe in 1830: Revolutions and Political Change* (London: George Allen and Unwin, 1983), 27.
5. Lewis Namier, *1848: The Revolution of the Intellectuals* (London: Oxford University Press, 1971).
6. Jacques Droz, *Europe Between Revolutions* (London: Fontana Press, 1985), 247.
7. *Gazette de France,* February 27, 1848, in *1848 in France,* ed. Roger Price (London: Thames and Hudson, 1975), 64.
8. Maurice Agulhon, *The Republican Experiment, 1848–1852,* trans. Janet Lloyd (Cambridge: Cambridge University Press, 1983), 57–58.
9. Alexis de Tocqueville, quoted in Namier, *1848,* 10.
10. Paul Ginsburg, *Daniele Manin and the Venetian Revolution of 1848–49* (Cambridge: Cambridge University Press, 1979), 90, 103.
11. Quoted in Sigrid Weigel, *Flugschriftenliteratur 1848 in Berlin* (Stuttgart: J. B. Metzlersche Verlagsbuchhandlung, 1979), 73.
12. Ludwig August Frankl, "Die Universität," in *Wiener Flugschriften zur sozialen Frage 1848* (Vienna: Europaverlag, 1980), 72.

Reading List

Aminzade, R. *Ballots and Barricades: Class Formation and Republican Politics.* Princeton: Princeton University Press, 1993. Artisans and industrial workers in nineteenth–century France.

Church, C. H. *Europe in 1830.* London: Allen and Unwin, 1983. Up–to–date survey of the revolutions of that year.

Dakin, D. *The Greek Struggle for Independence, 1821–1833.* Berkeley: University of California Press, 1973. Thorough study of the Greek revolt and its international ramifications.

Droz, J. *Europe Between Revolutions, 1815–1848.* Ithaca, N.Y.: Cornell University Press, 1980. The importance of socio–economic forces in shaping the temper of the time.

Hamerow, T. S. *Restoration, Revolution, Reaction.* Princeton, N.J.: Princeton University Press, 1958. Germany from the Vienna settlement to the formation of the German Empire in 1871.

Kissinger, H. *A World Restored.* Boston: Peter Smith, 1973. The effort to maintain the Vienna settlement through international conferences of the powers, by a leading international negotiator of the later twentieth century.

Kranzberg, M., ed. *1848: A Turning Point?* Lexington, Mass.: Heath, 1959. Conflicting assessments of the importance of the Revolutions of 1848.

Leslie, R. F. *Polish Politics and the Revolution of 1830.* London: Athlone Press, 1956. The anatomy of a revolution doomed by both its own internal divisions and the superior force marshaled against it.

Lynch, J. *Latin American Revolutions, 1808–1826: Old and New World Origins.* Norman: University of Oklahoma Press, 1994. Authoritative overview.

Namier, L. B. *1848: The Revolution of the Intellectuals.* New York: Anchor Books, 1964. Condemns liberal ideologues for their failure to provide adequate leadership.

Nicolson, H. *The Congress of Vienna.* New York: Harcourt Brace Jovanovich, 1970. Well–written analysis from a diplomat's point of view.

Pinkney, D. H. *The French Revolution of 1830.* Princeton, N.J.: Princeton University Press, 1970. Valuable study of the July Days and their aftermath.

Raeff, M. *The Decembrist Movement.* Englewood Cliffs, N.J.: Prentice Hall, 1966. Convincing account of the revolt of the children of privilege against Russian realities. See also the older but solid A. G. Mazour, *The First Russian Revolution* (Palo Alto, Calif.: Stanford University Press, 1937).

Robertson, P. *Revolutions of 1848.* Princeton, N.J.: Princeton University Press, 1952. Older narrative history emphasizing the central role of youth and students.

Salvemini, G. *Mazzini.* Palo Alto, Calif.: Stanford University Press, 1957. Life and thought of the Italian revolutionary leader.

Sauvigny, G. de. *Metternich and His Times.* Atlantic Highlands, N.J.: Humanities Press, 1962. Biography of the archconservative by a noted historian of the Restoration.

Sewell, W. H. *Work and Revolution in France.* Cambridge: Cambridge University Press, 1980. Useful analysis of the pressures on French workers that led to explosions like the June Days of 1848.

Sperber, J. *Rhineland Radicals: The Democratic Movement and the Revolution of 1848–1849.* Princeton, N.J.: Princeton University Press, 1991. Upsurge of revolution in western Germany, interpreted in its own terms but casting light on similar upheavals across Europe.

Talmon, J. L. *Romanticism and Revolt, 1815–1848.* New York: Norton, 1979. The cultural tone of the Age of Revolutions.

Thomas, M. I. *Threats of Revolution in Britain, 1789–1848.* London: Macmillan, 1977. Violent challenges to the status quo in even the most stable and liberal of the powers.

Venturi, F. *Roots of Revolution: A History of the Populist and Socialist Movements in Nineteenth Century Russia.* Translated by F. Haskell. London: Weidenfeld and Nicolson, 1960. Detailed study of the rise of Russia's revolutionary tradition, mostly in the second half of the century.

21

Blood and Iron
Reshaping the Nations

+Political Changes, East and West   +The Birth of Two New Nations
+The Evolving Americas   +The Drive for Social Change

The failure of the Revolutions of 1848 to transform Europe overnight did not end efforts at political change and social reform. Indeed, it was precisely the growing conviction that Western people *could* control their own destiny that gives unity to the complex half–century between 1848 and 1914.

A liberal Christian parliamentary leader like William Gladstone in Britain shared neither goals nor methods with the driven young *narodnik* terrorists who assassinated Russia's Czar Alexander II. What they and many others did have in common was a confidence that the system—whatever it was—*could* be changed, that institutions could be restructured, class or gender relations transformed, the nations themselves rebuilt by dedicated human effort. Contributors to this drive for change included Europeans of many persuasions—from conservatives to liberals, from nationalists to socialists, from reform–minded bureaucrats to the militant leaders of the growing labor and women's movements. Thanks to their often contradictory labors, the eighteenth–century Enlightenment dream of redesigning human society thus began to become a reality in the nineteenth century.

This chapter will look first at changes in four relatively stable European powers: Victorian Britain, France under Napoleon III and the Third Republic, the multinational Austrian empire, and czarist Russia. It will then turn to the appearance of two new great powers on the European stage: the newly unified states of Germany and Italy. A look at the Americas follows, where the Civil War in the United States and struggles between Latin American *caudillos,* or regional warlords, and central governments revealed the strength of the new American nations. The final section will focus on social problems and movements for social change as the century turned.

+Political Changes, East and West+

Though the West would never again seem so near to root–and–branch transformation from below as during the Revolutions of 1848, a healthy fear of another such upheaval undoubtedly moved European governments to undertake significant changes. The spread of industrialism and the ever–widening appeal of the nineteenth–century ideologies also stimulated demands for reform. Most of the resulting changes, however, were not the work of revolutionaries, but of establishment politicians with an eye to advancing their own interests.

The nineteenth century was Britain's "age of reform" through Parliament, especially between the 1860s and the 1890s. The latter half of the century also saw France evolve through a reform–minded emperor, Napoleon III (r. 1852–1870), to the democracy of the Third Republic (1870–1940). In the Russian and Austrian empires, finally, two autocracies reluctantly gave ground to demands for change.

Britain's Era of Reform

Britain was an outstanding exemplar of political progress in the later nineteenth century. The leaders of the rival Liberal and Conservative parties, William Gladstone (1809–1898) and Benjamin Disraeli (1804–1881), epitomized the modern politician, governing by the will of the voters and in the public interest as they conceived it. They fought each other tooth and nail through the later 1800s, but when the dust of battle cleared, Britain was a better place.

Gladstone was a strongly Christian statesman, eloquent and autocratic, a stiffly Victorian head of the Liberal party, into which the Whigs evolved around midcentury. Disraeli

The British Houses of Parliament, rebuilt in Gothic style in the nineteenth century, symbolize the oldest European representative government. The medieval origins of Parliament made a medieval style of architecture appropriate for these buildings. (Universal Pictorial Press and Agency, Ltd.)

Chronology 21: Political Changes and Challenges in Later Nineteenth Century

1859–1860	*Cavour engineers unification of Italy*
1860–1865	*Civil War in the United States*
1861	*Czar Alexander II abolishes serfdom in Russia*
1863	*Lincoln abolishes slavery in southern United States*
1870–1871	*Bismarck organizes unification of Germany*
1867	*Habsburg Dual Monarchy gives Hungary equality with Austria*
1867, 1884	*British industrial and agricultural workers get right to vote*
from 1869	*Labor unions legalized in various countries*
1871	*Republic established in France*
1880s	*Welfare legislation in Germany*
1881	*Narodniks assassinate liberal czar Alexander II*
1890s–1900s	*Women's suffrage campaigns in Britain*
1890s	*Anarchist terrorism in Europe*
1894–1906	*Dreyfus case divides France*

was a gaudy dresser and a popular novelist—an unlikely leader for a Conservative party still dominated by country squires and conventional Anglican clergymen.

From the 1860s into the 1890s, Gladstone worked for reform in government finances, for civil service examinations, for an end to religious tests for holding political office, for educational reform, and for many other changes. To one crucial line of political change, however, Gladstone and Disraeli both contributed: the expansion of the suffrage, the growth of democracy itself.

The Reform Bill of 1832, as noted in the last chapter, produced only a modest extension of political participation, opening the way for power sharing between the aristocracy and the middle classes. The Chartist agitation for the vote for all adult males was, as we have also seen, firmly suppressed in 1848. A start had been made, but those who enjoyed the right to vote and hold office were in no hurry to share it with those further down the social scale.

Twenty years on, however, the Reform Bill of 1867 did significantly expand the franchise, particularly for urban workers. The measure became law largely as the result of competition between the Conservative and Liberal leaders for workers' votes. The bill finally passed by Disraeli approximately doubled the number of British voters, from one to two million. The next step toward a truly democratic suffrage came almost two decades further on and was the work of Gladstone's Liberals. The Reform Bill of 1884 allowed most agricultural workers to vote, again doubling the number of legal voters to close to four and a half million. Perhaps three–quarters of British males could thus vote as the century turned.

One other major political reform of this period was the abolition of the House of Lords' veto power over legislation in 1911. This reform, bitterly resisted by Conservatives, decreed that any bill that passed the elected House of Commons three times became law even if the hereditary House of Lords opposed it. Slowly but surely, Britain was edging toward democracy.

France: The Second Empire and the Third Republic

In French history, the period between the revolution of 1848 and the outbreak of World War I in 1914 divides into two distinct eras. The first two decades comprise the Empire of

Napoleon III, who governed, first as president and then as emperor, from 1848 to 1870. The second was the Third Republic, which filled the last third of the nineteenth century—to be outlined here—and the first half of the twentieth.

France's Second Empire (1852–1870) comprised the reign of a single emperor: Napoleon III. Louis Napoleon Bonaparte demonstrated a remarkable capacity to win mass support from his startling victory in the 1848 presidential election to his landslides in the plebiscites called to ratify his coup of 1851 and his elevation to the title of "emperor" in 1852. Throughout his two decades in power, he combined the autocratic authority of a monarch with demagogic popular appeal. A one–time revolutionary and utopian thinker, he lowered food prices and sponsored public housing for the poor. In the 1860s, he moved toward granting real power to the people and had just instituted a new and more liberal constitution when he fell from power in 1870.

His reign is best known, however, for the most rapid period of industrial and financial growth in the nation's history. Big business came on with a rush, drawing on huge new financial institutions. French engineers constructed the Suez Canal in the 1860s, and the government itself built thousands of miles of railroads. Napoleon III also commissioned Baron Georges Haussmann (1809–1891) to rebuild substantial parts of Paris, producing a system of wide boulevards that not only added to the grandeur of the city but provided excellent avenues of fire in case of civil disturbances.

Unhappily, the new Napoleon also set out to win international prestige by breaking out of the containment imposed upon France in 1815. The result was a series of military misadventures that would have had his uncle, Napoleon I, shaking his head in disbelief.

Thus in the early 1850s, Napoleon III joined Britain in the Crimean War (1854–1856) with Russia, which he saw as the true power behind the Vienna settlement. France and Britain won, but gained little for their heavy casualties. In 1859, the French emperor supported Piedmont's prime minister Count Cavour against Austria and ended up providing a military shield behind which Cavour forged the new Kingdom of Italy—another great power for France to worry about.

Finally, in 1870, Napoleon allowed Prussia's master diplomat, Otto von Bismarck, to inveigle him into a war with Prussia. The result was a crushing defeat for France and the creation of a united German Empire that was immediately recognized as continental Europe's greatest power. Napoleon III's own ignominious surrender to the Prussians at Sedan in 1870 thus heralded the end of the long European leadership enjoyed by France and the beginning of the continental supremacy of Germany.

Aging and ill, Napoleon III abdicated and went into exile. A provisional republican government at Versailles negotiated a costly peace with the Germans and ushered in France's Third Republic. In Paris, meanwhile, more radical forces were at work. Inflamed with patriotic fervor and working–class discontent, the masses of the nation's capital mobilized as they had in the June Days of 1848, elected a radical municipal government called—as in the 1790s—the Commune, and defied both the Prussians and the provisional French government. From March to May of 1871, the Communards held out.

The *Paris Commune* drew upon many ideologies: nationalistic refusal to accept the recent defeat, the radical republican dream of reviving the Jacobin rigors of the 1790s, and the revolutionary socialist aspirations of ideologues like Karl Marx, who enthusiastically supported the Commune from his London exile. The radical regime, driven to extremities as the troops closed in, dynamited historic monuments, executed the archbishop of Paris, and generally horrified middle–class Europe. The French army, urged on by Bismarck, finally broke into the capital, slaughtered twenty–five thousand Frenchmen, and crushed the Commune.

For the rest of the century, the *Third Republic* ruled a France weary of revolutions yet haunted by the legacy of the revolutionary past. Supporters of the aristocracy, the church, and the monarchy abolished in 1871 feuded with liberals, socialists, and other advocates of change. The struggle, however, no longer took place in the streets, but in the political arena created by the Republic.

It was at least a stable regime, with a centralized bureaucracy of appointed prefects in the departments and mayors of the towns. It survived the Europewide depression that darkened the last quarter of the century. Middle–class French people, at least, remembered it as *la belle époque,* a period of prosperity and domestic tranquillity that was swept away by the Great War that began in 1914.

Austria and Russia: Autocracies under Pressure

In the old east European empires of Austria and Russia, autocratic monarchies still ruled, the influence of the church and the landed aristocracy remained strong, and conservative ideas prevailed. Industrial development came slowly and on a smaller scale, and middle–class liberals were less numerous and had much less political weight. Nationalists in Austria and socialists in Russia were seen as outright subversives, threatening the very survival of the state.

The long–lived Emperor Francis Joseph (r. 1848–1916) was the last real monarch Austria would ever have. Coming to the throne at the age of nineteen during the revolution of 1848, Francis Joseph presided over a long Indian summer of Viennese culture and gracious living. But his reign also saw a steady Habsburg retreat before the rising power of Prussia and Italy and the continuing advance of the isms Europe's autocrats thought they had buried in 1848.

Foreign affairs saw the empire most often on the defensive against the rise of Italian and German nationalism. In 1859, Austria lost its hegemony of Italy to Cavour's Piedmont, and in 1866 its predominance in the German states to Bismarck's Prussia. Through the rest of the century, the Habsburg regime survived in considerable part as the junior partner of a new German Empire whose capital was at Berlin rather than Vienna.

The great problem for the Habsburgs, however, was the rise of many nationalisms in their own empire. National feeling spread rapidly among the Magyars in Hungary and Czechs in Bohemia, the Poles, Slovaks, Slovenes, Croats, and other Slavic peoples, and the Italians of Venetia and Lombardy. Through the last half of the nineteenth century, Francis Joseph and his ministers labored to retain control. The emperor's greatest concession was the creation of the Austro–Hungarian *Dual Monarchy* in 1867, granting Hungary virtual parity with Austria under a common sovereign. But he continued to reject the demands of militant Czechs and other Slavic minorities for everything from schools in the regional language to local representative institutions.

The situation was made worse by the gradual disintegration of the equally multinational Ottoman Empire in the Balkans. After the successful Greek revolution of the 1820s, Serbia, Romania, and Bulgaria had gained their independence from the Ottomans. On the eve of World War I, a final series of Balkan Wars (1912–1913) freed the rest of the peninsula from Turkey. And these new nations stimulated inflammatory nationalism among the minority populations of the Habsburg realms.

The last decades of the nineteenth century were thus filled with demands for cultural autonomy and then for political independence. In the wake of World War I, these rival nationalisms would pull the Habsburg empire to pieces.

Russia, spared the upheavals of 1848, plunged into its own debacle less than a decade later in the Crimean War (1854–1856). This first European conflict between the great powers since 1815 pitted France, Britain, and Turkey against the vast but backward Russian Empire. Napoleon III sought to boost French prestige and win the support of French Catholics by challenging Russia's right to serve as official protector of the Turkish sultan's Christian subjects. Britain's goal was to discourage Russian expansionism which might threaten Britain's interests in India. The fighting, though largely limited to the Crimean peninsula in southern Russia, lasted for about a year.

Though the western European allies suffered disturbing casualties and gained little of substance, the war clearly demonstrated the material superiority of the more developed powers. Defeated Russia lost even the right to maintain a fleet on the Black Sea—a circumstance roughly comparable to a denial of the right of the United States to keep a fleet in the Caribbean! Humiliated and shaken, the giant nation that had turned back Napoleon retired to lick its wounds and contemplate the necessity for some drastic reforms.

As in the days of Peter and Catherine the Great, the goal once more was to catch up with the West. Czar Alexander II (r. 1855–1881), who inherited his throne in the middle of the war, took up the task of reform with such energy that he became known to history as "the czar emancipator."

Military reforms, including shorter terms of army enlistment to build larger reserves of trained men, came high on the agenda. Seeking popular support for the monarchy, Alexander II also introduced some local self–government, including provincial assemblies or *zemstvos* and municipal governing boards.

In 1861, Alexander II earned his label of "emancipator" by freeing the half of Russia's peasant population who were still serfs in the middle of the nineteenth century. Though the land allotments provided were too small to support a family, this was a major reform that raised wild hopes among Russia's liberal and radical minorities. Liberal country gentry, members of local governments, and professional employees of the *zemstvos* charged with care of roads and schools hoped to expand these beachheads of reform. Student radicals demonstrated for university reform, rights for women, democracy, and socialism. When a scandalized government closed down their universities, frustrated young radicals turned to secret societies and revolutionary dreams.

These *narodniki,* or Russian populists of the 1870s, developed peasant socialism. They declared that the traditional Russian village had been an essentially socialist institution and that the peasant majority of the population would provide the troops for a socialist revolution. The peasants, however, proved for the most part loyal to the czar. And when Alexander II punished student demonstrators and revolutionary agitators, the *narodniki* turned against him as well. After assassinating a number of czarist officials, the revolutionary People's Will society struck down the czar emancipator himself with a bomb in St. Petersburg in 1881.

Reaction closed over Russia for the next fifteen years. Alexander III (r. 1881–1894) took as his motto the three principles of "Autocracy, Orthodoxy, and Nationalism." His secret police, the notorious Third Section, filled the prisons and the Siberian labor camps with political dissidents. But the victory of reaction was only temporary. Like Habsburg Austria, Romanov Russia would fall to agitaters for one of the new ideologies early in the next century.

◆The Birth of Two New Nations◆

Britain's parliamentary reforms, France's Third Republic, Francis Joseph's Dual Monarchy, and the reforms of Alexander II brought major transformations to Europe's leading states. Two other nations, however, were even more drastically reshaped. After many centuries as "geographical expressions," Italy and Germany became united nations in the third quarter of the nineteenth century.

In each instance, the primary leadership came from a rapidly modernizing and ambitious nation—Prussia in Germany, Piedmont in Italy. In each, a shrewd, tough–minded minister of state gets most of the credit for the founding of the new nation—Bismarck in Prussia and Cavour in Piedmont. Both men were masters of *Realpolitik,* the hardboiled and unscrupulous political style that flourished after 1848. Cavour unified Italy in 1859–1860 and Bismarck brought Germany together in 1870–1871 through carefully orchestrated alliances and diplomatic "incidents".

Cavour and the Unification of Italy

Italy in 1849 was a land of shattered dreams. The Risorgimento lay in ruins, crushed by Austrian arms. The romantic Mazzinian revolutionaries, with all their plots and panache, had failed to break the Austrian yoke, free Italy from its petty despots, or unite the Italian people. There remained only one hope: the north Italian kingdom of Piedmont, with its ambitious king Victor Emmanuel II and its energetic, tirelessly scheming prime minister Count Cavour.

Piedmont, the only constitutional monarchy in Italy, was also a progressive nation, building railroads and pushing prosperity through free trade. The goal of Victor Emmanuel and Cavour was rather the aggrandizement of Piedmont than the liberation of Italy. But they had what the nationalists knew they had to have after 1848. "To defeat cannons and soldiers," a Lombard revolutionary explained, "cannons and soldiers are needed. . . . Piedmont has soldiers and cannon. Therefore I am Piedmontese."[1]

Plump, bespectacled, and frock–coated, a former entrepreneur turned politician, Count Camillo di Cavour (1810–1861) was a far less colorful character than the guerrilla leader Garibaldi—whom he recruited to his cause—or the conspirator Mazzini. But the pushy pragmatic prime minister was capable of some of the most daring diplomatic gambles of the century. He set to work to build a bigger Piedmont and ended by uniting most of Italy under the Piedmontese house of Savoy.

Cavour's prime instrument was Napoleon III of France. Too small to break the Austrian yoke alone, Piedmont needed the help of another great power. Cavour shrewdly exploited Napoleon III's longing to re–establish French greatness and gain some influence in the Italian peninsula. In a historic secret interview at Plombières in 1858, Cavour got Napoleon III to promise to support Piedmont in a war against Austria. Piedmont would gain the prosperous north Italian territories of Lombardy and Venetia from Austria; France would be compensated with the borderlands of Nice and Savoy. It was an opportunistic, hard–boiled, self–aggrandizing bargain, entirely in the mood of the new political realism of the post–1848 period. And it worked.

In 1859, Austria was maneuvered into attacking gallant little Piedmont. Napoleon III galloped to the rescue and defeated Austria. Cut off from Austrian support, the central Italian princes fled, opening the way for the establishment of pro–Piedmontese provisional

Unification of Italy, 1859–1870

governments. Cavour engineered plebiscites in which the people voted enthusiastically for union with victorious Piedmont. Then, in 1860, the guerrilla Garibaldi, secretly armed by Cavour himself, sailed to southern Italy with a thousand ragtag volunteers.

Giuseppe Garibaldi (1807–1882) had fought in the Italian revolutions of the 1830s and in 1848 and had even led partisan bands in South American revolts. Like Mazzini, he was committed, not only to Italian independence from Austrian control, but also to an Italian republic, free of the tyranny of kings. With his thousand *Redshirts*, so–called because this was the only uniform they had, he liberated first the island of Sicily, then most of the southern half of the Italian peninsula. It was an astonishing achievement for a handful of irregular soldiers.

But this victory by a republican revolutionary also threatened Cavour's determination to forge an Italian kingdom under Victor Emmanuel. Cavour, however, quickly regained the initiative. As the Redshirt advance faltered north of Naples, King Victor Emmanuel marched south. In a much publicized meeting, Victor Emmanuel won Garibaldi's acceptance of the Piedmontese ruler as king of the new Italy.

Cavour died in 1861, but Italy's new king, now Victor Emmanuel I (r. 1861–1878), and his ministers showed Cavourian astuteness in seizing diplomatic opportunities to complete the kingdom. A shrewdly timed alliance with Prussia in the Austro–Prussian War of 1866 brought Venetia to the new Italy. When France fell in its turn to Prussian arms in 1870, Italy occupied Rome as the French garrison fled north. Except for the tiny enclave of Vatican City, left to the pope, the task of the Risorgimento was largely complete.

The new Italy was not a democracy but a constitutional monarchy in which considerably less than 10 percent of the population could vote. As in the Third French Republic, a shifting oligarchy of liberals dominated the parliament, bartering votes and government favors for campaign contributions from the business community. And though the south remained an economic backwater, northern Italy at least continued to develop economically. The spirit of the new nation was thus much more that of the progressive but unscrupulous Cavour than that of ardent ideologues like Mazzini or Garibaldi.

Bismarck and the Unification of Germany

More conservative and autocratic than Piedmont, the Prussia of King William I still depended on the bureaucracy, the army, and the Junker aristocracy who staffed them. Economically and militarily, Prussia was also considerably more powerful than Piedmont. The north German great power enjoyed a booming industry, expanding trade, and leadership of the Zollverein, the customs union to which most German states belonged by midcentury. A recent Prussian army reform had reorganized the armed forces and adopted the latest weapons. A widespread railway network facilitated the deployment of troops at need. And in 1862 Bismarck was appointed the king's first minister.

Prince Otto von Bismarck (1815–1898) was no more a German nationalist than Cavour was an Italian one. Bismarck's goal, like Cavour's, was the aggrandizement of his own country. More conservative than Cavour, the Prussian chancellor tended to ignore the elected legislature for years at a time. Like the Italian, however, Germany's future "iron chancellor" was a shrewd opportunist, a "realist" of the hard–boiled new school of diplomacy. While he did not deliberately engineer the three wars that climaxed in the unification of Germany, he did demonstrate a masterly ability to play the cards history dealt him.

The road to German unification thus began with the Danish War of 1864, Bismarck's solution to the complex diplomatic tangle known as the Schleswig–Holstein question. To prevent Denmark's King Christian IX (r. 1863–1906) from annexing these two north German provinces—and to assert Prussia's leadership in defending German interests—Bismarck mobilized against the Danes. Austria insisted on joint action, and Denmark was quickly defeated, Schleswig and Holstein ceded to the two German powers.

The Austro–Prussian War of 1866 arose directly from the division of the spoils of this earlier conflict. In another brief summer war, Prussia's modern military machine overwhelmed the Austrian army at Sadowa. Prussia then annexed not only Schleswig and

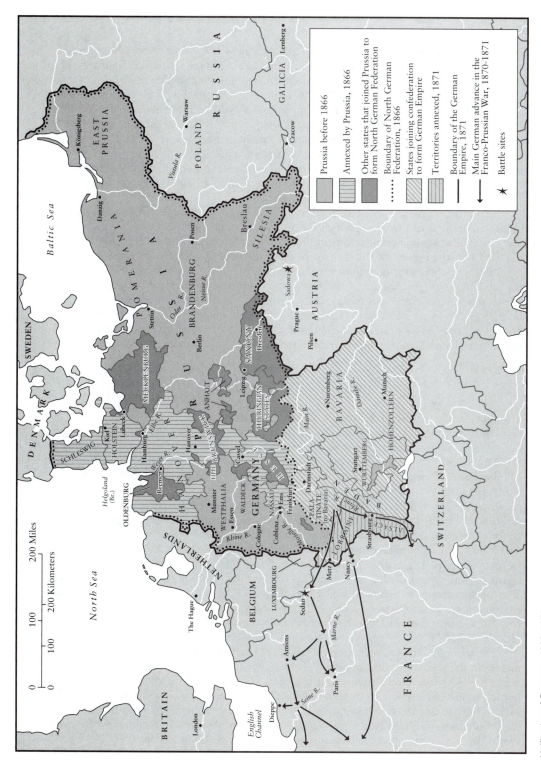

Legend

Unification of Germany, 1866–1871

- Prussia before 1866
- Annexed by Prussia, 1866
- Other states that joined Prussia to form North German Federation
- ······ Boundary of North German Federation, 1866
- States joining confederation to form German Empire
- Territories annexed, 1871
- —— Boundary of the German Empire, 1871
- → Main German advance in the Franco-Prussian War, 1870–1871
- ★ Battle sites

Map labels

RUSSIA

SWEDEN

Baltic Sea

DENMARK

North Sea

BRITAIN
- London

NETHERLANDS
- The Hague

BELGIUM
- LUXEMBOURG

FRANCE
- Sedan ★
- Amiens
- Paris
- Dieppe
- Metz
- Nancy
- Marne R.
- Seine R.

English Channel

SWITZERLAND

EAST PRUSSIA
- Königsberg
- Danzig

POMERANIA
- Stettin

POLAND
- Warsaw
- Posen
- Vistula R.

GALICIA
- Lemberg
- Cracow

BRANDENBURG
- Berlin
- Oder R.
- Neisse R.

SILESIA
- Breslau

SAXONY
- Dresden
- Leipzig

AUSTRIA
- Sadowa ★
- Prague
- Pilsen

BAVARIA
- Nuremberg
- Munich
- Danube R.
- Main R.

HOHENZOLLERN

WÜRTTEMBERG
- Stuttgart

BADEN

MECKLENBURG

HANOVER
- Hanover

ANHALT

THURINGIAN STATES

BRUNSWICK

WESTPHALIA
- Münster
- Essen

WALDECK

HESSE
- Cassel
- Darmstadt
- Frankfurt

NASSAU

UPPER HESSE

PALATINATE (to Bavaria)

LORRAINE

ALSACE
- Strasbourg

SCHLESWIG
- Kiel

HOLSTEIN

OLDENBURG

BREMEN
- Bremen
- Hamburg
- Lübeck

PRUSSIA

GERMANY

Helgoland (Br.)

Weser R.

Elbe R.

Rhine R.

Moselle R.

Ems R.

Cologne
- Coblenz

Scale

200 Miles
0   100   200

200 Kilometers
0   100   200

531

Unification of Germany, 1866–1871

Holstein but Hanover and other north German states as well. Most importantly, Bismarck also dissolved the Austrian–dominated German Confederation forged at Vienna in 1815 and organized a new North German Confederation dominated by Berlin.

The Franco–Prussian War of 1870–1871 climaxed this startling drive to power. Again, chance provided the opportunity. In a dispute over a possible Hohenzollern succession to the vacant throne of Spain, French politicians and journalists became alarmed over Hohenzollern "encirclement." The German claimant finally withdrew. But Bismarck turned this setback to his advantage by doctoring a dispatch from King William to sound as if his majesty had administered a stiff rebuke to the French. This *Ems Dispatch* (named for the resort town where the Prussian king made his remarks) enflamed French opinion and brought the war Bismarck had decided he needed.

Again the Prussian army performed like a well–oiled machine. Napoleon III, depending on tactics that had worked so well for his famous uncle half a century before, suffered one of the most ignominious defeats in French history at Sedan in the fall of 1870.

In 1871, the French ceded the two border provinces of Alsace and Lorraine and even agreed to pay a massive indemnity for the war Bismarck had started. More important, in the jubilation that greeted the Prussian triumph over France, the great national enemy, all the German states except Austria agreed to unification into a new German Empire to be headed by the king of Prussia. Declaration of the new empire by the assembled German princes at Louis XIV's palace of Versailles in the spring of 1871 dramatically signaled the end of one claim to Europewide preeminence and the birth of another.

Bismarck's Later Policies

The first decade of Bismarck's tenure as chief minister thus climaxed gloriously with the proclamation of the Hohenzollern empire. The next two decades were less dramatic but, by and large, no less successful for the German chancellor.

The Second Empire of the Germans—the first had been the medieval Holy Roman Empire—had a Reichstag, a legislature elected by universal male suffrage. Bismarck, however, kept a tight rein on this body, pressuring it or ignoring it at will. Liberal nationalists sometimes supported him and sometimes not; but he enjoyed the confidence of Emperor William I (r. 1871–1888), and that was what mattered. Bismarck's later struggles included famous battles against the Catholic church and the socialist parties of Germany, both of which he saw as adherents of international movements whose first loyalty was not to the German Empire. The *Kulturkampf* or spiritual struggle against Catholicism in southern Germany was typical of the anticlericalism of the time. It involved Bismarck's efforts to control church appointments, as well as attacks on Jesuits and conflicts over education and civil marriage. Despite some accommodations, however, the Kulturkampf was not a success: the German Catholic church stood firm and remained strong in the wake of the chancellor's onslaught.

The struggle with the socialists, on the other hand, looked more like a victory for Bismarck. In the wake of an attempt on William I's life for which they were blamed, the German socialist parties were suppressed for years. This accomplished, however, Bismarck himself sponsored a unique system of social welfare measures for German workers, the first such in Europe. He thus both suppressed and disarmed what he regarded as the "red menace." Socialism, too, however, survived the conservative leader's onslaught: by the eve of World War I, Germany had the largest block of socialist voters in Europe.

During the 1870s and 1880s, Bismarck also set himself the task of constructing a set of international alliances that would guarantee German security and, insofar as was possible, the peace of Europe. For twenty years, he did in fact keep France, the greatest enemy of the new Germany, diplomatically isolated. He also kept Austria and Russia, bitter rivals in the Balkans, from each others' throats. His most famous remark, like his spiked–helmet image, had a harsh and bloodthirsty tone: "The great questions of the day," he caustically explained to the legislature, "are not determined by speeches and majority votes, but by iron and blood."

We will return to Bismarck's alliance system when we examine its breakdown in the diplomatic reshuffling that led to World War I. In his own time, however, the iron chancellor did spend his later years working to keep the peace in a Europe in which there was at least one thoroughly satisfied power: the rich and powerful German Empire he had so largely forged himself.

◆The Evolving Americas◆

Nowhere were change and development more evident in the nineteenth century than in the new American nations across the Atlantic. Born in revolution, the United States and the Latin American countries continued to grow and to undergo drastic changes throughout the 1800s. The United States grew rapidly as it expanded across the continent and absorbed floods of immigrants in the 1800s. Federal victory in the American Civil War (1860–1865) solidified the Union, while the economic boom of the "gilded age" made the United States the world's most productive nation by 1900. The even newer nations of Latin America, meanwhile, developed less rapidly after independence in 1824. The southern republics faced a long period of political instability as local military leaders repeatedly rebelled against central governments.

Democracy and Division in the United States

A number of important issues dominated the history of the United States during the long first half of the nineteenth century, the six decades between the end of George Washington's presidency in 1797 and Abraham Lincoln's election in 1860. Among these were conflicts between national loyalty and sectionalism; the growth of political parties amid changing concepts of democracy; and such socio–economic trends as economic growth, territorial expansion, and a variety of social reform movements. Preeminent among the latter was the gnawing problem of black slavery in a nation that saw itself as a bastion of freedom in the world.

Three basic sections emerged: the industrial northeast, the plantation south, and the agrarian west. As the main industrial and financial center of the United States, the northeastern states supported a national bank and currency to encourage business activity, tariffs to protect American industry, and general economic integration—led by the northeast. In the southern states, growing demand for cotton to feed British and American textile mills produced a booming plantation economy, the so–called "cotton kingdom" worked by slave labor. Southerners therefore defended their "peculiar institution"—slavery—supported free trade with their British customers, and generally favored minimal federal interference in the affairs of the states. The largely agricultural west, finally, grew wheat, corn, tobacco, and livestock, both for its own use and for the northeastern regional market. Western interests therefore included free land for farmers in the endless western territories and improved transportation for access to eastern markets.

New England and the expanding west could agree on a grand compromise sometimes called the American System, an integrated economic structure with central financial institutions, a national currency (instead of a variety of currencies issued by local banks), federally financed turnpikes and canals, and tariff barriers to keep out cheap British imports. The south remained the odd man out, finding little in this compromise to suit its needs or satisfy its passion for the rights of separate states.

In the nation as a whole, meanwhile, the very concept of American democracy remained in flux during this period. As in Europe, the democratic ideal expanded to include a larger percentage of the American population. Thomas Jefferson (president 1801–1809), primary author of the Declaration of Independence and part of what was sometimes called the Virginia dynasty that produced Washington and other early leaders, envisioned a republic of independent landholding farmers. Because each freeholder would be able to support himself and his family on his own land, he would need little from the government and would be able to stand firm against tyranny. Andrew Jackson (president 1829–1837), a westerner and a hero of the War of 1812 against the British, enlarged this democratic vision. For Jackson, both the Virginia planters and the bankers and merchants of the northeast were American aristocrats. Jackson demanded a voice for "the common man," whom he saw as the true backbone of the nation. The crowds of rough frontier people, rude artisans, and ordinary farming folk who swarmed through the White House to celebrate his election looked far too democratic to supporters of the dignified republic of Washington and Jefferson.

Another major shift in the political system during the earlier 1800s was the emergence of political parties. The Constitution made no provision for them, and the founding fathers had deplored what they saw as factionalism. Yet as early as the 1790s, two factions were visible: Federalists supporting a strong central government and Jeffersonian Republicans, favoring minimal government power. By the 1820s, the Federalists were gone, and a party of Jacksonian Democrats had appeared, frankly committed to the *spoils system*, by which government jobs and other rewards naturally went to the party that won the election. In the 1850s, the Jeffersonian persuasion had given way to a new Republican party headed by Abraham Lincoln. Despite later changes, Democrats and Republicans would contest elections for the next century and a half. The *two–party system* found in many other English–speaking countries (as opposed to the multiparty system typical of continental European democracies) thus early took root in the United States.

During the 1830s and 1840s, which saw the revolutionary waves of 1830 and 1848 in Europe, militant campaigns for social reform also rocked the United States. There were drives for the reform of prisons and insane asylums, campaigns to limit the industrial working day to ten hours, and a sustained "temperance" campaign against drunkenness that succeeded in getting the sale of alcoholic beverages banned in a dozen states. Educational reformers like Horace Mann (1796–1859) convinced many states to establish systems of public higher education. And an early movement for equality between the sexes, led by Lucretia Mott (1793–1880) and Elizabeth Cady Stanton (1815–1902), convened the first Women's Rights Convention in Seneca Falls, New York, in 1848. The call of the *Seneca Falls convention* for basic property rights and improved education for women did lead to improvements in some states. But the convention's demand for political rights for women proved too radical even for the United States.

The most militant and divisive of these movements for social change, however, was the campaign for the abolition of slavery. One out of five Americans was a slave in 1800, and one out of seven remained enslaved at midcentury. Southern slaveowners saw the ancient institution as an economic necessity in the cotton kingdom. They also insisted that their slaves were better treated than northern factory workers, that the black race was naturally inferior and needed white supervision, and that their "hands" were quite happy with the simple tasks and pleasures of plantation life. *Abolitionists,* as agitators for the abolition of slavery became known, saw the use of slave labor as immoral, unchristian, and a blatant violation of the principles of freedom and equality for which the nation claimed to stand.

Leading abolitionists included fiery journalists like William Lloyd Garrison (1805–1879), escaped slaves like Frederick Douglass (1817–1895), Quakers, women's rights crusaders, and many others. Some abolitionists helped slaves escape to Canada via the *underground railway,* a chain of daring black liberators such as Harriet Tubman (c. 1820–1913) and northern sympathizers who hid the slaves and sent them on to freedom. Opponents and defenders of slavery fought in Congress and in the western territories over the admission of new states as "slave" or "free." In the 1850s, Harriet Beecher Stowe's (1811–1896) famous novel, *Uncle Tom's Cabin* (1851–1852), swung many into opposition to slavery. In 1859, a militant abolitionist named John Brown (1800–1859) attacked a federal arsenal at Harpers Ferry, Virginia, to secure weapons for a general slave revolt. Brown was captured and hanged, but to many he was a martyr to the abolitionist cause. And in the 1860s, what President Lincoln's secretary of state William H. Seward called "the irrepressible conflict" exploded into open civil war at last.

The Civil War and the Gilded Age

The United States came closest to a major midcentury reshaping in the Civil War of 1861–1865, the most costly of all American wars. Six hundred thousand Americans died in this ultimately fruitless attempt by the southern states to secede from the Union. In the aftermath, the south lay desolate, while the north roared into the greatest surge of industrialization and economic growth of the century, the gilded age of the later 1800s.

In 1860, Republican Abraham Lincoln, a lanky Illinois lawyer known for his antislavery views, was elected president of the United States. Southern leaders responded by declaring the secession of the South and the creation of a new nation, the Confederate States of America. Lincoln, determined to preserve the Union at all costs, refused to acknowledge the right of individual states to secede. When South Carolinians fired on Fort Sumter, a federal installation in Charleston harbor, the north mobilized to suppress the rebellion, the south to defend the Confederacy.

The south had many of the most skilled military commanders, the advantage of defending home ground, and a conviction that Britain and other countries where mills depended on southern cotton would support the Confederacy in the end. But the north had two or three times the population, wealth, factories, railroads, and ships. Britain did not rally to the south, but found other sources of cotton in its own vast empire. And in Abraham Lincoln, the north found one of the greatest leaders and most skilled politicians in American history.

Early southern victories could not overcome the north's massive advantages. The Union navy blockaded the coasts of the southern states, while Union armies wore down the Confederate forces. The high tide of Confederate fortunes came when Robert E. Lee (1807–1870), the south's commanding general, penetrated as far north as Gettysburg, Pennsylvania, in 1863, only to be turned back there in the bloodiest battle of the war. Southern armies soldiered on for two more years, but in 1865 Lee and other exhausted

Confederate generals surrendered, ending the attempt to divide the American nation into two sovereign states.

Within a week of Lee's surrender, President Lincoln was assassinated, leaving the country without his leadership during the disturbed period of "reconstruction" that followed the Civil War. During the struggle, the slaves had been freed, though without an allotment of land, so that most of them ended up working for low wages or a share of the crops on the same sort of southern plantation where they had once labored as slaves. The rest of the south, occupied and exploited by their northern conquerors, felt a bitterness and estrangement that lasted for generations. The south thus remained for the better part of a century the most underdeveloped and impoverished section of the country.

The rest of the United States, however, prospered after 1865. During the last third of the century, the northeast built an industrial system that became the most productive in the world, while the ongoing westward expansion swept triumphantly to the Pacific. Westward–moving pioneers had multiplied the amount of land under cultivation in the first half of the century. Further expansion brought new ore deposits as well as immense acreages of grazing and farming land into production as ranchers, miners, and homesteaders poured into the west. Railroads linked the nation from the Atlantic to the Pacific and became extremely profitable enterprises in their own right. The industrial, commercial, and financial growth of America's gilded age as a whole brought enormous wealth to tycoons like Andrew Carnegie (1835–1919) of U.S. Steel, John D. Rockefeller (1839–1937) of Standard Oil, and J. Pierpont Morgan (1837–1913), whose banking house attained international power. These captains of industry—some called them "robber barons"—often forced competitors into bankruptcy and drove their workers, many of them immigrants, as hard as they drove themselves. At the same time, however, the organizational and entrepreneurial skills of the Rockefellers and Carnegies did make a central contribution to the mushrooming wealth of the nation as a whole.

The end of the nineteenth century saw the United States become the world's leading agricultural and industrial power. Isolated still behind two oceans, the North American colossus was on the verge of asserting its preeminence as the twentieth century began.

Caudillos and Centralization in Latin America

The history of the Latin American republics to the south was in some ways similar to, in other ways quite different from, that of the United States. With the overthrow of Spanish rule in most of South and Middle America and the creation of a Brazilian Empire independent of Portugal, the southern half of the New World also seemed to be making a new start. As in North America and Europe, however, a change in government did not always mean a transformation of society. The Latin American Wars of Liberation (1810–1824) had eliminated the peninsular ruling class; but a victorious creole elite simply replaced European–born officials and church leaders as the ruling caste of the new republics. Commercial cities like Buenos Aires and Rio de Janeiro bred prosperous and increasingly powerful middle classes in the nineteenth century. Slavery was abolished in parts of South America before it was in the United States. But the large Indian, black, and peon elements in the population remained poor and exploited. The hacienda aristocracy of landowners and the Catholic church, with its unchallenged grip on the mind of the masses, retained their central place in Latin American society.

Economically, the Latin American countries continued to depend on the export of raw materials and agricultural goods and the importation of manufactured goods. Britain, rather than Spain or Portugal, was their most important trading partner. But this *dependency* on more developed nations remained a central feature of the Latin American economy.

New conflicts and new forces, however, did emerge from the Latin American revolutions. Many of the new countries, like the United States to the north, were torn by conflicts between central authority and local loyalties or regional powers. As in revolutionary France decades earlier, liberals tended to dominate the central governments, while traditional supporters of the church and the large landed estates called haciendas prevailed in the countryside. In sometimes bloody conflicts, constitutionalists and commercial elements in the capitals fought for strong government, while conservative landowners demanded autonomy for the distant provinces they dominated.

Out of the Wars of Liberation came perhaps the most distinctive feature of Latin American politics for the next century and a half: the power of the *caudillo*. The *caudillos* were war leaders, organizers of private armies of the sort that had defeated the royal troops during the revolutions. Often rooted in the local hacienda aristocracy, winning the support of the peons by personal favors and the promise of land, *caudillo* power nevertheless grew primarily out of the barrel of a gun. Most commonly rebels against the central governments, *caudillos* could become the most autocratic of dictators if their revolutions succeeded.

The major contribution of the *caudillos* to Latin American political history was to perpetuate the revolutionary tradition that saw bullets rather than ballots as the natural means of bringing about a change of government. In a larger socio–economic sense, however, these *caudillos* frequently spoke the language and sometimes advanced the interest of the rural masses more effectively than did the middle–class liberals of the cities. It was a dilemma that haunted Latin America thereafter: a conflict between liberal political institutions that ignored the economic needs of the majority, and the oppressive power of *caudillo* warlords, who often enjoyed the support of the *descamisados,* or "shirtless ones," the peasant masses of Latin America. Like the revolutionary ferment that began in Europe and North America in the decades around 1800, the Latin American Wars of Liberation were only a beginning to the two centuries of social change that followed.

♦The Drive for Social Change♦

Besides the reorganizing of central governments, the emergence of two new European great powers, and the development of the American republics, the 1800s produced a number of other broad efforts at restructuring Western society. Some of these drives for social change originated in governments, which now expanded drastically in size and assumed larger functions than ever before. Other movements for change, however, arose among the affected groups themselves, particularly among the growing numbers of industrial workers and increasingly militant women.

Such movements for change were to be found in all parts of Europe and the New World. Men gained the right to vote, women the right to work, and the poor access to public education. Whether instigated by a liberal like Gladstone or a conservative like Bismarck, by labor leaders or women's suffrage advocates, such efforts added up to a broad–gauge attempt to reorder Western society.

Social Reforms: Voting, Work, Education

We have already noted the extension of the suffrage to industrial and agricultural workers in Britain by the 1880s and the introduction of universal male suffrage in France as early as 1848. The new German Empire established universal manhood suffrage for its legislature in 1871, as did Austria in 1907, Italy in 1912, and a number of smaller countries during the same half–century.

The motives behind this key reform were often less ideological than practical and were sometimes purely opportunistic. Politicians of all persuasions favored an expanded suffrage when this expansion would give their own supporters—often factory workers or peasants— the right to vote. And many established political leaders saw the mass franchise as the only acceptable alternative to more violence in the streets.

Universal manhood suffrage, achieved in some places by the end of the century, did not transform the distribution of political power in the West. The working majority of Western people lacked the leisure, the money, and the knowledge and skills to plunge into politics. Middle– and upper–class leaders, often presenting themselves as the tribunes of the people, thus continued to fill most of the top spots in European government.

Still, the vote for the masses, coupled with memories of revolutions from 1789 to 1871, did make a difference. The massive political presence of "the people," enfranchised and increasingly organized politically, gave the rank–and–file citizenry an unprecedented weight in public discourse. In liberal western Europe, the votes of the people could make or break the careers of politicians, a fact that gave the people at least some veto power over the actions of their leaders.

Beyond suffrage reform, many of the new governmental functions involved intervention in the economic and social life of the state. In this, they represented a significant reversal of the laissez–faire policies of old–school liberalism, which had preached the virtues of strictly limited government. But humanitarian concerns on the one hand and fear of social upheaval on the other fostered a new spirit of activism in government. The problems created by industrialism, urban growth, and the population explosion required solutions that only the nation–state was in a position to provide. And the vast increase in state revenues generated by modern industrial society made an unheard–of level of public services financially affordable for the first time.

Government, for instance, moved to regulate working conditions in the new industrial system. Such intervention came first for children, then for women, and finally, around the end of the century, for men. Britain's pioneering Factory Act of 1833 prohibited the employment of children under nine in textile mills, and Britain made it illegal to employ women in mines in 1842. Not until 1909, however, did Britain legislate the eight–hour day for adult males, and then only for coal miners.

One new governmental function with an immense long–range potential for transforming Western life was public education. Traditionally, instruction in reading, writing, and arithmetic, normally accompanied by religious instruction, had gone primarily to favored groups in society—to aristocrats, guild members, or to those destined for the church. Most Europeans were thus illiterate at the beginning of the nineteenth century.

The new industrial economy, however, required more literate workers. Urbanization also encouraged mass education as a way of inculcating moral attitudes once taught by peasant families and village communities. Spreading secularism also shifted responsibility for education from the churches to the state, which valued schools as a means of fostering national loyalty.

Prussia created a system of primary schools as early as 1819, but most countries did not begin to require grammar schools in all communities until the 1870s. Tens of thousands of tax–supported public schools were built across Europe in the later nineteenth century. By 1900, free public education was almost universal in the more economically developed European nations. Secondary school and technical training institutions also flourished. The British private boarding school, the French *lycée*, and the German *Gymnasium* all provided rigorous classical educations for middle and upper–class children. Technical training in such Protestant countries as Prussia and Scotland produced large numbers of graduates with the skills needed for the industrial age.

Europe's universities, many of them medieval foundations, remained open only to a small minority of the social or intellectual elite. But education at this level, too, was more demanding than ever. German universities gained a special reputation for intellectual rigor. Enthusiasm for scholarly research spread from Germany, stimulating similar trends as far away as the United States.

The Labor Movement

Not all of these efforts to restructure important aspects of Western society, however, were the work of the governments. Two major drives for change surged up from the grass roots in the later nineteenth century: the labor movement and the women's movement.

The *labor movement,* or the organization of working people to defend their interests, was not an invention of the later nineteenth century, or even of the industrial age. Craft guilds established in the Middle Ages, though run by the guild masters, had channeled the militancy of working–class people even into the 1800s. Labor unions run by workers in the new industrial system had taken shape in the first half of the century, despite anticombination laws that made unions illegal in most places. Struggling against overwhelming odds to emancipate the laboring poor from brutal working conditions, ill health, and the hard life of slums or factory towns, early unions sometimes saw no hope for improvement without dismantling the entire system.

In the later 1800s, however, the situation changed. Labor unions were legalized in Germany in 1869, in Britain and Austria in the 1870s, in France in the 1880s, and even in Russia in 1906. Union membership grew rapidly during the depressed later decades of the century, giving workers' organizations more clout than ever before. In France, the number of unionized laborers grew from 140,000 in 1890 to over a million in 1912; in Britain, from 450,000 in 1876 to well over three million in 1912; and in Germany, from 300,000 in 1886 to 3,750,000 in 1912.

Paradoxically, as labor's power grew, its political militancy seemed to decline. Economically, the unions fought heroically for higher wages, shorter hours, and better working conditions. The number of strikes increased dramatically, and violence on both sides was not uncommon. But these "bread and butter" issues did increasingly replace the broader visions and wilder dreams of earlier decades. The moderate social democratic tendency among turn–of–the–century socialists was thus paralleled by more limited and practical goals in the labor movement. Labor leaders came to prefer a wage increase or safer working conditions today to dreams of a new social order tomorrow.

The labor movement thus entered the twentieth century still embattled and struggling. But it was bigger than it had ever been, and more willing to struggle within the prevailing social system for future gains.

The Women's Movement

The *women's movement,* meanwhile, was just building toward its major achievements as the nineteenth century ended. Organized later and drawing on an initially smaller pool of militants, workers for women's rights and female equality nevertheless laid the foundations of impressive gains in the next century.

Some basic progress was made simply through legal reform. Although a married woman's right to control property was granted in the U.S. state of Mississippi as early as 1839, most Western women did not get the basic legal right to control their own property until the 1880s. It was only after the turn of the century that a woman was legally permitted to sue for divorce on the same grounds as a man. Women also fought their way into European and American educational institutions during this period. Professional education for women training to become governesses for the children of the well–to–do was provided in Switzerland, Germany, and Britain in the 1840s. But male–dominated universities in many countries admitted women to their lecture halls only grudgingly in the later nineteenth century and in some cases refused to confer degrees on women for decades after they won the right to attend classes.

Beyond these rights to property and education, much of the women's movement of the later 1800s was a matter, not of organized pressure groups, but of decisions by determined individuals to break through the encrusted prejudice of centuries to achieve more rewarding lives for themselves. Careers in the professions, particularly law and medicine, were essentially closed to women at midcentury. By 1900, some women at least were earning degrees and practicing as lawyers and doctors. And yet, as late as 1913, Britain's chief medical journal rejected articles by women doctors as a matter of policy.

For some women, a new style of life accompanied these legal, educational, and economic breakthroughs. In Russia, the *"new woman"* emerged shortly after midcentury and became a European byword for up–to–the–minute radicalism. Earning her own living, dressing with defiant simplicity in an age of bustles and corsets, the Russian new woman smoked cigarettes and argued social and political questions over endless glasses of tea. She was also likely to be well represented in the ranks of the nihilists, *narodniki,* and other revolutionary groups, an ominous indication to conservatives of where the women's movement itself might lead.

The demand for a share of political power, however, required more than individual initiative and determination. Olympe de Gouges had demanded political rights for women in Europe as early as the 1790s. In the United States, the Seneca Falls Convention demanded the right to vote for women in 1848. In Latin America, Rosa Guerra championed "equality between both sexes" in her periodical *La Camelia* in the 1850s. "We are entering an era of liberty," she asserted confidently, "and there are no rights which exclude us!"[2]

The vote for women could be won only by the sort of organized pressure that was slowly winning that right for most Western males. Women's suffrage organizations emerged in Britain in the 1860s, in Germany, France, and elsewhere thereafter. Among Europe's outriders overseas, organized efforts began even earlier, in the United States as early as 1850, and not long thereafter in Australia.

The tactics of the *women's suffrage* crusade varied from country to country. In France, for instance, bourgeois women in quest of political rights early set a strategy based on commitment to the liberal Third Republic, to strict legality and "respectability." This approach did gain the French women activists more cooperation from male–run governments than other women's suffrage groups got. Such cooperation, however, stopped short of granting women the vote. In Germany, feminists cast their lot, not with liberalism and government, but with the socialist opposition—again, with poor results. Male German social democrats were no more likely than French republicans to match their egalitarian rhetoric with influential positions for women in the party. And like bourgeois liberal women in France, working–class socialist women in Germany often accepted the goals of the larger movement as primary. In Germany, the replacement of capitalism by socialism became the first objective, to which female political equality took second place. In practice, this meant little progress for women's suffrage.

In Britain, as in the United States, women fighters for political rights struck out on more militant and more single–mindedly feminist lines in the decades around 1900. The "suffragettes," as their opponents labeled them, began in the 1890s much as the Chartists had done before them, with public demonstrations, marches, and petitions to Parliament. After the turn of the century, however, the tactics of British suffragists became more militant. The public laughed when women's suffrage workers chained themselves to the House of Commons. But men waxed indignant when women interrupted political campaign speeches or debates in Commons to demand "Votes for Women!" And Victorian society in general was horrified when the suffragists smashed windows, dynamited buildings, or hurled themselves under the hooves of racing horses at the Grand National to draw attention to their cause. By focusing on feminist objectives and running their own movement, British women made a much more powerful impression than did women on the continent.

Before World War I, only New Zealand (1893), Finland (1906), and Norway (1913) had granted women the right to vote in national elections. Some state, provincial, or municipal voting rights had been granted in a number of countries, including Britain and the United States. And major victories for political equality did come in a rush immediately after World War I, accompanied by a new surge in women's social emancipation. But the organization and dedication had been mobilized in the nineteenth century, when most of the trends of the women's movement—legal, economic, social, and political—were laid down.

The Jews: Assimilation and Antisemitism

Another apparently fringe tendency with a terrible future was the rise of modern *antisemitism* in the later nineteenth century. A form of racism with deep roots in the past, prejudice against Jews in the Western world developed a disturbingly large popular following in the later 1800s.

Jewish history in the nineteenth century may be seen as two separate but oddly converging histories. In western and central Europe, Jewish history was an impressive success story. Jews found a congenial environment in the liberal capitalist society of the mid–nineteenth–century West. Many of them became prominent in business, the professions, and politics.

As they rose in society, some Western Jews ceased to practice their religion and sought assimilation into the German, Austrian, French, or other population among which they lived and prospered. Some modified their names, mixed with the best Gentile society, and even converted to Christianity. Other Jews clung to their cultural identity and even began to talk about returning to "Zion," their long–lost homeland in Palestine. Whether they moved toward assimilation or Zionism, however, these successful Jews remained an identifiable—and enviable—subgroup in Western society.

More strikingly distinct and far more alien–seeming to most Europeans were the large numbers of east European Jews, many of whom migrated into central and western Europe

Alfred Dreyfus, shown here in the uniform of the French army, survived his long years in France's penal colony on Devil's Island with remarkable courage and dignity. But the struggle between pro- and anti-Dreyfusards tore the fabric of French society. (Culver Pictures, Inc.)

from the 1880s on. Still forbidden to own land in Russia and Poland, Jews there had made their living as they could, as small-scale dealers, peddlers, or moneylenders to the peasantry. Their Christian neighbors in these regions often saw them, not only as hereditary foes of Christianity, but as exploiters who thrived off those to whom they sold cheap goods or lent money at substantial interest. In the 1880s, Christians blamed them for everything from the depression to the assassination of Czar Alexander II in 1881. And the reactionary Russian government of Alexander III (r. 1881–1894) launched a wave of persecution that confined Jews to a zone called the Pale of Residence in the Ukraine and White Russia, curtailed their educational opportunities, and sponsored pogroms—organized massacres of Jews.

Thus assaulted once more, many Jews packed up and moved west to settle in the urban ghettos of central and western Europe. Frequently speaking Yiddish—a mixture of Hebrew, Slavic, and German words—rather than the language of their new homelands, many of the new immigrants were rigorously orthodox in their religious practices, costume, and dietary regulations. These ghetto Jews further reinforced the popular impression of an alien presence among increasingly nationalistic Germans, French, and other Europeans.

The resulting antisemitic feeling took a variety of forms in the turn-of-the-century decades. Conservatives were still capable of seeing Jews as enemies of Christianity and of traditional values, as the secret force behind everything from anticlericalism to women's emancipation. Liberals saw Jewish defense of their cultural identity as a rejection of the liberal belief in the fundamental unity and similarity of all human beings. Socialists sometimes saw Jews as an embodiment of capitalist exploitation, whether as international financiers like the celebrated Rothschild family or as local pawnbrokers in some slum neighborhood. Most notoriously, racists added pseudoscientific charges of Jewish biological inferiority and fear of "race mixing" to the antisemitic brew. This redefining of a religious minority with a distinctive cultural tradition as a "race" reflected the popularity of racial analysis in an era of growing enthusiasm for biological and genetic studies. As we will see, it had terrible consequences in the next century.

In Russia in the nineteenth century, city mobs and illiterate peasants could still be roused to assaults on Jewish neighborhoods by such wild medieval charges as ritual murder of Christian children. In Austria, the very modern demagogue Mayor Karl Lüger of Vienna rode the antisemitic prejudices of his lower–middle–class and working–class constituents to power in the 1880s and 1890s. And in France, the most celebrated—and debated—instance of antisemitism of all split the nation through the 1890s: the Dreyfus affair.

The *Dreyfus case* was at one level a fascinating detective story. A Jewish officer in the French army, Captain Alfred Dreyfus (1859–1935) was convicted in 1894 of being a German spy, a crime for which he was sentenced to the living hell of the French penal colony of Devil's Island. Evidence subsequently emerged, however, that Dreyfus had been framed and that his conviction had been justified by forged documents. The forger committed suicide, and Dreyfus was pardoned, later exonerated, and even reinstated in the army. Meanwhile, however, the Third Republic had been brutally divided by the public struggle between Dreyfusards and anti–Dreyfusards.

Whether Captain Dreyfus's Jewishness was originally central to his persecution has been much debated in recent years. Anti–German feeling in France may well explain initial willingness to believe in German agents in the French military. But the long struggle that followed Dreyfus's first conviction clearly laid bare older prejudices. Supporters of the French Catholic church and the aristocratic French officer corps hated Dreyfus as a Jewish outsider. They saw his supporters, prominent among them the muckraking French novelist Emile Zola, as the vanguard of the anticlerical and unpatriotic elements in the Third Republic whom the right wing despised. Even historians who see antisemitism as less than central to the case admit that "Dreyfus was denied justice" in the long run "because he was Jewish."[3]

Racism in general and antisemitism in particular were on the rise in 1900. They were among the most bitter of the legacies of the nineteenth century to the twentieth.

Summary

The second half of the nineteenth century saw major political changes in all the great powers of the Western world. During the period between 1848 and 1914, Britain underwent a remarkable era of democratic and social reform, and the French Empire of Napoleon III was transformed into the Third French Republic. In addition, Austria loosened the reins on its multinational empire, and Russia survived a hectic period of reform and radical conspiracy under Alexander II, the czar who freed the serfs but was killed by a terrorist bomb.

Meanwhile, two new great powers emerged in Europe as Bismarck's Prussia unified Germany and Cavour's Piedmont orchestrated the unification of Italy. In the United States, however, an attempt by the southern states to secede from the Union was frustrated in a bloody Civil War. Latin America, for its part, experienced continuing conflict between central governments and provincial *caudillos.*

Democratic and social reforms proliferated during this half–century. The right to vote was extended to the brink of universal male suffrage, working conditions improved, and public education and pensions were made available to all citizens. The labor movement grew more powerful as unions were legalized, and the women's movement focused on demands for the right to vote that, in many parts of the Western world, was won early in the following century. Europe's Jewish minority faced both slow assimilation and intermittent persecution as the century ended.

Some Key Terms

abolitionists 535	*Kulturkampf* 532	Seneca Falls convention 534
antisemitism 541	labor movement 539	spoils system 534
caudillo 537	*narodnik* 527	Third Republic 526
dependency 537	new woman 540	two–party system 534
Dreyfus case 543	Paris Commune 525	underground railway 535
Dual Monarchy 526	*Realpolitik* 528	women's movement 540
Ems dispatch 532	Redshirts 529	women's suffrage 540

Notes

1. Quoted in Raymond Grew, *A Sterner Plan for Italian Unity: The Italian National Society in the Risorgimento* (Princeton, N.J.: Princeton University Press, 1963), 10.
2. Rosa Guerra, quoted in Lidia Falcon, *Mujer y Sociedad* (Barcelona: Fontanella, 1973), 186.
3. Robert L. Hoffman, *More Than a Trial: The Struggle over Captain Dreyfus* (New York: Free Press, 1980), 208.

Reading List

Beales, D. *The Risorgimento and the Unification of Italy.* London: Longman, Green, 1982. Judicious weighing of the factors involved. On Cavour's diplomatic intrigue, see A. Blumberg, *A Carefully Planned Accident: The Italian War of 1859* (Selingsgrove, N.J.: Susquehanna Press, 1990).

Bolt, C. *The Women's Movements in the United States and Britain from the 1790s to the 1930s.* Amherst: University of Massachusetts, 1993. Common issues and patterns of development. See also O. Banks, *Faces of Feminism: A Study of Feminism as a Social Movement* (New York: St. Martin's Press, 1981).

Chapman, G. *The Dreyfus Case: A Reassessment.* Westport, Conn.: Greenwood Press, 1979. Reexamines the complex of motives that turned a charge of espionage into an issue that divided a nation.

Coontz, S. *The Social Origins of Private Life: A History of American Families, 1600–1900.* New York: Verso, 1988. Penetrating survey of American families from colonial times through the nineteenth century.

Edwards, S. *The Paris Commune of 1871.* London: Eyre and Spottiswoode, 1971. The revolt that shocked the Western world—and that has been debated ever since.

Elwitt, S. *The Third Republic Defended: Bourgeois Reform in France, 1880–1914.* Baton Rouge:

Louisiana State University Press, 1988. Bourgeois reform as defense against social radicalism.

Hamerow, T. *The Birth of a New Europe: State and Society in the Nineteenth Century.* Chapel Hill: University of North Carolina Press, 1983. Impressive history of Europe between 1815 and 1914, building on economic and social foundations. For a good case study, see R. McLeod, ed., *Government and Expertise: Specialists, Administrators, and Professionals, 1860–1919* (New York: Cambridge University Press, 1988). On the growth of Victorian bureaucracy.

Holton, S. S. *Feminism and Democracy: Women's Suffrage and Reform Politics in Britain, 1900–1918.* New York: Cambridge University Press, 1986. Fits the women's movement into the pattern of the labor movement and other movements for social change. See also P. W. Romero, *E. Sylvia Pankhurst: Portrait of a Radical* (New Haven: Yale University Press, 1987), on the feminist leader, and, on posters and other movement art, L. Ticknor, *The Spectacle of Women: Imagery of the Suffrage Campaign, 1907–1914* (Chicago: University of Chicago Press, 1988).

Kaelble, H. *Industrialization and Social Inequality in Nineteenth Century Europe.* Translated by B. Little. New York: St. Martin's Press, 1986. Raises the question of whether the Industrial Revolution increased the gap between rich and poor. For a closer look at nineteenth-century slum life, see W. J. Fishman, *East End, 1888: Life in a London Borough Among the Laboring Poor* (Philadelphia: Temple University Press, 1988).

Lincoln, W. B. *The Great Reforms: Autocracy, Bureaucracy, and the Politics of Change in Imperial Russia.* DeKalb: Northern Illinois University Press, 1990. Analysis of the pattern of reform centering around Alexander II's emancipation of the serfs.

May, A. J. *The Habsburg Monarchy, 1867–1914.* Cambridge, Mass.: Harvard University Press, 1951. Older brief treatment. See also R. A. Kann, *The Multinational Empire* (New York: Octagon, 1964), which surveys the nationalities and Habsburg policies toward them.

Meinecke, F. *The German Catastrophe.* Boston: Beacon, 1963. Good German evaluation of "what went wrong" in the forging of the German state.

Mommson, W. J., and H. G. Husung, eds. *The Development of Trade Unionism in Great Britain and Germany, 1880–1914.* Boston: Allen and Unwin, 1985. Sees important similarities between labor unions in the leading industrial nations of Europe.

Neely, M. E. *The Last Best Hope of Earth: Abraham Lincoln and the Promise of America.* Cambridge: Harvard University Press, 1993. Highly praised brief study. For the Jackson era, see another short study, D. B. Cole, *The Presidency of Andrew Jackson* (Lawrence: University of Kansas Press, 1993).

Nord, P. G. *Paris Shopkeepers and the Politics of Resentment.* Princeton, N.J.: Princeton University Press, 1986. Lower middle–class political views, both reactionary and radical. Compare with D. Blackbourn and R. J. Evans, eds., *The German Bourgeoisie: Essays on the Social History of the German Middle Class from the Late Eighteenth to the Early Nineteenth Century* (London: Routledge, 1991). For an analytical comparative study of Germany, France, England, and the United States, see M. Mann, *The Sources of Social Power: The Rise of Classes and Nation States, 1760–1914* (New York: Cambridge University Press, 1993).

Pflanze, O. *Bismarck and the Development of Germany.* 3 vols. Princeton, N.J.: Princeton University Press, 1990. Major work on the iron chancellor. See also the older classic, E. Eyck, *Bismarck and the German Empire* (New York: Norton, 1964).

Schorske, C. E. *Fin-de-Siècle Vienna: Politics and Culture.* New York: Random House, 1981. Sophisticated analysis of the subtle interaction between cultural change and politics.

Smith, D. M. *Italy: A Modern History.* Ann Arbor: University of Michigan Press, 1959. Older but standard account. For the conflict between realist and idealist, see his *Cavour and Garibaldi* (Cambridge: Cambridge University Press, 1954).

Weber, E. *Peasants into Frenchmen: The Modernization of Rural France, 1870–1914.* Palo Alto, Calif.: Stanford University Press, 1976. Important contribution to the literature on the history of the peasantry in modern Europe.

Wertheimer, J. *Unwelcome Strangers: East European Jews in Imperial Germany.* New York: Oxford University Press, 1987. On the causes of Jewish migration, see I. M. Aronson, *Troubled Waters: The Origins of the 1881 Anti-Jewish Pogroms in Russia* (Pittsburgh: University of Pittsburgh Press, 1990).

22

Byron's Heart, Darwin's Ape, and Van Gogh's Ear

Romanticism, Materialism, and Nonrationalism

◆Romanticism: The Triumph of the Heart
◆Materialism: The Triumph of Reality   ◆The New Nonrationalism

Nineteenth–century culture both reflected and reacted against larger trends and currents in Western civilization. Three major movements may be detected in the 1800s: the rise of romanticism, which actually began as early as 1775; a materialist challenge that took shape around 1850; and a resurgence of romantic nonrationalism that was in full flower in the 1890s. Terms like "rise," "challenge," and "resurgence" reveal a pattern of conflict and cultural groping through the century—a search for forms and values appropriate to an age of bewildering change.

Romanticism began about the time of the American and French Revolutions as a revolutionary movement in the arts. At a basic level, it was a revolt of writers, artists, and composers who defied the classical rules that limited their artistic freedom. But these artistic rebels also reacted more generally against Enlightenment confidence in reason, urging the primacy of human feeling instead. Turning their backs on icy rationality, they thrilled to the beauty of nature and responded to both art and life with the powerful emotions we have come to call "romantic."

The emergence of philosophical materialism and of realism in the arts around midcentury corresponded with the rise of Darwinism and other scientific challenges to orthodox thinking. These related trends in art and thought also grew out of a more widespread awareness of the transforming effect of the Industrial Revolution on society. Novelists wrote about coal mines; artists painted railroad engines. Realistic authors and painters also self–consciously challenged what they saw as the sentimentality of their romantic predecessors.

The last decades of the century, finally, saw yet another upheaval in Western culture. Nonrationalists agreed with the romantics on the importance of emotionality, but, like the materialists, they saw human feelings rooted in human biology. The nonrationalists of the late nineteenth century were fascinated by Freud's assertion that the real source of human behavior lay in unconscious emotional drives and intrigued by Nietzsche's claim that God did not exist at all.

A violent, skewing seesaw of a cultural century, this hundred years will take us from Byron's poetic vision of a woman who "walks in beauty" through Darwin's biological view of humanity's ape–like ancestors to the hallucinatory paintings of Vincent van Gogh, known to generations of gallery–goers as the artist who cut off his own ear.

✦Romanticism: The Triumph of the Heart✦

Romanticism was a revolt in the arts that glorified the emotions and produced new attitudes toward the natural, social, and supernatural worlds in which we live. As one of the great cultural upheavals of modern times, the romantic movement—which we may date roughly as 1775–1850—produced colorful art, passionate music, and literature that challenged all the rules. Romantics exalted individual emotions, discovered modern social alienation, and felt themselves to be almost mystically in tune with the infinite. All these feelings, furthermore, carried over into later generations. If many of us today have a touch of the romantic in our makeup, we came by it honestly, as a major, living legacy from our nineteenth–century predecessors.

The Primacy of Emotion

The search for emotional understanding was central to the romantic view, which has been defined as "the spirit of seeking and adventure . . . overflowing all boundaries."[1] As a movement in the arts, romanticism was clearly a rebellion against some of the main currents of the preceding century. Romantics revolted against the eighteenth–century Enlightenment, with its classical rules for the arts, its admiration for science, and its underlying confidence in human reason. Romantic artists gloried in their originality and saw all true art as the product of a unique creative personality: classical rules and models, they declared, merely inhibited the free play of the individual genius.

Rationally formulated rules, furthermore, ran contrary to the emotional qualities romantics regarded as the essence of human nature. The mathematically defined natural laws of the scientific revolution thus failed to convince the romantic sensibility. Indeed, the fundamental rationalism of Western thought, from Plato to Newton, seemed to the romantics to be a dry, thin, thoroughly unsatisfying approach to understanding the pulsing realities of life in this world.

In place of reason as the primary instrument for comprehending the universe and our place in it, the romantic spirit preferred human feelings. Among the emotions that particularly moved them were "romantic" love, sensitivity to beauty, the human will, the melancholy spirit, and an all but indefinable longing for the infinite. Love between the sexes filled the poetry, plays, and fiction of the romantics and provided a theme for romantic painting and music. Indeed, love was so central a subject for romantic writers that the very word "romantic" has come to mean "of or pertaining to sexual love."

Enthusiasm for beauty, natural as well as artistic, was a scarcely less defining characteristic of the movement. Romantics gloried in poetry, music, and painting, yet also felt their hearts beat faster at the sight of a rainbow, a drifting cloud, or a field full of wildflowers. Some romantics also felt a powerful admiration for the power of a Napoleonic will to impose itself upon the world and sometimes saw in themselves a similar superhuman will power. Many were gripped by melancholy, a sadness or depression that might be triggered by personal misfortune—failure in love, for instance—or by disillusionment with the age in

Chronology 22: Romanticism, Materialism, Nonrationalism

1798	*Wordsworth's and Coleridge's* Lyrical Ballads *celebrate simple peasant hearts*
1818	*Byron's* Don Juan *incarnates hero as romantic wanderer*
1829	*Chopin's debut introduces new kind of romantic music*
1830	*Delacroix's* Liberty Leading the People, *a romantic painting hailing the Revolution of 1830*
1844	*Dumas's* Three Musketeers—*the romantic swashbucklers in action*
1847	*Emily Bronte's* Wuthering Heights—*lost romantic lovers in a wild romantic setting*
1850	*Courbet's* The Stonebreakers *realistically showcases life of the working poor*
1859	*Darwin's* Origin of Species *raises furor over theory of biological evolution*
1866	*Dostoyevsky's* Crime and Punishment *follows a youthful criminal into lower depths of St. Petersburg*
1871–1893	*Zola's* Rougon–Macquart *series traces lives of French people of all classes, seen as products of biology and environment*
1874	*First Impressionist show paints light, not things*
1885	*Nietzsche's* Zarathustra *announces the "death of god"*
1885–1890	*Van Gogh's major paintings reflect his tortured spirit*
1895	*Freud's* Studies on Hysteria *sees unconscious drives at heart of human psyche*

which they lived. Despite the anguish it brought, however, romantics valued melancholy as the sign of a sensitive soul, fully aware of the dark, even tragic side of life.

Most difficult to define of all, finally, was the romantic longing for "something more" than everyday life had to offer. The "something" might be distant lands—the Near East, North Africa, or the wilderness of the New World—or olden times, more likely the Renaissance or the Middle Ages than Greek or Roman antiquity. "Something more" could also be a better world than this, a free republic or a unified nation won on the barricades or a utopian socialist community to retreat to. Or it could be completely undefined, conceived of only symbolically as "the blue flower," the open road, or the spiritual core of the universe. Alienated from the grubby world of business, hating the official tyranny and corruption they saw on all sides, romantics felt themselves to be in tune with the cosmos if not with the times.

The Romantic Worldview

No single romantic heart could contain all these passions, at least not at one time. But taken together, they did give romantics a very different view of things. The world they wanted to live in—through art if not in reality—was a much more exciting one than that of the average getting–and–spending citizen. Bubbles on a brook and blowing flowers in a field, a moonlit forest, sunset flaming on Alpine crags or green islands in a southern sea all stirred the romantic heart. The color of a Near Eastern bazaar, the shimmering deserts of Africa, and the banks of the far Mississippi kindled a desire to escape from the everyday life of an increasingly bourgeois Europe. For the novelist Sir Walter Scott, it might be a medieval castle or a Scottish glen; for the poet Samuel Taylor Coleridge, it might be Xanadu, Kubla Khan's "pleasure dome" in far Cathay.

The people of those exotic places also inspired admiration in the romantic breast. Simple peasants and noble savages, Gypsies, bandits, Barbary pirates, and harem beauties populated romantic literature and art, crowding out the boringly respectable citizens one met in nineteenth–century drawing rooms. These were people who, in the romantic imagination at least, lived more virtuous or more exciting lives, who experienced life more directly through the emotions than the average nineteenth–century European. The naive vision of the peasant or the South Sea islander, the passions of the pirate or the pasha embodied the qualities romantics most admired and longed to share.

Around and beyond this world of the far away and long ago, there was for many romantics another world entirely: the mystical realm of the supernatural. Rejected as rank superstition by the Enlightenment, many forms of folk belief and spiritual vision were accepted by the romantic imagination as fit subjects for art and even as dimensions of reality. Ghosts and demons, nature spirits and fairy tale creatures had at least symbolic truth. From the Devil who tempted Goethe's Faust to the gods and mermaids of Wagner's *Ring* cycle of operas, from the deathless *Frankenstein* (1818) of Mary Wollstonecraft Shelley's (1797–1851) novel to the fairy tales collected in peasant cottages by the brothers Grimm, supernatural beings abounded in romantic literature and art. And some romantics experienced what they believed was a pantheistic spiritual presence infusing the natural world they loved, or felt the mystic presence of a transcendent God. Like William Blake (1757–1827), the late eighteenth–century mystical poet and artist, they longed:

> To see a World in a Grain of Sand,
> And a Heaven in a Wild Flower,
> Hold Infinity in the palm of your hand,
> And Eternity in an hour.[2]

The natural world, approached emotionally and intuitively rather than rationally, was thus a gateway to the infinite. Other such gateways were dreams, drug–induced experiences, and visionary trances, all seen, not as delusions, but as openings to a world beyond our own. Long before Freud laid out a scientific theory in which dreams were keys to self–understanding, the romantic movement was willing to entertain the ancient view that the dream life actually offered revelations of truths higher than those available to the waking mind.

Romantic Rebellion in Literature

The romantic movement is usually seen as beginning in the later eighteenth century and as flourishing throughout the first half of the nineteenth. Romanticism got its name from the fact that some early romantics were fascinated with the colorful chivalric romances of the Middle Ages. It was in fact an artistic insurrection, the first of an increasing number of such rebellions in the arts. Romanticism touched all the arts; but if the central medieval art was cathedral architecture and the most influential Renaissance artist a painter, so the archetypal romantic was a poet—a young lyric poet, pouring out his innermost feelings in passionate verse.

A galaxy of famous names from Germany, Britain, and France will illustrate the type. Such an overview will also indicate the extent to which history, as usual, defies such stereotyping.

Jean–Jacques Rousseau, one of the leading philosophes, published books with very romantic themes, exalting love in *The New Héloïse* (1761), nature in *Émile* (1762), and his own passionate life and towering ego in his *Confessions,* written in the later 1760s.

German central Europe produced a highly emotional literary upheaval, the *Sturm und Drang* (Storm and Stress) movement, beginning as early as the 1770s. Johann Wolfgang von Goethe's novel *The Sorrows of Young Werther* (1774) and Friedrich Schiller's play *The Robbers* (1781) exalted individual freedom, love, nature, and simple country people—all to be features of the romanticism of the next century. And while Goethe, "the Olympian," transcended any movement, his epic *Faust* (1808, 1831) is often cited as a masterful evocation of romantic passion, aspiration, and strife. The bargain the aged scholar Faust strikes with the Devil—Faust's soul in return for his youth restored, for love, beauty, and power—was one any romantic would gladly make.

The English romantic poets William Wordsworth (1770–1850) and Samuel Taylor Coleridge (1772–1834) published their most influential work, *Lyrical Ballads* (1798), while they were still in their twenties. Announcing a revolt against the high–flown poetic diction and rigorously patterned verse forms of the eighteenth century, Wordsworth and Coleridge dedicated themselves to exploring the beauties of nature and the uncorrupted hearts of country people. The English romantic poets of the next generation took up all these themes. They added sensitivity to the beauty of art itself, as in the work of John Keats (1795–1821), whose assertion that "beauty is truth" expressed an intense romantic conviction.

In George Gordon, Lord Byron (1780–1824), Britain produced the most admired of all the romantics. Handsome, brilliant, of noble birth, Byron also bore the mark of mortal suffering in a romantic limp. His poetry often featured "Byronic" heroes, mysterious, socially outcast young men, bearing a dark secret and doomed to an early death. Romantically linked with a number of ladies, a political radical who rejected "all existing governments," and a wanderer in exotic Mediterranean lands from Italy to Turkey, Byron himself lived a life that seemed to embody the love of nature, women, and freedom expressed in his epic *Don Juan* and in lyrics like "She Walks in Beauty":

> She walks in beauty, like the night
> Of cloudless climes and starry skies;
> And all that's best of dark and bright
> Meet in her aspect and her eyes.[3]

Like both Keats, who died of tuberculosis, and Shelley, who was drowned at sea, Byron did in fact die young of exposure and exhaustion in Greece, where he had gone to lend his support to the Greek revolution. It seemed to cap a defiantly romantic life with an ideal romantic death—fighting for freedom.

The remarkable Brontë sisters—Charlotte (1816–1855), Emily (1818–1848), and Anne (1820–1849)—who lived almost all their lives in the village parsonage of Haworth on the Yorkshire moors, were as wildly romantic in their way as the amoral, far–traveling Byron. Romantic elements filled their cloistered lives, reflected in the fairy tale realms they invented and chronicled endlessly in their childhood, the novels they published, and the poignant contrast between their trapped, isolated lives and early deaths and the soaring imaginations they nurtured in their tiny Yorkshire village.

The Brontës' novels were clearly infused with the spirit of nineteenth–century romanticism. Charlotte Brontë's *Jane Eyre* (1847) brings together such romantic characters and themes as an isolated, struggling governess for a heroine, a haunted Byronic hero, a mansion with a dark secret, madness, tragedy, and love finally triumphant. And in *Wuthering Heights* (1847), Emily Brontë forged a poetic and powerful fiction of the highest order. Deeply infused with a romantic sense of place and of the furious emotions of childhood, the book centers on the doomed love and tortured lives of the passionate Catherine and the outcast Heathcliff, two of the most vivid personalities in English literature—and both towering incarnations of the romantic spirit.

The romantic movement also flourished in France. The swashbuckling novels of Alexandre Dumas (1802–1870)—*The Three Musketeers* (1844), *The Count of Monte Cristo* (1845)—incarnated the romantic spirit of adventure for generations of readers. And the romantic novelist George Sand (1804–1876) filled her fiction with love of the countryside and simple village people that touched the heart of an international audience. But it was the wide–ranging genius of Victor Hugo (1820–1885) that dominated the French romantic movement through the 1830s and 1840s.

Victor Hugo managed to defy literary convention successfully in poetry, drama, and fiction throughout his long life. Hugo's immense drama *Cromwell* (1827)—significantly, about a revolutionary—included a preface denouncing the classical dramatic canons of unity of time, place, and action. His colorful *Hernani* (1830) set off violent altercations in the theater itself over its unconventional verse and structure. His novel *Notre Dame de Paris* (1831), familiar in English as *The Hunchback of Notre Dame,* evoked a colorful medieval world that never was, while his *Les Misérables* (1862) depicted the sufferings of the poor, the injustice of modern society, and the heroism of youthful revolutionaries. His lyric poetry, widely admired for its flowing beauty, also had political bite enough to get him expelled from France during the reign of Napoleon III, whom Hugo scathingly contrasted with his uncle the great Napoleon by dubbing him "Napoleon the little."

Art Full of Action and Color

In painting and music, romanticism blazed even more startling new trails toward the tumult of twentieth–century art. Even philosophy reflected the mood of these decades of emotional response to change.

Romantic artists rejected the classical emphasis on ancient or noble subjects, on balanced composition, and on meticulously accurate drawing with a decorous touch of color laid on as an afterthought. Instead, they found new excitement in medieval or "oriental" (Near Eastern or North African) themes and in contemporary or humble subjects. Stylistically, they emphasized rich color and dynamic composition, aiming at an art full of visual excitement and human feeling.

In France, Théodore Géricault (1791–1824) and Eugène Delacroix (1798–1863) vividly illustrated these trends. Both used swirling motion and bright colors to heighten the emotional impact of their work. Géricault's *Raft of the Medusa,* highlighting a tangled heap of human bodies on a life raft after a recent disaster at sea, and Delacroix's famous allegorical celebration of *Liberty Leading the People* over the barricades of 1830 probed subjects of powerful contemporary relevance in the vibrant new style. In Britain, the work of John Constable (1776–1837) and J. M. W. Turner (1775–1851) brought the natural world to life with a new conviction and brilliance. Constable's paintings of peaceful country scenes were not classic pastorals but living representations of fields, farms, hay wagons, and farm animals. Turner brought all the romantic enthusiasm for color and movement to his glowing images of sunsets or moonlight, storm or fire at sea. Indeed, luminous seascapes like *The Slave Ship* were studies of light itself, pointing the way to the impressionist movement to come.

Music from Beethoven to Bayreuth

Romanticism dominated music throughout the 1800s. In accomplishing their goal of stirring or shattering their hearers emotionally, romantic composers and performers expanded the range of sound production available to them, as painters were broadening the palette and writers the permissible forms of literature. The modern symphony orchestra emerged three times as large as the genteel eighteenth–century chamber orchestra, with woodwinds, brasses, and percussion instruments added to an expanded number of strings. The piano became the solo instrument par excellence, and mass–produced steel–stringed Steinways began to find their way into many middle–class homes. Operas were staged more splendidly than ever, and instrumental and choral music shifted from churches and aristocratic salons to large public concert halls, where the bourgeoisie could join the elite in being ravished by glorious sound. Outdoor "promenade" concerts, bandstands in public parks, and urban music halls made it possible for the masses to enjoy lighter music, from popular oom–pah–pah marches and Strauss waltzes to the operettas of Gilbert and Sullivan.

For concert goers and opera enthusiasts, the century produced some of the most splendid music in Western history. Ludwig van Beethoven (1770–1827) combined classical seriousness of purpose and intricacy of form with romantic range and passion to produce musical effects of unprecedented power. His music for strings and piano, his nine symphonies and single opera stunned contemporaries. Some of his music was so far ahead of its time that only later students could appreciate its innovative brilliance. Tragedy also struck Beethoven, as it did so many romantics: in his later years, he endured the ultimate catastrophe for a composer—deafness. With the Promethean courage of the great romantics, however, he defied his affliction and went on composing, overwhelming audiences with avalanches of sound that he himself would never hear.

Frédéric Chopin's (1810–1849) piano music was often composed in a frenzy of emotion, incorporating the longing and love he felt for his native Poland, from which he was exiled for much of his productive life. The *Lieder* (Songs) of Franz Schubert (1797–1828) evoked a wide range of emotions, though his dominant mode was one of melancholy and longing, the romantic's longing for "something more."

In opera, Giuseppe Verdi (1813–1901), Gioacchino Rossini (1792–1868), and Giacomo Puccini (1858–1924) epitomized the strong emotional and melodic appeal of the Italian school. You could hum their tunes on your way home from the opera house; Italians even sang them aloud in the streets. Verdi's themes—mysterious Egypt in *Aïda,* the hopeless love of a bourgeois youth for a doomed courtesan in *La Traviata*—had the romantic appeal of the colorful past and the wicked underside of contemporary life. In Richard Wagner (1813–1883), meanwhile, German opera produced a titan whose vast interlocking conceptions mingled all the arts in "musical dramas" beyond the reach of many, then or now. Drawing on the myths and legends of ancient or medieval Germans, Wagner's *Parsifal, Lohengrin,* and his immense cycle of operas *The Ring of the Niebelungs* found their ideal setting in the special theater that he built at Bayreuth, where his works are still staged, to international acclaim, today.

Philosophy in the Romantic Age

Religious thought, out of favor during the Enlightenment, found a new audience among the romantics, especially during the religious revival that occurred after 1815. The Danish Protestant thinker Soren Kierkegaard (1813–1855), though he criticized romanticism, was himself an emotionally tortured soul whose religious vision began with a dark view of the human condition. Kierkegaard was racked by the anguish and dread that the twentieth century called "existential," an anguish rooted in the nature of human existence itself. In Kierkegaard's view, humanity suffered from a spiritual disease that religious faith alone could cure. Arthur Schopenhauer (1788–1860) offered a different and even darker vision of the human condition. In Schopenhauer's godless universe, all things, including human beings, were creatures of irrational will. We are driven by the will to live, but also by obscure passions that life cannot in fact satisfy. For human will was pure desire, a compulsive psychological drive without any real end or object at all. Humans were thus condemned by their own desperate willfulness to a life of unsatisfied desire.

G. F. W. Hegel (1770–1831), Kant's greatest successor in the German idealist line of thought and author of such intricately reasoned works as *The Phenomenology of the Spirit* (1807) and *The Science of Logic* (1812–1816), is at one level the most rational of philosophers. But his central concern with human consciousness and human history, his focus on process and conflict, all have a strongly romantic ring. Conflict, for Hegel, was built into understanding, for every concept implied was in fact defined by its opposite: thus good is defined as the opposite of evil, reason itself as the opposite of the irrational. Change, too, was a key Hegelian principle: the Spirit of Reason that lay at the heart of history manifested itself in the process of historical change, actualizing its potential as it became aware of itself through history. A divine *becoming*, rather than a "divine being," thus dominated Hegel's metaphysics. Change, which Western thinkers since Plato had sought to overcome in a search for the still center of the turning world, was set at the core of the cosmos by the nineteenth century's most difficult philosopher.

♦ Materialism: The Triumph of Reality ♦

Around 1850, there came a sea of change in the European spirit. Through the third quarter of the century and beyond, romanticism gave way to a more materialistic worldview and to a clutch of related isms in thought and art. The following pages will outline the nature and origins of nineteenth–century materialism, its relation to the advancing sciences in the age of Darwin, and its impact on the arts in such styles as realism and naturalism. Again, we will probably encounter some familiar ideas. For like romanticism, materialism contributed to a *Weltanschauung,* or worldview, that continues to shape the attitudes and beliefs of the Western world today.

Philosophical Materialism

Philosophical *materialism* is the view that the world is composed entirely of matter—that there is no such thing as mind or spirit in the universe. Originally proposed by the Greek atomists, this theory had been revived by some scientists and philosophers during the scientific revolution and had found a handful of devotees in the Enlightenment. Finding a wider public in the age of Darwin, the materialist view was perceived as an attack on the religious assumptions that were central to the Judeo–Christian tradition. Nineteenth–century materialist philosophers did in fact attack Christianity with vigor, paving the way for a materialist view of history, religion, and truth.

Materialism was a worldview that emphasized, not unspoiled nature and faraway places, but belching smokestacks, throbbing dynamos, crowded, filthy slums, and the gaudy mansions of the newly rich. The people materialists admired were not poets and painters but scientists and engineers, not Byronic revolutionaries at the barricades but hard–boiled Bismarckian power politicians and modern mechanized armies. As materialists saw it, the romantics had lived in a world of dreams; materialists were concerned with realities.

The new materialism both reflected the spread of industrialism and affected the new ideologies. The spread of heavy industry and big business, the mechanization of transportation and communication, the sheer flood of material things produced by factories and displayed in department stores in the latter part of the century all loomed large in this consciousness. The tone of ideological protest in the second half of the century reflected this new materialist consciousness. Nationalists became less culturally oriented and more political and even chauvinistic, cheering their leaders on to patriotic wars and imperial conquests. Socialists turned from utopian ideals to Marxist "scientific socialism," which recognized the harsh realities of class conflict and preached class war. Liberals went beyond emphasis on the free individual to include analysis of the problems of industrial labor, slum living, and poverty generally, and began to legislate social reforms. Activist women took to the streets to force real concessions from society, and anarchists tried to destroy "the system" with bullets and bombs.

Scientific Breakthroughs in the Age of Darwin

The materialist view found one of its clearest avenues for expression in the continuing development of modern science. The scientific breakthroughs of the nineteenth century brought a vastly improved understanding of Planet Earth and the living things that inhabit it. The modern atomic theory, for instance, took shape in the nineteenth century, reducing the world to ninety–two clearly distinguishable elements of matter, weighed and arranged on the periodic table contrived by the Russian chemist Dmitri Mendeleyev (1834–1907). By the century's end, each atom was understood to be, not a minute lump of matter, but a miniature solar system of subatomic particles in motion. In the twentieth century, the number of known elements has grown to 107 and our understanding of the nature of subatomic particles has changed significantly, but the basic pattern remains that established by 1900.

Nineteenth–century geology, meanwhile, left little doubt in the minds of the scientifically inclined that the planet on which we live and the human race itself were far older than traditional reading of the Bible suggested. Studies of rock formations and the processes that govern geological change undertaken by the English geologist Charles Lyell (1797–1875) pushed the earth's age back millions of years. And in the second half of the century, the uncovering of the bones of cave–dwelling Neanderthal (1856) and Cro–Magnon (1868) people, in Germany and France respectively, gave humanity itself a prehistoric ancestry much farther back than Adam and Eve.

A series of biological discoveries made even greater contributions to this emerging materialistic image of humanity. The cellular composition of plant tissue had been recognized

This photograph of Charles Darwin, taken in his old age, projects a powerful impression of the English scientist whose theory of evolution changed the Western view of both nature and humanity. (Bettmann.)

as early as the seventeenth century; in the nineteenth century, cells were found to be basic to the composition of animal tissue also. Vaccination had been practiced in the eighteenth century, but it was only in the later nineteenth that the French scientist Louis Pasteur (1822–1895) and others developed the germ theory of disease. Once the mysterious process of infection was understood as the work of bacilli, microorganisms that could be killed, medical progress came rapidly—and the prestige of the physiological approach to understanding human nature rose as well.

The climax of nineteenth–century biological advance came with the theory of evolution propounded by the British naturalist Charles Darwin (1809–1882). Darwin's book *On the Origin of Species* (1859) was as epochal as Newton's discovery of the law of gravity in the seventeenth century or Copernicus's explanation of the solar system in the sixteenth.

A failure at the study of medicine and divinity, really interested only in hunting and collecting beetles, the young Darwin discovered his lifework on a five–year research voyage around the world. During his travels as a naturalist on the ship *Beagle,* from 1831 to 1836, Darwin was struck by the endless variety of species, each remarkably suited to its niche in nature. Seeking a general explanation for the fit between organs, functions, and environment, he formulated the principle of biological evolution through mutation, adaptation, and the *survival of the fittest.* Supported by evidence derived from comparative anatomy, embryology, paleontology, animal breeding, Malthusian population theory, and the geographical distribution of species, Darwin's *theory of evolution* offered a purely material explanation for human life on earth.

To begin with, Darwin noted that each species produced far more offspring than its niche in the natural world could possibly support. He remarked also that each individual differed, subtly or strikingly, from all other members of a given species. These variations—produced, as we now know, by random changes in the genes—sometimes produced individuals that were better adapted to survival than most members of the species. These better–adapted individuals tended to survive longer and to pass on their distinctive features to their descendants. Less well adapted members of the species, by contrast, tended not to live long enough to breed successfully. The result, over time, could be the gradual emergence of a new species. Such evolutionary change, Darwin declared, was in fact the source of all existing biological species—including the human race.

Roundly denounced by many for his rejection of traditional Christian belief in the divine creation of plants, animals, and especially of humanity, Darwin's theory of evolution nevertheless found ardent supporters. It seemed to give a scientific, materialistic explanation for the most complex of phenomena—the multitudinous forms of life itself.

Social Darwinism and Positivism

Although Darwin himself stuck to his specialty, the study of biology, others applied his ideas far more broadly. Such *social Darwinists* as T. H. Huxley (1825–1895), sometimes called "Darwin's bulldog," and Herbert Spencer (1820–1903) not only defended evolutionary biology but saw the theory of evolution at work in society as well. Spencer, especially, saw all human social institutions as products of social evolution from simpler to more complex forms. Human progress was thus built into nature, and a better or at least more complex future was assured.

During the later 1800s, social Darwinists also made use of the harsher elements of the theory of evolution to explain such trends of the times as big business, war, and imperialism. The emergence of huge industrial corporations through the destruction or absorption of smaller business rivals could thus be hailed as "the survival of the fittest" in the business world. War between nations was simply a healthy struggle for survival, Prussia's victory over France revealing the evolutionary superiority of Bismarck's Prussia over its rival. Even Western imperialism (see Chapter 23) could be justified as just another instance of the fittest coming out on top, the global empires of the British and the French representing the inevitable triumph of the "superior" white race over "lesser breeds" in other parts of the world.

There was, however, a larger philosophic significance to Darwinian evolution. As an aspect of the materialist reinterpretation, Darwinism amounted to a denial of human uniqueness. It seemed to reveal the human species as no special creation with dominion over bird and beast, but simply as one among many randomly evolving species. Like their anthropoid cousins in the zoo, it seemed to say, Western people—top hats and bustles, Victorian morality, romantic sensibility, and all—were merely the products of chance mutation interacting with the material environment.

Evolutionists patiently explained that Darwin had never claimed that people were descended from monkeys, merely that we were related to existing species of apes as cousins in the same family tree. It seemed a distinction without a difference to the multitudes who still shied away from the materialist world view.

A materialistic theory with clearer affirmative applications was the theory of knowledge, human nature, and society known as *positivism*. Positivists, impressed with the new scientific discoveries, revived the Enlightenment's conviction that scientific methods were the road to true understanding of the world. In this view, large accumulations of data scientifically gathered would in time reveal general laws of the social as well as the natural world. All other sources of truth—authority, abstract logic, even divine revelation—must be rejected as unsound. To achieve objective scientific understanding, human biases, needs, and wishful thinking must be set aside: absolute objectivity became the great positivist virtue.

Auguste Comte (1790–1857), a French social analyst and the founder of modern sociology, offered what he called a "positivist" interpretation of religious belief as a stage in human understanding of the world we live in. Religion, according to Comte, was a primitive attempt to explain the workings of the natural environment by peopling it with imaginary anthropomorphic deities. Philosophy, the next stage in the search for truth, replaced gods and goddesses with abstract principles or forces, like Platonic Ideas or Aristotelian entelechies. But only the modern "positive" approach, based on empirical scientific observation, could bring real understanding of the natural world. The German philosopher Ludwig Feuerbach (1804–1872)—like Marx, a materialist rebel against Hegel's abstruse rationalism—went still further. Feuerbach depicted deities as inventions designed to satisfy human psychological needs for "someone up there" who might care about human destiny. Man was not made in God's image, Feuerbach averred, but God in man's.

Challenges to Christianity emerged more openly as the century advanced. The French scholar Ernest Renan (1823–1892) wrote a life of Jesus that depicted him as human, not divine. During this third quarter of the century, scientists and popular philosophers presented the universe as a whole, empty of traditional religious meaning. For these materialist writers and lecturers, the cosmos was an endless, spiritually meaningless concatenation of what the philosopher Ludwig Büchner (1824–1899) called *Force and Matter* (1855). Magnificent in its scale and eternal scientific laws, such a universe nevertheless offered no support for human moral principles, no spiritual consolations to suffering humankind.

The positivist theory of human knowledge and human society could generate more affirmative visions, however. Comte was also the first prophet of what has been called "the religion of humanity." His version came complete with humanistic "sacraments" for each stage of life, months named for great human benefactors, and other paraphernalia intended to help the human race to worship the highest scientifically established form of life—humanity itself. More broadly applied, the religion of humanity in fact also permeated the nineteenth-century ideologies, exalting as they did human nature, rights, community, nationality, and other aspects of the human as opposed to the divine.

The most widespread form of positivism was the basic positivist theory of knowledge. Some large philosophical and religious questions might not be answerable at all by empirical, positivistic methods. But questions about the basic mechanics of things could certainly be answered in this way. The positivist standards of observation and objectivity in the study of the natural world thus promised scientific certainty, but—as their critics pointed out—at the price of closing the minds of positivists to philosophical, religious, and other traditional sources of truth.

Realism and Naturalism in Fiction

In literature and the arts, the middle of the century also marked a divide. Materialist influences were felt in the realist, naturalist, and even impressionist schools of the later 1800s.

Realism in literature, particularly in the novel, actually went back to the first half of the century. The novel, developed in the seventeenth and eighteenth centuries to satisfy the desire of the expanding middle class for a good story in a convincing setting, continued to provide these staples despite the romantic introduction of more colorful subject matter. Jane Austen (1775–1817), for instance, laughed at the romantic extravagances of her contemporaries and sounded like a "realist" to the romantic novelist Sir Walter Scott. Austen's half-dozen novels of the lives of country squires and their families, including *Sense and*

Sensibility (1811) and *Pride and Prejudice* (1813), offered a deft, ironic, but thoroughly convincing picture of the traditional social aspirations and fundamental humanity of the English "county family" of her time. Charles Dickens (1812–1870) presented a tour of midcentury England, with emphasis on town life, leading his readers from orphanage, workhouse, and slum to the business offices, the law courts, and the increasingly plushy homes of the well–to–do of the England of Queen Victoria.

In France, Honoré de Balzac (1799–1850) painted the world of the triumphant bourgeoisie on a huge canvas in the long series of stories and novels he came to call *The Human Comedy*. Focusing on the Paris of Louis Philippe (r. 1830–1848), Balzac's detailed and realistic descriptions of ambitious youth and exhausted age, of boardinghouse life and society balls, of criminals and literary coteries have the ring of the most accurate reportage. In later nineteenth–century France, Emile Zola (1840–1902) went considerably farther down this road. Zola developed the gritty style known as *naturalism*—the analysis of fictional characters in terms of genetic factors interacting with environment—to anatomize the France of Napoleon III (r. 1852–1870). Again, the author's range is phenomenal. From the slum dwellers of *The Drunkard* (1877), the sweating coal miners of *Germinal* (1885), and the narrow, grasping peasantry of *Earth* (1887), Zola takes us to the gaudy, corrupt society of the courtesan *Nana* (1880) and into the highest circles of government in *His Excellency* (1876). All in all, the twenty hefty volumes of his series about the Rougon and Macquart families, meticulously researched in their social milieus, constitute a searing exposé of the France of "Napoleon the little."

The nineteenth century also saw the birth of the great Russian novel. And despite a Russian flair for emotionalism and mysticism, the Russian novel flourished under the sign of realism. There is no better way to get to know the Russian aristocracy than through Count Leo Tolstoy's (1828–1910) family chronicle of the Napoleonic epoch, *War and Peace* (1865–1869) or his novel of passion and seduction among the nobility, *Anna Karenina* (1875–1877), both hailed as vivid and powerful evocations of those times and places. Ivan Turgenev's (1818–1883) *A Sportsman's Sketches* (1852) offer an equally convincing picture of country life and of the lives of serfs in the last years before their emancipation by Alexander II. And for all of its psychological aberrations and spiritual depths, the fiction of Fyodor Dostoyevsky (1821–1881) is dense with social detail. Dostoyevsky's *Crime and Punishment* (1866), the psychologically compelling story of the youthful nihilist Raskolnikov who murders a pawnbroker, is a vivid evocation of the sordid life of teahouses, taverns, and fetid tenements, the tangled streets and bridges of nineteenth–century St. Petersburg. One can follow Raskolnikov's vividly described wanderings through the grimy streets and along the dark canals of St. Petersburg today, with only a copy of *Crime and Punishment* for a guide.

There was a new realism in the theater, too. Its greatest exemplar was the Norwegian dramatist Henrik Ibsen (1828–1906), whose plays shocked contemporaries by exposing the hypocrisy and self–deception he detected in society. *A Doll's House* (1879) described a woman's bitterly won victory over an oppressive marriage, while *Ghosts* (1881) laid bare the shocking legacy of a supposed pillar of the community, a legacy most vividly embodied in hereditary venereal disease.

Some of the writers in the new mode saw a clear connection between their own work and the continuing advance of science. Contemporaries accused Balzac of "transforming the novel into 'moral chemistry.'"[4] Balzac had, in fact, been influenced by scientific disputes over heredity and had come to see human character as the product of a genetic inheritance operating within a given social environment. Even more committed to the materialist world view of his day, Zola opined that "the wind blows in the direction of science; . . . we are pushed toward the exact study of facts and things."[5]

Realism and Impressionism in Art

A similar combination of empirical observation and scientific theory lay behind the later nineteenth–century schools of painting called *realism* and *impressionism*. "It is necessary to be of one's time," said Gustave Courbet (1819–1877), who founded the realist movement in French painting in the early 1850s.[6] Courbet and his fellow realists rejected both academic classicism and romanticism, instead painting laborers and peasants at work and bourgeois men and women at play, the life of the boulevards and the crowds in the railway station. The realists painted their own time with a coolly objective accuracy that denied their subjects charm, picturesqueness, nobility, or any larger significance whatever. Often considered a radical, Courbet did characterize realism as "democracy in art."[7] Despite the artist's radical sympathies, however, his *Stone Breakers,* showing quarrymen at work, is no glorification of the nobility of labor, nor does his *Burial at Ornans,* depicting bored and chatty peasants burying a fellow villager, idealize the pious peasantry of romantic tradition. Both paintings are fundamentally exercises in telling it like it was in the France of the Second Empire.

The painters of the impressionist movement came together in the 1860s, had their first big exhibit in 1874, and scattered to more individual styles and careers in later years. The works of Claude Monet (1840–1926), Edgar Degas (1834–1917), Berthe Morisot (1841–1895), Auguste Renoir (1841–1919), and the American Mary Cassatt (1845–1926), with their shimmering color and deliberately rough and visible brush strokes, seem to have little in common with Courbet's meticulous painting. But the impressionists, like the realists, aimed at accurate representation of the contemporary scene. They did portraits and genre scenes, like Renoir's warm images of women, Degas's race track, circus, or ballet scenes, or Cassatt's oils and pastels of mothers and children. Though they often painted out of doors, they were as likely to do cityscapes as landscapes, and they frequently depicted such typically urban interiors as cafes or theaters.

But the impressionist goal had a scientific sound—to represent through color the play of ordinary light on trees and fields, streets, buildings, and other material objects. And Monet and his colleagues had in fact studied the latest optical theories of a French chemist who had discovered that "colors in proximity influence and modify one another" and had first proposed the principle of "optical mixture," that areas of "different dye appear to have a different color when seen together from a distance"—a key aspect of impressionist technique.[8] The impressionists, too, were thus followers of what they believed to be the latest scientific ideas as they explored the way the world really looked in the France of the Third Republic.

♦ The New Nonrationalism ♦

The last decades of the nineteenth century saw yet another change. The high culture that climaxed in the 1890s was partly a revival of romanticism, partly a rejection of materialism, and in many ways unique. For the decades to be discussed below were the years that produced Freud's disturbing depth psychology and the even more shocking philosophy of Nietzsche, the prophet of the death of God. This was the period that generated revolutionary painting like that of Van Gogh and Gauguin and admired such disturbing poetry as Baudelaire's *Flowers of Evil*. It was an era of strange visions and garish images, perversity, decadence and irrationalism.

Here we will use the term *nonrationalism* to characterize the culture of the decades around 1890. It is a word that emphasizes the rejection of reason without suggesting that such a rejection is *ir*rational or foolish. For like the romantics before them, the artistic rebels of the end of the century were rejecting a tradition that they thought failed utterly to define the world as they saw it.

The Rejection of Materialism

The reaction against materialism took many forms. There was a rejection of the secularizing policies of liberal governments, a resurgence of emotional commitment to God and country. Powerfully felt racism made the career of Mayor Lüger in Vienna and sent Captain Dreyfus to Devil's Island. There was a revival of romantic emotionalism in the arts that made Edmond Rostand's (1868–1918) poetic and swashbuckling *Cyrano de Bergerac* (1897) an instant success and that revived the myth of the romantic bohemian life of the artist in Puccini's melodic opera version of *La Bohème* (1896).

A major intellectual form of the revolt against materialistic science worship was the rejection of positivism by many serious thinkers. The notions that true objectivity is possible and that piles of data will reveal general truths had less and less appeal. Instead, new philosophers, social thinkers, and even scientists won fame by preaching the centrality of emotional factors and irrational forces in society and the universe. As the romantics rebelled against the Enlightenment for its exaggerated rationalism, so the new nonrationalists turned against the positivists of the generation that had preceded theirs.

In other ways, however, materialism still flourished. The public at large continued to be impressed by the progress of science and technology. The 1890s alone saw the discovery of X–rays by Wilhelm Roentgen, the discovery of radium by Marie and Pierre Curie, Henry Ford's first automobile, and the development of the first motion picture camera by the Lumière brothers. Freud was first and foremost a scientist, and even Nietzsche was a philosophical materialist, who publicly denied the existence of God.

In the end, there was a particular tone to the turn of the century that distinguished it from both romanticism and materialism. There was an off–key color about it, the green of absinthe in a Paris cafe, the glow of gaslight on lascivious faces. The 1880s and 1890s were the decades when, for sophisticates, love was replaced by sex, and sex meant night clubs like Paris's Moulin Rouge—or horrors like Jack the Ripper, who murdered prostitutes in foggy London alleys. The emotional release of these decades had a perverse, exotic, violent ambience that distinguished it clearly from all that had gone before.

Freud and Psychoanalysis

Perhaps the most controversial—and in the long run influential—of the champions of the new nonrationalism was a highly rational Viennese physician named Sigmund Freud (1856–1939) who proposed a radical new view of human nature in the 1890s. Seeking cures for the psychological illnesses that afflicted some citizens of the Habsburg capital at the century's end, Freud constructed a theory that explained such disorders as the product of nonrational forces in the human psyche.

For Freud, the conscious mind, reason, will, were all swept along by the ebb and flow of "libidinal" energies below the surface of consciousness. The *libido* was a fundamentally sexual urge, though it could find expression in nonsexual ways, including the purest devotion or the most soaring creativity. This central sex drive, Freud believed, was present even in infants and could take the form of incestuous desire for the parent of the opposite sex—the much–debated Oedipus and Electra complexes. Such compulsions were naturally rejected by the conscious mind and repressed into the portions of the mind Freud designated as the unconscious. The *unconscious* may be defined as the collection of accumulated and repressed mental experience that is not normally accessible to us because its contents are in some way dangerous or threatening—as uncontrolled drives could undermine such basic social institutions as the family. Repression itself, however, while suppressing dangerous impulses, also created psychic tensions that found painful expression in neurotic or psychotic symptoms.

In later years, Freud came to see such primal conflicts and pressures as the origins, on the negative side, of mental illness but also, on the positive side, of organized society, religion, and civilization itself. In free association, Freud found a cure for mental disorders. *Free association* is the technique by which a patient undergoing psychotherapy says everything that comes into his or her mind without restraint and the therapist endeavors to discover how these conscious ideas are associated in the patient's unconscious mind. Through this "talking cure," Freud tried to bring the secret longings and tensions that were causing problems to the surface, exorcise them, and free the patient from torments rooted in the unconscious.

According to Freud, unconscious drives could express themselves consciously through much more socially acceptable and even valuable channels. Thus through sublimation, sexual lust could be transmuted into the strong love that binds a couple or a family together, libidinal energies channeled into the creative energies of the artist, scientist, or philosopher. For many people at the turn of the century, however, a theory that detected sexuality in infants and suggested that incestuous desire was deeply rooted in the human psyche was as far beyond the pale as Darwinism had been, and just as horrifying.

Nietzsche and the Death of God

The 1880s, the decade before Freud first proposed his radical theories, had seen the climactic work of the even more notorious German philosopher Friedrich Nietzsche (1844–1900). As Freud seemed to undermine nineteenth–century views of human moral character, Nietzsche challenged orthodox belief in the God who had been the guarantor of morality for Western people for many centuries. And many sophisticated people read his books, for Nietzsche, rejecting the rigorously rational systems of metaphysics produced by other philosophers, wrote poetic prose glittering with imagery and caustic aphorisms published under such striking titles as *Beyond Good and Evil* (1886), *Antichrist* (1895), and *Thus Spake Zarathustra* (1885).

Raised in a strictly religious household and educated among nationalistic students in pre–Bismarckian Germany, Nietzsche became a classics professor at the Swiss University of Basel—and soon turned against religion, nationalism, and middle–class mores generally. For the unorthodox professor, all these nineteenth–century values were aspects of what he called the "slave morality" of his time. He blamed Christianity for cultivating a cowardly "herd mentality" by supporting the weak against the strong, the otherworldly fanatic against the healthy sensualist. Worst of all, Nietzsche declared, the God in whose name these doctrines had been promulgated had never really existed and had now died even in the hearts of those who still pretended to worship him. The result was the most hypocritical of societies, that of the modern West. The deluded masses of the Western world were in the grip of a morality designed for slaves, glorifying weakness and meekness out of envy of the strength and self–confidence of their superiors. The leaders of the West were rob-ber–baron capitalists, Bismarckian politicians, and callous generals, none of whom any longer believed in the God they all piously claimed to revere.

There was hope only for the distant future—hope, again, rooted in an irrational force. Some few individuals, whom Nietzsche called "supermen," would come on the scene who would be strong enough to defy this iniquitous system. In them would be born the *will to power*, a nonrational drive to master both themselves and their world. By defying the hypo-critical mores of his own time, a new Zarathustra[9] could open the way for new values suited to the new world that was slowly taking shape. For the immediate future, however, Niet-zsche saw only disillusionment, anguish, and madness in a godless world.

Nietzsche, whose mental balance was always delicate, went mad at the end of the 1880s and died in 1900. By then, though he could not know it, his Delphic iconoclasm had made him a cult figure for many intellectuals across Europe—and a shocking prophet of atheism to the century that was just beginning.

Nonrational Forces

An intellectual world in revolt against the dry statistics of the positivists and the dull me-chanical world of materialism produced other surging forces besides Freud's libidinal ener-gies and Nietzsche's will to power. Popular if sometimes esoteric prophets like Henri Berg-son, Georges Sorel, and Madame Blavatsky gave voice to a turn–of–the–century longing for deeper mystic meanings beneath the surface of human life and society.

Georges Sorel (1847–1922), convinced like the syndicalists that labor unions would play a key role in history, felt that social change could only come about through heroic pro-letarian struggle. Sorel's *Reflections on Violence* (1908) preached the value of a powerful so-cial myth, the dream of the general strike, in which all laboring people would strike at once, stopping society in its tracks and bringing governments to a halt. Whether the universal strike ever came or not, he urged, belief in it would galvanize workers for action against the system. Force and violence were also valuable in their own right as expressions of the heroic element in a weak and decadent bourgeois society.

Even more strikingly unpositivistic and antimaterialist, Henri Bergson's (1859–1940) *Creative Evolution* (1907) made the theory of *vitalism* available to those who had missed his public lectures on this mysterious but crucial power. The vital life force in humankind, Bergson declared, links humanity with the basic energy of the universe. It is this pulsing flow of energy that shapes each level of evolving matter; and the human mind, the highest achievement of creative evolution, is capable of making contact with the cosmic fountain-head from which it flows. Such contact, which would unleash a powerful surge of creativity in the individual, could only be made—once more—through a nonrational process. Only by intuition, not intellect, can we tap this ultimate source of power.

The Russian spiritualist Helena Petrovna Blavatsky (1831–1891), after years studying mysticism and traveling in Asia, founded the Theosophical Society to put humanity in touch with the ultimate spiritual powers of the universe. Establishing the headquarters of her movement first in New York and then in Madras, India, she claimed supernatural powers and became a focus of intense controversy. Her book, *Isis Unveiled* (1887), illustrates a wide interest in spiritualism, psychical research, and other unorthodox explorations. Across the Western world as the century turned, spirit mediums held dimly lit séances in which they claimed to serve as channels for communications by the spirits of the dead. Though psychical research societies often exposed such practitioners, the popularity of spiritualism was one more expression of the search for nonrational explanations and mystical realities that marked the end of the nineteenth century.

Fin–de–Siècle Art and Literature

Another label that captures much of the mood of this period is the French term *fin–de–siècle*—end of the century, end of the age. This elusive fin–de–siècle mood, felt by a sophisticated minority at the end of the nineteenth century, combined rejection of traditional values with affirmation of *decadence*. Decadence, in turn, meant a mixture of artificiality and eccentricity, of sensuousness and mysticism whose exponents often looked both abnormal and immoral to the majority of their fellow citizens. Particularly potent in art and literature, the decadent fin–de–siècle spirit was as irrational as romanticism, yet as cynical and worldly as materialism. Its overtones of perverse sexuality and cruelty, decadence and neurosis have given the European fin–de–siècle its distinctive tone and place in the history of Western culture.

Thus as the century drew to its end, a strange spirit seemed to be abroad in Europe. In 1889, the same year that Nietzsche went insane, Vincent Van Gogh (1853–1890), later to become the most popular of the postimpressionist painters, went into an insane asylum in southern France. Van Gogh, who sold almost no paintings in his own lifetime, daubed his dazzling canvases with glaringly visible brush strokes and bright colors that obviously owed much to his impressionist predecessors. The bright oranges and yellows of his sunflowers and glowing fields, however, like the intensely human feeling of his awkwardly drawn portraits, were his alone. And his sickly green and yellow cafes and swirling stars, the haunting cypresses and crows that darkened his later pictures hinted at the psychological problems that tormented him. In one surge of deep despair, he sliced off his own ear—and then painted a disturbing self–portrait of the bandaged results. He shot himself the year after he put himself under full–time psychological care.

There was plenty of other strange art around. In the 1890s, Van Gogh's friend Paul Gauguin (1848–1903) went off to Tahiti and painted dreamlike, darkly enigmatic pictures of the natives. The brooding figures and flat colors of his images from the South Seas earned him a reputation for plumbing mysteries too deep for civilized people to understand. Back in Paris, the dwarfish figure of Henri de Toulouse–Lautrec (1864–1901), crippled scion of an ancient noble family, lounged around night clubs like the Moulin Rouge, painting cabaret entertainers in a bright, assymetrical style learned from Japanese prints. In Britain, the *art nouveau* (new art) of Aubrey Beardsley (1872–1898), with its lyrical line, startling distortions, and unconcealed eroticism graced the pages of ultrasophisticated journals like the *Yellow Book*. In Freud's Vienna, the group of artists who called themselves the Secession outraged even the sophisticated Viennese. Among the paintings of sensually nude women produced by Secession leader Gustav Klimt (1862–1918), for instance, *Judith with the Head of Holofernes* shows only a small portion of the head of the slaughtered oppressor, focusing instead on Judith's almost voluptuously triumphant smile.

In the literature of this period as well, strange tones prevailed. Sexuality, violence, and hallucination, an emphasis on the perverse and the decadent were dominating themes in the poems and plays of Baudelaire and Rimbaud and the drama and fiction of Schnitzler and Oscar Wilde.

The French poet Charles Baudelaire (1821–1867) saw his *Flowers of Evil* (1857) condemned for blasphemy and flagrant immorality shortly after midcentury, before he himself succumbed to a life–shortening regimen of alcohol and drugs. The bohemian "cursed poet" Arthur Rimbaud (1854–1891) composed the nightmarish visions of his youthful *Season in Hell* in the 1870s and soon thereafter gave up writing shocking poetry to run guns in Africa. Oscar Wilde (1854–1900), comic dramatist, brilliant conversationalist, and the most admired wit of the period, punctured the pretensions of his time with elegantly phrased aphorisms that turned every pious cliche upside down. The very title of his most popular play, *The Importance of Being Earnest* (1895), was a sneer at Victorian seriousness. The year after this play was produced, Wilde was sent to prison for homosexuality, which was a criminal offense in Britain at that time.

The literature and art of the fin–de–siècle flowed with the new eroticism, with cruelty and sorrow, frequently framed with a sense of the world as dream or hallucination. Nonrational "forces" seemed to be loose in the mind of the West. They would do their part to make the new century even more shocking and more revolutionary than the old.

Summary

Romanticism, which flourished between 1775 and 1850, rejected classicism and the Enlightenment in favor of artistic freedom and the expression of strong feeling. Nineteenth–century romantic literature revolted against classical rules in favor of freer forms and powerfully felt emotions. Romantic painting was full of color, romantic music melodic, and both as full of excitement and feeling as Delacroix's *Liberty Leading the People* to victory over the barricades. Philosophers in the first half of the century saw metaphysical forces at work in history, from Hegel's unfolding Absolute Reason to Schopenhauer's objectless Will. For Western romantics, the heart had it's reasons which reason alone could never understand.

The second half of the century, however, saw realism and naturalism focusing on the grim realities of life rather than on emotional responses to it. After 1850, realistic novelists and painters tried to depict the world as it was, purged of sentiment and idealism, while impressionists simply tried to analyze the play of light on the material world. These artistic trends were rooted in a new surge of scientific discovery that seemed to challenge traditional religious and moral beliefs. Darwin's theory of evolution had enormous impact on the views of society and caused some to see human nature in terms of genes interacting with the environment. After midcentury, social Darwinist and materialist philosophers seemed to be reducing the whole world to matter and natural law.

By 1890, however, nonrationalism seemed to many to be seeking simply to shock rather than to expose realities or to express intense human feeling. Freud jolted Western thought by characterizing the psyche in terms of unconscious drives rather than rational decision making or moral principles. Around 1900, Bergson preached vitalism, Sorel extolled force and violence, and spiritualist séances won more converts than did metaphysical speculation. Postimpressionist painters like Van Gogh and Gauguin, meanwhile, gave expression to their own very untraditional visions of reality.

Some Key Terms

decadence   563
fin–de–siècle   563
free association   561
impressionism   559
libido   561
materialism   553

naturalism   558
nonrationalism   560
positivism   556
realism   557
romanticism   547
social Darwinism   556

survival of the fittest   555
theory of evolution   555
unconscious   561
vitalism   562
Weltanschauung   553
will to power   562

Notes

1. H. G. Schenk, *The Mind of the European Romantics* (Oxford: Oxford University Press, 1979), xxii.
2. William Blake, "Auguries of Innocence," in *Immortal Poems of the English Language,* ed. Oscar Williams (New York: Pocket Books, 1953), 227.
3. George Gordon, Lord Byron, "She Walks in Beauty," in Arthur Quiller–Couch, *The Oxford Book of English Verse 1250–1918* (Oxford: Clarendon Press, 1953), 707.

4. Linda Nochlin, *Realism* (Harmondsworth, England: Penguin Books, 1971), 42–44.
5. Emile Zola, quoted in ibid., 4.
6. Gustave Courbet, quoted in ibid., 28.
7. Ibid., 46.
8. Phoebe Pool, *Impressionism* (London: Thames and Hudson, 1967), 14.
9. In *Thus Spake Zarathustra,* Nietzsche speaks through the mouth of the fabled Persian prophet whose name is more commonly spelled Zoroaster.

Reading List

Austen, J. *Pride and Prejudice.* Edited by F. W. Bradbrook. New York: Oxford University Press, 1970. Wit and social portraits among England's country gentry.

Boyer, R. D. *Realism in European Theater and Drama, 1870–1920.* Westport, Conn.: Greenwood Press, 1979. Drama in the age of Ibsen. See also M. Bell, *The Sentiment of Reality* (London: Allen and Unwin, 1983), on realism in nineteenth–century fiction.

Brown, M. *The Shape of German Romanticism.* Ithaca, N.Y.: Cornell University Press, 1979. Scholarly overview.

Butler, M. *Romantics, Rebels, and Reactionaries.* Oxford: Oxford University Press, 1981. Romanticism in English literature. See also J. B. Twitchell, *Romantic Horizons* (New York: Columbia University Press, 1983), comparing English romantic poetry and painting.

Charlton, D. G., ed. *The French Romantics.* 2 vols. New York: Cambridge University Press, 1984. Personal and cultural imperatives move these romantics to speak to their times. See also W. J. Hemmings, *Culture and Society in France: 1789–1848* (New York: Scribner's, 1987).

Clark, K. *The Romantic Rebellion.* London: Omega, 1976. History of romantic painting by a leading art historian. See also the sumptuously illustrated volume by J. Clay, *Romanticism* (Oxford: Phaidon, 1981).

Cohen, G. A. *Karl Marx's Theory of History.* Oxford: Clarendon Press, 1978. Dialectical materialism at the heart of Marx's thought.

Cooke, M. G. *The Romantic Will.* New Haven: Yale University Press, 1976. Intriguing analysis of a key romantic quality.

Darwin, C. *The Darwin Reader.* Edited by M. Bates and P. S. Humphrey. New York: Scribner's, 1956. A good introduction to a very literate scientist.

Flaubert, G. *Madame Bovary.* Translated by F. Steegmuller. New York: Random House, 1957. Vivid psychological portrait set in sharply realized French provinces.

Gauguin. Oxford: Phaidon, 1978. A hundred pages of pictures. On Gauguin's famous flight to the South Seas. See also J. Teilet–Fisk, *Paradise Reviewed* (Epping, England: Bowker, 1983).

Gregory, F. *Scientific Materialism in Nineteenth–Century Germany.* Dordrecht: Reidel, 1977. Materialism finds a home in the new Germany.

Longyear, R. M. *Nineteenth Century Romanticism*

in Music. 2d ed. Englewood Cliffs, N.J.: Prentice Hall, 1973. The romantic element in Western music throughout the century.

Lukacs, G. *Studies in European Realism.* London: Merlin Press, 1972. Classic studies of European literary realists.

McGann, J. J. *The Romantic Ideology.* Chicago: University of Chicago Press, 1983. Romanticism as a worldview. See also H. Honour, *Romanticism* (London: Allen Lane, 1979), on the romantic style in art and civilization, and H. G. Schenk, *The Mind of the European Romantics* (Oxford: Oxford University Press, 1979), exploring the full range of romantic sensibilities.

Nalbantian, S. *Seeds of Decadence in the Late Nineteenth Century Novel.* London: Macmillan, 1983. Fictional attitudes in European literature after 1870.

Nietzsche, F. *Thus Spake Zarathustra.* Translated by W. Kaufmann. New York: Viking, 1966. Challenging introduction to the most poetic—and shocking—philosopher of the century.

Pierrot, J. *The Decadent Imagination.* Chicago: University of Chicago Press, 1981. French literary decadence.

Schamber, E. N. *The Artist as Politician.* London: University Press of America, 1984. Romanticism and politics in the first half of the nineteenth century.

Siegel, J. *Bohemian Paris: Culture, Politics, and the Boundaries of the Bourgeois Life, 1830–1930.* New York: Viking, 1986. Colorful myths and grimmer realities of the artistic life.

— 23 —

Empires on Which the Sun Never Sets

The Climax of Western Imperialism

*The New Imperialism   *The Western Predominance in Asia
*The Western Conquest of Africa   *Internal Imperialism
*The Impact of the New Imperialism

Ever since its beginnings in the Mediterranean basin, the Western world had been expanding across Europe and beyond the seas. In early modern times, the *old imperialism* of the sixteenth, seventeenth, and eighteenth centuries had imposed Western rule on North and South America and established Western commercial enclaves around the fringes of Asia and Africa. It was left to the *new imperialism* of the nineteenth century to bring Western expansion to its climax in the decades between 1870 and 1914. During these years, Western empire–builders partitioned Africa into colonies and carved up Asia into Western spheres of influence. Since Europe and both the Americas were already ruled by Western people, most of the globe lay, for a brief moment in time around 1900, under the control of the West.

The new imperialism thus produced a number of globe–girdling domains of unprecedented size. Poet Rudyard Kipling's description of Britain's quarter of the globe as "the empire on which the sun never sets" emphasized the striking fact that, since the British Empire stretched around the world, the sun was always shining on some portion of it. In a chronological sense too, few Europeans alive in 1900 dreamed that the sun would ever set on their enormous overseas empires.

This chapter will begin with an analysis of the forms, causes, and tools of this second wave of imperial expansion. It will then offer an overview of the spread of European hegemony over Asia and of the partitioning of Africa into European–ruled colonies. Thereafter, we will examine the "internal imperialism" of continental countries like the United States and Russia and conclude with a summary of the impact of the new imperialism on the world and the West.

At the beginning, it should be emphasized that the way we understand Western imperialism may depend very largely on whether our perspective on the subject is Western or non–Western. Even in the Western world, as we will see, the views of scholars differ on this complicated subject. No aspect of Western history, in fact, is more controversial than Western imperialism—or more worth exploring, both for its past significance and for its impact on the present and the future.

◆ The New Imperialism ◆

We will start with some generalities on the nature and causes of the upsurge of imperial conquest that boiled over in the decades after 1870. We will first survey the forms of imperial domination imposed by the West. We will then go over the causal factors at work, from the profit motive to missionary religiosity. Finally, we will look at the new tools, from iron–clad warships to quinine, which made this astonishing new wave of imperial conquests possible.

Forms of Imperialism

Three of the most common forms of the new imperialism of the nineteenth century may be easily distinguished. As we shall see, however, these do not exhaust the forms and broader definitions that historians of the subject have proposed.

The most obvious form of empire building is *colonization,* piling up colonies, as Spain had done in South America and Britain in North America during the era of the old imperialism. During the period of the new imperialism, almost the entire continent of Africa and important parts of Asia were annexed by European countries, governed by European administrators, and garrisoned by European troops. From the governor's mansion, the barracks, and the Europeanized colonial cities to the isolated district officer in the most distant village, colonies felt the transforming effect of imperialism more fully than the victims of any other form of Western hegemony.

It is possible simply to equate imperialism with colonialism and let it go at that. Most historians, however, would include less total forms of imperial control. Where a strong government already existed, for example, Western imperialists often simply established a *protectorate* over the reigning sultan or rajah. In return for financial aid and military support, the local ruler was expected to accept the guidance of a European "adviser" or "resident" in matters of interest to Europeans, such as trade policy or missionary activity. If the traditional ruler failed to heed European advice, his chief port or capital city might find itself under fire from a Western naval squadron. The protectorate gave Western powers less control, but it was also a much cheaper way of exerting significant influence beyond the seas.

A third and even more modest form of European imperialism was the *sphere of influence.* In this approach to imperial exploitation, most of the action took place in European board rooms and government offices, where commercial agreements and treaties were often negotiated and signed. The sphere of influence normally meant economic influence. It took the form of agreement by a non–Western state to grant businessmen from one or more Western powers the right to exploit raw material sources, build railways, or otherwise develop and profit from a slice of the non–Western world. Because the sphere of influence involved such limited control, European countries often resorted to this mode when the power of two or more imperial powers was so evenly matched that they chose to share rather than fight each other for paramountcy.

Other still broader conceptions of imperialism have gained considerable currency during the long twentieth–century post–mortem on nineteenth–century Western expansion. Some of these stress *economic imperialism,* detecting economic forces behind all forms of imperialism, portraying imperialism itself as a fundamentally economic relationship. Thus V. I. Lenin interpreted imperialism in Marxist terms, as a product of "the highest stage of

Chronology 23: The New Imperialism

1839–1842	*Opium War opens China to Western trade and influence*
1854	*U.S. Admiral Perry "opens" Japan to Western penetration*
1857	*Indian Mutiny challenges British rule in India*
1858	*British government takes over India from East India Company*
1860s–1890s	*Britain occupies Burma, Malaya*
1860s–1900	*Russians settle Siberia; Americans settle Far West*
1867	*Suez Canal opens short sea route from Europe to Asia*
1868	*Meiji Restoration begins Japan's drive to westernize in order to resist western penetration*
1870s–1890s	*France occupies Indochina*
1870s–1890s	*France seizes most of West Africa; Britain occupies most of East Africa*
1870–1914	*European great powers impose protectorates on Middle East*
1880s–1890s	*Germany, Italy, Belgium colonize parts of Africa*
1885	*Mahdi resists British imperialism in Sudan*
1900	*Boxer Rebellion tries to drive Westerners out of China*
1914	*Panama canal opens short sea route from Atlantic to Pacific*

capitalism" in need of markets, resources, and an "external proletariat" to provide cheap labor. More recently, Immanuel Wallerstein has characterized both old and new imperialism as stages in the development of a "world system" of economic exchange and exploitation, with the West at the center and the colonial areas as peripheral contributors.

Still another recent perspective draws more upon cultural anthropology than upon economics. Emphasizing *cultural imperialism,* this view focuses on the imposition of Western ideas, attitudes, high and popular culture, and styles of life on non–Western peoples. Cultural imperialism may take such forms as missionary religion seeking converts or Western popular music displacing native folk songs. More subtly, the sheer success of Western colonists may convince the indigenous population of the inferiority of their traditional ways of life to those of the West. This, it is suggested, may be the most insidious of all forms of Western imperialism: hegemony over the non–Western mind, heart, and soul.

Causes of the New Imperialism

If the new imperialism came in several forms, there were even more causes of this renewal of Western expansionism. Possible causes may include any or all of an array of economic and political needs, religious and humanitarian motives, and even nineteenth–century racial theories.

Economic factors were cited by enemies of imperialism like Lenin, but also by some of its defenders. "There are forty millions of people beyond the gateway to the Congo," opined journalist–turned–explorer H. M. Stanley, "and the cotton spinners of Manchester are waiting to clothe them."[1] The Industrial Revolution did in fact provide several motives for imperial expansion. Modern industry required raw materials not readily available in Europe, from rubber and oil to manganese and tungsten. Wherever these were available, colonial mines and plantations quickly appeared. The sheer productivity of the expanding industrial system created another powerful material motive—a need for new markets, like the forty million African customers Stanley saw waiting for Manchester textiles.

As industrial profits piled up, furthermore, Western financiers in search of new investment areas found that a higher rate of return could be earned financing main–line colonial railways than suburban lines in Europe. As unions gained leverage in the West, finally, manufacturers often found it cheaper to use lower–paid native labor in Asia or Africa.

Political and military factors also motivated some of the builders of Western empires in the nineteenth century. Nationalism filled British citizens with pride as they gazed at a world map, splashed with "cartographer's red," the color commonly assigned to Britain's global empire. Military leaders also sometimes demanded territorial annexations to provide naval bases and coaling stations for the new steam–powered fleets. The colonists themselves sometimes exerted political pressure for further land acquisitions to protect them from unfriendly neighbors or to open up new areas for exploitation.

Kipling offered the perfect phrase for the more idealistic motives that many imperialists claimed. It was, he said, *"the white man's burden"* to bring the benefits of Western civilization to the backward peoples of the rest of the earth. Preeminent among idealistic impulses was missionary zeal, which impelled many Protestant pastors and Catholic priests to spread the Christian Gospel from West Africa to the Far East. Secular humanitarianism also motivated many administrators and technicians to bring to non–Western peoples the presumed benefits of Western law, education, medicine, and government.

Nineteenth–century racist theories of Western superiority also very likely found an outlet in the imposition of Western rule on allegedly "inferior" races. "The white man," as a newspaper suggested in 1899, "being supported in his faith by the whole history of the world, believes firmly . . . that his color marks him out as belonging to the hereditary aristocracy of mankind."[2] By contrast, declared one famous proconsul of empire, "the typical African" was "happy, thriftless, excitable," a member of one of "the child–races of the world," in obvious need of Western tutelage.[3] More openly hostile evaluations of Africans and Asians depicted them as brutal, cunning, implacable foes of the superior Caucasian peoples, as foes who must be suppressed in order that the white race, self-defined as the hope of the human future, might prevail.

Some of the most exalted religious and humanitarian ideals may well have operated in combination with the most selfish economic and political concerns. Cecil Rhodes, Britain's most celebrated South African empire builder, was probably not far wrong when he defined imperial motivations as a mix of "money and noble notions."

The Tools of the New Imperialism

Why they did it, then, remains much disputed. How they got away with it—how they succeeded in imposing Western hegemony on most of the rest of the globe—seems to most historians to be a bit clearer.

From the broadest perspective, it appears that the West had, for a brief time, achieved a remarkable degree of political and economic superiority over other peoples. The rough parity in wealth and governmental structures that had prevailed between urban–imperial cultures from China to Europe had begun to tilt in Europe's favor as early as the fifteenth century. By the eighteenth, the Enlightenment's rationalization of government and the great breakthrough into modern industrialism had given the West massive advantages. In the nineteenth century, the Western peoples were clearly richer and more powerful than the ancient civilizations of China and Japan, India, and the Middle East, not to mention the prurban peoples of the world.

Some historians would also point to the discipline and morale of the Western troops who, when all is said and done, provided the ultimate sanction for Western domination. Again and again, the annals of the new imperialism recorded victories by small bodies of Western troops over much larger numbers of non–Western fighters. The discipline, rigorous training, and *esprit de corps* of these British or French regiments may help to explain their victories over Asian or African hosts.

In the final analysis, however, the heart of the matter was probably best summed up by the turn–of–the–century wit who wrote:

> Whatever happens, we have got
> The Maxim Gun, and they have not.[4]

It was above all the technology of the Industrial Revolution that gave later nineteenth–century Europeans their overwhelming advantage over the rest of the world. This advantage was not merely a matter of firepower. Steam railroads and ironclad steamships, the telegraph and the Suez Canal all contributed to the capacity of the West to impose its will on the rest of the globe. Quinine, by suppressing the fevers of malaria, opened the interior of tropical lands that had once been the white man's graveyard. A variety of technological innovations thus helped to make possible the Western hegemony of the world.

In the end, however, the weapons spoke loudest. New generations of field artillery, repeating rifles, the Maxim machine gun extolled above, and the heavy guns of ironclad warships ten times the size of the average Chinese junk proved irresistible. A British officer thus described the crushing impact of a single gunboat, the famous *Nemesis,* spearheading a drive up the Pearl River toward Canton in south China during the Opium War of 1839–1842:

> *Nemesis* . . . destroyed five forts, one battery, two military stations, and nine war junks, in which there were one hundred and fifteen guns . . . thus proving to the enemy that the British flag can be displayed throughout their inner waters wherever and whenever it is thought proper by us, against any mode they may adopt to prevent it.[5]

Rudyard Kipling himself honored the courage and sheer charging power of the Sudanese warriors who "broke a British square"—the traditional British defensive formation—and even admitted that, man for man, the African might be the better soldier. "It wasn't hardly fair," the bard of empire admitted, to turn the fury of European repeating rifles on such splendid fighting men.[6] But they did it all the same.

♦The Western Predominance in Asia♦

What the old imperialism had done in North and South America, the new imperialism attempted to do in Asia and Africa. This and the following section will outline the story of this monumental effort to bring two more continents under the sway of Western power during the later 1800s.

From ancient to early modern times, Asians had generally shown little interest in European trade goods, preferring to take precious metals in exchange for their own products. By the nineteenth century, however, the greatness of Western material power won increasing recognition in the East. As we will see in the following pages, Europeans conquered and colonized some Asian peoples, imposed protectorates and spheres of influence on oth-

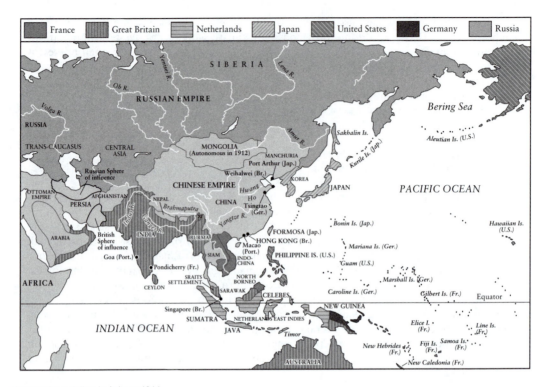

Western Imperialism in Asia, to 1914

ers. In the Middle East, in India and Southeast Asia, and even in far–off China and Japan, the looming Western predominance was felt as never before.

The Eastern Question

In the 1500s, the Ottoman Turkish Empire had been a fearful thing for Europeans to contemplate. One of the largest Muslim states ever assembled, the realms of the Ottoman sultan stretched from the Balkan peninsula and southern Russia down through Turkey and the Near East, then westward across North Africa to the Atlantic. Constantinople was the most powerful capital in western Eurasia, the Ottoman Empire a towering menace to Christendom.

In the 1700s and 1800s, however, Turkish power steadily declined. Among the political factors which combined to undermine the strength of the onetime superpower were weak sultans, ambitious chief ministers, and corrupt and inefficient officials. Broader problems included demands for local autonomy, a declining economy, and failure to keep up technologically with Europe. In the nineteenth century, Turkey was increasingly seen as "the sick man of Europe," the focus of a deathbed watch by all the powers—and the source of a whole new set of problems for the West. They called it the *Eastern Question;* and in the later nineteenth century, most answers to it seemed to involve Western imperial expansion.

At the core of this complex situation was the belief that if Turkey collapsed completely, Western power must flow into the resulting vacuum. This possibility, in turn, raised the question of whose power it would be and the consequent threat to the delicate balance of power on the eastern frontier of the Western world.

Everybody seemed to have a stake in the outcome. Russia was concerned because Turkey was on its southern borders and controlled the Straits that were the key to the Black Sea, Russia's only year–round access to the oceans of the world. Austria was involved because each new Balkan state that won its independence from the Ottoman Empire could inspire similar ambitions among the minority nationalities of the Habsburg Empire. France, from Napoleon I's Egyptian campaign of 1798–1799 through Napoleon III's opening of the Suez Canal in 1869, sought to carve out a French empire in realms that were at least nominally part of the Turkish Empire. Britain, which feared that growing Russian power in the Middle East would threaten its own Indian empire, soon became involved in colonial expansion in Ottoman Egypt. Even the new German Empire sought influence in Constantinople and dreamed of a lucrative Berlin–to–Baghdad railroad, while the new Italy reached for its own North African colonies in some territories nominally controlled by the Turks.

Beyond Turkey lay the equally moribund Persian Empire (Iran today), and beyond that the arid plateaus and mountains of Afghanistan, where the Khyber Pass led down into northwestern India. In the broadest sense, Persia and Afghanistan were part of the Eastern Question, too. At Teheran and Kabul, across these high plains and treeless slopes, Russian and British diplomats intrigued and generals fought proxy wars through feuding local factions. Nobody wanted to die in an Afghan war, but quite a few British and Russian soldiers did as their governments jockeyed for power on the road to India.

The end of the century saw no clear answer to the Eastern Question. Britain and Russia were carving out spheres of influence from Persia to the Indian borders. Britain and France were establishing their influence from Iraq and Syria through Palestine to Egypt, all still officially Ottoman provinces. In the Balkans, first Greece and Serbia, then Bulgaria, Romania, and others successfully rebelled against Ottoman Turkish rule. These revolts in turn kindled dreams of independence among the subject peoples of the Habsburg Austrian Empire—dreams that Austria's Russian rivals for influence in eastern Europe vigorously encouraged. And through it all the European powers alternately fought, bullied, and propped up what remained of Ottoman power rather than confront the problems that would have to be faced once the Ottomans were gone.

British India

Beyond the Middle East lay India, the heart of Britain's Asian empire. Here old–fashioned colonialism began, with all its color, its self–assured civilizing mission, its exploitation and brutality.

The huge Indian peninsula, second in population only to China, reached from the ice–bound Himalayas down through the teeming valley of the Ganges—India's historic heartland—and on south down the triangular Deccan peninsula to the large tropical island of Ceylon (Sri Lanka today). First reached by Portuguese traders just before 1500 and by the British and French East India Companies shortly after 1600, most of India remained subject to the emperors of the Mughal dynasty throughout the old imperial period. The British East India Company, however, had emerged as the real power in India following the defeat of the French there in 1763 and the rapid decline of Mughal authority thereafter.

This enormous sweep of lands and peoples was thus, in large part, run by a British commercial company through the first half of the nineteenth century. Profits, bribes, and other revenues continued to make company officials rich. The East India Company did attempt to bring some changes to Indian society, including road and canal building, the introduction of British education for the elite, and the suppression of the Hindu custom of *sati*, the self–immolation of a pious widow on her husband's pyre. For the most part, however, the company's interest was focused on maintaining political stability and high profits.

Then in 1857, resentment of foreign rule exploded in the great *Indian Mutiny*, a revolt by native troops that threatened to massacre or expel all the British on the subcontinent. The rebellion was touched off by the insensitive issuing of cartridges greased with beef and pork fat to Hindu and Muslim soldiers, though the cow was a sacred animal to Hindus, the pig unclean to Muslims. The convulsion that swept through India, however, revealed broader and deeper resentments of both Western exploitation and Western attempts to change Indian society, and there were horrifying atrocities on both sides before the uprising was suppressed.

During the second half of the century, India was taken over by the British government and run as a gigantic colony—"the jewel in the crown" of the British Empire. Fewer challenges to India's traditional culture were undertaken, though high–caste Indians continued to be educated in British schools and more Indians were incorporated into the colonial administration. More importantly, the *Raj*, as British rule in India was called, meant startling economic changes. Some of these, like the coming of the railroad, were distinct improvements. Others, such as the ruining of India's handloom cotton textile industry by British power–loom competition, were clearly economic disasters for India and major gains for Britain. When we add the large Indian army, which was soon serving outside India and giving Britain a land force to match that of Germany or France for the first time, the range of reasons for acquiring this particular colony is evident.

Colonizing Southeast Asia

The British had India to themselves in the nineteenth century. In Southeast Asia, however, the British had to share dominion with other Western powers.

Southeast Asia, which lies between India and China, is a region of mountains, jungles, and tropical rivers. The region divides into mainland and island areas: the large Indochinese peninsula and the long reach of tropical islands and seas that is today mostly Indonesia. The island realm, colonized by the Netherlands in the seventeenth century, remained the Dutch East Indies throughout the nineteenth. The Indochinese peninsula, however, the meeting place of Indian and Chinese cultures, had thus far escaped Western colonization. Then in the later nineteenth century, the British and the French parceled out most of this southeastern angle of the Asian mainland between them.

France acquired the eastern half of Indochina (today's Vietnam, Laos, and Cambodia) piecemeal between the 1860s and the 1890s, with increased activity after its defeat in the Franco–Prussian War in 1870, when French national pride badly needed a boost. The British, meanwhile, had moved into the western side of the area, particularly Burma (Myanmar) and the long, narrow Malay peninsula with the bustling port of Singapore at its southern tip. In the center of Indochina, meanwhile, the Kingdom of Siam (Thailand today) managed to accept aid from both the British and the French while becoming dependent on neither. For the Europeans, missionary activity and trade, railway building, rubber and tin were among the varied rewards of possessions in this sweltering corner of Asia.

Most of the islands of the Pacific, finally, were claimed by one or another of the Western imperial powers during the second half of the century. Invaded first by beachcombers and missionaries, then developed as naval bases or steppingstones to Eastern trade, these bare atolls and island paradises contributed little economically to the expanding Western hegemony. Yet they soon assumed a very special place in the Western vision of the non–Western world. From the days of Herman Melville's fiction and Paul Gauguin's paintings to our own time, Tahiti, Samoa, Hawaii, and similar "islands in the sun" have been imagined as latter–day Edens, the perfect escape from the pressures of modern civilization.

Opening Up China

Eastward still and northward from Southeast Asia flowed the China Seas and the thickly populated east coast of China, the world's oldest, largest, and most populous nation. Intermittently unified since before 200 BCE, the Chinese Empire was almost as large as all of Europe, had as varied a geography and a longer history.

China's historic center, like that of the United States, had been its east coast. The political core of the empire was in the northeast, where its current capital of Peking (now Beijing) was located; its commercial center was at Canton (now Guangzhou) in the southeast; and one of its major agricultural regions lay along the Yangtze (Chang today) River in between. China's huge population was densest in the coastal provinces and along its rivers. Its far western hinterlands, with their thin scattering of farmers and tent–dwelling nomads, contrasted as sharply with the urbanized east coast as the American "far west" did with the eastern states. Development along coasts and waterways was common among urban civilizations; China's coastal development, however, had the distinct disadvantage of bringing

Tz'u-Hsi, empress of China, is shown here seated on her throne in the Forbidden City in Peking (Beijing today). Can you see commitment to traditional ways in the face, pose, and setting of this photograph? (Bettmann.)

the nerve centers of the Chinese Empire within easy reach of Western naval power in the nineteenth century.

China had experienced its last great invasion in the seventeenth century, when Manchus already infused with some Chinese organizational and military skills had broken through the Great Wall of China from Manchuria. Ruling with great success through the seventeenth and eighteenth centuries, the earlier Manchu emperors presided over a last golden age of traditional Chinese culture. In the nineteenth century, however, Manchu power, like Mughal rule in India or Ottoman power in Turkey, was decaying. From the beginning of the great Western expansion, China had permitted only a few traders on the Pearl (now Zhu) River near Canton and a handful of Jesuit missionaries at the imperial court in Peking. In the 1800s, however, the dam burst, and the "Western barbarians" came pouring in.

It was a century of wars and revolutions, of massive Western penetration and crumbling Chinese institutions that by 1900 left the world's oldest and largest empire apparently on the verge of collapse and partition among the Western imperial powers. Equipped with heavily armed warships and smaller but devastatingly effective gunboats like *Nemesis,* the British and French defeated China in the Opium War of 1839–1842. This struggle, fought in part to compel the Chinese to open their frontiers to opium imports from British India, reveals the new imperialism at its least savory. The British and French attacked again in 1860, when they looted and burned the beautiful summer palace near Peking. In between, the empire was racked by a long and shattering civil war, the Taiping Rebellion, some of whose leaders were inspired by half-understood Christian doctrines—more evidence, in the eyes of the Chinese, of the subversive impact of the West.

At the end of the century, finally, came a second revolt, that of the Boxers. The Boxer Rebellion of 1900 was led by a religious society called the I Ho Chu'an or "Righteous Harmonious Fists"—roughly translated as "Boxers"—who believed their ancestral gods wanted them to expel all the foreigners whose presence polluted Chinese soil. The Boxers attacked Western missionaries and foreign legations, or diplomatic enclaves, in Chinese cities. In response, contingents of European, American, Japanese, and other colonial troops marched into China, smashed both the Boxers and the Chinese imperial army, and drove Tz'u–Hsi (1835–1908), the last Manchu empress of China, out of her own capital.

The net result of these wars and revolutions was to leave China all but helpless as the twentieth century began. After each defeat, the empire had been compelled to accept new *unequal treaties.* These agreements had given Westerners such rights as *extraterritoriality*—the privilege of being tried by Western laws and in Western courts for crimes committed in China. The treaties also opened up a large number of "treaty ports" to Western merchants and permitted European or American missionaries to travel and preach freely in China. In addition, the victorious Western powers carved colonies from the flanks of the dying Manchu Empire. These included not only traditional Chinese tributary states such as Burma (to Britain), Vietnam (to France), and Korea (to Japan), but also slices of China proper, including the island of Hong Kong, granted to Britain, and the Shantung peninsula, to Germany.

In the aftermath of China's humiliating defeat in the Boxer Rebellion, Western gunboats patrolled China's rivers, Western troops guarded their embassies, railroads, and other facilities, Christian missionaries flooded into the Chinese mission field, and European and American traders swarmed into the China market. With an Irishman running the Chinese customs service and the United States urging an "open door" for all Western powers to trade and invest in the Chinese Empire, China was as much the sick man of Asia as Turkey was the sick man of Europe.

Japan Joins the Imperialists

The reaction of the island empire of Japan to the Western challenge was almost diametrically opposed to that of China. Unique among non–Western nations, Japan not only avoided being colonized but acquired Western skills so rapidly that by the end of the nineteenth century the Japanese themselves had embarked on a notable campaign of imperialist expansion.

Living on islands farther off the shores of East Asia than Britain was from Europe, the Japanese had always been able to choose when and how much they would involve themselves in Asian affairs. They had borrowed from China a written language, Buddhist culture, and a cult of emperor worship roughly similar to Western divine–right monarchy. But they had also developed on their own a sophisticated merchant class and a distinctive urban culture, a militaristic *samurai* tradition comparable to European chivalry, and a system of government that put real power in the hands of the *shogun,* the military leader of the samurai, rather than in the hands of the figurehead emperor.

In the sixteenth century, Japan had eagerly bought guns from European traders and had at least tolerated Christian missionary activity. In the seventeenth, however, the Tokugawa dynasty of shoguns had emulated the Chinese emperors in closing Japan to Europeans, almost wiping out Japan's Christian converts, and leaving only a single port open for very limited Western imports.

Two centuries of self–imposed seclusion followed before the American commodore Matthew C. Perry arrived in Japan in 1853 demanding treaties and trade. After a look at the sleek black American warships, the government signed the treaties in 1854, and the country set to work to catch up with the latest in Western technology.

Fifteen years later, the fading power of the Tokugawa shoguns ended in a coup, which then restored the emperor to his ancient position of centrality. The Meiji emperor, Mutsuhito, sixteen at the time of the Meiji Restoration in 1868, presided over a drive to overtake the West that included educational, technological, commercial, and administrative reforms. Under a centralized government, the Japanese military armed itself with the latest weapons and even built a modern fleet of ironclad, steam–powered warships that brought all of East Asia within reach of Japanese ambition. Japan's merchant class also imitated Western methods, and Japanese businessmen were soon challenging Chinese and even Western traders in the East. This two–pronged assault, military and economic, would make Japan one of the world's leading powers in the course of the twentieth century.

The westernized military arm led the way, however. In 1895, Japan defeated its ancient mentor, China. The struggle, fought over control of the former Chinese tributary state of Korea, led to the shattering of China's old–fashioned army and navy and the temporary independence of Korea. In 1905, the Japanese military went on to humiliate one of the Western imperial powers in the Russo–Japanese War. In this conflict, triggered by Russian imperial penetration of Manchuria and Korea, Japanese forces defeated Russian armies and annihilated a Russian fleet that had sailed all the way around the world to meet its doom at the hands of Admiral Togo's (1846–1934) gleaming new naval squadron. Japan thus played its part in the chopping up of the Middle Kingdom, claiming China's Korean dependency and rivaling Russia in the economic development and exploitation of

Manchuria. Within a couple of generations, this heretofore closed society had absorbed enough Western techniques and technology, first to challenge the new imperialism in Asia, then to become a global economic power.

◆ The Western Conquest of Africa ◆

The so–called "scramble for Africa" during the later decades of the nineteenth century was the other great focus of the new imperialism. In some ways it was a good deal simpler than the spread of Western imperialism in the East. While the West imposed its will on Asia through a tangle of protectorates, spheres of influence, and evolving colonial dependencies, British, French, German, Italian, Belgian, and other imperial powers simply split up most of Africa into colonies, conquered or acquired by treaty and ruled thereafter by Europeans.

Before the rush to colonize Africa began around 1870, no more than a tenth of the continent was under European control. By 1900, scarcely a tenth remained free. The story of this partitioning of a continent is one of the most dramatic and disturbing in the centuries–long tale of Western imperial expansion.

The Pattern of Western Penetration

The pattern of Western penetration had a certain sameness around the continent of Africa. Frequently missionaries or explorers went into the interior well in advance of Western territorial claims, seeking souls to save or the headwaters of the Nile. Then came government expeditions, often pushing off from old coastal possessions once used for resupplying trading vessels on their way to the East or as holding pens for slaves. Marching inland, these expeditions signed treaties with local rulers, from the sophisticated Muslims of the north to the powerful Zulus of the south, offering military aid or financial help in return for submission to European powers. A third stage commonly involved the dispatching of troops to reaffirm the terms of treaties that some paramount chiefs had apparently not fully understood. The African rulers, who knew the local situation far better than the European interlopers did, were as often manipulating the French or British as the latter were duping them. In the end, however, Western firepower was likely to give the Europeans the better of any deal.

Within a few years, then, a European governor would take over the new colony. Imperial governors typically worked through a colonial administration with some African clerks and constables. Though they were sometimes aided by advisory councils that included members of prestigious African families, European officials ruled primarily in European interests. Under the protection of European troops, agents of European trading companies, miners, missionaries, and lonely district officers spread out through the bush, beginning the development, exploitation, and westernization of Africa.

British Indirect Rule: Cape to Cairo

By 1900 Britain, as behooved the world's most successful empire builder, controlled a sizable portion of Africa. And as befit representatives of one of Europe's most liberal states, British imperialists attempted to leave some authority in the hands of traditional rulers. Wherever British colonists settled in significant numbers, however, the power—and the profits—of empire quickly accrued to them.

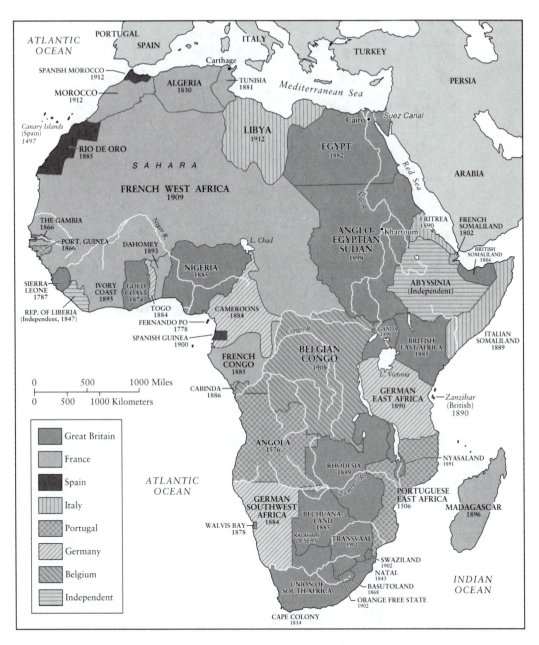

The Partition of Africa, to 1914

Britain's African holdings included an East African string of territories running from South Africa up to Egypt—from "the Cape [of Good Hope] to Cairo"—as well as a scattering of coastal enclaves in French–controlled West Africa. Egypt, still nominally part of

An African view of a Westerner traveling by river through the "dark continent," complete with parasol, pith helmet, and pipe. Do you think this is a realistic representation or a sarcastic caricature of the intruder? (Thomas Ona. Yoruba carving. Buscam Collection #26, Phoebe Hearst Museum of Anthropology, University of California at Berkeley)

the Ottoman Empire, fell first under French influence—an involvement that climaxed in the building of the Suez Canal in 1869—and then became a British protectorate. The arid plains of the Sudan further up the Nile was the scene of an epic struggle between the British and the Muslim religious leader Muhammad Ahmad (1844–1885), called the Mahdi ("the guided one" in Arabic). In 1885, the Mahdi's followers overwhelmed a British garrison at Khartoum and killed the famous British general Charles George ("Chinese") Gordon (b. 1833), so-called for his earlier service in China. Ten years later, however, a British punitive expedition shattered the Mahdi's host and added the Anglo–Egyptian Sudan to Britain's chain of dependencies.

Still further to the south, Britain acquired several black African colonies, of which Kenya became the best known. British farmers were soon shouldering aside indigenous African cultivators to make way for their own more productive acres, on which Africans became laborers. At the southern extremities of the continent, finally, aggressive British settlers swamped an older Dutch colony and, with some difficulty, defeated the mighty Zulus as well. The Dutch migrated into the interior of South Africa on the celebrated "Great Trek" (1835–1843); but when gold and diamonds were discovered in their new home, the British soon followed them. At the turn of the century, the Boer War (1899–1902) broke out between Britain and its rebellious Dutch subjects, called *Boers* from a Dutch word for "farmers." The Boers proved tough guerrilla fighters, and in the end the British had to send in massive reinforcements to defeat them. In order to cut the Boer forces off from civilian support, the British also developed the first concentration camps, where thousands of Boers died of disease.

In West Africa, finally, Britain acquired a small number of colonies, including Nigeria, which lies around the river Niger, and the Gold Coast (Ghana today). Fewer Britons settled in these lands of rain forest and arid plains, and these few British enclaves remained isolated in the French zone of Africa.

The British style of colonial rule did include an element of self–government. From the elected assemblies of the thirteen British North American colonies in earlier times to the increasingly democratic dominions of the nineteenth century—Canada, Australia, and New Zealand—a degree of self–rule had been Britain's policy. In Africa and Asia, however, this approach was watered down to a pattern of *indirect rule*. Indirect rule meant leaving a substantial sphere of delegated authority to paramount chiefs, emirs, sultans, and other traditional rulers. Among some African peoples, however, authority was not traditionally vested in a single ruler but was divided among age groups, heads of families, and other elements of village society. In such cases, it was sometimes deemed necessary to impose a chief with absolute power on the complex indigenous system simply to create a power center through which the British could rule "indirectly." Of course the colonial governor had the last word.

French Assimilation: West Africa

The French approached the colonization of Africa in a different spirit, but they, too, came to control a large part of the continent. Despite their losses to the British in Egypt and the Sudan, the French eventually ruled most of the huge bulge of West Africa as well as the large East African island of Madagascar.

The oldest French African colony, Algeria, had been seized under Charles X and Louis Philippe in the 1820s and 1830s. Lying just across the Mediterranean from southern France, it was soon filling up with French settlers and became a rich source of grain. In the later nineteenth century, the French added Tunisia and Morocco in North Africa and took over enormous tracts of sparsely settled grasslands and rain forest south of the Sahara. Grouped as French West Africa and French Equatorial Africa, these colonies—today encompassing more than a dozen independent nations—added up to a territory comparable in size to that of the continental United States.

The French invasion of West Africa met vigorous resistance from Africans, some of them led by descendants of the rulers of earlier African kingdoms. To suppress this resistance, French military commanders often governed these new colonies directly, imposing an autocratic discipline on "their" local chiefs that contrasted sharply with British indirect rule. The French colonial government's goal of *assimilation* was also different: France sought to assimilate all the colonized peoples of their empire, from Indochina to West Africa, into a larger French cultural community. For a few French–educated Africans, this could mean full rights of citizenship in the French Republic. In some distant future time, all these colonies were expected to relate to Paris just as did the departments of mainland France, as equal provinces of a single metropolis.

French assimilation, however, like British indirect rule, created as many problems as it solved. In the long run, it produced an African elite more imbued with French culture than with African culture—and thus cut off from their own people. The French policy also had the effect of spreading such Western ideologies as nationalism and socialism to Africa and producing generations of sophisticated African leaders prepared to use their knowledge against France itself.

Other African Colonies

Britain and France, in Africa as in the world at large, came out of the nineteenth century with the lion's share of empire. Most of the rest of Africa, however, was also partitioned among Western imperial powers. Some of these, like Portugal, were still managing colonies that had been established centuries before. Others, notably Germany, Italy, and Belgium, were latecomers to the imperial game. Little need be said about these more modest ventures individually except to stress the common pattern of colonial exploitation that all of them shared.

Portugal's large colonies in southern Africa, Angola and Mozambique, dreamed on under a tropical sun, scarcely remembering the days when Da Gama and Albuquerque had passed that way, sailing east to India. King Leopold II of Belgium (r. 1865–1909) personally annexed the huge central African area known as the Belgian Congo (today's Zaire) and soon became notorious for the savage treatment meted out to African laborers in his enormously lucrative Congo copper mines. Germany, hungry for its "place in the sun," acquired a number of African colonies, some of which, like Tanganyika (Tanzania today), had to be "pacified" by heavy deployment of military force. Italy determined on an empire in North Africa and the "horn" south of the Red Sea but was shatteringly defeated by the black African kingdom of Ethiopia. Ethiopia thus became the only sizable piece of Africa to remain completely free of Western control.

The central facts of Western aggression and exploitation thus underlay a variety of colonial ventures. Ethiopia in Africa, like Thailand in Asia, was among the rare corners of these two continents to escape the Western predominance that reached its climax around 1900. Elsewhere, east of Suez or from the Cape to Cairo, Western powers ruled as no other had ever done before.

✦ Internal Imperialism ✦

A thoroughly defensible survey of the new imperialism could stop here, with the Western hegemony of Asia and the partitioning of most of Africa. Yet there are other areas of Western advance that should be considered if we are to grasp the true scope of Western imperial expansion at its height. In several regions, what we may call *internal imperialism* occurred when Western settlers moved in large numbers into lands they had already claimed but had hitherto left largely to the indigenous non–Western inhabitants. The nations that best illustrate this pattern of Western imperialism were all continent–sized countries. Russia, the United States, and the large British dominion of Australia are outstanding examples. This section will show how, in the later 1800s, expanding Western peoples took possession of lands they had earlier only claimed and in so doing damaged or destroyed existing non–Western societies in these areas.

The Continental Countries

Geographically and historically, these widely dispersed lands had basic features in common. Scattered around the globe though they were, they reveal similarities in topography, population, and cultural background that do much to explain their common pattern of internal imperialism.

Geographically, all three were enormous countries, far larger than any western European nation. Russia sprawled all across the northern half of Eurasia, the United States stretched across North America from sea to sea, and Australia had a continent all to itself. All three also included within their borders large expanses of undeveloped land, much of it not obviously of productive value. Russian Siberia and central Asia, for example, encompassed Arctic wastes, deserts, and the sparse grasslands of the steppes. The United States included the plains of the far west, a slice of the Arctic in Alaska, and the deserts of the American southwest. Australia has been described as a ring of habitable land surrounding the vast arid interior Australians call the outback.

All three nations were clearly dominated by European–descended populations. These European elements, however, tended to be concentrated in one portion of each country. In the Russian Empire, this area was European Russia, west of the Urals. In the United States, it stretched down the east coast of North America. And in Australia, the original settlements were in New South Wales, in southeastern Australia.

Even these core populations of Europe's continental outliers, furthermore, were seen as less than ideal Europeans. "Scratch a Russian and you will find a Tatar," western Europeans opined darkly, referring to Muscovy's medieval centuries under the Golden Horde and the substantial Mongol element in its population. Americans were perceived as "Yankees," brash and vulgar, altogether too democratic and lacking in reverence for the wisdom of the Old World. Australians were provincials, slowly earning self–government within the British Empire but undisciplined and rough, perhaps revealing their convict ancestry whose first Australian homes had been penal colonies.

Large parts of all these nations, finally, were thinly inhabited by clearly non–Western peoples living at an earlier stage of social, economic, and political development than their European–descended neighbors. Those included the Muslim and Mongol peoples of Russian Siberia, central Asia, and the Caucasus; the Amerindians of the American midwest and far west; and the Aborigines of Australia's outback. Agriculturalists, herders, or hunters and gatherers, these peoples could offer little serious resistance to attacks mounted by the Westerners who already claimed their lands.

Conditions for Conquest

Among the causal factors that helped to trigger large–scale Western migrations into these territories were basic demographic, economic, and technological changes. In the second half of the nineteenth century, for instance, all three of these countries possessed large free–floating populations. The Australian gold rush of the 1850s and the American Homestead Act of 1862, offering 160 acres of free land to anyone who would farm it, both drew large numbers of immigrants. The lure of gold and land soon doubled the size of Australia's European population and combined with other factors to draw millions to the United States. Russia freed its serfs in 1861, and many, liberated with too little land to support them, turned their eyes eastward.

During this period also, important economic changes made increasing demands and opened up new possibilities for the exploitation of the "empty" lands east of the Urals, west of the Mississippi, or in the Australian outback. Under Alexander II (r. 1855–1881), the Industrial Revolution finally came to Russia, accelerating markedly under Nicholas II (r. 1894–1917). From the end of the American Civil War in 1865 onward, the United States plunged into its gilded age of booming industrial growth. And in Australia, a gold rush that began in the 1850s pointed toward more broadly based economic development to come. Markets for beef, wool, and grain, demands for metals and fuels sharply accentuated the lure of sheep ranching in the outback, mining in the Urals or the U.S. Mesabi range, herding cattle or farming on the great plains.

Technological advances, finally, once again gave these Western peoples the power they needed to take what they wanted. Railways knifed through the wilderness, carrying waves of immigrants out and their produce back to market. America's transcontinental railroad was completed in the 1860s, the Trans–Siberian Railway in the 1890s. The telegraph gave settlers instant communication, while barbed wire and new farming and mining equipment provided the tools to make the land pay as never before. Add repeating rifles like the Martini and the Winchester, Colt six–shooter pistols, and the self–confidence that went with these advantages, and the fate of the Amerindians, Aborigines, Mongols, and others was pretty much a foregone conclusion.

Destruction of Non–Western Societies

Russia's eastward expansion, the American westward movement, and Australian occupation of the central plains thus had a good deal in common. All these movements involved massive migrations, conflict, economic exploitation, and the destruction of non–Western societies that proved too fragile to stand the shock of the new imperialism. Americans, including many immigrants, moved westward across the Mississippi, the great plains, the Rockies, and the Sierra Nevadas after the Civil War. Millions of Russians, many of them former serfs, moved east of the Urals or south into central Asia or the mountainous Caucasus. Beginning from a smaller population base, lesser numbers of Australians moved into the arid interior where only Aboriginal food gatherers had once followed their prehistoric round.

Conflict was inevitable and frequently violent. American and Russian armies garrisoned isolated forts in Apache or Kazakh territories, staking out the ground for the new order. Australia's Aborigines were too few and too unorganized to provide real opposition, but border police and exasperated ranchers responded with lethal force to Aborigine poaching on what had once been their own hunting grounds. And once more, as earlier in the Americas, bacilli for which non–Westerners had no immunities took a larger toll than Western firearms did.

The invaders made the land more productive, but they also kept the profits of that productivity. Russian agriculture was not efficient by western European standards, but with irrigation and hard work it could make even central Asian lands bloom. American ranches and farms produced far more food and other products per square acre than the buffalo herds had provided for the Amerindians. Australian sheep ranching supported a much larger and more developed society than the food–gathering Aborigines had been able to construct. And besides farming and ranching, mining added a whole new dimension to the exploitation of the environment and brought new wealth to those who undertook it.

The original inhabitants survived their early losses in all three countries. Their numbers were least drastically cut in Russia, much more so in the United States. Nowhere, however, did native *cultures* survive this encounter with the industrialized West. Reservations and preserves did not really conserve the old Amerindian or Aboriginal way of life. Neither czarist occupiers nor the later soviet socialist republics ever intended to preserve indigenous cultures intact, seeking instead to modernize and then to sovietize underdeveloped minority peoples.

United States imperialist expansion led to the acquisition of a handful of small colonies outside the continental United States in the Spanish–American War of 1898, including the Philippines and Puerto Rico. Russia, as we have seen, was an active imperialist from Turkey and Afghanistan to China. But the most significant conquests of the two future superpowers, like those of Australia and similarly situated peoples in Canada, Brazil, and South Africa, were examples of internal imperialism, the physical occupation of lands that, though inhabited by non–Western peoples, were already Western on Western maps.

♦ The Impact of the New Imperialism ♦

Kipling–style imperialism—pith helmets and "dominion over palm and pine"—seems far in the past today. It produced some exciting headlines and generated fierce resentment among the colonized. But in the longer span of human history, do yesterday's empires really matter much?

In many ways, economic and political, social and cultural, the new Western imperialism did in fact have a profound long–term effect. We will look here at the ways in which the new imperialism did and did not benefit the West, at its transforming impact on non–Western peoples, and at the profoundly changed world it left behind.

Imperialism and the West

As we have seen, a widely accepted view of Western imperialism interprets it as a system designed to exploit the non–Western world in the interests of the capitalist West. We have already seen that economic incentives were indeed important causes of the new imperialism. But did the imperial powers in fact get rich off their colonies? It is a more difficult question to answer than we might expect.

Certainly the imperial powers did invest in and trade with their expanding overseas dependencies. The French, for instance, invested heavily in their overseas possessions—a total of well over five billion francs in public and private investment between 1880 and 1914. The British Empire at its greatest extent, around 1930, generated an annual trade flow of 300 million pounds worth of imports into Britain and almost 250 million pounds in exports to the colonies.

Further investigation, however, reveals that the business communities of the Western imperial powers actually invested more heavily in and traded more lavishly with lands *outside* their empires than within them. The British had less than half their overseas capital invested in imperial enterprises and only a little over one–quarter of its total commerce flowing between Britain and its colonies.

Such figures tend to indicate, at least to some interpreters, that Western capitalists normally preferred to deal with independent nations rather than with dependent colonies. The greatest flow of goods and capital in the nineteenth century was in fact within the emerging Atlantic community of nations, between Europe and the Americas—that is, within the expanding Western world itself.

The new imperialism also failed to fulfill other material expectations. Imperialistically minded political leaders who hoped to export surplus population to colonies without losing their services, for instance, must have been disappointed by the emigration statistics. Seventy percent of British emigrants settled outside the empire on which the sun never set.

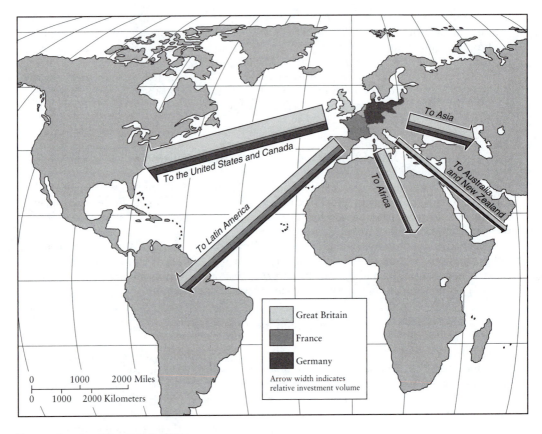

To Asia

To the United States and Canada

To Latin America

To Africa

To Australia and New Zealand

☐ Great Britain

☐ France

■ Germany

Arrow width indicates
relative investment volume

0   1000   2000 Miles

0   1000   2000 Kilometers

European Investment Overseas, to 1914

Of thirteen million Italians who left that overcrowded country between 1880 and 1914, only fifty–six thousand settled in Italian overseas possessions, the rest thronging to North and South America and other areas beyond the reach of the Italian flag.

Colonial populations, on the other hand, did make a significant contribution both to the labor force and to the military strength of the Western imperial powers. Labor was vastly cheaper on the colonial periphery. Most of it worked in plantation agriculture or in mining, but non–Europeans also labored on railroads and developed the beginnings of modern industry in such colonies as India or French Indochina. Large numbers of colonial people also served in Western armies, giving the West greater human resources for the global conflicts of the next century.

It is a mixed balance sheet, then, both economically and politically. When we add that colonial dependencies cost their rulers a good deal to operate, it is even harder to see them as having been a paying proposition. As we will see in the concluding pages of this chapter, there is a larger sense in which the West gained immeasurably from the creation of a global system of exchange and control. But the empires were probably not the sources of direct and massive profits dreamed of by imperialistic politicians and newspaper editors, by manufacturers and traders in Europe, and by European farmers, stock raisers, or mine operators in the colonies themselves.

Imperialism and the Non–Western World

Again, we may start with a common view, this time of the oppressive nature of imperialism as experienced by its targets. And certainly there is plenty of evidence that Western imperialists dealt brutally with colonized peoples. We may, for instance, remember the savagery of the Belgian Congo, where the hands of African laborers in the copper mines were cut off for theft. We may recall the "trail of tears," lined with the graves of Native Americans,

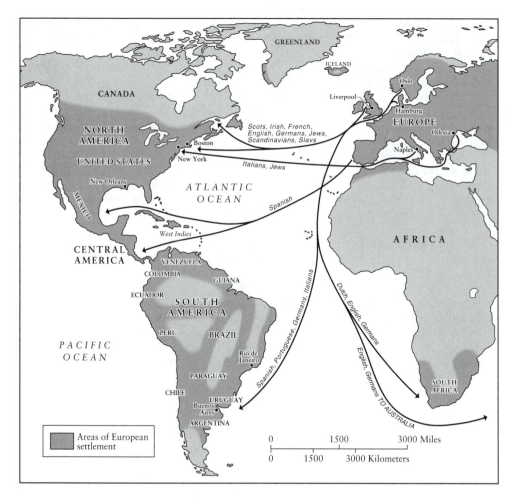

European Migration, 1820–1920

along which U.S. troops "removed" the Cherokee from their homes in the southeast to exile in Oklahoma. Such instances of civilized savagery were all part of the impact of the West on the non–West in the period of the new imperialism.

Western economic penetration also often had deeply destructive consequences. The copper and tin and petroleum Europeans siphoned out of non–Western lands would never return. The local industries that perished with the introduction of Western machine–made products would never revive. The rapid urbanization of village cultures began the process of undermining traditional ways of life, just as the lure of the city had undercut village life in Europe and America. The list of material shocks and strains to the social fabric caused by this massive Western intrusion into the non–Western world is long indeed.

Perhaps deepest of all were the intellectual, psychological, even spiritual consequences of the new imperialism for its victims. Basic features of Western civilization, as well as some of the newest Western worldviews, were communicated to at least an influential minority among the colonized. In government and mission schools across the non–Western world, Asian, African, and Amerindian elites learned English, French, Spanish, and other Western languages. Missionaries also made large numbers of Christian converts in the colonial world. Native languages and traditional religions survived, but the future belonged to those who had come to terms with Western tongues and faiths.

There were some advantages to the Western presence in the rest of the world, of course. Against the destruction of India's handloom industry we might weigh the building of India's continental system of railroads. Western science and technology, seen as the keys to both liberation from the West and the achievement of a Western standard of living, have been eagerly cultivated by non–Western peoples since independence. The Western languages spread by imperialism gave twentieth–century developing nations easier access to global trade, tourism, and other advantages. And Europeans did oppose some practices that Third World nations themselves have rejected since, such as painful footbinding for Chinese girls or the rigid discrimination against the "untouchable" classes imposed by India's caste system.

Western ideologies, as we will see in later chapters, made a special contribution to non–Western history. From Western liberalism, a few colonials learned to view themselves as equal to their rulers and as deserving the freedom that liberals said was a human birthright. From nationalism, they learned to see themselves as a national community, transcending traditional barriers of caste, clan, tribe, or religion. From socialism, even largely preindustrial peoples could borrow a special sensitivity to economic exploitation, as well as attitudes toward the role of government in economic development that would guide their thinking once independence was finally achieved. During the second half of the twentieth century, then, these European "isms" would play an important part, not only in Western history, but in the history of the world as a whole.

Summary

The new imperialism that reached its climax between 1870 and 1914 transformed most of Africa into European–ruled colonies, most of Asia into colonies, protectorates, or spheres of influence. By the end of the nineteenth century, the West had thus established an unprecedented political hegemony over most of the rest of the world.

The causes of this Western imperial expansion were complicated. Some causes were clearly economic. The complex industrial economies of the West drew resources from and exploited cheap labor in the non–Western world, while Western capitalists used less–developed regions of the globe as markets and as investment areas. Other causes of the new imperialism included the "white man's burden" theory that Western peoples had a duty to "civilize" the rest of the world, the well–established Western missionary impulse, and nineteenth–century assumptions of Western racial superiority.

This unprecedented surge of Western expansion was made possible by Western technological superiority in the first full century of the Industrial Revolution. Western weapons, tools, transportation, medicine, and other technological developments gave nineteenth–century empire builders insurmountable advantages over even the most sophisticated of non–Western empires.

Thus equipped and motivated, Europeans moved aggressively into Asia. Much of the Middle East was converted into European protectorates and spheres of interest. India became a gigantic British colony, and Britain and France parceled out mainland Southeast Asia between them. The Western powers seemed to be preparing to carve up the ancient Chinese Empire as

the century ended. Japan, however, rapidly modernized and actually joined the empire–builders at the end of the century.

Western nations also quickly divided Africa up into colonies after 1870. Thus British empire builders took over much of East Africa from Cairo to the Cape of Good Hope, while the French absorbed most of West Africa. The Belgians moved into Central Africa, and other European states seized other African territories.

Finally, large Western nations like the United States, Russia, and Australia seized this time to occupy territories long claimed but largely populated by non–Western peoples. The result was a further expansion of Western power in Asia, the Americas, and elsewhere.

The consequences of this unprecedented wave of imperial expansion were equally unparalleled. Westerners siphoned out resources, ruined local industries, and exploited foreign populations as laborers, soldiers, and in other ways. The new imperialism also spread many Western ideas among non–Western peoples, including ideological theories such as nationalism, that would prove as disruptive overseas as in Europe itself.

Some Key Terms

assimilation 581	Indian Mutiny 574	the Raj 574
Eastern Question 572	indirect rule 581	*samurai* 577
colonization 568	internal imperialism 582	*shogun* 577
cultural imperialism 569	new imperialism 567	sphere of influence 568
economic imperialism 568	old imperialism 567	"the white man's burden" 570
extraterritoriality 576	protectorate 568	unequal treaties 576

Notes

1. H. M. Stanley, quoted in Lance E. Davis and Robert A. Huttenback, *Mammon and the Pursuit of Empire: The Political Economy of British Imperialism, 1860–1912* (Cambridge: Cambridge University Press, 1986), 6.
2. *The Spectator,* August 19, 1899, quoted in John M. Mackenzie, *Imperialism and Popular Culture* (Manchester: Manchester University Press, 1986), 10.
3. Lord Lugard, quoted in J. A. Mangan, *The Games Ethic and Imperialism: Aspects of the Diffusion of an Ideal* (Harmondsworth, England: Viking, 1986), 112.
4. Hilaire Belloc, *The Modern Traveler* (London:

S. Swift, 1898), vi.

5. Commodore J. J. Gordon Bremmer to the Earl of Auckland, February 1841, quoted in Daniel R. Headrick, *The Tools of Empire: Technology and European Imperialism in the Nineteenth*

Century (New York: Oxford University Press, 1981), 50.

6. Rudyard Kipling, *A Kipling Pageant* (New York: Literary Guild, 1935), 908–909.

Reading List

Baumgart, W. *Imperialism.* Oxford: Oxford University Press, 1982. Theories of imperialism tested against the realities of English and French expansion. See also N. Etherington, *Theories of Imperialism* (London: Croom Helm, 1984).

Charlesworth, N. *British Rule and the Indian Economy.* London: Macmillan, 1982. Brief look at economic advantages and disadvantages of British rule for the Indian economy. See also M. H. Fisher, *Indirect Rule in India: Residents and the Residency System* (New York: Oxford University Press, 1991).

Cohen, W. B. *The French Encounter with Africa: White Response to Blacks, 1530–1880.* Bloomington: Indiana University Press, 1980. Cultures in conflict. See also his *Rulers of Empire: The French Colonial Services in Africa* (Stanford: Hoover Institution, 1971).

Fieldhouse, D. K. *The Colonial Empires: A Comparative Study from the Eighteenth Century.* London: Weidenfeld and Nicolson, 1966. Perhaps still the best available survey.

Headrick, D. R. *The Tools of Empire: Technology and European Imperialism in the Nineteenth Century.* New York: Oxford University Press, 1981. Discusses the role of steamships and quinine as well the superiority of European weapons.

Henderson, W. O. *Studies in German Colonial History.* Chicago: Quadrangle, 1962. Brief essays.

Kiernan, V. C. *From Conquest to Collapse: European Empires from 1815 to 1960.* New York: Pantheon, 1982. A dark picture of the new imperialism, stressing bloodshed, racism, and oppressive rule.

Lincoln, W. B. *The Conquest of a Continent: Siberia and the Russians.* New York: Random House, 1994. Vivid narrative history.

MacDonald, R. H. *The Language of Empire: Myths and Metaphors of Popular Imperialism, 1880–1918.* New York: Manchester University Press, 1994. Popular appeal of imperialism.

Manning, P. *Francophone Sub-Saharan Africa, 1880–1985.* New York: Cambridge University Press, 1988. Strong on the impact of contact with the West on African societies.

Morris, D. *The Washing of the Spears.* New York: Simon and Schuster, 1965. Monumental account of Britain's Zulu war. See also R. B. Edgerton, *Like Lions They Fought: The Zulu War and the Last Black Empire in South Africa* (New York: Free Press, 1988), based on new evidence, including survivors' diaries and interviews with combatants.

Pamuk, S. *The Ottoman Empire and European Capitalism, 1820–1913: Trade, Investment, and Production.* New York: Cambridge University Press, 1987. Statistical analysis of Western economic influence on the declining Ottoman realm.

Peckenham, T. *The Scramble for Africa: The White Man's Conquest of the Dark Continent from 1876 to 1912.* New York: Random House, 1992. Detailed political history of the new imperialism from the European perspective. See also A. J. Christopher, *Colonial Africa* (London: Croom Helm, 1984).

Phillips, A. *The Enigma of Colonialism: British Policy in West Africa.* Bloomington: Indiana University Press, 1989. Imperial efforts to establish capitalism in Britain's West African colonies.

Robinson, R. *Africa and the Victorians: The Official Mind of Imperialism.* 2d ed. London: Macmillan, 1981. Trailblazing monograph, revealing lack of enthusiasm for new colonies in the British Colonial Office. On racism as a motive, see P. Brantlinger, *Rule of Darkness: British Literature of Imperialism, 1830–1914* (Ithaca, N.Y.: Cornell University Press, 1988).

Rotberg, R. I. *The Founder: Cecil Rhodes and the Pursuit of Power.* New York: Norton, 1988. A convincing portrait of the archetypal British imperialist.

Slade, R. T. *King Leopold's Congo.* London: Oxford University Press, 1962. Best account in English of Belgian exploitation of the Congo.

Ward, A. *A Show of Justice.* Aukland: Aukland University Press, 1974. Impact of colonialism on the Maoris of New Zealand.

Wilson, H. S. *The Imperial Experience in Sub–Saharan Africa Since 1870*. Minneapolis: University of Minnesota Press, 1977. Excellent overview

of imperial impact on black Africa.

Wolf, E. R. *Europe and the People Without History*. Berkeley: University of California Press, 1982. Critical assessment of the impact of imperialism on colonized peoples.

PART VI
The Twentieth Century The West in a Changing World

In size, the Western world achieved its maximum extent in the first half of the twentieth century. The West sprawled across four continents in 1900—Europe, North and South America, and Australia—and Western–ruled empires encompassed most of Asia and Africa. The rest of the world waxed restless under Western rule, and in the second half of the century, these empires came tumbling down. But Western economic power, technological leadership, and even culture continued to play a predominant role in world history even in the later 1900s.

In political affairs, the first half of the twentieth century saw a widespread resurgence of autocratic government, ranging from the totalitarian regimes of Nazi Germany, Fascist Italy, and Communist Russia to personal dictatorships in many Latin American republics and a militarist takeover in increasingly westernized Japan. In international affairs, the West and much of the rest of the world were brutally ravaged by World War I (1914–1918) and World War II (1939–1945), the two most bloody and destructive wars in history.

After World War II and again after the cold war, liberal political institutions spread once more as former dictatorships moved toward working democracies. In international relations, the collapse of the Western overseas empires contributed many underdeveloped nations to the new "Third World," while the cold war divided the Western nations themselves into two armed camps led by the United States and the Soviet Union.

The economic centerpiece of the first half of the twentieth century was the Great Depression of the 1930s, which was triggered by the American Wall Street crash of 1929 and quickly spread to Europe and the rest of the world. During the half–century after World War II, however, free–market economies in the American camp, undergirded by substantial welfare nets, produced the highest standards of living in history. The state–run planned economies of the Soviet bloc, by contrast, fell steadily behind in productivity and collapsed at the end of the 1980s.

In terms of social and cultural history, middle–class Americans, western Europeans, and other Western peoples had enormous quantities of new consumer products to choose from. Increasingly also, Western women lived relatively independent lives, sharing educational and job opportunities once restricted to men. And in many parts of the Western world, young people became social arbiters, leading their elders into relatively amoral—some said immoral—new lifestyles. Modernism and postmodernism in the arts shared the apparent rejection of styles and values that characterized avant–garde thinking in this century.

As the twentieth century drew to a close, there were many problems still to be faced. These ran from racism, sexism, and aggressive nationalism to pollution, waste, overpopulation, and forms of poverty that seemed to be structural, built into a technologically developing world. The post–cold war 1990s seemed to be a time of new beginnings, but whether the end of the millennium pointed to an impressive "new world order" or yet another dangerous passage in the history of the West and the world, only time could tell.

Time Line: The West in a Changing World

from 1900   Modernism rejects society and experiments in art and literature

1905   Einstein's theory of relativity

1907–1914   Picasso invents cubism, reducing nature to abstract shapes

1910s–1920s   Rise of moving pictures as art and entertainment

1910s–1920s   Emergence of jazz as international musical form

1914   Sarajevo assassination triggers World War I

1914–1918   Trench warfare on the Western Front

1917   February Revolution overthrows the czar; October Revolution brings Bolshevik revolutionary leader Lenin to power

1919   Peace of Paris imposes harsh settlement on the Central Powers

1922   Mussolini's March on Rome succeeds

1928   Stalin emerges as leader of Soviet Union

1929   Wall Street crash brings Great Depression

1933   Hitler comes to power in Germany

1933–1939   Roosevelt's New Deal brings reforms in United States

1939–1945   World War II ravages Europe, parts of Asia and Africa

1940s   Big bang theory of origin of universe

1940s–1950s   Liberation of most Asian colonies

1940s–1950s   Existentialism asserts that "existence precedes essence"

1945–1949   Soviet satellite states established after World War II

1945–1974   Boom years in North America and Western Europe follow World War II

1947   Truman doctrine promises aid for nations threatened by Soviet expansionism; Marshall Plan offers economic aid

1949–1957   Military alliances (NATO, Warsaw Pact) and economic organizations (COMECON, Common Market) set up

1950s   DNA discovered, revealing key to genetic programming

1950–1953   Korean War

1950s   Pollock develops abstract expressionism, shifts international art center to New York

1950s   Emergence of Rock and Roll as international music

1950s   Color film again transforms motion pictures

1950s–1960s   Liberation of most African colonies

1956–1968   Civil rights movement in United States

from 1960s   Postmodernism rejects "the canon," modernist classics, and "great art" of any sort

1962   Cuban missile crisis threatens nuclear war

1965–1973   Vietnam War

1970s   Poststructuralism emphasizes use of ideas to dominate "discourse" and society

1970s–1990s   Women's movement pursues economic and political parity across Western world

1974–1990s   Economically depressed years across Western world

1989–1990   Soviet satellite states free; divided Germany reunited

1991   Soviet Union disintegrates

24

The Trenches and the Barricades

World War I and the Russian Revolution

This is a chapter about beginnings—the beginnings of the twentieth century and the beginnings of trends that would shape the next hundred years. We will begin therefore with the turn of the century, and with the importance of nationalism, socialism, and progressive reform in key countries around 1900.

Dated in terms of significant historical events, however, the twentieth century began not in 1900, but a decade and a half later, with the First World War (1914–1918) and the Russian Revolution of 1917. World War I was an unprecedented international disaster that cost millions of lives and left Western self–confidence badly shaken. The Russian Revolution brought a communist government to power that became a center of opposition to the status quo for most of the rest of the century. These two crises are the focus of the present chapter.

There had been wars that involved most of the great powers of the Western world before, including those of Louis XIV and Napoleon. None of these, however, could match the scale and ferocity of what participants in World War I called "the Great War." We will begin with an attempt to trace the causes of the catastrophe. Thereafter, a look at the conflict itself will show us something of the savagery of twentieth–century warfare. And an analysis of the peace the victorious Allies forced upon their enemies will provide a useful object lesson in how not to deal with a temporarily humbled foe.

The other central focus of this chapter will be the Russian Revolution that exploded toward the end of the First World War. Again, there had been epochal ideological revolutions in Europe before this—the English "century of revolution" that climaxed in 1688, for instance, and the French Revolution of 1789. But none made a greater difference to the future of the West and of the world than the Russian Revolution of 1917. From the success of the Russian Revolution sprang Joseph Stalin's "iron age," and the cold war that divided the Western world through the second half of the century.

♦The Turn of the Century♦

The West had never looked more successful and impressive than it did in 1900. Peace, prosperity, and progress seemed to have been achieved across most of the Western world.

But there were divisions much deeper than most people recognized in the political, social, and economic structure of the West. And looming larger than all the rest were three nations—Germany, Russia, and the United States—that would play dominant, often divisive roles in the tumultuous history of the twentieth century.

Society and Politics

Dining luxuriously at Maxim's in Paris or Delmonico's in New York, a silk–hatted gentleman and a long–gowned lady would have had every reason to feel smug in the early months of 1914. The most civilized of worlds seemed to be theirs as they savored rich sauces or richer desserts. Electric trolleys had replaced horsecars in the streets, and gleaming motor cars propelled by internal combustion engines chugged along amid the horse–drawn carriages and wagons. Americans were beginning to construct buildings so high they called them "skyscrapers," and a few daredevils in what looked like propeller–driven box kites were challenging the balloon's monopoly of the air. It was a wonderful time to be alive, at least for people who could afford to dine at Maxim's or Delmonico's.

It was a grimmer world than that, of course, as a stroll from a fancy restaurant to the slums of working–class Paris or the lower east side of New York might have revealed. There the urban poor, struggling to make ends meet, took a less enthusiastic view of the new century. And there were still many peasants for whom one century was much like another.

Aristocratic and middle–class citizens, in general, often shared a distrust of the new industrial laboring classes. In this sentiment, they were reinforced by another turn–of–the–century trend: the growth of an increasingly large white–collar class. Because their styles of work and life resembled those of their employers more than those of miners or assembly–line workers, white–collar workers eschewed unionization, rejected socialism, and thought of themselves as middle class rather than working class.

The size, aggressiveness, and power of the industrial proletariat itself varied considerably from one part of Europe to another. In southern and eastern Europe, industrialization had come later and a sizable proletariat was making its appearance for the first time. In Russia, there were three million industrial workers by the turn of the century, but by far the bulk of the population remained peasants on the land. In industrialized Britain, by contrast, nonagricultural workers were becoming the majority of the population. And in Germany the industrial working class constituted the largest single segment of the voting public.

In general, old–fashioned autocracy still dominated politics east of the Rhine. The aging emperor Francis Joseph (r. 1848–1916) of Austria–Hungary, perfectly embodied this conservatism as he struggled to hold onto power in the face of increasing demands from his Hungarian, Slavic, and other non–German subjects. Hoping that ancient traditional loyalty to the dynasty might outweigh more recently aroused nationalistic sentiments, the government in Vienna decided to give the vote to the peasant majority. Conflicting national loyalties, however, continued to divide the Habsburg realms, as each nationality demanded its own schools, official language, and other forms of autonomy.

In western Europe, liberals still passed reforms aimed at finishing off what remained of the conservative alliance of throne, church, and aristocracy. In France, for instance, liberals followed the vindication of Captain Dreyfus with a series of anticlerical laws intended to sever remaining ties between church and state. In Britain, the Liberal party undermined that bastion of aristocratic power, the House of Lords, which in 1911 lost its right to veto laws passed by the House of Commons.

Chronology 24: The First World War and the Russian Revolution

1879	*Dual Alliance binds Germany and Austria—the "Central Powers" diplomatically*
1904	*Entente Cordiale links Britain and France—"the Allies"*
1905–1906	*Revolution of 1905 forces Nicholas II to grant Duma (legislature) in Russia*
1905, 1911	*First and second Moroccan crisis divide France and Germany*
1908	*Bosnian crisis divides Austria and Russia*
1914	*Sarajevo assassination triggers World War I*
1914–1918	*Trench warfare on the Western Front*
1914–1917	*Russia suffers more than any other power from World War I; suffering builds opposition to government*
1915	*Italy enters war on Allied side; Gallipoli disaster for Allies*
1916	*Allied offensive fails on the Somme; German offensive fails at Verdun*
1917	*February Revolution overthrows Nicholas II, brings Duma leader Kerensky to power; October Revolution overthrows Kerensky, brings Bolshevik leader Lenin to power*
1917, 1918	*United States enters war on Allied side; Russia leaves the war, weakening Allies*
1918	*Armistice ends World War I*
1918–1921	*Russian Civil War—Bolsheviks successfully repel all rivals for power*
1919	*Peace of Paris imposes harsh settlement on the Central Powers*

Chauvinists in Germany, Bolsheviks in Russia

Three nations were to play central roles in the history of the twentieth century. In each of these nations, one of the major revolutionary ideologies of the nineteenth century played a crucial part in the twentieth. In Germany, that ism was racist nationalism; in Russia, it was revolutionary socialism; and in the United States, it was reformist liberalism.

The Germany that William II (r. 1888–1918) inherited was the product of two decades of remarkable political, economic, social, and military successes. Politically, the German people were unified as never before in their history in a centralized, efficiently administered modern state. Economically, the new Germany had leaped ahead in agricultural and industrial production until the German economy was challenging those of Britain and the United States. Altogether, it was easy to be patriotic in the Germany of the Second Empire.[1]

Unfortunately, German patriotism had evolved into a chauvinistic, even racist form of nationalism that brutally misdirected the course of German history through the first half of the twentieth century. Enthusiasm for the Prussian army, the core of the German army after unification in 1871, had never been higher. Emperor William II stimulated aggressive nationalism by issuing ringing announcements that Germany was embarking on a "New Course" and a "World Policy" to win its rightful "place in the sun" of overseas empire. The cult of the German national character or "folk soul" hardened into belief in a German "race" as the biological core of true Germanness. And Germans, like other Western peoples, increasingly condemned Jewish citizens as a different "race," as "un–German."

In Russia, Czar Nicholas II (r. 1894–1917) was an unaggressive man with none of his cousin William II's arrogant self–confidence. During his reign, he faced mounting opposition. The peasants liberated in 1861, still struggling with inadequate land allotments and heavy taxes, were prone to riot and local rebellion against oppressive officials. The economic reforms of Nicholas II's finance minister, Count Sergei Witte (1849–1915), had created an expanding industrial proletariat, underpaid and overworked, who were increasingly given to strikes and industrial disturbances. Liberal county officials and radical students demanded democratic institutions. And by 1900, a revolutionary socialist underground was plotting the overthrow of the czar himself.

Among these groups, the Social Revolutionaries followed in the *narodnik* peasant–socialist tradition, trying to rouse the peasantry to revolt. The Social Democrats, by contrast, were Russian Marxists who tried to mobilize the new proletariat. In 1903, the Marxists split into two feuding factions, the *Bolshevik* or "majority" party led by Vladimir Ilich Ulyanov (1870–1924), better known as Lenin, and the *Menshevik* or "minority" party, as Lenin shrewdly labeled them. Lenin and his Bolshevik faction took the old–fashioned Marxist view that reformist compromises were doomed to failure, that revolution was the only solution, and that only a tightly knit, rigidly disciplined core of professional revolutionaries could bring the revolution. But Bolsheviks like the exiled Lenin, arguing Marxist theory in the cheap cafes of Zurich, or like Stalin, languishing in czarist prisons or in Siberia, did not look particularly formidable as the century began.

In 1905, however, the revolution came—and failed. Russia's military disaster in the Russo–Japanese War triggered the Revolution of 1905. Russians of all classes were dismayed at the nation's failure to defeat the little island kingdom off the coast of East Asia. Many saw the defeat as evidence of the feebleness of Russian society as a whole. Peasants petitioned their "dear father czar" for reforms, and were fired on by the troops. Demonstrations mounted, and in some cities, working people's *soviets,* or "councils," took over the functions of government. In October 1905, Nicholas responded by issuing the *October Manifesto,* recognizing civil rights for Russians and granting an elected national legislature called the *Duma.* In 1906, however, he called out the troops once more and began to reinterpret the Manifesto, allowing only very limited authority to a Duma elected by a heavily class–weighted suffrage. Lenin and other hard–line Bolsheviks went back into exile to dream of "the next time."

The Progressive Movement in the United States

In the United States, turn–of–the–century problems began to find solutions in the Populist and Progressive movements, which loomed large in U. S. politics during the 1890s and the first two decades of the twentieth century.

American writers called *muckrakers* made the country vividly aware of the ruthlessness of some of the barons of U. S. business. Exploiting labor, driving rivals into bankruptcy, squeezing their customers, and bribing politicians to keep government off their backs, these industrial, commercial, and financial tycoons displayed little concern for the public interest. The growth of industrial technology also served to impoverish farmers and farm workers by keeping agricultural prices and wages low.

In the 1890s, the *Populist movement* rose from a fusion of farmers' and miners' groups determined on vigorous political action. The Populists blamed merchants, railroad magnates, financial manipulators, and corrupt politicians for all their woes. Populism produced some eloquent leaders. William Jennings Bryan (1860–1928), a passionate supporter of many Populist causes, was the Democratic presidential candidate in 1896 and again in 1900 and 1908. The Populist agitator Mary E. Lease (1850–1933) encouraged farmers to "raise less corn and more hell." Yet the raw, angry campaigns of the Populists accomplished little.

By 1900, however, a new, more broadly based, and more "respectable" reform tendency took shape in the movement called *Progressivism*. Progressives, whether Republicans or Democrats, tended to be liberal, middle–class Americans of older stock, often professional people. Shocked by the greed of the self–made millionaires and the corruption of urban political machines and state legislatures, they also apparently saw this new axis of power in the hands of industrial barons and political bosses as a challenge to their own traditional status. Their solution was government regulation, to be undertaken by respectable reformers like themselves. Running candidates first for local and state offices and after 1900 for the presidency itself, the Progressive movement produced two of the nation's most admired presidents: Republican Theodore Roosevelt (president 1901–1909) and Democrat Woodrow Wilson (president 1913–1921).

At the local level, Progressives pioneered such reforms as settlement houses to help slum dwellers, state regulation for railways, and state income taxes. They also developed the neutral city manager to replace urban machine politicians and drew academic experts into government, a practice that soon spread to Washington as well. Under bumptious Teddy Roosevelt's vigorous leadership, Progressive Republicans used the threat to "bust the trusts" to impose national regulation on the railroads, regulate the purity of food and drugs, and protect public lands from private exploitation. More stiff and preacherly, but no less inspiring to his followers, President Woodrow Wilson passed legislation against monopolies and reformed the currency through a system of federal reserve banks. During this period also, constitutional amendments provided for a federal income tax, and in the aftermath of World War I, doubled the size of the electorate by recognizing the right of American women to vote.

✦Origins of World War I✦

There have been many attempts to explain the outbreak of World War I. Both the *Allies,* mainly Britain, France, Russia, Italy, and later the United States, and the *Central Powers,* meaning primarily Germany and Austria, offered a variety of idealistic "war aims." The historical search for the long–range causes of the war, however, has led well back into the 1800s, to conflicts involving imperial rivalries, economic competition, the demands of military leaders, and the nationalistic passions of Europe's peoples. The quest for more immediate causes has concentrated on networks of international alliances and on a chain of crises building up to the sensational assassination of a Habsburg prince at Sarajevo in 1914—the political murder that precipitated the Great War.

Causes of Conflict

Among the more deeply rooted causes of the international tension that led to World War I, economic and imperial rivalries, arms races and militarism, rival nationalisms and rival alliances all seem to have made major contributions.

Industrial and commercial competition was particularly intense between Britain and Germany. Britain's long lead in the Industrial Revolution had evaporated in the second half of the nineteenth century, as British equipment grew dated. Germany's newer industrial plant and greater efficiency, by contrast, gave it a commercial advantage overseas that soon had the "made in Germany" label outselling the British label. Imperial conflicts also soured relations between powers. German leaders saw Britain as denying the new German Empire its legitimate "place in the sun" of worldwide colonial expansion. Franco–German imperial rivalry was intensified as well by the clash of the two nations over parts of North Africa.

Militarism and arms races also prepared both sides to fight a war on a scale unmatched in earlier history. By the end of the nineteenth century, enormous conscript armies and hugely expensive military hardware had accumulated in the Western nations. Military leaders worked out elaborate war plans, while civilian supporters of European armies and navies sparked enthusiasm for the military and demanded action when their "national honor" was challenged. Competitions in armaments also added to international tensions. Most important was the Anglo–German naval race, accurately characterized in a contemporary British cartoon in which a conservative explains: "Lord B– is right. We must build a bigger navy than the enemy will build when he hears we're building a bigger navy than he's building."[2]

Competing nationalisms also played a prime role in bringing on the war. French *revanchism,* a longing for revenge on Germany for the humiliation of 1870 and for recovery of the "lost provinces" of Alsace and Lorraine, certainly influenced the French decision to fight in 1914. Austrian fear of Balkan nationalism splitting their Danubian empire asunder drove them to issue the ultimatum to Serbia that set off the war. And Russian pan–Slavism, the view that Russia must support its little Slavic brothers, began the expansion of the conflict that drew all the great powers into the war in 1914.

Two Armed Camps

From a purely diplomatic perspective, finally, the simplest cause for the war was the rivalry of the two opposing alliance systems, the Allies and the Central Powers, that fought it. The binding and often secret agreements that committed the nations on each side to aid each other created fear and suspicion on both sides. In addition, treaty commitments dragged nations not involved in the initial quarrel into the war.

Paradoxically, Bismarck had begun building his system of international alliances after 1871 precisely to maintain the peace in Europe. The iron chancellor knew the French would long for revenge after their defeat in 1870; but he knew too that they would never dare attack Germany without allies. He therefore determined to isolate France diplomatically by binding as many other great powers as possible by treaty to Germany. By the time he retired in 1890, he had in fact woven a web of alliances that linked Germany with most of the other powers—Austria (by the Dual Alliance of 1879), Russia (by the Three Emperors League of 1873 and the Reinsurance Treaty of 1887), and Italy (by the Triple Alliance of 1882). Only Britain remained outside Bismarck's system, but he counted on Anglo–French colonial rivalries to prevent close ties between he two great imperial powers.

William II, however, lacked Bismarck's diplomatic vision. In the 1890s, the German emperor allowed Russia to slip out of the system. Thus turned loose in the international arena, Russian diplomats sought new friends and found them—in France and Britain. The result was a second system of treaties, the Triple Entente, which bound Britain, France, and Russia in a loose series of *ententes* (understandings) on military cooperation, imperial competition, and other matters.

Thus, seven years before the First World War broke out, Europe was divided into two armed camps. When war did come between two of the powers, the treaty obligations that bound allies pulled one great power after another into what thus became the First World War.

The Chain of Crises

Each of the twentieth century's world wars was preceded by a series of tense international crises. In each case, these preliminary confrontations were resolved short of war between the great powers. Yet they left a bitter legacy of mutual distrust, exhausted options, and determination on one or both sides to emerge victorious in the next such facedown.

Of the crises that led to World War I, two took place in North Africa, two in the Balkans. The Moroccan crises of 1905 and 1911 resulted from Germany's refusal to allow France to establish sovereignty over the Arab Kingdom of Morocco, just across the Strait of Gibraltar from Spain. An international conference and even a visit to Morocco by William II himself did not get Morocco for Germany. But these diplomatic maneuvers did leave both the Germans and the French suspicious and angry.

Austria precipitated the Bosnian crisis of 1908 by formally annexing Bosnia, a Balkan province of the crumbling Ottoman empire that Vienna had been informally administering for thirty years. Neighboring Serbia, which had hoped to absorb Bosnia itself, was outraged. Russia offered support to Serbia, but was forced to back down by German pressure. Again, the seeds of future conflict were sown.

The Balkan Wars of 1912–1913, finally, saw an alliance of small Balkan states attack the Ottoman Empire, seize what remained of its European holdings, and then turn on each other in a struggle over the spoils. Russia encouraged Serbia and its allies; but Austria intervened once more, denying Serbia its hoped–for Albanian territory.

The next year, in 1914, came the crisis that could not be resolved. This too was a confrontation in the Balkans involving Austria, Russia, and Serbia. But it would soon draw in Germany, France, and Britain as well.

Gavrilo Princip (1895–1918) was a nineteen–year–old Slavic advocate of Bosnian independence who had links with the super–patriotic Serbian secret society called Union or Death. This organization was dedicated to the liberation of all Slavs from Austrian control and the establishment of a South Slav nation ruled by Serbia. When the heir to the Habsburg throne, Archduke Francis Ferdinand (1863–1914), and his wife Sophie (1868–1914) embarked on a state visit to Sarajevo, capital of the newly acquired Habsburg territory of Bosnia, the Serbian secret society provided weapons for Princip and several other young Bosnian terrorists determined to strike a blow for Bosnian freedom.

A bomb hurled by one of the Bosnians missed its target, but bullets from Princip's Browning revolver killed both the archduke and his wife—and plunged Europe into the month–long crisis that brought on the war.

Austria's rulers, convinced of Serbian governmental complicity in the crime, issued a sweeping ultimatum to Belgrade demanding that Serbia put an end to anti–Austrian agitation, suppress nationalistic organizations, and punish all conspirators. Serbia accepted only some portions of the ultimatum and prepared for war. German leaders, aware that both

France and Russia were growing stronger every year, apparently decided that a war now would be better than a war later. Berlin therefore assured Vienna of its support, and Austria, thus reassured, declared war on Serbia a month after the assassination.

Russia mobilized to defend its Slavic ally, and the German Empire responded by declaring war on Russia. The French, eager to seize this opportunity for long–deferred revenge, announced their support for Russia. Germany, determined to deal with its more dangerous adversary first, then declared war on France as well. Britain hesitated, but German strategy quickly made up British minds. German war plans required the quickest possible strike at France—which meant through the neutral state of Belgium. This callous violation of Belgian neutrality tilted British opinion strongly against Germany, and Britain also declared war.

Others were sucked into the maelstrom in the coming months and years: Ottoman Turkey on the side of the Central Powers and Italy, Japan, and the United States on that of the Allies. Motives varied. Italy fought in large part for bits of "unredeemed" territory from Austria, while the United States fought to defend freedom of the seas against German submarines and to protect its war loans and military sales to the Allies. For one reason or another, all the great powers of the West were sucked into the cauldron of World War I before it was over.

♦ The Great War, 1914–1918 ♦

World War I was short on dazzling victories. It was to a considerable extent a defensive war, in which few great gains were made by anyone. Its effect was cumulative: a war of attrition, it bled all participants white over the years. Four years and millions of casualties later, it ended.

We will look rather briefly at the military campaigns that unfolded in western, eastern, and southern Europe, in the Middle East and beyond between 1914 and 1918. Special attention will be given to the nature and impact of trench warfare and of submarine war. We will also see how this first twentieth–century total war was fought out on the home front, as well as in the trenches. In the end, however, we will return to the battle fronts to trace the turning points of 1917 and the final massive campaigns of 1918 that brought the slaughter to an end.

Campaigns and Battles of World War I

It has been said that, thanks to excellent military training in the strategy and tactics of their predecessors, generals are often well prepared to fight the last war. So the Germans in 1914 had elaborate plans for a quick victory like that of the Franco–Prussian War forty–four years earlier. The Schlieffen Plan, drawn up under the direction of Germany's chief of staff, General Alfred von Schlieffen (1833–1913) during the 1890s, involved a quick passage through Belgium, with or without that country's consent, and a massive drive through northern France to seize Paris. Thereafter, Germany would be able to shift its victorious armies back across the German Empire to deal with the cumbersome Russian forces mobilizing to its east.

The German offensive of 1914 in fact netted more gains than any other drive of the war. By the end of August, German armies were at the Marne River in sight of Paris, and their long–range guns were dropping shells into the streets of the French capital. But the German commanders had weakened their own offensive by subtracting troops from the

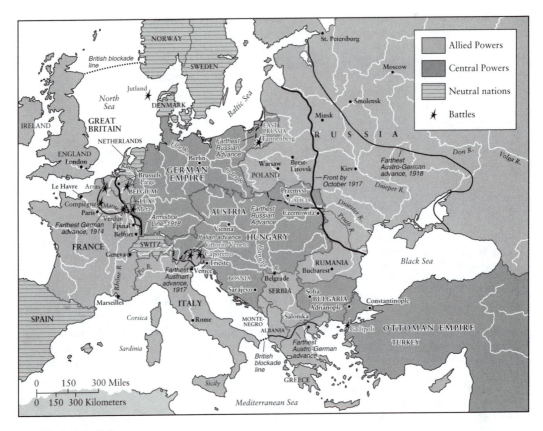

World War I, 1914–1918

crucial drive on Paris for redeployment to the Russian front. At the eleventh hour, the French poured troops into the first Battle of the Marne in September, many arriving straight from Paris in trucks, buses, and even taxis, and stemmed the German tide.

The French and British then launched their own offensive along the Marne, compelling the Germans to retreat from some of the territory they had occupied. The Allied offensive bogged down in its turn, however, and the opposing armies dug in for the winter. Although they did not know it, the trench lines they established that first autumn of the war were to be their homes for most of the next four years.

There were later offensives, immense efforts by one side or the other to break through by sheer weight of numbers and firepower. Perhaps the most devastating of all came in 1916, when the Germans concentrated massively on the French fortifications at Verdun (February–July) and the Allies countered on the river Somme (July–November). The Verdun offensive was immortalized by a French general's watchword, "They shall not pass." The Germans did not, in fact, break through, though it cost the French 350,000 casualties to make good the general's word. The subsequent British offensive on the Somme opened with casualties so huge that it has been described as "the blackest day in the history of the British army." Despite the sacrifice of 420,000 men, the army did not break through.

On the eastern front, German troops stopped Russia's initial drive into East Prussia in 1914. Thereafter the basic pattern of the war saw one Russian human–sea offensive after another sent reeling back by powerful counterattacks. A similar lack of major break-throughs characterized the war in Italy, which entered the conflict on the Allied side in 1915, and in Turkey, which joined on the side of the Central Powers. At Gallipoli, the Turks turned back a bloody Allied attempt to supply Russia through the Black Sea.

The struggle at sea featured attempts by both the British and the Germans to blockade each other's coasts. By and large, the Allies' blockade of the Central Powers held firm throughout the war, relentlessly tightening the bonds of hunger on their enemies. Germany used the recently developed submarine to keep shipping from reaching Britain and France, but this campaign had to be temporarily abandoned when neutrals, including the United States, protested atrocities like the 1915 sinking of the *Lusitania* with well over a thousand civilians on board.

Trench Warfare

As the years of struggle went by, a new image of warfare emerged. War was no longer a matter of flashing sabers and cavalry charges, but an inglorious way of dying in the shell craters of "no man's land" between the endless lines of trenches. War meant mud, cold, lice, dysentery, and the terrible certainty that only luck—not courage or loyalty or skill—could save you from becoming a random casualty in the next artillery barrage, in the carnage of the next offensive.

Technically, World War I was a "war of position" rather than a war of swift campaigns like those of Napoleon or Frederick the Great. Defensive tactics and weapons were simply more advanced in 1914 than those designed for offensive action. No one could break through anyone's defenses and maintain momentum for long.

Among the new weapons employed in this first twentieth–century war, the submarine, or U–boat, proved the most valuable. It was also one of the most reviled, particularly since the main function of the U–boat was to sink unarmed vessels bringing in supplies. The most admired of the new weapons were the first airplanes used in war. These propeller–driven biplanes, used for reconnaissance and for an occasional bombing mission, also engaged in aerial combats with each other. These "dogfights" earned for victorious "aces" the reputation of being the new knights of the air, jousting in the skies above the lines.

In the mud below, the first tanks appeared, snub–nosed monsters whose potential, like that of the warplane, was not fully realized until the next global conflict. More terrible in its effects was poison gas, which—when the wind was blowing right—could blind, sear, or asphyxiate enemy troops. Pictures of the faces of soldiers caught in mustard gas attacks without their gas masks have the power to turn even a late twentieth–century stomach.

Worst of all, however, were the everyday tools of *trench warfare:* barbed wire, machine guns, and the earth–shaking heavy guns. Most of the casualties were men scissored by shrapnel or torn apart by the concussion of high explosives, men punctured by a casual sniper's bullet or mowed down by streams of machine–gun fire as they lumbered under heavy packs toward the enemy's razor wire. These futile battlefields of the First World War were the first great killing grounds of the twentieth century. They would not be the last.

The Home Front

On the home front, World War I also wrought some striking transformations. Casualties were fewer and destruction behind the lines much less than in later twentieth–century wars, when the airplane had come into its own. But the impact on the structure of Western society was nonetheless great.

The First World War is often described as the first *total war,* the first war to mobilize all the resources and energies of whole peoples. Fought by conscript armies rather than by professionals, the 1914 war saw a military obligation imposed on all adult males who were not too old, physically disabled, or in a line of work essential to the war effort. Women were absorbed into war industries, making the shells and the ships needed to carry on the fight. The unparalleled wealth of the West was committed to the struggle, too, as high taxes and huge war loans were launched to pay for the ships and guns, the rains of shells and the streams of machine–gun bullets.

Total war also meant more sweeping government controls over the economy and over the lives of the people than ever before. Organizing all the resources of a modern nation for war necessitated government allocation of materials, produce, and labor, government controls over prices and wages, government rationing of consumer goods. It also required censorship of press reports and propaganda campaigns to stiffen the backbone of the nation for the struggle.

To fill the gaps left on the home front by the conscription of millions of men into the armies, millions of women took over jobs in industry, agriculture, and other sections of the economy. Laboring in munitions factories and shipyards, on farms, as trolley car conductors and subway workers, and in many other capacities, women made a major contribution to the war effort. As nurses, often close to the battle lines, women both shared the peril of the Great War and helped save many lives.

Some of these women workers were inspired by patriotism or by government propaganda urging them to "support their men" by war work. Others, including the many wives of servicemen trying to survive on meager government allotments, took men's jobs for economic reasons. Still others shared the view expressed by Vera Brittain in *Testament of Youth,* her harrowing account of her nursing service, that she should face the cataclysmic experience of her brother, fiancé, and friends at the front.

During the later years of the conflict, women also shared the growing disillusionment with the war. As the home front was increasingly starved even of basic necessities to support the war effort, women staged bread riots simply to feed their families. Some women, like the German socialist Rosa Luxemburg (1871–1919), actively tried to stir up working–class opposition to the war as a whole. Patriots and protesters, working women and women determined to accept their share of the common burden, they made the terrible war with which the century began part of their lives, too.

Turning Points

The year 1917 saw the turning points in World War I. That was the year both sides began to crack under the strain, the year the Russian Revolution brought that country's withdrawal from the conflict, and the year the United States entered the war.

The war was nearly three years old as the spring of 1917 began. The exultant patriotism with which many had greeted the guns of August 1914 was gone. There were mu-

Allied soldiers man a machine gun in what is left of a forest in northern France. The splintered trees gave little cover from the firepower that had destroyed them. (National Archives.)

tinies in the French army, and Italian troops began to desert in large numbers. Most important, 1917 was the year of the Russian Revolution; before the end of that year, the Bolsheviks announced that Russia would withdraw from the war entirely.

The other great reversal of 1917 was America's entry into the war. Early that year the Germans resumed unrestricted submarine warfare against the neutrals who kept the Allies so well supplied. The depredations of the U–boats finally tipped the scale in favor of American entry into the war.

President Wilson sympathized with Britain and France and dreamed of a world made "safe for democracy" by victory for the western European powers. The weight of American trade with the Allies and of war loans to them also influenced American opinion, as did fear that Germany might ally itself with Mexico, then torn by a revolution in which the United States more than once intervened. Germany's new submarine campaign was thus enough to bring a U. S. declaration of war.

The year 1918, then, saw the end of the Great War. Russia's new Bolshevik government signed a separate peace at Brest–Litovsk in March, and the Germans massed their troops on the western front for what they hoped would be the last offensive of the war. Advancing behind a curtain of earth–shaking artillery fire, the German army under General Erich Ludendorff (1865–1937) pushed once more to the Marne. The British and the French, however, had finally agreed to a unified command the preceding year, and the French general Ferdinand Foch (1851–1929) coordinated a successful defense. Reinforced by growing numbers of American troops under General John ("Black Jack") Pershing (1860–1948), a British counterattack spearheaded by hundreds of tanks pushed the Germans back almost to the Belgian border.

By November, Germany's generals knew that the army could not hold out much longer, while the home front was clearly crumbling under the pressure of hunger and news of repeated defeats. The Austro–Hungarian Empire, fissured by nationalist revolts, sought peace at the beginning of the month. In Germany, William II abdicated and fled into exile in Holland. And on November 11, 1918, a German provisional government signed an armistice that brought World War I to an end.

◆The Russian Revolution of 1917◆

While the Great War tore Europe apart, one of the most important revolutions in Western history exploded in Russia. We turn therefore from the mud and blood of the western front to the snowy streets of St. Petersburg and Moscow, where dedicated revolutionists and desperate masses of Russians tried once more to take the revolutionary road to social change. The road they started down in February, 1917 would bring the Communists to power in October and plunge the nation into the long and bloody Russian Civil War that lasted into the 1920s.

The February Revolution

V. I. Lenin, the Bolshevik leader who seized power in Russia in 1917, was a dedicated professional revolutionary, known for his combination of realism, tactical shrewdness, and total commitment to his cause. A dedicated Marxist, he also faced facts and sometimes adjusted theory to suit the realities of the situation. Sometimes flexible, sometimes table–banging and insistent, "the old man" with his balding head and narrow Tatar eyes was a force to be reckoned with.

Lenin's chief lieutenant in 1917 was Leon Trotsky (1879–1940), born Lev Bronstein. A cosmopolitan intellectual like Lenin, and an eloquent orator, Trotsky became the organizer of the Red Army, which successfully defended Lenin's revolution in the civil war. The much less well–known Joseph Stalin (1879–1953), however, had the most important future role to play. Born Joseph Dzhugashvili in the mountainous, bandit–ridden southern province of Georgia, he made his way in the movement as an organizer of "expropriations," bank robberies to support the cause.

The Bolsheviks did many things in the revolutionary year 1917, but one thing they did not do was overthrow the czar. The war and the Russian people did that, before Lenin and his colleagues reappeared on the scene at all.

From the crushing defeat at Tannenberg in 1914 onward, the war was a total disaster for Russia. The czar's commanders, fighting with tactics that dated back to Catherine the Great's time, were hopelessly unprepared to fight a modern war. Casualties mounted into the hundreds of thousands, dead and wounded, in a bad month. On the home front, the notoriously inefficient Russian bureaucracy could do nothing to control high prices, a collapsing transportation system, and shortages of housing, food, and fuel that left people freezing and hungry through the long Russian winters.

The Russian government itself, meanwhile, sank into a hopeless carnival of corruption. War profiteering, influence peddling, and even rumors of sabotage in high places combined with the pernicious influence of the peasant faith healer Grigori Rasputin (1873–1916). Because Rasputin, an ignorant and thoroughly corrupt man had a hypnotic power to ease the suffering of crown prince Alexis (1904–1918), a hemophiliac, Empress Alexandra saw him as a messenger sent from God to save the dynasty.

For the third time in sixty years, then, the autocratic Russian Empire faced and failed the test of warfare in the modern world. The loss of the Crimean War had brought Alexander II's emancipation of the serfs, and defeat in the Russo–Japanese War had pried the Oc-tober Manifesto out of Nicholas II. Failure in World War I finally brought the entire czarist regime down in ruins.

The so–called *February Revolution* actually happened in what the rest of the Western world called March; in 1917, the antiquated Julian calendar was still used in czarist Russia. Chaos was spreading through the country, demonstrators were swarming into the streets, and the troops sent to quell them refused to fire. A strike by women workers in a St. Pe-tersburg textile mill ignited popular protest in the capital itself. Leaders of the Duma and the army convinced Nicholas II that the country would no longer follow him and prevailed upon him to abdicate on March 15.

A Provisional Government of Duma politicians then took over in St. Petersburg. In the same building, a Workers' Soviet modeled on the 1905 revolutionary councils also set up shop. And a little over a month later, Lenin arrived at the Finland Station in the capital.[3]

The liberals in the Provisional Government, led by Alexander Kerensky (1881–1970), hoped to summon a constitutional convention and establish a liberal republic in Russia. Unfortunately, they were also determined to carry on the war. And this the hungry people of St. Petersburg and Moscow, as well as the soldiers who were already deserting, were in-creasingly unprepared to do.

The October Revolution

In the summer of 1917, the Provisional Government launched the "Kerensky offensive," which proved no more successful than its predecessors. The streets of the cities filled once more with deserters, strikers, demonstraters, while conservative military leaders threatened a right–wing coup. Attacked from left and right, Kerensky was on the ropes by November, when Lenin and his Bolsheviks moved against him.

The resulting *October Revolution* was made for a Hollywood epic. Across the wide squares and broad avenues of St. Petersburg, workers paraded or gathered in huge crowds to listen to Lenin or Trotsky. The Bolsheviks promised them, not a Marxist utopia, but simple basics: "Peace, Bread, and Land!" On November 7, 1917, Bolshevik military units and workers' platoons called Red Guards seized the Winter Palace and arrested most of the Provisional Government. Kerensky managed to escape; he fled into exile, and lived most of the rest of his life in California. In Moscow, Russia's second city, supporters of the govern-ment held the Kremlin, a walled compound of churches and palaces, against a Bolshevik siege that lasted a week. In other cities also, local Bolsheviks moved to seize power, often through domination of existing soviets or other local committees.

Enemies of the Revolution

Lenin and his colleagues—who were calling themselves the Communist Party from 1918 on—set to work at once to restructure Russian society. They moved the capital back to Moscow, the center of power before Peter the Great, which had the additional advantage of being farther from the war–torn frontiers. There they set up a Council of People's Com-missars, with Lenin as its chairman, to try to run the country.

Attempting to make good on his promises of peace, bread, and land, Lenin moved quickly. He sanctioned peasant seizures of land. He gathered grain—by confiscation when necessary—to feed the cities. And he signed a peace treaty with the Germans at

Brest–Litovsk in March 1918, surrendering a wide swath of the Russian Empire to get out of the war.

Democracy, however, was not a priority. When the Communists found themselves out-voted three to one in a hastily–called Constitutional Convention, Lenin promptly sent the military to close the convention down. As chairman of the Council of People's Commissars, he went back to governing with the power he had won in the streets.

He had many enemies and few friends. The peasant majority supported the Social Revolutionaries, who soon turned against the Bolsheviks. Czarist generals quickly took the field against the "Reds," as the Communists were called. Minority nationalities, from Poland and the Baltic states to the Ukraine, the Caucasus, and Central Asia—who had long resented czarist rule—seized this moment of turmoil in Russia to assert their independence, Poland and the Baltic states successfully. At Archangel in the far north and in Crimea in the south, meanwhile, American, French, and British troops arrived to prevent supplies intended for the war effort from falling into either German or Communist hands and provided active support for the White Russian armies.

Surrounded by enemies, the Communists made their real mark in history. Their great achievement was not so much seizing power—their predecessors had largely forfeited it—but hanging on to it through the long and brutal years of the Russian Civil War (1918–1921).

Civil War and Communist Victory

The years of civil war were stern and violent times all across the former Russian Empire. Lenin mastered mountains of detail, ran endless meetings, shouted at the crowds, his little beard jutting, his right hand chopping the air, his broad forehead and bald dome glistening with sweat. Taking no chances that the czar might prove a rallying point for counterrevolutionary forces, Lenin himself apparently ordered the killing of Nicholas II and his entire family, who were being held by a provincial soviet in Ekaterinburg.

Through the dark *taiga* forests of the north, through the rippling wheat fields of the Ukraine, bespectacled Trotsky roared in the armored train that was the mobile nerve center of the Red Army for two and a half years. He brought "greetings to all those who honestly and bravely defend the freedom and independence of the working class" and a "warning" for all others: "If any detachment retreats without orders, the first to be shot will be the [Communist] commissar, the next the commander. Cowards, scoundrels, and traitors will not escape the bullet."[4]

Lenin's policies through this prolonged crisis revealed a pragmatic mix of ideology, practicality, and traditional Russian authoritarianism. His basic policy of *war communism*, for example, had a clearly ideological ring. It meant taking control of commercial and financial institutions, nationalizing all sizable industrial plants, drafting people to work in labor battalions, confiscating grain. But it also meant legalizing peasant land seizures, though this strengthened the position of the peasantry as "agrarian capitalists." It meant allowing czarist officers to command Red Army units, albeit with commissars at their sides. Throughout, in fact, war communism had as much a practical as an ideological foundation.

Most significant for the future of Russia, the Communists in power quickly reverted to traditional Russian authoritarian methods in dealing with the crisis. The czarist civil service had been one of the primary pillars of the old order: the Communists established an even larger bureaucracy in their efforts to achieve their socialist aims. The czars had never hesitated to turn the Cossacks on rebellious peasants: now the Red Army, hammered together by Trotsky, proved absolutely essential to overcoming the Whites, the minority nationalities, the foreign invaders. The czar's secret police had been one of the scandals of Romanov Russia: but when the Social Revolutionaries in particular took up the gun once more, grievously wounding Lenin himself in August 1918, the Communists were more than ready to respond with their own secret police. The feared Cheka became the first of a long line of Soviet political police who would make Communist Russia one of the most rigidly totalitarian states of the first half of the twentieth century.

For the time being, however, these methods worked. Some of the rebellious minority nationalities—the Poles and the Baltic peoples—did maintain their independence. But the Polish invaders, the Japanese, the Czechs, and the Allies were all expelled from Russian soil. The Social Revolutionaries, the Whites, and the minority peoples of the Ukraine, the Caucasus, and elsewhere were suppressed or driven into exile. The Russian Communists were at last masters of the Russian Empire. In 1924, they approved a constitution for their new nation, subsequently known as the Union of Soviet Socialist Republics (USSR), or more briefly as the Soviet Union. For most of the rest of the new century, the new Soviet state would loom as a divisive force within the Western world.

◆The Peace of Paris◆

As postwar arrangements go, the *Peace of Paris* that followed the First World War was an unmitigated disaster. Many historians have since seen the peace treaties signed at Versailles and elsewhere around the French capital in 1919 as a prime cause of the Second World War, which followed only two decades later. Others see the Peace of Paris as little more than a truce in the "German wars" of the twentieth century. This section will survey the fall of the last European crowned heads and the disturbed state of the world in 1919, the negotiators who gathered in Paris, the peace they made, and the League of Nations they hoped would pick up the pieces.

The Fall of the Last Emperors

The Russian Romanovs were not the only imperial dynasty to collapse under the terrible strains of World War I. Across central and eastern Europe, the last emperors in the Western world—in Germany, Austria, and elsewhere—were overthrown, their empires fragmenting under the pounding of war and the revolutions unleashed by war.

In the German Empire, widespread hunger and demands for peace by liberals and socialists in the Reichstag combined with military mutinies and the threat of civil strife to end the war—and to bring down the government. As we have seen, William II abdicated and fled to neutral Holland two days before the armistice in November 1918. Civilian politicians, led by the Social Democrats, quickly formed a provisional government and proclaimed the German Republic. One of the first duties of the new government, unfortunately, was to sign the immensely unpopular Treaty of Versailles in the spring of 1919. The German Republic was thus stigmatized from the beginning for accepting the bad peace that followed the war the German Empire had lost.

In the Austro–Hungarian Dual Monarchy, defeat and hunger also unleashed domestic disorders. The minority nationalities of the Habsburg realm—Czechs, Yugoslavs, and others—their hopes stirred by President Wilson's ringing assertions of their rights to "national

Crumbling Empires After World War I

self–determination," declared their independence of Vienna. Under such pressures, the center could not hold. Old Francis Joseph, who had held his empire together since the revolutions of 1848, had died in 1916. His successor, Emperor Charles, abdicated in 1918, and the Austrian Republic, shorn of its Danubian Empire of minority nationalities, was proclaimed that same year.

Farther to the east, the empire of the Ottomans also melted in the fires of war. Never really European, the Ottoman Turkish Empire had nevertheless been a key player in European international relations throughout the modern period. The Balkan Wars of 1912 and

1913 had cost the Empire the remnants of its European holdings, and during World War I British–led Indian troops and Arab revolts fomented by the intrepid Englishman T. E. Lawrence (1888–1935), popularly known as "Lawrence of Arabia," had shattered the Ottoman Empire in the Near East. When Sultan Mohammed VI (r. 1917–1922) agreed to a humiliating postwar treaty, surrendering territory to Greeks, Italians, and his own Armenian subjects, a revolt at last toppled the seven–century–old dynasty. In 1922, a cabal of military officers called the Young Turks deposed the emperor, expelled the Italians and Greeks from formerly Ottoman territories, and massacred most of the Armenians. A Turkish Republic was thereupon founded under the chief of the Young Turks, Kemal Atatürk (1881–1938).

The fall of the last empires meant the end of monarchy as a real center of government in the West. But the dissolution of imperial holdings meant more. The fall of these multinational empires left a litter of new nations across eastern Europe and western Asia. From the Baltic states and Poland through the Balkans and the Near East, from Finland to Palestine, these small states came to play a significant role in twentieth–century history. Perhaps most important, they constituted a power vacuum, tempting larger neighbors to conquest or throwing up regional powers from among their own number. It was the beginning of a process of reorganization in eastern Europe and the Middle East.

In one place, it should be noted, the collapse of an imperial dynasty did not mean the disintegration of its empire. The emerging Soviet Union did lose a swath of czarist territory in 1918 but succeeded in reconquering other czarist acquisitions that rebelled at that time. In territorial terms, then, the USSR remained an old–style land empire. After World War II, the Soviet Union even reacquired the Baltic states—Estonia, Latvia, and Lithuania—and established hegemony over Poland. As we will see in a later chapter, this empire, too, collapsed before the end of the century, creating a new period of chaos in eastern Europe in the 1990s.

A War–Shaken World

The aftershocks of the war spread further still. The shattered fabric of Western—indeed world—society did not easily recover from those four years of death and destruction. A shaken generation had to face a revolution–torn world, a terrible plague—the influenza epidemic of 1918–1919—and the physical and psychological consequences of the Great War.

Thirteen million soldiers had been killed, and perhaps as many civilians. Many more were crippled, blinded, or suffering from other lifelong injuries. Others were troubled for years with the psychological aftereffects of their wartime experiences. These ranged from the emotional disturbance called "shell shock" to a number of antisocial attitudes, such as cynical disillusionment and a penchant for violence that made veterans easy recruits to totalitarian political parties. The best of a generation, it was often said, had died in the war, and Europe had to pay for it in the feeble leadership of the next two decades.

Destruction, too, was widespread. Many of the cities and villages of northern France, Belgium, northern Italy, and eastern Europe lay in ruins. Hunger still gripped the peoples of the Central Powers as the British blockade continued unrelenting until the peace treaty was signed. Honest German housewives were driven to stealing potatoes from farmers simply to put food on the table. The relief effort directed by the American engineer and future president Herbert Hoover (1874–1964) would come too late to prevent the worst of that scarring experience.

To add to these woes, the greatest plague since the Black Death of the Middle Ages struck a war–weakened world just at this time. The great influenza epidemic of 1918–1919 took twenty million more lives. Asian nations like India were especially hard hit, but many died in Europe and the United States as well before this virulent form of influenza had run its course.

There was, finally, no peace in the world as the peacemakers settled down to their work in Paris. Wars and revolutions still raged or were poised to break out in many places. The Russian Civil War continued to bleed that long–suffering land. In China, the last Manchu emperor had been deposed and a revolution had broken out that dragged on, with intervals of wary truce, from 1911 to 1949. Most disturbing to the Allied leaders gathering in Paris, rumors of communist revolution elsewhere in the world, inspired by the Bolshevik success in Russia, were widespread. In March 1919, Lenin founded the Third or Communist International—Comintern for short—dedicated to encouraging Bolshevik–style revolutions elsewhere. There were such insurrections in several places, but they proved unsuccessful. The left–wing Spartacist revolt in Germany, as we shall see, was quickly suppressed by the German army. The soviet–style government established in Hungary by Béla Kun (1886–1937), pressured by counterrevolutionary forces from within and by wars with other nationalistic east European states, collapsed in months. But fears of Marx's "world revolution" were rife that spring of 1919.

The Peacemakers

Meanwhile, hundreds of representatives of dozens of governments gathered in Paris in 1919 to draft peace treaties for the defeated Central Powers to sign. It was the largest such gathering since the Congress of Vienna more than a hundred years before. Among the peacemakers, however, only three nations and three men really mattered.

Georges Clemenceau (1841–1929), the French premier, was an old liberal and a passionate nationalist. A champion of the Third Republic in his earlier years, he had seen France twice invaded by Germans and was determined to prevent that from happening again. "Tiger" Clemenceau, a man in his seventies with a bristling white moustache, had announced his policy when he became premier in a single fierce phrase: "Home policy? I wage war! Foreign policy? I wage war! . . . All the time I wage war!"[5] He was still waging war on Germany when he sat down at the peace table in 1919.

The British prime minister, David Lloyd George (1863–1945), was a shrewd, silver–haired Welsh politician. A stalwart champion of the Asquith Liberal reform government of 1906, he had become prime minister himself in 1916. A genial fellow in private, Lloyd George had nonetheless run on a platform of revenge and restitution directed against Germany. Lloyd George would defend Britain's national interests and claims to compensation with vigor at Paris.

President Woodrow Wilson was perhaps the twentieth century's most celebrated case of an idealist in politics. Convinced of his own righteousness, he tended to ignore the opinions of others and to condemn those who disagreed with him as willful enemies of grace. He brought to Europe his now–famous Fourteen Points on which the peace settlement was to be based. These included "open covenants" (rather than secret treaties), freedom of the seas, free trade, national self–determination of peoples, limitations on armaments and colonization, and a "general association of nations" to keep the peace. He persuaded Europe to accept only the last of these in its entirety—and the United States itself promptly rejected that.

There was, finally, the endless complexity of dealing with so many of the world's problems in those hurried months of 1919. With the allied nations demanding their rewards, liberated peoples clamoring for land claimed by others, and supporters of many causes crying for a chance to be heard, the remarkable thing was perhaps not that a bad set of treaties was assembled, but that any treaties were assembled at all.

The Treaty of Versailles

The most important, and later the most condemned, of the treaties prepared at Paris in 1919 was the *Treaty of Versailles*. The embittered Germans were forced to sign this humiliating document in Louis XIV's great Hall of Mirrors, where the now–vanished German Empire had been proclaimed half a century before. By the terms of this treaty, Germany returned Alsace and Lorraine to France and ceded the Saar coal–mining region to that country for fifteen years. The defeated power also lost territory to other neighbors, including the "Polish corridor" that gave Poland access to the Baltic Sea and the Baltic port of Danzig, which was put under international administration. Once master of the most powerful military machine in Europe, Germany was permitted only a tiny army, lost most of its navy, and was prohibited from developing an air force. The new Germany was particularly forbidden to station military forces in the Rhineland, on the French frontier. In addition, the German government had to agree to a "war guilt" clause accepting responsibility for the war and consenting to pay reparations, which were subsequently fixed at what was then the unthinkable sum of 33 billion dollars.

The Versailles Treaty was intended to turn what had been Europe's most powerful nation into a second–class power incapable of future aggression. What it succeeded in doing was to envenom German politics, weaken the new German Republic which accepted the treaty, and sow the seeds of Hitler's war to come.

Separate treaties were imposed on the other Central Powers. Austria fared even worse than Germany, surrendering three–quarters of its lands and population—including many Germans—to the newly independent nations of Hungary, Czechoslovakia, Yugoslavia, and Poland. This former great power was thus also reduced to second–class status. Of the lesser Central Powers, Turkey, as indicated above, suffered a revolution over the territorially devastating terms imposed.

The Peace of Paris, like that of Vienna a century earlier, did redraw the map, not only of Europe, but of other parts of the world as well. Germany's colonies in Africa, Asia, and the Pacific, overrun early in the war by the Allies, were now turned over to them officially. Classified as "mandates," these areas were to be ruled and developed economically and politically until they were deemed ready for independence. The same sort of mandate tutelage was imposed on the former subject peoples of the Ottoman Empire, who were governed by the British and French between the wars. Japan, finally, asserted a less widely recognized "special interest" in China, and was angered when the Western powers refused to recognize the right of the Japanese to impose what amounted to a protectorate over its huge neighbor.

The League of Nations

Over the months, Woodrow Wilson had given in to his allies on one point of national interest after another. His great hope, however, remained a general association of nations to guide the course of international relations and keep the peace. From the balance–of–power politics of earlier centuries through the Concert of Europe in the nineteenth century, efforts had been made to impose some order on the jungle of international relations. The League of Nations laid out in 1919, however, was the first effort to institutionalize the process.

The League, with its headquarters at Geneva in neutral Switzerland, had three key institutions: an Assembly, a Council, and a permanent Secretariat. The Assembly brought together representatives of all member nations annually to discuss problems of war and peace as well as other matters of international concern. The Council, to consist of nine members, recognized the preeminent position of the great powers by offering permanent seats to Britain, France, Italy, Japan, and the United States, although the United States never took its seat. The Secretariat consisted of several hundred full–time officials charged with primarily administrative functions. Also affiliated with the League were the World Court and the International Labor Office. The World Court was composed of fifteen judges who ruled on violations of international law and volunteered to arbitrate international disputes. The International Labor Office drafted recommendations and international conventions regulating the terms and conditions of labor.

The League, as we shall see, did not prove to be an effective instrument for keeping peace among nations. It did do a better job of supervising some colonies, however, and it undertook a number of humanitarian programs. The League's control over colonies was limited to former territories of the defeated Central Powers, which were assigned as mandates to member nations. The latter were required to report annually on their custodianship of these peoples in the Middle East, Africa, and the Pacific; and League recommendations did influence the administration of these colonies for the better. The League also focused on such humanitarian concerns as international epidemics, the drug trade, and prostitution, and it offered some financial aid to member states in straitened circumstances.

The League of Nations had been Woodrow Wilson's dream. When Wilson returned home, however, he found that the League looked entirely too powerful for his countrymen, or at least for some of their elected leaders in the Senate. Leery of "entangling alliances" since Washington's day, the United States refused to join the new supranational organization.

The Great War was over, but the peace it left behind contributed significantly to the coming of a second global struggle only twenty years later. Defeated Germany and the new Soviet Union, pariahs among the Western nations in 1919, became the two most powerful and most dangerous nations in Europe. Altogether, it was not a propitious beginning for the twentieth century.

Summary

The Western world at the beginning of the twentieth century was politically divided into the more liberal nations of western Europe and the Americas and the more conservative states of central and eastern Europe. Three nations that played central roles in the history of the century were aggressively nationalistic Germany, Russia on the eve of take–over by revolutionary socialists, and the United States in the grip of a series of liberal reform movements.

A string of diplomatic crises climaxed

with the outbreak of the First World War in 1914. These crises involved rival European colonial claims and conflicts in the Balkans, where the assassination of the heir to the Austrian throne finally triggered a general European war.

World War I (1914–1918) was for the most part a grisly war of attrition in which neither the Allies—principally Britain, France, Italy, Russia, and later the United States—nor the Central Powers, most importantly Germany and Austria, were able to gain a decisive advantage. Machine guns, barbed wire, submarines, and poison gas made this the most costly war in history up to that time. After Russia had left the war and the United States had entered it, the struggle ended with the Central Powers in retreat and disintegration. The Peace of Paris imposed by the victorious Allies left Germany and a number of other nations embittered and paved the way to World War II.

In February, 1917, the terrible pounding Russia had taken in the war led to the overthrow of the czar. In October, Lenin and his Bolshevik revolutionaries seized power, withdrew Russia from the war, and began the Civil War to defend the power they had seized. In the early 1920s, the new Soviet Union emerged as the only communist power in the world.

Some Key Terms

Allies 598
Bolshevik 597
Central Powers 598
Duma 597
February Revolution 607
Menshevik 597

muckraker 597
October Manifesto 597
October Revolution 607
Peace of Paris 609
Populist movement 597
Progressivism 598

soviet 597
total war 604
Treaty of Versailles 613
trench warfare 603
war communism 608

Notes

1. The first empire was the Holy Roman Empire, founded in the tenth century, dominated by Austria since the later Middle Ages, and abolished by Napoleon in 1806.
2. Reprinted in P. M. Satterthwaite, *Bismarck to Brezhnev: Europe, 1870–1980* (Huddersfield, England: Schofield and Sims, 1984), 46.
3. Lenin reached Russia courtesy of the Germans, who correctly calculated that he would complete the breakdown of the Russian war effort and rushed him from Switzerland across Germany in a sealed train. He was, however, never a "German agent," as his enemies charged.
4. Leon Trotsky, quoted in Isaac Deutscher, *The Prophet Armed: Trotsky, 1879–1921* (New York: Oxford University Press, 1970), 419, 421.
5. Georges Clemenceau, quoted in John Williams, *The Home Fronts: Britain, France, and Germany, 1914–1918* (London: Constable, 1972), 221.

Reading List

Ascher, A. *The Revolution of 1905: Russia in Disarray.* Stanford: Stanford University Press, 1988. First of two volumes, looks likely to replace Sidney Harcave's *Russian Revolution of 1905* (1964) as standard work.

Bailey, T. *Woodrow Wilson and the Lost Peace.* Chicago: Quadrangle, 1963. The American president's contribution to the bad peace made at Paris.

Baldwin, H. *World War I.* New York: Harper and Row, 1962. By a leading military historian. See also C. Falls, *The Great War* (New York: Putnam, 1959).

Chamberlin, W. H. *The Russian Revolution, 1917–*

1921. New York: Grosset and Dunlap, 1965. An older but still standard account. See also E. H. Carr, *The Russian Revolution from Lenin to Stalin* (New York: Free Press, 1979).

Ferro, M. *October, 1917: A Social History of the Russian Revolution*. Translated by N. Stone. London: Routledge and Kegan Paul, 1980. Social dimensions of the Bolshevik seizure of power.

Fischer, F. *World Power Decline: The Controversy over Germany's Aims in the First World War*. Translated by L. L. Farrar, R. Kimber, and R. Kimber. New York: Norton, 1974. Revisionist views of Germany's responsibility for the coming of the Great War.

Fitzpatrick, S. *The Russian Revolution of 1917–1932*. New York: Oxford University Press, 1982. Analytical overview, from the 1917 Revolution to Stalin's rise to power.

Horne, A. *The Price of Glory: Verdun 1916*. London: Penguin, 1979. Disturbing factual account of the great battle.

Joll, J. *The Origins of the First World War*. New York: Longman, 1984. Very good summary of the extensive literature on the subject. See also L. Lafore, *The Long Fuse* (New York: Harper and Row, 1971).

Marwick, A. *War and Social Change in the Twentieth Century*. New York: St. Martin's Press, 1975. The transforming impact of the two world wars on Western society.

Millett, A. R., and W. Murray, eds. *Military Effectiveness*, vol. 1, *The First World War*. Boston: Allen and Unwin, 1988. Evaluates political, strategic, operational, and tactical effectiveness of the armies of each of the major powers.

Nicolson, H. G. *Peacemaking, 1919*. New York: Harcourt, Brace, 1939. A diplomat's assessment of the peace conference.

Raleigh, D. J. *Revolution on the Volga: 1917 in Sara-tov*. Ithaca, N.Y.: Cornell University Press, 1986. Bolshevik Revolution at the local level. See also O. Figes, *Peasant Russia, Civil War: The Volga Countryside in Revolution* (New York: Clarendon Press, 1989). On the civil war between peasants and Bolsheviks.

Reed, J. *Ten Days That Shook the World*. New York: Random House, 1960. Eyewitness account by an idealistic young American journalist.

Schapiro, L. *The Russian Revolution of 1917: The Origins of Modern Communism*. New York: Basic Books, 1984. Brings familiarity with the ideological dimension of modern revolutions to the subject.

Service, R. *Lenin: A Political Life*. 2 vols. Bloomington: Indiana University Press, 1985–1991. An ongoing impressive biographical study. Older, still valuable accounts include D. Shub, *Lenin* (London: Penguin, 1977).

Tuchman, B. *The Guns of August*. New York: Macmillan, 1962. Vivid account of the coming of World War I, by a leading popular historian.

Williams, J. *The Home Fronts: Britain, France, and Germany, 1914–1918*. London: Constable, 1972. The first total war and the civilian populations. See also J. J. Becker, *The Great War and the French People* (New York: St. Martin's Press, 1986).

Wohl, R. *The Generation of 1914*. Cambridge, Mass.: Harvard University Press, 1979. The war continues to shape the lives and thinking of the generation that fought it.

Wolfe, B. D. *Three Who Made a Revolution*. Boston: Beacon, 1956. Lenin, Trotsky, and Stalin, underground and in exile before 1917; still readable and intriguing. See also A. B. Ulam, *The Bolsheviks: The Intellectual and Political History of the Triumph of Communism in Russia* (New York: Macmillan, 1965).

25

Tomorrow the World
Depression and Dictatorship

*The Western Economy Between the Wars
*The Democracies Between the Wars   *Nazis and Fascists
*Communists, Militarists, and Other Dictators   *A Society of Subcultures

The twenty years between the Peace of Paris in 1919 and the German invasion of Poland in 1939 were in some ways as different as two decades can be. The 1920s were the jazz age, the decade of the Wall Street boom; the 1930s saw bread lines and the rise of Adolf Hitler. Both decades, however, illustrate two large trends. The first was the economic instability and collapse that became apparent with the Wall Street crash of 1929 and characterized the Great Depression that followed. The second was the political drift toward brutal dictatorship that brought Stalin to power in the Soviet Union in the late 1920s and Hitler to the German chancellorship in 1933.

This chapter will thus look at the Western economy between the wars in terms of a chronic economic instability that began in the 1920s and climaxed in the 1930s. It will survey the generally less–than–brilliant efforts of the democracies to deal with the resulting crisis. It will also examine the rise of the dictators of the interwar years—fascist, communist, militarist, and others—as a response to these troubled times. And it will provide a brief summary of Western society in the first half of the century, again full of conflicts and change.

We will look at the years between the wars, then, not as two contrasting decades, but in terms of trends that unify them. We will survey the evolution of the period as a whole, from the "roaring twenties" to the gathering darkness of the 1930s, gripped by depression and dictatorship, with worse yet on its way.

✦The Western Economy Between the Wars✦

Economic events are complicated things, hard to predict, hard even to explain after the fact. We are thus not as certain as we would like to be about the causes and essential character of even such a prominent economic event as the Great Depression of the 1930s. Nevertheless, some central features do seem to stand out. The pages that follow will outline a Western economy heavily dependent on the economic health of one nation. They will summarize the economic collapse of 1929, the nature of the depression that followed, and the increasingly desperate Western attempts at recovery through the following decade.

Overproduction and the World Economy

By the beginning of the twentieth century, Europe was buying large quantities of agricultural products and natural resources from outside Europe, both from colonies and from independent nations like the United States and Argentina. The Industrial Revolution had also spread to some of these regions, so that the United States was the world's most productive nation and a growing manufacturing capacity existed in such nations as Japan, India, and Brazil. And, thanks to steamships and railroads, global economic ties grew closer every year. This evolving global economy was a monumental achievement. It was also about to turn on its creators and on the rest of the world as well.

The fundamental fact about the world economy during this period was that it functioned entirely too well—it produced more than the world could consume. Technological advances, low wages outside the West, and capitalist competitiveness had overstimulated global productivity. World War I had further increased demand for overseas goods as European nations added war production to civilian demand and looked to the rest of the world to help make up the resulting production deficits. In response to this escalating demand, overseas suppliers had expanded their productive capacity still further. Then the war ended. Europe sought to return to full civilian production—and found the world awash in commodities and manufactured goods.

Throughout the two decades between 1919 and 1939, then, both the Western nations and their non–Western suppliers were struggling with a basic problem of overproduction. It could be overcome at some times, in some places, in some industries—but not everywhere, for everybody, all the time. Business and government alike tried desperately to juggle supply and demand, the conflicting needs of producers and consumers, under these crippling conditions. This continuing problem of overproduction was a major cause of the great economic depression that enveloped the world after 1929.

There were other basic problems, too, underlying the economic weakness of the period. Old industries like farming and textiles, coal and iron continued to decline, while such newer industries as chemicals, steel, electrical power, and petroleum continued to grow. The resulting dislocations were often devastating for regions and peoples who had gained their livelihoods from agriculture or coal mines. Some of the new industries, such as automobiles or radios, had immense potential for growth, but only as long as people had the money to pay for these products. Decline in one part of the economy could thus poison healthier economic sectors: the unemployed factory workers of the 1930s, for example, wanted cars and radios, but they could not pay for them. Many coal miners and farmers had not been able to afford them even in the 1920s.

The Role of the United States

Under these circumstances, U. S. economic strength became increasingly important in the 1920s. In a real sense, indeed, the United States became the powerhouse that drove the Western economy as a whole during that decade of dubious prosperity. In one area in particular, this role was pivotal: only U. S. money made possible the endlessly debated flow of war debts and reparations between the Western nations.

The Allies, determined to get some compensation for the long agony of the war, had imposed a virtually unpayable reparations bill on Germany. The United States, meanwhile, insisted on the repayment of the large war debts the Allies owed it, though its erstwhile

Chronology 25: The Great Depression and the Rise of Dictators

1920–1929	*United States economy booms, supports Western war debts and reparations*
1921–1928	*Lenin's New Economic Policy compromises with capitalism in the Soviet Union*
1922	*Mussolini's March on Rome brings Fascists to power in Italy*
1923	*Great inflation in Germany*
1924–1928	*Stalin takes over Communist party after Lenin's death*
1928–1939	*Stalin's first Five Year Plans collectivize Soviet economy*
1929	*Wall Street crash brings Great Depression*
1929–1939	*Great Depression across the Western world and beyond*
1930s–1945	*Militarists rule Japan*
1933	*Hitler appointed chancellor of Germany, crushes all rival parties*
1933–1945	*Roosevelt's New Deal brings reforms in United States; government spending during war brings economic recovery*
1934–1938	*Stalinist purge trials against class enemies in Soviet Union*

comrades in arms could no more afford to pay off their debts than the Germans could keep up their reparations payments. The solution was typical of the unreality of the prosperity of the 1920s. The United States lent money to Germany, which looked like a good economic investment in the long run. Germany paid a scaled–down version of its reparations bill to the Allies, who in turn tried to keep up with their war debt payments to the United States. It was a circular arrangement increasing nobody's actual wealth and largely dependent on a U. S. economy prosperous enough to continue pouring money into the pipeline.

The United States supported the fragile prosperity of the 1920s. Then came the Wall Street crash of 1929—and the roof fell in as the world was buried under the worst depression in history.

Some economic historians explain the Great Depression in terms of the ten–year business cycles of prosperity and hard times that had been recurring ever since the Industrial Revolution began. The Great Depression may thus be seen as an extremely deep cyclical depression. The depression of the 1930s also fits the more controversial "secular cycle," a cycle of good and bad times in which twenty–five year periods of prosperity alternate with a quarter–century eras of depressed conditions. Seen this way, the whole period between the wars can be seen as a secular downswing between two periods of prosperity, 1896–1914 and 1945–1974.

At the opposite extreme, it is possible to explain the Great Depression by focusing on a single event—an American event: the Wall Street stock–market *crash of 1929*. American stocks had been drastically inflated by speculation and often purchased on margin, that is, with as little as 10 percent cash investment, the rest being credit owed to brokerage houses and banks. The whole nation, in fact, was deeply in debt, living in mortgaged homes surrounded by labor–saving devices bought on credit. On October 29, 1929, a wild day of panic selling on Wall Street brought stock prices tumbling and wiped out millionnaire speculators and the life savings of small–town investors alike.

And there is the downward spiral effect so often noted. When their businesses went bankrupt, their employees lost their jobs. Unemployed men and women could not afford to buy the products of other factories, and these in turn shut down for lack of customers.

Out through the economy and across the seas the effect rippled, destroying the livelihoods of already hard–pressed farmers, ruining storekeepers who could not collect their bills and banks that could not collect on loans and mortgages. It is a dramatic and tragic picture, and one that economists seem to agree describes much of what happened.

On a global scale, this process can be more simply described. In 1929, the American economy, the great engine that had kept the system moving through the 1920s, finally ran out of steam—and the wheels of the international economy ground to a halt.

The U. S. market had finally reached the saturation point, the point where all the middle–class people who could afford to buy houses, cars, and labor–saving devices, even on credit, had them. When the American demand for goods and services was finally sated, the businesses that supplied that demand, the banks that financed those producers, the whole elaborate structure suddenly ran out of power. As a result, American financiers could no longer lend money to Germany; Germany could not pay its reparations to the rest of Europe; and Europe in turn defaulted on war debts to the United States. At the same time, European banks and businesses, deprived of U. S. capital, began to fail.

The West as a whole was thus shaken by the economic debacle in the United States. As the developed Western nations reeled, their colonies and other less–developed suppliers saw Western markets for their raw materials and agricultural products evaporate. Without the income from these commodity sales, the rest of the world could not afford to buy manufactured goods from America or Europe—causing further economic decline in the West. Hard–working people from Maine to Mandalay thus spiraled deeper and deeper down into the Great Depression of the 1930s.

The Great Depression

A few numbers will perhaps help us to visualize the impact of the *Great Depression*. During the years between 1929 and 1932, Germany's industrial production declined by 41 percent, that of the United States by 45 percent. Employment figures are equally grim. Ger-

Americans seek free food in a "soup kitchen" during the Great Depression of the 1930s. Why do you think the United States, despite the enormous suffering of its people, was able to survive this economic collapse without resorting to totalitarian measures? (AP/Wide World Photos.)

many with six million out of work and the United States with twelve million unemployed were the hardest hit, but other nations also had millions of men and women looking for jobs.

In human terms, the Depression meant successful middle–aged breadwinners losing businesses or executive positions. It meant young people who never found work at all, but subsisted on a meager dole in a shut–down company town through the years. It meant soup kitchens and bread lines, beggars on the streets and people sleeping under newspapers on park benches summer and winter, waiting for a break.

Various governments and sectors proposed a variety of ways for dealing with the Great Depression. One immediate response was a demand for welfare payments to workers deprived of their jobs by the collapse. Another immediate reaction was *economic nationalism,* a demand by farmers and businessmen for protective tariffs to keep out foreign competition. A third was a proposal to abandon the fixed gold standard for Western paper currencies, putting more paper money in circulation. All these approaches were tried, with varying degrees of success.

Two basic strategies, however, emerged. Many Western European capitalists tried to cut their labor bill in order to make their goods more competitive in the international market. Their governments also sought to pay only a modest dole to the unemployed, in order to keep the national debt as low as possible. A more radical solution was to subsidize lavish public works programs in order to put people to work and thus, by putting money in their pockets, to stimulate demand. Such large–scale, government–financed projects as Stalin's tractor factories, Hitler's network of superhighways, and Roosevelt's public works projects, to be discussed later, all had that much in common: they encouraged business growth by putting money in the hands of potential consumers.

Some recovery resulted. By and large, however, the world had to wait for the coming of World War II to put their people back to work in munitions factories and armies, thus ending the Great Depression at last.

♦The Democracies Between the Wars♦

The capitalist democracies emerged from World War I seriously damaged. A decade later, they were hit hard by the Great Depression. And throughout the interwar period they were challenged by the rise of powerful new dictatorships. Each of the democratic powers, furthermore, had its own particular problems to survive over these two decades. As we will see in this section, the United States responded with vigorous reform efforts under Franklin Roosevelt, while Britain, France, and other democracies essentially "muddled through." It seems fair to say that during this period, there was a great deal more drift than mastery among some of the freest and richest nations in the world.

FDR and the New Deal

The United States came out of World War I richer than it had ever been, and totally uninterested in political crusades. "The business of America is business" became the watchword of the 1920s. The United States was certainly ideally situated to do business. War production for the Allies and then for the United States itself had boosted the productivity of U. S. factories and farms. War loans had made the United States the world's greatest creditor nation. Through most of the decade, as noted above, the large and relatively affluent

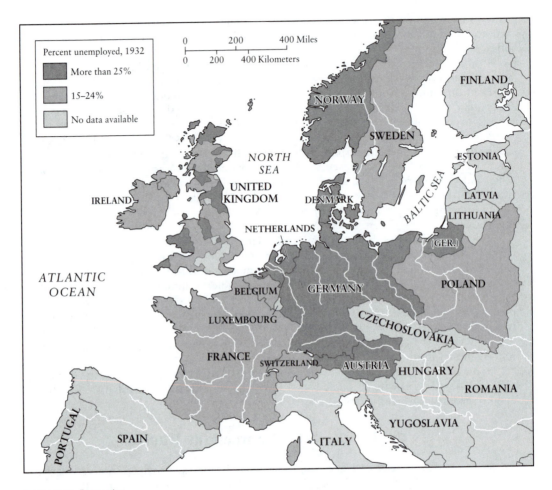

Europe in the Depression

U. S. population bought single–family houses and Ford Model–T cars and household appliances at an unrivaled rate. American factories responded to the demand, and by 1929 the United States was producing an astonishing 45 percent of the world's industrial goods, compared to Germany's 12 percent, Britain's 9, and France's 7.

On the frothy surface of the decade, things had never been better. Hedonistic youth flourished in the United States as nowhere else. It was a fad culture and a fun culture, dancing to Louis Armstrong's (1900–1971) jazz beat and cheering sports heroes like home–run slugger Babe Ruth (1895–1948) on to glory. Even the nation's greatest failure, the Eighteenth Amendment prohibiting the manufacture and sale of alcoholic beverages, had its colorful side: prohibition produced the illegal drinking places called "speakeasies" and turned brutal bootleggers like Al Capone (1899–1947) into Robin Hoods. And every American's heart could swell with pride as Charles Lindbergh (1902–1974), "the lone eagle," became the first person to fly solo across the Atlantic Ocean in 1927.

Then, in the last year of the decade, it all came apart in the stunning Wall Street crash. And a new and very different-seeming decade began.

When Franklin Roosevelt (president 1933–1945) told the American people, reeling from the Great Depression, that they had "nothing to fear but fear itself," he must have sounded like a cockeyed optimist. When he told his fellow citizens, many of whom were struggling just to stay afloat, that they had "a rendezvous with destiny," he ought to have gotten back a hollow laugh at best. Instead, he became the winningest president in U. S. history, elected and reelected four times, and commonly ranked with Washington and Lincoln by historians.

Democrat Franklin Delano Roosevelt, known to headline writers as FDR, was a cousin of former Republican president Teddy Roosevelt and an upstate New York country squire, the closest thing to aristocracy America had. Ambitious, pragmatic, charming, and wealthy, Franklin Roosevelt had it all—until he was stricken by polio and found himself bound to a wheelchair for the rest of his life. From the crippling disease, perhaps, came the one or two things he had not had before: a share of suffering that made him seem more human, and the demonstrated courage to fight his way back. Behind the big grin and the upwardly slanting cigarette holder was a man who knew what pain and struggle were about.

Roosevelt was fortunate also in marrying Anna Eleanor Roosevelt (1882–1962), a distant cousin of his and an intelligent and socially concerned woman whose political sympathies were slightly to the left of his own. Active in earlier years in advocating help for the slum–dwelling poor and in drawing women into politics, Eleanor Roosevelt became a supporter of organized labor and of the rights of black Americans in the 1930s. Setting out to go where her crippled husband could not, to be his eyes and ears in the world at large, she soon became a public personality in her own right and, for years after his death, America's most admired woman.

When this exceptional couple rode down Pennsylvania Avenue to the White House in March 1933, millions of Americans were jobless, farmers were losing their farms and businessmen their businesses, and banks were failing all across the country, taking the savings of their depositors with them into oblivion. What people need when the cards have gone this badly against them, said FDR, is a new deal. And Roosevelt's *New Deal* program of the 1930s became the most active and successful of any democracy's efforts to break the grip of the Depression. More than Progressivism or any earlier American reform effort, the New Deal made the U. S. government an active player, regulating, stimulating, and directing a fundamentally free–market economy toward recovery. Equally important, FDR began building a structure of welfare legislation and public services like those that had been growing in Europe for several generations. In this effort, he had the support of a unique "New Deal coalition" that brought him victory in four consecutive presidential elections. This Democratic alliance bound together blue–collar workers, African Americans, and the "solid south," where Democrats had dominated politics since the Civil War.

Under Roosevelt the federal government funded large public works programs such as the Works Projects Administration (WPA) to put men and women back to work. It guaranteed unionized labor's right to bargain collectively with employers, provided an aid package for farmers, insured bank deposits, and imposed stringent regulations on the stock market. A graduated income tax began a modest redistribution of the wealth, and the Social Security Act provided Americans with the beginning of a government–sponsored pension plan comparable to those introduced by Britain's Liberals decades before and by Bismarck in Germany a full half–century earlier.

Britain: A Diminishing Pie

Britain, sovereign of empire, trade, and the seas of the world in the nineteenth century, came out of the First World War with its global supremacy badly undermined. Britain had lost two–fifths of its merchant marine, had seen its profitable overseas investments turn to huge war debts, and had lost its commercial edge to the United States.

Through the intermittent prosperity of the 1920s and the deep depression of the 1930s, British management and labor, both hard hit, fought each other for larger shares of a diminishing pie. In 1926, Britain's unions resorted to the most powerful weapon in the labor arsenal: the general strike. Organized labor's attempt to shut the nation down to gain better wages for working people, however, failed in the face of determined middle–and upper–class opposition. Conservative industrial and commercial interests, meanwhile, urged protective tariffs combined with preferential trading agreements with Britain's colonies and with the self–governing dominions, such as Canada and Australia. British business, however, found the colonies and dominions unwilling to have their economies reshaped to suit the needs of the mother country.

The struggle spread to the political realm as well, as the British Labor party moved to replace the Liberals as the primary opposition party to the Conservatives. Under Ramsay MacDonald (1866–1937), Britain's socialists were actually in power for short periods in 1924 and 1931. Lacking a clear majority in the House of Commons, however, Labor had to depend on Liberal support. Labor also clearly lacked a mandate to try such socialist solutions to the nation's economic problems as government take–overs of ailing industries.

During most of the depression–ridden 1930s, then, the government was dominated by Conservatives. Their approach to a deteriorating economy included balancing the budget by cutting back on social services, depending on a meager dole to prevent worker unrest. Yet the Conservatives also had to abandon some of their favorite policies, taking Britain off the gold standard to encourage foreign trade and abandoning free trade in favor of protective tariffs.

Outside of the economic quagmire, however, British leaders continued to show some of their old flair for creative statesmanship and reform. Women finally got the vote in 1918. In 1931, the British Empire was restructured as the British Commonwealth of Nations, in which such developed dominions as Canada, Australia, and New Zealand obtained complete self–government.

Problems with Ireland, however, Britain's oldest colony, remained as intractable as ever. Militants of the Irish Republican Army had revolted in 1916 in the quickly suppressed Easter Rebellion and again in the 1920s, demanding complete freedom. Preoccupied with many postwar problems, Britain finally granted independence to the Irish Free State, comprising most of the island, which in 1948 became the Republic of Ireland. The six counties of Northern Ireland, or Ulster, however, were heavily settled by people of English descent and remained part of Britain, a source of further problems in later years.

France Muddles Through

Despite high wartime casualties and much war destruction, French economic recovery proceeded apace in the 1920s. Aided by reparations payments and the recovery of Alsace and Lorraine, France quickly rebuilt its industrial plant. In addition, major price inflation made French export goods cheap enough to boost its foreign trade one and a half times during the decade. An important result was that big industry and big labor unions, slow to materialize in France, finally began to replace individual artisans and small family–owned companies in the 1920s.

Still, France had more than its share of traditional family firms in the 1930s, and they, paradoxically, helped the nation ride out the Great Depression more easily than countries where industry was more concentrated. Exports continued relatively high, and unemployment ran relatively low. About one French worker in twenty was out of work, by contrast with one in five in Britain and one in three in the United States.

France, like Britain, had its first socialist governments in the interwar period, notably that of Léon Blum (1872–1950) in 1936–1937. Conservatives, however, dominated the government during both decades, as they did in Britain. And even the best of France's leaders—including the intensely nationalistic former liberal Raymond Poincaré (1860–1934), the intellectual Blum, and the eloquent socialist foreign minister Aristide Briand (1862–1932)—had limitations that prevented the nation from dealing effectively with new problems.

Thus Poincaré, one–time Dreyfusard turned ardent patriot, embodied French fear of Germany during the 1920s. When in 1923 the Germans could not meet the reparations schedule set by the Allies, Poincaré responded by sending the French army to occupy Germany's industrial Ruhr valley. Although the occupation did lead to a resumption of modified reparations payments, it also proved enormously costly to France. When Hitler's rise to power seemed to menace France in the 1930s, French politicians moved to build the hugely expensive Maginot line, a string of fortifications on the German frontier that, as we will see, failed disastrously during World War II.

Léon Blum and the socialists also suffered from a serious disability: the split in the European left as a whole over the Bolshevik Revolution in Russia. Some French socialists supported Lenin and his new Communist International (Comintern) founded in 1919, while others, including Blum, did not. This division prevented French socialists from taking unified action even when they were in power.

Weathering the Crisis

Smaller nations, too, suffered from the economically disturbed interwar decades. Some preserved their democratic institutions as Britain, France, and the United States did, in spite of urgings that more authoritarian governments might be better able to cope with the crisis.

Many of the Western countries that both survived economically and preserved liberal political institutions were in the northern and western zones of Europe. The Scandinavian countries, the Netherlands, Belgium, and Switzerland were among the democratic survivors. Outside Europe, members of the British Commonwealth, such as Canada and Australia, also preserved their hard–won democratic institutions.

In Eastern Europe, however, only the new state of Czechoslovakia, led by its intensely patriotic and liberal first president, Thomas Masaryk (1850–1937), really evolved into a functioning democracy between the wars. The Czechs had their problems, including a large German minority and the impact of the Depression on their well–developed industrial sector. Nevertheless, the little eastern European democracy did survive intact until the democratic powers of western Europe betrayed it into the hands of the greatest dictatorship of them all—Hitler's Germany—in 1938.

♦ Nazis and Fascists ♦

In some nations, as we have seen, the liberal political institutions forged in the nineteenth century demonstrated their ability to absorb the buffeting of both the First World War and the Great Depression. In other instances, however, desperate peoples opted for much more authoritarian—and, they hoped, stronger—forms of government.

Two of the most notorious beneficiaries of this trend were the Italian Fascist Benito Mussolini and the Nazi dictator Adolf Hitler. This section will outline Mussolini's rise and trace Hitler's emergence against the background of Italy's and Germany's enormous post-war problems. It will also analyze both cases as examples of the dense form of social control sometimes called totalitarianism.

Totalitarianism

Totalitarianism in the first half of the twentieth century meant dictators with more power over more people than any rulers in Western history. It meant the suppression of democratic institutions and individual rights, barrages of state propaganda, secret police, concentration camps, regimented populations, military aggression, and mass murder. In trying to explain the phenomenon, some scholars have distinguished an "authoritarian" or "totalitarian personality," which they see as particularly willing to accept such governments. Others have rejected the totalitarian label altogether, seeing fascism as the main culprit between the wars, and that as a product of economic and social developments. We will draw on these and other approaches in the following pages.

The totalitarian states of the early twentieth century were most often built around charismatic leaders, people capable of inspiring almost religious awe and devotion in the true believers who followed them. Both Hitler and Benito Mussolini called themselves "the Leader" (*Der Führer* and *Il Duce*), and even the considerably less colorful Stalin generated a massive "cult of the personality" focused on him as "the Lenin of today." Twentieth-century technology, with its floodlights and microphones, its radio and film, made it possible for a powerful personality to impose itself on more people than ever before.

Perhaps the most discussed feature of the modern totalitarian state, however, was the ideological party that supported the leader, controlled the weapons, and kept tabs on the bureaucracy. Whether its ideology was of the right or the left, the typical totalitarian party venerated the leader and made obedience the ultimate virtue. Totalitarianism stressed the unity of the party and the collectivity of the state over individual rights. And it saw the world outside as the scene of a life-and-death struggle in which the triumph of the party was both essential and inevitable.

Recently it has been suggested that this standard picture should be modified by a closer look at the masses themselves, the citizens of the fascist or communist totalitarian state. From the 1890s on, it has been urged, the fact of mass participation in political life conditioned and influenced the programs and policies of political leaders, including, after 1920, the architects of the totalitarian states. Hitler, though he promoted antisemitism vigorously, found the prejudice already widespread in Germany and elsewhere in Europe. Stalin did not invent the peasants' resentment of the better-off peasants he urged them to turn against. Rather, the leaders of totalitarian states shared and expressed these popular views and channeled them into terrible mass persecutions.

Mussolini and Fascist Italy

The first totalitarian dictator was the founder of fascism, Benito Mussolini (1883–1945), self–styled Duce of Italy between the wars. Easy to caricature with his big jaw and bulging stomach, given to operatic gestures and to haranguing the troops from balconies, Mussolini saw himself as an intellectual as well as a man of action. A socialist before World War I, he became a militant nationalist in 1914 and emerged from the war as a vigorous opponent of all left–wing groups.

Economic and political problems seemed to engulf Italy after World War I. The war cost well over half a million lives, gained no territory, and left the country awash in inflated prices and depressed wages. With the left controlling a third of the votes in the legislature and radicals occupying factories and forcing landowners to lower their rents, the situation was ripe for the emergence of a strongman capable of restoring "order"—meaning the conservative prewar status quo.

Mussolini began to organize fellow veterans into black–shirted paramilitary gangs called *squadristi di combattimento* (fighting squads) or *Blackshirts* to disrupt socialist rallies, smash radical presses, and generally attack the Italian left. His *Fascist party,* formally organized in 1921, took its name from the ax and bundle of rods (the fasces) carried ahead of an ancient Roman official, an image of authority and strength. After taking over several Italian cities, Mussolini mounted a "march on Rome" itself in the fall of 1922. Confronted with this challenge, King Victor Emmanuel III (r. 1900–1946) avoided trouble with the Blackshirts by inviting the Fascist leader to form a cabinet and govern Italy.

During the next few years, Fascist officials intimidated those who challenged them and even murdered the socialist leader of the opposition, Giacomo Matteotti (1885–1924). By the end of the decade, Mussolini had transformed the country. It became the model for later totalitarian dictatorships, at least of the right–wing, fascist stripe.

These young Italians were indoctrinated at an early age with love of Mussolini and with eagerness to fight for the Fascist cause. Can you imagine accepting such discipline and loyalty as prime virtues when you were a child?

Convinced that democracy was weak and decadent, the Duce preached the virtues of vigor, discipline, and strength. These he saw embodied in his own person as leader and in the Fascist party, which he soon expanded to include youth and even children's groups, all uniformed, drilled, and trained to revere the Duce.

The party in turn was believed to incarnate the disciplined virtue of the nation. There was, said Mussolini, no higher loyalty than allegiance to the Fascist state: "nothing above the state, nothing outside the state, nothing against the state." In the police state he put together, a restricted electorate voted on a party–prepared list of candidates, while Fascists held all positions in the cabinet and Mussolini was both chief of state and head of the party.

Economically, Mussolini restructured Italy along what he called "corporative" lines. Twenty–odd "corporations" were given official control over the nation's economic life, each containing representatives of business, labor, government, and the party. Mussolini remained friendly with the businessmen his *squadristi* had once supported and allowed them a good deal of say in the economic life of the nation. He also made peace with the Catholic church, long hostile to the Italian state, by turning Vatican City over to the pope and giving the church control of Italian education. As for the majority of Italians, the people's duty, he said, was "to believe, fight, and obey."[1]

The Rise of Hitler

Germany in the 1920s was, at least on paper, one of the most democratic countries in the world. Under the constitution of 1919, put together in the city of Weimar by the liberals and socialists who had dominated the Reichstag, the German *Weimar Republic* had an elected president, a chancellor (prime minister), a legislature, universal adult suffrage, and an exemplary bill of rights. This promising beginning, however, was fatally undercut by the bitter legacy of the war, by a series of intractable economic problems, and by political attacks from left and right that finally brought the Weimar Republic down.

Stripped of much territory and of its revered military establishment, saddled with reparations and war guilt, Germany faced the 1920s in dismay and disarray. And because the architects of the Weimar Republic had also signed the humiliating Versailles Treaty, many Germans had little use for the Republic from the beginning.

Economic problems, including waves of both inflation and depression, also proliferated. The great inflation of the early 1920s was rooted in the French occupation of the Ruhr in 1923. When German laborers in the area refused to work for the occupiers, Germany agreed to pay their lost salaries—by printing money. The resulting inflation sent prices skyrocketing, rendering the German mark virtually worthless and wiping out the life savings of countless solid German burghers.

The Dawes Plan, devised by American tycoon and politician Charles G. Dawes (1865–1951) in 1924, freed the Ruhr and scaled down German reparations. Then five years later came the Great Depression. In the early 1930s, with six million out of work, Germany was the hardest hit of all European nations. A people who could remember the days of the Hohenzollerns, when Germany had led the continent economically as well as militarily, had little respect for the Weimar Republic's management of the economy.

Politically, the German experiment in democracy looked like an even more obvious failure. From the beginning, the new government, whipsawed by militants of left and right, appeared to be incapable even of keeping peace in the streets. On the left were Bolshevik–inspired rebels like the Spartacists, who took their name from Spartacus, the leader of the famous Roman slave revolt. Led by revolutionary Marxists Rosa Luxembourg (1870–1919) and Karl Liebknecht (1871–1919), the Spartacists tried to seize power in 1919 but were suppressed by the army, who murdered Luxembourg and Liebknecht in the process.

Right–wing violence, however, was more common and more dangerous than that of the left. Right–wing groups, including paramilitary veterans' organizations, ultra–nationalists, and antisemitic elements, mounted more than one attempted *Putsch,* or seizure of power. Right–wing fanatics also assassinated government leaders including the internationally respected foreign minister Walther Rathenau (1867–1922), whose Jewish faith particularly outraged the antisemitic right. One of the least successful of these attempted seizures of power was the comic–opera "Beer Hall Putsch" of 1923, so called because the rebels gathered at a Munich beer hall before mounting their insurrection. A dozen of them were killed, and their leader, Adolf Hitler, drew a short prison term for his futile gesture.

Adolf Hitler (1889–1945), the future builder of Nazi Germany, was not German but Austrian by birth. A failed art student, he had developed a great enthusiasm for all things German and a virulent antisemitism. Emigrating to Germany on the eve of World War I, Hitler had served in the ranks, been wounded and decorated, and had finally found his true vocation in the violent ideological politics of postwar Germany.

Like Mussolini, Hitler was an ardent nationalist, assuring Germans that they would be great again, and a militant antileftist. His favorite scapegoat for all Germany's ills, however, was the Jewish community, whom he caricatured in the language of vulgar tabloid racism. He condemned Jews for their success in business and the professions and blamed them for Germany's defeat in the First World War. Above all, he defined Jews as a "race" rather than a religious denomination and preached a cosmic struggle between the Aryan "master race"—meaning Germans—and the Jewish "race," the *Untermenschen* or subhumans, for the future of civilization.

Through the 1920s, Hitler's German National Socialist Workers or *Nazi party* (*Nazi* was a modified abbreviation of the party name in German) evolved into a potent force in right–wing politics. His *Brownshirts*—the Nazi paramilitary force—fought in the streets with communist Red Flag militants, attacked Jews, and disrupted rallies. He used his time in prison after the Beer Hall Putsch to write his manifesto, *Mein Kampf* (My Struggle), and came out more popular than ever. And then, as the 1920s ended and the Depression closed in, the Weimar regime seemed more and more helpless, and things began to go Hitler's way at last.

The Weimar regime was paralyzed during the early 1930s. Since the Social Democratic party would not close ranks with the Communists, and old–fashioned conservatives would not form an alliance with the Nazis, neither the left nor the right could form a government. For three years after 1929, therefore, a cabal of conservatives prevailed upon President Paul von Hindenburg (1847–1934), the aging World War I hero, to rule by decree as provided in the constitution. Then the president's handlers decided to try to manipulate Hitler and his phenomenal voter appeal—the Nazis were now getting a solid third of the ballots—by naming him chancellor at the beginning of 1933.

Many Germans saw hope in Hitler in 1933. Lower–middle–class people voted for him out of fear of communism and their own dwindling social and economic status. Students loved his idealistic speches, and big businessmen gave funds to his party. Nationalists and antisemites of all classes supported him, and so did small–town monarchists longing for the return of the good old days of the Hohenzollerns.[2]

In the end, the man himself remains central. Hitler made the *Führer principle,* personal loyalty to the party's leader, a key element in Nazi ideology. "Long ago you heard the voice of a man," the leader's harsh voice would crackle into the microphones as he addressed a huge night rally bedecked with red swastika flags, "and it struck to your hearts, and it awakened you, and you followed this voice." And what did it say? "It is faith in our nation that has made us small people great, that has made us poor people rich, that has made us vacillating, dispirited, anxious people brave and courageous."[3] His Nazi followers in the Hitler Youth sang proudly of the future he had promised them:

> Today, Germany belongs to us
> Tomorrow, all the world.[4]

Hitler had made Germans feel good about themselves again, and many of them pinned their faith in the future he promised them.

Building the Thousand–Year Reich

Hitler moved at once to make himself master of Germany. He succeeded within a year. Genuinely fearful of a Communist Putsch, the new chancellor reacted to an attempt to burn down the Reichstag early in 1933—apparently the work of a feebleminded Dutch communist—by ordering a sweeping crackdown on the left. With not only German communists but Social Democratic leaders also in jail, Hitler prevailed upon rival conservative and nationalist parties to disband and support the Nazis in a united campaign against the left. In 1934, suspecting a plot by leaders of his own Brownshirt paramilitary force, he dispatched his new black–uniformed SS units and the feared secret police called the Gestapo to execute scores, perhaps hundreds, of leading Brownshirts and others whose loyalty was suspect.

Voted absolute power for four years, Hitler proceeded to solve the problems that had bedeviled the Weimar Republic by drawing upon a variety of models. He borrowed economic controls, for instance, from his socialist predecessors. Like Mussolini, he let business leaders have a major voice in running the economy, though under Nazi supervision. Like governments in other countries, Hitler launched major public works projects, including the world's first superhighways, the *Autobahns,* in order to put people back to work. Unlike the democracies, however, he also pumped up the economy and got the unemployed off the streets by embarking upon a crash program of rearmament.

The Führer, however, had larger goals. He was founding, he said, a *Third Reich* (Empire) following those of the Habsburgs and the Hohenzollerns. It was to be an empire that would last a thousand years.

Hitler surrounded himself with a group of ambitious, generally unscrupulous men. Hermann Goering (1893–1946), bluff, bull–necked, and ruthless, who had been a World War I flying ace, built the *Luftwaffe*—the German air corps—into the powerful force that swept the skies over Europe in the early years of World War II. Josef Goebbels (1897–1945), the Nazi minister of propaganda, devoted himself to glorifying the Führer and manipulating the news with minimal regard for the truth. The sinister Heinrich Himmler (1900–1945) headed Hitler's Praetorian Guard, the *SS* (*Schutzstaffel,* or "defense force"), which would later run the Nazi concentration camps, and the dreaded *Gestapo* (*Geheime Staatspolizei,* the secret police). These and others of Hitler's entourage, often self–aggrandizing and bitterly feuding among themselves, were nevertheless eager for the success of the Nazi cause that had made them the masters of Germany.

Like the Fascists in Italy, the Nazis moved to mobilize society as a whole in support of the new order. Uniformed organizations like the Hitler Youth inculcated veneration for the Führer and his cause. Women were encouraged to emulate the peasant wife, devoted to "the three Ks"—*Kinder, Kirche, Küche* (children, church, kitchen)—though during the crucial period of building the Nazi state, active participation in "the common task of achieving a National Socialist reconstruction" was expected.[5] Schoolbooks were rewritten to support Nazi racist theories, and universities were purged of books—and professors—who disagreed. Protestant churches were absorbed into a new Nazi Evangelical church; the Catholic church was forbidden to discuss politics. Censorship and propaganda combined with the ever-present secret police to ensure loyalty in thought, word, and deed.

Not everyone, however, was allowed to share in building the Thousand-Year Reich. Less favored "racial" types like Gypsies, Slavs, and above all Jews suffered active persecution from the earliest days of Hitler's rule.

By the *Nuremberg Laws* of 1935 and other Nazi edicts, Jews were forbidden to teach or study in schools or universities, to hold government jobs, to practice law or medicine, to work at other trades, to publish or perform in the arts. Mob violence against the Jews was officially encouraged, as in the notorious *Kristallnacht,* November 9, 1938, the "night of the broken glass," when Jews were attacked, Jewish windows were shattered, and synagogues were burned in many parts of Germany. A primary object of these measures was to force Jews to emigrate, leaving their property to the Nazi state. For the large majority who would not or could not afford to leave, however, a new policy was developed. By the early 1940s, the Nazis had begun to force Jews into ghettos and to intern them in concentration camps.

♦ Communists, Militarists, and Other Dictators ♦

Adolf Hitler was the most notorious of the new generation of dictators, but the Russian Communists and the militarists in Japan were equally important. Dictators of various stripes also rose to power in the less-developed parts of Europe, in Latin America, and in other parts of the world. But the Stalinists in Communist Russia were enough like the German and Italian states in terms of organization, ideological core, and sheer savagery to be called "totalitarian" also.

Stalin and the Five-Year Plans

The largest of Europe's totalitarian states, and the only one to survive past midcentury, was Soviet Russia. Under Joseph Stalin, who ruled the Soviet Union from the end of the 1920s to his death in 1953, the Soviet Communist regime was as all-encompassing and as repressive as the governments led by Hitler or Mussolini.

The years of the USSR's *New Economic Policy* (NEP) of the 1920s, like the Weimar period in German history, unconsciously paved the way for totalitarianism. The NEP was a compromise with capitalism introduced by Lenin in the early 1920s. Recognizing that the long ordeal of war, revolution, and civil strife had exhausted the country, Lenin decided to allow the nation time to recover. Under the NEP, the government owned the "commanding heights" of the economy, including large-scale manufacturing, banking, and international trade. But peasants were allowed to keep and work their own land. And small-business operators, so-called NEP-men, continued to function as small-scale capitalists through the period.

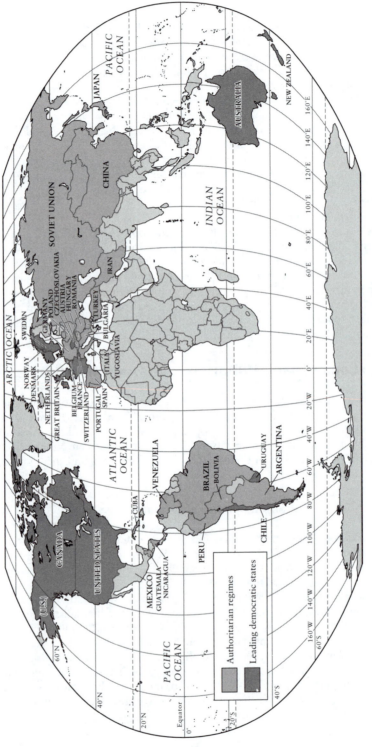

Democracies and Dictatorships, 1919–1939

Authoritarian regimes
Leading democratic states

The major events of the 1920s, however, were political. They included the premature death in 1924 of Lenin himself—who had never recovered from his 1918 injury by a Social Revolutionary assassin—and the resulting struggle for political supremacy between two of his lieutenants, Trotsky and Stalin.

Leon Trotsky, potent orator and an internationally known Marxist theorist, had helped organize both the Revolution of 1917 and victory in the Civil War. In the 1920s, he urged that for the Russian Revolution to succeed, it would have to be supported by similar revolutions in other countries—the "world revolution" that Marx had promised. Joseph Stalin, an agitator and organizer of bank robberies, had been sent to Siberia half a dozen times. He declared his faith in "socialism in one country"—that the Soviet Union could survive and prosper without international support.

What Stalin did have above all was organizational ability and a talent for exploiting others. Trotsky's dismissal of his rival as a mere *apparatchik,* or "machine man," was scathing; but a political machine was what the party was becoming—and Stalin had his hands on the levers of power. By 1929, Trotsky was on his way into exile overseas. He died, assassinated in Mexico in 1940, while Stalin, holding the unimpressive title of secretary of the Communist party, was hailed all over the Soviet Union as Lenin's successor.

Lenin had accomplished the political revolution. His power assured, Stalin announced his intention of achieving the economic revolution: the establishment of state socialism in the Soviet Union. In so doing, he brought full–fledged totalitarianism to Russia in the 1930s.

Stalin's decision to abandon the NEP and socialize the economy of the nation was partly rooted in his Marxist beliefs, which required abolition of private ownership of the means of production. Partly also, it was rooted in a Russian ambition, going back to Peter the Great, to "catch up with the West," which the Communists believed could best be accomplished through a state–run economy. It was probably also a decision rooted in fear of "capitalist encirclement," as illustrated first by Allied intervention in the Civil War, later by the vocal anti–communism of Hitler and Mussolini.

Finally, however, it was a political decision. More power for the government meant more power for the Communist party, which controlled the government. And victory on the economic front meant in particular triumph for Joseph Stalin, a vindication of his views and a glorious climax to his career.

To achieve this massive transformation of the national economy, the Russian Communists depended on state planning on an unprecedented scale. A Central Planning Committee laid out the major targets for each of a series of *Five Year Plans* for the nation as a whole. Regional and local committees developed their own plans within the framework of the national plan. Capital and resources were allocated and quotas set for every branch of the economy—for each province, factory, farm, and worker. As the Depression settled over the capitalist world, many watched the Soviet Union's "great experiment" in a planned economy with particular interest.

The three Five Year Plans that took Russia from Stalin's rise to power in 1928 to Hitler's invasion of Russia in 1941 had their greatest successes in heavy industry. Central planning worked pretty well when it was a question of setting up assembly–line factories to make trucks or tractors, building a steelworks or a hydroelectric dam, designing a prestige project like Moscow's elegant subway system, or hacking an entire industrial complex out of the frozen tundra east of the Urals. Heroic labors were accomplished, production rose rapidly, and—though Stalinist statistics are always dubious—quotas were sometimes achieved early. Rigorous industrial discipline had to be imposed on the new factory workers, many of them peasants who had never seen a machine or heard a factory whistle. But Stalin was never averse to imposing discipline.

He had much more difficulty in his efforts to collectivize agriculture. This he was determined to do in order to feed the workers in the cities and to sell grain overseas for export capital. As a Marxist, his ideological commitment was to the urban proletariat; he seems to have had little concern for the country's peasant majority.

In the early 1930s, then, the Soviet Union's peasant millions were moved from their small farms and ancient villages onto much larger collectively operated farms. Some of these large farms were owned in common by those who lived and worked there, sharing the profits; others were state owned, the workers thereon salaried employees of the government. Government–run machine tractor stations provided the collective farms with the use of agricultural machinery, with fertilizer, and with other services. Agricultural prices were set by the state, which was also the principal customer for the produce of the nation's farms.

There was trouble with the collectivization of agriculture from the start. The better–off peasants, called *kulaks,* meaning "tightfisted" exploiters of their neighbors, lost their land and were sent off to work camps. There they labored on canals or other large state projects—and died in large numbers. Many ordinary peasants resisted and had to be forced onto the collectives. Even when they were settled on the new socialized farms, many produced just enough grain for their own use. Stalin responded by simply ordering the confiscation of the produce the peasants had intended for themselves. This heavy–handed policy, combined with several bad growing seasons, created a major famine in the Soviet Union in the early 1930s. Perhaps three and one–half million peasants died in labor camps, as many as seven million more in the vast famine that accompanied collectivization.

Stalinist Terror: The Purges and the Gulag

Some historians have suggested that Stalin may have become increasingly paranoid as the years passed. As he thrust aside his rivals and stepped up pressure for forced–draft industrialization and compulsory collectivization, he soon had real enemies enough. In the later 1930s, using as his excuse the murder of a party leader, Stalin began to purge these "enemies of the people," real and fancied. The party *purge,* which had most commonly meant expelling inefficient or disloyal members from the party, now became a matter of exile, imprisonment, or execution.

During the 1930s, large numbers of Soviet citizens were arrested by the NKVD, the People's Commissariat of Internal Affairs, Stalin's secret police. The victims were confined in prisons, sent off to grueling Siberian work camps where many died, or simply executed outright. The victims were charged with being "Trotskyites," agents of capitalist powers, or "industrial saboteurs" whose plants had failed to meet their quotas. The better known among them were given show trials, where they were faced with shocking accusations, confronted by perjured testimony, and convicted by their own forced confessions. Prominent industrial managers, military commanders, and veteran party leaders—including Stalin's former rivals for the leadership—died in this way.

Writers and others who dared to express opinions and beliefs that differed from those of state were also sent to the camps. Under the reformer Mikhail Gorbachev in the 1980s, the files of the secret police itself revealed that it had convicted and sentenced a total of 3,778,234 people for such crimes and had executed 786,098 of them. Millions more probably died in the many *Gulag* zones, the "islands" of forced labor camps scattered across the Soviet Union. (*GULAG* is the Russian acronym for Chief Administration of Corrective Labor Camps.)

Stalinist communism also had its party organizations for children and youth, its cells among factory workers and collective farmers, its parades and mass rallies. Marxism–Leninism—in time expanded to Marxism–Leninism–Stalinism—became the country's official philosophy. The Russian Communists also made a determined effort to suppress religion, closing many local churches and drastically reducing membership in the Russian Orthodox church as a whole. Above all, Soviet citizens, like Germans, trembled in fear of the knock on the door after midnight, the discovery of "incriminating" papers and books, and the "little visit to the police station" from which one did not return.

Dictatorship Around the World

The Fascists in Italy, the Nazis in Germany, and the Communists in the Soviet Union were only the most notorious of these authoritarian regimes. Smaller, less–developed nations also produced dictatorial regimes in central, southern, and eastern Europe, in Latin America, and even in Japan. And though few were full–fledged totalitarian states, they were far from the democratic governments that Western liberals had expected.

Many of these regimes were in what we would call today economically underdeveloped areas. Primarily peasant lands, they often had only islands of industrial development, as in Austria and Argentina. They were also typically politically antiquated nations in which kings were often still at least viable candidates for national power or in which large landowners and established churches were still powerful in the countryside. In some countries, the military provided a traditional source of power. Even in developed Japan, a divine monarch and a strong samurai military tradition provided live alternatives to that nation's emerging representative institutions.

Through the 1920s and 1930s, these nations also had to face the aftereffects of World War I and the pressure of the Great Depression. Nationhood itself was a new experience for some of the eastern European peoples who had so recently been subjects of the Ottoman, Austrian, or Russian empires. In both Europe and Latin America, some had experimented with the forms of modern democracy but found them inadequate to the problems of economic and political modernization they faced.

A sampling of the troubled nations around the world who turned to authoritarian government under the pressures of the interwar years will both illustrate some common features and exemplify the variety of forms this great "flight from freedom" could take.

All across eastern Europe, democracy failed signally to take hold during the 1920s and 1930s. Poland, restored to the map of Europe after more than a century of partition and foreign rule, faced problems of bitterly disputed borders, unhappy minorities, and economic disarray—problems with which an unstable democratic government seemed unable to cope. In 1926 Marshal Josef Pilsudski (1867–1935) therefore led a "march on Warsaw" comparable to Mussolini's march on Rome that established Pilsudski as the country's autocratic ruler for the next decade.

Yugoslavia, an entirely new country formed of several three South Slav nationalities, including the Serbs, the Croats, and the Slovenes, was sharply divided by ethnic tensions, particularly between the Serbian rulers and the militant Croatian Peasant party. Facing violent agitation, threats of secession, and political assassinations, Yugoslavia's King Alexander

(r. 1921–1934) finally suspended democratic institutions and sought to impose an autocratic central government on his turbulent peoples. Alexander himself fell to an assassin's bullet in 1934, and an attempt was made to restore the fledgling democracy by constitutional reform in 1939. But World War II broke out before the end of the year, and Nazi occupation followed soon thereafter, replaced by communist autocracy after the war.

Elsewhere in the Balkans, unstable countries faced with devastating social, economic, and ethnic problems often drifted back to traditional authoritarian regimes. Bulgaria, battered by military coups, communist terrorists, and a pro–German Nazi party, sought refuge in the royal dictatorship of King Boris III (r. 1918–1943). In Romania, a Peasant party won redistribution of land and better relations with the Soviet Union, the antisemitic Iron Guard demanded a rapprochement with Nazi Germany, and kings Ferdinand (r. 1914–1927) and Carol II (r. 1930–1940) exercised sometimes autocratic power.

Dictatorships also emerged in the Iberian nations between the two world wars. Spain, nominally a constitutional monarchy under Alfonso XIII (r. 1912–1931) was actually ruled by military dictator General Miquel Primo de Rivera from 1923 to 1930. The country, however, was tormented by conflicts between an ancient landed aristocracy and an established Catholic church on the one hand and, on the other, an emerging industrial sector whose workers found aggressive leaders in liberal, socialist, and anarchist political parties. Spain also faced violent nationalist agitation, especially in the industrialized northern region of Catalonia. Following a bloody civil war (see next chapter) General Francisco Franco (1892–1973) seized power and ruled a one–party dictatorship for the rest of his life.

The Great Depression, with its severely depressed commodity prices, hit the southern American republics hard. In the early 1930s, more than half the twenty independent nations of Latin America responded to the resulting economic pressures with revolutions. The regimes that came to power were most commonly right–wing dictatorships, headed by conservatives, nationalists, or military leaders.

Thus the moderate–to–liberal Radical party that governed Argentina in the 1920s fell to a military coup in 1930. Under the so–called Conservative Republic, which ruled for the next dozen years, an alliance of militarists, nationalists, and other conservatives rigged elections and suppressed all political opposition. In Brazil, the nationalistic military leader Getulio Vargas (1883–1954) seized power in 1930 and ruled for the following fifteen years. Vargas governed by censorship and decree, outlawing opposition parties and even deploying the armed forces to impose his will. In Central America, the Somoza family came to power in the mid–1930s and ruled for two generations, savaging all political rivals. Like European authoritarian rulers, these Latin American dictators boasted of economic gains, including considerable industrial development; but their people, like central and eastern Europeans, paid a heavy price in human suffering.

Japan, on the other side of the world, developed, not a rigidly totalitarian system, but an amalgam of older and newer power structures dominated by military leaders and supported by passionate nationalism. Following its "opening" to the West by U. S. Commodore Matthew Perry (1794–1858) in 1853, the island empire had developed with unparalleled rapidity. Building on traditions of medieval samurai militarism and on sophisticated commercial cities built during the Tokugawa shogunate (1603–1868), Japan had produced a modern industrial system and a modernized army and navy capable of defeating China in 1895 and Russia in 1905. Yet Japan remained as much a peasant nation as either of these continental countries. Its impressive modernization, furthermore, had taken place after the Meiji Restoration of 1868, under the aegis of renewed loyalty to a divine emperor who became the focus of intense nationalism. Gripped by expansionist ambitions in Asia and resentful of Western refusal to recognize the legitimacy of those ambitions, Japan was a force to be reckoned with in the Far East and the Pacific in the first half of the twentieth century.

Through the 1920s, this new Asian great power was managed by a unique combination of often rivalrous groups. These included the emperor and his court; an alliance of big–business dynasties and politicians in Japan's Western–style legislature; and the leaders of the nation's admired new army and navy, which had thus far won all their wars.

In the 1930s, intensely nationalistic young army officers asserted Japan's right to dominate the East. They played upon traditional loyalty to the emperor and to the Japanese past and won the support of big business with its visions of vastly expanded markets. The militarists also cowed the politicians with assassinations like those in Germany a decade earlier, including the killing of a number of government leaders during the seizure of downtown Tokyo by a cabal of young army officers in 1936.

No totalitarian political party emerged, and both the ancient monarchy and Western representative institutions remained in existence. But real power was in the hands of the nation's military establishment in the 1930s, and Japanese nationalism provided an ideological cement as powerful as Nazism, Fascism or Communism in Europe.

♦A Society of Subcultures♦

Politically, the interwar decades saw the Western world increasingly divided between struggling democracies and resurgent authoritarian states. The social history of this period, however, reveals a contrasting tendency toward greater unity of experience. In an emerging consumer society, dominated by common work modes and mass culture, class and gender differences were beginning to be undercut by common life experiences and lifestyles. Even the great political differences between authoritarian and free societies were not sufficient to prevent middle– and working–class people, women and men, from having more in common than ever before. The social homogenization that would produce an increasingly uniform style of life across the Western world was getting under way.

The Consumer Society

The middle classes, who continued to dominate Western society in the twentieth century, defined themselves more and more by their style of life, by what they consumed rather than by what they produced. The lifestyle of this *consumer society* was less and less that of the stiff–collared nineteenth–century bourgeoisie, with its work ethic and its Victorian morality. The middle classes had often spent lavishly on material things, from velvet robes in the Middle Ages to overstuffed furniture in the nineteenth century. After the First World War, however, thanks to science and technology, they had some astonishing new things to buy.

Perhaps the single most transforming innovation for middle–class U. S. and western European consumers was the automobile. Owned by relatively few before World War I, cars became much more widely available in the 1920s, thanks particularly to American manufacturer Henry Ford (1863–1947), who developed assembly–line methods of production that brought autos within the price range of even lower–middle–class Americans. In Europe, such firms as Fiat in Italy, Renault in France, and the German Volkswagen (people's car) were soon following Ford's lead in producing cars that ordinary people could afford. The number of automobiles on the roads continued to grow through the 1920s. France produced 40,000 of them a year on the eve of World War I, and Germany only 10,000; in the late 1930s, the figures were 230,000 for France and 445,000 for Germany. Cars gave families mobility for a picnic or a Sunday drive and provided young people with wonderful privacy—"petting parlors on wheels," they were sometimes called. In the automobile the middle classes found the ultimate symbol of status and modernity.

For the household appliance market, electricity provided the greatest boon. The amount of electrical power generated expanded rapidly during the interwar years. In Britain it climbed from 8.5 million kilowatt hours in 1920 to 26 million in 1935; in the Soviet Union during the same period, it went from half a million to slightly over 26 million. This instant plug–in power made possible a growing number of labor–saving devices inside the home. Mass–marketed Hoover vacuum cleaners, washing machines, refrigerators, and telephones grew more common. Like automobiles, however, these new wonders of modern technology were affordable mostly to middle– and upper–class people and to more Americans than Europeans.

Work Modes and Mass Culture

We have already noted the shattering economic impact of the Great Depression on men and women who worked in factories and on farms. There were other changes in their working lives that should be noted here as well. And we should notice the extent to which the once diverse working populations of the West found themselves absorbed into a homogeneous *mass culture,* a single popular culture widely disseminated through the new media, during the interwar decades.

Important work–related changes that affected working people increasingly in this period were efforts to increase productivity, both by introducing new machinery and by increasing the amount of productive labor each worker contributed. In industry, "labor–saving" machinery continued to put laborers out of work even when the Depression did not. A newer tendency, emerging first in the United States but spreading to western Europe, was the attempt to get people to work harder through scientific management, efficiency studies, and "speedups." In the Soviet Union, so–called Stakhanovite programs—named for a legendary 1930s miner, Alexei Stakhanov—accomplished the same purpose by encouraging workers to exceed their official quotas.

As we have seen, American farmers and European peasants suffered from an agricultural depression in the 1920s as well as in the 1930s. Again, however, broader trends shaped their working lives as well. In the United States, exploitation by banks, railroads, and marketing firms was joined by the long–term effect of labor–saving farm machinery, which also eliminated jobs and drove many farm laborers to move to the cities, where unemployment was also endemic. In Europe, peasants lacked either capital or knowledge to take advantage of technological innovations and remained relatively unproductive and often embittered at changes they did not understand. And in the Soviet Union Stalinist agricultural collectivization not only brought famine in the 1930s but reduced productivity so greatly that what had been a grain–exporting nation under the czars depended on large imports of foreign grain for most of the rest of the century.

Both urban and rural workers, meanwhile, were undergoing another social transformation. In the twentieth century, consumerism and the media further invaded both small towns and close–knit neighborhoods with the growing appeal of mass culture. Radios, films, and ever cheaper consumer products reshaped the values of Western people, first in the middle and then in the lower classes. Indeed, while the Depression revived feelings of class antagonism, consumer products and the impact of the media undercut a sense of class, as well as ethnic and religious differences. It was a trend toward a one–culture society that, paradoxically, flourished in the troubled capitalist society of the United States more than in the avowedly egalitarian communist society of the Soviet Union.

Women in Democracies and Authoritarian States

During the 1920s and 1930s, what has been termed "the modern notion of womanhood" took shape in many Western countries. By and large, this new image of what a woman's life should be took root more solidly in the capitalist democracies than in more traditional or authoritarian societies.

In western Europe and America, this image of the ideal woman's life included "efficiency at home and work, energy in sports and sexual life, companionship with [rather than subservience to] her mate, and consumerism."[6] It was an image of home and work life merging which was rooted to some degree in changing social realities.

Widespread use of birth–control devices halved the number of children born between 1850 and 1950 in Britain, Germany, and Sweden and brought substantial declines elsewhere in Europe. To some degree, smaller families and increasing numbers of labor–saving appliances eased the burden of running a home and freed many women for other occupations and activities.[7]

Jobs outside the home in fact absorbed increasing numbers of middle–class women. Many became salespeople or clerical workers, teachers or telephone operators in the expanding service and white–collar sectors. Women also went into business for themselves, often opening small shops. By this time also, there were women doctors, dentists, lawyers, and university professors, though the numbers were not great.

Working women underwent two particularly traumatic experiences during the interwar years. The first came right after World War I, when large numbers were discharged from war industries when the troops returned looking for jobs. The second occurred a decade later when the Depression threw many women out of work. During these twenty years, fewer women worked outside the home than had done so before World War I.

Yet the overall contemporary impression of women's lives during these decades was one of greater freedom, variety, and excitement. After what the twentieth century saw as the stultifying respectability and hypocrisy of Victorian times, women emerged from whalebone corsets and heavy, floor–length gowns into the short skirts and boyish haircuts of the "flapper," the socially emancipated young woman of the jazz age.

Middle–class women at least were demanding and getting a new kind of freedom during these two decades: *social* emancipation. Besides dressing more lightly and comfortably, women went to social gatherings without male escorts and dined alone in restaurants. They took up vigorous outdoor sports, such as golf, tennis, and swimming, and were soon competing all the way up to the Olympic level.

Women who lived under more authoritarian regimes were also offered a new self–image and in some cases new legal rights. In most of these states, however, there was a counterbalancing reassertion of older values, notably an emphasis on home life and motherhood.

The fascist governments, glorifying male strength, virility, and force, assigned women a secondary role in society. The social revolutions Hitler and Mussolini proclaimed were embodied in goose–stepping phalanxes of uniformed men, and women's role was seen as primarily supportive. Above all, these leaders insisted, women could best serve their rejuvenated nations by bearing strong sons to further increase the military might of Fascist Italy or Nazi Germany.

Once in power, Hitler sponsored party organizations for girls and women but, as noted earlier, emphasized women's traditional roles in the nursery, the church, and the kitchen. As it became apparent that women workers outside the home would be needed to build the new German Reich, the Nazis, like the Fascists, fixed levels of remuneration for women workers well below men's wages.

The Soviet Union under Stalin offers a more complex picture. During Lenin's last years, women had gained legal equality, broader educational opportunities, liberalized divorce laws, legal abortions, and other changes widely seen as steps toward women's social emancipation. Under Stalin, however, many of these measures were watered down or abandoned. In the 1930s, demands for women's labor in industry and a contradictory desire to strengthen the family as a center of security against the strains of the new era combined to impose a heavy burden on Soviet women.

In the Stalin period, then, women did get more education and moved into jobs hitherto reserved for men, from medicine to heavy industrial labor. The result was what has been called the "double shift" for Soviet women, who were required to work a full day in the factory or the fields and then care for their families at night. Even though the Soviet Union did broaden the range of opportunities available to women, the material condition of most women was seldom improved thereby.

The Conflict of Generations

Educational reform was also a feature of the interwar years, from "progressive education" in the United States, which stressed preparation for citizenship, to the Montessori schools of Europe, which emphasized individual development over rote learning. In many places, nursery schools and kindergartens were introduced, freeing mothers for other work. University populations experienced rapid growth, particularly in the United States. U. S. institutions of higher learning doubled their enrollment, from half a million students in 1920 to over a million in 1930.

Cut off from parents and other adult role models in this expanding age-segregated educational system, young people generated their own *youth culture*. Finding mentors and models in the mass media, they became the quintessential radio and film fans, devotees of entertainers, athletes, and other celebrities. Greater middle-class prosperity and smaller families meant that youth enjoyed more attention and a higher material standard of living than earlier generations had. They bought huge quantities of phonograph records, movie and "true-romance" magazines, and clothing like that worn by their idols or their peers. The influence of American media spread as Hollywood feature films and the phonograph recordings of singers like Bing Crosby (1904–1977) flooded across the Western world and beyond.

As this youth culture grew, another form of social conflict also gained wider recognition between the wars: the *conflict of generations*. The phenomenon had been noticed in a political context in the nineteenth century: the barricade fighters and the bohemian artists always seemed to be young. In a larger cultural and social sense, however, the revolt of the younger generation was first widely noted in the 1920s and 1930s.

The first "lost generation" was that which came out of the First World War. Young Europeans, and later young Americans, returned home convinced that the war had proved nothing and achieved nothing; that it had in short been a swindle, they and their dead comrades its victims. This disillusionment with the war was the root of the "lost" quality widely noticed in the postwar generation. Allied politicians blamed the Germans for the catastrophe; but postwar youth noted that democracies as well as autocracies had sent their children off to the death fields in the name of some the same noble–sounding ideals—God, country, freedom, and civilization. A negative judgment on the war thus led some to a harsh rejection of Western civilization itself.

The most visible embodiment of this generational rebellion was the *flapper*. This very modern young woman wore her hair and skirts scandalously short, drank and smoked, and associated on a basis of complete social equality with young men. She also danced with them to the frenetic jazz beat or "cheek to cheek" to slower and even more disturbing rhythms from South America. She petted with them in parked cars and sometimes visited their apartments—or had them up to hers—unchaperoned. And if only well-off girls could afford the clothes or the boy friends with cars, working-class girls could read about their shocking behavior in novels, see them in films, and share vicariously their very un-Victorian romances.

The 1930s, finally, brought another sort of generational revolution to public attention. Under the impact of depression and authoritarian regimes, young people turned to political commitment once more. The totalitarian states had their youth corps—the Komsomol in the Soviet Union, the Hitler Youth in Germany, and Mussolini's Sons of the Wolf. These groups channeled their youthful political enthusiasm into the service of the leader and the state, eager to be part of the great crusade to build the Thousand-Year Reich or launch the World Revolution. In the democracies, youthful political passions included a militant antiwar movement in the early 1930s and a ground swell of pro–Soviet, antifascist feeling later. Young people demonstrated against war, joined the youth wing of the Communist party, or volunteered to fight against fascism in the Spanish Civil War. The coming of World War II would soon absorb all the energies of the young; but the world had not seen the last of the conflict of generations.

Summary

The economy of the Western world, apparently prosperous for most of the 1920s and deeply depressed in the 1930s, was actually unstable throughout the two decades between the world wars. The booming productivity of the United States powered the Western economy through the 1920s. After the Wall Street stock–market crash of 1929, however, the Great Depression swept from America to Europe and on to the rest of the world.

U. S. President Franklin Roosevelt's New Deal program, aimed at economic recovery, did much to provide a safety net of welfare services for the United States. Britain, France, and other Western nations stumbled through the Depression decade (1929–1939), but all these nations at least preserved their democratic institutions through the long crisis.

Dictatorships of various kinds, however, mushroomed in many parts of the world between the wars. The totalitarian regimes that emerged under Mussolini in Fascist Italy, under Hitler in Nazi Germany, and in Stalin's Soviet Union were the most powerful and oppressive of these authoritarian governments. In these states, dictators and their ideological parties used modern technology and bureaucracy to brutalize their own people and to launch premeditated aggressions against their neighbors.

In both democracies and dictatorships, however, society seemed to be moving toward a common experience that transcended class, gender, and generational divisions. Working–class and middle–class people shared an expanding mass culture, and women began to share the socially emancipated lifestyles of men, at least in more liberal countries. Young people in many lands shared jazz–age disillusionment in the 1920s, widespread joblessness and sometimes intense political commitment in the 1930s.

Some Key Terms

Blackshirts 627	Führer principle 629	New Economic Policy 631
Brownshirts 629	Gestapo 630	Nuremberg Laws 631
conflict of generations 640	Great Depression 620	purge 634
consumer society 637	*Gulag* 635	*Putsch* 629
crash of 1929 619	*Kristallnacht* 631	*SS* 630
economic nationalism 621	kulak 634	Third Reich 630
Fascist party 627	mass culture 638	totalitarianism 626
Five Year Plans 633	Nazi party 629	youth culture 640
flapper 641	New Deal 623	Weimar Republic 628

Notes

1. Benito Mussolini, quoted in Denis Mack Smith, *Mussolini* (London: Granada, 1983), 143.
2. Richard F. Hamilton, *Who Voted for Hitler?* (Princeton, N.J.: Princeton University Press, 1982); Eberhard Jäckel, *Hitlers Herrschaft: Vollzug einer Weltanschauung* (Stuttgart: Deutsche, 1986).
3. Adolf Hitler, quoted in Joachim C. Fest, *Hitler* (London: Weidenfeld and Nicolson, 1973), 511.
4. Peter H. Merkl, *Political Violence under the Swastika* (Princeton, N.J.: Princeton University Press, 1975), 469. For shifting theories of the causes of nazism, see Theodore S. Hamerow, "Guilt, Redemption, and Writing German History," *American Historical Review* 88(1983): 5–72.
5. Jill Stephenson, *Women in Nazi Society* (London: Croom Helm, 1975), 196, 143.
6. Bonnie G. Smith, *Changing Lives: Women in European Society Since 1700* (Lexington, Mass.: D.C. Heath, 1989), 411.
7. Labor–saving devices, however, did not always cut the number of hours housewives worked: they also sometimes raised standards and expectations and replaced servants, thereby making more work for the housewife.

Reading List

Allen, W. S. *The Nazi Seizure of Power*. New York: Franklin Watts, 1973. Detailed study of the Nazi take–over in a single town. See also I. Kershaw, *Inside Nazi Germany: Conformity, Opposition, and Racism in Everyday Life*, trans. R. Deveson (New Haven: Yale University Press, 1987). Lives of ordinary Germans.

Banner, L. W. *Women in Modern America: A Brief History*. New York: Harcourt Brace Jovanovich, 1974. Brief but very readable. See also W. H. Chafe, *The American Woman: Her Changing Social, Economic, and Political Role, 1920–1970* (New York: Oxford University Press, 1972), for a scholarly survey.

Bracher, K. *The German Dictatorship: The Origins, Structure, and Effects of National Socialism.* Translated by J. Steinberg. New York: Praeger, 1970. See also I. Kershaw, *The Nazi Dictator-*

ship: Problems and Perspectives of Interpretation (Baltimore: Edward Arnold, 1985).

Bullock, A. *Hitler: A Study in Tyranny.* New York: Harper and Row, 1971. Still widely recommended biography. See also N. Stone, *Hitler* (New York: Knopf, 1982), and an excellent German biography, J. C. Fest, *Hitler,* trans. R. and C. Winston (New York: Harcourt Brace Jovanovich, 1974).

Conquest, R. *The Great Terror: Stalin's Purge of the Thirties.* New York: Collier, 1973. The Stalinist police state. See also Conquest's *The Harvest of Sorrow: Soviet Collectivization and the Terror-Famine* (New York: Oxford University Press, 1986).

Eyck, E. *History of the Weimar Republic.* New York: Athenaeum, 1970. The German democracy that failed. For the political crisis that brought down the republic, see D. Harsch, *German Social Democracy and the Rise of Nazism* (Chapel Hill: University of North Carolina Press, 1993).

Galbraith, J. K. *The Great Crash.* New York: Avon, 1980. Lively account of the Wall Street crash of 1929 by a leading economist.

Graves, R., and A. Hodge. *The Long Weekend: A Social History of Great Britain, 1918–1939.* New York: Norton, 1963. Impressionistic but convincing social history. See also Graves's personal memoir of World War I and the lost generation, *Goodbye to All That,* rev. ed. (Garden City, N.Y.: Doubleday, 1957).

Greene, N. *From Versailles to Vichy: The Third Republic, 1919–1940.* Arlington Heights, Ill.: Harlan Davidson, 1970. France in the interwar years.

Kindleberger, C. P. *The World in Depression, 1929–1939.* London: Allen Lane, 1973. The larger picture, particularly good on Europe.

Leach, W. *Land of Desire: Merchants, Power, and the Rise of a New American Culture.* New York: Pantheon, 1993. The rise of consumer society in the United States, richly documented with examples.

Leuchtenburg, W. E. *Franklin D. Roosevelt and the New Deal, 1932–1940.* New York: Harper and Row, 1963. Focus on FDR's domestic policies. See also the older standard account, A. M.

Schlesinger, Jr., *The Age of Roosevelt* (Boston: Houghton Mifflin, 1957).

Mack Smith, D. *Mussolini.* New York: Viking, 1982. The maker of the first fascist state, by a leading historian of modern Italy. On Mussolini's rise to power, see A. Lyttleton, *The Seizure of Power: Fascism in Italy, 1919–1929,* 2d ed. (Princeton, N.J.: Princeton University Press, 1987), and on the impact of fascism, see E. R. Tannenbaum, *The Fascist Experience: Italian Society and Culture, 1922–1945* (New York: Basic Books, 1972).

Maier, C. S. *Recasting Bourgeois Europe: Stabilization in France, Germany, and Italy in the Decade after World War I.* Princeton, N.J.: Princeton University Press, 1975. Social history of the 1920s in three continental powers.

Muhlberger, D. *The Social Basis of European Fascist Movements.* New York: Methuen, 1987. Up-to-date essays note both diversity and similarities between fascist movements. On fascist ideology in Germany, Italy, and France, see E. Nolte, *Three Faces of Fascism,* trans. L. Vennewitz (New York: Holt, Rinehart and Winston, 1966).

Seton-Watson, H. *Eastern Europe Between the Wars, 1919–1941.* Hamden, Conn.: Archon, 1962. Older but still valuable survey.

Speer, A. *Inside the Third Reich.* Translated by R. and C. Winston. New York: Macmillan, 1970. Memoirs of a builder and organizer of German war production.

Thomas, H. *The Spanish Civil War.* Rev. ed. New York: Harper and Row, 1977. Authoritative study of the great liberal "lost cause" of the 1930s.

Tipton, F. B., and R. Aldrich. *An Economic and Social History of Europe,* vol. 1, *1890–1939.* Baltimore: Johns Hopkins University Press, 1987. Connects economic development with social and political changes.

Ulam, A. B. *Stalin: The Man and His Era.* New York: Viking, 1973. Good biography of the man who made the "second Russian revolution." An interesting comparative approach is A. Bullock's recent study of *Hitler and Stalin: Parallel Lives* (New York: Knopf, 1992).

—26—

From Blitzkrieg to Hiroshima
World War II Divides the Century

◆Aggression and Appeasement
◆Axis Victories, 1939–1942   ◆Allied Triumphs, 1942–1945
◆The Human Cost

War clouds had been gathering for a decade before the storm broke once more over Europe and the world. *The Gathering Storm* was the title Britain's prime minister Winston Churchill chose for the first volume of his account of the war through which he led his country. It is an image that effectively sums up the feeling that many thoughtful people had of a natural calamity building through the 1930s. And when it burst at last, it was a tempest unmatched in all the history of human warfare.

In many ways, World War II was very different from World War I. The First World War, for instance, was a war of position fought in the trenches; the Second World War was characterized by rapid mobility, with massive offensives sweeping over three continents and two oceans. Yet there are important similarities between the two also. In both, a large part of the globe was sucked into the struggle. In each case, the involvement of whole peoples turned the conflict into a modern total war. And in both world wars, modern technology raised casualty figures and the level of material destruction beyond those of any earlier struggle in human history.

This chapter will look at the causes and nature of World War II, at the sweep of its campaigns, and at its immediate consequences. It will trace the pattern of aggression and appeasement that led up to the war, outline the early Axis victories, and climax with the final Allied triumphs. In conclusion, the chapter will look at the terrible human cost of this most costly of all wars.

Much of the rest of this book will also be studded with references to this midcentury cataclysm. For if ever a war was a watershed, it was that which began in Poland in 1939 and ended six years later in Tokyo Bay.

◆Aggression and Appeasement◆

The simplest way to explain the causes of the Second World War is to call it "Hitler's war." Certainly his voice was loudest through the prewar period, blaring his demands, bullying other leaders and nations, laying down ultimatums to the world. But no event so vast and complicated as World War II can be explained simply by one man's ambitions. Like the First World War, the Second can only be explained by examining a complex pattern of long–range and more immediate causes. This section will focus on the former—on the deeper roots of war and on the string of international crises that finally triggered the great conflict.

Roots of War

Among the long–run causes of World War II were the resentments and dissatisfactions that the world inherited from the bad peace that ended World War I. The dissatisfied or *revisionist powers* included the principal losers: Austria, which had lost its Danubian Empire yet had been forbidden to associate itself with the other large German–speaking nation in central Europe; and Germany itself, stripped of lands and armed forces and saddled with reparations and war guilt. Also among the revisionists, however, were those of the winners who felt they had not been adequately compensated for their sacrifices. Thus Italy still clamored for bits of unredeemed Italian territory and made demands on the Balkans, the eastern Mediterranean, and Africa. And in the Far East, Japan found the Western powers unwilling to accept Japanese claims to a virtual protectorate over China or to recognize Japan as an equal partner in the councils of the great powers. As we will see, many of these resentments and diplomatic imperatives contributed to the coming of another war.

A second type of contributing diplomatic cause was the failure of interwar efforts to shore up the internationalist idealism embodied in the League of Nations. Nations apparently supported the international spirit of the League and Wilsonian idealism only when their own interests were not at stake. As a result, internationalism proved incapable of preventing another war.

The League of Nations itself did expand to include defeated Germany in 1926 and the Soviet Union in 1934. Through the League's Supreme Council, however, great–power interests dominated its deliberations and could paralyze the organization. And the United States, clearly one of the greatest powers, never joined at all.

There were other attempts to achieve the goal of world peace. In 1925, for example, the European great powers signed a series of agreements at Locarno, Switzerland, guaranteeing the border between France and Germany and bringing in other powers as guarantors. In 1928, the Kellogg–Briand Treaty further expanded on this *spirit of Locarno*. Negotiated by the American and French foreign ministers, and later signed by dozens of other countries, this peace pact rejected war altogether "as an instrument of national policy."

The Washington disarmament conference of 1921–1922 limited the size of the world's navies—the long–range weapons systems of the great powers—to a ratio in battleships and cruisers of 5 for Britain and the United States to every 3 for Japan to every 1.67 for France and Italy. But Britain was unhappy at granting parity to the United States, Japan equally unhappy at being excluded from the top category, and further attempts at disarmament failed.

Major economic and ideological factors also helped to bring on the Second World War of the century. The Great Depression of the 1930s was the main economic element, while a number of ideological commitments also predisposed the powers to fight.

The Depression not only helped bring dictators to power but strengthened them, as they seemed to provide strong leadership to face the economic crisis. At the same time, the Depression weakened the democracies by undermining both their economic strength and their self–confidence in the face of aggression.

Chronology 26.1: Aggression and Appeasement

1931	*Japan intervenes in Manchuria*
1935–1936	*Mussolini invades Ethiopia*
1936	*Hitler re–militarizes the Rhineland*
1936–1937	*Axis Alliance formed, linking Germany, Italy, and Japan*
1936–1939	*Spanish Civil War—Hitler and Mussolini support Franco*
1937–1945	*Japan invades China*
1938	*Hitler annexes Austria*
1938	*Munich crisis—Hitler annexes Czech lands*
1939	*Hitler–Stalin pact creates alliance between rival authoritarian powers*
1939	*Hitler invades Poland—World War II begins*

Among the ideological causes that played a part, nationalism flourished in Italy as Mussolini revived Roman territorial ambitions around the Mediterranean. Nationalism blazed up in Japan as its military leaders reached for hegemony of the East. And in Germany, Hitler revived national pride and conjured up a vision of a Third German Reich that would dominate Europe.

The ideological proclivities of the Soviet Union also helped make war possible. Marx had predicted a world revolution, and in 1919 the Soviets organized the Communist International (Comintern) to coordinate socialist parties around the world. When these efforts failed, Stalin did allow his idealistic foreign minister Maxim Litvinov (1876–1951) to call for a "popular front" with the democracies to guarantee their collective security against fascist aggression. But the Soviet Union's revolutionary rhetoric discouraged Britain and France from joining with the USSR against Hitler. At the same time, this Soviet stance provided Hitler and Mussolini with an excuse for the Axis "Anti–Comintern Pact" that sealed their alliance.

Aggression in China, Ethiopia, and Spain

The string of crises that climaxed on the Polish frontier in 1939 began with a series of aggressions as far away as southern Europe, northern Africa, and East Asia. The folly of the resulting pattern of diplomatic *appeasement*, pacifying aggressors by giving them what they demanded, was burned into the conscience of a generation.

The dynamism of Japan's growth and modernization made Japanese expansionism appealing to several segments of its population. Leading Japanese businessmen wanted to see their country economically predominant in Asia. But it was military leaders—especially younger, fanatically nationalistic army officers eager to advance Japanese interests by force—who seized the initiative in the 1930s. It was these young officers who assassinated westernized politicians and big businessmen and dragged the country into wars of conquest on the Asian mainland.

In 1931, young Japanese officers used a bomb explosion on the Japanese–built Manchurian Railway as an excuse to occupy the whole of Manchuria and convert it into the Japanese puppet state of Manchukuo. The League of Nations appointed a committee to investigate the matter but did nothing to stop it. In 1937, then, a much larger Japanese incursion began when an "incident" at the Marco Polo Bridge outside Peking (now Beijing) set off a full–scale Japanese invasion of China. The huge Chinese Republic was far less industrially developed than Japan and divided by a long civil war between a Nationalist party headed by General Chiang Kai–shek (1888–1975) and a Communist party led by Mao Zedong (1893–1976). Neither the Nationalist government nor Mao's Communist army could stand against the mechanized Japanese attack, which by the end of 1937 had overrun China's historic northern heartland around Peking, its breadbasket in the central Yangtze River valley, and the commercial centers along the coasts. Again, the League of Nations passed resolutions and did nothing.

Mussolini's invasion of Ethiopia in 1935 sought to erase the defeat Italy had suffered at the hands of the Ethiopians in 1896, to expand Italy's empire in the horn of northeastern Africa, and to create an overseas home for some of Italy's excess population. His goals also probably included providing a toughening experience for younger Fascists and some medals for older ones.

A conflict over a frontier water hole provided an excuse, and within six months, Mussolini's mobile army, employing bombers and poison gas against the Ethiopian cavalry, had conquered the last independent African country. Ethiopia's Christian emperor, Haile Selassie (1892–1975), pleaded his country's case before the League of Nations in person, but the economic sanctions the League voted did not include the one thing that would have stopped the Italian war machine: a ban on oil sales to Italy. Mussolini then occupied Albania, just across the Adriatic, and dispatched tens of thousands of troops to support the fascist cause in Spain.

The Spanish Civil War was a complicated tangle of overlapping problems, factions, and conflicts. A Spanish Republic had been established in the early 1930s and a left–liberal coalition had come to power in Madrid in February 1936. The Spanish Republic, however, was deeply divided between semifeudal landowners and medieval piety in the villages, communists and anarchists in industrial cities like Barcelona, and Catalonian nationalists demanding autonomy. The government's inability to find a consensus course through such a tangle opened the way for the fascist military revolt led by General Francisco Franco (1892–1975) that broke out in July 1936.

Hitler and Mussolini sent troops and planes to help Franco. Young volunteers came from many lands to defend the Republic, believing, as one put it, that "by fighting against fascism in Spain, we would be fighting against it in our own country, and in every other."[1] Delores Ibarruri (1895–1989), popularly known as *La Pasionaria* for her passionate speeches in defense of Spanish freedom, called for international support. The Soviet Union sent supplies and technical help for the republican side, but also sent ideological heretic hunters who spent as much time purging Trotskyites and anarchists as fighting the fascists. Britain and France refused to intervene in a civil struggle at all. As a result, Franco won. He destroyed the Republic and established a fascist dictatorship that would outlast all the others, ending only when he died in 1975.

Hitler in the Rhineland and Austria

The totalitarian ruler whose aggressive foreign policy did finally arouse sufficient opposition to ignite World War II was Adolf Hitler. A man whose motives, specific intentions, and even basic sanity have been endlessly debated, Hitler was, as we have seen, a fervent German nationalist and an Aryan racist. He wanted to build a German Reich that would include all Germans; he dreamed of territorial expansion, hegemony of Europe, perhaps even more. Germans, he said, needed more *Lebensraum,* or "living space," to breathe in, and the rest of the world must give way.

Europeans began to see Hitler as a threat to the peace and order of the continent soon after he came to power in January 1933. During the years between 1933 and 1935, he pulled Germany out of the League of Nations, unilaterally tore up the provisions of the Versailles Treaty limiting German military strength, and instituted a massive rearmament program and military conscription. In 1936, he unilaterally revoked another clause of the peace treaty—and tested the will of the Western powers to fight about it—by remilitarizing the Rhineland. In practice, this simply meant marching German troops into a strip of German land along the French frontier from which they had been banned by the treaty. The significance of the incursion lay in the fact that the French and British did nothing to prevent it. At the time Germany's rearmament was far from complete; the German troops could have been turned back, with considerable loss of face for the Führer. As it was, Hitler's prestige in Germany went up still further, as did his confidence that he could do as he pleased without fear of the consequences.

Hitler next moved to expand the Reich by incorporating all the German–speaking peoples of central Europe. A major first step was the annexation of Austria in 1938. An Austrian by birth, Hitler shared the feelings of many Austrians that their future lay in *Anschluss* or union with Germany. There was a Nazi party in Austria working energetically toward that end. Add Austria's troubled postwar history, including assassinations and attempted coups, and Austria looked unstable enough for easy plucking. In March 1938, after browbeating Austrian chancellor Kurt von Schuschnigg into capitulating, Hitler sent his troops in. Again, they marched in unopposed. The Führer himself made a triumphal entry into Vienna, and Austria was rapidly incorporated into the German Reich.

The Axis, Munich, and the Hitler–Stalin Pact

Through the earlier 1930s, Germany, Italy, and Japan had achieved a good deal by defiant aggression. In so doing, however, they had isolated themselves diplomatically, making enemies of many powers that did not dare to stand up to them. To overcome this isolation and advance their disparate interests, the three governments negotiated the so–called *Axis* alliance of 1936 and 1937. The core of the alliance was the Anti–Comintern Pact, signed by Hitler and Mussolini in 1936 and adhered to by Japan the following year. Officially an anticommunist agreement, the alliance allocated preeminent influence in Europe to Germany and Italy, predominance in Asia to Japan. The 1936 pact between the two European members created what many saw as a "Rome–Berlin axis" around which all European affairs turned, and the addition of Japan was deemed to have forged a global "Rome–Berlin–Tokyo axis"—hence the label of *Axis* alliance.

Thus fortified with allies, the German dictator in particular renewed aggressive demands for changes in the status quo. The Rhineland and Austria had both been German lands that welcomed German intervention. Now, however, Hitler began to demand freedom and reunification for German–speaking people living in non–German countries. He turned first to the Sudeten Germans of Czechoslovakia.

The Sudeten Germans were a substantial minority of more than three million German–speaking people, left in Slavic Czechoslovakia by the treaties of 1919. They lived in the mountainous Sudetenland, bordering Germany. In the 1930s, the Sudeten Germans organized their own Nazi party and began to call for freedom and unification with Germany. When Hitler demanded "self–determination" for his compatriots, Czech president Eduard Benes (1884–1948) refused, knowing that with those Germans he would lose not

British cartoonist David Low's famous cartoon of Hitler and Stalin greeting each other over the corpse of Poland has the rival dictators exchanging parodies of the insults they had hurled at each other through the 1930s. How long did this new-found friendship last? (David Low/Culver Pictures, Inc.)

only a sizable part of his country but its essential fortifications on the German borders. In taking this stand, Benes counted on French and British support for Czechoslovakia, eastern Europe's only functioning democracy. Neither the French nor the British, however, were willing to go to war over minority problems in eastern Europe.

In public speeches and in a series of tense conferences in the summer and fall of 1938, Hitler angrily demanded "his" Germans. He also assured British prime minister Neville Chamberlain (prime minister 1937–1940) and French premier Edouard Daladier (premier 1938–1940) that he would make no further territorial demands. After a final nerve–racking meeting between Hitler, Mussolini, Chamberlain, and Daladier at Munich in September 1938, the leaders of the two democratic powers gave way. They informed the Czechs that they would be better off without the "problem" of the Sudetenland to worry about, and German troops promptly occupied it. Chamberlain went home from the *Munich conference* to announce to cheering crowds that he brought them "peace in our time." The following March, Hitler's armies moved into Prague and set up a client state there, assigning smaller portions of the dismembered country to Poland and Hungary. "Munich" entered the diplomatic vocabulary of the West as shorthand for the ultimate act of appeasement.

The final crisis in a line that had left Europe punch–drunk with crises came a year after Munich, in September 1939, when Hitler set his sights on Poland. There were minority Germans to be reunited with the fatherland, particularly in the League–administered Baltic port of Danzig (Gdansk today). And Hitler wanted to reclaim the Danzig "Polish corridor," which the Versailles Treaty had created to give Poland access to the sea but which cut East Prussia off from the rest of Germany.

This time, however, when Hitler began to demand Danzig, Britain and France announced their intention to defend Polish sovereignty. Hitler, understandably, doubted their determination to do so. Then in late August, he confounded the democracies by announcing a pact with his archenemy on the other side of Poland, the Soviet Union.

The treaty, signed by the two foreign ministers, Joachim von Ribbentrop (1893–1946) and Vyacheslav Molotov (1890–1986), reversed a decade of bitter antagonism between Hitler and Stalin. For Hitler, it was an expedient move, guaranteeing him a free hand with Poland and opening up eastern Europe to him also. Stalin, who was still fearful of Germany and who, like Hitler, was convinced that the western Allies would never fight, had given up his efforts at a united front against fascism. In agreeing to the treaty, however, he apparently sought both time to prepare for a possible German attack and as much eastern European territory as he could get from an alliance with the Germans.

On September 1, 1939, a week after the Hitler–Stalin Pact, the German *Wehrmacht* (armed forces) knifed into Poland. On September 17, the Soviet Union invaded Poland from the east. In between these two events, Britain and France glumly declared war on Germany. The Second World War had begun.

♦ Axis Victories, 1939–1942 ♦

Through the first half of World War II, from the fall of 1939 well into 1942, the people of the Axis nations had plenty to cheer about. German and Japanese forces in particular seemed everywhere victorious. Flickering newsreels in movie theaters showed the home folks their field artillery jolting and belching smoke, their tanks roaring into battle, their troops advancing on every front. For the Allies, by contrast, it was a time of desperate retreats and jolting defeats, from Dunkirk to Pearl Harbor.

The trenches of World War I were a thing of the past. In their place was *Blitzkrieg,* "lightning war" at a pace that made Bismarck's summer wars seem like protracted conflicts by comparison. With petroleum–powered tanks and troop carriers instead of railroad transport, supported by dive bombers and strafing fighters, the armies of the Axis rolled to one rapid victory after another, while the ill–prepared Allies struggled to survive. During the first three years of the war, Germany and its allies thus brought almost all of Europe under their control, while Japan added Southeast Asia and the western half of the Pacific to its growing East Asian empire.

Hitler's Blitzkrieg

Hitler's invasion of Poland was the world's first glimpse of the new style of lightning war. Mechanized German troops poured across the frontier, while bombers ranged behind the lines as far as Warsaw. A little over two weeks later, Stalin sent his army across Poland's eastern frontiers. Before the month was out, the German Blitzkrieg had carried Hitler's forces to the Polish capital and Poland had fallen.

His object accomplished in the east, Hitler offered peace while he shifted his armies from Poland to the French frontier. The still–unprepared British and French limited themselves to naval engagements and border incursions—what the reporters called the "phony war." In the east, however, the Soviet Union was more active. There, the small nations of eastern Europe, from the Baltic to the Balkans, found themselves caught in a huge vise between the German Reich and the Soviet Union.

Chronology 26.2: World War II

1939	*German blitzkrieg crushes Poland*
1940	*German blitzkriegs overrun much of Scandinavia, Low Countries, and France*
1940–1941	*Battle of Britain—Germany fails to break Britain through aerial bombing*
1941	*Atlantic Charter binds United States to support Britain with aid*
1941	*Hitler invades Soviet Union*
1941	*Japan attacks United States bases in the Pacific, including Pearl Harbor*
1942	*British defeat German and Italian forces in North Africa at El Alamein*
1942–1943	*Soviets turn back German invasion at Stalingrad*
1943	*American and British forces invade Italy, force its surrender*
1943–1945	*U.S. Pacific "island–hopping" campaigns against Japan*
1944	*D–Day in Normandy—U.S., British, and Canadians liberate France*
1944–1945	*Soviets drive Germans out of Russia and Eastern Europe*
1945	*Yalta conference lays down debated terms for postwar order in Europe*
1945	*Allies invade Germany from east and west: Germany surrenders*
1945	*U.S. atom bombs Japan; Japan surrenders*

Stalin moved rapidly to recover czarist Russian lands lost in World War I and to push the frontiers of the Soviet Union as far west as possible. He annexed eastern Poland, incorporated the three Baltic states of Estonia, Latvia, and Lithuania, and invaded Finland, which after stubborn resistance, surrendered slices of territory near Leningrad for peace.

Hitler made even larger gains in eastern Europe. Besides most of Poland, he conquered or established satellite regimes in Hungary, Yugoslavia, Bulgaria, and Romania. And when an Italian invasion of Greece misfired badly, he came to Italy's aid, overran Greece, and even sent his paratroopers to capture the large island of Crete.

In the spring of 1940, meanwhile, western Europe itself finally faced the full fury of Hitler's Blitzkrieg. After three months of it, what was left of the western alliance looked to be on the verge of collapse.

Fearing a British attempt to turn his northern flank and cut him off from vitally needed iron ore in Scandinavia, Hitler struck that way first. Early in April, his troops crossed into Denmark, which offered no serious resistance. Norway, invaded by sea, held out for only a few weeks. In May, it was the turn of the Low Countries. Germany launched a massive invasion of the Netherlands, gutted the center of Rotterdam with the first sustained air raids focused on a single city, and broke the Dutch within a week. Belgium was sliced up by German motorized units spearheaded by tanks; it capitulated by the end of the month. Tiny Luxembourg was overwhelmed in a single day.

France's turn came next. Through the 1930s, France had based its defense policy on the Maginot line, a seemingly impregnable string of concrete underground fortifications, bunkers, and pillboxes, electrically lighted, linked by internal rail lines, and stretching the full length of the Franco–German frontier. Unfortunately, for financial reasons and in order not to insult friendly Belgium, the line had not been extended to cover the Franco–

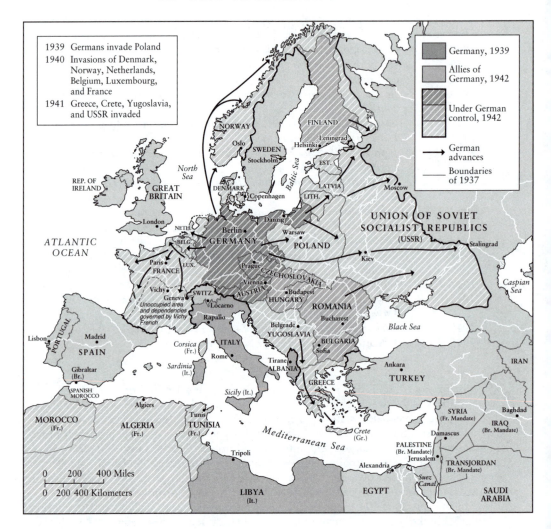

German Conquests in Europe, 1939–1942

Belgian border as well. And it was through shattered Belgium that the Germans burst into France in 1940.

The Allies—the French, a British expeditionary force, and what remained of the Belgians—were unprepared for the breakthrough and uncoordinated in their response. A daring German force, astonishing even the German high command, knifed into France, swung to the right behind the French and British lines, and raced to the Channel. The British evacuated their expeditionary force from the beaches at Dunkirk with the help of a plucky flotilla of private yachts and motorboats that crossed the English Channel to the rescue. Nevertheless, the Germans had expelled France's last ally from the continent.

The German army occupied Paris in June, and France signed an armistice before the end of the month. Hitler required that the signing take place in the identical railway car in which the Germans had been forced to sign the armistice terms in 1918. Thereafter, northern France was occupied by the Germans, while the southern part of the country was turned over to a collaborationist regime under the aged general Philippe Pétain (1856–1951) in Vichy. French soldiers who escaped to Britain, however, formed a Free French regime in exile headed by the strong–willed and highly intelligent general Charles de Gaulle (1890–1970).

The Battle of Britain

Hitler next turned his eyes toward Britain, but this time his intuition failed him, and he experienced his first setback. After the fall of France, the German ruler fully expected the disorganized British, who had left most of their military hardware behind them on the sands at Dunkirk, to sue for peace. But Britain had a new prime minister, the Conservative leader Winston Churchill (served for two terms 1940–1945, 1951–1955), who had no intention of surrendering.

The aristocratic Churchill had warned repeatedly of the Nazi menace through the 1930s. In the 1940s, he rallied the British to defend their island home. And despite his rotund figure, Churchill's "bulldog" jaw, thick cigar, and rolling eloquence made him an inspiring war leader for the British.

When the British refused to make terms, Hitler's air chief, Hermann Goering, set out to soften Britain up by intensive bombing from newly acquired bases in the Low Countries and France. In the resulting "Battle of Britain," whole sections of such cities as Coventry and London itself were leveled, while seaports and air bases came under heavy bombardment. But the Royal Air Force's Spitfire fighters, faster and more heavily armed than their German opponents, took a heavy toll of the German bombers. By the following spring, Hitler had abandoned both his invasion plans and the heaviest of the bombing. "Never," said Churchill of Britain's debt to its pilots, "have so many owed so much to so few."

The British prime minister, meanwhile, had been seeking help from nations of the Commonwealth and especially from the vast productive capacities of the United States. He found President Roosevelt more than willing to offer material aid. FDR both abhorred dictatorships and feared the economic threat of a world closed to American business—already badly shaken by the Depression—by German conquest of Europe and Japan's Co–Prosperity Sphere in Asia (discussed later). In addition, he was as determined as Theodore Roosevelt and Woodrow Wilson before him that America should be a prime architect of the twentieth–century global order and should therefore take a hand in winning the war and shaping the peace. FDR's interventionist tone, opposed by many Americans in the 1930s, found more support in the early 1940s for action short of war to turn the tide against authoritarianism in Europe before it reached America.

The United States therefore provided Britain with fifty U. S. destroyers in return for Caribbean naval bases. By the *Lend–Lease* Act of 1941, America offered war materiel and other aid to Britain or to any other nation whose defense was seen as vital to U. S. security. In the summer of that year, several months before Pearl Harbor, Churchill and Roosevelt met at sea to declare their joint hopes for a freer and happier postwar world.

By the summer of 1941, the Battle of Britain was won: Britain had survived the worst that Hitler could throw against it. By that time, however, the full weight of Hitler's war machine had been turned upon another great power—the Soviet Union.

The Invasion of Russia

In June 1941, the German Army drove into the Soviet Union in the operation code–named "Barbarossa" after the great medieval German warrior–emperor. It was Hitler's biggest gamble—and another major mistake.

The German invasion ended the period of Russo–German collaboration that had begun less than two years before. Hitler had long been convinced that Germany's destiny lay in the vast spaces and still underdeveloped resources of Slavic eastern Europe. Now, faced with a longer war, he had particular need of those resources. His earlier fear of bolshevism was also strengthened by Stalin's rapid expansion into the territories between the two great powers. In his melodramatic way, finally, Hitler seems to have believed that there must be a trial of strength between himself and Stalin. In the summer of 1941, he sent his soldiers to undergo that trial.

The bloody conflict between the German *Wehrmacht* and the Soviet Red Army was the most terrible theater of war in Europe. It claimed millions of lives and left much of European Russia devastated. It also, however, pinned down the largest part of the German Army throughout the war. And in the end, Hitler, like Napoleon before him, failed of his object in the face of Russian weather, Russian distances, and Russian determination—now armed with modern tools of war.

That summer of 1941, however, it looked to excited Germans as if the Leader was going to "pull it off again." His divisions powered their way rapidly across the western plains of the Soviet Union. By December, they had reached both of Russia's historic capitals, Moscow and Leningrad (now St. Petersburg) and had overrun much of the rich grainland of the Ukraine in the south. If neither Leningrad nor Moscow had actually fallen yet, their fate seemed sealed—at least to the cheering newsreel audiences far off in Germany.

Like the British, however, the Russians did not surrender. Stalin stayed on in Moscow even with German troops in the suburbs until he found a general, Marshal Georgi Zhukov (1896–1974), capable of revitalizing the Soviet defense. The citizens of Leningrad fought and froze and dynamited holes in the earth to bury their dead for nine hundred days in one of the epic sieges of history. But Leningrad, like London, survived.

Pearl Harbor

On the other side of the globe, the leaders of Germany's most powerful ally, Japan, made their greatest error. In December 1941, six months after the German invasion of the Soviet Union, Japan attacked the United States, thus bringing another great power into the war against the Axis. And yet in the Pacific, too, at first it looked like another smashing victory for the Axis powers.

The Japanese had taken advantage of the turmoil in Europe to reach for the hegemony of Asia so long denied them by the Western powers. In a clear economic challenge to the West, Tokyo announced the Greater East Asia Co–Prosperity Sphere, a plan for reorganizing Asian trade around Japan. The Japanese particularly needed Southeast Asian rubber and oil to continue their mechanized campaigns in China. Then, with Europe's major imperial powers either defeated or struggling to survive, Japan's military leaders under the leadership of General Hideki Tojo (premier 1941–1944) prepared to move in on Western colonial holdings in Asia. In all of these efforts, however, the United States seemed to stand in the way.

Roosevelt had opposed Japanese military adventures since the early 1930s, had urged the powers to refuse to recognize Japan's conquests, and viewed the Co–Prosperity Sphere as an act of economic aggression. By 1941, FDR was prepared to cut off Japanese supplies of raw materials from the United States and to freeze Japanese credits in America. Faced with growing American hostility, Tojo and the Japanese militarists decided to strike at U. S. strength in the East even as they reached for Europe's Asian territories.

On December 7, 1941, carrier–based Japanese planes struck the main U. S. naval base in the Pacific at Pearl Harbor, Hawaii, putting much of America's Pacific fleet out of action in a few hours of well–planned and meticulously executed bombing. Japanese troops also invaded and conquered the American–ruled Philippine Islands. At the same time, they occupied French Indochina and the Dutch East Indies and attacked British colonies from Hong Kong to Singapore, Malaya, and Burma. By the spring of 1942, Japan was master of an empire that included much of China and most of Southeast Asia.

But the United States, now more than ever convinced of the necessity for war after the attack on Pearl Harbor, was preparing itself to fight. And Hitler, committed by treaty to support Japan, had foolishly declared war on the United States, which brought America into the European war as well.

It looked grim to the western Allies those early months of 1942, as Germany launched new offensives in Russia and Australia braced itself for Japanese attack. In fact, the tide of battle in the biggest war in history was just about to turn.

◆Allied Triumphs, 1942–1945◆

From 1942 to 1945, the fortunes of war turned crushingly against the Axis powers. The Allies—the United States, the Soviet Union, and Britain—recovered from their initial setbacks, organized enormous drives over land and sea, and won the war. The story of these massive land campaigns in Europe, jungle fighting in Asia, naval warfare across the world's oceans, and aerial combat everywhere, is as dramatic as the tale of Axis triumphs with which the war began.

Turning Points

The military alliance that took shape in 1942 was headed by three remarkable men. Roosevelt, Churchill, and Stalin formed what Churchill, in his postwar memoirs, dubbed the "Grand Alliance," more commonly called simply the *Allies*, as in World War I. Roosevelt and Churchill consulted frequently and met with Stalin on several occasions. Churchill and Roosevelt, both aristocratic rulers of democracies, had much in common. But there was a great gap between the Anglo–American leaders and Stalin, the revolutionary ruler of a totalitarian state, who saw the men across the table as capitalists with no love for the Soviet Union.

Yet this disparate group of people did make some key decisions. As early as 1941, Churchill and Roosevelt signed the Atlantic Charter, first statement of Allied war aims, including national self–determination, freedom of the seas, free trade, arms reductions, and an international organization to maintain the peace. Some basic strategic matters were also established. The Soviets would have to continue to bear the brunt of the German war, though Stalin urged the western Allies to open a "second front" in Europe to pull large numbers of Germans out of Russia as soon as possible. The United States, meanwhile, was to be primarily responsible for the war against Japan in the Pacific, though the British committed themselves to carrying on the fight in the jungles of Southeast Asia.

Meanwhile, the Allies geared up for the coming effort. The United States had the world's largest industrial plant and most productive agriculture, most of it idling through the Depression at a fraction of full capacity. From 1942 on, machines hummed, reapers

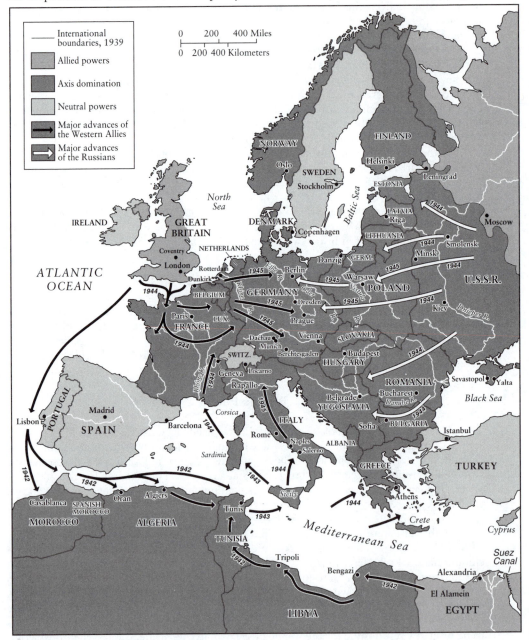

Allied Assault on Hitler's Europe, 1942–1945

churned through the fields of grain, "liberty ships" slid down the ways, and tanks and warplanes rolled off the assembly lines at a pace unmatched before. An efficient Anglo–American convoy system ferried these supplies across the Atlantic to Britain or around Scandinavia to Russia, in the teeth of German submarine and air attack.

Three major turning points in the war came during the period between the summer of 1942 and the following winter. They were the battles of El Alamein, Stalingrad, and Guadalcanal.

Hitler and his Italian allies had followed up their victories in the Balkans by crossing the eastern Mediterranean to attack the British in Egypt, the key to the Suez Canal and Britain's entire war effort in the East. The result was a two–year tank war in the sweltering sands of Britain's Egyptian colony. Germany's "desert fox," General Erwin Rommel (1891–1944), in overall command of the Axis troops, harried the British back toward the Nile delta and the canal beyond in the spring and summer of 1942. The British, however, dug in at El Alamein, 70 miles from Alexandria, and stopped the German advance (October–November 1942). In the fall, British forces under the aggressive command of General Bernard Montgomery (1887–1976), drove the Axis armies out of Egypt and occupied most of Libya. This victory, combined with the Anglo–American landings in North Africa that followed soon after, put the Axis clearly on the defensive at last.

On the Russian front, Hitler's armies had shifted their offensive south from Leningrad and Moscow, which were still stubbornly resisting German siege. Sweeping across the Ukraine toward the oil fields of the Caucasus, Hitler's armies came up against Stalingrad (Volgograd today), an industrial city on the Volga. From July 1942 to February of the following year, German troops fought to take the city, Russians to defend it—block by block, building by building, room by room. Meanwhile, Russian reinforcements encircled the Germans besieging the city, and the snows of a Russian winter closed over them all. Stalingrad was left a charred and gutted ruin. But the German army—what was left of it—surrendered. And the long German retreat from Russia began.

On the other side of the globe, finally, the United States turned the tide against the Japanese on the blue–green waters and jungle–clad islands of the Pacific. Japanese forces were closing in on Australia and cruising the central Pacific, west of Hawaii. In the summer of 1942, American forces turned back the Japanese with heavy losses in the Coral Sea northeast of Australia in May and in the central Pacific near Midway Island in June. In both cases, air power proved decisive, sometimes sinking Japanese warships while the two fleets were not only out of naval gunnery range but completely out of sight of each other. U. S. Marines, meanwhile, fought their way through the jungles of the Japanese–held island of Guadalcanal, off Australia, to a costly victory. This struggle between elite Marines and Japanese soldiers trained to the never–surrender samurai tradition set the pattern for similar bloody battles across the Pacific. But after 1942, the Japanese, like the Germans, were on the defensive.

Building Momentum: Russia, Africa, and Italy

The Allies had seized the initiative in 1942, but they were not yet capable of turning it into major breakthroughs. The heads of the Grand Alliance continued to meet to map broad strategy and basic war policy. From the Anglo–American Casablanca conference in 1943 flashed the famous V–for–Victory sign and the Allied demand of "unconditional surrender" from the Axis. Some feared that the unusual Allied requirement that the Axis surrender without negotiating terms might make the enemy fight on longer, but the demand did at least reassure Stalin that his western partners would not seek a separate peace. At

Teheran, later that same year, Roosevelt, Churchill, and Stalin sat down together to agree on the importance of a second front, the invasion of occupied France to relieve pressure on the USSR. They also agreed that the Soviet Union would declare war on Japan as soon as the European war ended.

Meanwhile, 1943 did see counteroffensives gathering momentum from the shores of the Mediterranean to the plains of Russia. In the north, the Russians took the offensive after their hard–won victory at Stalingrad. Taking as well as inflicting large casualties, they slowly pushed the Germans back. By the end of the year, they had crossed the Dnieper, liberated Smolensk, and trapped a German army in the Caucasus. The fighting was still on Russian soil, but it was now the Germans who were retreating as the Russian winter closed down once more.

In the crushing heat of North Africa, American troops under General Dwight Eisenhower (1890–1967) landed in the French colonies of Morocco and Algeria to join the British in the desert war against Rommel. Caught between the British pushing west from Egypt and the Americans driving east from Algeria, Rommel maneuvered with ingenuity and daring, but was finally extricated from an impossible situation by being recalled to Berlin. And in May 1943, more than a quarter of a million German and Italian troops surrendered in North Africa.

The Allies then embarked on an invasion of the weakest of the Axis partners—Italy, just across the narrow waist of the Mediterranean. An Anglo–American invasion and conquest of the island of Sicily in the summer of 1943 was followed by landings in southern Italy itself. With the Fascist dream of Mediterranean power in ruins, Italians lost all enthusiasm for Mussolini, who was overthrown in July 1943. Rescued by a detachment of Hitler's commandos, Mussolini was subsequently recaptured by Italian partisans and, in 1945, executed. He made his last appearance in history strung up by his heels over the pumps in a gas station in northern Italy.

Mussolini's German allies, however, moved quickly to shore up this crumbling southern bastion of Fortress Europe. Reinforcements were rushed to Italy, and the main Allied landings south of Naples were met by stiff German resistance. For the next two years, the Italian front was a slow, brutal contest as the British and Americans fought their way over rugged terrain up the peninsula toward the Alps.

D–Day in Western Europe

Elsewhere, things moved more rapidly for the Allies. In both eastern and western Europe, enormous offensives sent the Germans reeling back toward their own frontiers.

By the end of 1943, the Red Army had liberated two–thirds of the Soviet territory Hitler had overrun. In 1944, Russian troops broke the siege of Leningrad after that city had buried perhaps eight hundred thousand of its citizens. They drove the last German units in Russia back across Soviet frontiers, pushed on into Poland, and thrust down into the mountainous Balkans. Guerrilla attacks by partisans in Yugoslavia and Greece, combined with the approach of the Soviets, drove the Germans out of these countries. By the end of 1944 the Red Army was positioned to complete the conquest of eastern Europe and to drive on into Germany itself.

By that time also, the long–planned and repeatedly postponed second front had been opened on the beaches of Normandy in France. This combined American–British–Canadian venture was by far the largest seaborne invasion in history, involving thousands of ships and planes and hundreds of thousands of men. Carried out in the face of rough seas and German mines, wire, tank traps, artillery fire, and bunkers along the beaches, *D–Day*, June 6, 1944, was an epic achievement. The Germans held the Allies caged up among the hedgerows of the Normandy peninsula for more than a month before the invaders broke out and began to drive the Germans out of the country. Paris opened its doors to a combination of French underground uprising and Allied assault in mid–August.

By this time, aggressive Allied generals like Montgomery and the American George Patton (1885–1945) were vying with each other for the opportunity to get at the famous *Wehrmacht*. Tank–led American armored divisions racked up the kind of advances that had once been a German monopoly through the French countryside and into Belgium. In December 1944, the German counterattack in Belgium, called the Battle of the Bulge on the military maps, was contained in hard forest fighting in the snow. It was the last German effort in the west. The year 1945 began with the Allies poised on the Rhine as the Russians moved on East Prussia.

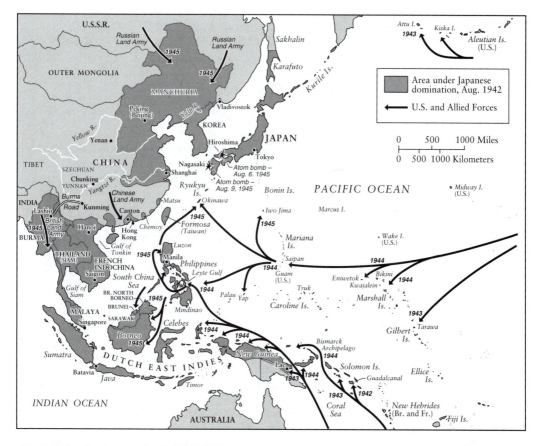

Allied Attack on the Japanese Empire, 1941–1945

Across the Pacific

In Asia, Japan also found itself within a tightening ring, though of a different sort. The enemies of the Japanese Empire closed in by sea and air rather than in tanks advancing across the land.

Naval victories gave the Americans firm control of the Pacific and paved the way for the recapture of the Philippines, America's large Southeast Asian colony, early in 1945. In the jungles of mainland Southeast Asia, meanwhile, British forces pushing down from India began to drive the Japanese out of Burma and Malaya. But it was at sea, on the islands of the Pacific, and in the skies over Japan itself that Japan's defeat was crafted.

To get near enough to the Japanese home islands to bomb and blockade them, the United States launched a series of crucial island campaigns in 1943 and 1944. Many Japanese soldiers fought to the last man rather than surrender to the Americans. The result was a string of bloody struggles over isolated rocks in the western Pacific with strange–sounding names like Tarawa (1943), Kwajalein (1944), and finally and most remembered, Iwo Jima and Okinawa (1945). At sea, Japanese *kamikaze* (divine wind) pilots deliberately crashed their bomb–laden planes into the American vessels.

Despite this determined resistance, in the early months of 1945 Japan was blockaded by sea and subject to regular bombing raids, fearsome incendiary attacks that were methodically reducing its lightly built cities to ashes. The end of the war was in sight on this side of the world also.

Unconditional Surrender, 1945

At Yalta in the liberated Crimea in February 1945, Roosevelt, Churchill, and Stalin began to discuss the postwar organization of Europe. There was agreement on the transformation of the wartime alliance into a global United Nations Organization, a project as dear to Roosevelt's heart as the League had been to Wilson's; on the division of Germany and Austria into zones of occupation; and on other matters. But the thorny question of the disposition of most of the eastern European nations remained undecided, leaving the relentless advance of the Red Army to make the final decision. Roosevelt was old and in failing health, in his fourth term and only months from his death; it has been suggested that a stronger man might have pushed harder for limits on Soviet hegemony of eastern Europe. In the last months of the war, however, Stalin had the cards: he would have been a hard man to talk out of some sort of Soviet hegemony in eastern Europe in any case.

In February 1945, then, the war moved into its final phase. In that month, American, British, and Allied troops crashed through the Siegfried line and drove eastward across Germany. On the other side of the shrinking Reich, the Russians under Marshal Zhukov pushed across East Prussia and on to Berlin, which the Red Army entered in April and captured in May 1945. With the Russians fighting their way through the streets, Adolf Hitler shot himself in his bunker under the bombed–out ruins of his capital. On May 8, 1945, the German high command signed an instrument of unconditional surrender.

By this time, Japan seemed to be preparing itself for a bitter last stand against the inevitable Allied invasion of the home islands. After the sanguinary struggles for Pacific atolls, American troops were not looking forward to it. Then from the air came the blow that suddenly and savagely ended the war in Asia. On August 6, 1945, the biggest secret weapon of the war, the first atomic bomb, was dropped on *Hiroshima*.

Exiled European scientists living in the United States, including Albert Einstein, had warned President Roosevelt as early as 1939 that an incredibly powerful explosion could theoretically be created by nuclear fission and that German scientists might be working on this awesome weapon. FDR had ordered a modest research program, which was radically upgraded after Pearl Harbor. Experiments carried on under the stadium at the University of Chicago and tests in the deserts of Los Alamos, New Mexico, produced a functional atomic bomb by the summer of 1945. When a U. S. B–29 bomber released the first A–Bomb over the southern Japanese city of Hiroshima, four and a half miles of the city was turned into an inferno, and seventy to eighty thousand people died.

There has been considerable discussion of the decision to use this fearsome weapon on a nation that was by then besieged by sea and was already being heavily bombed. President Harry Truman (president 1945–1953), who had succeeded Roosevelt on his death that spring, almost certainly had other motives, including ending the war before the Soviet Union could strengthen its position in the Far East. Perhaps most importantly, however, his military advisors had warned him that the Japanese, who had fought to the death for empty atolls like Iwo Jima and Okinawa, would resist the invasion of their home islands even more fiercely.

Two days after the Hiroshima bombing, Russia joined the war against Japan, and then the United States dropped a second atomic bomb on Nagasaki. The Japanese announced their willingness to surrender, making the single condition that they be allowed to retain their divine emperor, Hirohito, on the throne.

On September 2, 1945, a large fleet of Allied warships steamed into Tokyo Bay. The formal Japanese surrender document was signed on the American battleship *Missouri*, six years and one day after the most devastating war in history had begun with the German invasion of Poland in 1939.

◆The Human Cost◆

In a war that stretched over six years and three continents, numbers of casualties can be at best only estimates. Most authorities believe, however, that World War II took a total of between forty and fifty million human lives. We have seen that many fought and died in battle. We must now see how many others also made contributions to the war effort on the essential home front—or lost their lives as targets of aerial bombardment, in underground resistance movements, or in the Holocaust of the Jews.

The Home Front

On the home front total war looked much the same on both sides. New administrative agencies proliferated in Washington and London quite comparable to those in Berlin and Moscow. The War Production Board in the United States and Germany's Ministry of War Production fulfilled the same essential function of mobilizing a nation's resources for war. Subordinate boards, committees, commissions, and agencies directed the necessary allocation of ores and agricultural products, food, fuel, and transportation—all the elements of a complex economy. As in World War I, civilian consumption of scarce meat and sugar, shoes, clothing, gasoline, and other military essentials was strictly rationed. Prices were regulated, wages controlled, strikes prohibited, and other restrictions imposed. Again taxes went up and huge war debts accumulated to pay for the enormous conscript armies—America's reached twelve million—and the booming war industries.

Women in the embattled democracies flocked into war industries in the Second World War as they had in the First. "Rosie the Riveter," however, was not always a housewife working for the first time, but often a working woman who had held lower paid "women's jobs" before the war. The women's motives for taking jobs in war plants, while they certainly included patriotism, also involved a desire to get higher–paying jobs normally held by men. Although they were typically less well paid than male workers, women war workers nevertheless earned more than they ever had before. At the same time, they contributed greatly to the war effort, sometimes proving to be more meticulous and productive workers than the men they replaced.

A number of the warring nations also organized women's military auxiliaries and even fighting units. The United States and Britain, for instance, created women's branches of their military services which performed many essential functions in the immensely complex infrastructure of modern armies. In the Soviet Union, many thousands of women served as combat troops. And in both the USSR and the nations of occupied Europe, women joined underground resistance groups and partisan guerrilla bands to resist Axis leaders or disrupt the Axis occupation—a costly business, as we will see.

The Air War

On the home front as at the battle front, World War II took an unprecedented toll in human life and wrought unparalleled destruction across Europe, Asia, North Africa, and on the Atlantic and Pacific oceans. In this regard, the bombing plane proved to be the most feared and fearful of weapons. Bombers were used to support troops in action on the ground, somewhat as artillery had been (and continued to be) used. But other missions were also assigned to the new air forces. Strategic bombing was designed to shatter crucial economic and industrial support systems far behind the fighting lines. This kind of bombing destroyed munitions factories, oil refineries, shipyards, railway bridges—all the complicated infrastructure of mechanized warfare. Terror bombing targeted the civilian populations themselves, hoping to break their will to fight by indiscriminate bombing of cities. In this, it by and large failed: the citizens of London, Berlin, and Tokyo did not beg their governments to seek peace under even the most terrific bombardments. But the air war did succeed in gutting cities from Shanghai to Coventry.

People around the world saw the famous pictures: a baby lying alone in a bomb–blasted street in Shanghai after a Japanese attack, screaming; or St. Paul's cathedral in London wreathed in smoke, German bombs flickering behind it. Allied bombing made rapid progress, however, and soon proved more destructive than earlier Axis efforts. After months of bombing early in the war, most of London still stood. It took days of round–the–clock bombing to kindle the firestorm that leveled the great German industrial port city of Hamburg. But the ancient, lovely, and nonstrategic city of Dresden, jammed with war refugees, died in one night of massive incendiary bombing. And Hiroshima, hit in the last days of the war by an atomic bomb, was turned into a city–wide inferno in only a few seconds.

Repression and Resistance

Censorship, propaganda, and suspensions of civil rights for those suspected of aiding the enemy occurred in the most democratic states. So did large–scale internment of resident aliens. In Britain, recent immigrants from Nazi Germany, most of whom had fled the Nazi tyranny in the 1930s, were rounded up and interned during the war on the theory that German spies and saboteurs might be among them. Even more disturbing was the U. S. internment of tens of thousands of Japanese Americans for no more serious offense than that they or their ancestors had immigrated from Japan.

In the lands conquered by the Germans and Japanese particularly, governments who would collaborate with the conquerors were put into power. Some citizens of defeated countries, however, responded by organizing *resistance movements* to hurt the Axis, help the Allies, and hasten their own liberation. Organized in underground cells in cities or in partisan bands in the countryside, they collected intelligence for the Allies, smuggled out Allied prisoners, carried out sabotage or assassinations, or engaged in open guerrilla warfare. The Axis powers responded by arrest, torture, imprisonment in concentration camps, and execution. "The average 'life' of a female liaison officer," as one resistance leader remembered, "was no more than a few months."[2]

Hitler's "Final Solution"

Meanwhile, Hitler's pathological vision of a world locked in racial combat led him to what he called the "final solution" to the "Jewish problem": the physical extermination of all Europe's Jews. As his expanding power brought Jewish minorities in many countries within his reach, he decided to implement this "solution," apparently first formulated in his manifesto, *Mein Kampf,* in the 1920s. By the 1940s, there were others in the Führer's category of "subhumans" to be eliminated as well: Gypsies, Slavs, and homosexuals were high on his list. But Jews were the archvillains in Hitler's cosmology, and they were his prime targets.

As we have seen, Hitler had begun to exert pressure on the Jews immediately after he came to power. By the late 1930s and the early 1940s, Jews were no longer being urged to leave, but were being isolated within Hitler's growing empire instead.

Many Jews were herded into already existing ghettos—Jewish neighborhoods in cities—while others were sent to newly constructed concentration camps in the countryside. As the 1940s advanced, the ghettos, too, were emptied as Jews from all over conquered Europe were funneled into half a dozen large camps, most of them in occupied Poland. In these camps, the official explanation ran, the internees would be "resettled" and put to work for the good of the Reich. In fact, from 1941 on, the Nazis had determined to destroy the entire Jewish population of Europe. Thanks to the fanaticism of the party faithful, the discipline of guards and executioners, and the ghastly efficiency of modern bureaucracy and technology, this effort produced a harvest of death so great that a new term was coined to describe it—*genocide,* meaning an attempt to destroy an entire race of human beings.[3] This particular instance of genocide, the Nazi war against the Jews, is called the *Holocaust,* an ancient term meaning a mass sacrifice by fire.

The Holocaust

The massacre began in earnest as German armies drove deeper into eastern Europe, over-running Jewish villages and ghettos in Poland and the Soviet Union. Behind the advancing armies, special squads of SS troops—the Nazi party's own elite military arm—fanned out among the villages, rounding up large numbers of Jews and other "racial" enemies, including Gypsies and some Slavs. These groups were summarily executed, usually machine gunned after first being required to dig their own graves.

As hundreds of thousands and then millions of Jews from all parts of Europe fell into German hands, however, it became clear to Nazi leadership that more scientific methods of extermination were needed. It was for this purpose that the death camps at Auschwitz and elsewhere were built. These camps were equipped with gas chambers disguised as shower rooms and with large crematoria where the bodies of the dead were burned.

As the war raged around them, Jewish citizens of many countries were loaded onto special trains for shipment to the camps. Typically packed into freight cars without food or sanitary facilities, they often traveled for days to the heavily guarded camps in the east. Here the elderly, sick, feeble, and children were sent immediately to their deaths, while the strongest were often put to work in neighboring industrial facilities until they too grew too weak to be of use and were driven in their turn into the gas chambers. Overwork, meager rations, and disease due to overcrowding and unsanitary conditions in the camps also caused many deaths.

Accounts of the Holocaust have seared the conscience of the West ever since. The systematic savagery of execution squads, of troops who guarded or invaded ghettos, and above all of the death camp guards numb the imagination. Physical beatings, systematic starvation, and forced labor were accompanied by deliberate humiliation and degradation aimed at extinguishing the basic sense of humanity in the victims. For most, death came after having been ordered to strip and forced into concrete "shower rooms," where clouds of deadly hydrogen cyanide extinguished life in a few final minutes of horror. Even the dead were not spared degradation. Before they were cremated, long hair was cut off and gold fillings pulled from the teeth of the corpses—with their clothing, final contributions to Hitler's Reich.

In some places, against insurmountable odds, Jews who had heard rumors of the fate that awaited them resisted shipment to the camps. The Jews of the Warsaw ghetto took up

The combination of disbelief and terror in the faces of these Jewish women and children as they are led off by the Nazis who had crushed the 1943 Warsaw ghetto rebellion is a testament to the human capacity for unbridled evil. (United Press International Inc.)

arms against the German occupiers of the city and fought until they were crushed by overwhelming force. "Let it be known that every threshold in the ghetto . . . will . . . be a fortress," cried the Warsaw rebels, "that we may all perish in this struggle, but we will not surrender."[4] But the Nazis made every effort to deceive and confuse future victims. Many Jews could not believe that even the Nazis could be doing such a thing. In the end, there was no resisting the might of the Nazi murder machine.

In some cases, neighbors, fellow citizens, or others concealed or protected Jews from the Holocaust. Italian peasants hid Jews in their villages throughout the war, and Denmark as a nation saved almost all its Jewish citizens. But most often, people refused to see what was going on, refused to help, or actually collaborated in the massacre. People who lived near the reeking, groaning camps saw the trains empty month after month at their gates, knew that no one ever left, and said nothing. Allied governments refused the pleas of Jewish leaders overseas to bomb the camps, citing other military priorities as more important.

Of a European Jewish population of less than nine million, six million men, women, and children were massacred, along with several million Slavs, Gypsies, homosexuals, and other victims of the Nazi terror. Attempts to explain how civilized twentieth–century people could undertake such a genocidal assault on fellow human beings are many. Bureaucratic anonymity shielded officials who merely "did the paperwork" that routed the trains to the camps. The camp guards and SS murder squads often seem to have clung to the thought that they were merely "obeying orders," that their superiors bore the responsibility. And horrifyingly large numbers of Germans, like the Russians who sent the kulaks to their doom or executed "enemies of the people," may actually have believed that their victims were subhuman, deserving of the fate meted out to them. In the end, nothing can "explain" this, the worst atrocity in the most destructive war in the history of the Western world.

Summary

The internationalist idealism that had produced the League of Nations gave way in the 1930s to aggressive demands by the "revisionist" powers who felt dissatisfied with the Peace of Paris that had followed World War I. Japanese aggression in China, the Italian conquest of Ethiopia, and Hitler's absorption of Austria and most of Czechoslovakia were met by appeasement from the democratic powers. Only the German invasion of Poland in 1939 finally moved Britain and France to take up the challenge and plunged Europe into World War II.

From 1939 into 1942, German, Japanese, and other Axis forces went from victory to victory. Hitler's Blitzkrieg overwhelmed much of western Europe and established a hegemony over a substantial slice of eastern Europe as well. The Soviet Union, temporarily allied with Germany, also took its share of eastern Europe. At the other end of Eurasia, Japan absorbed most of Southeast Asia and a number of South Pacific islands while continuing to advance through China.

The tide turned in the second half of the war, 1942–1945, as Hitler's efforts to defeat Britain and conquer the Soviet Union both failed, while Japan's ill–considered attack on the United States at Pearl Harbor brought another great power into the war against the Axis. After Stalingrad, the Soviets liberated their own country and closed in on Germany from the east, while U. S. and British troops defeated the Axis in Africa and Italy, liberated France, and attacked Germany from the west. After a series of bloody island campaigns in the Pacific, meanwhile, the United States climaxed sustained bombing against Japan by dropping the first atomic bombs on Japanese cities. Germany and Japan both surrendered unconditionally in 1945.

The commitment of whole populations to "total war" led to massive bombing attacks on cities and to underground resistance movements and brutal repression. The fanatical Nazi effort to destroy Europe's Jewish population introduced new terms for crimes against humanity to the Western lexicon: *genocide* and the *Holocaust.*

Some Key Terms

Allies 655
Anschluss 648
appeasement 646
Axis 648
Blitzkrieg 650
D-Day 651

genocide 663
Hiroshima 661
Holocaust 663
kamikaze 660
Lebensraum 647
Lend-lease 653

Munich conference 649
resistance movements 663
revisionist powers 645
spirit of Locarno 645
Wehrmacht 650

Notes

1. Quoted in Raymond Carr, *The Spanish Tragedy: The Civil War in Perspective* (London: Weidenfeld and Nicolson, 1977), 142.
2. Henri Michel, *The Shadow War: Resistance in Europe, 1939–1945* (London: Corgi Books, 1975), 189.
3. The Jews of Europe did not of course constitute a separate race, but since the Nazis defined their victims in racial terms, the word *genocide* is commonly used in this connection.
4. Quoted in Golo Mann, *The History of Germany Since 1789,* trans. Marian Jackson (New York: Praeger, 1968), 338.

Reading List

Beck, E. B. *Under the Bomb: The German Home Front, 1942–1945.* Lexington: University Press of Kentucky, 1986. Sensitive account of the impact of total war on German civilians.

Bell, P. M. H. *The Origins of the Second World War in Europe.* New York: Longman, 1986. Solid, student–oriented summary of the causes of the war in Europe.

Bergamini, D. *Japan's Imperial Conspiracy.* New York: Morrow, 1971. Japanese expansionism in the Far East. See also A. Iriye, *After Imperialism: The Search for a New Order in the Far East, 1921–1931* (Cambridge, Mass.: Harvard University Press, 1965).

Bishop, E. *Their Finest Hour.* New York: Ballantine, 1968. The story of the aerial battle of Britain, briefly told. On the German air force, see W. Murray, *Luftwaffe* (London: Allen and Unwin, 1985).

Churchill, W. S. *The Second World War.* 6 vols. Boston: Houghton–Mifflin, 1948–1953. Eloquent account by the British war leader.

Deakin, F. W. *The Brutal Friendship: Mussolini, Hitler, and the Fall of Italian Fascism.* London: Weidenfeld and Nicolson, 1962. Relations between the European totalitarian leaders.

Eisenhower, D. D. *Crusade in Europe.* New York: Da Capo, 1977. World War II from the perspective of the supreme commander of the Allied forces in Europe.

Feis, H. *Churchill, Roosevelt, Stalin: The War They Waged and the Peace They Sought.* Princeton, N.J.: Princeton University Press, 1967. Older but still useful account of the Grand Alliance.

Haestrup, J. *Europe Ablaze.* Odense: Odense University Press, 1978. Wide–ranging survey of the resistance movements in Nazi–occupied Europe. See also the authoritative account by H. Michel, *The Shadow War: The European Resistance, 1939–1945* (New York: Harper and Row, 1972).

Hough, R. *The Longest Battle: The War at Sea,*

1939–1945. London: Weidenfeld and Nicolson, 1986. Stirring account of the naval side of World War II, with many firsthand reports by participants.

Levin, N. *The Holocaust: The Destruction of European Jewry, 1933–1945*. New York: Crowell, 1968. Hitler's Jewish policy, escalating to the "final solution." A searing case study of the Auschwitz death camp is O. Friedrich, *The End of the World: A History* (New York: Coward, McCann and Geoghegan, 1982), while M. R. Marrus, *The Holocaust in History* (Hanover, N.H.: University Press of New England for Brandeis University Press, 1987), sums up the scholarly literature.

Martel, G., ed. *The Origins of the Second World War Reconsidered*. Boston: Allen and Unwin, 1986. The dispute over A. J. P. Taylor's controversial revisionist claim in his *Origins of the Second World War* (London: Hamish Hamilton, 1961) that World War II was not "Hitler's war."

Millett, A. R., and W. Murray, eds. *Military Effectiveness*, vol. 3, *The Second World War*. Boston: Allen and Unwin, 1988. Rates the combatants on tactical, strategic, and political effectiveness.

O'Neill, W. *A Democracy at War: America's Fight at Home and Abroad in World War II*. New York: Free Press, 1993. Upbeat reading of America's part in the biggest war.

Seaton, A. *The Battle for Moscow, 1941–1942*. London: Hart–Davis, 1971. Outstanding narrative of a key battle.

Sontag, R. J. *A Broken World, 1919–1939*. New York: Harper and Row, 1971. International tensions during the twenty–year truce.

Taylor, T. *Munich: The Price of Peace*. New York: Doubleday, 1979. Insightful examination of a diplomatic crisis whose resolution has become synonymous with appeasement. See also the broader scope of A. L. Rowse, *Appeasement: A Study in Political Decline* (New York: Norton, 1963).

Toland, J. *The Rising Sun: The Decline and Fall of the Japanese Empire*. New York: Bantam, 1970. Gives the Japanese perspective on the war.

Weinberg, G. L. *A World at Arms: A Global History of World War II*. New York: Cambridge University Press, 1994. Impressive account of the war from Europe to the Pacific. For a leading military historian's view, see B. H. Liddell Hart, *The History of the Second World War* (New York: Putnam, 1971).

Wright, G. *The Ordeal of Total War, 1939–1945*. New York: Harper and Row, 1968. The impact of World War II on society, technology, and the collective psyche of the West.

27

A World Divided

The Cold War and the End of the Western Empires

•The Iron Curtain Descends •The Long Twilight Struggle
•Winding Down the Cold War •Colonies on the Eve of Independence
•The End of the Western Empires

The world emerged from World War II, as after World War I, into a peace that soon came to look almost as dangerous as the war just past. Two traumatic international trends quickly took shape. One was the long confrontation between the U. S. and the USSR and their allies that came to be known as the *cold war*. The other was the disintegration of the centuries–old Western overseas empires in a great wave of *colonial liberation movements*. Both the cold war and the end of the Western empires centered in the third quarter of the century, from 1945 to the 1970s, but neither reached a definitive ending until the 1990s.

The foreign relations of the Western nations after the Second World War were in large part structured by the "East–West" struggle called the cold war. This chapter will begin with a look at major sources of international tension and at the emergence of the Soviet bloc in eastern Europe and the American–led North Atlantic Treaty Organization. It will survey the triumph of communism in China, the struggles that left Korea and Vietnam divided, and the long series of clashes between the two global alliances, in eastern Europe and Latin America, Asia and Africa. It will then summarize steps toward detente and disarmament and outline the final collapse of the Soviet alliance in the years around 1990.

But this chapter will also attempt an overview of the other main trend of this period, the collapse of the European overseas empires which divided the world in another way— the wealthy "North" from the underdeveloped "South." The latter sections of the chapter will therefore seek the roots of revolt in colonial independence movements and their new leadership, survey the crumbling of Western power in Asia and Africa, and carry the story through to the collapse of the last "white settler" regime in South Africa in the early 1990s. Like the cold war, this great liberation is an epic story, and one whose consequences are, as we will see in later chapters, far from played out today.

◆The Iron Curtain Descends◆

In the wake of World War II, many people thought that the world was once again on the road to peace and progress. The dictators had been vanquished, and a vigorous policy of aid and trade would pull a shattered Europe out of its ruins. The newly organized United Nations would be the watchdog of peace for future generations.

This was not, however, what happened. The United Nations was duly established, and the war–battered nations, losers as well as winners, did recover economically with surprising rapidity. But peace was not at hand. Before the 1940s were over, world leaders were once again denouncing each other, armies were mobilized, and a new and much more terrible war seemed a very likely possibility—this time between the victorious Allies themselves.

In the pages that follow, we will look first at the United Nations as a force for peace. But we will focus most of our attention on the differing views and plans of Americans and Russians, the prime contestants in the cold war.

The United Nations

A vital expression of the new internationalism of the postwar period was the creation of a large number of not merely European but global organizations. Of these, the United Nations, successor to the League of Nations, was by far the most important.

The United Nations as we know it took shape toward the end of World War II and held its first meeting in San Francisco in 1945. Its permanent headquarters was built in New York City, though some of its agencies established their headquarters in Paris, Geneva, Rome, and elsewhere. The structure of the United Nations resembled that of the League, including a council, an assembly, and a secretariat, but the determination to make this new global organization work was considerably stronger than it had been a quarter of a century earlier.

The UN Security Council was dominated by five permanent members: the two new superpowers to come out of the war, the United States and the Soviet Union; the largest imperial powers in 1945, Britain and France; and China, which then as now included a large part of the population of the world. Each of these five nations had the right to veto any measure proposed for Council action. Like the League before it, the United Nations recognized the principles of national interest and great–power preeminence as necessary to ensure the participation of powerful nations that alone could make it work. The Soviet Union, certain to be outvoted by the United States and its allies, cast by far the majority of vetoes in the early years. The six additional members of the Security Council were elected from the general membership. During the first years, they normally supported the United States.

The General Assembly represented all countries and gave the less wealthy and less powerful a frequently utilized sounding board for their views. The size of the General Assembly grew when, as we will see, British, French, and other European empires broke up into the dozens of countries of the *Third World* during the postwar decades. These new "nonaligned" nations were not formally committed to either of the two great international alliances that grew up after the war, one led by the Americans (the so–called First World of affluent democracies) and the other by the Soviet Union (the communist nations of the less developed Second World). Nevertheless, the new countries frequently took an anti–imperialist stand that put them in opposition to the United States as well as to Britain, France, and other leading imperialist powers.

The complex, full–time Secretariat, headed by a secretary general, included agencies concerned with a variety of global problems, from world health and labor problems to cul-

Chronology 27.1: The Cold War

1945–1949	*Soviet satellite states established after World War II; Germany, Korea, and Vietnam divided*
1947	*Truman doctrine promises aid for nations threatened by Soviet expansionism; Marshall Plan offers economic aid*
1949–1957	*Military alliances (NATO, Warsaw Pact) and economic organizations (Common Market, COMECON) established*
1949	*Mao wins civil war in China, allies Communist China with Soviet Union*
1950–1953	*Korean War; U.S. repels North Korean attack on South Korea*
1956	*Hungarian revolt crushed*
1959	*Castro wins power in Cuba, allies with Soviet Union*
1962	*Cuban missile crisis threatens nuclear war*
1962–1975	*Vietnam War; U.S. withdraws; North Vietnamese victory reunifies Vietnam*
1968	*Czech revolt crushed*
1973	*Coup in Chile overthrows Allende regime*
1979–1990s	*Afghanistan War; Soviets withdraw; Muslim rebels seize control, fight among themselves*
1985–1991	*Gorbachev moves to reform communism, seeks ties with U.S. and western Europe*
1989–1990	*Soviet satellite states free; divided Germany reunited under west German leadership*
1991	*Soviet Union disintegrates, cold war ends*

tural projects. A useful advance beyond anything the League of Nations had attempted was the United Nations' role in peacekeeping around the globe. Activist secretaries general sought to negotiate truces in many wars, and members contributed troops to UN peacekeeping forces that took up positions between enemies to deter a resumption of hostilities.

Seen by some as a tool of big–power domination of small states, by others as a podium for irresponsible attacks on the larger states that paid the bills, the United Nations nevertheless did have its uses. Though in no sense a world government, the United Nations performed enough valuable functions that it survived, as its predecessor had not. It was at least the beginning of a framework beyond the international anarchy of earlier centuries. During the postwar decades, however, it was also, as we will see, a primary arena of international conflict.

A Split in the Western World

The roots of the mutual dislike and distrust that divided the United States and the Soviet Union were in large part ideological. Both the U. S. and the USSR had in fact exceptional traditions of commitment to systems of ideas and highly developed feelings about their own special place in history.

America's sense of its own uniqueness and dedication to higher ideals is often traced back to the seventeenth–century Pilgrims, zealous Puritans who crossed the ocean to build a New Jerusalem in the New England wilderness. The nation's eighteenth–century founding fathers were also true believers, committed to the new social ideas of the Enlightenment. The United States was thus a rare case of a nation founded in significant part on ideas. The republic that evolved over the next two centuries also took both political free-dom and free–enterprise capitalism very seriously. Woodrow Wilson at the beginning of the twentieth century embodied a basic American belief in the nation's destiny to spread democracy around the world. And so strong was America's commitment to free–market economics that the United States became one of the few Western countries that failed to produce any sizable socialist party in the twentieth century. Thus by the middle of this cen-tury the United States took for granted—and very seriously—its obligation to be the "leader of the free world." And many Americans saw in the Soviet Union the antithesis of American values: a socialistic dictatorship.

Russia also had a long–standing commitment to ideas, however, and a sense of its spe-cial role in history. From the emergence of the Muscovite state in the fifteenth century, czarist Russia had seen itself as the "third Rome," successor to both ancient Rome and me-dieval Byzantium as the center of the true faith, Orthodox Christianity. Traditionalist resis-tance to Peter the Great's reforms in the eighteenth century and the Slavophile tradition in the nineteenth had both developed this sense of the specialness of the Russian soul and of Russia's destiny to inaugurate a "Slavic age" in history. The Bolsheviks who seized power in 1917 simply substituted their version of revolutionary Marxism for the existing reli-gio–nationalist view of Russia's special role in history. The Union of Soviet Socialist Re-publics, like the United States, was thus founded on ideas: the Marxist dream of a global proletarian revolution and the Leninist conviction that Russia would be the vanguard of that revolution.

That these contrary visions of reality existed in the minds of Americans and Soviets at the time the cold war began seems established. How central these ideas were in shaping events, however, is another and equally important question, one that we will examine shortly.

The specific postwar intentions of the two superpowers, however, were rooted in prac-tical concerns as well as ideological considerations. In this area, too, there were striking dif-ferences between the powers.

American goals for the postwar period included the establishment of democratic gov-ernments in liberated Europe and the rapid economic recovery of that war–ravaged conti-nent. Another goal was free trade and the free passage of capital, both areas in which the United States was positioned to do well after the war. There were also those in America's postwar administrations who dreamed of undermining the Soviet hegemony of eastern Eu-rope and even destroying communism in the Soviet Union itself.

Moscow's plan for the postwar order of things gave Soviet recovery top priority. This meant squeezing reparations out of Germany and its wartime allies wherever possible. So-viet plans also almost certainly included the spread of Soviet influence wherever it could, especially in eastern Europe. Nineteenth–century Russian nationalists had seen themselves as the leaders of the other Slavic peoples and the dominant power in the region. Stalin, as we saw earlier, had used his pact with Hitler to recover the Baltic states and acquire slices of Poland and other eastern European countries. Two German invasions in the first half of the century made a buffer zone between the Soviet Union and western Europe seem es-sential.

These Soviet objectives, however, looked very different from the American side of the fence. U. S. opinion, for instance, saw the ruthless imposition of pro–Soviet and then com-munist regimes on neighboring countries after the war as a clear assault on democratic free-doms, not the building of a buffer zone. The overall impression in the United States was of a Stalinist expansionism that rivaled Hitler's.

What became the essential American response to this expansionism was described by George F. Kennan, then chief of the U. S. State Department's policy planning staff, as *containment*. This policy involved surrounding the Soviet Union with military alliances, a vigorous arms race, and other devices that we will discuss in later sections.

The long competition between the Soviet and American camps, then, quickly developed a momentum of its own. It spread far beyond Europe to Asia, Africa, Latin America—virtually everywhere that propaganda, economic aid, political alliances, or military intervention could reach. In the following pages we will attempt to reconstruct the events of the early years of the cold war, roughly 1945–1954, when what came to be called the *iron curtain* rolled down, dividing both the Western world and the world at large.

Stalin's Domination of Eastern Europe

There was no Congress of Vienna, no Peace of Paris after World War II. The war ended with complete military defeat of the Axis powers, essentially the "unconditional surrender" the Allies had demanded. At Nuremberg and elsewhere, some German and Japanese officials were tried and executed or imprisoned for such war crimes as the Nazi massacre of millions of Jews in Europe and the brutal mistreatment of civilians and prisoners of war by the Japanese military. Separate treaties were signed in the later 1940s and 1950s with Italy (1947), Japan (1952), and Austria (1955), as well as with Hitler's east European satellites. But the Grand Alliance—America, Britain, and Russia—broke apart so rapidly that the victorious Allies found it impossible to work together to impose any sort of new order on Europe or the world.

The most important postwar changes, however, involved Germany, Poland, and the Soviet Union, the countries where the war had begun. Conquered Germany, divided into four occupation zones, was soon reduced to two parts by the fusing of American, British, and French sectors into the new nation of West Germany (the Federal Republic of Germany) and the conversion of the Soviet zone into East Germany (the German Democratic Republic). In addition, the Germans lost to Poland a swath of territory that lay east of the Oder and Neisse rivers. Poland in turn ratified the Soviet Union's annexation of its own eastern territories. Thus in the wake of the war the Soviet Union expanded westward, Poland moved bodily to the west, and Germany was left shrunken and divided in the center of Europe. The Soviet Union also retained its other wartime annexations, including the Baltic states.

More disturbing to many western people than these territorial changes were the conflicts among the victors that sprang up after the war. Differences of principle arose between Roosevelt and Stalin. The American president believed that the liberated peoples of eastern Europe should be permitted to choose their own governments in free elections. Stalin, however, saw the matter differently: "Whoever occupies a territory," he declared, "also imposes his own social system. Everyone imposes his own system as far as his armies can reach. It cannot be otherwise."[1] Since the Red Army had overrun and occupied eastern Europe, there was not much the United States could do about it short of another war, a political impossibility in the wake of the one just ended.

Whatever its intentions and underlying motives, by 1949 Stalin's Soviet Union seemed to stand at the center of an empire that dwarfed those of Napoleon and Hitler. The Soviet dictator's achievements had come in waves. In alliance with Hitler, Stalin had recovered most of the territories Russia had lost in World War I, including the Baltic states of Estonia,

Latvia, and Lithuania as well as slices of Finland, Poland, and Romania. In alliance with Roosevelt and Churchill, the communist leader had achieved the czarist dream of Russian domination of eastern Europe, from East Germany and Poland south through Hungary and Czechoslovakia into the Balkans. In Asia, he had accomplished another Romanov imperialist goal by expelling Japan from Korea and establishing a Russian puppet state in the northern half of the peninsula. And when in 1949 the Chinese communists under Mao Zedong defeated Chiang Kai–shek and seized power in China (to be discussed later), it looked as though the world's most populous nation had been added to Stalin's empire.

The heart of the Soviet Union's expanding sphere of influence was the collection of *satellite states* in eastern Europe, the so–called "people's republics" ruled by client regimes who, in the early years, were little more than puppets of the Soviet leaders in the Kremlin. These states, as we will see, included East Germany, Poland, Hungary, Czechoslovakia, Romania, Bulgaria, and in the beginning Yugoslavia and Albania. In the typical satellite, local communists, usually trained in Moscow, had returned to their homeland soon after the Red Army overran it. The first postwar government was typically a coalition, including but not run by the local communist party. A second phase was reached when the communists achieved control but retained other political parties in the government to give at least the illusion of democracy. In the last stage, all other parties were abolished and a one–party communist regime was established with close ties to the Soviet Union. The new government proceeded to take control of industry, trade, and finance, often to collectivize agriculture, and always to impose censorship, police repression, and other Stalinist tactics.

The United States found it hard to object to the imposition of a pro–Soviet government on nations that had been members of the Axis alliance or to the elevation of anti–Nazi guerrilla leaders like Marshal Tito (Josip Broz) in Yugoslavia. In the two cases of Poland and Czechoslovakia, however, there was an outcry by the western Allies. The fall of the Czech government of Eduard Benes (1884–1948) and Jan Masaryk (1886–1948) to a Soviet–sponsored coup in 1948 caused particular dismay.

The eastern third of Germany, finally, was converted into the Soviet satellite state of East Germany in response to the formation of West Germany by the western Allies in 1949. The two Germanies became the center of the early cold war struggle. The tension was particularly high in Berlin, located in East Germany but occupied by all four Allied powers. As the western sectors of the city shared in the rapid economic recovery of West Germany, West Berlin became a showcase for the prosperity of the Federal Republic's "economic miracle," drawing large numbers of East Germans across the line.

As early as March 1946, less than a year after the end of the war in Europe, Winston Churchill warned that the Soviet Union was carving out a zone of Soviet domination in the eastern part of the continent from which Western influences were being rigidly excluded. "From Stettin in the Baltic to Trieste in the Adriatic," the British statesman declared in a speech in Fulton, Missouri, during a visit to the United States, "an iron curtain has descended across the continent." President Harry Truman's presence on the platform was apparently intended to indicate his approval of Churchill's view.

The following year, the American secretary of state, George C. Marshall, announced the Marshall Plan, which committed billions of U. S. dollars to aid European recovery, at least in part to prevent the spread of revolutionary Marxism. In Europe, opposition to Soviet expansionism stiffened, producing a series of setbacks for pro–Soviet elements in France, Italy, Greece, Yugoslavia, and Germany.

In the later 1940s, strong conservative leadership by Charles de Gaulle in France and Alcide de Gasperi (1881–1954) in Italy defeated the Communists at the polls. These defeats ended any chance of an electoral take–over by Communists in western Europe. Further east, Communist guerrillas in Greece, with support from Soviet satellite states, threatened the Greek constitutional monarch, while the Soviet Union pressured Turkey for expanded access to the Straits out of the Black Sea. In 1947, therefore, U. S. president Harry Truman (president 1945–1953) announced what became known as the Truman Doctrine, promising American aid to Greece, Turkey, and any other nation threatened by communist subversion. American assistance thereafter did contribute to the defeat of the Greek guerrillas, and the Soviets gave up their demands on Turkey.

In 1948, Stalin suffered another setback in the area when Tito's Yugoslavia seceded from the Soviet system of satellite states. The Yugoslavs, proud of having liberated themselves from Hitler, rallied round Marshal Tito (in power 1945–1980) when he rejected the Soviet model of socialist development, insisting that there were "many roads to socialism." Severing its ties with the eastern bloc, Yugoslavia thereafter considered itself "nonaligned," willing to accept aid from both Washington and Moscow but standing apart from both sides in the cold war.

The most dramatic confrontation of the postwar years, however, came in 1948 in isolated Berlin. Seeking to lever the western Allies out of the city, Soviet and East German authorities closed all land and water access to Berlin, hoping thus to compel the western garrisons to abandon the city. The United States, however, mounted the *Berlin airlift* of supplies into the western sectors of the city. After many months, the Soviets and East Germans gave up the effort, and West Berlin was politically integrated into the Federal Republic of (West) Germany created the following year. American, British, and French troops, however, remained to confront their counterparts in the Soviet sector of the city, which became the political capital of East Germany.

Mao's China, Korea and Vietnam Divided

In Asia, meanwhile, Soviet influence still seemed to be spreading as communists moved to seize power in China and Southeast Asia in the late 1940s and early 1950s. Again, American and other Western powers mobilized countervailing force and succeeded in winning at least a stalemate in the Far East. In this area, communist successes in China and French Indochina were balanced to some degree by Western victories in British and American Southeast Asian colonies, while the bruising Korean War ended with no discernible gains for either side.

The Communists came to power in China after a long and bloody struggle between the Chinese Communist leader Mao Zedong and the leader of the Chinese Nationalist party, Chiang Kai–shek. The Chinese Revolution had begun with the fall of the last imperial dynasty of China in 1911 and lasted until 1949. The United States had seen Chiang as an ally against Japan during World War II, but had come to see him as inefficient and corrupt after 1945. The Soviets, by contrast, supported Mao in the last years of the struggle. In the end, the Nationalists fled to the large offshore island of Taiwan, while Mao took power in Beijing (Peking) and began to establish one–party rule and a government–run economy on the Stalinist model.

In Washington, there was much recrimination over the "loss" of China, while the Soviet Union hastened to sign a treaty of friendship and offer aid to Mao's new People's Republic of China. When communists announced that "the East is Red," many in the West were unhappily inclined to agree with them.

Communist influence also appeared to be pushing down into Southeast Asia and further east into Korea. Here, however, western efforts were more successful in stopping the spread of Soviet power.

The Southeast Asian colonial revolts of the late 1940s and early 1950s—in Malaya, Vietnam, and elsewhere—will be discussed in a later section on the fall of Western overseas empires. Many of the organizers of these revolts, however, had read and been inspired by some of the writings of Marx and Lenin. Soviet leaders also saw these "national liberation struggles" in Leninist terms, as rebellions against an imperial extension of western capitalism. Though the Soviets could provide little or no concrete help so soon after their own devastating war, they did defend these movements at the United Nations and elsewhere. Some leaders of national liberation struggles also became communists, though very few rank–and–file guerrillas, fighting to drive the foreigners out of their villages and cities, had any knowledge of the *Communist Manifesto* or Lenin's doctrine that imperialism was "the highest stage of capitalism."

Ho Chi Minh (1890–1967), the chief leader of the Vietnamese struggle against the French in Indochina after the war, was a French–educated communist. Like Tito, he had fought the Axis—in Ho's case, the Japanese—and had impressed the Americans as someone worth supporting. The French, however, were not about to abandon the Indochinese colonies they had acquired in the latter part of the nineteenth century. As a result, Ho's revolt turned into a protracted guerrilla struggle, dragging on from the late 1940s to 1954. In the latter year, after putting all their prestige on the line in the defense of the isolated fortress of Dien Bien Phu—and losing it—the French agreed to liberate all their Indochinese holdings. In the Geneva settlement of 1954, however, Ho Chi Minh and his communist cadres got only North Vietnam, while Cambodia, Laos, and South Vietnam went to rulers whom the French felt they could continue to dominate. The struggle in Vietnam, however, was not over.

Elsewhere in Southeast Asia, communist–led guerrillas cropped up in the jungles of British–ruled Malaya and the American Philippines. In both cases, however, the western powers involved succeeded in suppressing the communists, the British before, the Americans after granting independence to the colonies.

The other major clash between American and allied forces and communists in Asia during the postwar period came in Korea. Like Germany, Korea had been divided by occupying armies at the end of World War II. Both the Soviets in the north and the Americans in the southern half of the Korean peninsula had sponsored local rulers, and rival republics of North and South Korea began to take shape. Then in 1950, the North Koreans invaded South Korea. Although earlier American pronouncements had made it sound as though Korea lay outside what the United States now regarded as its overseas defensive perimeter, President Truman took action. The United States succeeded in getting a United Nations resolution in favor of a "police action" to stop the aggression in Korea and sent in a largely American army under General Douglas MacArthur (1880–1964). MacArthur not only drove the North Koreans out of the south but overran most of North Korea itself. In doing so, however, MacArthur got too close to Korea's northern frontier with China. The communist leadership in Beijing thereupon dispatched regiments of Chinese "volunteers" into Korea—for centuries a Chinese tributary—and rolled the Americans back into South Korea once more. MacArthur, however, rallied, stopped the Chinese advance and pushed them back to a line very close to the original demarcation line between the two Koreas. There the war ended in 1953 with a truce that was still in force four decades later, with armies in place on both sides of the line.

Organizing the Cold War

If he could offer little material help to the North Vietnamese or the North Koreans, Stalin strove to consolidate his gains by organizing a new international communist organization, the Cominform. Truman and Western European leaders, apparently convinced of the danger of further Soviet communist expansion, organized militarily and economically for a long and bitter struggle.

In 1947, the Russians set up the Cominform, or Communist Information Bureau, a successor to the old Communist International, as a means of coordinating the activities of Communist parties in other countries. U. S. leaders, remembering how rigidly other Communist parties had followed the Stalinist line in the 1930s, saw the Cominform as a means of orchestrating international Communist subversion. The United States extended its influence in a different way, leasing sites for American military bases within reach of the Soviet Union and signing military alliances with governments in many parts of the world. This growing American presence around the fringes of the Soviet Union's Eurasian sphere looked like "capitalist encirclement" to the Soviet leadership.

In 1949, the United States, Canada, and their western European allies formed the North Atlantic Treaty Organization (*NATO*), a military alliance intended to prevent further Soviet expansion westward. By this means, the United States, twice sucked into great European wars in this century, sought to prevent another one by the classic strategy of redressing the balance of power against a potential aggressor. A large American army was stationed in Europe where, like the U. S. forces on the Soviet Union's other flank in Korea, it remained decade after decade. In 1955, the *Warsaw Pact* formalized the military alliance of the Soviet Union and its satellites in eastern Europe.

Separate European economic organizations also came into existence during the late 1940s and 1950s. The European Economic Community or Common Market in the west and Comecon, the Council for Mutual Economic Assistance, in the east, both had cold war implications, ratifying and strengthening the two alliances. By the early 1950s also, the Soviet Union had its own atomic and nuclear weapons, both developed soon after the American versions. A vigorous arms race ensued, another permanent feature of the cold war period in Western history.

A decade after the end of World War II, then, the world was clearly not at peace. Early in 1953, Truman's term in office ended and Stalin died later that same year. But the conflict they bequeathed to the divided Western world continued, growing more involuted and sometimes even more violent.

♦ The Long Twilight Struggle ♦

From the 1950s to the 1980s, the two superpowers remained on their guard, each charging the other with aggressive intentions. Each, however, was most likely to take up arms, not to expand further, but to suppress rebellion within its own sphere of influence—the Soviet Union in eastern Europe, the U. S. in Latin America. Where the great powers did reach beyond these recognized spheres, as in Vietnam and Afghanistan, neither succeeded.

What follows, then, is a brief summary of what U. S. President John F. Kennedy referred to in his 1961 inaugural address as the "long, twilight struggle," neither war nor peace, that divided the Western world for two generations.

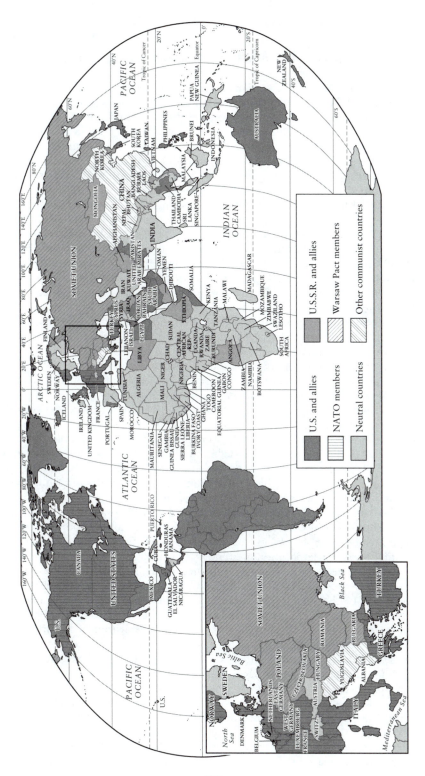

Cold War Alliances and Nonaligned Nations

Kennedy and Khrushchev: Hungary, Berlin, Cuba

During the later 1950s and the earlier 1960s, the Soviet leader Nikita Khrushchev (in power 1956–1964) faced two very different American presidents: former general Dwight Eisenhower (president 1953–1961) and dashing young John Kennedy (president 1961–1963). During these years, the Soviet Union had to deal with a crisis in Hungary, Kennedy confronted two in Cuba, and Berlin became once more a center of conflict.

The Soviet Union had faced abortive insurrections before. East Berliners, for example, had pelted Soviet tanks with stones to no avail in 1953. But things got drastically out of hand when Hungarians took up arms against the Soviet presence in 1956.

In that year, Khrushchev had delivered a shocking "secret speech" before the Soviet Communist Party Congress exposing the tyranny of Joseph Stalin, then only three years in his grave. Inspired in part by these revelations, young Hungarians took to the streets of Budapest. Rallying to the leadership of the reform–minded communist Imre Nagy (1895–1958), the Hungarian rebels hoped to establish more democratic institutions with less Soviet influence; they even talked of seceding from the Warsaw Pact. Khrushchev's liberalism did not extend, however, to allowing the basic Soviet military alliance to crumble. Late in 1956, he sent in Soviet tanks and crushed the Hungarian Revolt.

That year saw a number of other crises on both sides of the iron curtain. Poland was shaken by riots at Poznan in the spring of that year and by demands for the removal of Soviet troops from Polish soil in the fall. As the Hungarian crisis boiled over that autumn, the strongly nationalistic Polish communist leader Wladislav Gomulka (1905–1982), once imprisoned for anti–Russian attitudes, was restored to power. Gomulka negotiated the withdrawal of most Soviet forces and subsequently signed a treaty of friendship with the USSR that recognized a greater degree of parity than had yet obtained between the two communist countries.

Some of the NATO allies, meanwhile, were preoccupied with a problem of their own that fall of 1956, as the Suez crisis exploded in the Middle East. Egyptian president Gamal Abdel Nasser (1918–1970) had nationalized the British–run Suez Canal that summer. Britain had joined with France, which also had interests in the area, and with the new nation of Israel, which feared Nasser's anti–Israeli stance, to plan a coordinated assault intended to liberate the canal. The attack was launched in October and, though militarily successful, failed of its objective, due in part to U. S. refusal to sanction it. This old–fashioned imperialist intervention in Egypt, however, somewhat dulled the edge of the NATO condemnation of the Soviet invasion of Hungary that same fall.

The United States had repeatedly intervened in Latin American affairs in the early twentieth century, "policing" the Western Hemisphere and defending U. S. interests to the south. After 1950, the targets of American incursions were most often revolutionary regimes that espoused communist principles or sought help from the Soviet Union. U. S. intervention south of the border, however, was much less likely to take the form of invasion than of covert operations, usually in support of local conservative factions. Thus under Eisenhower, the American Central Intelligence Agency (CIA) supplied crucial help in the overthrow of Guatemalan president Jácobo Arbenz (1913–1971), whose policies appeared to be converging with those of Guatemalan communists.

President Kennedy faced a much more resilient foe in Cuba's Fidel Castro (1926–). The colorful Cuban guerrilla leader had overthrown the American–supported dictator Fulgencio Batista (1901–1973) in 1959, and had then announced that he was a communist and requested Soviet aid. During his first months in office in 1961, Kennedy allowed a CIA–trained expeditionary force of anti–Castro Cubans to attempt an invasion of the is-

The Cuban revolutionary leader Fidel Castro, shown here at his mountain guerrilla base, became a strong ally of the Soviet Union after his 1959 victory. To many Latin Americans Castro was not a communist threat but, in fact, a symbol of opposition to the U.S. political and economic predominance in the Americas. (AP/Wide World Photos.)

land. Partly because Kennedy refused to add air cover to the package of American support, the invaders were crushingly defeated on the beaches of Cuba's Bay of Pigs.

Kennedy and Khrushchev confronted each other directly in two major crises. The first involved the building of the *Berlin Wall* in 1961. The second was the Cuban missile crisis of 1962, the closest the two superpowers ever came to open war.

Divided Berlin, a source of contention since the 1948–1949 air lift, continued to be the center of a larger problem: the emigration of many thousands of East Germans to West Germany, often by way of Berlin. Unable to match the appeal of freedom and the "economic miracle" of West German recovery (see Chapter 28), the East Germans in 1961 moved to seal the frontier by building a concrete, barbed–wire–topped wall between the eastern and western zones. The United States protested loudly but could do nothing to stop this construction, which took place inside the eastern zone. The Berlin Wall did reduce the flow of emigration to a trickle, but it also proved to be a propaganda disaster for the Soviet side. What kind of people's republic, after all, had to build a wall to keep its people in?

The Cuban missile crisis of 1962 was an attempt by Khrushchev to strengthen his cold war hand by setting up Soviet nuclear missiles on the territory of his new ally, Cuba. The ploy could have put Soviet missiles even closer to the United States—only 90 miles off the American coast—than U. S. military bases in Europe were to the Soviet Union. When American military intelligence detected the sites in Cuba in the fall of 1962, however, President Kennedy peremptorily ordered the Soviets to withdraw missiles already in place and threatened to stop Soviet vessels bringing more of them on the high seas. For a few days, the world seemed to teeter on the brink of nuclear war. Because the United States at that time had a vastly larger nuclear arsenal than that of the Soviet Union, and because Kennedy also apparently sweetened his ultimatum with guarantees of no further attempts to invade Cuba, Khrushchev ordered the removal of the Soviet missiles.

Kennedy was assassinated the following year, Khrushchev deposed the year after that. The world had survived its closest brush with nuclear Armageddon. But the cold war went on.

Challenges in Czechoslovakia and Chile

Through the later 1960s and the 1970s, bushy browed Leonid Brezhnev (in power 1964–1982), faced a series of four American presidents, including Lyndon Johnson (president 1963–1969), and Richard Nixon (president 1969–1974). During these years, the Soviet Union confronted a major challenge in Czechoslovakia, while the United States opposed a communist government in Chile. The two superpowers also plunged into ill–conceived wars outside their respective spheres, the United States in Vietnam and the Soviet Union in Afghanistan.

Czechoslovakia, once the most democratic and economically developed of eastern European states, had since World War II been ruled by local Stalinists and had seen its economy hurt by the economic requirements the Soviet Union imposed on Soviet satellites. In 1968, the reform–minded communist Alexander Dubček (1921–) undertook the most far–reaching liberalization yet attempted in a communist state. During the "Prague spring" of that year, Dubček replaced censorship with freedom of expression, announced a policy of democratization within the Czech Communist party, and allowed others to voice aspirations for multiparty democracy and abandonment of the Warsaw Pact. It was probably the threat to the Warsaw Pact that led the Soviets, with the help of several satellite armies, to occupy Czechoslovakia with half a million troops in the fall of 1968. Dubček was compelled to undo most of his promising beginnings before being finally deposed the following year.

In democratic Chile in 1970, a decade–long movement by moderate political factions to advance the economic well–being of the population climaxed in the election to the presidency of Salvador Allende (president 1970–1973), a Marxist supported by both socialists

Cold War Interventions in the Americas

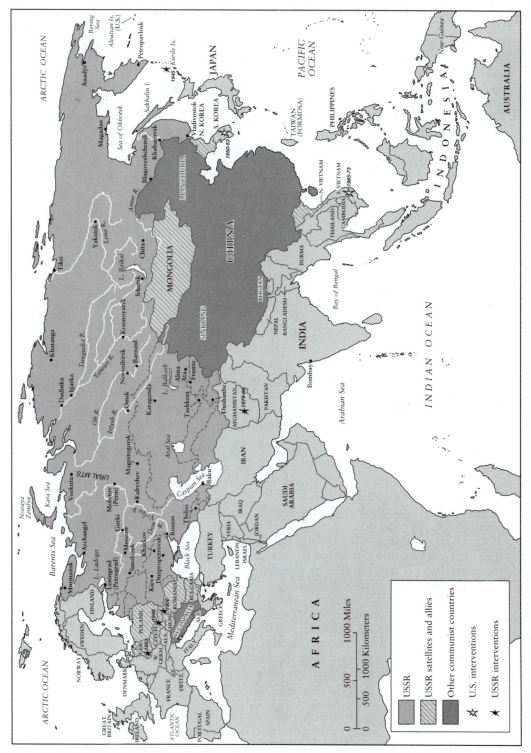

Cold War Interventions in Eurasia

and communists. Over the next three years, Allende moved to nationalize foreign–owned copper mines and other industries, to turn large estates over to peasant cooperatives, and to encourage workers to strike for higher wages. The Allende experiment in state socialism, however, also led to declining production and soaring inflation, alienating the middle classes. In the United States, the Nixon administration, deeply disturbed by the presence of a communist government, even an elected one, in the Western Hemisphere, provided covert support for Allende's opponents and discouraged foreign capital from investing in Chile. In 1973, a coup mounted by the Chilean military overthrew Allende, who died in a military assault on the presidential palace. The victorious junta proceeded to suppress all political parties and establish a brutal military dictatorship under General Augusto Pinochet (president 1973–1990).

Interventions in Vietnam and Afghanistan

The most costly and controversial cold war conflict of the 1960s and 1970s, however, was the American Vietnam War. This decade–long commitment began with the arrival of a handful of American military advisers in South Vietnam in the early 1960s and ended with a North Vietnamese victory over South Vietnam in 1975.

The former French Indochina was left fragmented after Ho Chi Minh's victory in 1954, Ho governing North Vietnam, the French–supported Ngo Din Diem (1901–1963) ruling South Vietnam, and Laos and Cambodia governed as independent countries. Diem refused to participate in scheduled Vietnam–wide elections, which Ho would almost certainly have won, and a North Vietnamese–supported guerrilla movement called the Viet Cong soon appeared in the jungles of South Vietnam. Under Eisenhower and Kennedy, the United States replaced France as the chief patron of the autocratic Diem regime, while the Soviet Union supported Ho Chi Minh in building a one–party state with a planned economy in the north.

Substantial amounts of U. S. financial aid and growing numbers of military advisers proved inadequate to suppress the Viet Cong guerrillas. President Johnson therefore decided on a dramatic escalation of the conflict, pouring in half a million American troops after 1965 and inaugurating a massive bombing campaign against North Vietnam itself. North Vietnam responded by sending regular army units into the south to support and, eventually, largely replace the South Vietnamese guerrillas. Under President Nixon, the United States intensified the bombing and spread the war to Cambodia to choke off the flow of North Vietnamese men and material to the south through that country. Diem was overthrown and in time replaced by a military ruler, General Nguyen Cao Ky (1930–) in 1963, but Ky's army, even with such large–scale U. S. help, could not win the war. In 1973, Nixon, pressured by widespread antiwar sentiment in America, negotiated the withdrawal of all American troops from Vietnam. Two years later, the North Vietnamese Army launched a major offensive which overwhelmed the army of South Vietnam and overran the south. The two halves of historic Vietnam were thus reunited under communist rule.

Vietnamese power also soon came to dominate neighboring Laos as well, while Cambodia fell to a local guerrilla movement called the Khmer Rouge (Red Khmer), communists who claimed to be the successors of the ancient Khmer Empire. Despite large amounts of aid and a massive military intervention in Vietnam and neighboring countries, the United States had failed to control events on the other side of the world.

The failure of the Soviet military incursion into Afghanistan, just across the southern frontier of the Soviet Union itself, provided further evidence of the limitations of military power as an instrument of cold war policy. Through the 1950s and 1960s, the Soviet Union had provided technical and economic aid and had cultivated pro–Soviet factions in this rugged, underdeveloped Muslim land. In 1973, the Afghan monarchy was overthrown, and in 1978 a pro–Soviet government under Nur Mohammed Taraki (1917–) came to power. Taraki's policies, from political centralization and collectivization of the economy to secularization of a strongly Islamic nation, triggered revolts by Muslim villagers and seminomadic clan chieftains all across the country. When the government in Kabul could not suppress the insurrection, the Soviet Army joined the conflict in 1979. The Soviets installed a new prime minister, Babrak Karmal (1929–), and turned modern tanks and air power loose on the mountain guerrillas. The United States provided covert aid for the Afghan rebels, just as the Soviets had supported North Vietnam. After ten years in Afghanistan, Soviet leader Mikhail Gorbachev, like President Nixon before him, withdrew his troops from the quagmire, completing the pullout in 1989. And in 1992 the Afghan rebels broke into Kabul as the North Vietnamese had marched into Saigon and toppled the unpopular pro–Soviet regime the Russians had left behind.

Continuing Conflict around the World

In the 1980s, two conservative American presidents, Ronald Reagan (president 1981–1989) and George Bush (president 1989–1993) faced three aging or ailing men in the Kremlin before the vigorous reformer Mikhail Gorbachev (in power 1985–1991), came to power in the middle of the decade. Through most of the 1980s, while the Afghanistan war dragged on, the U.S.SR became more modestly involved in Africa, and Poland simmered but did not explode. Presidents Reagan and Bush fought communism in Central America and the Caribbean. Then at the end of the decade the picture changed with dramatic suddenness as the cold war itself came to an unexpected conclusion.

On the Soviet side, Brezhnev's Afghanistan commitment was continued by his successors Yuri Andropov (1914–1985) and Konstantin Chernenko (1911–1985) and liquidated by Gorbachev. The aging Brezhnev had also offered Soviet support to several Middle Eastern and African countries. The latter included Angola, where Soviet aid and Cuban troops were deployed in support of the revolutionary Angolan communist government against American–backed guerrillas. Closer to home, however, the Soviets watched narrowly as Poland's communist regime dealt with a militantly independent labor movement called Solidarity. Under the energetic leadership of Lech Walesa (1943–), Solidarity gained international celebrity in the early 1980s with its demands for lower food prices and more democracy. The independent union was subsequently banned but continued underground, only to emerge once more at the end of the decade in a startling reversal of fortune—to be dealt with shortly.

The foreign policy of Presidents Reagan and Bush included determined efforts to smother left–wing guerrillas and governments in Central America and the Caribbean. In 1983, Reagan dispatched troops to crush a divided communist government on the tiny island of Grenada. Throughout the decade, Reagan gave lavish aid to the liberal government of Napoleón Duarte (1926–) in El Salvador in his struggle with guerrillas, though the United States showed less concern about the depredations of right–wing El Salvadoran vigilante "death squads." In the early 1990s, however, both leftist guerrilla attacks and death–squad killings seemed to fade away.

While supporting the government in El Salvador, the Reagan administration worked to subvert the Sandinista revolutionary government in neighboring Nicaragua, which had overthrown the repressive regime of Anastasio Somoza (1925–) in 1979. The Sandinistas accepted both Cuban and Soviet help and themselves supported the guerrillas in El Salvador. Reagan responded by arming and supplying the anti–Sandinista Contra guerrilla movement in Nicaragua. The Contras, however, proved able only to disrupt the country, not to overthrow its government. In 1987, a peace plan proposed by President Oscar Arias (1941–) of neighboring Costa Rica urged greater democracy in Nicaragua and an end to all foreign involvement. And in 1990, the anti–Sandinista leader Violeta Chamorro won a free election in her battered country, replacing the Sandinistas in power.

◆Winding Down the Cold War◆

While these crises came and went over the cold war decades, other factors acted to defuse the long confrontation. Those factors included intermittent efforts by both sides to defuse conflict through disarmament or diplomatic campaigns for "peaceful coexistence." Finally, after forty–five tense and draining years, the cold war ended with the collapse of both the Soviet bloc in eastern Europe and the Soviet Union itself.

Détente and Disarmament

Most of America's postwar leaders clearly preferred peace to war with a nuclear–armed Soviet Union. The Soviet leadership also, having seen its country twice devastated by world wars in the twentieth century, evidently had no desire for a nuclear confrontation. While neither side wished to give up its principles or its vital national interests, both were willing at least to talk peace.

In the 1950s, Nikita Khrushchev proposed a policy of *peaceful coexistence*. The essence of this doctrine was that, while competition between the two social systems would continue, a military clash between them was to be avoided at all costs. Khrushchev abolished the Cominform and made jocular tours of the United States during the Eisenhower years. A nuclear test–ban treaty attempted to control the development of new nuclear weapons. The world may have come close to nuclear war during the confrontation between Kennedy and Khruschev over Soviet missiles in Cuba in 1962, but the crisis was resolved, and a telecommunications link was installed between the White House and the Kremlin for use in future crises.

In the 1970s, while Leonid Brezhnev ruled the USSR, the diplomatic term *détente*, meaning a relaxation of strained relations between nations, was commonly used to describe what seemed an essentially stalemated cold war. Brezhnev's arms buildup gave the USSR rough parity with the United States in nuclear weaponry, and it seemed wiser to both sides to agree to disagree rather than risk a war that could only destroy them both. President Nixon traveled to the Soviet Union as well as to China, and Brezhnev visited the United States. The SALT Treaty, the outcome of the Strategic Arms Limitation Talks held in 1969 and 1970, put limits on the rival nuclear arsenals. Prudence and pragmatism dominated relations between the great powers in the 1970s.

The 1980s—the Reagan–Bush years—began with some strong verbal attacks on communism and the Soviets, and the decade saw the United States embark on an arms buildup of its own. Reagan equipped NATO armies with a controversial new generation of nuclear missiles and launched an even more controversial *Star Wars plan* to put defensive nuclear, laser, and other futuristic weapons into space. Yet Reagan, too, ended his two terms as president with a series of summit meetings, a visit to the Soviet Union, and the signing of a historic agreement not merely to limit testing or stockpiles, but actually to remove an entire category of nuclear weaponry from the field. Bush forged close ties with Gorbachev and then diplomatically stayed out of the way while the Soviet empire unraveled at the end of the 1980s.

Efforts to improve relations, then, paralleled the struggle from the 1950s on. Soviet–American summit meetings, bilateral discussions between western European leaders and their counterparts in the Soviet Union and other eastern European countries, and other East–West meetings were highlights of the quest for peace. Trade, Western loans, joint industrial ventures, and other economic ties became commonplace. Cultural and scientific exchanges, meetings between scholars and other unofficial types, and even growing Western tourism in the USSR all helped to defuse tensions. Perhaps most important, economic and political changes in China, the Soviet Union, and other communist countries gave many Western people hope for an end to basic differences between them. And then, at the end of the 1980s and the beginning of the 1990s, the "long, twilight struggle" came to an abrupt end.

The End of the Cold War

Between 1989 and 1991, pro–Soviet governments were overthrown in satellite states from East Germany to Bulgaria, the Soviet Union itself crumbled as most of its component republics rejected Moscow's authority, and Stalinist communism ceased to be a viable force in the Western world. Attempts to explain this dramatic end to the cold war stress various factors. The economic weakness of the communist system undoubtedly made a central contribution to its undoing. Popular opposition to a coercive political system was perhaps equally important. In the satellite states, nationalistic resentment of Soviet hegemony undoubtedly helps to explain what happened. U.S. President Reagan's announcement of a new round of arms competition with his "star wars" initiative, confronting the already strained Soviet economy with a challenge it could not meet, probably also encouraged Soviet retreat. And one other individual clearly played a key role: the Soviet communist reformer Mikhail Gorbachev.

As we will see in the next chapter, which focuses on the domestic history of the nations of the Western world in the later twentieth century, Gorbachev launched the first reform drive in the USSR since Khrushchev fell from power two decades earlier. But Gorbachev's efforts at greater openness in Soviet society and at social restructuring of the communist state not only plunged the Soviet Union into disarray but also stimulated demands for change in the Soviet satellites as well.

The satellite empire unraveled first, during the dramatic "Revolutions of 1989" that some compared to the revolutions of 1848 in significance. Across eastern Europe, subject peoples began once more to demand changes in their own countries and an end to Soviet domination. First in Poland and Hungary, which had already expanded contacts with western nations, and then in more rigidly communist states like East Germany and Czechoslovakia, citizens vigorously expressed their discontent. Record numbers of people fled to the west, while unprecedented mass demonstrations clamored for democratic government and economic reform in the streets of eastern capitals. And this time the Soviet Union did not move to suppress dissent in the satellites. Instead, Gorbachev urged client governments in the eastern bloc to make concessions and undertake reforms like those he had initiated in the USSR. And when the populace demanded that their Communist leaders resign, Soviet troops stationed in these Warsaw Pact states stayed in their barracks and let pro–Soviet regimes fall one after another. The Warsaw Pact itself collapsed, and Soviet troops began to retreat behind the borders of the USSR for the first time since World War II.

The Soviet Union, meanwhile, underwent changes that undermined its ability to sustain the cold war any longer. Gorbachev had launched his reforms with the idea of strengthening communism, but halfhearted economic reforms only increased the nation's economic problems, while greater "openness" encouraged demands for an end to one–party rule. And as the iron grip of the Kremlin relaxed, the long–suppressed nationalistic feelings of the many peoples who had been governed by the Russians since czarist times burst into the open, as they had during the Civil War of 1918–1921 and the German invasion of 1941–1942.

Under this multitude of pressures, as we will see in the next chapter, Gorbachev finally permitted three rebellious Soviet republics—the Baltic states of Lithuania, Latvia, and Estonia—to secede outright from the USSR. Thereafter, however, the accumulating resentments of hard–line Communists, would–be reformers, and inflamed nationalists combined to destroy the Soviet Union. Gorbachev himself, briefly overthrown in a right–wing coup in the summer of 1991, was rescued by Boris Yeltsin (1931–), the elected leader of the Russian Republic, who replaced Gorbachev as the most powerful man in the state in the fall of 1991. On all sides, meanwhile, other republics seceded from the USSR. The Soviet Union was dissolved, and the so–called Commonwealth of Independent States (CIS) engineered by Yeltsin had no real power. The fifteen former member states of the USSR sank into a chaos of economic decline, nationalistic feuding, and in some places open warfare between rival national groups.The cold war thus ended with the dissolution of the Soviet eastern European empire and the collapse of the Soviet Union itself. The schism that had divided the Western world for half a century was over.

✦Colonies on the Eve of Independence✦

The second great global trend of the decades after World War II was the disintegration of the European overseas empires that had once ringed the world with Western power. Where before World War II there stood half–a–dozen European world empires, in the years after the war scores of separate nations appeared on the map. Most of them, furthermore, declared themselves "nonaligned" with either side in the cold war, thus creating a new, third grouping of the world's nations, the so–called "Third World."

This section will survey the empires as they looked to colonized peoples in the early decades of the twentieth century. It will then examine the impact of World War II on the colonies and profile the leaders and movements that liberated much of the world from Western rule after 1945.

Development and Independence Movements

The new imperialism was never as firmly in place as the maps made it look. Color keyed— pink for Britain and its empire, green for France and its colonies, and so on—the Western colonial holdings seemed to span the globe. With protectorates and even hazier spheres of influence shaded in, not much of the world remained free of Western control. And the simple fact of being depicted on a map, like oceans and mountain ranges, made it all seem natural and permanent, part of the eternal order of things. Early rebellions had failed, and Western rule in Asia and Africa might be expected to last as long as European power in the Americas had done—several centuries at least. But new expectations of change had been stirred at the end of the First World War, and efforts were already being made to realize those hopes between the wars.

In the colonial world, hope centered on the *mandate system* and on efforts at colonial development generally. Under the League's mandate arrangement, the British and the French were to develop formerly German colonies or Ottoman provinces economically and politically to the point where they could function effectively in the modern world and then to grant them their independence. Many Europeans and colonial peoples as well thought that all colonies should be treated in this way. And in fact, efforts were made to introduce new crops, to improve harbors and build roads, and otherwise to make colonial areas more profitable, primarily for their imperial rulers, but also for professional, planter, shopkeeper, or civil service elites among the native populations.

In many of Europe's far–flung imperial territories, however, the native people were unwilling to wait and doubted very much that it would do them any good if they did. Violent rebellions like the Maji–Maji revolt in German East Africa (Tanzania today) or the resistance of the Mandinke people, who had ruled much of French West Africa in the 1880s and 1890s, were bloody failures in the face of superior Western firepower. The future belonged instead to organizations like the *Congress party* in British India. Established by Indian professionals and business people in the late nineteenth century, membership in the Congress party was limited to urban dwellers and the upper classes until, shortly after World War I, Gandhi came upon the scene. A British–educated lawyer who had been running a civil rights campaign in South Africa, Mohandas K. Gandhi (1869–1948) returned to his homeland in the 1920s and over the next two decades mobilized a genuinely national movement against British rule.

An unimpressive–looking man with a profound awareness of the traditions of his own people, Gandhi adopted the costume and lifestyle of a Hindu holy man, a *mahatma* or "great soul," in order to rally India's hundreds of millions of villagers to the cause. Thoroughly knowledgeable about British ways and institutions, from the law to the importance of newspaper publicity, Gandhi embarrassed his colonial overlords again and again with protest marches, civil disobedience, and hunger strikes. In particular, Gandhi adapted the classic Indian doctrine of *ahimsa* (nonviolence) to active campaigns of civil disobedience. Images of the Mahatma with his spinning wheel, making his own garments rather than buying British–made clothing, or leading swelling marches halfway across India to make salt illegally were flashed around the world by Western journalists. So were pictures of Indians beaten or even shot down in the streets. By the time the Second World War broke out in 1939, Gandhi was a living saint to the Indian masses and to many Western liberals as well, and the demand for freedom from British rule rumbled through the subcontinent.

Political movements with similar objectives existed in other colonies too. In the wake of World War II, they emerged with a roar all across the colonial world.

World War II and the Overseas Empires

World War II itself considerably improved colonial chances of success. The world changed greatly between 1939 and 1945, and many of these changes significantly weakened the prewar imperial system.

In Asia particularly, the Japanese conquest of European and American colonies showed once more that the West could be beaten. Japanese rule proved no more popular than Western rule had been. But even colonial peoples who had fought the Japanese, like Ho Chi Minh in French Indochina (Vietnam today), did not do so in order to submit once more to their returning European rulers. In some places, like the Dutch East Indies (today's Indonesia), the retreating Japanese left weapons behind that the indigenous peoples made good use of in the struggles for national liberation that soon followed.

On the other side of the world, meanwhile, Europe's imperial powers were digging themselves out of their ruins. In 1945 the Western powers scarcely had the resources to suppress determined revolts in Africa or Asia. And some of the powers, at least, no longer had the will. Many liberals and socialists opposed imperialism on ideological grounds. As these Europeans and Americans saw it, it was hypocritical to dictate to millions of non–Westerners around the world while practicing democracy at home. Such imperial disasters of the postwar period as the Suez crisis or the Algerian revolution aroused bitter opposition within the leading imperial nations.

Another major change was the emergence of the United States and the Soviet Union as the superpowers of the postwar era. Neither of these two nations, as it happened, had either the need or the desire for old–fashioned overseas empires. The Soviet Union's satellites were almost all within Europe itself, and the United States kept only a few Pacific island bases out of the lands its armies liberated from the Germans and Japanese. America's democratic traditions had moved Roosevelt to urge Churchill to liquidate the British Empire even during World War II, and the United States continued to put pressure on imperial powers to let their colonies go after the war. Lenin, the founder of the Soviet Union, had written one of the most widely read anti–imperialist classics, *Imperialism, the Highest Stage of Capitalism* (1916), and after 1945 the Soviet Union offered some direct aid and a great deal of verbal support to national liberation struggles both at the United Nations and in other forums.

The Japanese example, the decline of the imperial powers, and the rise of superpowers who sought no large overseas colonies all changed the situation after World War II. The stage was thus set for a new challenge to the Western imperial order.

A New Generation of Leaders

Revolutionary movements proliferated across two continents in the postwar decade, led by a new generation of anti–imperialist militants. Many of these are great names in the histories of their countries today, the George Washingtons and Simón Bolívars of the non–Western world. Before we plunge into another round of revolutions, then, a few generalizations about the leadership and their movements may be useful.

The typical colonial leader of a liberation movement was a westernized non–Western person. Usually from the higher ranks of their own societies, they had often either lived or studied in Britain, France, the United States, or some other Western nation. Ho Chi Minh learned his socialism in Paris and worked his way around the world on Western steamships. The African liberation leader Kwame Nkrumah studied in both Britain and the United States. Like Gandhi, these leaders bestrode two cultures and understood the West well enough to meet Western imperial officials on their own ground and beat them by their own rules. Across the colonial world, this new generation of leaders mobilized their peoples for struggle. Sometimes mobilization meant underground cells, as in Algeria, or guerrilla armies, as in French Indochina, that launched terrorist campaigns or open revolution.

More often, legal nonviolent organizations, like the Congress party in India, challenged colonial governors with political campaigns, economic boycotts, and other European–style opposition. Such national liberation parties went beyond prewar organizations by reaching out to the villages and down to the subliterate masses. Transcending traditional divisions of class and religion, clan and tribal affiliation, liberation parties also provided a basis for national unity when independence was won.

Colonial peoples in the second half of the twentieth century were as eager to be free as Italians, Germans, and Slavs had been in nineteenth–century Europe, or as French, English, and Americans in earlier centuries. And they made as large an impact on the history of their times.

◆ The End of the Western Empires ◆

The great liberation was a phenomenon as astonishing as the Western expansion that had forged the empires in the first place. In the two or three decades after the Second World War, more than fifty new nations and a billion people, a third of the population of the world at that time, gained their independence from foreign rule. Old imperialists retired to sip sundowners on their verandas and talk about the good days when being a *pukka sahib* (real master) meant something. For yesterday's colonial subjects, now free people, it was a time of jubilation and hope.

This final section will follow the liberation movements from India and Pakistan in the 1940s through Southeast Asia to Israel and the Arab nations. It will then move on to Algeria and French West Africa, Britain's West and East African colonies, the Belgian Congo, and South Africa, freed of Western rule only in the last decade of the century.

The Liberation of India and Pakistan

India, long groomed for autonomy if not for independence, had in its Congress party an organized liberation movement with strong and experienced leaders ready to take the helm. The British Labor party, governing Britain after World War II, was ready to let the huge colony go free. But there was a snag: the large minority of Muslim Indians, fearing oppression in a predominantly Hindu India, demanded a separate state of their own. Although both the British and the Congress party opposed partition, terrible riots between Muslims and Hindus, costing hundreds of thousands of lives, forced the creation of two new states in 1947: Hindu India and Muslim Pakistan. In 1948, the large southern island of Ceylon became an independent nation, later renamed Sri Lanka, and in 1971 the separate territory of East Pakistan claimed its own independence as Bangladesh.

Four generations of impressive leaders led India's hundreds of millions through the interwar liberation movement and their first four decades as an independent nation. Mahatma Gandhi, the prophet, shrewd strategist, and guru to his people, was assassinated by a Hindu extremist who thought Gandhi was making too many concessions to the Muslims at the moment of his triumph. At Gandhi's side, and carrying the torch after he fell, was the handsome, sophisticated Jawaharlal Nehru (1889–1964), who became India's first prime minister and a founder of the nonaligned movement among non–Western nations. Nehru's daughter Indira Gandhi (1917–1984), no relation to Mohandas Gandhi, became the country's next important ruler; autocratic mother of Mother India and probably the toughest of the lot, she was murdered by Sikh terrorists at the height of her power. Her son, Rajiv Gandhi (1945–1991), an airline pilot with no political ambitions, nevertheless took up the family tradition of Congress party leadership when his mother was killed—only to fall to an assassin's bomb in 1991. All three governed by consent of the governed in a huge nation with many economic problems that still prided itself on being the world's largest democracy.

Under Nehru and the Gandhis, mother and son, India faced many challenges. Holding together, developing, even feeding the world's second most populous country were notable achievements. But difficulties continued to mount. There were several wars with Pakistan and conflicts with China over disputed frontier areas. The Sikh separatist movement spread violence in the Punjab region of northwestern India. The "green revolution" of fertilizers and pesticides increased agricultural yields but could scarcely keep up with the seemingly uncontrollable birth rate. Nevertheless, as Mahatma Gandhi had said, they were at least India's problems now, not those of the country's foreign rulers.

End of Empire in Southeast Asia

Southeast Asia, divided among British, French, and Dutch colonies, also unraveled rapidly after the war. The French, as we have seen, fought a long war in Vietnam and lost it. The British freed Burma and Malaya more willingly, though they delayed the liberation of Malaya until they had suppressed a communist insurgency there. The Netherlands proved unable to reclaim its vast Dutch East Indies empire against determined opposition: under the leadership of the colorful Sukarno (1901–1970), Indonesia became a free nation in 1949. The Philippines, acquired by the United States in the Spanish–American War, was given its independence in 1946, though U. S. forces stayed on to help put down the communist–led Huk guerrillas there.

Southeast Asia continued to see its share of problems long after the independence struggles were over. Violence still ravaged the region. In the years to come, America's destructive Vietnam War and the North Vietnamese victory spread a pall over Indochina. Pol Pot, maximum leader of Cambodia's Khmer Rouge, turned Cambodia into one of the Century's bloodiest "killing fields," slaughtering perhaps a million of his compatriots because he saw them as too "western." Indonesia also saw more than one wave of political violence, including the massacre of tens of thousands of communists by the archipelago's Muslim population. In Southeast Asia, as elsewhere, independence did not bring the millennium; but it did turn the nations back over to the people who lived there.

Israel and the Arab Nations

Even in the 1980s, however, there were regions where Western and non–Western peoples came into conflict in situations that still looked, to non–Westerners at least, very much like imperialism. The two most disturbing of these ongoing conflicts were between Israel and the Arab states of the Middle East and between South Africa and the black Africans of that part of the continent. In each case, a rich and technologically sophisticated Western people strove to control a rebellious non–Western population while resisting attacks by hostile neighbors. There were substantial differences between the two situations, of course, but the basic confrontation remained the same.

The bulk of the Jewish population of Israel were newcomers to their ancient homeland, immigrants from Europe, America, and elsewhere. Some had come earlier, inspired by the turn–of–the–century Zionist movement, which had urged Jews to leave an inhospitable Europe and return to the land of their ancestors in the Middle East. At the time of World War I, Britain's Balfour Declaration (1917) recognized the right of Jewish settlement in what became Britain's Palestine mandate after the war. Following World War II,

Chronology 27.2: End of the Western Empires

1940s–1950s	*Liberation of most Asian colonies*
1947	*Britain frees India and Pakistan; Hindu–Muslin riots cost many lives*
1948	*Israel founded; Arab–Israeli wars begin*
1949	*Indonesia liberated by the Dutch*
1950s–1960s	*Liberation of most African colonies*
1950s–1980s	*South Africa imposes apartheid on African majority*
1954	*French Indochinese colonies freed after long French Vietnam War*
1957	*Britain frees Ghana*
1960	*Belgium frees Congo (Zaire); Congolese civil war follows*
1962	*French Algeria liberated after bloody guerrilla war*
1963	*Britain frees Kenya after Mau Mau resistance movement*
1990, 1995	*Apartheid ends in South Africa; resistance leader Mandela elected president*

Jewish survivors of the Holocaust poured into Palestine, once more for them the Promised Land.

The Muslim Palestinians resisted the Jewish influx, and the British tried to stem the flow. The United Nations prescribed partition as a solution. Jewish terrorist and guerrilla organizations fought both British and Palestinians and rejected the UN solution. In 1948, Jewish leaders in Palestine proclaimed the new state of Israel, and all the surrounding Arab states attacked it.

The Israelis won and established their new state, with David Ben–Gurion (1886–1973) as its first prime minister. They then set to work with Western technology, money, and infinite energy to make the hills and deserts of the ancient lands of David and Solomon bloom again. Beyond the frontiers, a million displaced Palestinians settled into refugee camps, waiting and working for the day when they could return and reconquer the land they still called Palestine.

The seeds of all that followed were thus there at the beginning: Jews and Palestinians claiming the same land, hostile Arabs eager to fight, Israelis refusing to give an inch. Conflict, internal and external, became the essence of Israel's modern history.

Israel fought half a dozen wars with nearby Arab states over the next forty years. The 1948 war won the Israelis their country, which, supported by the United States, was soon admitted to the United Nations and widely recognized. In 1956, seeking to undermine Egypt's aggressively anti–Israeli leader, Gamal Abdel Nasser (1918–1970), Israel joined Britain and France in a military attempt to seize the Suez Canal from Egypt, which had nationalized it earlier that year. The allies failed of their objective, due partly to American opposition, and Nasser came out of the crisis even more popular with his people. In 1967, however, Israel launched a preemptive strike of its own on several of its neighbors. In this famous Six Day War, Israel took the Sinai in the south from Egypt, the West Bank of the Jordan River from the Kingdom of Jordan, and, after hard fighting, the rugged Golan Heights from Syria in the north.

Things were never to go quite so gloriously again. Nasser died soon after his humiliation in the Six Day War. In 1973, however, his successor Anwar Sadat (1918–1981) launched a surprise attack of his own on Israel, the Yom Kippur War, so called because it began on that Jewish holiday. Sadat recaptured much of the Sinai before Israel rallied and counterattacked successfully. Not having gained as much as he had hoped, the Egyptian leader next turned to diplomacy, offering to break the solid Arab front against recognizing the legal existence of Israel in return for lost Egyptian territory and discussions of a home for the Palestinians. These agreements, formalized under the auspices of U. S. President Jimmy Carter at Camp David outside Washington, D.C., in 1978, looked like a hopeful turning point.

The exiled Palestinians, however, had organized their own terrorist groups under an umbrella association called the *Palestinian Liberation Organization* (PLO) headed by Yasir Arafat (1929–). The PLO and its affiliates regularly attacked Israeli soldiers and civilians, hijacked airplanes, and carried their violence as far as Europe. In 1982, Israel invaded Lebanon to destroy the PLO bases and settlements there, shattering Beirut and allowing Israel's local allies to massacre Palestinians in their camps. The PLO, routed and split, nevertheless survived and continued to seek support for what it now referred to as an independent Palestinian state, which would coexist with Israel rather than replace it.

The internal struggle grew more apparent in the later 1980s. Israel, with a population of three and a half million Jews, now ruled two million Palestinians, most of them in the territories conquered in the Six Day War, the West Bank and the Gaza Strip on the edge of the Sinai. Treated as second–class citizens and generally much less well off than the prosperous majority population, these Palestinians of the occupied territories began a resistance movement of their own in 1987. This *intifada* (uprising), led by stone–throwing youths, attempted to disrupt Israeli society and defy the authorities. Harsh Israeli countermeasures killed hundreds of Palestinians and cost the beleaguered country many friends overseas.

The first real break in the deadlock between Israelis and Palestinians came with peace deals brokered in Washington in the early 1990s between Israel and both the neighboring Arab kingdom of Jordan and Arafat's PLO. As Israel "traded land for peace" by agreeing to Palestinian rule over most of the remaining territories conquered in the 1967 war, hopes for a final deal between Israel and its last remaining hostile neighbor, Syria, grew. The assassination of Israeli prime minister Yitzak Rabin, a leading advocate of peace, and the election of Benjamin Netanyahu, a hardline opponent of concessions to the Arabs, seemed to put the trend toward compromise at risk in 1996. In the long run, however, most authorities saw no alternative to peace, even in this tortured corner of the globe.

Algeria and French West Africa

North and West Africa were in large part ruled by France before World War II. Coming out of their Vietnamese fiasco in the 1950s, the French strongly resisted the liberation of their largest North African colony, Algeria. Defeated again by the Algerian revolution, they made more politic arrangements for the amicable emancipation of their West African colonies south of the Sahara.

France negotiated full independence for its two North African protectorates, Morocco and Tunisia, with minimal conflict. Algeria, however, was a large colony just across the Mediterranean, with more than a million French settlers. When a rebellion erupted in the Casbah, or native quarter, of Algiers in 1954, the French fought back. The Algerian National Liberation Front launched a wave of urban terrorism that led to cruel repression. A settler vigilante group called the Secret Army slaughtered Algerians indiscriminately. In France, popular outrage at reports of torture and military brutality in Algeria brought the Fourth French Republic down and General Charles de Gaulle back to power. As one man whose patriotism was unquestionable, de Gaulle was able to negotiate independence for Algeria in 1962.

South of the shimmering Sahara, the colonies of French Equatorial and French West Africa filled almost the entire westward bulge of the continent. Here France at last took a more conciliatory line. And shrewd black African politicians like Léopold Senghor (1906–) of Senegal and Félix Houphouët–Boigny (1905–) of Ivory Coast were ready to seize the opportunity. Men who had French educations and knew Paris and its politics as well as they did the grasslands and rain forests of West Africa, these were leaders who could work with French liberals and socialists toward a peaceful transition. By 1960, a dozen new countries had been granted their independence. They got it, furthermore, within the framework of a French Community that included large amounts of aid for the often poverty–stricken new nations.

These sizable but barren and sparsely populated lands had a hard time thereafter. Their boundaries, drawn by nineteenth–century Europeans with little knowledge of African realities, divided peoples with long histories of unity and lumped very different peoples in the same colonies, which now became nations. The land was not productive, natural resources as basic as water were lacking, and the Sahara continued to expand southward every year, from time to time producing terrible famines.

Nevertheless, continuing French aid and technology and the entrepreneurial vigor of many of the people made success stories out of such countries as Senegal and Ivory Coast. With politicians as good at the power game as Houphouët–Boigny, who was always welcome in the Elysée Palace in Paris or the White House in Washington, there seemed to be hope even for the least naturally endowed regions of Africa.

British Africa—Ghana to Kenya

The British colonies in West Africa were mere enclaves along the Guinea Coast, jutting up into French West Africa. On the other side of the continent, however, Britain's holdings stretched up the coast of East Africa from the Cape of Good Hope to Cairo. Almost all these British colonies were freed in the 1950s and 1960s.

Britain's West African colonies, with their torrid tropical climates and dense coastal mangrove forests, had attracted only small settler populations. There was thus no powerful resident British resistance to turning the land back to its native inhabitants of the sort that developed in French Algeria. The first successful liberation leader in British Africa, Kwame Nkrumah (1909–1972) of the Gold Coast, was a charismatic speaker and indefatigable organizer whose Convention People's party soon stretched from the capital to the farthest village. A campaign of strikes, boycotts of British goods, and other challenges forced the British Colonial Office to speed up its timetable for emancipation, and the Gold Coast became the independent nation of Ghana in 1957. Nigeria and other British West African possessions gained their freedom soon thereafter.

The colonies of British East Africa achieved independence in the following decade. Here the situation was complicated by the substantial numbers of white settlers who had acquired title to rich farmland in Kenya, Tanganyika, and other colonies. Nervous already about their land and even their safety in a black African country, the settlers of Kenya in particular were made even more fearful by the depredations of the terrorist Mau Mau organization. Under the leadership of Jomo Kenyatta (1894–1978), who had studied at the London School of Economics and was known at home as "shadow of the burning spear," an amicable separation was worked out. Further south, Julius Nyerere (1922–), a Catholic and a socialist, led Tanganyika (Tanzania, after union with Zanzibar) to freedom as "the teacher" of his people. In both countries, white settlers were seen as economic assets and were urged to stay on; Western tourists, who brought money, were warmly welcomed to the game preserves.

All these former British colonies faced typical African problems. Populations composed of peoples with widely varying cultural backgrounds, languages, clan and tribal loyalties, and Muslim, Christian, or animist faiths could not always coexist. There were cruel civil wars, as in Nigeria. There were military take–overs, as in Ghana and Uganda, where the brutal buffoon Idi Amin (1926–) provided colorful copy for the Western press until Julius Nyerere's army drove him into exile. There were unmet high hopes, as in Kwame Nkrumah's dream of African unity: Nkrumah himself, deposed by his generals, died in exile. Still, struggling with their own problems and learning to play the international game of trade and aid, these new nations, too, began their independent histories.

The Congo and Southern Africa

The major colonies of central and southern Africa were Belgian, Portuguese, and, again, British. Freedom spread more slowly down the African stem, but, in the later decades of the century, it did come.

The Belgian Congo sprawled across the huge, heavily forested basin of the Congo River in the center of Africa. It was many times the size of Belgium itself and extremely valuable to that country, thanks particularly to large deposits of copper and uranium. At the end of the 1950s, however, Belgium, frightened by turmoil in other African colonies, abruptly conferred independence on the unprepared Congo. At the same time, however, the copper–rich province of Katanga seceded, looking to a continuation of its lucrative relationship with Belgian mining companies. A confused and bloody civil war followed, rendered bloodier by the resumption of tribal feuding and finally ended by a United Nations intervention and a military take–over. Out of the agony of the Congo came the new nation of Zaire, with a military ruler and a hard economic struggle still ahead.

Portugal, the oldest imperial power in Africa, had two large but underdeveloped colonies on opposite sides of the southern stem of Africa, Angola and Mozambique. Here, a tangle of rival guerrilla groups fought the Portuguese for years. As in Algeria, there was a revolutionary feedback into Europe. Young Portuguese officers, disturbed at the repression that they had been ordered to carry out in Africa, went home and helped overthrow the authoritarian regime established by António Salazar (1889–1970) in the 1920s. A free Portugal then liberated Mozambique in 1974 and Angola in 1975.

Two of Britain's colonies in southern Africa, Northern and Southern Rhodesia, named for the imperialist Cecil Rhodes, also gained independence in the 1960s and 1970s. Northern Rhodesia, rich in copper like its neighbor Zaire, was freed without much difficulty in 1964 as the new nation of Zambia. The following year, however, the white minority of Southern Rhodesia unilaterally declared their independence from Britain. A white settler regime headed by Ian Smith (1919–) thus circumvented British plans to secure a more adequate black representation in government before independence. For the next decade and a half, Smith and Rhodesia resisted guerrillas and international pressure before finally accepting majority black rule in 1980. The new country, Zimbabwe, also did its best to keep the white settlers, with their skills and capital, from leaving; and many, including Ian Smith, did stay on.

South Africa and Apartheid

The Republic of South Africa, rich in natural beauty, in fertile land, and in minerals including gold and diamonds was the last and longest holdout. But the Western people who ruled it in the postwar decades did not see themselves as interlopers. Some of them had been there for well over three centuries and considered themselves to be "the white tribe," as African as the black population. African blacks did not agree—understandably, in view of the oppressive conditions under which the black majority of South Africans lived.

After World War II, the country's *Afrikaaners,* the Boers and Dutch of earlier times, won control of the government from the English–speaking whites and imposed the rigorous system of racial segregation and oppression called *apartheid* (separation of the races) on the four–fifths of the population who were not of European descent. Strict Calvinists who believed that their religion forbade mixing of the races, the Afrikaaners passed laws imposing their views on the nation. Whites, blacks, "coloreds" (people of mixed parentage), and Asians, mostly from India, were to live, work, marry, study in school, or play on the beaches separately. Separate, politically autonomous "homelands" were to be set up for black South Africans. Blacks had to carry passes in white zones and could be arrested without formal charges and punished without trial.

Blacks responded by organizing protest marches and public meetings, and when troops and police fired on them, they went underground. They organized guerrilla raids from neighboring black African countries and domestic terrorism within South Africa. The most widely known of these groups, the *African National Congress* (ANC), resembled the Palestinian Liberation Organization in maintaining its headquarters in exile while serving as a rallying point for compatriots living under Western rule.

South Africa, like Israel, was also surrounded by enemies. Such "front–line states" as Angola and Mozambique provided bases for ANC guerrilla and terrorist attacks. South Africa reacted by repeated raids of its own into these countries, by supporting black guerrillas trying to overthrow the governments of these states, and by annexing the neighboring trusteeship area of Namibia and spreading apartheid there. The Republic of South Africa's most powerful weapon, however, was economic. Because it was Africa's most developed nation, it provided jobs in its mines and fields, not only for black South Africans, but for migrant workers from the front–line states themselves. Its railways and ports also served the rest of southern Africa as a vital means for getting export goods to the sea. South Africa's wealth seemed to be great enough that it could survive economic boycotts of various sorts imposed by the rest of the world in an effort to compel the government to change its policies. Desmond Tutu, a black African bishop, won the Nobel Peace prize, but there was no peace in South Africa.

A major breakthrough, finally, came at the end of the 1980s when a new president, F. W. De Klerk, offered peace to the African militants who had resisted apartheid for so

Nelson Mandela (left), long-imprisoned leader of South Africa's anti-apartheid movement, is shown here rejoining the leadership of the struggle after his release from prison by President F. W. de Klerk. (Sygma.)

long. De Klerk repealed the racial laws of apartheid, legalized the outlawed African National Congress, and in 1990 freed the ANC's leader, Nelson Mandela, after three decades in prison.

Years of delicate negotiations between De Klerk and Mandela followed, punctuated by outbreaks of renewed violence between whites and blacks and between rival black tribal groupings. But in 1995, South Africa held its first free elections, and the black majority elected Nelson Mandela president of Africa's richest and most powerful country. Many problems remained to be solved before South Africa's peoples could be sure of a future together, but the colonial liberation struggle did seem to be over at last.

Summary

Through the second half of the twentieth century, the Western world was split in two by the "long twilight struggle" called the cold war. This international rivalry pitted the United States and its allies against the Soviet bloc and a number of other communist states. The primary dividing line ran dow the middle of Europe, but the struggle also extended to Asia, Africa, and Latin America.

The "iron curtain" that divided the two sides rattled down in the decade after World War II, when Stalin imposed Russian control on eastern Europe and the United States organized the North Atlantic Treaty Organization—NATO. Communist regimes also rose to power in China, North Korea, and North Vietnam in these years. The struggle that followed saw revolts suppressed by the two superpowers in both eastern Europe and Latin America. Both superstates, however, failed outside their zones, most notably when America sent troops into Vietnam and Russia intervened in Afghanistan.

The long conflict proved enormously costly to both sides. It ended in the years around 1990 with the collapse of the eastern bloc and the disintegration of the Soviet Union itself.

Meanwhile, another global struggle also tore at the Western nations—the collapse of the vast overseas empires that had been growing for the past five centuries. During the decades following World War II, dozens of European colonies in Asia and Africa broke free of Western rule.

Growing desire for independence, the weakness of the Western imperialists after the war, and the skill of a new generation of westernized anti–Western colonial leaders all contributed to the success of these revolts. Sometimes Western powers willingly granted colonies their freedom, as did Britain in India and the United States in the Philippines. In other cases, long and bloody national liberation struggles were necessary, as in the French struggles to retain their colonies in Indochina and Algeria. By the mid–1990s, however, the last bastions of European rule in former colonies had fallen.

Some Key Terms

African National Congress   695
Afrikaaner   695
ahimsa   687
apartheid   695
Berlin airlift   674
Berlin Wall   679
cold war   668
colonial liberation
   movement   668

Congress party   687
containment   672
détente   684
intifada   692
iron curtain   672
mandate system   687
NATO   676
Palestine Liberation
   Organization   692

peaceful coexistence   684
satellite states   673
Star Wars plan   684
Third World   669
Warsaw Pact   676

Notes

1. Joseph Stalin, quoted in Milovan Djilas, *Conversations with Stalin,* trans. Michael Petrovich (New York: Harcourt Brace Jovanovich, 1962), 114.

Reading List

Aron, R. *The Imperial Republic: The United States and the World, 1945–1973.* Translated by F. Jellinek. Englewood Cliffs, N.J.: Prentice Hall, 1974. French view of America's global role.

Beschloss, M. R. *The Crisis Years: Kennedy and Khrushchev, 1960–1963.* New York: Harper Collins, 1992. The confrontations that came closest to the brink of war.

Boahen, A. A., ed. *General History of Africa,* vol. 7, *Africa Under Colonial Domination, 1880–1935* Berkeley and Los Angeles: University of California Press, 1985. UNESCO series volume on the period of the new imperialism and after.

Brown, J. M. *Gandhi: Prisoner of Hope.* New Haven: Yale University Press, 1989. Balanced account of the mature Gandhi's struggle for a free India. See also E. Erikson, *Gandhi's Truth: On the Origins of Militant Nonviolence* (New York: Norton, 1969). A psychoanalytical study of the Indian leader and his movement. For illuminating essays, see D. Dalton, *Mahatm Gandhi: Nonviolent Power in Action* (New York: Columbia University Press, 1993).

Darwin, J. *Britain and Decolonization: The Retreat from Empire in the Post–War World.* New York: St. Martin's Press, 1988. See also P. J. Cain and A. G. Hopkins, *British Imperialism: Crisis and Deconstruction* (New York: Longman, 1993).

Davison, W. P. *The Berlin Blockade.* Princeton, N.J.: Princeton University Press, 1958. Analysis of one of the most dangerous confrontations of the postwar period. On the Berlin Wall, see C. Cate, *The Ides of August: The Berlin Wall Crisis, 1961* (New York: Evans, 1979).

Gaddis, J. L. *Strategies of Containment.* New York: Oxford University Press, 1983. Major interpretation of U. S. cold war policies. See also his earlier *The United States and the Origins of the Cold War, 1941–1947* (New York: Columbia University Press, 1972).

Gifford, P., and W. R. Louis, eds. *Decolonization and African Independence: The Transfers of Power, 1960–1980.* New Haven: Yale University Press, 1988. Valuable essays, with some focus on roots of postcolonial decline.

Gormly, J. L. *The Collapse of the Grand Alliance,* *1945–1948.* Baton Rouge: Louisiana State University Press, 1987. Brief synthesis from a multinational perspective.

Herring, C. G. *America's Longest War: The United States and Vietnam, 1950–1975.* New York: Random House, 1979. A good survey. Views critical of American intervention include F. FitzGerald, *Fire in the Lake: The Vietnamese and the Americans in Vietnam* (New York: Random House, 1973), and D. Halberstam, *The Best and the Brightest* (New York: Fawcett, 1973).

Horowitz, D. *The Free World Colossus.* Rev. ed. New York: Hill and Wang, 1971. Sees the United States as an actively counterrevolutionary force in the world, rather than merely reacting to Soviet expansionism. An earlier proponent of this view is W. A. Williams, *The Tragedy of American Diplomacy,* 2d ed. (New York: Dell, 1972). Accounts emphasizing Soviet expansive tendencies include H. Feis, *From Trust to Terror: The Onset of the Cold War, 1945–1950* (New York: Norton, 1970) and Gaddis (1972), cited above.

Kaiser, R. G. *Why Gorbachev Happened: His Triumphs and His Failures.* New York: Simon and Schuster, 1991. An American journalist's view, based on years as a correspondent in Moscow.

Kaufman, B. I. *The Korean War: Challenges in Crisis, Credibility, and Command.* Philadelphia: Temple University Press, 1986. Political as well as military dimensions of the struggle between the two halves of divided Korea.

Kedourie, E., ed. *Nationalism in Asia and Africa.* New York: World Publishing Co., 1970. Analytical essays. See also R. Emerson, *From Empire to Nation: The Rise to Self–Assertion of Asian and African Peoples* (Cambridge, Mass.: Harvard University Press, 1960).

Kennan, G. *Russia and the West Under Lenin and Stalin.* Boston: Little, Brown, 1961. Diplomatic history by the architect of the U. S. containment policy.

Kennedy, D. *Islands of White: Settler Society and Culture in Kenya and Southern Rhodesia, 1890–1939.* Durham, N.C.: Duke University Press, 1987. Psychological study of reactionary settler communities in British Africa.

Lenczowski, G., ed. *The Political Awakening in the Middle East*. Englewood Cliffs, N.J.: Prentice Hall, 1970. Nationalism and anti–imperialism in Muslim lands. For an admired liberation leader, see J. Lacoutre, *Nasser* (New York: Knopf, 1973).

Maloba, W. O. *Mau Mau and Kenya: An Analysis of a Peasant Revolt*. Bloomington: Indiana University Press, 1993. Complex social movement analyzed in terms of nationalisms in conflict.

Thomas, H. *The Cuban Revolution*. London: Weidenfeld and Nicolson, 1986. Impressively researched treatment of a controversial subject. See also G. A. Geyer, *Guerrilla Prince: The Untold Story of Fidel Castro* (Boston: Little, Brown, 1991), a vivid journalistic portrait based on extensive interviews.

Ulam, A. *Expansion and Coexistence: The History of Soviet Foreign Policy, 1917–1967*. New York: Holt, Rinehart, 1974. Traces Soviet policy from the Revolution to the height of the cold war.

28

Fat Years, Lean Years

An Age of Affluence and Uncertainty

+Political Trends in the U.S. and Western Europe, 1940s–1990s
+Political Trends in the USSR and Eastern Europe, 1940s–1990s
+The Western Economy: Welfare Capitalism
+Western Society: Shifting Foundations

The domestic history of most of the Western nations in the second half of the twentieth century was quite different from that of the first half. On the political side, Western history from 1945 into the later 1990s was a story of democratic success in America and western Europe and authoritarian failure in eastern Europe—followed by confusion and disarray as the century ended. Economically, this half–century saw capitalism deliver fat years—the most affluent ever—and lean years, while communism went in for big projects, failed at consumer basics, and eventually collapsed.

We will look first at the political history of the major nations and regions of the Western world during these fifty years. This history shows a pattern of democracy surviving all challenges across the western half of the Western world. Toward the end of the century, furthermore, the eastern half also groped its way to representative government, though with what long–term success only the future could say.

Economically, the United States and western Europe advanced during the decades after 1945 to higher levels of productivity and affluence than they had ever known. After a quarter–century of growth, however, the Western economy experienced a significant downturn in the 1970s and 1980s. Eastern Europe, dominated by the Soviet Union, recovered more slowly from the war and advanced more slowly thereafter, only to shift course toward the free market and plunge into a painful transition period in the 1990s.

We will notice social problems during this era too, some of growing seriousness. Population growth came under control in the West, but migration from less economically favored parts of the world swelled, and the modern industrial city shifted toward the suburbs. Social conflict did not disappear, though youth revolts, the ongoing women's movement, and ethnic conflicts made more headlines than class struggle.

◆Political Trends in the U. S. and Western Europe, 1940s–1990s◆

In the United States, western Europe, and the Commonwealth countries, democratic governments were either well established or emerging after the war. As their economies boomed, the western democracies moved to expand their systems of government–supported social programs, from public health and higher education to unemployment compensation and substantial old–age pensions.

Country by country, it was a more varied pattern. The United States for the most part continued the reforms of the New Deal through the postwar decades, then veered to the right in the 1980s and 1990s. West Germany found strong leaders throughout this period as it became an exemplary democracy. France and Britain alternated socialist and conservative governments. Northern Europe prospered, southern Europe struggled to catch up, and the Commonwealth countries continued to face their problems and generally to solve them.

The United States: Fair Deal to Great Society

The United States remained the world's wealthiest and most powerful nation throughout this period. There were differences, however, between the earlier and later decades. The years between 1945 and 1968, under primarily Democratic leadership, were the most prosperous in U. S. history, and among the most prolific in social reforms. The 1970s and 1980s were dominated by Republicans and saw a reassertion of conservatism in the face of some difficult times for the country.

Franklin Roosevelt, his health undermined by guiding the nation through twelve of the most momentous years in American history, died suddenly in 1945, shortly after his re-election to an unexampled fourth term. His vice–president and successor, Harry Truman (president 1945–1953), a Missouri politician chosen to balance the ticket, turned out to be a feisty liberal who kept the New Deal in power for another seven years under the new rubric of *Fair Deal*. By the early 1950s, however, the country, disturbed by the growing power of the Soviet Union, chose former general Dwight Eisenhower (president 1953–1961), supreme commander of the Allied forces in Europe in the late war, as the first Republican president since the Depression. Though a Republican, "Ike" was not a partisan politician and made no effort to disassemble the New Deal.

The 1960s, the Kennedy–Johnson years, belonged to liberal Democrats again. Handsome, rich, sophisticated young John Kennedy (president 1961–1963), the first Catholic president, announced a stirring New Frontier of social change but found it difficult to get his program through Congress. Assassinated before the end of his term, Kennedy left more promises than accomplishments. Lyndon Johnson (president 1963–1969), an old New Dealer from Texas and an aggressive political operator, added substantially to the New Deal legacy of social legislation. By attempting to fight a war in Vietnam while building what he called the *Great Society* at home, however, Johnson both strained the nation's economy and stirred up a divisive antiwar movement. Thereafter, liberalism split among a variety of special–cause groups—ethnic, gender–related, environmental—allowing Republicans to dominate the White House for the next two decades.

The postwar years also saw a surge of anticommunist conservatism in the 1950s, when Senator Joseph McCarthy (1908–1957) and the House Un–American Activities Commit-

Chronology 28.1: The West in the Boom Years

1945–1974	Boom years in North America and Western Europe follow World War II
1945–1951	Atlee introduces the welfare state in Britain
1945–1953	Truman continues New Deal reforms
1948	Marshall Plan helps Western Europe rebuild after the war
1949–1963	Adenauer guides West Germany's "economic miracle"—postwar recovery—and builds democracy
1953–1964	Khruschev brings "thaw" to post–Stalin Soviet Union
1957	Common Market brings free trade and prosperity to western Europe
1956–1968	Civil rights movement in United States
1958–1969	De Gaulle founds Fifth French Republic
1963–1969	Johnson's Great Society reforms in United States
1968	Youth revolt at its height from Paris to Beijing

tee (HUAC) searched without much success for communists in government, the entertainment industry, the universities, and the military. At the same time, however, the period saw a substantial expansion of the American welfare state. Social security benefits were extended, while unemployment payments, food stamps for the poor, aid for mothers with dependent children, and aid for education all added to the structure of services. Harry Truman integrated the U. S. Army, the Supreme Court outlawed segregated education, and in the 1960s civil rights legislation sought to assure other basic rights for African Americans. A revival of the women's movement led in the 1970s and 1980s to an "affirmative action" campaign to require fair treatment for women in the workplace and elsewhere.

The most impressive grass–roots reform drive of the Kennedy–Johnson years was the African–American *civil rights movement* led by the Reverend Martin Luther King, Jr.

Martin Luther King, Jr., told the 1963 civil rights March on Washington, "I have a dream" of a racially integrated nation. The African American civil rights movement of the 1960s was the centerpiece of a decade of social activism in the United States.

(1929–1968), a gifted orator and crusader for black rights from Atlanta. During the 1960s King, a student of Mohandas Gandhi, the martyred leader of India's independence movement (see Chapter 27), resorted to nonviolent direct action. He and other African American civil rights leaders used boycotts, protest marches, sit–ins, and "freedom rides" into the segregationist south to compel the liberals in Washington to take action. Supported by white liberals and others, black Americans thus won their constitutional rights to equal access to public transportation, restaurants, housing, educational opportunities, and nondiscriminatory employment and promotion, as well as practical implementation of their basic right to vote.

In the 1960s also, some young white Americans, inspired by King and his youthful black cohorts, evolved a "new left" perspective on a broader front, triggering what became the largest wave of youthful political activism in American history. Young organizers supported President Johnson's "war on poverty" in the mid–1960s by trying to rally the poor themselves to demand reform. More successful, the youthful anti–Vietnam War movement of the later 1960s and early 1970s brought large numbers of students into the streets to protest U. S. involvement. In 1968, however, both Martin Luther King and Robert Kennedy (1925–1968), the slain president's brother and political heir, were murdered. After the election of the conservative Richard Nixon that year, followed by the winding down of the war in Vietnam, the youth revolt faded away.

The prosperity of the post–World War II period and the continuing Roosevelt coalition of blue–collar workers, blacks, and the solidly Democratic south kept the Democrats in power through the late sixties. For the next twenty years, however, prosperity gave way to an unsettled, sometimes deeply depressed economy. At the same time, the Democratic coalition fractured, and Republicans controlled the presidency.

America's Conservative Resurgence

American politics from the presidency of Richard Nixon through the administrations of Ronald Reagan and George Bush was dominated by national economic problems, personal enthusiasm for making money, and a revival of old–fashioned flag–waving patriotism and born–again Christian religious feeling. But there were some striking differences between the Nixon administration and the Reagan–Bush years.

Richard Nixon (president 1969–1974), who had been an anticommunist crusader in his early years in politics and as Eisenhower's vice–president in the 1950s, turned out to be a pragmatist in the White House. Through the early 1970s, he ended the Vietnam War and improved relations with both the Soviet Union and China. In domestic affairs, however, Nixon's struggle with the antiwar movement and with liberals in general led his subordinates to a variety of illegal actions against their political foes, including the planting of electronic listening devices in the Democratic party headquarters in the Watergate building in Washington. After the long *Watergate* crisis of the early 1970s, a combination of investigative journalism and congressional probes uncovered enough evidence to send many of the president's men to jail and to force Nixon himself to resign in order to escape impeachment.

Through the later 1970s, two thoroughly decent presidents, Republican Gerald Ford (president 1974–1977) and Democrat Jimmy Carter (president 1977–1981), restored some measure of faith in American government. But liberal political activists found little support for sixties–style crusades to win rights and recognition for women, homosexuals, blacks, Native Americans, Latinos, and other groups. And these new initiatives cost the American left support among middle– and working–class Americans.

Then in the 1980s, Ronald Reagan (president 1981–1989), a movie actor turned politician with an instinct for what the American public wanted to hear, presided over a re-birth of conservatism in the United States. The Roosevelt coalition collapsed entirely as blue–collar workers and white southerners moved to the right. A new alliance emerged, based on desire for rapid economic advancement, patriotism, religious revivalism, and "moral majority" demands for an end to legal abortions, a resumption of prayer in public schools, and suppression of sexually explicit fiction, films, and recordings. Larger conserva-tive goals such as cutting welfare services and whittling away both the size of the bureau-cracy and the cost of government had mixed success. Some benefits were cut, but the civil service did not shrink and the national debt skyrocketed due in large part to the huge cold war arms buildup mentioned in the previous chapter.

Reagan left to George Bush (president 1989–1993), his vice–president and successor, a reservoir of goodwill and a tangle of economic and social problems. The country was richer in 1990 than it had ever been—yet the national debt was so high that the govern-ment had little money to spend on multiplying national problems. The gap between rich and poor had also widened steadily during the 1970s and 1980s, creating dangerous social tensions. Economic growth had continued longer under Reagan than under any other president, yet there were more homeless Americans at the end of the 1980s than there had been since the Great Depression. Other major social problems included the scourge of drugs that ravaged the inner cities, bringing waves of violent crime, and the epidemic of AIDS (Acquired Immune Deficiency Syndrome), an almost invariably fatal disease spread primarily through sexual intercourse and intravenous drug use, for which no cure was known.

Sound and Fury in the 1990s

The early 1990s were a time of political confusion in the United States. Politicians—and non–politicians—of many stripes claimed a "mandate," but none held the attention of the voters for long. The Democratic party won little popular support for large–scale govern-ment intervention to deal with the nation's problems. The Republicans, on the other hand, seemed to generate more oppositionist sound and fury than unified conservative action.

The 1992 presidential campaign saw the victory of Democrat Bill Clinton, a young southern governor dedicated to social and economic reform who, with his wife, attorney Hillary Rodham Clinton, and youthful running mate Senator Al Gore, projected an image of youth and energy that reminded many of the Kennedy years. Activist government seemed to be popular in America once more, though the huge national debt inherited from the Reagan years and the continuing budget deficits of the 1990s made programs much more difficult to finance than they had once been.

The Republicans, however, succeeded in defeating a major Clinton health care pro-gram, and in 1994 won control of both houses of Congress. Under the energetic leader-ship of House Speaker Newt Gingrich, they then labored to pass a range of conservative anti–state measures, from a balanced budget amendment to the Constitution to the devo-lution of power from federal to state governments. On every side, angry voices thundered against welfare for the poor, affirmative action programs for minorities and women, the de-cline of the American family, and the "Washington insiders" who were held responsible.

President Clinton seemed to some to be abandoning the New Deal liberal tradition when he responded to Republican victories by offering moderately conservative measures of his own—and labeling Republican conservatism as "right-wing radicalism." Gingrich played into the president's hands by refusing to pass revenue measures, thus paralyzing the government. By 1995, a reviving economy and Clinton's conservatism pointed the way to his reelection.

The New Germany: Democracy and Prosperity

America's three leading allies in Europe—West Germany, France, and Britain—also experienced alternations between left- and right-wing rule in generally efficiently functioning democratic governments. Perhaps the biggest success, however, was that of West Germany, which in the second half of the century converted to democracy and emerged as one of the most economically productive states in the world.

The evolution of the Federal Republic of Germany from authoritarianism to democracy seems to have passed through four stages. The first was the fifteen-year period after the three western zones of occupation were fused in 1949, when democratic institutions were imposed by the Allies but run by the autocratic Konrad Adenauer (chancellor 1949–1963). Former anti–Nazi Catholic mayor of Cologne and head of the conservative Christian Democratic party, *der Alte* (the old man) projected the image of authority and strength that Germans needed to develop confidence in democracy. Adenauer and his finance minister Ludwig Erhard (1897–1977) also provided the stability and free–market stimulus that generated the nation's postwar "economic miracle." This amazing recovery was built on large reserves of managerial and technical skill, plenty of capital investment, and a booming foreign market for quality German manufactures, from cars to cameras. The resulting economic surge produced a sleekly modern new Germany rising on the ruins of the old.

The second stage in Germany's democratic evolution came in the 1960s, when younger Germans especially revealed a greater willingness to mobilize for political action, demonstrating more confidence in their democratic government. A youthful German assault on the right–wing periodical press proved at least that German democracy could cope with dissidents without turning back to totalitarian methods.

A third stage began in the 1970s. West Germany's largest problem remained its relations with "the other Germany" to the east. Deciding that "little steps" toward closer relations with East Germany were at least a beginning, Willy Brandt, a socialist who had been the anti–Stalinist mayor of West Berlin, embarked on a new *Ostpolitik* (Eastern policy) in the 1970s. Brandt arranged mutual recognition of the two Germanies, guarantees of access to Berlin, and acceptance of the German borders that had come out of World War II.

As in the United States, however, the 1980s and 1990s saw a conservative resurgence in Germany. The economic miracle was shaken by declining growth rates and rising unemployment, and radical terrorist gangs kidnapped German businessmen and planted bombs at NATO bases. In 1982, then, the Christian Democrats swept back into power under Helmut Kohl (chancellor 1982–), a big, plain–speaking man with the ability to empathize with the average German in the streets.

The conservative Kohl, strongly anti–Soviet, nevertheless took the lead in offering financial aid to encourage Mikhail Gorbachev's reforms in the later 1980s. And when the Berlin Wall came down in 1989, Kohl and his foreign minister Hans–Dietrich Genscher moved decisively to achieve West Germany's greatest foreign policy goal—reunification with East Germany. In the fall of 1990, the two Germanies were reunited and Helmut Kohl was elected chancellor of a German Republic united for the first time in half a century.

In the 1990s, Kohl turned his primary attention to greater unity for Europe as a whole. Working closely with the French Socialist president, François Mitterand, the German Chancellor labored to transform the western European customs union, popularly called the Common Market, into a European Union with a single currency, a free flow of capital and labor, a common passport, and stronger all–European governing institutions.

In the middle nineties, however, Germany faced serious economic problems, including an unemployment rate of 11 percent—twice as high as America's—and labor costs (including large fringe benefits) that rose 20 per cent in the first half of the decade—while their American competitors saw the labor bill decline by 10 percent. Other sources of mounting discontent included opposition to the high cost of rebuilding the East German provinces, and a resurgence of nationalistic resentment of foreign "guest workers" in Germany.

Germany was clearly Europe's strongest power. How effectively even Kohl could rebuild German confidence and bring an increasingly discontented Europe together, however, remained in doubt.

France: Gaullism to Socialism

French recovery was slower than Germany's. Once it came, however, France became the second most prosperous of European powers and shared with Germany a central role in European affairs. Under both conservatives like General De Gaulle and socialists like François Mitterand, France developed one of the most successful economies and full–service welfare states in Europe.

Humbled by its wartime experiences, France seemed to have little economic drive or political direction in the immediate postwar years. The post–1945 Fourth French Republic sank into a pattern of unstable coalition governments that seldom held power long enough to effect useful change. Two long and bloody wars that cost France its colonies in Indochina and Algeria further undermined the nation's self–confidence through the later 1940s and the 1950s. French industry, rebuilding after the war, did begin to move for the first time into modern production methods, while an accelerating French birth rate provided increased economic demand. But real revival did not come until the 1960s and 1970s under Charles de Gaulle (president 1944–1946, 1958–1969) and his successors.

De Gaulle, head of the Free French forces during World War II and a dedicated believer in the glory of the French nation, was as autocratic as Adenauer, and like him laid the foundations for confident democracy in his country. De Gaulle served as president briefly right after the war and was called back to power in 1958, when an Algerian revolt had kindled a settler reaction in the colony and filled the streets of Paris with antiwar demonstrators. De Gaulle gave France a new constitution, creating the Fifth Republic and giving real authority to the president rather than the premier. Through the 1960s, "the general" worked to rebuild French pride and to reestablish the nation's place in the world. Rejecting the leadership of both the United States and the Soviet Union, he charted an independent course for France. In particular, he worked with Adenauer to establish a close Franco––German working relationship that finally buried ancient enmities between the rivals across the Rhine.

In 1968, the French version of the world–wide youth revolt of the 1960s—a protest against France's rigidly centralized, dehumanizing educational system—took to the streets. The upheaval loosened de Gaulle's autocratic grip on the country, and he retired at the end of the 1960s. Through the 1970s, his political heirs ruled, coping as best they could with the economic problems of the decade. In 1981, however, the Gaullists lost to the Socialists, and François Mitterrand (president 1981–1995), a veteran of the French resistance and a thorough pragmatist, took over the leadership of the country.

Mitterand's socialist goals led him to nationalize leading French industries, to increase benefits for workers hurt by the economic downturn, and even for a time to take several communists into his cabinet. The economic decline that struck the West in the 1970s and 1980s, however, soon led Mitterrand to turn to policies of welfare austerity and encouragement of business growth not dissimilar to the policies of conservatives like Helmut Kohl in Germany and Margaret Thatcher in Britain. In foreign affairs, the French leader supported Reagan's firm stand on the defense of Europe and continued to cultivate the Franco–German friendship that made the two countries the twin pillars of the new Europe.

The 1989 national celebration of the two hundredth anniversary of the French Revolution revealed a prosperous, stylish, self–confident France. Economic and social problems, however, mounted during the earlier 1990s, as France faced an unemployment rate as high as 12 percent, twice America's. Popular resentment of Arab Muslim immigrants mounted, stimulated further by a 1995 rash of bombings apparently instigated by Islamist militants. When in 1995 Mitterand's conservative successor, Jacques Chirac, attempted to cut back

The Paris revolt of May, 1968, was in many ways the climax of the tumultuous youth revolts of the 1960s. Here the Paris police square off against demonstrators in one of the many melees that reestablished the city's reputation as the revolutionary capital of Europe. (Sygma.)

on the French welfare system, claiming that the government could no longer afford it, students demonstrated and striking workers paralyzed the country for weeks at a time.

Britain: Welfare State to Enterprise Culture

Britain's two most important leaders of the second half of the twentieth century were the Labor party head Clement Attlee (prime minister 1945–1951) who built the British welfare state in the 1940s, and the Conservative leader Margaret Thatcher (prime minister 1979–1990), who tore a good part of it down in the 1980s. In between, the nation that had once been the world's greatest imperial power, the founder of modern liberalism and the Industrial Revolution, struggled to keep its head above water.

Attlee nationalized such major industries as railroads, coal, and much of the steel industry, extended educational opportunities—and hence opportunities for successful careers—to more people, and established the British national health service that provided medical care for all Britons. Like Eisenhower, who left the New Deal in place when he became U. S. president, Winston Churchill and the Conservatives who returned to power in Britain in the 1950s left Labor's structure of state–owned industry and expanded welfare benefits pretty much alone. Problems, however, continued to beset the country. Bled white by the war and losing its empire in the decades that followed, the nation also faced declining productivity, many strikes, and the worst relationship between working–class and middle–class people anywhere in Europe. Britain was even torn by problems of race relations as immigrants from former colonies flooded into the country. Only with much hesitation did Britain join the Common Market, and it tended to cling to the original "special relationship" with America and to regard itself as outside the continent—while its living standards declined toward those of southern Europe.

Margaret Thatcher came to power in 1979 committed to changing and revitalizing the British economy by reemphasizing free enterprise. "The iron lady," as she was called, was tough and determined, condemned for her autocratic manner but admired for firmness and leadership. She worked diligently to slim down British industry to make it internationally competitive again, even though this meant unemployment levels comparable to those of the 1930s. She cracked down on high union wage demands and strikes that crippled the nation. She also tried to cut back on bureaucracy and on the cost of welfare services, to sell nationalized industries back to private owners, and generally to replace socialism with what she called the *enterprise culture*.

In international affairs, Thatcher fought and won what looked to critics like an imperialist war to protect a handful of British colonials in the Falkland Islands against a claim to sovereignty by nearby Argentina. Her conservative nationalism, however, also led her to resist the growth of European unity and the expansion of the Common Market. Her anticommunist political stance matched Reagan's, but she, like other European leaders, felt that she could "do business with Gorbachev" in the 1980s.

Like Reagan's America, Thatcher's Britain suffered from a deep divide between rich and poor, between the enterprise culture in the prosperous southeast around London and the large numbers of unemployed in the north. Margaret Thatcher finally fell from power in 1990, rejected by her own party and by much of the electorate over an unpopular tax policy. For a long decade, she had given Britain once again a leading voice in world affairs, but she had not solved her country's economic problems.

By 1996, then, her less dynamic Tory successor, John Major, faced the likelihood of defeat in the next election. The opposition had found a charismatic and tough–minded new leader in Tony Blair. Blair's Labor party had taken over the center of British politics, abandoning long–held socialist policies to speak for the average, deeply dissatisfied British voter. As in France, a change seemed likely—but this time from the more conservative to the more liberal party.

Western Europe: Prosperity and Problems North and South

The smaller states of western Europe flourished in the postwar period. The prosperous northern countries, from Scandinavia to the Netherlands, recovered from the Second World War, preserved or developed democratic institutions, and survived the depressed times of the 1970s and 1980s with relatively little difficulty. And even the poorer Mediterranean states in the south, such as Italy and Spain, developed more effective representative government and increased prosperity in the 1970s and 1980s.

Productive and prosperous, democratic, egalitarian, and boasting well–developed welfare services, the nations of northern Europe were some of the pleasantest places in the world to live in during this period. These included Scandinavia (Norway, Sweden, and Denmark, but also Finland and Iceland), the Benelux countries (the three neighboring states of Belgium, the Netherlands, and Luxembourg), and two Alpine states, Switzerland and Austria. Both the Scandinavian and Benelux countries had their own economic unions, though some of them also joined the Common Market. Sweden, Norway, and Austria experimented with participatory management, the participation by workers in the managing of factories and other industrial organizations, and succeeded in maintaining high employment even after the economy began to decline in the 1970s. All of them, however, preserved their capitalist economies and encouraged collaboration rather than conflict between labor unions and management.

Southern Europe, economically backward and ruled by despots before World War II (see Chapter 25), suddenly burst into the modern world in the 1970s. Italy's most striking achievement was this economic advance. From a European backwater, northern Italian industry, producing high–quality goods from automobiles to typewriters, pulled the rest of the country up and began to locate more manufacturing in the underdeveloped south. With a multiparty system dominated by the Social Democrats, Italy also had Europe's largest Communist party outside the Soviet bloc. The Italian Communists, however, were independent of Soviet influence and quite willing to oppose Moscow publicly over such matters as Soviet intervention in Czechoslovakia in 1968 or Afghanistan in 1979.

Revolutions toppled dictatorships in Greece and Portugal in 1974 and 1975, while Francisco Franco's death in the latter year turned Spain over to King Juan Carlos (r. 1975–), who proceeded to introduce democracy to that troubled country at last. Spain and Portugal particularly were soon experiencing rapid economic growth. The historic gap between the bustling north and the autocratic and somnolent south thus seemed to be narrowing in the 1990s.

The next two decades, however, saw many of the same problems that we have noticed in other Western lands appearing in these lesser European countries too. Higher unemployment, budget–busting increases in the cost of the welfare state, and resentment of foreign immigrants, especially from poorer countries in North Africa or the Middle East, all led to tensions and political strains. High prices and joblessness jolted Spain, Austria devel-

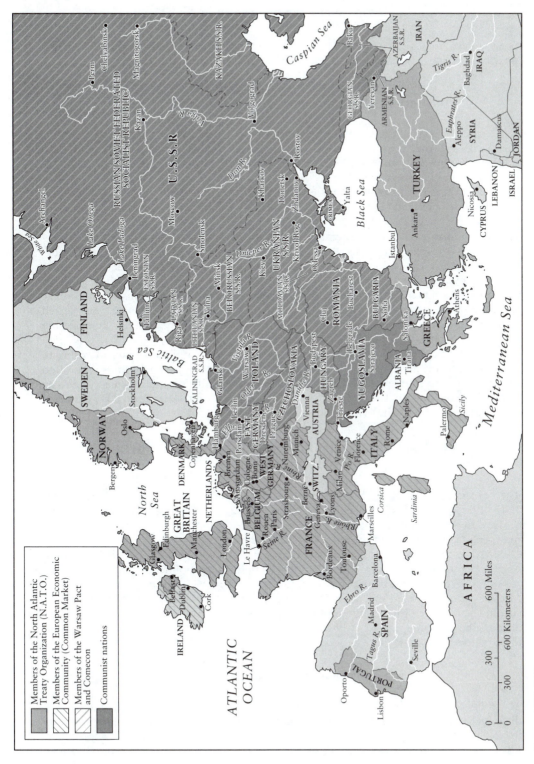

Members of the North Atlantic Treaty Organization (N.A.T.O.)

Members of the European Economic Community (Common Market)

Members of the Warsaw Pact and Comecon

Communist nations

ATLANTIC OCEAN

IRELAND
Dublin
Belfast
Cork

GREAT BRITAIN
Glasgow
Edinburgh
Manchester
London

North Sea

NORWAY
Bergen
Oslo

SWEDEN
Stockholm

DENMARK
Copenhagen

Baltic Sea

FINLAND
Helsinki

NETHERLANDS
Amsterdam
Le Havre
Rouen
Seine R.
Paris

BELGIUM
Brussels

Cologne
Bremen
Hamburg
Elbe R.
Berlin
Potsdam
EAST GERMANY
Dresden
WEST GERMANY
Bonn
Nuremberg
Munich
Prague
CZECHOSLOVAKIA

FRANCE
Strasbourg
Bordeaux
Toulouse
Lyons
Rhône R.
Marseilles
Geneva
Berne
SWITZ.
Milan
Po R.
Venice
Trieste
Florence
Rome
Naples
ITALY

Corsica

Sardinia

Sicily
Palermo

PORTUGAL
Oporto
Lisbon
Tagus R.

SPAIN
Madrid
Barcelona
Seville
Ebro R.

AFRICA

Mediterranean Sea

Bay of Biscay

White Sea
Archangel

Lake Onega
Lake Ladoga
Leningrad
Riga
LATVIAN S.S.R.
LITHUANIAN S.S.R.
ESTONIAN S.S.R.
Tallinn
KALININGRAD S.S.R.
Gdansk

POLAND
Warsaw
Vistula R.
Oder R.
Wroclaw

Perm
Chelyabinsk
Magnitogorsk
KAZAKH S.S.R.

U.S.S.R.
RUSSIAN SOVIET FEDERATED SOCIALIST REPUBLIC
Moscow
Kazan
Volga R.
Smolensk
Minsk
BELORUSSIAN S.S.R.
Kiev
Dnieper R.
UKRAINIAN S.S.R.
Lvov
Krivoi Rog
Odessa
MOLDAVIAN S.S.R.
Kharkov
Donetsk
Zhdanov
Rostov
Don R.
Volgograd

CRIMEA
Yalta

Black Sea
Istanbul

Caspian Sea
Baku
AZERBAIJAN S.S.R.
GEORGIAN S.S.R.
ARMENIAN S.S.R.
Yerevan

TURKEY
Ankara

Nicosia
CYPRUS

IRAN
Tigris R.
Baghdad
IRAQ
Euphrates R.
Aleppo
SYRIA
Damascus
LEBANON
ISRAEL
JORDAN

HUNGARY
Budapest
Vienna
AUSTRIA
Zagreb
Danube R.
Cluj
ROMANIA
Bucharest
Belgrade
YUGOSLAVIA
Sarajevo
Salonika
GREECE
Athens
ALBANIA
Tirana
BULGARIA
Sofia

600 Miles
600 Kilometers
300
300

Europe, 1945–1989

709

oped a quasi–fascist right–wing opposition, and Italy's government slid toward chaos in the wake of shocking revelations of widespread bribery of government leaders.

The Nations of the Commonwealth Face New Challenges

The leading nations of the Commonwealth—Canada, Australia, and New Zealand among them—had evolved into democracies in the preceding century and had generally been prosperous. They continued to do well in the postwar decades—generally considerably better than the mother country, in fact.

Canada became one of the seven leading capitalist nations in this period, but it traded so heavily with the United States that it became in many ways dependent on its prosperous and populous neighbor. The northern democracy also had problems with a separatist movement among the French–speaking people of Quebec province, a difficulty that not even Pierre Trudeau (premier 1969–1979, 1980–1984), who was of French–Canadian descent and became the nation's most internationally acclaimed prime minister, could put to rights. Australia, affluent before the war, approximated an American standard of living afterwards. Although it still clung to its European roots and its easygoing image, the country also began to come to terms with Asia. Australia traded on a large scale with Japan, eased its immigration restrictions to allow more Asians into the country, and took an increasing interest in the regional concerns of Southeast Asia.

In 1995, Canada's Quebec separatist movement came within a whisker of voting to leave, while Maori movement in New Zealand grew increasingly militant in its opposition to the rule of the white majority. The major Commonwealth countries seemed to be surviving the economic challenges of the nineties, but popular discontent voted governments out of office in both Australia and Canada.

◆ Political Trends in the USSR and Eastern Europe, 1940s–1990s ◆

The domestic history of the Soviet Union and the other nations of eastern Europe after 1945 differed markedly from that of the United States, western Europe, and some other U. S. allies. In the communist countries, one–party government and state control of the economy persisted through most of the second half of the century.

Even in the long decades when the bloc appeared most monolithic, however, there were in fact some steps toward liberalization, economic if not political, in these authoritarian eastern regions. And then in the later 1980s and early 1990s, under the leadership of Mikhail Gorbachev, both the Soviet Union and the bloc as a whole crumbled and slid into chaos. The collapse of the communist empire whose international ramifications were outlined in the preceding chapter will be considered here as part of the domestic history of these nations.

The Soviet Union: The Thaw and the Cadres

The political history of the Soviet Union since the Second World War has been the story of the long Stalinist hangover, the continuing impact of the cold war, and intermittent efforts to transcend both. Three names stand out: Khrushchev, Brezhnev, and Gorbachev. Khrushchev moved toward reform at home while crushing dissent in the bloc; Brezhnev brought political stability but economic paralysis; and Gorbachev's efforts at reform splintered the economy and brought the regime down in ruins.

At the Twentieth Party Congress in 1956, three years after Stalin's death, the new Communist party boss Nikita Khrushchev (in power 1956–1964) leveled some shocking charges at his predecessor. According to the new leader, Stalin's last years—the later 1940s and the early 1950s—were a harsh period of difficult recovery and grinding labor, a replay of the worst of the iron age of the 1930s. Khrushchev's "secret speech" was the beginning of a loosening of the reins that came to be known in the Soviet Union—a land used to long winters—as *the thaw*. The process of de–Stalinization thus begun included the freeing of large numbers of political prisoners, the posthumous rehabilitation of many others, the easing of censorship, and other manifestations of a freer spirit in Moscow than the country had known since the 1920s.

The thaw, however, proved to be premature. Khrushchev faced more problems than he could handle, some of them the results of de–Stalinization, some the results of the ongoing cold war, and some inherent in the communist system itself. A major domestic disappointment was the failure of Khrushchev's "virgin lands" scheme to rescue the Soviet Union's chronically underproductive collectivized agriculture by sending hordes of enthusiastic volunteers out to till marginal lands beyond the Ukrainian breadbasket, a plan apparently foiled by the soil, climate, and bureaucratic ineptitude. In 1964, Khrushchev was shuffled into early retirement by his enemies in the Kremlin.

He was nominally succeeded by Leonid Brezhnev (in power 1964–1982). Brezhnev had no interest in "the thaw" and soon went back to the status quo, an ossified regime of careerists, cronies, and corruption euphemistically described as "stability of cadres." There was comparatively little Stalinist brutality, and the camps were not refilled. But there was also little progress with the nation's problems. Agriculture continued to be woefully unproductive, and consumer goods were few and of much poorer quality than those available in western Europe. The Soviet Union's problems grew worse while party leaders acquired larger apartments, cars, and *dachas* (country cottages). The cadres were stable, but the country was stalled.

The Soviet Satellite States Survive

The Soviet Union's sphere of influence in eastern Europe tended to look much more monolithic to Americans, and more rigidly under the Soviet thumb, than it was. These nations tended increasingly to follow individual roads to socialism, and the Soviet Union's role in all of them was somewhat more limited than the barbed–wire image of enslaved peoples allows.

Most of eastern Europe, as we have seen, was historically a zone of peasant agriculture, with industrial development coming quite late outside of East Germany and Czechoslovakia. Nationalism was strong in all these countries, and many had minority nationalities of their own, like the two ethnic groups specified in the very name of Czechoslovakia—the Czechs and the Slovaks—or the six nationalities recognized in the federal structure of Yugoslavia.

The first generation of Soviet–sponsored rulers in eastern Europe were men who had spent years in the Soviet Union, who took some real loyalty to the Soviet Union as the "workers' fatherland" back with them to their own countries. However, Khrushchev's acceptance of the Titoist doctrine of "many roads to socialism" allowed for more freedom of operation within the bloc. More important, though, was the coming of a second generation of communist officials to power in eastern Europe itself. These men tended to be bureaucrats, economists, and planners with no revolutionary experience and with a purely national orientation, recognizing Soviet power but feeling no loyalty to the big brother of the communist world.

Eastern European countries run by such men acquired a good deal of autonomy over the years. Hungary, Czechoslovakia, and Poland all increased their trade with western Europe dramatically and put heavier emphasis on industrial development and consumer goods than the Soviet Union would have preferred. And in many eastern bloc nations, dissident movements grew up over the years.

The relatively depressed decades of the 1970s and 1980s, ending a period of unspectacular but steady economic growth and improved living standards in the eastern bloc, led to increased rumblings of discontent. Dissidents had already developed a vigorous underground *samizdat* literature, in which manuscripts passed from hand to hand to avoid government censorship of the press. After 1980, a host of groups surfaced demanding change in many areas. Poland's Solidarity labor union made international headlines by negotiating with the Polish Communist party itself as an equal, though it was subsequently driven underground for most of the 1980s.

Other groups also made inroads into state power, producing a "civil society" dedicated to such goals as peace, environmental controls, religious independence from the state, civil rights, and even a larger popular voice in government. The way was being prepared for the revolutionary transformation that would plunge eastern Europe into turmoil at the end of the 1980s.

The Gorbachev Revolution in the Soviet Union

As in the satellite states, the Soviet Union also began to experience changes in the later 1980s. When the Soviet leader Leonid Brezhnev died in 1982, he was succeeded by two men who lived to serve only a short time in office: Yuri Andropov (1914–1985) and Konstantin Chernenko (1911–1985), the first ailing, the latter elderly. In 1985 Mikhail Gorbachev maneuvered his way to power, and the Soviet Union was plunged into a new wave of reform that ended in the collapse of the Soviet state itself.

A compact, balding man who smiled easily, wore well–cut foreign suits, and had a natural flair for public relations, Gorbachev was a fresh wind in Soviet politics. Born in 1931, he represented a new generation coming to power. A passionate admirer of Lenin, he was still more willing than any Soviet leader before him to take a genuinely new look at the nation's problems and to take drastic action to solve them. A man who did not hesitate to tell the Central Committee that "the economy is a mess; we are behind in every area; we have forgotten how to work" and who tried to stop the Soviet people from drinking vodka was something new in Soviet politics.[1]

Gorbachev adopted two basic approaches to his country's problems: *glasnost,* or "openness," and *perestroika,* or "restructuring." Defying the Soviet tradition of silence and censorship, he demanded a candid exploration of all problems, in government, in the press, and in person on his tours from the Baltic states to the Soviet Far East. Citizens were encouraged to speak their minds, and dissidents like the Nobel Prize–winning physicist Andrei Sakharov (1921–1989) were brought back from Siberia and allowed to take part in political life. Crowds of nongovernment demonstrators appeared in the streets of Soviet cities for the first time since the Revolution.

Once problems were out in the open, Gorbachev demanded a radical restructuring of Soviet society in order to solve them. In two areas in particular, he saw a need for drastic change: the economy and political procedures. To improve the Soviet economy, he prescribed hard work and a dose of profit incentive and exposure to the free market. To revitalize Soviet politics, he allowed more than one candidate to run for each office for the first time in Soviet history. He even set out to streamline the party itself, cut down on the numbers of *apparatchiks* (bureaucrats), and give the Soviet Union less government instead of more.

The Revolutions of 1989 in the Satellite States

In the Soviet Union's client states in eastern Europe, people were already beginning to take action to get their governments off their backs. In a revolutionary contagion that recalled the revolutions of 1848, popular demonstrations erupted in one satellite state after another as the 1980s drew to a close. The nightly news on television was a sea of moving faces as eastern Europeans poured across frontiers into western Europe or paraded the streets of their own capitals demanding the resignation of their own communist governments. Signs and placards called for democratic elections, agitated speakers urged free–market economic reforms, and everyone seemed to want the Soviet troops garrisoned on their soil since World War II to pack up and go home.

To the astonishment of a watching world, the eastern European peoples got their way. The borders opened; the governments toppled. First in Poland and Hungary, already more open to western ideas, then in hard–line states like East Germany and Czechoslovakia, and finally in the least developed Balkan nations of Romania and Bulgaria, Soviet puppet regimes disappeared one by one. The opening of the Berlin Wall, symbol of a divided Europe for three decades, convinced most observers that Soviet domination of half the continent had effectively ended.

The Soviet reaction to these popular revolts was of course crucial to the success of the anticommunist movements. Gorbachev had unintentionally encouraged popular unrest in the satellites by urging fellow communist rulers to follow his example in undertaking political and economic reforms. Some U. S. and western European analysts felt that Gorbachev had really little choice but to allow the revolts to continue. The Soviet leader desperately needed an end to cold war spending and an infusion of western economic aid to help him "restructure." To achieve these goals, he had to convince Americans and western Europeans that the Soviet Union no longer constituted a threat, even to its eastern European neighbors. It was probably for such reasons that, as we saw in the last chapter, Gorbachev reversed the interventionist policies that had given the Soviets control of eastern Europe for half a century—and called his soldiers home.

The Disintegration of the Soviet Union, 1990–1991

In the USSR, meanwhile, Gorbachev's efforts had generated some changes, too. Under the pressure of lengthening lines in front of the shops and angry voices in the streets, the system began to come apart. The Communist party relinquished the monopoly of political power that went back to Lenin, and hundreds of local parties and other independent organizations sprang up across the country. Economic reformers demanded a complete abandonment of the planned economy and a return to private property and capitalist competition, though Gorbachev proceeded more slowly with economic than with political changes. A number of constituent republics, including the Baltic states of Estonia, Latvia, and Lithuania, demanded autonomy and then outright independence.

As the 1990s began, however, factions emerged to the left and right of the leader and pulled him down—along with the Soviet Union itself. On Gorbachev's left were rivals like Boris Yeltsin, elected president of the huge Russian Soviet Socialist Republic, which included half the population of the Soviet Union. Yeltsin demanded the devolution of power from Moscow to the separate republics and urged more free–market reforms. On the right, Communist party bigwigs, military brass, the KGB (the latest version of the secret police), and the entrenched managers of the state–run economy fiercely demanded a return to the iron fist to halt the disintegration of Soviet society.

In the summer of 1991, a group of inept communist conspirators attempted a coup to overthrow Gorbachev. Yeltsin, however, rallied the reformers and denounced the coup as illegal from the top of a tank sent to bully him into submission. The troops refused to fire on the people, the coup unraveled, and Gorbachev emerged from his brief captivity in the hands of the plotters safe and sound.

Yeltsin, however, seized the opportunity to have the Communist party declared illegal and to reorganize the Soviet Union itself into a loose confederation of sovereign states. That winter Gorbachev was forced to resign and Yeltsin, as president of the newly independent Russian Republic, became the most powerful leader in the collection of fifteen states that had once been the Soviet Union.

Yeltsin's efforts at economic reform antagonized the average Russian citizen as jobs disappeared and prices went through the ceiling. Yeltsin himself often showed signs of the authoritarian tendencies that were traditional in Russia. At one point he dealt with intransigent political opponents—and more threats of revolt—by sending in tanks to shell the legislature. When the small Caucasus region of Chechnya attempted to secede from Russia, Yeltsin sent in badly equipped, poorly led, and ill–trained troops who destroyed cities and villages and slaughtered tens of thousands of civilians in a desperate effort to crush the uprising—and ended by retreating anyway.

Russian society, meanwhile, degenerated rapidly into a carnival of gilded–age wealth and miserable poverty, corruption and violent crime. The Russian presidential election of 1996 pitted Boris Yeltsin against Gennady Zyuganov, head of the reborn Communist party. Yeltsin overcame an alcohol problem and heart trouble, asserted powerful control over the media, and mobilized his hand-picked administrators in the provinces to mount a victorious reelection campaign. But his health remained undependable, and the Russian political situation, like the economy and society, was still unproductive in the later 1990s.

◆ The Western Economy: Welfare Capitalism ◆

In the next two large sections, we will look at the broad contours of the economy and of Western society in the later twentieth century. Both these dimensions of the Western experience interacted with the political trends already traced. But both also have general characteristics that did much to define the lives of Western people between the 1940s and the 1990s.

Despite the political split in the Western world, economic recovery, as we have seen, proceeded surprisingly rapidly after World War II. The United States and western Europe put together an economic boom that lasted for a quarter of a century after 1945. In the 1970s and 1980s, however, the capitalist world experienced a serious depression followed by much more sluggish growth.

There was more international consultation over the direction of the economy than there had ever been before, and it was hoped that the powers would be able to halt further economic deterioration. For despite the ups and downs of the business cycle, the peoples of

The Revolutions of 1989

the Western world, with their houses, cars, electronic gadgetry, and eight–hour days were all what one authority labeled Americans—Peoples of Plenty.[2]

The United States and the European Postwar Recovery

The United States was by far the richest and most technologically advanced nation in the stricken world of 1945. The war had pulled America out of the Depression with a rush. The

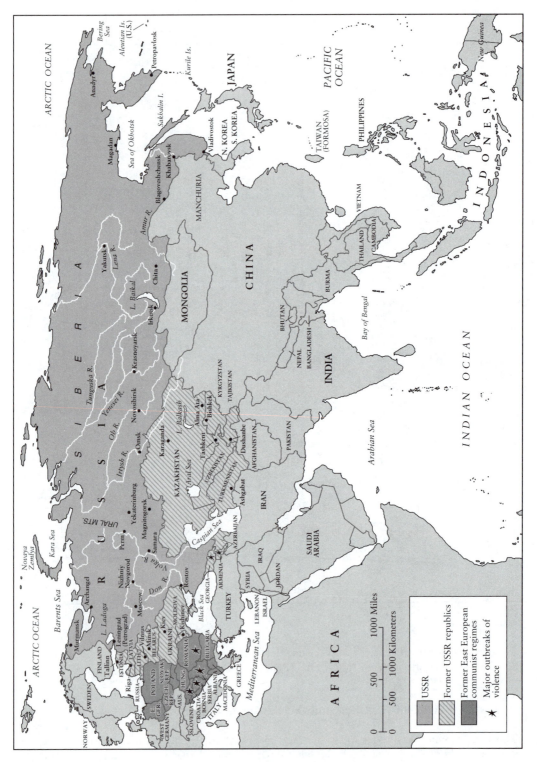

Collapse of the Soviet Empire, 1989–1991

battering Europe had taken opened the rest of the world to further American economic penetration. And none of America's industrial plant had ever been touched by a shell or a bomb.

Nevertheless, the United States could not function economically in a ruined world. American trade required developed trade partners. Swollen accumulations of American capital also saw excellent investment opportunities in Europe. It was therefore in American interests to help Europe get back on its feet as soon as possible. This rebuilding also seemed vital to accomplish before a shattered Europe became easy pickings for communist agitators. For these reasons, as well as from plain human compassion for a continent huddling in its ruins, the United States launched a massive program of postwar aid for European nations.

Help was first offered to Europe as a whole by U. S. secretary of state George Marshall in 1947. Because the communist leaders of the Soviet Union suspected that the real goal of the plan was to impose American economic suzerainty on Europe, the Soviets refused to accept the proffered aid or to allow the new Soviet client states in eastern Europe to do so either. As a result, *Marshall Plan* aid, American money to help Europe recover from the war, went only to the nations outside the Soviet orbit, from West Germany to the Atlantic.

Western Europe had been the more materially advanced half of the continent for centuries. It had deep reservoirs of technical skills, a half–demolished industrial plant that was in some cases not beyond salvaging, and even some wartime technological breakthroughs to draw upon. In addition, the Marshall Plan required the European countries to work together in planning their recovery. It was an approach that many Europeans approved of and that paid economic dividends for decades to come.

This North American–western European partnership across the Atlantic generated a remarkable recovery. These two major portions of the Western world, by working together, laid the foundations for the long postwar boom.

A broad framework for the reconstruction of the global economy had already been assembled in meetings held in the United States. A World Bank and an International Monetary Fund had established an international source of financing, and a General Agreement on Tariffs and Trade had laid the foundations for relatively free trade among nations. In place of the gold standard for all currencies, the U. S. dollar, the only sound currency left, became the standard to which others were pegged. Within this framework, the Marshall Plan offered capital, raw materials, and even food for hungry peoples. American private business also poured dollars into Europe by investing (at excellent rates of return), laying the foundations for some of the multinational business empires of the later twentieth century.

European governments and European businessmen put the money to a variety of uses, paying off crippling debts, rebuilding crucial industries, clearing up the ruins, and reestablishing the economy that had invented the Industrial Revolution in the first place. Within ten years western European nations were outproducing their prewar highs, and the biggest economic expansion in Western history was under way.

The Long Boom in the Capitalist West, 1950s–1970s

The economic growth of the Western capitalist countries during the 1950s and 1960s was stimulated by a surge of postwar demand. It was also leavened by a growing partnership between private business concerns and their governments, and by an innovative turn toward supranational economic organization.

Economic demand on both sides of the Atlantic had been building up to huge proportions during a decade and a half of depression and war. Flush with demobilization pay from the armed services or money earned in war industries or in the reviving postwar economy itself, many were able as well as eager to buy. Factories had to be retooled, cities had to be rebuilt, all of which meant more jobs, and more money to buy more things. Fueled by basic market forces, a boom thus rapidly developed.

Western governments also felt more responsibility than ever before to provide an environment that would ensure a rising standard of living for their people. Made confident by their success in organizing their economies for war, they turned to tinkering with the peacetime economy. Following the advice of liberal economist John Maynard Keynes (1883–1946), governments attempted to "fine–tune" successful economies to control the business cycle. In the second half of the century, they tried such devices as manipulation of interest rates and tax rates, state collaboration with business in securing foreign markets, even regulation of prices and wages to deal with inflation. When socialists were in power, many western European countries nationalized important industries: railroads and coal mines in Britain, chemicals and electricity in Germany, and banking, railways, and electricity in France. Subsidies for some industries and government regulation of others in the public interest were also part of this picture.

Most striking was the unparalleled amount of international economic cooperation and organization during the postwar period. The cooperative European administration of Marshall Plan aid gave governments growing confidence in such economic collaboration. Idealistic believers in the European community of nations urged further experiments, and a number of such cooperative organizations were forthcoming. The European Coal and Steel Community coordinated and regulated the production of these basic materials in western European nations. The European Atomic Energy Community (Euratom) began the European development of atomic energy. Joint ventures across national frontiers, like the Anglo–French collaboration that produced the Concorde, the world's fastest airliner, and a similar joint construction of a railroad tunnel under the English Channel, became more and more common.

The most important of all these international organizations was the European Economic Community, or *Common Market,* created by the Treaty of Rome in 1957. This organization aimed at coordinating and regulating production, commerce, currencies, migration, and other matters of mutual economic concern. As a customs union, the Common Market gave all members the right to trade in each others' countries, and it looked ahead to even greater economic and political integration in the future.

At the highest level, the last decades of the century saw regular annual meetings of the heads of the seven most highly developed nations in the capitalist world to coordinate the international economy. These meetings brought together the leaders of four European countries—Germany, France, Britain, and Italy—with those of the United States, Japan, and Canada. Such sessions fostered a cooperative climate within which national decisions might be made. They were certainly a far cry from the protectionist, mercantilist spirit that had pervaded the international economy in earlier decades and centuries.

This mix of economic policies produced a sophisticated capitalism that boosted production—and living standards—to unprecedented heights. During the two decades between the end of World War II and the mid–1960s, for instance, production grew by almost 5 percent per year in the Netherlands, 6 percent in Italy, and 7.5 percent in West Germany. Where the United States had stood alone above an economically prostrate world in 1945, three rivalrous centers of productivity thus came to dominate the globe in the later twentieth century: North America, western Europe, and Japan and the Pacific rim.

The Lean Years in the Capitalist West, 1970s–1990s

In the 1970s and 1980s, however, the long boom gave way to a sharp economic downturn. The wonder was that the effects were not much worse than they were for Western peoples who had grown used to a "helicopter economy," always going up.

The causes of the second worst depression of the century were various. In part, the insatiable postwar demand was finally sated as even these affluent generations found that they had piled up more debt than they could handle and would have to forgo a new car this year, or perhaps a new house forever. In part, too, foreign competition hurt Western economies, especially from Japan and such rapidly growing East Asian enclaves of capitalism as South Korea and Hong Kong. Another cause was the exporting of too many Western manufacturing jobs to these and other countries where labor was cheaper. Heavy industry thus declined in the West, including such former staples as coal, steel, and automobiles. And for every factory that shut down in the United States or Britain, hundreds of workers could not afford to buy a car, a washing machine, or a new suit of clothes, pushing the economy still further down.

But the precipitating catastrophe, comparable in its impact to the Wall Street crash of 1929, was the *oil shock* of 1973. A series of events in the Middle East, including continued U. S. support for Israel, led Middle Eastern oil producers to embargo oil sales to the West and then to jack up their prices drastically. Because of these decisions by the Arab–dominated petroleum producers' cartel, the Organization of Petroleum Exporting Countries, or OPEC, oil prices jumped from under \$2 a barrel in the early 1970s to \$30 a barrel in the early 1980s. Since petroleum was the most important power source in the industrial world, the entire international economy was thrown out of kilter by this jolting rise. Prices of goods and services shot up as the price of the basic energy source used in their production rose. Higher prices led inevitably to demands for higher wages—and the dreaded wage–price spiral of inflation. The result was a strange combination of economic stagnation and inflation sometimes called *stagflation*.

The consequence was a significant turnaround in the economic policies of Western governments. Frequently, conservative parties replaced liberal or socialist ones in power, and even where the left governed, as in France, the first concern was to restore the general health of the economy, not to nationalize industry or increase services. Everywhere, rough medicine was applied to stimulate renewed productivity and decrease inflation. In practice, deflating the economy meant depression, while increased "productivity" meant firing superfluous workers. The United States seemed willing to let heavy industry decay, hoping that high–tech industries like electronics and computers would power the economy back up. Britain encouraged the closing of inefficient factories and the pensioning off of "redundant" workers in order to become internationally competitive once more. In a number of countries, government–supported social services fell behind the needs of the population, while governments encouraged entrepreneurship and investment to rebuild their national economies.

Perhaps the most heartening aspect of the depressed 1970s and 1980s was the fact that they did not produce the kind of social and economic collapse that had occurred in the

Chronology 28.2: The Lean Years

1974–1990s	*Economically depressed years across the Western world*
1964–1982	*Brezhnev brings stability and stagnation to Soviet Union*
1969–1974	*American youth demonstrates against Vietnam War*
1970s–1990s	*Women's movement pursues economic and political parity across Western world*
1973–1974	*Arab oil price rise jolts Western economies*
1979–1990	*Thatcher advocates "enterprise culture" for Britain*
1980s	*Old "rust belt" industries give way to high tech, throwing many out of work*
1981–1989	*Reagan brings surging incomes for some Americans, de-"industrialization" for others*
1981–1995	*Mitterand moves from socialism to austerity in France*
1982–1990s	*Kohl re-unifies Germany as Europe's top power, but faces high cost of modernizing East Germany*
1985–1991	*Gorbachev's attempt to "restructure" Soviet Union leads to collapse of USSR*
1990s	*New leadership—Clinton in United States, Major in Britain, Chirac in France, Yeltsin in Russia—struggle with economic and political problems*

1930s. Relief agencies provided some safety net. When first Wall Street and then stock markets around the world crashed in October 1987, regulatory agencies limited the damage and the financial system absorbed the disaster with relative ease.

Nevertheless, the 1990s began with a widening gulf between the well–educated and affluent and the under–educated and poor. There were beggars in the streets of Western cities, as there had been fifty years earlier, and clamors for less free trade and more tariff protection against foreign competition. Meanwhile, governments also found that tax revenues could no longer support the welfare systems installed during the boom years after World War II. With the disappearance of jobs in heavy industry, many healthy young people found themselves in need of unemployment compensation. And with populations living considerably longer, demands on pensions, government medical care, and other programs were clearly going to increase even further in the near future.

The American economy seemed to some to be leading the West back out of the lean years. American businesses fought their way back into international competition by cutting out whole layers of "middle management." This however also spread the unemployment problem from blue–collar factory workers to white–collar management personnel. And while the American economy did generate millions of new jobs in the 1990s, they tended to be lower paid positions than those that had been lost.

The leaders of the European Community bet on even greater economic integration as a solution to economic problems. Changes in the Common Market provided for the free flow of capital, labor, and business and professional activity between nations, for common European passports and a European currency, making western Europe the largest affluent region in the world. Yet the continuing economic slowdown, highlighted by unemployment figures running above 10 percent, left many deeply worried. And many citizens clearly opposed reform plans which would put more power in the hands of the economic "Eurocrats" in Brussels, the administrative center of the European Community.

A High–Tech World

Whether the economy went up or down, however, the rapid growth of Western technology continued apace through the second half of the century. Technological growth was evident everywhere, from pocket calculators to the artificial satellites that orbited the planet in increasing profusion. Applied science and technology, key elements in Western history since the eighteenth century, played an even more important part in the history of the later twentieth.

Every individual life was touched every day by the new technology. Frozen foods relegated canned goods—the breakthrough of the nineteenth century—to the cheap shelves. Film achieved a dazzling level of visual realism, while television came into its own and devoured large chunks of the average Western person's day. Phonograph records gave way to tapes and then compact disks, calculators to personal computers, pinball machines to electronic games. A world criss–crossed by commercial jet service and linked by instant satellite phone connections seemed a far cry from the world of the Model–T Ford, let alone that of the horse and carriage.

Central heating and air conditioning at the touch of a thermostat, contact lenses to make your glasses invisible, pills to kill your pain, to help you sleep, to perk you up or slow you down—who could get through a day without a technological crutch? The Salk vaccine eliminated polio as other immunization techniques did other diseases, while such drugs as penicillin and other antibiotics destroyed many forms of infection. Machines were developed to perform bodily functions for people whose hearts, livers, and other organs were diseased. New surgical techniques were perfected to bypass clogged arteries, to replace ruined organs with transplanted ones, and to reattach body parts lost to accidents.

Of particular fascination to many was the so–called *space race* between the U. S. the USSR. The space race began in the later 1950s with artificial satellites, first unmanned and then with animal and human passengers, circling the earth. The first human to reach space in such a satellite was a Russian, Yuri Gagarin, in 1961. Further probes reached the moon—an American triumph, with Neil Armstrong, the first human to set foot on the lunar surface in 1969. Subsequent strides included unmanned voyages to nearby planets, fly-bys of more distant ones, and space probes moving on out toward the stars. Weather, communications, and spy satellites wheeled routinely around the earth, American "space shuttles" took off and returned after work in nearby space, and an orbital Soviet space station was manned and busy every day of the year. Late in the century, American astronauts and Russian cosmonauts began to collaborate, saving both some of the huge cost of space exploration.

The wide–ranging intrusion of applied science into human life also produced some serious problems, however. Such twentieth century stand–bys as the automobile, for example, caused tens of thousands of deaths every year and hundreds of thousands of injuries. It was widely recognized during this period that the planet's natural resources from petroleum to tin were being rapidly depleted. Industrial society polluted water, air, and soil as cars pumped noxious gases into the atmosphere, factories poured chemicals into rivers and lakes, damaged oil tankers coated the sea with petroleum, and developers destroyed hundreds of thousands of square miles of rain forest. Smog, acid rain, and other pollutants made the air of major cities frequently unbreathable, while damage to the earth's atmosphere threatened to overheat the great globe itself.

Terrible accidents like the unhappily paired *Challenger* and Chernobyl disasters of 1986 contributed to the feeling that science and technology were running out of control.

Early in that year the American space shuttle *Challenger* exploded in the air over Florida, killing all seven of the astronauts on board and grounding America's space program for years. The following summer, an accident at a Soviet nuclear reactor at Chernobyl caused dozens of deaths, led to the evacuation of a large area, and spread radiation poisoning over a broad swath of northern Europe.

Less than three centuries after the first industrial steam engines pumped water out of coal mines in the north of England, advanced technology was so woven into the warp and woof of modern civilization that there seemed to be no way of extricating ourselves from it. The West did seem at last to be alert to the dangers technology posed, and to be seeking solutions. But the answers themselves would have to be formulated within the framework of a highly technological society.

♦ Western Society: Shifting Foundations ♦

Western society in the second half of the twentieth century presented a variable and contradictory mix. Population growth, immigration from Third World countries, and changes in urban structure were important parts of the social scene. Social classes evolved in new directions, and class conflict seemed less intense. Racial, gender, and age–based differences, by contrast, were of more concern than they had been.

Population Growth, Migration, and the Changing City

Demographic changes begun centuries before continued, with variations, in the later twentieth century. Population grew, for a brief period, more rapidly than it had for generations. Migration patterns shifted significantly, while continuing urbanization produced both problems and progress.

The population explosion shifted its center to the non–Western world during the postwar period, but there was a population surge in the West as well. Overall, the population of Europe grew from 573 million in 1940 to 728 million in 1975, while that of the United States expanded from 134 million in 1941 to 250 million in 1990. The most rapid increase in births in both the United States and northwestern Europe came during the so–called *baby boom* of the 1950s and, in America, the 1960s. During this period, when people were no longer fearful of starting families in a great depression or a world war, birth rates were higher than they had been for generations. Western people also lived longer, thanks both to medical advances like new vaccines and antibiotics and to expanded public health services. Population thus grew at both ends, generating the surge of the third quarter of the century.

Another feature of the population history of these decades was a new wave of migration into both western Europe and America from Third World countries. Some of the migrants were political refugees, including Germans into West Germany after World War II and Cuban and Vietnamese refugees entering the United States after the Cuban Revolution and the Vietnam War. The largest number, however, were economically motivated. East and West Indians poured into Britain, Arabs and West Africans into France, Turks into Germany, and Mexicans, Puerto Ricans, and other Hispanic peoples into the United States, all in search of work. The more prosperous western European nations experienced increased immigration from the less–developed countries of southern Europe, including Spain, Portugal, and Italy.

Willing to work for lower wages and to do work that the indigenous population would not do, these migrants were often made to feel unwelcome. In particular, those whose legal status was shaky, such as undocumented Mexican immigrants into the United States or "guest workers" in Europe, were ill paid, badly housed, and set to demeaning or dangerous work by their employers. Newcomers were too often met by "Turkish jokes" in Germany or racist attacks on Vietnamese in the United States or on Pakistanis in Britain. Despite this resistance, however, the population mix of Western countries was evidently changing. And some immigrants, like Indians in Britain and East Asians in America, did exceedingly well in their new homes, contributing the sort of energy and ingenuity that had built the Western economy in the first place.

Cities, finally, were still the focal point for migration, whether from the surrounding countryside, from southern Europe, or from outside the West altogether. Urban trends in the later twentieth century included the rebuilding of shattered European cities, a middle–class emigration to the suburbs in the United States, and efforts to revitalize city centers in many parts of the Western world.

After the Second World War, many European cities had to be largely or totally rebuilt because of wartime damage. Gleaming modern metropolises sprang up across West Germany and elsewhere, and in countries as far apart as Britain and the Soviet Union, governments labored for years to erect housing blocks for low–income or blue–collar workers' families.

In America and more slowly in western Europe, meanwhile, the automobile made it possible for middle–class people to move out to leafy suburbs, sometimes called "bedroom communities" in the United States, and commute to the cities or to equally decentralized industrial parks. Shopping was increasingly done at malls or shopping centers located away from both work and residential neighborhoods. In the United States, everything from banking to buying a meal could be done without ever leaving your car.

Deprived of their tax base as both well–to–do homeowners and industry moved out, the inner cities deteriorated. In the 1970s and 1980s, however, a countertrend developed, a rediscovery of the sophisticated pleasures of urban living. City centers were rejuvenated by urban renewal programs, and rundown neighborhoods in New York, London, Paris, and elsewhere were "gentrified" to draw back upwardly mobile young people who would swell the tax rolls. These policies were often carried out at the expense of the poor, whose tenements were toppled by the wrecker's ball to make room for business blocks or condominiums; but they did bring money back to the cities, where it was sorely needed.

Growth of the Welfare State

As throughout the century, efforts were made to provide both welfare services for the neediest and social entitlements for all citizens. These benefits included public education, retirement incomes, public health care, and additional benefits for citizens with special problems, including the poor and the unemployed.

Britain had made a major commitment to "cradle to the grave" social services right after the war. Some of the most elaborate welfare systems were to be found in the Scandinavian countries, and Sweden became a model of democratic socialism. The United States, even after the New Deal and the social legislation of the Kennedy–Johnson years, had offered less in the way of welfare, though American attempts to legislate equal treatment for minority groups and women were more far–reaching than most. Social services, of course, cost the taxpayers money, cutting into the amount they had for discretionary spending. Thatcher in Britain and Reagan in America preferred individual saving and private charity to public spending for these purposes. Socialists and many liberals felt that the West was rich enough, even in its depressed periods, to afford basic services for all its people.

Educational opportunities increased. Enrollments in secondary schools expanded, and chances for advanced education grew, though they varied from country to country. France built additions to its national university system but still required the passing of difficult examinations at each level of the educational system as a prerequisite for admission to the next. At the opposite extreme, the United States offered a wide range of higher education, including two–year community colleges in many cities.

Educational reforms of various types were also popular. In the United States, "progressive education" for citizenship gave way to "open schools" designed to free the student from rote learning for self–development. In the 1980s, this trend in turn gave way to a "back to basics" emphasis on the classical liberal arts and solid social science subjects. In the 1990s, advocates of "multiculturalism" urged that Western countries provide a grounding in non–Western cultures for citizens with non–Western roots. Others demanded a return to traditional standards here too, with emphasis on a literary "canon" of great writers and patriotic history.

Middle Class, Working Class, Underclass

Social classes and the relations among them continued to evolve in the West. The middle classes, by now clearly the majority west of the iron curtain, did well for most of the second half of the century. Working–class organization remained strong in western Europe, but unions declined in the United States. In many places, finally, the later twentieth century spawned a growing underclass, often too uneducated to participate in a high–tech world, economically depressed, and socially dangerous.

In capitalist countries, a middle–class managerial elite had largely replaced the entrepreneurial owner–manager business class of earlier centuries. Industrial, commercial, and financial firms were now normally owned by stockholders but run by highly paid professional managers, usually with university degrees in management rather than long experience in a particular industry. Everywhere, government bureaucracy employed a large percentage of the working population. In the majority of European nations, east and west of the iron curtain, more than two–fifths of the work force was in government service by the 1960s.

Blue–collar jobs, like those of managers, required more training and a different sort of technical skill than the craft work or heavy manual labor of earlier times. There was still some heavy work to do in such trades as building construction, work on the docks, or garbage collection. But machinery, from fork lifts to automated assembly lines, made blue–collar work less onerous than it had been. Service work grew faster than manufacturing, so that fast–food restaurants, hotel chains, health care, and transportation absorbed an expanding share of the labor force. White–collar work also grew, providing teachers for the baby boom and clerical workers for expanding bureaucracies and postwar businesses.

During the postwar decades in particular, these working–class people shared in the new affluence. In western Europe, the United States, and elsewhere, this meant striking improvements, including comfortable apartments or private houses, automobiles, recreational vehicles, and month–long vacations.

There remained, however, a substantial segment of the population that was underemployed, unemployed, or even essentially unemployable. Especially later in the century, these people tended to be victims of changes in industry itself, notably the decline of heavy industry in the West and the rise of high–tech, as well as the overall shrinkage of manufacturing of all sorts and its replacement by service industries. It was often said that such changes created as many jobs as they eliminated; but the new jobs often involved very different skills, required moving to new areas, or paid a good deal less than the old ones. To these unemployed must be added the children of a "culture of poverty." Often members of minorities, these people were likely to be undereducated for most modern jobs, last hired and first fired, and trapped in a cycle of low ambition, low achievement, petty crime, and welfare checks.

This unemployable underclass, especially where its roots were in a different cultural community, could explode in violence like the "dangerous classes" of the nineteenth century. Drug related crime was endemic in such neighborhoods in the later twentieth century. Riots could also explode easily, whether in a black ghetto in America, an Arab suburb in France, or a German neighborhood penetrated by east European immigrants, Turkish "guest workers," or even Gypsies.

Ethnicity in the West

A growing source of social problems in the West was the increasing number of ethnic minorities to be found there. Varied ethnic patterns could greatly enrich Western culture, but they could and did lead to conflict also.

For most of its history, the western end of Eurasia had few minority populations, the most significant being the Jews. European imperial expansion to the New World, however, produced multi–racial societies in the Americas, combining European, African, and Native American peoples. And in the twentieth century, the economic success of the West drew floods of immigrants from Asia and Africa into Europe, and from Asia and Latin America to the United States.

Ethnic differences, or differences perceived as ethnic (both Jews and Arab, for instance, were caucasoids like other Europeans), had led to violence in the past, including pogroms against Jews in Europe and the lynching of African Americans in the United States. The later twentieth century saw no such large–scale horrors in the West. But subtler forms of persecution, from social prejudice to job discrimination and government policies aimed at forcing minorities to conform to majority norms did manifest themselves. And these in turn led to demoralization, social decay, and crime and rioting in minority neighborhoods across the West.

The West still claimed to be open to the world. Britain had opened its doors to immigrants from its former colonies after World War II, and Germany had faced a surge of immigrants from east Europe after the cold war. The United States absorbed millions of new immigrants in the 1980s and 1990s, the biggest influx since the beginning of the century, mostly from Asia and Latin America. Especially in economically insecure times, however, Western nations seemed to be saying that they could not add to the ethnic minorities among them—and sometimes could not even live in peace with those who were already there.

A Wider Choice for Women

Women worked outside the home in growing numbers after 1945. In western Europe and North America, working–class and even middle–class women had to seek employment outside to help maintain the quality of life the family wanted. Many middle–class women, however, sought work because they, like their male counterparts, wanted to build successful careers in business, the professions, or government. One result of this trend was to tap large amounts of hitherto unused talent. Another was to create a welter of new social problems and a reinvigorated women's movement demanding social change.

Women made perhaps the least visible progress in politics. There were still only a sprinkling of women in the representative assemblies and cabinets of Western countries. Some women did, however, beat the odds and rise to the top in politics, including Golda Meir (1898–1978), the Labor prime minister of Israel, and Margaret Thatcher, the Conservative prime minister of Britain. Many more women carved out distinguished careers for themselves in law, medicine, and academia, as well as in management and the boardrooms of major corporations.

Employers often discriminated against women in hiring, promotion, and pay. Working women who were also wives and mothers frequently discovered that they were expected to do most of the housework and child rearing also, leaving their husbands free to have a "real career." Where both partners took their careers seriously, they often found it necessary either to have no children or to neglect the ones they did have. And women who had no desire for families at all still sometimes found that they were disapproved of for having rejected the traditional female role.

Out of all these concerns, a revived women's movement took shape in the 1960s and 1970s. Admired mentors of the new movement included such celebrated intellectuals of an older generation as the existentialist Simone de Beauvoir (1908–1986), whose *oeuvre* included *The Second Sex* (1949–1950), a pathbreaking analysis of the female condition in modern times. The gurus of the new movement, however, were younger women, including such influential and subtle social analysts as Betty Friedan (1921–), author of *The Feminine Mystique* (1963), and Germaine Greer (1939–), whose *The Female Eunuch* (1970) offered an even more devastating critique of the psycho–social oppression of twentieth–century women in the West. Debunking "the happy housewife" as a male stereotype foisted upon women and the home that was "women's domain" as "a comfortable concentration camp," Friedan stirred a new wave of militance aimed at a new round of social reforms.

Under the influence of the new feminism, working women demanded equal pay for equal work and a fair shot at promotions. Those with families demanded maternity leaves and child care facilities. Unmarried women insisted on the right to sex lives as free as unmarried men's. And women's groups tried to show society as a whole that women should be free to do any kind of work that men did. Women newscasters and women war correspondents, women jockeys and women auto mechanics seemed to be changing the feminine image and opening the way to a wider choice of lives for the female half of the human race.

In the 1990s, some women did seem to be putting more emphasis on such traditional roles as those of wife and mother once more. Many young women firmly denied that they were "feminists"—though they also frequently expected the career opportunities that an older generation had won for women. The strain of holding a full–time job and raising children, especially without a husband or with one who had little time or inclination to share the housework, still proved daunting for many women. Other two–career couples adjusted their schedules, focused their energies, and coped.

The Youth: Militance and Withdrawal

Youth emerged as a widely recognized social subculture and sometimes as a conscious political force after 1945. Generational conflict became a widely discussed phenomenon, especially in the 1960s, the decade of the largest of all youth revolts.

The trend of the 1920s toward the emergence of a full–fledged subculture of the young crescendoed after 1945. Middle–class young people felt freer of traditional inhibitions than ever before, and both they and working–class youth had more money to spend. Beginning in the United States and spreading across Europe a "fun culture" of young people resulted. Whole industries grew up to feed youthful appetites for stylish clothes and haircuts, for high–fidelity sound systems and whatever the drug of choice might be that year. "Wheels" became a necessity—motorbikes more likely in Europe, automobiles in the United States. From the 1950s on, rock and roll was the most popular musical form with the young, and rock clubs in Europe and concerts that could fill a stadium on both sides of the ocean catered to this taste.

During the 1960s, the youth culture turned consciously against what many young people regarded as the corrupt world of their elders. This rebellion of the younger generation took two forms: militant protest seeking to change society, and countercultural withdrawal from it.

Organized political movements of students or youth flamed up in many parts of the world, from China and Japan to Algiers and Latin America. In the United States and Europe, these movements orchestrated mass demonstrations and even organized violence against "dehumanizing" educational systems, imperialism, racism, capitalism, war, atomic weapons, environmental damage, and other things. Youthful militance contributed significantly to the U. S. civil rights and anti–Vietnam War crusades, and youth movements shook the governments of leaders as powerful as America's Lyndon Johnson and France's Charles de Gaulle. The most exalted aspirations of young activists for a revolutionary new social order based on love and justice did not, however, succeed.

Another form of opposition to Western society during the 1960s was the cultural withdrawal of the "hippies," "flower children," or "street people" of what was sometimes called the *counterculture*. These youths simply turned away from a society they saw as materialistic and corrupt. Attempting to build their lives around love, music, drugs, and freedom from middle–class responsibilities, they escaped into oriental religions, a wandering street life, or country communes. Seeing no hope for changing the world, they sought to withdraw from it.

No similar surge of youthful revolt or withdrawal manifested itself between the early 1970s and the 1990s. By 1990, however, youthful dissidence once more seemed to be at least faintly detectable. Young people were disturbed by their own economic prospects, aroused against peoples of other ethnic, racial, religious, or other types, or gripped by some less clearly definable malaise. Some turned to violence, like the neo–Nazi German "skinheads"; others settled into counter–cultural depression, like the "grunge" American youth hailed by social commentators in the media as Generation X.

Beyond such mediagenic minorities, however, there did seem to be considerable discontent among the young as the nineties advanced. Cuts in government aid for university students, poor job prospects, and even fears that the welfare system would not be there for them in unemployment or old age probably contributed to renewed generational malaise. But much of the renewal of generational discord at the end of the century was as difficult for older people to understand as it always is. As so often over the preceding two hundred years, older and younger people had moved into different conceptual worlds once more, and nothing looked the same from the two sides of the generational divide.

Summary

During the half–century after 1945, the Western democracies alternated between periods of conservative rule and stretches of liberal or democratic socialist administrations. The former emphasized the free–market economic system that made the industrial capitalist nations the most economically productive countries in history. The latter channeled a proportion of this productivity into public education, health care, unemployment compensation, old age pensions, environmental protection, and other social welfare services for all citizens. Political life in the communist countries did provide stability and social order but was inflexible, unproductive, and drastically curtailed the rights of the individual.

In the second half of the twentieth century, as in the first half, the United States possessed the largest and most productive economy of any nation. With U.S. help, western Europe recovered rapidly from the devastation of World War II and built the European Economic Community, an immensely successfully customs union that brought unprecedented economic growth. Overall, the world's capitalist economies grew at record rates during the 1950s and 1960s, but slowed considerably from the mid–1970s well into the 1990s.

Social classes, genders, age groups, ethnic groups, and other subdivisions of Western society all experienced major changes in the second half of the twentieth century. Class conflict became less pronounced, ethnic differences perhaps more sharply distinguished. Women pushed closer to economic and political parity with men, and young people repeatedly begged to differ with their elders as generational conflict became a more and more common feature of world history.

Some Key Terms

baby boom 722
Common Market 718
civil rights movement 701
counterculture 727
enterprise culture 707
Fair Deal 700

glasnost 712
Great Society 700
Marshall Plan 717
oil shock 719
Ostpolitik 704
perestroika 712

samizdat literature 712
space race 721
stagflation 719
the thaw 711
Watergate 702

Notes

1. Mikhail Gorbachev, quoted in *Time,* January 4, 1988, p. 18.
2. David Potter, *People of Plenty: Abundance and the American Character* (Chicago: University of Chicago Press, 1954).

Reading List

Bothwell, R., et al. *Canada Since 1945: Power, Politics, and Provincialism.* Buffalo, N.Y.: University of Toronto Press, 1981. With Bothwell, I. Drummond, and J. English, *Canada, 1900–1945* (Buffalo, N.Y.: University of Toronto Press, 1987), provides a solid history of the emergence of twentieth–century Canada.

Chafe, W. H. *The American Woman: Her Changing Social, Economic, and Political Roles, 1920–1970.* New York: Oxford University Press, 1974. Good survey of the period between the suffrage movement and the renewed militance of the later 1900s.

Daniels, R. V. *The End of the Communist Revolution.* New York: Routledge, 1993. Gorbachev and the collapse of the Soviet Union, by an authority.

Flora, P., ed. *Growth to Limits: The Western European Welfare State Since World War II.* 4 vols. Berlin and New York: Walter de Gruyter and Co., 1986–1987. Pioneering studies of the development of "welfare rights" in the western European nations in the second half of the twentieth century. See also P. Baldwin, *The Politics of Social Solidarity: Class Bases of the European Welfare State, 1875–1975* (New York: Cambridge University Press, 1990), on the deeper roots of the welfare state in Europe.

Galbraith, J. K. *The Affluent Society.* 3d ed. New York: Mentor Books, 1978. Widely read view of American prosperity in the postwar decades.

Garrow, D. J. *Bearing the Cross: Martin Luther King, Jr., and the Southern Christian Leadership Conference.* New York: William Morrow, 1986. Effective portrait of the American civil rights leader and the movement he led.

Graubard, S., ed. *A New Europe?* Boston: Houghton Mifflin, 1964. A useful collection of essays on Europe recovered from World War II. On the newest "new Europe"—since the end of the cold war—a useful beginning is N. H. Wessell, *The New Europe: Revolution in East–West Relations* (New York: Academy of Political Science, 1991).

Hogan, M. J. *The Marshall Plan.* Cambridge: Cambridge University Press, 1987. How mutual need made this postwar relief measure a key step toward later economic integration.

Hough, J. *Russia and the West: Gorbachev and the Politics of Reform.* New York: Simon & Schuster, 1988. Challenging analysis of the policies of the Soviet reformer. On his successor, see J. Morrison, *Boris Yeltsin* (Harmondsworth, England: Penguin, 1992).

Jarausch, K. H. *The Rush to German Unity.* New York: Oxford University Press, 1994. Thoughtful analysis by an authority. See also P. H. Merkl, *German Unification in the European Context* (University Park: Pennsylvania State University Press, 1993).

McCormick, J. *Reclaiming Paradise: The Global Environmental Movement.* Bloomington: Indiana University Press, 1989. Pioneering history of environmentalism since the 1960s.

Rioux, J.–P. *The Fourth Republic, 1944–1958.* Translated by G. Rogers. New York: Cambridge University Press, 1987. Highly praised history of postwar France. On two major leaders since the war, see J. Lacouture, *De Gaulle,* 2 vols., trans. A. Sheridan (New York: Norton, 1992), and G. Ross, et al., *The Mitterrand Experiment* (New York: Oxford University Press, 1987). See also B. E. Brown, *Protest in Paris: Anatomy of a Revolt* (Morristown, N.J.: General Learning Press, 1974), on the 1968 youth revolt in Paris.

Rothschild, J. *Return to Diversity: A Political History of Eastern Europe Since World War II.* New York: Oxford University Press, 1989. A political scientist's explanation of the complex relations between the Soviet Union and the smaller eastern European states.

Schlesinger, A. M., Jr. *A Thousand Days.* Boston: Houghton Mifflin, 1965. The Kennedy years, by a historian who worked for the Kennedy administration.

Stokes, G. *The Walls Came Tumbling Down: The Collapse of Communism in Eastern Europe.* New York: Oxford University Press, 1993. Deep roots of the decline and fall of the communist empire. For the more immediate account of a journalist on the spot, see T. Garton Ash, *We the People: The Revolution of '89* (London: Granta Books, 1990).

Sullerot, E. *Women, Society, and Change.* New York: McGraw-Hill, 1971. Women in western Europe after World War II. Two books that inspired the later twentieth-century women's movement were B. Friedan, *The Feminine Mystique* (New York: Norton, 1963), and S. de

Beauvoir, *The Second Sex*, trans. H. M. Parshley (New York: Vintage, 1989).

Teaford, J. C. *The Twentieth Century American City: Problem, Promise, and Reality.* Baltimore: Johns Hopkins University Press, 1986. Scope and style recommend this survey to students.

Turner, H. A. *The Two Germanies Since 1975.* New Haven: Yale University Press, 1987. Brief political history of East and West Germany from their emergence to the eve of reunification.

Willis, F. R., ed. *European Integration.* New York: New Viewpoints, 1975. Europe's growing unity, social as well as economic. See also R. C. Mowat, *Creating the European Community* (New York: Barnes and Noble, 1973).

Young, H. *The Iron Lady: A Biography of Margaret Thatcher.* New York: Farrar, Straus and Giroux, 1989. Penetrating political analysis of the conservative British leader.

Zeigler, R. H. *American Workers, American Unions, 1920–1985.* Baltimore: Johns Hopkins University Press, 1986. Stresses uniqueness of U. S. unions, integrated into rather than battling capitalist society. On other aspects of work, see M. Crozier, *The World of the Office Worker,* trans. D. Landau (Chicago: University of Chicago Press, 1971), on the growth of the white–collar work force, and D. F. Noble, *Forces of Production: A Social History of Industrial Automation* (New York: Oxford University Press, 1986), on the rise of automated industry in the United States.

All Coherence Gone
A Revolution in Western Culture

♦The Second Scientific Revolution ♦Upheaval in Religion and Philosophy
♦Writers in Revolt ♦Artistic Experiments

The past three centuries have seen revolutions of many kinds in Western society, from political revolts to technological innovations to cultural and intellectual upheavals like the Enlightenment or the romantic movement. Not since the Renaissance, however, has Western culture seemed so eager to challenge artistic and intellectual conventions, so rebellious, original, and inventive, as in the past hundred years.

The present chapter will outline the amazing "second scientific revolution" of the twentieth century, with its astonishing breakthroughs in sciences from physics to biology. It will examine the bewildering upheaval in philosophy and religious thought that came on the heels of the new scientific insights. This chapter will also chronicle the rise and triumph of the startling artistic movement called modernism, which challenged accepted social views as well as traditional aesthetic values. And it will also look at the work of *post*modernist writers and artists, who dismissed even their modernist predecessors as part of the cultural establishment they had originally set out to subvert.

The intellectual and artistic turmoil of the twentieth century as a whole clearly constituted a massive revolution in Western culture. After Einstein and Picasso and Joyce, after existentialism and postmodernism and poststructuralism, the world looked to many like the early modern world of John Donne, "all coherence gone." It seemed unlikely that we could ever go home again to the calm and confident intellectual world our great–grandparents knew.

♦The Second Scientific Revolution♦

In one area of Western thought, the twentieth century produced uncontested—if still revolutionary—intellectual achievement of a high order. In the study of the material world, this age has been described as the century of the "second scientific revolution." As we will see in this section, scientists have probed the interior of the atom and the far limits of the universe, learning how stars are born and how living things are genetically programmed. But, as in Newton's or Darwin's day, scientific advance also created disturbing challenges to orthodox views. Einstein's theory of relativity was only the most striking jolt to both accepted scientific ideas and plain common sense.

Matter and Energy

Science in the twentieth century moved toward a new level of understanding of the structure and operation of the universe. Equipped with fantastic new instruments, scientists probed the subatomic world and analyzed the basic forces that governed the behavior of matter. The result was a world view radically different from the views of the Greeks or the scientific pioneers of the sixteenth and seventeenth centuries.

By the end of the nineteenth century, D. I. Mendeleyev's periodic table listed ninety–two elements of matter, arranged by their atomic weights. All elements were believed to be composed of three basic particles: negatively charged electrons orbiting a nucleus composed of positively charged protons and uncharged neutrons. In the course of the present century, the number of known elements and subatomic particles grew. The movement of the electrons was also redefined in terms of "shells" or orbital zones within which these minute particles of energy circle their nuclei.

The forces governing the behavior of matter were also reinterpreted. Where gravity had reigned as the sovereign force in the Newtonian universe, at least three forces emerged in the twentieth century: gravity, electromagnetism, and the strong nuclear force. Gravity was still the most far–reaching of these, for it bound all the large structures of the universe together. Within the atom, however, electromagnetic force linked the nucleus and its orbiting electrons through the attraction of positively and negatively charged subatomic particles. Within the nucleus, finally, the strong nuclear force held the positively charged protons together despite the electromagnetic repulsion of these similarly charged particles. The last frontier of physics seemed to be the creation of a unified field theory that might subsume this variety of forces under a single powerful explanatory principle.

What the new science offered was a physical world composed of tiny particles of pure energy spinning through vast reaches of empty space. The atom thus defined had little in common with the tiny nuggets of matter the Greeks and early modern scientists had called atoms. Even less material, however, was the mysterious world of radiant energy, explored by Marie Curie (1867–1934) in the early decades of the century.

Curie's experiments with radioactive materials brilliantly epitomized the work of the twentieth–century scientist—the meticulous researcher in an increasingly elaborate laboratory. Born in Poland, she came to Paris in the 1890s to study physics and, after earning her Ph.D., concentrated on the newly discovered phenomenon of radioactivity. Through a series of carefully conceived experiments, Curie was able to detect a tenth of a gram of the hitherto unknown element of radium in a solid ton of pitchblende ore. She discovered two new elements, radium and polonium. Most important, she explored the nature of radiation itself.

Radiation represents a startling phenomenon in nature, the transformation of matter into pure energy. As radio–active materials emit their powerful rays, Curie discovered, they lose atomic weight: matter disappears, turned into radiant energy. Marie Curie earned two Nobel prizes, one in physics, shared with her husband Pierre, and one in chemistry, making her the only person ever to earn Nobels for work in both sciences.

Chronology 29: Twentieth–Century Culture: from Relativity to Postmodernism

1898	*Curie discovers radium*
from 1900	*Modernism rejects society and experiments in art and literature*
1905	*Einstein formulates theory of relativity*
1907–1914	*Picasso invents cubism, reducing nature to abstract shapes*
1910s–1920s	*Rise of moving pictures as art and entertainment*
1910s–1920s	*Emergence of jazz as international musical form*
1916–1930s	*Dadaism rejects art and society; surrealism seeks inspiration in dreams, psychology*
1922	*Joyce's* Ulysses; *Eliot's* Wasteland
1927	*Woolf's* To the Lighthouse
1930s, 1950	*Sound film adds new dimension to movies; color film again transforms motion pictures*
1940s	*Big bang theory of origin of universe*
1940s–1950s	*Existentialism asserts that "existence precedes essence"*
1960s–1970s	*Structuralism seeks "deep structures"; poststructuralism emphasizes use of ideas to dominate "discourse" and society*
1967	*Garcia Marquez's* One Hundred Years of Solitude
from 1970s	*Postmodernism rejects "the canon," modernist classics, and "great art" of any sort*
1980s	*Deconstruction rejects "intent," probes for "subtext" beneath apparent message*

Relativity and Cosmology

The work of Albert Einstein (1879–1955) also broadened our understanding of the world we live in. Paradoxically, Einstein also joined a number of scientists who challenged the very possibility of scientific knowledge as it had traditionally been defined.

The physical world, Einstein suggested, should not be understood as an objective entity "out there"; it can only be understood relative to the eye of the beholder. Einstein's *theory of relativity* reinterpreted space and time, the fundamental force of gravity, and the structure of the universe itself.

Time, Einstein pointed out, is clearly relative to the viewpoint of the observer. The light from the stars that we see at night left those bodies of flaming gas thousands of years ago: what we see through a telescope "now" is the way they looked in the distant past. Space, too, Einstein insisted, is affected by the relationship between observer and observed. All motion must be measured relative to other objects—which are also in motion. Einstein also asserted that an object *expands* in the direction in which it is moving: thus a space ship moving at speeds approaching the velocity of light would grow longer. This would not be apparent to the astronauts within it, however, for they would also expand.

Einstein also redefined gravity, the linchpin of the Newtonian universe. Gravity was not a force of attraction between any two objects but a field of forces through which objects move and by which their motions were modified. This gravitational field, furthermore, affects not only matter, but energy as well. The sun's gravitational field, Einstein predicted, would bend the beams of light from distant stars passing near the sun enough to displace their apparent positions from their actual ones. Subsequent astronomical observations proved him right.

Albert Einstein, the most celebrated scientist of the twentieth century, won the Nobel Prize in Physics at the age of 42. Born in Germany, Einstein spent the latter part of his career in the United States, at the Institute for Advanced Study at Princeton University. (Karsh/Woodfin Camp & Associates.)

The whole universe had to be rethought under the aegis of relativity. Time, in Einstein's terms, ceased to be something distinct from space and became instead a fourth dimension of reality, after length, width, and depth. The universe became a space–time continuum, curving back upon itself under the tug of its own gravitational field. Because space itself curves, a beam of light—or a space ship setting out for the farthest reaches of the universe—would sooner or later return to its own starting point, having circumnavigated the curving space–time continuum without ever changing course at all!

On a more practical level, Einstein presented the world with perhaps the most famous formula in the history of physics: $E = mc^2$. Marie Curie had revealed that matter turned into pure energy in the laboratory. Einstein defined the relationship between matter and energy in mathematical terms, declaring that the amount of energy produced would be equal to the mass of the matter multiplied by the speed of light squared. Since the speed of light is a very large number—186,000 miles per second—a very small amount of matter could release an incredible amount of energy—as in fact happened in the atomic weapons and nuclear power plants of the later twentieth century.

The structure of the universe as a whole also looked more complex and more confusing as the twentieth century advanced. Larger and larger reflecting telescopes, radio telescopes, spectroscopes, and artificial satellites from which to carry out astronomical observations all added to our knowledge. Scientists analyzed the chemical content of distant stars and calculated the direction of stellar movement across the universe. From these studies came the central cosmological insight of the century, proposed by the physicist George Gamov (1904–1970) in the 1940s: the *big bang theory* of how the universe began.

According to this view, the universe began its history as a cosmic fireball, an incredibly condensed globe containing within itself all the matter and energy of the future cosmos. This fireball exploded, propelling radiant energy and dissociated subatomic particles outward like shrapnel from an exploding bomb. All the primary structures of the universe first took shape as the universe evolved. The strong nuclear force and electromagnetic energy pulled subatomic particles into atoms. Gravity drew swirling clouds of gas into the globular formations from which galaxies, stars, and circling systems of planets gradually emerged. And the expansion continues: the momentum of that primal explosion is still carrying all these structures outward into space.

The human race had just begun to probe the complexities and immensities of time and space as the twentieth century neared its end. At the end of 1995, Swiss and American astronomers began to report concrete evidence that planets revolved around other stars than our own sun. American and Russian astronauts, once competitors in space, were working together to produce platforms for further exploration of outer space. The Western peoples, who had wrought the first weapons of global destruction, had also taken the lead in reaching out into the infinite universe their ancestors had really begun to understand only three centuries before.

Biology and Psychology

Twentieth-century biology and psychology were in many ways expansions of Darwinian and Freudian ideas of the nineteenth century. In some ways, however, developments in both fields went far beyond their nineteenth-century precursors.

A major breakthrough was the discovery in the 1950s of DNA (deoxyribonucleicacid), the molecular compound that determines the form and growth of living tissues. This acid, a twisted double helix of hydrocarbon molecules, lies at the heart of the protoplasm of which all living matter is made. Yet each individual's DNA is unique, so completely different from any other's that in the 1990s detectives began to use DNA traces instead of fingerprints to identify criminals.

The latter half of the century also saw impressive progress in the study of animals in their normal habitats, where they understandably behave far more naturally than they do in laboratories or zoos. Jane Goodall (1934–) and Dian Fossey (1932–1985) set up camps in the African wilderness to observe the daily lives of troops of chimpanzees and mountain gorillas. From their pioneering studies came new insights into the ways in which the simple societies of humanity's nearest relatives resemble our own. Behavior patterns, from tool-making and social hierarchy to aggression and affection, turn out to be as characteristic of chimps foraging in the forest as of human beings in history.

Other students of animal behavior also argued the reverse hypothesis: that people are very like their animal kin, and that the roots of much human behavior lies in our animal natures. Sociobiologists like Edward O. Wilson (1929–) asserted that such human activities as defense of "our" territory, aggression, and even altruistic concern for others had genetic origins. Sociobiology thus emphasized humanity's animal nature—and challenged the view that human instincts are culturally conditioned rather than innate.

The study of mental functioning moved in new directions in the twentieth century. One trend was the further development of Freudian depth psychology. Another was the spread of behaviorism, the theory that human behavior is completely explainable in terms of external conditioning.

In his later years, Sigmund Freud proposed two primary human drives: the life instinct, which subsumed the sex drive, and the death instinct, which accounts for such orgies of destruction as World War I. Some of Freud's disciples struck out on their own, founding schools of psychology that focused on other allegedly basic human drives. Thus Carl Jung (1875–1961) declared that dreams reveal not only an individual's own unconscious, as Freud had said, but also a communal psychic life and a racial memory going back to earlier ages. The archetypal figures that appeared in dreams, Jung believed, were also to be found in mythology, religion, and various occult traditions. These archetypes symbolize basic human impulses of today and yesterday and can bring spiritual strength to an irreligious age.

The behaviorist school of psychology, by contrast, claimed that all human activity was the product of environmental conditioning. The Russian physiologist Ivan Pavlov (1849–1936) conditioned a dog to salivate at the sound of a bell by consistently ringing the bell just before presenting the dog's dinner. Other behaviorists, like B. F. Skinner (1904–1990), insisted that human beings too are conditioned by many material and social circumstances. Human behavior is the result, not of inner drives, but of child–rearing, education, and a lifelong barrage of subtle rewards and punishments conditioning us to behave as we do. Much twentieth–century education, advertising, and even government propaganda was based on this fundamental principle of behavioral conditioning.

Other students of the human mind penetrated the brain itself with surgical instruments, electrodes, and chemicals. From such experiments came a much more detailed understanding of the ways in which various parts of the brain interpret the signals that reach it from the sensory organs and direct the activity of the rest of the human organism. This physiological approach challenged both Freudian and behaviorist claims. The causes of such psychological illnesses as schizophrenia, students of the brain asserted, lay neither in deep drives nor cultural conditioning, but in body chemistry. This approach produced an array of mind–altering drugs to deal with manic, schizophrenic, and depressive disorders, as well as other psychological problems.

New Paradigms

Other theories examined the limits of scientific certainty and the role of the scientist in structuring truth. These theories further challenged old–fashioned notions of "objective knowledge" about the universe.

Some of these challenges to scientific certainty came from the empirical researches of the scientists themselves. Experimental results around the turn of the century, for instance, had indicated that there was simply no "right answer" to the long–debated question about whether light moves as a *wave* through space or as a series of separate *quanta* or particles of energy. Sometimes light behaves like a wave, sometimes like a particle, and it is after all really the *behavior* of light that interests scientists, not its "ultimate nature". The limits of scientific knowledge were more precisely defined by Werner Heisenberg (1901–1976) in his disquieting *uncertainty principle*. Heisenberg proposed that the process of scientific observation itself imposes limits on what we can ever know about the cosmos. For the introduction of an instrument of observation or measurement, even if it is only a beam of light, affects the area under observation. It might be possible to know the location of an electron, for instance, but not the speed with which it moves, or its speed but not its location, but never the two at the same time.

In general, many scientists began to feel that even scientific laws might best be defined as statistical probabilities, not ironclad rules determining the behavior of every particle of matter in the universe. Some experiments even showed that under certain circumstances matter actually behaves contrary to the accepted laws of physics. For brief moments of time and in very limited areas, for example, heat radiates from cooler objects to hotter ones instead of the other way around. Again, electrons leap from one orbit around the nucleus of the atom to another orbit—for no detectable reason at all. The statistical probabilities are still there, scientists concluded, but the ironclad "natural laws" of yore seemed to be fading.

Late in the twentieth century, the whole process of scientific investigation was called into question. Thomas Kuhn (1922–) advanced the view that scientific revolutions like those spearheaded by Copernicus or Darwin or Einstein were not simply the product of new empirical data, as had been believed. Instead, said Kuhn, a major change in scientific understanding was the result of looking at the evidence from a new perspective. It was this new point of view which drastically restructured the basic framework of scientific thought. Both perspective and intellectual restructuring, of course, came from the scientists themselves, not from the world "out there." Scientific progress was thus best understood, not as an accumulation of newly discovered facts, but as a series of interpretive frameworks.

Kuhn called these frameworks *paradigms* after the models of conjugations or other linguistic structures used in language study. Soon scholars in other fields were discovering paradigms in everything from history and the social sciences to literary criticism. More important, however, was the impact on Western attitudes toward scientific knowledge. To the dismayed layperson, at least, it looked as if all reality was relative, all scientific knowledge uncertain, and the scientist no longer an objective observer of the world but an inventor of paradigms with which to interpret it.

◆Upheaval in Religion and Philosophy◆

Formulating a convincing philosophical or religious view of such a world was not easy. In a Western culture where the sciences themselves seemed to reject absolute truth, all certainties were called in question. Seeking understanding in a world without firm intellectual foundations, Western philosophers and religious thinkers came up with a variety of worldviews, most of them freighted with ambiguities. We will look here at several such trends: at Christian thought in what some saw as a "post–Christian" world, at the grim worldview of existentialism, and at the radically subjective vision of structuralism, poststructuralism, and deconstruction.

Secularism and Salvation

Twentieth–century Western people were more willing than ever before in their history to adopt a purely secular, materialistic view of the world. Shortly before midcentury, the anti–Nazi priest Dietrich Bonhoeffer described the secularism of the age as a "great defection from God." Western humanity, he said,

> has learned to cope with all questions of importance without recourse to God as a working hypothesis. In questions regarding science, art, and even ethics, this [secular approach] has become an understood thing which one scarcely dares to tilt at any more.[1]

Historical criticism of the Bible continued to chip away at the literal interpretation of the Christian Scriptures. Even the Gospels were increasingly seen by scholars, not as eyewitness testimony, but as summaries of early Christian traditions about Christ written half a century or more after Christ's death. The famous Dead Sea scrolls, discovered in several sites around the Dead Sea in the 1940s and subsequent decades, vividly illustrated the religious ferment of Jesus' day but provided no new evidence concerning his own life and teachings.

Nevertheless, religion did influence the life of the Western mind in this as in other centuries. Christian churches could still claim more members than any other systematic Western philosophy of life. Judaism, though threatened by new waves of assimilation, also held its own and triumphed, surviving the Holocaust in the Old World and flourishing in the New. Both churches and synagogues strove to influence society and to console suffering humanity.

Both the political right and left benefited from such religious support. Europe's Christian Democratic parties, though they supported the rights of the governed as they understood them, opposed radicalism, socialism, and atheistic communism. The Christian right in America plunged into politics, championing family values and opposing what it saw as moral decay.

Other Christians threw themselves into liberal and radical movements. Christian socialism worked to advance the interests of working men and women in Europe through labor and welfare legislation. Catholic priests in Latin America developed the "liberation theology" of active commitment to social justice for peasants, Indians, and other oppressed groups. In the United States, as we have seen, preachers like Martin Luther King, Jr., were among the leaders of movements for African–American rights and peace in Vietnam.

There were other twentieth–century Christians, however, who detected in all this social involvement a retreat from what they saw as the central message of Christianity: its promise of eternal salvation. Their stress on the primarily spiritual mission of religion took a variety of forms. One was a literal interpretation of the Scriptures, a "born–again" theology that attempted to ignore or refute the historical analysis of biblical texts which had led mainstream churches to modify their views over the years. Insisting that every word of the Bible was divinely inspired, these *fundamentalists* found consolation for a hard life on earth in an eternity of bliss in heaven.

A more modern, if also more abstruse, formulation of the "eternal message" was that of Christian *neo–orthodoxy* preached by Carl Barth and by Reinhold and Richard Niebuhr. In this view, the spiritual anguish of modern times was rooted in the alienation of humanity from its divine Creator. The great sin of our times, in this view, was not the exploitation of one person by another, but the modern flight from religious faith. Until this yawning gulf between Creator and created was closed, the aching emptiness, the self–destructiveness and suffering that distinguished the human race would continue to torment us all.

Positivism and Pragmatism

Philosophers, like scientists and theologians, challenged their own traditional convictions in the twentieth century. The logical positivist school of thought insisted that philosophy should henceforth limit its efforts to serving as a handmaid to science, while the pragmatists called traditional definitions of truth itself into question.

The basis of *logical positivism* was the narrow definition of their own function espoused by many British and American philosophers. According to this school of thought, modern science had either taken over or rendered invalid most of the traditional quests of Western philosophy. Science, not metaphysics, would explain the ultimate nature of things, while absolute ethical standards had been proven impossible by the recognition that all such theories were relative, "true" only for the culture that formulated them. The real function of the philosopher, then, was simply to analyze the concepts of the modern sciences in order to render the conclusions of these disciplines more precise and accurate.

A related, distinctly American school of thought was *pragmatism* and the related instrumental approach to understanding. Pragmatism, developed in the nineteenth century by William James (1842–1910), sought to discover, not eternal meanings, but the *usefulness* of concepts. Truth was what James called the "cash value" of an idea, its use in life. Thus a sports team's belief that it can beat a rival has pragmatic value to the extent that this conviction makes it more likely that the team will in fact win. A statement is not inherently true, but becomes true: truth is something that *happens* to a statement in the hurly–burly of life and the rough interaction of ideas and realities.

In the twentieth century, James's successor John Dewey (1859–1952) produced a spinoff from pragmatism called instrumentalism. This approach put special stress on the impact of beliefs on the world. Ideas, said Dewey, were instruments. Working through the minds of human beings, they could accomplish great things in society. A leading educational reformer, he emphasized education for citizenship in a democratic society.

This pragmatic, instrumental approach became an important part of the Western temper in the twentieth century, serving often as a corrective to exaggerated commitment to ideological formulas.

Existentialism

Existentialism also traced its roots back to the nineteenth century, to Nietzsche's dark vision of "the death of God" or Dostoyevsky's sense of the radical irrationality of human life. Existentialists also accepted philosophical materialism, which denied the reality of spirit, and a scientific view of the universe that excluded divine purpose. "Existence," said Jean–Paul Sartre (1905–1980), the movement's guru in the years after World War II, "precedes essence." That is, the material existence of things is the one great given. Metaphysical essences, world–spirits, or the gods of religious creeds are figments of our imaginations. "The heavens are empty," Sartre declared, and there is no reason why any of us exist—we just "are."

Living through decades of totalitarianism and depression, war and cold war, thinkers like Martin Heidegger (1889–1976) in Germany and Sartre in France saw little to feel optimistic about. For them, all faiths, all ideologies had been proven mere human constructs. The teachings of Plato, Jesus, and Marx were all unprovable, and all alike served to distract us from the real task of the philosopher—facing the facts of life.

Beneath all systems of belief lay what Sartre called the *néant,* "nothingness," the void where significance ought to be. The consequence of this central absurdity of life was what the German existentialists termed *Angst,* usually translated as "anxiety" or "anguish." *Angst* was the spiritual malaise that lay always just below the level of consciousness, veiled by false happiness or a delusive understanding. Sartre described this malaise in the title of his most disturbing novel as *Nausea* (1938), a queasy, ever–present awareness of the meaninglessness of life.

Yet in a world without meaning, perceived only with anguish by the existential temper, a heroic existential life was also possible. For the person who truly perceived the valuelessness of the cosmos also perceived his duty in this empty world: the obligation to infuse value into it. For if we do not exercise this freedom to invent values, the universe will remain an empty husk, a dead thing without meaning or significance.

From Structuralism to Deconstruction

In the later twentieth century, the cult of existential anguish in the face of life's meaning-lessness gave way to a new concern in *avant–garde* thinking. This was *structuralism,* at the deepest level a passion to probe the meaning of meaning itself. Such explorations, French and American structuralists believed, could reveal "deep structures" beneath the random-ness of reality as experienced. Like existentialism, however, structural analysis seemed to undermine some of the most widely held beliefs of Western humanity.

Structuralists like anthropologist Claude Lévi–Strauss (1908–) saw the inner organi-zation of society in general as far more important than the specific detailed beliefs of any particular society. Structuralists thus compared the kinship relations in many societies, the common elements in myths, or the structure of all languages. This focus on the analysis of structures may be seen as a rebellion against existentialism. Defying existentialist condem-nation of system building, the structuralists tried "to reduce man's mental, social, and af-fective life to unconscious formal structures or patterns."[2]

What came to be called *poststructuralism,* as developed by thinkers like the French cul-tural historian Michel Foucault (1926–1984), turned the structuralist sense of underlying significances into a potent critique of all orthodoxies. Foucault analyzed society and culture in terms of language or "discourse." Whoever controls the words (or other systems of signs and symbols) we use to express ourselves, he declared, controls our very thoughts. By con-trolling the discourse, telling us which words or ideas are "valid," the powers that be pre-vent opposition to the status quo from even taking shape in the minds of the people. Radi-cal social critics in the later twentieth century seized upon this view to expose what they saw as an insidious cultural tyranny shaping society's treatment of minorities, or women, and other oppressed groups. For poststructuralists, there is no such thing as truth in an ab-solute sense, only "privileged discourse," signs and symbols arbitrarily defined as valid by ruling elites.

Deconstruction, as practiced by the philosopher Jacques Derrida (1930–), attempted an even more sweeping reduction. Concentrating on literature, apostles of deconstruction rejected the search for the "author's intention" that traditional scholars had investigated, focusing instead on the text before them. Disassembling a literary work into component

Jean-Paul Sartre and Simone de Beauvoir were pre-eminent French intellectuals of the mid-twentieth century. In their writings, which ranged from philosophy to fiction, they gave powerful expression to the existential world-view of the Western world after World War II. (Giansanti/Sygma.)

images, phrases, and concepts, deconstructionist critics reassembled it to present what they called the "subtext," the true underlying significance of the words, whether the author intended any such meanings or not. What mattered to the deconstructionist was the concealed, underlying pattern of meaning discovered beneath the surface of life by the anthropologist, philosopher, historian, or critic.

♦Writers in Revolt♦

The widespread cultural disaffection revealed by the drift of twentieth–century thought was even more powerfully expressed in literature and the arts. Much of the most critically acclaimed literature of our century has in fact been either a reaction against our times or an expression of the passion for artistic experimentation that characterized the age.

We will look here at the pioneering work of early modernists like James Joyce, Virginia Woolf, and T.S. Eliot. We will then have a brief glance at the dream–like world of dada and surrealism, at the mythology of socialist realism and the fairy–tale quality of magical realism. Finally, we will plunge into the relativism and nihilism of postmodern literature, which abandoned the quest for beauty and truth with a hollow laugh.

The Modernist Rebellion

The literary movement known as *modernism* embodied a strong critique of Western society, its values and institutions. The targets of this critical fiction included big business, the military, the churches, political leadership of all sorts, and bourgeois society in general. Serious twentieth–century writers tended to have little use for middle–class respectability, orthodox piety, flag–waving patriotism, and puritanical sexual mores. All of these qualities, many modern writers urged, were tainted with the exploitation and hypocrisy of the modern bourgeois world.

As important as this vigorous social critique was the experimentalism of twentieth–century writing. Like the modernist movement in other arts, modern literature tore up the rule book on how to produce a well–made play, a well–constructed novel, or a proper poem. The modernists launched a wide–ranging reassessment of all the elements of their craft, from plot and character to syntax and versification. Experimenting with all the elements of literary art, they produced works that left many readers baffled and alienated. Yet the modernists pressed on, convinced that art was more important than its audience, that being true to one's own vision often meant simply ignoring one's readers.

Literary modernism generated a host of separate schools and isolated individuals, all dedicated to self–expression, writing for themselves alone. In an atmosphere of militant manifestoes and defiant "little presses" publishing experimental writing for small coteries, many modernist writers believed that commercial success was in itself evidence of "selling out." To all, what mattered was the right word, the perfect phrase to express what they wanted to say—even if most of their fellow citizens had no idea what they were talking about.

Experimental Fiction

The history of literary modernism began in the late 1800s and continued through most of our own century. In this period, western nations large and small generated poets, dramatists, and writers of prose fiction who have enriched the literary heritage of the West.

Among the most celebrated, Germany produced the magisterial novelist Thomas Mann (1875–1955), whose *Buddenbrooks* (1901) and *The Magic Mountain* (1924) offered critical insights into European middle–class society. France gloried in Marcel Proust's (1871–1922) probing multivolume novel of French society in decay, *Remembrance of Things Past* (1913–1927). The United States clearly emerged as a literary center, producing such internationally known novelists as William Faulkner (1897–1962) and such experimental dramatists as Eugene O'Neill (1888–1953), whose work will be discussed below. Even the raw new Soviet Union generated the poetry of Anna Akhmatova (1889–1966) and Boris Pasternak (1890–1960), the poet–novelist whose *Dr. Zhivago* (1956) depicts the impact of the Russian Revolution on ordinary citizens with lyric feeling.

Virginia Woolf, pioneer of English literary modernism, was the center of the Bloomsbury set of British writers and artists. Though they were well educated and came from England's social elite, the Bloomsbury group prided themselves on unconventionality in life as in art. (National Portrait Gallery, London.)

It is too much to survey writer by writer or even country by country. Instead, we will try to illustrate the evolution of literary modernism in fiction through the work of three authors: Virginia Woolf, Franz Kafka, and James Joyce.

Virginia Woolf (1882–1941) was the central figure in the iconoclastic coterie of writers and artists known as the "Bloomsbury group" after the section of London where they lived. Woolf's primary contributions to modern fiction included an emphasis on the instability of the human character, the subtle blending of the inner lives of individuals with the flow of time itself, and a mingling of particular human lives with the larger flow of history. She was a pioneering practitioner of the *stream of consciousness* technique, in which an entire story is told through the stream of thoughts, feelings, and perceptions of the characters. Thus her novel *The Waves* (1931) offered only the flowing inner lives of six very different characters from early years to old age. And in *To the Lighthouse* (1927), perhaps her most complex and successful novel, she recreated a day at a summer house on the shore as perceived by wife and husband, parents and children, with a nuanced awareness of such harsh realities as domination, loss, and compromise.

The life of Franz Kafka (1883–1924), child of a middle–class Jewish family in Prague, himself a low–level functionary in the Austro–Hungarian bureaucracy, was dominated by his failure to please a domineering father. Kafka wrote with desperate conviction of human isolation, bringing his own anxieties and sense of guilt to such disturbing tales as *Metamorphosis* (1915), in which the hero is transformed into a giant insect, and *The Trial* (1925), which can be read as a terrifying exposé of modern bureaucracy—or as a revelation of the secret anxieties and guilts harbored by both Kafka and many of his readers.

In the fiction of the Irish writer James Joyce (1882–1941), stylistic innovations like those of Virginia Woolf joined a vision sometimes as hallucinatory as Kafka's to generate a uniquely modernist body of fiction. Joyce attained international celebrity with the publication of *Ulysses* (1922), a novel based on Homer's ancient epic, the *Odyssey*, but recounting the modern–day wanderings of Leopold Bloom, a Dublin advertising solicitor, from breakfast in the morning to the red–light district at night. Joyce's style also baffled readers. His last novel, *Finnegan's Wake* (1939), developed the mythic implications of the "night thoughts" of a hero, sound asleep in bed throughout the book, who expresses himself in an almost impenetrable "dream language" full of puns, allusions, and made–up words invented by the author himself.

Plays and Poetry in the Waste Land

Twentieth–century experimental drama sought to draw upon and develop all elements of the performing arts, from Greek tragedy to clowns and pantomimes. It dealt in challenging ways with social problems, with the human psyche, even with the nature of reality itself.

Some dramatists used the stage as a means of communicating their social commitments–often in defiantly untraditional ways. In plays like *Mother Courage and Her Children*, the German playwright Bertolt Brecht (1898–1956) deliberately tried to keep his audiences from identifying emotionally with his characters in order that they might remain aware of the social issues he was presenting. America's best–known playwright, Eugene O'Neill (1888–1953), veered from stark realism to far–out fantasy, adapting history and myth and manipulating masks, music, mime, and stage effects to give form to his protean dramatic vision. His *Mourning Becomes Electra* (1929–1931) drew on Greek myth and

Greek theater with its chorus, family focus, and echoes of Aeschylus' *Oresteia*. His *Emperor Jones* (1920), by contrast, involved the audience in a Caribbean voodoo ritual through the quickening beat of drums as the demagogic emperor is hunted to his death.

Modern theater often seemed to be as much about theater itself as about the world outside. The Italian dramatist Luigi Pirandello (1867–1936), for instance, wrote his celebrated *Six Characters in Search of an Author* (1922) as an exploration of the relations between the theater and the "real world," suggesting that theatrical illusion may actually be more real than the world we think we live in. Twentieth–century directors and impresarios also experimented with stagecraft and acting methods and tried to break down the barrier between spectators and actors. You might go to a hit musical comedy like *Starlight Express* in London and find yourself in the middle of a night–long race, with the actors whizzing through the audience on roller skates. Or you might attend a play staged by Jerzy Grotowsky (1933–) in Poland and find yourself *inside* the death camp at Auschwitz.

It was perhaps in poetry, however, that the modernist spirit in literature found its clearest expression. It seemed to many readers and critics that modern poetry was not so much exploring poetic forms as rejecting them out of hand. Such poetry sometimes substituted a flow of images for the verse patterns of earlier centuries. Yet the best of these writers did communicate some of the most exciting and most profound concerns of their times. The Irish poet William Butler Yeats (1865–1939), for example, mingled ancient Irish myths, a contemporary enthusiasm for esoteric "magic," and his own classical reading in his moving poems. Russia's Anna Akhmatova, whose career spanned the first half of the century, chiseled out powerful imagistic evocations of a sensitive individual and a whole nation struggling to survive through Stalin's iron age.

Perhaps the most celebrated of all the modernists poets, however, was the expatriate American T. S. Eliot (1888–1965), who lived most of his life in Britain. Eliot's demanding yet powerful condemnation of his own times, *The Waste Land* (1922), was often obscure to the casual reader. Yet he offered a disturbing commentary on what he saw as the soulless world in which he lived, a sordid and corrupt society without traditional or spiritual roots, without grace or greatness. And his enigmatic phrases became part of the vocabulary of the century. Many twentieth–century people came to see themselves as "the hollow men," their world as the "waste land" that it looked like to this thoroughly alienated modern poet.

The Dada–Surrealist Stream

A unique line of artistic development that involved both literature and the other arts was the dada–surrealist stream that lacerated traditional sensibilities between the world wars and influenced Western culture for the rest of the century. Like other modernist schools, both *dadaism* and *surrealism* rejected bourgeois social values, denounced traditional artistic practices, and appealed to nonrational forces—chance or the unconscious mind—to guide their creative impulses.

The dada movement (apparently named from the French word for "hobbyhorse"), created in the cabarets of neutral Switzerland during World War I, blamed Western civilization as a whole for the Great War, denouncing both Western art and Western social values. Dada impresario Tristan Tzara (1896–1963) and his cohorts defined dadaism as "art without sense" or even "anti–art," completely opposed to "honor, fatherland, the family, art . . . liberty . . . logic . . . discipline or religion."[3] Members of the new school staged cabaret performances that turned into riots and generally set out to shock the bourgeoisie.

André Breton (1896–1966), French poet and leader of the surrealist movement, which succeeded dadaism in the 1920s, defined surrealism as "pure psychic automatism . . . without any consideration for aesthetics or morality."[4] Breton and his fellow surrealists found their prophet in Sigmund Freud and his theory of dreams as expressions of the unconscious mind. The surrealist artist Salvador Dali (1904–1989) stirred uneasy feelings in viewers with his meticulously executed canvases of flaming giraffes, human bodies with drawers opening up in their chests, and the notorious melting clock faces, symbols of the failure of the bourgeois effort to impose order and reason on a fundamentally irrational world.

The dada–surrealist stream of Western art brought the nonrationalism of the romantic movement and the nineteenth–century *fin–de–siècle* back to the center of European culture. Nonrationalism would play an important part for the rest of the twentieth century.

From Socialist Realism to Magical Realism

The focus of most accounts of Western culture in the twentieth century remained in western Europe and—increasingly—North America. But there were interesting developments in eastern Europe and Latin America as well. In the Soviet Union, a determined effort was made to reject modernism and to mandate instead socialist realism—literature and art in the service of the revolutionary state. Latin American writers, by contrast, moved into the forefront of modernist fiction in the second half of the century with the unique style called magical realism.

The Russian Revolution at first kindled the enthusiasm of many Russian writers and artists, and the 1920s became a decade of cultural experiment in theater, film, and other arts. Writers like Vladimir Mayakovsky (1893–1930) urged modernists to give up their literary experiments and put their talents at the service of the Revolution. Organizations of proletarian writers and government organizations with jarring new labels like Agitprop (Agitation and Propaganda) encouraged working–class people to develop writing skills and tell their stories. By the 1930s, however, all this spontaneous activity had been taken over by the Communist party which dismissed modernism as decadent and reactionary.

Socialist realism demanded that literature offer a "concrete representation of reality in its revolutionary development" aimed at the "re–education of the working people in the spirit of socialism."[5] The result was most often uninspired novels of proletarian progress, featuring communist "positive heroes" saving idealized workers or peasants from the machinations of capitalist reactionaries or industrial saboteurs. Where impressive novels did take shape within these limiting parameters, they were most often written in the nineteenth–century realistic tradition, like Mikhail Sholokov's *And Quiet Flows the Don* (1926), depicting life among the Cossacks of the Don River region as they struggled to survive the Civil War.

Latin America produced a very different kind of "realism" during the Latin American literary flowering that began in the 1960s. Latin American *magical realism* combined traditional Hispanic interest in the peasantry—peons, gauchos, and Indians—with the latest modernist literary techniques.

An early transition figure was the Argentinian short story writer and poet Jorge Luis Borges (1899–1986). Borges, raised speaking English and educated in Europe, became the first Latin American writer to win an international reputation. His short, often fantastic tales, published as "fictions," sometimes sound more like literary puzzles or modern Arabian Nights entertainments than twentieth–century short stories.

It was Colombian writer Gabriel Garcia Márquez (1928–), however, who made magical realism a recognized style around the world. Garcia Márquez won international renown and a Nobel prize for literature with such novels as *One Hundred Years of Solitude* (1967) and *Autumn of the Patriarch* (1975). *One Hundred Years of Solitude* describes his fictional Colombian village of Macondo in his magical realist mix of naturalistic description and fantasy. This dreamlike combination of precise description, tongue–in–cheek humor, and bizarre and impossible events also leads the reader to accept fantastic occurrences as merely part of an enlarged human reality. The villagers marvel at the discovery of ice one day and watch flying carpets float down from the sky the next—all part of the magical–realist world of Macondo.

Late Modernism and Postmodernism

Modern writers continued to expose the shortcomings of Western society during the later twentieth century. In the United States, for instance, "beat" novelists like Jack Kerouac (1922–1969), author of the cult novel *On the Road* (1957), and poets like Allen Ginsberg (1926–), whose most celebrated poem was called *Howl* (1956), condemned the complacencies of Eisenhower's affluent America by "turning on" to drugs and "tuning out" of conventional life.

Like the modernists of the first half of the century, however, late modernist writers often turned from social concerns to psychodrama set inside the heads of individual characters, or to metaphysical meditations on the human condition. The latter was the course taken by the *theater of the absurd* in Europe following World War II. Perhaps the most famous absurdist play was Samuel Beckett's *Waiting for Godot* (1952), which might—or might not—be about the futility of waiting for God to manifest himself in a godless, meaningless world. This sort of literature made heavy demands on audiences—but rewarded them with challenging experiences. Most got the metaphysical message: "Godot" will never come to Beckett's characters, and their silliness and suffering will never lead to either salvation or damnation in a universe that simply does not care.

From the 1960s on, however, another new approach to creative endeavor emerged. Often called *postmodernism,* the new style rejected both realistic social fiction and the high–cultural pretensions of the modernists. Postmodernist writers deliberately subverted the stories they told by reminding readers that this was, after all, only a piece of fiction. They also abandoned conventional literary concerns like character development, realistic depiction of society, and even coherent narrative. "I began to write," declared the postmodern American author John Hawkes (1925–), "on the assumption that the true enemies of the novel were plot, character, setting, and themes."[6]

Postmodernist theorists rejected all distinctions between high culture and popular culture, good and bad art, deep thought and spontaneous fun. They had no use for the recognized literary standards that "centered" so–called classics and thrust vital popular genres to the periphery. For this postmodernist sensibility, fantasy and science fiction were as legitimate as the literature studied in English classes, and a film like *Star Wars* as worthy of admiration as either Homer's *Odyssey* or James Joyce's *Ulysses.*

At a deeper level, the postmodernists, like their dada predecessors, faulted both modernists and traditionalists for trying to reestablish order and meaning in an inherently chaotic and meaningless world. Postmodernist theorists condemned all "metafictional narratives," or narratives that saw point and meaning in human life, as efforts to conceal the true meaninglessness of the real world in which we live.

This grim view of life, often combined with isolation, depression, and substance abuse, took a heavy toll of twentieth–century writers. The taut, tragic life of the American poet Sylvia Plath (1932–1963) was highlighted by a disciplined effort to develop her immense talent and an intense but failed marriage to the English poet Ted Hughes. In the early 1960s, she drafted *The Bell Jar* (published 1971), a moving novel about her own nervous breakdown, and the luminous poems of her collection *Ariel* (1966). Her suicide at the age of thirty–one deprived modern poetry of a unique and powerful voice.

Other postmodernists, however, seemed to have a good time exposing the pointlessness of life. Such writers as the American Thomas Pynchon (1937–) filled works like *Gravity's Rainbow* (1975) with black humor, social satire, and sexual high jinks. Others, like the Italian writer Italo Calvino (1923–1985), mingled reality, fantasy, and enigmatic puzzles in indescribable books like *Invisible Cities* (1972). But Calvino did see serious problems beneath the new approach to literature and reality. He summed up the postmodern writer's predicament in the 1980s:

> Two contrasting conclusions . . . haunt the writer's mind. The one says: The world doesn't exist, only language exists. The other says: the common language has no meaning: the world is literally unspeakable.[7]

The French guru of 1980s postmodern analysis, Michel Foucault, summed the problem up with almost contemptuous ease:

> To all those who still . . . ask themselves questions about what man is in his essence, to all those who wish to take him as their starting point in their attempts to reach the truth . . . we can answer only with a philosophical laugh . . . .[8]

◆Artistic Experiments◆

Twentieth–century arts other than literature reflected many of the tendencies found in literary modernism. Analysis of forms, lack of concern for the audience, and rebellion against a modern society believed to be dominated by unappreciative philistines were among these similarities. This survey of the arts in an age of experimentation will offer an all-too-brief survey of modern painting, sculpture, architecture, music, dance, film, and other less categorizable arts.

Testing the Limits

Like literary modernists, modern artists rejected both contemporaneous taste and much of their heritage of Western values. Even more than modernist writers, the painters, sculptors, architects, composers, and dancers of the twentieth–century modernist movement set out to explore the formal elements of their arts. Yet they, too, in some ways clearly reflected the larger spirit of the age they rejected.

Formal elements had always been the building blocks of all the arts. Painters on cave walls or Greek vases, sculptors from ancient Rome to the Renaissance achieved their effects by manipulating line, shape, color, masses, surface textures, and other elements of form as opposed to the content of a statue or a painting. Premodern architects deployed precisely defined classic orders, and dancers in all times moved through carefully choreographed steps and gestures. All, in short, imposed some sort of formal order on the world.

Twentieth–century artists, however, made a full–time occupation out of testing the limits and possibilities of form. Their explorations and experiments in color, shape, patterned movement and sound, in enclosing space for living and working, and in the all–encompassing art of the motion picture were experiments undertaken for their own sake. The result was to give twentieth–century art a tone and texture to be found nowhere else in Western history.

The Evolution of Modernist Art

The history of twentieth–century painting began in the later nineteenth century with the postimpressionist painters. Thereafter the modernists followed a clear trajectory through the breakup of observed reality in the work of Picasso or its presentation for purely formal effects in Georgia O'Keeffe to the fully abstract art of such controversial twentieth–century masters as Jackson Pollock.

The life of Paul Gauguin (1848–1903) has seemed to many to illustrate the life of the modern artist in its essentially hostile relationship to modern society. A businessman with a wife and family through the first half of his life, Gauguin was thoroughly immersed in the bourgeois culture of the later nineteenth century. In his later, creative years, however, he turned from career and family to art, plunged into the Paris bohemia of the fin de siècle years, and finally took himself off to the South Seas to paint among the palm trees and un-materialistic Polynesians of Tahiti. His simply drawn Polynesians set in a dreamlike world of tropical beauty achieved a power and a mystery that seemed to go beyond the meticulously accurate academic painting of the time. The romantic enthusiasm for the "noble savage" here fused with the emerging modernist determination to go back to formal basics to grip the twentieth–century imagination.

The life of Georgia O'Keeffe (1887–1986) followed a very similar pattern several decades later on the other side of the Atlantic. O'Keeffe, too, moved from bourgeois respectability through New York's bohemia to self–exile from society, in the deserts of the American southwest. Better at drawing than Gauguin, she continued to paint her plant and animal forms in intimate detail. But she also chose and depicted her subjects—an open flower, the skull of a dead steer whitened on the desert—in ways carefully calculated to emphasize shapes, colors, and other formal qualities. O'Keeffe thus transformed these fragments of the natural world into abstractions without ever sacrificing their concrete reality.

Pablo Picasso (1881–1973), the century's most famous artist, moved from highly skilled academic and naturalistic painting to a devastating fragmentation of the world that went far beyond the simplifications of Gauguin and O'Keeffe. Picasso's great break with naturalism came just before World War I, when he invented the style that came to be called *cubism.*

Picasso and other cubist painters broke the subject up into shapes, planes, individual parts of the whole, then reduced these fragments to simple patterns, and finally, they rearranged these pieces in aesthetically pleasing compositions on the canvas. You can find the female forms in *Les Demoiselles d'Avignon* or the figures and instruments in *Three Musicians,* but it is the cubist composition that brings you back for a second look. This fragmented style could even enhance the impact of its subject as in Picasso's *Guernica,* which depicts the bombing of a market town in Spain during the Spanish Civil War with a sense of outrage that a more naturalistic picture would be hard put to convey.

New York emerged as the new center of modernist art after World War II. Preeminent among the leaders of what became known as the New York school stood the influential figure of Jackson Pollock (1912–1956), one of the many modernists who followed the formalist emphasis all the way to pure abstraction. Contemporaries raised their eyebrows as this leader of postwar *abstract expressionism* laid his huge canvases on the floor and walked all over them, dripping paint from the can in meandering, interweaving patterns across the surface. But Pollock thus achieved the implied object of the whole formalist movement: painting as pure as music, without any subject at all. He infused his patterns of line, not only with formal tensions, but with powerful expressions of emotion as well.

Subsequent developments in modernism included such styles as color field painting, minimalist or hard–edge art, and some striking personal statements almost too idiosyncratic for labels. Color field painting offered a strong emotional statement, as Pollock had, but through large areas of bright color rather than lyric patterns of line. The minimalist approach, by contrast, sought to avoid all emotional involvement, producing instead simple, geometric patterns of color set off by sharp boundaries, as in Josef Albers's (1888–1976) famous series, *Homage to the Square*. Such artists as Andy Warhol (1930–1987) and Roy Lichtenstein (1923–) returned to representational painting, but only to make fun of such popular icons as movie star Marilyn Monroe, Campbell's soup cans, and comic strips.

Other arts turned weirder, darker, and more violent as the century wore on. The rebellious urge to redefine art in outlandish ways, already expressed by the dadaists after World War I, surfaced again in the "performance art" of the 1990s. A performance artist might "make a statement" by taking off her clothes and smearing herself with chocolate, by destroying a musical instrument, burning money, or simply by going to sleep in a display case in a museum.

Still other artists carried on the modernist tradition of defying traditional morality by filling their work with sexual or violent material that still had power to shock. Robert Mapplethorpe's photographs of naked men and savage acts of self–mutilation led to the closing of museums that sponsored shows of his work. Christian religious subjects were displayed in ways that many religious people saw as blasphemous—and were regularly cited by those who sought to slash government funding for the arts.

Modern Sculpture and Architecture

Twentieth–century sculpture in stone, metal, and other materials also voyaged far from the Greek and Renaissance traditions of realistic representation, while architecture turned its back on all inherited traditions. Sculptors and builders often exploited new materials, creating impressions seldom or never seen before in these two arts.

Individualistic, experimental style became the distinguishing feature of modern sculpture, the art of carving, casting, and otherwise assembling three–dimensional works of art. Twentieth–century sculptors like Alberto Giacometti (1901–1966) and Henry Moore (1898–1986) imposed their own distinctive visions on the human figure. Giacometti's stark stick figures of rough metal were above all instantly recognizable as his. The English artist Henry Moore produced monumental female nudes, usually reclining and often with children, but always in a style that rejected realism in favor of massive interacting volumes and polished surfaces.

Other sculptors went further still. Some abandoned tradition and representation entirely, assembling pieces of metal and other materials into purely aesthetic compositions.

Thus Alexander Calder (1898–1976) created the "mobile," a work of art whose various parts, suspended on wires, rearrange themselves into new patterns with each passing breath of air. Others, like David Smith (1906–1965), welded stainless steel or "found objects" made of iron into carefully composed "constructs." Louise Nevelson (1900–1988) created artistic "environments" made of wooden boxes arranged in free–standing walls that became sought–after collectors' items in her own lifetime. Still others worked with the earth itself: the controversial Christo (1935–), for instance, specialized in reshaping the world around us by draping buildings in plastic, flinging curtains across canyons, or erecting clusters of giant umbrellas on opposite sides of the Pacific Ocean.

Architecture had already made some basic advances along the modernist road by the turn of the century. The strength of structural steel and poured concrete liberated architects from classic Western devices like the pillar and the arch. Their own modernist zeal for self–expression and innovation led twentieth–century builders like Frank Lloyd Wright (1867–1959) to set new goals for themselves and develop new styles to achieve these aims.

"Form follows function" was one such new ideal. *Functionalism* produced architecture that refused to imitate Greco–Roman or Gothic styles, creating instead environments for living that arranged spaces for the convenience and pleasure of the people who were to work or live there. Another approach emphasized fitting the building into its natural setting, integrating it with natural vegetation and landscape. Wright's famous house, *Taliesin West,* for instance, blended perfectly with both Native–American building styles and its Arizona desert setting.

Perhaps the most typical product of twentieth–century architecture, however, was that towering evocation of a technological age, the skyscraper. Based on a technology never available before, from steel girders to electrically operated elevators, skyscrapers soared to heights undreamed of in earlier ages. Raised first in the metropolises of the United States, these spires of steel and concrete spread to Europe and the rest of the world in the second half of the century. The skyscraper, reaching dozens of stories and hundreds of feet into the air, thus became the symbol of urban growth and life in our century, giving the cities of our times a profile undreamed of in earlier cycles of Western culture.

Architecture in the later twentieth century, finally, moved more consciously into the new postmodernist style than most other arts outside literature. Postmodernist architects abandoned functionalism and the clean–lined, poured–concrete structures of the international style, seeking inspiration instead in both past traditions and sometimes garish aspects of the present. Postmodernist architecture thus drew motifs from historic styles of building—sometimes tongue–in–cheek—or borrowed motifs from the neon–lit streets of Las Vegas. It also brought bright colors and even whimsy into building designs, making center cities much more colorful and interesting to look at.

Renzo Piano and Richard Rogers's *Pompidou Center* for the arts in Paris, for example, turns architecture inside out by putting usually concealed features like elevators and air ducts on the outside, coloring these pipes and beams bright blue, green, or red, and creating a cheerfully dotty "boiler room facade" that has outraged purists and drawn millions of visitors.

Modern Music and Dance

Nowhere did art acquire a more startling new look in the twentieth century than in perhaps the oldest of the arts: music and dance. This period launched an unprecedented reexamination of the basics in these arts that stripped both to the bone and developed startling new forms in musical composition and choreography.

In this century, composers offered such breakthroughs in sound as the twelve–tone scale in Europe, while African–American musicians in the United States forged the equally intricate but far more accessible form known as jazz. In the field of dance, Europeans perfected ballet while Americans again blazed new trails, notably in the development of modern dance.

Austrian–born Arnold Schoenberg (1874–1951), a classically trained composer and teacher, shook the world of classical music with his twelve–tone compositions of the 1920s. Breaking with normal compositional practice, Schoenberg began to use the entire twelve tones of the scale, arranged in an arbitrary "set," as the basis for a musical work. The result was music characterized by intricate mathematical structure but with no detectable "tune" at all. As a result, such works as his *Quartet for Winds* (1924), his first full–length piece in the new mode, sounded cacophonous to outraged audiences, though these works impressed and influenced a number of twentieth–century composers.

Combining this modern music with experimental dancing, modernistic sets, and some radically modern ideas could generate stunning theatrical experiences. *Rite of Spring,* composed by Igor Stravinsky (1882–1971) and staged by the Russian ballet master Sergei Diaghilev (1872–1929) in Paris in 1913, was such a miraculous moment. A puppetlike ballet, a dissonant score, and a theme based on primeval fertility cults and human sacrifice generated so much audience reaction that the dancers could hardly hear the orchestra. Only with the famous dancer and choreographer Vaslav Nijinsky (1890–1950) demonstrating the dance movements perched on a chair offstage were they able to get through one of the legendary opening nights in modern theatrical history.

In the second half of the century, John Cage (1912–1992), a pupil of Schoenberg's, tried to include a much wider range of sounds than those normally used in music. His controversial "indeterminist" compositions deployed randomly selected musical notes, used radios and tape recorders as "instruments," and in one celebrated case, offered four and a half minutes of complete silence as a concert piece.

Electronic technology, finally, transformed experimental composition. The Moog synthesizer made it possible to compose and perform music without any real instruments or human voices at all. Weird and even repulsive though the resulting audio experience might be to those accustomed to the mellower tones of old wood and human throats, electronic music seemed to be winning a recognized place in twentieth–century music.

Much more directly appealing were two musical forms to which America made major contributions—the popular idioms of jazz in the first half of the century and rock and roll in the second half. Jazz had its origins in African rhythms transmuted through the work songs of field hands and church spirituals into the popular musical forms of ragtime and the blues. From these modes, as performed in the American south around the turn of the century, jazz took shape. Reaching white America and then Europe in the 1920s—a period often called "the jazz age" in U. S. history—the new music evolved in the hands of such composers and performers as W. C. Handy (1873–1958), who was among the first to write down this music before the First World War. The brilliant trumpeter Louis Armstrong (1900–1971) epitomized the key part played by the soloist and the vital role of improvisation in the development of jazz. Edward ("Duke") Ellington (1899–1974), by contrast, was a meticulous composer and orchestrator, carefully integrating the talents of his musicians in the so–called big–band era of the 1930s. Popular rather than elitist, inspired and improvisational, the jazz creations of these African–American musicians found enthusiastic admirers around the world.

Another popular musical form that was born in America but spread widely across the Western world—and well beyond it—was rock and roll. Rock music took shape in the 1950s and won national and then international audiences through the work of such singers as Elvis Presley (1935–1977), the acknowledged "king" of the form in the early days. Outside the United States, British rock bands like the Beatles and the Rolling Stones gained international renown from the 1960s on. The Beatles evolved spectacularly through the sixties, from mop–topped teen idols crooning "I Wanna Hold Your Hand" through the astonishing new sounds of "Sergeant Pepper" into the mix of driving rock rhythms with musically exciting departures that characterized the best of later rock and roll. Building on a heavily accentuated beat, electronically amplified sound, and increasingly colorful staging, popular groups like the Stones filled sports stadiums with screaming fans on their elaborately mounted world tours.

Creative pioneers of *modern dance* like Martha Graham (1894–1991) refashioned this ancient art also. Classical ballet had become stereotyped and unexciting, limiting the freedom and self–expression of the dancer. The pioneers of modern dance, by contrast, reduced dance to its basic components of movement and gesture and stressed self–expression rather than mastery of traditional dance patterns. Thus modern dancers, like other modernists, emphasized formal elements and insisted above all on the freedom to innovate. Often reducing costume to the simple leotard and sets to the merest abstract indications, they gave dance a whole new look.

Thus rediscovering the potentialities of the human body as a vehicle for self–expression, such choreographers as Martha Graham could examine basic human relationships or cosmic problems through powerful nontraditional forms of dancing. Graham's often–expressed goal, "to give substance to things felt," incarnated the drive of modern dance toward the expression of inner feeling. In works like *Frontier* (1935), she exalted not only the American West but all the intensely felt frontiers of human life. In *Night Journey* (1947), her classic reworking of the Oedipus story from the point of view of his mother–wife Jocasta, she probed a human sensibility—and two fundamental human relationships—in a moment of anguished discovery.

The Emerging Art of the Film

The movies, as they are often called, were of course a popular art form from the beginning, but the motion picture has also produced art of the highest order. Born just before 1900, the cinema has become the quintessential art form of the twentieth century. The cinema film gave the impression of movement by projecting a series of still shots so rapidly that the human eye could not distinguish between the separate pictures and saw continuous motion instead. Through the first quarter of the century, movie makers perfected many of the techniques of cinematography. From the 1930s on sound films became common, and color and wide–screen projection came in after World War II.

The art of the film was international from the beginning. The best early film projectors were designed in France in the late nineteenth century, the most impressive studio sets in Germany in the 1920s. But it was in the Los Angeles suburb of Hollywood that the movies became a big business, purveyors of laughter, thrills, and dreams to millions of people around the world.

The medium's capacity for close–up intimacy made it a natural vehicle for love stories featuring screen idols like Rudolph Valentino (1895–1926), probably best known for his role as *The Sheik,* and Marlene Dietrich (1904–1992), the sultry nightclub entertainer of *The Blue Angel.* Comedy and tragedy were both intensified by vivid movie techniques, as in Mack Sennett's speeded–up "Keystone Cops" farces, full of slapstick physical humor, and the terrifying performances of Boris Karloff as the monster in *Frankenstein.* Sometimes comedy and tragedy were combined in the films of a genius like Charlie Chaplin (1889–1977), whose bowler–hatted tramp with the little mustache and liquid eyes was at one time the most universally recognized personality in the world.

While glamorous movie "stars" held the public's eye, directors were the presiding intelligences who transformed a popular entertainment medium into an art form. Among the most influential early directors were the American D. W. Griffith and Soviet film maker Sergei Eisenstein.

David Wark Griffith (1875–1948), an unsuccessful stage actor turned film director in the early days of movies, became the first great film maker. He led in developing such innovations as close–ups, long shots, fade–outs at the end of a scene, cross–cutting from one sequence of events to another to create excitement and suspense, and the alternation of short and long scenes for dramatic effect. He also made movie history with spectacular feats like the battle scenes in his first masterpiece, *Birth of a Nation* (1915). Despite its racist subject—the rise of the Ku Klux Klan—it showcased all of Griffith's new techniques with dazzling effect. It was "history written with lightning" across the screen, and with its release the cinema was established as an art form as well as a multi–million–dollar industry.

The Soviet film maker Sergei Eisenstein (1898–1948) began to make films in the heady experimental days after the Russian Revolution—and before the advent of Stalin. Young Eisenstein directed and produced film spectaculars in which "the people" as a whole shared the stage with the nominal hero. Thus *Battleship Potemkin* (1925) chronicled the revolt of ordinary seamen against the czarist navy, and *Alexander Nevsky* (1938) offered a pictorially stunning epic treatment of the medieval Russian hero that inspired Soviet audiences on the eve of World War II. Eisenstein's major addition to the emerging repertoire of film techniques was the art of *montage*—the art of splicing together short lengths of film to tell a story in vivid flashes of action, to suggest associations, to emphasize a central theme, or simply to create a powerful visual impact. Thus the famous "Odessa steps" scene in *Potemkin* tells the story of a czarist massacre by flashing from the advancing troops to the fleeing citizens and catching brief moments of horror—a baby carriage careening down the steps, the shattered lenses of a student's spectacles—to create a powerful visual impact.

The artistic development of the motion picture continued through the second half of the century. Italian new realism, with films like Roberto Rossellini's (1906–1977) *Open City* (1945), gave the world a gritty feel for life in the ruins of World War II. French new wave cinema added subtlety and complexity, developing the *auteur* approach, which emphasized the key role of the director, in films like Alain Robbe–Grillet's (1922–) *Last Year at Marienbad* (1961). Connoisseurs of the art film reveled in the dark vision of Swedish director Ingmar Bergman (1918–), whose *The Seventh Seal* (1956) combined brilliant ensemble acting with elaborate symbolism in a tale of disillusioned crusaders and the black death in medieval Europe. Japan's Akiro Kurosawa (1910–) baffled film buffs in many lands with challenging pictures like *Rashomon* (1950), in which three characters offered three different versions of a series of shocking events—and the audience was left to decide what "really" happened.

American directors also continued to make their contributions to the evolving new art. The U. S. film industry dominated the global popular market with action–adventure films and high production values, generally leaving to European and Asian directors the "art film" intended for small but discriminating audiences. Yet there was a high degree of artistry to the work of such American film makers as Francis Ford Coppola (1939–), maker of the trend–setting gangster film *The Godfather* (1972), George Lucas (1944–), creator of the *Star Wars* (1972) science fiction series, and Steven Spielberg (1947–), whose heart–warming *ET: The Extraterrestrial* (1982) set box–office records everywhere. At the same time, a few European productions, such as Britain's long–running "James Bond–007" spy series, coined money as efficiently as any Hollywood commercial movie.

As with music, technological advances combined with creative innovation to make the evolving film medium a fascinating and distinctively twentieth–century art form. The almost universal use of color and the wider screen, giving the image more depth, were key technical improvements in the second half of the century. Technicians and stunt men and women added amazing special effects, until there was almost literally nothing that could not be convincingly displayed on the screen. With these technical means at their disposal, film makers produced images of startling beauty, poignancy, horror, passion, and mystery.

Much of the popular appeal of movies was based on slapstick or risqué comedy, on such "sex and violence" staples as nude scenes and car chases, or on space–age special effects usually involving extraterrestrial threats to Planet Earth. But there were films with profounder goals and subtler artistic textures, and the motion picture remained perhaps the most fascinating of twentieth–century artistic accomplishments. That it was also in many ways the ultimate popular entertainment merely added to its protean quality as a medium that could appeal to all people.

The rapid spread of television across the Western world and the subsequent development of the video cassette further expanded the market and the possibilities for film makers. Television series, showing new adventures of the same characters every week, made international celebrities out of performers like comedians Lucille Ball (1911–1989) and Bill Cosby (1937–). The series format also allowed characters to develop and themes to be explored in ways that were impossible in a two–hour play or film.

Serious art had led the century–long assault on public sensibilities, but the popular arts—movies, television, popular music—were not far behind. Black "rap" music, reflecting the dangerous world of the slum–dwelling African–American male, characterized women as prostitutes and bitches and appeared to advocate drug use and various forms of mayhem. Television blossomed with new generations of ever more daring "situation comedies" full of sexual innuendo, of "talk shows" highlighted by confessions of exotic sexual behavior, and of films awash in violence.

The big cinema screen contributed its share of blood and sexual extravagance. The American film–maker for the nineties seemed to be Quentin Tarentino, whose *Reservoir Dogs* and *Pulp Fiction* joined a lengthening line of pictures that featured casual killing and shocking cruelty. Another long line of films with names like *Fatal Attraction* or *Basic Instinct* explored new sexual pathologies.

The public seemed to some to have had enough by the later 1990s. The religious right demanded censorship, television moved to regulate itself, and the public flocked to animated Walt Disney "family films" or to movies or television series based on the very un–explicit, generally un–paranoid nineteenth–century novels of Henry James, Edith Wharton, and even Jane Austen. Quality pictures like *Philadelphia* (about an AIDS victim) or *Forrest Gump* (about a mentally retarded young man) demonstrated that commonly shared values could be successfully explored in moving pictures. But there always seemed to be an international audience for another film full of violence, sex, and of course car chases.

Summary

During the last hundred years, "the second scientific revolution" introduced the public to such abstruse aspects of reality as radiation and relativity. Twentieth–century scientists also uncovered the basic forces that hold the universe together and the chemical compounds that program all living things. At a more theoretical level, cosmologists explained the origins of the cosmos in a "big bang" that generated the expanding universe in which we live. Yet emphasis on such terms as relativity and indeterminacy left many lay observers baffled at scientific disciplines that seemed to challenge their own most cherished principles.

Religious faith still provided the bedrock for many Western people, offering social reform and salvation for the individual believer. Philosophy, however, explored such secular and relativistic doctrines as pragmatism (stressing the usefulness of ideas rather than their truth), existentialism (asserting the primacy of raw existence over philosophic explanations of it), and the structuralist–poststructuralist view (which seemed to reduce reality to a tangle of conflicting discourses and paradigms).

Modernist and postmodernist literature, meanwhile, challenged tradition in both content and form. Serious twentieth–century novelists, dramatists, and poets rejected many of the values and institutions of the West. Perhaps even more important, however, modernism and later postmodernism rejected the traditional literary forms and plunged into a century of literary experimentation.

Formal explorations highlighted Western art in the twentieth century, too. Modern painters like Picasso broke reality up into abstract forms or, like Jackson Pollock, created pure patterns on canvas. Sculpture also followed this pattern, while architecture experimented with functionalism and new materials and music reached from electronically generated sound to improvisational and popular forms like jazz and rock and roll. The new art of the film combined technological wizardry and visual poetry to produce unprecedented effects on cinema screens around the world.

Some Key Terms

abstract expressionism 749
auteur theory 753
big bang theory 734
cubism 748
dadaism 744
deconstruction 740
existentialism 739
functionalism 750
fundamentalism 738

logical positivism 738
magical realism 745
modern dance 752
modernism 741
montage 753
neo–orthodoxy 738
paradigm 737
postmodernism 746
poststructuralism 740

pragmatism 739
radiation 732
socialist realism 745
stream of consciousness 743
structuralism 740
surrealism 744
theater of the absurd 746
theory of relativity 733
uncertainty principle 736

Notes

1. Dietrich Bonhoeffer, *Letters and Papers from Prison*, ed. E. Bethge (New York: Macmillan, 1966), 194–195.
2. Frederick Copleston, *A History of Philosophy*, vol. 9, *Maine de Biran to Sartre* (London: Search Press, 1975), 416.
3. Tristan Tzara, quoted in Anthony Esler, *Bombs Beards and Barricades* (New York: Stein and Day, 1971), 189–190.
4. André Breton, *Manifestoes of Surrealism*, trans. Richard Seaver and Helen R. Lane (Ann Arbor: University of Michigan Press, 1977), 26.
5. Statutes of the Union of Soviet Writers, in Michael T. Florinsky, *Russia: A Short History* (New York: Macmillan, 1964), 610.
6. John Hawkes, quoted in "John Hawkes: An Interview," *Wisconsin Studies in Contemporary Literature* 6 (1965): 143.
7. Italo Calvino, "The Written and the Unwritten Word," *New York Review of Books* (May 12, 1983), 38.
8. Michel Foucault, *The Order of Things* (New York: Vintage, 1973), 341.

Reading List

Arnason, H. H. *History of Modern Art*. New York: Abrams, 1969. Useful survey. For more recent scholarly essays on modernism in the arts, see M. Chefdor, R. Quinones, and A. Wachtel, eds., *Modernism* (Urbana: University of Illinois Press, 1986).

Beckett, S. *Waiting for Godot. (1952)* New York: Grove Press, 1954. Perhaps the most famous of the absurdist plays of the post–World War II period. On Beckett and others of this school, see M. Esslin, *The Theater of the Absurd* (Garden City, N.Y.: Doubleday, 1961).

DeMille, A. *Martha: The Life and Work of Martha Graham*. New York: Random House, 1991. Life of the founder of modern dance, by a lifelong friend and co–worker. For the work of a major modernist in music, see J. Cage, *Silence* (Cambridge, Mass.: MIT Press, 1969).

Derrida, J. *A Derrida Reader: Between the Blinds*. Edited by P. Kamuf. New York: Columbia University Press, 1991. Important selections from this enigmatic thinker, with useful introduction and notes.

Eliot, T. S. *Collected Poems*. Edited by F. Kermode. London: Faber, 1975. Good selection with valuable editing and introduction. On Eliot's place in the modernist canon, see L. Menand, *T. S. Eliot and His Context* (New York: Oxford University Press, 1987).

Gamov, G. *Thirty Years That Shook Physics*. Garden City, N.Y.: Anchor, 1966. A scientist's highly readable introduction to the second scientific revolution. On the "Newton" of the new movement, N. Calder, *Einstein's Universe* (London: British Broadcasting Company, 1979), is authoritative, readable, and even illustrated. For a provocative challenge to traditional views of how our understanding of the universe changes, see T. Kuhn's seminal essay, *The Structure of Scientific Revolutions* (Chicago: University of Chicago Press, 1962).

Garcia Márquez, G. *One Hundred Years of Solitude*. Translated by G. Rabassa. New York: Harper and Row, 1970. Epic of the Brazilian backlands, written in the neo–surrealist magical realist style of a number of post–World War II Latin American writers. On this Latin American renaissance, see D. F. Gallagher, *Modern Latin American Literature* (New York: Oxford University Press, 1973).

Gergardus, M. *Cubism and Futurism*. Oxford: Phaidon, 1979. Brief but well–illustrated coverage. On two other linked European movements, see M. Oesterreicher–Moellwo, *Surrealism and Dadaism* (Oxford: Phaidon, 1979), a well–illustrated treatment of the dada–surrealist stream in modern art. On abstract expressionism, consult I. Sandler, *The Triumph of American Painting* (New York: Praeger, 1970).

Giannetti, L. D. *Understanding Movies*. 4th ed. Englewood Cliffs, N.J.: Prentice Hall, 1987. Solid introduction to the art of the film.

Joyce, J. *Ulysses: The Corrected Text*. Edited by W. Gabler. Harmondsworth, England: Penguin, 1986. Controversial new edition of the modernist classic. For a picture of the author's early years, see his *Portrait of the Artist as a Young Man* (Harmondsworth, England: Penguin, 1976).

Quinn, S. *Marie Curie: A Life*. New York: Simon & Schuster, 1995. Recent and readable life of the pioneering scientist.

Safford, J. *Pragmatism and the Progressive Movement in the United States*. London: University Press of America, 1987. Views the spread of the pragmatic viewpoint in its political frame of reference and traces its influence.

Sartre, J. P. *No Exit and Three Other Plays*. New York: Random House, 1955. The emotional impact of existentialism, especially the postwar French variety, is best absorbed through Sartre's theater, or through such novels as A. Camus, *The Plague,* trans. G. Stuart (New York: Modern Library, 1948). For a close–up look at the Paris intellectuals after the war by one of them, see S. de Beauvoir, *The Mandarins,* trans. L. M. Friedman (New York: Meridian, 1960).

Schwartz, S. *The Matrix of Modernism*. Princeton, N.J.: Princeton Press, 1985. Readable recent account of literary modernism in its early phases. R. Williams, *The Politics of Modernism* (London: Verso, 1989), offers a recent cultural critic's analysis of the ideological sources of the movement.

Showalter, E. *Sexual Anarchy: Gender and Culture at the Fin de Siecle*. New York: Viking, 1990. Myths and metaphors of crisis and decline at the end of the nineteenth and twentieth centuries compared.

Skinner, B. F. *Reflections on Behaviorism and Society*. Englewood Cliffs, N.J.: Prentice Hall, 1978. Views of a leading behaviorist.

Tirro, F. *Jazz: A History*. New York: Norton, 1977. Overview of a major American contribution to Western culture. For the social context of the rise of the form, see A. Shaw, *The Jazz Age: Popular Music in the 1920s* (Oxford: Oxford University Press, 1987).

Wertenbaker, L. *The World of Picasso*. New York: Time–Life Books, 1967. Picasso and his contemporaries in modern art, well illustrated.

Wilson, E. O. *On Human Nature*. Cambridge, Mass.: Harvard University Press, 1978. Accessible presentation of the sociobiological thesis that nature is as important as nurture in determining human behavior. For both sides of the dispute, see A. L. Caplan, *The Sociobiology Debate* (New York: Harper and Row, 1976).

Woolf, V. *To the Lighthouse*. London: Hogarth Press, 1977. Masterpiece of early modernist writing. For Woolf's influential essays, see *The Common Reader* (London: Hogarth Press, 1984).

— 30 —

Towards 2000

The West and the World at the End of the Millennium

•The West and the Developing Nations
•The West and the Non-Western Powers •The West and a World in Disarray
•The West and a Planet at Risk •Toward a New World Order?

The West had been relating closely to the non–Western world for many centuries as the year 2000 approached. The roots of Western civilization lay in Greek city–states that had learned much from their Afro–Asian neighbors and in a Roman Empire that had once included at least small parts of Asia and Africa. During the Middle Ages, the West had reached out once more, however tentatively, toward Islamic lands in Crusades that were dress rehearsals for what was to come.

What came, of course, was the unparalleled Western overseas expansion of modern times. Over five centuries, between the late 1400s and the early 1900s, relentless European imperialism carried the West to mastery of most of the globe. By 1900, Europeans had reshaped North America, South America, and Australia in Europe's image, partitioned most of Africa into European colonies, and divided most of Asia into colonies, protectorates, and spheres of influence.

That world is gone today, collapsed in a rush during the decades after World War II. Dozens of new non–Western nations have emerged on the world stage and begun to play independent—and sometimes key—roles in our common history. As the year 2000 drew near, then, the West found itself as deeply involved in global affairs as ever, but now in a rapidly changing and increasingly challenging world.

This final chapter will survey the complexities of contemporary Western involvement with the rest of the world. It will look at Western relations with developing nations, many of which have needed our help, and with emerging economic powers on other continents, who have sometimes challenged our vital interests and our most cherished values. The chapter will also outline some of the global concerns we share with all the world's peoples, from economic and social problems to expanding populations, dwindling resources, and poisoned air and water.

A main theme of this book has been the West's historic entanglement with the world at large. This concluding chapter will survey our late twentieth–century involvement, evaluate the situation today, and try at least to resist the temptation to offer some risky predictions of the shape of things to come.

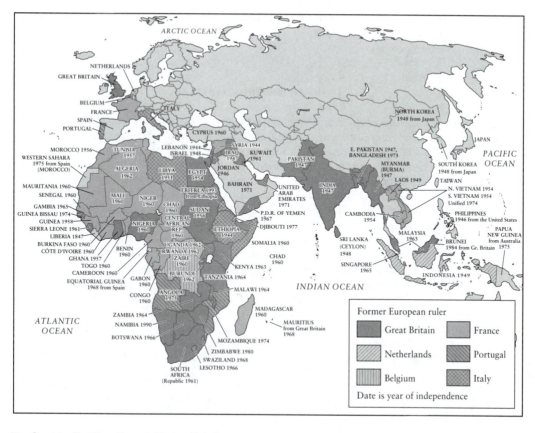

New Countries That Were Formerly Western Colonies

♦ The West and the Developing Nations ♦

As we saw in Chapter 28, a major global trend of the decades after World War II was the collapse of the extensive European overseas empires that once ringed the world with Western power. Where before World War II there stood half–a–dozen European world empires, now scores of separate nations appeared on the map. Most of them, furthermore, declared themselves "nonaligned" with either side in the cold war, thus creating a new, third grouping of nations, the so–called *Third World*.

In the following pages, we will look at the non–Western world as a whole in the later decades of the twentieth century. In so doing, we will have to distinguish between two types of non–Western country: *developing nations* on the one hand and the *emerging non–Western powers* on the other. In this section, we will look at the problem–racked majority, the developing countries of Africa, Asia, and Latin America. In the next section, we will study those non–Western countries, from the Middle Eastern oil nations to the booming East Asian rim, that experienced economic growth and became regional powers themselves before the end of the century. Everywhere, as we explore the "big picture" of the world in the later twentieth century, we will see continuing interaction between Western and non–Western peoples.

Defining the Third World

The developing nations of the Third World had many things in common: a shared colonial past, economic underdevelopment, generally authoritarian political structures, and pre-modern social and cultural formations. Their ties with the developed West not only did not vanish with political independence but in many ways grew stronger. The influence of the West on the rest of the world did not decline, but grew even after the political indepen-dence of their former colonies was established.

The umbrella term *non–Western nations* is very broad. During the later 1900s, the group of nations thus described included more than the former imperial dependencies in Asia and Africa. The label was sometimes used for the countries of Latin America as well, long independent and Western in political institutions and in social and cultural patterns but sharing many of the economic problems of the new nations of Africa and Asia. Other terms were also sometimes used for all three continents. Besides "Third World," "non-aligned," or "developing," the regional description *global south* was often used, referring to the tropical band of developing nations around the world. Just to complicate things fur-ther, the label "global south" was also sometimes applied to developing nations that were not in fact located in the southern hemisphere, such as China.

Economic and technological underdevelopment has often been cited as the defining characteristic of the global south. These are primarily agricultural countries with high levels of poverty, both urban and rural. They are village cultures, peasant societies, leavened by a scattering of modern metropolises ringed by shantytowns. They also have large and grow-ing populations to feed. The center of the population explosion has shifted from the West-ern world to Africa, Asia, and Latin America. Large populations, once seen as a source of strength, now multiplied the problems of the developing countries as they sought to raise the living standards of their people.

Many developing nations, like their Western counterparts a few decades earlier, turned to *authoritarian governments* to solve their multiple problems in the years after achieving independence. Some of these governments were surviving hereditary monarchies, as in a number of Muslim–ruled countries. Often they were one–party states governed by the charismatic leader and the mass party that had won their independence, as in many former African colonies. In other places, military leaders ruled through the army, a common pat-tern in Latin America ever since the nineteenth–century Wars of Liberation.

In many ways, the developing nations of Asia, Africa, and Latin America remained dis-tinctly non–Western cultures. Their religions—Muslim, Hindu, Buddhist, Catholic—were more likely to play central parts in their lives than were those of most Europeans. Clan and family ties, village traditions, and tribal affiliations were still very important in the global south. In many parts of the developing world, also, people claimed ties to civilizations older than that of the West, revering philosophers, poets, and ancient kings unknown to most Europeans or Americans.

These non–Western developing nations, finally, had a host of problems, some shared with Western developed countries, many particularly their own. Traditional education in the mosque or at the feet of village elders, for instance, was readily available; but literacy, technical training, and modern education in Western languages were often in shorter supply. An economic infrastructure of transport facilities, investment capital, and other requirements for economic growth was commonly lacking. Many former colonies were re-source poor. Agriculture was frequently inefficient, industry inadequate, poverty wide-spread. Epidemic diseases ravaged tropical populations.

Most of the colonies that became countries thus still had enormous problems left to solve when they celebrated their independence from their former imperial rulers. Technical training, economic infrastructure, modern industry, even export–oriented agriculture were still long–range goals rather than realities. And all of them required contact with the West-ern world, the primary source of technical know–how and money.

Old Agendas and Pressures for Change

There were some extremely impressive leaders in this part of the world, like Tanzania's Ny-erere and Ivory Coast's Houphouët–Boigny. But there were also some brutal dictatorships in the developing nations, like those of Idi Amin in Uganda, Pol Pot in Cambodia, or the notorious Somoza family in Nicaragua. Bloated bureaucracies could produce an immense amount of graft and corruption: Africans called top bureaucrats the *Wabenzi*—"the Mer-cedes–Benz people." Western powers sometimes supported dictatorships because their countries had something of value, such as the oil of Arabia, or were of political use, like the U.S. naval bases in the Philippines, or represented a thorn in the side of an antagonist, as Soviet–supported Cuba was to the United States.

The goals of the non–Western majority of humankind did include a number of objec-tives not rooted in Western contacts. The three continents where developing nations pre-dominated had their own histories, their own domestic tensions, and their own interna-tional rivalries. In Asia and Africa, the end of Western rule meant freedom to take up these suspended agendas once more. The Latin American nations had already been pursuing them for a century and a half.

These agendas included political ambitions, international conflicts, and religious en-thusiasms that predated the Western hegemony. Feuds within nations and between nations, suppressed by the Western conquerors, sprang up once again. Conflicts between peoples and tribal groupings ravaged Nigeria, Zaire, and other African nations soon after indepen-dence in the 1960s and did the same to Somalia and Rwanda as late as the 1990s. China re-vived its traditional claim to the predominant position in East Asia soon after Mao's victory in 1949, conquered Himalayan Tibet, fought border wars with India, and in the 1990s was still moving to reabsorb Hong Kong and threatening Taiwan with military action. Religion also resurfaced as a source of both strength and discord in the non–Western world. A far–reaching Muslim religious revival swept across western Asia and North Africa, restoring meaning to many lives but also contributing to a ferment of wars and revolutions. Hindu–Muslim violence kindled a series of military confrontations between India and Pakistan.

Westerners frequently failed to understand these non–Western priorities and impera-tives. Americans in particular were likely to see China's reassertion of its ancient claim to be the great power of East Asia as communist aggression, or to be outraged by the violent pas-sions unleashed by the Islamic revival in North Africa or the Middle East. Even a firm as-sertion of some rather puritanical Confucian values on the part of little Singapore, caning an American youth for vandalism, could seem cruel and unusual to some Westerners.

One overriding ambition, however, was shared by virtually all the new nations: the desire for rapid economic and technological development. Once political independence was achieved, this became the primary goal of the poor nations of the world. Much that we discuss in the following pages—political and economic links to the West, the willingness even to risk new imperialist exploitation—goes back to this determination to acquire standards of living and material power comparable to those already achieved by the Western peoples.

Capital, Trade, Aid, and Loans

Economic development was of central importance to the nations of the Third World as they struggled to provide better lives for their citizens. Over the second half of the twentieth century, the developing nations of non–Western world tried more than one tactic for economic development. Developing countries also depended heavily on the developed world for investment capital, trade, aid, and loans.

In the early years, many of the new nations, like revolutionary governments in Latin America, tried forms of state socialism. Revolutionary leaders had been accustomed to view capitalism as the economic system of their oppressors. Typically also, their countries lacked large amounts of private capital that might have stimulated development. The new rulers therefore often turned to government direction, state planning, controls on prices, marketing boards for export trade, and similar policies in the hope of moving rapidly from poverty to a better life. This approach did tend to prevent capitalist exploitation, but it could also produce bloated bureaucracies and graft. Even more disturbing, by limiting profits, it discouraged productivity and hence the economic growth it was supposed to generate.

In the later 1970s and the 1980s, therefore, many developing nations, like most communist countries, turned to free–market incentives to higher production. Growth rates did sometimes respond by rising. But high prices paid to producers meant inflation for consumers, and economic opportunity could nurture corruption as well as innovation. Above all, for already poor nations, the cancellation of price subsidies for items of daily consumption meant real suffering for the population. Thus both the socialist and capitalist systems, borrowed from the West, seemed to have limitations as solutions to the problems of the developing world.

Whichever approach was tried, foreign money was necessary to transform village cultures into modern societies. One source of this money was trade with the West. Developing nations sold what they had to offer the world market: agricultural products and raw materials. In exchange for these commodities, they imported manufactured goods. Both sides of this equation, unfortunately, had problems. Focusing their productive energies on export commodities, less–developed countries neglected basic subsistence agriculture; sometimes they had to import food into once self–sufficient economies in order to concentrate on growing coffee or cocoa for the export market. Both mines and large–scale farms, furthermore, were often owned by Western corporations, so that the profits from these exports did not stay within the developing nation. Commodity prices, finally, were not set by the sellers but in the free marketplace, and there were some disastrous declines in the 1970s and 1980s. Importing manufactured goods, finally, meant that developing nations did not make these things themselves, creating a dangerous industrial dependency on the developed West.

Western investment also became essential for development. Both private banks and foreign governments made investment capital available, as did the World Bank and regional investment banks. The *World Bank*, or International Bank for Reconstruction and Development, was an autonomous UN agency that lent money specifically for development. Such funds were often put into major projects, from railroads to hydroelectric dams. Both private and public investment sources, however, required that their investments earn some profit for them and their shareholders or taxpayers and, in the end, that they be paid back. And these things did not always happen in the poorer parts of the world.

If foreign trade and foreign investment failed to produce a developmental takeoff, there were other options: loans and aid. The *International Monetary Fund*, a pool of capital intended for emergency loans, provided money to help developing nations keep up with their debts and their projects. In return, however, the IMF required that the borrower "put its house in order," cutting waste in government and cutting back on subsidized prices for food and other necessities. Cuts in subsidies, however, could lead to a violent popular reaction that could end political careers or even overthrow governments.

A final source of help, which also failed to solve all problems, was economic aid. Foreign governments, concerned to help people and to bolster rickety alliances, offered financial help and technical assistance with everything from advanced engineering to modern agricultural techniques. The United States, Japan, and the Soviet Union, France, West Germany, and the Scandinavian countries were large sources of such aid. Groups like the U.S. Peace Corps and Britain's Volunteers in Service Overseas taught skills at the village level, while Soviet engineers labored over the Aswan Dam. But aid, too, ran out, and it could become addictive. Developing countries needed to find ways of standing on their own. Some, as we will see, were doing just that.

Women, Emancipation, and Poverty

Progress and poverty in the developing world had particular meaning for women. Some women challenged traditional taboos and began to dress, work, and live much as Western women did. For others, westernization made little difference or even increased the hardship of their lives.

Well–to–do Egyptian or Indian women, for instance, and many middle–class Latin American women were often as sophisticated and modern in culture and convictions as women from comparable strata of U.S. or western European society. Some took up charitable or educational work among poor or otherwise disadvantaged women, while others became vigorous advocates of women's rights in these traditional societies. So far as religious and cultural traditions allowed and male attitudes permitted, these women lived very much as their Western contemporaries did.

Considerably less affluent urban working women took the sort of jobs Western women had been taking for generations. Office and service jobs were increasingly open to women in developing countries, and changes in clothing and lifestyles often followed. Muslim women, for example, might lay aside the veil and the enveloping black robe for Western skirts and heels as they moved into the offices of modern business enterprises. Others resisted this sort of cultural westernization: Hindu women, for example, often continued to wear the traditional sari even in Western countries, and Muslim women sometimes returned to the old costume and customs after years of living in a more Western style.

In the village cultures of the developing world, meanwhile, economic growth and development programs too often hurt rather than helped the female half of the population. In the villages of rural Africa, for instance, foreign aid frequently encouraged the expansion of areas of productivity dominated by men, such as commercial agriculture or mining. Women, whose traditional work had a more local focus, were left out. Urbanization also drew men away from the villages for long periods if not for good, leaving women to support themselves and their families alone.

Even more than in the Western world, in short, there were great changes in the lives of the women of the developing countries in the last half of the twentieth century. They were not always changes for the better, though they did open wider vistas for those women who could take advantage of them.

The Roots of Non–Western Poverty

In many ways, then, the West remained a potent factor in the lives of non–Western peoples. As the generations who freed their countries from foreign rule grew gray in still underdeveloped lands, however, questions began to be heard in both the developing world and in the developed West. Was this new form of Western involvement, people on both sides wondered, ultimately in the interests of the developing nations at all?

For left–wing critics, Western policy toward the less developed was essentially nothing but *neoimperialism,* a new kind of imperialism through economic exploitation without the framework of colonial administration. *Deindustrialization* and *dependency* were two key charges leveled at the West in this context. The Western imperial powers, it was asserted, had destroyed or inhibited industrial development around the world, ruining the Indian handloom textile industry or undermining native African ironworks by introducing cheaper Western mass–produced goods. And even the independent countries of Latin America had always suffered from economic dependency on Europe and the United States, an exchange of commodities for manufactured products that undercut Latin America's own industrial development.

Criticism from the political right took a different view, claiming that the whole concept of Western support for developing societies was counterproductive. In this view, aid packages tended to encourage the governments of developing countries to ignore basic market forces and to try to direct the development of national wealth from above. This process, however well intended, could only slow economic growth and foster poverty. What was needed was to let developing nations find their own way to free–market capitalism without intervention from their own governments or the international community.

♦ The West and the Non–Western Powers ♦

Not all non–Western nations, however, fit patterns of underdevelopment, authoritarianism, and dependency. By the 1990s, a spectrum of degrees of development was increasingly evident in the non–Western world, which included a number of successful democracies. And the Western powers themselves were becoming increasingly aware of how dependent *they* were on at least some nations of the non–Western world.

We will survey the achievements of three such areas: Latin America, the Muslim Middle East, and the East Asian rim of the Pacific. In each case, relations with the West will be central to our inquiry. These three very different regions illustrate even more vividly than the underdeveloped areas how thoroughly interdependent the West and the world had become.

Latin American Development

Latin America had its wars of liberation in the nineteenth century, long before Africa and Asia, during the wave of democratic revolutions that also produced the United States. The political history of Latin America, however, was both more revolutionary and more authoritarian than that of the United States or Canada. And economically, it in many ways fitted the patterns of underdevelopment we have just sketched.

Politically, the two dozen republics of Central America, South America, and the Caribbean seemed to be moving out of the violent alternation of revolution and dictatorship and into a smoother succession of elected governments during the postwar period. The *caudillos* and military rulers of the nineteenth and earlier twentieth centuries were sometimes popular with large segments of the population—peasants or the urban poor, for instance—but they could also be savage to their opponents. All in all, Latin Americans seemed increasingly to prefer voting to revolution, and it was notable that in the 1990s, the majority of Latin American heads of state had been elected to office, rather than riding in on a tank.

In Mexico, for example, the Party of the Revolutionary Institutions (PRI) had ruled since the 1920s by offering something for everybody—business and labor, peasants and Indians, the generals and the politicos. But in this leading Hispanic nation, rapid population growth, unemployment, and one–party rule caused opposition to the PRI to grow. Although students were suppressed in the 1960s and early 1970s, in the later 1980s the PRI very nearly lost an election.

Brazil, the largest nation in South America, also appeared to be moving from authoritarian, or military, rule to constitutional government. Nevertheless, the economic and social problems of a country the size of the United States, facing widespread poverty and a mountain of foreign debt, were formidable indeed.

The two nations of South America's narrowing southern reaches had a mix of dictators and democratic regimes. Argentina was ruled during the decade after World War II by the colorful, quasi–fascistic Peróns, Juan (1895–1974) and Evita (1919–1952). Transcending Juan Perón's conservative and military support, the regime came to identify with the urban poor, the *descamisados* or "shirtless ones," and founded a movement that outlasted Evita's death and Juan's exile. Peronism, however, gave way to chaos, terrorism, and new military dictators. It was not until the 1980s, when Argentina's ruling generals lost a brief war with Britain over the Falkland (or Malvinas) Islands, that they were overthrown to be replaced by the freely elected government of Raul Alfonsín (1927–) and his successors.

Chile, stretching down the Pacific side of the continent, followed the opposite path, from a democratic tradition through the Allende attempt at radical social change to the brutal military dictatorship of General Augusto Pinochet (1915–). In 1988, however, after a decade and a half in power, Pinochet called a plebiscite to ratify another term for himself—and lost. Though the military was not likely to abandon all power in Chile, this country also seemed to be moving toward the Western pattern of democratic government.

Economically, Latin America often looked like a textbook case of underdevelopment, dependency, and neoimperialism. Its beef and wheat and bananas, copper and nitrates and bauxite were shipped to the United States and Europe, and many of its manufactured goods came from the same places. The region was heavily indebted to foreign bankers as a result of huge development loans in the 1970s, and the need to try to keep up with these debts made further economic progress almost impossible. The masses of rural and urban poor lived like the poor of the developing countries, in dusty villages and dirt–floored shantytowns.

Yet there were many signs of hope. Latin America's great cities—Rio de Janeiro and Buenos Aires, Caracas and Mexico City—had gracious nineteenth–century plazas and shining modern condominiums and business blocks to match those of North America and Europe. Mexico and Venezuela had enough oil to pay for a lot of development once petroleum prices steadied, and it was hard to dismiss Brazil, with its ultramodern capital at Brasília and its atomic power, as a backward country.

These nations of the southern half of the hemisphere were partially developed, halfway out of the developing world and into the developed category dominated by western Europe, North America, and the East Asian nations. How long it would take them to move the rest of the way remained to be seen.

Leadership and Conflict in the Middle East

The peoples of the Muslim Middle East were mostly, though not entirely, Arab in ancestry, language, and culture. The colonial period had been short there; most countries had experienced nothing more intrusive than the establishment of a European protectorate or sphere of influence. Liberated entirely after the Second World War, these nations, running from Pakistan to Egypt, were often grouped with the Arab lands of North Africa as a single cultural and political bloc. They were ruled by a variety of authoritarian governments: hereditary monarchies, military dictatorships, and in one case something very close to a theocracy, dominated for a decade by a Muslim holy man. These countries shared some common trends over the postwar decades. One was an ardent resurgence of Islamic religious faith. Another was an equally passionate wave of modern Arab nationalism. A third was a series of dangerous feuds between Muslim leaders, conflicts that made their contribution to war and revolution in the area.

The Ayatollah Khomeini, the militant Shiite Muslim leader who overthrew the last shah of Iran and attempted to restructure a slowly westernizing Iranian society according to Islamic religious law, dominated the lives and minds of his people throughout the 1980's.

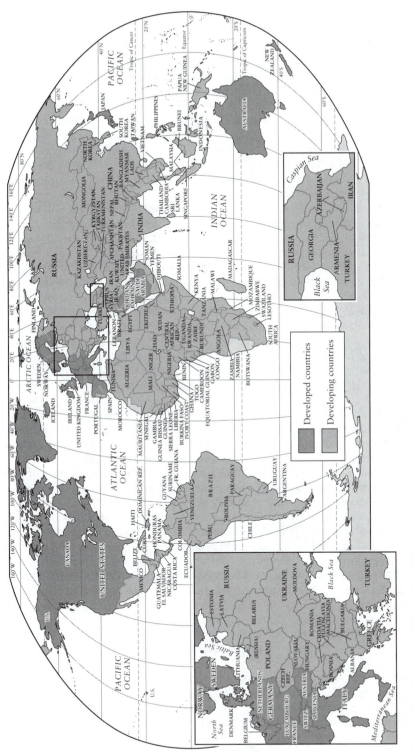

Developed and Developing Nations in the 1990s

Militarily, Israel remained the most powerful state in the Middle East. Beyond Israel, however, a triad of strong and very different Muslim nations dominated the region for much of the second half of the century: Egypt, Arabia, and Iran.

Egypt, after the overthrow of its last and very decadent king in the 1950s, was ruled by a succession of military men who transcended their military background to become internationally known, if controversial, statesmen. Gamal Abdel Nasser astonished the world by nationalizing the British–run Suez Canal in 1956 and getting away with it. Nasser's Egypt, as we have seen, became the leader of the anti–Israeli forces and accepted aid and advisers from the Soviet Union. His successor, Anwar Sadat, startled the world again by expelling the Soviets, accepting American aid instead, and becoming the first Muslim leader to make peace with Israel. Fearful of the direction in which Sadat was leading his country, Muslim fanatics assassinated him in 1981, but his successor Hosni Mubarak (1929–) continued to work for peace with Israel through settlement of the Palestinian problem.

The two primary rulers of Iran during this period, though both traditional Muslim power figures, were quite different from each other. Mohammad Reza Pahlavi, the last shah of Iran, ruled from 1941 until 1979. The Ayatollah Ruhollah Khomeini, an Islamic religious leader, toppled the shah that year in a nationwide outpouring of religious fervor and ruled the country until 1989. A non–Arab land dominated by Shiite rather than by traditional Sunni Muslims, Iran sought to exert a hegemony over the region as ancient Persia had done. The shah had ruled in imperial splendor and was a strong ally of the United States. The ayatollah defied the United States, holding the entire staff of the American Embassy hostage for a year. Khomeini also fought a long and ultimately futile war with neighboring Iraq over predominance in the oil–rich Persian Gulf. Both the shah's secret police and the ayatollah's Revolutionary Guards became feared symbols of the power their masters wielded.

Saudi Arabia, extremely conservative, religiously orthodox, and an American ally, controlled the world's largest oil reserves and presided over the Islamic holy places at Mecca and Medina. The Saudi sheiks opposed Shiite Iran, Israel, and, after Sadat's defection, Egypt as well. Arabia also dominated OPEC, the oil producers' cartel.

The larger importance of the Middle East to the rest of the world was of course its tremendous quantities of oil, which had become the most important industrial power source in the world in the twentieth century. The "*oil sheiks*," as they were sometimes called, used the threat of cutting off the flow of oil to discourage European powers from supporting Israel. From the early 1970s, Arab–dominated OPEC also limited production for commercial reasons in order to boost prices and profits. By the later 1980s, however, the West had cut back on its profligate use of petroleum, leading to an oversupply of oil that badly hurt OPEC. Nevertheless, the sheiks, who had invested their "petrodollars" lavishly in the industrialized world, still had plenty of economic clout. Again, ties between Western and non–Western states grew closer still as Muslim leaders bought into the future of the West.

Japan as an Economic Powerhouse

The non–Western world, in short, was not entirely an underdeveloped region. And the most dazzling example of rapid development outside the West was the oldest: Japan. Feared by its Western competitors as "Japan, Incorporated," the island kingdom was also a functioning democracy in the second half of the twentieth century.

The United States occupied Japan at the end of World War II, imposed a democratic constitution, and found the Japanese quick to learn the new rules. Business and elections were the American way, and they soon became the Japanese way, too. After Mao's victory in China and the stalemate in the Korean War, the United States turned to Japan as its chief ally in the Far East. This diplomatic revolution guaranteed Japan military protection and freed the Japanese to pour all their national energies into reconstruction and economic expansion. As in Mexico, one political party—the Liberal Democratic Party—won all the elections in Japan, but that party also represented the views of the majority of the conservative Japanese electorate. Japan, like South Korea, had one of the world's most volatile youth movements, ready to demonstrate for peace or against the nation's close ties with the United States. Most Japanese, however, put loyalty and hard work above rights and aggressive politics.

The Japanese, industrious, meticulous, highly educated, and energetic, were made for success in modern business. Instead of industrial strife and government as a countervailing force to big business, Japan cultivated close collaboration between management and labor, government and the business community. Workers did not make demands for higher wages or benefits; management guaranteed them employment even in hard times. Business accepted governmental guidance, and government helped big business to target and break into lucrative global markets.

In the early part of the century there was a time when Japanese goods were dismissed by Westerners as cheap imitations of quality goods. In the century's closing decades, however, the Japanese automobile and shipbuilding industries, Japanese electronics and computers were world leaders. Japan's robot assembly lines and its management techniques were admired and studied in the West. By the end of the 1980s, Japanese banks were the world's biggest, and Japan replaced the United States as the world's leading creditor nation. Japan even provided more aid for underdeveloped countries than any other nation in the world.

For a country with a limited population, few natural resources, and no petroleum at all, Japan had done very well indeed. And like the Arabs, the Japanese bought into the Western world, too, tightening still further the web of interdependence that bound the West to the rest of the globe.

The Tiger Economies: South Korea to Singapore

Japan was the most successful of the Pacific rim states, but there were others. These *"tiger"* economies included South Korea and Singapore and the islands of Taiwan (Formosa) and Hong Kong. South Korea and Taiwan had many ties with the United States, while the two city–states of Singapore and Hong Kong were current or former British colonies. Taiwan became Generalissimo Chiang Kai–shek's last home after Mao's victory in 1949. South Korea came out of the Korean War in 1953 as a shattered nation ruled by a series of political strongmen. However, these leaders did encourage rapid industrial growth, while popular demonstrations, often led by students, nudged the nation toward democracy. Building on its industrial and commercial boom, South Korea held increasingly free elections and, following the Seoul Olympics in 1988, announced readiness to discuss unification with the north.

All these East Asian countries followed essentially the same road to startling economic growth. For the most part lacking significant natural resources, they parlayed hard work and low wages through small workshops and light industry into the world market. "Made in Hong Kong" or Taiwan or South Korea at first meant cheap plastic junk to the rest of the world. But during the 1970s and 1980s, Hong Kong skyscrapers, South Korean cars, and Singapore Airlines—rated the world's best—became symbols of East Asian success. While oil–rich Arabs were investing in the West, only a very well off Western investor could afford to buy into Hong Kong at all.

The 1990s, furthermore, saw a "second generation" of Southeast Asian "tiger" economies rising. The vast Indonesian archipelago, bustling Malaysia, and even Vietnam were developing rapidly. As skyscrapers soared over Kuala Lumpur (Malaysia's capital) and Western investors pushed and shoved to "get in on the ground floor" in Hanoi (Vietnam's capital), it looked like boom times there too.

The Future of China and India

The two giant states of Asia, China and India, remained among the less–developed nations. But in the last decade of the twentieth century, these emerging non-western powers also seemed to be moving toward major free–market development.

The two had much in common. Among the oldest civilizations in the world, they were also among the poorest. They had the world's largest populations to feed, clothe, and house—more than a billion Chinese and three–quarters of a billion Indians. Both had gained control of their own destinies in the later 1940s and had turned to the then popular policies of government–directed economic development, including five–year plans and other trappings of Soviet–style planned economies. There were, however, important political differences: China had become a one–party communist state, while India emerged as the world's largest democracy.

China under communist rule generally fed its population, curtailed population growth, and stabilized an economy ravaged by a half–century of civil strife, albeit at a very basic level. Chairman Mao Zedong's more radical economic and social policies, however,

Indira Gandhi, strong-willed leader of India, is shown here addressing her people, the 700 million citizens of "the world's largest democracy." Religious passions boiling up from the past, however, led to her assassination by Sikh bodyguards in 1984. (UPI/Bettmann.)

proved disastrous failures. The "Great Leap Forward" did not turn peasant communes into productive dynamos, and the "Cultural Revolution" that unleashed youthful Red Guards on aging cadres, far from revitalizing the system, nearly destroyed it. The first spread starvation across the land, the second widespread violence. After Mao's death in 1975, China therefore turned in new and more promising directions for sustained economic growth.

Under Mao's old comrade, the diminutive and aging Deng Xiaoping, a policy of economic "*pragmatism*" was instituted. Pragmatism meant abandoning peasant communes and allowing entrepreneurially inclined peasants to build small, privately owned businesses. It meant permitting once–prosperous commercial and industrial cities like Shanghai and Guangzhou (Canton) to trade freely and profitably with the capitalist world once more. Pragmatism also meant importing foreign technology and encouraging foreign investment in joint ventures with Chinese business and industry and in "special economic zones" where productivity and profits shot up.

Democratic political reforms were not part of Deng's plan, however, and a wave of pro–democracy demonstrations centered in Tiananmen Square, Beijing, was ruthlessly suppressed in 1990. Economically, however, China under the leadership of the pragmatists seemed to some Western experts to be on the verge of rapid economic growth that could transform the lives of a quarter of the population of the globe. And developed nations from Japan to North America to Europe were eager to get in on that boom. American firms sold cars, Coke, and movie tickets to the Chinese, and total foreign investment in China grew from less than $3 billion to more than $80 billion in ten years. Supplying virtually anything to a quarter of the world's population couldn't help but be very profitable indeed for Western businesses.

India's economic progress was more modest, but India also pushed toward more rapid development as the century drew to a close. Torn by increasingly militant religious and nationalist groups—Hindus, Muslims, Sikhs in the north, and Tamils in the south—the subcontinent was held together by the Congress party and its leaders, the Nehru dynasty: Jawaharlal Nehru and Indira and Rajiv Gandhi. But neither a colonial legacy of early industrial development and a national railway system nor technological breakthroughs such as the "green revolution" of improved agricultural output could overcome India's deep village poverty and surging population growth. As in China, a government–run economy subsidized prices and guaranteed jobs but hamstrung economic growth.

A new willingness to try the free–market road to economic development appeared in the later 1980s, and after Rajiv Gandhi's assassination in 1991, his successors in the Congress party leadership launched a substantial wave of reforms. Under Prime Minister P. V. Narasimha Rao, India began to encourage free–market initiatives, from foreign trade to foreign investment to the spirit of entrepreneurship among India's own citizens. How far the changes would go and how successful they would be remained to be seen. But Deng Xiaoping's dictum in China—"to get rich is glorious!"—was echoed on the walls of India, where graffiti enthusiastically declared: "Freed from fetters, forward we go!"[1] Again, Western producers and investors hurried along to help and profit from India's economic growth.

◆ The West and a World in Disarray ◆

This global transformation sounds splendid—and yet to many it didn't feel that way. Neither the Western peoples who played such an essential part in this global transformation nor the citizens of developing or already developed non–Western states sounded happy in the later 1990s. After a sampling of the negative mood of those years, we will look at the specific economic, political, and social problems which beset the West and the world.

Anxieties, Fears—and Anger

It soon became apparent that many people, Western and non–Western, did not look upon the world of the late twentieth century with the enthusiasm one might expect. The world's economic, social, and political difficulties proved more intransigent than overly optimistic Western leaders expected. And Western peoples began to demand more attention to their own domestic problems and less to building a new world order. For their part, non–Western peoples continued to feel the strains of both deep poverty and dislocatingly rapid growth.

Domestic problems were certainly easy enough to find. But there was also a widespread malaise that seemed harder to explain.

The end of the cold war, for instance, seemed to some to deprive the Western world of its moral compass. Both communists and anti–communists had at least known who the villains were, and hence how to live a proper life themselves. The lean economic times during the last quarter of the century added to this sense of disorientation. Americans who had thought that loyalty and hard work guaranteed employment learned differently as their firms slimmed down to meet foreign competition. Eastern Europeans who had learned to barter their way through unproductive state–run economies were terrified to be flung into the uncertain world of the free market. Anxiety and fear multiplied, particularly among the young, who suspected they would never know even the basic security their parents had experienced.

Anxiety and fear were joined by anger. Peoples everywhere seemed prone to feel betrayed, oppressed, put upon, and mad. Americans whose incomes had scarcely risen in twenty years—but who still had houses and cars—were as angry as Russians whose economy had collapsed entirely. American religious conservatives were bitter over what they perceived as an anything–goes morality, including limits on public prayer, publicly funded abortion, and mass media awash in sex and violence. But Muslim fundamentalists were even more violently angry over the simple separation of church and state in their traditionally Islamic countries. Student demonstrators, striking workers, and voters choosing unlikely protest candidates in many lands—despite their differences—all shared a public mood of ill–contained outrage.

There was no way of telling how long this mood would last, or what it would lead to. But in the mid–1990s, it seemed to inflame political campaigns and public discourse everywhere. It was a mood that pointed toward an uncertain and possibly quite unhappy future.

Economic Problems

Beneath these national and international difficulties seemed to lie a broad spectrum of more general problems. These included economic dislocations, social dysfunctions, and inflamed ideological and religious creeds. The economic problems of the industrialized states differed significantly from those of the developing countries, but everybody had problems.

A major difficulty for the world's developed nations was commercial competition. Thus the trade imbalance between the world's two most dynamic economies, those of the United States and Japan, ran heavily in Japan's favor. Seemingly endless negotiations aimed at opening up Japanese markets to American goods strained the vital relationship between the two economic superpowers.

A pair of related problems were those of high unemployment and low wages in the industrialized Western nations. Some Western European countries, including Germany and France, faced unemployment levels well over 10 per cent in the 1990s. Other developed countries, like the United States, had unemployment rates only half that high—but many workers were trapped in low–pay, no–benefit service jobs, flipping hamburgers or bagging groceries in supermarkets. Some blamed both unemployment and low–wage jobs on competition from low–paid workers in developing countries. Others thought lack of education excluded many from well–rewarded jobs in increasingly high–tech economies.

The developing nations of the world continued to have their share of economic problems too. These included many difficulties that went back to independence and beyond into the colonial period.

International capital still shied away from the risks of investing in unstable poor countries. Powerful international loan agencies like the International Monetary Fund continued to require recipients to abolish inefficient state enterprises and cut subsidies on food and other basics. These policies cost jobs, raised food prices, and sometimes filled the streets with rioters—which further discouraged international investment in developing countries. Low international prices for the commodities they exported, as well as poor infrastructure and ill–educated populations further undercut development in the global South.

Social Difficulties

Many social problems also beset both new and developed nations. Migration, for instance, was a problem for rich and poor alike. Rich countries struggled to absorb waves of migrants—from Africa and Asia into Europe, from Latin America into the United States. Poor countries saw an accelerating flow of village people into the shanty–towns that ringed the cities. And the newcomers all too often added to the urban poverty, slum conditions, and competition for non–existent jobs that plagued Paris and Johannesburg, Los Angeles and Rio de Janeiro.

Social problems involving younger and older people also tormented both rich and poor countries. In the developing world, large families produced rapidly expanding populations, half of whose members were in their teens and twenties. Low–skilled younger generations drifted easily into unemployment, crime, and radical politics. In Western Europe, North America, and the developed East Asian rim, by contrast, populations who raised small families and benefited from modern medicine and high health standards grew older every year. Aging populations collected social security and had more medical expenses, imposing a heavy economic burden on society's working–age generations. Old people also made easy victims: in America, they were often mugged on the streets; in Russia, old people living alone were murdered for their apartments.

Shattered families also contributed to the social difficulties of the late twentieth century. In the United States, girls too young to raise children nevertheless had them, and unemployed fathers deserted families they could not support. In underdeveloped countries, men left their families in distant villages to find work in the cities, heaping a heavy burden of work and child–rearing on their wives. Both worlds tried to deal with the problems of decaying families and a fading sense of family responsibility. The United States ended government income support for mothers with dependent children, while Singapore moved to pass a "Sue Your Son" law allowing neglected elderly parents to take undutiful sons to court for non–support.

Creeds in Conflict

Ideas, however, could be as strong as social or economic problems in generating bitterness. Two particularly powerful sets of ideas capable of arousing passionate feeling in both developed and developing worlds were religion and nationalism.

Among the religious revival movements that suddenly emerged in many places, Islam was the most widely discussed in the Western world, which felt threatened by fundamentalist Islam. Militant Islamists demanded a return to the faith of their fathers, not only in religious matters, but in politics, economics, social life, the arts, and virtually every other aspect of human life. Other faiths also aroused people. India, once famous for its ability to absorb many faiths, was brutally divided between newly inflamed Hindus, Sikhs demanding their independence, and a Muslim minority. Catholics and Protestants in Northern Ireland, Fundamentalist Christians in the United States, and other vigorous crusaders made it clear that religion had not lost its power to stir the faithful to action.

Among the modern isms, the most aggressive was nationalism in its various forms. As state socialism receded in eastern Europe, it was replaced by local nationalisms. The peoples of the former Soviet satellites became ardent Poles, Hungarians, or Romanians once more, and Soviet citizens themselves rediscovered their Russian nationalism. A number of east European states split along national lines, including what commentators came to call the "former Czechoslovakia," "former Yugoslavia," and of course the former Soviet Union itself. Arabs, on the other hand, discovered a sweeping form of pan–Arabism, seeing their separate states as Western imperialist impositions and all Arabs as members of a single trans–national "Arab nation." Some of the most stable states still revealed strong national feeling, including such great powers as France, Japan, and the United States.

These impassioned creeds could have a variety of consequences. The U.S. considered a Constitutional amendment banning the desecration of the American flag. Japan took fifty years to apologize to its neighbors for World War II. The Basques of northern Spain assassinated politicians and the Irish Republican Army went back to sowing tourist London with bombs. "Former Yugoslavia" tore itself apart, adding the concept of "ethnic cleansing" to the vocabulary of twentieth–century horrors.

♦ The West and a Planet at Risk ♦

The planet itself, finally, seemed to some to be at serious risk at the end of the twentieth century. Swollen Third–World populations, intractable poverty, pollution, and the potential exhaustion of essential natural resources combined with looming environmental crises to add to the world's woes. And, once again, Western people, though they could not accept the full responsibility, felt a need to "do something" to save their planet.

The Population Explosion Roars On

The population explosion, which had begun as far back as the eighteenth century in the West, roared on across the developing world in the twentieth. Population curves in most of

Asia, Africa, and Latin America were all steeply up. Medical breakthroughs which checked the ravages of disease, and the "green revolution" which produced more food added to the numbers of people surviving. The demands of these mushrooming populations for education, jobs, housing, and in the end more food and more medical care could overwhelm any nation's efforts at development.

Experts foresaw a classic Malthusian collision between expanding populations and stagnating food supplies. Natural disasters, from floods and droughts to earthquakes and storms, could lead to disease and starvation. Wars and especially civil wars also acted as checks on further population growth.

But world populations continued to grow, jamming the cities of the Third World and flooding across the frontiers of the developed nations in search of work. The unrestrained overpeopling of the planet could be as paralyzing as a lack of natural resources or inadequate water supplies. The mere increase in numbers of citizens could overwhelm any developing nation's efforts at economic growth. Indian economic planners and political leaders, for instance, lamented that they had to run very hard just to stay in the same place—just to keep a low standard of living from deteriorating further—as the Indian population grew.

Pollution and Dwindling Resources

Two other linked natural problems affected both industrialized and developing countries. The pollution of the human environment was often worse in developing than in industrially developed nations because the latter at least attempted to regulate the production of pollutants. The slow exhaustion of key resources probably affected fully industrialized rich nations more than poor countries, since it was the affluent peoples who consumed the majority of all the world's production.

As far back as the eighteenth century, Western poets had lamented the dark clouds and ash filling the skies over the new industrial towns, the industrial chemicals staining rivers and streams. By the twentieth century, these blights had followed untrammeled industrialism to developing nations from Southeast Asia to eastern Europe. Mexico City gasped in danger–level smog more than two hundred days a year, and even Africa, once the unpolluted continent, saw garbage heaps growing along its roads and sewage seeping through its shanty towns. Oil spills brought silent springs to whole coastlines, and Los Angeles and Tokyo were not much closer to clean air than the cities of the global south.

The accelerating rate at which the world's growing and industrializing populations consumed irreplaceable resources also presented the world of 2000 CE with some terrifying prospects. Metals and minerals, petroleum and other fuels all existed in limited quantities in the earth's crust. As modern people burned countless gallons of oil in their private cars and tossed away millions of metal cans each day, stocks dwindled steadily. Science might find substitutes, but whether they would be as cheap as nature's versions was another question.

The Environmental Crisis

Among those who worried most were the scientists who foresaw coming environmental crises of various sorts. The long–term consequences of two centuries of exploiting the natural world without a thought for the damage we might be doing were all but upon us. Or so increasing numbers of experts seemed to be saying.

Environmental warnings multiplied through the later decades of the century. Pesticides used in farmers' fields could poison the food chain and bring "silent springs" where no birds sang. Industrial chemicals pumped into natural waterways could fill them with fish floating belly up. Clouds of airborne pollutants could bring "acid rain" destroying forests full of trees. Land developers, miners, loggers, and others destroyed the habitats of whole species, leading to their extinction.

Even the best–intentioned practices of modern economies could have unhappy environmental consequences. The tendency to cultivate only a limited number of species of plants and animals of particular value to humans today threatened the valuable diversity of uncultivated nature. For if something happened to our carefully cultivated grains or meat animals—a virus or blight—the world would no longer possess nature's variety from which to develop substitutes.

The most disturbing threats to the environment, however, seemed to focus on the invisible medium of all life, the atmosphere. Industrial gasses and fumes from home heating and gasoline engines poured into the earth's atmosphere day and night. The world's rain forests, which produced the oxygen we all breathe, grew smaller every year. Continent–sized holes appeared in the ozone layer, allowing destructive solar radiation to reach the earth's surface. Japanese citizens wore surgical masks in cities, and fair–skinned Scandinavians abandoned their beaches as the world braced itself for worse.

The worst might well lie ahead—the so–called *greenhouse effect* which threatened the earth with "global warming." This unhappy future involved the polluting of the upper atmosphere with thickening layers of gas which would turn back solar heat reflected from the earth's surface, just as the glass of a greenhouse contains the sun's heat. The result would be a slow but inexorable rise in global temperatures. Environmentalists saw the ice caps melting, coastal cities flooded by the sea, fertile farmlands turning into dustbowls.

Skeptics dismissed such concerns as alarmist and unproven. But countless millions of dollars were already being spent to clean up some of the worst polluted waters and lands. High–level international conferences gathered, heard scientific reports and agreed to try to limit the release of dangerous gasses into the air. The "tree–huggers" might be exaggerating the dangers, but there did seem to be a lot of long, hot summers in the nineties.

♦ Toward a New World Order? ♦

In the 1990s, in the aftermath of the cold war, many Western leaders saw a unique opportunity to redirect human energies toward a genuinely better world at last. Money saved from weapons could be spent on feeding, clothing, and housing the world's peoples. Former cold–war rivals could work together for the betterment of humankind. It was, for optimists at least, a heady moment.

It didn't last long. By the mid–nineties, the open road ahead for the West and the world seemed littered with international difficulties and mired in ideological differences. The present section will offer a glimpse of the high hopes that followed the cold war. Later sections will analyze the disturbingly negative public mood which challenged those dreams of a new world order. Finally, we will survey the many real problems that lay ahead. As we will see, early enthusiasm was soon tempered by recognition of the many unsolved problems still confronting both the West and the rest of the world's peoples.

A Watershed in Human Events

At the beginning of the 1990s, it looked to many as if the world were at a turning point in its history. A half–century of conflict was over, the fear of nuclear Armageddon apparently lifted. It looked like a watershed in human events.

In the aftermath of the cold war, American president George Bush began the 1990s looking forward to what he called a *new world order,* a world built on peace, freedom, and economic prosperity. Germany's Helmut Kohl, easily Europe's most powerful leader, pushed the continent toward greater economic and political integration. International civil servants at the United Nations looked for a larger role for the global organization, including more aggressive peace–keeping missions in the world's trouble spots. Among leaders, at least, hopes ran high for a restructured global order in which all people might enjoy peace and freedom, security, health, and even a decent material life for the first time in history.

One feature common to most of these schemes and dreams, however, was the assumption that the West would take the lead, and that Western ideals would guide the development of the new world order. In the short run, at least, continuing Western direction of the course of history seemed quite likely. Even more certain, however, was deep and continuing Western involvement in the affairs of the rest of the world.

The Pax Americana

The early 1990s did offer some impressive examples of Western, especially American, initiatives crowned with striking success. Militarily at least, the West was riding high in what pundits sometimes called the *Pax Americana,* the American peace which, like the *Pax Romana* to which it was compared, was built on American military strength.

The collapse of the Soviet Union left the world with only one superpower, and the United States proceeded to demonstrate this fact at once. On three continents, American troops moved in to carry out a variety of missions. In Panama, in Iraq, and in Bosnia, U.S. power was deployed effectively enough in the early 1990s to lend real weight to the claim that the world was now unipolar and that the United States was the leader of the re–united Western world.

In 1989, President George Bush massed American troops in Panama to overthrow Manuel Noriega, that country's dictator and former U.S. ally. A revolt against Noriega by his own people, which the United States had encouraged, had failed. Worse yet, America was facing a treaty obligation to turn the Panama Canal over to its host country, Noriega's Panama, before the end of the decade. With enormous superiority in firepower, the United States won a rapid and total victory, carrying Noriega back to the U.S. to be tried, convicted, and imprisoned for international drug dealing.

In Iraq's leader, Saddam Hussein, Bush faced a more formidable foe. In the summer of 1990 Saddam, another former U.S. ally, had invaded the oil–rich neighboring state of Kuwait. The U.S. president mobilized a strong alliance of Western and Arab states against

Saddam, massed a large, high–tech army in Arabia, and crushed the Iraqi forces in six weeks of aerial assault and a hundred hours of armored Blitzkrieg in the sands. Although Saddam survived the ordeal of "Operation Desert Storm," continuing to oppress the people of Iraq, the expedition was an impressive demonstration of Western military supremacy.

President Bill Clinton was less eager to send in the troops, but he did push hard to bring peace to a number of violence–torn regions of the world. By mobilizing but not injecting crack U.S. troops, he forced Haiti's military dictator into exile and restored democratically elected Jean–Bertrand Aristide to power. Thanks in considerable part to the efforts of American diplomats, real progress was made in the long confrontation between Israel and its Arab neighbors. Both King Hussein of neighboring Jordan and long–time Palestine Liberation Organization head Yassir Arafat signed peace agreements with Israel. Large tracts of occupied Palestinian land were turned over to Arafat. And even the assassination of Prime Minister Yitzak Rabin, the driving force behind Israel's peace effort, did not end ongoing negotiations with the last major Israeli foe in the region, President Assad of Syria.

Clinton was less successful in brokering peace between Catholic and Protestant factions in Ireland. But he did make what seemed like real progress for the first time in war–torn Bosnia. After four years of struggle among the peoples of the former Yugoslavia, Clinton prevailed upon the North Atlantic Treaty Organization to move at last. The high–tech airpower of the Western alliance focused on the Serbs who were widely held responsible for the long struggle in Bosnia and drove them to the bargaining table. There, U.S. negotiators pushed all parties to the most likely settlement yet—with a 60,000–man NATO force on the ground in Bosnia to encourage compliance.

Not everyone supported these military interventions, and it seemed likely that financial constraints in an uncertain global economy would limit such operations in the future. Moreover, many felt that military might was of less importance in a world where no great military threat remained. There was little question, however, that the Western powers, and the United States in particular, still dominated the globe in terms of traditional military strength.

The Coming Boom

Western involvement with the rest of the world economically looked a little more complicated in the 1990s. Powerful as the Western economies were, it looked to some economists as if the wealth of the West might depend on the health of the world economy as a whole.

The European economies, weighed down by costly worker benefits and welfare nets, remained sluggish, but the U.S. experienced steady growth through the earlier 1990s. In addition, there was a very real possibility that a long–term economic upswing was also under way. Some economists had detected a pattern of alternating twenty or twenty–five year periods of good and bad times in Western history going back to the beginning of the Industrial Revolution more than two centuries earlier. Such a "long wave" of economic growth, optimists asserted, might well be beginning in the middle nineties.

Under the heading of "The Coming Boom," London's prestigious *Economist* magazine predicted impressive global growth for the twenty years beginning in 1994. Surprisingly, the most rapid growth was likely to come in the developing nations rather than the mature industrial economies. This boom in the poor countries, however, would also stimulate growth in the already industrialized states, providing them with expanding markets for high–tech exports and lucrative new investment areas.

In 1992, seven of the ten largest economies in the world were in Europe or North America. By the year 2020, seven of the top ten might be in Asia. But the world as a whole, including the Western world, would also be a lot better off.

To facilitate this optimistic scenario, U.S. President Bill Clinton took the lead in developing systems for international free trade. He encouraged the building of regional and global commercial networks. In particular, he won Congressional ratification of two key international trade treaties, the revised General Agreement on Tariffs and Trade (GATT) and the new North American Free Trade Treaty (NAFTA). Whether a decades–long boom was coming or not, most economists agreed that free trade would stimulate the world economy as whole.

Shared Goals and Common Institutions

But there was broader evidence of a coming brave new world. Careful analysis seemed to reveal an emerging pattern of common political, economic, and social structures in the last decades of the twentieth century. It seemed at least possible that the profound differences of the past—between East and West in the cold war and between North and South in the global economic sweepstakes—were giving way to some shared goals and common institutions. And the source of many of those shared objectives was clearly the modern West, in particular that half of the Western world which had just won the cold war.

Politically, one–party states, military dictatorships, and other forms of authoritarian government appeared to be on the defensive. After 1989, the Eastern European countries replaced their self–perpetuating communist regimes with competing parties and free elec-

Two communist reformers meet in 1989, as Soviet leader Mikhail Gorbachev shakes hands with China's Deng Xiaoping. After loosening communism's grip on the USSR, Gorbachev fell from power; Deng's economic pragmatism led to the rapid spread of capitalism in Communist China. (AP/Wide World Photos.)

tions. Sometimes they re–elected people connected with the old Communist governments—but there was no talk of abrogating democracy again. In Latin America, the military rulers who had dominated politics for so long gave way to elected governments almost everywhere. At the beginning of 1995, only one un–elected ruler—Fidel Castro in Cuba—remained in the western hemisphere.

In Africa, some of the old liberation leaders allowed themselves to be voted out of office. In 1994, South Africa held its first democratic election and chose its first black African president, the remarkable Nelson Mandela. In Asia, freer elections in Korea, Taiwan, and elsewhere added strength to the Indian and Japanese examples of democratic governance.

There were still major exceptions. Deng Hsiaoping's Communist Party still ran China, and Boris Yeltsin's Russia was no model democracy. Many other authoritarian governments remained, especially in Africa and Asia. Still, some analysts saw long–term advantages to democracy that made this freer form of government look like the wave of the long–term future. Democratic governments, after all, did do a better job of protecting the rights of the governed. Elections provided periodic opportunities to replace corrupt, tyrannical, or ineffectual leaders. Democracies were also much more flexible than authoritarian regimes—a valuable feature in a rapidly changing world.

Economically, the 1980s and 1990s saw a widespread turn from state–run economies to free–market capitalism. First in the developing countries of the global South, then in the former communist countries of Eastern Europe and Asia, the economic theories of Adam Smith seemed to be replacing those of Karl Marx. In Russia, China, and many smaller nations, state planners and five–year–plans gave way to entrepreneurs and market forces like the law of supply and demand.

The basic reason for the shift appeared to be the markedly greater productivity of free markets over command economies. Western Europeans enjoyed a much higher standard of living than Eastern Europeans did, while Japan and the East Asian "tigers," including South Korea, Taiwan, Hong Kong, and Singapore, vastly outproduced communist China or North Korea. Third–world countries, after decades of following the communist model, decided to take a second look at capitalism—and began to change their ways too.

Socially, finally, there seemed to be general acceptance of the need for at least some sort of welfare safety net and for entitlements financed by taxes and administered by government. Public education, public health, retirement benefits, and some unemployment compensation were widely accepted government responsibilities. Many added aid for mothers with dependent children, job retraining in times of economic change, child care for working parents, and other supports. More than a hundred years of welfare reforms had made government—local, state, and national—an essential supplier of many basic services to all citizens.

There were challenges to this large welfare apparatus. Poor countries could hardly afford such services, yet their people demanded them. European and American governments found their highly developed welfare systems too expensive and began to consider cut–backs. In the United States, conservatives angrily demanded the repeal of some forms of aid—to unmarried mothers, for instance—though "entitlements" like social security and medical care for the aged were still widely supported. In general, citizens of both industrialized and less developed states wanted and needed modern welfare nets. And since democracy allowed the people to express their preferences by voting, it seemed unlikely that the world's social welfare programs would really be totally eliminated anytime soon.

Summary

The major concern of most non–Western states in the twentieth century was economic development aimed at achieving material standards of living comparable to those of the West. Many developing countries, plagued by lack of basic infrastructure, low commodity prices for what they produced, the difficulty of attracting capital investment, and their own unproductive economic policies, did not grow as fast as had been hoped. Some non–Western nations, however, parlayed resources like oil into real prosperity. Others, notably Japan and the "tigers," a string of smaller East and Southeast Asian countries, grew at phenomenal rates and rapidly achieved a Western–style standard of living.

Both Western and non–Western nations, however, faced some serious problems as the century ended. Economic problems, political challenges, and social difficulties afflicted all peoples in different ways. And all alike recognized increasingly the common danger of the physical deterioration of the planet on which they lived. To many experts, the world looked overpopulated, polluted, shorter on resources, and threatened by the very air its people breathed.

Both Western people and the peoples of the rest of the world thus faced a new century that offered its share of challenges to future generations. Boom times might be coming, but not all would share in the resulting rewards. Some Third World nations struggled to survive, while others were the fastest growing economies in the world. Many citizens of developed nations raged against their own governments, yet there were fewer brutal dictatorships in the world than there had been for a long time.

The Western world thus approached the end of the twentieth century in a situation that, despite many problems, might have generated considerable self-confidence. The cold-war split was ended. Western, particularly American, military power seemed unrivaled. And the world as a whole seemed to be moving toward some of the same political, economic, and social goals. Whether it would attain them remained to be seen.

Some Key Terms

authoritarian governments 760
deindustrialization 764
dependency 764
developing nations 759
emerging non–Western powers 759
global south 760
greenhouse effect 776
International Monetary Fund 763
neoimperialism 764
new world order 777
non–Western nations 760
"oil sheiks" 768
Pax Americana 777
"pragmatism" 771
Third World 759
"tigers" 769
World Bank 763

Note

1. Slogans quoted in *Economist,* June 6, 1992, p. 32, and May 23, 1992, p. 21.

Reading List

Attali, J. *Millennium: Winners and Losers in the Coming World Order.* Connors and N. Gardels. New York: Times Books, 1991. International relations in a post–cold war world. See also

C. W. Kegley, and E. R. Wittkopf, eds., *The Future of American Foreign Policy* (New York: St. Martin's Press, 1992) for essays on America's place in the new world order, and J. M. Rochester, *Waiting for the Millennium* (Columbia: University of South Carolina Press, 1993) on the role of the United Nations.

Austen, R. A. *African Economic History: Internal Development and External Dependency.* Portsmouth, N.H.: Heinemann, 1987. Offers a challenging synthesis of rival explanations for failures of development in independent Africa, with emphasis on failure of colonial developmental policies. See also P. Kennedy, *African Capitalism: The Struggle for Ascendancy* (New York: Cambridge University Press, 1988). On the shift from government-led economies to emergent capitalism.

Barnet, R. J. *Global Reach: The Power of the Multinational Corporations.* New York: Simon and Schuster, 1974. The multinational corporation as a key factor in the world economy. See also L. Solomon, *Multinational Corporations and the Emerging World Order* (Port Washington, N.Y.: Kennikat Press, 1978).

Boahen, A. A. ed., *General History of Africa,* vol. 7, *Africa Under Colonial Domination, 1880–1935* (Berkeley and Los Angeles: University of California Press, 1985). UNESCO series volume on the period of neoimperialism and after. Also valuable is M. Crowder, ed., *The Cambridge History of Africa,* vol. 8, *From c. 1940 to c. 1975* (New York: Cambridge University Press, 1984). Climactic volume of this series contains essays on Africa during the liberation period.

Brandt, W., et al. *North–South: A Program for Survival.* Cambridge, Mass.: MIT Press, 1980. Disturbing report on the differences between—and the interdependence of—rich and poor nations.

Brass, P. R. *The New Cambridge History of India,* vol. 4, *The Policies of India Since Independence.* New York: Cambridge University Press, 1990. Fragile democracy threatened by poverty, ethnic conflict, and religious feuds. See also K. Atul, ed., *India's Democracy: An Analysis of Changing State–Society Relations* (Princeton, N.J.: Princeton University Press, 1991). Essays seeking to explain the survival of democratic government in a poor Third World country.

Dittmer, L. *China's Continuous Revolution: The Post–Liberation Epoch, 1949–1981.* Berkeley and Los Angeles: University of California Press, 1987. Stimulating account of intraparty conflict and its impact on the nation during and after the Mao years. On the pragmatic trend in Chinese economic policies, see I. Hsu, *China Without Mao: The Search for a New Order* (New York: Oxford University Press, 1983).

Dwyer, D. J. *The City in the Third World.* New York: Barnes and Noble, 1974. Knowledgeable overview of rapid urbanization in developing countries. See also G. Breese, ed., *The City in Newly Developing Countries* (Englewood Cliffs, N.J.: Prentice Hall, 1972). Valuable essays on urbanization in the developing world.

Huntington, S. P. "The Clash of Civilizations?" *Foreign Affairs,* Vol. 72, No. 3 (Summer, 1993): pp. 22–49. Widely discussed thesis that after the cold war clash of ideologies will come conflict between historic civilizations—Western, Islamic, etc.

Huston, P. *Third World Women Speak Out.* New York: Praeger, 1979. Revealing interviews with women in six countries. See also C. Robertson and I. Berger, *Women and Class in Africa* (New York: Holmes and Meier, 1986). Essays tracing a decline in African women's social position under the impact of development.

Joekes, S. P. *Women in the World Economy.* New York: Oxford University Press, 1987. Brief cross–cultural survey of women in developed and less–developed economies.

Kedourie, E., ed. *Nationalism in Asia and Africa.* New York: World Publishing Co., 1970. Analytical essays. See also R. Emerson, *From Empire to Nation: The Rise to Self–Assertion of Asian and African Peoples* (Cambridge, Mass.: Harvard University Press, 1960).

Lenczowski, G., ed. *The Political Awakening in the Middle East.* Englewood Cliffs, N.J.: Prentice Hall, 1970. Nationalism and anti–imperialism in Muslim lands. For the life of an admired liberation leader, see J. Lacoutre, *Nasser* (New York: Knopf, 1973).

Lloyd, P. C., ed. *The New Elites of Tropical Africa.* London: Oxford University Press, 1966. Papers on how liberation and modernization throw up new ruling classes. For the other side of the coin, see J. Iliffe, *The African Poor: A History* (New York: Cambridge University Press, 1987). Suggests that random poverty of precolonial times has become a structural part of postcolonial African societies.

Lundestad, G. *East, West, North, South: Major Developments in International Politics, 1945–1986.* Translated by G. A. Kuam. Oslo: Norwegian University Press, 1986. Valuable overview of international relations, giving attention to Third World as well as to cold–war problems.

Mowoe, I. J., and R. Bjornson, eds. *Africa and the West: The Legacies of Empire.* Westport, Conn.: Greenwood, 1986. Essays illustrating the range and complexity of Western relations with African nations.

Quandt, W. B., F. Jabber, and A. M. Lesch. *The Politics of Palestinian Nationalism.* Berkeley: University of California Press, 1975. On the vexing question of a homeland for the Palestinians, see also views critical of Israel, including E. W. Said, *The Question of Palestine* (New York: Random House, 1980), and N. Chomsky, *The Fateful Triangle: The United States, Israel, and the Palestinians* (Boston: South End Press, 1983).

Rice, G. T. *The Bold Experiment: John F. Kennedy's Peace Corps.* Notre Dame: University of Notre Dame Press, 1985. Intriguing history of this sometimes undervalued effort to aid the new nations of the Third World.

Robertson, R. *Globalization: Social Theory and Global Culture.* London: Sage Publications, 1992. A leading sociological analyst of the globalization process summarizes sociological explanations for the increased interaction between peoples.

Tobias, M. *World War III: Population and the Biosphere at the End of the Millennium.* Santa Fe, NM: Bear and Co., 1994. Massive study of the impact of overpopulation on the environment.

Vogel, E. F. *Japan as Number One: Lessons for America.* Cambridge, Mass.: Harvard University Press, 1979. Widely debated discussion of Japanese economic and technological achievements, seen as a challenge to the West.

Glossary

abolitionist   American anti–slavery activist before the Civil War.

absolute monarch   European ruler claiming absolute authority over his or her people in the seventeenth and eighteenth centuries.

abstract expressionism   New York modernist painting style infusing non–representational art with strong personal feeling, as in the work of Jackson Pollock.

Act of Union   Official unification of England and Scotland in 1707.

African National Congress   Leading black African organization dedicated to bringing majority rule to South Africa in the later twentieth century.

Age of Reason   The era of the eighteenth–century Enlightenment; sometimes extended to include the philosophy and science of the seventeenth century.

agora   Marketplace in a Greek city–state.

Agricultural Revolution   Neolithic discovery of agriculture; eighteenth–century agricultural improvements in Western Europe.

ahimsa   Hindu Indian principle of non–violence, used for social protest by Gandhi and Martin Luther King, Jr.

Albigensian   Medieval French heretical sect, crushed in the savage twelfth–century Albigensian Crusade.

Allies   Two twentieth–century alliances against Germany and its partners: in World War I, primarily Britain, France, the United States, Russia, and Italy; in World War II, mainly the United States, Britain, and the Soviet Union.

Anabaptists   Sixteenth–century Protestant religious radicals, many of whom rejected infant baptism.

anarchism   Late nineteenth–century European ideology dedicated to destroying both government and private property.

ancien régime   The conservative social and political order in Europe before the French Revolution.

Anschluss   Annexation of Austria by Hitler's Germany in 1938.

Antigonid dynasty   Hellenistic rulers of Macedonia following the death of Alexander the Great.

antisemitism   Prejudice against Jews.

apartheid   Segregation of the races in South Africa in the later twentieth century.

appeasement   Western democracies' policy of allowing aggressors to have their way in order to avoid war during the 1930s.

archon   A chief magistrate in ancient Athens.

Areopagus   A prestigious court in ancient Athens.

Arians   Late Roman and early medieval Christian heretics, many of whom were barbarians later converted to Christianity.

assimilation   Nineteenth–century French colonial policy of imposing direct rule and French culture on colonized peoples.

atlatl   Spear thrower or throwing stick used to hurl a spear farther: the butt of the spear is caught in a thong or notch at one end of the *atlatl* while the thrower holds the other end.

atomism   Ancient Greek theory that all matter is made up of tiny uniform particles called atoms; revived in the seventeenth century by early modern scientists.

atra mors   The "dreadful death," Latin name for the medieval Bubonic Plague, mistranslated as the "Black Death."

audiencia   Spanish colonial advisory board in Latin America.

Augsburg confession   1530 statement of Lutheran religious views, urging reform of, not secession from, the Roman church.

Augustan Age   Period of Roman history when the restored empire was ruled by Augustus Caesar (r. 31 BCE–CE 14).

authority of the Bible Luther's view that the Bible is the sole source of revealed religious truth.

auto da fe "Act of faith," the public execution of lapsed heretics in medieval and early modern times.

autocrat Authoritarian ruler; one of the titles of the medieval Byzantine emperors.

Avignon papacy Popes resident in Avignon on the southern border of France during the late fourteenth and early fifteenth centuries.

Axis World War II alliance whose main members were Germany, Italy, and Japan.

Aztecs Imperial rulers of Mexico from the fifteenth to the early sixteenth centuries.

baby boom Rapid increase in family size following World War II, creating a large "younger generation" in the 1960s and a "greying" of the population at the end of the century.

balance of power Distribution of power among nations; diplomatic policy of constructing strong alliances to control powerful states, as in fifteenth-century Italy or eighteenth-century Europe.

baroque style Sixteenth- and seventeenth-century art style seeking to stir emotional response through movement, color, and scale.

bastard feudalism Late medieval corruption of the feudal system, exaggerating chivalric forms while replacing feudal loyalty with cash payments.

Bastille Royal prison destroyed in the French Revolution.

Benedictine Rule Basic medieval monastic rule, laid down by St. Benedict, prescribing poverty, chastity, and obedience.

benefice A post or appointment in the medieval or early modern church.

benefit of clergy Medieval Catholic rule that priests could be tried only in church courts.

Berlin airlift Supplying of Allied sectors of occupied Berlin by air during the Soviet-sponsored Berlin blockade of 1948.

Berlin Wall Wall dividing east and west Berlin, erected in 1961 to choke off flow of refugees from East Germany seeking jobs and freedom in West Germany.

big bang theory Twentieth-century theory that the universe was born in a cosmic explosion and has been expanding ever since.

Black Death Medieval plague that swept away a third of Europe's population.

black figure Ancient Greek style of vase painting in which the figures were drawn in black on the red clay of the vase.

black legend Account of the Spanish conquest of the New World emphasizing cruelty to the Native American population.

Blackshirts Mussolini's black-uniformed Fascist paramilitary forces in the 1920s and 1930s.

Blitzkrieg "Lightning war"—mechanized military assault characterized by rapid movement and crushing firepower, as mobilized by Bismarck in the nineteenth century and Hitler in the twentieth.

Bolshevik "Majority faction," the Leninist wing of the Russian Marxist party; after 1917, the Communist Party.

boule A legislative or administrative council in an ancient Greek city-state.

bourse Stock exchange, especially in early modern Europe.

boyar Russian nobility, especially medieval and early modern.

bread riot Public disturbance caused by high food prices.

Brownshirts Hitler's brown-uniformed Nazi storm troopers, his paramilitary force in the 1920s.

Burschenschaften Liberal nationalist German Student Unions during the early nineteenth century.

business cycle Alternation of economic booms and busts during the nineteenth and twentieth centuries.

Byzantine Empire The Eastern Roman Empire during the Middle Ages, from the fifth to the fifteenth century.

cabinet system Government by a prime minister and heads of government bureaus, all chosen from the majority party in the legislature; for example, the British government.

Caesarism Reform from the top by a strong ruler like Julius Caesar or Napoleon.

caesaropapism Church-state relationship in which the state is supreme, as developed in medieval Byzantium.

cahiers Lists of public grievances taken to the French Estates General in 1789.

caliph "Successor to the Prophet"—Muslim ruler combining political authority with religious sanction.

"calling of the princes" Summoning of Varangian (Viking) rulers to establish order in medieval Russian towns.

canon law   Legal code of the Roman Catholic church.

Carbonari   Revolutionary secret society in early nineteenth–century Italy.

Carolingian minuscule   Medieval style of writing in which lower–case as well as capital letters were used.

cartel   Agreement between nineteenth– and twentieth–century corporations to fix prices, assign quotas, or otherwise limit competition between them.

categorical imperative   Kant's view that we should always behave as we wish everyone else to behave.

cathedral   Church that serves as the seat of a bishop.

caudillo   Latin American warlord, building political power on the basis of peasant military force.

Celtic fringe   Celtic inhabitants of the western edge of Europe, especially Scotland, Ireland, and Wales.

Central Powers   Alliance of the central European great powers, Germany and Austria, from Bismarck's time through World War I.

chanson de geste   Medieval chivalric epic poem sung by minstrels glorifying the heroism of medieval knights.

Chartists   English suffrage reformers who demanded the vote for all male citizens in the 1830s and 1840s.

chauvinistic nationalism   Aggressive nationalistic policy, often advancing national interests by military means.

checks and balances   Montesquieu's Enlightenment theory that tyranny can be checked by a balanced division of governmental power among different institutions.

chivalric code   Code of conduct for medieval knights prescribing courage, loyalty, hospitality, and protection of ladies and the church.

church fathers   Leading thinkers in the early Christian church, including St. Augustine, St. Jerome, and Pope Gregory the Great.

Ciompi Revolt   Rebellion of wool workers in Renaissance Florence.

Cistercians   High medieval order of monks famed for spartan living and hard work.

civilization   Form of society usually characterized by urban and larger political units, central government, class structure, literacy, metal working, and other features.

classicism   Seventeenth–century style of literature and art prescribing ancient models and rules for creating beauty.

clientage   Relationship between Romans of higher and lower social class, in which the latter offered service and support in return for protection and economic benefits.

cold war   Struggle for global supremacy between alliances headed by the United States and the Soviet Union during the last half of the twentieth century.

coloni   Serf–like status of peasants in later Roman Empire.

colony   A settlement established by a people in a distant region, as by ancient Greeks around the Mediterranean and by modern Europeans around the world.

Comecon   Economic organization of communist eastern Europe, dominated by the Soviet Union, during the cold war.

Cominform   International communist information agency, established after World War II.

comitia centuriata   Roman "assembly of the centuries," in which male citizens met in their military units.

comitia tributa   Roman "assembly of the tribes" in which male citizens were grouped according to place of birth or residence.

commercial revolution   Revival of trade in the High Middle Ages, developing many modern business techniques.

Committee of Public Safety   Ruling committee of twelve leaders of the French Revolution during the period of the Terror.

Common Law   English traditional law, dating to medieval times and undergirding the legal systems of other English–speaking countries.

Common Market   The European Economic Community, a highly successful tariff union of western Europe established by the Treaty of Rome in 1957.

commune   Medieval and early modern town; socialistic community in nineteenth and twentieth centuries.

Concert of Europe   Attempt by the great powers to control and coordinate the international relations of Europe during the nineteenth century.

conciliar movement   Effort to resolve problems of the Great Schism in the fifteenth–century Catholic church through a series of church councils.

condottiere   Renaissance Italian commander of a mercenary military force.

conflict of generations   Differing world views and moral standards of people of different ages.

Congress of Vienna   Peace conference held in Vienna in 1814–1815 to reorganize Europe after the defeat of Napoleon.

Congress Party   Leading Indian party, founded in the nineteenth century to oppose British rule in India; led by Gandhi in first half of twentieth century, and ruled India in the second half.

conquistadors   "Conquerors," the Spanish soldiers who conquered much of the New World for Spain in the sixteenth century.

conservatism   Ideology emphasizing preservation of valuable ideals and institutions from the past.

consistory   Cooperative committee of Calvinist ministers and civic officials in sixteenth–century Geneva.

Constitution of 1791   First constitution of the French Revolution, replacing royal absolutism with constitutional monarchy.

constitutional monarchy   Royal government in which the monarch accepts legal limits on royal authority and shares power with legislative and other institutions.

consul   Highest–ranking Roman magistrate during the period of the Republic.

consumer society   Twentieth–century Western society seen as based primarily on the lavish consumption of goods and services.

containment   U.S. cold–war policy of preventing further expansion of the Soviet empire and limiting the spread of Soviet influence.

Continental System   Napoleon's plan to seal off his European empire from British trade.

corporation   Large business organization of the nineteenth and twentieth centuries.

Corpus Iuris Civilis   Justinian's Code, the sixth–century Byzantine codification of the Roman Law which became the foundation for a number of European law codes.

cortes   Spanish assembly or parliament, developed in early modern times.

cottage industry   Handicraft manufacturing organized by merchants but performed by peasants in their cottages.

Council of Trent   Catholic Reformation council convened in the 1540s, 1550s, and 1560s to re–examine doctrines and reform the church.

counterculture   1960s youth movement rejecting middle–class values in favor of a youth culture based on love, drugs, rock music, and communal living.

courtly love   Medieval doctrine urging knightly courtesy, tenderness, and romantic love for his lady as key parts of the chivalric code.

craft guild   Medieval organization of artisans practicing the same craft.

crash of 1929   Collapse of prices on the Wall Street Stock Exchange in New York, triggering the Great Depression.

Cro–Magnon   A paleolithic people first found in southwestern France, biologically identical with historic humanity.

Crusader state   Christian state established in the Muslim Near East during the High Middle Ages.

Crusades   Christian military expeditions against the Islamic Near East and North Africa, mostly dating from the late eleventh to the thirteenth centuries.

cubism   Style of modernist art developed by Picasso, fragmenting reality to reassemble it in aesthetically pleasing patterns.

cultural imperialism   Influence of a powerful nation's culture on those of other countries, especially weaker or poorer ones.

cultural nationalism   Earlier nineteenth-century nationalism, emphasizing language, literature, art, history, and other cultural sources of nationality.

curia regis   Medieval royal council.

Cynics   Hellenistic Greek philosophers who rejected Greek society and traditional values, preaching total self–sufficiency.

czar   Title of modern Russian monarchs, especially before Peter the Great took the title of emperor.

D–Day   June 6, 1944, the day of the Allied landings in Normandy in World War II.

dadaism   Post World War I "anti–art," ridiculing both traditional art and Western values.

dance of death   Theme in later medieval art showing Death leading all classes of society to their doom.

Danubian Empire   Habsburg territories centered on the Danube River valley and inhabited by non–German peoples, including Slavs, Magyars, and Italians.

Decembrists   Russian army officers who rebelled against the accession of Nicholas I in December, 1825.

Declaration of Independence   American colonial declaration of freedom from British rule.

Declaration of the Rights of Man   French Bill of Rights, stressing "liberty, equality, and brotherhood," promulgated in 1789.

deism   Enlightenment belief in a God who has created the universe and guaranteed its natural laws but who does not intervene further in its functioning.

Delian League   The fifth–century BCE Greek alliance against Persia, led by Athens, which evolved into the Athenian Empire.

deme   Administrative subdivision of ancient Athens and its hinterland.

descamisados   "Shirtless ones," the Latin American poor, whose support rulers often sought.

détente   In diplomacy, a stand–off or mutual acceptance of the status quo.

developed countries   Economically affluent and technologically advanced nations of the twentieth century.

developing countries   Nations, often newly emancipated from Western empires, which are less affluent or technologically advanced.

devotio moderna   Late medieval turn toward lay piety and mysticism, especially in the Netherlands and Germany.

diaspora   Dispersal of Jewish communities across the Western world, beginning in ancient times.

diet   Central or eastern European assembly of leading citizens, comparable to an early English parliament.

Directory   French government during the last stage of the Revolution.

divine sanction   Royal claim that monarchical government was divinely ordained.

division of labor   Separation of work into separate small tasks and the assigning of each to separate individuals or machines, as in modern industry.

Dominicans   Order of friars founded by St. Dominic in the thirteenth century.

Drang nach Osten   German "drive toward the east," into the Slavic lands of eastern Europe, begun in the Middle Ages.

Dreyfus case   Political upheaval in France centering on unjust 1894 conviction of Jewish army officer Alfred Dreyfus as a German spy.

Dual Monarchy   Austro–Hungarian governmental reform of 1867, granting Hungary parity with Austria under the Habsburgs.

Il Duce   "The Leader," Mussolini's title as head of the Italian Fascist party.

Duma   Russian political assembly between the Revolution of 1905 and that of 1917.

dynasty   Ruling family of a political state; by extension, any powerful family.

ecclesia   The citizens' assembly of ancient Athens.

economic demand   Desire for particular products by consumers; the force that drives a capitalist economy.

economic imperialism   Economic exploitation of another people to acquire resources, cheap labor, investment areas, or other material advantages.

Edict of Nantes   Henry IV's edict granting toleration to Protestants; revoked by Louis XIV.

émigrés   French emigrants, many of them aristocrats, who took refuge from the French Revolution in other countries.

Ems Dispatch   Telegram from the King of Prussia which, edited by Bismarck, helped cause the Franco–Prussian War.

enclosure   Agricultural practice of converting farm land into sheep pastures or commercial grain fields, often causing unemployment and dislocation of the peasants.

encomienda   Estate with Indian labor assigned to Spanish conquistadors in the New World.

England's Bill of Rights   Statement of the rights of Parliament and the English people imposed on William and Mary by England's "Glorious Revolution" of 1688.

enlightened absolutism   In the eighteenth–century, absolute rule by an enlightened ruler who claimed to use power in the interests of the people.

enquêteur   Medieval French royal official who oversaw the work of other royal officials in the provinces.

enragés Extremist fringe element in the French Revolution, popular with the *sans–culottes.*

Entente Cordiale "Cordiale Understanding," the series of agreements between Britain and France that led to their alliance in World War I.

enterprise culture British Prime Minister Thatcher's economic policy, emphasizing private enterprise and individual initiative.

ephor Chief magistrate in ancient Sparta.

Epicureans Hellenistic Greek and later Roman philosophers who saw pleasure and peace of mind as the goals of life.

equestrian Social class that challenged primacy of the patrician order in ancient Rome.

estates Legal classes of society in medieval and early modern Europe, usually including ecclesiastics, aristocrats, and commoners; the basis for early representative assemblies in Europe.

Estates General Early modern government assembly, particularly in France and the Netherlands.

evolution Darwin's theory of biological development through adaptation and the survival of the fittest.

existentialism Twentieth–century philosophy asserting that human existence is devoid of higher purpose or meaning.

extraterritoriality Imperialistic principle by which Western people lived under Western laws even in non–Western countries.

Fascist party Mussolini's totalitarian party and the model for similar authoritarian regimes in the 1920s and 1930s.

February Revolution The spontaneous upheaval in Russia early in 1917 which led to the abdication of Nicholas II and the emergence of the Kerensky government.

Federalist party Faction favoring strong central government during the Constitutional period and the early history of the United States.

Fenians Nineteenth–century Irish revolutionary nationalist organization.

feudal lord Medieval noble who could command the loyalty and service of vassal knights.

feudalism Medieval political system built on the exchange of military service for land and serf labor.

fief Land assigned to a vassal by his feudal lord.

fin de siècle "End of the century," term used for the 1890s, implying an unconventional or decadent break with the past.

First Triumvirate Informal political alliance of three ambitious Roman politicians, Julius Caesar, Pompey, and Crassus.

flying shuttle Eighteenth–century weaving machine that greatly increased cloth production in Britain.

Franciscans Order of wandering friars founded by St. Francis in the thirteenth century.

Frankfurt Assembly Convention of liberals from many German states which met in 1848 to try to forge a unified government for Germany.

free market Economic system emphasizing the power of consumer demand to generate production and de–emphasizing government regulation of the economy.

free trade movement Nineteenth–century businessmen's crusade to abolish customs duties in Britain.

the Fronde French revolutionary upheaval in the middle of the seventeenth century.

Führer principle Nazi emphasis on absolute commitment to the Leader, rather than to laws or institutions.

functionalism Modernist architectural theory that the form of a building should reflect its purpose or use.

general will Rousseau's theory that the best conscience of the people—not individual interests—should rule the state.

geocentric theory Ptolemy's view that the earth was the center of the universe.

Germanic peoples Preurban tribes who overran the Roman Empire in the fifth century and became the ancestors of many later European peoples, including the Germans, French, and English.

Gestapo Nazi secret police force in Hitler's Germany.

ghazi Muslim crusaders and raiders against Byzantium and Christian Europe.

ghetto Jewish section of a medieval or modern city.

Girondins Moderate faction among the leaders of the French Revolution.

glasnost Soviet leader Gorbachev's policy of "openness" in the 1980s, facing Soviet problems squarely instead of concealing difficulties.

globalization   Tendency of history, economics, art, and other things to become increasingly world–wide in scope in the twentieth century.

Glorious Revolution   English Revolution of 1688, establishing constitutional monarchy under William and Mary.

Golden Bull   Fourteenth–century decree by the Holy Roman Emperor granting unprecedented autonomy to the German princes.

Golden Horde   The Mongol khanate that ruled late medieval Russia.

golden mean   In Aristotelian ethics, virtue seen as the mean between extremes, "moderation in all things."

Gothic style   High medieval European art style, epitomized in Gothic cathedrals with their high pointed arches, stained glass windows, and flying buttresses.

Great Depression   Term use for both the long Western depression of the 1870s–1890s and the global depression of the 1930s.

Great Schism   Split in the Roman Catholic church (1378–1417) in which rival popes claimed headship of the church.

Greek (Eastern) Orthodox Church   Eastern European Christian church headed by the patriarch of Constantinople.

Gregorian reform   Medieval reform of the Roman Catholic church led by Pope Gregory VII.

gulag   Soviet system of labor camps scattered across the USSR.

hegemony   Domination of a country or region by another power.

heliaea courts   Large law courts in ancient Athens.

heliocentric theory   Copernicus's cosmological theory that the sun is the center of the universe.

Hellenes   Greek term for themselves, based on their belief that they were all descended from the mythical King Hellen of Thessaly.

Hellenistic Age   Period of Greek history from Alexander the Great in the fourth century BCE to the Roman conquest of the Mediterranean, completed in the first century BCE.

Hellenistic monarchies   Successor states to Alexander the Great's empire, characterized by autocratic power, courtly splendor, and claims of divinity.

Hellenization   Spread of Greek civilization, particularly to the Near East and North Africa during the Hellenistic period.

helot   A serf in ancient Sparta.

holding company   Form of nineteenth–century business organization which owned but did not direct a number of operating companies.

Holocaust   Massacre of six million Jews in Hitler's Europe during World War II.

Holy Roman Empire   Loosely organized German empire founded in the tenth century, expiring in the nineteenth.

homage and investiture   Medieval ceremony establishing a feudal relationship between lord and vassal.

hominid   The human family, including *homo erectus*, Neanderthal people, and Cro–Magnon people.

hoplite   Heavy infantry of ancient Greek citizen–soldiers.

humanism   Renaissance intellectual movement based on deep study of ancient culture.

Hundred Years War   Series of late medieval conflicts between England and France.

iconoclastic controversy   Dispute over use of icons in the Greek Orthodox church.

ideology   Nineteenth– or twentieth–century political, economic, or social theory offering a blueprint for changing society.

imperium   Political authority to command armies and punish citizens held by consuls in the Roman Republic and by emperors in the Roman Empire.

impressionism   Nineteenth–century French school of painting seeking to analyze light as the eye sees it.

Incas   Emperors of Peru and neighboring Andean regions in the late fifteenth and early sixteenth centuries.

Index of Forbidden Books   Catholic list of writings deemed immoral or irreligious by the church.

Indian Mutiny   Revolt of native troops against British rule of India in 1857.

indirect rule   British imperial policy of delegating authority to local rulers.

Indo–European peoples   Language group, probably originating on Eurasian steppes, spreading from India to Europe.

indulgences   Remission of punishment for sins granted in return for good works or monetary contribution to the church during medieval or Reformation times.

Industrial Revolution Emergence of modern industrial methods through steam power, the factory system, new methods of transportation and business organization beginning in the late eighteenth century, growing rapidly in the nineteenth.

Inquisition Medieval and early modern church court to uncover heresy.

intendant French government official dispatched to the provinces to impose authority of early absolutist monarchy.

interdict Papal ban on performing offices of Christian church.

interloper "Intruder," term used to describe English, French, and Dutch traders and colonizers who "intruded" into Spanish and Portuguese spheres of influence and empire in the seventeenth century.

internal imperialism Occupation of territory already formally claimed by nineteenth–century imperialist powers, as in U.S. westward movement and Russian advance into Siberia.

intifada Palestinian revolt against Israeli rule in later 1980s.

investiture controversy Dispute between medieval popes and secular rulers over who had power to invest bishops with their authority and lands.

Invincible Armada Spanish fleet that failed to conquer Elizabethan England.

iron curtain Dividing line between eastern and western Europe during the cold war.

Iron Lady Journalistic label for Britain's tough conservative prime minister in the 1980s.

Islam The religion and civilization of the Muslims, followers of the Prophet Muhammad, from the seventh century to the present.

ius gentium "Law of the peoples," legal principles originally applied to non-Roman subjects of the Roman Empire and later to citizens as well.

ius naturale "Natural law," the philosophical foundation for Roman legal system.

Jacobins Radical faction in the leadership of the French Revolution.

Jacquerie Peasant revolt in France at the time of the Hundred Years War.

janissary corps Christian converts serving Ottoman Turks in military and civil posts.

Jesuits The Society of Jesus, an order of friars organized by Loyola during the Catholic Reformation to combat heresy; also known for missionary and educational work.

jihad A Muslim holy war.

joint–stock company Form of business organization in which shares are distributed among a number of investors.

July Days Uprising in Paris during the French Revolution of 1830 in which the government of Charles X was overthrown.

Junkers Prussian aristocracy known for loyalty and efficiency.

Junta de noche Philip II's "night council" of special advisors in later sixteenth-century Spain.

justices of eyre Medieval English royal judges dispatched to try cases in the shires under Henry II.

Justices of the Peace English country gentry serving as royal officials.

kadi Muslim judge adjudicating disputes and trying cases according to Islamic law.

kamikaze Japanese suicide pilots who attacked U.S. ships during World War II.

Kievan Rus Medieval Russian state, centered in the southern steppes and ruled from Kiev by Varangian princes.

Koran The Muslim holy book, composed in the early seventh century by the Prophet Muhammad.

Kristallnacht The "night of the broken glass," Nazi–sponsored attack on German Jewish businesses and homes in 1938.

kulak Relatively successful Russian peasant of the sort purged by Stalin as "class enemies."

Kulturkampf Bismarck's campaign against the Catholic church in Germany.

labor movement Nineteenth– and twentieth–century movement to organize labor unions and advance the interests of workers.

laissez–faire Economic doctrine opposing government regulation of the free market.

latifundia Large slave–operated Roman estates.

League of Schmalkald Alliance of German Protestant princes organized in 1531 to defend Lutheran territories against the Catholic Holy Roman Emperor Charles V.

lebensraum "Living space," Hitler's goal in expanding his empire into eastern Europe.

lend–lease   U.S. policy of material aid to Britain at the beginning of World War II.

Levellers   Political democrats in the English Civil War who sought to "level" the social hierarchy.

Leviathan state   Hobbes's vision of the all–powerful state in the seventeenth century.

liberalism   Nineteenth– and twentieth–century ideology supporting political freedom and (in nineteenth century) free private enterprise.

libido   According to Freud, the unconscious energy behind sexual and other basic human feelings.

liege lord   Feudal overlord whose interests a vassal agrees to support first in any dispute.

linear A and B   Scripts ancestral to Greek used by the ancient Minoans and Mycenaeans.

liturgy   In ancient Greece, a wealthy person's material contribution to the service of the state; in the Christian church, a religious service.

logical positivism   Twentieth–century Anglo–American view that philosophy's function is largely limited to clarifying the meanings of terms.

Lombard League   Medieval alliance of northern Italian cities to resist German imperial intrusion.

Long March   Successful Chinese communist retreat from south China to a new base in north China in 1934–1935.

lugal   King of a Sumerian city–state.

Lumpenproletariat   In Marxist thought, criminal, mendicant, and other unemployed elements broken off from the working class.

ma'at   Egyptian principle of justice and order; the spirit in which the pharaohs ruled.

magical realism   Later twentieth–century Latin American school of literature mingling realism with fantasy.

Magna Carta   The "Great Charter" forced on King John in 1215 and seen as the foundation of later English liberties.

Malthusian ratios   Disturbing contrast between rapid population growth and the much slower growth in food supply pointed out by Malthus in 1798.

mandate system   Administration of former German colonies after World War I with avowed goal of development and liberation.

Manichaeans   Early Christian heretics who believed in the equal and opposite power of good and evil in the universe.

mannerism   Late Renaissance artistic style emphasizing elongated figures, sour colors, and startling lighting effects.

manor   Medieval farming village and surrounding land, run by a knight or noble and worked by serfs.

March on Versailles   Women's march that brought the royal family to Paris in the French Revolution.

Marxism   Influential variety of socialism propounded by Karl Marx, emphasizing economic determinism and class struggle.

mass culture   Popular forms of art and entertainment as developed in the twentieth century.

materialism   The philosophical view that only matter is real, ideas or spiritual phenomena being dismissed as illusions.

Menshevik   Faction of Russian Marxist underground who opposed Lenin, demanding a larger, more open party.

mercantilism   Early modern governmental economic policies seeking to control and develop the national economy.

merchant guild   Medieval organization of merchants and traders, often the dominant force in medieval cities.

Messiah   Among Jews, deliverer of the Jewish people foretold by the Prophets; among Christians, Jesus Christ seen as the savior of all humanity.

mestizo   Latin American ethnic group of mixed Spanish and Native American descent.

Methodism   Protestant religious sect founded in the eighteenth century, emphasizing emotional worship among the poor.

missi dominici   Royal emissaries sent out by Charlemagne to keep tabs on the provinces of his empire.

Model Parliament   First full Parliament in English history, including townsmen and knights as well as nobles and bishops, summoned by Edward I in 1295.

modernism   Twentieth–century movement in art and literature stressing formal values and often critical of modern society.

Mongols Militant pastoral nomads from the steppes; under Genghis Khan and his successors, they built an enormous Eurasian empire in the thirteenth and fourteenth centuries.

monopoly capitalism Control of the market, not by governments, but by gigantic corporations or cartels.

mosque Muslim house of worship.

muckraker American novelist or journalist who exposed abuses in business or government during the Progressive era.

Mughals Or Moguls, imperial rulers of India from the sixteenth through the eighteenth centuries.

multi–party system Form of democracy in which many parties compete for voter support.

Munich conference 1938 diplomatic conference in which Hitler secured British and French consent to his dismantling of Czechoslovakia.

mystery cults Near Eastern and North African religions offering ecstatic rites and personal salvation which found followers among Greeks and Romans.

Napoleonic Code Legal code introduced in France by Napoleon I.

narodnik Later nineteenth–century Russian revolutionary seeking to organize a socialist revolt among the peasants.

nationalism Nineteenth– and twentieth–century ideology stressing the importance of national identity, the national state, or the superiority of one nation over others.

natural rights Rights of human beings that government should not violate; particularly, the political rights urged by Locke and expanded by reformers of later centuries.

Nazi party Hitler's German National Socialist party, totalitarian rulers of Germany 1933–1945.

Neanderthal Prehistoric people originally discovered in the Neander valley in Germany; the immediate precursors of modern humans.

neoclassicism Eighteenth–century school of art even more devoted to models and rules than seventeenth–century classicism.

neoimperialism Continuing economic exploitation of former colonies and other developing nations by Western powers in the later twentieth century.

Neolithic Society of the New Stone Age, when human beings first settled into agricultural villages.

Neo–Orthodoxy Twentieth–century Christian stress on personal salvation, rather than social reform, as primary concern of the church.

Neoplatonism More mystical "New Platonism" developed by Plotinus of Alexandria in Roman times.

New Deal U.S. President Franklin Roosevelt's reform program during the 1930s.

New Economic Policy Lenin's compromise with small–scale capitalism in Russia during the 1920s.

New Frontier U.S. President Kennedy's program of reform; also used for his youthful, vigorous style of government.

new imperialism Second wave of Western imperialism, particularly between 1870 and 1914.

new monarchs Fifteenth– and sixteenth–century monarchs who revived royal power after late medieval decline.

Night of August 4 Surrender of many noble privileges by the French aristocracy at a meeting held August 4, 1789.

Ninety–five Theses Luther's list of arguments against the selling of indulgences that was published in 1517 and launched the Protestant Reformation.

nonrationalism Nineteenth–century romantic belief that emotions, intuitions, and other nonrational faculties—not reason—should be our main guide to understanding.

northern humanism Renaissance humanism north of Italy, characterized by special concern for Christian classics and morality, and providing background for the Reformation.

Nuremberg Laws Hitler's anti-Jewish laws of 1935.

October Manifesto Decree granting basic rights and a representative assembly extracted from Nicholas II during the Russian Revolution of 1905.

October Revolution Bolshevik revolt during the Russian Revolution of 1917, overthrowing the Kerensky government and bringing Lenin to power.

old imperialism First wave of Western overseas imperialism, from the fifteenth century to the eighteenth.

old regime European society before the French Revolution.

oligarchy Rule by a small group or by a particular social class; often by the middle classes, as in ancient

Greek or medieval European cities.

oprichniki   Marauding military order through which Ivan the Terrible imposed his will on sixteenth-century Russia.

Ostpolitik   West German Chancellor Brandt's policy of reconciliation with East Germany and eastern Europe.

Ottomans   Steppe nomads who conquered the Byzantine Empire in 1453 and founded the modern Ottoman Empire with its capital at Constantinople.

outback   The arid interior of Australia, "out back" of the settled areas along the coasts.

palace system   The Mycenaean structure of political and military power in ancient Greece.

Paleolithic   Society of the Old Stone Age, when people lived by food-gathering and hunting.

Palestine Liberation Organization   Anti-Israeli Palestinian guerrilla organization in the later twentieth century.

paradigm   Interpretive framework for understanding; applied to scientific revolutions, social thought, art and literary criticism, etc.

Paris Commune   Revolutionary government of the city of Paris, first in the 1790s, then in 1871 after the Franco-Prussian War.

parlement   French court of law; the Parlement of Paris had something of the prestige of the U.S. Supreme Court.

Parliament   Britain's two-house legislature, including the House of Lords (nobility and church leaders) and the elected House of Commons (country squires and middle-class citizens).

particularism   Commitment to the independence and interests of a region, state, or province in a larger political federation, as in the Holy Roman Empire.

patriarchs   Heads of the Eastern Orthodox church; comparable to popes in the Roman Catholic church.

patrician   The ancient Roman aristocracy, particularly powerful during the period of the Republic.

Pax Romana   The Roman Peace in the Western world during the first two centuries CE.

Peace of Paris   The 1919 peace settlement following World War I.

peaceful coexistence   Easing of cold-war tensions between the United States and the Soviet Union, particularly during the Khrushchev period.

Peasants Revolt   Late medieval rebellion in England.

Peloponnesian League   The Spartan-led alliance which fought Athens in the Peloponnesian Wars.

peons   Peasant laborers in Latin America, often Indians bound to hacienda labor by debt to the landowner.

perestroika   Soviet leader Gorbachev's proposed "restructuring" of the USSR in the 1980s.

perspective   Artistic technique for representing three-dimensionality convincingly on a flat surface.

Petrashevsky Circle   Mid-nineteenth century group of Russian radicals sent to Siberia for reading subversive western European books.

phalanstery   Fourier's model commune, one of several early "utopian" socialist schemes.

philosophes   Subversive eighteenth-century French thinkers; the leading intellectuals of the Enlightenment.

physiocrats   Eighteenth-century French economic reformers who saw the produce of the land as the real source of wealth.

Pietism   Eighteenth-century German Protestant movement stressing emotional commitment to religion.

plebeians   The urban lower classes in ancient Rome.

pneumonic plague   Virulent form of the Black Death affecting the lungs.

pogrom   Massacre of Jews, especially in eastern Europe.

polis   The ancient Greek city-state.

political nationalism   Form of nationalism emphasizing political unity or independence.

politique   Late sixteenth-century Europeans who favored religious compromise in order to restore political order.

Populist movement   U.S. political reform movement of the 1890s, emphasizing the plight of the farmers.

positivism   Nineteenth- and twentieth-century theory that scientific methods and objectivity are the only roads to truth.

postmodernism   Later twentieth-century approach to the arts rejecting "great" art and the search for a single "meaning" in art or life.

poststructuralism   Later twentieth-century philosophy rejecting all absolutes and seeing the world in terms of "discourse," the words or other symbols we use to describe our world.

power of the purse   Authority claimed by the elected House of Commons of the English Parliament to control royal revenues.

pragmatism   American philosophy, developed by William James, which judges the validity of an idea by its impact or usefulness.

predestination   Belief that each human soul has been predestined or assigned to heaven or hell; important particularly among Calvinist Protestants.

prévôt   Medieval French officials under the Capetians.

primogeniture   Inheritance of all property by the first-born son.

princeps   "First citizen," title of Augustus Caesar and other early Roman emperors.

principate   Early imperial period of Roman history when rulers avoided the imperial title by calling themselves "first citizens."

procurator   Head of the Russian Orthodox church under Peter the Great and his successors.

Progressivism   American political reform movement during the late nineteenth and early twentieth centuries.

prophets   Inspired holy men who both condemned and consoled the ancient Hebrews in God's name.

protectorate   Form of Western imperialism in which non-Western rulers continue to govern but accept the "advice" of a Western agent in return for protection and other rewards.

protoindustrialism   Early modern cottage industry organized by a merchant capitalist who provided raw material and picked up the finished product.

Ptolemaic dynasty   Macedonian dynasty that ruled Egypt from the fourth to the first century BCE.

Punic Wars   Wars between Rome and the Carthage in the third and second centuries BCE.

purge   Totalitarian practice of expelling or executing party members suspected of inefficiency, treason, or opposition to party policy.

Puritans   Sixteenth- and seventeenth-century English Protestants, many of them Calvinists, who opposed what they perceived as the immorality and Catholic leanings of the English established church.

putsch   Attempt to seize power by force, like Hitler's 1923 "Beer Hall Putsch."

Quadruple Alliance   Early nineteenth-century conservative alliance of Austria, Prussia, Russia, and France seeking to prevent resurgence of the revolutionary spirit.

racism   Belief that racial differences are crucial factors in history, and that some races are superior to others.

radiation   Conversion of matter into energy, as explored by Curie in connection with radium around 1900.

raison d'état   "Reason of state," the eighteenth-century principle justifying aggressive international behavior.

the Raj   British rule in India in the nineteenth and early twentieth centuries.

rationalism   Belief in the capacity of human reason to understand the world and solve human problems.

realism   Nineteenth- and twentieth-century school of literature and art describing society as it is, rejecting romantic dreams.

Realpolitik   Hardboiled, self-interested foreign policy style often associated with Bismarck.

Rechtsstaat   State ruled by laws rather than arbitrarily by a ruler.

reconquista   Spanish Christian "reconquest" of Spain from the Muslims in the Middle Ages.

red figure   Ancient Greek style of vase painting in which the surface of the vase was painted black except for the figures, which were left in the red color of the clay.

Redshirts   Garibaldi's troops in the liberation of Sicily and southern Italy.

Reform Bill of 1832   English electoral reform extending the vote to the middle classes and new industrial cities.

Reformation Parliament   English Parliament that enacted first Reformation laws under Henry VIII.

Reichstag   German legislative assembly.

Reign of Terror   Violently repressive period of the French Revolution between 1792 and 1794.

relational feminism   Nineteenth-century feminist view that women should define themselves in terms of their relations with—and duties to—husbands, children, and society at large.

relativity   Einstein's revolutionary theory that all aspects of the physical universe—even space and time—must be defined in relative terms.

Renaissance despot   Italian Renaissance ruler with no hereditary or religious claim on political power.

Renaissance person   Multitalented individual, especially in the Renaissance period.

resistance movements   Underground opposition to German occupation in conquered European countries during World War II.

Restoration   The attempt to re–establish the old regime in Europe after the defeat of Napoleon in 1815.

revisionist powers   The nations who were dissatisfied with the terms of the Peace of Paris after World War I, particularly Germany, Italy, and Japan.

los reyes católicos   The "Catholic kings," term for Ferdinand and Isabella of Spain.

Risorgimento   Nineteenth-century Italian unification movement.

robber baron   Negative characterization of late nineteenth–century businessmen, known to their admirers as "captains of industry."

rococo   Playful, decorative eighteenth–century art style.

Roman Civil War   The long struggle, combining class struggle with rivalry between ambitious Roman politicians that began with the reform attempts of the Gracchi in 133 and ended with Augustus's victory in 31 BCE.

Roman Empire   Rome from the end of the first century BCE to the fall of Rome in the fifth century CE, when ultimate political authority was held by the emperors.

Roman legion   Primary division of the Roman army consisting of 5000 men divided into ten cohorts.

Roman Republic   Rome from the fifth to the first century BCE, when its political life was dominated by the Senate, the assemblies, and elected magistrates.

romanticism   Cultural mood of the first half of the nineteenth century, urging the primacy of feeling over reason.

sacraments   Spiritual rites of passage in the Roman Catholic church: baptism, confirmation, marriage, ordination, penance, communion, last rites.

St. Bartholomew's Day Massacre   1572 Catholic massacre of Protestant Huguenots during the French wars of religion.

salon   Seventeenth– and eighteenth–century gathering of leaders of society and intellectual community to discuss art and (sometimes radical) ideas.

salonière   Hostess at an intellectual salon.

samizdat **literature**   Underground literature circulated in manuscript in eastern Europe during the communist period.

samurai   Japanese warriors in medieval and early modern times.

sans–culottes   Working–class people of Paris at the time of the French Revolution.

satellite state   East European client states of the Soviet Union during the later twentieth century.

satraps   Provincial governors in the Persian Empire.

scholasticism   High medieval philosophy and theology, rooted in rediscovery of Aristotle and seeking to explain faith in rational terms.

Second Triumvirate   Formal political alliance of three Roman rulers, Octavian, Antony, and Lepidus.

Seleucid monarchs   Macedonian dynasty that ruled Persia and Syria during the Hellenistic period.

Senate   Chief political assembly of ancient Rome, composed of heads of important families and men who had held the chief magistracies; upper house of U.S. Congress.

Seneca Falls Convention   Early American rights–for–women convention, held in 1848 at Seneca Falls, New York.

Sephardic Jews   Spanish Jews who forged a brilliant medieval culture under Muslim rule.

service nobility   Peter the Great's new class of Russian nobility whose high place depended on civil or military service to the state.

settlement empire   European colonies where Western people settled in significant numbers, as in the Americas.

Seven Years' War   Great–power struggle in the mid–eighteenth century, fought both in Europe (Prussia versus Austria) and overseas (British versus French empires).

sharia   Muslim law, based on Koran and Islamic traditions and administered by *kadis*.

shire   An English county.

shogun   War leader and de facto ruler of Japan in late medieval and early modern times.

simony   In the Christian church, the sin of selling positions in the church.

Slavophiles   Nineteenth–century Russian believers that Russia's future should be based on Slavic national character and Orthodox religiosity.

social contract   Formal or tacit agreement by which a people accept a particular government; Hobbes envisioned an absolutist contract, Locke a liberal one, and Rousseau a democratic one in which the best conscience of the people guides the state.

social Darwinism   Application of Darwinian biological concepts like "survival of the fittest" to such social practices and institutions as economic competition, war, and imperialism.

social democratic socialism   Form of socialism emphasizing social welfare measures and democratic control of the economy.

socialism   Nineteenth– and twentieth–century ideology focusing on public ownership of the means of production in order to insure fair distribution of goods and services.

socialist realism   Style of art favored by communist governments glorifying the workers and the Communist party.

Socratic method   Questioning and disputation in order to arrive at a higher level of understanding.

sophists   Fifth–century Greek philosophers, condemned for using tricky logic to prove that all things are relative and success alone matters.

sovereignty   Ultimate authority, particularly in an absolute monarchy.

sovereignty of God   Calvin's emphasis on divine omnipotence and the fundamental human duty of obedience to God's will.

soviet   Workers' councils during the 1905 and 1917 Russian Revolutions; structure of government throughout the Soviet period.

sphere of influence   Form of Western imperial domination, generally economic, through agreements with non–Western governments.

spinning jenny   Eighteenth–century machine that multiplied the number of threads that could be spun at one time.

spoils system   American term for use of government jobs to reward party faithful.

SS   The *Schutzstaffel*, Hitler's elite party troops of the 1930s and 1940s, notorious for their role in the Holocaust.

stadtholder   Chief magistrate of the Netherlands in early modern times.

Star Wars   U.S. President Reagan's plan to provide a space–age protective shield for the United States.

state of nature   The human condition outside of organized society and the political state, especially as described by seventeenth– and eighteenth–century political thinkers.

stigmata   The wounds of Christ appearing on the body of a saint or other mystic.

stoa   Columned portico used as a public meeting place in ancient Greece.

Stoicism   Hellenistic Greek and later Roman school of philosophy preaching the value of fortitude, duty, and the brotherhood of all rational beings.

stream of consciousness   Literary technique in which the story is told through the thoughts, feelings, and perceptions of characters.

structuralism   Twentieth–century social and cultural theory emphasizing underlying structures of ideas and institutions.

struggle of the orders   Conflict between patricians and plebeians in the early centuries of the Roman Republic.

Sturm und Drang   "Storm and Stress" pre–romantic literary movement in late eighteenth–century Germany.

supply and demand   Adam Smith's doctrine that economic demand will stimulate production in a self–governing free market system.

surrealism   Modernist literary and artistic movement seeking to give form to images summoned up from the unconscious mind, as through dreams or trances.

survival of the fittest   Darwinian biological concept, also applied to society; see *social Darwinism*.

syndicalism   Late nineteenth–century form of anarchism envisioning labor unions as the center of a free society.

tabula rasa   Locke's psychological theory that the human mind is a "blank slate" before experience inscribes ideas and attitudes there.

taille   Medieval French tax imposed on peasantry.

Tennis Court Oath   Oath taken by the French Estates General not to dissolve—despite royal pressure—until they had made a constitution for France.

Tetrarchy   Diocletian's restructuring of Roman government, dividing authority among two *Augusti* and two *Caesars*.

the Thaw   Khrushchev's reform efforts in the Soviet Union after Stalin's death in 1953.

theater of the absurd   Trend in drama following World War II, rejecting realism in favor of absurd events revealing the meaninglessness of life.

Theory of Ideas   Plato's philosophical theory that all material things are copies of archetypal Ideas, Forms, or Absolutes which exist in another realm of being.

Third Estate   The working majority in the medieval and early modern division of the population, excluding nobility and clergy and dominated by the bourgeoisie.

Third French Republic   Republican government established in 1871 after the Franco–Prussian War and lasting until Germany's World War II defeat of France in 1940.

Third World   Nonaligned nations, usually developing countries and former colonies, who refused to side with either superpower in the cold war.

Thirty Tyrants   Autocratic rulers installed in Athens by Sparta after Sparta's victory in the Peloponnesian War.

Tories   English Conservative party.

total war   Modern wars, especially World War I and World War II, requiring the commitment of all citizens and resources to the conflict.

totalitarianism   Twentieth–century form of authoritarian government, deploying technology and bureaucracy to impose rule by an ideological party and controlling all aspects of the lives of the population.

trading empire   European commercial expansion overseas, achieved through trading posts supported by political alliances and military force, as in India.

trench warfare   Static but brutal mode of fighting in World War I, with both sides dug into elaborate trench systems.

triangular trade routes   Imperial trade routes carrying manufactured goods to Africa, slaves to the Americas, and agricultural products to Europe.

tribune   Roman magistrate representing the interests of the common people.

trireme   Ancient Greek warship propelled by three banks of oars.

Turko–Mongol peoples   Nomadic steppe peoples, including Huns, Turks, and Mongols, who invaded Europe repeatedly from the east.

Twelfth–Century Renaissance   Cultural revival of the High Middle Ages, including scholastic philosophy and gothic art.

Twelve Tables   Earliest formulation of Roman law, inscribed on twelve wooden tablets in 450 BCE.

two–party system   Form of democracy in which two rival parties compete for voter support.

Unam Sanctam   Papal bull issued by Boniface VIII in 1302, claiming supremacy over all secular authorities.

unconscious   In Freud's psychology, the part of the mind of which we are not aware; home of basic drives and forgotten memories.

underground railway   American abolitionist organization dedicated to helping black slaves escape from the south before the Civil War.

Untermenschen   "Subhuman," the Nazi term for Jews.

urban patriciate   Commercial and financial aristocracy of the towns during medieval and early modern times.

utilitarianism   Nineteenth–century philosophy that evaluated institutions on the basis of social utility to achieve "the greatest happiness of the greatest number."

utopia   An ideal state or society, usually invented to point up injustice in existing societies; based on More's sixteenth–century book, *Utopia*.

utopian socialism   Form of nineteenth–century socialism urging communes in the healthy countryside.

vassal   In the feudal system, a knight who pledges military service and support for a more powerful feudal lord in exchange for land, serfs to work it, and the lord's protection.

veche   Municipal council in medieval Russian cities.

Versailles Treaty Peace treaty between the Allies and Germany following World War I; one of several treaties comprising the Peace of Paris in 1919.

Vienna settlement Reorganization of Europe by the Congress of Vienna, limiting French power and seeking to restore conservative institutions.

villas Late Roman agricultural estates in which peasantry surrendered their liberty in return for protection; precursors of medieval manors.

virtù Renaissance quality of character combining willpower and skill that made for success.

Volksgeist To nineteenth-century German nationalists, the "folk spirit" which incarnates the national character of a people.

War of the Austrian Succession Great-power struggle during the 1740s centering on the effort by Frederick the Great of Prussia to wrest Silesia from Maria Theresa's Austrian inheritance.

Wars of religion Wars and civil wars pitting Catholics against Protestants, at their height in the second half of the sixteenth century.

Wars of the Roses Civil war, 1455–1485, between rival houses of York and Lancaster for the throne of England.

Weimar Republic Liberal German government established by the Weimar Constitution and destroyed by Hitler in 1933.

weltanschauung "Worldview" of a religion, philosophy, or ideology.

westernization Increasing influence of western civilization on the rest of the world, especially in the nineteenth and twentieth centuries.

Whigs English liberal party during the eighteenth and earlier nineteenth centuries.

"white man's burden" Alleged duty of Western peoples to civilize "lesser breeds" in other parts of the world.

witch craze Widespread persecution of witches, mostly women believed to have supernatural powers and to be agents of Satan, between the fifteenth and seventeenth centuries.

witenagemot Anglo-Saxon royal council.

women's movement Campaign for legal rights, economic opportunities, and a share of political power for women during the later nineteenth and twentieth centuries.

women's suffrage The right of women to vote and hold political office, demanded in the nineteenth century and gained in the twentieth.

World Bank Global banking institution founded after World War II, increasingly dedicated to providing loans for economic development.

zemsky sobor Early modern Russian national assembly of notables, abandoned in the seventeenth century.

zemstvo Municipal council established in Russia in the later nineteenth century.

ziggurat Mesopotamian temple, pyramidal in shape with a shrine at the top.

Zollverein Nineteenth-century German customs union headed by Prussia.

Index

Rivera, Miquel Primo de, 636
Robber barons, 473
Robbers, The, 550
Robb-Grillet, Alain, 753
Robert, King of Naples, 259
Robespierre, Maximilien, 449, 450, 451
Rock and roll, 752
Rockefeller, John D., 473, 536
Rococo art, 414
Roentgen, Wilhelm, 560
Rogers, Richard, 750
Roland, Jeanne, 449, 451, 452
Roman Catholic church. *See also* Catholic Reformation; Christianity/Christian church
    Kulturkampf against, 532
    schism between Greek Orthodox church and, 193–94
    Ultra Catholics, 290
Roman Civil War, 89–95
Roman Empire, 102–26
    Augustan Age, 103–5
    chronology, 104
    decline and fall, 111–17
    economic expansion, 109–10
    emperors, first/second centuries, 105–7
    imperial government, 107–9
    Pax Romana, 103–11
    rise of Christianity, 117–24
    social life, 110–11
Romania, dictatorship in, 636
Roman legion, 92
Romanov, Michael, 310
Romanov dynasty, 310–11
Romanovna, Anastasia, 288
Roman Republic, 78–101
    Carthaginian wars, 85–88
    chronology, 80
    conquest: of the East, 88–89; of Italy, 84–85
    culture: 95–99; art, 99; engineering, 99; Hellenization of, 96; law, 98–99; literature, 96–97
    disorder/civil strife, 89–95
    early society, 81–83
    Etruscan influence, 81–82
    Mediterranean and, 80–81
    political institutions, 83
    Roman Civil War, 89, 90–95
    struggle of the orders, 83–84
Romanticism, 547–53
    chronology, 548
    defined, 547
    literary, 549–51
    primacy of emotion, 547–48
    romantic worldview, 548–49
Rome, Treaty of, 718
Rommel, Erwin, 657, 658
Roosevelt, Anna Eleanor, 623
Roosevelt, Franklin D., 621, 623, 653, 655, 658, 672, 700
Roosevelt, Theodore, 598
Rossellini, Roberto, 753
Rossini, Gioacchino, 552
Rostand, Edmond, 560
Rotten boroughs, 508
Rousseau, Jean-Jacques, 396, 399, 403, 404–5, 438, 550
Royal Society of London, 340
Rubens, Peter Paul, 328
Rump Parliament, 315
Rurik, 163
Russell, Lord John, 508
Russia
    antisemitism, 542, 543
    Crimean War, 527
    Duma, 597
    eastward expansion, 359–60

in 18th century, 377
internal imperialism, 582, 583, 584
modern, founding of, 311–12
"new woman," 540
reform era, 527
response to radicalism, 518–19
revolution of 1825, 502–3
Romanov dynasty, 310–11, 360
Russian Civil War, 608–9
Russian Revolution (1917), 419, 594
    communist victory, 608–9
    enemies of, 607–8
    February Revolution, 606–7
    October Revolution, 607
    war communism, 608
Russo-Japanese War, 577
Ruth, George Herman (Babe), 622

Sacraments, 195, 197
Sadat, Anwar, 691, 786
Sade, Marquis de, 380
Sailing to Byzantium (Yeats), 152
Saint-Just, Louis-Antoine, 450, 451
Sakharov, Andrei, 712
Salah ad-Din, 205
Salamis, naval battle at, 45
Salazar, António, 694
Salle, Robert Cavelier de La, 357
Salons/*Salonières*, 397, 399
SALT (Strategic Arms Limitation Talks) Treaty, 684
Salvation through faith, 271–72, 276
Samson Agonistes (Milton), 330
Samurai, 577
Sand, George, 551
San Martin, José de, 504
Sans-culottes, 443, 450
Sappho, 52, 53–54, 72
Sargon II, 13
Sargon of Akkad, 12
Sartre, Jean-Paul, 739
Sassanians, 112
Satellite states, Soviet Union, 673, 685–86, 711–12
    revolutions of 1989 in, 713
Satraps, 25
Saul, King of Israel, 27
Schiller, Friedrich, 550
Schlieffen, Alfred von, 601
Schlieffen Plan, 601
Schoenberg, Arnold, 751
Scholastics/scholasticism, 198–200
School of Athens, The (Raphael), 164
Schopenhauer, Arthur, 553
Schubert, Franz, 552
Schuschnigg, Kurt von, 648
Science
    ancient, 332–33
    Hellenistic, 72–73
Science of Logic, The (Hegel), 553
Scientific Revolution, 332–42, 400–401. *See also* Second scientific revolution
    Copernican breakthrough, 333–35
    impact of, 337–42
    Newton, 335–36
    new worldview, 341–42
    philosophers of, 338–40
    popularity of, 340–41
Scipio, Cornelius, 88
Scipio Aemilianus, 88
Scipio Africanus, 87–88
Sculpture
    baroque, 328–29
    classical Greek, 55–56
    Hellenistic, 69
    modernist, 749–50
    Renaissance, 265–66
    Roman Republic, 99
Season in Hell (Rimbaud), 564

Second Punic War, 87
Second scientific revolution, 731–37
    biology/psychology, 735–36
    matter/energy, 732
    new paradigms, 736–37
    relativity/cosmology, 733–35
Second Sex, The (Beauvoir), 726
Second Treatise of Government (Locke), 325, 404
Second Triumvirate, 95
Second World War. *See* World War II
Security Council, United Nations, 669
Selassie, Haile, emperor of Ethiopia, 647
Seleucid monarchies, 65, 117
Seleucus I, 65, 66
Seljuk Turks, 158, 204, 231
Senate (Roman Republic), 83, 84, 103
Seneca Falls convention, 534
Sénéchals, 185
Senghor, Léopold, 693
Sennacherib, 14
Sennett, Mack, 753
Sense and Sensibility (Austen), 558–59
Sentimentalism, Hellenistic, 69
Sephardic Jews, 202
September Massacres, 450
Serfdom, 141–42, 143
    abolition of, 475, 527
Servetus, Michael, 277
Service nobility, 311, 377
Settlement empires, 349
Seventeenth-century Europe, 297–344
    absolute monarchy, 303–12
    arts: 326–32; baroque, 327–29; classical, 329–30; for middle classes, 330–32
    chronology: Age of Louis XIV, 299; science/culture, 324
    constitutional government, 312–19
    famine/depression/disease, 301–2
    midcentury rebellions, 300–301
    scientific revolution. *See* Scientific Revolution
    sovereignty concept, 323
    Thirty Years' War, 289, 290, 297–300
    witch craze, 302–3
Seventh Seal, The, 753
Seven Years' War, 387, 389–92
Severus, Septimus, 111
Seward, William H., 535
Sforza, Caterina, 256
Shakespeare, William, 258, 260, 261
Sharia, 173
Shelley, Percy Bysshe, 550
She Walks in Beauty (Byron), 550
Shiite Muslims, 171, 172, 768
Shogunate, 577
Sholokov, Mikhail, 745
Sic et Non (Abelard), 200
Siemens, Karl Wilhelm, 470
Singapore, 769
Sisters of the Common Life, 227
Six Books on the Republic (Bodin), 323
Six Characters in Search of an Author (Pirandello), 744
Six Day War, 691
Skinner, B.F., 736
Slavery/slaves
    abolitionist movement, U.S., 534–35
    in fifth-century Greece, 46
    in Hellenistic Age, 66
Slave Ship, The (Turner), 552
Slavic peoples, 161–62
Slavophiles, Russian, 519
Smith, Adam, 396, 401, 405–7, 481, 482
Smith, David, 750